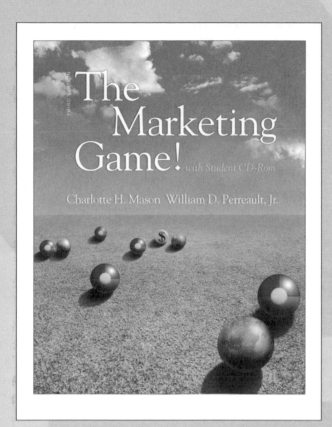

The Marketing Game!
with Student CD-Rom

Charlotte H. Mason William D. Perreault, Jr.

THE MARKETING GAME

The Marketing Game is a competitive marketing strategy simulation that allows students the opportunity to apply their marketing knowledge in a fun and interesting way.

   The Marketing Game is based on realistic marketing and realistic marketing relationships, and allows for maximum flexibility.

THE MOTIVATED LEARNER DVD SET

This four-DVD set of multimedia lecture for each chapter—8 hours in total—provides an opportunity to review the concepts of the text outside of the classroom. The video lectures combine slide shows, interactive graphics, and ad clips with helpful lecture voiceovers that will play on any DVD player and most PCs. The high quality means DVDs are the next best thing to live lectures. The DVDs also provide all of the **Basic Marketing** teaching videos and video cases (another 8 hours).

BASIC MARKETING

A GLOBAL-MANAGERIAL APPROACH

McGraw–Hill/Irwin Series in Marketing

Alreck & Settle
The Survey Research Handbook
Third Edition

Anderson, Beveridge, Lawton, & Scott
Merlin: A Marketing Simulation
First Edition

Arens
Contemporary Advertising
Ninth Edition

Arnould, Price & Zinkhan
Consumers
Second Edition

Bearden, Ingram, & LaForge
Marketing: Principles & Perspectives
Fourth Edition

Belch & Belch
Advertising & Promotion: An Integrated Marketing Communications Approach
Sixth Edition

Bingham & Gomes
Business Marketing
Third Edition

Cateora & Graham
International Marketing
Twelfth Edition

Cole & Mishler
Consumer and Business Credit Management
Eleventh Edition

Cravens & Piercy
Strategic Marketing
Seventh Edition

Cravens, Lamb & Crittenden
Strategic Marketing Management Cases
Seventh Edition

Crawford & Di Benedetto
New Products Management
Seventh Edition

Duncan
Principles of Advertising and IMC
Second Edition

Dwyer & Tanner
Business Marketing
Second Edition

Eisenmann
Internet Business Models: Text and Cases
First Edition

Etzel, Walker & Stanton
Marketing
Thirteenth Edition

Forrest
Internet Marketing Intelligence
First Edition

Futrell
ABC's of Relationship Selling
Eighth Edition

Futrell
Fundamentals of Selling
Eighth Edition

Gourville, Quelch, & Rangan
Cases in Health Care Marketing
First Edition

Hair, Bush & Ortinau
Marketing Research
Second Edition

Hawkins, Best & Coney
Consumer Behavior
Ninth Edition

Johansson
Global Marketing
Third Edition

Johnston & Marshall
Churchill/Ford/Walker's Sales Force Management
Seventh Edition

Johnston & Marshall
Relationship Selling and Sales Management
First Edition

Kerin, Hartley, & Rudelius
Marketing: The Core
First Edition

Kerin, Berkowitz, Hartley & Rudelius
Marketing
Seventh Edition

FIFTEENTH EDITION

BASIC MARKETING

A GLOBAL-MANAGERIAL APPROACH

William D. Perreault, Jr., Ph.D.
UNIVERSITY OF NORTH CAROLINA

E. Jerome McCarthy, Ph.D.
MICHIGAN STATE UNIVERSITY

McGraw-Hill
Irwin

Boston   Burr Ridge, IL   Dubuque, IA   Madison, WI   New York   San Francisco   St. Louis
Bangkok   Bogotá   Caracas   Kuala Lumpur   Lisbon   London   Madrid   Mexico City
Milan   Montreal   New Delhi   Santiago   Seoul   Singapore   Sydney   Taipei   Toronto

The McGraw·Hill Companies

McGraw Hill Irwin

BASIC MARKETING: A GLOBAL-MANAGERIAL APPROACH

ISBN 0-07-252523-1

Editorial director: *John E. Biernat*
Executive editor: *Linda Schreiber*
Coordinating editor: *Lin Davis*
Managing developmental editor: *Nancy Barbour*
Executive marketing manager: *Dan Silverburg*
Media producer: *Craig Atkins*
Senior project manager: *Christine A. Vaughan*
Manager, new book production: *Heather D. Burbridge*
Director of design BR: *Keith J. McPherson*
Photo research coordinator: *Jeremy Cheshareck*
Photo researcher: *Mike Hruby*
Lead supplement producer: *Cathy L. Tepper*
Senior digital content specialist: *Brian Nacik*
Interior design: *Kiera Pohl*
Cover Illustration: *Jeff Nishinaka/Bernstein & Andriulli*
Cover designer: *Keith J. McPherson*
Typeface: *10.5/12 Goudy*
Compositor: *GTS–Los Angeles, CA Campus*
Printer: *R. R. Donnelley*

Library of Congress Cataloging-in-Publication Data

Perreault, William D.
    Basic marketing: a global-managerial approach/William D. Perreault, Jr., E. Jerome
McCarthy.—15th ed.
        p. cm.—(McGraw-Hill/Irwin series in marketing)
    Includes bibliographical references and index.
    ISBN 0-07-252523-1 (alk. paper)
    1. Marketing—Management. I. McCarthy, E. Jerome (Edmund Jerome) II. Title. III.
Series.
HF5415.13.M369 2005
658.8—dc22
                                                                        2004040321

www.mhhe.com

About the Authors of *Basic Marketing, 15/e*

William D. Perreault, Jr.
is currently Kenan Professor at the University of North Carolina Kenan-Flagler Business School. He has also taught at Stanford University, the University of Georgia, and North Carolina State University and has been an invited speaker at over 80 universities. During 1997 he was the Arthur Andersen Distinguished Visitor at Cambridge University.

Dr. Perreault is the recipient of the two most prestigious awards in his field: the American Marketing Association Distinguished Educator Award and the Academy of Marketing Science Outstanding Educator Award. He also was selected for the Churchill Award, which honors career impact on marketing research. He was editor of the *Journal of Marketing Research* and has been on the review board of the *Journal of Marketing* and other journals. His research has also been published in many journals, and one *Journal of Marketing* article was recently voted one of the most influential articles on sales and sales management of the twentieth century.

The Decision Sciences Institute has recognized Dr. Perreault for innovations in marketing education, and at UNC he has received several awards for teaching excellence. His books include two other widely used texts: *Essentials of Marketing* and *The Marketing Game!*

Dr. Perreault is a past president of the American Marketing Association Academic Council and twice served on the AMA board. He was chair of an advisory committee to the U.S. Bureau of the Census, a trustee of the Marketing Science Institute, and on the Council of the Decision Sciences Institute. He is a Fellow of the Society for Marketing Advances. He has also worked as a consultant to organizations that range from GE and IBM to the Federal Trade Commission and Venezuelan Ministry of Education. He is on the advisory board for Copernicus: The Marketing Investment Strategy Group.

E. Jerome McCarthy
received his Ph.D. from the University of Minnesota. He has taught at the Universities of Oregon, Notre Dame, and Michigan State. He was honored with the American Marketing Association's Trailblazer Award in 1987, and he was voted one of the "top five" leaders in Marketing Thought by marketing educators.

He has been deeply involved in teaching and developing new teaching materials. Besides writing various articles and monographs, he is the author of textbooks on data processing and social issues in marketing.

Dr. McCarthy is active in making presentations to business meetings and academic conferences. He has worked with groups of teachers throughout the country and has addressed international conferences in South America, Africa, and India.

He was also a Ford Foundation Fellow in 1963–64, studying the role of marketing in global economic development. In 1959–60 he was a Ford Foundation Fellow at the Harvard Business School working on mathematical methods in marketing.

Besides his academic interests, Dr. McCarthy has been involved in consulting for, and guiding the growth of, a number of businesses—both in the U.S. and overseas. He has worked with top managers from Steelcase, Dow Chemical, 3M, Bemis, Grupo Industrial Alfa, and many other companies. He has also been active in executive education and is a director of several organizations. However, throughout his career his primary interests have been in (1) "converting" students to marketing and effective marketing strategy planning and (2) preparing teaching materials to help others do the same. This is why he has spent a large part of his career developing, revising, and improving marketing texts to reflect the most current thinking in the field.

Preface

Basic Marketing Is Designed to Satisfy Your Needs

This book is about marketing and marketing strategy planning. And, at its essence, marketing strategy planning is about figuring out how to do a superior job of satisfying customers. We take that point of view seriously and believe in practicing what we preach. So you can trust that this new edition of *Basic Marketing*—and all of the other teaching and learning materials that accompany it—will satisfy *your* needs. We're excited about this 15th edition of *Basic Marketing*, and we hope that you will be as well.

In developing this edition we've made hundreds of big and small additions, changes, and improvements in the text and all of the supporting materials that accompany it. We'll highlight some of those changes in this preface, but first it's useful to put this newest edition in a longer-term perspective.

Building on Pioneering Strengths

Basic Marketing pioneered an innovative structure—using the "four Ps" with a managerial approach—for the introductory marketing course. It quickly became one of the most widely used business textbooks ever published because it organized the best ideas about marketing so that readers could both understand and apply them. The unifying focus of these ideas was on how to make the marketing decisions that a manager must make in deciding what customers to focus on and how best to meet their needs.

Over many editions of *Basic Marketing* there has been constant change in marketing management and the marketing environment. Some of the changes have been dramatic, and others have been subtle. As a result, we have made ongoing changes to the text to reflect marketing's best practices and ideas. Throughout all of these changes, *Basic Marketing* and the supporting materials that accompany it have been more widely used than any other teaching materials for introductory marketing. It is gratifying that the four Ps has proved to be an organizing structure that has worked well for millions of students and teachers.

Continuous Innovation and Improvement

The success of *Basic Marketing* is not the result of a single strength—or one long-lasting innovation. Rather, the text's four Ps framework, managerial orientation, and strategy planning focus have proved to be foundation pillars that are remarkably robust for supporting new developments in the field and innovations in the text and package. Thus, with each new edition of *Basic Marketing* we have continued to innovate to better meet the needs of students and faculty. In fact, we have made ongoing changes in how we develop the logic of the four Ps and the marketing strategy planning process. As always, though, our objective is to provide a flexible, high-quality text and choices from comprehensive and reliable support materials—so that instructors and students can accomplish their learning objectives. For example, included with the other innovations and improvements for this new edition are

- Our *Motivated Learner Package,* a completely new concept for student learning—whether in distance learning or traditional environments—which includes a four-DVD set with an interesting video lecture on each chapter of the text as well as all of the *Basic Marketing* videos.

- Extensive revisions to the first three chapters, to introduce marketing orientation and customer value earlier and to introduce the marketing strategy planning process in the context of an integrative model that sets the stage for the rest of the text.

- Leaner, crisper, coverage throughout the whole text—resulting in 10 percent less text material for students to read while maintaining interesting and thorough coverage of all of the basics of marketing strategy planning.

- A new integrated treatment of macro-marketing topics and social issues with relevant marketing management topics throughout the text.

- A complete revision of the *Student CD to Accompany Basic Marketing* that comes with the text, with a new interface that integrates the rich variety of multimedia learning resources it includes.

- An updated and expanded archive of PowerPoint electronic lecture-support slides, with links to full-motion videos, ads, and photos, to provide instructors with flexible support for lectures and presentations.

- The *Instructor CD to Accompany Basic Marketing* that offers all of the text's teaching support materials in easy-to-use and electronic form and that features a refined new user interface to make it even faster to access materials.

- A sharper focus, throughout the text, on how the strategy planning process should lead to decisions about a target market and marketing mix that represents the best opportunity and competitive advantage for the firm and superior value for consumers.
- Interesting new video cases and teaching videos focused on current marketing issues.
- High-involvement Internet exercises integrated throughout each chapter of the text.

We Believe in Continuous Quality Improvement

As authors, we're committed to ongoing improvements—and we're both proud that we were implementing continuous quality improvements in preparing *Basic Marketing* long before the idea became popular in the world of business. We work to be creative in our coverage and approaches—because creativity is at the heart of the marketing spirit. The most creative teaching innovations are ones that meet students' needs and instructors' objectives. That's also why our first priority has always been, and always will be, producing quality materials that really work well for students and teachers. Students take the first marketing course only once. It is an investment and opportunity from which there should be a solid return. So we take it as a serious personal responsibility to support that investment with materials that are interesting and motivating—and that really build the skills and ideas that students need in their lives and careers.

Our belief that attention to continuous quality improvement in every aspect of the text and support materials *does make a difference* is consistently reaffirmed by the enthusiastic response of students and teachers alike to each new edition.

Leading Technology Innovations for Teaching and Learning

We take seriously our opportunity and responsibility to lead the marketing discipline in developing new, breakthrough approaches for teaching and learning in the first marketing course. Our thrust over the past two decades has been to use technology to provide better and easier options for teaching and richer and more interesting approaches for learning. Along with other innovations, we were the first to develop and offer spreadsheet-based computer-aided problems, custom-produced videos, a computerized test bank, a PC-based marketing simula-

tion, a hypertext reference, CD-based interactive versions of the text, PowerPoint presentation slides with linking by objectives, CD multimedia archives and presentation software for instructors, multimedia case support, and the multimedia CD for students. With this edition we continue these traditions of innovation with a redesigned *Student CD to Accompany Basic Marketing*, *myPowerWeb* online readings, an even easier-to-use and more comprehensive *Instructor CD to Accompany Basic Marketing*, the *Motivated Learner Package* (with lectures and videos on DVDs), and a host of new and improved teaching and learning materials available at the *Basic Marketing* website at www.mhhe.com/fourps.

Critically Revised, Updated, and Rewritten

This new edition of *Basic Marketing* is the highest-quality teaching and learning resource ever published for the introductory marketing course. The whole text and all of the supporting materials have been critically revised, updated, and rewritten. As in past editions, clear and interesting communication has been a priority. *Basic Marketing* is designed to make it easy, interesting, and fast for students to grasp the key concepts of marketing. Careful explanations provide a crisp focus on the important "basics" of marketing strategy planning. At the same time, we have thoroughly

- Researched and incorporated new concepts.
- Integrated hundreds of new examples that bring the concepts alive.
- Illustrated marketing ideas and "best practices" in a rich variety of contexts.

We have deliberately used marketing examples from a host of different contexts. Examples span large and small firms, profit and nonprofit organizations, organizations that have moved to e-commerce and those that have found other ways to innovate, domestic and international settings, purchases by organizations as well as by final consumers, services and ideas or "causes" as well as physical goods, and established products as well as new technologies—because this variety reinforces the point that effective marketing is critical to all organizations.

Clear Focus on Changes in Today's Dynamic Markets

This edition focuses special attention on changes taking place in today's dynamic markets. Throughout every chapter of the text we have integrated discussion and examples of

- Lifetime customer value and customer equity.
- Best practices in marketing, and how to avoid the mistakes of death-wish marketing (including

errors and omissions all too common among many failed dot-com operators).

- Effective e-commerce innovations and changes in marketing over the Internet.
- The costs and benefits of different approaches for customer acquisition and retention.
- Relationship building in marketing.
- Social impacts of marketing and macro-marketing.
- The importance of providing superior customer value as the means to achieve customer satisfaction and competitive advantage.
- International perspectives.
- Ethical issues and social impacts of marketing.

Similarly, we've also integrated new material on many important and fast-evolving topics. The following are but a sampling:

- Multichannel marketing.
- Integrated marketing communications, direct-response promotion, and customer-initiated interactive marketing communications.
- Promotional campaigns that build "buzz" among consumers.
- Impact of economic fluctuations, changes in international exchange rates, and other topics central to how the economy impacts marketing.
- The growth of business-to-business (B2B) exchanges on the Web and the expanding use of reverse auctions and interactive bidding.
- The circumstances when using a website for direct distribution or dual distribution makes sense and when it doesn't.
- The expanding role of sales technologies and self-service technology.
- The increasing channel power of large retail chains.
- Competitor analysis and how to develop competitive advantage.
- How to use flexible pricing and evaluate price sensitivity.
- Marketing control, including marketing cost analysis.

Driving Home Competitive Advantage

Throughout the 15th edition we've continued to put more emphasis on the *process* of marketing strategy planning. In today's dynamic markets it's not enough to simply figure out an attractive opportunity and an effective marketing mix. The real challenge is to quickly but logically zero in on the target market and marketing mix that is really best for the firm, while recognizing that strategies need to be refined and improved as market conditions change.

This highlights the need for breakthrough opportunities, the problems with me-too imitation, and the crucial role of competitive advantage in providing customers with superior value. In other words, we sharpen the focus on how to figure out the best blend of the four Ps and crush the mistaken view fostered by some texts that the marketing job is just coming up with *some* marketing mix.

Coupled with this, you'll learn how breakthroughs in information technology are driving changes in all aspects of marketing—whether it's e-commerce ordering, getting marketing information, preparing salespeople to interact with customers, or analyzing the "fire-hydrant" flow of data on sales and costs. We'll also highlight the many ways that relationships among marketing partners are changing—ranging from coordination of logistics to alliances among firms focused on the same market opportunity. You'll see how intense competition, both in the United States and around the world, is affecting marketing strategy planning. You'll see what it takes to transform an effective new-product development process into a profitable business.

Some other marketing texts are attempting to describe such changes. But that's not adequate. What sets *Basic Marketing* apart is that the explanations and examples equip students to see *why* these changes are taking place and what changes to expect in the future. That is an important distinction—because marketing is dynamic. Our objective is to prepare students to analyze marketing situations and develop exceptional marketing strategies—not just recite endless sets of lists.

A Fresh Design—to Make Important Concepts Even Clearer

Along with the new content, we've given the text a fresh design. The changes range from the new cover to hundreds of new photographs, ads, web pages, and illustrations. We've created many new exhibits—conceptual organizers, charts, and tables—and updated proven pieces from past editions, all with a fresh new design.

The aim of all this revising, refining, editing, and illustrating is to make important concepts and points even clearer to students. We want to make sure that each student really does get a good feel for a market-directed system and how he or she can help it—and some company—run better. We believe marketing is important and interesting—and we want every student who reads *Basic Marketing* to share our enthusiasm.

Twenty-Two Chapters—with an Emphasis on Marketing Strategy Planning

The emphasis of *Basic Marketing* is on marketing strategy planning. Twenty-two chapters introduce the important concepts in marketing management and help the student see marketing through the eyes of the marketing manager. The organization of the chapters and topics is carefully planned. But we took special care in writing so that

- It is possible to rearrange and use the chapters in many different sequences—to fit different needs.
- All of the topics and chapters fit together into a clear, overall framework for the marketing strategy planning process.

Broadly speaking, the chapters fall into two groupings. The first eight chapters introduce marketing and a broad view of the marketing strategy planning process. They cover topics such as segmentation, differentiation, the marketing environment, and buyer behavior, as well as how marketing information systems and research provide information about these forces to improve marketing decisions. The second half of the text goes into the details of planning the four Ps, with specific attention to the key strategy decisions in each area. Then we conclude with an integrative review and coverage of overarching topics such as implementation and control, marketing's link with other functional areas, and an assessment of marketing's challenges and opportunities.

The first chapter deals with the important role of marketing—focusing not only on how a marketing orientation guides a business or nonprofit organization in the process of providing superior value to customers but also on the role of macro-marketing and how a market-directed economy shapes choices and quality of life for consumers. Chapter 2 builds on these ideas with a focus on the marketing strategy planning process and why it involves narrowing down to selection of a specific target market and blending the four Ps into a marketing mix to meet the needs of those customers. With that foundation in place, the chapter introduces an integrative model of the marketing strategy planning process that serves as an organizing framework for the rest of the text.

Chapter 3 shows how analysis of the market and external market environment relate to segmentation and differentiation decisions as well as the criteria for narrowing down to a specific target market and marketing mix. This strategic view alerts students to the importance of evaluating opportunities in the external environments affecting marketing—and these are discussed in Chapter 4. This chapter also highlights the critical role of screening criteria for narrowing down from possible opportunities to those that the firm will pursue.

You have to understand customers to understand marketing and segment markets and satisfy target market needs. So the next three chapters take a closer look at customers. Chapter 5 introduces the demographic dimensions of the global consumer market and provides up-to-date coverage on important geodemographic trends. The next chapter studies the behavioral aspects of the final consumer market. Chapter 7 looks at how business and organizational customers—like manufacturers, channel members, and government purchasers—are using e-commerce and how they are similar to and different from final consumers.

Chapter 8 is a contemporary view of getting information—from marketing information systems and marketing research—for marketing management planning. This chapter includes discussion of how information technology—ranging from intranets to speedy collection of market research data—is transforming the marketing manager's job. This sets the stage for discussions in later chapters about how research and marketing information improve each area of marketing strategy planning.

The next group of chapters—Chapters 9 to 18—is concerned with developing a marketing mix out of the four Ps: Product, Place (involving channels of distribution, logistics, and distribution customer service), Promotion, and Price. These chapters are concerned with developing the "right" Product and making it available at the "right" Place with the "right" Promotion and the "right" Price—to satisfy target customers and still meet the objectives of the business. These chapters are presented in an integrated, analytical way—as part of the overall framework for the marketing strategy planning process—so students' thinking about planning marketing strategies develops logically.

Chapters 9 and 10 focus on product planning for goods and services as well as new-product development and the different strategy decisions that are required at different stages of the product life cycle. We emphasize the value of an organized new-product development process for developing really new products that propel a firm to profitable growth.

Chapters 11 through 13 focus on Place. Chapter 11 introduces decisions a manager must make about using direct distribution (for example, selling from the firm's own website) or working with other firms in a channel of distribution. We put special emphasis on the need for channel members to cooperate and coordinate to better meet the needs of customers. Chapter 12 focuses on the fast-changing arena of logistics and the strides that firms are making in using e-commerce to reduce the costs of storing, transporting, and handling products while improving the distribution service they provide customers. Chapter 13 provides a clear picture of retailers, wholesalers, and their strategy planning, including exchanges taking place via the Internet. This composite chapter helps students see why the big changes taking place in retailing are reshaping the channel systems for many consumer products.

Chapters 14 to 16 deal with Promotion. These chapters build on the concepts of integrated marketing communications, direct-response promotion, and customer-initiated digital communication, which are introduced in Chapter 14. Chapter 15 deals with the role of personal selling and sales technology in the promotion blend. Chapter 16 covers advertising and sales promotion, including the ways that managers are taking advantage of the Internet and other highly targeted media to communicate more effectively and efficiently.

Chapters 17 and 18 deal with Price. Chapter 17 focuses on pricing objectives and policies, including use of information technology to implement flexible pricing, pricing in the channel, and the use of discounts, allowances, and other variations from a list price. Chapter 18 covers cost-oriented and demand-oriented pricing approaches and how they fit in today's competitive environments. The careful coverage of marketing costs helps equip students to deal with the renewed cost-consciousness of the firms they will join.

Chapter 19 offers completely updated coverage of how information technology is reshaping marketing implementation and control. This chapter also details how quality management approaches can improve implementation, including implementation of better customer service.

Chapter 20 deals with the links between marketing and other functional areas. The marketing concept says that people in an organization should work together to satisfy customers at a profit. No other text has a chapter that explains how to accomplish the "working together" part of that idea. Yet it's increasingly important in the business world today; so that's what this important chapter is designed to do.

Chapter 21 reinforces the integrative nature of marketing management and reviews the marketing strategy planning process that leads to creative marketing plans and programs.

The final chapter considers how efficient the marketing process is. Here we evaluate the effectiveness of both micro- and macro-marketing—and we consider the competitive, technological, ethical, and social challenges facing marketing managers now and in the future. After this chapter, many students want to look at Appendix C—which is about career opportunities in marketing.

Careful Integration of Special Topics

Some textbooks treat "special" topics—like e-commerce, relationship marketing, international marketing, services marketing, marketing over the Internet, marketing for nonprofit organizations, marketing ethics, social issues, and business-to-business marketing—in separate chapters. We deliberatively avoid doing that because we are convinced that treating such topics separately leads to an unfortunate compartmentalization of ideas. We think they are too important to be isolated in

that way. For example, to simply tack on a new chapter on e-commerce or marketing applications on the Internet completely ignores the reality that these are not just isolated topics but rather must be considered broadly across the whole fabric of marketing decisions. In fact, the huge losses piled up by the collapse of thousands of dot-com firms a few years ago are evidence of what happens when managers fail to understand the need to integrate marketing strategy planning decisions and don't come to grips with issues such as competitor analysis, customer value, and the marketing concept. Conversely, there is virtually no area of marketing decision making where it's safe to ignore the impact of e-commerce, the Internet, or information technology. The same is true with other topics. So they are interwoven and illustrated throughout the text to emphasize that marketing thinking is crucial in all aspects of our society and economy. This edition is again packaged with a grid that shows, in detail, how and where specific topics are integrated throughout the text. Talk is cheap, especially when it comes to the hype from some publishers about how important topics are treated in a new text. But the grid offers proof that in *Basic Marketing* we have delivered on the promise of integrated treatment.

Students Get "How-to-Do-It" Skill and Confidence

Really understanding marketing and how to plan marketing strategies can build self-confidence—and it can help prepare a student to take an active part in the business world. To move students in this direction, we deliberately include a variety of frameworks, models, classification systems, cases, and "how-to-do-it" techniques that relate to our overall framework for marketing strategy planning. Taken together, they should speed the development of "marketing sense" and enable the student to analyze marketing situations and develop marketing plans in a confident and meaningful way. They are practical and they work. In addition, because they are interesting and understandable, they motivate students to see marketing as the challenging and rewarding area it is.

Basic Marketing Motivates High-Involvement Learning

So students will see what is coming in each *Basic Marketing* chapter, behavioral objectives are included on the first page of each chapter. And to speed student understanding, important new terms are shown in red and defined immediately. Further, a glossary of these terms is presented at the end of the book. Within chapters, major section headings and second-level headings (placed in the margin for clarity) immediately show how the material is organized *and* summarize key points in the text. Further, we have placed annotated photos and ads near the concepts they illustrate to provide a visual reminder of the ideas and to show vividly how they apply in the current business world. In each chapter we have integrated Internet exercises related to the concepts being developed. The focus of these exercises is on important marketing issues, not just on "surfing the Net."

All of these aids help the student understand important concepts and speed review before exams. End-of-chapter questions and problems offer additional opportunities. They can be used to encourage students to investigate the marketing process and develop their own ways of thinking about it. They can be used for independent study or as a basis for written assignments or class discussion.

Varied Types of Cases

Understanding of the text material can be deepened by analysis and discussion of specific cases. *Basic Marketing* features several different types of cases. Each chapter starts with an in-depth case study developed specifically to highlight that chapter's teaching objectives and the specific marketing decision areas covered in that chapter. Students are encouraged to reread the chapter-opening case after finishing the chapter—when they have a deeper understanding of the issues involved. In addition, each chapter features a special case report in a highlighted box. These thought-provoking cases illustrate how companies handle topics covered in that chapter. All of these cases provide an excellent basis for critical evaluation and discussion. And we've included relevant Internet addresses so that it is easy for students to quickly get updated information about the companies and topics covered in the cases. Of course, website addresses referenced in the cases may change. Some companies change their websites to get a fresh look, to take advantage of new Web capabilities, or just to update the information that's available. However, when that occurs, our *Basic Marketing* website at www.mhhe.com/fourps provides up-to-date links relevant to the chapters in the text. Our CDs also include links to the website so you can bookmark the site in your Internet browser.

In addition, there are several suggested cases at the end of each chapter. These suggested cases have been selected from the set of 35 cases that appear at the end of the book. The focus of these cases is on problem solving. They encourage students to apply, and really get involved with, the concepts developed in the text.

Each of the first 19 chapters also features a computer-aided problem. These case-based exercises stimulate a problem-solving approach to marketing strategy planning and give students hands-on experience that shows how logical analysis of alternative strategies can lead to improved decision making. For the convenience of students and faculty alike, printed versions of the cases for the computer-aided problems are incorporated in the book itself. Further, the award-winning spreadsheet software we developed specifically for use with these problems has been revised so that it is fully integrated with the other applications on the *Student CD* that comes with the text. With this edition a feature has been added in the software so that students can type their responses to questions on screen while viewing the computer spreadsheet—and then print both the comment and spreadsheet on one page.

New Multimedia Video Cases Are Integrative

In recent editions we've included a custom-produced set of exciting video cases. The response to them has been great, and this time we've expanded the set and updated some of the best from the previous set. Each of these combines a written case with an accompanying video. These 7 cases are a bit longer than the 35 text-only cases and open up the opportunity for students to analyze an organization's whole marketing program in more depth and with even greater integration. Marketing professors wrote the scripts for both the videos and text portions of the cases—so the videos reinforce real content while bringing a high-involvement multimedia dimension to the learning experience. And to assure consistency with all of the other *Basic Marketing* materials, we've carefully edited and coordinated the whole effort. These cases were developed so that they focus on different areas of the text, and thus they deal with a variety of issues:

- How a well-known company won profits and customer loyalty by developing a marketing mix that's carefully matched to the needs of its target market.
- New-product development for a major component part that is sold to producers who serve consumer markets.
- Shopping behavior and marketing strategy issues involved with a regional shopping mall.
- The growth strategy for a vineyard that is working to develop a major brand.
- The development of a new market awareness and strategy by a major nonprofit organization.
- A case on the promotional program for the introduction of an exciting new automobile.
- An integrated case on the marketing strategy for an innovative household appliance.

We designed these cases so that students can analyze them before or after seeing the video, or even without seeing the video at all. They can be used in a variety of ways, either for class discussion or individual assignments. To get the ball rolling, students can see clips from the video segments for the cases on their own *Student CD*. We're proud of these video cases, and we're sure that they will provide you with a valuable new way to learn about marketing.

Comprehensive, Current References for Independent Study

Some professors and students want to follow up on text readings. Each chapter is supplemented with detailed references—to both classic articles and current readings in business publications. These can guide more detailed study of the topics covered in a chapter.

Instructor Creates a System—with *Basic Marketing's P.L.U.S.*

Basic Marketing can be studied and used in many ways—the *Basic Marketing* text material is only the central component of our *Professional Learning Units Systems* (our *P.L.U.S.*) for students and teachers. Instructors (and students) can select from our units to develop their own personalized systems. Many combinations of units are possible, depending on course objectives. As a quick overview, in addition to the *Basic Marketing* text, the *P.L.U.S.* package includes a variety of new and updated supplements:

- A redesigned and updated *Student CD to Accompany Basic Marketing*, which includes clips for the video cases, a database of ads and annotations that illustrate key concepts for each chapter, a new version of our computer-aided problems (CAP) spreadsheet software, self-test quizzes (with two levels of questions), and narrated self-study PowerPoint electronic slide shows, to introduce students to what's ahead. The CD also includes a new edition of the *Basic Marketing Hypertext Reference* for use in developing marketing plans or reviewing for tests.

- An online learning center at our revised website (www.mhhe.com/fourps) for students and instructors, with features such as (constantly updated) links to just-published articles from myPowerWeb on topics in each chapter, chat rooms, software downloads, Internet website links, and other exciting features.

- A new and updated set of Interactive PowerPoint lecture slides, incorporating full-motion video clips, photos, ads, and interactive exercises to support the professor.

- An improved *Instructor CD to Accompany Basic Marketing*, which includes all of the instructor resources available for *Basic Marketing* in electronic form and a redesigned interface that makes it even easier to access the specific items the instructor wants to use.

In addition, we've completely revised and updated

- The *Multimedia Lecture Support Package*.
- The *Learning Aid* workbook.
- *Applications in Basic Marketing*, an annually updated book of marketing clippings from the popular press, free and shrinkwrapped with the text and, new to this edition, supplemented with myPowerWeb digital articles on the Web.
- Over 220 color acetates (also available as PowerPoint slides).
- Over 200 transparency masters (also available as PowerPoint slides).
- *Instructor's Manual*.
- Author-prepared *Manual of Tests*, accompanied by the *Diploma* test-generator software that supports both printed and online testing.
- A complete set of new and updated *teaching videos* and eight great video cases (all supported with a specially prepared *Instructor's Manual* to Accompany the Teaching Videos).
- A Windows version of *The Marketing Game!* (and instructor's manual) that offers password-protected digital plan and report files and supports working over the Internet.
- The totally new four-DVD set of video lectures (one per chapter) and videos that are the heart of the new *Basic Marketing Motivated Learner Package*.

We've been busy. You may not want to use all of this. Some people don't want any of it. But whatever you elect to use—and in whatever medium you like to work—the teaching and learning materials work well together. We've designed them that way.

Hypertext—a Marketing Knowledge Navigator

We introduced the innovative *Basic Marketing Hypertext Reference* with the 11th edition of *Basic Marketing* and have expanded its capabilities ever since. This easy-to-use Windows software puts almost all of the key concepts from *Basic Marketing* at your fingertips. It features hyperlinks, which means that when you are reading about a concept on screen you can instantly jump to more detail on that topic. You simply highlight the concept or topic and click with a mouse or press the enter key. Books assemble information in some specific order—but hypertext allows you to integrate thinking on any topic or combination of topics, regardless of where it is treated in the text.

The new version of the software provides an even clearer and easier way to search for ideas while developing a marketing plan. You can also use the software to review topics in "book order"—starting with learning objectives and then "paging" through each set of ideas. And when you're using *Hypertext* to help prepare ideas for a case study or marketing plan you can "bookmark" pages with key ideas and even add your own comments and annotations for later reference.

Free Applications Book—Updated Each Year

It is a sign of the commitment of our publisher to the introductory marketing course that it will publish a new edition of *Applications in Basic Marketing* every year and provide it free of charge shrinkwrapped with each new copy of the 15th edition of *Basic Marketing*. This annually updated collection of marketing "clippings"—from publications such as *The New York Times, Business Week, The Wall Street Journal, Advertising Age,* and *Fortune*—provides convenient access to short, interesting, and current discussions of marketing issues. Each edition features about 100 articles. There are a variety of short clippings related to each chapter in *Basic Marketing*. In addition, because we revise this collection each year, it includes timely material that is available in no other text.

Learning Aid—Deepens Understanding

There are more components to *P.L.U.S.* A separate *Learning Aid* provides several more units and offers further opportunities to obtain a deeper understanding of the material. The *Learning Aid* can be used by the student alone or with teacher direction. Portions of the *Learning Aid* help students to review what they have studied. For example, there is a brief introduction to each chapter, a list of the important new terms (with page numbers for easy reference), true-false questions (with answers and page numbers) that cover all the important terms and concepts, and multiple-choice questions (with answers) that illustrate the kinds of questions that may appear in examinations. In addition, the *Learning Aid* has cases, exercises, and problems—with clear instructions and worksheets for the student to complete. The *Learning Aid* also features computer-aided problems that build on the computer-aided cases in the text. The *Learning Aid* exercises can be used as classwork or homework—to drill on certain topics and to deepen understanding of others by motivating application and then discussion. In fact, reading *Basic Marketing* and working with the *Learning Aid* can be the basic activity of the course.

Compete and Learn—with *The Marketing Game!*, 3rd Edition

Another valuable resource is *The Marketing Game!*, a PC-based competitive simulation. It was developed specifically to reinforce the target marketing and marketing strategy planning ideas discussed in *Basic Marketing*. Students make marketing management decisions—blending the four Ps to compete for the business of different possible target markets. The innovative design of *The Marketing Game!* allows the instructor to increase the number of decision areas involved as students learn more about marketing. In fact, many instructors use the advanced levels of the game as the basis for a second course. *The Marketing Game!* is widely heralded as the best marketing strategy simulation available—and the new Windows edition widens its lead over the others available. Competitors don't even need to be on the same continent. It works great with password-protected decisions submitted over the Internet and reports returned the same way.

Multimedia Support for Preparation, Lectures, and Discussion

Basic Marketing and all of our accompanying materials have been developed to promote student learning and get students involved in the excitement and challenges of marketing management. Additional elements of *P.L.U.S.* have been specifically developed to help an instructor offer a truly professional course that meets the objectives he or she sets for students. Complete instructor's manuals accompany all of the *P.L.U.S.* components.

Electronic Presentation Slides with Many Uses

Basic Marketing is supported with a large variety of high-quality PowerPoint electronic slide presentations. This flexible package features a large number of PowerPoint graphics developed for every chapter in the text. An instructor can use the provided software to display the electronic slides with a computer-controlled video projector, in the order that they're provided or branching in whatever sequence is desired. Presentations can be based on composite slides, or the points on a slide can "build up" one point at a time.

Because we provide the native-format PowerPoint files, instructors can modify or delete any slide or add other slides by using their own copy of PowerPoint. And, of course, if electronic projection equipment isn't available, the instructor can print out the images to customized color acetates or black and white transparencies. All of the overhead masters are also available, in color, as PowerPoint slides.

While these slides are intended mainly for instructor use in class discussions and lectures, they are easy to use and can be placed on the Internet, on the school's computer network, or in a computer lab as a supplement for independent review by students. For distance education applications, narrated slide shows are available.

Complete Multimedia Lecture Support

With the PowerPoint electronic slide presentations we also provide detailed lecture notes, as well as lecture outlines. The PowerPoint slide show includes small versions of the slides for class handouts. All of these materials are packaged in our *Multimedia Lecture Support Package*. This supplement is also available in an electronic form on the *Instructor CD*, and that makes it even more convenient to use. It gives instructors a great deal of flexibility and saves time that can be spent on other teaching activities. Instructors who prefer to use materials like those that were in the past included with our *Lecture Guide* won't be disappointed either. The new package will provide that material as well—in both printed form and in the form of word-processing files (which makes it easier for instructors to electronically cut and paste and incorporate their own materials or to save time and effort in creating a website for the course).

In addition, the *Multimedia Lecture Support Package* is accompanied by a high-quality selection of overhead masters and color transparencies—over 420 in all. The manual provides detailed suggestions about ways to use them. All of these items are also available on the CD.

Exciting New Videos—Created by Marketing Experts

The newly revised and expanded *Basic Marketing Videos* are also available to all schools that adopt *Basic Marketing*. Half of the teaching videos are completely new—based on scripts written by expert marketing scholars and carefully linked to key topics in the text. In addition, several of the most popular video modules from the previous edition—the ones instructors and students said they most wanted to keep—have been thoroughly revised and updated. These new videos are really great, but it doesn't stop there! As we noted earlier, there are also seven great new videos to accompany the video cases. New with this edition, all of the videos are available on DVD as part of the *Motivated Learner Package* for independent student study.

Testing that Works for Faculty and Students

In addition, thousands of objective test questions— *written by the authors* to really work with the text—give instructors a high-quality resource. The *Diploma* program for Windows computers allows the instructor to select from any of these questions, change them as desired, or add new questions—and quickly print out a finished test customized to the instructor's course. As an added benefit, the instructor can publish questions to a website and students can take tests online.

The Responsibilities of Leadership

In closing, we return to a point raised at the beginning of this preface. *Basic Marketing* has been a leading textbook in marketing since its first edition. We take the responsibilities of that leadership seriously. We know that you want and deserve the very best teaching and learning materials possible. It is our commitment to bring you those materials—today with this edition and in the future with subsequent editions.

We recognize that fulfilling this commitment requires a process of continuous improvement. Improvements, changes, and development of new elements must be ongoing—because needs change. You are an important part of this evolution, of this leadership. We encourage your feedback. The most efficient way to get in touch with us is to send an e-mail message to Bill_Perreault@unc.edu. There's also a comment form built into the book's website, and if you prefer the traditional approach, send a letter to 2104 N. Lakeshore Dr., Chapel Hill, NC, 27514. Thoughtful criticisms and suggestions from students and teachers alike have helped to make *Basic Marketing* what it is. We hope that you will help make it what it will be in the future.

William D. Perreault, Jr.

E. Jerome McCarthy

Walkthrough

BASIC MARKETING HELPS YOU LEARN ABOUT MARKETING AND MARKETING STRATEGY PLANNING.

At its essence, marketing strategy planning is about figuring out how to do a superior job of satisfying customers. With that in mind, the 15th Edition of *Basic Marketing* was developed to satisfy your desire for knowledge and add value to your course experience. Not only will this text teach you about marketing and marketing strategy planning, but its design, pedagogy, and supplementary learning aids were developed to work well with the text and a variety of study situations.

Each person has a different approach to studying. Some may focus on reading that is covered during class, others prefer to prepare outside of the classroom and rely heavily on in-class interaction, and still others prefer more independence from the classroom. Some are more visual or more "hands on" in the way they learn and others just want clear and interesting explanations. To address a variety of needs and course situations, many hours went into creating the materials highlighted in this section. When used in combination with the text, these tools will elevate your understanding of marketing.

Take a moment now to learn more about all of the resources available to help you best prepare for this course—and for your future career.

BASIC MARKETING: AN INNOVATIVE MARKETING EXPERIENCE.

With twenty-two chapters that introduce the important concepts in marketing management, you will see all aspects of marketing through the eyes of the marketing manager. The first eight chapters introduce marketing and give you a framework for understanding marketing strategy planning in any type of organization, and then the second half of the text takes you into planning the four Ps of marketing (Product, Place, Promotion, and Price) with specific attention to the key strategy decisions in each area.

Basic Marketing pioneered the "four Ps" approach to organize and describe managerial marketing for introductory marketing courses. This new edition covers the dynamic changes taking place in marketing management and the marketing environment. Some of these changes have been dramatic, and others have been subtle. But the 15th Edition helps you understand the changes taking place and reflects today's best marketing practices and ideas.

Each chapter begins with a list of learning objectives that will help you understand and identify important terms and concepts covered in the chapter, and then provides an in-depth case study, developed specifically to motivate your interest and highlight real-life examples of the learning objectives and specific marketing decision areas covered in that chapter.

McDonald's pursues growth in a variety of ways including new product development efforts, like its Grilled Chicken Flatbread sandwich and McGriddles breakfast sandwich, to offer customers more reasons to eat at McDonald's.

Full-color photos and current ads are carefully placed in every chapter and annotated—to provide a visual emphasis on key concepts and ideas discussed in the text. These illustrations vividly show how companies apply marketing concepts in the modern business world.

INTERNATIONAL OPPORTUNITIES SHOULD BE CONSIDERED

It's easy for a marketing manager to fall into the trap of ignoring international markets, especially when the firm's domestic m[...] reasons to go to the trouble of looking elsewh[...]

The world is getting smaller

International trade is increasing all around [...] ing down. In addition, advances in e-comme[...] tions are making it easier and cheaper to re[...]

A variety of interesting exhibits— "conceptual organizers," charts, and tables—illustrate each chapter and focus your attention on key frameworks and ideas.

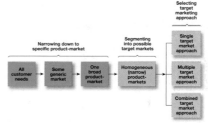

Exhibit 3-2
Narrowing Down to Target Markets

may be able to operate profitably. See Exhibit 3-2. No one firm can satisfy everyone's needs. So the naming—disaggregating—step involves brainstorming about very different solutions to various generic needs and selecting some broad areas—broad product-markets—where the firm has some resources and experience. This means that a car manufacturer would probably ignore all the possible opportunities in food and clothing markets and focus on the generic market, "transporting people in the world," and probably on the broad product-market, "cars, trucks, and utility vehicles for transporting people in the world."

Disaggregating, a practical rough-and-ready approach, tries to narrow down the marketing focus to product-market areas where the firm is more likely to have a competitive advantage or even to find breakthrough opportunities.

Market grid is a visual aid to market segmentation

Assuming that any broad product-market (or generic market) may consist of submarkets, picture a market as a rectangle with boxes that represent the smaller, more homogeneous product-markets.

Exhibit 3-3, for example, represents the broad product-market of bicycle riders. The boxes show different submarkets. One submarket might focus on people who want basic transportation, another on people who want exercise, and so on. Alternatively, in the generic "transporting market" discussed above, we might see different product-markets of customers for bicycles, motorcycles, cars, airplanes, ships, buses, and "others."

Segmenting is an aggregating process

Marketing-oriented managers think of **segmenting** as an aggregating process—clustering people with similar needs into a "market segment." A **market segment** is

Exhibit 3-3
A Market Grid Diagram with Submarkets

Broad product-market (or generic market) name goes here
(The bicycle-riders product-market)

| Submarket 1 (Exercisers) | Submarket 3 (Transportation riders) | Submarket 4 (Socializers) |
| Submarket 2 (Off-road adventurers) | Submarket 5 (Environmentalists) | |

66

problem. So she started SoapWorks and dev[...] products to pursue this opportunity. Unlike the big firms, she didn't have relations with grocery chains or money for national TV ads. To get around these weaknesses, she used inexpensive radio ads in local markets and touted SoapWorks as a company created for moms by a mom who cared about kids. She had a credible claim that the big corporations couldn't make. Her ads also helped her get shelf space because they urged other mothers to ask for SoapWorks products and to tell friends about stores that carried them. This wasn't the fastest possible way to introduce a new product line, but her cash-strapped strategy played to her unique strengths with her specific target market.[11]

INTERNET EXERCISE

Go to the SoapWorks website (www.soapworks.com) and click on the link for its store locator. Click your state on the map and see if there is a retailer in your area that carries SoapWorks products. Check several other states in different regions of the country. Why do you think that SoapWorks has distribution through retail stores in some states but not in others?

Internet exercises are integrated with the discussion of important ideas as they are developed to help you learn about marketing while you surf interesting websites.

Exhibit 2-10 focuses on planning each strategy carefully. Of course, this same approach works well when several strategies are to be planned. Then, having an organized evaluation process is even more important. It forces everyone involved to think through how the various strategies fit together as part of an overall marketing program.[12]

COLGATE BRUSHES UP ON MARKETING IN RURAL INDIA

Two-thirds of the people in India still live in rural farm areas. Many don't have life's basic comforts. For example, three out of four use wood as fuel to cook. Only about 40 percent have electricity, and less than 20 percent have piped water. Most can't afford a refrigerator. A person who works in the sugarcane fields, for example, only earns about $1 a day.

While these rural villagers do not have much money, there are about 1 *billion* of them. So they are an important potential market for basic products like toothpaste and shampoo. Marketing managers for Colgate know that. However, many rural Indians have never even held a tube of toothpaste. Rather, they clean their mouths with charcoal powder and the stem of a local plant. But Colgate can't rely on U.S.-style ads—or the local drugstore—to do the selling job. Half of the rural population can't read, and very few have a TV. They also don't go to stores. Rather, once a week the men go to a central market in a nearby village to get basic supplies they can't grow themselves.

In spite of these challenges, in the past decade Colgate has about doubled its sales—and rural Indians are now buying over 17,000 tons of toothpaste a year. What's the trick? Colgate sends a van that is equipped with a generator and video gear into a village on market day. Music attracts the shoppers, and then an entertaining half-hour video (infomercial) explains the benefits (including increased sex appeal!) of using Colgate toothpaste. The van reaches only about 100 people at a time, but many of those who see the video try the toothpaste. Of course, not many want to spend a day's wages to buy a standard tube. So Colgate offers a small (30 gram) tube for six rupees (about 18 cents). Colgate's approach is expensive, but managers in the firm are wisely thinking about the long-run return on the marketing investments.

Where did this idea come from? The video vans were first used in 1987 to spread propaganda for a political party that was denied airtime on state-run television. Between elections the vans were idle, so the owner decided to become a marketing specialist—and offered to rent the vans to firms like Colgate that wanted to reach rural consumers.[10]

So far, we have described how a market-directed macro-marketing system adjusts to become more effective and efficient by responding to customer needs. See Exhibit 1-3. As you read this book, you'll learn more about how marketing affects society and vice versa. You'll also learn more about specific marketing activities and be better informed when drawing conclusions about how fair and effective the macro-marketing system is. For now, however, we'll return to our general emphasis on micro-marketing and a managerial view of the role of marketing in individual organizations.

MARKETING'S ROLE HAS CHANGED A LOT OVER THE YEARS

It's clear that marketing decisions are very important to a firm's success. But marketing hasn't always been so complicated. In fact, understanding how marketing thinking has evolved makes the modern view clearer. So we will discuss five stages in marketing evolution: (1) the simple trade era, (2) the production era, (3) the sales era, (4) the marketing department era, and (5) the marketing company era. We'll talk about these eras as if they applied generally to all firms—but keep in mind that *some managers still have not made it to the final stages*. They are stuck in the past with old ways of thinking.

Specialization permitted trade—and middlemen met the need

When societies first moved toward some specialization of production and away from a subsistence economy where each family raised and consumed everything it produced, traders played an important role. Early "producers for the market" made products that were needed by themselves and their neighbors. As bartering became

15

Each chapter features a special case report in a highlighted box that illustrates how companies handle a topic of special interest covered in that chapter.

QUESTIONS AND PROBLEMS

1. List your activities for the first two hours after you woke up this morning. Briefly indicate how marketing affected your activities.

2. It is fairly easy to see why people do not beat a path to a mousetrap manufacturer's door, but would they be similarly indifferent if some food processor developed a revolutionary new food product that would provide all necessary nutrients in small pills for about $100 per year per person?

3. If a producer creates a really revolutionary new product and consumers can learn about it and purchase it at a website on the Internet, is any additional marketing effort really necessary? Explain your thinking.

4. Explain, in your own words, why this text emphasizes micro-marketing.

5. Distinguish between macro- and micro-marketing. Then explain how they are interrelated, if they are.

6. Refer to Exhibit 1-2, and give an example of a purchase you made recently that involved separation of information and separation in time between you and the producer. Briefly explain how these separations were overcome.

7. Describe a recent purchase you made. Indicate why that particular product was available at a store and, in particular, at the store where you bought it.

8. Define the functions of marketing in your own words. Using an example, explain how they can be shifted and shared.

9. Online computer shopping at websites on the Internet makes it possible for individual consumers to get direct information from hundreds of companies they would not otherwise know about. Consumers can place an order for a purchase that is then shipped to them directly. Will growth of these services ultimately eliminate the need for retailers and wholesalers? Explain your thinking, giving specific attention to what marketing functions are involved in these "electronic purchases" and who performs them.

10. Explain why a small producer might want a marketing research firm to take over some of its information-gathering activities.

11. Distinguish between how economic decisions are made in a planned economic system and how they are made in a market-directed economy.

12. Would the functions that must be provided and the development of wholesaling and retailing systems be any different in a planned economy from those in a market-directed economy?

13. Explain why a market-directed macro-marketing system encourages innovation. Give an example.

14. Define the marketing concept in your own words, and then explain why the notion of profit is usually included in this definition.

15. Define the marketing concept in your own words, and then suggest how acceptance of this concept might affect the organization and operation of your college.

16. Distinguish between production orientation and marketing orientation, illustrating with local examples.

17. Explain why a firm should view its internal activities as part of a total system. Illustrate your answer for (a) a large grocery products producer, (b) a plumbing wholesaler, (c) a department store chain, and (d) a cell phone service.

SUGGESTED CASES

COMPUTER-AIDED PROBLEM

3. Segmenting Customers

The marketing manager for Audiotronics Software Company is seeking new market opportunities. He is focusing on the voice recognition market and has narrowed down to three segments: the Fearful Typists, the Power Users, and the Professional Specialists. The Fearful Typists don't know much about computers—they just want a fast way to create e-mail messages, letters, and simple reports without errors. They don't need a lot of special features. They want simple instructions and a program that's easy to learn. The Power Users know a lot about computers, use them often, and want a voice recognition program with many special features. All computer programs seem easy to them—so they aren't worried about learning to use the various features. The Professional Specialists have jobs that require a lot of writing. They don't know much about computers but are willing to learn. They want special features needed for their work—but only if they aren't too hard to learn and use.

The marketing manager prepared a table summarizing the importance of each of three key needs in the three segments (see table below).

	Importance of Need (1 = not important; 10 = very important)		
Market Segment	Features	Easy to Use	Easy to Learn
Fearful typists	3	8	9
Power users	9	2	2
Professional specialists	7	5	6

Audiotronics' sales staff conducted interviews with seven potential customers who were asked to rate how important each of these three needs were in their work. The manager prepared a spreadsheet to help him cluster (aggregate) each person into one of the segments—along with other similar people. Each person's ratings are entered in the spreadsheet, and the clustering procedure computes a similarity score that indicates how similar (a low score) or dissimilar (a high score) the person is to the typical person in each of the segments. The manager can then "aggregate" potential customers into the segment that is most similar (that is, the one with the *lowest* similarity score).

a. The ratings for a potential customer appear on the first spreadsheet. Into which segment would you aggregate this person?

b. The responses for seven potential customers who were interviewed are listed in the table below. Enter the ratings for a customer in the spreadsheet and then write down the similarity score for each segment. Repeat the process for each customer. Based on your analysis, indicate the segment into which you would aggregate each customer. Indicate the size (number of customers) of each segment.

c. In the interview, each potential customer was also asked what type of computer he or she would be using.

THE LEARNING AID.

The *Learning Aid* helps you review and test yourself on material from each chapter—while also providing opportunities for you to obtain a deeper understanding of the material. The *Learning Aid* offers a hands-on way to develop a better understanding of the basics of marketing.

The *Learning Aid* provides a brief introduction to each chapter, a list of the important new terms (with page numbers for easy reference), true-false questions (with answers and page numbers) that cover all the important terms and concepts, and multiple-choice questions (with answers) that illustrate the kinds of questions that may appear in examinations.

Chapter 7

Business and organizational customers and their buying behavior

What This Chapter Is About

Chapter 7 discusses the buying behavior of the important business and organizational customers who buy for resale or for use in their own businesses. They buy more goods and services than final customers! There are many opportunities in marketing to producers, to middlemen, to government, and to nonprofit organizations—and it is important to understand how these organizational customers buy.

Organizations tend to be much more economic in their buying behavior than final consumers. Further, some must follow pre-set bidding and bargaining processes. Yet, they too have emotional needs. And sometimes a number of different people may influence the final purchase decision. Keep in mind that business and organizational customers are problem solvers too. Many of the ideas in Chapter 6 carry over, but with some adaptation.

This chapter deserves careful study because your past experience as a consumer is not as helpful here as it was in the last few chapters. Organizational customers are much less numerous. In some cases it is possible to create a separate marketing mix for each individual customer. Understanding these customers is necessary to plan marketing strategies for them. Try to see how they are both similar and different from final customers.

Important Terms

business and organizational customers, p. 184
purchasing specifications, p. 187
ISO 9000, p. 187
purchasing managers, p. 187
multiple buying influence, p. 188
buying center, p. 189
vendor analysis, p. 189
requisition, p. 191
new-task buying, p. 192
straight rebuy, p. 192

modified rebuy, p. 192
just-in-time delivery, p. 196
negotiated contract buying, p. 197
reciprocity, p. 198
competitive bids, p. 200
North American Industry Classification System
    (NAICS) codes, p. 206
open to buy, p. 210
resident buyers, p. 210
Foreign Corrupt Practices Act, p. 212

___	35.	Government buyers avoid the use of negotiated contracts whenever there are a lot of intangible factors.
___	36.	The Internet is not a very effective way to locate information on potential government target markets.
___	37.	In international markets, it is legal to make small grease money payments—if they are customary in that country.

Answers to True-False Questions

1. F, p. 184	14. F, p. 196	27. T, p. 208
2. T, p. 186	15. F, p. 197	28. F, p. 208
3. F, p. 186	16. T, p. 198	29. T, p. 209
4. T, p. 187	17. T, p. 199	30. T, p. 209
5. T, p. 188	18. T, p. 199-200	31. T, p. 210
6. F, p. 189	19. T, p. 200	32. F, p. 210
7. T, p. 189	20. T, p. 200	33. T, p. 210
8. T, p. 189	21. T, p. 201	34. F, p. 210
9. T, p. 190	22. T, p. 203	35. F, p. 211
10. T, p. 191	23. T, p. 203	36. F, p. 212
11. T, p. 192	24. T, p. 204	37. T, p. 212
12. F, p. 192	25. T, p. 205	
13. F, p. 193	26. T, p. 206-207	

Multiple-Choice Questions (Circle the correct response)

1. The bulk of all buying done in the United States is not by final consumers—but rather by business and organizational customers. Which of the following is a business or organizational customer?
   a.   a manufacturer.
   b.   a retailer.
   c.   a wholesaler.
   d.   a government agency.
   e.   All of the above are business and organizational customers.

2. In comparison to the buying of final consumers, the purchasing of organizational buyers:
   a.   is strictly economic and not at all emotional.
   b.   is always based on bids from multiple suppliers.
   c.   leans basically toward economy, quality, and dependability.
   d.   is even less predictable.
   e.   Both a and c are true statements.

3. Today, many agricultural commodities and manufactured items are subject to rigid control or grading. As a result, organizational buyers often buy on the basis of:
   a.   purchasing specifications.
   b.   negotiated contracts.
   c.   competitive bids.

Name: _____   Course & Section: _____

Exercise 7-3

Vendor analysis

This exercise is based on computer-aided problem number 7—Vendor Analysis. A complete description of the problem appears on page 214 of *Basic Marketing*, 14th edition.

1.   Supplier 2 is thinking about adding U.S. wholesalers to its channel of distribution. The supplier would ship in large, economical quantities to the wholesaler and the wholesaler would keep a stock of chips on hand. The wholesaler would charge CompuTech a higher price—1.90 a chip. But with the chips available from a reliable wholesaler CompuTech's inventory cost as a percent of its total order would only be 2 percent. In addition, the cost of transportation would only be $.01 per chip. Assuming CompuTech planned to buy 84,500 chips, what would its total costs be with and without the wholesaler? Should CompuTech encourage the supplier to add a wholesaler to the channel?

   Total Costs for Vendor Supplier 2, buying direct   _____

   Total Costs for Vendor Supplier 2, using wholesaler   _____

   _____

   _____

   _____

2.   Supplier 2 has explored the idea of adding wholesalers to the channel, but has found that it will take at least another year to find suitable wholesalers and develop relationships. As a result, if CompuTech deals with Supplier 2 its inventory cost as a percent of the total order would remain at 5.4 percent, and transportation cost would remain at $.03 per chip. But the supplier is still interested in improving its marketing mix now—so it can develop a strong relationship with CompuTech. Based on an analysis of CompuTech's needs, Supplier 2 has developed a new design for the electronic memory chips.

   The redesigned chips would have a built-in connector, so CompuTech would not have to buy separate connectors. In addition, the new design would make it faster and easier to replace a defective chip. The supplier estimates that with the new design it would cost CompuTech only $1.00 to replace a bad chip.

   The supplier has not yet priced the new chip, but it would cost the supplier an additional $.06 to produce each chip. If the supplier set the price of the chip at $1.93 each (the old price of $1.87 plus the additional $.06), how much would the new design cost CompuTech on an order of 84,500 chips. (Hint: compute CompuTech's total cost for the current design based on an order quantity of 84,500 chips, and then compute the total cost assuming the new price, the reduced cost of replacing a defective chip, and no cost for a connector.)

The *Learning Aid* also incorporates cases, problems, and exercises, including ones that build on the end-of-chapter computer-aided problems—with clear instructions and worksheets for you to complete for additional practice.

The *Marketing Game!* is a competitive marketing strategy simulation that allows you the opportunity to apply your marketing knowledge in a fun and interesting way. *The Marketing Game!* is applicable for all areas of marketing and all levels because the game is not based on just one simulation. Rather it is based on several simulations with one integrated framework. *The Marketing Game!* is based on realistic marketing and realistic marketing relationships, and allows for maximum flexibility.

MOTIVATED LEARNER PACKAGE

The 15th Edition of Perreault and McCarthy's *Basic Marketing* introduces yet another innovation for you as a beginning marketing student—the Motivated Learner Package.

The Motivated Learner Package contains the 15th Edition of the text, the free Student CD, and the newly created Motivated Learner DVD set. This DVD set includes the text's teaching videos, video cases (eight hours combined), and newly developed multimedia lectures for each chapter (an additional eight hours) in one, easy-to-use set. The multimedia lectures offer quality presentations by combining PowerPoint presentations with helpful lecture voiceovers in a DVD video format. These presentations are similar in quality to the narrated slide shows on the Student CD and are the next best thing to actually attending a live lecture.

FREE MULTIMEDIA STUDENT CD-ROM.

Each new copy of this book includes a custom-developed multimedia Student CD. Loaded with interesting and interactive tools, programs, videos, graphics, and illustrations, this CD will help you review and apply concepts from the 15th Edition of *Basic Marketing*. When used in combination with the text, the CD will enhance each lesson and engage you in real-world marketing situations.

Videos

Custom-produced video clips accompany cases printed in the text—to vividly illustrate points and start your creative juices flowing. These 7 video cases allow you to analyze an organization's whole marketing program in depth—giving you an opportunity to integrate and apply concepts from the course. Whether you enjoy the video clips on your own or later view and discuss the full videos in class, the video cases provide you with a valuable new way to learn about marketing.

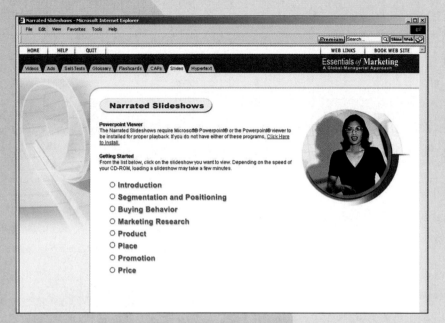

Narrated Slide Shows

Eight narrated slide shows provide an overview of key marketing concepts and reinforce how sections of the text fit together. They include full-motion video clips, photos, ads, and commentary that further illustrate ideas covered in lectures, class discussion, and independent reading.

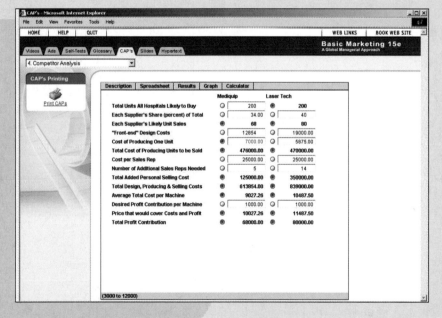

Computer-Aided Problems

Award-winning spreadsheets, pre-programmed specifically for ease of use with the computer-aided problems at the end of each chapter, are fully integrated with the other applications on the Student CD. This software allows you to enter your answers to questions on screen and then print out both the spreadsheet and answer. These interesting problems give you practice in working with marketing concepts to see how they impact a firm's overall profitability and effectiveness in serving customers.

ONLINE SUPPORT.

Understanding that you have a variety of classes and responsibilities to worry about, *Basic Marketing* offers flexible online study and support tools that will fit into any busy schedule. If you have a few moments in the library or when you're checking e-mail, you have enough time to visit the website to enhance your marketing education experience.

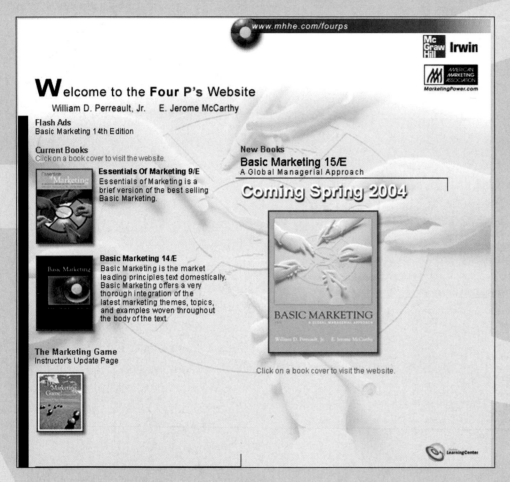

Website

Basic Marketing's website (www.mhhe.com/fourps) provides a cutting edge, interactive resource on marketing education.

Online Learning Center

The text's Online Learning Center features current events, downloadable supplements, chapter quizzes, and even videos of current commercials.

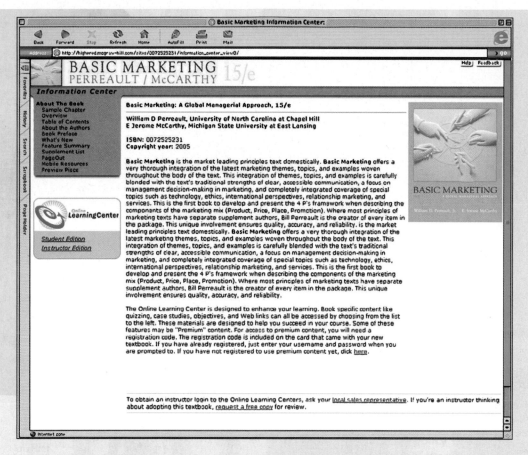

PowerWeb

Access PowerWeb through *Basic Marketing*'s site. It is constantly updated and offers links to just-published articles from the best business periodicals. Articles are keyed to the chapter lessons and PowerWeb provides interactive chat rooms, software updates, company Web links, and other exciting features.

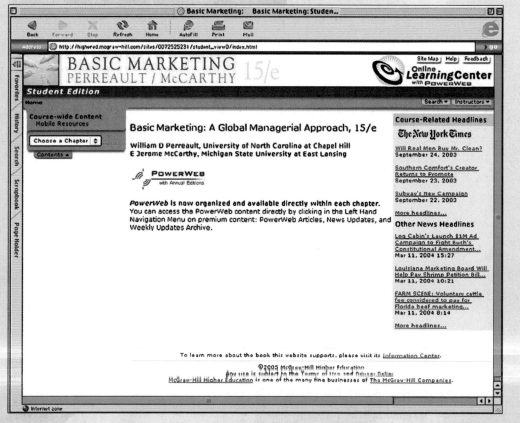

Acknowledgments

Basic Marketing has been influenced and improved by the inputs of more people than it is possible to list. We do, however, want to express our appreciation to those who have played the most significant roles, especially in this edition.

We are especially grateful to our many students who have criticized and made comments about materials in *Basic Marketing*. Indeed, in many ways, our students have been our best teachers.

We owe our greatest debt of gratitude to Lin Davis. The book probably wouldn't exist if it weren't for her—because without her help it would have been just too overwhelming and we'd have quit! Lin has been part of this team for about 20 years. During that time she has made contributions in every aspect of the text and package. For this edition she spent countless hours researching photos and case histories, and she critiqued thousands of manuscript pages through countless revisions of the text and all the accompanying materials. She has reviewed, edited, and critiqued every word we've written. Her hard work, positive attitude, and dedication to quality throughout the whole process is without match. We could not have asked for a better friend and colleague.

Many improvements in the current edition were stimulated by feedback from a number of colleagues around the country. Their feedback took many forms. In particular, we would like to recognize the helpful contributions of

Turina Bakker, University of Wisconsin

David Blackmore, University of Pittsburgh

Jonathan Bohlman, Purdue School of Management

Denny Bristow, St. Cloud State University

Derrell Bulls, Texas Women's University

Carmen Calabrese, University of North Carolina—Pembroke

Donald Caudill, Bluefield State College

Kenny Chan, California State University—Chico

E. Wayne Chandler, Eastern Illinois University

Paris Cleanthous, New York University—Stern School

Thomas Cline, St. Vincent College

Brian Connett, California State University—Northridge

J. Charlene Davis, Trinity University

Susan Higgins DeFago, John Carroll University

Les Dlabay, Lake Forest College

Glenna Dod, Wesleyan College

Michael Drafke, College of DuPage

Steven Engel, University of Colorado

Ken Fairweather, LeTourneau University

Lori S. Feldman, Purdue University

Richard Kent Fields, Carthage College

John Gaffney, Hiram College

Gary Grandison, Alabama State University

Mike Griffith, Cascade College

Khalil Hairston, Indiana Institute of Technology

Dorothy Harpool, Wichita State University

Lewis Hershey, University of North Carolina—Pembroke

Pamela Homer, California State University—Long Beach

Annette Jaiko, Triton College/College of DuPage

Fahri Karakaya, University of Massachusetts

Kathleen Krentler, San Diego State University

Kevin Lambert, Southeast Community College

Richard LaRosa, Indiana University of Pennsylvania

Lori Lohman, Augsburg College

Paul James Londrigan, Mott Community College

Richard Lutz, University of Florida

Rosalynn Martin, MidSouth Community College

Michele McCarren, Southern State Community College

Margaret Klayton Mi, Mary Washington College

Ed Mosher, Laramie Community College

Robert Montgomery, University of Evansville

David Oh, California State University—Los Angeles

Stephen Peters, Walla Walla Community College

Tracy Proulx, Park University

Daniel Ricica, Sinclair Community College

Jeremy Sierra, New Mexico State University

Lisa Simon, California Polytech—San Luis Obispo

Robert Smoot, Lees College

Don Soucy, University of North Carolina—Pembroke

Stephen Strange, Henderson Community College

Randy Stuart, Kennesaw State University

Uday Tate, Marshall University

Janice Taylor, Miami University

AJ Taylor, Austin Peay State University

Jeff Thieme, Syracuse University

Gary Tschantz, Walsh University

Fran Ucci, Triton College/College of DuPage

David Urban, Virginia Commonwealth University

Steve Vitucci, Tarleton State University

Fred Whitman, Mary Washington College

Judy Wilkinson, Youngstown State University

In addition, we appreciate people whose feedback on the previous two editions had an ongoing influence on this revision. They are

Mary Albrecht, Maryville University

David Andrus, Kansas State University at Manhattan

Turina Bakker, University of Wisconsin

Jonathan Bohlman, Purdue University

John Brennan, Florida State University

Linda Jane Coleman, Salem State College

Brent Cunningham, Jacksonville State University

Scott Davis, University of California at Davis

Phillip Downs, Florida State University

Michael Drafke, College of DuPage

Sean Dwyer, Louisiana Technical University

Lou Firenze, Northwood University

Thomas Giese, University of Richmond

J. Lee Goen, Oklahoma Baptist University

David Good, Central Missouri State University

Susan Gupta, University of Wisconsin at Milwaukee

John Hadjmarcou, University of Texas at El Paso

Bobby Hall, Wayland Baptist University

Dorothy Harpool, Wichita State University

Pamela Homer, California State University—Long Beach

Deborah Baker Hulse, University of Texas at Tyler

Timothy Johnston, University of Tennessee at Martin

Eileen Kearney, Montgomery County Community College

James Kellaris, University of Cincinnati

Jean Laliberte, Troy State University

Debra Laverie, Texas Tech University

W. J. Mahony, Southern Wesleyan University

James McAloon, Fitchburg State University

Michael Mezja, University of Las Vegas

Robert Montgomery, University of Evansville

Todd Mooradian, College of William and Mary

Marlene Morris, Georgetown University

Brenda Moscool, California State University—Bakersfield

Reza Motameni, California State University—Fresno

Thomas Myers, University of Richmond

Philip S. Nitse, Idaho State University at Pocatello

J. R. Ogden, Kutztown University

Sam Okoroafo, University of Toledo

Esther S. Page-Wood, Western Michigan University

Daniel Rajaratnam, Baylor University

Catherine Rich-Duval, Merrimack College

Lee Richardson, University of Baltimore

Carlos Rodriguez, Governors State University

Robert Roe, University of Wyoming

Joel Saegert, University of Texas at San Antonio

Charles Schwepker, Central Missouri State University

Kenneth Shamley, Sinclair College

Doris Shaw, Kent State University

Donald Shifter, Fontbonne College

J. Taylor, Austin Peay University

Janice Taylor, Miami University

Kimberly Taylor, Florida International University

Jeff Thieme, Syracuse University

Scott Thompson, University of Wisconsin—Oshkosh

David Urban, Virginia Commonwealth University

Jane Wayland, Eastern Illinois University

M.G.M. Wetzeis, Universiteit Maastrict, The Netherlands

Robert Witherspoon, Triton College

Joyce H. Wood, N. Virginia Community College

Newell Wright, James Madison University

We've always believed that the best way to build consistency and quality into the text and the other *P.L.U.S.* units is to do as much as possible ourselves. With the growth of multimedia technologies, it's darn hard to be an expert on them all. But we've had spectacular help in that regard.

We're especially indebted to David Urban for his creative work on the lecture-support PowerPoint presentation slides, the interactive exercises, and the Motivated Learner Package lecture videos for this edition. David is a great teacher and a great collaborator in sharing his insights and skills with us and others who use *Basic Marketing* for teaching and learning. Milt Pressley and Lewis Hershey partici-

pated in PowerPoint work on the previous editions and their influence is still felt. It's rare to find world-class marketing professors who also have their skill and experience with teaching technologies, so we are certainly fortunate that they've shared their brainwaves on this project.

John Gayle worked with us to redesign and program the new version of the CD. John also provided creative support on the PowerPoint slides. Nick Childers at Arthur Scott Productions has been the guru behind the scenes in production work on the video package for many editions. He also worked with us in developing the first versions of our CDs. Nick Childers and Debra Childers continue to play an important role not only in the videos but in multimedia innovations such as the Motivated Learner Package.

For several editions Judy Wilkinson has played a big role as producer of the video series for the book. In that capacity she worked closely with us to come up with ideas, and she provided guidance to the talented group of marketing professors and managers who created or revised videos for this edition. Judy also is the author of several outstanding video segments. Too much of the video footage used at all levels of education is full of glitz but devoid of content—because the people who produce it too often don't know the content. We've been able to conquer that challenge, but only because of the contributions made by Judy and other outstanding colleagues who have converted their marketing insights to the video medium. More specifically, we express respect for and deep appreciation to other authors of the video series:

James Burley

David Burns

Debra Childers

W. Davis Folsom

Douglas Hausknecht

Bart Kittle

Bill Levy

Don McBane

J. R. Montgomery

Deborah Owens

George Prough

Peter Rainsford

Jane Reid

Roger Schoenfeldt

Thomas Sherer

Of course, like other aspects of *Basic Marketing*, the video series has evolved and improved over time, and its current strength is partly due to the insights of Phil Niffenegger, who served as producer for our early video efforts. The video series also continues to benefit from the contributions of colleagues who developed videos in earlier editions. They are

Gary R. Brockway, Murray State University

Martha O. Cooper, Ohio State University

Carolyn Costley, University of Miami

Scott Johnson, University of Louisville

Gene R. Lazniak, Marquette University

Charles S. Madden, Baylor University

W. Glynn Mangold, Murray State University

Robert Miller, Central Michigan University

Michael R. Mullen, Florida Atlantic University

Phillip Niffenegger, Murray State University

Thomas G. Ponzurick, West Virginia University

Jeanne M. Simmons, Marquette University

Rollie O. Tillman, University of North Carolina at Chapel Hill

Robert Welsh, Central Michigan University

Holt Wilson, Central Michigan University

Poh-Lin Yeou, University of South Carolina

Faculty and students at our current and past academic institutions—Michigan State University, University of North Carolina, Notre Dame, University of Georgia, Northwestern University, University of Oregon, University of Minnesota, and Stanford University—have significantly shaped the book. Professor Andrew A. Brogowicz of Western Michigan University contributed many fine ideas to early editions of the text and supplements. Neil Morgan, Charlotte Mason, Val Zeithaml, John Workman, Nicholas Didow, and Barry Bayus have provided a constant flow of helpful suggestions. Joe Cannon's suggestions, insights, and contributions have been particularly helpful.

We are also grateful to the colleagues with whom we collaborate to produce international adaptations of the text. In particular, Stan Shapiro, Ken Wong, and Pascale G. Quester have all had a significant impact on *Basic Marketing*.

The designers, artists, editors, and production people at McGraw-Hill/Irwin who worked with us on this edition warrant special recognition. All of them have shared our commitment to excellence and brought their own individual creativity to the project. First we should salute Christine Vaughan, who has done a great (and patient) job as production manager for the project. Without her adaptive problem solving we could not have succeeded with a (very) rapid-response production schedule—which is exactly what it takes to be certain that teachers and students get the most current information possible. In the same vein, Cathy Tepper continues as our hardworking, "can-do" supplements editor for this edition. We appreciate her dedication to all of the details involved in bringing such a complex project to market.

Nancy Barbour has been the developmental editor on the project through a number of editions. Her consistent support and belief in our quality objectives have been an ongoing influence. Our projects create an enormous amount of work for her, and we appreciate what she does, especially now that her skills have been recognized with broader responsibilities for managing other development editors. Linda Schreiber is due special recognition. She serves as executive editor (and commander-in-chief) for this edition and has handled those responsibilities in the midst of many other professional challenges, including expanded responsibilities for a new publishing list acquired while this edition was under way as well as work signing up other new marketing talent.

Keith McPherson is a long-term, creative, and valuable contributor to the look and feel of *Basic Marketing*.

He again took the creative lead in designing an attractive cover and inside for the book; he also put his personal touch on every piece of art and all of the illustrations in the text. These are enormously time-consuming efforts, but what a talent he is and what patience he exhibits in bringing it all together to create a book that not only discusses but really illustrates best practices in marketing! We also appreciate Mike Hruby, who again tracked down permissions for photos and ads we selected to use to illustrate important ideas.

Dan Silverburg is our new marketing manager for the project. He has already jumped into the position with gusto and brought great ideas and hard work to the team. He is not only taking initiative for promotion of this new edition but also showing all the right instincts to do the type of longer-term marketing strategy planning that is as important to a text as it is with any other product offering. We also owe a debt of gratitude to Mark Christianson, Charles Pelto, Victoria Bryant, Damian Moshak, and especially Craig Atkins, who have taken the internal lead at McGraw-Hill in producing all of the *Basic Marketing* technology initiatives.

Rob Zwettler, Merrily Mazza, David Littlehale, John Biernat, and Jerry Saykes have all found time in their busy executive schedules to share their publishing insights—and they also gave us crucial top-management support. Steve Patterson is living proof that it is possible to survive and prosper after years as editor of this project, and his ongoing friendship and support is still much appreciated.

Our families have been patient and consistent supporters through all phases in developing *Basic Marketing*. The support has been direct and substantive. Pam Perreault has provided valuable assistance and more encouragement than you could imagine through many editions of the text. And Will and Suzanne Perreault continue to provide valuable suggestions and ideas as well as encouragement and support while their dad is too often consumed with a never-ending set of deadlines.

We are indebted to all the firms that allowed us to reproduce their proprietary materials here. Similarly, we are grateful to associates from our business experiences who have shared their perspectives and feedback and enhanced our sensitivity to the key challenges of marketing management. In that regard, we especially acknowledge Kevin Clancy, Peter Krieg, and their colleagues at Copernicus: The Marketing Investment Strategy Group. The combination of pragmatic experience and creative insight they bring to the table is very encouraging. If you want to see great marketing, watch them create it.

A textbook must capsulize existing knowledge while bringing new perspectives and organization to enhance it. Our thinking has been shaped by the writings of literally thousands of marketing scholars and practitioners. In some cases it is impossible to give unique credit for a particular idea or concept because so many people have played important roles in anticipating, suggesting, shaping, and developing it. We gratefully acknowledge these contributors—from the early thought-leaders to contemporary authors and researchers—who have shared their creative ideas. We respect their impact on the development of marketing and more specifically this book.

To all of these persons—and to the many publishers who graciously granted permission to use their materials— we are deeply grateful. Responsibility for any errors or omissions is certainly ours, but the book would not have been possible without the assistance of many others. Our sincere appreciation goes to all who contributed.

William D. Perreault, Jr.

E. Jerome McCarthy

Contents

CHAPTER THREE

Focusing Marketing Strategy with Segmentation and Positioning

CHAPTER FOUR

Evaluating Opportunities in the Changing Marketing Environment

CHAPTER FIVE

Demographic Dimensions of Global Consumer Markets

CHAPTER SIX

Behavioral Dimensions of the Consumer Market

CHAPTER SEVEN

Business and Organizational Customers and Their Buying Behavior

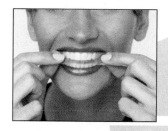

CHAPTER EIGHT

Improving Decisions with Marketing Information

CHAPTER NINE

Elements of Product Planning for Goods and Services

CHAPTER TEN

Product Management and New-Product Development

CHAPTER ELEVEN

Place and Development of Channel Systems

CHAPTER TWELVE

Distribution Customer Service and Logistics

CHAPTER THIRTEEN

Retailers, Wholesalers, and Their Strategy Planning

Price Setting in the Business World

Pricing Objectives and Policies

Implementing and Controlling Marketing Plans: Evolution and Revolution

CHAPTER TWENTY

Managing Marketing's Link with Other Functional Areas

CHAPTER TWENTY-ONE

Developing Innovative Marketing Plans

CHAPTER TWENTY-TWO

Ethical Marketing in a Consumer-Oriented World: Appraisal and Challenges

BASIC MARKETING
A GLOBAL-MANAGERIAL APPROACH

1. Know what marketing is and why you should learn about it.

2. Understand the difference between micro-marketing and macro-marketing.

3. Know the marketing functions and why marketing specialists—including intermediaries and facilitators—develop to perform them.

4. Understand what a market-driven economy is and how it adjusts the macro-marketing system.

5. Know what the marketing concept is—and how it should guide a firm or nonprofit organization.

6. Understand what customer value is and why it is important to customer satisfaction.

7. Know how social responsibility and marketing ethics relate to the marketing concept.

8. Understand the important new terms (shown in red).

CHAPTER ONE

Marketing's Value to Consumers, Firms, and Society

When it's time to roll out of bed in the morning, does your Sony alarm clock wake you with a buzzer—or by playing your favorite radio station? Is the station playing rock, classical, or country music—or perhaps a Red Cross ad asking you to contribute blood? Will you slip into your Levi's jeans, your shirt from Abercrombie and Fitch, and your Nikes, or does the day call for your Brooks Brothers interviewing suit? Will breakfast be Lender's Bagels with cream cheese or Kellogg's Frosted Flakes—made with grain from America's heartland—or some extra-large eggs and Oscar Mayer bacon cooked in a Panasonic microwave oven imported from Japan? Will you mix up some Tang instant juice and brew a pot of Maxwell House coffee—or is this a day to meet a friend at the local Starbucks, where you'll pay someone else to fix you a Frappuccino

while you use the Internet connection to log on to MSN.com to check your e-mail? After breakfast, will you head off to school or work in a Toyota Scion, on your Rollerblade inline skates, or on the bus that the city bought from General Motors?

When you think about it, you can't get very far into a day without bumping into marketing—and what the whole marketing system does for you. It affects every aspect of our lives—often in ways we don't even consider.

In other parts of the world, people wake up each day to different kinds of experiences. A family in China may have little choice about what food they will eat or where their clothing will come from. A consumer in a large city like Tokyo may have many choices but not be familiar with products that have names like Oscar Mayer and Brooks Brothers.

What's more, each element in the descriptions above could be viewed in more detail and through a different lens. Consider, for example, that visit to Starbucks. What exactly is it about Starbucks that makes so many customers so satisfied with the experience? Why do they come back time and again when they could get a cup of coffee almost anywhere, at half the price? Do loyal customers use the Starbucks card because it allows them to participate in sweepstakes and get e-mail notices of in-store promotions and new products? Or is it because the card makes it fast and easy to order and pay? Why does Starbucks offer Internet wireless hot spots at many locations—and, by the way, who dreamed up the idea of calling that tasty icy thing a Frappuccino? Twenty years ago, Starbucks was just another tiny company in Seattle; now it operates over 5,000 coffee bars, has expanded into distribution through supermarkets, and is one of the best-known brand names in the world (yes, even in Tokyo). If this is such a simple (and profitable) business idea, why didn't somebody else think of it earlier? And if the idea is easy to copy now, what does Starbucks do so differently that makes it one of the "Ten Most Admired Companies in America"? And if you were going to build your own marketing success, what would it be and how would you do it?[1]

In this text, we'll answer questions like these. In this chapter, you'll see what marketing is all about and why it's important to you as a consumer. We'll also explore why it is so crucial to the success of individual firms and nonprofit organizations and the impact that it has on the quality of life in different societies.

MARKETING—WHAT'S IT ALL ABOUT?

Marketing is more than selling or advertising

Many people think that marketing means "selling" or "advertising." It's true that these are parts of marketing. But *marketing is much more than selling and advertising.*

How did all those bicycles get here?

To illustrate some of the other important things that are included in marketing, think about all the bicycles being peddled with varying degrees of energy by bike riders around the world. Most of us don't make our own bicycles. Instead, they are made by firms like Schwinn, Performance, Huffy, and Murray.

Most bikes do the same thing—get the rider from one place to another. But a bike rider can choose from a wide assortment of models. They are designed in different sizes and with or without gears. Off-road bikes have large knobby tires. Kids and older people may want more wheels—to make balancing easier. Some bikes need baskets or even trailers for cargo. You can buy a basic bike for less than $50. Or you can spend more than $2,500 for a custom frame.

This variety of styles and features complicates the production and sale of bicycles. The following list shows some of the things a firm should do before and after it decides to produce and sell a bike.

1. Analyze the needs of people who might buy a bike and decide if they want more or different models.
2. Predict what types of bikes—handlebar styles, type of wheels, brakes, and materials—different customers will want and decide which of these people the firm will try to satisfy.
3. Estimate how many of these people will want to buy bicycles, and when.
4. Determine where in the world these bike riders will be and how to get the firm's bikes to them.
5. Estimate what price they are willing to pay for their bikes and if the firm can make a profit selling at that price.
6. Decide which kinds of promotion should be used to tell potential customers about the firm's bikes.

Selling and advertising are important parts of marketing, but modern marketing involves more. For example, to better satisfy its customers' needs and make traveling more enjoyable, this French railroad's service includes door-to-door delivery of the passenger's luggage. The ad says, "Your luggage is old enough to travel by itself. It's up to us to ensure you'd rather go by train."

7. Estimate how many competing companies will be making bikes, what kind, and at what prices.
8. Figure out how to provide warranty service if a customer has a problem after buying a bike.

The above activities are not part of **production**—actually making goods or performing services. Rather, they are part of a larger process—called *marketing*—that provides needed direction for production and helps make sure that the right goods and services are produced and find their way to consumers.

You'll learn much more about marketing activities in the next chapter. For now, it's enough to see that marketing plays an essential role in providing consumers with need-satisfying goods and services and, more generally, in creating customer satisfaction. Simply put, **customer satisfaction** is the extent to which a firm fulfills a customer's needs, desires, and expectations.

Marketing's crucial role in customer satisfaction

Some people think that if you just produce a good product, customers will be satisfied and your business will be a success. This attitude is reflected in the old saying: "Make a better mousetrap and the world will beat a path to your door."

The "better mousetrap" idea probably wasn't true in Grandpa's time, and it certainly isn't true today. In modern economies, the grass grows high on the path to the Better Mousetrap Factory—if the new mousetrap is not properly marketed.

Production and marketing are both important parts of a total business system aimed at providing consumers with need-satisfying goods and services. Together, production and marketing supply five kinds of economic utility—form, task, time, place, and possession utility—that are needed to provide consumer satisfaction. Here, **utility** means the power to satisfy human needs. See Exhibit 1-1.

Customer needs determine utility

Form utility is provided when someone produces something tangible—for instance, a bicycle. **Task utility** is provided when someone performs a task for someone else—for instance, when a bank handles financial transactions. But just producing bicycles or handling bank accounts doesn't result in consumer satisfaction. The product must be something that consumers want or there is no need to be satisfied—and no utility.

This is how marketing thinking guides the production side of business. Marketing focuses on what customers want and should guide what is produced and offered. It doesn't make sense to try to sell goods and services consumers don't want when there are so many things they do want. Let's take our "mousetrap" example a step further.

Exhibit 1-1
Types of Utility and How
They Are Provided

Some customers don't want *any kind* of mousetrap. They may want someone else to exterminate the mice for them, or they may live where mice are not a problem.

Even when marketing and production combine to provide form or task utility, consumers won't be satisfied until time, place, and possession utility are also provided.

Time utility means having the product available *when* the customer wants it. And **place utility** means having the product available *where* the customer wants it. Bicycles that stay at a factory don't do anyone any good. Time and place utility are very important for services too. For example, neighborhood health care clinics are very popular because people can walk in as soon as they feel sick, not a week later when their doctor can schedule an appointment.

Possession utility means obtaining a good or service and having the right to use or consume it. Customers usually exchange money or something else of value for possession utility.

We'll look at all the ways that marketing provides utility later.

MARKETING IS IMPORTANT TO YOU

Marketing is important to every consumer

As a consumer, you pay for the cost of marketing activities. In advanced economies, marketing costs about 50 cents of each consumer dollar. For some goods and services, the percentage is much higher. Marketing affects almost every aspect of your daily life. All the goods and services you buy, the stores where you shop, and the radio and TV programs paid for by advertising are there because of marketing. Even your job résumé is part of a marketing campaign to sell yourself to some employer! Some courses are interesting when you take them but never relevant again once they're over. Not so with marketing—you'll be a consumer dealing with marketing for the rest of your life.

Marketing will be important to your job

Another reason for studying marketing is that it offers many exciting and rewarding career opportunities. Throughout this book you will find information about opportunities in different areas of marketing.

Even if you're aiming for a nonmarketing job, knowing something about marketing will help you do your own job better. Throughout the book, we'll discuss ways that marketing relates to other functional areas—and Chapter 20 focuses on those issues. Further, marketing is important to

> **Marketing Manager for Consumer Electronics**
>
> We've got a new opportunity that should help our business grow into the next decade. Put your college degree and experience in marketing consumer durables to work. Come help us analyze our markets and plan our marketing mix in a logical, creative, and enthusiastic way. This job offers income above industry standards, dynamic colleagues, relocation to desirable midwest suburb, and fast-track upward mobility. Check our website for more detail or reply in confidence, with a copy of your resume, to Box 4953.

the success of every organization. The same basic principles used to sell soap are also used to "sell" ideas, politicians, mass transportation, health care services, conservation, museums, and even colleges.[2]

Marketing affects standard of living and economic growth

An even more basic reason for studying marketing is that marketing plays a big part in economic growth and development. One key reason is that marketing encourages research and **innovation**—the development and spread of new ideas, goods, and services. As firms offer new and better ways of satisfying consumer needs, customers have more choices among products and this fosters competition for consumers' money. This competition drives down prices. Moreover, when firms develop products that really satisfy customers, fuller employment and higher incomes can result. The combination of these forces means that marketing has a big impact on consumers' standard of living—and it is important to the future of all nations.[3]

HOW SHOULD WE DEFINE MARKETING?

Micro- or macro-marketing?

In our bicycle example, we saw that a producer of bicycles has to perform many customer-related activities besides just making bikes. The same is true for an insurance company, an art museum, or a family-service agency. This supports the idea of marketing as a set of activities done by an individual organization to satisfy the customers that it serves.

On the other hand, people can't survive on bicycles and art museums alone! In advanced economies, it takes goods and services from thousands of organizations to satisfy the many needs of society. A typical Wal-Mart supercenter carries more than 120,000 different items. A society needs some sort of marketing system to organize the efforts of all the producers and middlemen needed to satisfy the varied needs of all its citizens. So marketing is also an important social process.

INTERNET EXERCISE

You can check out the online shopping experience of Wal-Mart on the Web by going to the Wal-Mart home page (www.walmart.com) and clicking on a tab for one of the product categories. How many different manufacturers' products are shown? Would consumers be better off if each manufacturer just sold directly from its own website?

So *marketing is both a set of activities performed by organizations and a social process.* In other words, marketing exists at both the micro and macro levels. Therefore, we will use two definitions of marketing—one for micro-marketing and another for macro-marketing. Micro-marketing looks at customers and the organizations that serve them. Macro-marketing takes a broad view of our whole production–distribution system.

Micro-marketing defined

Micro-marketing is the performance of activities that seek to accomplish an organization's objectives by anticipating customer or client needs and directing a flow of need-satisfying goods and services from producer to customer or client.

Let's look at this definition.[4]

Applies to profit and nonprofit organizations

Marketing applies to both profit and nonprofit organizations. Profit is the objective for most business firms. But other types of organizations may seek more members—or acceptance of an idea. Customers or clients may be individual consumers, business firms, nonprofit organizations, government agencies, or even foreign nations.

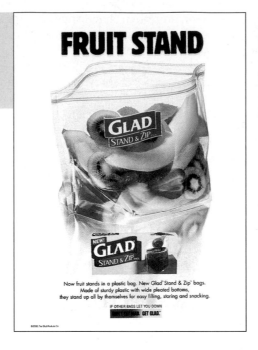

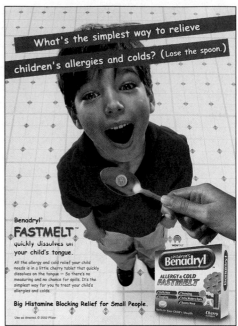

While most customers and clients pay for the goods and services they receive, others may receive them free of charge or at a reduced cost through private or government support.

More than just persuading customers

Marketing isn't just selling and advertising. Unfortunately, many executives still think it is. They feel that the job of marketing is to "get rid of" whatever the company happens to produce. In fact, the aim of marketing is to identify customers' needs and meet those needs so well that the product almost "sells itself." This is true whether the product is a physical good, a service, or even an idea. If the whole marketing job has been done well, customers don't need much persuading. They should be ready to buy. And after they do buy, they'll be satisfied and ready to buy the same way again the next time.

Begins with customer needs

Marketing should begin with potential customer needs—not with the production process. Marketing should try to anticipate needs. And then marketing, rather than production, should determine what goods and services are to be developed—including decisions about product design and packaging; prices or fees; credit and collection policies; use of middlemen; transporting and storing policies; advertising and sales policies; and, after the sale, installation, customer service, warranty, and perhaps even disposal policies.

Does not do it alone

This does not mean that marketing should try to take over production, accounting, and financial activities. Rather, it means that marketing—by interpreting customers' needs—should provide direction for these activities and try to coordinate them.

Marketing involves exchanges

The idea that marketing involves a flow of need-satisfying offerings from a producer to a customer implies that there is an exchange of the need-satisfying offering for something else, such as the customer's money. Marketing focuses on facilitating exchanges. In fact, *marketing doesn't occur unless two or more parties are willing to exchange something for something else.* For example, in a **pure subsistence economy**—when each family unit produces everything it consumes—there is no need to exchange goods and services and no marketing is involved. (Although each producer-consumer unit is totally self-sufficient in such a situation, the standard of living is typically relatively low.)

Builds a relationship with the customer

Keep in mind that a marketing exchange may be part of an ongoing relationship, not just a single transaction. When marketing helps everyone in a firm really meet the needs of a customer before and after a purchase, the firm doesn't just get a single sale. Rather, it has a sale and an ongoing *relationship* with the customer. Then, in the future, when the customer has the same need again—or some other need that the firm can meet—other sales will follow. Often, the marketing *flow* of need-satisfying goods and services is not just for a single transaction but rather is part of building a long-lasting relationship that benefits both the firm and the customer.

The focus of this text—management-oriented micro-marketing

Since you are probably preparing for a career in management, the main focus of this text will be on micro-marketing. We will see marketing through the eyes of the marketing manager.

The marketing ideas we will be discussing throughout this text apply to a wide variety of situations. They are important for new ventures started by one person as well as big corporations, in domestic and international markets, and regardless of whether the focus is on marketing physical goods, services, or an idea or cause. They are equally critical whether the relevant customers or clients are individual consumers, businesses, or some other type of organization. For editorial convenience, we will sometimes use the term *firm* as a shorthand way of referring to any type of organization, whether it is a political party, a religious organization, a government agency, or the like. However, to reinforce the point that the ideas apply to all types of organizations, throughout the book we will illustrate marketing concepts in a wide variety of situations.

Although micro-marketing is the primary focus of the text, marketing managers must remember that their organizations are just small parts of a larger macro-marketing system. Therefore, next we will briefly look at the macro view of marketing. Then, we will develop this idea more fully in later chapters.

MACRO-MARKETING

Macro-marketing is a social process that directs an economy's flow of goods and services from producers to consumers in a way that effectively matches supply and demand and accomplishes the objectives of society.[5]

Emphasis is on whole system

With macro-marketing we are still concerned with the flow of need-satisfying goods and services from producer to consumer. However, the emphasis with macro-marketing is not on the activities of individual organizations. Instead, the emphasis is on *how the whole marketing system works*. This includes looking at how marketing affects society and vice versa.

Every society needs a macro-marketing system to help match supply and demand. Different producers in a society have different objectives, resources, and skills. Likewise, not all consumers share the same needs, preferences, and wealth. In other words, within every society there are both heterogeneous (highly varied) supply capabilities and heterogeneous demands for goods and services. The role of a macro-marketing system is to effectively match this heterogeneous supply and demand *and* at the same time accomplish society's objectives.

An effective macro-marketing system delivers the goods and services that consumers want and need. It gets products to them in the right time, in the right place, and at a price they're willing to pay. It keeps consumers satisfied after the sale and brings them back to purchase again when they are ready. That's not an easy job—

Most consumers who drink tea live far from where it is grown. To overcome this spatial separation, someone must first perform a variety of marketing functions, like standardizing and grading the tea leaves, transporting and storing them, and buying and selling them.

(Tea-Java) Simply, Pure Tea From Java

especially if you think about the variety of goods and services a highly developed economy can produce and the many kinds of goods and services consumers want.

Separation between producers and consumers

Effective marketing in an advanced economy is difficult because producers and consumers are often separated in several ways. As Exhibit 1-2 shows, exchange between producers and consumers is hampered by spatial separation, separation in time, separation of information and values, and separation of ownership. You may love your MP3 player, but you probably don't know when or where it was produced or how it got to you. The people in the factory that produced it don't know about you or how you live.

In addition, most firms specialize in producing and selling large amounts of a narrow assortment of goods and services. This allows them to take advantage of mass production with its **economies of scale**—which means that as a company produces larger numbers of a particular product, the cost of each of these products goes down. Yet most consumers only want to buy a small quantity; they also want a wide assortment of different goods and services. These "discrepancies of quantity" and "discrepancies of assortment" further complicate exchange between producers and consumers (Exhibit 1-2). That is, each producer specializes in producing and selling large amounts of a narrow assortment of goods and services, but each consumer wants only small quantities of a wide assortment of goods and services.[6]

Marketing functions help narrow the gap

The purpose of a macro-marketing system is to overcome these separations and discrepancies. The "universal functions of marketing" help do this.

The **universal functions of marketing** are buying, selling, transporting, storing, standardization and grading, financing, risk taking, and market information. They must be performed in all macro-marketing systems. *How* these functions are performed—and *by whom*—may differ among nations and economic systems. But they are needed in any macro-marketing system. Let's take a closer look at them now.

Any kind of exchange usually involves buying and selling. The **buying function** means looking for and evaluating goods and services. The **selling function** involves promoting the product. It includes the use of personal selling, advertising, and other direct and mass selling methods. This is probably the most visible function of marketing.

The **transporting function** means the movement of goods from one place to another. The **storing function** involves holding goods until customers need them.

Standardization and grading involve sorting products according to size and quality. This makes buying and selling easier because it reduces the need for inspection and sampling. **Financing** provides the necessary cash and credit to produce, transport, store, promote, sell, and buy products. **Risk taking** involves bearing the uncertainties that are part of the marketing process. A firm can never be sure that

Exhibit 1-2   Marketing Facilitates Production and Consumption

Production Sector
Specialization and division of labor result in heterogeneous supply capabilities

Discrepancies of Quantity. Producers prefer to produce and sell in large quantities. Consumers prefer to buy and consume in small quantities.

Discrepancies of Assortment. Producers specialize in producing a narrow assortment of goods and services. Consumers need a broad assortment.

Marketing needed to overcome discrepancies and separations

Spatial Separation. Producers tend to locate where it is economical to produce, while consumers are located in many scattered locations.

Separation in Time. Consumers may not want to consume goods and services at the time producers would prefer to produce them, and time may be required to transport goods from producer to consumer.

Separation of Information. Producers do not know who needs what, where, when, and at what price. Consumers do not know what is available from whom, where, when, and at what price.

Separation in Values. Producers value goods and services in terms of costs and competitive prices. Consumers value them in terms of economic utility and ability to pay.

Separation of Ownership. Producers hold title to goods and services that they themselves do not want to consume. Consumers want goods and services that they do not own.

Consumption Sector
Heterogeneous demand for form, task, time, place, and possession utility to satisfy needs and wants

customers will want to buy its products. Products can also be damaged, stolen, or outdated. The **market information function** involves the collection, analysis, and distribution of all the information needed to plan, carry out, and control marketing activities, whether in the firm's own neighborhood or in a market overseas.

Producers, consumers, and marketing specialists perform functions

Producers and consumers sometimes handle some of the marketing functions themselves. However, exchanges are often easier or less expensive when a marketing specialist performs some of the marketing functions. For example, both producers and consumers may benefit when an **intermediary** (or a **middleman**)—someone who specializes in trade rather than production—plays a role in the exchange process. In Chapters 12–13 we'll cover the variety of marketing functions performed by the two basic types of middlemen: retailers and wholesalers. However, you don't need to think about it very long to imagine what it would be like to shop at many different factories for the wide variety of brands of packaged foods that you like rather than at a well-stocked local grocery store. While middlemen must charge for services they provide, this charge is usually offset by the savings of time, effort, and expense that would be involved without an intermediary. So these middlemen can help to make the whole macro-marketing system more efficient and effective.

A wide variety of other marketing specialists may also help smooth exchanges between producers, consumers, or middlemen. These specialists are **facilitators**— firms that provide one or more of the marketing functions other than buying or selling. These facilitators include advertising agencies, marketing research firms, independent product-testing laboratories, Internet service providers, public warehouses, transporting firms, communications companies, and financial institutions (including banks).

Some marketing specialists perform all the functions. Others specialize in only one or two. Marketing research firms, for example, specialize only in the market information function. Further, technology may make a certain function easier to

Intermediaries and facilitators develop and offer specialized services that facilitate exchange between producers and customers.

perform. For example, the buying process may require that a customer first identify relevant sellers and where they are. Even though that might be accomplished quickly and easily with an online search of the Internet, the function hasn't been cut out.

New specialists develop to fill market needs

As the Internet example suggests, new types of marketing specialists develop or evolve when new opportunities arise for someone to make exchanges between producers and consumers more efficient or effective. Such changes can come quickly, as is illustrated by the speed with which firms have adopted e-commerce. **E-commerce** refers to exchanges between individuals or organizations—and activities that facilitate these exchanges—based on applications of information technology. New types of Internet-based intermediaries—like Amazon.com and eBay.com—are helping to cut the costs of many marketing functions. Similarly, Internet service providers like MSN.com and AOL.com that also operate websites are a new type of facilitator. They make it easier for many firms to satisfy their customers with Web-based information searches or transactions. Collectively, these developments have had a significant impact on the efficiency of our macro-marketing system. At the same time, many individual firms take advantage of these innovations to improve profitability and customer satisfaction.[7]

Through innovation, specialization, or economies of scale, marketing intermediaries and facilitators are often able to perform the marketing functions better—and at a lower cost—than producers or consumers can. This allows producers and consumers to spend more time on production, consumption, or other activities—including leisure.

Functions can be shifted and shared

From a macro-marketing viewpoint, all of the marketing functions must be performed by someone—an individual producer or consumer, an intermediary, a facilitator, or, in some cases, even a nation's government. No function can be completely eliminated. *However, from a micro viewpoint, not every firm must perform all of the functions. Rather, responsibility for performing the marketing functions can be shifted and shared in a variety of ways. Further, not all goods and services require all the functions at every level of their production.* "Pure services"—like a plane ride—don't need storing, for example. But storing is required in the production of the plane and while the plane is not in service.

Regardless of who performs the marketing functions, in general they must be performed effectively and efficiently or the performance of the whole macro-marketing system will suffer. With many different possible ways for marketing functions to be performed in a macro-marketing system, how can a society hope to arrive at a combination that best serves the needs of its citizens? To answer this question, we can look at the role of marketing in different types of economic systems.

THE ROLE OF MARKETING IN ECONOMIC SYSTEMS

All societies must provide for the needs of their members. Therefore, every society needs some sort of **economic system**—the way an economy organizes to use scarce resources to produce goods and services and distribute them for consumption by various people and groups in the society.

How an economic system operates depends on a society's objectives and the nature of its political institutions.[8] But regardless of what form these take, all economic systems must develop some method—along with appropriate economic institutions—to decide what and how much is to be produced and distributed by whom, when, to whom, and why.

There are two basic kinds of economic systems: planned systems and market-directed systems. Actually, no economy is entirely planned or market-directed. Most are a mixture of the two extremes.

Government planners may make the decisions

In a **planned economic system**, government planners decide what and how much is to be produced and distributed by whom, when, to whom, and why. Producers generally have little choice about what goods and services to produce. Their main task is to meet their assigned production quotas. Prices are set by government planners and tend to be very rigid—not changing according to supply and demand. Consumers usually have some freedom of choice—it's impossible to control every single detail! But the assortment of goods and services may be quite limited. Activities such as market research, branding, and advertising usually are neglected. Sometimes they aren't done at all.

Government planning may work fairly well as long as an economy is simple and the variety of goods and services is small. It may even be necessary under certain conditions—during wartime, drought, or political instability, for example. However, as economies become more complex, government planning becomes more difficult. It may even break down. Countries such as China, North Korea, and Cuba still rely primarily on planned economic systems. Even so, around the world there is a broad move toward market-directed economic systems—because they are more effective in meeting consumer needs.

A market-directed economy adjusts itself

In a **market-directed economic system**, the individual decisions of the many producers and consumers make the macro-level decisions for the whole economy. In a pure market-directed economy, consumers make a society's production decisions when they make their choices in the marketplace. They decide what is to be produced and by whom—through their dollar "votes."

Price is a measure of value

Prices in the marketplace are a rough measure of how society values particular goods and services. If consumers are willing to pay the market prices, then apparently they feel they are getting at least their money's worth. Similarly, the cost of labor and materials is a rough measure of the value of the resources used in the production of goods and services to meet these needs. When consumer needs that can be served profitably—not just the needs of the majority—will probably be met by some profit-minded businesses.

Exhibit 1-3
Model of a Market-Directed
Macro-Marketing System

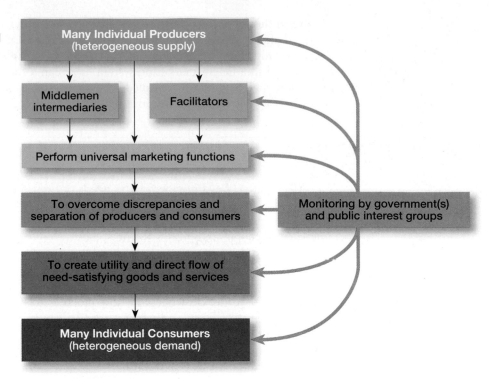

Greatest freedom of choice

Consumers in a market-directed economy enjoy great freedom of choice. They are not forced to buy any goods or services, except those that must be provided for the good of society—things such as national defense, schools, police and fire protection, highway systems, and public-health services. These are provided by the community—and the citizens are taxed to pay for them.

Similarly, producers are free to do whatever they wish—provided that they stay within the rules of the game set by government *and* receive enough dollar "votes" from consumers. If they do their job well, they earn a profit and stay in business. But profit, survival, and growth are not guaranteed.

The role of government

The American economy and most other Western economies are mainly market-directed—but not completely. Society assigns supervision of the system to the government. For example, besides setting and enforcing the "rules of the game," government agencies control interest rates and the supply of money. They also set import and export rules that affect international competition, regulate radio and TV broadcasting, sometimes control wages and prices, and so on. Government also tries to be sure that property is protected, contracts are enforced, individuals are not exploited, no group unfairly monopolizes markets, and producers deliver the kinds and quality of goods and services they claim to be offering.[9]

Is a macro-marketing system effective and fair?

The effectiveness and fairness of a particular macro-marketing system must be evaluated in terms of that society's objectives. Obviously, all nations don't share the same objectives. For example, Swedish citizens receive many "free" services—like health care and retirement benefits. Goods and services are fairly evenly distributed among the Swedish population. By contrast, North Korea places little emphasis on producing goods and services for individual consumers—and more on military spending. In India the distribution of goods and services is very uneven—with a big gap between the have-nots and the elite haves. Whether each of these systems is judged "fair" or "effective" depends on the objectives of the society.

COLGATE BRUSHES UP ON MARKETING IN RURAL INDIA

Two-thirds of the people in India still live in rural farm areas. Many don't have life's basic comforts. For example, three out of four use wood as fuel to cook. Only about 40 percent have electricity, and less than 20 percent have piped water. Most can't afford a refrigerator. A person who works in the sugarcane fields, for example, only earns about $1 a day.

While these rural villagers do not have much money, there are about 1 *billion* of them. So they are an important potential market for basic products like toothpaste and shampoo. Marketing managers for Colgate know that. However, many rural Indians have never even held a tube of toothpaste. Rather, they clean their mouths with charcoal powder and the stem of a local plant. But Colgate can't rely on U.S.-style ads—or the local drugstore—to do the selling job. Half of the rural population can't read, and very few have a TV. They also don't go to stores. Rather, once a week the men go to a central market in a nearby village to get basic supplies they can't grow themselves.

In spite of these challenges, in the past decade Colgate has about doubled its sales—and rural Indians

are now buying over 17,000 tons of toothpaste a year. What's the trick? Colgate sends a van that is equipped with a generator and video gear into a village on market day. Music attracts the shoppers, and then an entertaining half-hour video (infomercial) explains the benefits (including increased sex appeal!) of using Colgate toothpaste. The van reaches only about 100 people at a time, but many of those who see the video try the toothpaste. Of course, not many want to spend a day's wages to buy a standard tube. So Colgate offers a small (30 gram) tube for six rupees (about 18 cents). Colgate's approach is expensive, but managers in the firm are wisely thinking about the long-run return on the marketing investments.

Where did this idea come from? The video vans were first used in 1987 to spread propaganda for a political party that was denied airtime on state-run television. Between elections the vans were idle, so the owner decided to become a marketing specialist—and offered to rent the vans to firms like Colgate that wanted to reach rural consumers.[10]

So far, we have described how a market-directed macro-marketing system adjusts to become more effective and efficient by responding to customer needs. See Exhibit 1-3. As you read this book, you'll learn more about how marketing affects society and vice versa. You'll also learn more about specific marketing activities and be better informed when drawing conclusions about how fair and effective the macro-marketing system is. For now, however, we'll return to our general emphasis on micro-marketing and a managerial view of the role of marketing in individual organizations.

MARKETING'S ROLE HAS CHANGED A LOT OVER THE YEARS

It's clear that marketing decisions are very important to a firm's success. But marketing hasn't always been so complicated. In fact, understanding how marketing thinking has evolved makes the modern view clearer. So we will discuss five stages in marketing evolution: (1) the simple trade era, (2) the production era, (3) the sales era, (4) the marketing department era, and (5) the marketing company era. We'll talk about these eras as if they applied generally to all firms—but keep in mind that *some managers still have not made it to the final stages.* They are stuck in the past with old ways of thinking.

Specialization permitted trade—and middlemen met the need

When societies first moved toward some specialization of production and away from a subsistence economy where each family raised and consumed everything it produced, traders played an important role. Early "producers for the market" made products that were needed by themselves and their neighbors. As bartering became

15

more difficult, societies moved into the **simple trade era**—a time when families traded or sold their "surplus" output to local middlemen. These specialists resold the goods to other consumers or distant middlemen. This was the early role of marketing—and it is still the focus of marketing in many of the less-developed areas of the world. In fact, even in the United States, the United Kingdom, and other more advanced economies, marketing didn't change much until the Industrial Revolution brought larger factories a little over a hundred years ago.

From the production to the sales era

From the Industrial Revolution until the 1920s, most companies were in the production era. The **production era** is a time when a company focuses on production of a few specific products—perhaps because few of these products are available in the market. "If we can make it, it will sell" is management thinking characteristic of the production era. Because of product shortages, many nations—including China and many of the post-communist republics of Eastern Europe—continue to operate with production era approaches.

By about 1930, most companies in the industrialized Western nations had more production capability than ever before. Now the problem wasn't just to produce—but to beat the competition and win customers. This led many firms to enter the sales era. The **sales era** is a time when a company emphasizes selling because of increased competition.

To the marketing department era

For most firms in advanced economies, the sales era continued until at least 1950. By then, sales were growing rapidly in most areas of the economy. The problem was deciding where to put the company's effort. Someone was needed to tie together the efforts of research, purchasing, production, shipping, and sales. As this situation became more common, the sales era was replaced by the marketing department era. The **marketing department era** is a time when all marketing activities are brought under the control of one department to improve short-run policy planning and to try to integrate the firm's activities.

To the marketing company era

Since 1960, most firms have developed at least some managers with a marketing management outlook. Many of these firms have even graduated from the marketing department era into the marketing company era. The **marketing company era** is a time when, in addition to short-run marketing planning, marketing people develop long-range plans—sometimes five or more years ahead—and the whole company effort is guided by the marketing concept.

WHAT DOES THE MARKETING CONCEPT MEAN?

The **marketing concept** means that an organization aims *all* its efforts at satisfying its *customers*—at a *profit*. The marketing concept is a simple but very important idea. See Exhibit 1-4.

The marketing concept is not a new idea—it's been around for a long time. But some managers show little interest in customers' needs. These managers still have a **production orientation**—making whatever products are easy to produce and *then* trying to sell them. They think of customers existing to buy the firm's output rather than of firms existing to serve customers and—more broadly—the needs of society.

Well-managed firms have replaced this production orientation with a marketing orientation. A **marketing orientation** means trying to carry out the marketing concept. Instead of just trying to get customers to buy what the firm has produced, a marketing-oriented firm tries to offer customers what they need.

Three basic ideas are included in the definition of the marketing concept: (1) customer satisfaction, (2) a total company effort, and (3) profit—not just sales—as an objective. These ideas deserve more discussion.

Customer satisfaction guides the whole system

"Give the customers what they need" seems so obvious that it may be hard for you to see why the marketing concept requires special attention. However, people don't always do the logical—especially when it means changing what they've done in the past. In a typical company 40 years ago, production managers thought mainly about getting out the product. Accountants were interested only in balancing the books. Financial people looked after the company's cash position. And salespeople were mainly concerned with getting orders for whatever product was in the warehouse. Each department thought of its own activity as the center of the business. Unfortunately, this is still true in many companies today.

Exhibit 1-4
Organizations with a Marketing Orientation Carry Out the Marketing Concept

Work together to do a better job	Ideally, all managers should work together as a team. Every department may directly or indirectly impact customer satisfaction. But some managers tend to build "fences" around their own departments. There may be meetings to try to get them to work together—but they come and go from the meetings worried only about protecting their own turf.

We use the term *production orientation* as a shorthand way to refer to this kind of narrow thinking—and lack of a central focus—in a business firm. But keep in mind that this problem may be seen in sales-oriented sales representatives, advertising-oriented agency people, finance-oriented finance people, directors of nonprofit organizations, and so on. It is not a criticism of people who manage production. They aren't necessarily any more guilty of narrow thinking than anyone else.

The fences come down in an organization that has accepted the marketing concept. There may still be departments because specialization often makes sense. But the total system's effort is guided by what customers want—instead of what each department would like to do.

In Chapter 20, we'll go into more detail on the relationship between marketing and other functions. Here, however, you should see that the marketing concept provides a guiding focus that *all* departments adopt. It should be a philosophy of the whole organization, not just an idea that applies to the marketing department. |
| **Survival and success require a profit** | Firms must satisfy customers. But keep in mind that it may cost more to satisfy some needs than any customers are willing to pay. Or it may be much more costly to try to attract new customers than it is to build a strong relationship with—and repeat purchases from—existing customers. So profit—the difference between a firm's revenue and its total costs—is the bottom-line measure of the firm's success and ability to survive. It is the balancing point that helps the firm determine what needs it will try to satisfy with its total (sometimes costly!) effort. |

ADOPTION OF THE MARKETING CONCEPT HAS NOT BEEN EASY OR UNIVERSAL

	The marketing concept was first accepted by consumer products companies such as General Electric and Procter & Gamble. Competition was intense in their markets—and trying to satisfy customers' needs more fully was a way to win in this competition. Widespread publicity about the success of the marketing concept at these companies helped spread the message to other firms.[11]

Producers of industrial commodities—steel, coal, paper, glass, and chemicals—have accepted the marketing concept slowly if at all. Similarly, many traditional retailers have been slow to accept the marketing concept. |
| **Service industries are catching up** | Service industries—including airlines, power and telephone companies, banks, investment firms, lawyers, physicians, accountants, and insurance companies—were slow to adopt the marketing concept, too. But in recent years this has changed dramatically. This is partly due to changes in government regulations that forced many of these businesses to be more competitive.

Banks used to be open for limited hours that were convenient for bankers—not customers. Many closed during lunch hour! But now banks stay open longer and also offer more services for their customers—automated teller machines, banking over the Internet, or a "personal banker" to give financial advice.[12] |
| **It's easy to slip into a production orientation** | The marketing concept may seem obvious, but it's very easy to slip into a production-oriented way of thinking. For example, a company might rush a new product to market—rather than first finding out if it will fill an unsatisfied need. |

Exhibit 1-5 Some Differences in Outlook between Adopters of the Marketing Concept and the Typical Production-Oriented Managers

Topic	Marketing Orientation	Production Orientation
Attitudes toward customers	Customer needs determine company plans.	They should be glad we exist, trying to cut costs and bringing out better products.
An Internet website	A new way to serve customers.	If we have a website customers will flock to us.
Product offering	Company makes what it can sell.	Company sells what it can make.
Role of marketing research	To determine customer needs and how well company is satisfying them.	To determine customer reaction, if used at all.
Interest in innovation	Focus is on locating new opportunities.	Focus is on technology and cost cutting.
Importance of profit	A critical objective.	A residual, what's left after all costs are covered.
Role of packaging	Designed for customer convenience and as a selling tool.	Seen merely as protection for the product.
Inventory levels	Set with customer requirements and costs in mind.	Set to make production more convenient.
Focus of advertising	Need-satisfying benefits of goods and services.	Product features and how products are made.
Role of sales force	Help the customer to buy if the product fits customer's needs, while coordinating with rest of firm.	Sell the customer, don't worry about coordination with other promotion efforts or rest of firm.
Relationship with customer	Customer satisfaction before and after sale leads to a profitable long-run relationship.	Relationship ends when a sale is made.
Costs	Eliminate costs that do not give value to customer.	Keep costs as low as possible.

Many firms in high-technology businesses fall into this trap. Consider the thousands of new dot-com firms that failed. They may have had a vision of what the technology could do, but they didn't stop to figure out all that it would take to satisfy customers or make a profit. Imagine how parents felt when eToys.com failed to deliver online purchases of Christmas toys on time. If you had that experience, would you ever shop there again? What would you tell others?

Take a look at Exhibit 1-5. It shows some differences in outlook between adopters of the marketing concept and typical production-oriented managers. As the exhibit suggests, the marketing concept forces the company to think through what it is doing—and why. And it motivates the company to develop plans for accomplishing its objectives.

THE MARKETING CONCEPT AND CUSTOMER VALUE

Take the customer's point of view

A manager who adopts the marketing concept sees customer satisfaction as the path to profits. And to better understand what it takes to satisfy a customer, it's useful to take the customer's point of view.

A customer may look at a market offering from two views. One deals with the potential benefits of that offering; the other concerns what the customer has to give up to get those benefits. Consider a student who has just finished an exam and is thinking about getting a cup of mocha latte from Starbucks. Our coffee lover might see this as a great-tasting snack, a personal reward, a quick pick-me-up, and even as a way to get to know an attractive classmate. Clearly, different needs are associated with these different benefits. The cost of getting these benefits would include the price of the coffee and any tip, but there might be other nondollar costs. For example, how difficult it will be to park is a convenience cost. Slow service would be an aggravation. And you might worry about another kind of cost if the professor whose exam you have the next day sees you "wasting time" at Starbucks.

Customer value reflects benefits and costs

As this example suggests, both benefits and costs can take many different forms, perhaps ranging from economic to emotional. They also may vary depending on the situation. However, it is the customer's view of the various benefits and costs that is important. This leads us to the concept of **customer value**—the difference between the benefits a customer sees from a market offering and the costs of obtaining those benefits. A consumer is likely to be more satisfied when the customer value is higher—when benefits exceed costs by a larger margin. On the other hand, a consumer who sees the costs as greater than the benefits isn't likely to become a customer.

Some people think that low price and high customer value are the same thing. But that may not be the case at all. A good or service that doesn't meet a consumer's needs results in low customer value, even if the price is very low. Yet a high price may be more than acceptable when it obtains the desired benefits. Think again about our Starbucks example. You can get a cup of coffee for a much lower price, but Starbucks offers more than *just* a cup of coffee.

Customer may not think about it very much

It's useful for a manager to evaluate ways to improve the benefits, or reduce the costs, of what the firm offers customers. However, this doesn't mean that customers stop and compute some sort of customer value score before making each purchase. If they did, there wouldn't be much time in life for anything else. So a manager's objective and thorough analysis may not accurately reflect the customer's impressions. Yet it is the customer's view that matters—even when the customer has not thought about it.

Where does competition fit?

You can't afford to ignore competition. Consumers usually have choices about how they will meet their needs. So a firm that offers superior customer value is likely to win and keep customers. See Exhibit 1-6.

Exhibit 1-6
Customer Value and Competition

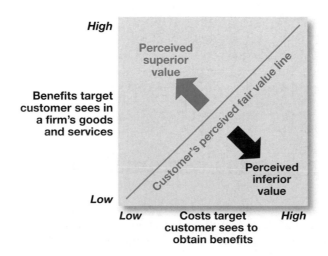

20

Often the best way to improve customer value, and beat the competition, is to be first to satisfy a need that others have not even considered.

The competition between Pepsi and Coke illustrates this. Coke and Pepsi were spending millions of dollars on promotion—fighting head-to-head for the same cola customers. They put so much emphasis on the cola competition that they missed other opportunities. That gave firms like Snapple the chance to enter the market and steal away customers. For these customers, the desired benefits—and the greatest customer value—came from the variety of a fruit-flavored drink, not from one more cola.

Build relationships with customer value

Firms that embrace the marketing concept seek ways to build a profitable long-term relationship with each customer. Even the most innovative firm faces competition sooner or later. And trying to get new customers by taking them away from a competitor is usually more costly than retaining current customers by really satisfying their needs. Satisfied customers buy again and again. This makes their buying job easier, and it also increases the selling firm's profits.

Building relationships with customers requires that everyone in a firm work together to provide customer value before *and after* each purchase. If there is a problem with a customer's bill, the accounting people can't just leave it to the salesperson to straighten it out or, even worse, act like it's "the customer's problem." The long-term relationship with the customer—and the lifetime value of the customer's future purchases—is threatened unless everyone works together to make things right for the customer. Similarly, the firm's advertising people can't just develop ads that try to convince a customer to buy once. If the firm doesn't deliver on the benefits promised in its ads, the customer is likely to go elsewhere the next time the need arises. And the same ideas apply whether the issue is meeting promised delivery dates, resolving warranty problems, giving a customer help on how to use a product, or even making it easy for the customer to return a purchase made in error.

In other words, any time the customer value is reduced—because the benefits to the customer decrease or the costs increase—the relationship is weakened.[13]

Exhibit 1-7 summarizes these ideas. In a firm that has adopted the marketing concept, everyone focuses on customer satisfaction. They offer superior customer value.

Exhibit 1-7
Satisfying Customers with Superior Customer Value to Build Profitable Relationships

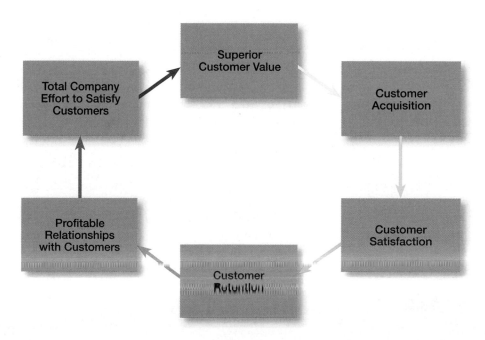

That helps attract customers in the first place—and keeps them satisfied after they buy. Because customers are satisfied, they want to purchase from the firm again. The relationship with customers is profitable, so the firm is encouraged to find better ways to offer superior customer value. In other words, when a firm adopts the marketing concept, it wins and so do its customers.

L. L. Bean delivers superior value

L. L. Bean illustrates these ideas. It is a firm that builds enduring relationships with its customers. It offers good customer value to consumers who are interested in enjoying the outdoors. Bean's quality products are well suited to a wide variety of outdoor needs—whether it's clothing for hikers or equipment for campers. The firm field-tests all its products—to be certain they live up to the firm's "100% satisfaction" guarantee. Although Bean operates a retail store in Freeport, Maine, its Internet website (www.llbean.com) and catalogs reach customers all over the world. Bean's computers track what each customer is buying, so new catalogs are mailed directly to the people who are most interested. Customers can call toll-free 24 hours a day—and get whatever advice they need because the salespeople are real experts on what they sell. Bean also makes it easy for consumers to return a product. Bean's prices are not low, but Bean retains its loyal customers because they like the benefits of the relationship.[14]

INTERNET EXERCISE

The L. L. Bean website (www.llbean.com) offers consumers a lot of information, including an "Explore the Outdoors" section with information about international and national parks. Do you think that this helps Bean to build relationships with its target customers?

THE MARKETING CONCEPT APPLIES IN NONPROFIT ORGANIZATIONS

Newcomers to marketing thinking

The marketing concept is as important for nonprofit organizations as it is for business firms. In fact, marketing applies to all sorts of public and private nonprofit organizations—ranging from government agencies, health care organizations, educational institutions, and religious groups to charities, political parties, and fine arts organizations.

Support may not come from satisfied "customers"

As with any business firm, a nonprofit organization needs resources and support to survive and achieve its objectives. Yet support often does not come directly from those who receive the benefits the organization produces. For example, the World Wildlife Fund protects animals. If supporters of the World Wildlife Fund are not satisfied with its efforts—don't think the benefits are worth what it costs to provide them—they will, and should, put their time and money elsewhere.

Just as most firms face competition for customers, most nonprofits face competition for the resources and support they need. The Air Force faces a big problem if it can't attract new recruits. A shelter for the homeless may fail if supporters decide to focus on some other cause, such as AIDS education.

What is the "bottom line"?

As with a business, a nonprofit must take in as much money as it spends or it won't survive. However, a nonprofit organization does not measure "profit" in the

Marketing is now widely accepted by many nonprofit organizations, including the Girl Scouts organization. This ad reminds girls, their families, volunteers, and other stakeholders that its programs are fun, up-to-date, and important in helping "girls grow strong."

same way as a firm. And its key measures of long-term success are also different. The YMCA, colleges, symphony orchestras, and the post office, for example, all seek to achieve different objectives and need different measures of success.

Profit guides business decisions because it reflects both the costs and benefits of different activities. In a nonprofit organization, it is sometimes more difficult to be objective in evaluating the benefits of different activities relative to what they cost. However, if everyone in an organization agrees to *some* measure(s) of long-run success, it helps serve as a guide to where the organization should focus its efforts.

May not be organized for marketing

Some nonprofits face other challenges in organizing to adopt the marketing concept. Often no one has overall responsibility for marketing activities. Even when some leaders do the marketing thinking, they may have trouble getting unpaid volunteers with many different interests to all agree with the marketing strategy. Volunteers tend to do what they feel like doing![15]

Nonprofits achieve objectives by satisfying needs

A simple example shows how marketing thinking helped a small town reduce robberies. Initially the chief of police asked the town manager for a larger budget—for more officers and patrol cars. Instead of a bigger budget, the town manager suggested a different approach. She put two officers in charge of a community watch program. They helped neighbors to organize and notify the police of any suspicious situations. They also set up a program to engrave ID numbers on belongings. And new signs warned thieves that a community watch was in effect. Break-ins all but stopped—without increasing the police budget. What the town *really* needed was more effective crime prevention—not just more police officers.

Throughout this book, we'll be discussing the marketing concept and related ideas as they apply in many different settings. Often we'll simply say "in a firm" or "in a business"—but remember that most of the ideas can be applied in *any* type of organization.

THE MARKETING CONCEPT, SOCIAL RESPONSIBILITY, AND MARKETING ETHICS

Society's needs must be considered

The marketing concept is so logical that it's hard to argue with it. Yet when a firm focuses its efforts on satisfying some consumers—to achieve its objectives—there may be negative effects on society. For example, producers and consumers making free choices can cause conflicts and difficulties. This is called the **micro-macro dilemma**. What is "good" for some firms and consumers may not be good for society as a whole.

For example, many Americans want the convenience of disposable products and products in easy-to-use, small-serving packages. But these same "convenient" products and packages often lead to pollution of the environment and inefficient use of natural resources. Should future generations be left to pay the consequences of pollution that is the result of free choice by today's consumers?

Socially responsible marketing managers are concerned about the environmental impact of their decisions, and some firms are finding innovative ways to both help the environment and improve customer satisfaction at the same time.

Questions like these are not easy to answer. The basic reason is that many different people may have a stake in the outcomes—and social consequences—of the choices made by individual managers *and* consumers in a market-directed system. This means that marketing managers should be concerned with **social responsibility**—a firm's obligation to improve its positive effects on society and reduce its negative effects. As you read this book and learn more about marketing, you will also learn more about social responsibility in marketing—and why it must be taken seriously. You'll also see that being socially responsible sometimes requires difficult trade-offs.

Consider, for example, the environmental problems created by CFCs, chemicals that were used in hundreds of critical products, including fire extinguishers, cooling systems, and electronic circuit boards. When it was learned that CFCs deplete the earth's ozone layer, it was not possible to immediately stop producing and using all CFCs. For many products critical to society, there was no feasible short-term substitute. Du Pont and other producers of CFCs worked hard to balance these conflicting demands until substitute products could be found. Yet you can see that there are no easy answers for how such conflicts should be resolved.[16]

The issue of social responsibility in marketing also raises other important questions—for which there are no easy answers.

Should all consumer needs be satisfied?

Some consumers want products that may not be safe or good for them in the long run. Some critics argue that businesses should not offer high-heeled shoes, alcoholic beverages, or sugar-coated cereals because they aren't "good" for consumers in the long run.

Similarly, bicycles and roller blades are among the most dangerous products identified by the Consumer Product Safety Commission. Who should decide if these products will be offered to consumers?

What if it cuts into profits?

Being more socially conscious often seems to lead to positive customer response. For example, many consumers praise Wal-Mart as a "safe haven" for kids to shop because it does not carry CDs that are not suitable for children, lewd videos, plastic guns that look authentic, and video games judged to be too violent. Green Mountain has had a very good response to electric power produced with less pollution (even though the price is higher). And some consumers buy only from firms that certify that their overseas factories don't rely on child labor.[17]

Yet as the examples above show, there are times when being socially responsible conflicts with a firm's profit objective. Concerns about such conflicts have prompted critics to raise the basic question: Is the marketing concept really desirable?

Many socially conscious marketing managers are trying to resolve this problem. Their definition of customer satisfaction includes long-range effects—as well as immediate customer satisfaction. They try to balance consumer, company, *and* social interests.

The marketing concept guides marketing ethics

Certainly some concerns about social responsibility and marketing arise because some individual firm or manager was intentionally unethical and cheated the market. Of course, a manager cannot be truly consumer-oriented and at the same time intentionally unethical. However, at times, problems and criticism may arise because a manager did not fully consider the ethical implications of a decision. In either case, there is no excuse for sloppiness when it comes to **marketing ethics**—the moral standards that guide marketing decisions and actions. Each individual develops moral standards based on his or her own values. That helps explain why opinions about what is right or wrong often vary from one person to another, from one society to another, and among different groups within a society. It is sometimes difficult to say whose opinions are "correct." Even so, such opinions may have a very real influence on whether an individual's (or a firm's) marketing decisions and actions are accepted or rejected. So marketing ethics are not only a philosophical issue, they are also a pragmatic concern.

Problems may arise when some individual manager does not share the same marketing ethics as others in the organization. One person operating alone can damage a firm's reputation and even survival.

To be certain that standards for marketing ethics are as clear as possible, many organizations have developed their own written codes of ethics. These codes usually state—at least at a general level—the ethical standards that everyone in the firm should follow in dealing with customers and other people. Many professional societies also have such codes. For example, the American Marketing Association's code of ethics—see Exhibit 1-8—sets specific ethical standards for many aspects of marketing.[18]

Throughout the text, we will be discussing the types of ethical issues individual marketing managers face. But we won't be moralizing and trying to tell you how you should think on any given issue. Rather, by the end of the course we hope that *you* will have some firm personal opinions about what is and is not ethical in micro-marketing activities.[19]

Fortunately, the prevailing practice of most businesspeople is to be fair and honest. However, not all criticisms of marketing focus on ethical issues.

Marketing has its critics

We must admit that marketing—as it exists in the United States and other developed societies—has many critics. Marketing activity is especially open to criticism because it is the part of business most visible to the public.

A number of typical complaints about marketing are summarized in Exhibit 1-9. Think about these criticisms and whether you agree with them or not. What complaints do you have that are not covered by one of the categories in Exhibit 1-9?

Such complaints should not be taken lightly. They show that many people are unhappy with some parts of the marketing system. Certainly, the strong public

Exhibit 1-8   Code of Ethics, American Marketing Association

CODE OF ETHICS

Members of the American Marketing Association (AMA) are committed to ethical professional conduct. They have joined together in subscribing to this Code of Ethics embracing the following topics:

Responsibilities of the Marketer

Marketers must accept responsibility for the consequences of their activities and make every effort to ensure that their decisions, recommendations, and actions function to identify, serve, and satisfy all relevant publics: customers, organizations and society.

Marketers' professional conduct must be guided by:

1. The basic rule of professional ethics: not knowingly to do harm;

2. The adherence to all applicable laws and regulations;

3. The accurate representation of their education, training and experience; and

4. The active support, practice and promotion of this Code of Ethics.

Honesty and Fairness

Marketers shall uphold and advance the integrity, honor, and dignity of the marketing profession by:

1. Being honest in serving consumers, clients, employees, suppliers, distributors and the public;

2. Not knowingly participating in conflict of interest without prior notice to all parties involved; and

3. Establishing equitable fee schedules including the payment or receipt of usual, customary and/or legal compensation for marketing exchanges.

Rights and Duties of Parties in the Marketing Exchange Process

Participants in the marketing exchange process should be able to expect that:

1. Products and services offered are safe and fit for their intended uses;

2. Communications about offered products and services are not deceptive;

3. All parties intend to discharge their obligations, financial and otherwise, in good faith; and

4. Appropriate internal methods exist for equitable adjustment and/or redress of grievances concerning purchases.

It is understood that the above would include, but is not limited to, the following responsibilities of the marketer:

In the area of product development and management,

- disclosure of all substantial risks associated with product or service usage;

- identification of any product component substitution that might materially change the product or impact on the buyer's purchase decision;

- identification of extra-cost added features.

In the area of promotions,

- avoidance of false and misleading advertising;

- rejection of high pressure manipulations, or misleading sales tactics;

- avoidance of sales promotions that use deception or manipulation.

In the area of distribution,

- not manipulating the availability of a product for purpose of exploitation;

- not using coercion in the marketing channel;

- not exerting undue influence over the reseller's choice to handle a product.

In the area of pricing,

- not engaging in price fixing;

- not practicing predatory pricing;

- disclosing the full price associated with any purchase.

In the area of marketing research,

- prohibiting selling or fund raising under the guise of conducting research;

- maintaining research integrity by avoiding misrepresentation and omission of pertinent research data;

- treating outside clients and suppliers fairly.

Organizational Relationships

Marketers should be aware of how their behavior may influence or impact on the behavior of others in organizational relationships. They should not demand, encourage or apply coercion to obtain unethical behavior in their relationships with others, such as employees, suppliers or customers.

1. Apply confidentiality and anonymity in professional relationships with regard to privileged information;

2. Meet their obligations and responsibilities in contracts and mutual agreements in a timely manner;

3. Avoid taking the work of others, in whole, or in part, and represent this work as their own or directly benefit from it without compensation or consent of the originator or owner;

4. Avoid manipulation to take advantage of situations to maximize personal welfare in a way that unfairly deprives or damages the organization or others.

Any AMA member found to be in violation of any provision of this Code of Ethics may have his or her Association membership suspended or revoked.

Exhibit 1-9 Sample Criticisms of Marketing

- Advertising is everywhere, and it's often annoying, misleading, or wasteful.
- The quality of products is poor and often they are not even safe.
- There are too many unnecessary products.
- Packaging and labeling are often confusing and deceptive.
- Middlemen add too much to the cost of distribution and just raise prices without providing anything in return.
- Marketing serves the rich and exploits the poor.

- Service stinks, and when a consumer has a problem nobody cares.
- Marketing creates interest in products that pollute the environment.
- Private information about consumers is collected and used to sell them things they don't want.
- Marketing makes people too materialistic and motivates them toward "things" instead of social needs.
- Easy consumer credit makes people buy things they don't need and can't afford.

support for consumer protection laws proves that not all consumers feel they are being treated like royalty.

As you consider the various criticisms of marketing, keep in mind that not all of them deal with the marketing practices of specific firms. Some of the complaints about marketing really focus on the basic idea of a market-directed macro-marketing system—and these criticisms often occur because people don't understand what marketing is—or how it works.[20] As you go through this book, we'll discuss some of these criticisms. Then in our final chapter, we will return to a more complete appraisal of marketing in our consumer-oriented society.

CONCLUSION

In this chapter, we highlighted the value of marketing for consumers, firms, and society. There are two levels of marketing: micro-marketing and macro-marketing. Micro-marketing focuses on the activities of individual firms. Macro-marketing is concerned with the way the whole marketing system works in a society or economy. We discussed the functions of marketing and who performs them, including marketing specialists who serve as intermediaries between producers and consumers and other specialists who are facilitators. We explained how a market-directed economy works, through the macro-marketing system, to provide consumers with choices. We introduced macro-marketing in this chapter, and we'll consider macro-marketing issues throughout the text. But the major thrust of this book is on micro-marketing.

The marketing concept provides direction to a marketing-oriented firm. The marketing concept stresses that the company's efforts should focus on satisfying some target customers—at a profit. Production-oriented firms tend to forget this. The various departments

within a production-oriented firm let their natural conflicts of interest get in the way of customer satisfaction. Satisfaction relates to customer value, and superior customer value is crucial in attracting customers and in building beneficial long-term relationships with them.

We also covered ways that social responsibility and marketing ethics relate to the marketing concept, and ended with the criticisms of marketing—both of the way individual firms work and of the whole macro system.

By learning more about market-oriented decision making, you will be able to make more efficient and socially responsible decisions. This will help improve the performance of individual firms and organizations (your employers). And eventually it will help our macro-marketing system work better. In the next chapter, we introduce a marketing strategy planning process that is the framework for ideas developed throughout the rest of the text—and that will guide your marketing thinking in the future.

KEY TERMS

production, 5

customer satisfaction, 5

utility, 5

form utility, 5

task utility, 5

time utility, 6

QUESTIONS AND PROBLEMS

1. List your activities for the first two hours after you woke up this morning. Briefly indicate how marketing affected your activities.

2. It is fairly easy to see why people do not beat a path to a mousetrap manufacturer's door, but would they be similarly indifferent if some food processor developed a revolutionary new food product that would provide all necessary nutrients in small pills for about $100 per year per person?

3. If a producer creates a really revolutionary new product and consumers can learn about it and purchase it at a website on the Internet, is any additional marketing effort really necessary? Explain your thinking.

4. Explain, in your own words, why this text emphasizes micro-marketing.

5. Distinguish between macro- and micro-marketing. Then explain how they are interrelated, if they are.

6. Refer to Exhibit 1-2, and give an example of a purchase you made recently that involved separation of information and separation in time between you and the producer. Briefly explain how these separations were overcome.

7. Describe a recent purchase you made. Indicate why that particular product was available at a store and, in particular, at the store where you bought it.

8. Define the functions of marketing in your own words. Using an example, explain how they can be shifted and shared.

9. Online computer shopping at websites on the Internet makes it possible for individual consumers to get direct information from hundreds of companies they would not otherwise know about. Consumers can place an order for a purchase that is then shipped to them directly. Will growth of these services ultimately eliminate the need for retailers and wholesalers? Explain your thinking, giving specific attention to what marketing functions are involved in these "electronic purchases" and who performs them.

10. Explain why a small producer might want a marketing research firm to take over some of its information-gathering activities.

11. Distinguish between how economic decisions are made in a planned economic system and how they are made in a market-directed economy.

12. Would the functions that must be provided and the development of wholesaling and retailing systems be any different in a planned economy from those in a market-directed economy?

13. Explain why a market-directed macro-marketing system encourages innovation. Give an example.

14. Define the marketing concept in your own words, and then explain why the notion of profit is usually included in this definition.

15. Define the marketing concept in your own words, and then suggest how acceptance of this concept might affect the organization and operation of your college.

16. Distinguish between production orientation and marketing orientation, illustrating with local examples.

17. Explain why a firm should view its internal activities as part of a total system. Illustrate your answer for (a) a large grocery products producer, (b) a plumbing wholesaler, (c) a department store chain, and (d) a cell phone service.

18. Give examples of some of the benefits and costs that might contribute to the customer value of each of the following products: (*a*) a wristwatch, (*b*) a weight-loss diet supplement, (*c*) a cruise on a luxury liner, and (*d*) a checking account from a bank.

19. Give an example of a recent purchase you made where the purchase wasn't just a single transaction but rather part of an ongoing relationship with the seller. Discuss what the seller has done (or could do better) to strengthen the relationship and increase the odds of you being a loyal customer in the future.

20. Discuss how the micro-macro dilemma relates to each of the following products: high-powered engines in cars, nuclear power, bank credit cards, and pesticides that improve farm production.

21. A committee of the American Marketing Association defined marketing as "the process of planning and executing the conception, pricing, promotion, and distribution of ideas, goods, and services to create exchanges that satisfy individual and organizational objectives." Does this definition consider macro-marketing? Explain your answer.

SUGGESTED CASES

1. McDonald's "Seniors" Restaurant

2. Healthy Foods, Inc.

COMPUTER-AIDED PROBLEM

1. Revenue, Cost, and Profit Relationships

RESOURCE REMINDER

This problem introduces you to the computer-aided problem (CAP) software—which is on the CD that accompanies this text—and gets you started with the use of spreadsheet analysis for marketing decision making. This problem is simple. In fact, you could work it without the software. But by starting with a simple problem, you will learn how to use the program more quickly and see how it will help you with more complicated problems. Instructions for the software are available at the end of this text.

Sue Cline, the business manager at Magna University Student Bookstore, is developing plans for the next academic year. The bookstore is one of the university's non-profit activities, but any "surplus" (profit) it earns is used to support the student activities center.

Two popular products at the bookstore are the student academic calendar and notebooks with the school name. Sue Cline thinks that she can sell calendars to 90 percent of Magna's 3,000 students, so she has had 2,700 printed. The total cost, including artwork and printing, is $11,500. Last year the calendar sold for $5.00, but Sue is considering changing the price this year.

Sue thinks that the bookstore will be able to sell 6,000 notebooks if they are priced right. But she knows that many students will buy similar notebooks (without the school name) from stores in town if the bookstore price is too high.

Sue has entered the information about selling price, quantity, and costs for calendars and notebooks in the spreadsheet program so that it is easy to evaluate the effect of different decisions. The spreadsheet is also set up to calculate revenue and profit, based on

$$\text{Revenue} = (\text{Selling price}) \times (\text{Quantity sold})$$

$$\text{Profit} = (\text{Revenue}) - (\text{Total cost})$$

Use the program to answer the questions below. Record your answers on a separate sheet of paper.

a. From the Spreadsheet Screen, how much revenue does Sue expect from calendars? How much revenue from notebooks? How much profit will the store earn from calendars? From notebooks?

b. If Sue increases the price of her calendars to $6.00 and still sells the same quantity, what is the expected revenue? The expected profit? (Note: Change the price from $5.00 to $6.00 on the spreadsheet and the program will recompute revenue and profit.) On your sheet of paper, show the calculations that confirm that the program has given you the correct values.

c. Sue is interested in getting an overview of how a change in the price of notebooks would affect revenue and profit, assuming that she sells all 6,000 notebooks she is thinking of ordering. Prepare a table—on your sheet of paper—with column headings for three variables: selling price, revenue, and profit. Show the value for revenue and profit for different possible selling prices for a notebook—starting at a minimum price of $1.60 and adding 8 cents to the price until you reach a maximum of $2.40. At what price will selling 6,000 notebooks contribute $5,400.00 to profit? At what price would notebook sales contribute only $1,080.00? (Hint: Use the What If analysis feature to compute the new values. Start by selecting "selling price" for notebooks as the value to change, with a minimum value of $1.60 and a maximum value of $2.40. Select the revenue and profit for notebooks as the values to display.)

For additional questions related to this problem, see Exercise 1-5 in the *Learning Aid for Use with Basic Marketing*, 15th edition.

CHAPTER TWO

Marketing Strategy Planning

As you saw in Chapter 1, marketing and marketing management are important in our society—and in business firms and nonprofit organizations. To get you thinking about the marketing strategy planning ideas we will be developing in this chapter and the rest of the book, let's consider Dell Computers.

As a freshman in college, Michael Dell started buying and reselling computers from his dorm room. At that time, the typical marketing mix for PCs emphasized distribution through specialized computer stores that sold to business users and some final consumers. Often the dealers' service quality didn't justify the high prices they charged, the features of the PCs they had in stock didn't match what customers wanted, and repairs were a hassle.

Dell decided there was a target market of price-conscious customers who would respond to a different marketing mix. He used direct-response advertising in computer magazines—and customers called a toll-free number to order a computer with the exact features

they wanted. Dell built computers to match the specific orders that came in and used UPS to quickly ship orders directly to the customer. Prices were low, too—because the direct channel meant there was no retailer markup and the build-to-order approach reduced inventory costs. This approach also kept Dell in constant contact with customers. Problems could be identified quickly and corrected. Dell also implemented the plan well—with constant improvements—to make good on its promise of reliable machines and superior service. For example, Dell pioneered a system of guaranteed on-site service—within 24 hours. Dell also set up ongoing programs to train all employees to work together to please customers.

Of course, it's hard to satisfy everyone all of the time. For example, profits fell when one of Dell's laptop designs didn't measure up. Customers simply didn't see them as a good value. However, smart marketers learn from and fix mistakes. Dell quickly got its product line back on the bull's eye.

As sales grew, Dell put more money into advertising. Its ad agency crafted ads to position Dell in consumers' minds as an aggressive, value-oriented source of computers. At the same time, Dell added a direct sales force to call on big government and corporate buyers—because they expected in-person selling and a relationship, not just a telephone contact. And when these important customers said they wanted Dell to offer high-power machines to run their corporate networks, Dell put money into R&D to create what they needed.

Dell also saw the prospect for international growth. Many firms moved into Europe by exporting. But Dell set up its own operations there. Dell knew it would be tough to win over skeptical European buyers. They had never bought big-ticket items such as PCs on the phone. Yet in less than five years, sales in Europe grew to 40 percent of Dell's total revenue and Dell pushed into Asian markets for more growth. That also posed challenges, so Dell's advertising manager invited major ad agencies to make presentations on how Dell could be more effective with its $80 million global advertising campaign.

By the mid 1990s, IBM and other firms were trying to imitate Dell's direct-order approach. However, the retailers who were selling the bulk of IBM's PCs were not happy about facing price competition from their own supplier! So IBM couldn't simply copy Dell's strategy. It was in conflict with the rest of IBM's marketing program.

As computer prices fell, many firms were worried about how to cope with slim profits. But Dell saw an opportunity for profitable growth by extending its direct model to a website (www.dell.com). Moreover, online selling lowered expenses and reduced supply and inventory costs. For example, when a customer ordered a PC produced in one factory and a monitor

produced in another, the two pieces were brought together enroute to the customer. This cost cutting proved to be especially important when the economy softened and demand for PCs fell off. Building on its strengths, Dell cut prices in what many competitors saw as an "irrational" price war. But the design of Dell's website and sales system allowed it to charge different prices to different segments to match demand with supply. For example, high-margin laptops were priced lower to educational customers—to stimulate demand—than to government buyers who were less price sensitive. Similarly, if the supply of new 17-inch flat-screen monitors fell short, Dell could use an online promotion for 19-inch monitors and shift demand. To earn more profit from existing customers, Dell also put more emphasis on selling extended-care service agreements.

As PC sales taper off, Dell is seeking new growth with strategies that will enhance its marketing program. For example, Dell's new kiosks in retail stores and malls should reach new customers who want to shop and buy "in person." And product-development efforts include new lines of printers, handhelds, and network servers. In contrast, after screening the opportunity for new tablet computers, Dell decided *not* to be one of the earliest firms in that market.[1]

We've mentioned only a few of many decisions marketing managers at Dell had to make in developing marketing strategies, but you can see that each of these decisions affects the others. Further, making marketing decisions is never easy and strategies may need to change. Yet knowing what basic decision areas to consider helps you to plan a more successful strategy. This chapter will get you started by giving you a framework for thinking about marketing strategy planning—which is what the rest of this book is all about.

THE MANAGEMENT JOB IN MARKETING

In Chapter 1 you learned about the marketing concept—a philosophy to guide the whole firm toward satisfying customers at a profit. From the Dell case, it's clear that marketing decisions are very important to a firm's success. So let's look more closely at how a marketing manager helps a firm to achieve its objectives. Because the marketing manager is a manager, let's look at the marketing management process.

The **marketing management process** is the process of (1) *planning* marketing activities, (2) directing the *implementation* of the plans, and (3) *controlling* these plans. Planning, implementation, and control are basic jobs of all managers—but here we will emphasize what they mean to marketing managers.

Exhibit 2-1 shows the relationships among the three jobs in the marketing management process. The jobs are all connected to show that the marketing management process is continuous. In the planning job, managers set guidelines for the implementing job and specify expected results. They use these expected results in the control job to determine if everything has worked out as planned. The link from the control job to the planning job is especially important. This feedback often leads to changes in the plans or to new plans.

Marketing managers should seek new opportunities

Marketing managers cannot be satisfied just planning present activities. Markets are dynamic. Consumers' needs, competitors, and the environment keep changing. Consider Parker Brothers, a company that seemed to have a "Monopoly" in family

Exhibit 2-1
The Marketing Management Process

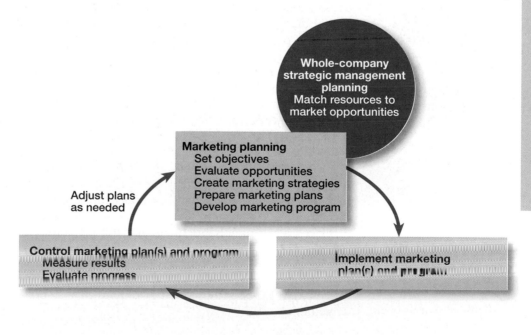

games. While it continued selling board games, firms like Sega, Sony, and Nintendo zoomed in with video game competition. Of course, not every opportunity is good for every company. Really attractive opportunities are those that fit with what the whole company wants to do and is able to do well.

Strategic management planning concerns the whole firm

The job of planning strategies to guide a whole company is called **strategic (management) planning**—the managerial process of developing and maintaining a match between an organization's resources and its market opportunities. This is a top-management job. It includes planning not only for marketing but also for production, finance, human resources, and other areas. In Chapter 20, we'll look at links between marketing and these areas.

Although marketing strategies are not whole-company plans, company plans should be market-oriented. And the marketing plan often sets the tone and direction for the whole company. So we will use *strategy planning* and *marketing strategy planning* to mean the same thing.[2]

WHAT IS MARKETING STRATEGY PLANNING?

Marketing strategy planning means finding attractive opportunities and developing profitable marketing strategies. But what is a "marketing strategy"? We have used these words rather casually so far. Now let's see what they really mean.

What is a marketing strategy?

A **marketing strategy** specifies a target market and a related marketing mix. It is a big picture of what a firm will do in some market. Two interrelated parts are needed:

1. A **target market**—a fairly homogeneous (similar) group of customers to whom a company wishes to appeal.
2. A **marketing mix**—the controllable variables the company puts together to satisfy this target group.

The importance of target customers in this process can be seen in Exhibit 2-2, where the target customer—the "C"—is at the center of the diagram. The customer is surrounded by the controllable variables that we call the "marketing mix." A typical marketing mix includes some product, offered at a price, with some promotion to tell potential customers about the product, and a way to reach the customer's place.

The marketing strategy for The Learning Company's software aims at a specific group of target customers: young parents who have a computer at home and want their kids to learn while playing. The strategy calls for a variety of educational software products—like *Reader Rabbit* and *Where in the World Is Carmen Sandiego?* The firm's software is designed with entertaining graphics and sound, and it's tested on kids to be certain that it is easy to use. To make it convenient for target customers to buy the software, it can be ordered from the firm's own website (www.learningcompany.com) or from other retailers like Toys "R" Us. Promotion has helped build customer interest in the software. For example, when marketing managers released *Where in Time Is Carmen Sandiego?* they not only placed ads in family-oriented computer magazines but also sent direct-mail flyers or e-mail to registered customers of the firm's other products. Some firms sell less-expensive games for kids, but parents are loyal to The Learning Company brand because it caters to their needs and offers first-class customer service—including a 90-day, no-questions-asked guarantee that assures the buyer of good customer value.[3]

Target marketing is not mass marketing

Note that a marketing strategy specifies some *particular* target customers. This approach is called "target marketing" to distinguish it from "mass marketing." **Target marketing** says that a marketing mix is tailored to fit some specific target customers. In contrast, **mass marketing**—the typical production-oriented approach—vaguely aims at "everyone" with the same marketing mix. Mass marketing assumes that everyone is the same—and it considers everyone to be a potential customer. It may help to think of target marketing as the "rifle approach" and mass marketing as the "shotgun approach." See Exhibit 2-3.

Mass marketers may do target marketing

Commonly used terms can be confusing here. The terms *mass marketing* and *mass marketers* do not mean the same thing. Far from it! *Mass marketing* means trying to sell to "everyone," as we explained above. *Mass marketers* like Kraft Foods and Wal-Mart are aiming at clearly defined target markets. The confusion with mass marketing occurs because their target markets usually are large and spread out.

Target marketing can mean big markets and profits

Target marketing is not limited to small market segments—only to fairly homogeneous ones. A very large market—even what is sometimes called the "mass market"—may be fairly homogeneous, and a target marketer will deliberately aim at it. For example, a very large group of parents of young children are homogeneous on many dimensions—including their attitudes about changing baby diapers. In the United States alone, this group spends about $4 billion a year on disposable diapers—so it should be no surprise that it is a major target market for companies like Kimberly-Clark (Huggies) and Procter & Gamble (Pampers).

The basic reason to focus on some specific target customers is so that you can develop a marketing mix that satisfies those customers' *specific* needs better than they are satisfied by some other firm. For example, E*trade uses an Internet site (www.etrade.com) to target knowledgeable investors who want a convenient, low-cost way to buy and sell stocks online without a lot of advice (or pressure) from a salesperson.

When a firm carefully targets its marketing mix, it is less likely to face direct competitors. So superior customer value is achieved with the benefits provided by the whole marketing mix rather than just by relying on a lower price. Whole Foods Market

Exhibit 2-3
Production-Oriented and Marketing-Oriented Managers Have Different Views of the Market

Production-oriented manager sees everyone as basically similar and practices "mass marketing"

Marketing-oriented manager sees everyone as different and practices "target marketing"

(WFM) is a good example. Most grocery stores sell the same brands—so they compete on price and profits tend to be weak. In contrast, WFM makes attractive profits with a differentiated marketing mix that delights its target customers. WFM sees itself as a buying agent for its customers and not the selling agent for manufacturers—so it evaluates the ingredients, freshness, safety, taste, nutritive value, and appearance of all the products it carries. It hires people who love food. They don't just sell food—but rather help their customers appreciate the difference natural and organic products can make in the quality of their lives. Service is attentive, friendly, and offered with some flair, which helps make the store fun and inviting. Customers often socialize while they shop. Not everyone wants the marketing mix that WFM offers; but its target customers love shopping there—and they spread the word to others.

DEVELOPING MARKETING MIXES FOR TARGET MARKETS

There are many marketing mix decisions

There are many possible ways to satisfy the needs of target customers. A product might have many different features. Customer service levels before or after the sale can be adjusted. The package, brand name, and warranty can be changed. Various advertising media—newspapers, magazines, cable, the Internet—may be used. A company's own sales force or other sales specialists can be used. The price can be changed, discounts can be given, and so on. With so many possible variables, is there any way to help organize all these decisions and simplify the selection of marketing mixes? The answer is yes.

The four "Ps" make up a marketing mix

It is useful to reduce all the variables in the marketing mix to four basic ones:

Product.
Place.
Promotion.
Price.

It helps to think of the four major parts of a marketing mix as the "four Ps." Exhibit 2-4 emphasizes their relationship and their common focus on the target customer—"C."

Exhibit 2-4
A Marketing Strategy—Showing the Four Ps of a Marketing Mix

Customer is not part of the marketing mix

The customer is shown surrounded by the four Ps in Exhibit 2-4. Some students assume that the customer is part of the marketing mix—but this is not so. The customer should be the *target* of all marketing efforts. The customer is placed in the center of the diagram to show this. The C stands for some specific customers—the target market.

Exhibit 2-5 shows some of the strategy decision variables organized by the four Ps. These will be discussed in later chapters. For now, let's just describe each P briefly.

Product—the good or service for the target's needs

The Product area is concerned with developing the right "product" for the target market. This offering may involve a physical good, a service, or a blend of both. Keep in mind that Product is not limited to physical goods. For example, the Product of H & R Block is a completed tax form. The Product of a political party is the set of causes it will work to achieve. The important thing to remember is that your good or service should satisfy some customers' needs.

Along with other Product-area decisions like branding, packaging, and warranties, we will talk about developing and managing new products and whole product lines.

Exhibit 2-5
Strategy Decision Areas
Organized by the Four Ps

Product	Place	Promotion	Price
Physical good	Objectives	Objectives	Objectives
Service	Channel type	Promotion blend	Flexibility
Features	Market exposure	Salespeople	Level over
Benefits	Kinds of	Kind	product life
Quality level	middlemen	Number	cycle
Accessories	Kinds and	Selection	Geographic terms
Installation	locations of	Training	Discounts
Instructions	stores	Motivation	Allowances
Warranty	How to handle	Advertising	
Product lines	transporting	Targets	
Packaging	and storing	Kinds of ads	
Branding	Service levels	Media type	
	Recruiting	Copy thrust	
	middlemen	Prepared by	
	Managing	whom	
	channels	Sales promotion	
		Publicity	

Place—reaching the target

Place is concerned with all the decisions involved in getting the "right" product to the target market's Place. A product isn't much good to a customer if it isn't available when and where it's wanted.

A product reaches customers through a channel of distribution. A **channel of distribution** is any series of firms (or individuals) that participate in the flow of products from producer to final user or consumer.

Sometimes a channel system is quite short. It may run directly from a producer to a final user or consumer. This is especially common in business markets and in the marketing of services. The channel is direct when a producer uses an online website to handle orders by target customers, whether the customer is a final consumer or an organization. So direct channels have become much more common since the development of the Internet.

On the other hand, often the channel system is much more complex—involving many different retailers and wholesalers. See Exhibit 2-6 for some examples. When

A firm's product may involve a physical good, a service, or a combination of both.

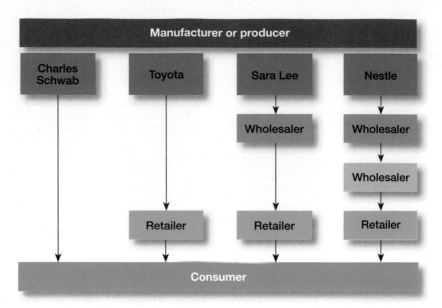

a marketing manager has several different target markets, several different channels of distribution may be needed.

We will also see how physical distribution service levels and decisions concerning logistics (transporting, storing, and handling products) relate to the other Place decisions and the rest of the marketing mix.

Promotion—telling and selling the customer

The third P—Promotion—is concerned with telling the target market or others in the channel of distribution about the "right" product. Sometimes promotion is focused on acquiring new customers, and sometimes it's focused on retaining current customers. Promotion includes personal selling, mass selling, and sales promotion. It is the marketing manager's job to blend these methods of communication.

Personal selling involves direct spoken communication between sellers and potential customers. Personal selling usually happens face-to-face, but sometimes the communication occurs over the telephone or even via a video conference over the Internet. Personal selling lets the salesperson adapt the firm's marketing mix to each potential customer. But this individual attention comes at a price; personal selling can be very expensive. Often this personal effort has to be blended with mass selling and sales promotion.

Mass selling is communicating with large numbers of customers at the same time. The main form of mass selling is **advertising**—any *paid* form of nonpersonal presentation of ideas, goods, or services by an identified sponsor. **Publicity**—any *unpaid* form of nonpersonal presentation of ideas, goods, or services—is another important form of mass selling. Mass selling may involve a wide variety of media, ranging from newspapers and billboards to the Internet.

Sales promotion refers to those promotion activities—other than advertising, publicity, and personal selling—that stimulate interest, trial, or purchase by final customers or others in the channel. This can involve use of coupons, point-of-purchase materials, samples, signs, contests, catalogs, novelties, and circulars.

Price—making it right

In addition to developing the right Product, Place, and Promotion, marketing managers must also decide the right Price. Price setting must consider the kind of competition in the target market and the cost of the whole marketing mix. A manager must also try to estimate customer reaction to possible prices. Besides this, the manager must know current practices as to markups, discounts, and other terms of sale. And if customers won't accept the Price, all of the planning effort is wasted.

LIFETIME VALUE OF CUSTOMERS CAN BE VERY HIGH— OR VERY LOW

Investors lost millions when stock market values of dot-com firms collapsed after an initial, frenzied run up. But why did values get so high in the first place, especially when most dot-coms were not yet profitable? The stock went up because many investors expected that the firms would earn profits in the future as more consumers went online and the early dot-coms accumulated customers. These hopes were fueled by dot-coms that made optimistic predictions about the lifetime value of the customers they were acquiring. The lifetime value of the customer concept is not new. For decades General Motors has known that a consumer who buys a GM car and is satisfied is likely to buy another one the next time. If that happens again and again, over a lifetime the happy customer would spend $250,000 on GM cars. Of course, this only works if the firm's marketing mix attracts the target customers and the relationship keeps them satisfied before, during, and after every purchase. If you don't satisfy and retain customers they don't have high lifetime value and don't generate sales. Of course, sales revenue alone does not guarantee profits. For example, a firm can't give away products—or spend so much on promotion to acquire new customers (or keep the ones it has)—that the revenue will never be able to offset the costs. Unfortunately, that is what happened with many of the dot-coms. They saw how the financial arithmetic might work—*assuming* that new customers kept buying and costs came under control. But without a sensible marketing strategy, that assumption was not realistic.[4]

Each of the four Ps contributes to the whole

All four Ps are needed in a marketing mix. In fact, they should all be tied together. But is any one more important than the others? Generally speaking, the answer is no— all contribute to one whole. When a marketing mix is being developed, all (final) decisions about the Ps should be made at the same time. That's why the four Ps are arranged around the customer (C) in a circle—to show that they all are equally important.

Let's sum up our discussion of marketing mix planning thus far. We develop a *Product* to satisfy the target customers. We find a way to reach our target customers' *Place*. We use *Promotion* to tell the target customers (and others in the channel) about the product that has been designed for them. And we set a *Price* after estimating expected customer reaction to the total offering and the costs of getting it to them.

Strategy jobs must be done together

It is important to stress—it cannot be overemphasized—that selecting a target market *and* developing a marketing mix are interrelated. Both parts of a marketing strategy must be decided together. It is *strategies* that must be evaluated against the company's objectives—not alternative target markets or alternative marketing mixes.

Understanding target markets leads to good strategies

The needs of a target market often virtually determine the nature of an appropriate marketing mix. So marketers must analyze their potential target markets with great care. This book will explore ways of identifying attractive market opportunities and developing appropriate strategies.

These ideas can be seen more clearly with an example in the children's fashion market.

Market-oriented strategy planning at Toddler University

The case of Jeff Silverman and Toddler University (TU), Inc., a shoe company he started, illustrates the strategy planning process. During high school and college, Silverman worked as a salesperson at local shoe stores. He also gained valuable experience during a year working for Nike. From these jobs he learned a lot about customers' needs and interests. He also realized that some parents were not satisfied when it came to finding shoes for their preschool children.

Silverman thought that there was a large, but hard to describe, mass market for general-purpose baby shoes—perhaps 60 or 70 percent of the potential for all kinds

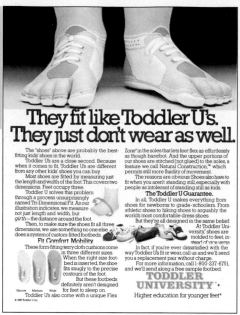

They fit like Toddler U's. They just don't wear as well.

The "shoes" above are probably the best-fitting kids' shoes in the world.

Toddler U's are a close second. Because when it comes to fit, Toddler U's are different from any other kids' shoes you can buy.

Most shoes are fitted by measuring just the length and width of the foot. This covers two dimensions. Feet occupy three.

Toddler U solves this problem through a process unsurprisingly named Tri-Dimensional Fit. As our illustration indicates, we measure not just length and width, but *girth*—the distance around the foot.

Then, to make sure the shoes fit all three dimensions, we use something no one else does: a system of custom-fitted footbeds.

Fit Comfort Mobility

These form-fitting terry cloth cushions come in three different sizes. When the right size footbed is inserted, the shoe fits snugly to the precise contours of the foot.

But these footbeds definitely aren't designed for feet to sleep on.

Toddler U's also come with a unique Flex

Zone® in the soles that lets feet flex as effortlessly as though barefoot. And the upper portions of our shoes are stitched (not glued) to the soles, a feature we call Natural Construction,™ which permits still more fluidity of movement.

The reasons are obvious: Shoes also have to fit when you aren't standing still, especially with people as intolerant of standing still as kids.

The Toddler U Guarantee.

In all, Toddler U makes everything from shoes for newborns to grade-schoolers. From athletic shoes to hiking shoes to arguably the world's most comfortable dress shoes.

But they're all designed in the same belief.

At Toddler University, shoes are molded to feet, instead of vice versa.

In fact, if you're ever dissatisfied with the way Toddler U's fit or wear, call us and we'll send you a replacement pair without charge.

For more information, call 1-800-237-6751, and we'll send along a free sample footbed.

TODDLER UNIVERSITY

Higher education for younger feet

To smuggle durable, custom-fitted shoes into a kid's wardrobe, disguise them as sneakers.

Toddler University presents a great leap forward for children's feet.

It's called the Higher Education™ Sneaker. And while its playful exterior may look like other sneakers, there the resemblance ends.

Because what you see here is footwear that gives kids who live in sneakers a significantly higher standard of living.

For instance, most companies that make lightweight shoes take the issue of fit all too lightly. Toddler U's come with custom-fitted footbeds that mold shoes to every contour of your child's feet. An exclusive process we call Tri-Dimensional Fit.

Other sneaker soles are surprisingly inflexible when it comes to bending. But

our Higher Education soles allow a child's feet to bend almost as easily as if they were barefoot, thanks to their pliant Flex Zones.

And since destroying sneakers is among every kid's favorite sports, ours come with thicker leathers, molded rubber toe guards, and sturdy T.U. Custom Canvas.™

Making them the first sneakers specifically designed to finish last.

In other words, Higher Education is anything but a sneaker of the old school.

To see the complete line in a brilliant array of styles and colors, phone 1-800-237-6751 for the Toddler U dealer near you.

TODDLER UNIVERSITY

Higher education for younger feet

of baby shoes. Silverman did not focus on this market because it didn't make sense for his small company to compete head on with many other firms where he had no particular advantage. However, he identified four other markets that were quite different. In the following description of these markets, note that useful marketing mixes come to mind immediately.

The *Traditionalists* seemed to be satisfied with a well-manufactured shoe that was available from "quality" stores where they could seek help in selecting the right size and fit. They didn't mind if the design was old-fashioned and didn't change. They wanted a well-known brand that had a reputation for quality, even if it was a bit more expensive.

Many of the *Economy Oriented* parents were in the lower income group. They wanted a basic shoe at a low price. They saw baby shoes as all pretty much the same—so a "name" brand didn't have much appeal. They were willing to shop around to see what was on sale at local discount, department, or shoe stores.

The *Fashion Conscious* were interested in dressing up baby in shoes that looked like smaller versions of the latest styles that they bought for themselves. Fit was important, but beyond that a colorful design is what got their attention. They were more likely to look for baby-size shoes at the shop where they bought their own athletic shoes.

The *Attentive Parents* wanted shoes that met a variety of needs. They wanted shoes to be fun and fashionable and functional. They didn't want just a good fit but also design and materials that were really right for baby play and learning to walk. These well-informed, upscale shoppers were likely to buy from a store that specialized in baby items. They were willing to pay a premium price if they found the right product.

Silverman thought that Stride Rite and Buster Brown were meeting the needs of the Traditionalists quite well. The Economy Oriented and Fashion Conscious customers were satisfied with shoes from a variety of other companies, including Nike. But Silverman saw a way to get a toe up on the competition by targeting the Attentive Parents with a marketing mix that combined, in his words, "fit and function with fun and fashion." He developed a detailed marketing plan that attracted financial backers, and at age 24 his company came to life.

TU didn't have its own production facilities, so Silverman contracted with a producer in Taiwan to make shoes with his brand name and to his specs. And his specs were different—they improved the product for his target market. Unlike most rigid high-topped infant shoes, he designed softer shoes with more comfortable rubber soles. The shoes lasted longer because they are stitched rather than glued. An extrawide opening made fitting easier on squirming feet. He also patented a special insert so parents could adjust the width. This change also helped win support from retailers. Since there are 11 sizes of children's shoes—and five widths—retailers usually need to stock 55 pairs of each model. TU's adjustable width reduced this stocking problem and made it more profitable for retailers to sell the line. It also made it possible for TU to resupply soldout inventory faster than competitors. Silverman's Product and Place decisions worked together well to provide customer value and also to give him a competitive advantage.

For promotion, Silverman developed print ads with close-up photos of babies wearing his shoes and informative details about their special benefits. Creative packaging also helped promote the shoe and attract customers in the store. For example, he put one athletic-style shoe in a box that looked like a gray gym locker. Silverman also provided the stores with "shoe rides"—electric-powered rocking replicas of its shoes. The rides not only attracted kids to the shoe department, but since they were coin-operated, they paid for themselves in a year.

TU priced most of its shoes at $35 to $40 a pair. This is a premium price, but with today's smaller families, the Attentive Parents are willing to spend more on each child.

In just four years, TU's sales jumped from $100,000 to over $40 million. To keep growth going, Silverman expanded distribution to reach new markets in Europe. To take advantage of TU's relationship with its satisfied target customers, he also added shoes for older kids to the Toddler University product assortment. Then Silverman made his biggest sale of all: He sold his company to Genesco, one of the biggest firms in the footwear business.[5]

THE MARKETING PLAN IS A GUIDE TO IMPLEMENTATION AND CONTROL

Marketing plan fills out marketing strategy

As the Toddler University case illustrates, a marketing strategy sets a target market and a marketing mix. It is a big picture of what a firm will do in some market. A marketing plan goes farther. A **marketing plan** is a written statement of a marketing strategy *and* the time-related details for carrying out the strategy. It should spell out the following in detail: (1) what marketing mix will be offered, to whom (that is, the target market), and for how long; (2) what company resources (shown as costs) will be needed at what rate (month by month perhaps); and (3) what results are expected (sales and profits perhaps monthly or quarterly, customer satisfaction levels, and the like). The plan should also include some control procedures—so that whoever is to carry out the plan will know if things are going wrong. This might be something as simple as comparing actual sales against expected sales—with a warning flag to be raised whenever total sales fall below a certain level.

In Chapter 21 we will take a closer look at what is in a marketing plan. At that point, you will have learned about all of the major strategy decision areas (Exhibit 2-5) and how to blend them into an innovative strategy.

Implementation puts plans into operation

After a marketing plan is developed, a marketing manager knows *what* needs to be done. Then the manager is concerned with **implementation**—putting marketing plans into operation.

Strategies work out as planned only when they are effectively implemented. Many **operational decisions**—short-run decisions to help implement strategies—may be needed.

Managers should make operational decisions within the guidelines set down during strategy planning. They develop product policies, place policies, and so on

Exhibit 2-7 Relation of Strategy Policies to Operational Decisions for Baby Shoe Company

Marketing Mix Decision Area	Strategy Policies	Likely Operational Decisions
Product	Carry as limited a line of colors, styles, and sizes as will satisfy the target market.	Add, change, or drop colors, styles, and/or sizes as customer tastes dictate.
Place	Distribute through selected "baby-products" retailers that will carry the full line and provide good in-store sales support and promotion.	In market areas where sales potential is not achieved, add new retail outlets and/or drop retailers whose performance is poor.
Promotion	Promote the benefits and value of the special design and how it meets customer needs.	When a retailer hires a new salesperson, send current training package with details on product line; increase use of local newspaper print ads during peak demand periods (before holidays, etc.).
Price	Maintain a "premium" price, but encourage retailers to make large-volume orders by offering discounts on quantity purchases.	Offer short-term introductory price "deals" to retailers when a new style is first introduced.

as part of strategy planning. Then operational decisions within these policies probably will be necessary—while carrying out the basic strategy. Note, however, that as long as these operational decisions stay within the policy guidelines, managers are making no change in the basic strategy. If the controls show that operational decisions are not producing the desired results, however, the managers may have to reevaluate the whole strategy—rather than just working harder at implementing it.

It's easier to see the difference between strategy decisions and operational decisions if we illustrate these ideas using our Toddler University example. Possible four-P or basic strategy policies are shown in the left-hand column in Exhibit 2-7, and examples of operational decisions are shown in the right-hand column.

It should be clear that some operational decisions are made regularly—even daily—and such decisions should not be confused with planning strategy. Certainly, a great deal of effort can be involved in these operational decisions. They might take a good part of the sales or advertising manager's time. But they are not the strategy decisions that will be our primary concern.

Our focus in this text is on developing marketing strategies. But eventually marketing managers must control the marketing plans that they develop and implement.[6]

Control is analyzing and correcting what you've done

The control job provides the feedback that leads managers to modify their marketing strategies. To maintain control, a marketing manager uses a number of tools—like computer sales analysis, marketing research surveys, and accounting analysis of expenses and profits. Chapter 19 considers the important topic of controlling marketing plans and programs.

In addition, as we talk about each of the marketing decision areas, we will discuss some of the control problems. This will help you understand how control keeps the firm on course—or shows the need to plan a new course.

All marketing jobs require planning and control

At first, it might appear that only high-level management or large companies need be concerned with planning and control. This is not true. Every organization needs planning—and without control it's impossible to know if the plans are working.

Several plans make a whole marketing program

Most companies implement more than one marketing strategy—and related marketing plan—at the same time. They may have several products—some of them quite different—that are aimed at different target markets. The other elements of

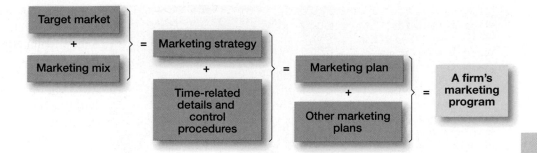

Exhibit 2-8
Elements of a Firm's
Marketing Program

the marketing mix may vary too. Gillette's Right Guard deodorant, its Mach3 razor blades, and its Duracell Ultra batteries all have different marketing mixes. Yet the strategies for each must be implemented at the same time.[7]

A **marketing program** blends all of the firm's marketing plans into one "big" plan. See Exhibit 2-8. This program, then, is the responsibility of the whole company. Typically, the whole *marketing program* is an integrated part of the whole-company strategic plan we discussed earlier.

We will emphasize planning one marketing strategy at a time, rather than planning—or implementing—a whole marketing program. This is practical because it is important to plan each strategy carefully. Too many marketing managers fall into sloppy thinking. They try to develop too many strategies all at once—and don't develop any very carefully. However, when new strategies are evaluated, it makes sense to see how well they fit with the existing marketing program. And, we'll talk about merging plans into a marketing program in Chapter 21.

Marketing strategy planning may be very important to you soon—maybe in your present job or college activities. In Appendix C on marketing careers, we present some strategy planning ideas for getting a marketing job.

THE IMPORTANCE OF MARKETING STRATEGY PLANNING

We emphasize the planning part of the marketing manager's job for a good reason. The "onetime" strategy decisions—the decisions that decide what business the company is in and the strategies it will follow—usually determine success, or failure. An extremely good plan might be carried out badly and still be profitable, while a poor but well-implemented plan can lose money. The case history that follows shows the importance of planning and why we emphasize marketing strategy planning throughout this text.

Time for new strategies in the watch industry

The conventional watchmakers—both domestic and foreign—had always aimed at customers who thought of watches as high-priced, high-quality symbols to mark special events, like graduations or retirement. Advertising was concentrated around Christmas and graduation time and stressed a watch's symbolic appeal. Expensive jewelry stores were the main retail outlets.

This commonly accepted strategy of the major watch companies ignored people in the target market that just wanted to tell the time and were interested in a reliable, low-priced watch. So the U.S. Time Company developed a successful strategy around its Timex watches and became the world's largest watch company. Timex completely upset the watch industry—both foreign and domestic—not only by offering a good product (with a one-year repair or replace guarantee) at a lower price, but also by using new, lower-cost channels of distribution. Its watches were widely available in drugstores, discount houses, and nearly any other retail stores that would carry them.

TIMEX
LIFE IS TICKING

Marketing managers at Timex soon faced a new challenge. Texas Instruments, a new competitor in the watch market, took the industry by storm with its low-cost but very accurate electronic watches—using the same channels Timex had originally developed. But other firms quickly developed a watch that used a more stylish liquid crystal display for the digital readout. Texas Instruments could not change quickly enough to keep up, and the other companies took away its customers. The competition became so intense that Texas Instruments stopped marketing watches altogether.

While Timex and others were focusing on lower-priced watches, Japan's Seiko captured a commanding share of the high-priced gift market for its stylish and accurate quartz watches by obtaining strong distribution. All of this forced many traditional watchmakers—like some of the once-famous Swiss brands—to close their factories.

Then Switzerland's Swatch launched its colorful, affordable plastic watches and changed what consumers see when they look at their watches. Swatch promoted its watches as fashion accessories and set them apart from those of other firms, whose ads squabbled about whose watches were most accurate and dependable. Swatch was also able to attract new retailers by focusing its distribution on upscale fashion and department stores. The total size of the watch market increased because many consumers bought several watches to match different fashions.

The economic downturn in the early 1990s brought more changes. Consumers were more cost conscious and less interested in expensive watches like those made by Rolex that were the "in" status symbol a few years earlier. The reemergence of value-seeking customers prompted Timex to return to its famous advertising tagline of the 1960s: "It takes a licking and keeps on ticking." Its position as the inexpensive-but-durable choice has helped it strengthen its distribution and has given it a leg up in getting shelf space for new products, such as its Indiglo line of watches.

By the turn of the century, the total market for watches was growing at only about 5 percent a year. To spark higher sales of its lines, Timex pushed to introduce more watches that combine time-telling and other needs. For example, Timex watches include heart-rate monitors, GPS systems to compute a runner's distance and speed, personal digital assistant functions (including data links to a computer), and Internet messenger capabilities so a watch can receive short text messages, like an alert from the wearer's stockbroker that it's time to sell. Of course, all the new features can make a watch more complicated to use, so Timex has promoted its I-control technology, which makes its watches "ridiculously easy to use." However, the competition is on the move as well. For example, Fossil, Inc., and Citizen Watch Company were the first watch companies to incorporate Microsoft's new operating system for SPOT (Small Personal Objective Technology). These watches connect to a wireless network to provide a variety of information services, including traffic and weather reports. With such changes always underway, marketing strategies at Timex must be constantly updated and revised.[8]

CREATIVE STRATEGY PLANNING NEEDED FOR SURVIVAL

Dramatic shifts in strategy—like those described above—may surprise conventional, production-oriented managers. But such changes should be expected. Managers who embrace the marketing concept realize that they cannot just define their line of business in terms of the products they currently produce or sell. Rather, they have to think about the basic consumer needs they serve, how those needs may change in the future, and how they can improve the value they offer to customers. If they are too nearsighted, they may fail to see what's coming until too late.

Creative strategy planning is becoming even more important. Domestic and foreign competition threatens those who can't provide superior customer value and find ways to build stronger relationships with customers. New markets, new customers, and new ways of doing things must be found if companies are to operate profitably in the future—and contribute to the macro-marketing system.

Focus on "best practices" for improved results

The case studies and concepts in this chapter highlight effective marketing thinking. Throughout the text, we will continue with this thrust—focusing on marketing frameworks and concepts that produce good results. Some of these are new and innovative, and others are well established. What they have in common is that they all work well.

Sometimes we will warn you about marketing errors—so you can avoid them. But we won't just give you laundry lists of different approaches and then leave it to you to guess what might work. Rather, our focus will be on "best-practices" marketing.

There is an important reason for this approach. In too many firms, managers do a poor job planning and implementing marketing strategies and programs. And, as shown in Exhibit 2-9, this type of "death-wish" marketing is both costly and ineffective. In fact, you can see that even the average marketing program isn't producing great results—and that accounts for the majority of firms!

Exhibit 2-9 was developed by experts at Copernicus, one of the premier marketing research and consulting firms in the world. As these experts indicate in the chart, some managers are creating marketing programs that produce exceptional results for their companies. This book will help you do exactly that.

WHAT ARE ATTRACTIVE OPPORTUNITIES?

Effective marketing strategy planning matches opportunities to the firm's resources (what it can do) and its objectives (what top management wants to do). Successful strategies get their start when a creative manager spots an attractive market opportunity. Yet an opportunity that is attractive for one firm may not be attractive for another. Attractive opportunities for a particular firm are those that the firm has some chance of doing something about—given its resources and objectives.

Exhibit 2-9 Distribution of Different Firms Based on Their Marketing Performance

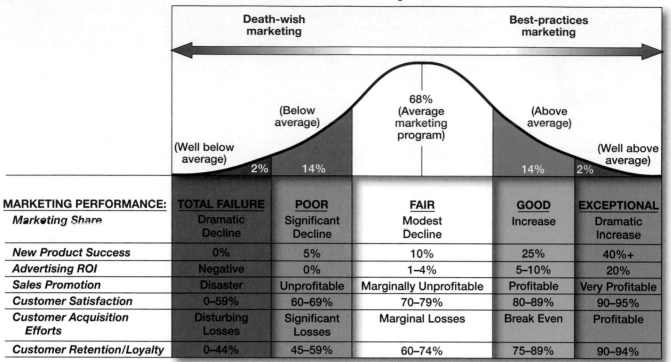

MARKETING PERFORMANCE:	TOTAL FAILURE	POOR	FAIR	GOOD	EXCEPTIONAL
Marketing Share	Dramatic Decline	Significant Decline	Modest Decline	Increase	Dramatic Increase
New Product Success	0%	5%	10%	25%	40%+
Advertising ROI	Negative	0%	1–4%	5–10%	20%
Sales Promotion	Disaster	Unprofitable	Marginally Unprofitable	Profitable	Very Profitable
Customer Satisfaction	0–59%	60–69%	70–79%	80–89%	90–95%
Customer Acquisition Efforts	Disturbing Losses	Significant Losses	Marginal Losses	Break Even	Profitable
Customer Retention/Loyalty	0–44%	45–59%	60–74%	75–89%	90–94%

Breakthrough opportunities are best

Throughout this book, we will emphasize finding **breakthrough opportunities**—opportunities that help innovators develop hard-to-copy marketing strategies that will be very profitable for a long time. That's important because there are always imitators who want to "share" the innovator's profits—if they can. It's hard to continuously provide *superior* value to target customers if competitors can easily copy your marketing mix.

Competitive advantage is needed—at least

Even if a manager can't find a breakthrough opportunity, the firm should try to obtain a competitive advantage to increase its chances for profit or survival. **Competitive advantage** means that a firm has a marketing mix that the target market sees as better than a competitor's mix. A competitive advantage may result from efforts in different areas of the firm—cost cutting in production, innovative R&D, more effective purchasing of needed components, or financing for a new distribution facility. Similarly, a strong sales force, a well-known brand name, or good dealers may give it a competitive advantage in pursuing an opportunity. Whatever the source, an advantage only succeeds if it allows the firm to provide superior value and satisfy customers better than some competitor.

Sometimes a firm can achieve breakthrough opportunities and competitive advantage by simply fine-tuning its current marketing mix(es) or developing closer relationships with its customers. Other times it may need new facilities, new people in new parts of the world, and totally new ways of solving problems. But every firm needs some competitive advantage—so the promotion people have something unique to sell and success doesn't just hinge on offering lower and lower prices.[9]

Avoid hit-or-miss marketing with a logical process

You can see why a manager *should* seek attractive opportunities. But that doesn't mean that everyone does—or that everyone can turn an opportunity into a successful strategy. As Exhibit 2-9 shows, too many firms settle for the sort of death-wish marketing that doesn't satisfy customers or make a profit—to say nothing about achieving a breakthrough or providing superior value. It's all too easy for a well-intentioned manager to react in a piecemeal way to what appears to be an opportunity. Then by the time the problems are obvious, it's too late.

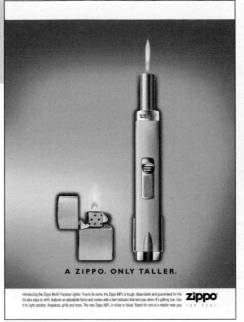

Developing a successful marketing strategy doesn't need to be a hit-or-miss proposition. And it won't be if you learn the marketing strategy planning process developed in this text. Exhibit 2-10 summarizes the marketing strategy planning process we'll be developing throughout the rest of the chapters.

MARKETING STRATEGY PLANNING PROCESS HIGHLIGHTS OPPORTUNITIES

We've emphasized that a marketing strategy requires decisions about the specific customers the firm will target and the marketing mix the firm will develop to appeal to that target market. We can organize the many marketing mix decisions (review Exhibit 2-5) in terms of the four Ps—Product, Place, Promotion, and Price. Thus, the "final" strategy decisions are represented by the target market surrounded by the four Ps. However, the idea isn't just to come up with *some* strategy. After all, there are hundreds or even thousands of combinations of marketing mix decisions and target markets (i.e., strategies) that a firm might try. Rather, the challenge is to zero in on the best strategy.

Process narrows down from broad opportunities to specific strategy

As Exhibit 2-10 suggests, it is useful to think of the marketing strategy planning process as a narrowing-down process. Later in this chapter and in the next two chapters we will go into more detail about strategy decisions relevant to each of the terms in this figure. Then, throughout the rest of the book, we will present a variety of concepts and "how to" frameworks that will help you improve the way you make these strategy decisions. As a preview of what's coming, let's briefly overview the general logic of the process depicted in Exhibit 2-10.

The process starts with a broad look at a market—paying special attention to customer needs, the firm's objectives and resources, and competitors. This helps to identify new and unique opportunities that might be overlooked if the focus is narrowed too quickly.

Segmentation helps pinpoint the target

A key objective of marketing is to satisfy the needs of some group of customers that the firm serves. Broadly speaking, then, in the early stages of a search for opportunities we're looking for customers with needs that are not being satisfied as well as they

Exhibit 2-10
Overview of Marketing
Strategy Planning Process

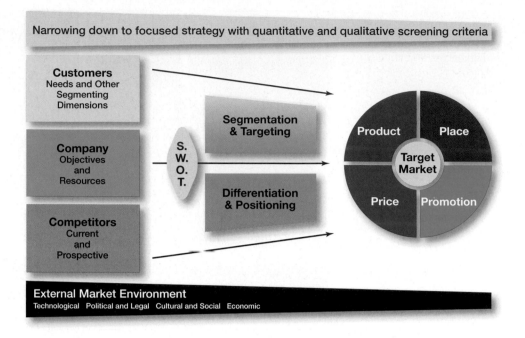

might be. Of course, potential customers are not all alike. They don't all have the same needs—nor do they always want to meet needs in the same way. Part of the reason is that there are different possible types of customers with many different characteristics. For example, individual consumers often have different needs than organizations, and people with certain attitudes or interests have different preferences for how they spend their time, what shows they watch, and the like. In spite of the many possible differences, there often are subgroups (segments) of consumers who are similar and could be satisfied with the same marketing mix. Thus, we try to identify and understand these different subgroups—with market segmentation. We will explain approaches for segmenting markets later in Chapter 3. Then, in Chapters 5 to 7, we delve into the many interesting aspects of customer behavior. For now, however, you should know that really understanding customers is at the heart of using market segmentation to narrow down to a specific target market. In other words, segmentation helps a manager decide to serve some segment(s)—subgroup(s) of customers—and not others.

Narrow down to a superior marketing mix

A marketing mix must meet the needs of target customers, but a firm isn't likely to get a competitive advantage if it *just* meets needs in the same way as some other firm. So in evaluating possible strategies, the marketing manager should think about whether there is a way to differentiate the marketing mix. **Differentiation** means that the marketing mix is distinct from and better than what is available from a competitor. Sometimes the difference is based mainly on one important element of the marketing mix—say, an improved product or faster delivery. However, differentiation often requires that the firm fine-tune all of the elements of its marketing mix to the specific needs of a distinctive target market. Differentiation is also more obvious to target customers when there is a consistent theme integrated across the four Ps decision areas. That emphasizes the difference so target customers will think of the firm as being in a unique position to meet their needs. For example, in Norway many auto buyers are particularly concerned about safety in the snow. So Audi offers a permanent four-wheel drive system, called quattro, that helps the car to hold the road. Audi ads emphasize this differentiation. Rather than show the car, however, the ads feature things that are very sticky (like bubblegum!) and the only text is the headline "sticks like quattro" and the Audi brand name. Of course, handling is not Audi's only strength, but it is an important one in helping to position Audi as

This Norwegian ad for the Audi Quattro simply says, "Sticks like quattro." Although it doesn't show the car at all, it helps to differentiate the Audi and its four-wheel drive system that holds the road especially well, even in the snow.

Sticks like quattro*

Audi
Vorsprung durch Technik

better than competing brands with this target market. In contrast, consider General Motors' decision to discontinue the 100-year-old Oldsmobile line. In spite of repeated efforts, marketers for Oldsmobile were no longer able to develop a differentiated position in the crowded U.S. auto market. And when target customers don't see an advantage with a firm's marketing mix, they just move on.[10]

In Chapter 3, we'll introduce concepts relevant to this sort of positioning. Then, in Chapters 9 to 18, we'll cover the many ways in which the four Ps of the marketing mix can be differentiated. For now you can see that the thrust is to narrow down from all possible marketing mixes to one that is differentiated to meet target customers' needs particularly well. Of course, finding the best differentiation requires that we understand competitors as well as customers.

Screening criteria make it clear why you select a strategy

There are usually more different opportunities—and strategy possibilities—than a firm can pursue. Each one has its own advantages and disadvantages. Trends in the external market environment may make a potential opportunity more or less attractive. These complications can make it difficult to zero in on the best target market and marketing mix. However, developing a set of specific qualitative and quantitative screening criteria can help a manager define what business and markets the firm wants to compete in. It can also help eliminate potential strategies that are not well suited for the firm. We will cover screening criteria in more detail in Chapter 4. For now, you should realize that the criteria you select in a specific situation grow out of an analysis of the company's objectives and resources.

S.W.O.T. analysis highlights advantages and disadvantages

A useful aid for identifying relevant screening criteria and for zeroing in on a feasible strategy is **S.W.O.T. analysis**—which identifies and lists the firm's strengths and weaknesses and its opportunities and threats. The name S.W.O.T. is simply an abbreviation for the first letters of the words strengths, weaknesses, opportunities, and threats. A good S.W.O.T. analysis helps the manager focus on a strategy that takes advantage of the firm's opportunities and strengths while avoiding its weaknesses and threats to its success. These can be compared with the pros and cons of different strategies that are considered.

The marketing strategy developed by Amilya Antonetti illustrates the basic ideas behind a S.W.O.T. analysis. Her son was allergic to the chemicals in standard detergents—and her research showed that many other children had the same problem. So she started SoapWorks and developed a line of hypoallergenic cleaning products to pursue this opportunity. Unlike the big firms, she didn't have relations with grocery chains or money for national TV ads. To get around these weaknesses, she used inexpensive radio ads in local markets and touted SoapWorks as a company created for moms by a mom who cared about kids. She had a credible claim that the big corporations couldn't make. Her ads also helped her get shelf space because they urged other mothers to ask for SoapWorks products and to tell friends about stores that carried them. This wasn't the fastest possible way to introduce a new product line, but her cash-strapped strategy played to her unique strengths with her specific target market.[11]

INTERNET EXERCISE

Go to the SoapWorks website (www.soapworks.com) and click on the link for its store locator. Click your state on the map and see if there is a retailer in your area that carries SoapWorks products. Check several other states in different regions of the country. Why do you think that SoapWorks has distribution through retail stores in some states but not in others?

Exhibit 2-10 focuses on planning each strategy carefully. Of course, this same approach works well when several strategies are to be planned. Then, having an organized evaluation process is even more important. It forces everyone involved to think through how the various strategies fit together as part of an overall marketing program.[12]

TYPES OF OPPORTUNITIES TO PURSUE

Some alert marketers seem to be able to spot attractive opportunities everywhere they look. This seems reasonable when you recognize that most people have unsatisfied needs. Unfortunately, many opportunities seem "obvious" only after someone else identifies them. So, early in the marketing strategy planning process it's useful for marketers to have a framework for thinking about the broad kinds of opportunities they may find. Exhibit 2-11 shows four broad possibilities: market penetration, market development, product development, and diversification. We will look at these separately, but some firms pursue more than one type of opportunity at the same time.

Market penetration

Market penetration means trying to increase sales of a firm's present products in its present markets—probably through a more aggressive marketing mix. The firm may try to strengthen its relationship with customers to increase their rate of use or repeat purchases, or try to attract competitors' customers or current nonusers. Coleman got a 50 percent increase in sales of its outdoor equipment, like camping lanterns and stoves, by reaching its target market with special promotional displays at outdoor events like concerts, fishing tournaments, and NASCAR races. For example, about 250,000 auto racing fans camp on-site at NASCAR races each year—so a display at the campground is an effective way to reach customers when they have leisure time to browse through product displays and demos.[13]

New promotion appeals alone may not be effective. A firm may need to make it easier for customers to place repeat orders on the Internet. Or it may need to add more stores in present areas for greater convenience. Short-term price cuts or coupon offers may help.

Many firms try to increase market penetration by developing closer relationships with customers so that they will be loyal. Frequent buyer clubs use this approach. Similarly, firms often analyze customer databases to identify "cross-selling" opportunities. For example, when a customer goes online to register Adobe's Photoshop, the web page promotes other related products, including its popular Acrobat Reader.

Exhibit 2-11
Four Basic Types of
Opportunities

	Present products	New products
Present markets	Market penetration	Product development
New markets	Market development	Diversification

Market development

Market development means trying to increase sales by selling present products in new markets. This may involve searching for new uses for a product. E-Z-Go, a producer of golf carts, has done this. Its carts are now a quiet way for workers to get around malls, airports, and big factories. The large units are popular as utility vehicles on farms, at outdoor sports events, and at resorts. E-Z-Go even fits carts with ice compartments and cash drawers so they can be used for mobile food services.

Firms may also try advertising in different media to reach new target customers. Or they may add channels of distribution or new stores in new areas, including overseas. For example, to reach new customers, McDonald's has opened outlets in airports, zoos, casinos, and military bases. And it's rapidly expanded into international markets with outlets in places like Russia, Brazil, and China.[14]

Product development

Product development means offering new or improved products for present markets. By knowing the present market's needs, a firm may see new ways to satisfy customers. For example, kids are the big consumers of ketchup. So Heinz figured out how ketchup could be more fun. Producing ketchup in gross green and funky purple colors—in an EZ Squirt dispenser molded to fit little hands—increased sales so much that the factory had to run 24/7. Ski resorts have developed trails for hiking and biking to bring their winter ski customers back in the summer. Nike moved beyond shoes and sportswear to offer its athletic target market a running watch, digital audio player, and even a portable heart-rate monitor. And of course Intel boosts sales by developing newer and faster chips.[15]

Diversification

Diversification means moving into totally different lines of business—perhaps entirely unfamiliar products, markets, or even levels in the production-marketing system. Products and customers that are very different from a firm's current base may look attractive to the optimists—but these opportunities are usually hard to evaluate. That's why diversification usually involves the biggest risk. McDonald's, for example, opened two hotels in Switzerland. The plan was to serve families on the weekend, but business travelers were the target during the week. Business travelers are not the group that McDonald's usually serves, and an upscale hotel is also very different from a fast-food restaurant. This helps to explain why operation of the Golden Arch hotels was taken over by a hospitality management company after two years. On the other hand, diversification can be successful—especially when the new strategy fits well with the firm's resources and marketing program.[16]

Which opportunities come first?

Usually firms find attractive opportunities fairly close to markets they already know. This may allow them to capitalize on changes in their present markets—or more basic changes in the external environment. Moreover, many firms are finding that the easiest way to increase profits is to do a better job of hanging onto the customers that they've already won—by meeting their needs so well that they wouldn't consider switching to another firm.

For these reasons, most firms think first of greater market penetration. They want to increase profits where they already have experience and strengths. On the other hand, many firms are proving that market development—including the move into new international markets—is another profitable way to take advantage of current strengths.

So many flavors melted together. So little time.

Get into McDonald's now for the Grilled Chicken Flatbread Sandwich.
Tender grilled chicken, zesty pepper jack cheese, fresh lettuce and tomato
all wrapped up in warm toasty flatbread. It's an incredible blend of flavors waiting just for you.
But hurry, it's only here for a little time.

A returning favorite on our New Tastes Menu!

Weird. But a good kind of weird.

New McGriddles. Inside: Your choice of savory bacon or sausage, with eggs and cheese.
Outside: Two warm, golden griddle cakes with the sweet taste of maple syrup baked right in.
So good together, you'll wonder why nobody thought of it before. New McGriddles.
Only from McDonald's. They may sound weird, but we know you'll like 'em.

New McGriddles

McDonald's pursues growth in a variety of ways including new product development efforts, like its Grilled Chicken Flatbread sandwich and McGriddles breakfast sandwich, to offer customers more reasons to eat at McDonald's.

INTERNATIONAL OPPORTUNITIES SHOULD BE CONSIDERED

It's easy for a marketing manager to fall into the trap of ignoring international markets, especially when the firm's domestic market is prosperous. Yet there are good reasons to go to the trouble of looking elsewhere for opportunities.

The world is getting smaller

International trade is increasing all around the world, and trade barriers are coming down. In addition, advances in e-commerce, transportation, and communications are making it easier and cheaper to reach international customers. With an Internet website and e-mail, even the smallest firm can provide international customers with a great deal of information—and easy ways to order—at very little expense. E-commerce ordering can be fast and efficient whether the customer is a mile away or in another country. Around the world, potential customers have needs and money to spend. The real question is whether a firm can effectively use its resources to meet these customers' needs at a profit.

Develop a competitive advantage at home and abroad

If customers in other countries are interested in the products a firm offers—or could offer—serving them may improve economies of scale. Lower costs (and prices) may give a firm a competitive advantage both in its home markets *and* abroad. Black and Decker, for example, uses electric motors in many of its tools and appliances. By selling overseas as well as in the United States, it gets economies of scale and the cost per motor is very low.

Marketing managers who are only interested in the "convenient" customers in their own backyards may be rudely surprised to find that an aggressive, low-cost foreign producer is willing to pursue those customers—even if doing it is not convenient. Many companies that thought they could avoid the struggles of international competition have learned this lesson the hard way. The owner of Purafil, a small firm in Atlanta that makes air purification equipment, puts it this way: "If I'm not [selling to an oil refinery] in Saudi Arabia, somebody else is going to solve their problem, then come attack me on my home turf."[17]

Get an early start in a new market

Different countries are at different stages of economic and technological development, and their consumers have different needs at different times.

Lipton is pursuing new customers and growth in over 100 countries. For example, its multilingual website in Belgium explains how to make exotic cocktails from Ice Tea, and in Asia it encourages consumer trial with free samples.

A company facing tough competition, thin profit margins, and slow sales growth at home may get a fresh start in another country where demand for its product is just beginning to grow. A marketing manager may be able to transfer marketing know-how—or some other competitive advantage—the firm has already developed. Consider JLG, a Pennsylvania-based producer of equipment used to lift workers and tools at construction sites. Faced with tough competition, JLG's profits all but evaporated. By cutting costs, the company improved its domestic sales. But it got an even bigger boost from expanding overseas. By 2000 its international sales were greater than its total sales five years before. Now JLG is adding distribution in China. So international sales could soon account for half of its business.[18]

Find better trends in variables

Unfavorable trends in the marketing environment at home—or favorable trends in other countries—may make international marketing particularly attractive. For example, population growth in the United States has slowed and income is leveling off. In other places in the world, population and income are increasing rapidly. Many U.S. firms can no longer rely on the constant market growth that once drove increased domestic sales. Growth—and perhaps even survival—will come only by aiming at more distant customers. It doesn't make sense to casually assume that all of the best opportunities exist "at home."[19]

Screening must consider risks as well as benefits

International opportunities should be considered in the strategy planning process, but they don't always survive as the most attractive ones that are turned into strategies. As with local opportunities, managers should consider international opportunities relative to the firm's objectives and resources—as well as its strengths and weaknesses.

Screening criteria for international market development may include a variety of factors ranging from expected rate of population growth or cultural challenges to political instability or other economic risks. Risks are often higher with international opportunities. For example, while the 9/11 attack on the World Trade Center shows that horrible terrorist acts are not limited to overseas markets, most managers find it more difficult to protect a firm's employees—and its financial interests—in a remote market if the political structure, laws, resources, and culture are very different.

CONCLUSION

The marketing manager must constantly study the market environment—seeking attractive opportunities and planning new strategies. A marketing strategy specifies a target market and the marketing mix the firm will offer to provide that target market with superior cus-

tomer value. A marketing mix has four major decision areas: the four Ps—Product, Place, Promotion, and Price.

There are usually more opportunities than a firm can pursue, so possible target markets must be matched with marketing mixes the firm can offer. Then attractive strategies—really, whole marketing plans—are chosen for implementation. Controls are needed to be sure that the plans are carried out successfully. If anything goes wrong along the way, continual feedback should cause the process to be started over again—with the marketing manager planning more attractive marketing strategies. Thus, the job of marketing management is one of continuous planning, implementing, and control.

Firms need effective strategy planning to survive in our increasingly competitive markets. The challenge isn't just to come up with *some* strategy, but to zero in on the strategy that is best for the firm given its objectives and resources—and taking into consideration its strengths and weaknesses and the opportunities and threats that it faces. To improve your ability in this area, this chapter introduces a framework for marketing strategy planning. The rest of this text is organized to deepen your understanding of this framework and how to use it to develop profitable marketing mixes for clearly defined target markets. After several chapters on analyzing target markets, we will discuss each of the four Ps in greater detail.

While market-oriented strategy planning is helpful to marketers, it is also needed by financial managers, accountants, production and personnel people, and all other specialists. A market-oriented plan lets everybody in the firm know what ballpark they are playing in and what they are trying to accomplish.

We will use the term *marketing manager* for editorial convenience, but really, when we talk about marketing strategy planning, we are talking about the planning that a market-oriented manager should do when developing a firm's strategic plans. This kind of thinking should be done—or at least understood—by everyone in the organization. And this means even the entry-level salesperson, production supervisor, retail buyer, or personnel counselor.

KEY TERMS

marketing management process, 35	mass selling, 40	breakthrough opportunities, 48
strategic (management) planning, 36	advertising, 40	competitive advantage, 48
marketing strategy, 36	publicity, 40	differentiation, 50
target market, 36	sales promotion, 40	S.W.O.T. analysis, 51
marketing mix, 36	marketing plan, 43	market penetration, 52
target marketing, 37	implementation, 43	market development, 53
mass marketing, 37	operational decisions, 43	product development, 53
channel of distribution, 39	marketing program, 45	diversification, 53
personal selling, 40		

QUESTIONS AND PROBLEMS

1. Distinguish clearly between a marketing strategy and a marketing mix. Use an example.

2. Distinguish clearly between mass marketing and target marketing. Use an example.

3. Why is the customer placed in the center of the four Ps in the text diagram of a marketing strategy (Exhibit 2-4)? Explain, using a specific example from your own experience.

4. If a company sells its products only from a website, which is accessible over the Internet to customers from all over the world, does it still need to worry about having a specific target market? Explain your thinking.

5. Explain, in your own words, what each of the four Ps involves.

6. Evaluate the text's statement, "A marketing strategy sets the details of implementation."

7. Distinguish between strategy decisions and operational decisions, illustrating for a local retailer.

8. Distinguish between a strategy, a marketing plan, and a marketing program, illustrating for a local retailer.

9. Outline a marketing strategy for each of the following new products: (*a*) a radically new design for a toothbrush, (*b*) a new fishing reel, (*c*) a new wonder drug, and (*d*) a new industrial stapling machine.

10. Provide a specific illustration of why marketing strategy planning is important for all businesspeople, not just for those in the marketing department.

11. Exhibit 2-9 shows that only about three out of every four customers are, on average, satisfied by a firm's marketing programs. Give an example of a purchase you made where you were not satisfied and what the firm could have changed to satisfy you. If customer satisfaction is so important to firms, why don't they score better in this area?

12. Distinguish between an attractive opportunity and a breakthrough opportunity. Give an example.

13. Explain how new opportunities may be seen by defining a firm's markets more precisely. Illustrate for a situation where you feel there is an opportunity—namely, an unsatisfied market segment—even if it is not very large.

14. In your own words, explain why the book suggests that you should think of marketing strategy planning as a narrowing down process.

15. Explain the major differences among the four basic types of growth opportunities discussed in the text and cite examples for two of these types of opportunities.

16. Explain why a firm may want to pursue a market penetration opportunity before pursuing one involving product development or diversification.

17. In your own words, explain several reasons why a marketing manager should consider international markets when evaluating possible opportunities.

18. Give an example of a foreign-made product (other than an automobile) that you personally have purchased. Give some reasons why you purchased that product. Do you think that there was a good opportunity for a domestic firm to get your business? Explain why or why not.

SUGGESTED CASES

4. Computer Support Services
5. ResinTech

29. Custom Castings, Inc.

COMPUTER-AIDED PROBLEM

2. Target Marketing

RESOURCE REMINDER

Marko, Inc.'s managers are comparing the profitability of a target marketing strategy with a mass marketing "strategy." The spreadsheet gives information about both approaches.

The mass marketing strategy is aiming at a much bigger market. But a smaller percent of the consumers in the market will actually buy this product—because not everyone needs or can afford it. Moreover, because this marketing mix is not tailored to specific needs, Marko will get a smaller share of the business from those who do buy than it would with a more targeted marketing mix.

Just trying to reach the mass market will take more promotion and require more retail outlets in more locations—so promotion costs and distribution costs are higher than with the target marketing strategy. On the other hand, the cost of producing each unit is higher with the target marketing strategy—to build in a more satisfying set of features. But because the more targeted marketing mix is trying to satisfy the needs of a specific target market, those customers will be willing to pay a higher price.

In the spreadsheet, "quantity sold" (by the firm) is equal to the number of people in the market who will actually buy one each of the product—multiplied by the share of those purchases won by the firm's marketing mix. Thus, a change in the size of the market, the percent of people who purchase, or the share captured by the firm will affect quantity sold. And a change in quantity sold will affect total revenue, total cost, and profit.

a. On a piece of paper, show the calculations that prove that the spreadsheet "total profit" value for the target marketing strategy is correct. (Hint: Remember to multiply unit production cost and unit distribution cost by the quantity sold.) Which approach seems better—target marketing or mass marketing? Why?

b. If the target marketer could find a way to reduce distribution cost per unit by $.25, how much would profit increase?

c. If Marko, Inc., decided to use the target marketing strategy and better marketing mix decisions increased its share of purchases from 50 to 60 percent—without increasing costs—what would happen to total profit? What does this analysis suggest about the importance of marketing managers knowing enough about their target markets to be effective target marketers?

For additional questions related to this problem, see Exercise 2-4 in the *Learning Aid for Use with Basic Marketing*, 15th edition.

1. Know about defining generic markets and product-markets.

2. Know what market segmentation is and how to segment product-markets into submarkets.

3. Know three approaches to market-oriented strategy planning.

4. Know dimensions that may be useful for segmenting markets.

5. Know a seven-step approach to market segmentation that you can do yourself.

6. Know what positioning is and why it is useful.

7. Understand the important new terms (shown in red).

CHAPTER THREE

Focusing Marketing Strategy with Segmentation and Positioning

If you wanted to take a picture to give to a friend, what would you do? Would you buy some Kodak Gold film for your 35 mm camera, shoot a few pictures, have the local drugstore send the film to Kodak for processing, and then mail your friend the best print? Or would you snap a few pictures with your new Hewlett-Packard (HP) digital camera, insert the camera's memory card in your HP PhotoSmart printer, and print the best photo on the spot? If your friend later wanted a copy, would she make it on her HP scanner or send it to Kodak for a reprint?

How is it that Kodak, long famous for those "Kodak moments," now finds itself competing with HP for a share of the wallet of customers who want to capture photographic images? These firms serve similar customer needs, but the products (and whole marketing mixes)

with which they compete are very different. Further, the group of customers who prefer Kodak's offering is probably different—on a variety of characteristics—from the segment of people who prefer HP's offering.

To understand HP's marketing program, and how its strategies have become more focused with market segmentation, let's take a longer-term look at how its strategy has evolved.

In the early 1980s, most people used a typewriter to prepare letters and reports. With the introduction of the PC, however, word processing changed—and

presented new printing needs. The early dot-matrix printers were fast enough to work with computers, but the output was of poor quality. Most businesses wanted both high speed and high quality.

HP responded to this need with its initial LaserJet printer. It printed text pages quickly, used a variety of typefaces for a quality look, could handle a variety of graphics, and was designed to handle big print jobs. However, it was difficult to set up and use — so HP sold it through a select group of computer dealers that could provide customers with technical support. Even at a price of $3,000, the basic LaserJet provided superior customer value for many business customers. It even handled jobs that previously required typesetting by a printing service—and the market expanded rapidly as more customers realized the benefits of desktop publishing.

By the time other firms introduced basic laser printers, HP was a few steps ahead of them. It improved the speed and quality of its basic printer but also fine-tuned different strategies for different customer groups. For example, it developed high-capacity models that could be shared on corporate networks and that had special accessories like envelope feeders. At the same time, it came out with low-cost models to attract home-office users and expanded distribution into outlets such as Office Depot to reach them.

As the Windows operating system became popular, HP saw the need for low-cost color printing and moved quickly to introduce a limited line of inkjet printers. They were not as fast as lasers for text, but they offered color graphics at a reasonable cost. HP quickly developed different marketing mixes for different target markets. For example, wide-format DeskJet printers, available through office supply stores, were popular with managers even though they were pricey—because they could print presentations or big spreadsheets on oversized paper. The price was much lower and features were simpler on basic models targeted at individual consumers. However, sales of replacement color print cartridges were very profitable—and demand grew as consumers used their printers for more different purposes, ranging from homemade greeting cards to holiday letters. So HP worked to expand distribution to make replacement cartridges easy to buy—even in grocery stores and drugstores—and offered free software that made it even easier for consumers to use the printers in more different ways.

As the popularity of the Internet and digital photography grew, so did the demand for low-cost color printing. However, firms like Epson, Lexmark, and Canon increased competition with similar models and put downward pressure on prices—especially in the consumer market. To keep its lead, HP needed to update its strategy—with more segmenting. Regardless of other needs, most final consumers were price sensitive, so HP started by redesigning its printers to cut the cost of features that did not add value to final consumers. For example, the older models, originally designed with business users in mind, were so sturdy that you could stand on them. That was more heavy-duty than most consumers needed, and it also made the printers heavier and more costly to ship to stores. But HP didn't want to just produce one inexpensive model to appeal to the budget-oriented buyers. Rather, the new-product designers used knowledge of the needs of different segments of consumers to create an entirely new line of more than 50 consumer products—inkjet printers, printers for digital cameras, "all in one" printer/fax/copier/scanners, portable printers for notebooks, and more. With the PhotoSmart line of printers, for example, a digital camera user can quickly and easily print pictures without even using a computer.

It's costly to produce so many different models for different segments. However, each segment is large enough that it is profitable to develop a specialized strategy that earns a larger share of purchases. Further, by innovating to meet the needs of new segments, HP isn't just taking market share away from other brands of printers. Rather, it is expanding the market. For example, some photographers will switch from using traditional photo processing precisely because HP's PhotoSmart printers offer a simple new way to get pictures from a digital camera onto paper. It is the ease-of-use benefit that determines why they pick an HP PhotoSmart instead of some other brand.

Of course, competitors will continue to try to copy what HP does—and some will come up with innovations of their own. However, HP's targeted strategy planning helps to explain why two out of every three printers in use today is an HP.[1]

SEARCH FOR OPPORTUNITIES CAN BEGIN BY UNDERSTANDING MARKETS

Find breakthrough opportunities

The marketing strategy planning process involves careful evaluation of the market opportunities available before narrowing down to focus on the most attractive target market and marketing mix (review Exhibit 2-10). As the HP case illustrates, a manager who develops an understanding of the needs and characteristics of specific groups of target customers within the broader market may see new, breakthrough opportunities. But it's not always obvious how to identify the real needs of a target market—or the marketing mix that those customers will see as different from, and better than, what is available from a competitor. This chapter covers concepts and approaches that will help you to succeed in the search for those opportunities.

What is a company's market?

Identifying a company's market is an important but sticky issue. In general, a **market** is a group of potential customers with similar needs who are willing to exchange something of value with sellers offering various goods or services—that is, ways of satisfying those needs. However, within a general market, marketing-oriented managers develop marketing mixes for *specific* target markets. Getting the firm to focus on specific target markets is vital.

Don't just focus on the product

Some production-oriented managers don't understand this narrowing-down process. They get into trouble because they ignore the tough part of defining markets. To make the narrowing-down process easier, they just describe their markets in terms of *products* they sell. For example, producers and retailers of greeting cards might define their market as the "greeting-card" market. But this production-oriented approach ignores customers—and customers make a market. This also leads to missed opportunities. Hallmark isn't missing these opportunities. Instead, Hallmark aims at the "personal-expression" market. Hallmark stores offer all kinds of products that can be sent as "memory makers"—to express one person's

The Olympus pocket camera competes directly with other 35 mm cameras, but it may also compete in a broader product-market against Vivitar's digital camera for kids or even Samsung's innovative DigitAll mobile phone that takes photos with a built-in digital camera and then wirelessly sends them by email.

feelings toward another. And as opportunities related to these needs change, Hallmark changes too. For example, at the Hallmark website (www.hallmark.com) it is easy to get shopping suggestions from an online "gift assistant," to order flowers, or to personalize an electronic greeting card to send over the Internet.[2]

From generic markets to product-markets

To understand the narrowing-down process, it's useful to think of two basic types of markets. A **generic market** is a market with *broadly* similar needs—and sellers offering various, *often diverse,* ways of satisfying those needs. In contrast, a **product-market** is a market with *very* similar needs and sellers offering various *close substitute* ways of satisfying those needs.[3]

A generic market description looks at markets broadly and from a customer's viewpoint. Entertainment-seekers, for example, have several very different ways to satisfy their needs. An entertainment-seeker might buy a TiVo digital video recorder and plasma screen TV, sign up for a cruise on the Carnival Line, or reserve season tickets for the symphony. Any one of these *very different* products may satisfy this entertainment need. Sellers in this generic entertainment-seeker market have to focus on the need(s) the customers want satisfied—not on how one seller's product (digital TV system, vacation, or live music) is better than that of another producer.

It is sometimes hard to understand and define generic markets because *quite different product types may compete with each other.* For example, a person on a business trip to Italy might want a convenient way to record memories of the trip. Minolta's digital camera, Sony's video camcorder, Kodak's PalmPix digital accessory for a Palm, and even postcards from local shops may all compete to serve our traveler's needs. If customers see all these products as substitutes—as competitors in the same generic market—then marketers must deal with this complication.

Understanding the geographic boundaries of a market can suggest new opportunities.

Suppose, however, that our traveler decides to satisfy this need with a digital camera. Then—in this product-market—Minolta, Kodak, HP, Nikon, and many other brands may compete with each other for the customer's dollars. In this product-market concerned with digital cameras *and* needs to conveniently record memories, consumers compare similar products to satisfy their image needs.

Broaden market definitions to find opportunities

Broader market definitions—including both generic market definitions and product-market definitions—can help firms find opportunities. But deciding *how* broad to go isn't easy. Too narrow a definition limits a firm's opportunities—but too broad a definition makes the company's efforts and resources seem insignificant. Consider, for example, the mighty Coca-Cola Company. It has great success and a huge market share in the U.S. cola-drinkers' market. On the other hand, its share of all beverage drinking worldwide is very small.

Here we try to match opportunities to a firm's resources and objectives. So the *relevant market for finding opportunities* should be bigger than the firm's present product-market—but not so big that the firm couldn't expand and be an important competitor. A small manufacturer of screwdrivers in Mexico, for example, shouldn't define its market as broadly as "the worldwide tool users market" or as narrowly as "our present screwdriver customers." But it may have the production or marketing potential, or both, to consider "the handyman's hand-tool market in North America." Carefully naming your product-market can help you see possible opportunities.

NAMING PRODUCT-MARKETS AND GENERIC MARKETS

Some managers think about markets just in terms of the product they already produce and sell. But this approach can lead to missed opportunities. For example, think about all of the minivans and SUVs that you see and how many cars they've replaced on the road. If Chrysler had been thinking only about the "car" market, the minivan opportunity might have been missed altogether. And as we highlighted in the HP case, photographic film is being replaced with digital pictures, just as digital video recorders (DVRs) are replacing VCRs, MP3 players are replacing portable CD players, and cell phones are replacing phone booths.

As this suggests, when evaluating opportunities, product-related terms do not—by themselves—adequately describe a market. A complete product-market definition includes a four-part description.

What:	1. Product type (type of good and type of service)
To meet what:	2. Customer (user) needs
For whom:	3. Customer types
Where:	4. Geographic area

We refer to these four-part descriptions as product-market "names" because most managers label their markets when they think, write, or talk about them. Such a four part definition can be clumsy, however, so we often use a nickname. And the nickname should refer to people—not products—because, as we emphasize, people make markets!

Product type should meet customer needs

Product type describes the goods and/or services that customers want. Sometimes the product type is strictly a physical good or strictly a service. But marketing managers who ignore the possibility that *both* are important can miss opportunities.

Customer (user) needs refer to the needs the product type satisfies for the customer. At a very basic level, product types usually provide functional benefits such as nourishing, protecting, warming, cooling, transporting, cleaning, holding, saving time, and so forth. Although we need to identify such "basic" needs first, in advanced economies, we usually go on to emotional needs—such as needs for fun, excitement, pleasing appearance, or status. Correctly defining the need(s) relevant to a market is crucial and requires a good understanding of customers. We discuss these topics more fully in Chapters 6 and 7. As a brief example, however, a buyer might want a small van to handle various cargo- and people-moving needs. The marketer would need to consider related needs such as economy in use, flexibility and convenience in changing the seat arrangement, comfort for the driver and passengers, and perhaps the image the driver wants to project.

Customer type refers to the final consumer or user of a product type. Here we want to choose a name that describes all present (possible) types of customers. To define customer type, marketers should identify the final consumer or user of the product type, rather than the buyer—if they are different. For instance, producers should avoid treating middlemen as a customer type—unless middlemen actually use the product in their own business.

The *geographic area* is where a firm competes, or plans to compete, for customers. Naming the geographic area may seem trivial, but understanding the geographic boundaries of a market can suggest new opportunities. A firm aiming only at the domestic market, for example, may want to expand into world markets.

No product type in generic market names

A generic market description *doesn't include any product-type terms*. It consists of only three parts of the product-market definition—without the product type. This emphasizes that any product type that satisfies the customer's needs can compete in a generic market. Exhibit 3-1 shows the relationship between generic market and product-market definitions.

Later we'll study the many possible dimensions for segmenting markets. But for now you should see that defining markets only in terms of current products is not the best way to find new opportunities. Instead, the most effective way to find opportunities is to use market segmentation.

Exhibit 3-1
Relationship between
Generic and Product-Market
Definitions

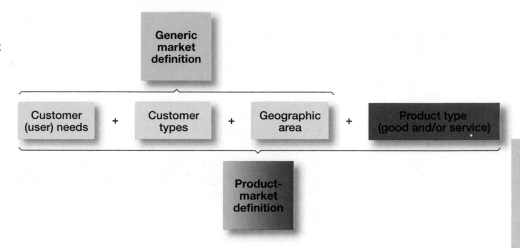

MARKET SEGMENTATION DEFINES POSSIBLE TARGET MARKETS

Market segmentation is a two-step process

Market segmentation is a two-step process of (1) *naming* broad product-markets and (2) *segmenting* these broad product-markets in order to select target markets and develop suitable marketing mixes.

This two-step process isn't well understood. First-time market segmentation efforts often fail because beginners start with the whole mass market and try to find one or two demographic characteristics to divide up (segment) this market. Customer behavior is usually too complex to be explained in terms of just one or two demographic characteristics. For example, not all elderly men buy the same products or brands. Other dimensions usually must be considered—starting with customer needs.

Naming broad product-markets is disaggregating

The first step in effective market segmentation involves naming a broad product-market of interest to the firm. Marketers must break apart—disaggregate—all possible needs into some generic markets and broad product-markets in which the firm

Initially the Clorox brand name became well known as laundry bleach, but now the brand is used with other products related to the broader product-market for household cleaning needs.

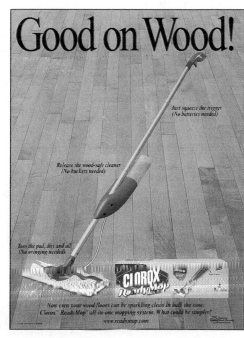

Exhibit 3-2
Narrowing Down to Target
Markets

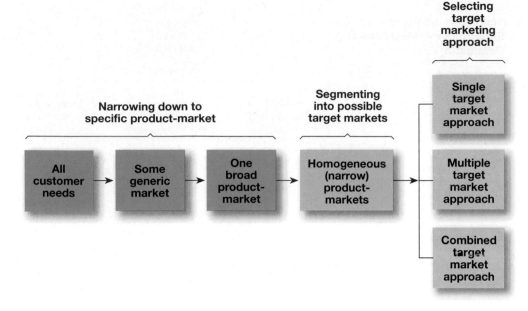

may be able to operate profitably. See Exhibit 3-2. No one firm can satisfy every-one's needs. So the naming—disaggregating—step involves brainstorming about very different solutions to various generic needs and selecting some broad areas—broad product-markets—where the firm has some resources and experience. This means that a car manufacturer would probably ignore all the possible opportunities in food and clothing markets and focus on the generic market, "transporting people in the world," and probably on the broad product-market, "cars, trucks, and utility vehicles for transporting people in the world."

Disaggregating, a practical rough-and-ready approach, tries to narrow down the marketing focus to product-market areas where the firm is more likely to have a competitive advantage or even to find breakthrough opportunities.

Market grid is a visual aid to market segmentation

Assuming that any broad product-market (or generic market) may consist of sub-markets, picture a market as a rectangle with boxes that represent the smaller, more homogeneous product-markets.

Exhibit 3-3, for example, represents the broad product-market of bicycle riders. The boxes show different submarkets. One submarket might focus on people who want basic transportation, another on people who want exercise, and so on. Alternatively, in the generic "transporting market" discussed above, we might see different product-markets of customers for bicycles, motorcycles, cars, airplanes, ships, buses, and "others."

Segmenting is an aggregating process

Marketing-oriented managers think of **segmenting** as an aggregating process—clustering people with similar needs into a "market segment." A **market segment** is

Exhibit 3-3
A Market Grid Diagram with
Submarkets

Broad product-market (or generic market) name goes here
(The bicycle-riders product-market)

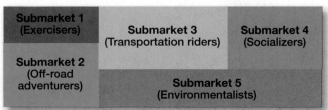

Exhibit 3-4

Every Individual Has His or Her Own Unique Position in a Market—Those with Similar Positions Can Be Aggregated into Potential Target Markets

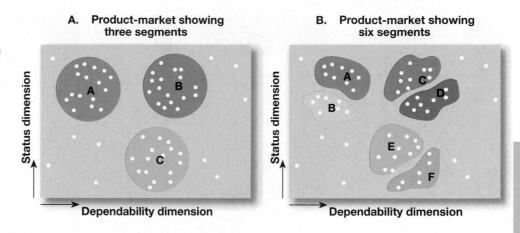

A. Product-market showing three segments

B. Product-market showing six segments

a (relatively) homogeneous group of customers who will respond to a marketing mix in a similar way.

This part of the market segmentation process (see Exhibit 3-2) takes a different approach from the naming part. Here we look for similarities rather than basic differences in needs. Segmenters start with the idea that each person is one of a kind but that it may be possible to aggregate some similar people into a product-market.

Segmenters see each of these one-of-a-kind people as having a unique set of dimensions. Consider a product-market in which customers' needs differ on two important segmenting dimensions: need for status and need for dependability. In Exhibit 3-4A, each dot shows a person's position on the two dimensions. While each person's position is unique, many of these people are similar in terms of how much status and dependability they want. So a segmenter may aggregate them into three (an arbitrary number) relatively homogeneous submarkets—A, B, and C. Group A might be called "status-oriented" and Group C "dependability-oriented." Members of Group B want both and might be called the "demanders."

How far should the aggregating go?

The segmenter wants to aggregate individual customers into some workable number of relatively homogeneous target markets and then treat each target market differently.

Look again at Exhibit 3-4A. Remember we talked about three segments. But this was an arbitrary number. As Exhibit 3-4B shows, there may really be six segments. What do you think—does this broad product-market consist of three segments or six?

Another difficulty with segmenting is that some potential customers just don't fit neatly into market segments. For example, not everyone in Exhibit 3-4B was put into one of the groups. Forcing them into one of the groups would have made these segments more heterogeneous and harder to please. Further, forming additional segments for them probably wouldn't be profitable. They are too few and not very similar in terms of the two dimensions. These people are simply too unique to be catered to and may have to be ignored—unless they are willing to pay a high price for special treatment.

The number of segments that should be formed depends more on judgment than on some scientific rule. But the following guidelines can help.

Criteria for segmenting a broad product-market

Ideally, "good" market segments meet the following criteria:

1. *Homogeneous (similar) within*—the customers in a market segment should be as similar as possible with respect to their likely responses to marketing mix variables *and* their segmenting dimensions.

2. *Heterogeneous (different) between*—the customers in different segments should be as different as possible with respect to their likely responses to marketing mix variables and their segmenting dimensions.

3. *Substantial*—the segment should be big enough to be profitable.

4. *Operational*—the segmenting dimensions should be useful for identifying customers and deciding on marketing mix variables.

It is especially important that segments be *operational*. This leads marketers to include demographic dimensions such as age, sex, income, location, and family size. In fact, it is difficult to make some Place and Promotion decisions without such information.

Avoid segmenting dimensions that have no practical operational use. For example, you may find a personality trait such as moodiness among the traits of heavy buyers of a product, but how could you use this fact? Salespeople can't give a personality test to each buyer. Similarly, advertising couldn't make much use of this information. So although moodiness might be related in some way to previous purchases, it would not be a useful dimension for segmenting.

Target marketers aim at specific targets

Once you accept the idea that broad product-markets may have submarkets, you can see that target marketers usually have a choice among many possible target markets.

There are three basic ways to develop market-oriented strategies in a broad product-market.

1. The **single target market approach**—segmenting the market and picking one of the homogeneous segments as the firm's target market.
2. The **multiple target market approach**—segmenting the market and choosing two or more segments, then treating each as a separate target market needing a different marketing mix.
3. The **combined target market approach**—combining two or more submarkets into one larger target market as a basis for one strategy.

Note that all three approaches involve target marketing. They all aim at specific, clearly defined target markets. See Exhibit 3-5. For convenience, we call people who follow the first two approaches the "segmenters" and people who use the third approach the "combiners."

Combiners try to satisfy "pretty well"

Combiners try to increase the size of their target markets by combining two or more segments. Combiners look at various submarkets for similarities rather than differences. Then they try to extend or modify their basic offering to appeal to these

Exhibit 3-5
Target Marketers Have
Specific Aims

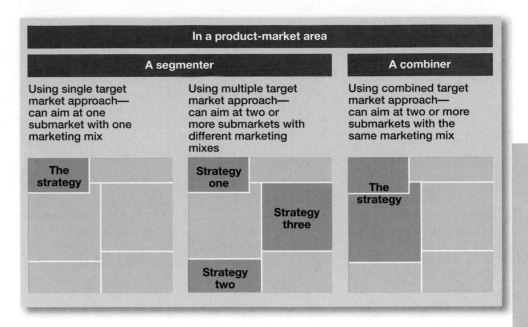

"combined" customers with just one marketing mix. See Exhibit 3-5. For example, combiners may try a new package, more service, a new brand, or new flavors. But even if they make product or other marketing mix changes, they don't try to satisfy unique smaller submarkets. Instead, combiners try to improve the general appeal of their marketing mix to appeal to a bigger "combined" target market.

A combined target market approach may help achieve some economies of scale. It may also require less investment than developing different marketing mixes for different segments—making it especially attractive for firms with limited resources.

Too much combining is risky

It is tempting to aim at larger combined markets instead of using different marketing mixes for smaller segmented markets. But combiners must be careful not to aggregate too far. As they enlarge the target market, individual differences within each submarket may begin to outweigh the similarities. This makes it harder to develop marketing mixes that can satisfy potential customers.

A combiner faces the continual risk of innovative segmenters chipping away at the various segments of the combined target market—by offering more attractive marketing mixes to more homogeneous submarkets. ATI Technologies, a firm that is a leader in making graphics chips for PCs, saw this happen. It produced high-quality products with features desired by a very wide variety of computer users. But then ATI lost business to more specialized competitors like Nvidia Corp. Nvidia focused on the needs of video-game lovers who don't want to compromise when it comes to realistic special effects. Nvidia developed chips that did fewer things, but by doing those specialized things really well it captured much of the video-game lovers' business—until ATI did more segmenting.

Segmenters try to satisfy "very well"

Segmenters aim at one or more homogeneous segments and try to develop a different marketing mix for each segment. Segmenters usually adjust their marketing mixes for each target market—perhaps making basic changes in the product itself—because they want to satisfy each segment very well.

Instead of assuming that the whole market consists of a fairly similar set of customers (like the mass marketer does) or merging various submarkets together (like the combiner), a segmenter sees submarkets with their own demand curves—as shown in Exhibit 3-6. Segmenters believe that aiming at one, or some, of these smaller markets makes it possible to provide superior value and satisfy them better. This then provides greater profit potential for the firm.

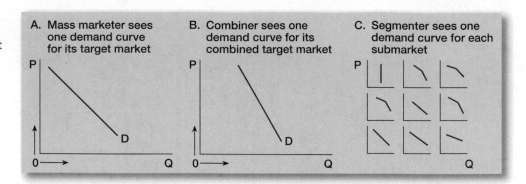

A. Mass marketer sees one demand curve for its target market

B. Combiner sees one demand curve for its combined target market

C. Segmenter sees one demand curve for each submarket

Segmenting may produce bigger sales

Note that segmenters are not settling for a smaller sales potential or lower profits. Instead, they hope to increase sales by getting a much larger share of the business in the market(s) they target. A segmenter that really satisfies the target market can often build such a close relationship with customers that it faces no real competition. A segmenter that offers a marketing mix precisely matched to the needs of the target market can often charge a higher price that produces higher profits.

Consider the success of the Aeron desk chair developed by Herman Miller (HM), a 75-year-old company that makes office furniture. Most firms that sell office furniture offered similar lines of executive desk chairs that were padded for comfort and conveyed the look of success. Marketing managers at HM realized that some customers felt that these traditional chairs were boring. Further, in an e-commerce world, even top executives sit at computers and want a chair that provides both good support and good looks. So to satisfy this upscale segment, HM designed a new type of chair from scratch. There's no fabric or padding, but everything about it adjusts to your body. It's so comfortable that HM positions it as "the chair you can wear." With a price tag close to $1,000, the Aeron chair became a status symbol for high-tech managers and has been as profitable as it is popular.[4]

Should you segment or combine?

Which approach should a firm use? This depends on the firm's resources, the nature of competition, and—most important—the similarity of customer needs, attitudes, and buying behavior.

In general, it's usually safer to be a segmenter—that is, to try to satisfy some customers *very* well instead of many just *fairly* well. That's why many firms use the single or multiple target market approach instead of the combined target market approach. Procter & Gamble, for example, offers many products that seem to compete directly with each other (e.g., Tide versus Cheer or Crest versus Gleem). However, P&G offers tailor-made marketing mixes to each submarket large and profitable enough to deserve a separate marketing mix. Though extremely effective, this approach may not be possible for a smaller firm with more limited resources. A smaller firm may have to use the single target market approach—focusing all its efforts at the one submarket niche where it sees the best opportunity.[5]

Kaepa, Inc., is a good example. Sales of its all-purpose sneakers plummeted as larger firms like Nike and Reebok stole customers with a multiple target market approach. They developed innovative products and aimed their promotion at specific needs—like jogging, aerobics, cross-training, and walking. Kaepa turned things around by catering to the needs of cheerleaders. Cheerleading squads can order Kaepa shoes with custom team logos and colors. The soles of the shoes feature finger grooves that make it easier for cheerleaders to build human pyramids. The Kaepa website (www.kaepa.com) attracts the cheerleader target market with links to a host of other cheering sites. Kaepa also carefully targets its market research and promotion. Kaepa salespeople attend the cheerleading camps that each summer draw 40,000 enthusiasts. Kaepa even arranges for the cheering teams it sponsors to do

Toothpaste marketers often fine-tune their marketing mixes to appeal to the specific needs of different target market segments.

demos at retail stores. This generates publicity and pulls in buyers, so retailers put more emphasis on the Kaepa line.[6]

Profit is the balancing point

In practice, cost considerations probably encourage more aggregating—to obtain economies of scale—while demand considerations suggest less aggregating—to satisfy needs more exactly.

Profit is the balancing point. It determines how unique a marketing mix the firm can afford to offer to a particular group.

WHAT DIMENSIONS ARE USED TO SEGMENT MARKETS?

Segmenting dimensions guide marketing mix planning

Market segmentation forces a marketing manager to decide which product-market dimensions might be useful for planning marketing strategies. The dimensions should help guide marketing mix planning. Exhibit 3-7 shows the basic kinds of dimensions we'll be talking about in Chapters 5 and 6—and their probable effect on the four Ps. Ideally, we want to describe any potential product-market in terms

Exhibit 3-7 Relation of Potential Target Market Dimensions to Marketing Strategy Decision Areas

Potential Target Market Dimensions	Effects on Strategy Decision Areas
1. Behavioral needs, attitudes, and how present and potential goods and services fit into customers' consumption patterns.	Affects *Product* (features, packaging, product line assortment, branding) and *Promotion* (what potential customers need and want to know about the firm's offering, and what appeals should be used).
2. Urgency to get need satisfied and desire and willingness to seek information, compare, and shop.	Affects *Place* (how directly products are distributed from producer to customer, how extensively they are made available, and the level of service needed) and *Price* (how much potential customers are willing to pay).
3. Geographic location and other demographic characteristics of potential customers.	Affects size of *Target Markets* (economic potential), *Place* (where products should be made available), and *Promotion* (where and to whom to target advertising and personal selling).

Exhibit 3-8 Possible Segmenting Dimensions and Typical Breakdowns for Consumer Markets

Behavioral

Needs	Economic, functional, physiological, psychological, social, and more detailed needs.
Benefits sought	Situation specific, but to satisfy specific or general needs.
Thoughts	Favorable or unfavorable attitudes, interests, opinions, beliefs.
Rate of use	Heavy, medium, light, nonusers.
Purchase relationship	Positive and ongoing, intermittent, no relationship, bad relationship.
Brand familiarity	Insistence, preference, recognition, nonrecognition, rejection.
Kind of shopping	Convenience, comparison shopping, specialty, none (unsought product).
Type of problem-solving	Routinized response, limited, extensive.
Information required	Low, medium, high.

Geographic

Region of world, country	North America (United States, Canada), Europe (France, Italy, Germany), and so on.
Region in country	(Examples in United States): Pacific, Mountain, West North Central, West South Central, East North Central, East South Central, South Atlantic, Middle Atlantic, New England.
Size of city	No city; population under 5,000; 5,000–19,999; 20,000–49,999; 50,000–99,999; 100,000–249,999; 250,000–499,999; 500,000–999,999; 1,000,000–3,999,999; 4,000,000 or over.

Demographic

Income	Under $5,000; $5,000–9,999; $10,000–14,999; $15,000–19,999; $20,000–29,999; $30,000–39,999; $40,000–59,999; $60,000 and over.
Sex	Male, female.
Age	Infant; under 6; 6–11; 12–17; 18–24; 25–34; 35–49; 50–64; 65 or over.
Family size	1, 2, 3–4, 5 or more.
Family life cycle	Young, single; young, married, no children; young, married, youngest child under 6; young, married, youngest child over 6; older, married, with children; older, married, no children under 18; older, single; other variations for single parents, divorced, etc.
Occupation	Professional and technical; managers, officials, and proprietors; clerical sales; craftspeople; foremen; operatives; farmers; retired; students; housewives; unemployed.
Education	Grade school or less; some high school; high school graduate; some college; college graduate.
Ethnicity	Asian, Black, Hispanic, Native American, White, multiracial.
Social class	Lower-lower, upper-lower, lower-middle, upper-middle, lower-upper, upper-upper.

Note: Terms used in this table are explained in detail later in the text.

of all three types of customer-related dimensions—plus a product type description—because these dimensions help us develop better marketing mixes.

Many segmenting dimensions may be considered

Customers can be described by many specific dimensions. Exhibit 3-8 shows some dimensions useful for segmenting consumer markets. A few are behavioral dimensions, others are geographic and demographic. Exhibit 3-9 shows some additional dimensions for segmenting markets when the customers are businesses, government agencies, or other types of organizations. Regardless of whether customers are final consumers or organizations, segmenting a broad product-market *usually* requires using several different dimensions at the same time.[7]

What are the qualifying and determining dimensions?

To select the important segmenting dimensions, think about two different types of dimensions. **Qualifying dimensions** are those relevant to including a customer type in a product-market. **Determining dimensions** are those that actually affect the customer's purchase of a specific product or brand in a product-market.

Exhibit 3-9
Possible Segmenting
Dimensions for Business/
Organizational Markets

Kind of relationship	Weak loyalty → strong loyalty to vendor Single source → multiple vendors "Arm's length" dealings → close partnership No reciprocity → complete reciprocity
Type of customer	Manufacturer, service producer, government agency, military, nonprofit, wholesaler or retailer (when end user), and so on.
Demographics	Geographic location (region of world, country, region within country, urban → rural); Size (number of employees, sales volume); Primary business or industry (North American Industry Classification System); Number of facilities
How customer will use product	Installations, components, accessories, raw materials, supplies, professional services
Type of buying situation	Decentralized → centralized Buyer → multiple buying influence Straight rebuy → modified rebuy → new-task buying
Purchasing methods	Vendor analysis, purchasing specifications, Internet bids, negotiated contracts, long-term contracts, e-commerce websites

Note: Terms used in this table are explained in detail later in the text.

A prospective car buyer, for example, has to have enough money—or credit—to buy a car and insure it. Our buyer also needs a driver's license. This still doesn't guarantee a purchase. He or she must have a real need—like a job that requires "wheels" or kids who have to be carpooled. This need may motivate the purchase of *some* car. But these qualifying dimensions don't determine what specific brand or model car the person might buy. That depends on more specific interests—such as the kind of safety, performance, or appearance the customer wants. Determining dimensions related to these needs affect the specific car the customer purchases. If safety is a determining dimension for a customer, a Volvo wagon that offers side impact protection, air bags, and all-wheel drive might be the customer's first choice.

Any hiking boot should repel water, and a product that doesn't meet that "qualifying need" probably wouldn't appeal to many hikers. Sorel wants its target customers to know that its boots go further in keeping feet dry because that difference may determine which brand of boot they buy.

Exhibit 3-10 Finding the Relevant Segmenting Dimensions

| Segmenting dimensions become more specific to reasons why the target segment chooses to buy a particular brand of the product |

All potential dimensions	Qualifying dimensions	Determining dimensions (product type)	Determining dimensions (brand specific)
Dimensions generally relevant to purchasing behavior	Dimensions relevant to including a customer type in the product-market	Dimensions that affect the customer's purchase of a specific type of product	Dimensions that affect the customer's choice of a specific brand

Determining dimensions may be very specific

How specific the determining dimensions are depends on whether you are concerned with a general product type or a specific brand. See Exhibit 3-10. The more specific you want to be, the more particular the determining dimensions may be. In a particular case, the determining dimensions may seem minor. But they are important because they *are* the determining dimensions.

Marketers at General Mills know this. Lots of people try to check e-mail or drive a car while eating breakfast or lunch. General Mills has figured out that for many of these target customers the real determining dimension in picking a snack is whether it can be eaten "one-handed."[8]

Qualifying dimensions are important too

The qualifying dimensions help identify the "core features" that must be offered to everyone in a product-market. Qualifying and determining dimensions work together in marketing strategy planning.

Different dimensions needed for different submarkets

Note that each different submarket within a broad product-market may be motivated by a different set of dimensions. In the snack food market, for example, health food enthusiasts are interested in nutrition, dieters worry about calories, and economical shoppers with lots of kids may want volume to "fill them up."

Ethical issues in selecting segmenting dimensions

Marketing managers sometimes face ethical decisions when selecting segmenting dimensions. Problems may arise if a firm targets customers who are somehow at a disadvantage in dealing with the firm or who are unlikely to see the negative effects of their own choices. For example, some people criticize shoe companies for targeting poor, inner-city kids who see expensive athletic shoes as an important status symbol. Many firms, including producers of infant formula, have been criticized for targeting consumers in less-developed nations. Encyclopedia publishers have been criticized for aggressive selling to less-educated parents who don't realize that the "pennies a day" credit terms are more than they can afford. Some nutritionists criticize firms that market soft drinks, candy, and snack foods to children.

Sometimes a marketing manager must decide whether a firm should serve customers it really doesn't want to serve. For example, banks sometimes offer marketing mixes that are attractive to wealthy customers but that basically drive off low-income consumers.

People often disagree about what segmenting dimensions are ethical in a given situation. A marketing manager needs to consider not only his or her own view but also the views of other groups in society. Even when there is no clear "right" answer, negative publicity may be very damaging. This is what Amazon.com encountered when it was revealed that it was charging some regular customers higher prices than new customers at its site.[9]

International marketing requires even more segmenting

Success in international marketing requires even more attention to segmenting. There are over 228 nations with their own unique cultures! And they differ greatly in language, customs (including business ethics), beliefs, religions, race, and income distribution patterns. (We'll discuss some of these differences in Chapters 5 and 6.) These additional differences can complicate the segmenting process. Even worse, critical data is often less available—and less dependable—as firms move into international markets. This is one reason why some firms insist that local operations and decisions be handled by natives. They, at least, have a feel for their markets.

There are more dimensions—but there is a way

Segmenting international markets may require more dimensions. But one practical method adds just one step to the approach discussed above. First, marketers segment by country or region—looking at demographic, cultural, and other characteristics, including stage of economic development. This may help them find regional or national submarkets that are fairly similar. Then—depending on whether the firm is aiming at final consumers or business markets—they apply the same basic approaches discussed earlier.

A BEST PRACTICE APPROACH TO SEGMENTING PRODUCT-MARKETS

Most marketing managers embrace the idea of using market segmentation to narrow down from a broad set of opportunities to a specific target market and marketing strategy (review Exhibit 2-10). There are also hundreds of books and articles about different approaches and tools for market segmentation that a manager might consider. Yet many managers don't do a good job with market segmentation. One reason is that they are often unclear where to start or how to fit the ideas together. So that you don't have this knowledge gap, here we introduce a logical seven-step approach to market segmentation. Later in Chapter 8 you'll learn more about how marketing research can help to fine-tune some of the decisions made with this approach. But even without additional research, *this approach works*—and it has led to successful strategies. It is especially useful for finding the determining dimensions for product types. However, when you want to find dimensions for specific brands—especially when there are several competing brands—you may need more sophisticated techniques.

To be sure you understand this approach, we will review each step separately and use an ongoing example to show how each step works. The example concerns people who need a place to stay—in particular, the market for motel guests in a big urban area.

1: Name the broad product-market

First, decide what broad product-market the firm wants to be in. This may be stated in the firm's objectives. Or if the firm is already successful in some product-market, its current position might be a good starting point. Try to build on the firm's strengths and avoid its weaknesses and competitors' strengths. Available resources, both human and financial, will limit the possibilities—especially if the firm is just getting started.

Example

A firm has been building small motels around the edges of a large city and renting rooms to travelers. A narrow view—considering only the firm's current products and markets—might lead the firm to think only of more small motels. A bigger view might see such motels as only a small part of the larger "overnight lodging needs" market in the firm's geographic area. Taking an even bigger view, the firm could consider expanding to other geographic areas—or moving into other kinds of products (like apartment buildings, retirement centers, or even parks for people who travel in their own recreational vehicles).

There has to be some balance between naming the product-market too narrowly (same old product, same old market) and naming it too broadly (the whole world and all its needs). Here the firm decides on the whole market of motel users in one city—because this is a city where the number of visitors is growing and where the firm has some experience.

2: List potential customers' needs

Write down as many relevant needs as you can—considering all of the potential customers in the broad product-market. This is a brainstorming step. The list doesn't have to be complete yet, but it should provide enough input to help stimulate your thinking in the next steps. To see possible needs, think about *why* some people buy the present offerings in this broad product-market. At this point, focus on the basic needs—but begin to consider what a company could offer to meet those needs.

Example

In the broad motel guest market, you can easily list some possible needs: privacy (including a private room and furnishings), safety and security (security guards, lighted parking lots with video coverage), comfort (a good bed and nice furnishings), space for activities (exercise, work, socializing), entertainment (TV, radio, video games), convenience (registration, check-out, reservations, access to highways), economy (costs), communicating (phone, messages, fax, voice mail, Internet service), and the like.

3: Form homogeneous submarkets—narrow product-markets

Assuming that some people have (or emphasize) different needs than others, form different submarkets based on each submarket's specific needs. Start by forming one submarket around some typical type of customer (perhaps even yourself), and then aggregate similar people into this segment as long as they can be satisfied by the same marketing mix. Write down the important need dimensions and customer-related characteristics (including demographic characteristics) of each submarket to help you decide whether each new customer type should be included in the first segment. This will also help later—when you name the submarkets.

For example, if the people in one market are young families looking for a good place to stay on vacation, this will help you understand what they want and why—and will help you name the market (perhaps as "family vacationers").

Put people who are not homogeneous—who don't fit in the first segment—in a new submarket. List their different need dimensions on another line. Continue this classifying until three or more submarkets emerge.

Example

A young family on a vacation probably wants a motel to provide a clean room large enough for adults and children, convenient parking, a location near tourist attractions, a pool for recreation with a lifeguard for safety, entertainment in the room (a TV and video movies), and perhaps a refrigerator or vending machine for snacks. A traveling executive, on the other hand, has quite different interests—a room with a desk, but *also* a nice restaurant, fast transportation to and from an airport, more services (room service, dry cleaning, a way to send and receive a fax, and fast check-in)—without distracting noise from children. See Exhibit 3-11.

4: Identify the determining dimensions

Review the list of need dimensions for each possible segment and identify the determining dimensions (perhaps by putting an asterisk beside them). Although the qualifying dimensions are important—perhaps reflecting "core needs" that should be satisfied—they are not the *determining* dimensions we are seeking now.

Nickname of Product-Market	Need Dimensions (benefits sought)	Customer-Related Characteristics
1 Family vacationers	Comfort, security, privacy, *family fun, recreation (playground, pool), entertainment (video games, movies), child care, and snacks*	Couples and single parents with children who want a fun family experience: young, active, and energetic.
2 Upscale executives	Comfort, security, privacy, *distinctive furnishings, attentive staff, prestige status, easy access to airport and business meetings, express check-in and check-out, quality dining, business services (copying, fax, wi-fi Internet)*	Senior business executives with a big expense account who want to be pampered with "very important person" service and accommodations; often repeat guests.
3 Budget-oriented travelers	Comfort, security, privacy, *economy, (no extras that increase cost), convenience (to low-cost restaurants, highways), free parking*	Young people, retirees, and salespeople who travel by car, pay their own expenses, and want a simple place for one night—before moving on.
4 Long-stay guests	Comfort, security, privacy, *homelike amenities (kitchenette, separate living room), laundry and exercise facilities, pleasant grounds, entertainment, staying "connected" (e-mail, etc.)*	Businesspeople, out-of-town visitors, and others who stay in the same motel for a week or more; want many of the comforts they have at home.
5 Event-centered visitors	Comfort, security, privacy, *socializing (lounges and public areas), conference facilities (including catering of group meals), message and transportation services*	Individuals who are attending events scheduled at the motel (a business meeting or conference, family reunion, wedding, etc.) often for several days.
6 Resort seekers	Comfort, security, privacy, *relaxation (golf, whirlpool bath), pleasure (fine dining, nice views), fun, variety information (arrangements for theater, activities)*	Sophisticated couples with leisure time to relax and have "adult" fun; they want to show their individuality and have discretionary income to spend.

Note: Comfort, security, and privacy are core qualifying needs. Determining dimensions for each segment are in italic.

To help identify the determining dimensions, think carefully about the needs and attitudes of the people in each possible segment. They may not seem very different from market to market, but if they are determining to those people then they *are* determining!

Example

With our motel customers, basic comfort needs (heating and cooling, a good bed, a clean bathroom), a telephone for communicating, and safety and security are probably not determining. Everyone has these qualifying needs. Looking beyond these common needs helps you see the determining dimensions—such as different needs with respect to recreation, restaurant facilities, services, and so on. See the needs highlighted in italic in Exhibit 3-11.

5: Name (nickname) the possible product-markets

Review the determining dimensions—market by market—and name (nickname) each one based on the relative importance of the determining dimensions (and aided by your description of the customer types). A market grid is a good way to help visualize this broad product-market and its narrow product-markets.

Draw the market grid as a rectangle with boxes inside representing smaller, more homogeneous segments. See Exhibit 3-11. Think of the whole grid as representing the broad product-market and each of the rows as a different (narrower) product-market. Since the markets within a broad product-market usually require very different segmenting dimensions, don't try to use the same dimensions to name every submarket. Then label each segment with its nickname.

Example

Exhibit 3-11 identifies the following overnight guest submarkets: (1) family vacationers, (2) upscale executives, (3) budget-oriented travelers, (4) long-stay guests, (5) event-centered visitors, and (6) resort seekers. Note that each segment has a different set of determining dimensions (benefits sought) that follow directly from customer type and needs.

6: Evaluate why product–market segments behave as they do

After naming the markets as we did in step 5, think about what else you know about each segment to see how and why these markets behave the way they do. Different segments may have similar, but slightly different, needs. This may explain why some competitive offerings are more successful than others. It can also mean you have to split and rename some segments.

Example

The resort seekers might have been treated as family vacationers in step 5 because the "family" characteristic did not seem important. But with more thought, we see that while some of the resort seekers are interested in the same sort of fun and recreation as the family vacationers, resort seekers focus on adult fun—not activities with children. For them, getting away from the family vacationer's children may be part of the escape they want. Further, although the resort seekers are a higher income group who are similar to the upscale executives, they have different needs than the executives and probably should be treated as a separate market. The point is that you might discover these market differences only in step 6. At this step you would name the "resort seekers" market—and create a related row in the grid to describe the new segment.

7: Make a rough estimate of the size of each product–market segment

Remember, we are looking for profitable opportunities. So now we must try to tie our product-markets to demographic data—or other customer-related characteristics—to make it easier to estimate the size of these markets. We aren't trying to estimate our likely sales yet. Sales depend on the competition as well as the particulars of the marketing mix. Now we only want to provide a basis for later forecasting and marketing mix planning. The more we know about possible target markets, the easier those jobs are.

Fortunately, we can obtain a lot of data on the size of markets—especially demographic data. And bringing in demographics adds a note of economic reality. Some possible product-markets may have almost no market potential. Without hard facts, we risk aiming at such markets.

To refine the market grid, you might want to change the height of the rows so that they give a better idea of the size of the various segments. This will help highlight the larger, and perhaps more attractive, opportunities. Remember, the relative sizes of the markets might vary depending on what geographic areas you consider. The market sizes might vary from city to city or from one country to another.

Example

We can tie the family vacationers to demographic data. Most of them are between 21 and 45. The U.S. Census Bureau publishes detailed data by age, family size, and related information. Moreover, a state tourist bureau or city Chamber of Commerce might be able to provide estimates of how many families vacation in a specific city during a year and how long they stay. Given this information, it's easy to estimate the total number of nights family vacationers will need motel rooms in a certain city.

Market dimensions suggest a good mix

Once we follow all seven steps, we should be able to outline the kinds of marketing mixes that would appeal to the various markets. For example, based on the determining dimensions (benefits sought) in Exhibit 3-11, a motel designed to appeal to the upscale executives might offer rooms with quality furniture (including a desk and chair for reading and an extra comfortable bed with special luxury sheets and pillows), a high-quality restaurant with all-hours room service, special business services (copying, fax, wireless Internet access) on an extra-cost basis, limousine pickup at the airport, someone to help with travel problems, and precleared check-in and check-out. The motel might also provide a quiet bar and exercise room and extras such as thick bath towels and a valet service for free shoe shines. It might also offer a business library for after-hours reading and a free copy of *The Wall Street Journal* delivered every morning. Of course, the price could be high to pay for this special treatment. It's also useful to think about what the executives would *not* want: noisy facilities shared by families with young children!

While the discussion above focuses on the upscale executives, profitable marketing mixes can be developed for the other segments as well. For example, Super 8 has done very well by targeting budget-oriented travelers. Similarly, Residence Inns cater to the needs of long-stay guests with kitchens and grocery shopping services, fireplaces, and convenient recreation areas. Courtyard by Marriott has been successful with facilities designed for event-centered visitors. During the week, many of its customers are there for business conferences, but on the weekend the focus often shifts to family events—such as meals and receptions related to a wedding or family reunion.[10]

Improve the marketing mix for current customers

Our motel example highlights an approach to identify new target market and marketing mix opportunities. However, the same approaches provide a basis for identifying new ways to serve existing customers and strengthen the relationship with them. Too often, firms let their strategies get stagnant. For example, special business services related to the determining needs of upscale executives (like voice mail) might initially help a motel win this business with superior customer value. However, the motel loses its competitive edge if other motels start to offer the same benefits. Or the benefit might disappear if customer needs change; executives who carry a cell phone don't need voice mail at the motel. Then the determining dimensions change. To retain the base of customers it has built or attract new ones, the motel needs to find new and better ways to meet the executives' needs. Reevaluating the need dimensions and customer-related characteristics, perhaps in greater detail, may point to new opportunities. For example, our motel might equip rooms with a wireless access point to a high-speed Internet connection.

MORE SOPHISTICATED TECHNIQUES MAY HELP IN SEGMENTING

Marketing researchers and managers often turn to computer-aided methods for help with the segmenting job. A detailed review of the possibilities is beyond the scope of this book. But a brief discussion will give you a flavor of how computer-aided methods work. In addition, the computer-aided problem for this chapter (3, Segmenting Customers) on the Student CD that accompanies the text gives you a hands-on feel for how managers use them.

Clustering usually requires a computer

Clustering techniques try to find similar patterns within sets of data. Clustering groups customers who are similar on their segmenting dimensions into homogeneous segments. Clustering approaches use computers to do what previously was done with much intuition and judgment.

The data to be clustered might include such dimensions as demographic characteristics, the importance of different needs, attitudes toward the product, and past buying behavior. The computer searches all the data for homogeneous groups of people. When it finds them, marketers study the dimensions of the people in the groups

to see why the computer clustered them together. The results sometimes suggest new, or at least better, marketing strategies.[11]

A cluster analysis of the toothpaste market, for example, might show that some people buy toothpaste because it tastes good (the sensory segment), while others are concerned with the effect of clean teeth and fresh breath on their social image (the sociables). Still others worry about decay or tartar (the worriers), and some are just interested in the best value for their money (the value seekers). Each of these market segments calls for a different marketing mix—although some of the four Ps may be similar.

Customer database can focus the effort

A variation of the clustering approach is based on customer relationship management methods. With **customer relationship management (CRM)**, the seller fine-tunes the marketing effort with information from a detailed customer database. This usually includes data on a customer's past purchases as well as other segmenting information. For example, an auto-repair garage that keeps a database of customer oil changes can send a reminder postcard when it's time for the next oil change. Similarly, a florist that keeps a database of customers who have ordered flowers for Mother's Day or Valentine's Day can call them in advance with a special offer. Firms that operate over the Internet may have a special advantage with these database-focused approaches. They are able to communicate with customers via a website or e-mail, which means that the whole effort is not only targeted but also very inexpensive. Further, it's fast and easy for a customer to reply.[12]

Amazon.com takes this even further. When a customer orders a book, the Amazon CRM system at the website recommends other related books that have been purchased by other customers who bought that book.

INTERNET EXERCISE

Visit the website for onContact Software (www.oncontact.com), and from the demo link at the top of the page select "screenshot tour" (*note:* the interactive tour requires that you register). Select the links to review the different examples of the firm's client management software. Give several examples of how this software could help a salesperson be more effective in working with customers.

CDW TARGETS THE SMALL BUSINESS SEGMENT WITH UNCOMMON SERVICE

Sellers in business markets often rely on customer size as a key segmentation dimension. When potential profit from serving a big customer is high, the selling firm may even treat that customer as a "segment of one"—and develop a unique marketing mix targeted to win and keep its business. Even if a unique marketing mix isn't justified, big customers in these segments often get volume discounts, extra services, and personalized attention. By contrast, smaller customers are often left to get information and handle orders themselves—at a seller's website. This can be efficient, reduce costs for both the seller and customer, and serve the need. But that is not always the case.

CDW is a wholesaler that sells all sorts of computer gear produced by many manufacturers. Most of its 360,000 business customers are too small to command much attention from equipment manufacturers. Yet they also have smaller IT departments and know less about buying IT equipment. CDW has enjoyed rapid growth because it offers a marketing mix that is atypical for these customers. Even the smallest customer gets a dedicated account manager (AM). These salespeople

don't just take orders; they go through months of CDW training so that they really understand a customer's needs and can help the buyer make the right purchases. The AM is a single point-of-contact with the account over time and is encouraged to act almost as an extension of the client's IT department. This relationship helps the AM anticipate client needs; the AM is also supported with customer relationship management databases that help predict when an upgrade is needed—rather than wait for the customer to ask. This is especially helpful to small customers who don't have backup systems in place to tide them over if something goes wrong. This is also why CDW fills orders fast—usually on the same day they are received. To provide that level of service with 17,000 orders a day, CDW operates a 450,000-square-foot distribution center and keeps about $130 million in inventory on hand. CDW's "high-touch" strategy is costly, but high volume keeps its prices competitive. And CDW's sales volume is high because CDW delivers superior customer value that wins a large share of its target customers' business.[13]

DIFFERENTIATION AND POSITIONING TAKE THE CUSTOMER POINT OF VIEW

Differentiate the marketing mix—to serve customers better

As we've emphasized throughout, the reason for focusing on a specific target market—by using marketing segmentation approaches or tools such as cluster analysis or CRM—is so that you can fine-tune the whole marketing mix to provide some group of potential customers with superior value. By *differentiating* the marketing mix to do a better job meeting customers' needs, the firm builds a competitive advantage. When this happens, target customers view the firm's position in the market as uniquely suited to their preferences and needs. Further, because everyone in the firm is clear about what position it wants to achieve with customers, the Product, Promotion, and other marketing mix decisions can be blended better to achieve the desired objectives.

Although the marketing manager may want customers to see the firm's offering as unique, that is not always possible. Me-too imitators may come along and copy the firm's strategy. Further, even if a firm's marketing mix is different, consumers may not know or care. They're busy and, simply put, the firm's product may not be that important in their lives. Even so, in looking for opportunities it's important for the marketing manager to know how customers *do* view the firm's offering. It's also important for the marketing manager to have a clear idea about how he or she would like for customers to view the firm's offering. This is where another important concept, *positioning*, comes in.

Firms often use promotion to help "position" how a marketing mix meets target customers' specific needs. For example, Bic ads along the roadside in Thailand highlight an ultraclose shave. In the United States, Target wants consumers to remember not only its fashions and other soft goods but also its houseware lines.

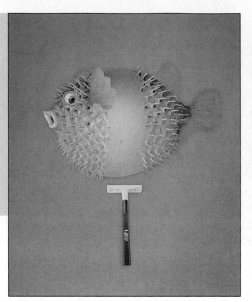

Positioning is based on customers' views

Positioning refers to how customers think about proposed or present brands in a market. A marketing manager needs a realistic view of how customers think about offerings in the market. Without that, it's hard to differentiate. At the same time, the manager should know how he or she *wants* target customers to think about the firm's marketing mix. Positioning issues are especially important when competitors in a market appear to be very similar. For example, many people think that there isn't much difference between one brand of TV and another. But Sony wants TV buyers to see its Wega flatscreen as offering the best picture and brightest colors.

Once you know what customers think, then you can decide whether to leave the product (and marketing mix) alone or reposition it. This may mean *physical changes in the product* or simply *image changes based on promotion*. For example, most cola drinkers can't pick out their favorite brand in a blind test—so physical changes might not be necessary (and might not even work) to reposition a cola. Yet ads that portray Pepsi drinkers in funny situations help position "the Joy of Pepsi." Conversely, 7Up reminds us that it is the uncola with no caffeine, "never had it and never will."

INTERNET EXERCISE

For many years, Michelin's marketing mix emphasized the safety of Michelin tires. To highlight that positioning, scores of ads showed the "Michelin baby" surrounded by a tire with the tagline "because so much is riding on your tires." Ads still use this tagline, but the baby is no longer used. Now most promotion highlights another icon, the "Michelin Man." Go to the Michelin website (www.michelin.com), select the country where you live, and review the site. Does the website reinforce the safety positioning suggested by the tagline? Explain your thinking.

Figuring out what customers really think about competing products isn't easy, but there are approaches that help. Most of them require some formal marketing

Exhibit 3-12
"Product Space" Representing Consumers' Perceptions for Different Brands of Bar Soap

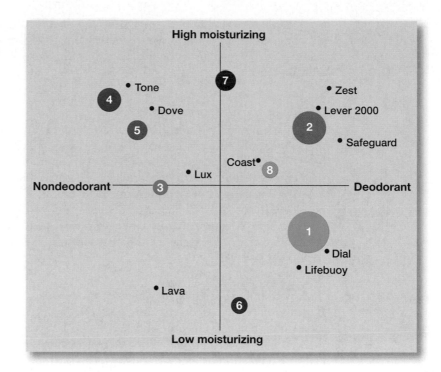

research. The results are usually plotted on graphs to help show how consumers view the competing products. Usually, the products' positions are related to two or three product features that are important to the target customers.

Managers make the graphs for positioning decisions by asking consumers to make judgments about different brands—including their "ideal" brand—and then use computer programs to summarize the ratings and plot the results. The details of positioning techniques—sometimes called *perceptual mapping*—are beyond the scope of this text. But Exhibit 3-12 shows the possibilities.[14]

Exhibit 3-12 shows the "product space" for different brands of bar soap using two dimensions—the extent to which consumers think the soaps moisturize and deodorize their skin. For example, consumers see Dove as quite high on moisturizing but low on deodorizing. Dove and Tone are close together—implying that consumers think of them as similar on these characteristics. Dial is viewed as different and is further away on the graph. Remember that positioning maps are based on *customers' perceptions*—the actual characteristics of the products (as determined by a chemical test) might be different!

Each segment may have its own preferences

The circles in Exhibit 3-12 show different sets (submarkets) of consumers clustered near their ideal soap preferences. Groups of respondents with a similar ideal product are circled to show apparent customer concentrations. In this graph, the size of the circles suggests the size of the segments for the different ideals.

Ideal clusters 1 and 2 are the largest and are close to two popular brands—Dial and Lever 2000. It appears that customers in cluster 1 want more moisturizing than they see in Dial. However, exactly what this brand should do about this isn't clear. Perhaps Dial should leave its physical product alone—but emphasize moisturizing more in its promotion to make a stronger appeal to those who want moisturizers. A marketing manager talking about this approach might simply refer to it as "positioning the brand as a good moisturizer." Of course, whether the effort is successful depends on whether the whole marketing mix delivers on the promise of the positioning communication.

Note that ideal cluster 7 is not near any of the present brands. This may suggest an opportunity for introducing a new product—a strong moisturizer with some deodorizers. A firm that chooses to follow this approach would be making a segmenting effort.

Combining versus segmenting

Positioning analysis may lead a firm to combining—rather than segmenting—if managers think they can make several general appeals to different parts of a "combined" market. For example, by varying its promotion, Coast might try to appeal to segments 8, 1, and 2 with one product. These segments are all quite similar (close together) in what they want in an ideal brand. On the other hand, there may be clearly defined submarkets—and some parts of the market may be "owned" by one product or brand. In this case, segmenting efforts may be practical—moving the firm's own product into another segment of the general market area where competition is weaker.

Positioning as part of broader analysis

A positioning analysis helps managers understand how customers see their market. It is a visual aid to understanding a product-market. The first time such an analysis is done, managers may be shocked to see how much customers' perceptions of a market differ from their own. For this reason alone, positioning analysis may be crucial. But a positioning analysis usually focuses on specific product features and brands that are close competitors in the product-market. Thus, it is a product-oriented approach. Important *customer*-related dimensions—including needs and attitudes—may be overlooked.

Premature emphasis on product features is dangerous in other ways as well. As our bar soap example shows, starting with a product-oriented definition of a market and how bar soaps compete against other bar soaps can make a firm miss more basic shifts in markets. For example, bars have lost popularity to liquid soaps. Other products, like bath oils or body shampoos for use in the shower, are now part of the relevant competition also. Managers wouldn't see these shifts if they looked only at alternative bar soap brands—the focus is just too narrow.

It's also important to realize that the way consumers look at a product isn't just a matter of chance. Let's return to our bar soap example. While many consumers do think about soap in terms of moisturizing and deodorizing, other needs shouldn't be overlooked. For example, some consumers are especially concerned about wiping out germs. Marketers for Dial soap recognized this need and developed ads that positioned Dial as "the choice" for these target customers. This helped Dial win new customers, including those who switched from Lifebuoy—which was otherwise similar to Dial (see Exhibit 3-12). In fact, what happened to Lifebuoy highlights what happens if managers don't update their marketing strategy as customer needs and competition change. Lifebuoy was the first deodorant soap on the market; it was a leading brand for over 100 years. But it gradually lost sales to competitors with stronger marketing mixes (clearer differentiation, better positioning, and superior customer value) until 2002, when Lever stopped selling it.

As we emphasize throughout the text, you must understand potential needs and attitudes when planning marketing strategies. If customers treat different products as substitutes, then a firm has to position itself against those products too. Customers won't always be conscious of all of the detailed ways that a firm's marketing mix might be different, but careful positioning can help highlight a unifying theme or benefits that relate to the determining dimensions of the target market. Thus, it's useful to think of positioning as part of the broader strategy planning process—because the purpose is to ensure that the whole marketing mix is positioned for competitive advantage.

CONCLUSION

Firms need creative strategy planning to survive in our increasingly competitive markets. In this chapter, we saw that carefully defining generic markets and product-markets can help find new opportunities. We stressed the shortcomings of a too narrow, product-oriented view of markets.

We also discussed market segmentation—the process of naming and then segmenting broad product-markets to find potentially attractive target markets. Some people try to segment markets by starting with the mass market and then dividing it into smaller submarkets based on a few dimensions. But this can lead to poor results. Instead, market segmentation should first focus on a broad product-market and then group similar customers into homogeneous submarkets. The more similar the potential customers are, the larger the submarkets can be. Four criteria for evaluating possible product-market segments were presented.

Once a broad product-market is segmented, marketing managers can use one of three approaches to market-oriented strategy planning: (1) the single target market approach, (2) the multiple target market approach, and (3) the combined target market approach. In general, we encouraged marketers to be segmenters rather than combiners.

We also discussed some computer-aided approaches—clustering techniques, CRM, and positioning.

In summary, good marketers should be experts on markets and likely segmenting dimensions. By creatively segmenting markets, they may spot opportunities—even breakthrough opportunities—and help their firms succeed against aggressive competitors offering similar products. Segmenting is basic to target marketing. And the more you practice segmenting, the more meaningful market segments you will see.

KEY TERMS

market, 61

generic market, 62

product-market, 62

market segmentation, 65

segmenting, 66

market segment, 66

single target market approach, 68

multiple target market approach, 68

combined target market approach, 68

combiners, 68

segmenters, 69

qualifying dimensions, 72

determining dimensions, 72

clustering techniques, 79

customer relationship management (CRM) , 80

positioning, 82

QUESTIONS AND PROBLEMS

1. Distinguish between a generic market and a product-market. Illustrate your answer.

2. Explain what market segmentation is.

3. List the types of potential segmenting dimensions, and explain which you would try to apply first, second, and third in a particular situation. If the nature of the situation would affect your answer, explain how.

4. Explain why segmentation efforts based on attempts to divide the mass market using a few demographic dimensions may be very disappointing.

5. Illustrate the concept that segmenting is an aggregating process by referring to the admissions policies of your own college and a nearby college or university.

6. Review the types of segmenting dimensions listed in Exhibits 3-8 and 3-9, and select the ones you think

should be combined to fully explain the market segment you personally would be in if you were planning to buy a new watch today. List several dimensions and try to develop a shorthand name, like "fashion-oriented," to describe your own personal market segment. Then try to estimate what proportion of the total watch market would be accounted for by your market segment. Next, explain if there are any offerings that come close to meeting the needs of your market. If not, what sort of a marketing mix is needed? Would it be economically attractive for anyone to try to satisfy your market segment? Why or why not?

7. Identify the determining dimension or dimensions that explain why you bought the specific brand you did in your most recent purchase of a *(a)* soft drink, *(b)* shampoo, *(c)* shirt or blouse, and *(d)* larger, more ex-

pensive item, such as a bicycle, camera, or boat. Try to express the determining dimension(s) in terms of your own personal characteristics rather than the product's characteristics. Estimate what share of the market would probably be motivated by the same determining dimension(s).

8. Consider the market for off-campus apartments in your city. Identify some submarkets that have differ-

ent needs and determining dimensions. Then evaluate how well the needs in these market segments are being met in your geographic area. Is there an obvious breakthrough opportunity waiting for someone?

9. Explain how positioning analysis can help a marketing manager identify target market opportunities.

SUGGESTED CASES

7. Lilybank Lodge

30. Deluxe Foods, Ltd.

COMPUTER-AIDED PROBLEM

3. Segmenting Customers

RESOURCE REMINDER

The marketing manager for Audiotronics Software Company is seeking new market opportunities. He is focusing on the voice recognition market and has narrowed down to three segments: the Fearful Typists, the Power Users, and the Professional Specialists. The Fearful Typists don't know much about computers—they just want a fast way to create e-mail messages, letters, and simple reports without errors. They don't need a lot of special features. They want simple instructions and a program that's easy to

learn. The Power Users know a lot about computers, use them often, and want a voice recognition program with many special features. All computer programs seem easy to them—so they aren't worried about learning to use the various features. The Professional Specialists have jobs that require a lot of writing. They don't know much about computers but are willing to learn. They want special features needed for their work—but only if they aren't too hard to learn and use.

The marketing manager prepared a table summarizing the importance of each of three key needs in the three segments (see table below).

Market Segment	Importance of Need (1 = not important; 10 = very important)		
	Features	Easy to Use	Easy to Learn
Fearful typists	3	8	9
Power users	9	2	2
Professional specialists	7	5	6

Audiotronics' sales staff conducted interviews with seven potential customers who were asked to rate how important each of these three needs were in their work. The manager prepared a spreadsheet to help him cluster (aggregate) each person into one of the segments— along with other similar people. Each person's ratings are entered in the spreadsheet, and the clustering procedure computes a similarity score that indicates how similar (a low score) or dissimilar (a high score) the person is to the typical person in each of the segments. The manager can then "aggregate" potential customers into the segment that is most similar (that is, the one with the *lowest* similarity score).

a. The ratings for a potential customer appear on the first spreadsheet. Into which segment would you aggregate this person?

b. The responses for seven potential customers who were interviewed are listed in the table below. Enter the ratings for a customer in the spreadsheet and then write down the similarity score for each segment. Repeat the process for each customer. Based on your analysis, indicate the segment into which you would aggregate each customer. Indicate the size (number of customers) of each segment.

c. In the interview, each potential customer was also asked what type of computer he or she would be using. The responses are shown in the table along with the ratings. Group the responses based on the customer's segment. If you were targeting the Fearful Typists segment, what type of computer would you focus on when developing your software?

d. Based on your analysis, which customer would you say is least like any of the segments? Briefly explain the reason for your choice.

For additional questions related to this problem, see Exercise 3-4 in the *Learning Aid for Use with Basic Marketing,* 15th edition.

Potential Customer	Importance of Need (1 = not important; 10 = very important)			
	Features	Easy to Use	Easy to Learn	Type of Computer
A.	8	1	2	Dell laptop
B.	6	6	5	IBM desktop
C.	4	9	8	Apple
D.	2	6	7	Apple
E.	5	6	5	IBM desktop
F.	8	3	1	Dell laptop
G.	4	6	8	Apple

1. Know the variables that shape the environment of marketing strategy planning.

2. Understand why company objectives are important in guiding marketing strategy planning.

3. See how the resources of a firm affect the search for opportunities.

4. Know how the different kinds of competitive situations affect strategy planning.

5. Understand how the economic and technological environment can affect strategy planning.

6. Know why you might be sent to prison if you ignore the political and legal environment.

7. Understand how to screen and evaluate marketing strategy opportunities.

8. Understand the important new terms (shown in red).

CHAPTER FOUR

Evaluating Opportunities in the Changing Marketing Environment

UPS is on a roll. But if you think it's just those clean brown trucks or sleek European delivery cycles that are moving, think again. Important marketing strategy changes are underway—and they don't end with the new logo or the TV ads that ask "What can Brown do for you?" Top management's objective isn't just to be the leader in delivering packages; it's also to be the world leader in delivering services and information to help corporate clients pare shipping, inventory, and handling costs while improving customer satisfaction. To achieve these objectives, marketing managers at UPS are developing completely new marketing strategies for new services and markets, like logistics consulting and handling of digital invoices and payments.

UPS faces tough competition from package delivery rivals FedEx and DHL, but the new UPS strategies mean that now it also competes with a host of other firms that market information technology solutions for business problems. But UPS has resources and strengths that help in this competition. It has already earned the trust of many business customers with whom it has close working relationships. Its experience and expertise are also a competitive advantage. UPS began to make huge investments in information systems over a decade ago, mainly to make its own operations more efficient. Then UPS quickly took advantage of the Internet to give customers access to UPS package-tracking databases (www.ups.com). For many business customers, knowing precisely where stuff was meant saving millions of dollars in inventory costs. That opened customers' eyes to the possibilities. Then UPS set up a special sales force to help firms link their e-commerce websites directly to UPS shipping data. That gave it more opportunities to see ways that UPS could improve a customer's

distribution system. Now, for example, if you order a pair of Air Jordans at Nike.com, the order is instantly filled by UPS from Nike inventory maintained at a UPS warehouse in Kentucky—and UPS delivers the sneakers directly to you the next day. In fact, if there is any problem and you call the toll-free number on Nike's website, it's a UPS employee at a call center in San Antonio who answers your call.

Sometimes UPS logistics solutions don't even rely on UPS trucks. For example, Ford Motor Company gave UPS a contract to manage the transportation and distribution of over four million cars and trucks a year—from 21 different factories to 6,000 dealers across North America. With the system, a Ford dealer who wanted to find a metallic blue Mustang convertible could instantly do it online. The UPS system also reduced transit time for a new car and saved millions of dollars a year in inventory carrying costs.

These successes are earning profits for UPS, but it still must cope with the challenges of a weakened economy. However, even when demand for package deliveries is low, UPS has a profit advantage over competitors who are less efficient. A weak economy may even help the UPS strategic business unit that offers logistics consulting services because customer firms have an even greater need to pare costs. That is one reason the market for logistics-consulting services is expected to double by 2007. Moreover, the trend toward free trade is helping UPS expand revenue from both international airfreight and the broker services it now offers to help firms cope with international customs laws.

On the other hand, the growth of international trade also means more competition at home, especially from DHL (which is owned by Deutsche Post AG, the German postal system). To speed its growth in the United States, DHL acquired the ground operations of Airborne Express. However, U.S. law restricts foreign ownership of airlines that fly between U.S. cities. So the U.S Department of Transportation held hearings on the ownership of the DHL Airways. While UPS cannot control either the legal or competitive environment that it faces, the decisions made by the DOT will have an important influence. UPS may need to further refine its marketing strategy to address changes in the marketing environment that it faces.[1]

THE MARKETING ENVIRONMENT

The UPS case shows that a marketing manager must analyze customer needs and choose marketing strategy variables within the framework of the marketing environment and how it is changing.

A large number of forces shape the marketing environment. To help organize your thinking, it's useful to classify the various forces as falling into either (1) the direct market environment or (2) the external market environment. The direct environment includes customers, the company, and competitors. The external market environment is broader and includes four major areas:

1. Economic environment.
2. Technological environment.
3. Political and legal environment.
4. Cultural and social environment.

The marketing manager can't control the variables of the marketing environment. That's why it's useful to think of them as uncontrollable variables. On the other hand, the marketing manager should carefully analyze the environmental variables when making decisions that can be controlled. For example, a manager can select a strategy that leads the firm into a product-market where competition is not yet strong. In this chapter, we'll look at the marketing environment variables in more detail. We'll see how they shape opportunities—limiting some possibilities and making others more attractive.

OBJECTIVES SHOULD SET FIRM'S COURSE

A company must decide where it's going, or it may fall into the trap expressed so well by the quotation: "Having lost sight of our objective, we redoubled our efforts." Company objectives should shape the direction and operation of the whole business.

It is difficult to set objectives that really guide the present and future development of a company. The marketing manager should be heard when the company is setting objectives. But setting whole-company objectives—within resource limits—is ultimately the responsibility of top management. Top management must look at the whole business, relate its present objectives and resources to the external environment, and then decide what the firm wants to accomplish in the future.

Three basic objectives provide guidelines

The following three objectives provide a useful starting point for setting a firm's objectives. They should be sought *together* because in the long run a failure in even one of the three areas can lead to total failure of the business. A business should

1. Engage in specific activities that will perform a socially and economically useful function.
2. Develop an organization to carry on the business and implement its strategies.
3. Earn enough profit to survive.[2]

Should be socially useful

The first objective isn't just a "do-gooder" objective. Businesses can't exist without the approval of consumers. If a firm's activities appear to be contrary to the consumer "good," the firm can be wiped out almost overnight by political or legal action—or consumers' own negative responses.[3]

Should earn some profit

A firm must make a profit to survive. But just saying that a firm should try to make a profit isn't enough. Management must specify the time period involved since many plans that maximize profit in the long run lose money during the first few years. Thousands of new dot-com firms went belly-up after a year or two of losses because they could not even cover their expenses in the short run.

On the other hand, seeking only short-term profits may steer the firm from opportunities that would offer larger long-run profits. For example, Fruit of the Loom struggled to maximize profits with its men's underwear and other clothing lines, but in those intensely competitive markets the maximum possible profit margins were so thin that it ultimately had to reorganize under the bankruptcy law. In a situation like this, it might be better to set a *target* rate of profit that will lead the firm into areas with more promising possibilities.

A mission statement helps set the course

Our three general objectives provide guidelines, but a firm should develop its own objectives. This is important, but top executives often don't state their objectives clearly. If objectives aren't clear from the start, different managers may hold unspoken and conflicting objectives.

Many firms try to avoid this problem by developing a **mission statement,** which sets out the organization's basic purpose for being. For example, the mission of the Fort Smith Public Library (www.fspl.lib.ar.us) is "to serve the minds of the citizens in our community by providing easy access to resources that meet their informational and recreational needs." A good mission statement should focus on a few key goals rather than embracing everything. It should also supply guidelines when managers face difficult decisions. For example, if an employee of the library is trying to decide whether or not to write a proposal for the funding of a Spanish language story time or new computers that provide Internet access, it should be clear that these services are within the scope of the library's stated mission. A mission statement may need to be revised as new market needs arise or as the marketing environment changes. But this would be a fundamental change and not one that is made casually.[4]

The whole firm must work toward the same objectives

A mission statement is important, but it is not a substitute for more specific objectives that provide guidance in screening possible opportunities. For example, top management might set objectives such as "earn 25 percent annual return on investment" and "introduce at least three innovative and successful products in the next two years."

Of course, when there are a number of specific objectives stated by top management, it is critical that they be compatible. For example, the objective of introducing new products is reasonable. However, if the costs of developing and introducing the new products cannot be recouped within one year, the return on investment objective is impossible.[5]

Company objectives should lead to marketing objectives

To avoid such problems, the marketing manager should at least be involved in setting company objectives. Company objectives guide managers as they search for and evaluate opportunities—and later plan marketing strategies. Particular *marketing* objectives should be set within the framework of larger company objectives. As shown in Exhibit 4-1, firms need a hierarchy of objectives—moving from company objectives to marketing department objectives. For each marketing strategy, firms also need objectives for each of the four Ps—as well as more detailed objectives. For example, in the Promotion area, we need objectives for advertising, sales promotion, *and* personal selling.

Exhibit 4-1 A Hierarchy of Objectives

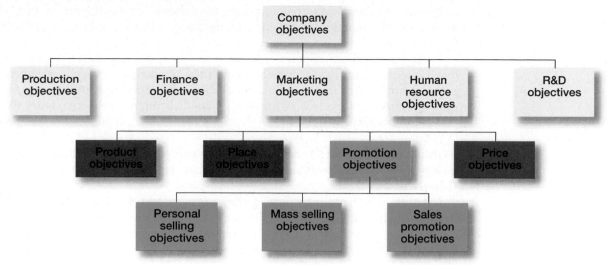

Toyota provides a good example. One of its company objectives is to achieve high customer satisfaction. So the R&D people design vehicles to meet specific reliability objectives. Similarly, the production people work to cut manufacturing defects. The marketing department, in turn, sets specific customer satisfaction objectives for every product. That leads to specific promotion objectives to ensure that the sales and advertising people don't promise more than the company can deliver. Dealers' service people, in turn, work to fix any problem the first time it's reported.

Both company objectives and marketing objectives should be realistic and achievable. Overly ambitious objectives are useless if the firm lacks the resources to achieve them.

COMPANY RESOURCES MAY LIMIT SEARCH FOR OPPORTUNITIES

Every firm has some resources—hopefully some unique ones—that set it apart. Breakthrough opportunities—or at least some competitive advantage—come from making use of these strengths while avoiding direct competition with firms having similar strengths.

To find its strengths, a firm must evaluate its functional areas (production, research and engineering, marketing, general management, and finance) as well as its present products and markets. The knowledge of people at the firm can also be a unique resource. By analyzing successes or failures in relation to the firm's resources, management can discover why the firm was successful—or why it failed—in the past.

Harley-Davidson's motorcycle business was on the ropes, and it was losing customers to Japanese competitors. Studying the Japanese firms helped Harley identify ways to produce higher quality motorcycles at lower cost. With these resource-use problems resolved, Harley was again on the road to achieving its objectives. As its sales and reputation grew, its close relationship with Harley owners became a resource that helped Harley introduce a profitable line of accessories. The

Harley case highlights both manufacturing quality and relationships with existing customers as resources. Other resources that should be considered as part of an evaluation of strengths and weaknesses are discussed in the following sections.[6]

Financial strength

Some opportunities require large amounts of capital just to get started. Money may be required for R&D, production facilities, marketing research, or advertising before a firm makes its first sale. And even a really good opportunity may not be profitable for years. So lack of financial strength is often a barrier to entry into an otherwise attractive market.

Producing capability and flexibility

In many businesses, the cost of producing and selling each unit decreases as the quantity increases. Therefore, smaller firms can be at a great cost disadvantage if they try to win business from larger competitors.

On the other hand, new—or smaller—firms sometimes have the advantage of flexibility. They are not handicapped with large, special-purpose facilities that are obsolete or poorly located. Large steel producers once enjoyed economies of scale. But today they have trouble competing with producers using smaller, more flexible plants.

Some firms are finding that they have the greatest flexibility by not having any "in house" manufacturing at all. Sara Lee, the company that markets brands like Hanes and L'Eggs, is a good example. Sara Lee sold its manufacturing facilities for many of these textile-related markets. Sara Lee says it doesn't have a competitive advantage in manufacturing. Further, as its needs change in various markets around the world it will buy products from whatever suppliers are best able to meet its specifications.

Marketing strengths

Our marketing strategy planning framework (Exhibit 2-10) helps in analyzing current marketing resources. In the product area, for example, a familiar brand can be a big strength. Starbucks is famous for its coffee beverages. When Starbucks introduced its Coffee Ice Cream, many people quickly tried it because they knew what Starbucks flavor meant.[7] A new idea or process may be protected by a *patent*. A patent owner has a 20-year monopoly to develop and use its new product, process, or material. If one firm has a strong patent, competitors may be limited to second-rate offerings—and their efforts may be doomed to failure.[8]

Hurd faces many large competitors that mass produce windows in large quantities, so Hurd wants customers who are building a new home to see that its strength is that it creates each individual window with care.

Good relations with established middlemen—or control of good locations—can be important resources. When marketing managers at Microsoft decided to introduce the Xbox game console, Microsoft software and computer accessories had already proved profitable for retailers like Best Buy and Wal-Mart that could reach the target market. So these retailers were willing to give the new product shelf space even if they were already carrying competing products from Nintendo or Sony.[9]

Similarly, existing computer systems that effectively share information in the channel, speed delivery of orders, and control inventory can be a big advantage. When P&G adds a new type of detergent, the systems to manage distribution are already in place.

Promotion and price resources must be considered too. Fidelity Investments already has a skilled sales force. Marketing managers know these sales reps can handle new products and customers. And expertise to create an Internet website for online orders may enable a firm to expand its market and undercut competitors' prices.

Finally, thorough understanding of a target market can give a company an edge. Many companies fail in new product-markets because they don't really understand the needs of the new customers or the new competitive environment.

ANALYZING COMPETITORS AND THE COMPETITIVE ENVIRONMENT

Choose opportunities that avoid head-on competition

The **competitive environment** affects the number and types of competitors the marketing manager must face and how they may behave. Although marketing managers usually can't control these factors, they can choose strategies that avoid head-on competition. And where competition is inevitable, they can plan for it.

Economists describe four basic kinds of market (competitive) situations: pure competition, oligopoly, monopolistic competition, and monopoly. Understanding the differences among these market situations is helpful in analyzing the competitive environment, and our discussion assumes some familiarity with these concepts. (For a review, see Exhibit A-11 and the related discussion in Appendix A, which follows Chapter 22.)

Most product-markets head toward pure competition—or oligopoly—over the long run. In these situations, competitors offer very similar products. Because

Dutch Boy wants to provide superior value and avoid head-on competition by illustrating that its paint is in a container that is easier to open, hold, and pour than competitors' paint cans. Dirt Devil wants to convince customers that its Scorpion Hand Vac has more power than competitors, so its ad gives the specific amp and watt rating. However, a consumer who does not know the ratings for other brands may not know that this is an advantage.

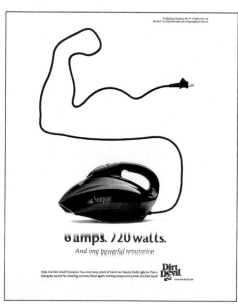

customers see the different available products (marketing mixes) as close substitutes, managers just compete with lower and lower prices, and profit margins shrink. Sometimes managers do this much too quickly, without really thinking through the question of how to add more customer value. The marketing mix that offers the best customer value is not necessarily the one with the lowest price.

Avoiding pure competition is sensible and certainly fits with our emphasis on target marketing and the need to find a competitive advantage on which to differentiate the firm's marketing mix. This is why effective target marketing is fundamentally different from effective decision making in other areas of business. Accounting, production, and financial managers for competing firms can learn about and use the same standardized approaches—and they will work well in each case. By contrast, marketing managers can't just adopt the same "good" marketing strategy being used by other firms. That just leads to head-on competition and a downward spiral in prices and profits. So target marketers try to offer a marketing mix better suited to customers' needs than competitors' offerings.

Competitor-free environments are rare

Most marketing managers would like to have such a strong marketing mix that customers see it as uniquely able to meet their needs. This competitor-free ideal guides the search for breakthrough opportunities. Yet monopoly situations, in which one firm completely controls a broad product-market, are rare in market-directed economies. Further, governments commonly regulate monopolies. For example, in many parts of the world prices set by utility companies must be approved by a government agency. Although most marketing managers can't expect to operate with complete control in an unregulated monopoly, they can move away from head-on competition.

Monopolistic competition is typical—and a challenge

In monopolistic competition, a number of different firms offer marketing mixes that at least some customers see as different. Each competitor tries to get control (a monopoly) in its "own" target market. But competition still exists because some customers see the various alternatives as substitutes. Most marketing managers in developed economies face monopolistic competition.

In monopolistic competition, marketing managers sometimes try to differentiate very similar products by relying on other elements of the marketing mix. For example, Clorox Bleach uses the same basic chemicals as other bleaches. But marketing managers for Clorox may help to set it apart from other bleaches by offering an improved pouring spout, by producing ads that demonstrate its stain-killing power, or by getting it better shelf positions in supermarkets. Yet such approaches may not work, especially if competitors can easily imitate each new idea.

Analyze competitors to find a competitive advantage

The best way for a marketing manager to avoid head-on competition is to find new or better ways to satisfy customers' needs and provide value. The search for a breakthrough opportunity—or some sort of competitive advantage—requires an understanding not only of customers but also of competitors. That's why marketing managers turn to **competitor analysis**—an organized approach for evaluating the strengths and weaknesses of current or potential competitors' marketing strategies.

The basic approach to competitor analysis is simple. You compare the strengths and weaknesses of your current (or planned) target market and marketing mix with what competitors are currently doing or are likely to do in response to your strategy.

The initial step in competitor analysis is to identify potential competitors. It's useful to start broadly and from the viewpoint of target customers. Companies may offer quite different products to meet the same needs, but they are competitors if customers see them as offering close substitutes. For example, disposable diapers, cloth diapers, and diaper rental services all compete in the same generic market concerned with baby care. Identifying a broad set of potential competitors helps marketing managers understand the different ways customers are currently meeting needs and sometimes points to new opportunities. For example, even parents who

usually prefer the economy of cloth diapers may be interested in the convenience of disposables when they travel.

Usually, however, marketing managers quickly narrow the focus of their analysis to the set of **competitive rivals**—firms that will be the closest competitors. Rivals offering similar products are usually easy to identify. However, with a really new and different product concept, the closest competitor may be a firm that is currently serving similar needs with a different type of product. Although such firms may not appear to be close competitors, they are likely to fight back—perhaps with a directly competitive product—if another firm starts to take away customers.

Anticipate competition that will come

A successful strategy attracts copycats who jump in for a share of the profit. Sometimes a creative imitator figures out a way to provide customers with superior value. Then sales may disappear before the pioneer even knows what's happened.

Finding a sustainable competitive advantage requires special attention to competitor strengths and weaknesses. For example, it is very difficult to dislodge a firm that is already a market leader simply by attacking with a similar strategy. The leader can usually defend its position by quickly copying the best parts of what a new competitor is trying to do. On the other hand, an established competitor may not be able to defend quickly if it is attacked where it is weak. For example, Sony Walkman CD players had a large market share. When RCA added a new feature to its CD players that enabled them to also handle MP3 files, Sony was slow to respond. Sony executives were worried that more widespread use of MP3 files would hurt profits from the firm's music recording business.[10]

Watch for competitive barriers

In a competitor analysis, you also consider **competitive barriers**—the conditions that may make it difficult, or even impossible, for a firm to compete in a market. Such barriers may limit your own plans or, alternatively, block competitors' responses to an innovative strategy.

For example, Exhibit 4-2 summarizes a competitor analysis in the Japanese market for disposable diapers. P&G was about to replace its original Pampers, which were selling poorly, with a new version that offered improved fit and better absorbency. Kao and Uni-Charm, the two leading Japanese producers, both had better distribution

	P&G's Current and Planned Strategy	Kao's Strengths (+) and Weaknesses (−)	Uni-Charm's Strengths (+) and Weaknesses (−)
Target Market(s)	Upscale, modern parents who can afford disposable diapers	Same as for P&G	Same as for P&G, but also budget-conscious segment that includes cloth diaper users (+)
Product	Improved fit and absorbency (+); brand name imagery weak in Japan (−)	Brand familiarity (+), but no longer the best performance (−)	Two brands—for different market segments—and more convenient package with handles (+)
Place	Distribution through independent wholesalers to both food stores and drugstores (+), but handled by fewer retailers (−)	Close relations with and control over wholesalers who carry only Kao products (+); computerized inventory reorder system (+)	Distribution through 80% of food stores in best locations (+); shelf space for two brands (+)
Promotion	Heaviest spending on daytime TV, heavy sales promotion, including free samples (+); small sales force (−)	Large efficient sales force (+); lowest advertising spending (−) and out-of-date ad claims (−)	Advertising spending high (+), effective ads that appeal to Japanese mothers (+)
Price	High retail price (−), but lower unit price for larger quantities (+)	Highest retail price (−), but also best margins for wholesalers and retailers (+)	Lowest available retail price (+); price of premium brand comparable to P&G (−)
(Potential) Competitive Barriers	Patent protection (+), limits in access to retail shelf space (−)	Inferior product (−), excellent logistics support system (+)	Economies of scale and lower costs (+); loyal customers (+)
Likely Response(s)	Improve wholesaler and retailer margins; faster deliveries in channel; change package to require less shelf space	Press retailers to increase in-store promotion; change advertising and/or improve product	Increase short-term sales promotions; but if P&G takes customers, cut price on premium brand

networks. Kao also had a better computer system to handle reorders. Because most Japanese grocery stores and drugstores are very small, frequent restocking by wholesalers is critical. So getting cooperation in the channel was a potential competitive barrier for P&G. To overcome this problem, P&G changed its packaging to take up less space and offered wholesalers and retailers better markups.[11]

Seek information about competitors

A marketing manager should actively seek information about current or potential competitors. Although most firms try to keep the specifics of their plans secret, much public information may be available. Sources of competitor information include trade publications, alert sales reps, middlemen, and other industry experts. In business markets, customers may be quick to explain what competing suppliers are offering.

The Internet is a powerful way to get information about competitors. A firm that puts all of its marketing information on a website for customers also makes it readily available to competitors. Similarly, it's easy to search through thousands of online publications and databases for any mention of a competitor. It's also increasingly common to specify what you want and instruct a software "robot" to send you a copy as soon as it's available.

INTERNET EXERCISE

If you were a new marketing manager at Rubbermaid, you might be interested in finding out more about Tupperware, an important competitor in some markets. What type of relevant information could you get by going to the Tupperware website (www.tupperware.com)?

Ethical issues may arise

The search for information about competitors sometimes raises ethical issues. For example, people who change jobs and move to competing firms may have a great deal of information about the competitor, but is it ethical for them to use it? Similarly, some firms have been criticized for going too far—like waiting at a landfill for competitors' trash to find copies of confidential company reports. And the high-tech version of that occurs when computer "hackers" use the Internet to break into a competitor's computer network.

Beyond the moral issues, spying on competitors to obtain trade secrets is illegal. Damage awards can be huge. The courts ordered competing firms to pay Procter & Gamble about $125 million in damages for stealing secrets about its Duncan Hines soft cookies.[12]

Competition may vary from country to country

A firm that faces very stiff competition may find that the competitive environment—and the opportunities—are much better in another region or country. For instance, eight years of slow growth and deregulation made the Japanese market extremely competitive. So the Iris Ohyama Company, a maker of plastic storage containers, started exporting to North America. Within three years, its sales to U.S. retailers like Staples were $60 million.[13]

Direct competition cannot always be avoided

Despite the desire to avoid highly competitive situations, a firm may find that it can't. Some firms are already in an industry before it becomes intensely competitive. For example, Rubbermaid was one of the first firms to introduce sturdy, low-cost plastic housewares. Now it is a respected brand name but faces competition from hundreds of other firms. As competitors fail, new firms enter the market, possibly because they don't see more attractive alternatives. This is a common pattern with small retailers and wholesalers in less-developed economies. New entrants may not even know how competitive the market is—but they stick it out until they run out of money.

THE ECONOMIC ENVIRONMENT

The **economic and technological environment** affects the way firms—and the whole economy—use resources. We will treat the economic and technological environments separately to emphasize that the technological environment provides a *base* for the economic environment. Technical skills and equipment affect the way companies convert an economy's resources into output. The economic environment, on the other hand, is affected by the way all of the parts of a macro-economic system interact. This then affects such things as national income, economic growth, and inflation. The economic environment may vary from one country to another, but economies around the world are linked.

Economic conditions change rapidly

The economic environment can, and does, change quite rapidly. The effects can be far-reaching and require changes in marketing strategy.

Even a well-planned marketing strategy may fail if a country or region goes through a rapid business decline. As consumers' incomes drop, they must shift their spending patterns. They may simply have to do without some products. When this happens, many businesses collapse or have big losses. You can see how quickly this happens by considering what happened in Thailand in the late 1990s. In a few months, the buying power of Thai money (the baht) was cut by half. Imagine how *your* life would change if you suddenly had half as much money. If this happened to you and most of the people you know, what would its effect be on businesses where you buy?

Economic changes are not always this dramatic. Consider the recent cooling off of the U.S. economy. The growth of the economy leading up to 2000 created a strong job market, increased incomes, and focused attention on the rising value of

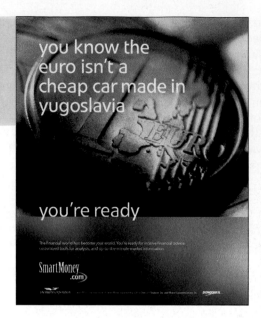

investments. Many consumers felt like they were well off. Purchases of pricey items and luxuries trended up because of this "wealth effect." This behavior quickly disappeared when the economy turned, but for most products demand declined more gradually. Even so, many companies aren't strong enough to survive such downturns.

Interest rates and inflation affect buying

Changes in the economy are often accompanied by changes in the interest rate—the charge for borrowing money. Interest rates directly affect the total price borrowers must pay for products. So the interest rate affects when, and if, they will buy. This is an especially important factor in some business markets. But it also affects consumer purchases of homes, cars, and other items usually bought on credit.

Interest rates usually increase during periods of inflation, and inflation is a fact of life in many economies. In some Latin American countries, inflation has exceeded 400 percent a year in recent years. In contrast, recent U.S. levels—3 to 20 percent—seem low. Still, inflation must be considered in strategy planning. When costs are rising rapidly and there are no more cost-cutting measures to take, a marketing manager may have to increase prices.

The global economy is connected

The economies of the world are connected—and changes in one economy quickly affect others. One reason for this is that the amount of international trade is increasing—and it is affected by changes in and between economies. For example, International Harvester (IH) was very successful selling its earth-moving equipment in Asia when construction was booming. However, when an economic downturn spread across Asia, many customers could no longer make payments. IH faced big losses—and the cost of retrieving equipment that was 13,000 miles away!

Changes in the *exchange rate*—how much one country's money is worth in another country's money—have an important effect on international trade. When the dollar is strong, it's worth more in foreign countries. This sounds good—but it makes U.S. products more expensive overseas and foreign products cheaper in the United States. New domestic competition arises as foreign products gain a competitive edge with lower prices. A country's whole economic system can change as the balance of imports and exports shifts—affecting jobs, consumer income, and national productivity.

Marketing managers must watch the economic environment carefully. In contrast to the cultural and social environment, economic conditions can move rapidly and require immediate strategy changes.[14]

Your car will be watching the road, even if you're not.

We all know how important it is to pay attention to the road but, once in a while, your mind wanders. We are working on ways to help prevent your car from wandering too. We're also developing the 'electronic eye', which may recognize obstacles on the road. And bring your car to a stop if necessary. Now do we have your attention? Find out more about the 'Vision of Accident free Driving' at www.daimlerchrysler.com.

DAIMLERCHRYSLER
Answers for questions to come.

THE TECHNOLOGICAL ENVIRONMENT

Technology affects opportunities

Technology is the application of science to convert an economy's resources to output. Technology affects marketing in two basic ways: with new products and with new processes (ways of doing things). For example, advances in information technology make it possible for people in different parts of the world to communicate with satellite video-conferencing and to send complex design drawings over the Internet. Websites enable sophisticated e-commerce exchanges between remote firms. These process changes are accompanied by an exciting explosion of high-tech products—from genome-based medicines to cars that contact the police if they are stolen.

Technology transfer is rapid

New technologies have created important industries that didn't even exist a few years ago. Ten years ago eBay didn't exist. Now it's one of the best known firms in the world. With such big opportunities at stake, you can also see why there is such rapid transfer of technology from one part of the world to another. But technology transfer is not automatic. Someone—perhaps you—has to see the opportunity.

Internet technologies are reshaping marketing

Many of the big advances in business have come from early recognition of new ways to do things. There is perhaps no better example of this than the World Wide Web and the Internet. The **Internet** is a system for linking computers around the world. The idea of linking computers in a network is not new. Even so, the Internet expands the network concept to include any computer anywhere and the World Wide Web makes the exchange of information easy. As a result, this technology is radically changing just about every aspect of marketing. We'll be discussing these changes in more detail throughout the text, but for now we'll just illustrate the impact.

Consider the arena of promotion. The invention of TV changed marketing because it suddenly made it possible for a sponsor to broadcast a vivid message to millions of people at the same time. Now, the Internet makes it possible for that sponsor to select any of millions of messages and to simultaneously narrowcast any of them to millions of different individuals. It is just as easy for customers to request the information in the first place, or to respond electronically once they have it. Thus, the Internet's capability radically changes our ideas about how firms communicate with customers, and vice versa. Similarly, the Internet is creating totally different approaches to pricing. Airlines run online auctions of seats that might otherwise go unsold. If you sell every seat to the highest bidder, you are really pricing precisely to match supply and demand. To check out an online auction, go to www.ebay.com.

In hindsight, new approaches such as these seem obvious—given that the technology is available. But they are not obvious up front—unless you're really looking for them.[15]

Technology also poses challenges

Technological change opens up new opportunities, but it also poses challenges for marketers. For some firms, success hinges on how quickly new ideas can be brought to market. But it's easy for a firm to slip into a production orientation in the flush of excitement that comes from a new idea or R&D discovery. That makes it more important than ever for marketing thinking to guide the production process—starting at the beginning with decisions about what customers will really value and where development efforts should be focused.

Technology and ethical issues

Marketers often must help their firms decide what technological developments are ethically acceptable. For example, many firms track information about who "hits" the company web page and what website they came from. The firm can then sell this information to whoever wants to use it to send promotional e-mail. Yet uninvited e-mail is just another form of invasion of privacy.

Some attractive technological developments may be rejected because of their long-run effects on the environment. Aseptic drink boxes, for example, are convenient but difficult to recycle. In a case like this, what's good for the firm and some customers may not be good for the cultural and social environment or acceptable in the political and legal environment. Being close to the market should give marketers a better feel for current trends and help firms avoid serious mistakes.[16]

THE POLITICAL ENVIRONMENT

The attitudes and reactions of people, social critics, and governments all affect the political environment. Consumers in the same country usually share a common political environment, but the political environment can also affect opportunities at a local or international level. Some business managers have become very successful by studying the political environment and developing strategies that take advantage of opportunities related to changing political dimensions.

Nationalism can be limiting in international markets

Strong sentiments of **nationalism**—an emphasis on a country's interests before everything else—affect how macro-marketing systems work. They can affect how marketing managers work as well. Nationalistic feelings can reduce sales—or even block all marketing activity—in some international markets. For many years, Japan has made it difficult for outside firms to do business there—in spite of the fact that Japanese producers of cars, TVs, digital cameras, and other products have established profitable markets in the United States, Europe, and other parts of the world.

The "Buy American" policy in many government contracts and business purchases reflects this same attitude in the United States. There is broad support for protecting U.S. producers—and jobs—from foreign competition.[17]

Nationalistic feelings can determine whether a firm can enter markets because businesses often must get permission to operate. In some political environments, this is only a routine formality. In others, a lot of red tape and personal influence are involved, and bribes are sometimes expected. This raises ethical issues for marketing managers—and legal issues too, since it's illegal for U.S. firms to offer such

Adero wants marketers to keep in mind that a website that can attract prospects from all over the world won't be successful in turning them into customers if it ignores nationalism and cultural differences.

オワリダ

THAT'S JAPANESE FOR "YOU'RE TOAST" IF YOUR WEBSITE CAN'T ACCOMMODATE OUR LANGUAGE AND CURRENCY.

THINK YOU'RE READY TO DO E-BUSINESS WITH A COMPLETELY DIFFERENT CULTURE? ARE YOU SPEAKING THE RIGHT LANGUAGE? USING THE RIGHT CURRENCY? BEFORE DIVING INTO ANY FOREIGN MARKET, YOU'VE GOT TO MAKE SURE YOUR BUSINESS APPROACH IS APPROPRIATE AND ON TARGET. ADERO CAN HELP. FROM TOKYO TO PARIS, ADERO'S WORLDWIDE NETWORK ROUTES THE RIGHT WEB CONTENT TO THE RIGHT PEOPLE. THAT WAY, YOU WON'T GET BURNED.

adero›
The world wants your business.™

WWW.ADERO.COM

bribes. Clearly, that can make it difficult for a U.S. firm to compete with a company from a country that doesn't have similar laws.

Regional groupings are becoming more important

Important dimensions of the political environment are likely to be similar among nations that have banded together to have common regional economic boundaries. The move toward the unification of Europe and free trade among the nations of North America are outstanding examples of this sort of regional grouping.

The unification of European markets

In the past, each country in Europe had its own unique trade rules and regulations. These differences made it difficult and expensive to move products from one country to the others. Now, the member countries of the European Union (EU) are reducing conflicting laws, taxes, and other obstacles to trade within Europe. This, in turn, is reducing costs and the prices European consumers pay and creating new jobs. Even bigger changes may come if Britain decides to join other countries that have moved to the euro, a new unified money system for the EU. With the currencies of countries in the euro-zone phased out, transactions no longer involve the extra uncertainty and cost of converting payments from one currency to another.

Although Europe is becoming the largest unified market in the world, marketers will still encounter differences among European countries. What happened to Lands' End, the Wisconsin-based Internet and mail-order retailer, illustrates the issues. To better reach European consumers, Lands' End set up shop in England and Germany. As in the United States, its promotion and website touted the unconditional lifetime guarantee that is a key part of its strategy. However, German consumer protection rules prohibited promotion of the guarantee; the Germans argued that the promotion was a misleading gimmick (on the logic that the cost of the guarantee was "hidden" in higher prices that consumers would pay). German officials wanted this ban to apply even if the German consumer purchased the product from a Lands' End website in England. If quirky local rules like this are allowed to prevail, small companies that want to use e-commerce to efficiently reach the whole European market will have to comply with all of the different laws in every country. This could erode benefits that should come from more European unification.[18]

| NAFTA is building trade cooperation | The international competition fostered by the moves to unify Europe provided impetus for the United States, Mexico, and Canada to develop more cooperative trade agreements. The **North American Free Trade Agreement (NAFTA)** lays out a plan to reshape the rules of trade among the United States, Canada, and Mexico. NAFTA basically enlarges the free-trade pact that had already knocked down most barriers to U.S.–Canada trade, and over a 15-year period it will eliminate most such barriers with Mexico. It also establishes a forum for resolving future trade disputes. |

The long-term economic impact of NAFTA is yet to be seen. However, tariffs that have already dropped are having a significant impact on specific businesses. For example, Raychem Corp., a small producer of telecommunications equipment, no longer faces a 25 percent tariff on exports to Mexico. That is leveling its competitive playing field and creating new opportunities. On the other hand, many firms have moved production—and jobs—to Mexico where labor is cheaper. NAFTA is creating a free-trade region that encompasses over 400 million people and three economies that produce over $9 trillion worth of goods and services annually. Thus, the changes that result from NAFTA may ultimately be as significant as those in Europe. Talks are underway to explore the concept of expanding NAFTA to create a free-trade zone for 34 countries across North, South, and Central America.

Of course, removal of some economic and political barriers—whether across all of the Americas or Europe—will not eliminate the need to adjust strategies to reach submarkets of consumers. Centuries of cultural differences will not disappear overnight. Some may never disappear.[19]

Some dramatic changes in the political environment—like the fall of communism in Eastern Europe—happen fast and are hard to predict. Yet many important political changes—both within and across nations—evolve more gradually. The development of consumerism is a good example.

| Consumerism is here—and basic | **Consumerism** is a social movement that seeks to increase the rights and powers of consumers. In the last 40 years, consumerism has emerged as a major political force. Although the consumer movement has spread to many different countries, it was born in America. |

The basic goals of modern consumerism haven't changed much since 1962, when President Kennedy's "Consumer Bill of Rights" affirmed consumers' rights to safety, to be informed, to choose, and to be heard.

Forty years ago, U.S. consumerism was much more visible. Consumers staged frequent boycotts and protest marches and attracted much media attention. Today, consumer groups provide information and work on special projects like product safety standards. Publications like *Consumer Reports* provide product comparisons and information on other consumer concerns.

Clearly, top management—and marketing managers—must continue to pay attention to consumer concerns. The old, production-oriented ways of doing things are no longer acceptable.[20]

THE LEGAL ENVIRONMENT

Changes in the political environment often lead to changes in the legal environment and in the way existing laws are enforced. The legal environment sets the basic rules for how a business can operate in society. The legal environment may severely limit some choices, but changes in laws and how they are interpreted also create new opportunities. To illustrate the effects of the legal environment, we will discuss how it has evolved in the United States. However, laws often vary from one country to another.

Law	Product	Place	Promotion	Price
Sherman Act (1890) Monopoly or conspiracy in restraint of trade	Monopoly or conspiracy to control a product	Monopoly or conspiracy to control distribution channels		Monopoly or conspiracy to fix or control prices
Clayton Act (1914) Substantially lessens competition	Forcing sale of some products with others— tying contracts	Exclusive dealing contracts (limiting buyers' sources of supply)		Price discrimination by manufacturers
Federal Trade Commission Act (1914) Unfair methods of competition		Unfair policies	Deceptive ads or selling practices	Deceptive pricing
Robinson-Patman Act (1936) Tends to injure competition		Prohibits paying allowances to "direct" buyers in lieu of middlemen costs (brokerage charges)	Prohibits "fake" advertising allowances or discrimination in help offered	Prohibits price discrimination on goods of "like grade and quality" without cost justification, and limits quantity discounts
Wheeler-Lea Amendment (1938) Unfair or deceptive practices	Deceptive packaging or branding		Deceptive ads or selling claims	Deceptive pricing
Antimerger Act (1950) Lessens competition	Buying competitors	Buying producers or distributors		
Magnuson-Moss Act (1975) Unreasonable practices	Product warranties			

Trying to encourage competition

American economic and legislative thinking is based on the idea that competition among many small firms helps the economy. Therefore, attempts by business to limit competition are considered contrary to the public interest.

Starting in 1890, Congress passed a series of antimonopoly laws. Exhibit 4-3 shows the names and dates of these laws. Although the specific focus of each law is different, in general they are all intended to encourage competition.

Antimonopoly law and marketing mix planning

In later chapters, we will specifically apply antimonopoly law to the four Ps. For now you should know what kind of proof the government must have to get a conviction under each of the major laws. You should also know which of the four Ps are most affected by each law. Exhibit 4-3 provides such a summary—with a phrase following each law to show what the government must prove to get a conviction.

Prosecution is serious—you can go to jail

Businesses and *individual managers* are subject to both criminal and civil laws. Penalties for breaking civil laws are limited to blocking or forcing certain actions— along with fines. Where criminal law applies, jail sentences can be imposed. For example, several managers at Beech-Nut Nutrition Company were fined $100,000 each and sent to jail. In spite of ads claiming that Beech-Nut's apple juice was 100 percent natural, they tried to bolster profits by secretly using low-cost artificial ingredients.[21]

Consumer protection laws are not new

Although antimonopoly laws focus on protecting competition, the wording of the laws in Exhibit 4-3 has, over time, moved toward protecting consumers. Some consumer protections are also built into the English and U.S. common law systems. A seller has to tell the truth (if asked a direct question), meet contracts, and stand behind the firm's product (to some reasonable extent). Beyond this, it is expected that vigorous competition in the marketplace will protect consumers—*so long as they are careful*.

Yet focusing only on competition didn't protect consumers very well in some areas. So the government found it necessary to pass other laws. For example, various laws regulate packaging and labels, credit practices, and environmental issues. Usually, however, the laws focus on specific types of products.

Foods and drugs are controlled

Consumer protection laws in the United States go back to 1906 when Congress passed the Pure Food and Drug Act. Unsanitary meat-packing practices in the Chicago stockyards stirred consumer support for this act. This was a major victory for consumer protection. Before the law, it was assumed that common law and the old warning "let the buyer beware" would take care of consumers.

Later acts corrected some loopholes in the law. The law now bans the shipment of unsanitary and poisonous products and requires much testing of drugs. The Food and Drug Administration (FDA) attempts to control manufacturers of these products. It can seize products that violate its rules—including regulations on branding and labeling.

Product safety is controlled

The Consumer Product Safety Act (of 1972), another important consumer protection law, set up the Consumer Product Safety Commission. This group has broad power to set safety standards and can impose penalties for failure to meet these standards. There is some question as to how much safety consumers really want—the commission found the bicycle the most hazardous product under its control!

But given that the commission has the power to *force* a product off the market—or require expensive recalls to correct problems—it is obvious that safety must be considered in product design. And safety must be treated seriously by marketing managers. There is no more tragic example of this than the recent recalls of Firestone tires used as original equipment on Ford's Explorer SUV. Hundreds of consumers were killed or seriously injured in accidents.[22]

INTERNET EXERCISE

The Consumer Product Safety Commission sometimes requires automakers to issue recalls. However, not all consumers learn about the recalls. Go to the *Consumer Reports* website (www.consumerreports.org) and select the link for recalls. Then check to see if there has been a recall on a year and model of car or truck that is of interest to you (say, one owned by your family).

State and local laws vary

Besides federal legislation—which affects interstate commerce—marketers must be aware of state and local laws. There are state and city laws regulating minimum prices and the setting of prices, regulations for starting up a business (licenses, examinations, and even tax payments), and in some communities, regulations

Exhibit 4-4   Some Important U.S. Federal Regulatory Agencies

Agencies	Responsibilities
Federal Trade Commission (FTC)	Enforces laws and develops guidelines regarding unfair business practices
Food and Drug Administration (FDA)	Enforces laws and develops regulations to prevent distribution and sale of adulterated or misbranded foods, drugs, cosmetics, and hazardous consumer products
Consumer Product Safety Commission (CPSC)	Enforces the Consumer Product Safety Act—which covers any consumer product not assigned to other regulatory agencies
Federal Communications Commission (FCC)	Regulates interstate wire, radio, television, and telephone
Environmental Protection Agency (EPA)	Develops and enforces environmental protection standards

prohibiting certain activities—such as telephone selling or selling on Sundays or during evenings.

Know the laws—follow the courts and federal agencies

Often laws are vaguely phrased—to convey intent but not specific detail. Then it's up to the courts and government agencies to spell out the details. As a result, a law may be interpreted and enforced differently over time. For example, during the late 1970s and 1980s, many U.S. government agencies regulated businesses less zealously and instead focused more on encouraging competition. Attention to regulation was swinging the other way in the 1990s—in part to correct abuses such as those that occurred in the savings and loan industry.

It was in this sort of political environment that the U.S. Justice Department, and the attorneys general in a number of states, brought charges against Microsoft. Many government officials, competitors, and consumer interest groups felt that Microsoft violated the antimonopoly laws, and at one point a judge declared that Microsoft would be broken up into two or more competing companies. However, the court case dragged on for over five years, and by the time of the national elections in 2000 the political climate was swinging toward less aggressive enforcement of the laws. As this very visible and important case shows, how the laws are interpreted and enforced can be even more important than the wording of the law when it was originally written.[23]

Because legislation must be interpreted by federal agencies and the courts, marketing managers need to study both legislative developments and the thinking of the courts and agencies. See Exhibit 4-4 for a description of some important federal regulatory agencies that should be considered in marketing strategy planning.

Consumerists and the law say "let the seller beware"

The old rule about buyer–seller relations—*let the buyer beware*—has changed to *let the seller beware*. The current shift to proconsumer laws and court decisions suggests that lawmakers are more interested in protecting consumers. This may upset production-oriented managers. But times have changed—and managers must adapt to this new political and legal environment.[24]

THE CULTURAL AND SOCIAL ENVIRONMENT

The **cultural and social environment** affects how and why people live and behave as they do—which affects customer buying behavior and eventually the economic, political, and legal environment. Many variables make up the cultural and social environment. Some examples are the languages people speak, the type of education they have, their religious beliefs, what type of food they eat, the style of clothing and housing they have, and how they view work, marriage, and family. Because

Realizing that more and more consumers are interested in the benefits of a healthy diet, Kellogg uses humor to remind consumers that its Nutri-Grain bar is a healthy (and not so fattening) choice for breakfast. Similarly, Orville Redenbacher's Smart Pop reminds snackers that "now you can eat all you want" because its new flavor is 94 percent fat free.

the cultural and social environment has such broad effects, most people don't stop to think about it, or how it may be changing, or how it may differ for other people.

A marketing manager can't afford to take the cultural and social environment for granted. Although changes tend to come slowly, they can have far-reaching effects. A marketing manager who sees the changes early may be able to identify big opportunities. Further, within any broad society, different subgroups of people may be affected by the cultural and social environment in different ways. In most countries, the trend toward multiculturalism is making such differences even more important to marketers. They require special attention when segmenting markets. In fact, dealing with these differences is often one of the greatest challenges managers face when planning strategies, especially for international markets.

Since we will discuss details of how the cultural and social environment relates to buying behavior in Chapters 5 through 7, here we will just use an example to illustrate its impact on marketing strategy planning.

Changing women's roles

The shifting roles of women in society illustrate the importance of the cultural and social environment on marketing strategy planning. Fifty years ago, most people in the United States felt that a woman's role was in the home—first and foremost as a wife and mother. Women had less opportunity for higher education and were completely shut out of many of the most interesting jobs. Obviously, there have been big changes in that stereotyped thinking. With better job opportunities, more women are delaying marriage, and once married they are likely to stay in the workforce and have fewer children. For example, in 1950, only 24 percent of wives worked outside the home. Now that figure is over 60 percent. Among women in the 35–44 age group, the percentage is already over 70. Not everything has changed, though. The median income for women lags and is only 73 percent of men's.

Still, the flood of women into the job market boosted economic growth and changed U.S. society in many other ways. Many in-home jobs that used to be done primarily by women—ranging from family shopping to preparing meals to doing volunteer work—still need to be done by someone. Husbands and children now do some of these jobs, a situation that has changed the target market for many products. Or a working woman may face a crushing "poverty of time" and look for help elsewhere, creating opportunities for producers of frozen meals, child care centers, dry cleaners, financial services, and the like.

HYBRID CARS PLUG INTO A PITCH FOR CONVENIENCE AND POWER

For 100 years, gasoline-powered vehicles have been the king of the road. And unlike in some cultures, people in the United States drive everywhere they go. Yet this has created problems. The high cost of gasoline, its environmental impact, and reliance on oil from the politically volatile Middle East long ago led to federal laws that required automakers to improve gas mileage. In response, during the 1980s and 90s automakers redesigned vehicles to improve mileage. Even so, progress was slow. Many consumers preferred big gas-guzzler SUVs that were a better match for their suburban lifestyles. A decade ago, to help curb smog in cities like Los Angeles, desperate California lawmakers even told automakers that by 2003, 10 percent of the autos and trucks they sell must produce zero emissions. To nudge toward that target, a few manufacturers offered electric vehicles. Yet battery-powered cars, like GM's EV1, were very costly, had a drive-range less than 100 miles, and were generally underpowered. A few wealthy celebrities drove them for publicity or to make an environmental "statement." But for most consumers, electric cars were too expensive and the need to plug them into an electric outlet was a real obstacle.

Now sales of hybrid vehicles (which combine power from gasoline and electric motors) are beginning to grow. Competition among producers is encouraging innovations based on this new technology. Costs are lower, mileage is higher, and power is better. For example, both Toyota and Honda enjoyed a dramatic jump in sales when they introduced their new Prius and Civic hybrids. This jump occurred in spite of a weak economy—when many consumers postpone big purchases. Initial sales might have been even higher if it were not for a problem that was revealed by Toyota's marketing research. Even after thousands of hybrids were on the road, about half of all consumers wrongly believed that you still have to plug in a hybrid (or said that they just didn't know). In light of this, Toyota worked with its ad agency to develop promotions to constantly remind consumers that "you never have to plug it in." Yet many consumers are still not very motivated to pay extra to buy a "green" vehicle. This may explain why Ford's promotion focuses on the increased power of its new hybrid SUVs and trucks rather than on an environmental appeal.[25]

Although there is still a big wage gap between men and women, the income working women generate gives them new independence and purchasing power. For example, women now purchase about half of all cars. Not long ago, many car dealers insulted a woman shopper by ignoring her or suggesting that she come back with her husband. Now car companies have realized that women are important customers. It's interesting that Japanese car dealers, especially Mazda and Toyota, were the first to really pay attention to women customers. In Japan, fewer women have jobs or buy cars—the Japanese society is still very much male-oriented. Perhaps it was the extreme contrast with Japanese society that prompted these firms to pay more attention to women buyers in the United States.[26]

Women's changing role has created opportunities for marketing but also complications. A marketing mix targeted at women, for example, may require a real balancing act. Advertising showing a woman at the office may attract some customers but alienate housewives who feel that their job doesn't command as much status as it should. Conversely, an ad that shows a woman doing housework might be criticized for encouraging stereotypes.

Changes come slowly   Most changes in basic cultural values and social attitudes come slowly. An individual firm can't hope to encourage big changes in the short run. Instead, it should identify current attitudes and work within these constraints—as it seeks new and better opportunities.[27]

A progressive firm constantly looks for new opportunities. Once the opportunities are identified, the firm must screen and evaluate them. Usually, a firm can't pursue all available opportunities, so it must try to match its opportunities to its resources and objectives. First, management must quickly screen out obvious mismatches so other opportunities can be analyzed more carefully. Let's look at some approaches for screening and evaluating opportunities.

Developing and applying screening criteria

After you analyze the firm's resources (for strengths and weaknesses), the environmental trends the firm faces, and the objectives of top management, you merge them all into a set of product-market screening criteria. These criteria should include both quantitative and qualitative components. The quantitative components summarize the firm's objectives: sales, profit, and return on investment (ROI) targets. (Note: ROI analysis is discussed briefly in Appendix B, which comes after Chapter 22.) The qualitative components summarize what kinds of businesses the firm wants to be in, what businesses it wants to exclude, what weaknesses it should avoid, and what resources (strengths) and trends it should build on.[28]

Developing screening criteria is difficult but worth the effort. They summarize in one place what the firm wants to accomplish—in quantitative terms—as well as roughly how and where it wants to accomplish it. When a manager can explain the specific criteria that are relevant to selecting (or screening out) an opportunity, others can understand the manager's logic. Thus, marketing decisions are not just made or accepted based on intuition and gut feel.

The criteria should be realistic—that is, they should be achievable. Opportunities that pass the screen should be able to be turned into strategies that the firm can implement with the resources it has.

Exhibit 4-5 illustrates some product-market screening criteria for a small retail and wholesale distributor. These criteria help the firm's managers eliminate unsuitable opportunities and find attractive ones to turn into strategies and plans.

Whole plans should be evaluated

You need to forecast the probable results of implementing a marketing strategy to apply the quantitative part of the screening criteria because only implemented plans generate sales, profits, and return on investment. For a rough screening, you only need to estimate the likely results of implementing each opportunity over a logical planning period. If a product's life is likely to be three years, for example, a good strategy may not produce profitable results for 6 to 12 months. But evaluated over the projected three-year life, the product may look like a winner. When evaluating the potential of possible opportunities (product-market strategies), it is important to evaluate similar things—that is, *whole* plans.

Opportunities that pass the screening criteria should be evaluated in more detail before being accepted as *the* product-market strategic plans for implementation. Usually, a firm has more opportunities than resources and has to choose among them—to match its opportunities to its resources and objectives. The following approaches help firms select among possible plans.

Total profit approach can help evaluate possible plans

In the total profit approach, management forecasts potential sales and costs during the life of the plan to estimate likely profitability.

Managers may evaluate the prospects for each plan over a five-year planning period, using monthly and/or annual sales and cost estimates. This is shown graphically in Exhibit 4-6.

Note that managers can evaluate different marketing plans at the same time. Exhibit 4-6 compares a much improved product and product concept (Product A)

Exhibit 4-5 An Example of Product-Market Screening Criteria for a Small Retail and Wholesale Distributor ($10 million annual sales)

1. **Quantitative criteria**
   a. Increase sales by $1,500,000 per year for the next five years.
   b. Earn ROI of at least 25 percent before taxes on new ventures.
   c. Break even within one year on new ventures.
   d. Opportunity must be large enough to justify interest (to help meet objectives) but small enough so company can handle with the resources available.
   e. Several opportunities should be pursued to reach the objectives—to spread the risks.

2. **Qualitative criteria**
   a. Nature of business preferred.
      (1) Should take advantage of our Internet order system and website promotion.
      (2) New goods and services for present customers to strengthen relationships and revenue.
      (3) "Quality" products that do not cannibalize sales of current products.
      (4) Competition should be weak and opportunity should be hard to copy for several years.
      (5) There should be strongly felt (even unsatisfied) needs—to reduce promotion costs and permit "high" prices.
   b. Constraints.
      (1) Nature of businesses to exclude.
         (a) Manufacturing.
         (b) Any requiring large fixed capital investments.
         (c) Any requiring many support people who must be "good" all the time and would require much supervision.
      (2) Geographic.
         (a) United States, Mexico, and Canada only.
      (3) General.
         (a) Make use of current strengths.
         (b) Attractiveness of market should be reinforced by more than one of the following basic trends: technological, demographic, social, economic, political.
         (c) Market should not be bucking any basic trends.

with a "me-too" product (Product B) for the same target market. In the short run, the me-too product will make a profit sooner and might look like the better choice—if managers consider only one year's results. The improved product, on the other hand, will take a good deal of pioneering—but over its five-year life will be much more profitable.

Return-on-investment (ROI) approach can help evaluate possible plans too

Besides evaluating the profit potential of possible plans, firms may also calculate the return on investment of resources needed to implement plans. ROI analyses can be useful for selecting among possible plans because equally profitable plans may require vastly different resources and offer different rates of return on investment. One plan may require a heavy investment in advertising and channel development, for example, while another relies primarily on lower price. Some firms are very concerned with ROI, especially those that borrow money for working capital. There is little point in borrowing to implement strategies that won't return enough to meet the cost of borrowing.

Exhibit 4-6
Expected Sales and Cost Curves of Two Strategies over Five-Year Planning Periods

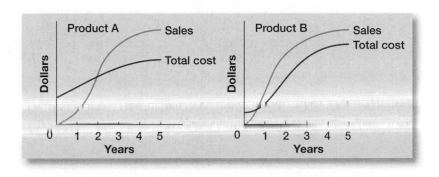

PLANNING GRIDS HELP EVALUATE A PORTFOLIO OF OPPORTUNITIES

When a firm has many possibilities to evaluate, it usually has to compare quite different ones. This problem is easier to handle with graphical approaches—such as the nine-box strategic planning grid developed by General Electric and used by many other companies. Such grids can help evaluate a firm's whole portfolio of strategic plans or businesses.

General Electric looks for green positions

General Electric's strategic planning grid—see Exhibit 4-7—forces company managers to make three-part judgments (high, medium, and low) about the business strengths and industry attractiveness of all proposed or existing product-market plans. As you can see from Exhibit 4-7, this approach helps a manager organize information about the company's marketing environments (discussed earlier in this chapter) along with information about its strategy and translate it into relevant screening criteria.

The industry attractiveness dimension helps managers answer the question: Does this product-market plan look like a good idea? To answer that question, managers have to judge such factors (screening criteria) as the size of the market and its growth rate, the nature of competition, the plan's potential environmental or social impact, and how laws might affect it. Note that an opportunity may be attractive for *some* company—but not well suited to the strengths (and weaknesses) of a particular firm. That is why the GE grid also considers the business strengths dimension.

The business strengths dimension focuses on the ability of the company to pursue a product-market plan effectively. To make judgments along this dimension, a manager evaluates whether the firm has people with the right talents and skills to implement the plan, whether the plan is consistent with the firm's image and profit objectives, and whether the firm could establish a profitable market share given its technical capability, costs, and size. Here again, these factors suggest screening criteria specific to this firm and market situation.

GE feels opportunities that fall into the green boxes in the upper left-hand corner of the grid are its best growth opportunities. Managers give these opportunities high marks on both industry attractiveness and business strengths. The red boxes in the lower right-hand corner of the grid, on the other hand, suggest a no-growth policy. Existing red businesses may continue to generate earnings, but they no longer deserve much investment. Yellow businesses are borderline cases—they can go either way. GE may continue to support an existing yellow business but will probably reject a proposal for a new one. It simply wouldn't look good enough on the relevant screening criteria.

Exhibit 4-7
General Electric's Strategic Planning Grid

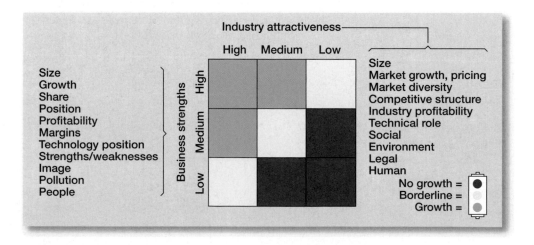

GE's "stoplight" evaluation method is a subjective, multiple-factor approach. It avoids the traps and possible errors of trying to use oversimplified, single-number criteria—like ROI or market share. Instead, top managers review detailed written summaries of many different screening criteria that help them make summary judgments. Then they can make a collective judgment. This approach helps everyone understand why the company supports some new opportunities and not others.[29]

General Electric considers factors that reflect its objectives. Another firm might modify the evaluation to emphasize other screening criteria—depending on its objectives and the type of product-market plans it is considering.

MULTIPRODUCT FIRMS HAVE A DIFFICULT STRATEGY PLANNING JOB

Multiproduct firms, like General Electric, obviously have a more difficult strategic planning job than firms with only a few products or product lines aimed at the same target markets. Multiproduct firms have to develop strategic plans for very different businesses. And they have to balance plans and resources so the whole company reaches its objectives. This means they must approve plans that make sense for the whole company—even if it means getting needed resources by milking some businesses and eliminating others.

Details on how to manage a complicated multiproduct firm are beyond our scope. But you should be aware that the principles in this text are applicable—they just have to be extended. For example, some multiproduct firms form strategic business units (SBUs), and some use portfolio management.

Strategic business units may help

A **strategic business unit (SBU)** is an organizational unit (within a larger company) that focuses on some product-markets and is treated as a separate profit center. By forming SBUs, a company formally acknowledges its very different activities. One SBU of Sara Lee, for example, produces baked goods for consumers and restaurants; another produces and markets Hanes brand T-shirts and underwear.

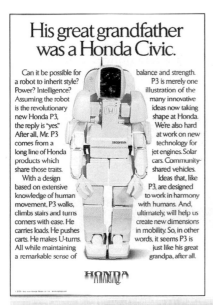

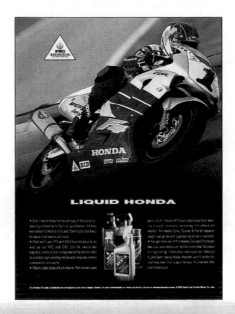

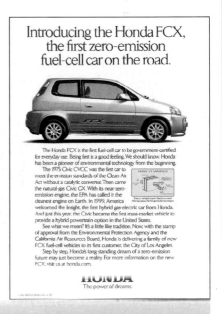

Large multiproduct firms, like Honda, evaluate and pursue a varied portfolio of strategic opportunities all around the world.

Some SBUs grow rapidly and require a great deal of attention and resources. Others produce only average profits and should be *milked*—that is, allowed to generate cash for the businesses with more potential. Product lines with poor market position, low profits, and poor growth prospects should be dropped or sold.

Some firms use portfolio management

Some top managements handle strategic planning for a multiproduct firm with an approach called **portfolio management**—which treats alternative products, divisions, or strategic business units as though they were stock investments, to be bought and sold using financial criteria. Such managers make trade-offs among very different opportunities. They treat the various alternatives as investments that should be supported, milked, or sold off—depending on profitability and return on investment. In effect, they evaluate each alternative just like a stock market trader evaluates a stock.[30]

This approach makes some sense if alternatives are really quite different. Top managers feel they can't become very familiar with the prospects for all of their alternatives. So they fall back on the easy-to-compare quantitative criteria. And because the short run is much clearer than the long run, they place heavy emphasis on *current* profitability and return on investment. This puts great pressure on the operating managers to deliver *in the short run*—perhaps even neglecting the long run.

Neglecting the long run is risky—and this is the main weakness of the portfolio approach. This weakness can be overcome by enhancing the portfolio management approach with market-oriented strategic plans. They make it possible for managers to more accurately evaluate the alternatives' short-run and long-run prospects.

EVALUATING OPPORTUNITIES IN INTERNATIONAL MARKETS

Evaluate the risks

The approaches we've discussed so far apply to international markets just as they do to domestic ones. But in international markets it is often harder to fully understand the marketing environment variables. This may make it harder to see the risks involved in particular opportunities. Some countries are politically unstable; their governments and constitutions come and go. An investment safe under one government might become a takeover target under another.

To reduce the risk of missing some basic variable that may help screen out a risky opportunity, marketing managers sometimes need a detailed analysis of the market

Some products, like industrial motors made by Baldor, are used the same way all over the world. Other products are much more sensitive to cultural differences.

Exhibit 4-8
Continuum of
Environmental Sensitivity

Insensitive		Sensitive
Industrial products	Basic commodity-type consumer products	Consumer products that are linked to cultural variables

environment they are considering entering. Such an analysis can reveal facts about an unfamiliar market that a manager in a distant country might otherwise overlook. Further, a local citizen who knows the marketing environment may be able to identify an "obvious" problem ignored even in a careful analysis. Thus, it is very useful for the analysis to include inputs from locals—perhaps cooperative middlemen.[31]

Risks vary with environmental sensitivity

The farther you go from familiar territory, the greater the risk of making big mistakes. But not all products, or marketing mixes, involve the same risk. Think of the risks as running along a "continuum of environmental sensitivity." See Exhibit 4-8.

Some products are relatively insensitive to the economic and cultural environment they're placed in. These products may be accepted as is—or they may require just a little adaptation to make them suitable for local use. Most industrial products are near the insensitive end of this continuum.

At the other end of the continuum, we find highly sensitive products that may be difficult or impossible to adapt to all international situations. Consumer products closely linked to other social or cultural variables are at this end. For example, some cultures view dieting as unhealthy; that explains why products like Diet Pepsi that are popular in the United States have done poorly there. "Faddy" type consumer products are also at this end of the continuum. It's sometimes difficult to understand why such products are well accepted in a home market. This, in turn, makes it even more difficult to predict how they might be received in a different environment.

This continuum helps explain why many of the early successes in international marketing were basic commodities such as gasoline, soap, transportation vehicles, mining equipment, and agricultural machinery. It also helps explain why some consumer products firms have been successful with basically the same promotion and products in different parts of the globe.

Yet some managers don't understand the reason for these successes. They think they can develop a global marketing mix for just about *any* product. They fail to see that firms producing and/or selling products near the sensitive end of the continuum should carefully analyze how their products will be seen and used in new environments—and plan their strategies accordingly.[32]

What if risks are still hard to judge?

If the risks of an international opportunity are hard to judge, it may be wise to look first for opportunities that involve exporting. This gives managers a chance to build experience, know-how, and confidence over time. Then the firm will be in a better position to judge the prospects and risks of taking further steps.

CONCLUSION

Businesses need innovative strategy planning to survive in our increasingly competitive markets. In this chapter, we discussed the variables that shape the environment of marketing strategy planning and how they may affect opportunities. First we looked at how the firm's own resources and objectives may help guide or limit the search for opportunities. Then we went on to look at the need to understand competition and how to do a competitive analysis. Then we shifted our focus to the external market environments. They are important because changes in these environments present new opportunities, as well as problems, that a marketing manager must deal with in marketing strategy planning.

The economic environment—including chances of recessions or inflation—also affects the choice of strategies. And the marketer must try to anticipate, understand, and deal with these changes—as well as changes in the technology underlying the economic environment.

The marketing manager must also be aware of legal restrictions and be sensitive to changing political climates. The acceptance of consumerism has already forced many changes.

The cultural and social environment affects how people behave and what marketing strategies will be successful.

Developing good marketing strategies within all these environments isn't easy. You can see that marketing management is a challenging job that requires integration of information from many disciplines.

Eventually, managers need procedures for screening and evaluating opportunities. We explained an approach for developing qualitative and quantitative screening criteria—from an analysis of the strengths and weaknesses of the company's resources, the environmental trends it faces, and top management's objectives. We also discussed ways for evaluating and managing quite different opportunities—using the GE strategic planning grid, SBUs, and portfolio management.

Now we can go on in the rest of the book to discuss how to turn opportunities into profitable marketing plans and programs.

KEY TERMS

mission statement, 92

competitive environment, 95

competitor analysis, 96

competitive rivals, 97

competitive barriers, 97

economic and technological environment, 99

technology, 101

Internet, 101

nationalism, 102

North American Free Trade Agreement (NAFTA), 104

consumerism, 104

cultural and social environment, 107

strategic business unit (SBU), 113

portfolio management, 114

QUESTIONS AND PROBLEMS

1. Do you think it makes sense for a firm to base its mission statement on the type of product it produces? For example, would it be good for a division that produces electric motors to have as its mission: "We want to make the best (from our customers' point of view) electric motors available anywhere in the world"?

2. Explain how a firm's objectives may affect its search for opportunities.

3. Specifically, how would various company objectives affect the development of a marketing mix for a new type of Internet browser software? If this company were just being formed by a former programmer with limited financial resources, list the objectives the programmer might have. Then discuss how they would affect the development of the programmer's marketing strategy.

4. Explain how a firm's resources may limit its search for opportunities. Cite a specific example for a specific resource.

5. Discuss how a company's financial strength may have a bearing on the kinds of products it produces. Will it have an impact on the other three Ps as well? If so, how? Use an example in your answer.

6. In your own words, explain how a marketing manager might use a competitor analysis to avoid situations that involve head-on competition.

7. The owner of a small hardware store—the only one in a medium-sized town in the mountains—has just learned that a large home improvement chain plans to open a new store nearby. How difficult will it be for the owner to plan for this new competitive threat? Explain your answer.

8. Discuss the probable impact on your hometown if a major breakthrough in air transportation allowed foreign producers to ship into any U.S. market for about the same transportation cost that domestic producers incur.

9. Will the elimination of trade barriers between countries in Europe eliminate the need to consider submarkets of European consumers? Why or why not?

10. Which way does the U.S. political and legal environment seem to be moving (with respect to business-related affairs)?

11. Why is it necessary to have so many laws regulating business? Why hasn't Congress just passed one set of laws to take care of business problems?

12. What and who is the U.S. government attempting to protect in its effort to preserve and regulate competition?

13. For each of the *major* laws discussed in the text, indicate whether in the long run the law will promote or restrict competition (see Exhibit 4-3). As a consumer without any financial interest in business, what is your reaction to each of these laws?

14. Are consumer protection laws really new? Discuss the evolution of consumer protection. Is more such legislation likely?

15. Explain the components of product-market screening criteria that can be used to evaluate opportunities.

16. Explain the differences between the total profit approach and the return-on-investment approach to evaluating alternative plans.

17. Explain General Electric's strategic planning grid approach to evaluating opportunities.

18. Distinguish between the operation of a strategic business unit and a firm that only pays lip service to adopting the marketing concept.

SUGGESTED CASES

2. Healthy Foods, Inc.

6. Valley Steel Company

COMPUTER-AIDED PROBLEM

4. Competitor Analysis

RESOURCE REMINDER

Mediquip, Inc., produces medical equipment and uses its own sales force to sell the equipment to hospitals. Recently, several hospitals have asked Mediquip to develop a laser-beam "scalpel" for eye surgery. Mediquip has the needed resources, and 200 hospitals will probably buy the equipment. But Mediquip managers have heard that Laser Technologies—another quality producer—is thinking of competing for the same business. Mediquip has other good opportunities it could pursue—so it wants to see if it would have a competitive advantage over Laser Tech.

Mediquip and Laser Tech are similar in many ways, but there are important differences. Laser Technologies already produces key parts that are needed for the new laser product—so its production costs would be lower. It would cost Mediquip more to design the product—and getting parts from outside suppliers would result in higher production costs.

On the other hand, Mediquip has marketing strengths. It already has a good reputation with hospitals—and its sales force calls on only hospitals. Mediquip thinks that each of its current sales reps could spend some time selling the new product and that it could adjust sales territories so only four more sales reps would be needed for good coverage in the market. In contrast, Laser Tech's sales reps call on only industrial customers, so it would have to add 14 reps to cover the hospitals.

Hospitals have budget pressures—so the supplier with the lowest price is likely to get a larger share of the business. But Mediquip knows that either supplier's price will be set high enough to cover the added costs of designing, producing, and selling the new product—and leave something for profit.

Mediquip gathers information about its own likely costs and can estimate Laser Tech's costs from industry studies and Laser Tech's annual report. Mediquip has set up a spreadsheet to evaluate the proposed new product.

a. The initial spreadsheet results are based on the assumption that Mediquip and Laser Tech will split the business 50/50. If Mediquip can win at least 50 percent of the market, does Mediquip have a competitive advantage over Laser Tech? Explain.

b. Because of economies of scale, both suppliers' average cost per machine will vary depending on the quantity sold. If Mediquip had only 45 percent of the market and Laser Tech 55 percent, how would their costs (average total cost per machine) compare? What if Mediquip had 55 percent of the market and Laser Tech only 45 percent? What conclusion do you draw from these analyses?

c. It is possible that Laser Tech may not enter the market. If Mediquip has 100 percent of the market, and quantity purchases from its suppliers will reduce the cost of producing one unit to $6,500, what price would cover all its costs and contribute $1,125 to profit for every machine sold? What does this suggest about the desirability of finding your own unsatisfied target markets? Explain.

For additional questions related to this problem, see Exercise 4-4 in the *Learning Aid for Use with Basic Marketing,* 15th edition.

1. Know about population and income trends in global markets—and how they affect marketers.

2. Understand how population growth is shifting in different areas and for different age groups.

3. Know about the distribution of income in the United States.

4. Know how consumer spending is related to family life cycle and other demographic dimensions.

5. Know why ethnic markets are important—and why increasingly they are the focus of multicultural marketing strategies.

6. Understand the important new terms (shown in red).

CHAPTER FIVE

Demographic Dimensions of Global Consumer Markets

When Charles Schwab started the financial services company that bears his name, investors who wanted to direct their own investments—without a lot of advice or pressure from a broker—didn't have many alternatives. Schwab's firm filled that need with no-frills service and a discount price. But of course the firm's innovative and targeted marketing strategies didn't stop there. In the 1980s, just as the large group of middle-age baby boomers were beginning to worry about investing for retirement, Schwab's firm was the first to give them a lot of choices in a big "supermarket" of mutual funds. Then in the 1990s, Schwab's marketing team pioneered low-cost website-based trading and Schwab quickly became the top online broker (www.schwab.com).

Marketing managers at Schwab have continued to find ways to satisfy many different types of customers,

but they don't just see all investors as one big market. Rather, they develop different marketing mixes to meet different needs. Consider, for example, the senior citizen group. Americans over 65 control about 70 percent of the country's investment assets, but Internet use among this group is low compared to younger people. To better meet the needs of this group—and others who prefer personal contact—Schwab supplemented its online services by adding more call-in advisors as well as opening new branch investment centers in high-growth areas. Schwab also added a new division that specializes in estate planning—another financial issue of special concern to older, more affluent clients.

Affluent investors, with the most wealth to manage, often have special needs when it comes to expert advice, objective research, and a personal relationship. To provide this group with the choices they want, the firm developed its targeted Schwab Private Client service. It provides these high-income clients with the attention they deserve while allowing them to stay involved and in control.

Similarly, Schwab has distinct strategies to reach fast-growing ethnic markets. It's no accident that branch offices in cities like San Francisco and New York have investment consultants who speak Mandarin and Cantonese. The firm has found that many Chinese Americans, even long-term residents of the U.S., like to converse with an advisor in their native language— and these customers are a key target market. While Chinese Americans are a small percentage of the total U.S. population, the median income of their households is much higher than the typical American household and they are more likely to have a college degree and own their own businesses. To attract Chinese American investors who prefer online trading, Schwab provides investors with a fully integrated website that offers trading, news, research, and account management, all in Chinese. (chinese.schwab.com).

Schwab has also developed strategies to sharpen its focus on the growing number of women who manage their own investments. Importantly, the needs and interests of these women are sometimes different. To better reach this group, Schwab offers investment seminars and events specifically for, and taught by, women. These seminars avoid jargon and include topics of special concern to women, such as how to handle finances after a divorce. Schwab also developed promotion targeted specifically at women. For example, one of the early advertising efforts was a clever TV commercial featuring Sarah Ferguson, the Duchess of York and a divorced mom, telling a little girl a bed-time tale about a young woman who is whisked away by a knight to a castle, married, and given her every wish "forever and ever." But then the ad ended with a shot of Ms. Ferguson saying, "Of course, if it doesn't work out you'll need to understand the difference between a P/E ratio and a dividend yield."

Schwab's strategies and success have not gone unnoticed by competitors. For example, E*Trade, which started on the Web, has opened financial centers with "relationship advisors" in major cities and E*Trade financial ATMs in many locations. And firms like Fidelity Investments are putting multilingual brokers in many offices. So, as competition and customer needs change, Schwab will need to continue seeking markets with new growth opportunities.[1]

TARGET MARKETERS FOCUS ON THE CUSTOMER

Target marketers believe that the *customer* should be the focus of all business and marketing activity. These marketers hope to develop unique marketing strategies by finding unsatisfied customers and offering them superior value with more attractive marketing mixes. They want to work in less-competitive markets with more inelastic demand curves. Finding these attractive opportunities takes real knowledge of potential customers and what they want. This means finding those market dimensions that make a difference—in terms of population, income, needs, attitudes, and buying behavior.

Marketers need to answer three important questions about any potential market:

1. What are its relevant segmenting dimensions?
2. How big is it?
3. Where is it?

The first question is basic. Management judgment—perhaps aided by analysis of existing data and new findings from marketing research—is needed to pick the right dimensions.

To help build your judgment regarding buying behavior, this chapter and the next two will discuss what we know about various kinds of customers and their buying behavior. Keep in mind that we aren't trying to make generalizations about average

Information about demographic characteristics of consumer markets is readily available and can help marketing managers plan more successful strategies.

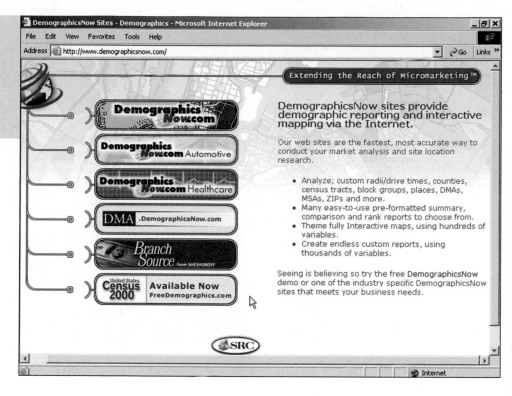

customers or how the mass market behaves—but rather how *some* people in *some* markets behave. You should expect to find differences.

In this chapter we focus on demographic dimensions. Demographic dimensions provide marketing managers with critical information about the size, location, and characteristics of target markets. Marketing managers must also be alert to demographic trends. They often provide an early warning about new opportunities—or the need to adjust existing strategies.

Get the facts straight—for good marketing decisions

Everybody "knows" that there is a vast and largely untapped market in China and that many people in Somalia live in desperate poverty. It's also clear that demographic dimensions vary within countries: Lots of retired people live in Florida, many Californians speak Spanish, and the population in the Sun Belt states is growing fast. Generalities like these may be partly true—but "partly true" isn't good enough when it comes to making marketing strategy decisions.

Fortunately, much useful information is available on the demographic dimensions of consumer markets around the world. Most of it is free because it has been collected by government agencies. With valid data available, managers have no excuse for basing their decisions on guesses. Look at the data in the next few chapters in terms of selecting relevant market dimensions—and estimating the potential in different market segments. Also, check your own assumptions against these data. Now is a good time to get your facts straight!

PEOPLE WITH MONEY MAKE MARKETS

Markets consist of people with money to spend. So it makes sense to start with a broad view of how population, income, and other key demographic dimensions vary for different countries around the world. This will help you to see why so many firms pursue opportunities in international markets. And our examples will illustrate why companies can't depend on half-truths in increasingly competitive international markets.

SONY

WALKMAN

Marketers search for growing markets

Some marketing managers never consider opportunities outside of their own country. That may make sense in some cases, but it may also lead to missed opportunities. For example, crowded cities in the United States may seem to offer great potential, but the U.S. population makes up less than 5 percent of the total world population, which is now over 6 billion.

Although a country's current population is important, it provides only a snapshot of the market. The population trend is also important.

Between 1950 and 2000, world population doubled. Early in that period, global population growth was over 2 percent per year. Now it's down to about 1.2 percent. Exhibit 5-1 shows where long-term world population growth will come from. Notice the expected growth of countries in the Middle and Far East. India (with a population of over 1 billion) and China (with a population of almost 1.3 billion) are getting even larger. You can see why so many firms from all over the world want to reach consumers in these countries now that trade barriers are relaxing. Although many of the countries in South America and Africa have much smaller populations, they too are growing at a rapid rate.[2]

Exhibit 5-1 shows that over the long term population growth is expected in most countries. But how rapidly? And will output and income increase faster than population? These are important questions for marketers. The answers affect how quickly a country moves to higher stages of development and becomes a new market for different kinds of products.

Population, income, and other demographic dimensions help to answer these questions. Exhibit 5-2 on pages 126–127 summarizes current data for representative countries from different regions around the world. Note that population growth varies dramatically from country to country. In general, less-developed countries experience the fastest rate of growth. The populations of Pakistan, Nicaragua, Nigeria, and Saudi Arabia are expected to nearly double by 2025. The population of the United States will grow by only about 22 percent in that time period. Population growth is even slower in Canada, Japan, and the European countries.[3]

Population is becoming more concentrated

The population in some countries is spread over a very large area. Population density is important to marketers. If the population is very spread out, as it is in many of the African countries, it is difficult and expensive for marketers to adjust

For firms interested in pursuing international markets, the growing concentration of population and income in major cities often simplifies Place and Promotion strategy decisions.

time and place discrepancies between producers and consumers. This is especially a problem in countries without efficient highway and rail systems. Similarly, a widely spread population may make promotion more difficult, especially if there are language differences or communication systems are poor. Of course, even in countries with low population density, major cities may be packed with people.

The extent to which a country's population is clustered around urban areas varies a lot. In the United Kingdom, Argentina, Australia, Israel, and Singapore, for example, more than 85 percent of people live in urban areas. (See Exhibit 5-2.) By contrast, in Ethiopia, Nepal, and Uganda less than 17 percent of the people live in major urban areas.

People everywhere are moving off the farm and into industrial and urban areas. Shifts in population—combined with already dense populations—have led to extreme crowding in some parts of the world. And the crowding is likely to get worse.

The worldwide trend toward urbanization has prompted increased interest in international markets. For many firms, the concentration of people in major cities simplifies Place and Promotion strategy decisions, especially for major cities in the wealthiest nations. Affluent, big-city consumers often have similar lifestyles and needs. Thus, many of the products successful in Toronto, New York, or Paris are likely to be successful in Caracas and Tokyo. The spread of the Internet, satellite TV, and other communication technologies will accelerate this trend.

However, keep in mind that many of the world's consumers—whether crowded in cities or widely spread in rural areas—live in deplorable conditions. These people have little hope of escaping the crush of poverty. They certainly have needs—but they don't have the income to do anything about the needs.

There's no market when there's no income

Profitable markets require income—as well as people. The amount of money people can spend affects the products they are likely to buy. When considering international markets, income is often one of the most important demographic dimensions.

There are a variety of different measures of national income. One widely used measure is **gross domestic product (GDP)**—the total market value of all goods and services provided in a country's economy in a year by both residents and nonresidents of that

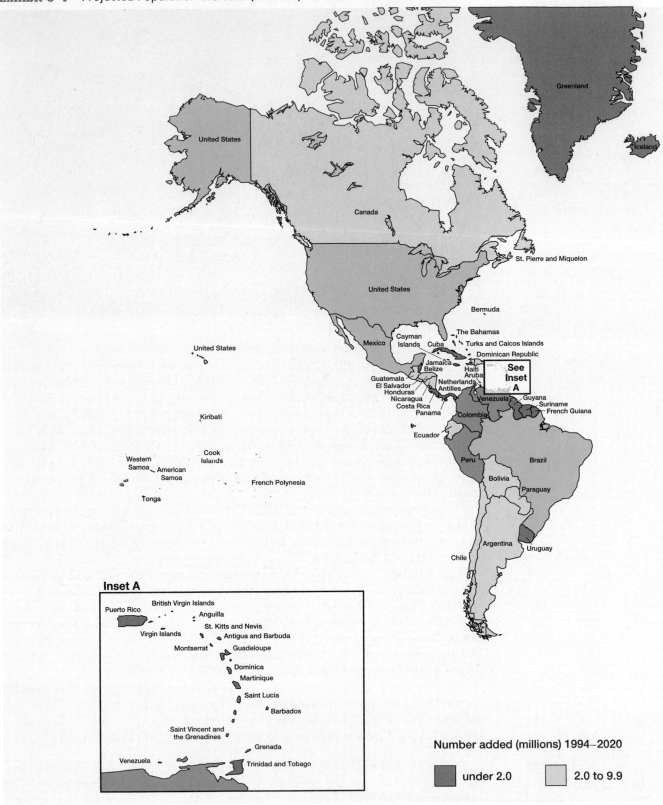

Inset A

Number added (millions) 1994—2020

under 2.0   2.0 to 9.9

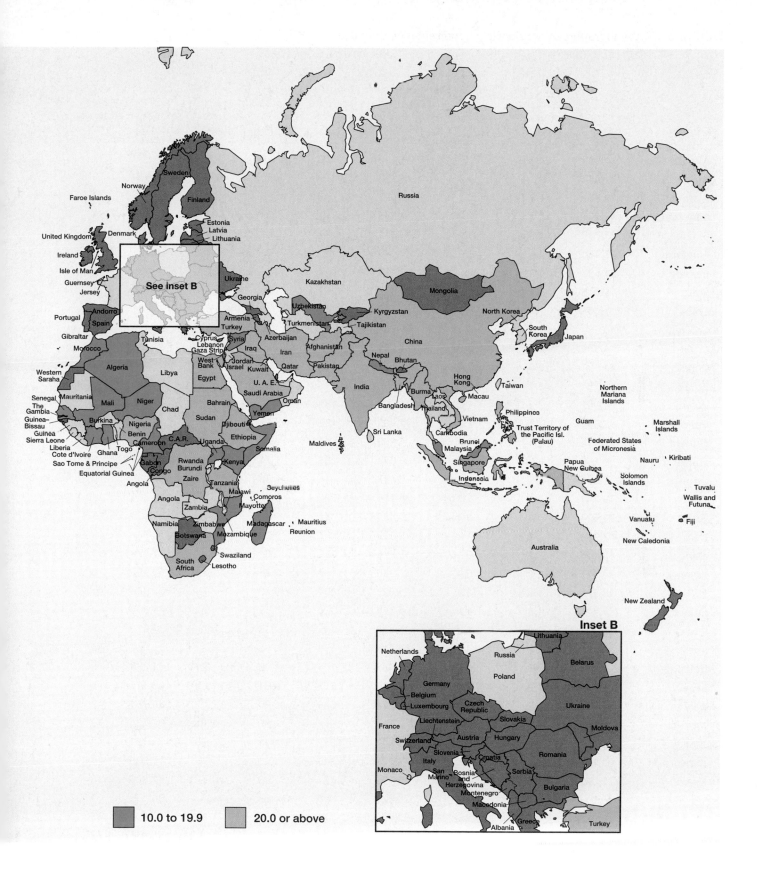

10.0 to 19.9	20.0 or above

Inset B

Netherlands
Germany
Belgium
Luxembourg
France
Liechtenstein
Switzerland
Monaco
Italy
San Marino
Lithuania
Russia
Poland
Czech Republic
Austria
Slovenia
Croatia
Slovakia
Hungary
Bosnia and Herzegovina
Serbia
Montenegro
Macedonia
Albania
Greece
Belarus
Ukraine
Moldova
Romania
Bulgaria
Turkey

Exhibit 5-2   Demographic Dimensions for Representative Countries

Country	2001 Population (000s)	1990–2000 Percent Population Growth	2000–2010 Percent Population Growth	2025 Projected Population (000s)	2001 Population Density (people/ square mile)	2001 Percent of Population in Urban Areas	2001 GNI per Capita	2001 GDP (millions of $U.S.)	2001 Illiteracy Percent
Algeria	31,736	2.1	1.6	44,270	35	49	1,650	54,680	32
Argentina	37,917	1.3	1.0	45,757	35	90	6,940	268,638	3
Australia	19,358	1.2	0.9	23,023	7	85	19,900	368,726	0
Bangladesh	132,975	1.7	2.0	204,539	2,539	23	360	46,706	59
Brazil	177,753	1.5	1.1	217,825	53	81	3,070	502,509	13
Cameroon	15,110	2.4	1.9	22,440	87	48	580	8,501	28
Canada	31,593	1.2	0.9	38,165	9	78	21,930	694,475	0
Chile	15,328	1.4	1.0	18,532	53	86	4,590	66,450	4
China	1,271,085	1.0	0.6	1,448,447	354	38	890	1,159,031	14
Colombia	40,349	1.9	1.5	55,065	101	71	1,890	82,411	8
Croatia	4,334	−0.5	0.5	4,569	199	54	4,550	20,260	2
Cuba	11,184	0.6	0.3	11,831	261	75	—	—	3
Ecuador	13,184	2.2	1.8	19,154	123	61	1,080	17,982	8
Egypt	71,902	2.2	1.8	103,353	181	43	1,530	98,476	44
Ethiopia	63,959	2.7	1.8	91,205	152	15	100	6,233	60
Finland	5,176	0.4	0.1	5,208	44	61	23,780	120,855	0
France	59,658	0.5	0.4	63,085	283	74	22,730	1,390,807	0
Germany	82,281	0.3	0.0	80,637	614	86	23,560	1,846,069	0
Ghana	19,843	2.4	1.3	25,365	224	37	290	5,301	27
Greece	10,624	0.4	0.1	10,490	210	59	11,430	117,169	3
Haiti	7,288	1.7	1.8	11,083	655	35	480	3,737	49
Hungary	10,106	−0.2	−0.3	9,276	283	64	4,830	51,926	1
Iceland	278	0.8	0.4	300	7	93	28,910	7,702	0
India	1,018,504	1.8	1.4	1,361,625	897	28	460	477,342	42
Indonesia	227,741	1.8	1.4	300,277	324	39	690	145,306	13
Iran	66,791	1.4	1.1	85,480	105	66	1,680	114,052	23
Iraq	23,332	2.2	2.7	40,418	139	68	—	—	60
Ireland	3,841	0.8	0.9	4,438	144	58	22,850	103,298	0
Israel	5,938	2.6	1.3	7,612	757	91	16,750	108,325	5
Italy	57,845	0.2	0.1	56,234	508	90	19,390	1,088,754	2
Jamaica	2,666	0.7	0.7	3,250	638	50	2,800	7,784	13
Japan	126,892	0.3	0.0	120,001	832	78	35,610	4,141,431	0
Kenya	30,777	2.4	1.0	35,271	140	20	350	11,396	17
Kuwait	2,042	−0.8	3.5	4,175	297	100	18,270	32,806	18
Libya	5,241	2.1	2.3	8,323	8	86	—	34,137	19
Madagascar	15,983	3.0	3.0	32,966	71	22	260	4,604	33
Malaysia	22,229	2.2	1.8	33,065	175	57	3,330	88,041	12

Country	2001 Population (000s)	1990–2000 Percent Population Growth	2000–2010 Percent Population Growth	2025 Projected Population (000s)	2001 Population Density (people/ square mile)	2001 Percent of Population in Urban Areas	2001 GNI per Capita	2001 GDP (millions of $U.S.)	2001 Illiteracy Percent
Mexico	101,879	1.7	1.4	133,835	137	74	5,530	617,820	9
Morocco	30,645	2.0	1.6	42,553	178	55	1,190	34,219	50
Mozambique	17,142	2.9	0.5	17,496	64	28	210	3,607	55
Nepal	25,284	2.5	2.2	39,918	479	11	250	5,562	57
Netherlands	15,981	0.6	0.4	17,250	1,220	62	24,330	380,137	0
Nicaragua	4,918	2.8	1.9	7,269	106	57	370	2,068	33
Nigeria	127,120	2.9	2.4	206,398	360	36	290	41,373	35
North Korea	21,940	0.8	0.9	25,755	473	59	—	—	—
Norway	4,503	0.5	0.4	4,951	38	74	35,630	166,145	0
Pakistan	144,617	2.2	1.9	213,338	481	33	420	58,668	56
Panama	2,879	1.7	1.3	3,676	97	62	3,260	10,171	8
Peru	27,484	2.1	1.5	37,487	56	72	1,980	54,047	10
Philippines	81,370	2.1	1.8	118,686	720	47	1,030	71,438	5
Poland	38,634	0.1	0.0	38,011	329	62	4,230	176,256	0
Romania	22,364	−0.2	−0.2	20,854	251	55	1,720	38,718	2
Russia	145,470	−0.1	−0.3	135,952	22	73	1,750	309,951	0
Saudi Arabia	22,757	3.3	3.3	48,517	27	83	8,460	186,489	23
Singapore	4,300	3.2	3.3	8,316	17,849	100	21,500	85,648	7
Somalia	7,489	0.8	3.1	14,862	31	28	—	—	—
South Africa	42,573	1.3	−0.4	34,045	92	54	2,820	113,274	14
South Korea	47,619	1.0	0.6	51,801	1,264	79	9,460	422,167	2
Spain	40,087	0.2	0.1	39,578	208	64	14,300	581,823	2
Sri Lanka	19,409	1.1	0.8	22,594	776	30	880	15,911	8
Sudan	36,080	2.8	2.6	61,339	39	27	340	12,525	41
Sweden	8,875	0.4	0.0	8,929	56	84	25,400	209,814	0
Switzerland	7,283	0.6	0.2	7,359	474	68	38,330	247,091	0
Syria	16,729	2.7	2.3	26,548	235	50	1,040	19,495	25
Tanzania	34,583	2.7	2.0	52,813	106	22	270	9,341	24
Thailand	63,007	1.2	0.9	73,260	313	31	1,940	114,681	4
Turkey	66,494	1.6	1.1	82,205	223	66	2,530	147,683	14
Uganda	24,170	3.1	3.0	48,040	311	16	260	5,675	32
Ukraine	48,760	−0.5	−0.6	43,293	209	67	720	37,588	0
United Kingdom	59,723	0.3	0.3	63,819	639	90	25,120	1,424,094	0
United States	284,797	1.2	0.9	349,666	79	75	34,280	10,065,265	0
Venezuela	23,917	2.0	1.4	32,061	70	87	4,760	124,948	7
Vietnam	79,544	1.6	1.3	104,436	636	24	410	32,723	7
Zimbabwe	12,332	1.8	0.6	12,773	76	32	480	9,057	11

China has the largest population in the world, and its culture and economy are undergoing rapid changes. For example, consumers in China buy more cell phones than in any other country. Their Internet use is also growing; it is predicted that by 2007, Chinese will be the number one language on the Web. Managers who ignore such changes may miss out on attractive opportunities.

country. *Gross national income (GNI)* is a measure that is similar to GDP, but GNI does not include income earned by foreigners who own resources in that nation. By contrast, GDP does include foreign income. (Note: Until recently, GNI was called gross national product or GNP, so many government documents still include that label.)

When you compare countries with different patterns of international investment, the income measure you use can make a difference. For example, Ford has a factory in Thailand. The GDP measure for Thailand would include the profits from that factory because they were earned in that country. However, Ford is not a Thai firm and most of its profit will ultimately flow out of Thailand. Thus, the Thai GNI would not include those profits. You should see that using GDP income measures can give the impression that people in less-developed countries have more income than they really do. In addition, in a country with a large population the income of the whole nation must be spread over more people. So GNI *per capita* (per person) is a useful figure because it gives some idea of the income level of people in the country.

Developed economies have most of the income

Exhibit 5-2 gives an estimate of GNI per capita and GDP for each country listed. You can see that the more developed industrial nations—including the United States, Japan, and Germany—account for the biggest share of the world's GDP. In these countries the GNI per capita is also quite high. This explains why so much trade takes place between these countries—and why many firms see them as the more important markets. In general, markets like these offer the best potential for products that are targeted at consumers with higher income levels. As a point of comparison, the GNI per capita in the United States is $34,280.[4]

Many managers, however, see great potential—and less competition—where GNI per capita is low. For example, Mars is making a big push to promote its candy in the countries of Eastern Europe. As with many other firms, it hopes to establish a relationship with consumers now, and then turn strong brand loyalty into profitable growth as consumer incomes increase.

A business and a human opportunity

The large number of countries with low GNI per capita is a stark reminder that much of the world's population lives in extreme poverty. You see some sign of this even among some countries with large overall GDP. For example, GNI per capita in China is only about $890 per year (in U.S. dollars) and in India it is about half that at $460.

Many countries are in the early stages of economic development. Most of their people work on farms and live barely within the money economy. At the extreme, in Ethiopia GNI per capita per year is only about $100. To put this in perspective, 60 percent of the world's population—in 61 countries—receives only about 6 percent of the world's total income, or about $2 a day.

These people, however, have needs, and many are eager to improve themselves. But they may not be able to raise their living standards without outside help. This presents a challenge and an opportunity to the developed nations—and to their business firms. Some companies are trying to help the people of less-developed countries. Corporations such as Pillsbury, Monsanto, and Coca-Cola have developed nutritious foods that can be sold cheaply, but still profitably, in poorer countries.[5]

What do Third World consumers really need?

Marketing managers from developed nations sometimes face an ethical dilemma about whether their products help or hurt consumers in less-developed nations. For example, a United Nations report criticized Coke and Pepsi for expanding their soft-drink sales in the Philippines. The study concluded that consumers had shifted to soft drinks from local beverages—such as a mixture of lime juice and coconut water—that provided needed vitamins.

In another much publicized case, producers of infant formula were criticized for giving free samples to hospitals. Nestlé and other big suppliers in this market say that they only gave the free samples to children who were in need—and at the request of hospitals. But critics argued that the practice encouraged new mothers to give up breast feeding. Away from the hospital, mothers would rely on unsanitary water supplies. Such improper use of the formula could lead to malnutrition and other illnesses. So Nestlé and the others pledged to stop giving away free samples. Although that step stopped some misuse, now the formula is not available to many people who really need it. For example, over a million babies have been infected with AIDS from breast feeding. To help fight this staggering epidemic, Nestlé said it was willing to donate formula, but not unless the World Health Organization agreed that it was not a violation of its pledge.

In cases like these, a marketing manager may need to weigh the benefits and risks of trying to serve Third World markets. For example, in the United States, Quicksilver Enterprises sells its 250-pound aluminum and fiberglass "ultralight" airplanes—which look like go-carts with wings—to wealthy hobbyists. However, Quicksilver found a growing market for ultralights in developing nations, where farmers use them for crop dusting. They help farmers increase production of much needed foods. So what's the problem? In the U.S. the government bans ultralights as not being safe enough for crop dusting. Some critics argue that a firm shouldn't sell its products in foreign markets if they are illegal in the U.S. But ultimately, the marketing manager often must decide what to do.[6]

Reading, writing, and marketing problems

The ability of a country's people to read and write has a direct influence on the development of its economy—and on marketing strategy planning. The degree of literacy affects the way information is delivered, which in marketing means promotion. Unfortunately, only about three-fourths of the world's population can read and write. Data on illiteracy rates is inexact because different countries use different measures. Even so, you may be surprised by the high illiteracy rates for some of the countries in Exhibit 5-2.

Illiteracy sometimes causes difficulties with product labels and instructions, for which we normally use words. This was one issue in the infant formula conflict. In an even more extreme case, some producers of baby food found that consumers misinterpreted a baby's picture on their packages. Illiterate natives believed that the product was just that—a ground up baby! Many companies meet this lack of literacy with instructions that use pictures instead of words. Singer used this approach with its sewing machines.

Even in Latin America—which has generally higher literacy rates than Africa or Asia—a large number of people cannot read and write. Marketers have to use symbols, colors, and other nonverbal means of communication if they want to reach the masses.[7]

Much segmenting may be required

Marketers can learn a great deal about possible opportunities in different countries by studying available demographic data and trends. The examples we considered here give you a feel, but much more useful data is available. For example, *The World Factbook* is prepared by the Central Intelligence Agency (CIA) for the use of U.S. government officials, but it is available to everyone. It gives facts and statistics on each country in the world. This book can be accessed at the CIA's website (www.odci.gov/cia/publications/factbook). The World Bank publishes *The World Development Indicators*, another excellent source for statistics on individual countries. It is available at the World Bank's website (www.worldbank.org/data/wdi). The International Programs Center of the U.S. Census Bureau also publishes an analysis on world population and related topics called *World Population Profile*. You can also access useful statistics for individual countries at the Census Bureau's website (www.census.gov/ipc).

INTERNET EXERCISE Visit the website for the CIA (www.odci.gov). Scroll down to "Library and Reference" and click on "The World Factbook." Compare the profile data for Canada and Australia. How are they similar and how are they different?

After finding some countries or regions of possible interest (and eliminating unattractive ones), much more segmenting may be required. To illustrate how useful demographic dimensions can be in this effort, we will consider specific characteristics of the U.S. market in some detail. For additional data on the U.S. market, you can go to the Census Bureau's website (www.census.gov). Similar ideas apply to other markets around the world.

POPULATION TRENDS IN THE U.S. CONSUMER MARKET

Where does your state stand?

Exhibit 5-3 is a map of the U.S. showing the relative population for each state. The "high areas" on this map emphasize the concentration of population in different geographic regions. Note that California is the most populated state, with Texas a distant second. New York, in third place, still has almost as large a population as Texas, but Texas's population is more spread out. More generally, the heavy concentration of people in the Northeast makes this market larger than the whole West Coast.

As is the case in many countries, the most populated U.S. areas developed near inexpensive water transportation—on ocean harbors (East and West Coasts), along major rivers (like the Mississippi), or in the Great Lakes region. Obviously, these markets are attractive to many marketers. But this can also mean tough competition, as in the big urban East and West Coast markets.

Marketers anxious to avoid the extremely competitive East and West Coast markets often view the midwestern and southern states as unique target markets. Note, too, the few people in the plains and mountain states, which explains why some national marketers pay less attention to these areas.

Exhibit 5-3 Map of U.S. Showing Population by State (all figures in thousands)

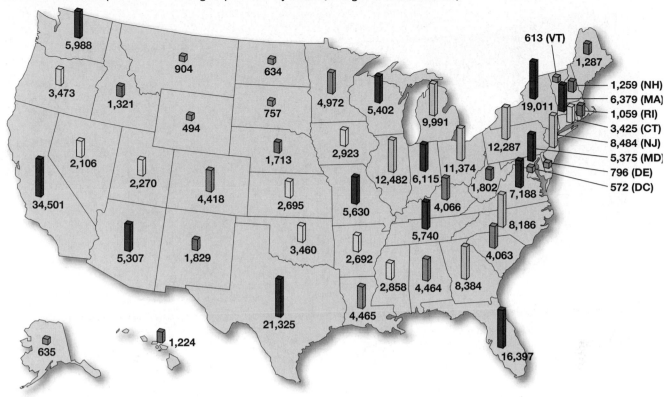

2001 Population: ■ 0–1,000 ■ 1,001–2,000 □ 2,001–4,000 ■ 4,001–5,000 ■ 5,001–8,000 □ 8,001–15,000 ■ Over 15,000
Note: The height of the block in each state shows its relative population level.

Where are the people today and tomorrow?

Population figures for a single year don't show the dynamic aspects of markets. Currently, U.S. population is over 288 million (up from about 285 million in 2001). By 2025, the U.S. population could rise to about 350 million. But it is important to remember that the population will grow at different rates in different places. Marketers always look for fast-growing markets. They want to know where growth has occurred recently—and where growth is likely to occur in the future.

Exhibit 5-4 shows the percentage growth in population in different regions of the country. The states with the blue and green shading are growing at the fastest rate. Note that the greatest growth is in the West—in states such as Nevada, Arizona, Colorado, Utah, and Idaho. Growth continues in the Sun Belt states of the South as well, with Georgia leading the way with 26 percent, and other Sun Belt states like Florida, Texas, and North Carolina growing rapidly.

Notice that some of the most populated areas in Exhibit 5-3 are not growing the fastest. The population of New York, for example, grew at 5.5 percent during the last decade. Other states like Connecticut and Pennsylvania grew less than 4 percent. In fact, the West is growing at almost four times the rate of the Northeast.

These different rates of growth are especially important to marketers. Sudden growth in one area may create a demand for many new shopping centers—while retailers in declining areas face tougher competition for a smaller number of customers. In growing areas, demand may increase so rapidly that profits may be good even in poorly planned facilities.

These maps summarize state-level data to give the big picture. However, much more detailed population data are available. You can obtain detailed census data or updated estimates—for very small geographic areas. Just as we mapped population

Exhibit 5-4   Percent Change in Population by State, 1990–2000

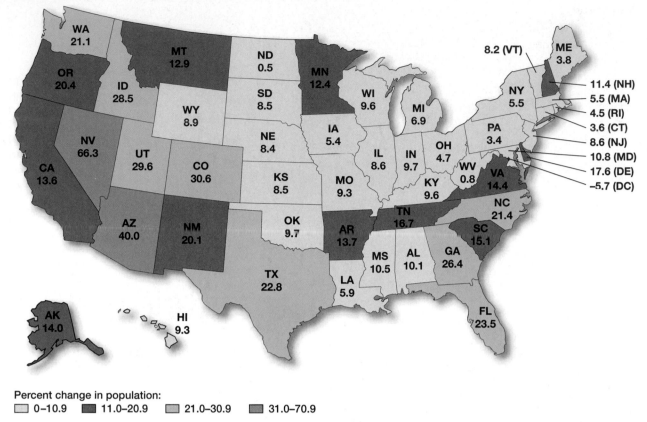

Percent change in population:
▢ 0–10.9   ■ 11.0–20.9   ■ 21.0–30.9   ■ 31.0–70.9

changes at the state level, a local marketer can divide a big metropolitan area into many smaller areas to see where the action is. As this decade continues, census data may become outdated—but by then local and state government planning groups may be able to provide updates.

Population will keep growing, but . . .

Despite the large increases, the *rate* of population growth in the U.S. has slowed dramatically—to about 1 percent a year during the last decade. In fact, many U.S. marketers who enjoyed rapid and profitable growth in the 1970s and 1980s know that the domestic picnic is over. They now turn to international markets where population—and sales revenues—continue to grow.

In the U.S., most of our future growth is expected to come from immigration. In fact, even now the total U.S. population would start to decline if immigration stopped. Let's look at some of these trends and what they mean to marketing managers.[8]

Birthrate—boom or bust?

The U.S. **birthrate**—the number of babies born per 1,000 people—fluctuated greatly in the last 50 years. Exhibit 5-5 shows a clear pattern. A post–World War II baby boom began as returning soldiers started families, and it lasted about 15 years into the early 1960s. In the 1970s, the situation changed to a "baby bust" as more women stayed in the workforce and couples waited longer to have children. When you see the dip in the birthrate—and think about the declining market for baby products—you can understand why Johnson & Johnson promotes its baby shampoo to adults who want a gentle product. You can also understand why Johnson & Johnson looks for opportunities in Asia and Latin America where the birthrate is higher.

The U.S. birthrate hit a low in 1976 and then rose again—but only slightly. From 1980 to 1990 the birthrate was between 15 and 17. It is starting to drop again now, and this trend should continue—with an estimated birthrate of about 14.1

Exhibit 5-5
Changes in the U.S.
Birthrate, 1935–2005

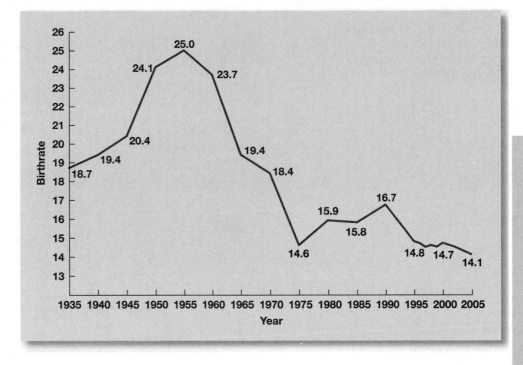

around the year 2005. These shifts are easy to explain. As the baby boom generation entered its child-bearing years, there were more women to have babies. However, as the boomers aged this baby "boomlet" passed and turned to what some have called a "baby bust." In addition, American couples are having fewer children. There may be more demand for small apartments, in-home entertainment, travel, and smaller food packages.

With fewer children, parents can spend more money on each child. For example, expensive bikes, video game consoles, MP3 players, and designer clothes for children have all sold well in recent years because parents can indulge one or two children more easily than a houseful.[9]

Highly targeted advertising media are proving especially effective at targeting messages to specific demographic groups. For example, TBS Superstation targets its Comedy Block to a particular group, and *Automobile Magazine* targets people who love cars.

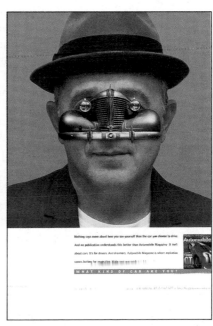

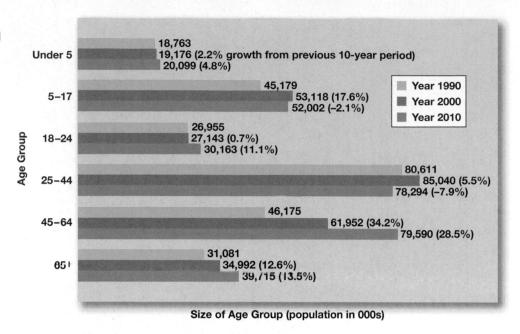

Size of Age Group (population in 000s)

The graying of America

Because our population is growing slowly, the average age is rising. In 1970, the average age of the population was 28—but by the year 2001 the average age jumped to about 36.

Stated another way, the percentage of the population in different age groups is changing. Exhibit 5-6 shows the number of people in different age groups in 1990 and 2000—and how the size of these groups will look in 2010. Note the big increases in the 45–64 age group from 1990 to 2000 and also 2000 to 2010.

The major reason for the changing age distribution is that the post–World War II baby boom produced about one-fourth of the present U.S. population. This large group crowded into the schools in the 1950s and 60s—and then into the job market in the 1970s. In the 1980s, they swelled the middle-aged group. And early in the 21st century, they will reach retirement—still a dominant group in the total population. According to one population expert, "It's like a goat passing through a boa constrictor."

Some of the effects of this big market are very apparent. For example, recording industry sales exploded—to the beat of rock and roll music and the Beatles—as the baby boom group moved into their record-buying teens. Soon after, colleges added facilities and faculty to handle the surge—then had to cope with excess capacity and loss of revenue when the student-age population dwindled. To relieve financial strain many colleges now add special courses and programs for adults to attract the now-aging baby boom students. On the other hand, the fitness industry and food producers who offer low-calorie foods are reaping the benefit of a middle-aged "bulge" in the population.

Medical advances help people live longer and are also adding to the proportion of the population in the senior citizen group. Note from Exhibit 5-6 that the over-65 age group will grow another 13.5 percent by 2010. Even more dramatic, with life expectancy increasing the over-65 group will double in size by 2030 and they will be 20 percent of the total U.S. population. This ongoing growth creates new opportunities for such industries as tourism, health care, and financial services.[10]

The teen cycle has started again

While society—and many marketers—has been fixated on the aging baby boomers, the ranks of teenagers have started to grow again. This is in part reflected in the 17.6 percent growth of the 5–17 age group between 1990 and 2000 and the 11.1 percent growth rate of the 18–24 age group in this decade (see Exhibit 5-6).

HOW TO GET A BOOST IN MOBILE PHONE SALES TO TEENS

When cell phones first came out 30 years ago they were pricey tools for high-income executives. They were sold at prices around $800 (with $1-a-minute service plans) by dealers who could explain their value and close the deal. Even at those prices, service was often limited to big metro business areas. Of course, that quickly changed as costs came down; before long, mass-merchandisers were giving away phones to customers who would sign a one-year service contract or a family plan. And companies like Sprint and AT&T even bypassed the retailer with credit card sales from their own websites. Yet until recently, wireless carriers have had trouble hooking up with Generation Y—the group of "tweens," teens, and twenty-somethings born between 1977 and 1995. Gen Y is famed for its skepticism, and they have proved a difficult target market to woo. The calling plans offered by the big firms left them cold, and most didn't yet have the income (or credit rating) required by firms like AT&T and Cingular.

Now, however, Boost Mobile has figured out how to crack the code and get sales penetration with this group. In its initial efforts in California and Nevada, for example, Boost is adding 40,000 customers a month—almost all of them under 30. No, the phone itself is not the big sell—they're pretty much like the others available. But Boost ignores traditional distribution channels and instead focuses on selling in surf shops, record stores, and other youth hangouts. Binding contracts and credit checks are gone, too. Instead, Boost relies on a pay-as-you-go plan, and rather than a monthly bill customers can buy a chunk of prepaid airtime from retailers like 7-Eleven or Target or online (www.boostmobile.com). Boost promotion isn't traditional either. It targets Gen Y with advertising in *Surfer* magazine and by sponsoring events like skateboarding competitions. Boost customers don't use their phones like their parents do. A third of their minutes are used with a $1-a-day unlimited-use walkie-talkie feature—to talk with nearby friends—and they send a lot of text messages. When Boost started this push only about one-third of all U.S. teens owned a mobile phone. Boost won't reel in all of the remaining 25 million or so teen prospects—competitors like Virgin Mobile are taking their share—but Boost's strategy promises to generate more growth.[11]

But the coming changes are even bigger than this suggests. For 15 years, there was a steady decline in the number of teenagers. Now that has reversed. Between 1995 and 2005, the teenage group will grow at close to twice the rate of the overall population. By the time the number of teens peaks in 2010, the size of this group will top the baby boom–fueled teen explosion of the 1970s. In 2010, there will be over 35 million U.S. teens—and along the way a new teen-oriented culture will reshape society and markets. However, marketers who simultaneously try to appeal to aging baby boomers and to teens may find themselves right in the middle of a real clash of cultures.[12]

Household composition is changing

Many people incorrectly think of the "typical" American household as a married couple with two children—living in the suburbs. This never was true and is even less true now. Less than 24 percent of households consist of a husband, wife, and children under 18. Another 28 percent of households involve married couples, but ones without children living at home. Moreover, kids don't always have a mom and dad at home. Today, one-third of the babies in the U.S. are born to a single parent.

Although about 85 percent of all Americans marry, they are marrying later, delaying child bearing, and having fewer children. And couples don't stay together as long as they used to. The U.S. has the highest divorce rate in the world—about 50 percent of marriages end in divorce. That helps to explain why more than 12 percent of U.S. households are now families headed by a single woman. Yet divorce does not seem to deter people from marrying again. Over 80 percent of divorced people remarry in what is described as "the triumph of hope over experience." Still, even with all this shifting around, at any given time only about 60 percent of all adults are married.

A firm that is effective in targeting one demographic segment may find that other demographic groups dislike its marketing mix. For example, the ad shown here, created by DiMassimo Brand Advertising, shows what the agency believes many 40+ women think about much of the advertising that they see.

"IF YOU WANT MY MONEY, STOP SHOWING ME PICTURES OF MY DAUGHTER IN UNDERWEAR."

And stop pretending you think she's me. That's not "aspirational," that's obnoxious. It's your decision.

Nonfamily households are increasing

Many households are not families in the traditional sense. There are now about 5.5 million unmarried couples who live together. That's a whopping 70 percent increase during the last decade. Some of these arrangements are temporary—as in college towns or in large cities where recent graduates go for their first "real" job. But the majority are older couples who choose not to get married. The number of these nontraditional households is still relatively small. But marketers pay special attention to them because they are growing at a much higher rate than the traditional family households. And they have different needs and attitudes than the stereotypical American family. To reach this market, some banks changed their policies about loans to unmarried couples for homes, cars, and other major purchases. And some insurance companies designed coverage for unmarried couples.

Single-adult households are also on the rise, and they account for over one-fourth of all households—almost 27 million people! These include young adults who leave home when they finish school, as well as separated, divorced, or widowed people who live alone. In some big cities, the percentage of single-person households is even higher—around 30 percent in New York and Washington, D.C. These people need smaller apartments, smaller cars, smaller food packages, and, in some cases, less-expensive household furnishings because many singles don't have much money. Other singles have ample discretionary income and are attractive markets for top-of-the-line clothing, expensive electronic gadgets, status cars, travel, nice restaurants, and trendy bars.[13]

The shift to urban and suburban areas

Migration from rural to urban areas has been continuous in the United States since 1800. In 1920, about half the population lived in rural areas. By 1950, the number living on farms dropped to 15 percent—and now it is less than 2 percent. We have become an urban and suburban society.[14]

Since World War II, there has been a continuous flight to the suburbs by middle-income consumers. By 1970, more people lived in the suburbs than in the central cities. Retailers moved too—following their customers. Lower-income consumers—

often with varied ethnic backgrounds—moved in, changing the nature of markets in the center of the city.

Industries too have been fleeing the cities, moving many jobs closer to the suburbs. Today's urban economic system is not as dependent on central cities. A growing population must go somewhere—and the suburbs can combine pleasant neighborhoods with easy transportation to higher-paying jobs nearby or in the city.

Purchase patterns are different in the suburbs. For example, a big city resident may not need or own a car. But with no mass transportation, living carless in the suburbs is difficult. And in some areas, it almost seems that an SUV or a minivan—to carpool kids and haul lawn supplies or pets—is a necessity.

Local political boundaries don't define market areas

These continuing shifts—to and from urban and suburban areas—mean that the usual practice of reporting population by city and county boundaries can result in misleading descriptions of markets. Marketers are more interested in the size of homogeneous *marketing* areas than in the number of people within political boundaries. To meet this need, the U.S. Census Bureau has developed a separate population classification based on metropolitan statistical areas. Much data is reported on the characteristics of people in these areas. The technical definition of these areas has changed over time. But basically a **Metropolitan Statistical Area (MSA)** is an integrated economic and social unit with a large population nucleus. Generally, an MSA centers on one city or urbanized area of 50,000 or more inhabitants and includes bordering urban areas.

The largest MSAs—basically those with a population of more than a million—are called Consolidated Metropolitan Statistical Areas. Almost 80 percent of all Americans live in MSAs, and over 41 percent live in the 19 largest CMSAs. More detailed data is available for areas within these sprawling, giant urban areas.

Big targets are attractive—but very competitive

Some national marketers sell only in these metro areas because of their large, concentrated populations. They know that having so many customers packed into a small area can simplify the marketing effort. They can use fewer middlemen and still offer products conveniently. One or two local advertising media—a city newspaper or TV station—can reach most residents. If a sales force is needed, it will incur less travel time and expense because people are closer together.

Metro areas are also attractive markets because they offer greater sales potential than their large population alone suggests. Consumers in these areas have more money to spend because wages tend to be higher. In addition, professionals—with higher salaries—are concentrated there. But remember that competition for consumer dollars is usually stiff in an MSA.[15]

The mobile ones are an attractive market

Of course, none of these population shifts is necessarily permanent. People move, stay awhile, and then move again. In fact, about 16 percent of Americans move each year. Although about 6 out of 10 moves are within the same county, both the local and long-distance mobiles are important market segments.

Often people who move in the same city trade up to a bigger or better house or neighborhood. They tend to be younger and better educated people on the way up in their careers. Their income is rising—and they have money to spend. Buying a new house may spark many other purchases too. The old sofa may look shabby in the new house. And the bigger yard may require a new lawn mower, or even a yard service.

Many long-distance moves are prompted by the search for a better lifestyle. Many affluent retirees, for example, move to find a more comfortable life. Young people also hop from place to place, attracted by better job opportunities. This applies to graduates moving to high-paying, new-economy jobs as well as recent immigrants whose only choice may be a low-wage service job.

Regardless of why someone moves, many market-oriented decisions have to be made fairly quickly after a move. People must find new sources of food, clothing, medical and dental care, and household products. Once they make these basic buying decisions, they may not change for a long time. Alert marketers try to locate these potential customers early—to inform them of offerings before they make their purchase decisions. Retail chains, "national" brands, and franchised services available in different areas have a competitive advantage with mobiles. The customer who moves to a new town may find a familiar CVS or Blockbuster sign down the street and never even try their local competitors.[16]

INCOME DIMENSIONS OF THE U.S. MARKET

So far, we have been concerned mainly with the *number* of different types of people—and *where* they live.

More people are in middle and upper income levels

Earlier in this chapter you saw how GNI figures can be helpful in analyzing markets. But GNI figures are more meaningful to marketing managers when converted to family or household income and its distribution. Family incomes in the U.S. generally increased with GNI. But even more important to marketers, the *distribution* of income changed drastically over time.

Fifty years ago, the U.S. income distribution looked something like a pyramid. Most families were bunched together at the low end of the income scale—just over a subsistence level—to form the base of the income pyramid. There were many fewer families in the middle range, and a relative handful formed an elite market at the top. This pattern still exists in many nations.

By the 1970s, real income (buying power) in the U.S. had risen so much that most families—even those near the bottom of the income distribution—could afford a comfortable standard of living. And the proportion of people with middle incomes was much larger. Such middle-income people enjoyed real choices in the marketplace.

This revolution broadened markets and drastically changed the U.S. marketing system. Products viewed as luxuries in most parts of the world sell to "mass" markets

Marketers are very aware that spending varies with income and other demographic dimensions.

Exhibit 5-7
Median Family Income over
Time (in 2001 dollars)

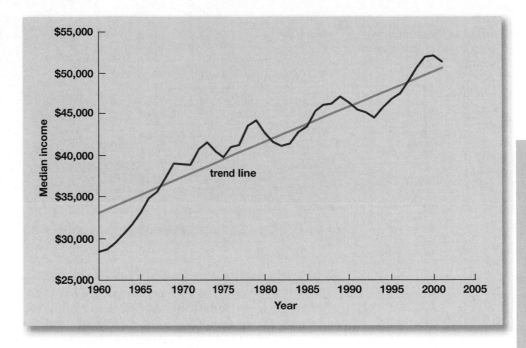

in the United States. And these large markets lead to economies of scale, which boost our standard of living even more. Similar situations exist in Canada, many Western European countries, Australia, New Zealand, and Japan.

Real income growth has slowed—but for how long?

Trends in median family income from 1960 to 2001 reflect this upward shift in the income distribution—and the increased number of families with more money to spend. See Exhibit 5-7. Note, though, that (real) median income stopped its continuous rise during the inflation-ridden 1970s. Since then it has gone through periods of both upswings and decreases, but the changes in recent years have not been as great as they were a few decades ago.

There is heated debate about what will happen to consumer incomes—and income distribution—in the future. Some business analysts feel that the lack of significant income growth signals worse things to come. They think that a decline in the manufacturing sector of the economy threatens America's middle-class standard of living. These analysts argue that in industries with traditionally high wages, firms are replacing workers with technology—to be able to compete with low-cost foreign producers. At the same time, new jobs are coming from growth of the lower-paying service industries. But other analysts are not so pessimistic. They agree that the percentage of the workforce earning middle-income wages has declined recently—but they think this is a temporary shift, not a long-term trend, and that over time the efficiencies that come from new information technologies will "lift" the whole economy.

What happens to income levels will be critical to you and to American consumers in general. It is easy for both consumers and marketing managers to be lulled by the promise of a constantly increasing standard of living. Both consumer thinking and marketing strategy will have to adjust if growth does not resume.

The higher-income groups receive a big share

Higher-income groups in the U.S. receive a very large share of total income, as you can see in Exhibit 5-8, which divides all families into five equal-sized groups—from lowest income to highest. Note that although the median income of U.S. families in 2001 was about $51,407, the top 20 percent of the families—those with incomes over $94,150—received almost 48 percent of the total income. This gave them extra buying power, especially for luxury items like memberships in country

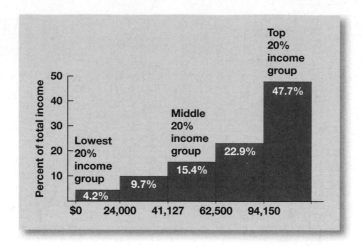

clubs and yachts. Well-to-do families with incomes over $164,104—the top 5 percent nationally—got 21 percent of the total income.

At the lower end of the scale, almost 15 million families had less than $24,000 income. They account for 20 percent of all families but receive only 4.2 percent of total income. Even this low-income group is an attractive market for some basic commodities, especially food and clothing—even though almost half of them live below the poverty level of $18,022 for a family of four. These consumers may receive food stamps, medicare, and public housing, which increases their buying power. Some marketers target this group, usually with a lower-price marketing mix.

How much income is "enough?"

We can't stress the importance of income distribution too much. Many companies make serious marketing strategy errors by overestimating the amount of income in various target markets. Marketers can easily make such errors because of the natural tendency for people to associate with others like themselves and to assume that almost everyone lives like they do. A marketing manager who earns $135,000 a year may have no clue what life is like for a family that lives on $25,000 a year.

The 2001 median family income of about $51,407 is a useful reference point because some college graduates start near this level. And a young working couple together can easily go way over this figure. This may seem like a lot of money at first—but it is surprising how soon needs and expenses rise and adjust to available income. America's middle-income consumers have been hit hard by the spiraling costs of health care, housing, energy, cars, taxes, and tuition bills. More than ever, these consumers look for purchases that offer good value for the money spent. Some high-living marketers may not understand that these consumers *need* to pinch their pennies, but that practical reality now explains much of the buying behavior of lower and middle-income markets in the U.S.[17]

Can low-income consumers protect themselves?

In considering statistics such as these, it is important for all of us to think about the enormous problems of poverty that low-income consumers face. There are 33 million people in the U.S. who live in poverty, and their lives are often hard. They often can't afford enough to eat, insurance or proper medical care, clothing for their children, or even a safe place to live. In market-directed economies, consumers are free to make choices in the marketplace. But with little income, education, or opportunity to become informed, many consumers in the lowest income groups have few real choices. Some marketing managers struggle over whether to serve these markets. A credit company, for example, may find customers willing to pay a high finance charge to borrow money. And the high rate may be needed to cover the risk of unpaid loans. But is it exploitation to charge a higher rate to those who can least afford it and who really have no other choice?[18]

SPENDING VARIES WITH INCOME AND OTHER DEMOGRAPHIC DIMENSIONS

We've been using the term *family income* because consumer budget studies show that many consumers spend their incomes as part of family or household units. They usually pool their incomes when planning major expenditures. So most of our discussion will concern how families or households spend their income.

Disposable income is what you get to spend

Families don't get to spend all of their income. **Disposable income** is what is left after taxes. Out of this disposable income—together with gifts, pensions, cash savings, or other assets—the family makes its expenditures. Some families don't spend all their disposable income—they save part of it. Therefore, when trying to estimate potential sales in target markets, we should distinguish among income, disposable income, and what consumers actually spend.

Discretionary income is elusive

Most families spend a good portion of their income on such "necessities" as food, rent or house payments, car and home furnishings payments, and insurance. A family's purchase of "luxuries" comes from **discretionary income**—what is left of disposable income after paying for necessities.

Discretionary income is an elusive concept because the definition of necessities varies from family to family and over time. It depends on what they think is necessary for their lifestyle. A cable TV service might be purchased out of discretionary income by a lower-income family but be considered a necessity by a higher-income family. But if many people in a lower-income neighborhood subscribe to cable TV, it might become a "necessity" for the others—and severely reduce the discretionary income available for other purchases.

The majority of U.S. families do not have enough discretionary income to afford the lifestyles they see on TV and in other mass media. On the other hand, some young adults and older people without family responsibilities have a lot of discretionary income. They may be especially attractive markets for electronic gear, digital cameras, new cars, foreign travel, designer fashions, and various kinds of recreation—tennis, skiing, boating, concerts, and fine restaurants.[19]

Exhibit 5-9 Stages in Modern Family Life Cycles

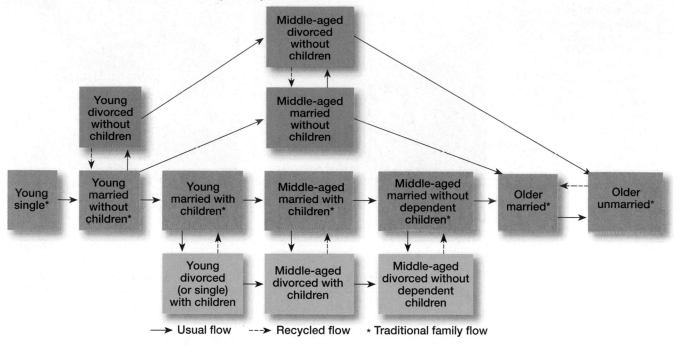

→ Usual flow   ---▶ Recycled flow   * Traditional family flow

Spending varies over the family life cycle

Income has a direct bearing on spending patterns, but many other demographic dimensions are also useful in understanding consumer buying. Marital status, age, and the age of any children in the family have an especially important effect on how people spend their income. Put together, these dimensions tell us about the life-cycle stage of a family. Exhibit 5-9 shows a summary of stages in the family life cycle. In our discussion, we will focus on the traditional flow from one stage to the next—as shown in the middle of the diagram. However, as shown at the top and bottom of the exhibit, divorce does interrupt the flow for many people; after a divorce, they may recycle through earlier stages.[20]

Young people and families accept new ideas

Singles and young couples seem to be more willing to try new products and brands—and they are careful, price-conscious shoppers. Younger people often earn less than older consumers, but they spend a greater proportion of their income on discretionary items because they don't have the major expenses of home ownership, education, and family rearing. Although many young people are waiting longer to marry, most do tie the knot eventually. These younger families—especially those with no children—are still accumulating durable goods, such as automobiles and home furnishings. They spend less on food. Only as children arrive and grow does family spending shift to soft goods and services, such as education, medical, and personal care. This usually happens when the family head reaches the 35–49 age group. To meet expenses, people in this age group often make more purchases on credit, and they save less of their income.

Divorce—increasingly a fact of American life—disrupts the family life-cycle pattern. Divorced parents don't spend like other singles. The mother usually has custody of the children, and the father may pay child support. The mother and children typically have much less income than two-parent families. Such families spend a larger percent of their income on housing, child care, and other necessities—with little left for discretionary purchases. If a single parent remarries, the family life cycle may start over again.[21]

Reallocation for teenagers

Once children become teenagers, further shifts in spending occur. Teenagers eat more, want to wear expensive clothes, and develop recreation and education needs that are hard on the family budget. The parents—or increasingly, the single parent—

may be forced to reallocate expenditures to cover these expenses—spending less on durable goods, such as appliances, automobiles, household goods, and housing. The fast-rising expense of sending a son or daughter to college can create a major financial crisis.

For many firms, teens are an important and attractive market. The amount of money involved may surprise you. America's teens currently spend over $170 billion a year and spending is growing at double-digit rates. Further, in today's families with a single parent or with two wage earners, teens play an increasingly important role in shopping and shaping family purchases. With teens spending more money, they are a target for many firms. For example, Siemens added an MP3 player to its wireless phone to help it win teen preference away from Nokia. Similarly, MasterCard is targeting teens with its credit card promotions and Bausch & Lomb's contact-lens sales hit record levels when the firm refocused its marketing efforts on teens.[22]

Selling to the empty nesters

Another important category is the **empty nesters**—people whose children are grown and who are now able to spend their money in other ways. Usually these people are in the 50–64 age group. But this is an elusive group because some people marry later and are still raising a family at this age. And in recent years lots of empty nesters have been surprised when adult singles move back in to avoid the big costs of housing.

Empty nesters are an attractive market for many items. Often they have paid for their homes, and the big expenses of raising a family are behind them. They are more interested in travel, sports cars, and other things they couldn't afford before. Much depends on their income, of course. But this is a high-income period for many workers, especially white-collar workers.[23]

Senior citizens are a big market

Finally, marketers should not neglect the **senior citizens**—people over 65. The number of people over 65 is increasing rapidly because of modern medicine, improved sanitary conditions, and better nutrition. This group now makes up over 12 percent of the population.

Our senior citizens are more prosperous than ever before. Their income is lower than in their peak earning years, but most do have money to spend. They don't just squeak by on Social Security. Such prosperity is a dramatic change. In 1960, about a third of all senior citizens had incomes below the poverty level. Now, only about 10 percent are considered "poor"—lower than the 11.7 percent figure for all adults.

Older people also have very different needs. Many firms already cater to senior citizens—and more will be serving this market. For example, some companies have developed housing and "life care" centers designed to appeal to older people. Casio makes a calculator with large, easy-to-read numbers. Publix Super Markets, a big Florida chain, trains employees to cater to older customers. Checkout clerks, for example, give older customers two light bags instead of one heavier one. Some travel agents find that senior citizens are an eager market for expensive tours and cruises. Other companies offer diet supplements and drug products, often in special easy-to-open packages. And senior citizen discounts at drugstores are more than just a courtesy—the elderly make up the biggest market for medicines.

Keep in mind, however, that older people are not all the same. With a group this large, generalities and stereotypes can be dangerous. Different senior citizen target markets have different needs and require different marketing strategies.[24]

ETHNIC DIMENSIONS OF THE U.S. MARKET

Do ethnic groups buy differently?

America may be called the melting pot, but ethnic groups deserve special attention when analyzing markets. One basic reason is that people from different ethnic groups may be influenced by very different cultural variables. They may have quite

Many firms are developing new strategies to appeal to fast-growing ethnic markets in the U.S. For example, the "Got Milk?" campaign targets Hispanic consumers with this Spanish language ad that features celebrity Lili Estefan.

different needs and their own ways of thinking. Moreover, Americans are beginning to recognize the value of multicultural diversity. The U.S. is becoming a multicultural market. As a result, rather than disappearing in a melting pot, some important cultural and ethnic dimensions are being preserved and highlighted. This creates both opportunities and challenges for marketers.

Some important ethnic differences are obvious. For example, more than 1 out of 5 families in the U.S. speaks a language other than English at home. Some areas have a much higher rate. In Miami and San Antonio, for example, about one out of three families speaks Spanish. This obviously affects promotion planning. Similarly, brand preferences vary for some ethnic groups. For example, cosmetic companies offer products tailored to different skin tones. But ethnic groups don't just differ in the color of their skin. Differences in attitudes, experiences, and values, as well as where they shop and what advertising appeals they attend to, come together to shape differences in buying behavior.

INTERNET EXERCISE

Visit the website for Ethnic Grocer (www.ethnicgrocer.com), select "Shop by Country," and then "Mexico." Next, select "Beverages, Coffees, & Tea," and then "Carbonated Beverages." Are any of the carbonated beverages listed for Mexico likely to become popular in the U.S.? Why or why not?

Stereotypes are common—and misleading

A marketer needs to study ethnic dimensions very carefully because they can be subtle and fast-changing. This is also an area where stereotyped thinking is the most common—and misleading. Many firms make the mistake of treating all consumers in a particular ethnic group as homogeneous. For example, some marketing managers treat all 36 million African American consumers as "the black market," ignoring the great variability among African American households on other segmenting dimensions. Income variability is a good example. While the median income of black families is still lower than for the whole population, that is changing. Today, 51 percent of black couples have an income of at least $50,000—and 23 percent have an income of $75,000 or more. These affluent consumers are also a relatively youthful market and a larger percentage (compared with white consumers) are in earlier stages of the life cycle and therefore a better market for certain products—especially durable goods like cars, furniture, home appliances, and electronic equipment.

Ethnic markets are becoming more important

More marketers pay attention to ethnic groups now because the number of ethnic consumers is growing at a much faster rate than the overall society. Much of this growth results from immigration. In addition, however, the median age of Asian Americans, African Americans, and Hispanics is much lower than that of whites—and the birthrate is higher.

In combination, these factors have a dramatic effect. The Hispanic population in the U.S., now almost 39 million and about 13.5 percent of the total population, surged by more than 60 percent since 1990. To put this in perspective, the Hispanic population in the U.S. is nearly as large as the population of Spain and 20 percent larger than the population of Canada. There are now more Hispanics in the U.S. than African Americans, previously the largest minority group. Hispanics are on average 10 years younger than the overall population, which helps to explain why one out of every five babies born in the U.S. is Hispanic. So it's not surprising that Nickelodeon's bilingual *Dora the Explorer* is the number two preschool show on commercial TV. You can see why strong Hispanic influences among the youth culture will be even greater in the years ahead. Already the surge of growth in the Hispanic population has changed the fabric of life in the U.S., influencing everything from food on grocery shelves to popular music.

While there are fewer Asian Americans (about 12.7 million, or 4.4 percent of the total population), the number has tripled since 1980—the fastest growth rate for any ethnic segment of the population. It is because of growth like this that companies as varied as Southwest Airlines and Sears are targeting these consumers, especially in local markets where the Asian American population is concentrated.

The buying power of ethnic submarkets is also increasing rapidly. Estimates suggest that African American consumers now spend about $646 billion a year, Hispanics more than $581 billion a year, and Asian Americans more than $296 billion a year. It's also important to marketers that much of this buying power is concentrated in certain cities and states, which makes targeted promotion and distribution more efficient. For example, over 20 percent of San Francisco's residents are Asians.

Strategy changes may be needed

These ethnic shifts are changing the face of the American market. Already more than 36 percent of American children are African American, Hispanic, or Asian. Longer term, whites are expected to become a minority by 2050. Many companies will need separate strategies for these ethnically or racially defined markets. Some may only require changes in Place and Promotion. But many companies have had difficulty developing strategies and segmenting ethnic submarkets. For example, Asian Americans emigrated from China, Japan, the Philippines, India, Korea, Vietnam, Laos, and Cambodia. Many come from very different backgrounds with no common language, religion, or culture. That adds to the marketing challenge; it means marketers must really understand the basic needs that motivate specific target markets to think and act as they do. This is important with any consumer market, regardless of people's ethnic or racial background or where in the world they live. We'll deal with that important issue in more detail in the next chapter.[25]

CONCLUSION

In this chapter, we studied population, income, and other demographic dimensions of consumer markets. Getting the facts straight on how over 6 billion people are spread over the world is important to marketing managers. We learned that the potential of a given market cannot be determined by population figures alone. Geographic location, income, stage in life cycle, ethnic background, and other factors are important too. We talked about some of the ways these dimensions—and changes in them—affect marketing strategy planning.

We also noted the growth of urban areas in countries around the world. The high concentration of population and spending power in large metropolitan areas of the U.S. has already made them attractive target markets. However, competition in these markets is often tough.

One of the outstanding characteristics of U.S. consumers is their mobility. Managers must pay attention to changes in markets. High mobility makes even relatively new data suspect. Data can only aid a manager's judgment—not replace it.

U.S. consumers are among the most affluent in the world. They have more discretionary income and can afford a wide variety of products that people in other parts of the world view as luxuries. However, in the U.S., as in most other societies, income is distributed unevenly among different groups. Consumers at the top income levels have a disproportionately large share of the total buying power.

The kind of data discussed in this chapter can be very useful for estimating the market potential within possible target markets. But, unfortunately, it is not very helpful in explaining specific customer behavior—why people buy *specific* products and *specific* brands. Yet such detailed forecasts are important to marketing managers. Better forecasts can come from a better understanding of consumer behavior—the subject of the next chapter.

KEY TERMS

gross domestic product (GDP), 123

birthrate, 132

Metropolitan Statistical Area (MSA), 137

disposable income, 141

discretionary income, 141

empty nesters, 143

senior citizens, 143

QUESTIONS AND PROBLEMS

1. Drawing on data in Exhibit 5-2, do you think that Romania would be an attractive market for a firm that produces home appliances? What about Finland? Discuss your reasons.

2. Discuss the value of gross domestic product and gross national income per capita as measures of market potential in international consumer markets. Refer to specific data in your answer.

3. Discuss how the worldwide trend toward urbanization is affecting opportunities for international marketing.

4. Discuss how slower population growth will affect businesses in your local community.

5. Discuss the impact of the new teen cycle on marketing strategy planning in the U.S.

6. Name three specific examples of firms that developed a marketing mix to appeal to senior citizens. Name three examples of firms that developed a marketing mix to appeal to teenagers.

7. Some demographic characteristics are more important than others in determining market potential. For each of the following characteristics, identify two products for which this characteristic is *most* impor-

tant: *(a)* size of geographic area, *(b)* population, *(c)* income, *(d)* stage of life cycle.

8. Name three specific examples (specific products or brands—not just product categories) and explain how demand in the U.S. will differ by geographic location *and* urban–rural location.

9. Explain how the continuing mobility of U.S. consumers—as well as the development of big metropolitan areas—should affect marketing strategy planning in the future. Be sure to consider the impact on the four Ps.

10. Explain why the concept of the Metropolitan Statistical Area was developed. Is it the most useful breakdown for retailers?

11. Explain why mobile consumers can be an attractive market.

12. Explain how the redistribution of income in the U.S. has affected marketing planning thus far and its likely impact in the future.

13. Why are marketing managers paying more attention to ethnic dimensions of consumer markets in the U.S.?

14. Name three categories of products marketed in the U.S. that are influenced by Hispanic culture.

SUGGESTED CASES

8. Marie's Ristorante
10. Murphy's Ice Land

30. Deluxe Foods, Ltd.

COMPUTER-AIDED PROBLEM

5. Demographic Analysis

RESOURCE REMINDER

Stylco, Inc., is a producer of specialty clothing. To differentiate its designs and appeal to its African American target market, Stylco uses authentic African prints. Originally, it just focused on designs targeted at adults in the 35–44 age range. However, in the late 1990s, when sales to these middle-aged adults started to level off, Stylco added a more conservative line of clothes for older consumers. Most buyers of the conservative styles are in the 45–59 age group.

Stylco has focused on distributing its products through select fashion boutiques in metropolitan market areas with the highest concentrations of African American consumers. This approach has reduced Stylco's personal selling expense; as a result, however, only a percentage of the total black population is served by current Stylco retailers. For example, about half of the consumers in the 35–44 age group are in the market areas served by Stylco retailers.

In the fall of 2004, Naomi Davis, Stylco's marketing manager, read an article about the "graying of America." This left her wondering how shifts in the age distribution might affect her market and sales.

To get a long-run view of these trends, she looked at census data on black consumers by age group. She also looked up estimates of the expected percent rate of change in the size of each group through the year 2005. By multiplying these rates by the size her target markets were in 2000, she can estimate how large they are likely to be in the year 2005. Further, from analysis of past sales data, she knows that the number of units the firm sells is directly proportional to the size of each age group. Specifically, the ratio of units sold to target market size has been about 5 units per 1,000 people (that is, a ratio of .005). Finally, she determined the firm's average unit profit for each of the lines. To see how changes in population are likely to affect Stylco units sold and future profits from each line, Davis programmed all of these data, and the relationships discussed above, into a spreadsheet.

a. Briefly compare the profit data for 2000 and estimated profit for 2005 as it appears on the initial spreadsheet. What is the basic reason for the expected shift? What are the implications of these and other data in the spreadsheet for Stylco's marketing strategy planning?

b. The rate of growth or decline for different age groups tends to vary from one geographic region to another. Davis thinks that in the market areas that Stylco serves the size of the 35–44 age group may decrease by as much as 10 to 12 percent by 2005. However, the Census Bureau estimates that the decline of the black 35–44 age group for the whole country will only be about −1.7 percent. If the decline in the target market size for Davis' market areas turns out to be −1.7 percent rather than the −10.1 she has assumed, what is the potential effect on profits from the young adult line? On overall profits?

c. Because more firms are paying attention to fast-growing ethnic markets, Davis thinks competition may increase in lines targeted at affluent African Americans in the 45–59 age group. Because of price competition, the line targeted at this group already earns a lower average profit per unit. Further, as more firms compete for this business, she thinks that her "ratio of units sold to market size" may decrease. Use the what-if analysis to prepare a table showing how percent of profit from this group, as well as total profit, might change as the ratio of units sold to market size varies between a minimum of .001 and a maximum of .010. Explain the implications to the firm.

For additional questions related to this problem, see Exercise 5-4 in the *Learning Aid for Use with Basic Marketing,* 15th edition.

1. Understand the economic-buyer model of buyer behavior.

2. Understand how psychological variables affect an individual's buying behavior.

3. Understand how social influences affect an individual's and household's buying behavior.

4. See why the purchase situation has an effect on consumer behavior.

5. Know how consumers use problem-solving processes.

6. Have some feel for how a consumer handles all the behavioral variables and incoming stimuli.

7. Understand the important new terms (shown in red).

CHAPTER SIX

Behavioral Dimensions of the Consumer Market

In the 1970s, yogurt was a popular food in Europe but for the most part unknown in the U.S. culture. Most American consumers were not aware of it, had never tried it, and didn't know if they would like it. All of that changed when Dannon and other firms began to promote and distribute yogurt in the United States. Sales grew slowly at first, but that changed in the 1980s as more adults became interested in healthy eating. For lots of on-the-go workers, yogurt was an economical lunch that tasted good and saved time. It didn't require preparation or cleanup, and it could be eaten almost anywhere. All you needed was a plastic spoon.

By the 1990s, many brands and flavors of yogurt were on the market. Most consumers couldn't tell the difference between brands. When it was time to buy, they just picked up their routine brand or perhaps whatever was on sale. Most marketers felt that growth in the yogurt category was pretty much tapped out. But by carefully studying consumer behavior, Ian Friendly and others on his marketing team at Yoplait changed all of that. Their marketing plan for a new product, Go-Gurt, racked up $100 million in sales in the first year. Much of that represented new demand in the yogurt category because the percentage of kids eating yogurt doubled. That was no accident. They created Go-Gurt to have kid appeal.

Kids need nutritious food, but research showed that what they want in snacks is great taste, convenience, and fun. Traditional yogurt was convenient, but it still took one hand for the spoon and one to hold the carton. And a carton of yogurt didn't exactly impress the other kids as a cool thing to eat. Go-Gurt took care of that. It did away with the spoon by put-

ting the yogurt in a 9-inch-long, one-handed squeeze tube. The creaminess of the product was adjusted to make it just right for on-the-go eating. Kids didn't have a very positive attitude about most standard yogurt flavors, so the foil-embossed Go-Gurt tube was filled with flavors kids could learn to love—like Strawberry Splash and Watermelon Meltdown.

Go-Gurt's introductory ads were placed on media like Nickelodeon so they'd reach kids directly. Then it was up to them to ask their parents to buy Go-Gurt at the store. The ads positioned Go-Gurt not just as a food but as a lifestyle accessory for kids. To build awareness of the benefits of the package and interest in the product, the ads conveyed the idea that it was OK to play with your food. For example, in one spot, a young skateboarder holding a Go-Gurt blasts past another kid who looks bored eating from a carton of yogurt as the announcer asks, "Why eat yogurt like this when you can eat with your hands, not a spoon? Go-Gurt comes in a totally cool squeeze tube you can squeeze and slurp, grab and glurp." The Go-Gurt slurping skateboarder tells the other boy, "Hey, lose the spoon."

To follow up on the awareness and interest generated by the ads, a heavy sampling program played a crucial role in building product trial. No, the samples were not distributed at the grocery store. Kids on skateboards and scooters passed out samples from backpacks at festivals, theme parks, soccer games, and local parks.

Other food companies quickly imitated Yoplait's tube packaging. Yet none was able to copy Go-Gurt's big success. Hunt's Squeez 'n Go pudding, Mott's Fruit Blasters apple sauce, and Skippy peanut butter in a tube were among the brands that did not sell well. Why? Moms complained that the tubes created a big mess on kids' clothes and furniture, so retailers lost interest and would not provide shelf-space support. One critic argued that the costly failures could have been avoided—because the "knee-jerk reaction" to imitate Go-Gurt resulted in products that were rushed to market without adequate research to gather insights from consumers.[1]

CONSUMER BEHAVIOR—WHY DO THEY BUY WHAT THEY BUY?

In the last chapter, we discussed basic data on population, income, and consumer spending patterns. This information can help marketers predict basic *trends* in consumer spending patterns. For example, the average person in the U.S. or Canada consumes 5 times more than a Mexican person, 10 times more than a Chinese person, and 30 times more than a person from India. Unfortunately, when many firms sell similar products, demographic analysis isn't much help in predicting which specific products and brands consumers will purchase—and why. Our Go-Gurt case shows that many other variables can influence consumers and their buying behavior.

To better understand why consumers buy as they do, many marketers turn to the behavioral sciences for help. In this chapter, we'll explore some of the thinking from economics, psychology, sociology, and the other behavioral disciplines.

Specific consumer behaviors vary a great deal for different products and from one target market to the next. In today's global markets, the variations are countless. That makes it impractical to catalog all the possibilities for every different situation. For example, how and why a given consumer buys a specific brand of cookies may be very different from how that same consumer buys a DVD recorder; and customers in different countries may have very different reactions to either product. But there are *general* behavioral principles—frameworks—that marketing managers can apply to learn more about their specific target markets. Our approach focuses on developing your skill in working with these frameworks.

Economic needs affect many buying decisions, but for some purchases the behavioral influences on a consumer are more important.

THE BEHAVIORAL SCIENCES HELP YOU UNDERSTAND THE BUYING PROCESS

Economic needs affect most buying decisions

Most economists assume that consumers are **economic buyers**—people who know all the facts and logically compare choices to get the greatest satisfaction from spending their time and money. A logical extension of the economic-buyer theory led us to look at consumer income patterns. This approach is valuable because consumers must at least have income to be in a market. Further, most consumers don't have enough income to buy everything they want, so they must make choices.

This view assumes that economic needs guide most consumer behavior. **Economic needs** are concerned with making the best use of a consumer's time and money—as the consumer judges it. Some consumers look for the lowest price. Others will pay extra for convenience. And others may weigh price and quality for the best value. Some economic needs are

1. Economy of purchase or use.
2. Convenience.
3. Efficiency in operation or use.
4. Dependability in use.
5. Improvement of earnings.

Clearly, marketing managers must be alert to new ways to appeal to economic needs. Most consumers appreciate firms that offer them improved economic value for the money they spend. But improved value does not just mean offering lower and lower prices. For example, products can be designed to work better, require less service, or last longer. Promotion can inform consumers about product benefits in terms of measurable factors like operating costs, the length of the guarantee, or the time a product will save. Carefully planned Place decisions can make it easier and faster for customers who face a poverty of time to make a purchase.

Economic value is an important factor in many purchase decisions. But most marketing managers think that buyer behavior is not as simple as the economic-buyer model suggests. A product that one person sees as a good value—and is eager to

Exhibit 6-1
A Model of Buyer Behavior

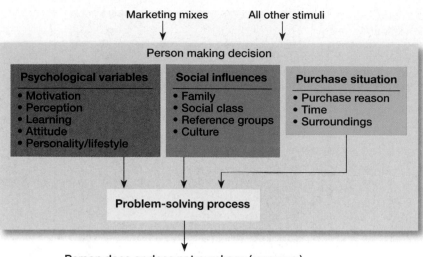

Marketing mixes | All other stimuli

Person making decision

Psychological variables
- Motivation
- Perception
- Learning
- Attitude
- Personality/lifestyle

Social influences
- Family
- Social class
- Reference groups
- Culture

Purchase situation
- Purchase reason
- Time
- Surroundings

Problem-solving process

Person does or does not purchase (response)

buy—is of no interest to someone else. So we can't expect to understand buying behavior without taking a broader view.

How we will view consumer behavior

Many behavioral dimensions influence consumers. Let's try to combine these dimensions into a model of how consumers make decisions. Exhibit 6-1 shows that psychological variables, social influences, and the purchase situation all affect a person's buying behavior. We'll discuss these topics in the next few pages. Then we'll expand the model to include the consumer problem-solving process.

PSYCHOLOGICAL INFLUENCES WITHIN AN INDIVIDUAL

Here we will discuss some variables of special interest to marketers—including motivation, perception, learning, attitudes, and lifestyle. Much of what we know about these *psychological (intrapersonal) variables* draws from ideas originally developed in the field of psychology.

Needs motivate consumers

Everybody is motivated by needs and wants. **Needs** are the basic forces that motivate a person to do something. Some needs involve a person's physical well-being, others the individual's self-view and relationship with others. Needs are more basic than wants. **Wants** are "needs" that are learned during a person's life. For example, everyone needs water or some kind of liquid, but some people also have learned to want Clearly Canadian's raspberry-flavored sparkling water on the rocks.

When a need is not satisfied, it may lead to a drive. The need for liquid, for example, leads to a thirst drive. A **drive** is a strong stimulus that encourages action to reduce a need. Drives are internal—they are the reasons behind certain behavior patterns. In marketing, a product purchase results from a drive to satisfy some need.

Some critics imply that marketers can somehow manipulate consumers to buy products against their will. But marketing managers can't create internal drives. Most marketing managers realize that trying to get consumers to act against their will is a waste of time. Instead, a good marketing manager studies what consumer drives, needs, and wants already exist and how they can be satisfied better.

Consumers seek benefits to meet needs

We're all a bundle of needs and wants. Exhibit 6-2 lists some important needs that might motivate a person to some action. This list, of course, is not complete. But thinking about such needs can help you see what *benefits* consumers might seek from a marketing mix.

Exhibit 6-2 Possible Needs Motivating a Person to Some Action

Types of Needs	Specific Examples			
Physiological needs	Hunger Sex Rest	Thirst Body elimination	Activity Self-preservation	Sleep Warmth/coolness
Psychological needs	Aggression Family preservation Nurturing Playing-relaxing Self-identification	Curiosity Imitation Order Power Tenderness	Being responsible Independence Personal fulfillment Pride	Dominance Love Playing-competition Self-expression
Desire for . . .	Acceptance Affiliation Comfort Esteem Knowledge Respect Status	Achievement Appreciation Leisure Fame Prestige Retaliation Sympathy	Acquisition Beauty Distance—"space" Happiness Pleasure Self-satisfaction Variety	Affection Companionship Distinctiveness Identification Recognition Sociability Fun
Freedom from . . .	Fear Pain Harm	Depression Stress Ridicule	Discomfort Loss Sadness	Anxiety Illness Pressure

When a marketing manager defines a product-market, the needs may be quite specific. For example, the food need might be as specific as wanting a Domino's thick-crust pepperoni pizza—delivered to your door hot and ready to eat.

Several needs at the same time

Consumer psychologists often argue that a person may have several reasons for buying—at the same time. Maslow is well known for his five-level hierarchy of needs. We will discuss a similar four-level hierarchy that is easier to apply to consumer behavior. Exhibit 6-3 illustrates the four levels along with an advertising slogan showing how a company has tried to appeal to each need. The lowest-level needs are physiological. Then come safety, social, and personal needs. As a study aid, think of the PSSP needs.[2]

Most products must fill more than one need at the same time.

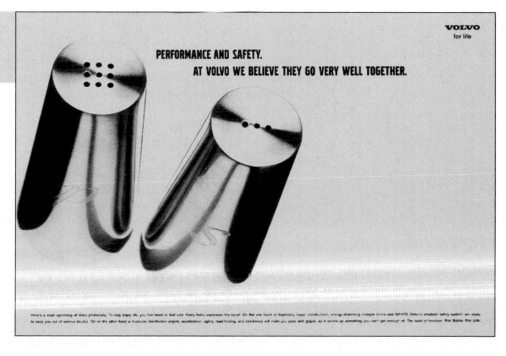

Exhibit 6-3 The PSSP Hierarchy of Needs

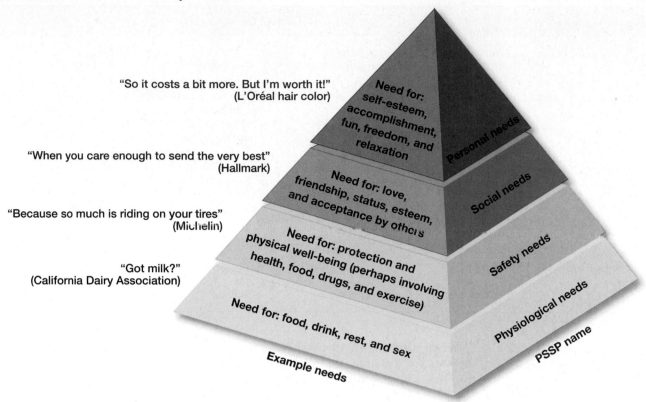

"So it costs a bit more. But I'm worth it!"
(L'Oréal hair color)

"When you care enough to send the very best"
(Hallmark)

"Because so much is riding on your tires"
(Michelin)

"Got milk?"
(California Dairy Association)

Need for: self-esteem, accomplishment, fun, freedom, and relaxation

Need for: love, friendship, status, esteem, and acceptance by others

Need for: protection and physical well-being (perhaps involving health, food, drugs, and exercise)

Need for: food, drink, rest, and sex

Personal needs

Social needs

Safety needs

Physiological needs

PSSP name

Example needs

Physiological needs are concerned with biological needs—food, drink, rest, and sex. **Safety needs** are concerned with protection and physical well-being (perhaps involving health, food, medicine, and exercise). **Social needs** are concerned with love, friendship, status, and esteem—things that involve a person's interaction with others. **Personal needs**, on the other hand, are concerned with an individual's need for personal satisfaction—unrelated to what others think or do. Examples include self-esteem, accomplishment, fun, freedom, and relaxation.

Motivation theory suggests that we never reach a state of complete satisfaction. As soon as we get our lower-level needs reasonably satisfied, those at higher levels become more dominant. This explains why marketing efforts targeted at affluent consumers in advanced economies often focus on higher-level needs. It also explains why these approaches may be useless in parts of the world where consumers' basic needs are not being met.

It is important to see, however, that a particular product may satisfy more than one need at the same time. In fact, most consumers try to fill a *set* of needs rather than just one need or another in sequence.

Obviously marketers should try to satisfy different needs. Yet discovering these specific consumer needs may require careful analysis. Consider, for example, the lowly vegetable peeler. Marketing managers for OXO International realized that many people, especially young children and senior citizens, have trouble gripping the handle of a typical peeler. OXO redesigned the peeler with a bigger handle that addressed this physical need. OXO also coated the handle with dishwasher-safe rubber. This makes cleanup more convenient—and the sharp peeler is safer to use when the grip is wet. The attractively designed grip also appeals to consumers who get personal satisfaction from cooking and who want to impress their guests. Even though OXO priced the peeler much higher than most kitchen utensils, it has sold very well because it appeals to people with a variety of needs. Since that initial

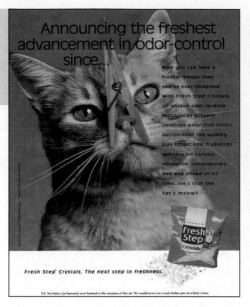

How consumers perceive a product or marketing communication may depend on consumer interest and the urgency of the need.

success, OXO has redesigned many everyday utensils, including its new scoop colander. The colander's long handle makes it safe and easy to scoop and drain cooked pasta—without handling a hot pan or boiling water.[3]

Perception determines what consumers see and feel

Consumers select varying ways to meet their needs sometimes because of differences in **perception**—how we gather and interpret information from the world around us.

We are constantly bombarded by stimuli—ads, products, stores—yet we may not hear or see anything. This is because we apply the following selective processes:

1. **Selective exposure**—our eyes and minds seek out and notice only information that interests us. How often have you closed a pop-up ad at a website without even noticing what it was for?

2. **Selective perception**—we screen out or modify ideas, messages, and information that conflict with previously learned attitudes and beliefs.

3. **Selective retention**—we remember only what we want to remember.

These selective processes help explain why some people are not affected by some advertising—even offensive advertising. They just don't see or remember it! Even if they do, they may dismiss it immediately. Some consumers are skeptical about any advertising message.

These selective processes are stronger than many people realize. For example, to make their positioning efforts memorable, many companies use a common slogan ("tag line") on all of their ads. However, when researchers showed consumers the tag lines for 22 of the biggest advertisers (over $100 million a year), only 6 were recognized by more than 10 percent of the consumers. Three slogans were not recognized by anyone in the sample. One of those was Circuit City's "We're with you" slogan that had been running in ads for two years. (Wal-Mart's "Always low prices, Always," with 64 percent recognition, was the only slogan recognized by more than half of the sample.)[4]

Our needs affect these selective processes. And current needs receive more attention. For example, Goodyear tire retailers advertise some sale in the newspaper almost weekly. Most of the time we don't even notice these ads—until we need new tires. Only then do we tune in to Goodyear's ads.

Marketers are interested in these selective processes because they affect how target consumers get and retain information. This is also why marketers are interested in how consumers *learn*.

Learning determines what response is likely

Learning is a change in a person's thought processes caused by prior experience. Learning is often based on direct experience: A little girl tastes her first cone of Ben & Jerry's Uncanny Cashew flavor ice cream, and learning occurs! Learning may also be based on indirect experience or associations. If you watch an ad that shows other people enjoying Ben & Jerry's Chocolate Fudge Brownie low-fat frozen yogurt, you might conclude that you'd like it too.

Consumer learning may result from things that marketers do, or it may result from stimuli that have nothing to do with marketing. Either way, almost all consumer behavior is learned.[5]

Experts describe a number of steps in the learning process. We've already discussed the idea of a drive as a strong stimulus that encourages action. Depending on the **cues**—products, signs, ads, and other stimuli in the environment—an individual chooses some specific response. A **response** is an effort to satisfy a drive. The specific response chosen depends on the cues and the person's past experience.

Reinforcement of the learning process occurs when the response is followed by satisfaction—that is, reduction in the drive. Reinforcement strengthens the relationship between the cue and the response. And it may lead to a similar response the next time the drive occurs. Repeated reinforcement leads to development of a habit—making the individual's decision process routine. Exhibit 6-4 shows the relationships of the important variables in the learning process.

The learning process can be illustrated by a thirsty person. The thirst *drive* could be satisfied in a variety of ways. But if the person happened to walk past a vending machine and saw a Mountain Dew sign—a *cue*—then he might satisfy the drive with a *response*—buying a Mountain Dew. If the experience is satisfactory, positive *reinforcement* occurs, and our friend may be quicker to satisfy this drive in the same way in the future. This emphasizes the importance of developing good products that live up to the promises of the firm's advertising. People can learn to like or dislike Mountain Dew—reinforcement and learning work both ways. Unless marketers satisfy their customers, they must constantly try to attract new ones to replace the dissatisfied ones who don't come back.

Good experiences can lead to positive attitudes about a firm's product. Bad experiences can lead to negative attitudes that even good promotion won't be able to change.

Exhibit 6-4
The Learning Process

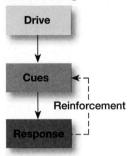

Positive cues help a marketing mix

Sometimes marketers try to identify cues or images that have positive associations from some other situation and relate them to their marketing mix. Many people associate the smell of lemons with a fresh, natural cleanliness. So companies often add lemon scent to household cleaning products—Clorox bleach and Pledge furniture polish, for example—because it has these associations. Similarly, firms like Calvin Klein use ads suggesting that people who use their products have more appeal to the opposite sex. Simple cues may even be important for a big purchase. Some consumers draw conclusions about the quality of a car at a dealer's showroom from the "thunk" of the door when it closes. Luxury-car makers try for a "new car smell" with an aroma of leather and wood, even though the car would really smell more like metal and adhesives as it comes off the production line in a factory.[6]

Many needs are culturally learned

Many needs are culturally (or socially) learned. The need for food, for instance, may lead to many specific food wants. Many Japanese enjoy sushi (raw fish), and their children learn to like it. Fewer Americans, however, have learned to enjoy it.

Some critics argue that marketing efforts encourage people to spend money on learned wants totally unrelated to any basic need. For example, Europeans are less concerned about perspiration, and many don't buy or use antiperspirants. Yet Americans spend millions of dollars on such products. Advertising says that using Ban deodorant "takes the worry out of being close." But is marketing activity the cause of the difference in the two cultures? Most research says that advertising can't convince buyers of something contrary to their basic attitudes.

156

Many consumers (and retailers) still think of Keds as white sneakers. This ad is trying to change that perception by showcasing the brand's expansion into colorful new styles, such as slides, mules, and thongs. While the Keds marketing mix has changed, sometimes it takes time to change what and how consumers think.

Attitudes relate to buying

An **attitude** is a person's point of view toward something. The "something" may be a product, an advertisement, a salesperson, a firm, or an idea. Attitudes are an important topic for marketers because attitudes affect the selective processes, learning, and eventually the buying decisions people make.

Because attitudes are usually thought of as involving liking or disliking, they have some action implications. Beliefs are not so action-oriented. A **belief** is a person's opinion about something. Beliefs may help shape a consumer's attitudes but don't necessarily involve any liking or disliking. It is possible to have a belief—say, that Listerine PocketPak strips have a medicinal taste—without really caring what they taste like. On the other hand, beliefs about a product may have a positive or negative effect in shaping consumers' attitudes. For example, promotion for Splenda, a new no-cal sweetener in a yellow packet, informs consumers that it's "made from sugar so it tastes like sugar." A dieter who believes that Splenda will taste better because it is made from sugar might try it instead of just routinely rebuying another brand, like Equal. On the other hand, a person with diabetes might believe that he should avoid Splenda—like he avoids other products made from sugar—even though Splenda is actually suitable for people with diabetes.[7]

In an attempt to relate attitude more closely to purchase behavior, some marketers stretched the attitude concept to include consumer "preferences" or "intention to buy." Managers who must forecast how much of their brand customers will buy are particularly interested in the intention to buy. Forecasts would be easier if attitudes were good predictors of intentions to buy. Unfortunately, the relationships usually are not that simple. A person may have positive attitudes toward Jacuzzi whirlpool bathtubs but no intention of buying one.

Try to understand attitudes and beliefs

Research on consumer attitudes and beliefs can sometimes help a marketing manager get a better picture of markets. For example, consumers with very positive attitudes toward a new product idea might provide a good opportunity—especially if they have negative attitudes about competitors' offerings. Or they may have beliefs that would discourage them from buying a product.

Marketing managers for Purina Dog Chow faced this challenge. Research showed that one segment of consumers thought that Purina was a great dog food, but they didn't buy it all of the time. They believed that their dogs would get bored with it. After all, people don't like eating the same thing all of the time. But dogs are not people. Vets have found dogs benefit from a good, consistent diet. So Purina devel-

Marketing managers for new Olay Cleansing Cloths (and other Olay skin care products) wanted to take advantage of the familiar Oil of Olay brand name, but realized that many consumers didn't have a positive association between "oil" and beauty. So the brand name was updated to just Olay and the logo of a woman's figure was changed slightly to appeal to younger women.

oped an ad campaign to convince these dog owners that what they believed was not true. Each ad gave a dog's-eye-view reaction to being fed a different dog food. In one ad, after taking a few bites, the dog looks into the camera with a pained expression and walks away. He returns with a packet of antacid, which he drops in his water bowl. Advertising research and sales results both showed that the soft-sell ad hit the bull's-eye in convincing occasional customers that switching foods was not good. Many bought Purina more regularly, and Dog Chow sales increased by $36 million. Consumer beliefs—right or wrong—can have a significant impact on whether a strategy succeeds.[8]

Most marketers work with existing attitudes

Purina's efforts were successful in changing beliefs. But marketers generally try to understand the attitudes of their potential customers and work with them. Because attitudes tend to be enduring, it's usually more economical to work with consumer attitudes than to try to change them.

Changing negative attitudes may be necessary

Yet changing present attitudes—especially negative ones—is sometimes necessary. Consider the plight of auto companies that rely heavily on revenue from sales of minivans. It's hard to find a vehicle that is less hip than a minivan; most people associate them with carpooling, hauling groceries, and other not-so-glamorous activities. It's no wonder that lots of buyers who need passenger space have opted for the more rugged sport-utility vehicles. Even if they don't need a rugged vehicle, it helps their self-image. That may help explain why GM now refers to its minivans as "crossover sports vans" and why Nissan is pushing to make its minivan more sexy. Its recently redesigned Quest sports a lush interior and stylish lines, the ride is smoother, the handling is better, and ads position it as not just for moms, but for hot mamas. One two-page ad says "Passion built it. Passion will fill it up." Perhaps these efforts will help differentiate Quest from other minivans. And if other firms continue to spruce up their minivans attitudes may slowly change. But this is likely to be a slow, expensive effort. Changing negative attitudes is probably the most difficult job marketers face.[9]

Ethical issues may arise

Part of the marketing job is to inform and persuade consumers about a firm's offering. An ethical issue sometimes arises, however, if consumers have *inaccurate* beliefs. For example, many consumers are confused about what foods are really healthy. Marketers for a number of food companies have been criticized for packaging and

158

WOULD YOU LIKE THOSE PEANUTS WITH SUGAR AND CREAM?

Marketing managers for Planters' peanuts wanted a new package that would keep peanuts fresh. They also wanted the package to be a cue to promote freshness to consumers. They thought that they had the right idea when they put Planters Fresh Roast Salted Peanuts in a vacuum-packed bric-pac, like the ones that coffee comes in. They were confident that when consumers saw the vacuum-packed peanuts it would remind them that they were fresh roasted, just like with fresh-roasted coffee. To reinforce that message, Planters put the words "Fresh Roast" in large print on the front of the package—right under the Planters name and over the words "salted peanuts." The familiar Mr. Peanut trademark character was there too. He looked dapper with his top hat and cane pointing toward the words "Fresh Roast." This all seemed like a good idea, but it didn't work as planned.

One problem was that the peanuts weren't the same size and shape as coffee, so the bags were pretty lumpy. That made the words harder to read on supermarket shelves. The bags were supposed to be resealable. But that didn't work well because of the lumps. So once the bag was opened, the peanuts got stale. Consumers who expected extra freshness were disappointed. But other shoppers had a bigger surprise before they even left the store.

Some consumers opened the bag and put the contents into the grocery store's coffee grinder. You can imagine the gooey peanut butter mess that made. You can also imagine that the store manager was not happy with Planters. Were the consumers trying to make peanut butter? No. Everything on the bag made it clear that it was peanuts. However, the link of the bag with coffee was so strong that consumers didn't stop to think about it. Moreover, the new package came out at about the same time that flavored coffees were just becoming popular. Hey, if some ad is telling you to try hazelnut-flavored coffee, why not peanut-flavored coffee too? No, Planters doesn't want to compete with Starbucks, so this package is off the market.[10]

promotion that take advantage of inaccurate consumer perceptions about the meaning of the words *lite* or *low-fat*. A firm's lite donuts may have less fat or fewer calories than its other donuts—but that doesn't mean that the donut is *low* in fat or calories. Similarly, promotion of a "children's cold formula" may play off parents' fears that adult medicines are too strong—even though the basic ingredients in the children's formula are the same and only the dosage is different. And when Lance Armstrong's winning smile appears in a Subaru ad, it's easy to forget that he's paid for his endorsement.

Marketers must also be careful about promotion that might encourage false beliefs, even if the advertising is not explicitly misleading. For example, ads for Ultra Slim-Fast low-fat beverage don't claim that anyone who buys the product will lose all the weight they want or look like the slim models who appear in the ads—but some critics argue that the advertising gives that impression.[11]

Meeting expectations is important

Attitudes and beliefs sometimes combine to form an **expectation**—an outcome or event that a person anticipates or looks forward to. Consumer expectations often focus on the benefits or value that the consumer expects from a firm's marketing mix. This is an important issue for marketers because a consumer is likely to be dissatisfied if his or her expectations are not met. For example, when Dryel home dry-cleaning kits were introduced, ads portrayed Dryel as an alternative to expensive dry-cleaner services. Many consumers who tried it were disappointed because it failed to get out some stains and clothing still needed to be pressed.[12]

A key point here is that consumers may evaluate a product not just on how well it performs, but on how it performs *relative to their expectations*. A product that otherwise might get high marks from a satisfied consumer may be a disappointment if there's a gap between what the consumer gets and what the consumer expects. Promotion that overpromises what the rest of the marketing mix can really deliver leads to problems in this area. Finding the right balance, however, can be difficult. Consider the challenge faced by marketing managers for Van Heusen shirts. A few years ago Van Heusen came up with a new way to treat its shirts so that they look better when they come out of the wash than previous wash-and-wear shirts. Van Heusen promoted these shirts as "wrinkle-free" and the label showed an iron stuffed in a garbage can. Most people agree that the new shirt is an improvement. Even so, consumers who buy a shirt expecting it to look as crisp as if it had just been ironed are disappointed. For them, the improvement is not enough.[13]

Personality affects how people see things

Many researchers study how personality affects people's behavior, but the results have generally been disappointing to marketers. A trait like neatness can be associated with users of certain types of products—like cleaning materials. But marketing managers have not found a way to use personality in marketing strategy planning.[14] As a result, they've stopped focusing on personality measures borrowed from psychologists and instead developed lifestyle analysis.

Psychographics focus on activities, interests, and opinions

Psychographics or **lifestyle analysis** is the analysis of a person's day-to-day pattern of living as expressed in that person's Activities, Interests, and Opinions—sometimes referred to as AIOs. Exhibit 6-5 shows a number of variables for each of the AIO dimensions—along with some demographics used to add detail to the lifestyle profile of a target market.

Lifestyle analysis assumes that marketers can plan more effective strategies if they know more about their target markets. Understanding the lifestyle of target customers has been especially helpful in providing ideas for advertising themes. Let's see how it adds to a typical demographic description. It may not help Toyota marketing managers much to know that an average member of the target market for a Highlander SUV is 34.8 years old, married, lives in a three-bedroom home, and has 2.3 children. Lifestyles help marketers paint a more human portrait of the target market. For example, lifestyle analysis might show that the 34.8-year-old is also a community-oriented consumer with traditional values who especially enjoys spectator sports and spends much time in other family activities. An ad might show the Highlander being used by a happy family at a ball game so the target market could really identify with the ad. And the ad might be placed on an ESPN show whose viewers match the target lifestyle profile.[15]

Marketing managers for consumer products firms who are interested in learning more about the lifestyle of a target market sometimes turn to outside specialists for help. For example, SRI Consulting Business Intelligence (SRIC-BI), a research firm, offers a service called geoVALS (VALS is an abbreviation for values, attitudes, and lifestyles). GeoVALS uses psychographics to show where customers live and why

Exhibit 6-5
Lifestyle Dimensions (and some related demographic dimensions)

Dimension	Examples		
Activities	Work	Vacation	Surfing Web
	Hobbies	Entertainment	Shopping
	Social events	Club membership	Sports
Interests	Family	Community	Food
	Home	Recreation	Media
	Job	Fashion	Achievements
Opinions	Themselves	Business	Products
	Social issues	Economics	Future
	Politics	Education	Culture
Demographics	Income	Geographic area	Occupation
	Age	Ethnicity	Family size
	Family life cycle	Dwelling	Education

The Harley-Davidson marketing mix often emphasizes the lifestyle and psychographics of its target customers, not just the features of its popular motorcycles.

SOMEWHERE ON AN AIRPLANE A MAN IS TRYING TO RIP OPEN A SMALL BAG OF PEANUTS.

they behave as they do; it is especially useful for targeting direct-mail ad campaigns. With another VALS service, SRIC-BI describes a firm's target market in terms of a set of typical VALS lifestyle groups (segments). An advantage of this approach is that SRIC-BI has developed very detailed information about the various VALS groups. For example, the VALS approach has been used to profile consumers in the United Kingdom, Germany, Japan, and Canada as well as the United States. However, the disadvantage of VALS—and other similar approaches—is that it may not be very specific to the marketing manager's target market.[16]

INTERNET EXERCISE

Go to the SRIC-BI Internet site (www.sric-bi.com), click on VALS survey, and then click on "Take the Survey" to review the VALS questionnaire. If you wish, complete the short questionnaire online. If you provide your e-mail address, SRIC-BI will provide you with your VALS profile.

SOCIAL INFLUENCES AFFECT CONSUMER BEHAVIOR

We've been discussing some of the ways needs, attitudes, and other psychological variables influence the buying process. Now we'll see that these variables—and the buying process—are often affected by relations with other people too. We'll look at how the individual interacts with family, social class, and other groups who may have influence.

Who is the real decision maker in family purchases?

Relationships with other family members influence many aspects of consumer behavior. We saw specific examples of this in Chapter 5 when we considered the effects of the family life cycle on family spending patterns. Family members may also share many attitudes and values, consider each other's opinions, and divide various buying tasks. In years past, most marketers in the United States targeted the wife as the family purchasing agent. Now, with sex-role stereotypes changed and with night and weekend shopping more popular, men and older children take more

responsibility for shopping and decision making. In other countries, family roles vary. For example, in Norway women still do most of the family shopping.

Although only one family member may go to the store and make a specific purchase, when planning marketing strategy it's important to know who else may be involved. Other family members may have influenced the decision or really decided what to buy. Still others may use the product.

You don't have to watch much Saturday morning TV to see that Kellogg's knows this. Cartoon characters like Tony the Tiger tell kids about the goodies found in certain cereal packages and urge them to remind Dad or Mom to pick up that brand at the store. Similarly, the box for Post's Oreo O's cereal looks like the wrapper on the cookies, to get kids' attention in the store. Kids also influence grown-up purchases—to the tune of $300 billion a year. Surveys show that kids often have a big say in a family's choice of products such as apparel, cars, vacations, electronics, and health and beauty aids. For example, 82 percent of parents say they choose vacations based on kids' opinions.

Family considerations may overwhelm personal ones

A husband and wife may jointly agree on many important purchases, but sometimes they may have strong personal preferences. However, such individual preferences may change if the other spouse has different priorities. One might want to take a family vacation to Disneyland—when the other wants a new Sony DVD recorder and high-definition large-screen TV. The actual outcome in such a situation is unpredictable. The preferences of one spouse might change because of affection for the other or because of the other's power and influence.

Buying responsibility and influence vary greatly depending on the product and the family. A marketer trying to plan a strategy will find it helpful to research the specific target market. Remember, many buying decisions are made jointly, and thinking only about who actually buys the product can misdirect the marketing strategy.[17]

Social class affects attitudes, values, and buying

Up to now, we've been concerned with individuals and their family relationships. Now let's consider how society looks at an individual and perhaps the family—in terms of social class. A **social class** is a group of people who have approximately equal social position as viewed by others in the society.

Almost every society has some social class structure. In most countries, social class is closely related to a person's occupation, but it may also be influenced by education, community participation, where a person lives, income, possessions, social skills, and other factors—including what family a person is born into. Because of such differences, people in different social classes tend to have different beliefs and feelings.

In most countries—including the United States—there is *some* general relationship between income level and social class. But the income level of people within the same social class can vary greatly, and people with the same income level may be in different social classes. So income by itself is usually not a good measure of social class. And people in different social classes may spend, save, and borrow money in very different ways. For example, spending for clothing, housing, home furnishings, and leisure activities, as well as choices of where and how to shop, often vary with social class.

The U.S. class system is far less rigid than those in most countries. Children start out in the same social class as their parents—but they can move to a different social class depending on their educational levels or the jobs they hold. By contrast, India's social structure is much more rigid, and individuals can't easily move up in the class system.

Reference group influence is usually more important when others will be able to see which product a consumer is using. Jockey wants young people to view its underwear as in fashion and encourages them to "Let 'em know you're Jockey."

Marketers want to know what buyers in various social classes are like. In the United States, simple approaches for measuring social class groupings are based on a person's *occupation, education,* and *type and location of housing.* By using marketing research surveys or available census data, marketers can get a feel for the social class of a target market.

What do these classes mean?

Many people think of America as a middle-class society. In fact, when asked to classify themselves, most people just say that they're middle class or working class. But social class studies suggest that in many marketing situations the social class groups are more distinct than that suggests. Various classes shop at different stores. They prefer different treatment from salespeople. They buy different brands of products—even though prices are about the same. And they have different spending–saving attitudes, even when they have the same income level.

Reference groups are relevant too

A **reference group** is the people to whom an individual looks when forming attitudes about a particular topic. People normally have several reference groups for different topics. Some they meet face-to-face. Others they just wish to imitate. In either case, they may take values from these reference groups and make buying decisions based on what the group might accept.

We're always making comparisons between ourselves and others. So reference groups are more important when others will be able to "see" which product or brand we're using. Influence is stronger for products that relate to status in the group. For one group, owning an expensive fur coat may be a sign of "having arrived." A group of animal lovers might view it as a sign of bad judgment. In either case, a consumer's decision to buy or not buy a fur coat might depend on the opinions of others in that consumer's reference group.[18]

Reaching the opinion leaders who are buyers

An **opinion leader** is a person who influences others. Opinion leaders aren't necessarily wealthier or better educated. And opinion leaders on one subject aren't necessarily opinion leaders on another. For example, you may have a friend who is ahead of the curve in knowing about computer products, but you might not want that friend's opinion about new clothing styles and cosmetics. On the other hand, sometimes a leader in one area earns respect in another. Arnold

The original Betty, 1936

1965

1980

1972

1986

Betty Crocker 1996

General Mills has changed "Betty Crocker's" appearance as consumer attitudes and lifestyles have changed. The face of the newest Betty Crocker reflects her multicultural background.

Schwarzenegger became influential as an entertainer, but then he became an opinion leader in politics.

Each social class and age group tends to have its own opinion leaders. Some marketing mixes aim especially at these people since their opinions affect others and research shows that they are involved in many product-related discussions with "followers." Favorable word-of-mouth publicity from opinion leaders can really help a marketing mix. But the opposite is also true. If opinion leaders aren't satisfied, they're likely to talk about it and negatively influence others.[19]

Culture surrounds the other influences

Culture is the whole set of beliefs, attitudes, and ways of doing things of a reasonably homogeneous set of people. In Chapters 4 and 5, we looked at the broad impact of culture.

We can think of the American culture, the French culture, or the Latin American culture. People within these cultural groupings tend to be more similar in outlook and behavior. But often it is useful to think of subcultures within such groupings. For example, within the American culture, there are various religious and ethnic subcultures; also different cultural forces tend to prevail in different regions of the country.

Failure to consider cultural differences, even subtle ones, can result in problems. To promote their product and get people to try it, marketers for Pepto-Bismol often provide free samples at festivals and street fairs. Their idea is that people tend to overindulge at such events. However, when they distributed sample packets at a festival in San Francisco's Chinatown, they insulted many of the people they wanted to influence. Booths with Chinese delicacies lined the streets, and many of the participants interpreted the sample packets (which featured the word "Nauseous" in large letters) as suggesting that Chinese delicacies were nauseating. The possibility of this misinterpretation may seem obvious in hindsight, but if it had been that obvious in advance the whole promotion would have been handled differently.[20]

Culture varies in international markets

Planning strategies that consider cultural differences in international markets can be even harder—and such cultures usually vary more. Each foreign market may need to be treated as a separate market with its own submarkets. Ignoring cultural differences—or assuming that they are not important—almost guarantees failure in international markets.

For example, Japanese consumers tend to snap up the latest gadgets, but only about 7 percent of Japanese households have a dishwasher (compared to about 50 percent in the U.S.). Appliance manufacturers who have tried to export their standard models to Japan have met with failure. One reason is that Japanese kitchens are much too small for units that are standard in the U.S. Another problem is that fermented soybeans and other common Japanese foods tend to be very sticky. A standard dishwasher won't clean the dishes well. To address these cultural differences, manufacturers have developed small countertop machines with powerful jets to do the cleaning. But another obstacle remains. Many traditional Japanese feel that it is the woman's duty to wash the dishes. For many housewives, the guilt of having dishes done by a machine is worse than the aggravation of doing the job. Foreign firms had missed that, but Matsushita, a Japanese firm, got big increases in sales by focusing its promotion on conserving hot water and hygiene—rather than convenience—as the important reasons to buy a dishwasher.[21]

From a target marketing point of view, a marketing manager probably wants to aim at people within one culture or subculture. A firm developing strategies for two cultures often needs two different marketing plans.[22]

The attitudes and beliefs that we usually associate with culture tend to change slowly. Consider something as unemotional as a cup of tea. For a long time, tea has been a basic part of British culture. Taking a break for a cup of hot tea is tradition— a social moment with friends. In striking contrast, few British consumers ever drink iced tea. Lipton, Nestea, and other iced-tea makers would like to change that. They look at the 330 million gallons of iced tea routinely purchased by Americans each year and ask, "Why not in Britain?" But they face tough odds—and it's not just the cooler weather in England. Consumers there associate iced tea with the dregs left in the bottom of the teapot after it's cooled off. It's not an appealing image, and it isn't likely to change quickly. Iced-tea sales won't pick up until it does.[23]

Because cultural forces tend to change slowly, marketers can often avoid problems by getting help from someone who already has a good understanding of the culture of the target customers. This helps to avoid problems. Then the marketers should be able to focus on the more dynamic variables discussed above.

INDIVIDUALS ARE AFFECTED BY THE PURCHASE SITUATION

Needs, benefits sought, attitudes, motivation, and even how a consumer selects certain products all vary depending on the purchase situation. So different purchase situations may require different marketing mixes—even when the same target market is involved. Let's briefly consider some of the ways that the purchase situation can vary.

Purchase reason can vary

Why a consumer makes a purchase can affect buying behavior. For example, a student buying a pen to take notes might pick up an inexpensive Bic. But the same student might choose a Cross pen as a gift for a friend. And a gadget-lover with some free time on his hands might buy a digital pen that transfers handwritten notes to a tablet computer—just for the fun of trying it.

Time affects what happens

Time influences a purchase situation. *When* consumers make a purchase—and the time they have available for shopping—will influence their behavior. A leisurely dinner or socializing with friends at a Starbucks induces different behavior than grabbing a quick cup of 7-Eleven coffee on the way to work.

The urgency of the need is another time-related factor. A sports buff who needs a digital video recorder with an "instant replay" feature in time for the Super Bowl—that evening—might spend an hour driving across town in heavy traffic to get the right unit. In a different circumstance, the same person might order a unit online from a website and figure that the extra time for it to be shipped is well worth the money saved.

On the other hand, how long something takes may be relative. Our online shopper might be frustrated by a web page that takes two minutes to load and abandon

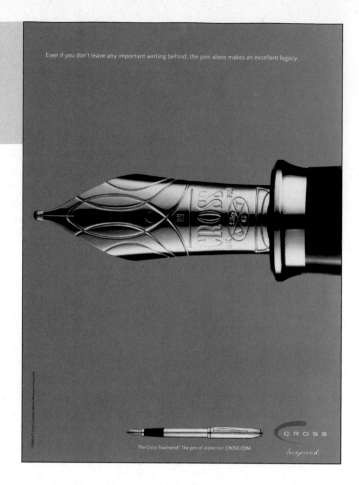

Even if you don't leave any important writing behind, the pen alone makes an excellent legacy.

The Cross Townsend.® The pen of distinction. CROSS.COM

CROSS

Inspired.

his virtual shopping cart after the digital video recorder is already selected. This happens all of the time online. On the other hand, you don't often see a consumer walk away from a shopping cart because of a two-minute wait in a checkout line at a store.

Surroundings affect buying too

Surroundings can affect buying behavior. The excitement at an on-site auction may stimulate impulse buying. Checking out an auction online might lead to a different response.

Surroundings may discourage buying too. For example, some people don't like to stand in a checkout line where others can see what they're buying—even if the other shoppers are complete strangers.[24]

CONSUMERS USE PROBLEM-SOLVING PROCESSES

The variables discussed affect *what* products a consumer finally decides to purchase. Marketing managers also need to understand *how* buyers use a problem-solving process to select particular products.

Most consumers seem to use the following five-step problem-solving process:

1. Becoming aware of, or interested in, the problem.
2. Recalling and gathering information about possible solutions.
3. Evaluating alternative solutions—perhaps trying some out.
4. Deciding on the appropriate solution.
5. Evaluating the decision.[25]

Exhibit 6-6
An Expanded Model of the Consumer Problem-Solving Process

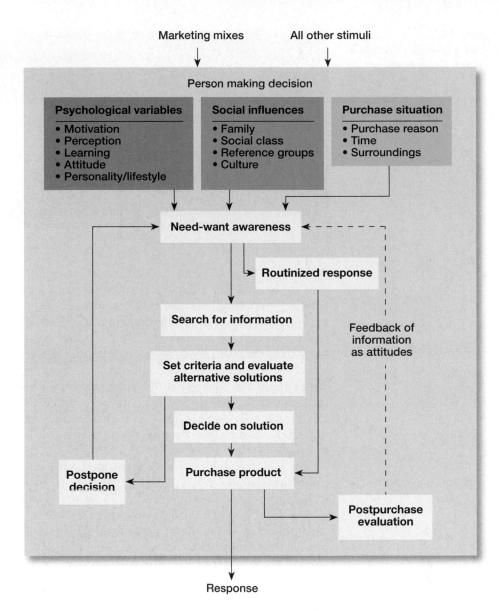

Exhibit 6-6 presents an expanded version of the buyer-behavior model shown in Exhibit 6-1. Note that this exhibit integrates the problem-solving process with the whole set of variables we've been reviewing.

When consumers evaluate information about purchase alternatives, they may weigh not only a product type in relation to other types of products but also differences in brands within a product type *and* the stores where the products may be available. This can be a very complicated evaluation procedure, and, depending on their choice of criteria, consumers may make seemingly irrational decisions. If convenient service is crucial, for example, a buyer might pay list price for an unexciting car from a very convenient dealer. Marketers need a way to analyze these decisions.

Grid of evaluative criteria helps

On the basis of studies of how consumers seek out and evaluate product information, researchers suggest that marketing managers use an evaluative grid showing features common to different products (or marketing mixes). For example, Exhibit 6-7 shows some of the features common to three different cars a consumer might consider.

Exhibit 6-7
Grid of Evaluative Criteria
for Three Car Brands

Brands	Common features			
	Gas mileage	Ease of service	Comfortable interior	Styling
Nissan	[−]	+	+	−
Saab	+	[−]	+	+
Subaru	+	+	[+]	[−]

Note: Pluses and minuses indicate a consumer's evaluation of a feature for a brand.

The first thing to notice about this sample grid is that it lists information about only a few cars. For a marketer, making it into a consumer's **consideration set**—the list of potential choices that a consumer will actually consider buying—can be critically important. When making purchase decisions, even important ones, consumers often save time and effort by first narrowing down to a few alternatives that they will evaluate more carefully. Sometimes they just narrow down based on a familiar brand name or because they remember an interesting ad. Other times a product might be suggested by a friend or get attention because it is displayed by a local retailer or shows up in an Internet search for information. But brands that don't at least make it into the consumer's consideration set are not likely to get close attention—or in the end be what the consumer chooses to buy.

The grid in Exhibit 6-7 encourages marketing managers to view each product in the consideration set as a bundle of features or attributes. The pluses and minuses in Exhibit 6-7 indicate one consumer's attitude toward each feature of each car. If members of the target market don't rate a feature of the marketing manager's brand with pluses, it may indicate a problem. The manager might want to change the product to improve that feature or perhaps use more promotion to emphasize an already acceptable feature. The consumer in Exhibit 6-7 has a minus under gas mileage for the Nissan. If the Nissan really gets better gas mileage than the other cars, promotion might focus on mileage to improve consumer attitudes toward this feature and toward the whole product.

Some consumers will reject a product if they see *one* feature as substandard—regardless of how favorably they regard the product's other features. The consumer in Exhibit 6-7 might avoid the Saab, which he saw as less than satisfactory on ease of service, even if it were superior in all other aspects. In other instances, a consumer's overall attitude toward the product might be such that a few good features could make up for some shortcomings. The comfortable interior of the Subaru (Exhibit 6-7) might make up for less exciting styling—especially if the consumer viewed comfort as really important.

Of course, most consumers don't use a grid like this. However, constructing such a grid helps managers think about what evaluative criteria target consumers consider really important, what consumers' attitudes are toward their product (or marketing mix) on each criteria, and how consumers combine the criteria to reach a final decision. Having a better understanding of the process should help a manager develop a better marketing mix.[26]

Three levels of problem solving are useful

The basic problem-solving process shows the steps consumers may go through trying to find a way to satisfy their needs—but it doesn't show how long this process will take or how much thought a consumer will give to each step. Individuals who

Exhibit 6-8 Problem-Solving Continuum

Low involvement
Frequently purchased
Inexpensive
Little risk
Little information needed

| Routinized response behavior | Limited problem solving | Extensive problem solving |

High involvement
Infrequently purchased
Expensive
High risk
Much information desired

have had a lot of experience solving certain problems can move quickly through some of the steps or almost directly to a decision.

It is helpful, therefore, to recognize three levels of problem solving: extensive problem solving, limited problem solving, and routinized response behavior. See Exhibit 6-8. These problem-solving approaches are used for any kind of product. Consumers use **extensive problem solving** for a completely new or important need—when they put *much* effort into deciding how to satisfy it. For example, a music lover who wants to download music might decide to buy an MP3 player—but not have any idea what model to buy. After talking with friends to find out about their experiences with different models, she might do a search on the Internet to see if highly recommended models were still available, to get the details about features, and even to look for published product reviews. She might also compare prices listed by firms selling the players over the Internet. After thinking about her needs some more, she might want to visit a local dealer to listen to a Sony unit with an optional memory card to hold more tracks. And if she likes the sound—and the store has a good extended service guarantee at the right price—she'll buy it. This is not exactly an impulse purchase!

Consumers use **limited problem solving** when they're willing to put *some* effort into deciding the best way to satisfy a need. Limited problem solving is typical when a consumer has some previous experience in solving a problem but isn't certain which choice is best at the current time. If our music lover also wanted some new compact discs for her car CD player, she would already know what type of music she enjoys. She might go to a familiar store and evaluate what new CDs they had in stock for her favorite types of music.

Consumers use **routinized response behavior** when they regularly select a particular way of satisfying a need when it occurs. Routinized response behavior is typical when a consumer has considerable experience in how to meet a need and has no need for additional information. For example, our music lover might routinely buy the latest recording by her favorite band as soon as it's available.

Most marketing managers would like their target consumers to buy their products in this routinized way. Some firms provide special services for frequent buyers, encourage repeat business with discounts, or do other things to build a good relationship so that the customer purchases from them in a routinized way.

Routinized response behavior is also typical for **low-involvement purchases**—purchases that have little importance or relevance for the customer. Let's face it, buying a box of salt is probably not one of the burning issues in your life.[27]

Problem solving is a learning process

The reason problem solving becomes simpler with time is that people learn from experience—both positive and negative things. As consumers approach the problem-solving process, they bring attitudes formed by previous experiences and social training. Each new problem-solving process may then contribute to or modify this attitude set.

New concepts require an adoption process

When consumers face a really new concept, their previous experience may not be relevant. These situations involve the **adoption process**—the steps individuals go through on the way to accepting or rejecting a new idea. Although the adoption

process is similar to the problem-solving process, learning plays a clearer role and promotion's contribution to a marketing mix is more visible.

In the adoption process, an individual moves through some fairly definite steps:

1. *Awareness*—the potential customer comes to know about the product but lacks details. The consumer may not even know how it works or what it will do.

2. *Interest*—if the consumer becomes interested, he or she will gather general information and facts about the product.

3. *Evaluation*—a consumer begins to give the product a mental trial, applying it to his or her personal situation.

4. *Trial*—the consumer may buy the product to experiment with it in use. A product that is either too expensive to try or isn't available for trial may never be adopted.

5. *Decision*—the consumer decides on either adoption or rejection. A satisfactory evaluation and trial may lead to adoption of the product and regular use. According to psychological learning theory, reinforcement leads to adoption.

6. *Confirmation*—the adopter continues to rethink the decision and searches for support for the decision—that is, further reinforcement.[28]

PepsiCo had to work with the adoption process when it introduced Pepsi One, a low-calorie cola. Many consumers are interested in staying trim, but diet sodas have an image of bad taste. In light of that, Pepsi's initial ads didn't directly say that Pepsi One was a diet drink. Rather, they used the slogan "True Cola Taste. One Calorie." But that confused a lot of consumers who couldn't tell what made it different from Diet Pepsi. As a result, consumer interest was not as great as Pepsi had expected. Because awareness and interest were low among consumers, retailers didn't devote much shelf space to Pepsi One, so it often wasn't even there for a consumer to consider. Even after a year on the market, trial was low. To help more consumers through the adoption process, Pepsi made changes. To build awareness and interest, new ads explained that Pepsi One was using a new sweetener, recently approved by the government, which tasted better than the sweetener used in other diet drinks. The ads showed consumers drinking Pepsi One and not being able to taste the difference from a regular cola; they used the tagline "Too good to be one calorie, but it is." Pepsi also changed the packaging graphics to put more emphasis on the sweetener at the point of purchase. To generate more trial, Pepsi pushed to get Pepsi One promoted in special end-aisle displays and stepped up its sampling program with taste-testing booths on campuses, in office cafeterias, and at movie theaters. Of course, consumers who tried Pepsi One would seek it out again only if they were satisfied with the taste.[29]

INTERNET EXERCISE

To make it easier for consumers to visualize how certain fashions will look, the Lands' End website (www.landsend.com) has an interactive "virtual model" feature. Go to the Lands' End website, click on "My Model," and check out this feature. Do you think that it makes it easier to evaluate a potential purchase?

Dissonance may set in after the decision

A buyer may have second thoughts after making a purchase decision. The buyer may have chosen from among several attractive alternatives—weighing the pros and cons and finally making a decision. Later doubts, however, may lead to **dissonance**—tension caused by uncertainty about the rightness of a decision. Dissonance may lead a buyer to search for additional information to confirm the wisdom of the decision and so reduce tension. Without this confirmation, the adopter might buy something else next time or not comment positively about the product to others.[30]

SEVERAL PROCESSES ARE RELATED AND RELEVANT TO STRATEGY PLANNING

Exhibit 6-9 shows the interrelation of the problem-solving process, the adoption process, and learning. It is important to see this interrelation and to understand that promotion can modify or accelerate it. Also note that the potential buyers' problem-solving behavior should affect how firms design their distribution systems. Similarly, customers' attitudes may determine how price sensitive they are and what price the firm should charge. Knowing how target markets handle these processes helps companies with their marketing strategy planning.

Exhibit 6-9
Relation of Problem-Solving Process, Adoption Process, and Learning (given a problem)

Problem-solving steps	Adoption process steps	Learning steps
1. Becoming aware of or interested in the problem	Awareness and interest	Drive
2. Gathering information about possible solutions	Interest and evaluation	Cues
3. Evaluating alternative solutions, perhaps trying some out	Evaluation, maybe trial	Reinforcement
4. Deciding on the appropriate solution	Decision	Response
5. Evaluating the decision	Confirmation	

In Saudi Arabia, McDonald's modifies its marketing mix to adapt to the local culture. For example, the McDonald's in Riyadh is segregated by sex with a separate section for women and children.

CONSUMER BEHAVIOR IN INTERNATIONAL MARKETS

All the influences interact—often in subtle ways

You're a consumer, so you probably have very good intuition about the many influences on consumer behavior that we've been discussing. For many different purchase situations you also know from experience which variables are most important. That's good, but it's also a potential trap—especially when developing marketing mixes for consumers in international markets. The less a marketing manager knows about the *specific* social and intrapersonal variables that shape the behavior of target customers, the more likely it is that relying on intuition or personal experience will be misleading. We all have a tendency to try to explain things we don't understand by generalizing from what we do know. Yet when it comes to consumer behavior, many of the specifics do not generalize from one culture to another.

Cadbury's effort to develop a Japanese market for its Dairy Milk Chocolate candy bar illustrates the point. Cadbury marketing managers conducted marketing research to find out more about candy preferences among Japanese consumers. The consumers said that they didn't like the high milk-fat content of Cadbury's bar. Cadbury's managers, however, reasoned that this reaction must be from lack of opportunity to become accustomed to the candy. After all, in most other countries it's the rich taste of the candy that turns consumers into "chocoholics." When Cadbury introduced the bar in Japan, it was a real flop. Taste preferences in other countries simply didn't generalize to Japan. It also wasn't just a matter of opportunity. The whole diet in Japan is different enough that eating the candy was unpleasant. By contrast, Dannon was successful because it took similar research findings to heart and dramatically modified its yogurt dairy desserts until they satisfied Japanese tastes.[31]

Sometimes an understanding of local cultural influences points to new ways to blend the four Ps. For example, Nestlé knew that free samples would be a good way to kick start the adoption process when it wanted to introduce a new line of food flavorings in Brazil. In the United States, it's common to distribute samples at stores. But local Nestlé managers knew a more effective approach. In Brazil, cooks rely on stoves that run on gas rather than electricity, so local deliverymen regularly bring canisters of gas into consumers' kitchens. Nestlé paid the deliverymen to offer their customers samples of the flavorings and explain how to use them. Consumers showed more interest in the samples when they were offered by someone they knew and trusted—and the conversation usually took place right by the stove where the flavorings would be used.[32]

Watch out for stereotypes, and change

Consumers in a foreign culture may be bound by some similar cultural forces, but that doesn't mean that they are all the same. So it's important to watch out for oversimplifying stereotypes. Further, changes in the underlying social forces may make outdated views irrelevant.

Many Westerners believe that the typical Japanese executive works very long hours and devotes very little time to family life. That stereotype has been highlighted in the Western media. It's still partly true. Yet many young Japanese executives now want a more balanced family life; they don't want to continue the almost total dedication to business accepted by the previous generation. A marketer who didn't recognize this change probably wouldn't fully understand these people, their needs, or buying behavior in their families.

Developing a marketing mix that really satisfies the needs of a target market takes a real understanding of consumer behavior and the varied forces that shape it. That holds whether the target market is local or half way around the world. So when planning strategies for international markets, it's best to involve locals who have a better chance of understanding the experience, attitudes, and interests of your customers. Many companies, even very sophisticated ones, have faltered because they failed to heed that simple advice.

CONCLUSION

In this chapter, we analyzed the individual consumer as a problem solver who is influenced by psychological variables, social influences, and the purchase situation. All of these variables are related, and our model of buyer behavior helps integrate them into one process. Marketing strategy planning requires a good grasp of this material.

Assuming that everyone behaves the way you do—or even like your family or friends do—can lead to expensive marketing errors.

Consumer buying behavior results from the consumer's efforts to satisfy needs and wants. We discussed some reasons why consumers buy and saw that consumer behavior can't be fully explained by only a list of needs.

We also saw that most societies are divided into social classes, a fact that helps explain some consumer

behavior. And we discussed the impact of reference groups and opinion leaders.

We presented a buyer behavior model to help you interpret and integrate the present findings—as well as any new data you might get from marketing research. As of now, the behavioral sciences can only offer insights and theories, which the marketing manager must blend with intuition and judgment to develop marketing strategies.

Companies may have to use marketing research to answer specific questions. But if a firm has neither the money nor the time for research, then marketing managers have to rely on available descriptions of present behavior and guesstimates about future behavior. Popular magazines and TV shows often reflect the public's shifting attitudes. And many studies of the changing consumer are published regularly in the business and trade press. That material—coupled with the information in this book—will help your marketing strategy planning.

Remember that consumers—with all their needs and attitudes—may be elusive, but they aren't invisible.

Research has provided more data and understanding of consumer behavior than business managers generally use. Applying this information may help you find your breakthrough opportunity.

KEY TERMS

economic buyers, 151
economic needs, 151
needs, 152
wants, 152
drive, 152
physiological needs, 154
safety needs, 154
social needs, 154
personal needs, 154
perception, 155
selective exposure, 155

selective perception, 155
selective retention, 155
learning, 156
cues, 156
response, 156
reinforcement, 156
attitude, 157
belief, 157
expectation, 159
psychographics, 160
lifestyle analysis, 160

social class, 162
reference group, 163
opinion leader, 163
culture, 164
consideration set, 168
extensive problem solving, 169
limited problem solving, 169
routinized response behavior, 169
low-involvement purchases, 169
adoption process, 169
dissonance, 171

QUESTIONS AND PROBLEMS

1. In your own words, explain economic needs and how they relate to the economic-buyer model of consumer behavior. Give an example of a purchase you recently made that is consistent with the economic-buyer model. Give another that is not explained by the economic-buyer model. Explain your thinking.

2. Explain what is meant by a hierarchy of needs and provide examples of one or more products that enable you to satisfy each of the four levels of need.

3. Cut out or photocopy two recent advertisements: one full-page color ad from a magazine and one large display from a newspaper. In each case, indicate which needs the ads are appealing to.

4. Explain how an understanding of consumers' learning processes might affect marketing strategy planning. Give an example.

5. Briefly describe your own *beliefs* about the potential value of wearing automobile seat belts, your *attitude* toward seat belts, and your *intention* about using a seat belt the next time you're in a car.

6. Give an example of a recent purchase experience in which you were dissatisfied because a firm's marketing mix did not meet your expectations. Indicate how the purchase fell short of your expectations—and

also explain whether your expectations were formed based on the firm's promotion or on something else.

7. Explain psychographics and lifestyle analysis. Explain how they might be useful for planning marketing strategies to reach college students, as opposed to average consumers.

8. A supermarket chain is planning to open a number of new stores to appeal to Hispanics in southern California. Give some examples that indicate how the four Ps might be adjusted to appeal to the Hispanic subculture.

9. How should social class influences affect the planning of a new restaurant in a large city? How might the four Ps be adjusted?

10. Illustrate how the reference group concept may apply in practice by explaining how you personally are influenced by some reference group for some product. What are the implications of such behavior for marketing managers?

11. Give two examples of recent purchases where the specific purchase situation influenced your purchase decision. Briefly explain how your decision was affected.

12. Give an example of a recent purchase in which you used extensive problem solving. What sources of information did you use in making the decision?

13. On the basis of the data and analysis presented in Chapters 5 and 6, what kind of buying behavior would you expect to find for the following products: *(a)* a haircut, *(b)* a shampoo, *(c)* a digital camera, *(d)* a tennis racket, *(e)* a dress belt, *(f)* a cell phone, *(g)* life insurance, *(h)* an ice cream cone, and *(i)* a new checking account? Set up a chart for your answer with products along the left-hand margin as the row headings and the following factors as headings for the columns: *(a)* how consumers would shop for these products, *(b)* how far they would travel to buy the product, *(c)* whether they would buy by brand, *(d)* whether they would compare with other products, and *(e)* any other factors they should consider. Insert short answers—words or phrases are satisfactory—in the various boxes. Be prepared to discuss how the answers you put in the chart would affect each product's marketing mix.

14. Review the Go-Gurt case that introduces this chapter, and identify the key terms (that appear in red) from the text of the chapter that you think are illustrated in the case. Write down each key term you identify and briefly explain how it is illustrated.

SUGGESTED CASES

1. McDonald's "Seniors" Restaurant
3. Pillsbury's Häagen-Dazs

9. SleepEasy Motel
11. Joggers Universe

COMPUTER-AIDED PROBLEM

6. Selective Processes

RESOURCE REMINDER

Submag, Inc., uses direct-mail promotion to sell magazine subscriptions. Magazine publishers pay Submag $3.12 for each new subscription. Submag's costs include the expenses of printing, addressing, and mailing each direct-mail advertisement plus the cost of using a mailing list. There are many suppliers of mailing lists, and the cost and quality of different lists vary.

Submag's marketing manager, Shandra Debose, is trying to choose between two possible mailing lists. One list has been generated from phone directories. It is less expensive than the other list, but the supplier acknowledges that about 10 percent of the names are out-of-date (addresses where people have moved away.) A competing supplier offers a list of active members of professional associations. This list costs 4 cents per name more than the phone list, but only 8 percent of the addresses are out-of-date.

In addition to concerns about out-of-date names, not every consumer who receives a mailing buys a subscription. For example, *selective exposure* is a problem. Some target customers never see the offer—they just toss out junk mail without even opening the envelope. Industry studies show that this wastes about 10 percent of each mailing—although the precise percentage varies from one mailing list to another.

Selective perception influences some consumers who do open the mailing. Some are simply not interested. Others don't want to deal with a subscription service. Although the price is good, these consumers worry that they'll never get the magazines. Submag's previous experience is that selective perception causes more than half of those who read the offer to reject it.

Of those who perceive the message as intended, many are interested. But *selective retention* can be a problem. Some people set the information aside and then forget to send in the subscription order.

Submag can mail about 25,000 pieces per week. Shandra Debose has set up a spreadsheet to help her study effects of the various relationships discussed above and to choose between the two mailing lists.

a. If you were Debose, which of the two lists would you buy based on the initial spreadsheet? Why?

b. For the most profitable list, what is the minimum number of items that Submag will have to mail to earn a profit of at least $3,500?

c. For an additional cost of $.01 per mailing, Submag can include a reply card that will reduce the percent of consumers who forget to send in an order (Percent Lost—Selective Retention) to 45 percent. If Submag mails 25,000 items, is it worth the additional cost to include the reply card? Explain your logic.

For additional questions related to this problem, see Exercise 6-3 in the *Learning Aid for Use with Basic Marketing*, 15th edition.

1. Know who the business and organizational customers are.

2. See why multiple influence is common in business and organizational purchase decisions.

3. Understand the problem-solving behavior of organizational buyers.

4. Understand the different types of buyer–seller relationships and their benefits and limitations.

5. Know the basic e-commerce methods used in organizational buying.

6. Know about the number and distribution of manufacturers and why they are an important customer group.

7. Know how buying by service firms, retailers, wholesalers, and governments is similar to—and different from—buying by manufacturers.

8. Understand the important new terms (shown in red).

CHAPTER SEVEN

Business and Organizational Customers and Their Buying Behavior

METOKOTE CORP. SPECIALIZES IN PROTECTIVE COATING APPLICATIONS, LIKE POWDER-COAT AND LIQUID PAINT, THAT OTHER MANUFACTURERS NEED FOR THE PARTS AND EQUIPMENT THEY MAKE. FOR EXAMPLE, WHEN YOU SEE JOHN DEERE AGRICULTURAL, CONSTRUCTION, OR LAWN AND GROUNDS-CARE

equipment, many of the components have likely been coated (painted) in a MetoKote facility. In fact, Deere & Company and MetoKote have a close buyer–seller relationship. While Deere uses a variety of methods to identify suppliers and get competitive bids for many items it needs, it's different with MetoKote. Deere isn't going to switch to some other supplier just because other options provide cheaper coatings. MetoKote not only provides protective coatings for many John Deere products, it has built facilities right next to some Deere plants. When it's time for a component to be coated, a conveyer belt moves the part out of the John Deere plant and into the MetoKote facility. A short time later it's back—and it's green or yellow.

Deere favors this type of arrangement. It lets MetoKote's experts keep up with all of the environmental regulations and new technologies for coatings.

For a manufacturer, this type of relationship allows its facilities to be smaller and less costly to build and maintain, as the space isn't required for large spray booths. With MetoKote's facilities located nearby, newly-coated parts for Deere do not have to be shipped, resulting in fewer scratches and dents—

which results in higher quality parts with less rework required.

The decision to purchase coating services this way wasn't made casually. And it takes ongoing cooperation and good communication by many people in both organizations to make the relationship work. The decision additionally indicates that the choice of vendor rests on a variety of operational responsibilities within an organization—not exclusively with the purchasing department, but with finance, quality control, and in some cases even the production employees themselves.

John Deere needs high-quality protective finishes because its customers want durable, long-lasting equipment. Like John Deere, they want good value. Upholding Deere & Company's long reputation for quality service is equally as important as the company's reputation for a quality product.

For example, if a huge commercial farm in Brazil needs a repair part, workers can contact the local John Deere dealer or at any hour, visit the company's website (www.johndeere.com) to access JDParts.com (www.jdparts.com), the online service that allows

customers to learn which dealers have a needed part in inventory, check the price, and place an order for fast delivery. But helping John Deere customers and dealers earn better profits doesn't stop there.

For example, some John Deere farm equipment now includes a global positioning device that tracks exactly where the equipment goes when it is plowing, seeding, or cutting. The company's GreenStar™ system, which can easily be moved from machine to machine, uses advanced technology to measure average farm and field yields, and facilitate documentation of tillage practices, planting, spraying, weather, and more. These Deere innovations can help a farmer make better management decisions, increase productivity, and provide better value to the entire operation. Of course, a farmer who wants to buy a new tractor with global positioning may want a Deere dealer to take used equipment in trade. To help its dealers sell trade-ins, Deere launched Used Xpress™, a website that tracks used equipment its dealers have for sale. If a customer wants a used machine that the local dealer doesn't have, the local dealer can quickly find it at another Deere dealer. And dealers who are not worrying about getting rid of used inventory can focus more on sales of new equipment. Customers can also access several other online resources to find used John Deere equipment across all of its divisions. It is benefits like these that make Deere the supplier of choice for many business customers.[1]

BUSINESS AND ORGANIZATIONAL CUSTOMERS—A BIG OPPORTUNITY

Most of us think about individual final consumers when we hear the term *customer*. But many marketing managers aim at customers who are not final consumers. In fact, more purchases are made by businesses and other organizations than by final consumers. As the John Deere case illustrates, the buying behavior of these organizational customers can be very different from the buying behavior of final consumers. Developing marketing strategies for these markets requires a solid understanding of who these customers are and how they buy. That is the focus of this chapter.

What types of customers are involved?

Business and organizational customers are any buyers who buy for resale or to produce other goods and services. Exhibit 7-1 shows the different types of customers in these markets. As you can see, not all of the organizational customers in these markets are business firms. Even so, to distinguish them from the final consumer market, managers sometimes refer to them collectively as the "business-to-business" market, or simply the *B2B market*.

Many characteristics of buying behavior are common across these varied types of organizations. That's why the different kinds of organizational customers are sometimes loosely called "business buyers," "intermediate buyers," or "industrial buyers." As we discuss organizational buying, we will intermix examples of buying by many different types of organizations. Later in the chapter, however, we will highlight some of the specific characteristics of the different customer groups.

Exhibit 7-1
Examples of Different Types
of Business and
Organizational Customers

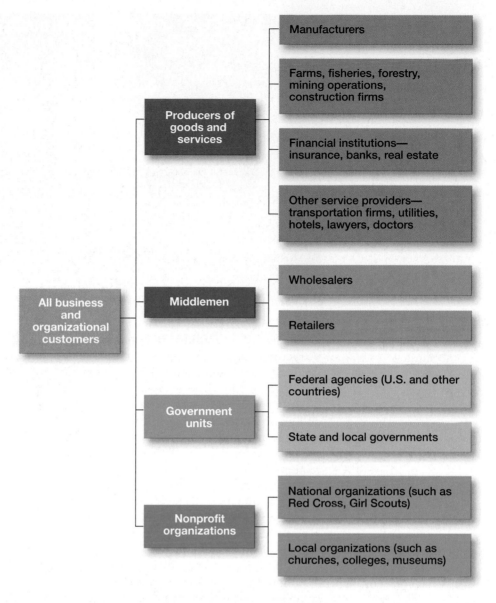

ORGANIZATIONAL CUSTOMERS ARE DIFFERENT

Organizations buy for a basic purpose

Like final consumers, organizations make purchases to satisfy needs. But it's often easier to understand an organization's needs because most organizations make purchases for the same basic reason. They buy goods and services that will help them meet the demand for the goods and services that they in turn supply to their markets. In other words, their basic need is to satisfy their own customers and clients. A producer buys because it wants to earn a profit by making and selling goods or services. A wholesaler or retailer buys products it can profitably resell to its customers. A town government wants to meet its legal and social obligations to citizens. Similarly, a country club wants to help its members enjoy their leisure time.

Basic purchasing needs are economic

Organizational buyers are usually less emotional in their buying than final consumers. They typically focus on economic factors when they make purchase decisions.

When the yield is there at the end, odds are Lorsban was there in the beginning.

Buyers try to consider the total cost of selecting a supplier and its particular marketing mix, not just the initial price of the product. For example, a hospital that needs a new type of digital X-ray equipment might look at both the original cost and ongoing costs, how it would affect doctor productivity, and of course the quality of the images it produces. The hospital might also consider the seller's reliability and general cooperativeness; the ability to provide speedy maintenance and repair, steady supply under all conditions, and reliable and fast delivery; and any past and present relationships (including previous favors and cooperation in meeting special requests).

The matter of dependability deserves further emphasis. An organization may not be able to function if purchases don't arrive when they're expected. For example, there's nothing worse to a manufacturer than shutting down a production line because sellers haven't delivered the goods. Dependable product quality is important too. For example, a bug in e-commerce software purchased by a firm might cause the firm's online order system to shut down. The costs of finding and correcting the problem—to say nothing about the cost of the lost business—could be completely out of proportion to the original cost of the software.

Even small differences are important

Understanding how the buying behavior of a particular organization differs from others can be very important. Even seemingly trivial differences in buying behavior may be important because success often hinges on fine-tuning the marketing mix.

Sellers often approach each organizational customer directly, usually through a sales representative. This gives the seller more chance to adjust the marketing mix for each individual customer. A seller may even develop a unique strategy for each individual customer. This approach carries target marketing to its extreme. But sellers often need unique strategies to compete for large-volume purchases.

In such situations, the individual sales rep takes much responsibility for strategy planning. The sales rep often coordinates the whole relationship between the supplier and the customer. That may involve working with many people—including top management—in both firms. This is relevant to your career planning since these interesting jobs are very challenging, and they pay well too.

Serving customers in international markets

Many marketers discover that there are good opportunities to serve business customers in different countries around the world. Specific business customs do vary from one country to another—and the differences can be important. For

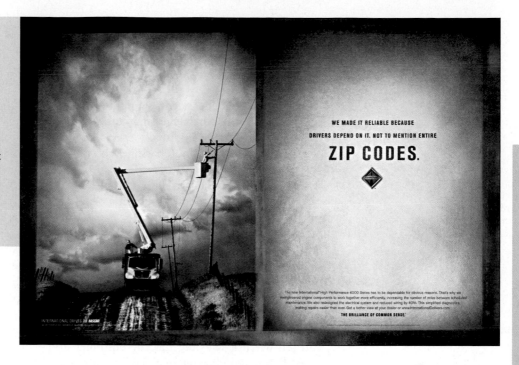

example, a salesperson working in Japan must know how to handle a customer's business card with respect. Japanese consider it rude to write notes on the back of a card or put it in a wallet while the person who presented it is still in the room. But the basic approaches marketers use to deal with business customers in different parts of the world are much less varied than those required to reach individual consumers.

This is probably why the shift to a global economy has been so rapid for many firms. Their business customers in different countries buy in similar ways and can be reached with similar marketing mixes. Moreover, business customers are often willing to work with a distant supplier who has developed a superior marketing mix.

Specifications describe the need

Organizational buyers often buy on the basis of a set of **purchasing specifications**— a written (or electronic) description of what the firm wants to buy. When quality is highly standardized, as is often the case with manufactured items, the specification may simply consist of a brand name or part number. With products like agricultural commodities, where there is more variation, the specification may include information about the grade of the product. Often, however, the purchase requirements are more complicated; then the specifications may set out detailed information about the performance standards the product must meet. Purchase specifications for services tend to be detailed because services are less standardized and usually are not performed until after they're purchased.

Customers may expect quality certification

Organizational customers considering a new supplier or one from overseas may be concerned about product quality. However, this is becoming less of an obstacle because of ISO 9000. **ISO 9000** is a way for a supplier to document its quality procedures according to internationally recognized standards.

ISO 9000 assures a customer that the supplier has effective quality checks in place, without the customer having to conduct its own costly and time consuming audit. Some customers won't buy from any supplier who doesn't have it. To get ISO 9000 certified, a company basically must prove to outside auditors that it documents in detail how the company operates and who is responsible for quality every step of the way.[2]

MANY DIFFERENT PEOPLE MAY INFLUENCE A DECISION

Purchasing managers are specialists

Many organizations, especially large ones, rely on specialists to ensure that purchases are handled sensibly. These specialists have different titles in different firms (such as procurement officer, supply manager, purchasing agent, or buyer), but basically they are all **purchasing managers**—buying specialists for their employers. In large organizations, they usually specialize by product area and are real experts.

Some people think purchasing is handled by clerks who sit in cubicles and do the paperwork to place orders. That view is out-of-date. Today, most firms look to their procurement departments to help cut costs and provide competitive advantage. In this environment, purchasing people have a lot of clout. And there are good job opportunities in purchasing for capable business graduates.

Salespeople often have to see a purchasing manager first—before they contact any other employee. These buyers hold important positions and take a dim view of sales reps who try to go around them. Rather than being "sold," these buyers want salespeople to provide accurate information that will help them buy wisely. They like information on new goods and services, and tips on potential price changes, supply shortages, and other changes in market conditions. Sometimes all it takes for a sales rep to keep a buyer up-to-date is to send an occasional e-mail. But a buyer can tell when a sales rep has the customer firm's interest at heart.

Although purchasing managers usually coordinate relationships with suppliers, other people may also play important roles in influencing the purchase decision.[3]

Multiple buying influence in a buying center

Multiple buying influence means that several people—perhaps even top management—share in making a purchase decision. Possible buying influences include

1. *Users*—perhaps production line workers or their supervisors.
2. *Influencers*—perhaps engineering or R&D people who help write specifications or supply information for evaluating alternatives.

A person who works on a utility firm's high-power wires needs safe, durable climbing gear. A number of different people may influence the decision about which gear the firm should buy.

3. *Buyers*—the purchasing managers who have the responsibility for working with suppliers and arranging the terms of the sale.
4. *Deciders*—the people in the organization who have the power to select or approve the supplier—often a purchasing manager but perhaps top management for larger purchases.
5. *Gatekeepers*—people who control the flow of information within the organization—perhaps a purchasing manager who shields users or other deciders. Gatekeepers can also include receptionists, secretaries, research assistants, and others who influence the flow of information about potential purchases.

An example shows how the different buying influences work. Suppose Electrolux, the Swedish firm that produces vacuum cleaners, wants to buy a machine to stamp out the various metal parts it needs. An assistant to the purchasing manager does an Internet search to identify possible vendors. However, the list that the assistant (a gatekeeper) prepares for the manager excludes a few vendors on the basis of an initial evaluation of information from their websites. The manager e-mails a description of the problem to vendors on the list. It turns out that each of them is eager to get the business and submits a proposal. Several people (influencers) at Electrolux help to evaluate the vendors' proposals. A finance manager worries about the high cost and suggests leasing the machine. The quality control people want a machine that will do a more accurate job—although it's more expensive. The production manager is interested in speed of operation. The production line workers and their supervisors want the machine that is easiest to use so workers can continue to rotate jobs.

The company president (the decider) asks the purchasing department to assemble all the information but retains the power to select and approve the supplier. The purchasing manager's assistant schedules visits for salespeople. After all these buying influences are considered, one of the purchasing agents for the firm (the buyer) will be responsible for making recommendations and arranging the terms of the sale.

It is helpful to think of a **buying center** as all the people who participate in or influence a purchase. Different people may make up a buying center from one decision to the next. This makes the marketing job difficult.

The salesperson must study each case carefully. Just learning who to talk with may be hard, but thinking about the various roles in the buying center can help. See Exhibit 7–2.

The salesperson may have to talk to every member of the buying center—stressing different topics for each. This not only complicates the promotion job but also lengthens it. Approval of a routine order may take anywhere from a day to several

Exhibit 7-2
Multiple Influence and Roles in the Buying Center

months. On very important purchases—a new computer system, a new building, or major equipment—the selling period may take a year or more.[4]

Vendor analysis considers all of the influences

Considering all of the economic factors and influences relevant to a purchase decision is sometimes complex. A supplier or product that is best in one way may not be best in others. To try to deal with these situations, many firms use **vendor analysis**—a formal rating of suppliers on all relevant areas of performance. The purpose isn't just to get a low price from the supplier on a given part or service. Rather, the goal is to lower the *total costs* associated with purchases. Analysis might show that the best vendor is the one that helps the customer reduce costs of excess inventory, retooling of equipment, or defective parts.[5]

Behavioral needs are relevant too

Vendor analysis tries to focus on economic factors, but purchasing in organizations may also involve many of the same behavioral dimensions we discussed in Chapter 6. Purchasing managers and others involved in buying decisions are human, and they want friendly relationships with suppliers.

The purchasing people in some firms are eager to imitate progressive competitors or even to be the first to try new products. Such "innovators" deserve special attention when new products are being introduced.

The different people involved in purchase decisions are also human with respect to protecting their own interests and their own position in the company. That's one reason people from different departments may have different priorities in trying to influence what is purchased. Similarly, purchasing managers may want to avoid taking risks that might reflect badly on their decisions. They have to buy a wide variety of products and make decisions involving many factors beyond their control. If

A seller's marketing mix may need to consider both the needs of the customer company as well as the needs of individuals who influence the purchase decision.

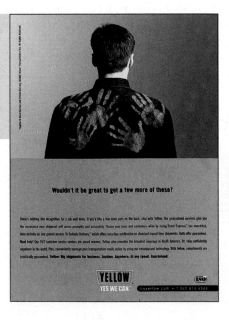

Exhibit 7-3
Overlapping Needs of
Individual Influencers and
the Customer Organization

Risk
Job security
Comfort
Individual's needs
Career advancement
Money / Rewards
Other needs

Overlap in needs

Innovation
Survival
Customer satisfaction
Company's needs
Growth
Profit
Other needs

a new source delivers late or quality is poor, you can guess who will be blamed. Marketers who can help the buyer avoid risk have a definite appeal. In fact, this may make the difference between a successful and unsuccessful marketing mix.

A seller's marketing mix should satisfy *both* the needs of the customer company as well as the needs of individuals who influence the purchase. Therefore, sellers need to find an overlapping area where both can be satisfied. See Exhibit 7-3 for a summary of this idea.

Ethical conflicts may arise

Although organizational buyers are influenced by their own needs, most are serious professionals who are careful to avoid a conflict between their own self-interest and company outcomes. Marketers must be careful here. A salesperson who offers one of his company pens to a prospect may view the giveaway as part of the promotion effort—but the customer firm may have a policy against any employee accepting *any* gift from a supplier. For example, General Motors developed an ethics policy that forbids employees from accepting anything of value from a vendor. It specifically includes entertainment—like a golf outing, a steak dinner, or tickets to a sporting event.

Most organizational buyers do their work ethically and expect marketers to do the same. Yet there have been highly publicized abuses. For example, some members of the site selection committee for the 2000 Olympic Games asked for personal gifts that may have influenced where the games were held. In another case, the telephone company that serves New York found out that some of its buyers were giving contracts to suppliers who offered them vacation trips and other personal favors. Abuses of this sort have prompted many organizations to set up policies that prohibit a buyer or other employees from accepting anything from a potential supplier.

Marketers need to take concerns about conflict of interest very seriously. Part of the promotion job is to persuade different individuals who may influence an organization's purchase. Yet the whole marketing effort may be tainted if it even *appears* that a marketer has encouraged a person who influences a decision to put personal gain ahead of company interest.[6]

Purchasing may be centralized

If a large organization has facilities at many locations, much of the purchasing work may be done at a central location. With centralized buying, a sales rep may be able to sell to facilities all over a country—or even across several countries—without leaving a base city. Wal-Mart handles most of the purchase decisions for stores in its retail chain from its headquarters in Arkansas. Many purchasing decisions for agencies of the U.S. government are handled in Washington, D.C.

Many firms also have centralized controls on who can make purchases. A person who needs to purchase something usually completes a **requisition**—a request to buy

Exhibit 7-4
Organizational Buying
Processes

Characteristics	Type of Process		
	New-Task Buying	Modified Rebuy	Straight Rebuy
Time Required	Much	Medium	Little
Multiple Influence	Much	Some	Little
Review of Suppliers	Much	Some	None
Information Needed	Much	Some	Little

something. This is frequently handled online to cut time and paper shuffling. Even so, there may be delays before a supervisor authorizes the requisition and a purchasing manager can select the "best" seller and turn the authorization into a purchase order. The process may take a few hours for a simple purchase—but it may turn into months for a complex purchase.

ORGANIZATIONAL BUYERS ARE PROBLEM SOLVERS

Three kinds of buying processes are useful

In Chapter 6, we discussed problem solving by consumers and how it might vary from extensive problem solving to routine buying. In organizational markets, we can adapt these concepts slightly and work with three similar buying processes: a new-task buying process, a modified rebuy process, or a straight rebuy.[7] See Exhibit 7-4.

New-task buying occurs when an organization has a new need and the customer wants a great deal of information. New-task buying can involve setting product specifications, evaluating sources of supply, and establishing an order routine that can be followed in the future if results are satisfactory. Multiple buying influence is typical in new-task buying.

A **straight rebuy** is a routine repurchase that may have been made many times before. Buyers probably don't bother looking for new information or new sources of supply. Most of a company's small or recurring purchases are of this type—but they take only a small part of an organized buyer's time. Important purchases may be made this way too—but only after the firm has decided what procedure will be "routine."

The **modified rebuy** is the in-between process where some review of the buying situation is done—though not as much as in new-task buying. Sometimes a competitor will get lazy enjoying a straight rebuy situation. An alert marketer can turn these situations into opportunities by providing more information or a better marketing mix.

New-task buying requires information

Customers in a new-task buying situation are likely to seek information from a variety of sources. See Exhibit 7-5. Keep in mind that many of the impersonal sources are readily available in electronic form online as well as in other formats. How much information a customer collects depends on the importance of the purchase and the level of uncertainty about what choice might be best. The time and expense of searching for information may not be justified for a minor purchase. But a major purchase often involves real detective work by the buyer.

Of course, the flip side of the new-task buying situation is that a seller's promotion has much more chance to have an impact. At the very least, the marketer

Exhibit 7-5
Major Sources of
Information Used by
Organizational Buyers

	Marketing sources	Nonmarketing sources
Personal sources	• Salespeople • Others from supplier firms • Trade shows	• Buying center members • Outside business associates • Consultants and outside experts
Impersonal sources	• Advertising in trade publications • Sales literature • Sales catalogs • Web page	• Rating services • Trade associations • News publications • Product directories • Internet news pointcasts

needs to be certain that his or her firm will turn up in the buyer's search. In this regard, a good website is a crucial piece of insurance. Later we will talk more about the role of e-commerce at this stage, but for now you should see that even a simple website is likely to turn up in a buyer's Internet search.[8]

What buying procedure becomes routine is critical

Once a buying firm gets beyond the early stages of a new-task buying decision, it needs to make important decisions about how it is going to deal with one or more suppliers to meet its needs. At one extreme, a buyer might want to rely on competition among all available vendors to get the best price on each and every order it places. At the other extreme, it might just routinely buy from one vendor with whom it already has a good relationship. In practice, there are many important and common variations between these extremes. To better understand the variations—and why firms rely on different approaches in different situations—let's take a closer look at the benefits and limitations of different types of buyer–seller relationships. That will also help you to see why new e-commerce developments in business markets have become so important.

BUYER–SELLER RELATIONSHIPS IN BUSINESS MARKETS

Close relationships may produce mutual benefits

There are often significant benefits of a close working relationship between a supplier and a customer firm. And such relationships are becoming common. Many firms are reducing the number of suppliers with whom they work—expecting more in return from the suppliers that remain. The best relationships involve real partnerships where there's mutual trust and a long-term outlook.

Closely tied firms can often share tasks at lower total cost than would be possible working at arm's length. Costs are sometimes reduced simply by reducing uncertainty and risk. A supplier is often able to reduce its selling price if a customer commits to larger orders or orders over a longer period of time. A large sales volume may produce economies of scale and reduce selling costs. The customer benefits from lower cost and also is assured a dependable source of supply.

A firm that works closely with a supplier can resolve joint problems. For example, it may cost both the supplier and the customer more to resolve the problems of a defective product after it is delivered than it would have cost to prevent the problem. But without the customer's help it may be impossible for the supplier to identify a solution to the problem. As the head of purchasing at Motorola puts it, "Every time we make an error it takes people at both ends to correct it."

The partnership between AlliedSignal and Betz Laboratories shows the benefits of a good relationship. A while back, Betz was just one of several suppliers that sold Allied chemicals to keep the water in its plants from gunking up pipes and rusting machinery. But Betz didn't stop at selling commodity powders. Teams of Betz experts and Allied engineers studied each plant to find places where water was being wasted.

In less than a year a team in one plant found $2.5 million in potential cost reductions. For example, by adding a few valves to recycle the water in a cooling tower, Betz was able to save 300 gallons of water a minute, which resulted in savings of over $100,000 a year and reduced environmental impact. Because of ideas like this, Allied's overall use of water treatment chemicals decreased. However, Betz sales to Allied doubled because it became Allied's sole supplier.[9]

Relationships may not make sense

Although close relationships can produce benefits, they are not always best. A long-term commitment to a partner may reduce flexibility. When competition drives down prices and spurs innovation, the customer may be better off letting suppliers compete for the business. It may not be worth the customer's investment to build a relationship for purchases that are not particularly important or made that frequently.

It may at first appear that a seller would *always* prefer to have a closer relationship with a customer, but that is not so. Some customers may place orders that are too small or require so much special attention that the relationship would never be profitable for the seller. Also, in situations where a customer doesn't want a relationship, trying to build one may cost more than it's worth. Further, many small suppliers have made the mistake of relying too heavily on relationships with too few customers. One failed relationship may bankrupt the business.[10]

Relationships have many dimensions

Relationships are not "all or nothing" arrangements. Firms may have a close relationship in some ways and not in others. Thus, it's useful to know about five key dimensions that help characterize most buyer–seller relationships: cooperation, information sharing, operational linkages, legal bonds, and relationship-specific adaptations. Purchasing managers for the buying firm and salespeople for the supplier usually coordinate the different dimensions of a relationship. However, as shown in Exhibit 7-6, close relationships often involve direct contacts between a number of people from other areas in both firms.[11]

Cooperation treats problems as joint responsibilities

In cooperative relationships, the buyer and seller work together to achieve both mutual and individual objectives. This doesn't mean that the buyer (or seller) will always do what the other wants. Rather, the two firms treat problems that arise as a joint responsibility.

National Semiconductor (NS) and Siltec, a supplier of silicon wafers, have found clever ways to cooperate and cut costs. For example, workers at the NS plant used

Exhibit 7-6
Key Dimensions of
Relationships in Business
Markets

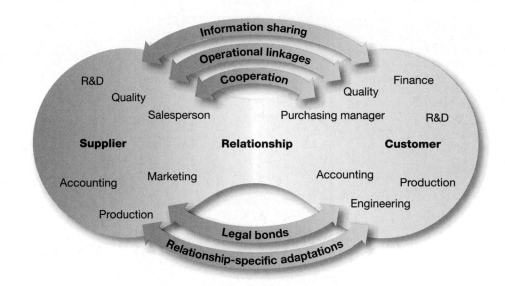

to throw away the expensive plastic cassettes that Siltec uses to ship the silicon wafers. Now Siltec and NS cooperate to recycle the cassettes. This helps the environment and also saves more than $300,000 a year. Siltec passes along most of that to NS as lower prices.[12]

Shared information is useful but may be risky

Some relationships involve open sharing of information that is useful to both the buyer and seller. This might include the exchange of proprietary cost data, discussion of demand forecasts, and joint work on new product designs. Information might be shared through information systems or over the Internet. This is often a key facet of relationships that involve e-commerce.

Many firms share information by providing relationship partners with access to password-protected websites. One big advantage of this approach is that it is fast and easy to update the information. A customer can trust information that is the same information used by someone inside the supplier company. In addition, it provides easy "click-here" self-service access for customers who might have very different computer systems in their own firms. It also saves time. A customer can check detailed product specs or the status of a job on the production line without having to wait for a sales rep or someone else to answer the question.

Information sharing can lead to better decisions, reduced uncertainty about the future, and better planning. However, firms don't want to share information if there's a risk that a partner might misuse it. For example, some suppliers claim that General Motors' former purchasing chief showed blueprints of their secret technology to competing suppliers. Such violations of trust in a relationship are an ethical matter and should be taken seriously. However, as a practical matter, it makes sense to know a partner well before revealing all.

Operational linkages share functions between firms

Operational linkages are direct ties between the internal operations of the buyer and seller firms. These linkages usually involve formal arrangements and ongoing coordination of activities between the firms. Shared activities are especially important when neither firm, working on its own, can perform a function as well as the two firms can working together. John Deere's relationship with MetoKote, described at the start of this chapter, involves operational linkages.

Operational linkages are often required to reduce total inventory costs. Business customers want to maintain an adequate inventory—certainly enough to prevent stock-outs or keep production lines moving. On the other hand, keeping too much inventory is expensive. Providing a customer with inventory when it's needed may require that a supplier be able to provide **just-in-time delivery**—reliably

getting products there *just* before the customer needs them. We'll discuss just-in-time systems in more detail in Chapter 12. For now, it's enough to see that just-in-time relationships between buyers and sellers usually require operational linkages (as well as information sharing). For example, Wal-Mart might want a producer of socks to pack cartons so that when they are unloaded at a Wal-Mart distribution facility all of the cartons for a certain store or district are grouped together. This makes it easier and faster for forklifts to "cross dock" the pallets and load them onto an outbound truck. This also reduces Wal-Mart's costs because the cartons only need to be handled one time. However, it means that the supplier's production and packing of socks in different colors and sizes must be closely linked to the precise store in the Wal-Mart chain that places each order.

Operational linkages may also involve the routine activities of individuals who almost become part of the customer's operations. Design engineers, salespeople, and service representatives may participate in developing solutions to ongoing problems, conduct regular maintenance checks on equipment, or monitor inventory and coordinate orders. Consider the relationship between Johnson Controls, the supplier that makes instrument panels for Jeep's Liberty SUV, and its customer. When the Liberty was still in the planning stages, teams of people from both firms worked together to develop a special system of racks to move the instrument panels from JC's plant to the Jeep production line. Similar equipment was installed at the instrument panel plant and at the receiving dock for Jeep's assembly line. When the instrument panels get to the end of their own assembly line, the equipment automatically rolls them onto the racks in a waiting truck. The truck hauls the panels to the Jeep plant, and they are automatically unloaded, in sequence to match the next Liberty on the production line. [13]

Linkages may be customized to a particular relationship, as in the Jeep example, or they may be standardized and operate the same way across many exchange partners. For example, in the channel of distribution for grocery products many different producers are standardizing their distribution procedures and coordinating with retail chains to make it faster and cheaper to replenish grocery store shelves.

When a customer's operations are dependent on those of a supplier, it may be difficult or expensive to switch to another supplier. So buyers sometimes avoid a relationship that would result in these "switching costs."

Contracts spell out obligations

Many purchases in business markets are simple transactions. The seller's basic responsibility is to transfer title to goods or perform services, and the buyer's basic responsibility is to pay the agreed price. However, in some buyer–seller relationships the responsibilities of the parties are spelled out in a detailed legal contract. An agreement may apply only for a short period, but long-term contracts are also common.

For example, a customer might ask a supplier to guarantee a 6 percent price reduction for a particular part for each of the next three years and pledge to virtually eliminate defects. In return, the customer might offer to double its orders and help the supplier boost productivity. This might sound attractive to the supplier but also require new people or facilities. The supplier may not be willing to make these long-term commitments unless the buyer is willing to sign a contract for promised purchases. The contract might spell out what would happen if deliveries are late or if quality is below specification.

Sometimes the buyer and seller know roughly what is needed but can't fix all the details in advance. For example, specifications or total requirements may change over time. Then the relationship may involve **negotiated contract buying,** which means agreeing to a contract that allows for changes in the purchase arrangements. In such cases, the general project and basic price is described but with provision for changes and price adjustments up or down. Or a supplier may be asked to accept a contract that provides some type of incentive—such as full coverage of costs plus a fixed fee or full costs plus a profit percentage tied to costs.

When a contract provides a formal plan for the future of a relationship, some types of risk are reduced. But a firm may not want to be legally locked in when the future is unclear. Alternatively, some managers figure that even a detailed contract isn't a good substitute for regular, good-faith reviews to make sure that neither party gets hurt by changing business conditions.

Harley-Davidson used this approach when it moved toward closer relationships with a smaller number of suppliers. Purchasing executives tossed out detailed contracts and replaced them with a short statement of principles to guide relationships between Harley and its suppliers. This "operate on a handshake" approach is typical of relationships with Japanese firms. Many other firms have adopted it. It's great when it works, and a disaster when it doesn't.

Specific adaptations invest in the relationship

Relationship-specific adaptations involve changes in a firm's product or procedures that are unique to the needs or capabilities of a relationship partner. Industrial suppliers often custom design a new product for just one customer; this may require investments in R&D or new manufacturing technologies. Donnelly Corp. is an extreme example. It had been supplying Honda with mirrors for the interiors of its cars. Honda's purchasing people liked Donnelly's collaborative style, so they urged Donnelly to supply exterior mirrors as well. Donnelly had never been in that business—so it had to build a factory to get started.

Buying firms may also adapt to a particular supplier; a computer maker may design around Intel's Pentium chip, and independent photo processors say "We use Kodak paper for the good look" in their advertising. However, buyers are often hesitant about making big investments that increase dependence on a specific supplier. Typically, they do it only when there isn't a good alternative—perhaps because only one or a few suppliers are available to meet a need—or if the benefits of the investment are clear before it's made. On the other hand, sometimes a buyer will invest in a relationship because the seller has already demonstrated a willingness to do so.[14]

The relationship between Flex-N-Gate and Toyota illustrates relationship-specific adaptations. Flex-N-Gate had a contract to supply some of the rear bumpers Toyota needed for its U.S. facilities. After a while, however, Toyota's quality control people were unhappy about the number of minor defects in the bumpers. Further, Flex-N-Gate's deliveries were not as dependable as Toyota's production people required. Rather than just end the relationship, Toyota and Flex-N-Gate both made investments to improve it. Toyota sent a team of experts who spent a lot of time figuring out the reasons for the problems and then showing Flex-N-Gate how to build better bumpers faster and cheaper. Following the advice of Toyota's experts, Shahid Khan (Flex-N-Gate's owner) reorganized equipment in his factory. He also had to retrain his employees to do their jobs in new ways. The changes were so complicated that two of Khan's six production supervisors quit in frustration. But the trouble was worth the effort. Productivity went up 60 percent, the number of defects dropped by 80 percent, and Flex-N-Gate got a larger share of Toyota's business. Toyota got something it wanted, too: a committed supplier that could meet its standards and a big price reduction on bumpers.[15]

A seller may have more incentive to propose new ideas that save the customer money when the firms have a mutual investment in a long-term relationship. The customer firm usually rewards the seller with more orders or a larger share of its business, and this encourages future suggestions and loyalty by the supplier. In contrast, buyers who use a competitive bid system exclusively—either by choice or necessity, as in some government and institutional purchasing—may not be offered much beyond basic goods and services. They are interested primarily in price.

Powerful customer may control the relationship

Although a marketing manager may want to work in a cooperative partnership, that may be impossible with large customers who have the power to dictate how the relationship will work. For example, Duall/Wind, a plastics producer, was a supplier of small parts for Polaroid instant cameras. But when Duall/Wind wanted to raise its prices to cover increasing costs, Polaroid balked. Polaroid's purchasing manager demanded that Duall/Wind show a breakdown of all its costs, from materials to labor to profit. As Duall/Wind's president said, "I had a tough time getting through my head that Polaroid wanted to come right in here and have us divulge all that." But Polaroid is a big account—and it got the information it wanted. Polaroid buyers agreed to a price increase only after they were confident that Duall/Wind was doing everything possible to control costs.[16]

Buyers may still use several sources to spread their risk

Even if a marketing manager develops the best marketing mix possible and cultivates a close relationship with the customer, the customer may not give *all* of its business to one supplier. Buyers often look for several dependable sources of supply to protect themselves from unpredictable events such as strikes, fires, or floods in one of their suppliers' plants. A good marketing mix is still likely to win a larger share of the total business—which can prove to be very important. From a buyer's point of view, it may not seem like a big deal to give a particular supplier a 30 percent share of the orders rather than a 20 percent share. But for the seller that's a 50 percent increase in sales![17]

Reciprocity may influence relationship

We've emphasized that most buyer–seller relationships are based on reducing the customer's total procurement costs. However, for completeness we should mention that some relationships are based on reciprocity. **Reciprocity** means trading sales for sales—that is, "if you buy from me, I'll buy from you." If a company's customers also can supply products that the firm buys, then the sales departments of both buyer and seller may try to trade sales for sales. Purchasing managers generally resist reciprocity but often face pressure from their sales departments.

When prices and quality are otherwise competitive, an outside supplier seldom can break a reciprocity relationship. The outside supplier can only hope to become an alternate source of supply and wait for the competitor to let its quality slip or prices rise.

Reciprocity is often a bigger factor in other countries than it is in the United States. In Japan, for example, reciprocity is very common.[18]

We've been discussing some of the differences in how customer firms and their suppliers relate to each other. How a customer uses e-commerce is also related to these differences.

INTERNET E-COMMERCE IS RESHAPING MANY BUSINESS MARKETS

The Internet and new types of B2B e-commerce websites have changed the way that many purchase decisions are made. The Web is making it possible for all types of information to flow back and forth between buyers and sellers much more quickly and efficiently. This lowers the cost of the search for market information and, in many cases, the cost of transactions. For example, online order systems can cut out paper-shuffling bottlenecks, speed the delivery of purchases, and reduce inventory costs. We'll discuss distribution service related issues in more detail in Chapter 12.

Here, we'll consider basic e-commerce website resources that many buyers use and the role that they play. We'll describe them separately, but often one website (or linked set of websites) combines them.

Community sites mainly offer digital information

Like online trade magazines (or online trade associations), community sites offer information and communications of interest for specific industries. A website may focus on a single "community" or feature different sections for different industries. Community sites were among the first on the Web because many just put in digital form information that was already being distributed in other ways. Initially they relied on advertising revenue to operate, but now some of them charge fees or try to earn commissions based on sales referrals.

Catalog sites make it convenient to search for products

Catalog sites, as the name implies, offer digital product catalogs, usually for a number of different sellers. For example, PlasticsNet.com focuses on polymers and resins used in the plastics industry. The basic benefit of catalog sites is that they make it easy for industrial buyers to search for a product and do one-stop shopping. For example, Grainger.com features a vast array of supply items that are used across many different industries. Catalog sites are upgrading their service to make it easier for a buyer to place an order, track delivery status, and update inventory information. Many are improving the quality of the information available. For instance, rather than just give a basic description of an electric motor, a site might also provide a link so the buyer can download detailed engineering drawings and electrical details.

Exchanges bring buyers and sellers together

Exchanges operate much like a stock exchange (for example, the New York Stock Exchange) by bringing buyers and sellers together to agree on prices for commodities such as energy or chemicals (see, for example, www.chemconnect.com). Exchanges are sometimes independent intermediaries or they may be backed by major firms in the industry. Either way, an exchange must maintain a neutral role and not favor either buyers or sellers if it expects return visits.

Procurement hubs operate for the benefit of buyers

Procurement hub sites direct suppliers to particular companies (or divisions of a company) that need to make purchases. In some industries, recognized leaders have banded together to create procurement hubs. The big three automakers in the U.S. are doing this. These hubs make it easier for a larger number of suppliers to find out about the purchasing needs of customers in target industries. As a result, the number of suppliers competing for a buyer's business increases, and this tends to drive down selling prices or provide benefits to the buyer with respect to other terms of the sale. On the other hand, procurement hubs are a way for a seller to find out about and pursue sales opportunities with new customers (or new markets) without a lot of additional research or selling expense.

Interactive competitive bidding systems drive down prices

Most procurement hubs incorporate an interactive system to get competitive bids. **Competitive bids** are the terms of sale offered by different suppliers in response to the purchase specifications posted by the buyer. Usually, the focus is on the supplier's price. Firms have used the competitive bidding process for a long

The Internet is making it fast and easy for customers to communicate their needs to a larger number of suppliers and to use competitively based bid pricing or reverse auctions.

time. However, before the Internet it was usually too slow and too inconvenient to go through several rounds of bids. Now, however, it is fast and easy for a customer firm to run a *reverse auction*. Vendors are invited (via e-mail or at the procurement hub) to place a bid for a purchase with a given specification. Usually the bidding still focuses on price, but sometimes other terms of sale (like warranty period or delivery time) are considered as well. Each bid, and who made it, is typically visible to all potential bidders via the website. That way, other bidders can decide whether or not to offer the customer a lower price. Depending on the preferences of the customer, the bidding can be limited by a specific deadline.

Best Buy, the big retail chain, negotiates with longtime vendors to purchase most of the consumer electronics gear that it sells. Best Buy's customers expect to find the right brands and hot new products at its stores. But when buying operating supplies and services (like construction materials and rebate-fulfillment services), Best Buy uses sites like FreeMarkets (www.freemarkets.com) to solicit competitive bids. In a period of about a year it spent $100 million on purchases this way. But a purchasing manager for Best Buy reported that getting bids online helped Best Buy save over $12 million in the same time period. Further, getting bids the old way took weeks, but now he may get 100 bids in an hour. [19]

Auction sites focus on unique items

Auction sites tend to be more seller-driven and are especially popular for used items, surplus inventory, and perishable products (such as unsold advertising space or produce) that are unique and only available for sale once. For example, www.avbid.new runs auctions related to aircraft parts and services. At these auctions the seller lists and describes what's for sale, and potential buyers place their bids (what they would pay) at a website. Auctions use a variety of formats, but in general the highest bidder (prior to the deadline) purchases the product. Some auction sites also handle reverse auctions for the benefit of buyers. FreeMarkets (www.freemarkets.com) is a popular site that operates this way.

Collaboration hubs support cooperation

Collaboration hubs go beyond matching buyers and sellers for a one-time transaction and instead are designed to help firms work together. The collaboration might involve design, manufacturing, and distribution. Many of these sites focus on the needs of smaller firms, usually within a vertical industry. For instance, Citadon (www.citadon.com) provides a single online workplace for construction contractors to collaborate with architects, store blueprints, work through building permit requirements, and purchase building materials.

Websites within and across industries

As the examples above suggest, some B2B e-commerce websites are specialized for firms at different levels of production and distribution within a particular industry. For example, one of these "vertical" sites that specializes in the plastics industry might be of interest to firms that make the basic chemicals from which plastics are formed, firms that create plastic injection molding equipment, and firms that use that equipment to make finished goods. On the other hand, some websites are designed to serve a broad ("horizontal") cross section of firms from different industries. For example, a horizontal site might serve manufacturers regardless of whether they produce bearings, truck frames, or construction equipment. See Exhibit 7-7.

Exhibit 7-7

Examples of Different B2B E-Commerce Sites Used by Organizational Buyers and Sellers

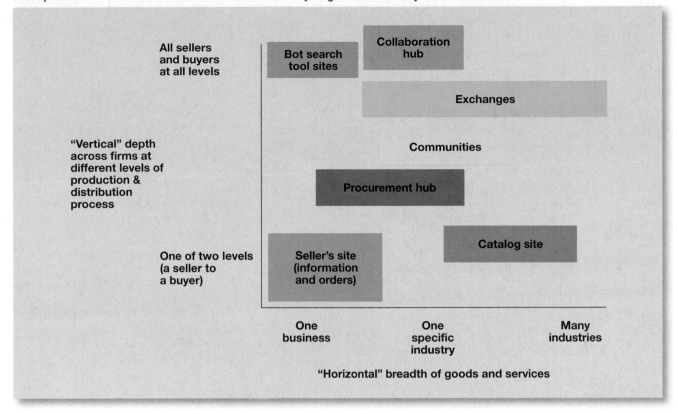

Because of the differences in focus, several sites often compete to be *the* online central market that serves a group of buyers and sellers. This competition is why many B2B websites that were established just a few years ago have already merged or gone out of business. Even so, in some industries there are still several sites that traders might use. Instead of simplifying the exchange process, this can make it more complicated. For example, a seller who posts an auction on the wrong site may get no bids, although serious buyers, in turn, might waste time checking other sites not included in the seller's efforts.

Internet (ro)bots search for products—by description

Purchasing managers often use Internet search engines to find what they need. For example, if a purchasing manager can specify a certain model of a product the search "bot" (short for *robot*) looks for websites where that product is mentioned. Some bots take things further and assemble price comparisons or e-mail distribution lists.

Bots can also help purchasing people figure out exactly how to describe what they want. By searching for descriptions of products in a broad product category, it is often possible to develop a better understanding not only of what alternatives exist but also of what specs are best for the particular need.

Some purchasing managers are using this basic approach to locate hard-to-find, off-the-shelf products that eliminate the need for custom-produced items. For example, Allstates Rubber & Tools in the suburbs of Chicago is a small firm, but it got a $1,000 order for rubber grommets (tiny rings used to protect electric wires) from a company in Saudi Arabia. If the customer had not been able to locate Allstates' website on the Internet it probably would have paid higher prices to have the grommets custom-produced—and Allstates would have missed the business.[20]

Linking Buyers, Products, and Distributors

NATIONAL SEMICONDUCTOR DESIGNED its Web site to serve several key audiences. Purchasers from large customers who buy directly from the company's salespeople have private extranets with tailored information. National's other customers buy through distributors, but they can use National's site to research products and link directly to distributors' sites to buy. National also allows engineers and purchasing agents to look at information in ways that suit their individual needs.

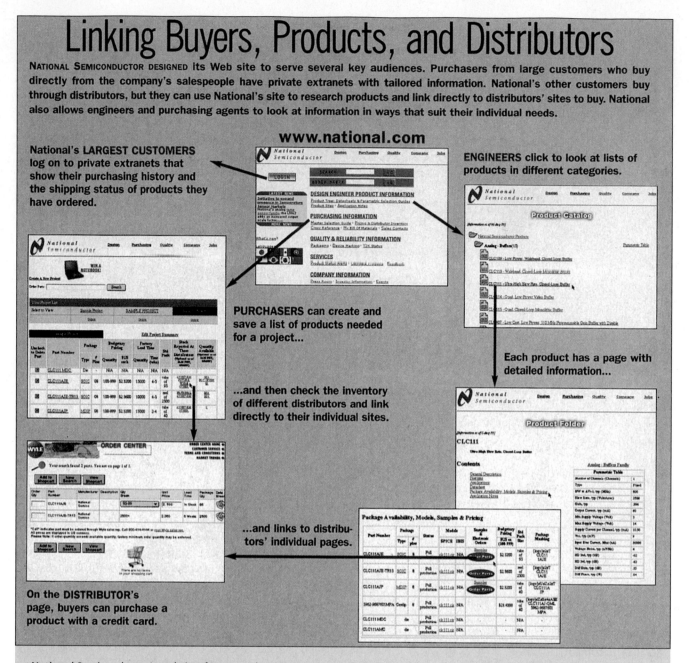

National's LARGEST CUSTOMERS log on to private extranets that show their purchasing history and the shipping status of products they have ordered.

www.national.com

ENGINEERS click to look at lists of products in different categories.

PURCHASERS can create and save a list of products needed for a project...

...and then check the inventory of different distributors and link directly to their individual sites.

Each product has a page with detailed information...

...and links to distributors' individual pages.

On the **DISTRIBUTOR's** page, buyers can purchase a product with a credit card.

National Semiconductor's website, for example, creates easy e-commerce links between its customers, products, and distributors.

More progress is needed

When everything else about a supplier's marketing mix is the same, a buyer would obviously prefer low prices. But "everything else" is not always the same. We considered examples of this earlier when we reviewed why a buyer might prefer closer relationships with fewer sellers. So Internet tools that focus primarily on lowering the purchase price do not necessarily lower total purchasing costs or provide a benefit in all types of purchases.

On the other hand, many firms are developing websites and Internet-based systems that help buyers and sellers work together in more efficient and effective relationships. National Semiconductor's website, for example, creates easy links

GE LIGHTS THE WAY FOR E-COMMERCE

General Electric is a true pioneer in e-commerce—and its successes provide evidence of what is possible. Even so, some of its early efforts didn't work. When it first tried to solicit bids from vendors over the Internet, it only focused on price. So it got a lot of lowball quotes from firms that didn't have the ability to fill orders. By 1995 GE was on a smarter track. It developed an Internet-based system called the Trading Process Network (TPN) that eliminated the delays of traditional purchasing approaches still using paper documents and snail mail. With TPN, a buyer for GE's lighting division could search the Net to find possible suppliers for the custom-made machine tools it needed. To eliminate the paper shuffle, electronic blueprints could be sent with a bid request via e-mail. As a GE purchasing manager put it, they could "simply point and click and send out a bid package to suppliers around the world." Suppliers could respond quickly, too. So a bid process that previously took about a month could be reduced to only days, or even hours.

When GE executives saw how e-commerce was improving their purchasing, they decided to offer the TPN service to outside companies. A small firm could try the TPN Web (www.getradeweb.com) for a fee of only $65 a month. However, the monthly fee for a large company was $70,000. That pricing gives a hint of the kind of savings big purchasers could reap—and why GE's Global eXchange Services (GXS) division pushed to develop a full-service Internet portal. GSX quickly grew to become one of the largest B2B e-commerce networks in the world—linking 100,000 trading partners involved in 1 billion exchanges a year worth $1 trillion in goods and service.

In 2002, GE sold GSX (except for a 10 percent share) for a whopping $800 million and now it operates as an independent e-commerce service provider. But GE has continued to drive down its own purchasing costs with e-commerce. To put this in perspective, in the first six months that GE used real-time, online competitive bidding, GE saved $480 million. However, GE does not purchase everything this way. And even when it relies on online competitive bidding it does not always select the lowest bid. A supplier with a higher bid may get the business when it offers a service or other value that meets GE's needs.[21]

between its customers, products, and distributors. Large customers get special services, like access to a secure website that shows specific purchase histories and production or shipping status of their orders. Smaller customers can get all the product information they need and then link directly to the order page for the distributor that serves them. This system does not go as far as some, but it illustrates how shared information and cooperation over the Internet is helping to create better relationships.[22]

E-commerce order systems are common

We've been discussing ways that managers use the Web. But some e-commerce computer systems *automatically* handle a large portion of routine order-placing. Buyers program decision rules that tell the computer how to order and leave the details of following through to the computer. For example, when an order comes in that requires certain materials or parts, the computer system automatically orders them from the appropriate suppliers, the delivery date is set, and production is scheduled.

If economic conditions change, buyers modify the computer instructions. When nothing unusual happens, however, the computer system continues to routinely rebuy as needs develop—electronically sending purchase orders to the regular supplier.

Obviously, it's a big sale to be selected as the major supplier that routinely receives all of a customer's electronic orders for the products you sell. Often this type of customer will be more impressed by an attractive marketing mix for a whole line of products than just a lower price for a particular order. Further, it may be too expensive and too much trouble to change the whole buying system just because somebody is offering a low price on a particular day.

| It pays to have an ongoing relationship | In this sort of routine order situation, it's very important to be one of the regular sources of supply. For straight rebuys, the buyer (or computer) may place an order without even considering other potential sources. However, if a buyer believes that there are several suppliers who could meet the specs, the buyer may request competitive bids. If different suppliers' quality, dependability, and delivery schedules all meet the specs, the buyer will select the low-price bid. But a creative marketer needs to look carefully at the purchaser's specs—and the need—to see if other elements of the marketing mix could provide a competitive advantage. |

Sellers' sales reps (and perhaps whole teams of people) regularly call on these customers, but *not* to sell a particular item. Rather, they want to maintain relations, become a preferred source, or point out new developments that might cause the buyer to reevaluate the present straight rebuy procedure and give more business to the sales rep's company.

| Variations in buying by customer type | We've been discussing aspects of relationships and e-commerce that generally apply with different types of customer organizations—in both the U.S. and internationally. However, it's also useful to have more detail about specific types of customers. |

MANUFACTURERS ARE IMPORTANT CUSTOMERS

| There are not many big ones | One of the most striking facts about manufacturers is how few there are compared to final consumers. This is true in every country. In the United States, for example, there are about 355,000 factories. Exhibit 7-8 shows that the majority of these are quite small—over half have less than 10 workers. But output from these small firms accounts for less than 3 percent of manufacturing value. In small plants, the owners often do the buying. And they buy less formally than buyers in the relatively few large manufacturing plants—which employ most of the workers and produce a large share of the value added by manufacturing. For example, less than 4 percent of all plants have 250 or more employees, yet they employ nearly half of the production employees and produce about 61 percent of the value added by manufacturers. |

In other countries, the size distribution of manufacturers varies. But across different countries, the same general conclusion holds: Marketers often segment industrial markets on the basis of customer size because large firms do so much of the buying.

| Customers cluster in geographic areas | In addition to concentration by company size, industrial markets are concentrated in certain geographic areas. Internationally, industrial customers are concentrated in countries that are at the more advanced stages of economic development. From all the talk in the news about the U.S. shifting from an industrial economy to a service and information economy you might conclude that the U.S. is an exception—that the industrial market in this country is shrinking. But that's a myth. The U.S. is still the world's leading industrial economy. What's more, manufacturing output is higher than at any other time in the nation's history. So in a global sense, there is a high concentration of manufacturers in the U.S. |

Within a country, there is often further concentration in specific areas. In the U.S., many factories are concentrated in big metropolitan areas—especially in New York, Pennsylvania, Ohio, Illinois, Texas, and California.[23]

Exhibit 7-8
Size Distribution of Manufacturing Establishments

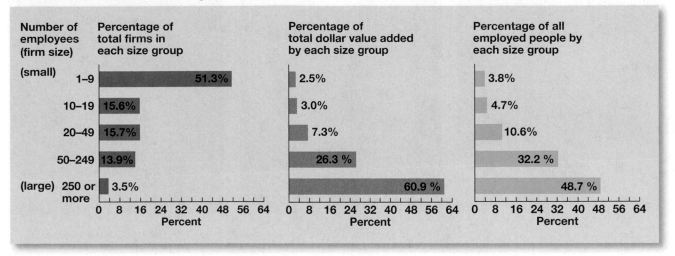

There is also concentration by industry. In Germany, for example, the steel industry is concentrated in the Ruhr Valley. Similarly, U.S. manufacturers of high-tech electronics are concentrated in California's famous Silicon Valley near San Francisco and also along Boston's Route 128.

Business data often classifies industries

The products an industrial customer needs to buy depend on the business it is in. Because of this, sales of a product are often concentrated among customers in similar businesses. For example, apparel manufacturers are the main customers for zippers. Marketing managers who can relate their own sales to their customers' type of business can focus their efforts.

Detailed information is often available to help a marketing manager learn more about customers in different lines of business. The U.S. government collects and publishes data by the **North American Industry Classification System (NAICS) codes**—groups of firms in similar lines of business. (NAICS is pronounced like "nakes.") The number of establishments, sales volumes, and number of employees—broken down by geographic areas—are given for each NAICS code. A number of other countries collect similar data, and some of them try to coordinate their efforts with an international variation of the NAICS system. However, in many countries data on business customers is incomplete or inaccurate.

The NAICS is a recent development. The U.S. adopted it as a standard in 1997. However, it is being phased in over time. The phase-in makes it easier to use the system because in the past data were reported using Standard Industrial Classification (SIC) codes. Many of the codes are similar; check the website at www.naics.com for details. However, the move to the new system is helping business marketers. The NAICS system is suited for identifying new or fast-changing industries—and for marketers that spells opportunity. NAICS is also more detailed than SIC and works better for services such as financial institutions, health care providers, and firms in the entertainment business. The general logic of NAICS and SIC is similar. So let's take a closer look at how the NAICS codes work.

The NAICS code breakdowns start with broad industry categories such as construction (23), manufacturing (31), wholesale trade (42), finance and insurance (52), and so on. Within each two-digit industry breakdown, much more detailed data may be available for three-digit industries (that is, subindustries of

A firm like Alcoa Aluminum is likely to find that the majority of its customers are concentrated within a few industries that it can identify by North American Industry Classification System code number.

the two-digit industries). For example, within the two-digit manufacturing industry (code 31) there are manufacturers of food (311), beverages and tobacco (312), and others, including apparel manufacturers (315). Then each three-digit group of firms is further subdivided into more detailed four-, five-, and six-digit classifications. For instance, within the three-digit (315) apparel manufacturers there are four-digit subgroups for knitting mills (3151), cut and sew firms (3152), and producers of apparel accessories (3159). Exhibit 7-9 illustrates that breakdowns are more detailed as you move to codes with more digits. However, detailed data (say, broken down at the four-digit level) isn't available for all industries in every geographic area. The government does not provide detail when only one or two plants are located in an area.

INTERNET EXERCISE

Comprehensive information about NAICS codes is available online (www.naics.com). At the website select "NAICS Code Search" and when the search page appears submit a query for the keyword "welding." If your firm was interested in selling its lasers to manufacturers of laser welding equipment, what is the NAICS code of the industry for which you would want to get a list of manufacturers?

Many firms find their *current* customers' NAICS codes and then look at NAICS-coded lists for similar companies that may need the same goods and services. Other companies look at which NAICS categories are growing or declining to discover new opportunities.

If companies aiming at business target markets in the United States know exactly who they are aiming at, readily available data organized by NAICS codes can be valuable. Most trade associations and private organizations that gather data on business markets also use these codes.

The NAICS codes are an improvement over the old approach, but they are not perfect. Some companies have sales in several categories but are listed in only one—the code with the largest sales. In addition, some businesses don't fit any of the categories very well. So although a lot of good information is available, the codes must be used carefully.[24]

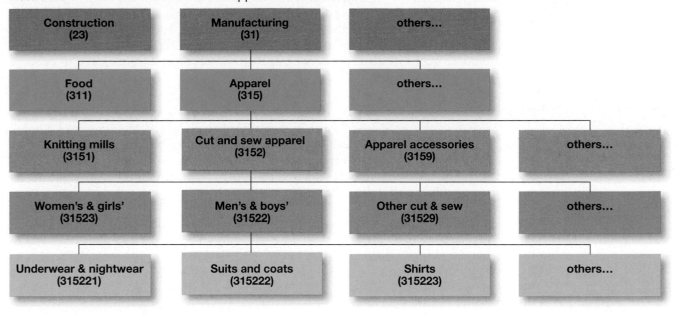

PRODUCERS OF SERVICES—SMALLER AND MORE SPREAD OUT

The service side of the U.S. economy is large and has been growing fast. Service operations are also growing in some other countries. There are many good opportunities to provide these service companies with the products they need to support their operations. But there are also challenges.

The United States has about 2.5 million service firms—over six times as many as it has manufacturers. Some of these are big companies with international operations. Examples include AT&T, Hilton Hotels, Prudential Insurance, CitiGroup,

Many firms are developing new strategies to target small businesses, a fast-growing sector of the economy. For example, Hertz offers double Frequent Flyer Miles and a free year of Club Gold membership to small businesses. Kinko's, FedEx, and American Express work together to provide customers who pay with an American Express Business Card a 10 percent discount on Kinko's purchases and on shipments made from FedEx Express drop boxes located at most Kinko's locations.

and EDS (Electronic Data Systems). These firms have purchasing departments that are like those in large manufacturing organizations. But as you might guess given the large number of service firms, most of them are small. They're also more spread out around the country than manufacturing concerns. Factories often locate where transportation facilities are good, raw materials are available, and it is less costly to produce goods in quantity. Service operations, in contrast, often have to be close to their customers.

Buying may not be as formal

Purchases by small service firms are often handled by whoever is in charge. This may be a doctor, lawyer, owner of a local insurance agency, or manager of a hotel. Suppliers who usually deal with purchasing specialists in large organizations may have trouble adjusting to this market. Personal selling is still an important part of promotion, but reaching these customers in the first place often requires more advertising. And small service firms may need much more help in buying than a large corporation.

Canon, the familiar name in office copiers, was very successful serving the needs of smaller service firms like law offices. Canon developed promotion materials to help first-time buyers understand differences in copiers. It emphasized that its machines were easy to use and maintain. And Canon also used retail channels to make the copiers available in smaller areas where there wasn't enough business to justify using a sales rep.[25]

RETAILERS AND WHOLESALERS BUY FOR THEIR CUSTOMERS

Most retail and wholesale buyers see themselves as purchasing agents for their target customers—remembering the old saying that "Goods well bought are half sold." Typically, retailers do *not* see themselves as sales agents for particular manufacturers. They buy what they think they can profitably sell. For example, the buying specialist at Walgreens Drugstores who handles products targeted at ethnic consumers is a real expert. He knows what ethnic customers want and won't be persuaded by a sales rep for a manufacturer who can't provide it. Of course, there is a place for collaboration, as when the Walgreens buyer works with people at Soft Sheen Products to develop a new product for the African American target market. That's profitable for both firms.

Similarly, wholesalers buy what they think their retailers can sell. In other words, they focus on the needs and attitudes of *their* target customers. For example, Super Valu—a leading food distributor in the U.S.—calls itself "the retail support company." As a top manager at Super Valu put it, "Our mandate is to try to satisfy our retailer customers with *whatever it takes*."[26]

Committee buying is impersonal

Some buyers—especially those who work for big retail chains—are annoyed by the number of wholesalers' and manufacturers' representatives who call on them. Space in their stores is limited, and they simply are not interested in carrying every product that some salesperson wants them to sell. Consider the problem facing grocery chains. In an average week, 150 to 250 new items are offered to the buying offices of a large chain like Safeway. If the chain accepted all of them, it would add 10,000 new items during a single year! Obviously, these firms need a way to deal with this overload.[27]

Decisions to add or drop lines or change buying policies may be handled by a *buying committee*. The seller still calls on and gives a pitch to a buyer—but the buyer does not have final responsibility. Instead, the buyer prepares forms

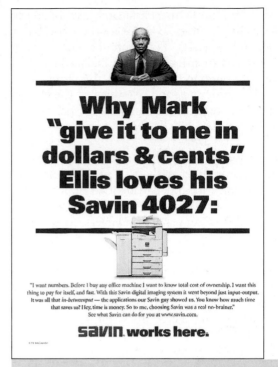

In a smaller service organization, purchases may be made by the person who is in charge rather than a person with full-time responsibility for purchasing. Retailers, on the other hand, often rely on buying specialists who buy what they think the retailer can profitably resell to its customers.

summarizing proposals for new products and passes them on to the committee for evaluation. The seller may not get to present her story to the buying committee in person. This rational, almost cold-blooded approach certainly reduces the impact of a persuasive salesperson. On the other hand, it may favor a firm that has hard data on how its whole marketing mix will help the retailer to attract and keep customers.

Buyers watch computer output closely

Most larger firms now use sophisticated computerized inventory replenishment systems. Scanners at retail checkout counters keep track of what goes out the door—and computers use this data to update the records. Even small retailers and wholesalers use automated control systems that create daily reports showing sales of every product. Buyers with this kind of information know, in detail, the profitability of the different competing products. If a product isn't moving, the retailer isn't likely to be impressed by a salesperson's request for more in-store attention or added shelf space.

Reorders are straight rebuys

Retailers and wholesalers usually carry a large number of products. A drug wholesaler, for example, may carry up to 125,000 products. Because they deal with so many products, most middlemen buy their products on a routine, automatic reorder basis—straight rebuys—once they make the initial decision to stock specific items. Automatic computer ordering is a natural outgrowth of computerized checkout systems. Sellers to these markets must understand the size of the buyer's job and have something useful to say and do when they call.

Some are not "open to buy"

Retail buyers are sometimes controlled by a miniature profit and loss statement for each department or merchandise line. In an effort to make a profit, the buyer tries to forecast sales, merchandise costs, and expenses. The figure for "cost of merchandise" is the amount buyers have budgeted to spend over the budget period. If the money has not yet been spent, buyers are **open to buy**—that is, the buyers have budgeted funds that can be spent during the current period. However, if the budget has been spent, they are no longer in the market and no amount of special promotion or price-cutting is likely to induce them to buy.[28]

Buying and selling are closely related

In wholesale and retail firms, there is usually a very close relationship between buying and selling. Buyers are often in close contact with their firm's salespeople and with customers. The housewares buyer for a local department store, for example, may even supervise the salespeople who sell housewares. Salespeople are quick to tell the buyer if a customer wants a product that is not available—especially if the salespeople work on commission.

Resident buyers may help a firm's buyers

Resident buyers are independent buying agents who work in central markets (New York City, Paris, Rome, Hong Kong, Chicago, Los Angeles) for several retailer or wholesaler customers based in outlying areas or other countries. They buy new styles and fashions and fill-in items as their customers run out of stock during the year.

Resident buying organizations fill a need. They help small channel members (producers and middlemen) reach each other inexpensively. Resident buyers usually are paid an annual fee based on their purchases.

THE GOVERNMENT MARKET

Size and diversity

Some marketers ignore the government market because they think that government red tape is more trouble than it's worth. They probably don't realize how big the government market really is. Government is the largest customer group in many

Government agencies are important customers for a wide variety of products.

I AM A POLICE OFFICER.

I HAVE X-RAY VISION. I HAVE THE POWER TO SEE A BANK ROBBERY FROM ACROSS TOWN. I HAVE THE POWER TO SEE HOW MANY PEOPLE ARE ROBBING THE BANK. I EVEN HAVE THE POWER TO SEE WHICH ONE IS WEARING THE SKI MASK. I AM MORE THAN A POLICE OFFICER.

I AM A NETWORK.

I AM THE X-RAY GLASSES. I AM A WIRELESS NETWORK. I HAVE THE POWER TO SEND VIDEO AND DATA WITHOUT THE USE OF WIRES. I HAVE THE POWER TO LINK A BANK'S SURVEILLANCE CAMERA TO A SQUAD CAR EN ROUTE TO A ROBBERY. I HAVE THE POWER TO SHOW COPS WHAT THEY'RE UP AGAINST. I AM HERE TO PROTECT AND SERVE. I AM MORE THAN A NETWORK.

CISCO SYSTEMS

THIS IS THE POWER OF THE NETWORK. NOW.

cisco.com/powernow

countries—including the United States. About 30 percent of the U.S. gross domestic product is spent by various government units; the figure is much higher in some economies. Different government units in the United States spend about $2,952,000,000,000 (think about it!) a year to buy almost every kind of product. They run not only schools, police departments, and military organizations, but also supermarkets, public utilities, research laboratories, offices, hospitals, and even liquor stores. These huge government expenditures cannot be ignored by an aggressive marketing manager.

Competitive bids may be required

Government buyers in the United States are expected to spend money wisely—in the public interest—so their purchases are usually subject to much public review. To avoid charges of favoritism, most government customers buy by specification using a mandatory bidding procedure. Often the government buyer must accept the lowest bid that meets the specifications. You can see how important it is for the buyer to write precise and complete specifications. Otherwise, sellers may submit a bid that fits the specs but doesn't really match what is needed. By law, a government unit might have to accept the lowest bid—even for an unwanted product.

Writing specifications is not easy—and buyers usually appreciate the help of well-informed salespeople. Salespeople *want* to have input on the specifications so their product can be considered or even have an advantage. One company may get the business—even with a bid that is not the lowest—because the lower bids don't meet minimum specifications.

Rigged specs are an ethical concern

At the extreme, a government customer who wants a specific brand or supplier may try to write the description so that no other supplier can meet all the specs. The buyer may have good reasons for such preferences—a more reliable product, prompt delivery, or better service after the sale. This kind of loyalty sounds great, but marketers must be sensitive to the ethical issues involved. Laws that require government customers to get bids are intended to increase competition among suppliers, not reduce it. Specs that are written primarily to defeat the purpose of these laws may be viewed as illegal bid rigging.

The approved supplier list

Specification and bidding difficulties aren't problems in all government orders. Some items that are bought frequently—or for which there are widely accepted standards—are purchased routinely. The government unit simply places an order at a previously approved price. To share in this business, a supplier must be on the list of approved suppliers. The list is updated occasionally, sometimes by a bid procedure. Government units buy school supplies, construction materials, and gasoline this way. Buyers and sellers agree on a price that will stay the same for a specific period—perhaps a year.

Negotiated contracts are common too

Contracts may be negotiated for items that are not branded or easily described, for products that require research and development, or in cases where there is no effective competition. Depending on the government unit involved, the contract may be subject to audit and renegotiation, especially if the contractor makes a larger profit than expected.

Negotiation is often necessary when there are many intangible factors. Unfortunately, this is exactly where favoritism and influence can slip in. And such influence is not unknown—especially in city and state government. Nevertheless, negotiation is an important buying method in government sales—so a marketing mix should emphasize more than just low price.[29]

Learning what government wants

In the United States, there are more than 87,900 local government units (school districts, cities, counties, and states) as well as many federal agencies that make purchases. Keeping on top of all of them is nearly impossible. Potential suppliers should focus on the government units they want to cater to and learn the bidding methods of those units. Then it's easier to stay informed since most government contracts are advertised. Target marketing can make a big contribution here—making sure the marketing mixes are well matched with the different bid procedures. In addition, good timing can be very important—because an agency may not be able to make a purchase if money isn't already set aside in its budget. Agencies often plan their budgets before the start of a new fiscal year. For federal agencies in the U.S., that is often in October. On the other hand, at the end of a fiscal year an agency may have some flexibility to use leftover funds to make purchases.

A marketer can learn a lot about potential government target markets from various government publications and by using the Internet. For example, the General Services Administration handles vendor contracts for off-the-shelf goods and services; information for vendors is available at www.gsa.gov. There is an online resource center for government contracting at www.govcon.com. Similarly, the site at www.fbodaily.com (which is an abbreviation for *Federal Business Opportunities Daily*) recently replaced the *Commerce Business Daily* as the official listing of all federal government contract opportunities and awards over $25,000. The Small Business Administration (www.sba.gov) offers many resources, including the *U.S. Purchasing, Specifications, and Sales Directory*. It explains government procedures to encourage competition for such business. Various state and local governments also offer guidance, as do government units in many other countries.

Trade magazines and trade associations provide information on how to reach schools, hospitals, highway departments, park departments, and so on. These are unique target markets and must be treated as such when developing marketing strategies.

Dealing with foreign governments

Selling to government units in foreign countries can be a real challenge. In many cases, a firm must get permission from the government in its own country to sell to a foreign government. Moreover, most government contracts favor domestic suppliers if they are available. Even if such favoritism is not explicit, public sentiment may make it very difficult for a foreign competitor to get a contract. Or the government bureaucracy may simply bury a foreign supplier in so much red tape that there's no way to win.

Is it unethical to "buy help"?

In some countries, government officials expect small payments (grease money) just to speed up processing of routine paperwork, inspections, or decisions from the local bureaucracy. Outright influence peddling—where government officials or their friends request bribe money to sway a purchase decision—is common in some markets. In the past, marketers from some countries have looked at such bribes as a cost of doing business. However, the **Foreign Corrupt Practices Act**, passed by the U.S. Congress in 1977, prohibits U.S. firms from paying bribes to foreign officials. A person who pays bribes, or authorizes an agent to pay them, can face stiff penalties. However, the law was amended in 1988 to allow small grease money payments if they are customary in a local culture. Further, a manager isn't held responsible if an agent in the foreign country secretly pays bribes. An ethical dilemma may arise if a marketing manager *thinks* that money paid to a foreign agent might be used, in part, to bribe a government official. However, most U.S. businesses have learned to live with this law—and in general they comply with its intent.[30]

CONCLUSION

In this chapter, we considered the number, size, location, and buying behavior of various types of organizational customers—to try to identify logical dimensions for segmenting markets and developing marketing mixes. We looked at who makes and influences organizational buying decisions, and how multiple influence may make the marketing job more difficult. We also saw that the nature of the buyer and the buying situation are relevant and that the problem-solving models of buyer behavior introduced in Chapter 6 apply here, with modifications.

Buying behavior—and marketing opportunities—may change when there's a close relationship between a supplier and a customer. However, close relationships are not an all-or-nothing thing. There are different ways that a supplier can build a closer relationship with its customers. We identified key dimensions of relationships and their benefits and limitations.

We also looked at how buyers use e-commerce in the buying process. Some capabilities, like interactive competitive bidding, have already had a major impact. And much progress is underway toward fostering more efficient relationships.

The chapter focuses on aspects of buying behavior that often apply to different types of organizational customers. However, we discussed some key differences in the manufacturer, services, intermediary, and government markets.

A clear understanding of organizational buying habits, needs, and attitudes can aid marketing strategy planning. And since there are fewer organizational customers than final consumers, it may even be possible for some marketing managers (and their salespeople) to develop a unique strategy for each potential customer.

This chapter offers some general principles that are useful in strategy planning—but the nature of the products being offered may require adjustments in the plans. Different product classes are discussed in Chapter 9. Variations by product may provide additional segmenting dimensions to help a marketing manager fine-tune a marketing strategy.

KEY TERMS

business and organizational customers, 178

purchasing specifications, 181

ISO 9000, 181

purchasing managers, 182

multiple buying influence, 182

buying center, 183

vendor analysis, 184

requisition, 185

new-task buying, 186

straight rebuy, 186

modified rebuy, 186

just-in-time delivery, 189

negotiated contract buying, 191

reciprocity, 192

competitive bids, 193

North American Industry Classification System (NAICS) codes, 199

open to buy, 204

resident buyers, 204

Foreign Corrupt Practices Act, 206

QUESTIONS AND PROBLEMS

1. In your own words, explain how buying behavior of business customers in different countries may have been a factor in speeding the spread of international marketing.

2. Compare and contrast the buying behavior of final consumers and organizational buyers. In what ways are they most similar and in what ways are they most different?

3. Briefly discuss why a marketing manager should think about who is likely to be involved in the buying center for a particular purchase. Is the buying center idea useful in consumer buying? Explain your answer.

4. If a nonprofit hospital were planning to buy expensive MRI scanning equipment (to detect tumors), who might be involved in the buying center? Explain

your answer and describe the types of influence that different people might have.

5. Describe the situations that would lead to the use of the three different buying processes for a particular product—lightweight bumpers for a pickup truck.

6. Why would an organizational buyer want to get competitive bids? What are some of the situations when competitive bidding can't be used?

7. How likely would each of the following be to use competitive bids: (a) a small town that needed a road resurfaced, (b) a scouting organization that needed a printer to print its scouting handbook, (c) a hardware retailer that wants to add a new lawn mower line, (d) a grocery store chain that wants to install new checkout scanners, and (e) a sorority that

wants to buy a computer to keep track of member dues? Explain your answers.

8. Discuss the advantages and disadvantages of just-in-time supply relationships from an organizational buyer's point of view. Are the advantages and disadvantages merely reversed from the seller's point of view?

9. Explain why a customer might be willing to work more cooperatively with a small number of suppliers rather than pitting suppliers in a competition against each other. Give an example that illustrates your points.

10. Would a tool manufacturer need a different marketing strategy for a big retail chain like Home Depot than for a single hardware store run by its owner? Discuss your answer.

11. How do you think a furniture manufacturer's buying habits and practices would be affected by the specific type of product to be purchased? Consider fabric for upholstered furniture, a lathe for the production line, cardboard for shipping cartons, and lubricants for production machinery.

12. Discuss the importance of target marketing when analyzing organizational markets. How easy is it to isolate homogeneous market segments in these markets?

13. Explain how NAICS codes might be helpful in evaluating and understanding business markets. Give an example.

14. Considering the nature of retail buying, outline the basic ingredients of promotion to retail buyers. Does it make any difference what kinds of products are involved? Are any other factors relevant?

15. The government market is obviously an extremely large one, yet it is often slighted or even ignored by many firms. Red tape is certainly one reason, but there are others. Discuss the situation and be sure to include the possibility of segmenting in your analysis.

16. Some critics argue that the Foreign Corrupt Practices Act puts U.S. businesses at a disadvantage when competing in foreign markets with suppliers from other countries that do not have similar laws. Do you think that this is a reasonable criticism? Explain your answer.

SUGGESTED CASES

5. ResinTech

6. Valley Steel Company

COMPUTER-AIDED PROBLEM

7. Vendor Analysis

RESOURCE REMINDER

CompuTech, Inc., makes circuit boards for microcomputers. It is evaluating two possible suppliers of electronic memory chips.

The chips do the same job. Although manufacturing quality has been improving, some chips are always defective. Both suppliers will replace defective chips. But the only practical way to test for a defective chip is to assemble a circuit board and "burn it in"—run it and see if it works. When one chip on a board is defective at that point, it costs $2.00 for the extra labor time to replace it. Supplier 1 guarantees a chip failure rate of not more than 1 per 100 (that is, a defect rate of 1 percent). The second supplier's 2 percent defective rate is higher, but its price is lower.

Supplier 1 has been able to improve its quality because it uses a heavier plastic case to hold the chip. The only disadvantage of the heavier case is that it requires CompuTech to use a connector that is somewhat more expensive.

Transportation costs are added to the price quoted by either supplier, but Supplier 2 is further away so transportation costs are higher. And because of the distance, delays in supplies reaching CompuTech are sometimes a problem. To ensure that a sufficient supply is on hand to keep production going, CompuTech must maintain a backup inventory—and this increases inventory costs. CompuTech figures inventory costs—the expenses of finance and storage—as a percentage of the total order cost.

To make its vendor analysis easier, CompuTech's purchasing agent has entered data about the two suppliers on a spreadsheet. He based his estimates on the quantity he thinks he will need over a full year.

a. Based on the results shown in the initial spreadsheet, which supplier do you think CompuTech should select? Why?

b. CompuTech estimates it will need 100,000 chips a year if sales go as expected. But if sales are slow, fewer chips will be needed. This isn't an issue with Supplier 2; its price is the same at any quantity. However, Supplier 1's price per chip will be $1.95 if CompuTech buys less than 90,000 during the year. If CompuTech only needs 84,500 chips, which supplier would be more economical? Why?

c. If the actual purchase quantity will be 84,500 and Supplier 1's price is $1.95, what is the highest price at which Supplier 2 will still be the lower-cost vendor for CompuTech? (Hint: You can enter various prices for Supplier 2 in the spreadsheet—or use the analysis feature to vary Supplier 2's price and display the total costs for both vendors.)

For additional questions related to this problem, see Exercise 7-3 in the *Learning Aid for Use with Basic Marketing,* 15th edition.

CHAPTER EIGHT

Improving Decisions with Marketing Information

When you see the array of products—strips, gels, swabs, and more—on drugstore shelves to make your smile whiter and brighter, it's easy to forget that just a few years ago this category of products—for a combination of oral care and beauty needs—didn't exist. Movie stars would pay Hollywood dentists thousands of dollars for special whitening treatments, but the rest of us would just envy their pearly smiles.

That changed after research convinced marketing managers for Crest oral care products that this unmet need was a big opportunity. A variety of marketing research firms, including National Opinion Research and Semaphore, helped with the research. For example, focus group interviews suggested that consumers would be excited about a do-it-yourself whitening treatment that was effective, simple to use, and affordable. Responses by representative samples of consumers to survey questionnaires confirmed that this

was a large market. Online product concept tests revealed that there would be demand even at a price around $50, which would cover development and introductory promotion costs. On the other hand, research also revealed that dentists, who are influential in recommending oral care products, were concerned that the product might eat into their business.

When the R&D people came up with the idea of using a clear, tape-like strip that works by sticking to the teeth, product effectiveness tests confirmed that consumers could see a difference in whiteness. Research also showed that 30 minutes was the consumer limit for wearing the strips. Research even helped in selecting a brand name, Crest Whitestrips, and in focusing the positioning with advertising copy on "easy to use" and "superior whitening versus toothpaste" benefits.

Rather than work with traditional test markets in retail stores, marketing managers used infomercials and ads in consumer magazines to explain the product and direct consumers to a website (www.whitestrips.com) where they could buy Whitestrips. That approach not only produced sales quickly but also showed retailers that there was strong demand, even at a $44 retail price. Moreover, by doing studies on the Internet, researchers were able to deliver consumer test market input to marketing managers within days. For example, when researchers found that 80 percent of customers were female rather than the 50/50 split of men and women that was expected, the ad agency refined the focus of the advertising media.

When Whitestrips went into national distribution, the new product launch was one of the most successful in 20 years. Within a year, sales of Whitestrips surpassed $200 million and the product became the category leader. A professional version of Whitestrips for dentists to sell contributed to this success. Some dentists reported that the strips even helped increase interest in other types of cosmetic dentistry.

Competitors weighed in quickly with entries such as Mentadent's Tooth Whitening System and Colgate's Simply White, and that increased price competition. But research continues to play a crucial role in shaping Whitestrips marketing. For example, three years after introducing the original Whitestrips, research data from Information Resources, Inc., showed that Crest Whitestrips was still the leader in the category with more than half of total sales. To maintain that lead, Crest introduced new products. One was Crest Night Effects, a lower-priced product, which is dabbed on the teeth and worn while sleeping. The other was a premium version of Whitestrips. It has a higher concentration of the whitening ingredient, but perhaps the bigger selling point is that it works in half the time. Many retailers took shelf space away from Mentadent to stock all three of Crest's whitening products. Based on internal sales data, they knew that Mentadent was losing sales to both Colgate and Crest.[1]

The Whitestrips case shows that successful marketing strategies require information about potential target markets and their likely responses to marketing mixes as well as about competition and other marketing environment variables. Managers also need information for implementation and control. Without good information, managers are left to guess—and in today's fast-changing markets, that invites failure.

RADICAL CHANGES ARE UNDERWAY IN MARKETING INFORMATION

Marketing managers for some companies make decisions based almost totally on their own judgment—with very little hard data. The manager may not even know that he or she is about to make the same mistake that the previous person in that job already made! When it's time to make a decision, they may wish they had more information. But by then it's too late, so they do without.

MIS makes information available and accessible

Many firms realize that it doesn't pay to wait until you have important questions you can't answer. They anticipate the information they will need. They work to develop a *continual flow of information* that is available and quickly accessible when it's needed.

A **marketing information system (MIS)** is an organized way of continually gathering, accessing, and analyzing information that marketing managers need to make decisions.

New developments in computer networks, software, and information technology are making it easier for companies to gather and analyze marketing information.

We won't cover all of the technical details of planning for an MIS. But you should understand what an MIS is so you know some of the possibilities. So we'll be discussing the elements of a complete MIS as shown in Exhibit 8-1. As part of that review, we'll highlight how technology is changing MIS use.

Get more information—faster and easier

Basic MIS concepts are not very different today than they were 20 years ago. However, advances in information technology have ushered in *radical* improvements. Now it is easy to set up and use an MIS. A short time ago, exchanging data among remote computers was very difficult. Now, it's standard. Managers have access to much more information. It's instantly available, and often just a mouse click away.

The *type* of information available is also changing dramatically. Until recently, marketing managers relied on computers mainly for number crunching. The multimedia revolution in computing lifted that limitation. Now it doesn't matter whether marketing information takes the form of a report, spreadsheet, database, presentation, photo, graphic, video, or table of statistics. It is all being created on computer. So it

Exhibit 8-1
Elements of a Complete Marketing Information System

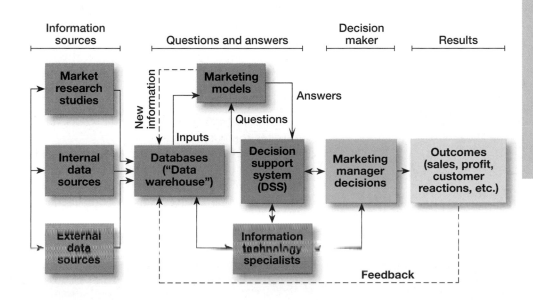

can be easily stored and accessed by computer. When we talk about a "database" of marketing information, it may include all types of information, not just numbers.

An intranet is easy to update

Many firms, even very small ones, have their own **intranet**—a system for linking computers within a company. An intranet works like the Internet. However, to maintain security, access to websites or data on an intranet is usually limited to employees. Even so, information is available on demand. Further, it's a simple matter to "publish" new information to a website as it becomes available.

In any case, you seldom have all the information you need. Both customers and competitors can be unpredictable. Getting the precise information you want may cost too much or take too long. For example, data on international markets is often incomplete, outdated, or difficult to obtain. So a manager often must decide what information is really critical and how to get it.

Marketing managers must help develop an MIS

Computers are getting easier to use, but setting up and supporting an MIS still requires technical skill. In fact, converting an existing MIS to take advantage of Internet capabilities can be a real challenge. So in some companies, an MIS is set up by a person or group that provides *all* departments in the firm with information technology support. Or it may be set up by marketing specialists.

These specialists are important, but the marketing manager should play an important role, too. Marketing managers know what data they've routinely used or needed in the past. They can also foresee what types of data might be useful. They should communicate these needs to the specialists so the information will be there when they want it and in the form they want it.

Decision support systems put managers online

An MIS system organizes incoming information into a **data warehouse**—a place where databases are stored so that they are available when needed. You can think of a data warehouse as a sort of electronic library, where all of the information is indexed extremely well. Firms with an MIS often have information technology specialists who help managers get specialized reports and output from the warehouse. However, to get better decisions, most MIS systems now provide marketing managers with a decision support system. A **decision support system (DSS)** is a computer program that makes it easy for a marketing manager to get and use information *as he or she is making decisions*.

A decision support system usually involves some sort of **search engine**—a computer program that helps a marketing manager find information that is needed. For example, a manager who wants sales data for the previous week or day might search for any database or computer file that references the term *unit sales* as well as the relevant data. The search engine would identify any files where that term appeared. If there were many, the manager could narrow the search further (say by specifying the product of interest).

When the search is focused on numerical data, simply finding the information may not go far enough. Thus, a DSS typically helps change raw data—like product sales for the previous day—into more *useful information*. For example, it may draw graphs to show relationships in data—perhaps comparing yesterday's sales to the sales on the same day in the last four weeks. The MIS that managers at Frito-Lay use illustrates the possibilities.

All of Frito-Lay's salespeople are equipped with hand-held computers. Throughout the day they input sales information at the stores they visit. In the evening they send all the data over telephone lines to a central computer, where it is analyzed. Within 24 hours marketing managers at headquarters and in regional offices get reports and graphs that summarize how sales went the day before—broken down by brands and locations. The information system even allows a manager to zoom in and take a closer look at a problem in Peoria or a sales success in Sacramento.[2]

Some decision support systems go even further. They allow the manager to see how answers to questions might change in various situations. For example, a manager at Kraft Foods may want to estimate how much sales will increase if the firm uses a certain type of promotion in a specific market area. The DSS will ask the manager for a *personal* judgment about how much business could be won from each competitor in that market. Then, using this input and drawing on data in the database about how the promotion had worked in other markets, the system will make a sales estimate using a marketing model. A **marketing model** is a statement of relationships among marketing variables.

In short, the decision support system puts managers online so they can study available data and make better marketing decisions—faster.[3]

Information for planning, implementation, and control

Once marketing managers use an MIS—and perhaps a DSS—they are eager for more information. They realize that they can improve all aspects of their planning—blending individual Ps, combining the four Ps into mixes, and developing and selecting plans. Further, they can monitor the implementation of current plans, comparing results against plans and making necessary changes more quickly. For example, LensCrafters is one of the largest chains of eyewear stores in the United States and Canada. Each of its 850 stores carries a very large selection of frame styles, lenses, and sunglasses tailored not only to the age, gender, and ethnic makeup of the local market but also to what is selling at that particular store. Shifts in eyewear fashions can come fast. So managers at LensCrafters routinely analyze sales data available in the firm's marketing information system. By breaking down sales by product, store, and time period, they can spot buying trends early and plan for them.[4] (Note: The sales and cost analysis techniques discussed in Chapter 18 are often used in an MIS.)

Many firms are not there yet

Of course, not every firm has a complete MIS system. And in some firms that do, managers don't know how to use what's there. A major problem is that many managers are used to doing it the old way—and they don't think through what information they need.

One sales manager thought he was progressive when he asked his assistant for a report listing each sales rep's sales for the previous month and the current month. The assistant quickly found the relevant information on the firm's intranet, put it into an Excel spreadsheet, and printed out the report. Later, however, she was surprised to see the sales manager working on the list with a calculator. He was figuring the percentage change in sales for the month and ranking the reps from largest increase in sales to smallest. The spreadsheet software could have done all of that—instantly—but the sales manager got what he *asked for*, not what he really needed. An MIS can provide information—but only the marketing manager knows what problem needs solving. It's the job of the manager—not the computer or the MIS specialist—to ask for the right information in the right form.

MIS use is growing rapidly

Some people think that only large firms can develop an effective MIS. In fact, just the opposite may be true. Big firms with complicated marketing programs often face a challenge trying to develop an MIS from scratch. And once a large firm has a system in place it may be very costly to switch to something better. It can be easier for small firms because they are often more focused. They can get started with a simple system and then expand it as needs expand. There is a lot of opportunity in this area for students who are able and willing to apply computer skills to solve real marketing problems.[5]

New questions require new answers

MIS systems tend to focus on recurring information needs. Routinely analyzing such information can be valuable to marketing managers. But it shouldn't be their only source of information for decision making. They must try to satisfy ever-changing needs in dynamic markets. So marketing research must be used—to supplement data already available and accessible through the MIS.

WHAT IS MARKETING RESEARCH?

Research provides a bridge to customers

The marketing concept says that marketing managers should meet the needs of customers. Yet today, many marketing managers are isolated in company offices—far from potential customers.

This means marketing managers have to rely on help from **marketing research**—procedures to develop and analyze new information to help marketing managers make decisions. One of the important jobs of a marketing researcher is to get the "facts" that are not currently available.

Who does the work?

Most large companies have a separate marketing research department to plan and carry out research projects. These departments often use outside specialists—including interviewing and tabulating services—to handle technical assignments. Further, they may call in specialized marketing consultants and marketing research organizations to take charge of a research project.

Small companies (those with less than $4 or $5 million in sales) usually don't have separate marketing research departments. They often depend on their salespeople or managers to conduct what research they do.

Some nonprofit organizations have begun to use marketing research—usually with the help of outside specialists. For example, many politicians rely on research firms to conduct surveys of voter attitudes.[6]

Ethical issues in marketing research

The basic reason for doing marketing research is to get information that people can trust in making decisions. But research often involves many hidden details. A person who wants to misuse marketing research to pursue a personal agenda can often do so.

Perhaps the most common ethical issues concern decisions to withhold certain information about the research. For example, a manager might selectively share only those results that support his or her viewpoint. Others involved in a decision might never know that they are getting only partial truths. Or during a set of interviews, a researcher may discover that consumers are interpreting a poorly worded question many different ways. If the researcher doesn't admit the problem, an unknowing manager may rely on meaningless results.

Another problem involves more blatant abuses. It is unethical for a firm to contact consumers under the pretense of doing research when the real purpose is to sell something. For example, some political organizations have been criticized for surveying voters to find out their attitudes about various political candidates and issues.

Then, armed with that information, someone else calls back to solicit donations. Legitimate marketing researchers don't do this!

The relationship between the researcher and the manager sometimes creates an ethical conflict. Managers must be careful not to send a signal that the only acceptable results from a research project are ones that confirm their existing viewpoints. Researchers are supposed to be objective, but that objectivity may be swayed if future jobs depend on getting the "right" results.[7]

Effective research usually requires cooperation

Good marketing research requires cooperation between researchers and marketing managers. Researchers must be sure their research focuses on real problems.

Marketing managers must be able to explain what their problems are and what kinds of information they need. They should be able to communicate with specialists in the specialists' language. Marketing managers may only be "consumers" of research. But they should be informed consumers—able to explain exactly what they want from the research. They should also know about some of the basic decisions made during the research process so they know the limitations of the findings.

For this reason, our discussion of marketing research won't emphasize mechanics but rather how to plan and evaluate the work of marketing researchers.[8]

THE SCIENTIFIC METHOD AND MARKETING RESEARCH

The scientific method—combined with the strategy planning framework we discussed in Chapter 2—can help marketing managers make better decisions.

The **scientific method** is a decision-making approach that focuses on being objective and orderly in *testing* ideas before accepting them. With the scientific method, managers don't just *assume* that their intuition is correct. Instead, they use their intuition and observations to develop **hypotheses**—educated guesses about the relationships between things or about what will happen in the future. Then they test their hypotheses before making final decisions.

A manager who relies only on intuition might introduce a new product without testing consumer response. But a manager who uses the scientific method might say, "I think (hypothesize) that consumers currently using the most popular brand will prefer our new product. Let's run some consumer tests. If at least 60 percent of the consumers prefer our product, we can introduce it in a regional test market. If it doesn't pass the consumer test there, we can make some changes and try again."

The scientific method forces an orderly research process. Some managers don't carefully specify what information they need. They blindly move ahead—hoping that research will provide "the answer." Other managers may have a clearly defined problem or question but lose their way after that. These hit-or-miss approaches waste both time and money.

FIVE-STEP APPROACH TO MARKETING RESEARCH

The **marketing research process** is a five-step application of the scientific method that includes:

1. Defining the problem.
2. Analyzing the situation.
3. Getting problem-specific data.
4. Interpreting the data.
5. Solving the problem.

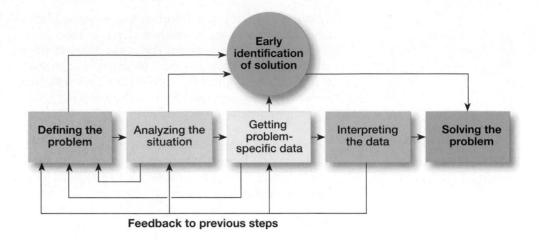

Exhibit 8-2 shows the five steps in the process. Note that the process may lead to a solution before all of the steps are completed. Or as the feedback arrows show, researchers may return to an earlier step if needed. For example, the interpreting step may point to a new question—or reveal the need for additional information—before a final decision can be made.

DEFINING THE PROBLEM—STEP 1

Defining the problem is often the most difficult step in the marketing research process. But it's important for the objectives of the research to be clearly defined. The best research job on the wrong problem is wasted effort.

Finding the right problem level almost solves the problem

The strategy planning framework introduced in Chapter 2 can be useful here. It can help the researcher identify the real problem area and what information is needed. Do we really know enough about our target markets to work out all of the four Ps? Do we know enough to decide what celebrity to use in an ad or how to handle a price war in New York City or Tokyo? If not, we may want to do research rather than rely on intuition.

The importance of understanding the problem—and then trying to solve it—can be seen in the introduction of Fab One Shot, a laundry product developed to clean, soften, and reduce static cling all in one step. Marketing managers were sure that Fab One Shot was going to appeal to heavy users—especially working women with large families. Research showed that 80 percent of these women used three different laundry products for the family wash, but they were looking for more convenience.

When marketing managers found that other firms were testing similar products, they rushed Fab One Shot into distribution. To encourage first-time purchases, they offered introductory price discounts, coupons, and rebates. And they supported the sales promotion with heavy advertising on TV programs that research showed the heavy users watched.

However, research never addressed the problem of how the heavy user target market would react. After the introductory price-off deals were dropped, sales dropped off too. While the product was convenient, heavy users weren't willing to pay the price—about 25 cents for each washload. For the heavy users, price was a qualifying dimension. And these consumers didn't like Fab's premeasured packets because they had no control over how much detergent they could put in. The competing firms recognized these problems at the research stage and decided not to introduce their products.

After the fact, it was clear that Fab One Shot was most popular with college students, singles, and people living in small apartments. They didn't use much—so the convenience benefit offset the higher price. But the company never targeted those segments. It just assumed that it would be profitable to target the big market of heavy users.[9]

The moral of this story is that our strategy planning framework is useful for guiding the problem definition step—as well as the whole marketing research process. First, a marketing manager should understand the target market and what needs the firm can satisfy. Then the manager can focus on lower-level problems—namely, how sensitive the target market is to a change in one or more of the marketing mix ingredients. Without such a framework, marketing researchers can waste time, and money, working on the wrong problem.

Don't confuse problems with symptoms

The problem definition step sounds simple—and that's the danger. It's easy to confuse symptoms with the problem. Suppose a firm's MIS shows that the company's sales are decreasing in certain territories while expenses are remaining the same—resulting in a decline in profits. Will it help to define the problem by asking: How can we stop the sales decline? Probably not. This would be like fitting a hearing-impaired patient with a hearing aid without first trying to find out *why* the patient was having trouble hearing.

It's easy to fall into the trap of mistaking symptoms for the problem. When this happens, the research objectives are not clear, and researchers may ignore relevant questions—while analyzing unimportant questions in expensive detail.

Setting research objectives may require more understanding

Sometimes the research objectives are very clear. A manager wants to know if the targeted households have tried a new product and what percent of them bought it a second time. But research objectives aren't always so simple. The manager might also want to know *why* some didn't buy or whether they had even heard of the product. Companies rarely have enough time and money to study everything. A manager must narrow the research objectives. One good way is to develop a list of research questions that includes all the possible problem areas. Then the manager can consider the items on the list more completely—in the situation analysis step—before narrowing down to final research objectives.

ANALYZING THE SITUATION—STEP 2

What information do we already have?

When the marketing manager thinks the real problem has begun to surface, a situation analysis is useful. A **situation analysis** is an informal study of what information is already available in the problem area. It can help define the problem and specify what additional information, if any, is needed.

Pick the brains around you

The situation analysis usually involves informal talks with informed people. Informed people can be others in the firm, a few good middlemen who have close contact with customers, or others knowledgeable about the industry. In industrial markets—where relationships with customers are close—researchers may even call the customers themselves.

Situation analysis helps educate a researcher

The situation analysis is especially important if the researcher is a research specialist who doesn't know much about the management decisions to be made or if the marketing manager is dealing with unfamiliar areas. They both must be sure they understand the problem area—including the nature of the target market, the marketing mix, competition, and other external factors. Otherwise, the researcher may rush ahead and make costly mistakes or simply discover facts that management already knows. The following case illustrates this danger.

A marketing manager at the home office of a large retail chain hired a research firm to do in-store interviews to learn what customers liked most, and least, about some of its stores in other cities. Interviewers diligently filled out their questionnaires. When the results came in, it was apparent that neither the marketing manager nor the researcher had done their homework. No one had even talked with the local store managers! Several of the stores were in the middle of some messy remodeling—so all the customers' responses concerned the noise and dust from the construction. The research was a waste of money.

Secondary data may provide the answers—or some background

The situation analysis should also find relevant **secondary data**—information that has been collected or published already. Later, in Step 3, we will cover **primary data**—information specifically collected to solve a current problem. Too often researchers rush to gather primary data when much relevant secondary information is already available—at little or no cost! See Exhibit 8-3.

Much secondary data is available

Ideally, much secondary data is already available from the firm's MIS. Data that has not been organized in an MIS may be available from the company's files and reports. Secondary data also is available from libraries, trade associations, government agencies, and private research organizations; increasingly, these organizations are putting their information online. So one of the first places a researcher should look for secondary data is on the Internet.

Search engines find information on the Internet

Although much information relevant to your situation analysis may be on the Internet, it won't do you much good if you can't find it. Fortunately, there are a number of good tools for searching on the Internet and reference books that explain the details of the different tools. However, the basic idea is simple. And, usually, the best way to start is to use a search engine.

Most popular Internet browsers, like Netscape Navigator and Microsoft Internet Explorer, have a menu selection or button to activate an Internet search. In addition, there are hundreds of more specialized search engines. In general, a user specifies words or a phrase to find and the search engine produces a list of hyperlinks to websites where that search string is found. Usually, all you do is click on the

Exhibit 8-3   Sources of Secondary and Primary Data

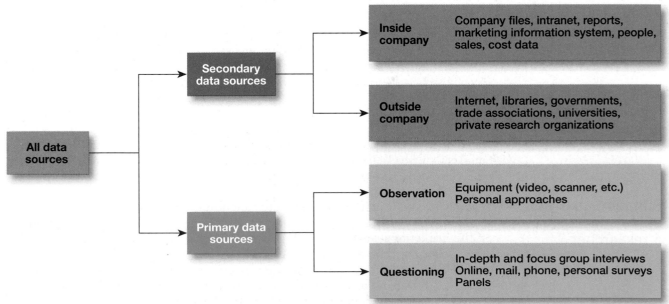

The Internet is dramatically changing how marketing managers get both primary and secondary data.

hyperlink of interest and the browser shows the relevant page on screen. If you want, you can go back to the list and check out other links.

 One of the most popular and useful search engines is at the website for Google (www.google.com). It is especially good at searching for web pages. Another very useful search engine is at the AltaVista website (www.altavista.com); it does a good job of classifying online documents that include the search string. A search engine that is particularly useful for locating specific people or businesses is at www.hotbot.lycos.com. The Northern Light search engine (www.northernlight.com) is very good at identifying published articles on the search topic. Keep in mind, however, that these are just a few of the popular search engines. In fact, if you want to get an idea of how many are available—and how they are different—go to www.yahoo.com and do a search on the term *search engine*.[10]

Most computerized database and index services are now available over the Internet. Some of these are provided by libraries and private firms. For instance, for a fee a user can use Dow Jones' interactive news retrieval system (www.djnr.com) to search the full text of hundreds of publications, including newspapers from around the world. ProQuest Direct, at www.proquest.com, is another valuable research tool. It provides access to one of the world's largest collections of information, including summaries of articles from over 5,000 publications. Many articles are available in full text, full image format.

INTERNET EXERCISE

Assume that your boss has asked you to do a customer satisfaction survey. As part of a situation analysis, you want to get ideas about what others have done in this area. Go to the website for the Google search engine (www.google.com). In the dialogue box type 'customer satisfaction survey' (include the single quote marks) and click on Google search. Look at some of the websites identified. How helpful is this? How could it be improved?

Government data is inexpensive

Federal and state governments publish data on many subjects. Government data is often useful in estimating the size of markets. In Chapter 5 we gave a number of examples of the different types of data that are available and suggested some websites.

Distribution of government data is not limited to the Internet, however. Almost all government data is available in inexpensive publications. Much of it is also available in computer form ready for further analysis.

Sometimes it's more practical to use summary publications for leads to more detailed reports. For the U.S. market, one of the most useful summary references is the *Statistical Abstract of the United States*. Like an almanac, it is issued in print form each year and gives 1,500 summary tables from more than 200 published sources. Detailed footnotes guide readers to more specific information on a topic. The abstract and much of the source material on which it is based are available online at www.census.gov. Similarly, the *United Nations Statistical Yearbook* is one of the finest summaries of worldwide data; like many other international statistical references, it is available on CD-ROM and online (www.un.org/depts/unsd).

Secondary data is very limited on some international markets. However, most countries with advanced economies have government agencies that help researchers get the data they need. For example, Statistics Canada (www.statcan.ca) compiles a great deal of information on the Canadian market. Eurostat (europa.eu.int/comm/eurostat), the statistical office for the European Union countries, and the Organization for Economic Cooperation (in Paris) offer many publications packed with data on Europe. In the United States, the Department of Commerce (www.doc.gov) distributes statistics compiled by all other federal departments. Some city and state governments have similar agencies for local data. The Yahoo website (www.yahoo.com) provides an index to a large amount of information about different governments.

Private sources are useful too

Many private research organizations—as well as advertising agencies, newspapers, and magazines—regularly compile and publish data. A good business library is valuable for sources such as *Sales & Marketing Management*, *Advertising Age*, *Journal of Global Marketing*, and the publications of the National Industrial Conference Board.

The *Encyclopedia of Associations* lists 75,000 U.S. and international trade and professional associations that can be a good source of information. For example, the American Marketing Association (www.ama.org) has an information center with many marketing publications.

Most trade associations compile data from and for their members. Some also publish magazines that focus on important topics in the industry. *Chain Store Age*, for example, has much information on retailing (www.chainstoreage.com).

Standard & Poor's Industry Surveys is another source of information on whole industries. And the local telephone company or your library usually has copies of the Yellow Pages for many cities; Yellow Page listings are also available on the Internet. Similarly, a number of firms sell computer CD-ROMs that include all of the businesses in the country. Resources such as these may be a big help in estimating the amount of competition in certain lines of business and where it is located.[11]

Situation analysis yields a lot—for very little

The virtue of a good situation analysis is that it can be very informative but takes little time. And it's inexpensive compared with more formal research efforts—like a large-scale survey. Situation analysis can help focus further research or even eliminate the need for it entirely. The situation analyst is really trying to determine the exact nature of the situation and the problem.

Determine what else is needed

At the end of the situation analysis, you can see which research questions—from the list developed during the problem definition step—remain unanswered. Then you have to decide exactly what information you need to answer those questions and how to get it.

This may require discussion between technical experts and the marketing manager. Often companies use a written **research proposal**—a plan that specifies what information will be obtained and how—to be sure no misunderstandings occur later. The research plan may include information about costs, what data will be collected, how it will be collected, who will analyze it and how, and how long the process will take. Then the marketing manager must decide if the time and costs involved are worthwhile. It's foolish to pay $100,000 for information to solve a $50,000 problem!

GETTING PROBLEM-SPECIFIC DATA—STEP 3

Gathering primary data

The next step is to plan a formal research project to gather primary data. There are different methods for collecting primary data. Which approach to use depends on the nature of the problem and how much time and money are available.

In most primary data collection, the researcher tries to learn what customers think about some topic or how they behave under some conditions. There are two basic methods for obtaining information about customers: *questioning* and *observing*. Questioning can range from qualitative to quantitative research. And many kinds of observing are possible.

Qualitative questioning—open-ended with a hidden purpose

Qualitative research seeks in-depth, open-ended responses, not yes or no answers. The researcher tries to get people to share their thoughts on a topic—without giving them many directions or guidelines about what to say.

A researcher might ask different consumers, "What do you think about when you decide where to shop for food?" One person may talk about convenient location, another about service, and others about the quality of the fresh produce. The real advantage of this approach is *depth*. Each person can be asked follow-up questions so the researcher really understands what *that* respondent is thinking. The depth of the qualitative approach gets at the details—even if the researcher needs a lot of judgment to summarize it all.

Some types of qualitative research don't use specific questions. For example, a consumer might simply be shown a product or an ad and be asked to comment.

Focus groups stimulate discussion

The most widely used form of qualitative questioning in marketing research is the **focus group interview**, which involves interviewing 6 to 10 people in an informal group setting. The focus group also uses open-ended questions, but here the interviewer wants to get group interaction—to stimulate thinking and get immediate reactions.

A skilled focus group leader can learn a lot from this approach. A typical session may last an hour, so participants can cover a lot of ground. Sessions are often videotaped (or broadcast over the Internet or by satellite) so different managers can form their own impressions of what happened. Some research firms create electronic focus groups in which participants log onto a specified website and with others participate in a chat session; each person types in comments that are shared on the computer screen of each of the other participants. What they type is the record of the session.[12]

Focus groups are also popular in business markets. For example, IBM used 27 focus groups as part of its research to better identify who in large companies makes buying decisions for e-commerce equipment and how they thought about the issues of selecting a vendor.[13]

Regardless of how a focus group is conducted, conclusions reached from a session usually vary depending on who watches it. A typical problem—and serious

Focus groups are popular, and well-run groups can provide a lot of useful information. As with any type of marketing research, a marketing manager should be aware of both the advantages and limitations of this approach when drawing conclusions and making decisions.

limitation—with qualitative research is that it's hard to measure the results objectively. The results seem to depend largely on the viewpoint of the researcher. In addition, people willing to participate in a focus group—especially those who talk the most—may not be representative of the broader target market.

Focus groups can be conducted quickly and at relatively low cost—an average of about $3,500 each. This is part of their appeal. But focus groups are probably being overused. It's easy to fall into the trap of treating an idea arising from a focus group as a "fact" that applies to a broad target market. For example, it's trendy for food product firms in Japan to do focus groups with teenage girls. The logic is that girls will be brutally honest about what they think and that they are good at predicting what will be a hit. So based on a girl's comments in a focus group, Meiji Milk Products substituted oolong tea for fruit juice in a new drink it was developing. The suggested change might or might not be a good one. But there's no way to know if one girl's point of view is representative.[14]

To avoid this trap, some researchers use qualitative research to prepare for quantitative research. For example, the Jacksonville Symphony Orchestra wanted to broaden its base of support and increase ticket sales. It hired a marketing research firm to conduct focus group interviews. These interviews helped the marketing managers refine their ideas about what these target "customers" liked and did not like about the orchestra. The ideas were then tested with a larger, more representative

sample. When the managers planned their promotion and the orchestra's program on the basis of research, ticket sales nearly doubled.[15]

Qualitative research can provide good ideas—hypotheses. But we need other approaches—perhaps based on more representative samples and objective measures—to *test* the hypotheses.

Structured questioning gives more objective results

When researchers use identical questions and response alternatives, they can summarize the information quantitatively. Samples can be larger and more representative, and various statistics can be used to draw conclusions. For these reasons, most survey research is **quantitative research**—which seeks structured responses that can be summarized in numbers, like percentages, averages, or other statistics. For example, a marketing researcher might calculate what percentage of respondents have tried a new product and then figure an average score for how satisfied they were.

Fixed responses speed answering and analysis

Survey questionnaires usually provide fixed responses to questions to simplify analysis of the replies. This multiple-choice approach also makes it easier and faster for respondents to reply. Simple fill-in-a-number questions are also widely used in quantitative research. Fixed responses are also more convenient for computer analysis, which is how most surveys are analyzed.

Quantitative measures of attitudes too

One common approach to measuring consumers' attitudes and opinions is to have respondents indicate how much they agree or disagree with a questionnaire statement. A researcher interested in what target consumers think about frozen pizzas, for example, might include a statement like "I add extra topppings when I prepare frozen pizza." The respondent might check off a response such as (1) strongly disagree, (2) disagree, (3) agree, or (4) strongly agree.

Another approach is to have respondents *rate* a product, feature, or store. For example, a questionnaire might ask consumers to rate the taste of a pizza as *excellent, good, fair,* or *poor.*

Surveys come in many forms

Decisions about what specific questions to ask and how to ask them usually depend on how respondents will be contacted—by mail (or electronic mail), via a website, on the phone, or in person. What question and response approach is used may also affect the survey. There are many possibilities. For example, whether the survey is self-administered or handled by an interviewer, the questionnaire may be on paper or in

In head-to-head ice cream tests, online panel beats mall intercept

When an ice cream manufacturer wanted consumers to pick the favorite of 48 proposed flavor names, they backed up a mall intercept with a quantitative online study. Both methods produced the same favorite flavor—but online was faster and more cost-efficient. Saving time and money are just some of the ways that Greenfield Online research beats the old-fashioned kind. Put our expert consultants and advanced technology to work for you.
www.greenfield.com
877.213.8642

Greenfield Online
Leading the Research Revolution™

• Quantitative Studies
• Qualitative Studies
• Media Research
• Self-Directed Research
• Syndicated Studies
• Website Evaluations

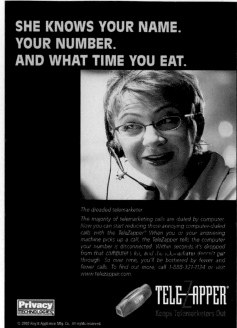

SHE KNOWS YOUR NAME.
YOUR NUMBER.
AND WHAT TIME YOU EAT.

The dreaded telemarketer
The majority of telemarketing calls are dialed by computer. Now you can start reducing those annoying computer-dialed calls with the TeleZapper.® When you or your answering machine picks up a call, the TeleZapper tells the computer your number is disconnected. Within seconds, it's dropped from that computer list, and the telemarketer doesn't get through. So over time, you'll be bothered by fewer and fewer calls. To find out more, call 1-888-321-1134 or visit www.telezapper.com.

Privacy TECHNOLOGIES

TELE ZAPPER
Keeps Telemarketers Out

© 2002 Royal Appliance Mfg. Co. All rights reserved.

an interactive computer format (perhaps distributed on a CD or disk or displayed on a website). The computer can be programmed to skip certain questions, depending on answers given. Computerized questionnaires also allow the research to show pictures or play audio/video clips (for example, to get reactions to an advertising jingle). In an automated telephone interview, questions may be prerecorded on an audio tape or computer and the subject responds by pushing touch-tone buttons on the phone.

Mail and online surveys are common and convenient

A questionnaire distributed by mail, e-mail, or online is useful when extensive questioning is necessary. Respondents can complete the questions at their convenience. They may be more willing to provide personal information—since a questionnaire can be completed anonymously. But the questions must be simple and easy to follow since no interviewer is there to help. If the respondent is likely to be a computer user, it may be possible to send the questionnaire on a disk (or put it on a website) and include a help feature with additional directions for people who need them.

A big problem with questionnaires is that many people don't complete them. The **response rate**—the percentage of people contacted who complete the questionnaire—is often low and respondents may not be representative. There is particular concern about the representativeness of people who complete online questionnaires. The response rates tend to be even lower than by mail. In addition, online respondents may be younger, better educated, or different in other ways that impact how they answer. Mail, e-mail, and online surveys are economical if a large number of people respond. But they may be quite expensive if the response rate is low. Worse, the results may be misleading if the respondents are not representative.

Distributing questionnaires by e-mail, or at a website, is popular. It is quick, and the responses come back in computer form. Surveys sent by regular mail usually take a lot longer. In business markets, questionnaires can sometimes be sent by fax.

Regardless of how quickly a questionnaire is distributed, it often takes a month or more to get the data back. That is too slow for some decisions. Moreover, it is difficult to get respondents to expand on particular points. In markets where illiteracy is a problem, it may not be possible to get any response. In spite of these limitations, the convenience and economy of self-administered surveys makes them popular for collecting primary data.

Telephone surveys—fast and effective

Telephone interviews are also popular. They are effective for getting quick answers to simple questions. Telephone interviews allow the interviewer to probe and really learn what the respondent is thinking. In addition, with computer-aided telephone interviewing, answers are immediately recorded on a computer, resulting in fast data analysis. On the other hand, many consumers find calls intrusive—and about a third refuse to answer any questions. Moreover, respondents can't be certain who is calling or how personal information might be used.

Personal interview surveys—can be in-depth

A personal interview survey is usually much more expensive per interview than e-mail, mail, or telephone surveys. But it's easier to get and keep the respondent's attention when the interviewer is right there. The interviewer can also help explain complicated directions and perhaps get better responses. For these reasons, personal interviews are commonly used for research on business customers. To reduce the cost of locating consumer respondents, interviews are sometimes done at a store or shopping mall. This is called a mall intercept interview because the interviewer stops a shopper and asks for responses to the survey.

Researchers have to be careful that having an interviewer involved doesn't affect the respondent's answers. Sometimes people won't give an answer they consider embarrassing. Or they may try to impress or please the interviewer. Further, in some cultures people don't want to give any information. For example, many people in Africa, Latin America, and Eastern Europe are reluctant to be interviewed. This is also a problem in many low-income, inner-city areas in the United States; even Census Bureau interviewers have trouble getting cooperation.[16]

Sometimes questioning has limitations. Then observing may be more accurate or economical.

Observing—what you see is what you get

Observing—as a method of collecting data—focuses on a well-defined problem. Here we are not talking about the casual observations that may stimulate ideas in the early steps of a research project. With the observation method, researchers try to see or record what the subject does naturally. They don't want the observing to *influence* the subject's behavior.

A museum director wanted to know which of the many exhibits was most popular. A survey didn't help. Visitors seemed to want to please the interviewer and usually said that all of the exhibits were interesting. Putting observers near exhibits—to record how long visitors spent at each one—didn't help either. The curious visitors stood around to see what the observer was recording, and that messed up the measures. Finally, the museum floors were waxed to a glossy shine. Several weeks later, the floors around the exhibits were inspected. It was easy to tell which exhibits were most popular—based on how much wax had worn off the floor!

In some situations, consumers are recorded on video. This may be in a store, at home, or out with friends. Later, researchers can study the tape by running the film at very slow speed or actually analyzing each frame. Researchers use this technique to study the routes consumers follow through a grocery store or how they select

Data from electronic scanners helps retailers decide what brands are selling and helps their suppliers plan ahead so that products arrive at the store in time to prevent stock-outs.

products in a department store. Similarly, firms that have online shopping services on the Internet can use software to "watch" how consumers use the website, how much time they spend at each display, and the like.

Similarly, many franchise companies use the observation method to check how well a franchisee is performing. Krispy Kreme hires people to go to different Krispy Kreme stores and act like normal customers. Then these "secret shoppers" report back to Krispy Kreme on how they were treated, the quality of the service and food, and the cleanliness of the store. The report may include digital pictures or videos that are instantly sent over the Internet from a laptop computer.

Observing is common in advertising research

Observation methods are common in advertising research. For example, Nielsen Media Research (www.nielsenmedia.com) uses a device called the "people meter" that adapts the observation method to television audience research. This device is attached to the TV set in the homes of selected families. It records when the set is on and what station is tuned in. The fact that the TV networks sometimes criticize Nielsen's "counts" of audience size is a reminder that conclusions based on observing are sometimes subject to interpretation, even when a device of some sort is involved.

Checkout scanners see a lot

Computerized scanners at retail checkout counters, a major breakthrough in observing, help researchers collect very specific, and useful, information. Often this type of data feeds directly into a firm's MIS. Managers of a large chain of stores can see exactly what products have sold each day and how much money each department in each store has earned. But the scanner also has wider applications for marketing research.

Information Resources, Inc. (www.infores.com), and ACNielsen (acnielsen.com) use **consumer panels**—a group of consumers who provide information on a continuing basis. Whenever a panel member shops for groceries, he or she gives an ID card to the clerk, who scans the number. Then the scanner records every purchase—including brands, sizes, prices, and any coupons used. In a variation of this approach, consumers use a hand-held scanner to record purchases once they get home. For a fee, clients can evaluate actual customer purchase patterns and answer questions. For example, if a consumer switched from another brand, did she go back to her old brand the next time?

Some members of the consumer panel are also tied into a special TV cable system. With this system, a company can direct advertisements to some houses and not others. Then researchers can evaluate the effect of the ads by comparing the purchases of consumers who saw the ads with those who didn't.

The use of scanners to "observe" what customers actually do has changed consumer research methods. Companies can turn to firms like Information Resources

WHIRLPOOL HEATS UP SALES WITH MARKETING RESEARCH

Marketing managers at Whirlpool want to satisfy customers. So they do a lot of research to find out how satisfied customers really are. For example, each year Whirlpool sends an appliance satisfaction survey to 180,000 households. Respondents rate all of their appliances on dozens of dimensions. When a competing product scores higher, Whirlpool engineers take it apart to see why and build the best ideas into their new models. However, they don't just wait for competitors to figure things out first.

A recently introduced oven, now one of Whirlpool's hottest sellers, illustrates their approach. A survey showed that consumers wanted an oven with easy-to-clean controls. That didn't seem consistent with previous sales patterns; the firm's MIS showed that models with knobs consistently outsold models with easier-to-clean push buttons. Rather than disregard the survey, Whirlpool designed a range with touch pad controls by listening to consumers at every step along the way. Consumers who played with computer simulations of the touch pad explained what they liked and didn't like. Videos of consumers who tried prototype models in mall intercept interviews provided ideas to further refine the design. The result is a touch pad

control that is easy to clean and so easy to use that consumers don't even need to read the manual.

Consumer research has been an even more important factor in Whirlpool's growth overseas. For example, until recently only about one-third of European households had a microwave oven. Whirlpool researchers learned that more people would buy a microwave oven if it could crisp food as it heated the food. Whirlpool designed a microwave with a broiler coil and other innovations. The result is an oven that is popular in Britain for frying bacon and eggs and in Italy for crisping pizza crusts.

Research also guided the design of a washing machine that sells for under $200 in developing nations. In Brazil, for example, workers earn an average of $220 a month, so few households have been able to afford a washer until now. Researchers who visited homes and observed manual washing realized that many Brazilians do laundry frequently and in small batches. As a result, automatic washers could be small, less powerful, and less costly to produce. However, focus groups revealed many low-income consumers saw the washer as a status symbol, so Whirlpool used stylish, colorful trim, four legs rather than the usual boxy styling, and a clear plastic lid that allows people to watch the washer operate.[17]

---

as a *single source* of complete information about customers' attitudes, shopping behavior, and media habits.

For example, Ocean Spray was seeing sales slip to competitors. Analysis of panel data revealed that households with kids are the heaviest purchasers of juice. Yet they purchased Ocean Spray on a less frequent basis. Further research with these panel members revealed this was due to its "too tart" taste and tendency to stain. To combat this, the company focused its energies on developing White Cranberry Juice Drinks by harvesting the berries before they develop their traditional red color and pungent taste. An ad for the new product depicted a mom and her small son enjoying the taste of the new White Cranberry juice. When the boy accidentally spills it on the floor, it's also clear that it doesn't stain.[18]

Data captured by electronic scanners is equally important to e-commerce in business-to-business markets. Increasingly, firms mark their shipping cartons and packages with computer-readable bar codes that make it fast and easy to track inventory, shipments, orders, and the like. As information about product sales or shipments becomes available, it is instantly included in the MIS and accessible over the Internet.[19]

Experimental method controls conditions

A marketing manager can get a different kind of information—with either questionnaire or observing—using the experimental method. With the **experimental method,** researchers compare the responses of two (or more) groups that are similar except on the characteristic being tested. Researchers want to learn if the specific

Simmons' ad agency used an experiment to improve a new print ad for the Beautyrest mattress. Groups of consumers saw two different ads. The ads were the same, except that one featured a father holding a baby and the other featured a mother. The ad with the father earned higher recall scores.

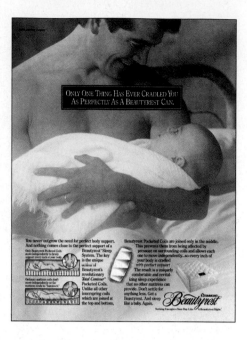

characteristic—which varies among groups—*causes* differences in some response among the groups. For example, a researcher might be interested in comparing responses of consumers who had seen an ad for a new product with consumers who had not seen the ad. The "response" might be an observed behavior—like the purchase of a product—or the answer to a specific question—like "How interested are you in this new product?" See Exhibit 8-4.

Marketing managers for Mars—the company that makes Snickers candy bars—used the experimental method to help solve a problem. They wanted to know if making their candy bar bigger would increase sales enough to offset the higher cost. To decide, they conducted a marketing experiment in which the company carefully varied the size of candy bars sold in *different* markets. Otherwise, the marketing mix stayed the same. Then researchers tracked sales in each market area to see the effect of the different sizes. They saw a big difference immediately: The added sales more than offset the cost of a bigger candy bar.

Exhibit 8-4   Illustration of Experimental Method in Comparing Effectiveness of Two Ads

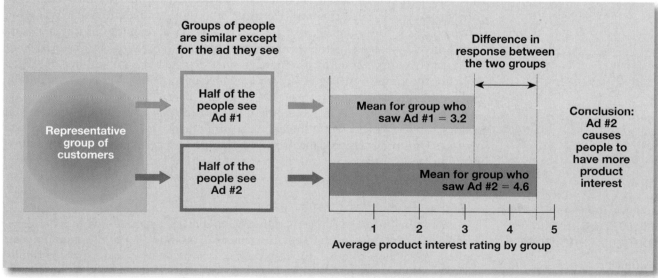

A firm's own data on customers' past purchases, if properly analyzed, can be an important source of information for evaluating new opportunities.

Test-marketing of new products is another type of marketing experiment. In a typical approach, a company tries variations on its planned marketing mix in a few geographic market areas. The results of the tests help to identify problems or refine the marketing mix—before the decision is made to go to broader distribution. However, alert competitors may disrupt such tests—perhaps by increasing promotion or offering retailers extra discounts. To avoid these problems, firms sometimes conduct tests in foreign markets.

Researchers don't use the experimental method as often as surveys and focus groups. Many managers don't understand the valuable information they can get from this method. Further, they don't like the idea of some researcher "experimenting" with their business.[20]

Syndicated research shares data collection costs

Some private research firms specialize in collecting data and then sell it to managers in many different client firms. Often the marketing manager subscribes to the research service and gets regular updates. About 40 percent of marketing research spending is for syndicated research, and this helps explain why it can be an economical approach when marketing managers from many different firms need the same type of data. For example, Market Facts (www.marketfacts.com) sells access to its surveys on home appliances and electronics, retail banking and insurance, and other product categories. Simmons Market Research Bureau (www.smrb.com) does extensive research on consumer media habits and then sells its data to many advertising agencies. Many different auto producers use J. D. Power's (www.jdpa.com) surveys of customer satisfaction—often as the basis for

advertising claims. Subscription data services are available for many different industries—ranging from food service to prescription drugs to micro electronic devices.[21]

INTERPRETING THE DATA—STEP 4

What does it really mean?

After someone collects the data, it has to be analyzed to decide what it all means. In quantitative research, this step usually involves statistics. **Statistical packages**—easy-to-use computer programs that analyze data—have made this step easier. As we noted earlier, some firms provide *decision support systems* so managers can use a statistical package to interpret data themselves. More often, however, technical specialists are involved at the interpretation step.

Cross-tabulation is one of the most frequently used approaches for analyzing and interpreting marketing research data. It shows the relationship of answers to two different questions. Exhibit 8-5 is an example. The cross-tab analysis showed that customers who had moved in the last year were much more likely than nonmovers to have adopted "Caller ID" on their phones at home.

There are many other approaches for statistical analysis—the best one depends on the situation. The details of statistical analysis are beyond the scope of this book.

Exhibit 8-5
Cross-Tabulation Breakdown of Responses to a Phone Company Consumer Survey

		Have You Moved in the Last Year?		
	Answers:	No	Yes	Total
Do you have "Caller ID" on your phone at home?	Yes	10.2%	23.4%	15.5%
	No	89.8	76.6	84.5
	Total	100.0%	100.0%	100.0%

Interpretation: 15.5 percent of people in the survey said that they had "Caller ID" on their phone at home. However, the percentage was much higher (23.4%) among people who had moved in the last year, and lower (10.2%) among people who had not moved.

But a good manager should know enough to understand what a research project can and can't do.[22]

Is your sample really representative?

It's usually impossible for marketing managers to collect all the information they want about everyone in a **population**—the total group they are interested in. Marketing researchers typically study only a **sample,** a part of the relevant population. How well a sample *represents* the total population affects the results. Results from a sample that is not representative may not give a true picture.

The manager of a retail store might want a phone survey to learn what consumers think about the store's hours. If interviewers make all of the calls during the day, consumers who work outside the home during the day won't be represented. Those interviewed might say the limited store hours are "satisfactory." Yet it would be a mistake to assume that *all* consumers are satisfied.

Random samples tend to be representative

You can see that getting a representative sample is very important. One method of doing so is **random sampling,** where each member of the population has the same chance of being included in the sample. Great care must be used to ensure that sampling is really random, not just haphazard.

If a random sample is chosen from a population, it will tend to have the same characteristics and be representative of the population. "Tend to" is important because it is only a tendency—the sample is not exactly the same as the population.

Much marketing research is based on nonrandom sampling because of the high cost and difficulty of obtaining a truly random sample. Sometimes nonrandom samples give very good results—especially in industrial markets where the number of customers may be relatively small and fairly similar. But results from nonrandom samples must be interpreted, and used, with care.

Research results are not exact

An estimate from a sample, even a representative one, usually varies somewhat from the true value for a total population. Managers sometimes forget this. They assume that survey results are exact. Instead, when interpreting sample estimates, managers should think of them as *suggesting* the approximate value.

If random selection is used to develop the sample, researchers can use various methods to help determine the likely accuracy of the sample value. This is done in terms of **confidence intervals**—the range on either side of an estimate that is likely to contain the true value for the whole population. Some managers are surprised to learn how wide that range can be.

Consider a wholesaler who has 1,000 retail customers and wants to learn how many of these retailers carry a product from a competing supplier. If the wholesaler randomly samples 100 retailers and 20 say yes, then the sample estimate is 20 percent. But with that information the wholesaler can only be 95 percent confident that the percentage of all retailers is in the confidence interval between 12 and 28 percent.[23]

The larger the sample size, the greater the accuracy of estimates from a random sample. With a larger sample, a few unusual responses are less likely to make a big difference.

Validity problems can destroy research

Even if the sampling is carefully planned, it is also important to evaluate the quality of the research data itself.

Managers and researchers should be sure that research data really measures what it is supposed to measure. Many of the variables marketing managers are interested in are difficult to measure accurately. Questionnaires may let us assign numbers to consumer responses, but that still doesn't mean that the result is precise. An interviewer might ask "How much did you spend on soft drinks last week?" A respondent may be perfectly willing to cooperate—and be part of the representative sample— but just not be able to remember.

Validity concerns the extent to which data measures what it is intended to measure. Validity problems are important in marketing research because many people will try to answer even when they don't know what they're talking about. Further, a poorly worded question can mean different things to different people and invalidate the results. Often, pretests of a research project are required to evaluate the quality of the questions and measures and to ensure that potential problems have been identified.

Poor interpretation can destroy research

Besides sampling and validity problems, a marketing manager must consider whether the analysis of the data supports the *conclusions* drawn in the interpretation step. Sometimes technical specialists pick the right statistical procedure—their calculations are exact—but they misinterpret the data because they don't understand the management problem. In one survey, car buyers were asked to rank five cars in order from "most preferred" to "least preferred." One car was ranked first by slightly more respondents than any other car so the researcher reported it as the "most liked car." That interpretation, however, ignored the fact that 70 percent of the respondents ranked the car *last*!

Interpretation problems like this can be subtle but crucial. Some people draw misleading conclusions on purpose to get the results they want. Marketing managers must decide whether *all* of the results support the interpretation and are relevant to their problem.

Marketing manager and researcher should work together

Marketing research involves many technical details. But you can see that the marketing researcher and the marketing manager must work together to be sure that they really do solve the problem facing the firm. If the whole research process has been a joint effort, then the interpretation step can move quickly to decision making— and solving the problem.

SOLVING THE PROBLEM—STEP 5

The last step is solving the problem

In the problem solution step, managers use the research results to make marketing decisions.

Some researchers, and some managers, are fascinated by the interesting tidbits of information that come from the research process. They are excited if the research

reveals something they didn't know before. But if research doesn't have action implications, it has little value and suggests poor planning by the researcher and the manager.

When the research process is finished, the marketing manager should be able to apply the findings in marketing strategy planning—the choice of a target market or the mix of the four Ps. If the research doesn't provide information to help guide these decisions, the company has wasted research time and money.

We emphasize this step because it is the reason for and logical conclusion to the whole research process. This final step must be anticipated at each of the earlier steps.

INTERNATIONAL MARKETING RESEARCH

Research contributes to international success

Marketing research on overseas markets is often a major contributor toward international marketing success. Conversely, export failures are often due to a lack of home office expertise concerning customer interests, needs, and other segmenting dimensions as well as environmental factors such as competitors' prices and products. Effective marketing research can help to overcome these problems.

Avoid mistakes with local researchers

Whether a firm is small and entering overseas markets for the first time or already large and well established internationally, there are often advantages to working with local market research firms. They know the local situation and are less likely to make mistakes based on misunderstanding the customs, language, or circumstances of the customers they study.

Many large research firms have a network of local offices around the world to help with such efforts. Similarly, multinational or local advertising agencies and middlemen can often provide leads on identifying the best research suppliers.

| Some coordination and standardization makes sense | When a firm is doing similar research projects in different markets around the world, it makes sense for the marketing manager to coordinate the efforts. If the manager doesn't establish some basic guidelines at the outset, the different research projects may all vary so much that the results can't be compared from one market area to another. Such comparisons give a home office manager a better chance of understanding how the markets are similar and how they differ. |

Companies with operations in various countries often attempt to centralize some market research functions. One reason is to reduce costs or achieve research economies of scale. The centralized approach also improves the firm's ability to transfer experience and know-how from one market area or project to another. For example, one of Eastman Kodak's International Divisions appointed a market research specialist in each subsidiary company throughout the Asian region. The specialists report to local marketing managers but also receive research direction from expert research managers in the head office in the U.S.

There is even greater opportunity and need to standardize and coordinate elements of a marketing information system in an international marketing operation. Computer databases and information systems are most useful when they are designed to include the same variables organized consistently over time. Without this, it is impossible for the manager to go into much depth in comparing and contrasting data from different markets.[24]

HOW MUCH INFORMATION DO YOU NEED?

What is the value of information?

We have been talking about the benefits of good marketing information, but dependable information can be expensive. For example, the continuing research available from companies such as Information Resources, Inc., can cost a company well over $100,000 a year.

The high cost of good information must be balanced against its probable value to management. Managers never get all the information they would like to have. Very detailed surveys or experiments may be "too good" or "too expensive" or "too late" if all the company needs is a rough sampling of retailer attitudes toward a new pricing plan by tomorrow. Money is also wasted if research shows that a manager's guesses are wrong and the manager ignores the facts.

Marketing managers must take risks because of incomplete information. That's part of their job and always will be. But they must weigh the cost of getting more data against its likely value. If the risk is not too great, the cost of getting more information may be greater than the potential loss from a poor decision. A decision to expand into a new territory with the present marketing mix, for example, might be made with more confidence after a $50,000 survey. But just sending a sales rep into the territory for a few weeks to try to sell potential customers would be a lot cheaper. And, if successful, the answer is in and so are some sales.[25]

CONCLUSION

Marketing managers face difficult decisions in selecting target markets and managing marketing mixes. And managers rarely have all the information they would like to have. This problem is usually worse for managers who work with international markets. But they don't have to rely only on intuition. They can usually obtain good information to improve the quality of their decisions.

Both large and small firms are taking advantage of the Internet and intranets to set up marketing information systems (MIS)—to be certain that routinely needed data is available and accessible quickly.

Marketing managers deal with rapidly changing environments. Available data is not always adequate to answer the detailed questions that arise. Then a marketing research project may be required to gather new information.

Marketing research should be guided by the scientific method. The scientific approach to solving marketing problems involves five steps: defining the problem, analyzing the situation, obtaining data, interpreting data, and solving the problem. This objective and orga-

nized approach helps to keep research on target—reducing the risk of doing costly research that isn't necessary or doesn't solve the problem.

Our strategy planning framework can be helpful in finding the real problem. By finding and focusing on the real problem, the researcher and marketing manager may be able to move quickly to a useful solution—without the cost and risks of gathering primary data in a formal research project. With imagination, they may even be able to find the answers in their MIS or in other readily available secondary data.

KEY TERMS

marketing information system (MIS), 212

intranet, 214

data warehouse, 214

decision support system (DSS), 214

search engine, 214

marketing model, 215

marketing research, 216

scientific method, 217

hypotheses, 217

marketing research process, 217

situation analysis, 219

secondary data, 220

primary data, 220

research proposal, 223

qualitative research, 223

focus group interview, 223

quantitative research, 225

response rate, 226

consumer panels, 229

experimental method, 229

statistical packages, 232

population, 233

sample, 233

random sampling, 233

confidence intervals, 234

validity, 234

QUESTIONS AND PROBLEMS

1. Discuss the concept of a marketing information system and why it is important for marketing managers to be involved in planning the system.

2. In your own words, explain why a decision support system (DSS) can add to the value of a marketing information system. Give an example of how a decision support system might help.

3. If a firm's intranet and marketing decision support system do not include a search engine, would they still be useful to a marketing manager? Why?

4. Discuss how output from a marketing information system (MIS) might differ from the output of a typical marketing research department.

5. Discuss some of the likely problems facing the marketing manager in a small firm that has just purchased a personal computer with a cable modem to search the Internet for information on competitors' marketing plans.

6. Explain the key characteristics of the scientific method and show why these are important to managers concerned with research.

7. How is the situation analysis different from the data collection step? Can both these steps be done at the same time to obtain answers sooner? Is this wise?

8. Distinguish between primary data and secondary data and illustrate your answer.

9. With so much secondary information now available free or at low cost over the Internet, why would a firm ever want to spend the money to do primary research?

10. If a firm were interested in estimating the distribution of income in the state of California, how could it proceed? Be specific.

11. If a firm were interested in estimating sand and clay production in Georgia, how could it proceed? Be specific.

12. Go to the library (or get on the Internet) and find (in some government publication or website) three marketing-oriented "facts" on international markets that you did not know existed or were available. Record on one page and show sources.

13. Explain why a company might want to do focus group interviews rather than individual interviews with the same people.

14. Distinguish between qualitative and quantitative approaches to research—and give some of the key advantages and limitations of each approach.

15. Define response rate and discuss why a marketing manager might be concerned about the response rate achieved in a particular survey. Give an example.

16. Prepare a table that summarizes some of the key advantages and limitations of mail, e-mail, telephone, and personal interview approaches for administering questionnaires.

17. Would a firm want to subscribe to a shared cost data service if the same data were going to be available to competitors? Discuss your reasoning.

18. Explain how you might use different types of research (focus groups, observation, survey, and experiment) to forecast market reaction to a new kind of dispos- able baby diaper, which is to receive no promotion other than what the retailer will give it. Further, assume that the new diaper's name will not be associated with other known products. The product will be offered at competitive prices.

19. Marketing research involves expense—sometimes considerable expense. Why does the text recommend the use of marketing research even though a highly experienced marketing executive is available?

20. A marketing manager is considering opportunities to export her firm's current consumer products to several different countries. She is interested in getting secondary data that will help her narrow down choices to countries that offer the best potential. The manager then plans to do more detailed primary research with consumers in those markets. What suggestions would you give her about how to proceed?

21. Discuss the concept that some information may be too expensive to obtain in relation to its value. Illustrate.

SUGGESTED CASES

8. Marie's Ristorante

9. SleepEasy Motel

COMPUTER-AIDED PROBLEM

8. Marketing Research

RESOURCE REMINDER

Texmac, Inc., has an idea for a new type of weaving machine that could replace the machines now used by many textile manufacturers. Texmac has done a telephone survey to estimate how many of the old-style machines are now in use. Respondents using the present machines were also asked if they would buy the improved machine at a price of $10,000.

Texmac researchers identified a population of about 5,000 textile factories as potential customers. A sample of these were surveyed, and Texmac received 500 responses. Researchers think the total potential market is about 10 times larger than the sample of respondents. Two hundred twenty of the respondents indicated that their firms used old machines like the one the new machine was intended to replace. Forty percent of those firms said that they would be interested in buying the new Texmac machine.

Texmac thinks the sample respondents are representative of the total population, but the marketing manager realizes that estimates based on a sample may not be exact when applied to the whole population. He wants to see how sampling error would affect profit estimates. Data for this problem appears in the spreadsheet. Quantity estimates for the whole market are computed from the sample estimates. These quantity estimates are used in computing likely sales, costs, and profit contribution.

a. An article in a trade magazine reports that there are about 5,200 textile factories that use the old-style machine. If the total market is really 5,200 customers—not 5,000 as Texmac originally thought—how does that affect the total quantity estimate and profit contribution?

b. Some of the people who responded to the survey didn't know much about different types of machines. If the actual number of old machines in the market is really 200 per 500 firms—not 220 as estimated from survey responses—how much would this affect the expected profit contribution (for 5,200 factories)?

c. The marketing manager knows that the percentage of textile factories that would actually buy the new machine might be different from the 40 percent who said they would in the survey. He estimates that the proportion that will replace the old machine might be as low as 36 and as high as 44 percent—depending on business conditions. Use the analysis feature to prepare a table that shows how expected quantity and profit contribution change when the sample percent varies between a minimum of 36 and a maximum of 44 percent. What does this analysis suggest about the use of estimates from marketing research samples? (Note: Use 5,200 for the number of potential customers and use 220 as the estimate of the number of old machines in the sample.)

For additional questions related to this problem, see Exercise 8-3 in the *Learning Aid for Use with Basic Marketing,* 15th edition.

1. Understand what "Product" really means.

2. Know the key differences between goods and services.

3. Know the differences among the various consumer and business product classes.

4. Understand how the product classes can help a marketing manager plan marketing strategies.

5. Understand what branding is and how to use it in strategy planning.

6. Understand the importance of packaging in strategy planning.

7. Understand the role of warranties in strategy planning.

8. Understand the important new terms (shown in red).

CHAPTER NINE

Elements of Product Planning for Goods and Services

The Segway™ Human Transporter (HT) isn't just a new product, it's a new product concept. A design engineer is likely to be excited by the Segway HT's unique features. Under the power of its rechargeable batteries, its onboard computers and five gyroscopes automatically balance the two-wheel superscooter as its rider glides down the sidewalk at up to 12 mph. Even the two-tone plastic fenders that sit above the wheels are unique. They are coated with Sollx, a high-quality chemical film developed by General Electric; Sollx gleams like colorful paint, but it resists scratches.

Of course, most customers don't dwell on technical features like Sollx, gyroscopes, or central processors; instead, they think about the benefits and satisfaction that might come from using the product. The benefits that the Segway HT offers depend to some extent on

whether it is sold as a consumer product or a business product. For example, a firm might buy a unit because it provides a fast, safe, and nonpolluting way for workers to get around inside a sprawling distribution center. Similarly, the Post Office has evaluated it as a way to cut costs as mail carriers go from house to house. Alternatively, upscale consumers who live in congested urban areas might see it as a fun, quiet, and flexible way to get around without worrying about traffic, parking, or fill-ups at a gas station. It costs only about ten cents a day to charge the battery.

Before the Segway HT was introduced, the new product development process was wrapped in secrecy. Rumors even spread on the Internet that it might be some sort of hovercraft. This created some unrealistic expectations, but it also stimulated media coverage, publicity, and initial sales at Amazon.com. Thousands of units sold that way. Now Segway's website (www.segway.com) lists the names and locations of Segway dealers. This is still a selective distribution effort. Distribution through dealers makes sense for this sort of product. A customer who visits a local dealer can inspect the different models in the Segway product line and a salesperson can answer questions. In addition, before spending $4,500 on a Segway HT, a customer is likely to ask "where do I get warranty service if I have a problem?" In fact, some customers were reminded of such after-the-sale service issues when Segway announced a voluntary product recall. The Consumer Product Safety Commission encouraged the recall to head off tipping-over problems that could occur if a rider ignored warning messages or the unit lacked power for a maneuver.

While Segway has had its share of publicity, the Segway HT is still an unsought product for many consumers. They don't know what someone might do with a "human transporter." In some places, the device may continue to be unsought if pedestrian groups fight the idea of sharing sidewalks with Segway HTs. But Dean Kamen, Segway HT's inventor, likes to compare it to the Stanley Steamer and early automobiles. When the automobile was first available, it was a curiosity that only the rich could afford. At that time, a horse and carriage was cheaper and more reliable. No one was predicting that 25 years later there would be no more horses in cities. And who could have anticipated that those early automobiles would spark 100 years of sales growth and hundreds of competing brands—ranging from Hummers and PT Cruisers to BMW Z8s and Lexus sedans—for a variety of needs. So what do *you* think? Will the Segway HT pioneer growth of a new type of product market? Or, instead, will it just become an interesting collector's item?[1]

THE PRODUCT AREA INVOLVES MANY STRATEGY DECISIONS

The Segway case highlights some important topics we'll discuss in this chapter and the next. Here we'll start by looking at how customers see a firm's product. Then we'll talk about product classes to help you better understand marketing strategy planning. We'll also talk about branding, packaging, and warranties. As shown in Exhibit 9-1, there are many strategy decisions related to the Product area.

WHAT IS A PRODUCT?

Customers buy satisfaction, not parts

When Nikon sells a Coolpix digital camera, is it just selling a certain number of switches and buttons, a plastic case, a lens, and megapixels of memory?

When Air Jamaica sells a ticket for a flight to the Caribbean, is it just selling so much wear and tear on an airplane and so much pilot fatigue?

The answer to these questions is *no*. Instead, what these companies are really selling is the satisfaction, use, or benefit the customer wants.

All consumers care about is that their Coolpix cameras make it easy to take cool pictures. And when they take a trip on Air Jamaica, they really don't care how hard it is on the plane or the crew. They just want a safe, comfortable trip. In the same way, when producers and middlemen buy a product, they're interested in the profit they can make from its purchase—through use or resale.

Product means the need-satisfying offering of a firm. The idea of "Product" as potential customer satisfaction or benefits is very important. Many business managers

Exhibit 9-1
Strategy Planning for
Product

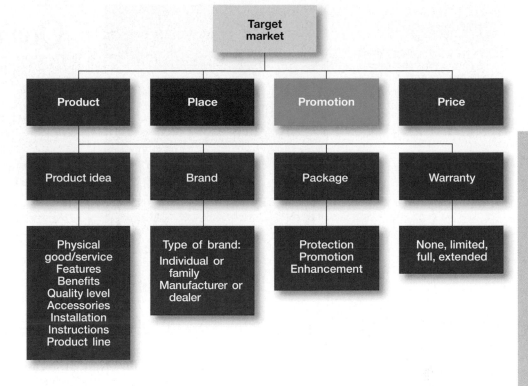

get wrapped up in the technical details involved in producing a product. But that's not how most customers view the product. Most customers think about a product in terms of the total satisfaction it provides. That satisfaction may require a "total" product offering that is really a combination of excellent service, a physical good with the right features, useful instructions, a convenient package, a trustworthy warranty, and perhaps even a familiar name that has satisfied the consumer in the past.

Product quality is not always a life or death matter, but a firm that provides customers with superior customer value is likely to have a competitive advantage.

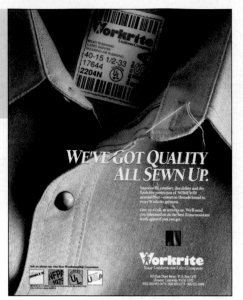

Product quality and customer needs

Product quality should also be determined by how customers view the product. From a marketing perspective, **quality** means a product's ability to satisfy a customer's needs or requirements. This definition focuses on the customer—and how the customer thinks a product will fit some purpose. For example, the "best" satellite TV service may not be the one with the highest number of channels but the one that includes a local channel that a consumer wants to watch. Similarly, the best-quality clothing for casual wear on campus may be a pair of jeans, not a pair of dress slacks made of a higher-grade fabric.

Among different types of jeans, the one with the strongest stitching and the most comfortable or durable fabric might be thought of as having the highest grade or *relative quality* for its product type. Marketing managers often focus on relative quality when comparing their products to competitors' offerings. However, a product with better features is not a high-quality product if the features aren't what the target market wants.

Quality and satisfaction depend on the total product offering. If potato chips get stale on the shelf because of poor packaging, the consumer will be dissatisfied. A broken button on a shirt will disappoint the customer—even if the laundry did a nice job cleaning and pressing the collar. A full-featured TiVo digital video recorder is a poor-quality product if it's hard for a consumer to program a recording session.[2]

Goods and/or services are the product

You already know that a product may be a physical *good* or a *service* or a *blend* of both. Yet, it's too easy to slip into a limited, physical-product point of view. We want to think of a product in terms of the needs it satisfies. If a firm's objective is to satisfy customer needs, service can be part of its product—or service alone may *be* the product—and must be provided as part of a total marketing mix.

Exhibit 9-2 shows this bigger view of Product. It shows that a product can range from a 100 percent emphasis on physical goods—for commodities like steel pipe—to a 100 percent emphasis on service, like Internet access from EarthLink. Regardless of the emphasis involved, the marketing manager must consider most of the same elements in planning products and marketing mixes. Given this, we usually won't make a distinction between goods and services but will call all of them *Products*. Sometimes, however, understanding the differences in goods and services can help fine-tune marketing strategy planning. So let's look at some of these differences next.

Exhibit 9-2
Examples of Possible Blends of Physical Goods and Services in a Product

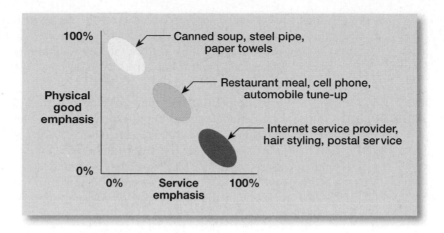

- 100% — Canned soup, steel pipe, paper towels
- Physical good emphasis — Restaurant meal, cell phone, automobile tune-up
- Internet service provider, hair styling, postal service
- 0%
- 0% — Service emphasis — 100%

DIFFERENCES IN GOODS AND SERVICES

How tangible is the product?

Because a good is a physical thing, it can be seen and touched. You can try on a pair of Timberland shoes, thumb through the latest issue of *Rolling Stone* magazine, or smell Colombian coffee as it brews. A good is a *tangible* item. When you buy it, you own it. And it's usually pretty easy to see exactly what you'll get.

On the other hand, a **service** is a deed performed by one party for another. When you provide a customer with a service, the customer can't keep it. Rather, a service is experienced, used, or consumed. You go see a DreamWorks Pictures movie, but afterward all you have is a memory. You ride on a ski lift in the Alps, but you don't own the equipment. Services are not physical—they are *intangible*. You can't "hold" a service. And it may be hard to know exactly what you'll get when you buy it.

Most products are a combination of tangible and intangible elements. A Domino's pizza is tangible, but the fast home delivery is not.

Is the product produced before it's sold?

Goods are usually produced in a factory and then sold. A Sony flat-screen TV may be stored in a warehouse or store waiting for a buyer. By contrast, services are often sold first, then produced. And they're produced and consumed in the same

State Farm knows that customers often want to have personal contact with an insurance agent, so its marketing mix relies on local agents and its promotion says "we live where you live." Orbitz offers many services to its customers including e-mail updates on airline schedules. Service is a key element of the product offered by both State Farm and Orbitz.

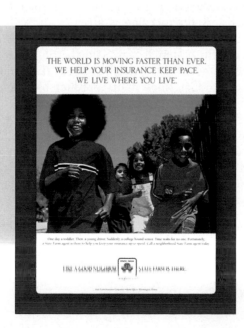

time frame. Thus, goods producers may be far away from the customer, but service providers often work in the customer's presence.

A worker in a Sony TV factory can be in a bad mood—and customers will never know. But a rude bank teller can drive customers away.

Services can't be stored or transported

Services are perishable—they can't be stored. This makes it harder to balance supply and demand. An example explains the problem.

MCI sells long-distance telephone services. Even on Mother's Day when demand is high, customers expect the service to be available. They don't want to hear "Sorry, all lines are busy." So MCI must have enough equipment and employees to deal with peak demand times. But when customers aren't making many calls, MCI's facilities are idle and the unused capacity (equipment and people) can't be saved and sold later.

It's often difficult to have economies of scale when the product emphasis is on service. *Services often have to be produced in the presence of the customer.* So service suppliers often need duplicate equipment and staff at places where the service is actually provided. Merrill Lynch sells investment advice along with financial products worldwide. That advice could, perhaps, be produced more economically in a single building in New York City and made available only on its website. But Merrill Lynch has offices all over the world. Many customers want a personal touch from the stockbroker telling them how to invest their money.[3]

Think about the whole product

Providing the right product—when and where and how the customer wants it— is a challenge. This is true whether the product is primarily a service, primarily a good, or as is usually the case, a blend of both. Marketing managers must think about the "whole" Product they provide, and then make sure that all of the elements fit together and work with the rest of the marketing strategy. Sometimes a single product isn't enough to meet the needs of target customers. Then assortments of different products may be required.

WHOLE PRODUCT LINES MUST BE DEVELOPED TOO

A **product assortment** is the set of all product lines and individual products that a firm sells. A **product line** is a set of individual products that are closely related. The seller may see the products in a line as related because they're produced or operate in a similar way, sold to the same target market, sold through the same types of outlets, or priced at about the same level. Sara Lee, for example, has many product lines in its product assortment—including coffee, tea, luncheon meats, desserts, snacks, hosiery, sportswear, lingerie, and shoe polish. But Enterprise has one product line—different types of vehicles to rent. An **individual product** is a particular product within a product line. It usually is differentiated by brand, level of service offered, price, or some other characteristic. For example, each size and flavor of a brand of soap is an individual product. Middlemen usually think of each separate product as a stock-keeping unit (SKU) and assign it a unique SKU number.

Each individual product and target market may require a separate strategy. For example, Sara Lee's strategy for selling its Café Pilão coffee in Brazil is different from its strategy for selling Hanes men's underwear in the United States. We'll focus mainly on developing one marketing strategy at a time. But remember that a marketing manager may have to plan *several* strategies to develop an effective marketing program for a whole company.

PRODUCT CLASSES HELP PLAN MARKETING STRATEGIES

You don't have to treat *every* product as unique when planning strategies. Some product classes require similar marketing mixes. These product classes are a useful starting point for developing marketing mixes for new products and evaluating present mixes.

Product classes start with type of customer

All products fit into one of two broad groups—based on the type of customer that will use them. **Consumer products** are products meant for the final consumer. **Business products** are products meant for use in producing other products.

The same product—like Bertolli Olive Oil—*might* be both a consumer product and a business product. Consumers buy it to use in their own kitchens, but food processing companies and restaurants buy it in large quantities as an ingredient in

the products they sell. Selling the same product to both final consumers and business customers requires (at least) two different strategies.

There are product classes within each group. Consumer product classes are based on *how consumers think about and shop for products*. Business product classes are based on *how buyers think about products and how they'll be used*.

CONSUMER PRODUCT CLASSES

Consumer product classes divide into four groups: (1) convenience, (2) shopping, (3) specialty, and (4) unsought. *Each class is based on the way people buy products.* See Exhibit 9-3 for a summary of how these product classes relate to marketing mixes.[4]

Convenience products—purchased quickly with little effort

Convenience products are products a consumer needs but isn't willing to spend much time or effort shopping for. These products are bought often, require little service or selling, don't cost much, and may even be bought by habit. A convenience product may be a staple, impulse product, or emergency product.

Staples are products that are bought often, routinely, and without much thought—like breakfast cereal, canned soup, and most other packaged foods used almost every day in almost every household.

Exhibit 9-3   Consumer Product Classes and Marketing Mix Planning

Consumer Product Class	Marketing Mix Considerations	Consumer Behavior
Convenience products		
Staples	Maximum exposure with widespread, low-cost distribution; mass selling by producer; usually low price; branding is important.	Routinized (habitual), low effort, frequent purchases; low involvement.
Impulse	Widespread distribution with display at point of purchase.	Unplanned purchases bought quickly.
Emergency	Need widespread distribution near probable point of need; price sensitivity low.	Purchase made with time pressure when a need is great.
Shopping products		
Homogeneous	Need enough exposure to facilitate price comparison; price sensitivity high.	Customers see little difference among alternatives, seek lowest price.
Heterogeneous	Need distribution near similar products; promotion (including personal selling) to highlight product advantages; less price sensitivity.	Extensive problem solving; consumer may need help in making a decision (salesperson, website, etc.).
Specialty products	Price sensitivity is likely to be low; limited distribution may be acceptable, but should be treated as a convenience or shopping product (in whichever category product would typically be included) to reach persons not yet sold on its specialty product status.	Willing to expend effort to get specific product, even if not necessary; strong preferences make it an important purchase; Internet becoming important information source.
Unsought products		
New unsought	Must be available in places where similar (or related) products are sought; needs attention-getting promotion.	Need for product not strongly felt; unaware of benefits or not yet gone through adoption process.
Regularly unsought	Requires very aggressive promotion, usually personal selling.	Aware of product but not interested; attitude toward product may even be negative.

Many consumers shop for plates and other tableware as if they were homogeneous products, but Crate & Barrel wants customers to see its distinctive offerings as heterogeneous shopping products, or perhaps even specialty items.

The average person spends 26 years finding the right partner. 13 months finding the right church. 8 months finding the right caterer. And 6 months finding the right honeymoon spot. Which just may explain why the average person often ends up with the wrong plates.

Crate&Barrel

Impulse products are products that are bought quickly—as *unplanned* purchases—because of a strongly felt need. True impulse products are items that the customer hadn't planned to buy, decides to buy on sight, may have bought the same way many times before, and wants right now. If the buyer doesn't see an impulse product at the right time, the sale may be lost.[5]

Emergency products are products that are purchased immediately when the need is great. The customer doesn't have time to shop around when a traffic accident occurs, a thunderstorm begins, or an impromptu party starts. The price of the ambulance service, raincoat, or ice cubes won't be important.

Shopping products— are compared

Shopping products are products that a customer feels are worth the time and effort to compare with competing products. Shopping products can be divided into two types, depending on what customers are comparing: (1) homogeneous or (2) heterogeneous shopping products.

Homogeneous shopping products are shopping products the customer sees as basically the same and wants at the lowest price. Some consumers feel that certain sizes and types of computers, television sets, washing machines, and even cars are very similar. So they shop for the best price. For some products, the Internet has become a way to do that quickly.

Firms may try to emphasize and promote their product differences to avoid head-to-head price competition. For example, Rustoleum says that its spray paint goes on smoother and does a better job of preventing rust. But if consumers don't think the differences are real or important in terms of the value they seek, they'll just look at price.

Heterogeneous shopping products are shopping products the customer sees as different and wants to inspect for quality and suitability. Furniture, clothing, and membership in a spa are good examples. Often the consumer expects help from a knowledgeable salesperson. Quality and style matter more than price. In fact, once the customer finds the right product, price may not matter as long as it's reasonable. For example, you may have asked a friend to recommend a good dentist without even asking what the dentist charges.

Branding may be less important for heterogeneous shopping products. The more carefully consumers compare price and quality, the less they rely on brand names or labels. Some retailers carry competing brands so consumers won't go to a competitor to compare items.

Specialty products— no substitutes please!

Specialty products are consumer products that the customer really wants and makes a special effort to find. Shopping for a specialty product doesn't mean comparing—the buyer wants that special product and is willing to search for it. It's the customer's *willingness to search*—not the extent of searching—that makes it a specialty product.

Any branded product that consumers insist on by name is a specialty product. Marketing managers want customers to see their products as specialty products and ask for them over and over again. Building that kind of relationship isn't easy. It means satisfying the customer every time. However, that's easier and a lot less costly than trying to win back dissatisfied customers or attract new customers who are not seeking the product at all.

Unsought products—need promotion

Unsought products are products that potential customers don't yet want or know they can buy. So they don't search for them at all. In fact, consumers probably won't buy these products if they see them—unless Promotion can show their value.

There are two types of unsought products. **New unsought products** are products offering really new ideas that potential customers don't know about yet. Informative promotion can help convince customers to accept the product, ending its unsought status. Dannon's yogurt, Litton's microwave ovens, and Netscape's browser are all popular items now, but initially they were new unsought products.

Regularly unsought products are products—like gravestones, life insurance, and encyclopedias—that stay unsought but not unbought forever. There may be a need, but potential customers aren't motivated to satisfy it. For this kind of product, personal selling is *very* important.

Many nonprofit organizations try to "sell" their unsought products. For example, the Red Cross regularly holds blood drives to remind prospective donors of how important it is to give blood.

One product may be seen several ways

The same product might be seen in different ways by different target markets at the same time. For example, a product viewed as a staple by most consumers in the United States, Canada, or some similar affluent country might be seen as a heterogeneous shopping product by consumers in another country. The price might be much higher when considered as a proportion of the consumer's budget, and the available choices might be very different. Similarly, a convenient place to shop often means very different things in different countries. In Japan, for example, retail stores tend to be smaller and carry smaller selections of products.

BUSINESS PRODUCTS ARE DIFFERENT

Business product classes are also useful for developing marketing mixes—since business firms use a system of buying related to these product classes.

Before looking at business product differences, however, we'll note some important similarities that affect marketing strategy planning.

One demand derived from another

The big difference in the business products market is **derived demand**—the demand for business products derives from the demand for final consumer products. For example, car manufacturers buy about one-fifth of all steel products. But if demand for cars drops, they'll buy less steel. Then even the steel supplier with the best marketing mix is likely to lose sales.[6]

Price increases might not reduce quantity purchased

Total *industry* demand for business products is fairly inelastic. Business firms must buy what they need to produce their own products. Even if the cost of basic silicon doubles, for example, Intel needs it to make computer chips. However, sharp business buyers try to buy as economically as possible. So the demand facing *individual sellers* may be extremely elastic—if similar products are available at a lower price.

Businesses buy the goods and services they need to produce products for their own customers, so the demand for GE's special plastic resins, used to make lightweight and impact-resistant body panels, is derived from consumer demand for VW's unique car.

Tax treatment affects buying too

How a firm's accountants—and the tax laws—treat a purchase is also important to business customers. An **expense item** is a product whose total cost is treated as a business expense in the year it's purchased. A **capital item** is a long-lasting product that can be used and depreciated for many years. Often it's very expensive. Customers pay for the capital item when they buy it, but for tax purposes the cost is spread over a number of years. This may reduce the cash available for other purchases.

BUSINESS PRODUCT CLASSES—HOW THEY ARE DEFINED

Business product classes are based on how buyers see products and how the products will be used. The classes of business products are (1) installations, (2) accessories, (3) raw materials, (4) components, (5) supplies, and (6) professional services. Exhibit 9-4 relates these product classes to marketing mix planning.

Installations—a boom-or-bust business

Installations—such as buildings, land rights, and major equipment—are important capital items. One-of-a-kind installations—like office buildings and custom-made machines—generally require special negotiations for each sale. Negotiations often involve top management and can stretch over months or even years. Standardized major equipment is treated more routinely.

Installations are a boom-or-bust business. During growth periods, firms may buy installations to increase capacity. But during a downswing, sales fall off sharply.[7]

Specialized services are needed as part of the product

Suppliers sometimes include special services with an installation at no extra cost. A firm that sells (or leases) equipment to dentists, for example, may install it and help the dentist learn to use it.

Accessories—important but short-lived capital items

Accessories are short-lived capital items—tools and equipment used in production or office activities—like Canon's small copy machines, Rockwell's portable drills, and Steelcase's filing cabinets.

Since these products cost less and last a shorter time than installations, multiple buying influence is less important. Operating people and purchasing agents, rather

Exhibit 9-4   Business Product Classes and Marketing Mix Planning

Business Product Classes	Marketing Mix Considerations	Buying Behavior
Installations	Usually requires skillful personal selling by producer, including technical contacts, or understanding of applications; leasing and specialized support services may be required.	Multiple buying influence (including top management) and new-task buying are common; infrequent purchase, long decision period, and boom-or-bust demand are typical.
Accessory equipment	Need fairly widespread distribution and numerous contacts by experienced and sometimes technically trained personnel; price competition is often intense, but quality is important.	Purchasing and operating personnel typically make decisions; shorter decision period than for installations; Internet sourcing.
Raw materials	Grading is important, and transportation and storing can be crucial because of seasonal production and/or perishable products; markets tend to be very competitive.	Long-term contract may be required to ensure supply; online auctions.
Component parts and materials	Product quality and delivery reliability are usually extremely important; negotiation and technical selling typical on less-standardized items; replacement after market may require different strategies.	Multiple buying influence is common; online competitive bids used to encourage competitive pricing.
Maintenance, repair, and operating (MRO) supplies	Typically require widespread distribution or fast delivery (repair items); arrangements with appropriate middlemen may be crucial.	Often handled as straight rebuys, except important operating supplies may be treated much more seriously and involve multiple buying influence.
Professional services	Services customized to buyer's need; personal selling very important; inelastic demand often supports high prices.	Customer may compare outside service with what internal people could provide; needs may be very specialized.

than top managers, may make the purchase decision. As with installations, some customers may wish to lease or rent—to expense the cost.

Accessories are more standardized than installations. And they're usually needed by more customers. For example, IBM sells its robotics systems, which can cost over $2 million, as custom installations to large manufacturers. But IBM's Thinkpad computers are accessory equipment for just about every type of modern business all around the world.

Raw materials become part of a physical good

Raw materials are unprocessed expense items—such as logs, iron ore, and wheat—that are moved to the next production process with little handling. Unlike installations and accessories, *raw materials become part of a physical good and are expense items*.

There are two types of raw materials: (1) farm products and (2) natural products. **Farm products** are grown by farmers—examples are oranges, sugar cane, and cattle. **Natural products** are products that occur in nature—such as timber, iron ore, oil, and coal.

The need for grading is one of the important differences between raw materials and other business products. Nature produces what it will—and someone must sort and grade raw materials to satisfy various market segments.

Most buyers of raw materials want ample supplies in the right grades for specific uses—fresh vegetables for Green Giant's production lines or logs for Weyerhaeuser's paper mills. To ensure steady quantities, raw materials customers often sign long-term contracts, sometimes at guaranteed prices.

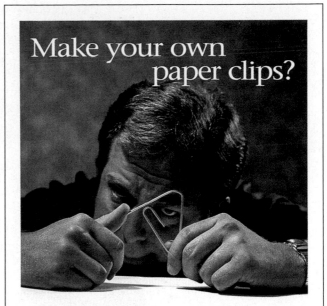

PerkinElmer produces component parts used by aircraft engine original equipment manufacturers (OEMs). It also sells airplane owners the maintenance, repair, and operating (MRO) supplies they need. The marketing mix for the two target markets is different, but the firm wants MRO customers to know that they are dealing with the same team of experts who sold the original equipment. ADP, by contrast, sells professional services. It wants potential customers to see that it makes sense to have ADP handle human resource administrative tasks that might otherwise be handled by a firm's own employees.

Component parts and materials must meet specifications

Components are processed expense items that become part of a finished product. Component *parts* are finished (or nearly finished) items that are ready for assembly into the final product. ATI's graphics cards included in personal computers, TRW's air bags in cars, and Briggs and Stratton's engines for lawn mowers are examples. Component *materials* are items such as wire, plastic, or textiles. They have already been processed but must be processed further before becoming part of the final product. Quality is important with components because they become part of the firm's own product.

Components are often produced in large quantity to meet standard specifications. However, some components are custom-made. Then teamwork between the buyer and seller may be needed to arrive at the right specifications. So a buyer may develop a close partnership with a dependable supplier. And top management may be involved if the price is high or the component is extremely important to the final product. In contrast, standardized component materials are more likely to be purchased online using a competitive bidding system.

Since component parts go into finished products, a replacement market often develops. This after market can be both large and very profitable. Car tires and batteries are two examples of components originally sold in the OEM (*original equipment market*) that become consumer products in the after market. The target markets are different—and different marketing mixes are usually necessary.[8]

Service Master helps hospitals improve a new mom's satisfaction with the hospital by serving "celebration meals." Many companies outsource computer technical support work to outside service providers.

Supplies for maintenance, repair, and operations

Supplies are expense items that do not become part of a finished product. Buyers may treat these items less seriously. When a firm cuts its budget, orders for supplies may be the first to go. Supplies can be divided into three types: (1) maintenance, (2) repair, and (3) operating supplies—giving them their common name: MRO supplies.

Maintenance and small operating supplies are like convenience products. The item will be ordered because it is needed—but buyers won't spend much time on it. Branding may become important because it makes buying easier for such "nuisance" purchases. Breadth of assortment and the seller's dependability are also important. Middlemen usually handle the many supply items. They are often purchased via online catalog sites.[9]

Important operating supplies, like coal and fuel oil, receive special treatment. Usually there are several sources for such commodity products—and large volumes may be purchased at global exchanges on the Internet.

Professional services—pay to get it done

Professional services are specialized services that support a firm's operations. They are usually expense items. Engineering or management consulting services can improve the plant layout or the company's efficiency. Information technology services can maintain a company's networks and websites. Design services can suggest a new look for products or promotion materials. Advertising agencies can help promote the firm's products. And food services can improve morale.

Managers compare the cost of buying professional services outside the firm (*outsourcing*) to the cost of having company people do them. Further, many firms try to cut costs by downsizing the number of people that they employ. In many cases, work that was previously done by an employee is now purchased from an independent supplier. Clearly, the number of service specialists is growing in our complex economy.

BRANDING NEEDS A STRATEGY DECISION TOO

There are so many brands—and we're so used to seeing them—that we take them for granted. But branding is an important decision area, so we will treat it in some detail.

What is branding?

Branding means the use of a name, term, symbol, or design—or a combination of these—to identify a product. It includes the use of brand names, trademarks, and practically all other means of product identification.

Brand name has a narrower meaning. A **brand name** is a word, letter, or a group of words or letters. Examples include America Online (AOL), WD-40, 3M Post-its, and PT Cruiser.

Trademark is a legal term. A **trademark** includes only those words, symbols, or marks that are legally registered for use by a single company. A **service mark** is the same as a trademark except that it refers to a service offering.

The word *FedEx* can be used to explain these differences. The FedEx overnight delivery service is branded under the brand name FedEx (whether it's spoken or printed in any manner). When "FedEx" is printed in a certain kind of script, however, it becomes a trademark. A trademark need not be attached to the product. It need not even be a word—it can be a symbol. Exhibit 9-5 shows some common trademarks.

These differences may seem technical. But they are very important to business firms that spend a lot of money to protect and promote their brands. Sometimes a firm's brand name is the only element in its marketing mix that a competitor can't copy.

Brands meet needs

Well-recognized brands make shopping easier. Think of trying to buy groceries, for example, if you had to evaluate each of 25,000 items every time you went to a supermarket. Many customers are willing to buy new things—but having gambled and won, they like to buy a sure thing the next time.

Brand promotion has advantages for branders as well as customers. A good brand reduces the marketer's selling time and effort. Good brands can also improve the company's image—speeding acceptance of new products marketed under the same name. For example, many consumers quickly tried Listerine PocketPaks breath fresheners when they appeared because they already knew they liked Listerine mouthwash.[10]

CONDITIONS FAVORABLE TO BRANDING

Can you recall a brand name for file folders, bed frames, electric extension cords, or nails? As these examples suggest, it's not always easy to establish a respected brand.

The following conditions are favorable to successful branding:

1. The product is easy to label and identify by brand or trademark.
2. The product quality is easy to maintain and the best value for the price.
3. Dependable and widespread availability is possible. When customers start using a brand, they want to be able to continue using it.
4. Demand is strong enough that the market price can be high enough to make the branding effort profitable.
5. There are economies of scale. If the branding is really successful, costs should drop and profits should increase.
6. Favorable shelf locations or display space in stores will help. This is something retailers can control when they brand their own products.

In general, these conditions are less common in less-developed economies, and that may explain why efforts to build brands in less-developed nations often fail.

ACHIEVING BRAND FAMILIARITY IS NOT EASY

The earliest and most aggressive brand promoters in America were the patent medicine companies. They were joined by the food manufacturers, who grew in size after the Civil War. Some of the brands started in the 1860s and 1870s (and still going strong) are Borden's Condensed Milk, Quaker Oats, Pillsbury's Best Flour, and Ivory Soap. Today, familiar brands exist for most product categories, ranging from crayons (Crayola) to real estate services (Century 21). However, what brand is familiar often varies from one country to another.

Brand acceptance must be earned with a good product and regular promotion. **Brand familiarity** means how well customers recognize and accept a company's brand. The degree of brand familiarity affects the planning for the rest of the marketing mix—especially where the product should be offered and what promotion is needed.

Five levels of brand familiarity

Five levels of brand familiarity are useful for strategy planning: (1) rejection, (2) nonrecognition, (3) recognition, (4) preference, and (5) insistence.

Some brands have been tried and found wanting. **Brand rejection** means that potential customers won't buy a brand unless its image is changed. Rejection may suggest a

It takes time and money to build brand awareness, so sometimes brands can be extended to new product offerings and different product categories. Dove has recently introduced new products that benefit from its well-recognized brand name.

Nutrition Bar

WHAT COLOR COLA WOULD YOU LIKE?

Marketing managers for Pepsi Bottling are seeking new customers. The traditional competition with Coke and retailers' private-label colas continues to be a challenge. However, another battle is brewing over the new generation of youthful soda drinkers—the "heavy users." They are less homogeneous than in the past. Many don't find big brands as appealing, and some don't see *any* cola as "their" drink. They want something different. So Pepsi developed a number of new products to appeal to different segments of this market. One of these was Code Red, a cherry-flavored, caffeine-loaded, extension of Pepsi's Mountain Dew brand. The new-product team relied on a form of marketing experiment to develop Code Red. A large sample of consumers—including urban youth from different ethnic groups, computer geeks, and others in the target market—tested and rated different combinations of product features over time. This helped to fine-tune Code Red's packaging, candy-red color, and cherry taste. Then, before Code Red was even available in stores, Pepsi used grassroots promotion to build brand awareness and word-of-mouth publicity.

For example, an online game, "Mission: Code Red," gave players the chance to win free samples; similarly, a million samples were handed out at youth-oriented events like the Winter X Games and college basketball games.

Efforts like these helped Code Red achieve first-year sales that were even bigger than expected. So Pepsi quickly introduced other brand extensions, including lemon-flavored Pepsi Twist, Vanilla Pepsi, and Pepsi Blue. The taste of Pepsi Blue, described as a "berry/cola fusion," and its Windex-like color were selected because they appealed to youth who were bored with ordinary cola.

It will take time to see if Pepsi's efforts to target niche markets will be profitable. One risk is that these brand extensions will just siphon shelf space and sales away from regular Pepsi and Mountain Dew. Initially, about one-fourth of Code Red sales came from Mountain Dew. In addition, this is not the first time that Pepsi has tried to introduce new products under its well-known family brand. In the 1990s, Pepsi Crystal, a clear-colored soda, and Pepsi AM both lost their fizz after the introductory promotion ended.[11]

change in the product or perhaps only a shift to target customers who have a better image of the brand. Overcoming a negative image is difficult and can be very expensive.

Brand rejection is a big concern for service-oriented businesses because it's hard to control the quality of service. A business traveler who gets a dirty room in a Hilton Hotel in Caracas, Venezuela, might not return to a Hilton anywhere. Yet it's difficult for Hilton to ensure that every maid does a good job every time.

Some products are seen as basically the same. **Brand nonrecognition** means final consumers don't recognize a brand at all—even though middlemen may use the brand name for identification and inventory control. Examples include school supplies, inexpensive dinnerware, many of the items that you'd find in a hardware store, and thousands of dot-coms on the Internet.

Brand recognition means that customers remember the brand. This may not seem like much, but it can be a big advantage if there are many "nothing" brands on the market. Even if consumers can't recall the brand without help, they may be reminded when they see it in a store among other less familiar brands.

Most branders would like to win **brand preference**—which means that target customers usually choose the brand over other brands, perhaps because of habit or favorable past experience.

Brand insistence means customers insist on a firm's branded product and are willing to search for it. This is an objective of many target marketers.

The right brand name can help

A good brand name can help build brand familiarity. It can help tell something important about the company or its product. Exhibit 9-6 lists some characteristics of a good brand name. Some successful brand names seem to break all these rules, but many of them got started when there was less competition.

257

Exhibit 9-6
Characteristics of a Good
Brand Name

- Short and simple
- Easy to spell and read
- Easy to recognize and remember
- Easy to pronounce
- Can be pronounced in only one way
- Can be pronounced in all languages (for international markets)

- Suggestive of product benefits
- Adaptable to packaging/labeling needs
- No undesirable imagery
- Always timely (does not go out-of-date)
- Adaptable to any advertising medium
- Legally available for use (not in use by another firm)

Companies that compete in international markets face a special problem in selecting brand names. A name that conveys a positive image in one language may be meaningless in another. Or, worse, it may have unintended meanings. GM's Nova car is a classic example. GM stuck with the Nova name when it introduced the car in South America. It seemed like a sensible decision because *nova* is the Spanish word for star. However, Nova also sounds the same as the Spanish words for "no go." Consumers weren't interested in a no-go car, and sales didn't pick up until GM changed the name.[12]

A respected name builds brand equity

Because it's costly to build brand recognition, some firms prefer to acquire established brands rather than try to build their own. The value of a brand to its current owner or to a firm that wants to buy it is sometimes called **brand equity**—the value of a brand's overall strength in the market. For example, brand equity is likely to be higher if many satisfied customers insist on buying the brand and if retailers are eager to stock it. That almost guarantees ongoing profits.

The financial value of the Yahoo brand name illustrates the brand equity idea. In 1994, Yahoo was just a tiny start-up trying to make it with a directory site on the Internet. Most people had never heard the name, and few even knew what the Internet was or why you'd need a directory site. As interest in the Internet grew, Yahoo promoted its brand name on TV and in magazines. It was often the only website name that newcomers to the Web knew, so for many it was a good place from which to start their surfing. Within a few years, Yahoo was attracting 30 million different people a month. Since Yahoo charged fees to advertisers eager to reach these users, the familiarity of its brand translated directly into ad revenues.[13]

PROTECTING BRAND NAMES AND TRADEMARKS

U.S. common law and civil law protect the rights of trademark and brand name owners. The **Lanham Act** (of 1946) spells out what kinds of marks (including brand names) can be protected and the exact method of protecting them. The law applies to goods shipped in interstate or foreign commerce.

The Lanham Act does not force registration. But registering under the Lanham Act is often a first step toward protecting a trademark to be used in international markets. That's because some nations require that a trademark be registered in its home country before they will register or protect it.

You must protect your own

A brand can be a real asset to a company. Each firm should try to see that its brand doesn't become a common descriptive term for its kind of product. When this happens, the brand name or trademark becomes public property—and the owner loses all rights to it. This happened with the names cellophane, aspirin, shredded wheat, and kerosene.[14]

Counterfeiting is accepted in some cultures

Even when products are properly registered, counterfeiters may make unauthorized copies. Many well-known brands—ranging from Levi's jeans to Rolex watches to Zantax ulcer medicine—face this problem. Of course, pirated digital copies of songs, movies, and books are also routinely shared over the Internet. Counterfeiting is especially common in developing nations. In China, for example, many DVDs, CDs, and software programs are bootleg copies. Counterfeiting can be big business, so efforts to stop it may meet with limited success. There are also differences in cultural values. In South Korea, for example, many people don't see counterfeiting as unethical.[15]

WHAT KIND OF BRAND TO USE?

Keep it in the family

Branders of more than one product must decide whether they are going to use a **family brand**—the same brand name for several products—or individual brands for each product. Examples of family brands are Keebler snack food products and Sears' Kenmore appliances.

The use of the same brand for many products makes sense if all are similar in type and quality. The main benefit is that the goodwill attached to one or two products may help the others. Money spent to promote the brand name benefits more than one product, which cuts promotion costs for each product.

A special kind of family brand is a **licensed brand**—a well-known brand that sellers pay a fee to use. For example, the familiar Sunkist brand name has been licensed to many companies for use on more than 400 products in 30 countries.[16]

Individual brands for outside and inside competition

A company uses **individual brands**—separate brand names for each product— when it's important for the products to each have a separate identity, as when products vary in quality or type.

If the products are really different, such as Elmer's glue and Borden's ice cream, individual brands can avoid confusion. Some firms use individual brands with similar products to make segmentation and positioning efforts easier. For example, when General Mills introduced a line of organic cereals, it used the Cascadian Farms name and the Big G logo was not on the box. The rationale was that consumers who try to avoid additives might not trust a big corporate brand.[17]

As these trade ads suggest, both Del Monte and GE want retailers to remember that many consumers already know and trust their brand names.

Generic "brands"

Products that some consumers see as commodities may be difficult or expensive to brand. Some manufacturers and middlemen have responded to this problem with **generic products**—products that have no brand at all other than identification of their contents and the manufacturer or middleman. Generic products are usually offered in plain packages at lower prices. They are quite common in less-developed nations.[18]

WHO SHOULD DO THE BRANDING?

Manufacturer brands versus dealer brands

Manufacturer brands are brands created by producers. These are sometimes called *national brands* because the brand is promoted all across the country or in large regions. Note, however, that many manufacturer brands are now distributed globally. Such brands include Nabisco, Campbell's, Whirlpool, Ford, and IBM. Many creators of service-oriented firms—like McDonald's, Orkin Pest Control, and Bank of America—promote their brands this way too.

Dealer brands, also called **private brands,** are brands created by middlemen. Examples of dealer brands include the brands of Kroger, Ace Hardware, Radio Shack, Wal-Mart, and Sears. Some of these are advertised and distributed more widely than many national brands. For example, national TV ads helped Original Arizona Jeans (by JCPenney) and Canyon River Blues (by Sears) compete with Levi's and Wrangler.

From the middleman's perspective, the major advantage of selling a popular manufacturer brand is that the product is already presold to some target customers. The major disadvantage is that manufacturers normally offer lower gross margins than the middleman might be able to earn with a dealer brand. In addition, the manufacturer maintains control of the brand and may withdraw it from a middleman at any time. Customers, loyal to the brand rather than to the retailer or wholesaler, may go elsewhere if the brand is not available.

Dealer branders take on more responsibility and must promote their own product. They must be able to arrange a dependable source of supply and usually have to buy in fairly large quantities. This increases their risk and cost of carrying inventory. However, these problems are easier to overcome if the middleman deals in a large sales volume, as is the case with many large retail chains.

Who's winning the battle of the brands?

The **battle of the brands,** the competition between dealer brands and manufacturer brands, is just a question of whose brands will be more popular and who will be in control.

At one time, manufacturer brands were much more popular than dealer brands. Now sales of both kinds of brands are about equal—but sales of dealer brands are expected to continue growing. Middlemen have some advantages in this battle. With the number of large retail chains growing, they are better able to arrange reliable sources of supply at low cost. They can also give the dealer brand special shelf position or promotion.

Consumers benefit from the battle. Competition has already narrowed price differences between manufacturer brands and well-known dealer brands. And big retailers like Wal-Mart are constantly pushing manufacturers to lower prices—because national brands at low prices bring in even more customers than store brands.[19]

Innovative packaging turns Ariel's "Liquitabs" into a more convenient product. The copy on this French ad says "all the power of Ariel in a single dose."

THE STRATEGIC IMPORTANCE OF PACKAGING

Packaging involves promoting, protecting, and enhancing the product. Packaging can be important to both sellers and customers. See Exhibit 9-7. It can make a product more convenient to use or store. It can prevent spoiling or damage. Good packaging makes products easier to identify and promotes the brand at the point of purchase and even in use.

Packaging can enhance the product

A new package can make *the* important difference in a new marketing strategy—by meeting customers' needs better. Sometimes a new package makes the product easier or safer to use. For example, most drug and food products now have special seals to prevent product tampering. And clever packaging is an important part of a new effort by Campbell's Soup to pump new life into an old product—soup. Campbell's developed its Soup at Hand with a package that doesn't require a can opener or a stirring pot and instead is microwavable. Soup at Hand is just right for today's on-the-go consumers who want a portable meal solution, so it also helps Campbell's get distribution in convenience stores and vending machines. Consumers value convenience, so the Soup at Hand price of $1.49 (versus $.79 for a traditional can of soup) also produces attractive profits.[20]

Packaging sends a message

Packaging can tie the product to the rest of the marketing strategy. Packaging for Energizer batteries features the pink bunny seen in attention-getting TV ads and reminds consumers that the batteries are durable. A good package sometimes gives a firm more promotion effect than it could get with advertising. Customers see the package in stores, when they're actually buying.

Exhibit 9-7 Some Ways Packaging Benefits Consumers and Marketers

Opportunity to Add Value	Some Decision Factors	Examples
Promotion	Link product to promotion	The bunny on the Energizer battery package is a reminder that it "keeps going and going."
	Branding at point of purchase or consumption	Coke's logo greets almost everyone each time the refrigerator is opened.
	Product information	Kraft's nutrition label helps consumers decide which cheese to buy, and a UPC code reduces checkout time and errors.
Protection	For shipping and storing	Sony's MP3 player is kept safe by Styrofoam inserts.
	From spoiling	Tylenol's safety seal prevents tampering.
	From shoplifting	Cardboard hang-tag on Gillette razor blades is too large to hide in hand.
Enhance product	The environment	Tide detergent bottle can be recycled.
	Convenience in use	Squeezable tube of Yoplait Go-Gurt is easy to eat on the go and in new situations.
	Added product functions	Plastic tub is useful for refrigerator leftovers after the Cool Whip is gone.

Packaging may lower distribution costs

Better protective packaging is very important to manufacturers and wholesalers. They sometimes have to pay the cost of goods damaged in shipment. Retailers need protective packaging too. It can reduce storing costs by cutting breakage, spoilage, and theft. Good packages also save space and are easier to handle and display.[21]

Universal product codes speed handling

To speed handling of fast-selling products, government and industry representatives have developed a **universal product code (UPC)** that identifies each product with marks readable by electronic scanners. A computer then matches each code to the product and its price. These codes speed the checkout process and reduce the need to mark the price on every item. They also reduce errors by cashiers and make it easy to control inventory and track sales of specific products.[22]

WHAT IS SOCIALLY RESPONSIBLE PACKAGING?

Laws reduce confusion and clutter

In the United States, consumer criticism finally led to the passage of the **Federal Fair Packaging and Labeling Act** (of 1966)—which requires that consumer goods be clearly labeled in easy-to-understand terms—to give consumers more information. The law also calls on industry to try to reduce the number of package sizes and make labels more useful. Since then there have been further guidelines. The most far-reaching are based on the Nutrition Labeling and Education Act of 1990. It requires food manufacturers to use a uniform format that allows consumers to compare the nutritional value of different products.[23]

INTERNET EXERCISE

The FDA's website has a quiz to test your food-label knowledge. Go to that quiz at Internet address www.cfsan.fda.gov/label.html and click on the box that reads: "Quiz yourself! Test your Food Label Knowledge." Try the five questions. Did you learn anything?

A study by the Internet Advertising Bureau showed that firms, like Kimberly-Clark (the producer of the Kleenex brand) and Colgate, are able to develop more brand awareness and purchase preference when they shift some of their ad budgets to online media.

Current laws also offer more guidance on environmental issues. Some states require a consumer to pay a deposit on bottles and cans until they're returned. These laws mean well, but they can be a challenge. Channels of distribution are usually set up to distribute products, not return empty packages.[24]

Ethical decisions remain

Although various laws provide guidance on many packaging issues, many areas still require marketing managers to make ethical choices. For example, some firms have been criticized for designing packages that conceal a downsized product, giving consumers less for their money. Similarly, some retailers design packages and labels for their private-label products that look just like, and are easily confused with, manufacturer brands. Are efforts such as these unethical, or are they simply an attempt to make packaging a more effective part of a marketing mix? Different people will answer differently.

Empty packages litter our streets, and some plastic packages will lie in a city dump for decades. But some consumers like the convenience that accompanies these problems. Is it unethical for a marketing manager to give consumers with different preferences a choice? Some critics argue that it is. Others praise firms that give consumers choices.

Many critics feel that labeling information is too often incomplete or misleading. For example, what does it really mean if a label says a food product is "organic" or "low fat"? Do consumers really understand the nutritional information required by law? Further, some consumers want information that is difficult, perhaps even impossible, to provide. For example, how can a label accurately describe a product's taste or texture? But the ethical issues usually focus on how far a marketing manager should go in putting potentially negative information on a package. For example, should Häagen-Dazs affix a label that says "this product will clog your arteries"? That sounds extreme, but what type of information *is* appropriate?[25]

Unit-pricing is a possible help

Some retailers, especially supermarkets, make it easier for consumers to compare packages with different weights or volumes. They use **unit pricing**—which involves placing the price per ounce (or some other standard measure) on or near the product. This makes price comparison easier.[26]

WARRANTY POLICIES ARE A PART OF STRATEGY PLANNING

Warranty puts promises in writing

A **warranty** explains what the seller promises about its product. A marketing manager should decide whether to offer a specific warranty, and if so what the warranty will cover and how it will be communicated to target customers. This is an area where the legal environment—as well as customer needs and competitive offerings—must be considered.

U.S. common law says that producers must stand behind their products—even if they don't offer a specific warranty. A written warranty provided by the seller may promise more than the common law provides. However, it may actually *reduce* the responsibility a producer would have under common law.

The federal **Magnuson-Moss Act** (of 1975) says that producers must provide a clearly written warranty if they choose to offer any warranty. The warranty does not have to be strong. However, Federal Trade Commission (FTC) guidelines try to ensure that warranties are clear and definite and not deceptive or unfair. A warranty must also be available for inspection before the purchase.

A company has to make it clear whether it's offering a full or limited warranty—and the law defines what *full* means. Most firms offer a limited warranty if they offer one at all. In recent years, many firms have reduced the period of warranty coverage. Apple's popular iPod music player and Sony's Clie handheld organizer, for example, only have 90-day warranties. However, the Clie warranty is extended to one year if the owner registers the product.

Warranty may improve the marketing mix

Some firms use warranties to improve the appeal of their marketing mix. They design more quality into their goods or services and offer refunds or replacement, not just repair, if there is a problem. Xerox Corp. uses this approach with its copy machines. Its three-year warranty says that a customer who is not satisfied with a copier—for *any* reason—can trade it for another model. A strong warranty sends consumers a signal about brand quality. A few years ago, Hyundai, the South Korean car maker, pushed to improve quality. Yet among consumers its old reputation lingered. That changed after Hyundai put a 10-year warranty on its cars and used TV ads to tout it as "America's best warranty."

In a competitive market, a product warranty or a service guarantee can be the critical difference in a firm's marketing mix.

Service guarantees

Customer service guarantees are becoming more common as a way to attract, and keep, customers. Pizza Hut guarantees a luncheon pizza in five minutes or it's free. General Motors set up a fast-oil-change guarantee to compete with fast-lube specialists who were taking customers away from dealers. If the dealer doesn't get the job done in 29 minutes or less, the next oil change is free. The Hampton Inn motel chain guarantees "100% satisfaction." If you're not totally satisfied with your stay, you're not expected to pay.

There's more risk in offering a service guarantee than a warranty on a physical product. An apathetic employee or a service breakdown can create a big expense. However, without the guarantee, dissatisfied customers may just go away mad without ever complaining. When customers collect on a guarantee, the company can fix the problem.

Warranty support can be costly

The cost of warranty support ultimately must be covered by the price that consumers pay. This has led some firms to offer warranty choices. The basic price for a product may include a warranty that covers a short time period or that covers parts but not labor. Consumers who want more or better protection pay extra for an extended warranty or a service contract.[27]

CONCLUSION

In this chapter, we looked at Product very broadly. We saw that a firm's Product is *what satisfies the needs of its target market.* A product may be a physical good, a service, or some combination.

We introduced consumer product and business product classes and showed their effect on planning marketing mixes. Consumer product classes are based on consumers' buying behavior. Business product classes are based on how buyers see the products and how they are used.

Branding and packaging can create new and more satisfying products. Packaging offers special opportunities to promote the product and inform customers. Variations in packaging can make a product attractive to different target markets.

Customers see brands as a guarantee of quality, and this leads to repeat purchasing. For marketers, such routine buying means lower promotion costs and higher sales.

Marketing managers use individual or family brands. In the end, however, customers express their approval or disapproval of the whole Product (including the brand). The degree of brand familiarity is a measure of the marketing manager's ability to carve out a separate market. And brand familiarity affects Place, Price, and Promotion decisions.

Warranties are also important in strategy planning. A warranty need not be strong—it just has to be clearly stated. But some customers find strong warranties attractive.

Product is concerned with much more than physical goods and services. To succeed in our increasingly competitive markets, the marketing manager must also be concerned about packaging, branding, and warranties.

KEY TERMS

product, 242
quality, 244
service, 245
product assortment, 246
product line, 246
individual product, 246
consumer products, 247
business products, 247
convenience products, 248

staples, 248
impulse products, 249
emergency products, 249
shopping products, 249
homogeneous shopping products, 249
heterogeneous shopping products, 249
specialty products, 249

unsought products, 250
new unsought products, 250
regularly unsought products, 250
derived demand, 250
expense item, 251
capital item, 251
installations, 251
accessories, 251
raw materials, 252

QUESTIONS AND PROBLEMS

1. Define, in your own words, what a Product is.

2. Discuss several ways in which physical goods are different from pure services. Give an example of a good and then an example of a service that illustrates each of the differences.

3. What products are being offered by a shop that specializes in bicycles? By a travel agent? By a supermarket? By a new car dealer?

4. What kinds of consumer products are the following: *(a)* watches, *(b)* automobiles, and *(c)* toothpastes? Explain your reasoning.

5. Consumer services tend to be intangible, and goods tend to be tangible. Use an example to explain how the lack of a physical good in a pure service might affect efforts to promote the service.

6. How would the marketing mix for a staple convenience product differ from the one for a homogeneous shopping product? How would the mix for a specialty product differ from the mix for a heterogeneous shopping product? Use examples.

7. Give an example of a product that is a *new* unsought product for most people. Briefly explain why it is an unsought product.

8. In what types of stores would you expect to find *(a)* convenience products, *(b)* shopping products, *(c)* specialty products, and *(d)* unsought products?

9. Cite two examples of business products that require a substantial amount of service in order to be useful.

10. Explain why a new law office might want to lease furniture rather than buy it.

11. Would you expect to find any wholesalers selling the various types of business products? Are retail stores required (or something like retail stores)?

12. What kinds of business products are the following: *(a)* lubricating oil, *(b)* electric motors, and *(c)* a firm that provides landscaping and grass mowing for an apartment complex? Explain your reasoning.

13. How do raw materials differ from other business products? Do the differences have any impact on their marketing mixes? If so, what specifically?

14. For the kinds of business products described in this chapter, complete the following table (use one or a few well-chosen words).

   1. *Kind of distribution facility(ies) needed and functions they will provide.*
   2. *Caliber of salespeople required.*
   3. *Kind of advertising required.*

Products	1	2	3
Installations			
Buildings and land rights			
Major equipment			
Standard			
Custom-made			
Accessories			
Raw materials			
Farm products			
Natural products			
Components			
Supplies			
Maintenance and small operating supplies			
Operating supplies			
Professional services			

15. Is there any difference between a brand name and a trademark? If so, why is this difference important?

16. Is a well-known brand valuable only to the owner of the brand?

17. Suggest an example of a product and a competitive situation where it would *not* be profitable for a firm to spend large sums of money to establish a brand.

18. List five brand names and indicate what product is associated with the brand name. Evaluate the strengths and weaknesses of the brand name.

19. Explain family brands. Should Best Buy carry its own dealer brands to compete with some of the popular manufacturer brands it carries? Explain your reasons.

20. In the past, Sears emphasized its own dealer brands. Now it is carrying more well-known manufacturer brands. What are the benefits to Sears of carrying more manufacturer brands?

21. What does the degree of brand familiarity imply about previous and future promotion efforts? How does the degree of brand familiarity affect the Place and Price variables?

22. You operate a small hardware store with emphasis on manufacturer brands and have barely been breaking even. Evaluate the proposal of a large wholesaler who offers a full line of dealer-branded hardware items at substantially lower prices. Specify any assumptions necessary to obtain a definite answer.

23. Give an example where packaging costs probably *(a)* lower total distribution costs and *(b)* raise total distribution costs.

24. Is it more difficult to support a warranty for a service than for a physical good? Explain your reasons.

SUGGESTED CASES

1. McDonald's "Seniors" Restaurant

13. Paper Products, Inc.

COMPUTER-AIDED PROBLEMS

9. Branding Decision

RESOURCE REMINDER

Wholesteen Dairy, Inc., produces and sells Wholesteen brand condensed milk to grocery retailers. The overall market for condensed milk is fairly flat, and there's sharp competition among dairies for retailers' business. Wholesteen's regular price to retailers is $8.88 a case (24 cans). FoodWorld—a fast-growing supermarket chain and Wholesteen's largest customer—buys 20,000 cases of Wholesteen's condensed milk a year. That's 20 percent of Wholesteen's total sales volume of 100,000 cases per year.

FoodWorld is proposing that Wholesteen produce private label condensed milk to be sold with the FoodWorld brand name. FoodWorld proposes to buy the same total quantity as it does now, but it wants half (10,000 cases) with the Wholesteen brand and half with the FoodWorld brand. FoodWorld wants Wholesteen to reduce costs by using a lower-quality can for the FoodWorld brand. That change will cost Wholesteen $.01 less per can than it costs for the cans that Wholesteen uses for its own brand. FoodWorld will also provide preprinted labels with its brand name—which will save Wholesteen an additional $.02 a can.

Wholesteen spends $70,000 a year on promotion to increase familiarity with the Wholesteen brand. In addition, Wholesteen gives retailers an allowance of $.25 per case for their local advertising which features the Wholesteen brand. FoodWorld has agreed to give up the advertising allowance for its own brand, but it is only willing to pay $7.40 a case for the milk that will be sold with the FoodWorld brand name. It will continue under the old terms for the rest of its purchases.

Sue Glick, Wholesteen's marketing manager, is considering the FoodWorld proposal. She has entered cost and revenue data on a spreadsheet—so she can see more clearly how the proposal might affect revenue and profits.

a. Based on the data in the initial spreadsheet, how will Wholesteen profits be affected if Glick accepts the FoodWorld proposal?

b. Glick is worried that FoodWorld will find another producer for the FoodWorld private label milk if Wholesteen rejects the proposal. This would immediately reduce Wholesteen's annual sales by 10,000 cases. FoodWorld might even stop buying from Wholesteen altogether. What would happen to profits in these two situations?

c. FoodWorld is rapidly opening new stores and sells milk in every store. The FoodWorld buyer says that next year's purchases could be up to 25,000 cases of Wholesteen's condensed milk. But Sue Glick knows that FoodWorld may stop buying the Wholesteen brand and want all 25,000 cases to carry the FoodWorld private label brand. How will this affect profit? (Hint: enter the new quantities in the "proposal" column of the spreadsheet.)

d. What should Wholesteen do? Why?

For additional questions related to this problem, see Exercise 9-5 in the *Learning Aid for Use with Basic Marketing,* 15th edition.

WHEN YOU FINISH
THIS CHAPTER,
YOU SHOULD

1. Understand how
   product life cycles
   affect strategy
   planning.

2. Know what is
   involved in designing
   new products and
   what "new products"
   really are.

3. Understand the new-
   product development
   process.

4. See why product
   liability must be
   considered in
   screening new
   products.

5. Understand the need
   for product or brand
   managers.

6. Understand the
   important new terms
   (shown in red).

CHAPTER TEN

Product Management and New-Product Development

MOTOROLA IS A LARGE COMPANY, BUT IT DIDN'T BEGIN THAT WAY. IT STARTED 75 YEARS AGO AS A TINY INNOVATOR IN ELECTRIC RADIOS WHEN BROADCAST COMMUNICATIONS WERE IN THEIR INFANCY. THEN IT CONTINUED TO GROW AS IT DEVELOPED RADIOS FOR "MOTOR CARS" (HENCE THE

Motorola name) and next moved on to become a pioneer in color TV. Later, Motorola continued to enjoy profit growth from its role in developing the market for semiconductors—and in more recent times, Motorola has been a dominant brand in the explosive growth of the cell phone market. Now, however, Motorola is no longer involved in radios or TVs, parts of its semiconductor business are being sold off, and even its cell phone business is fighting for market share and profits against a host of worldwide competitors. It is still developing new and improved cell phones, but that is required just to stay in the game.

Firms that identify breakthrough market opportunities create exciting growth, but over time that growth is also what attracts competitors. Competition puts pressure on price levels and ultimately on profits. That's why Motorola's newest product development efforts are focused on meeting needs that other firms have not yet addressed. For example, Motorola is working on creating electronic display screens made out of thin plastic film. Plastic-based "organic light-emitting diodes" may ultimately lead to inexpensive TV and computer displays that are the size of a wall and

applied like wallpaper. Another recent effort led to development of a "wearable" electronic device (similar to a wireless PDA) with its display screen built into the frame of a set of stylish eyewear. This device incorporates a heads-up display, digital camera, and an ear bud. The person wearing it can view 800 × 600 displays while simultaneously staying in touch with his or her surroundings. For example, a surgeon might use it to watch a display of a patient's MRI while doing sensitive surgery, or a test pilot could see a tutorial on the cockpit controls while flying a new airplane. Or later—if economies of scale bring down costs—kids might use it to watch music videos or play video games.

Motorola is a big company with technical strengths. But new-product development is equally important to smaller firms. Consider the case of Plantronics, a telephone headset maker. Revenues from sales to its core target market, operators in corporate call centers, were falling. Many customer firms were switching from human operators to digital voice mail systems. To offset the lost revenues, Plantronics looked at trends in the market to identify new opportunities. For example, when drivers using cell phones became a safety issue, Plantronics developed a hands-free headset and worked with cell phone retailers to promote it. Now it is pursuing a similar initiative in England, which recently passed a hands-free law.

Customer satisfaction with the comfort, sound quality, and freedom of movement of Plantronics cell phone headsets has led to an opportunity to expand its product line into new products for home offices. Plantronics is also promoting its headsets to business firms—as a way to improve productivity and relieve stress among office workers.

Plantronics marketing managers have also capitalized on demographic trends like an aging population and diversified into products for the hearing impaired.

However, most of Plantronics new-product development efforts stick close to needs it already understands and capabilities it has in place. For example, it has developed a headset to be used with Microsoft's Xbox video console. Similarly, the growing use of multifunction wireless PDAs with built-in cell phones and cameras is another opportunity. Some consumers will prefer to use a headset with these devices because they are larger than a normal cell phone and awkward to hold up to your ear. Who knows, at some point in the future Plantronics may need to develop a headset with a microphone and a Bluetooth communications link that works with Motorola's heads-up display goggles.[1]

MANAGING PRODUCTS OVER THEIR LIFE CYCLES

The life and death cycle seen in our Motorola case is being repeated over and over again in product-markets worldwide. Cell phones are replacing shortwave radios and CBs and also making it possible for people to communicate from places where it was previously impossible. Cellular linkups over the Internet are coming on strong. Cassette tapes replaced vinyl records, and now CDs, digital minidiscs, and VHS tapes are challenged by DVD and downloaded MP3 digital files stored on miniature memory cards.

These innovations show that products, markets, and competition change over time. This makes marketing management an exciting challenge. Developing new products and managing existing products to meet changing conditions is important to the success of every firm. In this chapter, we will look at some important ideas in these areas.

Revolutionary products create new product-markets. But competitors are always developing and copying new ideas and products—making existing products out-of-date more quickly than ever. Products, like consumers, go through life cycles.

Product life cycle has four major stages

The **product life cycle** describes the stages a really new product idea goes through from beginning to end. The product life cycle is divided into four major stages: (1) market introduction, (2) market growth, (3) market maturity, and (4) sales decline. The product life cycle is concerned with new types (or categories) of products in the market, not just what happens to an individual brand.

A particular firm's marketing mix usually must change during the product life cycle. There are several reasons why customers' attitudes and needs may change over

Exhibit 10-1
Typical Life Cycle of a New Product Concept

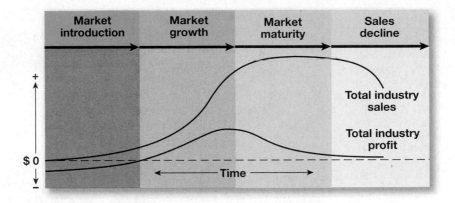

the product life cycle. The product may be aimed at entirely different target markets at different stages. And the nature of competition moves toward pure competition or oligopoly.

Further, total sales of the product—by all competitors in the industry—vary in each of its four stages. They move from very low in the market introduction stage to high at market maturity and then back to low in the sales decline stage. More important, the profit picture changes too. These general relationships can be seen in Exhibit 10-1. Note that sales and profits do not move together over time. *Industry profits decline while industry sales are still rising.*[2]

Market introduction—investing in the future

In the **market introduction** stage, sales are low as a new idea is first introduced to a market. Customers aren't looking for the product. Even if the product offers superior value, customers don't even know about it. Informative promotion is needed to tell potential customers about the advantages and uses of the new product concept.

Even though a firm promotes its new product, it takes time for customers to learn that the product is available. Most companies experience losses during the introduction stage because they spend so much money for Promotion, Product, and Place development. Of course, they invest the money in the hope of future profits.

Market growth—profits go up and down

In the **market growth** stage, industry sales grow fast—but industry profits rise and then start falling. The innovator begins to make big profits as more and more customers buy. But competitors see the opportunity and enter the market. Some just copy the most successful product or try to improve it to compete better. Others try to refine their offerings to do a better job of appealing to some target markets. The new entries result in much product variety. So monopolistic competition—with down-sloping demand curves—is typical of the market growth stage.

This is the time of biggest profits *for the industry*. It is also a time of rapid sales and earnings growth for companies with effective strategies. *But it is toward the end of this stage when industry profits begin to decline* as competition and consumer price sensitivity increase. See Exhibit 10-1.

Some firms make big strategy planning mistakes at this stage by not understanding the product life cycle. They see the big sales and profit opportunities of the early market growth stage but ignore the competition that will soon follow. When they realize their mistake, it may be too late. This happened with many dot-coms during the late 1990s. Marketing managers who understand the cycle and pay attention to competitor analysis are less likely to encounter this problem.

Market maturity sales level off, profits continue down

The **market maturity** stage occurs when industry sales level off and competition gets tougher. Many aggressive competitors have entered the race for profits—except in oligopoly situations. Industry profits go down throughout the market maturity

Innovative products, like Samsung's new 63-inch plasma high-definition TV and Transitions' new lens technology, are likely to get to the market growth stage of the product life cycle more quickly if customers see them as superior to products currently in use.

stage because promotion costs rise and some competitors cut prices to attract business. Less efficient firms can't compete with this pressure—and they drop out of the market. There is a long-run downward pressure on prices.

New firms may still enter the market at this stage—increasing competition even more. Note that late entries skip the early life-cycle stages, including the profitable market growth stage. And they must try to take a share of the saturated market from established firms, which is difficult and expensive. The market leaders have a lot at stake, so they fight hard to defend their share. Customers who are happy with their current relationship won't switch to a new brand. So late entrants usually have a tough battle.

Persuasive promotion becomes even more important during the market maturity stage. Products may differ only slightly. Most competitors have discovered effective appeals or just copied the leaders. As the various products become almost the same in the minds of potential consumers, price sensitivity is a real factor.[3]

The video game market vividly illustrates these competitive forces. By the time Microsoft introduced its Xbox game console, Nintendo's GameCube and Sony's PlayStation were already established leaders in the maturing market. Microsoft hoped to grab market share with a superior product designed to sell at a competitive price. To tout the advantages of the Xbox, it spent heavily on promotion. The others fought back with costly promotion of their own. Then Sony took advantage of its economies of scale and slashed the PlayStation II price by a third soon after Xbox hit the market. Nintendo followed with its own cuts. Experts estimate that, after matching the lower prices, Microsoft *lost* about $100 on each unit it sold. All the low prices did prompt renewed growth in unit sales. As the market leader, the added volume helped Sony make up for revenue lost from its price cut. However, for Microsoft, the expanded volume resulted in even greater total costs of coming into the market late. Time will tell if Microsoft's strengths will help it recoup profits by capturing share in video game software, a market that is still growing.[4]

In the United States, the markets for most cars, boats, and many household appliances are in market maturity. This stage may continue for many years—until a basically new-product idea comes along—even though individual brands or models come and go. For example, high-definition digital TV (HDTV) is coming on now, and over time it will make obsolete not only the old-style TVs but also the broadcast systems on which they rely.

| Sales decline—a time of replacement | During the **sales decline** stage, new products replace the old. Price competition from dying products becomes more vigorous—but firms with strong brands may make profits until the end because they have successfully differentiated their products. |

As the new products go through their introduction stage, the old ones may keep some sales by appealing to their most loyal customers or those who are slow to try new ideas. These conservative buyers might switch later—smoothing the sales decline.

PRODUCT LIFE CYCLES SHOULD BE RELATED TO SPECIFIC MARKETS

Remember that product life cycles describe industry sales and profits for a *product idea* within a particular product-market. The sales and profits of an individual brand may not, and often do not, follow the life-cycle pattern. They may vary up and down throughout the life cycle—sometimes moving in the opposite direction of industry sales and profits. Further, a product idea may be in a different life-cycle stage in different markets.

Individual brands may not follow the pattern

A given firm may introduce or drop a specific product during *any* stage of the product life cycle. A "me-too" brand introduced during the market growth stage, for example, may never get sales at all and suffer a quick death. But market leaders may enjoy high profits during the market maturity stage—even though industry profits are declining. Weaker products, on the other hand, may not earn a profit during any stage of the product life cycle. Sometimes the innovator brand loses so much in the introduction stage that it has to drop out just as others are reaping big profits in the growth stage.

Strategy planners who naively expect sales of an individual product to follow the general product life-cycle pattern are likely to be rudely surprised. In fact, it might be more sensible to think in terms of "product-market life cycles" rather than product life cycles—but we will use the term *product life cycle* because it is commonly accepted and widely used.

Marketing managers for Colgate have found many opportunities for new growth in international markets.

Each market should be carefully defined

How we see product life cycles depends on how broadly we define a product-market. For example, over 80 percent of all U.S. households own microwave ovens. Although they are at the market maturity stage here, in many other countries they're still early in the growth stage. Even in European countries like Denmark, Italy, and Spain, fewer than 20 percent of all households own microwave ovens.[5] As this example suggests, a firm with a mature product can sometimes find new growth in international markets.

How broadly we define the needs of customers in a product-market also affects how we view product life cycles—and who the competitors are. Consider the needs related to storing and preparing foods. Wax paper sales in the United States started to decline when Dow introduced Saran Wrap. Then sales of Saran Wrap (and other similar products) fell sharply when small plastic storage bags became popular. However, sales picked up again later when microwave cooking became popular. Then resealable bags like those from Ziploc took over because they can be used in both the freezer and the microwave.

If a market is defined broadly, there may be many competitors—and the market may appear to be in market maturity. On the other hand, if we focus on a narrow submarket—and a particular way of satisfying specific needs—then we may see much shorter product life cycles as improved product ideas come along to replace the old.

PRODUCT LIFE CYCLES VARY IN LENGTH

How long a whole product life cycle takes—and the length of each stage—varies a lot across products. The cycle may vary from 90 days—in the case of toys like the Ghostbusters line—to possibly 100 years for gas-powered cars.

The product life-cycle concept does not tell a manager precisely *how long* the cycle will last. But a manager can often make a good guess based on the life cycle for similar products. Sometimes marketing research can help too. However, it is more important to expect and plan for the different stages than to know the precise length of each cycle.

Some products move fast

A new-product idea will move through the early stages of the life cycle more quickly when it has certain characteristics. For example, the greater the *comparative advantage* of a new product over those already on the market, the more rapidly its

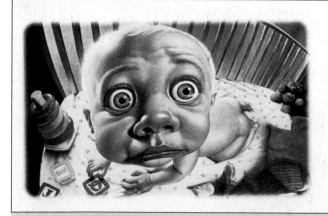

New products that do a better job of meeting the needs of specific target customers are more likely to move quickly and successfully through the introductory stage of the product life cycle.

274

sales will grow. Sales growth is also faster when the product is *easy to use* and if its advantages are *easy to communicate*. If the product *can be tried* on a limited basis—without a lot of risk to the customer—it can usually be introduced more quickly. Finally, if the product is *compatible* with the values and experiences of target customers, they are likely to buy it more quickly.

The fast adoption of DVD players is a good example. The concept of renting or buying movies to view at home was already compatible with consumer lifestyles, but many consumers hesitated before buying a DVD player. They wanted to see if DVD movies would be readily available. As movies appeared, DVD player sales took off because they had advantages over VHS tape players. Consumers could clearly tell that the picture and audio quality were better from a store demo—without buying anything. Further, ads highlighted DVD extras such as deleted scenes and interviews with directors. DVD players also met music listening needs because they worked with music CDs. Even though there is now high penetration of DVD players, many consumers still tape TV shows. However, now that the price of DVD recorders is falling, they will probably drive VHS recorders into the market decline stage of the product life cycle. Note, however, that DVD player adoption has not been as fast in less-developed countries. DVD players do not have the same comparative advantages in places where TV penetration is still low, movies are not available, and the costs are higher relative to consumer income.[6]

INTERNET EXERCISE

A number of software, hardware, and programming firms are working on products that deliver Internet information via TV. Explore the MSN TV website (www.msntv.com) to find out about one aspect of this idea and take the MSN Tour. How does MSN TV stack up when you consider the characteristics of an innovation reviewed earlier?

Product life cycles are getting shorter

Although the life of different products varies, in general product life cycles are getting shorter. This is partly due to rapidly changing technology. One new invention may make possible many new products that replace old ones. Tiny electronic microchips led to thousands of new products—from Texas Instruments calculators in the early days to microchip-controlled heart valves now.

Patents for a new product may not be much protection in slowing down competitors. Competitors can often find ways to copy the product idea without violating a specific patent. Worse, some unethical firms simply disregard the patent. This can be a big problem, especially for firms that rely on unique technology for competitive advantage. For example, Cisco Systems became suspicious when it learned that a Chinese competitor was selling computer network hardware that was similar. Even the model numbers and software commands were the same. It took a sting operation and six more months of detective work for Cisco to prove that its patent was being violated. In this case, the competitor took the product off the market and claimed the violation was unintentional. However, in other situations a product's life may be over before a case can get through patent-court bottlenecks. By then, the copycat competitor may even be out of business. These problems are even more severe in international cases because different governments, rules, and court systems are involved. The patent system, in the United States and internationally, needs significant improvement if it is to really protect firms that develop innovative ideas.[7]

Although life cycles keep moving in the developed economies, many advances bypass most consumers in less-developed economies. These consumers struggle at the subsistence level, without an effective macro-marketing system to stimulate innovation. However, some of the innovations and economies of scale made possible in the advanced societies do trickle down to benefit these consumers. Inexpensive antibiotics and drought-resistant plants, for example, are making a life-or-death difference.

The early bird usually makes the profits

The product life cycle means that firms must be developing new products all the time. Further, they must try to have marketing mixes that will make the most of the market growth stage—when profits are highest.

During the growth stage, competitors are likely to rapidly introduce product improvements. Fast changes in marketing strategy may be required here because profits don't necessarily go to the innovator. Sometimes fast copiers of the basic idea win in the market growth stage. General Motor's electric car, the EV1, was the first zero-emission vehicle on the market when it was first sold in California. However, Toyota and Honda leapfrogged past GM when they introduced hybrid vehicles powered by a combination of gas engine and electric motor. Their hybrids did not eliminate all emissions, but they met other needs better. They have more power, don't need to be plugged in, and are less expensive. With these changes, the market for low-emission hybrids is growing rapidly, and other producers are getting into the act. However, GM is still playing catch up. In fact, some experts think that it will continue to trail its Japanese competitors because they are faster in adapting to market needs, even when they get their start by imitating an innovator. Marketers need to be innovative, but at the same time they must be flexible in adapting to the needs and attitudes of their target markets.[8]

The short happy life of fashions and fads

The sales of some products are influenced by **fashion**—the currently accepted or popular style. Fashion-related products tend to have short life cycles. What is currently popular can shift rapidly. A certain color or style of clothing—baggy jeans, miniskirts, or four-inch-wide ties—may be in fashion one season and outdated the next. Marketing managers who work with fashions often have to make really fast product changes.

How fast is fast enough? Zara, a women's fashion retailer based in Spain, takes only about two weeks to go from a new fashion concept to having items on the racks of its stores. Zara's market-watching designers get a constant flow of new fashion ideas from music videos, fashion shows, and magazines. Zara quickly produces

A certain color or style may be in fashion one season and outdated the next. Zara, a fashion retailer, puts its catalog on its website (www.zara.com) so it can be updated quickly each season.

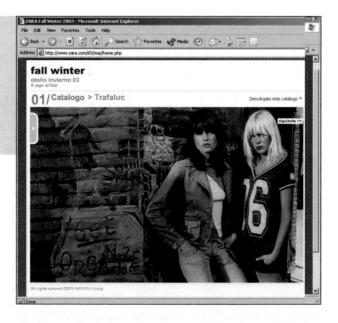

276

just enough of a design to test the waters and then sends it out for overnight delivery to some of its 449 stores around the world. Stores track consumer preferences every day through point-of-sale computers and designers get online summaries of what's selling and where. If an item is hot, more is produced and shipped. Otherwise it's dropped. With this system items are rarely on the shelves of Zara stores for more than a few weeks.[9]

It's not really clear why a particular fashion becomes popular. Many present fashions are adaptations or revivals of previously popular styles. Designers are always looking for styles that will satisfy fashion innovators who crave distinctiveness. Lower-cost copies of the popular items may then catch on with other groups and survive for a while. Yet the constant changes increase the cost of producing and marketing fashion products and the costs to consumers. Fashion changes are a luxury that most people in less-developed countries simply can't afford.

A **fad** is an idea that is fashionable only to certain groups who are enthusiastic about it. But these groups are so fickle that a fad is even more short lived than a regular fashion. Many toys—whether it's a Hasbro *Lord of the Rings* plastic figure or a Toymax Paintball pack—are fads but do well during a short-lived cycle.[10]

PLANNING FOR DIFFERENT STAGES OF THE PRODUCT LIFE CYCLE

Length of cycle affects strategy planning

Where a product is in its life cycle—and how fast it's moving to the next stage—should affect marketing strategy planning. Marketing managers must make realistic plans for the later stages. Exhibit 10-2 shows the relationship of the product life cycle to the marketing mix variables. The technical terms in this figure are discussed later in the book.

Introducing new products

Exhibit 10-2 shows that a marketing manager has to do a lot of strategy planning to introduce a really new product. Money must be spent developing the new product. Even if the product is unique, this doesn't mean that everyone will immediately come running to the producer's door. The firm will have to build channels of distribution—perhaps offering special incentives to win cooperation. Promotion is needed to build demand *for the whole idea* not just to sell a specific brand. Because all this is expensive, it may lead the marketing manager to try to "skim" the market—charging a relatively high price to help pay for the introductory costs.

The correct strategy, however, depends on how quickly the new idea will be accepted by customers—and how quickly competitors will follow with their own versions of the product. When the early stages of the cycle will be fast, a low initial (penetration) price may make sense to help develop loyal customers early and keep competitors out.

Pioneer may need help from competitors

Sometimes it's not in the best interest of the market pioneer for competitors to stay out of the market. Building customer interest in a really new-product idea—and obtaining distribution to make the product available—can be too big a job for a single company. Two or more companies investing in promotion to build demand may help to stimulate the growth of the whole product-market. Similarly, a new product may languish if it is not compatible with other products that customers rely on. This is what happened with Digital Video Express (Divx) video disks. When Divx came out, many consumer-electronics firms were launching DVD format products. Divx had advantages over DVD, but it was not compatible with many of the

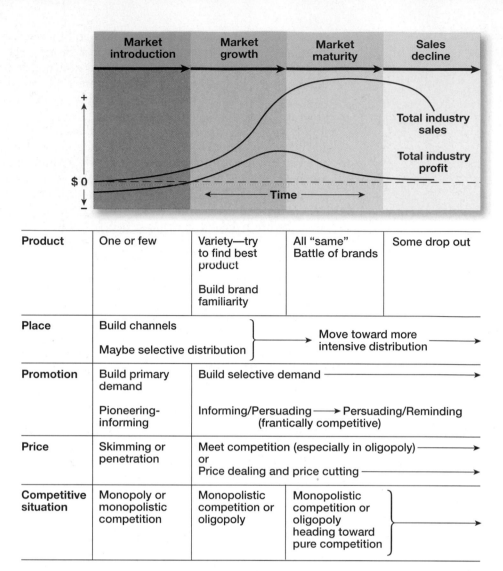

	Market introduction	Market growth	Market maturity	Sales decline
Product	One or few	Variety—try to find best product Build brand familiarity	All "same" Battle of brands	Some drop out
Place	Build channels Maybe selective distribution	Move toward more intensive distribution		
Promotion	Build primary demand Pioneering-informing	Build selective demand Informing/Persuading → Persuading/Reminding (frantically competitive)		
Price	Skimming or penetration	Meet competition (especially in oligopoly) → or Price dealing and price cutting →		
Competitive situation	Monopoly or monopolistic competition	Monopolistic competition or oligopoly	Monopolistic competition or oligopoly heading toward pure competition	

ordinary DVD players that were already on the market. Video stores didn't want to stock movies in both formats so Divx fizzled.[11]

New product sales may not take off

Not all new-product ideas catch on. Customers or middlemen may not be satisfied with the marketing mix, or other new products may meet the same need better. But the success that eludes a firm with its initial strategy can sometimes be achieved by modifying the strategy. David Mintz invented a soy-based frozen dessert and started Tofutti Brands, Inc., to sell it. Tofutti was especially appealing to people who could not eat dairy products. To quickly reach his target market, Mintz's strategy was to offer a limited number of flavors and partner with a big company that already had national distribution in supermarkets. Häagen-Dazs agreed to the plan but wanted exclusive distribution rights. Sales grew quickly at first but then plummeted when conflicts between Mintz and Häagen-Dazs ended the relationship. To keep consumers interested in Tofutti while he slowly rebuilt distribution through a dozen specialized wholesalers, Mintz had to constantly offer new flavors.[12]

How quickly a firm can change its strategy as the life cycle moves on is also relevant. Some firms are very flexible. They can compete effectively with larger, less adaptable competitors by adjusting their strategies more frequently.

Some companies continue to do well in market maturity by improving their products or by finding new uses and applications. DuPont Textiles & Interiors' LYCRA® has expanded from personal apparel to furniture upholstery and Lipton has developed a cold brew tea.

Managing maturing products

It's important for a firm to have some competitive advantage as it moves into market maturity. Even a small advantage can make a big difference—and some firms do very well by carefully managing their maturing products. They are able to capitalize on a slightly better product or perhaps lower production or marketing costs. Or they are simply more successful at promotion—allowing them to differentiate their more or less homogeneous product from competitors. For example, graham crackers were competing in a mature market and sales were flat. Nabisco used the same ingredients to create bite-sized Teddy Grahams and then promoted them heavily. These changes captured new sales and profits for Nabisco.[13]

Industry profits are declining in market maturity. Top managers must see this, or they will expect the attractive profits that are no longer possible. If top managers don't understand the situation, they may place impossible burdens on the marketing department—causing marketing managers to think about deceptive advertising or some other desperate attempt to reach impossible objectives.

Product life cycles keep moving. But that doesn't mean a firm should just sit by as its sales decline. There are other choices. A firm can improve its product or develop an innovative new product for the same market. Or it can develop a strategy for its product (perhaps with modifications) targeted at a new market. For example, it might find a market in a country where the life cycle is not so far along, or it might try to serve a new need. Or the firm can withdraw the product before it completes the cycle and refocus on better opportunities. See Exhibit 10-3.

Improve the product or develop a new one

When a firm's product has won loyal customers, it can be successful for a long time—even in a mature or declining market. However, continued improvements may be needed as customers' needs shift. An outstanding example is Procter &

Exhibit 10-3
Examples of Three Marketing Strategy Choices for a Firm in a Mature Product-Market

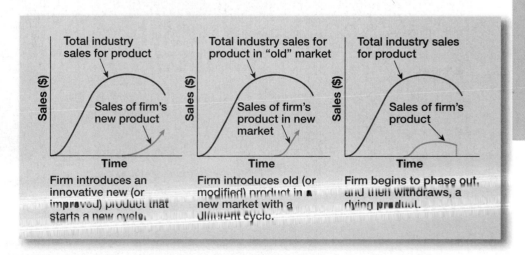

Gamble's Tide. Introduced in 1947, Tide led to a whole new generation of powdered laundry products that cleaned better with fewer suds. But Tide continues to change because of new washing machines and fabrics. The Tide sold today has had at least 55 modifications.

Do product modifications—like those made with powdered Tide—create a wholly new product that should have its own product life cycle? Or are they technical adjustments of the original product idea? We will take the latter position—focusing on the product idea rather than changes in features. This means that some of these Tide changes were made in the market maturity stage. But this type of product improvement can help to extend the product life cycle.

On the other hand, a firm that develops an innovative new product may move to a new product life cycle. For example, by 1985 new liquid detergents like Wisk were moving into the growth stage, and sales of powdered detergents were declining. To share in the growth-stage profits for liquid detergents and to offset the loss of customers from powdered Tide, Procter & Gamble introduced Liquid Tide.

Even though regular powdered detergents are in the decline stage, traditional powdered Tide continues to sell well because it still does the job for some consumers. But sales growth is likely to come from liquid detergents and the new low-suds detergents.[14]

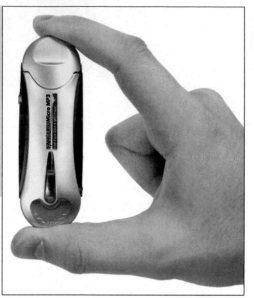

Develop new strategies for different markets

In a mature market, a firm may be fighting to keep or increase its market share. But if the firm finds a new use for the product, it may stimulate overall demand. DuPont's Teflon fluorocarbon resin is a good example. It was developed more than 50 years ago and has enjoyed sales growth as a nonstick coating for cookware

and as a lining for chemically resistant equipment. But marketing managers for Teflon are not waiting to be stuck with declining profits in those mature markets. They are constantly developing strategies for new markets. For example, Teflon is now selling well as a special coating for the wires used in high-speed communications between computers and as an additive that improves bathroom cleaning products.[15]

Phasing out dying products

Not all strategies have to be exciting growth strategies. If prospects are poor in some product-market, a phase-out strategy may be needed. The need for phasing out becomes more obvious as the sales decline stage arrives. But even in market maturity, it may be clear that a particular product is not going to be profitable enough to reach the company's objectives. In any case, it is wise to remember that marketing plans are implemented as ongoing strategies. Salespeople make calls, inventory moves in the channel, advertising is scheduled for several months into the future, and so on. So the firm usually experiences losses if managers end a plan too abruptly. Because of this, it's sometimes better to phase out the product gradually.

Phasing out a product may involve some difficult implementation problems. But phase-out is also a *strategy*—and it must be market-oriented to cut losses. In fact, it is possible to milk a dying product for some time if competitors move out more quickly and there is ongoing (though declining) demand. Some customers are willing to pay attractive prices to get their old favorite.

NEW-PRODUCT PLANNING

In most markets, progress marches on. So it is essential for a firm to develop new products or modify its current products to meet changing customer needs and competitors' actions. Not having an active new-product development process means that consciously, or subconsciously, the firm has decided to milk its current products and go out of business. New-product planning is not an optional matter. It has to be done just to survive in today's dynamic markets.

What is a new product?

In discussing the introductory stage of product life cycles, we focused on the types of really new product innovations that tend to disrupt old ways of doing things. However, each year firms introduce many products that are basically refinements of existing products. So a **new product** is one that is new *in any way* for the company concerned.

A product can become "new" in many ways. A fresh idea can be turned into a new product and start a new product life cycle. For example, Alza Corporation's time-release skin patches are replacing pills and injections for some medications.

Variations on an existing product idea can also make a product new. For example, Logitech has improved the lowly computer mouse by making it wireless and Gatorade has made its bottle easier to grip. Even small changes in an existing product can make it new.[16]

FTC says product is "new" only six months

A firm can call its product new for only a limited time. Six months is the limit according to the **Federal Trade Commission (FTC)**—the federal government agency that polices antimonopoly laws. To be called new, says the FTC, a product must be entirely new or changed in a "functionally significant or substantial respect."

Ethical issues in new-product planning

New-product decisions—and decisions to abandon old products—often involve ethical considerations. For example, some firms (including firms that develop drugs) have been criticized for holding back important new-product innovations until patents run out, or sales slow down, on their existing products.

At the same time, others have been criticized for "planned obsolescence"—releasing new products that the company plans to soon replace with improved new versions. Similarly, wholesalers and middlemen complain that producers too often keep their new-product introduction plans a secret and leave middlemen with dated inventory that they can sell only at a loss.

Companies also face ethical dilemmas when they decide to stop supplying a product or the service and replacement parts to keep it useful. An old model of a Cuisinart food processor, for example, might be in perfect shape except for a crack in the plastic mixing bowl. It's sensible for the company to improve the design if the crack is a frequent problem, but if consumers can't get a replacement part for the model they already own, they're left holding the bag.

Criticisms are also leveled at firms that constantly release minor variations of products that already saturate markets. Consider what happened with disposable diapers. Marketing managers thought that they were serving some customers' needs better when they offered diapers in boys' and girls' versions and in a variety of sizes, shapes, and colors. But many retailers felt that the new products were simply a ploy to get more shelf space. Further, some consumers complained that the bewildering array of choices made shopping difficult. Some people would level the same criticism at Huggies Little Swimmers Disposable Swimpants. But unlike other disposables, this product doesn't swell in the water. They have been a success because they seem to fill a different need.

Different marketing managers might have very different reactions to such criticisms. However, product management decisions often have a significant effect on customers and middlemen. A too-casual decision may lead to a negative backlash that affects the firm's strategy or reputation.[17]

AN ORGANIZED NEW-PRODUCT DEVELOPMENT PROCESS IS CRITICAL

Identifying and developing new-product ideas—and effective strategies to go with them—is often the key to a firm's success and survival. But the costs of new-product development and the risks of failure are high. Experts estimate that consumer packaged-goods companies spend at least $20 million to introduce a new brand—and 70 to 80 percent of these new brands flop. That's a big expense—and a waste. In the service sector, the front-end cost of a failed effort may not be as high, but it can have a devastating long-term effect if dissatisfied consumers turn elsewhere for help.[18]

INTERNET EXERCISE

Marketing Intelligence Service, Ltd., is a U.S.-based firm that tracks new consumer packaged-goods—both successes and failures. Enter its website (www.productscan.com) and click on the *What's New* button, then review its selections for new product innovations of the year. Do you think that these products offer customers superior value, or are they just me-too imitations?

A new product may fail for many reasons. Most often, companies fail to offer a unique benefit or underestimate the competition. Sometimes the idea is good but the company has design problems—or the product costs much more to produce than was expected. Some companies rush to get a product on the market without developing a complete marketing plan.[19]

But moving too slowly can be a problem too. With the fast pace of change for many products, speedy entry into the market can be a key to competitive advantage. Marketing managers at Xerox learned this the hard way. Japanese competitors

Generating innovative and profitable new products requires an understanding of customer needs—and an organized new-product development process.

were taking market share with innovative new models of copiers. It turned out that the competitors were developing new models twice as fast as Xerox and at half the cost. For Xerox to compete, it had to slash its five-year product development cycle. Many other companies—ranging from auto manufacturers like DaimlerChrysler to Internet service firms like E*Trade—are working to speed up the new-product development process.[20]

To move quickly and also avoid expensive new-product failures, companies should follow an organized new-product development process. The following pages describe such a process, which moves logically through five steps: (1) idea generation, (2) screening, (3) idea evaluation, (4) development (of product and marketing mix), and (5) commercialization.[21] See Exhibit 10-4.

The general process is similar for both consumer and business markets—and for both goods and services. There are some significant differences, but we will emphasize the similarities in the following discussion.

Process tries to kill new ideas— economically

An important element in the new-product development process is continued evaluation of a new idea's likely profitability and return on investment. The hypothesis tested is that the new idea will *not* be profitable. This puts the burden on the new

Exhibit 10-4   New-Product Development Process

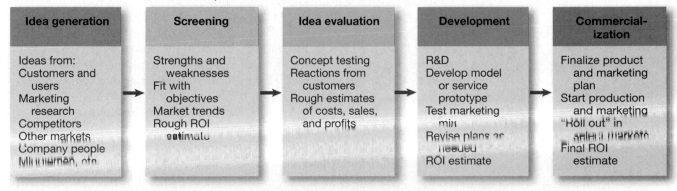

Idea generation	Screening	Idea evaluation	Development	Commercial- ization
Ideas from: Customers and users Marketing research Competitors Other markets Company people Middlemen, etc.	Strengths and weaknesses Fit with objectives Market trends Rough ROI estimate	Concept testing Reactions from customers Rough estimates of costs, sales, and profits	R&D Develop model or service prototype Test marketing mix Revise plans as needed ROI estimate	Finalize product and marketing plan Start production and marketing "Roll out" in select markets Final ROI estimate

idea—to prove itself or be rejected. Such a process may seem harsh, but experience shows that most new ideas have some flaw. Marketers try to discover those flaws early, and either find a remedy or reject the idea completely. Applying this process requires much analysis of the idea *before* the company spends money to develop and market a product. This is a major departure from the usual production-oriented approach— in which a company develops a product first and then asks sales to "get rid of it."

Step 1: Idea generation

Finding new-product ideas can't be left to chance. Instead, firms need a formal procedure to generate a continuous flow of ideas. New ideas can come from a company's own sales or production staff, middlemen, competitors, consumer surveys, or other sources such as trade associations, advertising agencies, or government agencies. By analyzing new and different views of the company's markets and studying present consumer behavior, a marketing manager can spot opportunities that have not yet occurred to competitors or even to potential customers. For example, ideas for new service concepts may come directly from analysis of consumer complaints.

No one firm can always be first with the best new ideas. So companies should pay attention to what competitors are doing. Some firms use what's called *reverse engineering*. For example, new-product specialists at Ford Motor Company buy other firms' cars as soon as they're available. Then they take the cars apart to look for new ideas or improvements. British Airways talks to travel agents to learn about new services offered by competitors. Many other companies use similar approaches.[22]

Many firms now "shop" in international markets for new ideas. For instance, food companies in Europe are experimenting with an innovation recently introduced in Japan—a clear, odorless, natural film for wrapping food. Consumers don't have to unwrap it; when they put the product in boiling water or a microwave, the wrapper vanishes.[23]

Research shows that many new ideas in business markets come from customers who identify a need they have. Then they approach a supplier with the idea and perhaps even with a particular design or specification. These customers become the lead users of the product, but the supplier can also pursue the opportunity in other markets.[24]

Step 2: Screening

Screening involves evaluating the new ideas with the type of S.W.O.T analysis described in Chapter 2 and the product-market screening criteria described in Chapter 4. Recall that these criteria include the combined output of a resources (strengths and weaknesses) analysis, a long-run trends analysis, and a thorough understanding of the company's objectives. See Exhibit 2-10 and Exhibit 4-5. Further, a "good" new idea should eventually lead to a product (and marketing mix) that will give the firm a competitive advantage—hopefully, a lasting one.

The life-cycle stage at which a firm's new product enters the market has a direct bearing on its prospects for growth. So screening should consider how the strategy for a new product will hold up over the whole product life cycle.

Thinking about the strengths and weaknesses of a new-product idea from both a short- and long-term perspective can be a challenge. However, decisions about how the firm brings a new product to market often shape future market opportunities (and threats). A classic example is IBM's decision to license the operating system for the IBM PC when it was introduced. At that time, designing a PC to use an existing operating system (like the one then available from Microsoft) was a fast and low-cost way to get to market. However, the operating system ultimately produced more profit for Microsoft than the hardware did for IBM.

Some companies screen based on consumer welfare

Screening should also consider how a new product will affect consumers over time. Ideally, the product should increase consumer welfare, not just satisfy a whim. Exhibit 10-5 shows different kinds of new-product opportunities. Obviously, a

Independent product testing labs, like Underwriters Laboratories (UL) and CSA International, give consumers added confidence that products are safe.

socially responsible firm tries to find desirable opportunities rather than deficient ones. This may not be as easy as it sounds, however. Some consumers want pleasing products and give little thought to their own long-term welfare. And some competitors will offer consumers whatever they will buy.

Safety must be considered

Real acceptance of the marketing concept prompts managers to screen new products on the basis of how safe they are. Safety is not a casual matter. The U.S. **Consumer Product Safety Act** (of 1972) set up the Consumer Product Safety Commission to encourage safety in product design and better quality control. The commission has a great deal of power. It can set safety standards for products. It can order costly repairs or return of unsafe products. And it can back up its orders with fines and jail sentences. The Food and Drug Administration has similar powers for food and drugs.

Exhibit 10-5
Types of New-Product
Opportunities

		Immediate satisfaction	
		High	Low
Long-run consumer welfare	High	Desirable products	Salutary products
	Low	Pleasing products	Deficient products

Product safety complicates strategy planning because not all customers—even those who want better safety features—are willing to pay more for safer products. Some features cost a lot to add and increase prices considerably. These safety concerns must be considered at the screening step because a firm can later be held liable for unsafe products.

Products can turn to liabilities

Product liability means the legal obligation of sellers to pay damages to individuals who are injured by defective or unsafe products. Product liability is a serious matter. Liability settlements may exceed not only a company's insurance coverage but its total assets!

Relative to most other countries, U.S. courts enforce a very strict product liability standard. Sellers may be held responsible for injuries related to their products no matter how the items are used or how well they're designed. In one widely publicized judgment, McDonald's paid a huge settlement to a woman who was burned when her coffee spilled. The court concluded that there was not enough warning about how hot the coffee was.

Cases and settlements like this are common. Some critics argue that the U.S. rules are so tough that they discourage innovation and economic growth. In contrast, Japan may be too slack. Japan's system discourages consumers from filing complaints because they are required to pay a percentage of any damages they seek as court costs—regardless of whether they win or lose.

Sometimes there is incentive for lawyers to push liability cases to take a share of the payments. Juries sometimes give huge settlements based on an emotional reaction to the case rather than scientific evidence. That seems to have happened in lawsuits over silicon breast implants.

Product liability is a serious ethical and legal matter. Many countries are attempting to change their laws so that they will be fair to both firms and consumers. But until product liability questions are resolved, marketing managers must be even more sensitive when screening new-product ideas.[25]

ROI is a crucial screening criterion

Getting by the initial screening criteria doesn't guarantee success for the new idea. But it does show that at least the new idea is in the right ballpark *for this firm*. If many ideas pass the screening criteria, a firm must set priorities to determine which ones go on to the next step in the process. This can be done by comparing the ROI (return on investment) for each idea—assuming the firm is ROI-oriented. The most attractive alternatives are pursued first.

Step 3: Idea evaluation

When an idea moves past the screening step, it is evaluated more carefully. Note that an actual product has not yet been developed—and this can handicap the firm in getting feedback from customers. For help in idea evaluation, firms use **concept testing**—getting reactions from customers about how well a new-product idea fits their needs. Concept testing uses market research—ranging from informal focus groups to formal surveys of potential customers.

Companies can often estimate likely costs, revenue, and profitability at this stage. And market research can help identify the size of potential markets. Even informal focus groups are useful—especially if they show that potential users are not excited about the new idea. If results are discouraging, it may be best to kill the idea at this stage. Remember, in this hypothesis-testing process, we're looking for any evidence that an idea is *not* a good opportunity for this firm and should be rejected.

Product planners must think about wholesaler and retailer customers as well as final consumers. Middlemen may have special concerns about handling a proposed product. A Utah ice-cream maker was considering a new line of ice-cream novelty products—and he had visions of a hot market in California. But he had to drop his idea when he learned that grocery store chains wanted payments of $20,000 each just to stock his frozen novelties in their freezers. Without the payment, they didn't want to risk using profitable freezer space on an unproven product. This is not an unusual case. At the idea evaluation stage, companies often find that other members of the distribution channel won't cooperate.[26]

Idea evaluation is often more precise in business markets. Potential customers are more informed—and their needs focus on the economic reasons for buying rather than emotional factors. Further, given the derived nature of demand in business markets, most needs are already being satisfied in some way. So new products just substitute for existing ones. This means that product planners can compare the cost advantages and limitations of a new product with those currently being used. And by interviewing well-informed people, they can determine the range of product requirements and decide whether there is an opportunity.

For example, you've probably noticed that most new car designs use low-profile headlights. They allow sleeker styling and better gas mileage. Yet these lights were initially only used on high-priced cars. That's because the GE development team worked with engineers at Ford when they were first developing the bulbs for these headlights. Together they determined that the switch to the new bulb and head-light assembly would add about $200 to the price of a car. That meant that the bulb was initially limited to luxury cars—until economies of scale brought down the costs.[27]

Whatever research methods are used, the idea evaluation step should gather enough information to help decide whether there is an opportunity, whether it fits with the firm's resources, *and* whether there is a basis for developing a competitive advantage. With such information, the firm can estimate likely ROI in the various market segments and decide whether to continue the new-product development process.[28]

Step 4: Development

Product ideas that survive the screening and idea evaluation steps must now be analyzed further. Usually, this involves some research and development (R&D) and engineering to design and develop the physical part of the product. In the case of a new service offering, the firm will work out the details of what training, equipment, staff, and so on will be needed to deliver on the idea. Input from a firm's earlier efforts helps guide this technical work.

New computer-aided design (CAD) systems are sparking a revolution in design work. Designers can develop lifelike 3-D color drawings of packages and products. Changes can be made almost instantly. They can be sent by e-mail to managers all

over the world for immediate review. They can even be put on a website for marketing research with remote customers. Then once the designs are finalized, they feed directly into computer-controlled manufacturing systems. Companies like Motorola and Timex have found that these systems cut their new-product development time in half—giving them a leg up on many competitors.

Even so, it is still useful to test models and early versions of the product in the market. This process may have several cycles. A manufacturer may build a model of a physical product or produce limited quantities; a service firm may try to train a small group of service providers. Product tests with customers may lead to revisions—*before* the firm commits to full-scale efforts.

With actual goods or services, potential customers can react to how well the product meets their needs. Focus groups, panels, and larger surveys can react to specific features and to the whole product idea. Sometimes that reaction kills the idea. For example, Coca-Cola Foods believed it had a great idea with Minute Maid

Four other car companies have already bought one. Whatever do you suppose they want them for?

Porsche 968: The next evolution.

Squeeze-Fresh, frozen orange juice concentrate in a squeeze bottle. In tests, however, Squeeze-Fresh bombed. Consumers loved the idea but hated the product. It was messy to use, and no one knew how much concentrate to squeeze in the glass.[29]

In other cases, testing can lead to revision of product specifications for different markets. Sometimes months or even years of research may be necessary to focus on precisely what different market segments will find acceptable. For example, Gillette's Mach3 razor blade took over a decade and $750 million in development and tooling costs.[30]

Firms often use full-scale market testing to get reactions in real market conditions or to test variations in the marketing mix. For example, a firm may test alternative brands, prices, or advertising copy in different test cities. Note that the firm is testing the whole marketing mix, not just the product. For example, a hotel chain might test a new service offering at one location to see how it goes over.

Test-marketing can be risky because it may give information to competitors. In fact, a company in Chicago—Marketing Intelligence Services—monitors products in test markets and then sells the information to competing firms. Similar firms monitor markets in other countries.

But *not* testing is risky too. Frito-Lay was so sure it understood consumers' snack preferences that it introduced a three-item cracker line without market testing. Even with network TV ad support, MaxSnax met with overwhelming consumer indifference. By the time Frito-Lay pulled the product from store shelves, it had lost $52 million.[31]

Market tests can be very expensive. Yet they can uncover problems that otherwise might go undetected and destroy the whole strategy. After the market test, the firm can estimate likely ROI for various strategies to determine whether the idea moves on to commercialization.

Some companies don't do market tests because they just aren't practical. In fashion markets, for example, speed is extremely important, and products are usually just tried in market. And durable products—which have high fixed production costs and long production lead times—may have to go directly to market. In these cases, it is especially important that the early steps be done carefully to reduce the chances for failure.[32]

Step 5: Commercialization

A product idea that survives this far can finally be placed on the market. Putting a product on the market is expensive, and success usually requires cooperation of the whole company. Manufacturing or service facilities have to be set up. Goods have to be produced to fill the channels of distribution, or people must be hired and trained to provide services. Further, introductory promotion is costly—especially if the company is entering a very competitive market.

Because of the size of the job, some firms introduce their products city by city or region by region—in a gradual "rollout"—until they have complete market coverage. Sprint used this approach in introducing its broadband wireless service that included a rooftop transmission device. Detroit, Phoenix, and San Francisco were targeted first. Rollouts also permit more market testing, but the main purpose is to do a good job implementing the marketing plan. But marketing managers also need to pay close attention to control—to ensure that the implementation effort is working and that the strategy is on target.

NEW-PRODUCT DEVELOPMENT: A TOTAL COMPANY EFFORT

We've been discussing the steps in a logical, new-product development process. However, as shown in Exhibit 10-6, many factors can impact the success of the effort.

Top-level support is vital

Companies that are particularly successful at developing new goods and services seem to have one key trait in common: enthusiastic top-management support for new-product development. New products tend to upset old routines that managers of established products often try in subtle but effective ways to maintain. So someone with top-level support, and authority to get things done, needs to be responsible for new-product development.[33]

Put someone in charge

In addition, rather than leaving new-product development to someone in engineering, R&D, or sales who happens to be interested in taking the initiative, successful companies put someone in charge. It may be a person, department, or team. But it's not a casual thing. It's a major responsibility of the job.

A new-product development team with people from different departments helps ensure that new ideas are carefully evaluated and profitable ones are quickly brought to market. It's important to choose the right people for the job. Overly

Exhibit 10-6 New-Product Development Success Factors

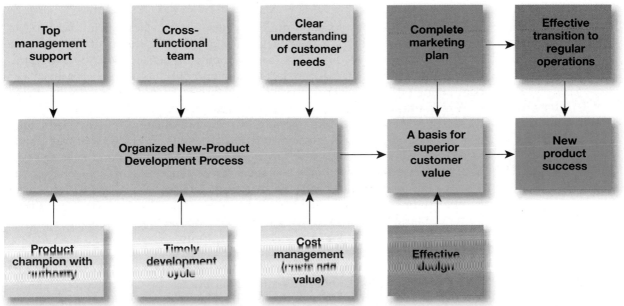

conservative managers may kill too many, or even all, new ideas. Or committees may create bureaucratic delays that make the difference between a product's success or failure.

Market needs guide R&D effort

Many new-product ideas come from scientific discoveries and new technologies. In many firms the new-product R&D effort is handled by scientists, engineers, and other technical specialists. Even service firms have technical specialists who help in development work. For example, a bank thinking about offering customers a new set of investment alternatives must be certain that it can deliver on its promises. Skillful R&D work can give a firm a competitive advantage—especially if it competes in high-tech markets. However, technical creativity by itself is not enough. The R&D effort must be guided by the type of market-oriented new-product development process we've been discussing.

From the idea generation stage to the commercialization stage, the R&D specialists, the operations people, and the marketing people must work together to evaluate the feasibility of new ideas. They may meet in person, or communicate with e-mail or intranet sites, or perhaps via teleconferencing or some other technology. There are many ways to share ideas. So it isn't sensible for a marketing manager to develop elaborate marketing plans for goods or services that the firm simply can't produce—or produce profitably. It also doesn't make sense for R&D people to develop a technology or product that does not have potential for the firm and its markets. Clearly, a balancing act is involved here. But the critical point is the basic one we've been emphasizing throughout the whole book: Marketing-oriented firms seek to satisfy customer needs at a profit with an integrated, whole company effort.

Steps should not be skipped

Even with a careful development process, many new products do fail—usually because a company skips some steps in the process. Because speed can be important, it's always tempting to skip needed steps when some part of the process seems to indicate that the company has a "really good idea." But the process moves in steps—gathering different kinds of information along the way. By skipping steps, a firm may miss an important aspect that could make a whole strategy less profitable or actually cause it to fail.

NEED FOR PRODUCT MANAGERS

Product variety leads to product managers

Eventually, the new product is no longer new—it becomes just another product. In some firms, at this point the new-product people turn the product over to the regular operating people and go on to developing other new ideas. In other firms, the person who was the new-product champion continues with the product, perhaps taking on the broader responsibility for turning it into a successful business.

When a firm has only one or a few related products, everyone is interested in them. But when a firm has products in several different product categories, management may decide to put someone in charge of each category, or each brand, to be sure that attention to these products is not lost in the rush of everyday business. **Product managers** or **brand managers** manage specific products—often taking over the jobs formerly handled by an advertising manager. That gives a clue to what is often their major responsibility—Promotion—since the products have already been developed by the new-product people. However, some brand managers start at the new-product development stage and carry on from there.

Product managers are especially common in large companies that produce many kinds of products. Several product managers may serve under a marketing manager. Sometimes these product managers are responsible for the profitable operation of a particular product's whole marketing effort. Then they have to coordinate their

HOW TO BE INNOVATIVE WHEN YOU'RE A HUNDRED YEARS OLD

3M is a 100-year-old company that has discovered its own "fountain of youth." Yet it is no secret what it does to constantly renew itself. 3M is fast and successful in spinning out new products that offer innovative and practical solutions to customers' problems. This doesn't happen by chance. It is an ongoing priority of top managers. For example, 3M's chief set an objective that 30 percent of sales should come from products that didn't exist four years earlier. You can see the emphasis on innovation in even the quickest visit to 3M's website (www.3m.com). Current 3M innovations include respirators (for Department of Homeland Security "first responders"), radiant light film (for uses ranging from brighter cell phone displays to glittery signage), elastomers (which seal in aggressive chemicals in high-temperature settings), and Filtrete electrostatic fibers (which filter dust out of heating vents). Everywhere you look there are past 3M innovations that are still being improved, including brands like Post-it Notes, Thinsulate outdoor wear, and Scotch Pop-Up Tape Strips.

3M motivates innovation by staying close to customers, rewarding new-product champions, and sharing ideas among divisions. Teams from marketing, operations, and R&D screen new-product concepts for the ones with the highest profit potential. Then everyone works to bring the best ones to market fast. 3M's Scotch-Brite Never Rust Wool Soap Pads show how this approach can succeed. Consumers told 3M marketing researchers that they wanted an improved soap pad. Ordinary steel wool pads leave rust stains on sinks and tiny metal splinters in dishpan hands. 3M screens new products for their environmental impact, so the R&D people developed a pad using plastic fibers from recycled plastic bottles. Experts from 3M's abrasives division figured out how to coat the fibers with fine abrasives and biodegradable soap. Further marketing research refined the shape of the pads, and test markets evaluated details of the marketing plan. For example, tests confirmed that consumers liked the colorful package made from recycled paper and would pay more for Never Rust pads than they did for Brillo.

The managers varied the marketing plan for different countries. In mature markets such as the U.S. and Brazil where steel wool pads already had a large consumer base, the objective was to capture share. In Japan, where steel wool is not commonly used, the objective was to pioneer the market and attract new customers. In a firm renowned for innovation, the launch of Never Rust pads was one of 3M's most profitable ever.

3M is also serious about how its innovations affect consumer welfare. When managers learned that traces of a chemical in 3M's Scotchgard fabric protector might persist in the environment, they didn't wait for scientists to do more tests. They voluntarily pulled the popular product off the market—before they even knew if R&D could find a substitute chemical.[34]

Consumer packaged-goods companies, like Nabisco, usually assign brand managers who are responsible for individual products. However, when there are a number of products in the same product category, there is often a higher-level manager who ensures that the marketing program for the whole category is effective.

efforts with others, including the sales manager, advertising agencies, production and research people, and even channel members. This is likely to lead to difficulties if product managers have no control over the marketing strategy for other related brands or authority over other functional areas whose efforts they are expected to direct and coordinate.

To avoid these problems, in some companies the product manager serves mainly as a "product champion"—concerned with planning and getting the promotion effort implemented. A higher-level marketing manager with more authority coordinates the efforts and integrates the marketing strategies for different products into an overall plan.

The activities of product managers vary a lot depending on their experience and aggressiveness and the company's organizational philosophy. Today, companies are emphasizing marketing *experience*—because this important job takes more than academic training and enthusiasm. But it is clear that someone must be responsible for developing and implementing product-related plans, especially when a company has many products.[35]

CONCLUSION

New-product planning is an increasingly important activity in a modern economy because it is no longer very profitable to just sell me-too products in highly competitive markets. Markets, competition, and product life cycles are changing at a fast pace.

The product life-cycle concept is especially important to marketing strategy planning. It shows that a firm needs different marketing mixes—and even strategies—as a product moves through its cycle. This is an important point because profits change during the life cycle—with most of the profits going to the innovators or fast copiers.

We pointed out that a product is new to a firm if it is new in any way or to any target market. But the Fed-eral Trade Commission takes a narrower view of what you can call "new."

New products are so important to business survival that firms need some organized process for developing them. We discuss such a process and empha-size that it requires a total company effort to be successful.

The failure rate of new products is high—but it is lower for better-managed firms that recognize product development and management as vital processes. Some firms appoint product managers to manage individual products and new-product teams to ensure that the process is carried out successfully.

KEY TERMS

product life cycle, 270

market introduction, 271

market growth, 271

market maturity, 271

sales decline, 273

fashion, 276

fad, 277

new product, 281

Federal Trade Commission (FTC) , 281

Consumer Product Safety Act, 285

product liability, 286

concept testing, 286

product managers, 290

brand managers, 290

QUESTIONS AND PROBLEMS

1. Explain how industry sales and industry profits be-have over the product life cycle.

2. Cite two examples of products that you feel are cur-rently in each of the product life-cycle stages. Con-sider services as well as physical goods.

3. Explain how you might reach different conclusions about the correct product life-cycle stage(s) in the worldwide automobile market.

4. Explain why individual brands may not follow the product life-cycle pattern. Give an example of a new brand that is not entering the life cycle at the market introduction stage.

5. Discuss the life cycle of a product in terms of its prob-able impact on a manufacturer's marketing mix. Il-lustrate using personal computers.

6. What characteristics of a new product will help it to move through the early stages of the product life cy-cle more quickly? Briefly discuss each characteristic—illustrating with a product of your choice. Indicate how each characteristic might be viewed in some other country.

7. What is a new product? Illustrate your answer.

8. Explain the importance of an organized new-product development process and illustrate how it might be used for *(a)* a new hair care product, *(b)* a new chil-dren's toy, and *(c)* a new subscribers-only cable tele-vision channel.

9. Discuss how you might use the new-product devel-opment process if you were thinking about offering some kind of summer service to residents in a beach resort town.

10. Explain the role of product or brand managers. When would it make sense for one of a company's current brand managers to be in charge of the new-product development process? Explain your thinking.

11. If a firm offers one of its brands in a number of different countries, would it make sense for one brand manager to be in charge, or would each country require its own brand manager? Explain your thinking.

12. Discuss the social value of new-product development activities that seem to encourage people to discard products that are not all worn out. Is this an economic waste? How worn out is all worn out? Must a shirt have holes in it? How big?

SUGGESTED CASES

3. Pillsbury's Häagen-Dazs
12. Applied Chemistry Corporation

20. Leisure World, Inc.

COMPUTER-AIDED PROBLEM

10. Growth Stage Competition

RESOURCE REMINDER

AgriChem, Inc., has introduced an innovative new product—a combination fertilizer, weed killer, and insecticide that makes it much easier for soybean farmers to produce a profitable crop. The product introduction was quite successful, with 1 million units sold in the year of introduction. And AgriChem's profits are increasing. Total market demand is expected to grow at a rate of 200,000 units a year for the next five years. Even so, AgriChem's marketing managers are concerned about what will happen to sales and profits during this period.

Based on past experience with similar situations, they expect one new competitor to enter the market during each of the next five years. They think this competitive pressure will drive prices down about 6 percent a year. Further, although the total market is growing, they know that new competitors will chip away at AgriChem's market share—even with the 10 percent a year increase planned for the promotion budget. In spite of the competitive pressure, the marketing managers are sure that familiarity with AgriChem's brand will help it hold a large share of the total market and give AgriChem greater economies of scale than competitors. In fact, they expect that the ratio of profit to dollar sales for AgriChem should be about 10 percent higher than for competitors.

AgriChem's marketing managers have decided the best way to get a handle on the situation is to organize the data in a spreadsheet. They have set up the spreadsheet so they can change the "years in the future" value and see what is likely to happen to AgriChem and the rest of the industry. The starting spreadsheet shows the current situation with data from the first full year of production.

a. Compare AgriChem's market share and profit for this year with what is expected next year—given the marketing managers' current assumptions. What are they expecting? (Hint: Set number of years in the future to 1.)

b. Prepare a table showing AgriChem's expected profit, and the expected industry revenue and profit, for the current year and the next five years. Briefly explain what happens to industry sales and profits and why. (Hint: Do an analysis to vary the number of years in the future value in the spreadsheet from a minimum of 0—the current year—to a maximum of 5. Display the three values requested.)

c. If market demand grows faster than expected—say, at 280,000 units a year—what will happen to AgriChem's profits and the expected industry revenues and profits over the next five years? What are the implications of this analysis?

For additional questions related to this problem, see Exercise 10-3 in the *Learning Aid for Use with Basic Marketing,* 15th edition.

1. Understand what product classes suggest about Place objectives.

2. Understand why some firms use direct channel systems while others rely on intermediaries and indirect systems.

3. Understand how and why marketing specialists develop to make channel systems more effective.

4. Understand how to develop cooperative relationships and avoid conflict in channel systems.

5. Know how channel members in vertical marketing systems shift and share functions to meet customer needs.

6. Understand the differences between intensive, selective, and exclusive distribution.

7. Understand the important new terms (shown in red).

CHAPTER ELEVEN

Place and Development of Channel Systems

STEVE KENDAL'S FIRM CREATES VIDEO GAMES. GROWTH SEEMED EASY DURING HIS FIRST FIVE YEARS IN BUSINESS. A FEW GOOD WHOLESALERS HELPED GET HIS INITIAL GAMES INTO VIDEO GAME SHOPS, GAMERS LIKED THEM, AND THEY SPREAD THE WORD. BUT THE MARKET FOR VIDEO GAMES

was maturing. Competition was intense among game producers and also at the retail level. More retailers had started to sell video games at low prices. Many of the small shops were going out of business or joining chains. Kendal thought it was time to change his strategy, including his Place arrangements. He got the idea to shift his focus to *educational* video games from his wife, a teacher. She had told him about the surging popularity of products, like Disney's Baby Einstein videos, that targeted upscale parents who wanted ways to make their kids smarter. Kendal knew he could develop games that were fun, involving, and educational. Those benefits would make parents less price sensitive—and attract interest from retailers who wanted profitable new sales in the game category. When Kendal saw an article that Barnes & Noble, the big book store chain and Internet site, had bought a controlling interest in the chain of GameStop stores, he decided it was time to act. Most game developers would have glossed over that news, but in his previous job Kendal had gotten a taste of what that might mean.

Kendal had been a manager for the Cozy Bookshop, a family-owned store that for decades had been *the* place to buy books in his college-town market. Kendal moved on to start his video game business before Cozy had its final inventory clearance sale. But its fate seemed clear because sales of books through independent bookshops dropped by over 25 percent in the 1990s. Like Cozy, many of these shops went out of business because of changes in the channels of distribution for books. Many of the small publishers with whom these shops worked also had troubles.

Competitors had emerged and slowly chipped away at Cozy's sales over the years. The mail-order book clubs, the religious book store that opened in town, and the used-textbook brokers all ate into business. But the coffin nail was driven by the growth of big national chains. They had buying clout with publishers and could demand lower prices for larger quantities. They also had aggressive marketing programs to woo consumers. Cozy had lost some customers to the frequent-buyer discount and special-order service at Walden Books. Others went to Barnes & Noble for the selection—and the coffee bar. The local Costco store carried only a few best-sellers, but its low prices turned shoppers into impulse buyers. Some of Cozy's ex-customers were no longer shopping in any store. Rather, they were buying from Amazon.com or from other online sellers who were able to sell at even lower prices than Amazon by linking their order systems to big wholesalers like Ingram Book Company that efficiently handled all of the logistics.

Kendal could see that the same changes were unfolding in channel systems for video games. Like many retailers with whom it was competing, Barnes & Noble had already scrambled its product lines and added music and entertainment products, including video games. Further, Barnes & Noble's role in GameStop meant that the 1,400 stores in that chain would be adopting the same effective customer service, inventory, shipping, and order systems that Barnes & Noble already had in place. Kendal knew that working with these powerful chains would be a challenge, but he thought that his educational games would appeal to customers they were already serving. Kendal even considered developing a line of educational games that GameStop could sell exclusively with its own brand name. Barnes & Noble had already published and sold some books that way. Kendal's new strategy would mean breaking off relations with the small shops that helped him get started, but from the experience of his bookseller days he was worried that many members of that channel were not going to survive.[1]

PLACE DECISIONS ARE AN IMPORTANT PART OF MARKETING STRATEGY

This case shows that offering customers a good product at a reasonable price is not the whole story. Managers must also think about **Place**—making goods and services available in the right quantities and locations—when customers want them. And when different target markets have different needs, a number of Place

Puma coordinates its promotion efforts with Lady Foot Locker, the retail chain, so that consumers will know where they can buy Puma's popular shoes. Ads for Esprit eyewear often list the names of stores where they are available.

Exhibit 11-1
Strategy Decision Areas
in Place

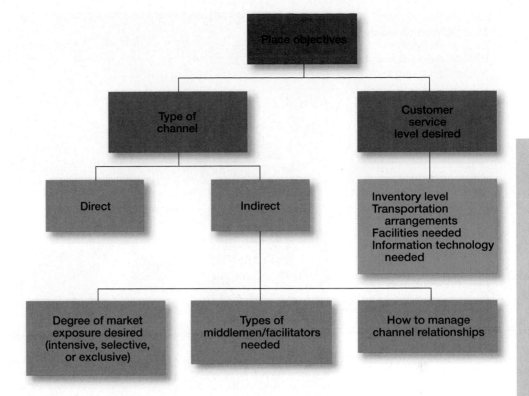

variations may be required. Our opening case also makes it clear that new Place arrangements can dramatically change the competition in a product-market. This is especially important in business today because many firms are using information technology, including websites and e-commerce, to reach customers more efficiently.

In the next three chapters, we'll deal with the many important strategy decisions that a marketing manager must make concerning Place. Exhibit 11-1 gives an overview. We'll start in this chapter with a discussion of the type of channel that's needed to meet customers' needs. We'll show why specialists are often involved and how they come together to form a **channel of distribution**—any series of firms or individuals who participate in the flow of products from producer to final user or consumer. We'll also consider how to manage relations among channel members to reduce conflict and improve cooperation.

In Chapter 12, we'll expand our coverage of Place to include decisions that a marketing manager makes to decide what level of distribution service to offer—and why he or she must coordinate storing and transporting activities—providing the desired service at a reasonable cost. Then, in Chapter 13, we'll take a closer look at the many different types of retailing and wholesaling firms. We'll consider their role in channels as well as the strategy decisions they make to satisfy their own customers.

PLACE DECISIONS ARE GUIDED BY "IDEAL" PLACE OBJECTIVES

All marketing managers want to be sure that their goods and services are available in the right quantities and locations—when customers want them. But customers may have different needs with respect to time, place, and possession utility as they make different purchases.

Most pet food companies focus on distribution through grocery stores, but Science Diet brand premium pet foods reach consumers in the U.S., Japan, France, and Italy through a different channel—veterinary offices and pet stores. Because Science Diet has developed cooperative relationships with members of this channel, Science Diet products often get special promotion support at the point of purchase. In addition, as shown in this ad, the package reminds customers that Science Diet is "Veterinarian Recommended."

Product classes suggest Place objectives

In Chapter 9 we introduced the product classes, which summarize consumers' urgency to have needs satisfied and willingness to seek information, shop, and compare. Now you should be able to use the product classes to handle Place decisions.

Exhibit 9-3 shows the relationship between consumer product classes and ideal Place objectives. Similarly, Exhibit 9-4 shows the business product classes and how they relate to customer needs. Study these exhibits carefully. They set the framework for making Place decisions. In particular, the product classes help us decide how much market exposure we'll need in each geographic area.

Place system is not automatic

Several different product classes may be involved if different market segments view a product in different ways. Thus, marketing managers may need to develop several strategies, each with its own Place arrangements. There may not be one Place arrangement that is best.

Place decisions have long-run effects

The marketing manager must also consider Place objectives in relation to the product life cycle; see Exhibit 10-2. Place decisions often have long-run effects. They're usually harder to change than Product, Price, and Promotion decisions. Many firms that thought they could quickly establish effective websites for direct online sales, for example, found that it took several years and millions of dollars to work out the kinks. It can take even longer and cost more to develop effective working relationships with others in the channel. Legal contracts with channel partners may limit changes. And it's hard to move retail stores and wholesale facilities once they are set up. Yet as products mature, they typically need broader distribution to reach different target customers.

The distribution of premium pet foods followed this pattern. A decade ago, supermarkets wouldn't carry specialized pet foods because there wasn't much demand. So marketing managers for Science Diet products concentrated on getting distribution through pet shops and veterinary offices. Science Diet's sales in this channel grew rapidly. What's more, profit margins on the specialty foods were much higher than on traditional fare. Seeing this growth, Purina, Kal Kan, and other producers developed new products and worked with their supermarket channels to set up special "nutrition centers" on the pet food aisle. As market growth continued, P&G bought Iams and pushed for distribution in pet superstores, at mass-merchandisers, and online. But Science Diet is still competing well in its own channel. It's using the same approach in pet stores in Japan, France, and Italy.[2]

CHANNEL SYSTEM MAY BE DIRECT OR INDIRECT

One of the most basic Place decisions producers must make is whether to handle the whole distribution themselves—perhaps by relying on direct-to-customer e-commerce selling—or use wholesalers, retailers, and other specialists (see Exhibit 11-1). Middlemen, in turn, must select the producers they'll work with.

Why a firm might want to use direct distribution

Many firms prefer to distribute directly to the final customer or consumer because they want to control the whole marketing job. They may think that they can serve target customers at a lower cost or do the work more effectively than middlemen. Since middlemen often carry products of several competing producers, they might not give any one item the special emphasis its producer wants.

The Internet makes direct distribution easier

Website-based e-commerce systems give many firms direct access to customers whom it would have been impossible to reach in the past. Even small, specialized firms may be able to establish a web page and draw customers from all over the world. Of course, there are limitations. If a customer wants a salesperson to demonstrate a product, then a "virtual store" may not be adequate. However, distribution via the Internet is still evolving. Some firms now use live camera "feeds" while talking with the customer over an Internet video phone. Other innovations are being tested. Regardless, if it's with the help of technology or by other more traditional means, there often *are* great advantages in selling directly to the final user or consumer.

Direct contact with customers

If a firm is in direct contact with its customers, it is more aware of changes in customer attitudes. It is in a better position to adjust its marketing mix quickly

In the U.S. and many other developed nations, Unilever relies primarily on indirect distribution through a variety of wholesalers and retailers. However, in Spain it delivers frozen foods directly to consumer homes, and in Vietnam a mobile store brings products to local consumers. And now some products are sold direct to consumers from an Internet website.

because there is no need to convince other channel members to help. If a product needs an aggressive selling effort or special technical service, the marketing manager can ensure that salespeople receive the necessary training and motivation.

Suitable middlemen are not available

A firm may have to go direct if suitable middlemen are not available or will not cooperate. For example, Apple is again opening its own stores in hopes of getting more in-store promotional emphasis on what's different about its iMac computers. SoBe, the firm that produces distinctive drinks targeted at the health and fitness crowd, went direct for a different reason. It was obtaining distribution in retail outlets in most areas with the help of beverage wholesalers. However, SoBe ran into difficulties when Snapple, a rival drink company, bought out SoBe's main wholesaler in New Jersey. SoBe tried to find another good wholesaler but none were available. That left SoBe with very limited distribution. So marketers for SoBe had little choice but to sell directly to retailers. Getting retailer cooperation and good shelf space was still a challenge, but it was easier when SoBe provided retailers with its own bright-colored, lizard-decorated coolers.[3]

Middlemen who have the best contacts with the target market may be hesitant to add unproven vendors or new products, especially really new products that don't fit well with their current business. Many new products die because the producer can't find willing middlemen and doesn't have the financial resources to handle direct distribution.

In the United States, the Census Bureau publishes detailed data concerning wholesalers and retailers, including breakdowns by kind of business, product line, and geographic territory. Similar information is available for Canada and many other countries, including most of those in the European Union. Most of this data is available online. It can be very valuable in strategy planning—especially to learn whether potential channel members are serving a target market. You can also learn what sales volume current middlemen are achieving.

Common with business customers and services

Many business products are sold direct-to-customer. Alcan sells aluminum to General Motors direct. And Honda sells its motors direct to lawn mower producers. This is understandable since in business markets there are fewer transactions, orders are larger, and customers may be concentrated in one geographic area. Further, once relationships are established, e-commerce systems can efficiently handle orders, inventory replenishment, and routine information (such as delivery schedules).

Service firms often use direct channels. If the service must be produced in the presence of customers, there may be little need for middlemen. An accounting firm like PricewaterhouseCoopers, for example, must deal directly with its customers. However, many firms that produce physical goods turn to middlemen specialists to help provide the services customers expect. Maytag may hope that its authorized dealers don't get many repair calls, but the service is available when customers need it. Here the middleman produces the service.[4]

Some consumer products are sold direct

Many companies that produce consumer products have websites where a consumer can place a direct order. But for most consumer products this is still a small part of total sales. Most consumer products are sold through middlemen.

INTERNET EXERCISE

Gateway is a computer company that uses direct distribution to its customers in the U.S. Go to the Gateway website (www.gateway.com) and think about how it is organized. Is the website organized well to help Gateway reach different segments of customers in the U.S.?

Of course, some consumer products are sold direct to consumers where they live or work. Mary Kay and Avon cosmetics, Electrolux vacuum cleaners, Amway household products, and Sara Lee are examples. These firms and many others are finding that this is a good way to crack open international markets ranging from India and China to Brazil and the U.K. Most of these firms rely on direct selling, which involves personal sales contact between a representative of the company and an individual consumer. However, most of these "salespeople" are *not* company employees. Rather, they usually work as independent middlemen, and the companies that they sell for refer to them as *dealers, distributors, agents,* or some similar term. So in a strict technical sense, this is not really direct producer-to-consumer distribution.[5]

Don't be confused by the term *direct marketing*

Even though most consumer products are sold through middlemen, an increasing number of firms rely on **direct marketing**—direct communication between a seller and an individual customer using a promotion method other than face-to-face personal selling. Sometimes direct marketing promotion is coupled with direct distribution from a producer to consumers. Park Seed Company, for example, sells the seeds it grows directly to consumers with a mail catalog and website. However, many firms that use direct marketing promotion distribute their products through middlemen. So the term *direct marketing* is primarily concerned with the Promotion area, not Place decisions. We'll talk about direct marketing promotion in more detail in Chapter 14.[6]

When indirect channels are best

Even if a producer wants to handle the whole distribution job, sometimes it's simply not possible. Customers often have established buying patterns. For example, Square D, a producer of electrical supplies, might want to sell directly to electrical contractors. It can certainly set up a website for online orders or even open sales offices in key markets. But if contractors like to make all of their purchases in one convenient stop—at a local electrical wholesaler—the only practical way to reach them is through a wholesaler.

Consumers want convenience

Similarly, consumers are spread throughout many geographic areas and often prefer to shop for certain products at specific places. Some consumers, for instance, see Sears as *the* place to shop for tires, so they'll only buy the brands that Sears carries. This is one reason most firms that produce consumer products rely so heavily on indirect channels (see Exhibit 2-6).[7]

Until recently, Levi Strauss jeans were not distributed by Wal-Mart. However, many shoppers prefer to buy their jeans at Wal-Mart and other mass-merchandisers. To reach this segment, Levi Strauss created the Signature line. It features lighter-weight denim and less detailing and is now available at Wal-Mart, Target, and Kmart.

Middlemen may invest in inventory

Direct distribution usually requires a significant investment in facilities, people, and information technology. A company that has limited financial resources or that wants to retain flexibility may want to avoid that investment by working with established middlemen.

Middlemen may further reduce a producer's need for working capital by buying the producer's output and carrying it in inventory until it's sold. If customers want a good "right now," there must be an inventory available to make the sale. And if customers are spread over a large area, it will probably be necessary to have widespread distribution.

Middlemen may reduce credit risk

Some middlemen play a critical role by providing credit to customers at the end of the channel. A middleman who knows local customers can help reduce credit risks. As sales via the Internet grow, sellers are looking for faster and better ways to check the credit ratings of distant customers. It's an unhappy day when the marketing manager learns that a customer who was shipped goods based on an online order can't pay the invoice.

The most important reason for using an indirect channel of distribution is that an intermediary can often help producers serve customer needs better and at lower cost. Remember that we discussed this briefly in Chapter 1. Now we'll go into more detail.

CHANNEL SPECIALISTS MAY REDUCE DISCREPANCIES AND SEPARATIONS

The assortment and quantity of products customers want may be different from the assortment and quantity of products companies produce. Producers are often located far from their customers and may not know how best to reach them.

Office Depot, a large office supplies chain, accumulates products from many producers at its distribution center and then breaks bulk to provide the convenient assortments that consumers expect to find at individual Office Depot stores.

Customers in turn may not know about their choices. Specialists develop to adjust these discrepancies and separations.[8]

Middlemen may supply needed information

Specialists often help provide information to bring buyers and sellers together. For example, most consumers don't know much about the wide variety of home and auto insurance policies available. A local independent insurance agent may help them decide which policy, and which insurance company, best fits their needs.

Middlemen who are close to their customers are often able to anticipate customer needs and forecast demand more accurately. This information can help reduce inventory costs in the whole channel—and it may help the producer smooth out production.

Most producers seek help from specialists when they first enter international markets. Specialists can provide crucial information about customer needs and insights into differences in the marketing environment.

Discrepancies of quantity and assortment

Discrepancy of quantity means the difference between the quantity of products it is economical for a producer to make and the quantity final users or consumers normally want. For example, most manufacturers of golf balls produce large quantities—perhaps 200,000 to 500,000 in a given time period. The average golfer, however, wants only a few balls at a time. Adjusting for this discrepancy usually requires middlemen—wholesalers and retailers.

Producers typically specialize by product—and therefore another discrepancy develops. **Discrepancy of assortment** means the difference between the lines a typical producer makes and the assortment final consumers or users want. Most golfers, for example, need more than golf balls. They want golf shoes, gloves, clubs, a bag, and, of course, a golf course to play on. And they usually don't want to shop for each item separately. So, again, there is a need for wholesalers and retailers to adjust these discrepancies.

Channel specialists adjust discrepancies with regrouping activities

Regrouping activities adjust the quantities or assortments of products handled at each level in a channel of distribution.

There are four regrouping activities: accumulating, bulk-breaking, sorting, and assorting. When one or more of these activities is needed, a marketing specialist may develop to fill this need.

Adjusting quantity discrepancies by accumulating and bulk-breaking

Accumulating involves collecting products from many small producers. Much of the coffee that comes from Colombia is grown on small farms in the mountains. Accumulating the small crops into larger quantities is a way of getting the lowest transporting rate and making it more convenient for distant food processing companies to buy and handle it. Accumulating is especially important in less-developed countries and in other situations, like agricultural markets, where there are many small producers.

Accumulating is also important with professional services because they often involve the combined work of a number of individuals, each of whom is a specialized producer. A hospital makes it easier for patients by accumulating the services of a number of health care specialists, many of whom may not actually work for the hospital.

Many middlemen who operate from Internet websites focus on accumulating. Specialized sites for everything from Chinese art to Dutch flower bulbs bring together the output of many producers.

Bulk-breaking involves dividing larger quantities into smaller quantities as products get closer to the final market. The bulk-breaking may involve several levels of middlemen. Wholesalers may sell smaller quantities to other wholesalers or directly to retailers. Retailers continue breaking bulk as they sell individual items to their customers.

Adjusting assortment discrepancies by sorting and assorting

Different types of specialists adjust assortment discrepancies. They perform two types of regrouping activities: sorting and assorting.

To reach its place objectives, Sprint sells PCS phones and its wireless services through 12,000 outlets, including retail chains like Staples and its own Sprint PCS Stores.

Sorting means separating products into grades and qualities desired by different target markets. For example, an investment firm might offer its customers shares in a mutual fund made up only of stocks for companies that pay regular dividends. Similarly, a wholesaler that specializes in serving convenience stores may focus on smaller packages of frequently used products.

Assorting means putting together a variety of products to give a target market what it wants. This usually is done by those closest to the final consumer or user—retailers or wholesalers who try to supply a wide assortment of products for the convenience of their customers. Thus, a wholesaler selling Yazoo tractors and mowers to golf courses might also carry Pennington grass seed and Scott fertilizer.

Watch for changes

Sometimes these discrepancies are adjusted badly, especially when consumer wants and attitudes shift rapidly. When cell phones suddenly became popular, an opportunity developed for a new specialist. Cell phone dealers came on the scene to help customers figure out what type of cell phone and service would meet their needs. It cost the sellers of cell services about $300 per customer to sell through dealers. However, as the market grew, competition for customers heated up and electronics stores wanted a piece of the action. They were willing to take a smaller markup. Now that the market is established, cell service providers are finding it cheaper to sell from a website or use their own salespeople.[9]

Specialists should develop to adjust discrepancies *if they must be adjusted*. But there is no point in having middlemen just because that's the way it's been done in the past. Sometimes a breakthrough opportunity can come from finding a better way to reduce discrepancies. Some manufacturers of business products can now reach more customers in distant markets with an Internet website than it was previously possible for them to reach with independent manufacturers' reps who sold on commission (but otherwise left distribution to the firm). The website cost advantage can translate to lower prices and a marketing mix that is a better value for some target segments.[10]

CHANNEL RELATIONSHIP MUST BE MANAGED

Marketing manager must choose type of channel relationship

Middlemen specialists can help make a channel more efficient. But there may be problems getting the different firms in a channel to work together well. How well they work together depends on the type of relationship they have. This should be carefully considered since marketing managers usually have choices about what type of channel system to join or develop.

A channel captain can improve the performance of the whole channel—by developing strategies that help everyone in the channel do a better job of meeting the needs of target customers at the end of the channel.

The whole channel should have a product-market commitment

Ideally, all of the members of a channel system should have a shared *product-market commitment*—with all members focusing on the same target market at the end of the channel and sharing the various marketing functions in appropriate ways. When members of a channel do this, they are better able to compete effectively for the customer's business. Unfortunately, many marketing managers overlook this idea because it's not the way their firms have traditionally handled channel relationships.

Traditional channel systems involve weak relationships

In **traditional channel systems,** the various channel members make little or no effort to cooperate with each other. They buy and sell from each other—and that's the extent of their relationship. Each channel member does only what it considers to be in its own best interest. It doesn't worry about other members of the channel. This is shortsighted, but it's easy to see how it can happen. The objectives of the various channel members may be different. For example, General Electric wants a wholesaler of electrical building supplies to sell GE products. But a wholesaler who works with different producers may not care whose products get sold. The wholesaler just wants happy customers and a good profit margin.

Traditional channel systems are still typical, and very important, in some industries. The members of these channels have their independence, but they may pay for it too. As we will see, such channels are declining in importance—with good reason.[11]

Conflict gets in the way

Specialization can make a channel more efficient—but not if the specialists are so independent that the channel doesn't work smoothly. Because members of traditional channel systems often have different objectives—and different ideas about how things should be done—conflict is common.

There are two basic types of conflict in channels of distribution. Vertical conflicts occur between firms at different levels in the channel of distribution. A vertical conflict may occur if a producer and a retailer disagree about how much shelf space or promotion effort the retailer should give the producer's product. For example, when Wherehouse Entertainment (a large retail music chain) started to sell used CDs—at about half the price of new ones—several recording companies said that they would halt cooperative advertising payments to any retailer that sold used CDs. The recording companies felt that the used CDs hurt their sales.[12]

Horizontal conflicts occur between firms at the same level in the channel of distribution. For example, a furniture store that keeps a complete line of furniture on display isn't happy to find out that a discount chain store down the street is offering customers lower prices on special orders of the same items. The discounter is getting a free ride from the competing store's investment in inventory. And nothing gets an independent retailer more charged up than finding out that a chain store is selling some product for less than the wholesale price the independent pays.

Cooperative relationships share common objectives

Usually the best way to avoid conflict is to get everyone in the channel working together in a cooperative relationship that is focused on the same basic objective—satisfying the customer at the end of the channel. This leads us away from traditional channels to cooperative channel relationships and the channel captain concept.

Channel captain can guide channel relationships

Each channel system should act as a unit, where each member of the channel collaborates to serve customers at the end of the channel. In this view, cooperation is everyone's responsibility. However, some firms are in a better position to take the lead in the relationship and in coordinating the whole channel effort. This situation calls for a **channel captain**—a manager who helps direct the activities of a whole channel and tries to avoid or solve channel conflicts.

For example, when Harley-Davidson wanted to expand sales of fashion accessories, it was difficult for motorcycle dealers to devote enough space to all of the different styles. Harley considered selling the items directly from its own website, but that would take sales away from dealers who were working hard to help Harley sell both cycles and fashions. So Harley's president asked a group of dealers and Harley managers to work together to come up with a plan they all liked. The result was a website that sells Harley products through the dealer that is closest to the customer.[13]

The concept of a single channel captain is logical. But most traditional channels don't have a recognized captain. The various firms don't act as a coordinated system. Yet firms are interrelated, even if poorly, by their policies. So it makes sense to try to avoid channel conflicts by planning for channel relations. The channel captain arranges for the necessary functions to be performed in the most effective way.

The situation faced by Goodyear is a good example. The Goodyear brand was sold almost exclusively through its own stores and its 2,500 independent tire dealers. But sales were falling. There were many reasons. France's Michelin and Japan's Bridgestone had aggressively expanded distribution in North America. Moreover, many consumers were shopping at discount outlets. Goodyear decided it had no choice but to expand distribution and sell Goodyear tires to Kmart's Penske autocenters and other big retail chains. To reach the discount shoppers, Goodyear also converted many of its own autocenters to no-frills stores operated under the Just Tires name. However, to reduce the conflict that these changes caused with its independent dealers, Goodyear introduced the new Aquatred line and other specialized tires that appealed to the dealers' target market. Goodyear also increased advertising and created the Gemini brand name to help promote service by Goodyear dealers. Because of this channel leadership, Goodyear's sales increased and so did the sales of its dealers.[14]

Some producers lead their channels

As the Goodyear case suggests, in the U.S. producers frequently take the lead in channel relations. Middlemen often wait to see what the producer intends to do

Exhibit 11-2 How Channel Functions May Be Shifted and Shared in Different Channel Systems

A. How strategy decisions are handled in a producer-led channel

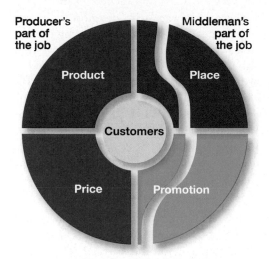

B. How strategy decisions are handled in a retailer-led channel

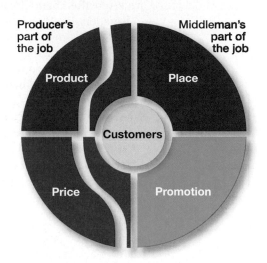

and wants them to do. Then they decide whether their roles will be profitable and whether they want to join in the channel effort.

Exhibit 11-2A shows this type of producer-led channel system. Here the producer has selected the target market and developed the Product, set the Price structure, done some consumer and channel Promotion, and developed the Place setup. Middlemen are then expected to finish the Promotion job in their respective places. Of course, in a retailer-dominated channel system, the marketing jobs would be handled in a different way.

Some middlemen are channel captains

Sometimes wholesalers or retailers do take the lead. They are closer to the final user or consumer and are in an ideal position to assume the channel captain role. These middlemen analyze their customers' needs and then seek out producers who

can provide these products at reasonable prices. With the growth of powerful chains, like Wal-Mart and Toys "R" Us, retailers now dominate the channel systems for many products in the United States. In Japan, very large wholesalers (trading companies) are often the channel captains.

Retailers like Sears and wholesalers like Ace Hardware who develop their own dealer brands in effect act like producers. They specify the whole marketing mix for a product and merely delegate production to a factory. Exhibit 11-2B shows how marketing strategy might be handled in this sort of retailer-led channel system.

Some strong middlemen use their power to control channel relationships. For example, buyers for Wal-Mart look at the value added by a wholesaler. If they think Wal-Mart can be efficient without the wholesaler, they tell the producer that the chain will only buy direct—usually at a lower price than was paid to the wholesaler.[15]

VERTICAL MARKETING SYSTEMS FOCUS ON FINAL CUSTOMERS

Many marketing managers accept the view that a coordinated channel system can help everyone in the channel. These managers are moving their firms away from traditional channel systems and instead developing or joining vertical market systems. **Vertical marketing systems** are channel systems in which the whole channel focuses on the same target market at the end of the channel. Such systems make sense, and are growing, because if the final customer doesn't buy the product, the whole channel suffers. There are three types of vertical marketing systems—corporate, administered, and contractual. Exhibit 11-3 summarizes some characteristics of these systems and compares them with traditional systems.

Corporate channel systems shorten channels

Some corporations develop their own vertical marketing systems by internal expansion or by buying other firms, or both. With **corporate channel systems**—corporate ownership all along the channel—we might say the firm is going "direct." But actually the firm may be handling manufacturing, wholesaling, *and* retailing—so it's more accurate to think of the firm as a vertical marketing system.

Corporate channel systems may develop by **vertical integration**—acquiring firms at different levels of channel activity. Bridgestone, for example, has rubber plantations in Liberia, tire plants in Ohio, and wholesale and retail outlets all over the world. In England, most of the quaint local pubs are now actually owned and operated by the large beer breweries.

Exhibit 11-3
Characteristics of Traditional and Vertical Marketing Systems

| | | Type of Channel | | |
| | | Vertical Marketing Systems | | |
Characteristics	Traditional	Administered	Contractual	Corporate
Amount of cooperation	Little or none	Some to good	Fairly good to good	Complete
Control maintained by	None	Economic power and leadership	Contracts	Ownership by one company
Examples	Typical channel of "independents"	General Electric, Miller Beer, O.M. Scott & Sons (lawn products)	McDonald's, Holiday Inn, Ace Hardware, Super Valu, Coca-Cola, Chevrolet	Florsheim Shoes, Sherwin-Williams, Mothers Work

MUSIC FIRMS FIDDLE AROUND WHILE CUSTOMERS SEARCH FOR DIGITAL TUNES

The music industry knew that its target market was the Internet generation, but it doggedly stuck to distribution of music on CDs through its traditional channels of distribution. Selling digital downloads was, at best, a piecemeal effort. With this head-in-the-sand approach, the Internet became a threat rather than an opportunity.

Napster's file-sharing service kick-started the digital media revolution and attracted 60 million avid fans who downloaded pirated digital songs for free. Even after Napster was forced into liquidation in 2002, few music firms had come up with effective plans of their own for digital distribution. A year later, Napster was reinvented as a subscription service. For $9.95 a month, a user could legally download songs for 99 cents each.

However, by then Apple's iTunes online music jukebox and pay-per-song store had a head start. It had distribution agreements with most music labels. Also, iTunes was designed to be easy to use, but only with Apple's popular iPod MP3 player (although the iPod software was updated to reach Windows users later). Apple even formed an alliance with America Online so that AOL's 25 million users would be steered to iTunes.com for music purchases and billed directly on their AOL accounts for downloads. However, competition from new intermediaries for digital content is heating up, so consumers are likely to have many available choices not only for music but for movies, books, and other items.[16]

Corporate channel systems are sometimes started by retailers. Mothers Work is a good example. It started as a mail-order catalog specializing in maternity clothes. Now it sells more than a third of all maternity clothes in the U.S. Vertical integration has been a key factor in its ability to give its customers what they want. It has over 700 company-run stores, its own designers, fabric-cutting operations, warehouses, and information systems to tie them all together.[17]

Vertical integration has potential advantages—stable sources of supplies, better control of distribution and quality, greater buying power, and lower executive overhead. Provided that the discrepancies of quantity and assortment are not too great at each level in a channel, vertical integration can be profitable. However, many managers have found that it's hard to be really good at running manufacturing, wholesaling, and retailing businesses that are very different from each other. Instead, they try to be more efficient at what they do best and focus on ways to get cooperation in the channel for the other activities.

Administered and contractual systems may work well

Firms can often gain the advantages of vertical integration without building a costly corporate channel. A manager can develop administered or contractual channel systems instead. In **administered channel systems**, the channel members informally agree to cooperate with each other. They can agree to routinize ordering, share inventory and sales information over computer networks, standardize accounting, and coordinate promotion efforts. In **contractual channel systems**, the channel members agree by contract to cooperate with each other. With both of these systems, the members retain some of the flexibility of a traditional channel system.

The opportunities to reduce costs and provide customers with superior value are growing in these systems because of help from information technology. For example, Costco has a system that it calls "vendor managed inventory" in which key suppliers take over responsibility for managing a set of products, often a whole product category. Costco uses this approach with Kimberly-Clark (KC), the firm that makes Huggies. Every day, an analyst at KC's headquarters studies Costco's online data that details Huggies' sales and inventory at every Costco store. The analyst studies how much is sold of each item in each store in the average week. If inventory is getting

Wal-Mart uses real-time data and works with vendors to ensure that the right assortment of products is always on hand, while reducing inventory levels and virtually eliminating lost sales because of out-of-stock items. Such cooperation among channel members can reduce costs and result in lower prices to the final consumer.

low, a new order is placed and shipping is scheduled. Shipping cartons with computer-readable bar codes track the status of shipments and reduce errors. This system reduces buying and selling costs, inventory management, lost sales from inventory stock-outs, and the consumer frustration that creates. Because KC does this job well, it makes more money and so does Costco. Costco could do the job itself, but it handles such a wide assortment of products that it would be costly to do all the work required in every high-volume category.[18]

Vertical marketing systems—dominant force in the marketplace

Vertical systems in the consumer products area have a healthy majority of retail sales and should continue to increase their share in the future. Vertical marketing systems are becoming the major competitive units in the U.S. distribution system—and they are growing rapidly in other parts of the world as well.[19]

Short-term alliances are also popular

Firms that cooperate to build vertical marketing systems typically share a longer-term commitment. Sometimes, however, what a firm wants is a short-term collaboration to accomplish a specific objective. This may lead to an alliance, a partnership (usually informal) in which firms agree to work together to achieve an objective. An alliance may involve two firms, or a whole network of firms. The firms may be at the same level in the channel or at different levels. For example, a number of hardware, software, and service firms in the computer business have formed alliances to build a market for the Linux operating system. Some of these firms are even competitors (at least in some of their product-markets). Nevertheless, without the alliance it would be difficult for any of them to compete with Microsoft.[20]

THE BEST CHANNEL SYSTEM SHOULD ACHIEVE IDEAL MARKET EXPOSURE

You may think that all marketing managers want their products to have maximum exposure to potential customers. This isn't true. Some product classes require much less market exposure than others. **Ideal market exposure** makes a product available widely enough to satisfy target customers' needs but not exceed them. Too much exposure only increases the total cost of marketing.

To make products more readily available, a manufacturer may need to recruit additional middlemen and also be certain that it is convenient for consumers to purchase online.

Ideal exposure may be intensive, selective, or exclusive

Intensive distribution is selling a product through all responsible and suitable wholesalers or retailers who will stock or sell the product. **Selective distribution** is selling through only those middlemen who will give the product special attention. **Exclusive distribution** is selling through only one middleman in a particular geographic area. As we move from intensive to exclusive distribution, we give up exposure in return for some other advantage—including, but not limited to, lower cost.

In practice, this means that Wrigley's chewing gum is handled, through intensive distribution, by about a million U.S. outlets. Rolls-Royces are handled, through exclusive distribution, by only a limited number of middlemen across the country.

Intensive distribution—sell it where they buy it

Intensive distribution is commonly needed for convenience products and business supplies—such as laser printer cartridges, ring binders, and copier paper—used by all offices. Customers want such products nearby.

The seller's intent is important here. Intensive distribution refers to the desire to sell through *all* responsible and suitable outlets. What this means depends on customer habits and preferences. If customers preferred to buy Panasonic portable TVs only at electronics stores, you would try to sell through all electronics stores to achieve intensive distribution. Today, however, many customers buy small portable TVs at a variety of convenient outlets—including Eckerd drugstores, a local Target, over the phone from the Sharper Image catalog, or perhaps from a website on the Internet. This means that an intensive distribution policy requires use of all these outlets, and more than one channel, to reach one target market.

Rayovac batteries were not selling well even though their performance was very similar to other batteries. Part of that was due to heavier advertising for Duracell and Energizer. But consumers usually don't go shopping for batteries. They're purchased on impulse 83 percent of the time. To get a larger share of purchases, Rayovac had to be in more stores. It offered retailers a marketing mix with less advertising and a lower price. In three years, the brand moved from being available in 36,000 stores to 82,000 stores—and that increase gave sales a big charge.[21]

Selective distribution—sell it where it sells best

Selective distribution covers the broad area of market exposure between intensive and exclusive distribution. It may be suitable for all categories of products. Only the better middlemen are used here. Companies commonly use selective distribution to gain some of the advantages of exclusive distribution—while still achieving fairly widespread market coverage.

Reduce costs and get better partners	A selective policy might be used to avoid selling to wholesalers or retailers that (1) place orders that are too small to justify making calls, (2) make too many returns or request too much service, (3) have a poor credit rating, or (4) are not in a position to do a satisfactory job.

A selective policy might be used to avoid selling to wholesalers or retailers that (1) place orders that are too small to justify making calls, (2) make too many returns or request too much service, (3) have a poor credit rating, or (4) are not in a position to do a satisfactory job.

Selective distribution is becoming more popular than intensive distribution as firms see that they don't need 100 percent coverage of a market to support national advertising. Often the majority of sales come from relatively few customers—and the others buy too little compared to the cost of working with them. This is called the 80/20 rule—80 percent of a company's sales often come from only 20 percent of its customers *until it becomes more selective in choosing customers.*

Esprit—a producer of women's clothing—was selling through about 4,000 department stores and specialty shops in the United States. But Esprit's sales analysis showed that sales in Esprit's own stores were about four times better than sales in other outlets. Profits increased when Esprit cut back to about half as many outlets and opened more of its own stores and a website. Over time, competition from retailers like The Gap and Abercrombie & Fitch increased in the United States, so in recent years Esprit has selectively focused on building profitability in 600 directly managed shops and 2,000 franchised shops in Europe and Asia.[22]

Get special effort from channel members

Selective distribution can produce greater profits not only for the producer but for all channel members. Wholesalers and retailers are more willing to promote products aggressively if they know they're going to obtain the majority of sales through their own efforts. They may carry wider lines, do more promotion, and provide more service—all of which lead to more sales.

Selective often moves to intensive as market grows

In the early part of the life cycle of a new unsought good, a producer may have to use selective distribution. Well-known middlemen may have the power to get such a product introduced, but sometimes on their own terms. That often means limiting the number of competing wholesalers and retailers. The producer may be happy with such an arrangement at first but dislike it later when more retailers want to carry the product.

Exclusive distribution sometimes makes sense

Exclusive distribution is just an extreme case of selective distribution—the firm selects only one middleman in each geographic area. Besides the various advantages of selective distribution, producers may want to use exclusive distribution to help control prices and the service offered in a channel.

Retailers of shopping products and specialty products often try to get exclusive distribution rights in their territories. Fast-food franchises often have exclusive distribution—and that's one reason they're popular. Owners of McDonald's franchises pay a share of sales and follow McDonald's strategy to keep the exclusive right to a market.

Unlike selective distribution, exclusive distribution usually involves a verbal or written agreement stating that channel members will buy all or most of a given product from the seller. In return, these middlemen are granted the exclusive rights to that product in their territories.

Is limiting market exposure legal?

Exclusive distribution is a vague area under U.S. antimonopoly laws. Courts currently focus on whether an exclusive distribution arrangement hurts competition.

Horizontal arrangements among competitors are illegal

Horizontal arrangements—among *competing* retailers, wholesalers, or producers—to limit sales by customer or territory have consistently been ruled illegal by the U.S. Supreme Court. Courts consider such arrangements obvious collusion that reduces competition and harms customers.

Vertical arrangements may or may not be legal

The legality of vertical arrangements—between producers and middlemen—is not as clear-cut. A 1977 Supreme Court decision (involving Sylvania and the distribution of TV sets) reversed an earlier ruling that it was always illegal to set up vertical relationships limiting territories or customers. Now courts can weigh the possible good effects against the possible restrictions on competition. They look at competition between whole channels rather than just focusing on competition at one level of distribution.

The Sylvania decision does not mean that all vertical arrangements are legal. Rather, it says that a firm has to be able to legally justify any exclusive arrangements.

Thus, firms should be extremely cautious about entering into *any* exclusive distribution arrangement. The courts can force a change in relationships that were expensive to develop. And even worse, the courts can award triple damages if they rule that competition has been hurt.

The same cautions apply to selective distribution. Here, however, less formal arrangements are typical—and the possible impact on competition is more remote. It is now more acceptable to carefully select channel members when building a channel system. Refusing to sell to some middlemen, however, should be part of a logical plan with long-term benefits to consumers.[23]

CHANNEL SYSTEMS CAN BE COMPLEX

Trying to achieve the desired degree of market exposure can lead to complex channels of distribution. Firms may need different channels to reach different segments of a broad product-market or to be sure they reach each segment. Sometimes this results in competition between different channels.

Consider the different channels used by a company that publishes computer books. See Exhibit 11-4. This publisher sells through a general book wholesaler who in turn sells to Internet book retailers and independent book retailers. The publisher may have some direct sales of its best-selling books to a large chain or even to consumers who order directly from its website. However, it might also sell through a computer supplies wholesaler that serves electronics superstores like Best Buy. This can cause problems because different wholesalers and retailers want different markups. It also increases competition, including price competition. And the competition among different middlemen may result in conflicts between the middlemen and the publisher.

Multichannel distribution systems may be needed

Multichannel distribution (sometimes called **dual distribution**) occurs when a producer uses several competing channels to reach the same target market—perhaps using several middlemen in addition to selling directly. Multichannel distribution is becoming more common. For instance, big retail chains want large quantities and low prices. A producer may sell directly to retail chains and rely on wholesalers to sell to smaller accounts. Some established middlemen resent this because they don't appreciate *any* competition—especially price competition set up by their own suppliers.

Other times, producers are forced to use multichannel distribution because their present channels are doing a poor job or aren't reaching some potential customers. For example, Reebok International had been relying on local sporting goods stores to sell its shoes to high school and college athletic teams. But Reebok wasn't getting much of the business. When it set up its own team-sales department to sell directly to the schools, it got a 30,000-unit increase in sales.[24]

Exhibit 11-4 An Example of Multichannel Distribution by a Publisher of Computer Books

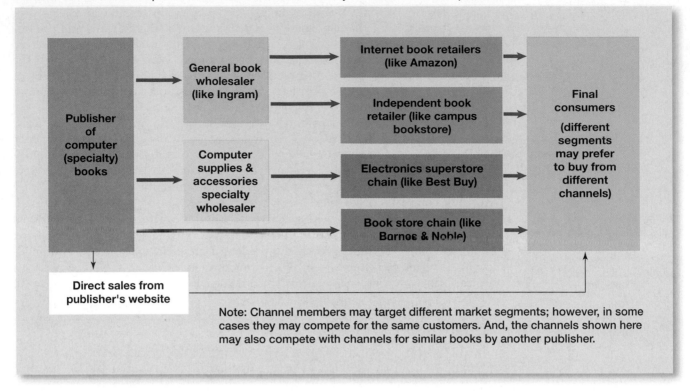

Note: Channel members may target different market segments; however, in some cases they may compete for the same customers. And, the channels shown here may also compete with channels for similar books by another publisher.

Ethical decisions may be required

If competition changes or customers' Place requirements shift, the current channel system may not be effective. The changes required to serve customer needs may hurt one or more members of the channel. Ethical dilemmas in the channels area arise in situations like this—because not everyone in the channel can win.

For example, wholesalers and the independent retailers that they serve in a channel of distribution may trust a producer channel-captain to develop marketing strategies that will work for the whole channel. However, the producer may decide that consumers, and its own business, are best served by a change (say, dropping current middlemen and selling directly to big retail chains). A move of this sort, if implemented immediately, may not give current middlemen-partners a chance to make adjustments of their own. The more dependent they are on the producer, the more severe the impact is likely to be. It's not easy to determine the best or most ethical solution in these situations. However, marketing managers must think carefully about the consequences of Place strategy changes for other channel members. In channels, as in any business dealing, relationships of trust must be treated with care.[25]

INTERNET EXERCISE

Avon Products, Inc., has created a separate "mark" line of cosmetics and other beauty products that is targeted at young women. Avon sells mark at a website and through independent sales reps (agents), including college students who sell to their friends. Review the mark website (www.meetmark.com). Do you think that mark reps would view the website as competing for their customers' purchases and a source of conflict, or would they think that it helps them promote mark and identify new prospects? Explain your thinking.

Reverse channels should be planned

Most firms focus on getting products to their customers. But some marketing managers must also plan for **reverse channels**—channels used to retrieve products that customers no longer want. The need for reverse channels may arise in a variety of different situations. Toy companies, automobile firms, drug companies, and others sometimes have to recall products because of safety problems. A firm that makes an error in completing an order may have to take returns. If a Viewsonic computer monitor breaks while it's still under warranty, someone needs to get it to the repair center. Soft-drink companies may need to recycle empty bottles. Similarly, used inkjet and laser toner catridges are often recycled and reused. And, of course, consumers sometimes buy something in error and want to return it. This is common with online purchases where consumers can't see, touch, or try the product before purchasing it.[26]

Another problem arises from products that are damaged in shipping or discontinued. Most manufacturers take them back. A grocery products trade group says

that the cost of such unsalable products, in total, may be as much as $4 billion a year. To reduce such costs, P&G has adopted a no-returns policy and instead gives retailers a payment for damaged items. Some retailers don't like P&G's policy, but it is important to see that it is a specific plan and part of an overall strategy.

When marketing managers don't plan for reverse channels, the firm's customers may be left to solve "their" problem. That usually doesn't make sense. So a complete plan for Place may need to consider an efficient way to return products—with policies that different channel members agree on. It may also require specialists who were not involved in getting the product to the consumer. But if that's what it takes to satisfy customers, it should be part of marketing strategy planning.[27]

CONCLUSION

In this chapter, we discussed the role of Place and noted that Place decisions are especially important because they may be difficult and expensive to change.

Marketing specialists, and channel systems, develop to adjust discrepancies of quantity and assortment. Their regrouping activities are basic in any economic system. And adjusting discrepancies provides opportunities for creative marketers.

Channel planning requires firms to decide on the degree of market exposure they want. The ideal level of exposure may be intensive, selective, or exclusive. They also need to consider the legality of limiting market exposure to avoid having to undo an expensively developed channel system or face steep fines.

The importance of planning channel systems was discussed—along with the role of a channel captain. We stressed that channel systems compete with each other and that vertical marketing systems seem to be winning.

In this broader context, the "battle of the brands" is only a skirmish in the battle between various channel systems. And we emphasized that producers aren't necessarily the channel captains. Often middlemen control or even dominate channels of distribution.

KEY TERMS

place, 296
channel of distribution, 297
direct marketing, 301

discrepancy of quantity, 303
discrepancy of assortment, 303
regrouping activities, 303

accumulating, 303
bulk-breaking, 303
sorting, 304

QUESTIONS AND PROBLEMS

1. Review the case at the beginning of the chapter and discuss the competitive advantages that Barnes & Noble would have over a small bookshop. What advantages does a small bookshop have?

2. Give two examples of service firms that work with other channel specialists to sell their products to final consumers. What marketing functions is the specialist providing in each case?

3. Discuss some reasons why a firm that produces installations might use direct distribution in its domestic market but use middlemen to reach overseas customers.

4. Explain discrepancies of quantity and assortment using the clothing business as an example. How does the application of these concepts change when selling steel to the automobile industry? What impact does this have on the number and kinds of marketing specialists required?

5. Explain the four regrouping activities with an example from the building supply industry (nails, paint, flooring, plumbing fixtures, etc.). Do you think that many specialists develop in this industry, or do producers handle the job themselves? What kinds of marketing channels would you expect to find in this industry, and what functions would various channel members provide?

6. Insurance agents are middlemen who help other members of the channel by providing information and handling the selling function. Does it make sense for an insurance agent to specialize and work exclusively with one insurance provider? Why or why not?

7. Discuss the Place objectives and distribution arrangements that are appropriate for the following products (indicate any special assumptions you have to make to obtain an answer):

   a. A postal scale for products weighing up to 2 pounds.
   b. Children's toys: (1) radio-controlled model airplanes costing $80 or more, (2) small rubber balls.

   c. Heavy-duty, rechargeable, battery-powered nut tighteners for factory production lines.
   d. Fiberglass fabric used in making roofing shingles.

8. Give an example of a producer that uses two or more different channels of distribution. Briefly discuss what problems this might cause.

9. Explain how a channel captain can help traditional independent firms compete with a corporate (integrated) channel system.

10. Find an example of vertical integration within your city. Are there any particular advantages to this vertical integration? If so, what are they? If there are no such advantages, how do you explain the integration?

11. What would happen if retailer-organized channels (either formally integrated or administered) dominated consumer product marketing?

12. How does the nature of the product relate to the degree of market exposure desired?

13. Why would middlemen want to be exclusive distributors for a product? Why would producers want exclusive distribution? Would middlemen be equally anxious to get exclusive distribution for any type of product? Why or why not? Explain with reference to the following products: candy bars, batteries, golf clubs, golf balls, steak knives, televisions, and industrial woodworking machinery.

14. Explain the present legal status of exclusive distribution. Describe a situation where exclusive distribution is almost sure to be legal. Describe the nature and size of competitors and the industry, as well as the nature of the exclusive arrangement. Would this exclusive arrangement be of any value to the producer or middleman?

15. Discuss the promotion a new grocery products producer would need in order to develop appropriate channels and move products through those channels. Would the nature of this job change for a new producer of dresses? How about for a new, small producer of installations?

SUGGESTED CASES

COMPUTER-AIDED PROBLEM

11. Intensive versus Selective Distribution

RESOURCE REMINDER

Hydropump, Inc., produces and sells high-quality pumps to business customers. Its marketing research shows a growing market for a similar type of pump aimed at final consumers—for use with Jacuzzi-style tubs in home remodeling jobs. Hydropump will have to develop new channels of distribution to reach this target market because most consumers rely on a retailer for advice about the combination of tub, pump, heater, and related plumbing fixtures they need. Hydropump's marketing manager, Robert Black, is trying to decide between intensive and selective distribution. With intensive distribution, he would try to sell through all the plumbing supply, bathroom fixture, and hot-tub retailers who will carry the pump. He estimates that about 5,600 suitable retailers would be willing to carry a new pump. With selective distribution, he would focus on about 280 of the best hot-tub dealers (2 or 3 in the 100 largest metropolitan areas).

Intensive distribution would require Hydropump to do more mass selling—primarily advertising in home renovation magazines—to help stimulate consumer familiarity with the brand and convince retailers that Hydropump equipment will sell. The price to the retailer might have to be lower too (to permit a bigger markup) so they will be motivated to sell Hydropump rather than some other brand offering a smaller markup.

With intensive distribution, each Hydropump sales rep could probably handle about 300 retailers effectively. With selective distribution, each sales rep could handle only about 70 retailers because more merchandising help would be necessary. Managing the smaller sales force and fewer retailers, with the selective approach, would require less manager overhead cost.

Going to all suitable and available retailers would make the pump available through about 20 times as many retailers and have the potential of reaching more customers. However, many customers shop at more than one retailer before making a final choice—so selective distribution would reach almost as many potential customers. Further, if Hydropump is using selective distribution, it would get more in-store sales attention for its pump and a larger share of pump purchases at each retailer.

Black has decided to use a spreadsheet to analyze the benefits and costs of intensive versus selective distribution.

a. Based on the initial spreadsheet, which approach seems to be the most sensible for Hydropump? Why?

b. A consultant points out that even selective distribution needs national promotion. If Black has to increase advertising and spend a total of $100,000 on mass selling to be able to recruit the retailers he wants for selective distribution, would selective or intensive distribution be more profitable?

c. With intensive distribution, how large a share (percent) of the retailers' total unit sales would Hydropump have to capture to sell enough pumps to earn $200,000 profit?

For additional questions related to this problem, see Exercise 11-3 in the *Learning Aid for Use with Basic Marketing,* 15th edition.

CHAPTER TWELVE

Distribution Customer Service and Logistics

If you want a Coca-Cola, there's usually one close by—no matter where you might be in the world. And that's no accident. An executive for the best-known brand name in the world stated the objective simply: "Make Coca-Cola available within an arm's reach of desire." To achieve that objective, Coke works with many different channels of distribution. But that's just the start. Think about what it takes for a bottle, can, or cup of Coke to be there whenever you're thirsty. In warehouses and distribution centers, on trucks, in gyms and sports arenas, and thousands of other retail outlets, Coke handles, stores, and transports more than 400 billion servings of the soft drink a year. Getting all of that product to consumers could be a logistical nightmare, but Coke does it effectively and at a low cost. Think about it: A can of Coke at the store costs

only about 15 cents more than it costs you to have the Post Office deliver a letter.

Fast information about what the market needs helps keep Coke's distribution on target. Coke uses an Internet-based data system that links about one million retailers and other sellers to Coke and its bottlers. The system lets Coke bottlers and retailers exchange purchase orders, invoices, and pricing information online. Orders are processed instantly—so sales to consumers at the end of the channel aren't lost because of stock-outs. Similarly, computer systems show Coke managers exactly what's selling in each market; they can even estimate the effects of promotions as they plan inventories and deliveries. And Coke products move efficiently through the channel. In Cincinnati, for example, Coke built the beverage industry's first fully automated distribution center. Forklifts were replaced with automatically guided vehicles that speed up the product flow and reduce labor costs. And when Coke's truck drivers get to the retail store, they efficiently stock the shelves.

Coke's strategies in international markets rely on many of the same ideas. But the stage of market development varies in different countries, so Coke's emphasis varies as well. To increase sales in France, for example, Coke installed thousands of soft-drink coolers in French supermarkets. In Great Britain, Coke emphasizes multi-packs because it wants to have more inventory at the point of consumption—in consumers' homes. In Japan, by contrast, Coke has relied heavily on an army of truck drivers to constantly restock one million Coke vending machines, more per capita than anywhere else in the world. Coke is even testing vending machines that raise the price when it's hot or when few cans are left. And, in Australia, some Coke vending machines have built-in cell phone systems; a press of a button makes a call so customers can charge the Coke to their cell phone accounts.

In less-developed areas, the Place system is not always so sophisticated. In China, for example, Coke has done well in big cities, but most of the population lives in outlying areas, where high transportation costs made Coke too expensive. So Coke built more local bottling facilities in these areas and set up systems to recycle glass bottles. With these changes, a serving of Coke is now only about 12 cents. The market potential for Coke in India is also huge, but the per capita consumption of soft drinks at present is only about seven 8-oz servings per year. So, in India, Coke is increasing promotion and gearing up to handle more demand by investing $150 million to expand its bottling and distribution network.

Coke is also working to increase fountain-drink sales in domestic and international markets. As part of that effort, Coke equips restaurants and food outlets with Coke dispensers. Once a Coke dispenser is installed, the retailer usually doesn't have room for a competitor's dispenser. And when a consumer wants a fountain drink, Coke isn't just "the real thing," it's the only thing. The number of fountain outlets has grown so rapidly that one Coke account rep serves as many as 1,000 retail customers in a geographic area. That means that the little guys could get lost in the shuffle. However, to give them the service they need at a reasonable cost, Coke launched Coke.net, a password-protected web portal where fountain customers can access account managers online, track syrup orders, request equipment repairs, or download marketing support materials.

Of course, Pepsi is a tough competitor and isn't taking all of this sitting down. It has added more noncola products, and its edgy ads for Code Red and other products are helping it gain market share—which means it gets more shelf space and more Pepsi stocked at the point of purchase. Coke is pushing on new fronts as well. So the competition is becoming even more intense. It's not just the "Cola Wars" any more but rather the wars for cola, juice, water, sports drinks, tea, and many other beverages. And who wins customers and profits in this broader competition will depend on overall marketing programs—but clearly Place has an important role to play.[1]

PHYSICAL DISTRIBUTION GETS IT TO CUSTOMERS

Choosing the right channel of distribution is crucial in getting products to the target market's Place. But as the Coke case shows, that alone is usually not enough to ensure that products are available at the right time and in the right quantities. Whenever the product includes a physical good, Place requires logistics decisions. **Logistics** is the transporting, storing, and handling of goods to match target customers' needs with a firm's marketing mix—both within individual firms and along a channel of distribution. **Physical distribution (PD)** is another common name for logistics. PD provides time and place utility and makes possession utility possible. The physical distribution system must meet customers' needs with an acceptable service level and cost.

Logistics costs are very important to both firms and consumers. These costs vary from firm to firm and, from a macro-marketing perspective, from country to country. However, for many physical goods, firms spend half or more of their total marketing dollars on physical distribution activities. The total amount of money involved is so large that even small improvements in this area can have a big effect on a whole macro-marketing system and consumers' quality of life. For example, during the 1990s many supermarket chains and producers that supply them collaborated to create a system called Efficient Consumer Response (ECR) that cut grocers' costs, and prices, by about 11 percent. That translated to savings of about $30 *billion* a year for U.S. consumers! The basic idea of ECR involves paperless, computerized links between grocers and their suppliers, which leads to continuous replenishment of shelves based on what actually sells each day. Although the ECR movement started in the U.S. and Canada, it quickly spread across Europe and in other regions.[2]

PHYSICAL DISTRIBUTION CUSTOMER SERVICE

From the beginning, we've emphasized that marketing strategy planning is based on meeting customers' needs. Planning for logistics and Place is no exception. So let's start by looking at logistics through a customer's eyes.

Logistics activities are often invisible to consumers, but a breakdown in distribution customer service can result in dissatisfied consumers and lost business.

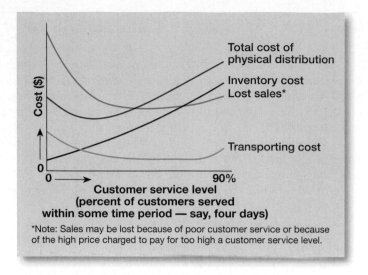

Exhibit 12-1
Trade-Offs among Physical
Distribution Costs, Customer
Service Level, and Sales

*Note: Sales may be lost because of poor customer service or because of the high price charged to pay for too high a customer service level.

Customers want products, not excuses

Customers don't care how a product was moved or stored or what some channel member had to do to provide it. Rather, customers think in terms of the physical distribution **customer service level**—how rapidly and dependably a firm can deliver what they, the customers, want. Marketing managers need to understand the customer's point of view.

What does this really mean? It means that Toyota wants to have enough windshields delivered to make cars *that* day—not late so production stops *or* early so there are a lot of extras to move around or store. In turn, it means that the Toyota dealer wants the car when it's due so that salespeople are not left making lame excuses to the customer who ordered it. It means that business executives who rent cars from Hertz want them to be ready when they get off their planes. It means that when you order a blue shirt at the Lands' End website you receive blue, not pink. It means you want your Tostitos to be whole when you buy a bag at the snack bar—not crushed into crumbs from rough handling in a warehouse.

Physical distribution is invisible to most consumers

PD is, and should be, a part of marketing that is "invisible" to most consumers. It only gets their attention when something goes wrong. At that point, it may be too late to do anything that will keep them happy.

In countries where physical distribution systems are inefficient, consumers face shortages of the products they need. By contrast, most consumers in the United States and Canada don't think much about physical distribution. This probably means that these market-directed macro-marketing systems work pretty well—that a lot of individual marketing managers have made good decisions in this area. But it doesn't mean that the decisions are always clear-cut or simple. In fact, many trade-offs may be required.

Trade-offs of costs, service, and sales

Most customers would prefer very good service at a very low price. But that combination is hard to provide because it usually costs more to provide higher levels of service. So most physical distribution decisions involve trade-offs between costs, the customer service level, and sales.

If you want a new HP computer and the Best Buy store where you would like to buy it doesn't have it on hand, you're likely to buy it elsewhere; or if that model HP is hard to get you might just switch to some other brand. Perhaps the Best Buy store could keep your business by guaranteeing two-day delivery of your computer—by using airfreight from HP's factory. In this case, the manager is trading the cost of storing inventory for the extra cost of speedy delivery—assuming that the computer is available in inventory *somewhere* in the channel. In this example, missing one sale may not seem that important, but it all adds up. A few years ago a

322

The physical distribution customer service level—including fast and reliable delivery of whatever assortment is needed—is critical to many business customers.

computer company lost over $500 million in sales because its computers weren't available when and where customers were ready to buy them.

Exhibit 12-1 illustrates trade-off relationships like those highlighted in the HP example. For example, faster but more expensive transportation may reduce the need for a costly inventory of computers. If the service level is too low, customers will buy elsewhere and sales will be lost. Alternatively, the supplier may hope that a higher service level will attract more customers. But if the service level is higher than customers want or are willing to pay for, sales will be lost to competitors.

The trade-offs that must be made in the PD area can be complicated. The lowest-cost approach may not be best—if customers aren't satisfied. If different target markets want different customer service levels, several different strategies may be needed.[3]

Many firms are trying to address these complications with e-commerce. Information technology can improve service levels and cut costs at the same time. Better information flows make it easier to coordinate activities, improve efficiency, and add value for the customer.

PHYSICAL DISTRIBUTION CONCEPT FOCUSES ON THE WHOLE DISTRIBUTION SYSTEM

The physical distribution concept

The **physical distribution (PD) concept** says that all transporting, storing, and product-handling activities of a business and a whole channel system should be coordinated as one system that seeks to minimize the cost of distribution for a given customer service level. Both lower costs and better service help to increase customer value. It may be hard to see this as a startling development. But until just a few years ago, even the most progressive companies treated physical distribution functions as separate and unrelated activities.

Within a firm, responsibility for different distribution activities was spread among various departments—production, shipping, sales, warehousing, and others. No one person was responsible for coordinating storing and shipping decisions or customer service levels. It was even more rare for different firms in the channel to collaborate. Each just did its own thing. Unfortunately, in too many firms old-fashioned ways persist—with a focus on individual functional activities rather than the whole physical distribution system.[4]

Decide what service level to offer

With broader adoption of the physical distribution concept, this is changing. Firms work together to decide what aspects of service are most important to customers at the end of the channel. Then they focus on finding the least expensive way to achieve the target level of service.

Exhibit 12-2 shows a variety of factors that may influence the customer service level (at each level in the channel). The most important aspects of customer service depend on target market needs. Xerox might focus on how long it takes to deliver copy machine repair parts once it receives an order. When a copier breaks down, customers want the repair "yesterday." The service level might be stated as "we will deliver 90 percent of all emergency repair parts within 24 hours." This might require that commonly needed parts be available on the service truck, that order processing be very fast, and that parts not available locally be sent by airfreight. Obviously, supplying this service level will affect the total cost of the PD system. But it may also beat competitors.

Exhibit 12-2
Examples of Factors that Affect PD Service Levels

- Advance information on product availability
- Time to enter and process orders
- Backorder procedures
- Where inventory is stored
- Accuracy in filling orders
- Damage in shipping, storing, and handling
- Online status information

- Advance information on delays
- Time needed to deliver an order
- Reliability in meeting delivery date
- Complying with customer's instructions
- Defect-free deliveries
- How needed adjustments are handled
- Procedures for handling returns

Fast PD service can be critical for retailers that appeal to consumers who are eager to get a new product that is in hot demand—the latest CD or DVD release, a best-selling book, or a popular toy or video game. For instance, most of the sales of a new video game may be in the first few months. Stores like Wal-Mart and Best Buy can sell games at a low price, but it may take a while for a large shipment to come, work through their distribution centers, and get to store shelves. By then, a retailer like Babbages that has paid for airfreight and direct delivery to stores may have been able to completely sell out to those consumers who are willing to pay a higher price to avoid the wait.[5]

Increasing service levels may also be very profitable in highly competitive situations where the firm has little else to differentiate its marketing mix. Marketing managers at Clorox, for example, must do everything they can to develop and keep strong partnerships with middlemen. Many other firms sell products with precisely the same ingredients and are constantly trying to steal customers. Yet Clorox's high standards for customer service help it obtain a competitive advantage. For example, when the bleach buyer for a major retail chain went on vacation, the chain's central distribution center almost ran out of Clorox liquid bleach. But Clorox people identified the problem themselves—because of a computer system that allowed Clorox to access the chain's inventory records and sales data for Clorox products. Clorox rearranged production to get a shipment out fast enough to prevent the chain, and Clorox, from losing sales. In the future when another bleach supplier tells buyers for the chain that "bleach is bleach," they'll remember the distribution service Clorox provides.[6]

Find the lowest total cost for the right service level

In selecting a PD system, the **total cost approach** involves evaluating each possible PD system and identifying *all* of the costs of each alternative. This approach uses the tools of cost accounting and economics. Costs that otherwise might be ignored—like inventory carrying costs—are considered. The possible costs of lost sales due to a lower customer service level may also be considered. The following example clarifies why the total cost approach is important.

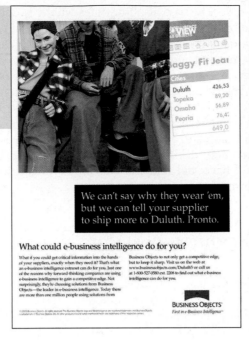

A cost comparison of alternative systems

The Good Earth Vegetable Company was shipping produce to distant markets by train. The cost of shipping a ton of vegetables by train averaged less than half the cost of airfreight so the company assumed that rail was the best method. But then Good Earth managers did a more complete analysis. To their surprise, they found the airfreight system was faster and cheaper.

Exhibit 12-3 compares the costs for the two distribution systems—airplane and railroad. Because shipping by train was slow, Good Earth had to keep a large inventory in a warehouse to fill orders on time. And the company was also surprised at the extra cost of carrying the inventory in transit. Good Earth's managers also found that the cost of spoiled vegetables during shipment and storage in the warehouse was much higher when they used rail shipping.

In this case, total cost analyses showed that airfreight, while more costly by itself, provided better service than the conventional means—and at a lower total

Exhibit 12-3
Comparative Costs of Airplane versus Rail and Warehouse

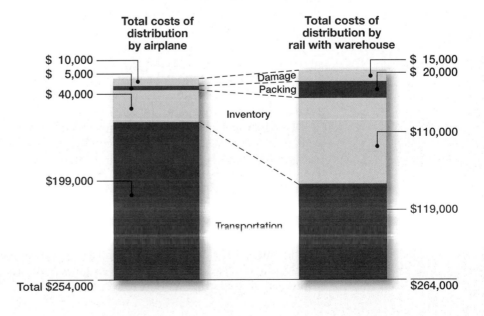

	Total costs of distribution by airplane	Total costs of distribution by rail with warehouse
	$ 10,000	$ 15,000
Damage	$ 5,000	$ 20,000
Packing	$ 40,000	
Inventory		$110,000
	$199,000	$119,000
Transportation		
Total	**$254,000**	**$264,000**

distribution cost. The case also illustrates why it is important to get beyond a focus on individual functional elements of PD and instead consider the costs and service level of a whole system. This broader focus should consider how the whole channel operates, not just individual firms.

Many firms are now applying this type of thinking to improve value to customers and profits. For example, applying the total cost approach, National Semiconductor cut its standard delivery time in half, reduced distribution costs 2.5 percent, and increased sales by 34 percent. In the process, it shut down six warehouses around the globe and started to airfreight microchips to its worldwide customers from a new 125,000-square-foot distribution center in Singapore. In advance of these changes, no one would have said that this was an obvious thing to do. But it proved to be the smart thing.[7]

COORDINATING LOGISTICS ACTIVITIES AMONG FIRMS

Functions can be shifted and shared in the channel

As a marketing manager develops the Place part of a strategy, it is important to decide how physical distribution functions can and should be divided within the channel. Who will store, handle, and transport the goods—and who will pay for these services? Who will coordinate all of the PD activities?

There is no right sharing arrangement. Physical distribution can be varied endlessly in a marketing mix and in a channel system. And competitors may share these functions in different ways—with different costs and results.

How PD is shared affects the rest of a strategy

How the PD functions are shared affects the other three Ps—especially Price. The sharing arrangement can also make (or break) a strategy. Consider Channel Master, a firm that wanted to take advantage of the growing market for the dish-like antennas used to receive TV signals from satellites. The product looked like it could be a big success, but the small company didn't have the money to invest in a large inventory. So Channel Master decided to work only with wholesalers who were willing to buy (and pay for) several units—to be used for demonstrations and to ensure that buyers got immediate delivery.

In the first few months Channel Master earned $2 million in revenues—just by providing inventory for the channel. And the wholesalers paid the interest cost of carrying inventory—over $300,000 the first year. Here the wholesalers helped share the risk of the new venture, but it was a good decision for them too. They won many sales from a competing channel whose customers had to wait several months for delivery. And by getting off to a strong start, Channel Master became a market leader.

A coordinated effort reduces conflict

PD decisions interact with other Place decisions, the rest of the marketing mix, and the whole marketing strategy. If firms in the channel do not plan and coordinate how they will share PD activities, PD is likely to be a source of conflict rather than a basis for competitive advantage. Holly Farms' problems in introducing a new product illustrate this point.

Marketers at Holly Farms were encouraged when preroasted chicken performed well in a market test. But channel conflict surfaced when they moved to broader distribution. The Holly Farm label indicated a date by which the chicken should be sold. Many grocers refused to buy the roast chicken because they had only a few days after it was delivered to sell it. They didn't want it to spoil, at their expense, on the shelf.

The source of the problem was that it took too long to ship roast chicken from the plant to stores. Coupled with slow turnover, that didn't leave grocers enough selling time. To address the problem, Holly Farms used faster transportation and developed new packaging that allowed grocers to store the chicken longer. Holly Farms also shifted its promotion budget to put more emphasis on in-store promotions

ETOYS.COM FINDS OUT THAT MANAGING DISTRIBUTION SERVICE ISN'T ALWAYS FUN

When you see a Toys "R" Us ad with Geoffry the Giraffe touting the huge selection of toys at every store, it's no surprise that Toys "R" Us has crushed many local toy shops. When eToys.com was founded in 1997, its aspiration was to do the same to Toys "R" Us. The eToys.com dream was to be the premier site on the Internet for the kids' product-market. Many investors shared its vision of unlimited growth. At one time, eToys' stock market value was 35 percent greater than that of Toys "R" Us, even though eToys never earned any profit. eToys did deliver in producing a slick e-commerce website where parents could search for toys by age group or theme or product and then quickly place an order.

But eToys underestimated how competitors would react to its plan to take most of their customers, which is what it would have taken to cover eToys' costs. Toys "R"

Us quickly teamed up with Amazon. Wal-Mart copied some of eToys' best ideas but already had the buying clout to create its own brands and sell toys cheaper. eToys also assumed customers would be loyal once it attracted them with huge spending on ads. However, when 5 percent of eToys' orders didn't go out on time during the 1999 holiday season, every parent who let a kid down told everyone they knew. Then, when eToys tried to improve its distribution systems, costs spiraled out of control because of the hassles of storing and handling breakable toys that come in all sorts of sizes and shapes. eToys went out of business when it became clear that it would take years of constant sales growth just to cover its total costs. A great website doesn't eliminate the need to offer effective distribution service at a cost that can be profitable.[8]

to speed up sales once the chicken arrived. With these changes, Holly Farms won cooperation in the channel and established its product in the market.[9]

JIT requires a close, cooperative relationship

We introduced the concept of just-in-time (JIT) delivery in Chapter 7. Now that you know more about PD alternatives, it's useful to consider some of the marketing strategy implications of this approach.

A key advantage of JIT for business customers is that it reduces their PD costs—especially storing and handling costs. However, if the customer doesn't have any backup inventory, there's no security blanket if a supplier's delivery truck gets stuck in traffic, there's an error in what's shipped, or there are any quality problems. Thus, a JIT system requires that a supplier have extremely high quality control in every PD activity.

A JIT system usually requires that a supplier respond to very short order lead times and the customer's production schedule. Thus, e-commerce order systems and information sharing over computer networks are often required. JIT suppliers often locate their facilities close to important customers. Trucks may make smaller and more frequent deliveries—perhaps even several times a day.

A JIT system shifts greater responsibility for PD activities backward in the channel. If the supplier can be more efficient than the customer could be in controlling PD costs—and still provide the customer with the service level required—this approach can work well for everyone in the channel. However, JIT is not always the best approach. It may be better for a supplier to produce and ship in larger, more economical quantities—if the savings offset the distribution system's total inventory and handling costs.[10]

Chain of supply may involve even more firms

In our discussion, we have taken the point of view of a marketing manager. This focuses on how logistics should be coordinated to meet the needs of customers at the end of the channel of distribution. Now, however, we should broaden the picture somewhat because the relationships within the distribution channel are sometimes part of a broader network of relationships in the **chain of supply**—the complete set

To help a manufacturer of soccer balls reduce its logistics costs, CNF ships the balls to Europe uninflated and then pumps them up before the last leg of their journey to individual outlets.

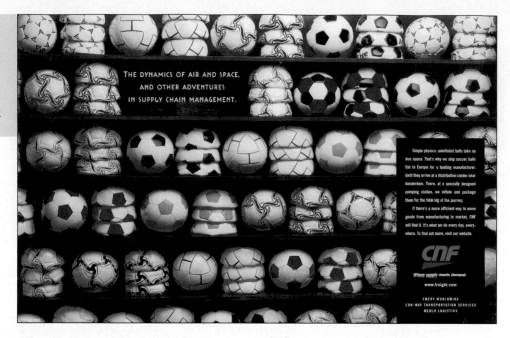

THE DYNAMICS OF AIR AND SPACE, AND OTHER ADVENTURES IN SUPPLY CHAIN MANAGEMENT.

Simple physics: uninflated balls take up less space. That's why we ship soccer balls flat to Europe for a leading manufacturer. Until they arrive at a distribution center near Amsterdam. There, at a specially designed pumping station, we inflate and package them for the final leg of the journey.

If there's a more efficient way to move goods from manufacturing to market, CNF will find it. It's what we do every day, everywhere. To find out more, visit our website.

CNF

Where supply meets demand.

www.freight.com

EMERY WORLDWIDE
CON-WAY TRANSPORTATION SERVICES
MENLO LOGISTICS

of firms and facilities and logistics activities that are involved in procuring materials, transforming them into intermediate or finished products, and distributing them to customers. For example, Toyota not only works with dealers and customers but also with the supplier firms from which it buys parts. Those firms, in turn, coordinate with their own suppliers. What happens at each link can impact the whole chain. If the firm that produces seats for Toyota doesn't get the fabric from its supplier on time, the seats will be delayed in route to Toyota and the car will be slow getting to the dealer and consumer.

Ideally, all of the firms in the chain of supply should work together to meet the needs of the customer at the very end of the chain. That way, at each link along the chain the shifting and sharing of logistics functions and costs are handled to result in maximum value for the final customer. Further, all of the firms in the whole chain of supply are able to do a better job of competing against competitors who are involved in other chains of supply.

It's still difficult for a manager in any one company to know what kind of logistics sharing arrangement will work best, or even be possible, in a whole series of other companies. Because of that, many firms turn to outside experts for help. For example, specialists may design the e-commerce computer systems that link all of the firms in a chain of supply or figure out the best way to shift logistics functions among firms. Firms sometimes outsource the whole job of planning *and* implementing their logistics systems.[11]

INTERNET EXERCISE

Large corporations often turn to other firms that specialize in logistics—transportation and warehousing services, consultants, developers of software for e-commerce, and the like—to help implement the physical distribution aspects of their marketing strategies. The website of the Virtual Logistics Directory (www.logisticdirectory.com) lists many logistics specialists and what they do. Go to the website and select the *Integrated Logistics* category. Review the descriptions of some of the firms listed, and then pick one. Explain why a large corporation with a logistics problem might seek its help rather than just trying to tackle the problem internally.

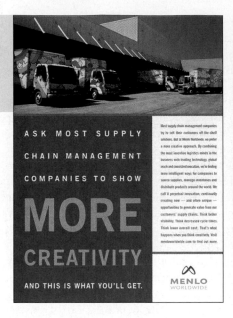

Better information helps coordinate PD

Coordinating all of the elements of PD has always been a challenge—even in a single firm. Trying to coordinate orders, inventory, and transportation throughout the whole supply chain is even tougher. But information shared over the Internet and at websites has been important in finding solutions to these challenges. Physical distribution decisions will continue to improve as more firms are able to have their computers "talk to each other" directly and as websites help managers get access to up-to-date information whenever they need it.

Electronic data interchange sets a standard

Until recently, differences in computer systems from one firm to another hampered the flow of information. Many firms attacked this problem by adopting **electronic data interchange (EDI)**—an approach that puts information in a standardized format easily shared between different computer systems. In many firms, purchase orders, shipping reports, and other paper documents were replaced with computerized EDI. With EDI, a customer transmits its order information directly to the supplier's computer. The supplier's computer immediately processes the order and schedules production, order assembly, and transportation. Inventory information is automatically updated, and status reports are available instantly. The supplier might then use EDI to send the updated information to the transportation provider's computer. In fact, most international transportation firms rely on EDI links with their customers.

EDI systems were originally developed before the Internet gained widespread use. Traditional EDI systems are expensive to develop and rely on proprietary computer networks to exchange data securely. Newer alternatives to this approach that rely on the Internet and a standard format, called XML, for exchanging data are gaining popularity.[12]

Improved information flow and better coordination of PD activities is a key reason for the success of Pepperidge Farm's line of premium cookies. Most of the company's delivery truck drivers use hand-held computers to record the inventory at each stop along their routes. They use the Internet to instantly transmit the information into a computer at the bakeries, and cookies in short supply are produced. The right assortment of fresh cookies is quickly shipped to local markets, and delivery trucks are loaded with what retailers need that day. Pepperidge Farm moves cookies from its bakeries to store shelves in about three days; more could be produced take about 10 days. That means fresher cookies for consumers and helps to support Pepperidge Farm's high-quality positioning and premium price.[13]

Ethical issues may arise

Most of the ethical issues that arise in the PD area concern communications about product availability. For example, some critics say that Internet sellers too often take orders for products that are not available or which they cannot deliver as quickly as customers expect. Yet a marketing manager can't always know precisely how long it will take before a product will be available. It doesn't make sense for the marketer to lose a customer if it appears that he or she can satisfy the customer's needs. But the customer may be inconvenienced or face added cost if the marketer's best guess isn't accurate. Similarly, some critics say that stores too often run out of products that they promote to attract consumers to the store. Yet it may not be possible for the marketer to predict demand, or to know when placing an ad that deliveries won't arrive. Different people have different views about how a firm should handle such situations. Some retailers just offer rain checks.

Some suppliers criticize customers for abusing efforts to coordinate PD activities in the channel. For example, some retailers hedge against uncertain demand by telling suppliers that they plan to place an order, but then they don't confirm the order until the last minute. This shifts the uncertainty to the supplier. Is this unethical? Some think it is. However, the firm's order policies can reduce such problems—if the cost of providing the service customers want is higher than what they will pay. [14]

Now that you see why the coordination of physical distribution activities is so important, let's take a closer look at some of the PD decision areas.

THE TRANSPORTING FUNCTION ADDS VALUE TO A MARKETING STRATEGY

Transporting aids economic development and exchange

Transporting is the marketing function of moving goods. Transportation provides time and place utilities—at a cost. But the cost is less than the value added to products by moving them or there is little reason to ship in the first place.

Transporting can help achieve economies of scale in production. If production costs can be reduced by producing larger quantities in one location, these savings may more than offset the added cost of transporting the finished products to customers. Without low-cost transportation, both within countries and internationally, there would be no mass distribution as we know it today.

The cost of transportation adds little to the total cost of products—like pharmaceuticals—that are already valuable relative to their size and weight. But transporting costs can be a large part of the total cost for heavy products that are low in value, like sheet aluminum.

Exhibit 12-4
Transporting Costs as a
Percent of Selling Price for
Different Products

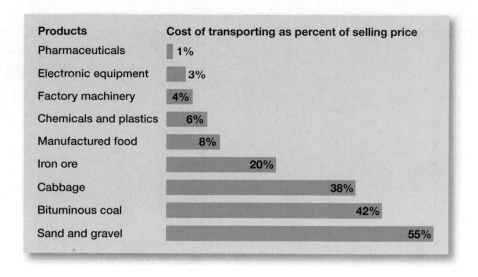

Products	Cost of transporting as percent of selling price
Pharmaceuticals	1%
Electronic equipment	3%
Factory machinery	4%
Chemicals and plastics	6%
Manufactured food	8%
Iron ore	20%
Cabbage	38%
Bituminous coal	42%
Sand and gravel	55%

Transporting can be costly

Transporting costs limit the target markets a marketing manager can serve. Shipping costs increase delivered cost—and that's what really interests customers. Transport costs add little to the cost of products that are already valuable relative to their size and weight. A case of medicine, for example, might be shipped to a drugstore at low cost. But transporting costs can be a large part of the total cost for heavy products of low value—like many minerals and raw materials. You can imagine that shipping a massive roll of aluminum to a producer of soft-drink cans is an expensive proposition. Exhibit 12-4 shows transporting costs as a percent of total sales dollars for several products.[15]

Governments may influence transportation

Government often plays an important role in the development of a country's transportation system, including its roads, harbors, railroads, and airports. And different countries regulate transportation differently, although regulation has in general been decreasing.

For example, as part of their move toward unification, most European countries are reducing their transporting regulations. The construction of the tunnel under the English Channel is a dramatic example of the changes taking place. The "chunnel" allows trains to speed between England and the rest of Europe.

As regulations decreased in the U.S., competition in the transportation industry increased. As a result, a marketing manager generally has many carriers in one or more modes competing for the firm's transporting business. Or a firm can do its own transporting. So knowing about the different modes is important.[16]

WHICH TRANSPORTING ALTERNATIVE IS BEST?

Transporting function must fit the whole strategy

The transporting function should fit into the whole marketing strategy. But picking the best transporting alternative depends on the product, other physical distribution decisions, and what service level the company wants to offer. The best alternative should provide the level of service (for example, speed and dependability) required at as low a cost as possible. Exhibit 12-5 shows that different modes of transportation have different strengths and weaknesses. You can find more detail at the website of the Bureau of Transportation Statistics (www.bts.gov). Low transporting cost is *not* the only criterion for selecting the best mode.[17]

Exhibit 12-5   Benefits and Limitations of Different Transport Modes

| | | | **Transporting Features** | | | |
Mode	Cost	Delivery Speed	Number of Locations Served	Ability to Handle a Variety of Goods	Frequency of Scheduled Shipments	Dependability in Meeting Schedules
Truck	High	Fast	Very extensive	High	High	High
Rail	Medium	Average	Extensive	High	Low	Medium
Water	Very low	Very slow	Limited	Very high	Very low	Medium
Air	Very high	Very fast	Extensive	Limited	High	High
Pipeline	Low	Slow	Very limited	Very limited	Medium	High

Railroads—large loads moved at low cost

Railroads are still the workhorse of the U.S. transportation system. They carry more freight over more miles than any other mode. However, they account for less than 10 percent of transport revenues. They carry heavy and bulky goods—such as coal, steel, and chemicals—over long distances at relatively low cost. For example, in the United States the average cost to ship by rail runs about 2 to 3 cents a ton-mile. Because railroad freight usually moves more slowly than truck shipments, it is not as well suited for perishable items or those in urgent demand. Railroads are most efficient at handling full carloads of goods. Less-than-carload (LCL) shipments take a lot of handling, which means they usually move more slowly and at a higher price per pound than carload shipments.[18]

Trucks are more expensive, but flexible and essential

The flexibility and speed of trucks make them better at moving small quantities of goods for shorter distances. They can travel on almost any road. They go where the rails can't. They are also reliable in meeting delivery schedules, which is an essential

Mercedes recently introduced a new, smaller truck that is designed to be more flexible in making deliveries in congested cities like Istanbul, where this ad appeared.

DHL offers a full range of logistics services, sometimes coordinating shipments across several modes of transportation, to better meet the needs of its clients.

requirement for logistics systems that provide rapid replenishment of inventory after a sale. In combination these factors explain why at least 75 percent of U.S. consumer products travel at least part of the way from producer to consumer by truck. And in countries with good highway systems, trucks can give extremely fast service. Trucks compete for high-value items. This is reflected in their rates, which average about 27 cents per ton-mile in the United States. Critics complain that trucks congest traffic and damage highways. But trucks are essential to our present macro-marketing system.[19]

Ship it overseas, but slowly

Water transportation is the slowest shipping mode, but it is usually the lowest-cost way of shipping heavy freight. Water transportation is very important for international shipments and often the only practical approach. This explains why port cities like Boston, New York City, Rotterdam, Osaka, and Singapore are important centers for international trade.

Inland waterways are important too

Inland waterways (such as the Mississippi River and Great Lakes in the United States and the Rhine and Danube in Europe) are also important, especially for bulky, nonperishable products such as iron ore, grain, and gravel. However, when winter ice closes freshwater harbors, alternate transportation must be used.

Pipelines move oil and gas

Pipelines are used primarily to move oil and natural gas. So pipelines are important both in the oil-producing and oil-consuming countries. Only a few major cities in the United States, Canada, Mexico, and Latin America are more than 200 miles from a major pipeline system. However, the majority of the pipelines in the United States are located in the Southwest, connecting the oil fields and refineries.

Airfreight is expensive, but fast and growing

The most expensive cargo transporting mode is airplane—but it is fast! Airfreight rates are on average three times higher than trucking rates—but the greater speed may offset the added cost.

High-value, low-weight goods—like high-fashion clothing and parts for the electronics industry—are often shipped by air. Perishable products that previously could not be shipped are now being flown across continents and oceans. Flowers and bulbs from Holland, for example, now are jet flown to points all over the world. And airfreight has become very important for small emergency deliveries, like repair parts, special orders, and business documents that must be somewhere the next day.

But airplanes may cut the total cost of distribution

Using planes may reduce the cost of packing, unpacking, and preparing goods for sale and may help a firm reduce inventory costs by eliminating outlying warehouses. Valuable benefits of airfreight's speed are less spoilage, theft, and damage. Although the *transporting* cost of air shipments may be higher, the *total cost* of distribution may be lower. As more firms realize this, airfreight firms—like DHL Worldwide Express, FedEx, and Emery Air Freight—have enjoyed rapid growth.

These firms play an especially important role in the growth of international business. While the bulk of international cargo moves on ships, the speed of airfreight opens up global markets for many businesses that previously had only domestic opportunities. For example, DHL Worldwide Express offers 24-hour delivery service from Tokyo to Los Angeles, New York to Rome, and London to Chicago. For a firm whose products are valuable relative to their weight and size, the cost of air deliveries may seem trivial when compared to the sales potential of competing in new markets.[20]

Put it in a container— and move between modes easily

Products often move by several different modes and carriers during their journey. This is especially common for international shipments. Japanese firms, like Sony, ship stereos to the United States, Canada, and Europe by boat. When they arrive at the dock, they are loaded on trains and sent across the country. Then the units are delivered to a wholesaler by truck or rail.

To better coordinate the flow of products between modes, transportation companies like CSX offer customers a complete choice of different transportation modes. Then CSX, not the customer, figures out the best and lowest-cost way to shift and share transporting functions between the modes.[21]

Loading and unloading goods several times used to be a real problem. Parts of a shipment would become separated, damaged, or even stolen. And handling the goods, perhaps many times, raised costs and slowed delivery. Many of these problems are reduced with **containerization**—grouping individual items into an economical shipping quantity and sealing them in protective containers for transit to the final destination. This protects the products and simplifies handling during shipping. Some containers are as large as truck bodies.

A change in the way that a product is packaged can help reduce shipping, storing, and product handling costs while at the same time improving benefits and value to the final consumer.

Piggyback—a ride on two or more modes

Piggyback service means loading truck trailers—or flatbed trailers carrying containers—on railcars to provide both speed and flexibility. Railroads now pick up truck trailers at the producer's location, load them onto specially designed rail flatcars, and haul them as close to the customer as rail lines run. The trailers are then hooked up to a truck tractor and delivered to the buyer's door. Similar services are offered on oceangoing ships—allowing door-to-door service between cities around the world.

Transportation choices affect environmental costs too

Marketing managers must be sensitive to the environmental effects of transportation decisions. Some say trucks cause air pollution in already crowded cities. People who live near airports suffer from noise pollution. A damaged pipeline can spew thousands of gallons of oil before it can be repaired. The Exxon *Valdez* oil spill in Alaska is a dramatic example of the kind of environmental disaster that can happen when a transportation accident occurs.

Many firms are taking steps to reduce these problems. For example, Conoco is building ships with double hulls to reduce the risk of leaks. FedEx and UPS are revamping their fleets to reduce emissions. Some trucking and railroad firms have elaborate safety procedures for dealing with toxic cargo. Today, the public *expects* companies to manufacture, transport, sell, and dispose of products in an environmentally sound manner. Companies are even more sensitive to these issues in an era of terrorism. However, all these efforts increase the cost of distribution.[22]

ECONOMIES OF SCALE IN TRANSPORTING

Most transporting rates—the prices charged for transporting—are based on the idea that large quantities of a good can be shipped at a lower transport cost per pound than small quantities. Whether a furniture producer sends a truck to deliver one sofa or a full carload, the company still has to pay for the driver, the truck, the gas, and other expenses like insurance.

Transporters often give much lower rates for quantities that make efficient use of their transport facilities. Thus, transport costs per pound for less-than-full carloads or truckloads are often twice as high as for full loads. These quantity rate differences are one important reason for the development of some wholesalers. They buy in large quantities to get the advantage of economies of scale in transporting. Then they sell in the smaller quantities their customers need.

Freight forwarders accumulate economical shipping quantities

Freight forwarders combine the small shipments of many shippers into more economical shipping quantities. Freight forwarders do not own their own transporting facilities—except perhaps for delivery trucks. Rather, they wholesale air, ship, rail, and truck space. They accumulate small shipments from many shippers and reship in larger quantities to obtain lower transporting rates.

Freight forwarders are especially useful in arranging international shipping. They handle 75 percent of the general cargo shipped from U.S. ports to foreign countries. They are also very helpful for handling international airfreight.[23]

Should you do it yourself?

To cut transporting costs or get more control, some marketing managers do their own transporting rather than buy from specialists. Large producers, like Levi Strauss, often buy or lease their own truck fleets. Shell Oil and other large petroleum, iron ore, and gypsum rock producers have their own ships. Some firms now buy their own planes for airfreight.[24]

THE STORING FUNCTION AND MARKETING STRATEGY

Store it and smooth out sales, increase profits and consumer satisfaction

Storing is the marketing function of holding goods. It provides time utility. **Inventory** is the amount of goods being stored.

Maintaining the right inventory level is difficult when it's hard to forecast likely demand. Even so, a firm that is stocked out when customers are ready to buy may not only lose the sale but also damage the relationship and the possibility of future

When consumers buy in large quantities and keep the product inventory near the point of consumption they take over some of the inventory carrying costs— and they may consume more.

GE provides logistics-related services that help firms reduce costs and improve customer service.

sales. Kmart ran into this problem. Many consumers decided it was no longer a convenient place to shop when stores repeatedly ran out of basic staples that consumers expected to find.

Storing is necessary when production of goods doesn't match consumption. This is common with mass production. Nippon Steel, for example, might produce thousands of steel bars of one size before changing the machines to produce another size. It's often cheaper to produce large quantities of one size, and store the unsold quantity, than to have shorter production runs. Thus, storing goods allows the producer to achieve economies of scale in production.

Some buyers purchase in large quantities to get quantity discounts from the producer or transporter. Then the extra goods must be stored until there is demand. And goods are sometimes stored as a hedge against future price rises, strikes, shipping interruptions, and other disruptions.

Storing varies the channel system

Storing allows producers and middlemen to keep stocks at convenient locations, ready to meet customers' needs. In fact, storing is one of the major activities of some middlemen.

Most channel members provide the storing function for some length of time. Even final consumers store some things for their future needs. Which channel members store the product, and for how long, affects the behavior of all channel members. For example, the producer of Snapper lawn mowers tries to get wholesalers to inventory a wide selection of its machines. That way, retailers can carry smaller inventories since they can be sure of dependable local supplies from wholesalers. And the retailers might decide to sell Snapper—rather than Toro or some other brand that they would have to store at their own expense.

If final customers "store" the product, more of it may be used or consumed. Coke wants customers to buy six packs and 2-liter bottles. Then consumers have an "inventory" in the refrigerator when thirst hits. Of course, consumers aren't always willing to hold the inventory. In China, for example, Coke had little success until it gave up pushing 2-liter bottles and switched to single-serving 75 ml bottles. Only

Exhibit 12-6 Many Expenses Contribute to Total Inventory Cost

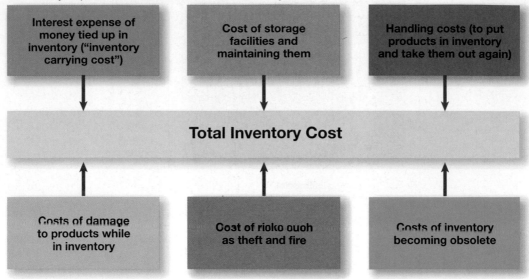

1 out of 10 Chinese families has a refrigerator—so they didn't have a good way to store a bottle once it was open.

Goods are stored at a cost

Storing can increase the value of goods, but *storing always involves costs* too. Different kinds of cost are involved. See Exhibit 12-6. Car dealers, for example, must store cars on their lots—waiting for the right customer. The interest expense of money tied up in the inventory is a major cost. In addition, if a new car on the lot is dented or scratched, there is a repair cost. If a car isn't sold before the new models come out, its value drops. There is also a risk of fire or theft—so the retailer must carry insurance. And, of course, dealers incur the cost of leasing or owning the display lot where they store the cars.

In today's competitive markets, most firms watch their inventories closely. Taken in total, the annual direct and indirect costs of inventory are typically 20 to 40 percent of the average value of the inventory. Firms try to cut unnecessary inventory because it can make the difference between a profitable strategy and a loser. On the other hand, a marketing manager must be very careful in making the distinction between unnecessary inventory and inventory needed to provide the distribution service customers expect.[25]

Rapid response cuts inventory costs

Many firms are finding that they can cut inventory costs and still provide the desired customer service—if they can reduce the time it takes to replace items that are sold. This is one important reason that JIT and ECR approaches have been widely adopted. The firms involved use EDI, the Internet, and similar computerized approaches to share information and speed up the order cycle and delivery process.

Information from JIT and ECR systems can also help firms see the benefit of dropping some of the items that they stock and sell. P&G is a vivid example. Between 1991 and 1996 it introduced many new products but cut its total number of SKUs (individual stock-keeping units) by 34 percent, mainly by cutting the number of sizes and colors for some of its brands. After the cuts, sales of the remaining products went up and costs came down. With fewer products, P&G put more marketing effort behind those it kept, and its retailers were more willing to push products that turn over quickly. Reducing the number of SKUs does reduce consumer choice, but there is a point where the value of additional choice doesn't justify the extra cost.[26]

SPECIALIZED STORING FACILITIES MAY BE REQUIRED

New cars can be stored outside on the dealer's lot. Fuel oil can be stored in a specially designed tank. Coal and other raw materials can be stored in open pits. But most products must be stored inside protective buildings. Often, firms can choose among different types of specialized storing facilities. The right choice may reduce costs and serve customers better.

Private warehouses are common

Private warehouses are storing facilities owned or leased by companies for their own use. Most manufacturers, wholesalers, and retailers have some storing facilities either in their main buildings or in a separate location. A sales manager often is responsible for managing a manufacturer's finished-goods warehouse, especially if regional sales branches aren't near the factory.

Firms use private warehouses when a large volume of goods must be stored regularly. Yet private warehouses can be expensive. If the need changes, the extra space may be hard, or impossible, to rent to others.

Public warehouses fill special needs

Public warehouses are independent storing facilities. They can provide all the services that a company's own warehouse can provide. A company might choose a public warehouse if it doesn't have a regular need for space. For example, Tonka Toys uses public warehouses because its business is seasonal. Tonka pays for the space only when it is used. Public warehouses are also useful for manufacturers that must maintain stocks in many locations, including foreign countries.

In most countries, public warehouses are located in all major metropolitan areas and many smaller cities. See Exhibit 12-7 for a comparison of private and public warehouses.[27]

Warehousing facilities cut handling costs too

The cost of physical handling is a major storing cost. Goods must be handled once when put into storage and again when removed to be sold. To reduce these costs, modern one-story buildings away from downtown traffic have replaced most old multistory warehouses. They eliminate the need for elevators and permit the use of power-operated lift trucks, battery-operated motor scooters, roller-skating order pickers, electric hoists for heavy items, and hydraulic ramps to speed loading and unloading. Bar codes and UPC (uniform product code) numbers make it easy for

Exhibit 12-7   A Comparison of Private Warehouses and Public Warehouses

Characteristics	Type of Warehouse	
	Private	Public
Fixed investment	Very high	No fixed investment
Unit cost	High if volume is low Very low if volume is very high	Low: charges are made only for space needed
Control	High	Low managerial control
Adequacy for product line	Highly adequate	May not be convenient
Flexibility	Low: fixed costs have already been committed	High: easy to end arrangement

Many firms are using innovative technologies to more quickly and accurately track the flow of products through distribution channels. For example, this scanner, worn on a worker's hand like a ring, uses Bluetooth wireless technology so that information in a bar code can be instantly transmitted to a firm's information system.

computers to monitor inventory, order needed stock, and track storing and shipping costs. Increasingly, this information flows over wireless networks and takes advantage of radio frequency identification (RFID) tags that precisely track where items are. Some warehouses have computer-controlled order-picking systems or conveyor belts that speed the process of locating and assembling the assortment required to fill an order.[28]

THE DISTRIBUTION CENTER—A DIFFERENT KIND OF WAREHOUSE

Is storing really needed?

Discrepancies of assortment or quantity between one channel level and another are often adjusted at the place where goods are stored. It reduces handling costs to regroup and store at the same place—*if both functions are required*. But sometimes regrouping is required when storing isn't.

Don't store it, distribute it

A **distribution center** is a special kind of warehouse designed to speed the flow of goods and avoid unnecessary storing costs. Anchor Hocking moves over a million pounds of its housewares products through its distribution center each day. Faster inventory turnover and easier bulk-breaking reduce the cost of carrying inventory.

Today, the distribution center concept is widely used by firms at all channel levels. Many products buzz through a distribution center without ever tarrying on a shelf; workers and equipment immediately sort the products as they come in and then move them to an outgoing loading dock and the vehicle that will take them to their next stop.

Managers must be innovative to provide customers with superior value

More competitive markets, improved technology, coordination among firms, and efficient new distribution centers are bringing big improvements to the PD area. Yet the biggest challenges may be more basic. As we've emphasized here, physical distribution activities transcend departmental, corporate, and even national boundaries. So taking advantage of ways to improve often requires cooperation all along the channel system. Too often, such cooperation doesn't exist—and changing ingrained ways of doing things is hard. But marketing managers who push for innovations in these areas are likely to win customers away from firms and whole channel systems that are stuck doing things in the old way.[29]

CONCLUSION

This chapter deals with logistics activities and how they provide *time* and *place* utility to improve value to the customer. We looked at the customer service level and why it is important.

We emphasized the relation between customer service level, transporting, and storing. The physical distribution concept focuses on coordinating all the storing, transporting, and product handling activities into a smoothly working system—to deliver the desired service level and customer value at the lowest cost.

Marketing managers often want to improve service and may select a higher-cost alternative to improve their marketing mix. The total cost approach might reveal that it is possible *both* to reduce costs and to improve service—perhaps by identifying creative new distribution alternatives.

We discussed various modes of transporting and their advantages and disadvantages. We also discussed ways to reduce inventory costs. We explained why distribution centers are an important way to cut storing and handling costs, and we explained how computerized information links—within firms and among firms in the channel—are increasingly important in blending all of the activities into a smooth-running system.

Effective marketing managers make important strategy decisions about physical distribution. Creative strategy decisions may result in lower PD costs while maintaining or improving the customer service level. And production-oriented competitors may not even understand what is happening.

KEY TERMS

logistics, 321

physical distribution (PD), 321

customer service level, 322

physical distribution (PD) concept, 323

total cost approach, 324

chain of supply, 327

electronic data interchange (EDI), 329

transporting, 330

containerization, 334

piggyback service, 335

freight forwarders, 336

storing, 336

inventory, 336

private warehouses, 339

public warehouses, 339

distribution center, 340

QUESTIONS AND PROBLEMS

1. Explain how adjusting the customer service level could improve a marketing mix. Illustrate.

2. Briefly explain which aspects of customer service you think would be most important for a producer that sells fabric to a firm that manufactures furniture.

3. Briefly describe a purchase you made where the customer service level had an effect on the product you selected or where you purchased it.

4. Discuss the types of trade-offs involved in PD costs, service levels, and sales.

5. Give an example of why it is important for different firms in the chain of supply to coordinate logistics activities.

6. Discuss some of the ways computers are being used to improve PD decisions.

7. Explain why a just-in-time delivery system would require a supplier to pay attention to quality control. Give an example to illustrate your points.

8. Discuss the problems a supplier might encounter in using a just-in-time delivery system with a customer in a foreign country.

9. Review the list of factors that affect PD service level in Exhibit 12-2. Indicate which ones are most likely to be improved by EDI links between a supplier and its customers.

10. Explain the total cost approach and why it may cause conflicts in some firms. Give examples of how conflicts might occur between different departments.

11. Discuss the relative advantages and disadvantages of railroads, trucks, and airlines as transporting methods.

12. Discuss why economies of scale in transportation might encourage a producer to include a regional merchant wholesaler in the channel of distribution for its consumer product.

13. Discuss some of the ways that air transportation can change other aspects of a Place system.

14. Explain which transportation mode would probably be most suitable for shipping the following goods to a large Los Angeles department store:

   a. 300 pounds of Maine lobster.

   b. 15 pounds of screwdrivers from Ohio.

   c. Three dining room tables from High Point, North Carolina.

   d. 500 high-fashion dresses from the fashion district in Paris.

   e. A 10,000-pound shipment of exercise equipment from Germany.

   f. 600,000 pounds of various appliances from Evansville, Indiana.

15. Indicate the nearest location where you would expect to find large storage facilities. What kinds of products would be stored there? Why are they stored there instead of some other place?

16. When would a producer or middleman find it desirable to use a public warehouse rather than a private warehouse? Illustrate, using a specific product or situation.

17. Discuss the distribution center concept. Is this likely to eliminate the storing function of conventional wholesalers? Is it applicable to all products? If not, cite several examples.

18. Clearly differentiate between a warehouse and a distribution center. Explain how a specific product would be handled differently by each.

19. If a retailer operates only from a website and ships all orders by UPS, is it freed from the logistics issues that face traditional retailers? Explain your thinking.

SUGGESTED CASES

16. Matisse Company

26. Riverside Packers, Inc.

COMPUTER-AIDED PROBLEM

12. Total Distribution Cost

RESOURCE REMINDER

Proto Company has been producing various items made of plastic. It recently added a line of plain plastic cards that other firms (such as banks and retail stores) will imprint to produce credit cards. Proto offers its customers the plastic cards in different colors, but they all sell for $40 per box of 1,000. Tom Phillips, Proto's product manager for this line, is considering two possible physical distribution systems. He estimates that if Proto uses airfreight, transportation costs will be $7.50 a box, and its cost of carrying inventory will be 5 percent of total annual sales dollars. Alternatively, Proto could ship by rail for $2 a box. But rail transport will require renting space at four regional warehouses—at $26,000 a year each. Inventory carrying cost with this system will be 10 percent of total annual sales dollars. Phillips prepared a spreadsheet to compare the cost of the two alternative physical distribution systems.

a. If Proto Company expects to sell 20,000 boxes a year, what are the total physical distribution costs for each of the systems?

b. If Phillips can negotiate cheaper warehouse space for the rail option so that each warehouse costs only $20,000 per year, which physical distribution system has the lowest overall cost?

c. Proto's finance manager predicts that interest rates are likely to be lower during the next marketing plan year and suggests that Tom Phillips use inventory carrying costs of 4 percent for airfreight and 7.5 percent for railroads (with warehouse cost at $20,000 each). If interest rates are in fact lower, which alternative would you suggest? Why?

For additional questions related to this problem, see Exercise 12-3 in the *Learning Aid for Use with Basic Marketing,* 15th edition.

CHAPTER THIRTEEN

Retailers, Wholesalers, and Their Strategy Planning

Frieda's, Inc., is a family-owned wholesale firm that each year supplies supermarkets and food-service distributors with $30 million worth of exotic fruits and vegetables. It was started by Frieda Caplan in 1962; now, her daughters Karen and Jackie run the company.

It is a sign of the marketing savvy of these women that kiwi fruit, artichokes, Chinese donut peaches, alfalfa sprouts, spaghetti squash, pearl onions, and mushrooms no longer seem very exotic. All of these crops were once viewed as unusual. Few farmers grew them, and consumers didn't know about them. Supermarkets and traditional produce wholesalers didn't want to handle them because they had a limited market. Frieda's helped to change all that.

Caplan realized that some supermarkets wanted to put more emphasis on their produce departments.

Because of her efforts, most supermarkets now carry kiwi, which has become a major crop for California farmers.

Because demand has grown, many larger wholesalers now handle kiwi. But that doesn't bother the Caplans. When one of Frieda's specialty items becomes a commodity with low profit margins, another novel item replaces it. In a typical year, Frieda's introduces about 40 new products. The Frieda's label is now on 500 products—like Asian pears, kiwano melons, sun-dried yellow tomatoes, and hot Asian chiles.

A few years ago, some skeptics said that specialty wholesalers like Frieda's would bite the dust because online market exchanges, like Produce.com, would make them obsolete. However, Produce.com is out of business and Frieda's is growing faster than ever, by taking advantage of its own website and by providing value-adding services that get supermarket buyers to think beyond just getting the lowest bid on some commodity.

The Caplans recently established an online retail operation, Shop@Friedas, that offers many of the firm's specialty items and a limited line of gift selections like the "Chile Lover's Basket." Pictures and descriptions of the different products are on the firm's website at

These retailers were targeting consumers who were less price-sensitive and wanted more choices in the hard-to-manage produce department. So she looked for products that would help her retailer-customers meet this need. For example, the funny looking, egg-shaped kiwi fruit with its fuzzy brown skin was popular in New Zealand but virtually unknown to consumers in other parts of the world. Caplan worked with small farmer-producers to ensure that she could provide her retailer-customers with a steady supply. The packaged kiwi with interesting recipes and promoted kiwi *and* her brand name to consumers.

www.friedas.com, where consumers can order online. The website also has a Club Frieda section, where consumer-members get recipes and advance information about new products and local promotions. The website also invites consumers to be the "eyes and ears of the company" and send in ideas about interesting new products. Building relationships with consumers isn't new at Frieda's. Earlier the Caplans developed a database with detailed information about preferences and buying habits of 100,000 consumers. These consumers wrote the company in response to an invitation on Frieda's label.

Frieda's continues to have an advantage with many supermarkets because consumers love its products and it offers many special services. It was the first to routinely use airfreight for orders and to send produce managers a weekly "hot sheet" about the best sellers. The Caplans also use seminars and press releases to inform produce buyers about how to improve sales. For example, one attention-getting story was about Frieda's "El Mercado de Frieda" line, which helps retailers do a better job attracting and serving Hispanic customers—a growth segment in many locales. Now that more consumers are eating out, Frieda's is looking beyond the grocery store channel. It has established a separate division to serve the special needs of food-service distributors. Frieda's has been successful for a long time because it constantly finds new ways to add value in the channel.[1]

WHOLESALERS AND RETAILERS PLAN THEIR OWN STRATEGIES

Understand how retailing and wholesaling are evolving

In Chapter 11, we discussed the vital role that wholesalers and retailers perform in channel systems. Now, we'll look at the decisions that retailers and wholesalers make in developing their own strategies. We'll also highlight how their strategies have evolved.

Understanding the how and why of these changes will help you know what to expect in the future. It will also make it clear that it is the whole strategy, not just one aspect of it, that ultimately is a success or failure. This may seem obvious, but it's a point that many people have ignored—at great cost.

Consider the dramatic changes prompted by the Internet. A few years ago many people were proclaiming that it would quickly change everything we thought about successful retailing. Yet many creative ideas for online retailing bombed precisely because managers of dot-coms failed to understand why retailing has evolved as it has. For many consumers and many types of purchases, it won't matter that an online retailer posts low prices for an incredible assortment if there's no way to get customer service, products are not actually available, or it's a hassle to return a green shirt that looked blue on the website. *You* want to avoid the trap of this sort of incomplete thinking!

So in this chapter we'll focus on decisions that apply to all retailers and wholesalers, while highlighting how their strategies are changing.

THE NATURE OF RETAILING

Retailing covers all of the activities involved in the sale of products to final consumers. Retailers range from large chains of specialized stores, like Toys "R" Us, to individual merchants like the woman who sells baskets from an open stall in the central market in Ibadan, Nigeria. Some retailers operate from stores and others operate without a store—by selling online, on TV, with a printed catalog, from vending machines, or even in consumers' homes. Most retailers sell physical goods produced by someone else. But in the case of service retailing—like dry cleaning, fast food, tourist attractions, online bank accounts, or one-hour photo processing—the retailer is also the producer. Because they serve individual consumers, even the largest retailers face the challenge of handling small transactions. And the total number of transactions with consumers is much greater than at other channel levels.

Retailing is crucial to consumers in every macro-marketing system. For example, consumers spend $3.7 *trillion* (that's $3,700,000,000,000!) a year buying goods and services from U.S. retailers.

The nature of retailing and its rate of change are generally related to the stage and speed of a country's economic development. In the U.S., retailing is more varied and dynamic than in most other countries. By studying the U.S. system, you will better understand where retailing is headed in other parts of the world.

PLANNING A RETAILER'S STRATEGY

Retailers interact directly with final consumers—so strategy planning is critical to their survival. If a retailer loses a customer to a competitor, the retailer is the one who suffers. Producers and wholesalers still make *their* sale regardless of which retailer sells the product.

Consumers have reasons for buying from particular retailers

Different consumers prefer different kinds of retailers. But many retailers either don't know or don't care why. All too often, beginning retailers just rent a store and assume customers will show up. As a result, in the U.S. about three-fourths of new retailing ventures fail during the first year. Even an established retailer will quickly lose if its customers find a better way to meet their needs. To avoid this fate, a retailer should carefully identify possible target markets and try to understand why these people buy where they do. That helps the retailer finetune its marketing mix to the needs of specific target markets.[2]

Retailer's whole offering is its Product

Most retailers in developed nations sell more than one kind of product. So the brands and product assortment they carry can be critical to success. Yet it's best to take a broader view in thinking about the Product strategy decisions for a retailer's marketing mix. The retailer's *whole* offering—assortment of goods and services, advice from salesclerks, convenience, and the like—is its "Product."

Different consumers have different needs—and needs vary from one purchase situation to another. Which retailer's Product offers the best customer value depends on the needs that a customer wants to satisfy. Whatever the effect of other consumer needs, economic needs are usually very important in shaping the choice of a retailer. Social and individual needs may also come into play. Our discussion of consumer behavior in Chapter 6 applies here.

It's best of think of a retailer's Product as its whole offering—including its assortment of goods and services, advice from salespeople, the convenience of shopping, and hours it is available.

Features of offering relate to needs

Features of a retailer's offering that relate to economic needs include
- *Convenience* (available hours, finding needed products, fast checkout, location, parking).
- *Product selection* (width and depth of assortment, quality).
- *Special services* (special orders, home delivery, gift wrap, entertainment).
- *Fairness in dealings* (honesty, correcting problems, return privileges, purchase risks).
- *Helpful information* (courteous sales help, displays, demonstrations, product information).
- *Prices* (value, credit, special discounts, taxes or extra charges).

Some features that relate to social and emotional factors include
- *Social image* (status, prestige, "fitting in" with other shoppers).
- *Shopping atmosphere* (comfort, safety, excitement, relaxation, sounds, smells).

In later chapters we'll go into much more detail on the price and promotion decisions that all firms, including retailers and wholesalers, make.

Strategy requires carefully set policies

In developing a strategy a retailer should consciously make decisions that set policies on *all* of the factors above. Each of them can impact a customer's view of the costs and benefits of choosing that retailer. And in combination they differentiate one retailer's offering and strategy from another. If the combination doesn't provide superior value to some target market, the retailer will fail.

Consumer needs relate to segmentation and positioning

Segmentation and positioning decisions are important to retailers. And ignoring either economic or social and emotional values in those decisions can lead to serious errors in a retailer's strategy planning.

Consider, for example, how the shopping atmosphere may have an emotional effect on a consumer's view of a retailer. How merchandise is displayed, what decorations, colors, and finishes are used, and even the temperature, sounds, and smell of a store all contribute to its "atmospherics" and store image. The right combination may attract more target customers and encourage them to spend more. Tiffany's,

In spite of consumer interest in Western products and new retailing formats, most retailing in Asia is still handled by small limited-line stores, like this Chinese electronics store.

for example, offers luxury surroundings and inventive displays to attract upscale consumers. But Tiffany's may also appeal to consumers who get an ego boost from Tiffany's prestige image and very attentive staff. Of course, interesting surroundings are usually costly, and the prices that consumers pay must cover that expense. An online jewelry retailer avoids those costs but offers a completely different shopping experience and deals with a different set of needs. So a retailer's atmosphere and image may be a plus or a minus, depending on the target market. And there's no single right answer about which target market is best. Like Tiffany's, Dollar General has been very profitable. But it has a "budget" image and atmosphere that appeals to working-class customers, many of whom just prefer to shop where they don't feel out of place.[3]

Different types of retailers emphasize different strategies

Retailers have an almost unlimited number of ways in which to alter their offerings—their marketing mixes—to appeal to a target market. Because of all the variations, it's oversimplified to classify retailers and their strategies on the basis of a single characteristic—such as merchandise, services, sales volume, or even whether they operate in cyberspace. But a good place to start is by considering basic types of retailers and some differences in their strategies.

Let's look first at conventional retailers. Then we'll see how other retailers successfully modify conventional offerings to better meet the needs of *some* consumers. Think about *why* the changes take place. That will help you identify opportunities and plan better marketing strategies.

CONVENTIONAL RETAILERS—TRY TO AVOID PRICE COMPETITION

Single-line, limited-line retailers specialize by product

A hundred and fifty years ago, **general stores**—which carried anything they could sell in reasonable volume—were the main retailers in the United States. But with the growing number of consumer products after the Civil War, general stores couldn't offer enough variety in all their traditional lines. So some stores began specializing in dry goods, apparel, furniture, or groceries.

Now, most conventional retailers are **single-line** or **limited-line stores**—stores that specialize in certain lines of related products rather than a wide assortment. Many specialize not only in a single line, such as clothing, but also in a *limited line* within

Exhibit 13-1   Types of Retailers and the Nature of Their Offerings

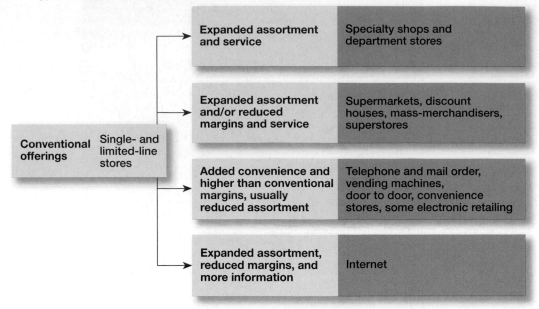

the broader line. Within the clothing line, a retailer might carry *only* shoes, formal wear, or even neckties but offer depth in that limited line.

Single-line, limited-line stores are being squeezed

The main advantage of limited-line retailers is that they can satisfy some target markets better. Perhaps some are just more conveniently located. But most adjust to suit specific customers. They build a relationship with their customers and earn a position as *the* place to shop for a certain type of product. But these retailers face the costly problem of having to stock some slow-moving items in order to satisfy their target markets. Many of these stores are small—with high expenses relative to sales. So they try to keep their prices up by avoiding competition on identical products.

Conventional retailers like this have been around for a long time and are still found in every community. They are a durable lot and clearly satisfy some people's needs. In fact, in most countries conventional retailers still handle the vast majority of all retailing sales. However, this situation is changing fast. Nowhere is the change clearer than in the United States. Conventional retailers are being squeezed by retailers who modify their mixes in the various ways suggested in Exhibit 13-1. Let's look closer at some of these other types of retailers.

EXPAND ASSORTMENT AND SERVICE—TO COMPETE AT A HIGH PRICE

Specialty shops usually sell shopping products

A **specialty shop**—a type of conventional limited-line store—is usually small and has a distinct "personality." Specialty shops sell special types of shopping products, such as high-quality sporting goods, exclusive clothing, cameras, or even antiques. They aim at a carefully defined target market by offering a unique product assortment, knowledgeable salesclerks, and better service.

Catering to certain types of customers whom the management and salespeople know well simplifies buying, speeds turnover, and cuts costs due to obsolescence and style changes. Specialty shops probably will continue to be a part of the retailing scene as long as customers have varied tastes and the money to satisfy them.[4]

Department stores combine many limited-line stores and specialty shops

Department stores are larger stores that are organized into many separate departments and offer many product lines. Each department is like a separate limited-line store and handles a wide variety of shopping products, such as men's wear or housewares. They are usually strong in customer services, including credit, merchandise return, delivery, and sales help.

Department stores are still a major force in big cities. But in the U.S., the number of department stores, the average sales per store, and their share of retail business has declined continuously since the 1970s. Well-run limited-line stores compete with good service and often carry the same brands. In the U.S. and many other countries, mass-merchandising retailers have posed an even bigger threat.[5]

EVOLUTION OF MASS-MERCHANDISING RETAILERS

Mass-merchandising is different from conventional retailing

So far we've been describing retailers primarily in terms of their product *assortment*. This reflects traditional thinking about retailing. We could talk about supermarkets, discount houses, or online retailers in these terms too. But then we would miss some important differences—just as some conventional retailers did when mass-merchandising retailers first appeared.

Conventional retailers think that demand in their area is fixed—and they have a "buy low and sell high" philosophy. Many modern retailers reject this idea. They accept the **mass-merchandising concept**—which says that retailers should offer low prices to get faster turnover and greater sales volumes—by appealing to larger markets. The mass-merchandising concept applies to many types of retailers, including both those that operate stores and those that sell online. But to understand mass-merchandising better, let's look at its evolution from the development of supermarkets and discounters to modern mass-merchandisers like Wal-Mart in the U.S., Tesco in the U.K., and Amazon.com on the Internet.

Supermarkets started the move to mass-merchandising

From a world view, most food stores are relatively small limited-line operations. Shopping for food is inconvenient and expensive. Many Italians, for example, still go to one shop for pasta, another for meat, and yet another for milk. This may seem outdated, but many of the world's consumers don't have access to **supermarkets**—large stores specializing in groceries with self-service and wide assortments.

The basic idea for supermarkets developed in the U.S. during the 1930s Depression. Some innovators introduced self-service to cut costs but provided a broad assortment in large bare-bones stores. Profits came from large-volume sales, not from high traditional markups.[6]

Newer supermarkets carry 40,000 product items and stores average around 45,000 square feet. To be called a supermarket, a store must have annual sales of at least $2 million, but the average supermarket sells about $17 million a year. In the U.S., there are about 32,000 supermarkets, and in most areas they are at the saturation level and competition is intense. In many other countries, however, they are just becoming a force.[7]

To outsell competitors, supermarkets try to differentiate their offerings. Some have better produce, lower prices, a cleaner store, and so forth. But there are many things they all have to offer—like milk and eggs and cereal. In fact, an average family gets about 80 percent of its needs from only about 150 SKUs. The rub is that the particular 150 SKUs vary from family to family. In the end, a consumer makes a single choice in deciding to shop at a particular supermarket. But to come out on top in *that* choice, the supermarket must offer consumers many thousands of choices and at the same time keep costs low.[8]

Modern supermarkets are planned for maximum efficiency. Scanners at checkout make it possible to carefully analyze the sales of each item and allocate more shelf

Although U.S. supermarkets were the first mass-merchandisers, the mass-merchandising concept has now been introduced by many retailers. Single-line mass-merchandisers like Office Depot offer selections and prices that make it difficult for traditional retailers to compete.

space to faster-moving and higher-profit items. *Survival* depends on efficiency. Net profits in supermarkets usually run a thin 1 percent of sales *or less!*

Some supermarket operators have opened "super warehouse" stores. These 50,000- to 100,000-square-foot stores carry more items than supermarkets, but they usually put less emphasis on perishable items like produce or meat. These efficiently run, warehouse-like facilities sell groceries at about 25 percent off the typical supermarket price.[9]

Discount houses upset some conventional retailers

After World War II, some retailers started to focus on discount prices. These **discount houses** offered "hard goods" (cameras, TVs, appliances) at substantial price cuts to customers who would go to the discounter's low-rent store, pay cash, and take care of any service or repair problems themselves. These retailers sold at 20 to 30 percent off the list price being charged by conventional retailers.

In the early 1950s, with war shortages finally over, manufacturer brands became more available. The discount houses were able to get any brands they wanted and to offer wider assortments. At this stage, many discounters turned respectable—moving to better locations and offering more services and guarantees. It was from these origins that today's mass-merchandisers developed.

Mass-merchandisers are more than discounters

Mass-merchandisers are large, self-service stores with many departments that emphasize "soft goods" (housewares, clothing, and fabrics) and staples (like health and beauty aids) but still follow the discount house's emphasis on lower margins to get faster turnover. Mass-merchandisers, like Wal-Mart and Target, have checkout counters in the front of the store and little sales help on the floor. Today, the average mass-merchandiser has nearly 60,000 square feet of floor space, but many new stores are 100,000 square feet or more. Mass-merchandisers grew rapidly—and they've become the primary place to shop for many frequently purchased consumer products.

By itself, Wal-Mart handles 30 percent or more of the total national sales for whole categories of products. Even if you don't shop at Wal-Mart, Sam Walton (who started the company) has had a big impact on your life. He pioneered the use of high-tech systems to create electronic links with suppliers and take inefficiencies

out of retailing logistics. That brought down costs *and* prices and attracted more customers, which gave Wal-Mart even more clout in pressuring manufacturers to lower prices. Other retailers are still scrambling to catch up. It was competition from Wal-Mart on staples such as health and beauty aids and household cleaning products that prompted firms in the supermarket supply chain to start the Efficient Consumer Response movement we discussed in Chapter 12.

Although these mass-merchandisers are the driving force in much of retailing in the U.S. today, in many areas they're no longer just taking customers from conventional retailers but instead are locked in head-to-head competition with each other. Kmart, once the largest retailer in the U.S., had to close many unprofitable stores in its struggle to stay in business. Because their growth rate in the U.S. has slowed substantially, for future growth, they're expanding internationally.[10]

Supercenters meet all routine needs

Some supermarkets and mass-merchandisers have moved toward becoming **supercenters (hypermarkets)**—very large stores that try to carry not only food and drug items but all goods and services that the consumer purchases *routinely*. These superstores look a lot like a combination of the supermarkets, drugstores, and mass-merchandisers from which they have evolved, but the concept is different. A supercenter is trying to meet *all* the customer's routine needs at a low price. Supercenter operators include Meijer, Fred Meyer, Super Target, and Wal-Mart. In fact, Wal-Mart's supercenters have turned it into the largest food retailer in the U.S.

Supercenters average more than 150,000 square feet and carry about 50,000 items. Their assortment in one place is convenient, but many time-pressured consumers think that the crowds, lines, and "wandering around" time in the store are not.[11]

New mass-merchandising formats keep coming

The warehouse club is another retailing format that quickly gained popularity. Sam's Club and Costco are two of the largest. Consumers usually pay an annual membership fee to shop in these large, no-frills facilities. Among the 3,500 items per store, they carry food, appliances, yard tools, tires, and other items that many consumers see as homogeneous shopping items and want at the lowest possible price. The growth of

Many retailers are looking for ways to make shopping faster and more convenient. With self-service scanners, shoppers save time and grocers save money. With Mobil's SpeedPass system, a miniature electronic device identifies the driver and turns on the pump; the customer doesn't even need a credit card.

these clubs has also been fueled by sales to small-business customers. That's why some people refer to these outlets as wholesale clubs. However, when half or more of a firm's sales are to final consumers, it is classified as a retailer, not a wholesaler.[12]

Single-line mass-merchandisers are coming on strong

Since 1980, some retailers focusing on single product lines have adopted the mass-merchandisers' approach with great success. Toys "R" Us pioneered this trend. Similarly, Ikea (furniture), Home Depot (home improvements), Circuit City (electronics), and Office Depot attract large numbers of customers with their large assortment and low prices in a specific product category. These stores are called *category killers* because it's so hard for less specialized retailers to compete.[13]

It's reasonable to think about the move to 24-hours-a-day online selling—by the established retailers, new firms that never relied on stores, or both—as a next step in the evolution of mass-merchandising. But we'll have a more complete basis for evaluating the strengths and limitations of selling and shopping on the Web if we first look at some retailers who have targeted consumers who want more convenience, even if the price is higher.

SOME RETAILERS FOCUS ON ADDED CONVENIENCE

Convenience (food) stores must have the right assortment

Convenience (food) stores are a convenience-oriented variation of the conventional limited-line food stores. Instead of expanding their assortment, however, convenience stores limit their stock to pickup or fill-in items like bread, milk, beer, and eat-on-the-go snacks. Many also sell gas. Stores such as 7-Eleven and Stop-N-Go aim to fill consumers' needs between trips to a supermarket, and many of them are competing with fast-food outlets. They offer convenience, not assortment, and often charge prices 10 to 20 percent higher than nearby supermarkets. However, as many other retailers have expanded their hours, intense competition is driving down convenience store prices and profits.[14]

Vending machines are convenient

Automatic vending is selling and delivering products through vending machines. Vending machine sales account for only about 1.5 percent of total U.S. retail sales. Yet for some target markets this retailing method can't be ignored.

The major disadvantage to automatic vending is high cost. The machines are expensive to buy, stock, and repair relative to the volume they sell. So vendors must charge higher prices.[15]

Shop at home, in a variety of ways

In-home shopping in the U.S. started in the pioneer days with **door-to-door selling**—a salesperson going directly to the consumer's home. Variations on this approach are still important for firms like Amway and Mary Kay. It meets some consumers' need for convenient personal attention. It is also growing in popularity in some international markets, like China, where it provides salespeople with a good income. In the U.S., it now accounts for less than 1 percent of retail sales. It's getting harder to find someone at home during the day.

On the other hand, time-pressured, dual-career families are a prime target market for **telephone and direct-mail retailing** that allow consumers to shop at home—usually placing orders by mail or a toll-free long-distance telephone call and charging the purchase to a credit card. Typically, catalogs and ads on TV let customers see the offerings, and purchases are delivered by UPS. Some consumers really like this convenience, especially for products not available in local stores.

This approach reduces costs by using computer mailing lists to target specific customers and by using warehouse-type buildings and limited sales help. And shoplifting—a big expense for most retailers—isn't a problem. In recent years, many of these firms have faced increased competition, slower sales growth, and lower profits. As we will discuss, however, the Internet is opening up new growth opportunities for many of these firms.[16]

Put the catalog on cable TV or computer

QVC, Home Shopping Network, and others are succeeding by devoting cable TV channels to home shopping. The explosion in the number of available cable channels and new interactive cable services will make sales from this approach grow even faster. In addition, QVC has opened a major website on the Internet. However, selling on the Internet is turning into something much more than just a variation of selling on TV or from a catalog.[17]

RETAILING ON THE INTERNET

Most mass-merchandisers now sell on the Web, so one could view that development as just another aspect of how low-margin sellers try to appeal to a large target market with wide assortments at discount prices. Or one might view the Internet as just another way to add convenient in-home shopping, with an electronic catalog and ordering on a remote computer. After all, that's the way most people saw earlier pre-Internet dial-up systems such as Prodigy—a joint venture between Sears and IBM that fizzled because it was too complicated.

Yet both of these views are incomplete and probably misleading. Rather than just treat it as a new way that some types of retailers are incrementally varying their old strategies, let's look at what is *really* different about it.

It's still in its infancy

Internet retailing is still in the growth stages. On the one hand, Internet usage continues to rise and consumer e-commerce sales have grown at a fast rate. In 1997, consumers spent about $2.7 billion on the Internet. To put that in perspective, it took about 3 percent of Wal-Mart's stores to rack up the same sales. By 2003 that number leaped to over $50 billion, and that does not include spending for travel or financial services, which more than double the amount. But don't confuse the effect that the Internet may have on retailing with the reality of its immediate economic impact. So far, it accounts for less than 2 percent of retailing sales dollars. So in absolute dollars, retailing on the Internet is in its infancy. Thus, it's useful to consider what's different about it today and how it will evolve. See Exhibit 13-2.

Moving information versus moving goods

Stripped to its essence, the Internet dramatically lowers the cost of communication and makes it faster. The Internet produces the biggest gains in businesses where better information flows result in more efficiency. That's what happens in much online B2B e-commerce. On the other hand, Place decisions for consumer markets need to deal with the challenge of getting many small purchases to the *consumer's* place. Much of the investment in Internet retailing systems has been directed toward moving information (like orders), not physical goods. It takes, for example,

Exhibit 13-2 Some Illustrative Differences between Online and In-Store Shopping

Characteristics	Online Shopping	In-Store Shopping
Customer characteristics	Younger, better educated, more upscale	Cross section; depends on store
Day-of-week emphasis	Higher percent of purchases during weekdays	Higher percent of purchases on the weekend
Customer service	Weak but improving	Varies, but usually better than online
Products purchased	More emphasis on one-time purchases	More emphasis on routine purchases
Availability of product	Not available for inspection or immediate use	Usually available for inspection and immediate use
Comparative information about products	Much more extensive, but sometimes poorly organized	Often weak (for example, limited to what is on packages)
Entertainment value	A media experience	Often a social experience
Charges	Product prices often lower, but shipping and handling costly	Product prices and taxes higher, but usually no delivery expense
Shopping hours and preparation	Completely flexible if online access is available	Depends on store and available transportation to store

about $25 million to build a world-class website for consumer e-commerce. But it costs about $150 million to build a distribution center and systems to support a large-scale consumer web operation. Therefore, much of the attention so far has been on the "front door" of the Internet "store" and not on the back end of retailing operations where more of the big costs accumulate.

The investments and innovations will come into balance over time, just as they have with other retailing innovations. But demand is what will shape investments in new supply capabilities. So far, the basic patterns of consumer demand have not changed that much.

Convenience takes on new meanings

Traditional thinking about retail stores looked at shopping convenience from the perspective of product assortments and location. On the Internet, by contrast, a consumer can get to a very wide assortment, perhaps from different sellers, by clicking from one website to another. The assortment moves toward being unlimited.

Buyarock.com created a website with a tongue-in-cheek 1950s design, animations, and information about buying a diamond ("Buyarock 101") to help appeal to male shoppers searching for an engagement ring. However, some shoppers are hesitant to make any big purchase online.

AND THE WINNING BIDDER IS EBAY

There have been lots of retailing innovations, but most people wouldn't put flea markets or estate auctions in that category. Yet if you combine those ideas, attract about 28 million active buyers and sellers, use a state-of-the-art website to help them all complete exchanges worth $20 billion a year, then you'll have eBay. And given that eBay takes a cut of the $700 worth of deals that get made *every second,* it is not only an innovation but a very profitable one.

At the eBay.com "department store," sellers offer products ranging from one-of-a-kind antique collector cars or comic books to the latest designer wedding dresses (used only once!) and plasma screen HDTVs. And most of the time there's somebody, somewhere, who wants to buy what's listed. Imagine how managers at eBay must feel; they have little control over their vendors or who their target customers are. However, it is all about the customers. eBay is a self-directed marketplace where customer bids determine what will sell (and it also has "Buy It Now" items for customers who don't want to bid).

Of course, eBay has learned some things from traditional retailers. It doesn't have "greeters," but it has 2,000 customer service reps. It also constantly improves product categories so it is easier for shoppers to find what they want. eBay will even handle the bidding automatically and then link the buyer to PayPal to securely transfer payment to the seller. Of course, some sellers don't want to hassle with eBay. So for them eBay offers links to "trading assistants," independent specialists who handle eBay selling on a fee basis, much like an old-fashioned consignment shop.[18]

But the Internet makes shopping inconvenient in other ways. You have to plan ahead. You can't touch a product. When you buy something, you've actually just ordered it and you don't have it to use. Someone else has to deliver it, and that involves delays and costs.

Surfing around the Internet is convenient for people who are facile with computers, but many consumers are not. At present, people who actually shop on the Web are better educated, younger, and more well-to-do. It should be no surprise that the majority of retail dollars spent on the Internet so far are for computer-related stuff. That target market visits the Internet store. But many people don't.

Of course, use of the Internet is growing. Cable and telephone companies are in a race to provide more consumers with faster access. Costs will continue to come down.

More and less information at the same time

On the Internet a consumer can't really inspect a product. Many consumers see that as a disadvantage. On the other hand, in a retail store it's often hard to get good information. At a website detailed product information is just a mouse-click away.

It's also possible to access a much broader array of information. Ziff-Davis Publishing, for example, has a comprehensive website (www.zdnet.com) with product reviews, feature comparisons, and performance tests on many computer-related products. Similar sites exist for everything from automobiles to vitamins. Better information can make many consumers better shoppers, even if they buy in a store rather than online. That's what many web surfers do now. That reduces the risk of buying the wrong thing and the hassles of returning it if there's a problem.

More powerful computers are also opening up many more possibilities for multimedia information—pictures, product-demo videos, and audio explanations. The Internet is also a good medium for messaging and video conferencing. Many computers now come with an inexpensive videocam. So in the future it will be easier for consumers to get help from a real person while at a website. Many failed dot-com retailers figured out too late that cutting costs by dropping human customer service support was a big mistake. They ignored the lessons learned by mass-merchandisers when they tried to do the same thing in their early days.

Many established retailers, like Barnes & Noble, are combining "clicks and bricks" to meet consumers' needs better than would be possible with only an online website or a store.

Lost in the "aisles" of the Internet

If you know what you want, you can usually find it fast on the Internet. You can look for "Revo sunglasses" and get a list of sellers and see pictures of every style made. However, you may get too much information or the wrong information when you do a search. So there is a need for better "virtual malls"—databases with lots of information that can be viewed lots of ways—to make it easier to get information you want and avoid irrelevant clutter. Retailers like Amazon have improved their websites to make progress on this front.

INTERNET EXERCISE

INTERSHOP Communications develops and sells software that companies use to create "virtual stores" for Internet retailing. For example, it allows a seller to create an online catalog that is easy for consumers to use, and it has tools for analyzing sales and keeping track of customers. Go to the firm's website (www.intershop.com) and select *Products* and then *Enfinity MultiSite*. Review the information provided. Do you think it would be easier for consumers if all Internet sellers used a common system, such as this one, rather than coming up with many different arrangements? Briefly explain your thinking.

The costs are still deceptive

The Internet makes it easy to compare products and prices from different sellers. That has put price pressure on Internet sellers who have not figured out how else to differentiate what they offer. For more expensive items, a discount price may offset delivery costs. That often isn't the case with less expensive items. Low-cost ways of handling post-purchase deliveries need to be developed for the Internet to be really practical for everyday purchases. We'll return to this issue at the end of the chapter. For now, though, we should note that a large number of people are working on that problem. For example, Tesco in England sells groceries from a website and delivers them within 24 hours. But other firms, like Webvan, collapsed under the problems of trying to do that in a way that satisfies consumers' needs.

Exhibit 13-3 A Three-Dimensional View of the Market for Retail Facilities and the Probable Position of Some Present Offerings

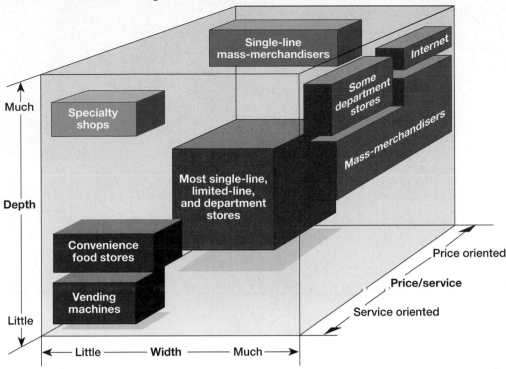

Another cost occurs if a product must be returned. That, of course, assumes you get what you order. The Internet is the ultimate weapon for fly-by-night operators. Fraud is already a big problem.

Competitive effects will influence other retailers

Retailers of every type are experimenting with selling on the Internet. They range from department stores like Bloomingdale's to discounters like Target to limited-line retailers like Virtual Vineyards (wine) to service providers like FTD (flower deliveries).

None of these retailers knows what longer-term impact Internet selling will have on their market. However, as new retailing formats and concepts are refined, they increase the competitive pressure on existing companies.[19]

RETAILING TYPES ARE EXPLAINED BY CONSUMER NEEDS FILLED

We've talked about many different types of retailers and how they evolved. No single characteristic provides a good basis for classifying all of them. However, Exhibit 13-3 positions different types of retailers in terms of three consumer-oriented dimensions: (1) width of assortment desired, (2) depth of assortment desired, and (3) a price/service combination. Price and service are combined because they are often indirectly related. Services are costly to provide. So retailers with a lot of service must charge prices that cover the added costs.

We can position most existing retailers within this three-dimensional market diagram. Exhibit 13-3, for example, suggests the *why* of vending machines. Some people—in the front upper left-hand corner—have a strong need for a specific item and are not interested in width of assortment or price. Note where Internet retailers are placed in the diagram. Does that position make sense to you?

Some manufacturers have always had outlet stores near their factories, but outlet malls are emerging as a new retailing format that is popular with some consumers.

WHY RETAILERS EVOLVE AND CHANGE

The wheel of retailing keeps rolling

The **wheel of retailing theory** says that new types of retailers enter the market as low-status, low-margin, low-price operators and then, if successful, evolve into more conventional retailers offering more services with higher operating costs and higher prices. Then they're threatened by new low-status, low-margin, low-price retailers—and the wheel turns again. Department stores, supermarkets, and mass-merchandisers went through this cycle. Some Internet sellers are on this path.

The wheel of retailing theory, however, doesn't explain all major retailing developments. Vending machines entered as high-cost, high-margin operations. Convenience food stores are high-priced. Suburban shopping centers don't emphasize low price. Current retailers who are adding websites are likely to face competitors who cut operating expenses even deeper.

Scrambled merchandising— mixing product lines for higher profits

Conventional retailers tend to specialize by product line. But most modern retailers are moving toward **scrambled merchandising**—carrying any product lines they think they can sell profitably. Supermarkets and drugstores sell anything they can move in volume—panty hose, phone cards, one-hour photo processing, motor oil, potted plants, and computer software. Mass-merchandisers don't just sell everyday items but also cell phones, computer printers, and jewelry.[20]

Product life-cycle concept applies to retailer types too

Consumers' needs help explain why some kinds of retailers developed. But we can apply the product life-cycle concept to understand this process better. A retailer with a new idea may have big profits—for a while. But if it's a really good idea, the retailer can count on speedy imitation and a squeeze on profits. Other retailers will copy the new format or scramble their product mix to sell products that offer them higher margins or faster turnover. That puts pressure on the original firm to change or lose its market.

Some conventional retailers are in decline as these life and death cycles continue. Recent innovators, like the Internet merchants, are still in the market growth stage.

Exhibit 13-4   Retailer Life Cycles—Timing and Years to Market Maturity

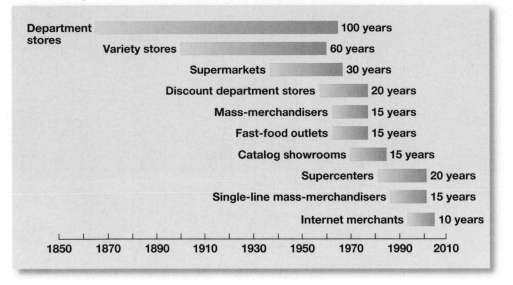

See Exhibit 13-4. Some retailing formats that are mature in the United States are only now beginning to grow in other countries.

Ethical issues may arise

Most retailers face intense competitive pressure. The desperation that comes with such pressure has pushed some retailers toward questionable marketing practices.

Critics argue, for example, that retailers too often advertise special sale items to bring price-sensitive shoppers into the store or to a website but then don't stock enough to meet demand. Other retailers are criticized for pushing consumers to trade up to more expensive items. What is ethical and unethical in situations like these, however, is subject to debate. Retailers can't always anticipate demand perfectly, and deliveries may not arrive on time. Similarly, trading up may be a sensible part of a strategy—if it's done honestly.

The marketing concept should guide firms away from unethical treatment of customers. However, a retailer on the edge of going out of business may lose perspective on the need to satisfy customers in both the short and the long term.[21]

RETAILER SIZE AND PROFITS

A few big retailers do most of the business

The large number of retailers (1,113,600) might suggest that retailing is a field of small businesses. To some extent this is true. As shown in Exhibit 13-5, when the last census of retailers was published over 62 percent of all the retail stores in the United States had annual sales of less than $1 million. But that's only part of the story. Those same retailers accounted for only about 10 cents of every $1 in retail sales!

The larger retail stores—those selling more than $5 million annually—do most of the business. Less than 10 percent of the retail stores are this big, yet they account for over 65 percent of all retail sales. Many small retailers are being squeezed out of business.[22]

Big chains are building market clout

The main way for a retailer to achieve economies of scale is with a corporate chain. A **corporate chain** is a firm that owns and manages more than one store— and often it's many. Chains have grown rapidly and now account for about half of

Exhibit 13-5   Distribution of Stores by Size and Share of Total U.S. Retail Sales

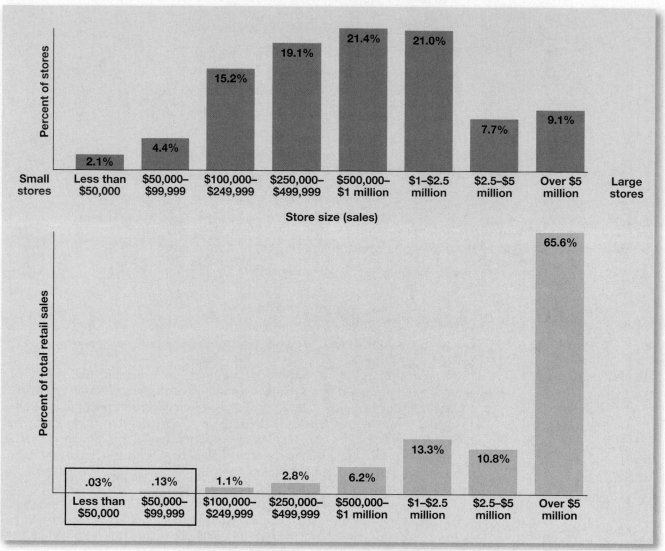

all retail sales. You can expect chains to continue to grow and take business from independent stores.

Large chains use central buying for different stores. They take advantage of quantity discounts and develop their own efficient distribution centers. They can use computer networks to control inventory costs and stock-outs. They may also spread promotion, information technology, and management costs to many stores. Retail chains also have their own dealer brands. Many of these chains are becoming powerful members, or channel captains, in their channel systems. In fact, the most successful of these big chains, like Home Depot and Wal-Mart, control access to so many consumers that they have the clout to dictate almost every detail of relationships with their suppliers.[23]

Independents form chains too

Competitive pressure from corporate chains encouraged the development of both cooperative chains and voluntary chains. **Cooperative chains** are retailer-sponsored groups—formed by independent retailers—that run their own buying organizations and conduct joint promotion efforts. Cooperative chains face a tough battle. Some, like True Value Hardware, are still adapting as they identify the weakness of corporate

Ich freue mich auf meinen grossen Auftritt im Streichelzoo vom 11.–23.2.

SHOPPI&TIVOLI
S p r e i t e n b a c h

Shoppi Tivoli is a shopping mall in Switzerland. The ad says: "I'm looking forward to my gig at the petting zoo between February 11 and 23." Shopping centers around the world are adding entertainment to draw customers and make shopping more enjoyable.

chains. For example, ads remind consumers that they don't need to waste a half-hour lost in a big store to pick up some simple item.

Voluntary chains are wholesaler-sponsored groups that work with "independent" retailers. Some are linked by contracts stating common operating procedures and requiring the use of common storefront designs, store names, and joint promotion efforts. Examples include SuperValu in groceries and Ace in hardware.

Franchisors form chains too

In a **franchise operation,** the franchisor develops a good marketing strategy, and the retail franchise holders carry out the strategy in their own units. Each franchise holder benefits from its relationship with the larger company and its experience, buying power, promotion, and image. In return, the franchise holder usually signs a contract to pay fees and commissions and to strictly follow franchise rules designed to continue the successful strategy.

Franchise holders' sales account for about half of all retail sales. One reason is that franchising is especially popular with service retailers, a fast-growing sector of the economy.[24]

DIFFERENCES IN RETAILING IN DIFFERENT NATIONS

New ideas spread across countries

New retailing approaches that succeed in one part of the world are often quickly adapted to other countries. Self-service approaches that started with supermarkets in the United States are now found in retail operations worldwide. The supercenter concept, on the other hand, initially developed in Europe.

Mass-merchandising requires mass markets	The low prices, selections, and efficient operations offered by mass-merchandisers might be attractive to consumers everywhere. But consumers in less-developed nations often don't have the income to support mass distribution. The small shops that survive in these economies sell in very small quantities, often to a small number of consumers.
Some countries block change	The political and legal environment severely limits the evolution of retailing in some nations. Japan is a prime example. For years its Large Store Law—aimed at protecting the country's politically powerful small shopkeepers—has been a real barrier to retail change. The law restricts development of large stores by requiring special permits, which are routinely denied.

Japan is taking steps to change the Large Store Law. One such change allowed Toys "R" Us to move into the Japanese market. Even so, most experts believe that it will be years before Japan moves away from its system of small, limited-line shops. Many countries in other parts of Asia and South America impose similar restrictions. On the other hand, the European Union is prompting member countries to drop such rules.[25] |

WHAT IS A WHOLESALER?

It's hard to define what a wholesaler is because there are so many different wholesalers doing different jobs. Some of their activities may even seem like manufacturing. As a result, some wholesalers describe themselves as "manufacturer and dealer." Some like to identify themselves with such general terms as *merchant*, *agent*, *dealer*, or *distributor*. And others just take the name commonly used in their trade—without really thinking about what it means.

To avoid a long technical discussion on the nature of wholesaling, we'll use the U.S. Bureau of the Census definition:

Wholesaling is concerned with the *activities* of those persons or establishments that sell to retailers and other merchants, or to industrial, institutional, and commercial users, but that do not sell in large amounts to final consumers.

So **wholesalers** are firms whose main function is providing wholesaling activities. Wholesalers sell to all of the different types of organizational customers shown in Exhibit 7-1.

Wholesaling activities are just variations of the basic marketing functions—gathering and providing information, buying and selling, grading, storing, transporting, financing, and risk taking—we discussed in Chapter 1. You can understand wholesalers' strategies better if you look at them as members of channels. They add value by doing jobs for their customers and for their suppliers.

WHOLESALING IS CHANGING WITH THE TIMES

A hundred years ago wholesalers dominated distribution channels in the United States and most other countries. The many small producers and small retailers needed their services. This situation still exists in less-developed economies. However, in the developed nations, as producers became larger many bypassed the wholesalers. Similarly, large retail chains often take control of functions that had been handled by wholesalers. Now e-commerce is making it easier for producers and consumers to "connect" without having a wholesaler in the middle of the exchange.

In light of these changes, many people have predicted a gloomy future for wholesalers. In the 1980s that seemed to be the pattern. Now, however, many wholesalers

The Internet has helped many wholesalers expand their market opportunities. For example, databases at ImporterUSA.com list wholesale importers and distributors of machinery in the U.S. This type of information helps producers identify a wholesaler that might be a good channel partner and helps customers find the right wholesaler-supplier.

are adapting rapidly and finding new ways to add value in the channel. For example, some of the biggest B2B e-commerce sites on the Internet are wholesaler operations, and many wholesalers are enjoying significant growth.

Producing profits, not chasing orders

Progressive wholesalers are becoming more concerned with their customers and with channel systems. Many are using technology to offer better service. Others develop voluntary chains that bind them more closely to their customers.

Modern wholesalers no longer require all customers to pay for all the services they offer simply because certain customers use them. Many offer a basic service at minimum cost—then charge additional fees for any special services required. They've also streamlined their operations to cut unnecessary costs and improve profits. In fact, wholesalers pioneered many of the recent logistics innovations we discussed in Chapter 12. They use computers to track inventory and reorder only when it's really needed. Computerized sales analysis helps them identify and drop unprofitable products and customers. This sometimes leads to a selective distribution policy—when it's unprofitable to build relationships with too many small customers. Then they can fine-tune how they add value for their profitable customers.

Perhaps good-bye to some

Not all wholesalers are progressive, and less efficient ones will fail. Some wholesalers will disappear as the functions they provided in the past are shifted and shared in different ways in the channel. Cost-conscious buyers for Wal-Mart, Lowe's, and other chains are refusing to deal with some of the middlemen who represent small producers. They want to negotiate directly with the producer. Similarly, producers see advantages in having closer direct relationships with fewer suppliers—and they're paring out weaker vendors. Efficient delivery services like UPS and Federal Express are also making it easy for many producers to ship directly to their customers, even ones in foreign markets. The Internet is putting pressure on wholesalers whose primary role is providing information to bring buyers and sellers together.[26]

Is it an ethical issue?

All of this is squeezing some wholesalers out of business. Some critics, including many of the wounded wholesalers, argue that it's unethical for powerful suppliers or customers to simply cut out wholesalers who spend money and time, perhaps decades, developing markets. Contracts between channel members and laws sometimes define what is or is not legal. But the ethical issues are often more ambiguous.

Exhibit 13-6 U.S. Wholesale Trade by Type of Wholesale Operation

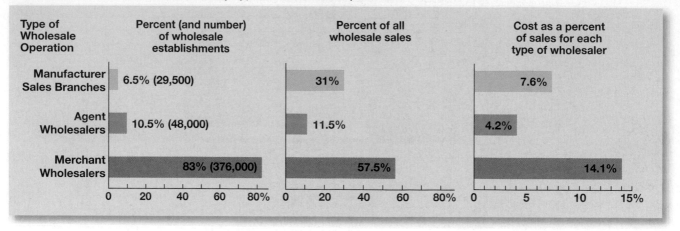

Type of Wholesale Operation	Percent (and number) of wholesale establishments	Percent of all wholesale sales	Cost as a percent of sales for each type of wholesaler
Manufacturer Sales Branches	6.5% (29,500)	31%	7.6%
Agent Wholesalers	10.5% (48,000)	11.5%	4.2%
Merchant Wholesalers	83% (376,000)	57.5%	14.1%

For example, Amana notified Cooper Distributing Co. that it intended to cancel their distribution agreement in 10 days. Cooper had handled Amana appliances for 30 years, and Amana products represented 85 percent of Cooper's sales. Amana's explanation to Cooper? "We just think we can do it better."

Situations like this arise often. They may be cold-hearted, but are they unethical? We argue that it isn't fair to cut off the relationship with such short notice. But most wholesalers realize that their business is *always* at risk—if they don't perform channel functions better or cheaper than their suppliers or customers can do themselves.[27]

Survivors will need effective strategies

The wholesalers who do survive will need to be efficient, but that doesn't mean they'll all have low costs. Some wholesalers' higher operating expenses result from the strategies they select, including the special services they offer to *some* customers.

WHOLESALERS ADD VALUE IN DIFFERENT WAYS

Exhibit 13-6 compares the number, sales volume, and operating expenses of some major types of wholesalers. The differences in operating expenses suggest that each of these types performs, or does not perform, certain wholesaling functions. But which ones and why? And why do manufacturers use merchant wholesalers—costing 14.1 percent of sales—when agent middlemen cost only 4.2 percent?

To answer these questions, we must understand what these wholesalers do and don't do. Exhibit 13-7 gives a big-picture view of the major types of wholesalers we'll be discussing. There are lots more specialized types, but our discussion will give you a sense of the diversity. Note that a major difference between merchant and agent wholesalers is whether they *own* the products they sell. Before discussing these wholesalers, we'll briefly consider producers who handle their own wholesaling activities.

Manufacturers' sales branches are considered wholesalers

Manufacturers who just take over some wholesaling activities are not considered wholesalers. However, when they have **manufacturers' sales branches**—warehouses that producers set up at separate locations away from their factories—they're classified as wholesalers by the U.S. Census Bureau and by government agencies in many other countries.

In the United States, these manufacturer-owned branch operations account for about 6.5 percent of wholesale facilities—but they handle 31 percent of total wholesale sales. One reason sales per branch are so high is that the branches are usually

Exhibit 13-7 Types of Wholesalers

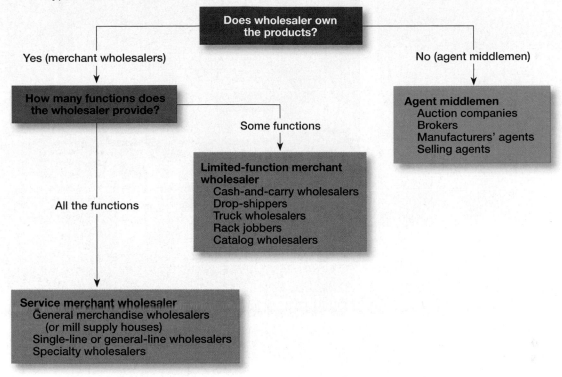

placed in the best market areas. This also helps explain why their operating costs, as a percent of sales, are often lower. It's also easier for a manufacturer to coordinate information and logistics functions with its own branch operations than with independent wholesalers.[28]

MERCHANT WHOLESALERS ARE THE MOST NUMEROUS

Merchant wholesalers own (take title to) the products they sell. They often specialize by certain types of products or customers. For example, Fastenal is a wholesaler that specializes in distributing threaded fasteners used by a variety of manufacturers. It owns (takes title to) the fasteners for some period before selling to its customers. If you think all merchant wholesalers are fading away, Fastenal is proof that they can serve a needed role. In the last decade Fastenal's profits have grown at about the same pace as Microsoft's.[29]

INTERNET EXERCISE

Check out the different aspects of the Fastenal website (www.fastenal.com). Give examples of ways that the website is intended to help Fastenal's customers and suppliers.

Exhibit 13-6 shows that over 80 percent of the wholesaling establishments in the United States are merchant wholesalers—and they handle over 57 percent of wholesale sales. Merchant wholesalers are even more common in other countries. Japan is an extreme example. Products are often bought and sold by a series of merchant wholesalers on their way to the business user or retailer.[30]

Merchant wholesalers in Africa are often smaller, carry narrower product lines, and deal with fewer customers than their counterparts in North America.

Service wholesalers provide all the functions

Service wholesalers are merchant wholesalers that provide all the wholesaling functions. Within this basic group are three types: (1) general merchandise, (2) single-line, and (3) specialty.

General merchandise wholesalers are service wholesalers that carry a wide variety of nonperishable items such as hardware, electrical supplies, furniture, drugs, cosmetics, and automobile equipment. With their broad line of convenience and shopping products, they serve hardware stores, drugstores, and small department stores. *Mill supply houses* operate in a similar way, but they carry a broad variety of accessories and supplies to serve the needs of manufacturers.

Single-line (or general-line) wholesalers are service wholesalers that carry a narrower line of merchandise than general merchandise wholesalers. For example, they might carry only food, apparel, or certain types of industrial tools or supplies. In consumer products, they serve the single- and limited-line stores. In business products, they cover a wider geographic area and offer more specialized service.

Specialty wholesalers are service wholesalers that carry a very narrow range of products and offer more information and service than other service wholesalers. A consumer products specialty wholesaler might carry only health foods or oriental foods instead of a full line of groceries. Some limited-line and specialty wholesalers are growing by helping independent retailer-customers find better ways to compete with mass-merchandisers. But in general, many consumer-products wholesalers have been hit hard by the growth of retail chains that set up their own distribution centers and deal directly with producers.

A specialty wholesaler of business products might limit itself to fields requiring special technical knowledge or service. Richardson Electronics is an interesting example. It specializes in distributing replacement parts, such as electron tubes, for old equipment that many manufacturers still use on the factory floor. Richardson describes itself as "on the trailing edge of technology," but many of its customers operate in countries where new technologies are not yet common. Richardson gives them easy access to information from its website (www.rell.com) and makes its products available quickly by stocking them in locations around the world.[31]

3M produces 1,600 products that are used by auto body repair shops in the U.S., Europe, Japan, and other countries. To reach this target market, 3M works with hundreds of specialty wholesalers.

Limited-function wholesalers provide some functions

Limited-function wholesalers provide only *some* wholesaling functions. In the following paragraphs, we briefly discuss the main features of these wholesalers. Although less numerous in some countries, these wholesalers are very important for some products.

Cash-and-carry wholesalers want cash

Cash-and-carry wholesalers operate like service wholesalers—except that the customer must pay cash. In the U.S., big warehouse clubs have taken much of this business. But cash-and-carry operators are common in less-developed nations where very small retailers handle the bulk of retail transactions. Full-service wholesalers often refuse to grant credit to small businesses that may have trouble paying their bills.

Drop-shippers do not handle the products

Drop-shippers own (take title to) the products they sell—but they do *not* actually handle, stock, or deliver them. These wholesalers are mainly involved in selling. They get orders and pass them on to producers. Then the producer ships the order directly to the customer. Drop-shippers commonly sell bulky products (like lumber) for which additional handling would be expensive and possibly damaging. Drop-shippers in the U.S. are already feeling the squeeze from buyers and sellers connecting directly via the Internet. But the progressive ones are fighting back by setting up their own websites and getting fees for referrals.

Truck wholesalers deliver—at a cost

Truck wholesalers specialize in delivering products that they stock in their own trucks. Their big advantage is that they promptly deliver perishable products that regular wholesalers prefer not to carry. A 7-Eleven store that runs out of potato chips on a busy Friday night doesn't want to be out of stock all weekend! They help retailers keep a tight rein on inventory, and they seem to meet a need.

Rack jobbers sell hard-to-handle assortments

Rack jobbers specialize in hard-to-handle assortments of products that a retailer doesn't want to manage—and rack jobbers usually display the products on their own wire racks. For example, a grocery store or mass-merchandiser might rely on a rack jobber to decide which paperback books or magazines it sells. The wholesaler knows which titles sell in the local area and applies that knowledge in many stores.

Catalog wholesalers reach outlying areas

Catalog wholesalers sell out of catalogs that may be distributed widely to smaller industrial customers or retailers that might not be called on by other middlemen. Customers place orders at a website or by mail, e-mail, fax, or telephone. These wholesalers sell lines such as hardware, jewelry, sporting goods, and computers. For example, Inmac uses a catalog that is printed in six languages and a website (www.inmac.com) to sell a complete line of computer accessories. Many of its

Innovative wholesalers are using multilingual bar codes to reduce costs and errors in overseas markets.

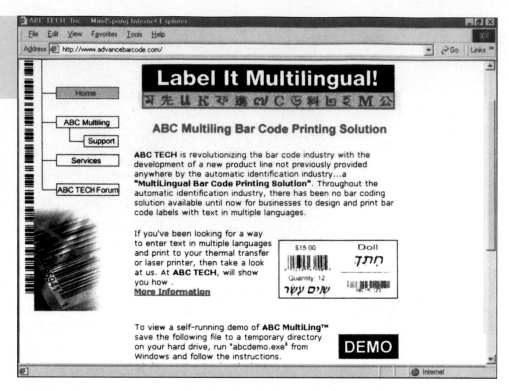

customers don't have a local wholesaler, but they can place orders from anywhere in the world. Most catalog wholesalers quickly adapted to the Internet. It fits what they were already doing and makes it easier. But they're facing more competition too; the Internet allows customers to compare prices from more sources of supply.[32]

AGENT MIDDLEMEN ARE STRONG ON SELLING

They don't own the products

Agent middlemen are wholesalers who do *not* own the products they sell. Their main purpose is to help in buying and selling. Agent middlemen normally specialize by customer type and by product or product line. But they usually provide even fewer functions than the limited-function wholesalers. They operate at relatively low cost—sometimes 2 to 6 percent of their selling price—or less in the case of website-based agents who simply bring buyers and sellers together. Worldwide, the role of agent middlemen is rapidly being transformed by the Internet. Those who didn't get on board this fast-moving train were left behind.

They are important in international trade

Agent middlemen are common in international trade. Many markets have only a few well-financed merchant wholesalers. The best many producers can do is get local representation through agents and then arrange financing through banks that specialize in international trade.

Agent middlemen are usually experts on local business customs and regulations in their own countries. Sometimes a marketing manager can't work through a foreign government's red tape without the help of a local agent.

Manufacturers' agents— freewheeling sales reps

A **manufacturers' agent** sells similar products for several noncompeting producers—for a commission on what is actually sold. Such agents work almost as members of each company's sales force, but they're really independent middlemen. More than half of all agent middlemen are manufacturers' agents.

A few years ago, auctions were used for only a few specialized product categories, but now online services like eBay are making auctions a convenient and popular approach for buying and selling many different types of products (both new and used).

Their big plus is that they already call on some customers and can add another product line at relatively low cost—and at no cost to the producer until something sells! If an area's sales potential is low, a company may use a manufacturers' agent because the agent can do the job at low cost. Small producers often use agents everywhere because their sales volume is too small to justify their own sales force.

Agents can be especially useful for introducing new products. For this service, they may earn 10 to 15 percent commission. (In contrast, their commission on large-volume established products may be quite low—perhaps only 2 percent.) A 10 to 15 percent commission rate may seem small for a new product with low sales. Once a product sells well, however, a producer may think the rate is high and begin using its own sales reps. Agents are well aware of this possibility. That's why most try to work for many producers and avoid being dependent on only one line.

Export or import agents are basically manufacturers' agents who specialize in international trade. These agent middlemen operate in every country and help international firms adjust to unfamiliar market conditions in foreign markets.

Manufacturers' reps will continue to play an important role in businesses that need an agent to perform order-getting tasks. But manufacturers' reps everywhere are feeling pressure when it comes to routine business contacts. More producers are turning to telephone selling, websites, e-mail, teleconferencing, and faxes to contact customers directly.[33]

Brokers provide information

Brokers bring buyers and sellers together. Brokers usually have a *temporary* relationship with the buyer and seller while a particular deal is negotiated. They are especially useful when buyers and sellers don't come into the market very often. The broker's product is information about what buyers need and what supplies are available. If the transaction is completed, they earn a commission from whichever party hired them. **Export and import brokers** operate like other brokers, but they specialize in bringing together buyers and sellers from different countries. Smart brokers quickly saw new opportunities to expand their reach by using the Internet. As the Internet causes consolidation, it will also provide more value. A smaller number of cyberbrokers will cut costs and dominate the business with larger databases of buyers and sellers.

Selling agents—almost marketing managers

Selling agents take over the whole marketing job of producers—not just the selling function. A selling agent may handle the entire output of one or more producers, even competing producers, with almost complete control of pricing, selling, and advertising. In effect, the agent becomes each producer's marketing manager.

Financial trouble is one of the main reasons a producer calls in a selling agent. The selling agent may provide working capital but may also take over the affairs of the business. But selling agents also work internationally. A **combination export manager** is a blend of manufacturers' agent and selling agent—handling the entire export function for several producers of similar but noncompeting lines.

Auction companies speed up the sale

Auction companies provide a place where buyers and sellers can come together and bid to complete a transaction. Traditionally they were important in certain lines—such as livestock, fur, tobacco, and used cars—where demand and supply conditions change rapidly.

Auto Auction Network Limited (Aucsat), based in New Zealand, is a good example of a progressive auction company that put the bid process on the Internet. Its very successful used-car auction runs from a website (www.aucsat.co.nz). It provides bidders with a thorough online rating of the quality of each car. In the past, most auction companies said "What you see is what you get." Because the ratings add value and are credible, Aucsat attracts more dealers. The Internet has spurred growth of all sorts of auction companies in lines of business where auctions have previously not been common.[34]

WHAT WILL HAPPEN TO RETAILERS AND WHOLESALERS IN THE FUTURE?

A common theme in this chapter—and the two before it—is that channels of distribution are in the midst of dynamic changes. There have been dramatic improvements in logistics, the Internet, and e-commerce. But before all of this, the evolution of retailing and wholesaling was ongoing. Middlemen that find new and better ways to add value prosper.

A variety of firms are trying to figure out how to have a presence on the Web. Many are reshaping competition in the product-markets in which they compete. On the other hand, much of the initial change has simply been an adjustment to what was done in the past. The catalog becomes electronic. E-mail supplements toll-free phone orders. A retailer opens a new website instead of a new store. The technology is revolutionary and exciting, but much of what firms are doing with it so far is evolutionary.

In time, more revolutionary change may come. Imagine, for example, what it would take for you—and everyone you know—to do most of your routine shopping on the Internet. What new marketing functions would be needed, and who would provide them? Let's consider one scenario.

After you put products in your virtual shopping basket at several websites, the seller assembles your items in a carton with a bar code for your personal name, address, and account. Then that carton and cartons for all of the other orders that come into that website would be quickly taken in large economical batches to an intermediary. The computer-controlled sorting system going into the intermediary's five-acre facility would scan each carton's bar code and route it to the sorting area for a truck that serves you and each of your neighbors. After a night of accumulating all the cartons that are directed to you from different sellers, the intermediary would place the cartons on a delivery vehicle in the right sequence so they can be efficiently unloaded as the truck passes each customer on its route.[35]

Something like this probably isn't far off. Specialists will develop to make distribution *after* an Internet purchase more efficient, just as middlemen developed to make distribution more efficient *prior* to purchases in retail stores. What is described above isn't very different from what UPS does now, but the cost per package is much higher than it would be if everybody got deliveries everyday.

If the after-purchase distribution problem is handled, who will the seller be? Will the Internet merchants of tomorrow be an evolved form of the retailers of today? Or will current-day wholesalers be in a better position to catch that prize? Some wholesalers are already working with very large assortments. Or, in a world where you can conveniently surf from one specialized seller to another, will the breadth of assortment from any one seller be irrelevant? That could put producers in a stronger position. Perhaps none of these traditional forms of business will lead the way, but rather it will be a unique new type of specialist that is born on the Internet. The answers to these questions will take time, but already new intermediaries are coming on the scene.

Let's admit it. You can only speculate about where e-commerce will lead. But perhaps it's good to speculate a little. The way markets work in the future will depend on creative innovations that people like you imagine, analyze, and ultimately turn into profitable marketing strategies.

CONCLUSION

Modern retailing is scrambled—and we'll probably see more changes in the future. In such a dynamic environment, a producer's marketing manager must choose very carefully among the available kinds of retailers. And retailers must plan their marketing mixes with their target customers' needs in mind—while at the same time becoming part of an effective channel system.

We described many types of retailers—and we saw that each has its advantages and disadvantages. We also saw that modern retailers have discarded conventional practices. The old "buy low and sell high" philosophy is no longer a safe guide. Lower margins with faster turnover is the modern philosophy as more retailers move into mass-merchandising. But even this is no guarantee of success as retailers' life cycles move on.

Growth of chains and scrambled merchandising will continue as retailing evolves to meet changing consumer demands. But important breakthroughs are possible—perhaps with the Internet—and consumers probably will continue to move away from conventional retailers.

Wholesalers can provide functions for those both above and below them in a channel of distribution. These services are closely related to the basic marketing functions. There are many types of wholesalers. Some provide all the wholesaling functions—while others specialize in only a few. Eliminating wholesalers does not eliminate the need for the functions they now provide, but technology is helping firms to perform these functions in more efficient ways.

Merchant wholesalers are the most numerous and account for the majority of wholesale sales. Their distinguishing characteristic is that they take title to (own) products. Agent middlemen, on the other hand, act more like sales representatives for sellers or buyers—and they do not take title.

Despite dire predictions, wholesalers continue to exist. The more progressive ones are adapting to a changing environment. But some less progressive wholesalers will fail. The Internet is already taking its toll. On the other hand, new types of intermediaries are evolving. Some are creating new ways of helping producers and their customers achieve their objectives by finding new ways to add value.

KEY TERMS

QUESTIONS AND PROBLEMS

1. What sort of a "product" are specialty shops offering? What are the prospects for organizing a chain of specialty shops?

2. Distinguish among discount houses, price-cutting by conventional retailers, and mass-merchandising. Forecast the future of low-price selling in food, clothing, and appliances. How will the Internet affect that future?

3. Discuss a few changes in the marketing environment that you think help to explain why telephone, mail-order, and Internet retailing have been growing so rapidly.

4. What are some advantages and disadvantages to using the Internet for shopping?

5. Apply the wheel of retailing theory to your local community. What changes seem likely? Will established retailers see the need for change, or will entirely new firms have to develop?

6. What advantages does a retail chain have over a retailer who operates with a single store? Does a small retailer have any advantages in competing against a chain? Explain your answer.

7. Many producers are now seeking new opportunities in international markets. Are the opportunities for international expansion equally good for retailers? Explain your answer.

8. Discuss how computer systems affect wholesalers' and retailers' operations.

9. Consider the evolution of wholesaling in relation to the evolution of retailing. List several changes that are similar, and several that are fundamentally different.

10. Do wholesalers and retailers need to worry about new-product planning just as a producer needs to have an organized new-product development process? Explain your answer.

11. How do you think a retailer of Maytag washing machines would react if Maytag set up a website, sold direct to consumers, and shipped direct from its distribution center? Explain your thinking.

12. What risks do merchant wholesalers assume by taking title to goods? Is the size of this risk about constant for all merchant wholesalers?

13. Why would a manufacturer set up its own sales branches if established wholesalers were already available?

14. What is an agent middleman's marketing mix?

15. Why do you think that many merchant middlemen handle competing products from different producers, while manufacturers' agents usually handle only noncompeting products from different producers?

16. What alternatives does a producer have if it is trying to expand distribution in a foreign market and finds that the best existing merchant middlemen won't handle imported products?

17. Discuss the future growth and nature of wholesaling if chains, scrambled merchandising, and the Internet continue to become more important. How will wholesalers have to adjust their mixes? Will wholesalers be eliminated? If not, what wholesaling functions will be most important? Are there any particular lines of trade where wholesalers may have increasing difficulty?

SUGGESTED CASES

11. Joggers Universe
14. Multimedia Corral

15. Growth Enterprises
16. Matisse Company

COMPUTER-AIDED PROBLEM

13. Selecting Channel Intermediaries

RESOURCE REMINDER

Art Glass Productions, a producer of decorative glass gift items, wants to expand into a new territory. Managers at Art Glass know that unit sales in the new territory will be affected by consumer response to the products. But sales will also be affected by which combination of wholesalers and retailers Art Glass selects. There is a choice between two wholesalers. One wholesaler, Giftware Distributing, is a merchant wholesaler that specializes in gift items; it sells to gift shops, department stores, and some mass-merchandisers. The other wholesaler, Margaret Degan & Associates, is a manufacturers' agent that calls on many of the gift shops in the territory.

Art Glass makes a variety of glass items, but the cost of making an item is usually about the same—$5.20 a unit. The items would sell to Giftware Distributing at $12.00 each—and in turn the merchant wholesaler's price to retailers would be $14.00—leaving Giftware with a $2.00 markup to cover costs and profit. Giftware Distributing is the only reputable merchant wholesaler in the territory, and it has agreed to carry the line only if Art Glass is willing to advertise in a trade magazine aimed at retail buyers for gift items. These ads will cost $8,000 a year.

As a manufacturers' agent, Margaret Degan would cover all of her own expenses and would earn 8 percent of the $14.00 price per unit charged the gift shops. Individual orders would be shipped directly to the retail gift shops by Art Glass, using United Parcel Service (UPS). Art Glass would pay the UPS charges at an average cost of $2.00 per item. In contrast, Giftware Distributing would anticipate demand and place larger orders in advance. This would reduce the shipping costs, which Art Glass would pay, to about $.60 a unit.

Art Glass' marketing manager thinks that Degan would only be able to sell about 75 percent as many items as Giftware Distributing—since she doesn't have time to call on all of the smaller shops and doesn't call on any department stores. On the other hand, the merchant wholesaler's demand for $8,000 worth of supporting advertising requires a significant outlay.

The marketing manager at Art Glass decided to use a spreadsheet to determine how large sales would have to be to make it more profitable to work with Giftware and to see how the different channel arrangements would contribute to profits at different sales levels.

a. Given the estimated unit sales and other values shown on the initial spreadsheet, which type of wholesaler would contribute the most profit to Art Glass Productions?

b. If sales in the new territory are slower than expected, so that the merchant wholesaler was able to sell only 3,000 units—or the agent 2,250 units—which wholesaler would contribute the most to Art Glass' profits? (Note: Assume that the merchant wholesaler only buys what it can sell; that is, it doesn't carry extra inventory beyond what is needed to meet demand.)

c. Prepare a table showing how the two wholesalers' contributions to profit compare as the quantity sold varies from 3,500 units to 4,500 units for the merchant wholesaler and 75 percent of these numbers for the manufacturers' agent. Discuss these results. (Note: Use the analysis feature to vary the quantity sold by the merchant wholesaler, and the program will compute 75 percent of that quantity as the estimate of what the agent will sell.)

For additional questions related to this problem, see Exercise 13-4 in the *Learning Aid for Use with Basic Marketing,* 15th edition.

1. Know the advantages and disadvantages of the promotion methods a marketing manager can use in strategy planning.

2. Understand the integrated marketing communications concept and why most firms use a blend of different promotion methods.

3. Understand the importance of promotion objectives.

4. Know how the communication process affects promotion planning.

5. Understand how direct-response promotion is helping marketers develop more targeted promotion blends.

6. Understand how new customer-initiated interactive communication is different.

7. Know how typical promotion plans are blended to get an extra push from middlemen and help from customers in pulling products through the channel.

8. Understand how promotion blends typically vary over the adoption curve and product life cycle.

9. Understand how to determine how much to spend on promotion efforts.

10. Understand the important new terms (shown in red).

CHAPTER FOURTEEN

Promotion— Introduction to Integrated Marketing Communications

The classic MINI Cooper was a pop icon in England in the 1960s. John Lennon and Paul McCartney were MINI owners when they wrote "Baby, You Can Drive My Car." But the quirky MINI never made a splash in the U.S. (only 10,000 classic MINIs were sold from 1960–67). Now, however, all of that has changed— with the help of effective promotion.

After the BMW Group took ownership of the MINI brand, a new-product development team designed a new model. They gave it updated styling and high-tech features (including six standard airbags, Corner Brake Control, Dynamic Stability Control, ABS, heated seats, and a six-speaker CD stereo). Tiny compacts were already popular in Europe. Yet in the U.S., where SUVs rule the road, the new MINI was the smallest car on the American road. The BMW Group hoped that the U.S.

launch of the MINI would attract a segment of adventurous, fun-loving innovators who would change that. Kerri Martin, the Marketing Communications Manager for MINI U.S.A., planned the promotion to make that happen. Her team faced several challenges. The MINI brand had to be launched independently of any BMW brand association, so promotion had to simultaneously launch a new brand, two models, and a new small car segment. Further, Martin's team didn't have the big promotion budget typical for high-volume cars because first year production was limited to 20,000 units.

Martin needed distinctive promotion to appeal to prospects who saw the unique MINI as a form of self-expression, not just as a way to get to work. She selected the Crispin Porter + Bogusky (CPB) ad agency to help.

They were creative—and not scared off by her warning to avoid costly TV campaigns and traditional ads.

Before the MINI'S introduction, they staged a series of sales promotion events to give the MINI a personality—and draw traffic to the newly created website. For example, they mounted a MINI on top of a jumbo SUV and drove it to auto shows and around major metropolitan cities like New York and San Francisco. A sign on the SUV said, "What are you doing for fun this weekend?" The big idea was that your fun stuff always goes on top, whether it be your skiis, mountain bikes, or your MINI Cooper. Next they tore out seats at the Superdome in New Orleans and put a MINI right in with the fans for a game. The publicity stunts drew national TV coverage, including coverage on Monday

Night Football. To get as much attention from TV ads would have cost millions of dollars. Before the rollout to dealers, CPB started to add cheeky billboard messages, like the one on the side of an urban parking garage that showed a picture of the MINI and the simple copy "Parking. How sad." Other ads just featured a simple headline such as "The SUV backlash officially starts now," its "LET'S MOTOR" tagline, and the address for its website at www.MINIUSA.com.

In response to these attention-getting efforts, over 125,000 consumers flocked to the website—before cars even hit dealer showrooms. Thousands played the interactive video games and e-mailed electronic MINI greeting cards to friends—which helped spread the buzz. "MINI Insiders" signed up to receive e-mail newsletters about the MINI, and many used the dealer locator to find out where to see a MINI in person and take a test drive. MINI dealers added personal selling to the promotion blend. MINI Motoring Advisors (MINI doesn't use the term salesmen) explained MINI's options, negotiated prices, completed orders, and arranged for deliveries. Each MINI is delivered with a mint on the seat and a wrap on the steering wheel indicating that "Your MINI has been thoroughly inspected from boot to bonnet." Boot is a British term for a trunk and a bonnet is a hood.

Once cars were on dealer lots, CPB broadened the reach of the MINI message with more billboards, magazine ads and inserts, and 60-second ads in movie theaters. Some dealers ran the theater ads on local TV. CPB created custom ads for some magazines taking advantage of the unique editorial environments. That was more expensive than just repeating the same ad month after month, but it generated much higher interest and ad recall. For example, an ad in *Playboy* featured a MINI in a centerfold format (along with a tongue-in-cheek list of "likes and dislikes" and a data sheet). An insert in another magazine allowed readers to customize their own MINI with accessory stickers.

By the end of the year, 56 percent of U.S. consumers were aware of the MINI. More importantly, dealers had orders for 20 percent more MINIs than were available. The MINI was even named the 2003 "North American Car of the Year." However, the successful introduction doesn't ensure that the MINI will become a long-run success. So promotion for the MINI will need to evolve with changes in the marketing environment while it remains true to the motoring spirit of the brand.[1]

SEVERAL PROMOTION METHODS ARE AVAILABLE

Promotion is communicating information between seller and potential buyer or others in the channel to influence attitudes and behavior. The marketing manager's main promotion job is to tell target customers that the right Product is available at the right Place at the right Price.

As the Mini Cooper example shows, a marketing manager can choose from several promotion methods—personal selling, mass selling, and sales promotion (see

Scholastic, Inc., the distributor of the Harry Potter series of books, generated national publicity when it released the latest book. Kids and their parents waited at bookstores, at midnight, to be the first to get a copy.

Exhibit 14-1). Further, because the different promotion methods have different strengths and limitations, a marketing manager usually uses them in combination. And, as with other marketing mix decisions, it is critical that the marketer manage and coordinate the different promotion methods as an integrated whole, not as separate and unrelated parts.

Personal selling—flexibility is its strength

Personal selling involves direct spoken communication between sellers and potential customers. Salespeople get immediate feedback, which helps them to adapt. Although some personal selling is included in most marketing mixes, it can be very expensive. So it's often desirable to combine personal selling with mass selling and sales promotion.

Mass selling involves advertising and publicity

Mass selling is communicating with large numbers of potential customers at the same time. It's less flexible than personal selling, but when the target market is large and scattered, mass selling can be less expensive.

Advertising is the main form of mass selling. **Advertising** is any *paid* form of nonpersonal presentation of ideas, goods, or services by an identified sponsor. It includes the use of traditional media like magazines, newspapers, radio and TV, signs, and direct mail as well as new media such as the Internet. While advertising must be paid for, another form of mass selling—publicity—is "free."

Publicity avoids media costs

Publicity is any *unpaid* form of nonpersonal presentation of ideas, goods, or services. Of course, publicity people are paid. But they try to attract attention to the firm and its offerings *without having to pay media costs*. For example, movie studios try to get celebrities on TV talk shows because this generates a lot of interest and sells tickets to new movies without the studio paying for TV time.

Exhibit 14-1
Basic Promotion Methods and Strategy Planning

Publicity generated for *Harry Potter and the Order of the Phoenix* is a classic example. There was already huge interest in the Potter series. Every new book had increased sales. But Scholastic, Inc., the distributor of the books, got an even bigger bang—and worldwide media coverage—by keeping the plot shrouded in secrecy and notifying bookstores and the media that no store could sell the book before 12:01 A.M. Saturday, June 21. Print runs and deliveries were scheduled to make that stick. As word of the secrecy spread, national media picked up on the story and devoted a huge amount of attention to it. For example, the week the book came out, Harry was on the cover of *Time* and a feature article explained all of the reasons it was going to be one of the fastest-selling books in history. Local newspapers got in on the action with their own stories on late-night Harry parties planned by local retailers. With publicity like that, even people who had never heard of the series wanted to find out what they were missing.[2]

If a firm has a really new message, publicity may be more effective than advertising. Trade magazines, for example, may carry articles featuring the newsworthy products of regular advertisers—in part because they *are* regular advertisers. The firm's publicity people write the basic copy and then try to convince magazine editors to print it. A consumer might carefully read a long magazine story but ignore an ad with the same information.

Some companies prepare videotapes designed to get free publicity for their products on TV news shows. For example, after learning that Seattle Mariner Jay Buhner loves Cheerios, a General Mills marketing manager had 162 boxes of the cereal stuffed into his spring-training locker and videotaped Buhner's surprise on opening his locker. TV news programs in 12 major markets showed the video. It would have cost hundreds of thousands of dollars to get as much attention with advertising.[3]

One problem with publicity is that the media don't always say or show what the firm intends. Heinz ran into this problem when it introduced Blastin' Green EZ Squirt Ketchup. The media covered it earlier than Heinz intended, so in-store displays were not yet stocked and there wasn't enough inventory to fill the orders that flowed in from retailers. Heinz also wanted publicity to focus more on the bottle's design and how it was easy for kids to use, but the green color got the attention. In Heinz' case, the media coverage was still a positive.[4] That isn't always the case. When Segway got an order from the vice president of the United States, it seemed like a perfect opportunity for publicity. It looked even better at the White House when President Bush got on to take a ride—until he fell off the Segway with photographers snapping pictures.[5]

Sales promotion tries to spark immediate interest

Sales promotion refers to promotion activities—other than advertising, publicity, and personal selling—that stimulate interest, trial, or purchase by final customers or others in the channel. Sales promotion may be aimed at consumers, at middlemen,

Exhibit 14-2
Example of Sales Promotion Activities

Aimed at final consumers or users	Aimed at middlemen	Aimed at company's own sales force
Contests	Price deals	Contests
Coupons	Promotion	Bonuses
Aisle displays	allowances	Meetings
Samples	Sales contests	Portfolios
Trade shows	Calendars	Displays
Point-of-purchase	Gifts	Sales aids
materials	Trade shows	Training materials
Banners and	Meetings	
streamers	Catalogs	
Frequent buyer	Merchandising aids	
programs	Videos	
Sponsored events		

Many different specialists help firms with special sales promotion needs. For example, Featherlite sells special trailers for use with event marketing and FloorGraphics helps firms with point-of-sale ads on the floors of retail stores.

or at a firm's own employees. Examples are listed in Exhibit 14-2. Relative to other promotion methods, sales promotion can usually be implemented quickly and get results sooner. In fact, most sales promotion efforts are designed to produce immediate results.

Less is spent on advertising than personal selling or sales promotion

Many people incorrectly think that promotion money gets spent primarily on advertising—because advertising is all around them. The many ads you see on the Web, in magazines and newspapers, and on TV are impressive—and costly. But all the special sales promotions—coupons, sweepstakes, trade shows, and the like—add up to even more money. Similarly, much personal selling goes on in the channels and in other business markets. In total, firms spend less money on advertising than on personal selling or sales promotion.

We'll talk about individual promotion methods in more detail in the next two chapters. First, however, you need to understand the role of the whole promotion blend—personal selling, mass selling, and sales promotion combined—so you can see how promotion fits into the rest of the marketing mix.

SOMEONE MUST PLAN, INTEGRATE, AND MANAGE THE PROMOTION BLEND

Each promotion method has its own strengths and weaknesses. In combination, they complement each other. Each method also involves its own distinct activities and requires different types of expertise. As a result, it's usually the responsibility of specialists—such as sales managers, advertising managers, and promotion managers—to develop and implement the detailed plans for the various parts of the overall promotion blend.

Sales managers manage salespeople

Sales managers are concerned with managing personal selling. Often the sales manager is responsible for building good distribution channels and implementing

Place policies. In smaller companies, the sales manager may also act as the marketing manager and be responsible for advertising and sales promotion.

Advertising managers work with ads and agencies

Advertising managers manage their company's mass-selling effort—in television, newspapers, magazines, and other media. Their job is choosing the right media and developing the ads. Advertising departments within their own firms may help in these efforts—or they may use outside advertising agencies. The advertising manager may handle publicity too. Or it may be handled by an outside agency or by whoever handles **public relations**—communication with noncustomers, including labor, public interest groups, stockholders, and the government.

Sales promotion managers need many talents

Sales promotion managers manage their company's sales promotion effort. In some companies, a sales promotion manager has independent status and reports directly to the marketing manager. If a firm's sales promotion spending is substantial, it probably *should* have a specific sales promotion manager. Sometimes, however, the sales or advertising departments handle sales promotion efforts—or sales promotion is left as a responsibility of individual brand managers. Regardless of who the manager is, sales promotion activities vary so much that many firms use both inside and outside specialists.

Marketing manager talks to all, blends all

Although many specialists may be involved in planning for and implementing specific promotion methods, determining the blend of promotion methods is a strategy decision—and it is the responsibility of the marketing manager.

The various promotion specialists tend to focus on what they know best and their own areas of responsibility. A creative web page designer or advertising copywriter in New York may have no idea what a salesperson does during a call on a wholesaler. In addition, because of differences in outlook and experience, the advertising, sales, and sales promotion managers often have trouble working with each other as partners. Too often they just view other promotion methods as using up budget money they want.

The marketing manager must weigh the pros and cons of the various promotion methods, then devise an effective promotion blend—fitting in the various departments and personalities and coordinating their efforts. Then the advertising, sales, and sales promotion managers should develop the details consistent with what the marketing manager wants to accomplish.

Send a consistent and complete message with integrated marketing communications

Effective blending of all of the firm's promotion efforts should produce **integrated marketing communications**—the intentional coordination of every communication from a firm to a target customer to convey a consistent and complete message.

The Mini Cooper case at the start of this chapter is a good example of integrated marketing communications. Different promotion methods handle different parts of the job. Yet the methods are coordinated so that the sum is greater than the parts. The separate messages are complementary, but also consistent.

INTERNET EXERCISE

Sony produces a very wide variety of products. Does the information available on its website (www.sony.com) appear to be part of an integrated marketing communications effort? Explain your thinking.

It seems obvious that a firm's different communications to a target market should be consistent. However, when a number of different people are working on different promotion elements, they are likely to see the same big picture only if a marketing

Stanley Works depends on a blend of integrated marketing communications, including sales presentations and product demonstration tours, trade ads focused on retailers, ads targeted at end-users, and a website that provides information on the whole line.

manager ensures that it happens. Getting consistency is harder when different firms handle different aspects of the promotion effort. For example, different firms in the channel may have conflicting objectives.

To get effective coordination, everyone involved with the promotion effort must clearly understand the plan for the overall marketing strategy. They all need to understand how each promotion method will contribute to achieve specific promotion objectives.[6]

Exhibit 14-3
Promotion Seeks to Shift
the Demand Curve

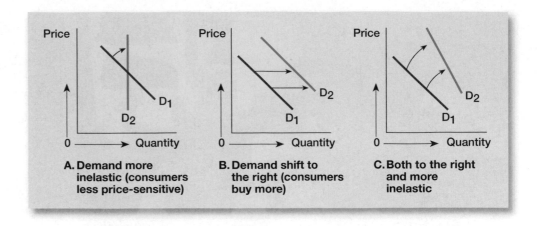

A. Demand more inelastic (consumers less price-sensitive)

B. Demand shift to the right (consumers buy more)

C. Both to the right and more inelastic

WHICH METHODS TO USE DEPENDS ON PROMOTION OBJECTIVES

Overall objective is to affect behavior

The different promotion methods are all different forms of communication. They should encourage customers to choose a *specific* product. Therefore, promotion must (1) reinforce present attitudes or relationships that might lead to favorable behavior or (2) actually change the attitudes and behavior of the firm's target market.

In terms of demand curves, promotion may help the firm make its present demand curve more inelastic, or shift the demand curve to the right, or both. These possibilities are shown in Exhibit 14-3. The buyer behavior model introduced in Chapter 6 showed the many influences on buying behavior. You saw there that affecting buyer behavior is a tough job—but that is exactly the objective of Promotion.

Informing, persuading, and reminding are basic promotion objectives

Promotion objectives must be clearly defined—because the right promotion blend depends on what the firm wants to accomplish. It's helpful to think of three basic promotion objectives: *informing*, *persuading*, and *reminding* target customers about the company and its marketing mix. All try to affect buyer behavior by providing more information.

It's also useful to set more specific promotion objectives that state *exactly who* you want to inform, persuade, or remind, and *why*. This is unique to each company's strategy—and specific objectives vary by promotion method. We'll talk about more specific promotion objectives in the next two chapters. Here we'll focus on the three basic promotion objectives and how you can reach them.

Informing is educating

Potential customers must know something about a product if they are to buy at all. A firm with a really new product may not have to do anything but inform consumers about it and show that it meets consumer needs better than other products.

Persuading usually becomes necessary

When competitors offer similar products, the firm must not only *inform* customers that its product is available but also persuade them to buy it. A *persuading* objective means the firm will try to develop a favorable set of attitudes so customers will buy, and keep buying, its product. A persuading objective often focuses on reasons why one brand is better than others. To convince consumers to buy Brawny paper towels, ads position Brawny as the towel that's best for tough cleanup jobs.

Reminding may be enough, sometimes

If target customers already have positive attitudes about a firm's marketing mix—or a good relationship with a firm—a *reminding* objective might be suitable. This objective can be extremely important. Customers who have been attracted and sold once are still targets for competitors' appeals. Reminding them of their past satisfaction may keep them from shifting to a competitor. Campbell realizes that most people know about its soup—so much of its advertising is intended to remind.

This trade ad for Simply White Clear Whitening Gel informs potential channel members that the new product is available and that market testing gives evidence that it will be profitable for the retailer. With its ad Beech-Nut wants to persuade parents that its natural baby food is superior to other products.

Promotion objectives relate to adoption process

In Chapter 6, we looked at consumer buying as a problem-solving process in which buyers go through steps on the way to adopting (or rejecting) an idea or product. The three basic promotion objectives relate to these steps. See Exhibit 14-4. *Informing* and *persuading* may be needed to affect the potential customer's knowledge and attitudes about a product and then bring about its adoption. Later promotion can simply *remind* the customer about that favorable experience and confirm the adoption decision.

The AIDA model is a practical approach

The basic promotion objectives and adoption process fit very neatly with another action-oriented model—called AIDA—that we will use in this and the next two chapters to guide some of our discussion.

The **AIDA model** consists of four promotion jobs: (1) to get *Attention*, (2) to hold *Interest*, (3) to arouse *Desire*, and (4) to obtain *Action*. (As a memory aid, note that the first letters of the four key words spell AIDA, the well-known opera.)

Exhibit 14-4 shows the relationship of the adoption process to the AIDA jobs. Getting attention is necessary to make consumers aware of the company's offering. Holding interest gives the communication a chance to build the consumer's interest in the product. Arousing desire affects the evaluation process, perhaps building preference. And obtaining action includes gaining trial, which may lead to a purchase decision. Continuing promotion is needed to confirm the decision and encourage an ongoing relationship and additional purchases.

Exhibit 14-4
Relation of Promotion Objectives, Adoption Process, and AIDA Model

Promotion Objectives	Adoption Process	AIDA Model
Informing	Awareness	Attention
	Interest	Interest
Persuading	Evaluation	Desire
	Trial	
	Decision	Action
Reminding	Confirmation	

Exhibit 14-5
The Traditional
Communication Process

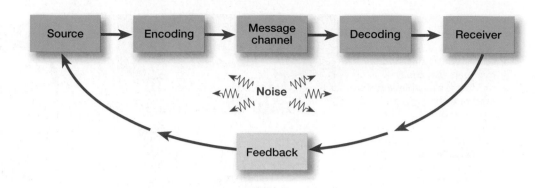

PROMOTION REQUIRES EFFECTIVE COMMUNICATION

Communication can break down

Promotion is wasted when it doesn't communicate effectively. There are many reasons why a promotion message can be misunderstood or not heard at all. To understand this, it's useful to think about a whole **communication process**—which means a source trying to reach a receiver with a message. Exhibit 14-5 shows the elements of the communication process. Here we see that a **source**—the sender of a message—is trying to deliver a message to a **receiver**—a potential customer. Customers evaluate both the message and the source of the message in terms of trustworthiness and credibility. For example, American Dental Association (ADA) studies show that Listerine mouthwash helps reduce plaque buildup on teeth. Listerine mentions the ADA endorsement in its promotion to help make the promotion message credible.

A major advantage of personal selling is that the source—the seller—can get immediate feedback from the receiver. It's easier to judge how the message is being received and to change it if necessary. Mass sellers usually must depend on marketing research or total sales figures for feedback—and that can take too long. Many marketers include toll-free telephone numbers and website addresses as ways of building direct-response feedback from consumers into their mass-selling efforts.

The **noise**—shown in Exhibit 14-5—is any distraction that reduces the effectiveness of the communication process. Conversations and snack-getting during TV ads are noise. The clutter of competing ads on the Internet is noise. Advertisers who plan messages must recognize that many possible distractions—noise—can interfere with communications.

Encoding and decoding depend on a common frame of reference

Exhibit 14-6

This Same Message May Be Interpreted Differently

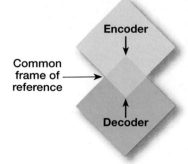

The basic difficulty in the communication process occurs during encoding and decoding. **Encoding** is the source deciding what it wants to say and translating it into words or symbols that will have the same meaning to the receiver. **Decoding** is the receiver translating the message. This process can be very tricky. The meanings of various words and symbols may differ depending on the attitudes and experiences of the two groups. People need a common frame of reference to communicate effectively. See Exhibit 14-6. Maidenform encountered this problem with its promotion aimed at working women. The company ran a series of ads depicting women stockbrokers and doctors wearing Maidenform lingerie. The men in the ads were fully dressed. Maidenform was trying to show women in positions of authority, but some women felt the ad presented them as sex objects. In this case, the promotion people who encoded the message didn't understand the attitudes of the target market and how they would decode the message.[7]

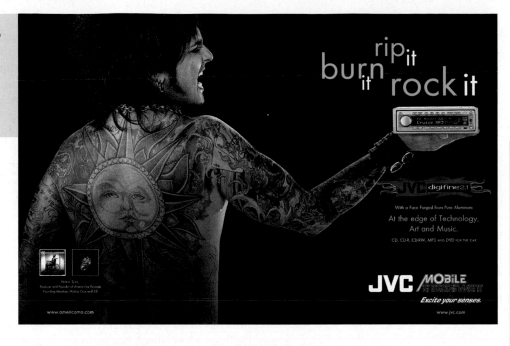

JVC's ad for its mobile stereo gear features tattooed rock star Nikki Sixx and appears in print media that are specially tuned to its youthful, music-loving target market.

Message channel is important too

The communication process is complicated even more because the message is coming from a source through some **message channel**—the carrier of the message. A source can use many message channels to deliver a message. The salesperson does it in person with voice and action. Advertising must do it with media such as magazines, TV, e-mail, or Internet websites. A particular message channel may enhance or detract from a message. A TV ad, for example, can *show* that Dawn dishwashing detergent "takes the grease away"; the same claim might not be convincing if it arrived in a consumer's e-mail. On the other hand, a receiver may attach value to a product if the message comes in a well-respected magazine. For instance, many people who are interested in herbal supplements have concerns about safety since the government does not regulate them like it does drugs. Some of these consumers might buy herbal supplements that advertise in *Good Housekeeping* magazine— because they have faith in its seal.[8]

The same message may be interpreted differently

Different audiences may interpret a message differently. Such differences are common in international marketing when cultural differences or translation are problems. In Taiwan, the translation of the Pepsi slogan "Come alive with the Pepsi Generation" came out as "Pepsi will bring your ancestors back from the dead." Worse, a campaign for Schweppes Tonic Water in Italy translated the name into Schweppes Toilet Water. Many firms run into problems like this.[9]

Problems occur even when there is no translation. For example, a new children's cough syrup was advertised as extra strength. The advertising people thought they were assuring parents that the product worked well. But moms and dads avoided the product because they feared that it might be too strong for their children.

Ethical issues in marketing communications

Promotion is one of the most often criticized areas of marketing. Many criticisms focus on whether communications are honest and fair. Marketers must sometimes make ethical judgments in considering these charges and in planning their promotion.

For example, when a TV news program broadcasts a video publicity release, consumers don't know it was prepared to achieve marketing objectives. They think the news staff is the source. That may make the message more credible, but is it fair? Many say yes—as long as the publicity information is truthful. But gray areas still remain.

Critics raise similar concerns about the use of celebrities in advertisements. A person who plays the role of an honest and trustworthy person on a popular TV series may be a credible message source in an ad, but is using such a person misleading to consumers? Some critics believe it is. Others argue that consumers recognize advertising when they see it and know celebrities are paid for their endorsements.

The most common criticisms of promotion relate to exaggerated claims. If an ad or a salesperson claims that a product is the "best available," is that just a personal opinion or should every statement be backed up by proof? What type of proof should be required? Some promotions do misrepresent the benefits of a product. However, most marketing managers want relationships with, and repeat purchases from, their customers. They realize that customers won't come back if the marketing mix doesn't deliver what the promotion promises. Further, many consumers are skeptical about all the claims they hear and see. As a result, most marketing managers work to make promotion claims specific and believable.[10]

INTEGRATED DIRECT-RESPONSE PROMOTION IS VERY TARGETED

The challenge of developing promotions that reach *specific* target customers has prompted many firms to turn to direct marketing—direct communication between a seller and an individual customer using a promotion method other than face-to-face personal selling. Most direct marketing communications are designed to prompt immediate feedback—a direct response—by customers. That's why this type of communication is often called *direct-response promotion.*

Early efforts in the direct-response area focused on direct-mail advertising. A carefully selected mailing list—perhaps from the firm's customer relationship management (CRM) database—allowed advertisers to reach customers with specific

Overture helps firms to reach customers who are actively searching for their products on the Internet.

interests. And direct-mail advertising proved to be very effective when the objective was to get a direct response from the customer.

Now it's more than direct-mail advertising

Achieving a measurable, direct response from specific target customers is still the heart of direct promotion. But direct-response media now include telephone, print, e-mail, a website, broadcast, and even interactive video. The customer's response may be a purchase (or donation), a question, or a request for more information. At a website, the response may be a simple mouse-click to link to more information, a click to put an item in a virtual shopping cart, or a click to purchase.

Often the customer responds by calling a toll-free telephone number or, in the case of business markets, by sending a fax or an e-mail. Then a salesperson calls and follows up. That might involve filling an order or scheduling a personal visit with a prospect. There are, however, many variations on this approach. For example, some firms route incoming information-request calls to a computerized answering system. The caller indicates what information is required by pushing a few buttons on the telephone keypad. Then the computer instantly sends requested information to the caller's fax machine.

Direct-response promotion is often an important component of integrated marketing communications programs and is closely tied to other elements of the marketing mix. However, what distinguishes this general approach is that the marketer targets more of its promotion effort at specific individuals who respond directly.[11] A promotion campaign developed by BMW illustrates these ideas. BMW and other car companies have found that videotapes are a good way to provide consumers with a lot of information about a new model. However, it's too expensive to send tapes to everyone. To target the mailing, BMW first sends likely car buyers (high-income consumers who own a BMW or competing brand) personalized direct-mail ads that offer a free videotape. Interested consumers send back a return card. Then BMW sends the advertising tape and updates its database so a dealer will know to call the consumer.

Target customer directly with a CRM database

Direct-response promotion usually relies on a customer relationship management (CRM) database to target specific prospects. The computerized database includes customers' names and addresses (or telephone numbers) as well as past purchases and other segmenting characteristics. Greenpeace and the Cousteau Society send mail advertisements to people interested in environmental issues. They ask for donations or other types of support. Individuals (or segments) who respond to direct promotion are the target for additional promotion. For example, a customer who buys lingerie from a catalog or a website once is a good candidate for a follow-up. The follow up might extend to other types of clothing.

Direct-response methods raise ethical concerns

Direct-response promotion and CRM database targeting have become an important part of many marketing mixes. But critics argue that thousands of acres of trees are consumed each week just to make the paper for direct-response "junk mail" that consumers don't want. In addition, many consumers don't like getting direct-promotion telephone solicitations at any time, but especially during evening meal times when these calls are particularly frequent. Similarly, most e-mail users resent that they need to waste time dealing with a constant flow of "spam" that floods their e-mail boxes; there's so much spam that it slows down the whole Internet. Worse, some firms have been criticized for creating websites that secretly install "spyware" on customers' computers; then, unknown to the user, the program gathers information about the user and sends it back to the firm over the Internet. There are many other privacy issues related to how a direct-response database might be used, especially if it includes details of a consumer's purchases.

Most firms that use direct-response promotion are very sensitive to these concerns and take steps to address them. However, many people feel that solutions to these problems require other steps, and laws in these areas are changing. For example, most states have passed laws prohibiting automatic calling systems that use pre-recorded messages rather than a live salesperson. Many states have their own "do not call" laws and federal laws are under review. A host of new regulations concerning consumer privacy are also being considered by lawmakers. So marketers who do not heed warnings about consumer concerns in this area may find themselves in trouble—not only with customers but in the courts.[12]

THE CUSTOMER MAY INITIATE THE COMMUNICATION PROCESS

Traditional thinking about promotion—and for that matter about the communication process—has usually been based on the idea that it's the seller ("source") who initiates the communication. Of course, for decades consumers have been looking in the Yellow Pages for information or asking retail salespeople for help. Similarly, it's not news that organizational buyers contact potential vendors to ask questions or request bids.

In the past, a marketer usually viewed the buyer as a passive message receiver—at least until the marketer has done something to stimulate attention, interest, and desire. That's one reason that targeting is so important—so that the promotion expense isn't wasted on someone who isn't interested. Moreover, most mass-selling messages are based on the idea that you can get a customer's attention and interest for only a minute or two. Even with direct-response promotion, the marketer typically has taken the first step.

New electronic media enable interactive communication

However, this is changing. Buyers can now access a great deal of information (including pictures, video, and audio, as well as text) and place an order without the seller having been directly involved at all. The interactive technologies enabling this change take many different forms. Some of the most important are websites,

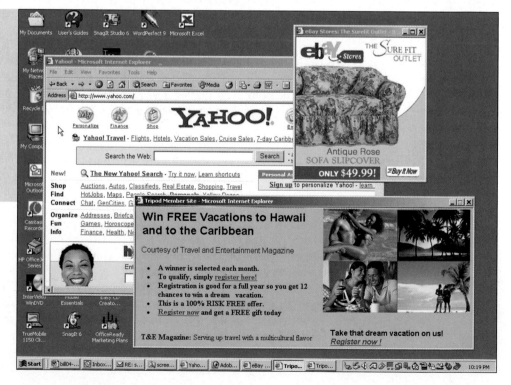

When a web surfer uses the search engine at Yahoo, one or more pop-up ads may appear. The advertising revenue pays for the service that Yahoo provides free to users, and some consumers click on interesting ads to get more information. However, some critics argue that pop-ups are too obtrusive.

390

e-mail list-servers, caller-controlled fax-on-demand, computerized telephone voice-messaging systems, video kiosks in malls, CD and DVD disks on personal computers, and MSN TV.

For example, England has had interactive cable TV for over a decade. Consumers can use a standard TV and remote control to get information that ranges from local weather to specials at the local supermarket. Similar systems are becoming more available in other countries as government regulations change and as cable companies upgrade their equipment.

Work is underway on interactive cable systems in which icons will appear on-screen as consumers watch a program or movie. For example, an icon might appear on a jacket worn by a talk show guest. A consumer who is interested in the product will be able to press a button on a remote control to pause the show and get more information about the product and where to buy it—or even to place an order. The same concept is already implemented on DVDs for some movies. When this type of system is available via cable (or with streaming video over the Internet), it will reshape the way many marketing communications are handled.

Consider the simple model of customer ("receiver") initiated interactive communication shown in Exhibit 14-7. At first it doesn't seem very different from the traditional communication model we considered earlier (Exhibit 14-5). However, the differences are significant.

Consumer initiates communication with a search process

In the model in Exhibit 14-7, a customer initiates the communication process with a decision to search for information in a particular message channel. The most far-reaching message channel to search is the Internet. The message channel is still the carrier of the message, as was the case before, but "searchable" message channels usually feature an archive of existing messages on a number of topics. There may be many available topics—even millions.

Exhibit 14-7
A Model of Customer-Initiated Interactive Communication

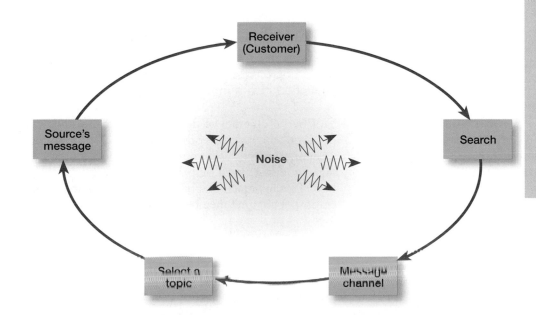

In the next step, the consumer selects one specific topic on which to receive a message. Selecting a topic might be done in one of a variety of ways, depending on the message channel. The most typical approaches involve using a mouse, remote control device, or keypad to highlight a selection from an initial list (like a table of contents or index). Of course, other approaches are common. Many dial-up telephone systems use voice-recognition. Or, in the case of the Internet, you might type a phrase and have the computer search for a list of topics that include it.

Consumer decides how much information to get

Once a specific topic is selected, the message for that topic is displayed. Typically, the message is brief. But it may include a simple way to get more detailed information, select another related topic, return to the original selection process, or quit the search. Thus, after each message the consumer can decide whether to search further (say, to get more detail). This interactive approach makes it easy for the consumer to get as much information as desired. However, noise may still be a problem. For example, a consumer may waste time and still not find what is needed—because it is not available or is too hard to find. So some firms offer consumers a website choice that establishes communication with a real person at a 24-hour-a-day service center. Some of these systems use instant messaging so that the consumer and a customer service person can chat online. With other systems, like AT&T's "Interactive Answers" approach, a service person immediately phones the customer to provide the information or help needed. Other firms are using variations of this approach, including live teleconferencing or messaging over the Internet.

Action, including purchase, may be immediate

The action required to make a purchase by interactive media is usually fast and easy. At many Internet sites, for example, a consumer can click on an item to place it in a virtual shopping cart, charge it to a credit card, and arrange for shipping.

Custom communications will be more personalized

The traditional principles of communication discussed earlier in the chapter are still important in customer-initiated interactive communication. At the same time, the interactive approach allows the marketer to customize communication to the needs and responses of the consumer. As new approaches develop in this arena, we are seeing more promotion targeted at single-person "segments."[13]

HOW TYPICAL PROMOTION PLANS ARE BLENDED AND INTEGRATED

There is no one right blend

There is no one *right* promotion blend for all situations. Each one must be developed as part of a marketing mix and should be designed to achieve the firm's promotion objectives in each marketing strategy. So let's take a closer look at typical promotion blends in different situations.

Get a push in the channel with promotion to middlemen

When a channel of distribution involves middlemen, their cooperation can be crucial to the success of the overall marketing strategy. **Pushing** (a product through a channel) means using normal promotion effort—personal selling, advertising, and sales promotion—to help sell the whole marketing mix to possible channel members. This approach emphasizes the importance of securing the wholehearted cooperation of channel members to promote the product in the channel and to the final user.

Producers usually take on much of the responsibility for the pushing effort in the channel. However, wholesalers often handle at least some of the promotion to retailers. Similarly, retailers often handle promotion in their local markets. The overall effort is most likely to be effective when all of the individual messages are carefully integrated.

The Hanes ad (on the left) is targeted at parents and kids and designed to stimulate demand and help pull Hanes' popular products through the channel of distribution. The Hanes trade ad (on the right) is targeted at retailers and designed to inform them about the consumer promotion and encourage them to carry Hanes brand products.

Promotion to middlemen emphasizes personal selling

Salespeople handle most of the important communication with middlemen. Middlemen don't want empty promises. They want to know what they can expect in return for their cooperation and help. A salesperson can answer questions about what promotion will be directed toward the final consumer, each channel member's part in marketing the product, and important details on pricing, markups, promotion assistance, and allowances. A salesperson can also help the firm determine when it should adjust its marketing mix from one middleman to another.

When suppliers offer similar products and compete for attention and shelf space, middlemen usually pay attention to the one with the best profit potential. So sales promotions targeted at middlemen usually focus on short-term arrangements that will improve the middleman's profits. For example, a soft-drink bottler might offer a convenience store a free case of drinks with each two cases it buys. The free case improves the store's profit margin on the whole purchase.

Firms run ads in trade magazines to recruit new middlemen or to inform channel members about a new offering. Trade ads usually encourage middlemen to contact the supplier for more information, and then a salesperson takes over.

Push within a firm— with promotion to employees

Some firms emphasize promotion to their own employees—especially salespeople or others in contact with customers. This type of *internal marketing* effort is basically a variation on the pushing approach. One objective of an annual sales meeting is to inform reps about important elements of the marketing strategy—so they'll work together as a team to implement it. Some firms use promotion to motivate employees to provide customer service or achieve higher sales. This is typical in services where the quality of the employees' efforts is a big part of the product. Some ads, for example, use the theme "we like to see you smile." The ads communicate to customers, but also remind employees that the service they provide is crucial to customer satisfaction.

Pulling policy— customer demand pulls the product through the channel

Most producers focus a significant amount of promotion on customers at the end of the channel. This helps to stimulate demand and pull the product through the channel of distribution. **Pulling** means getting customers to ask middlemen for the product.

Pulling and pushing are usually used in combination. See Exhibit 14-8. However, if middlemen won't work with a producer—perhaps because they're already carrying a competing brand—a producer may try to use a pulling approach by itself. This involves highly aggressive promotion to final consumers or users—perhaps using coupons or samples—temporarily bypassing middlemen. If the promotion works, the

Exhibit 14-8
Promotion May Encourage
Pushing in the Channel,
Pulling by Customers, or
Both

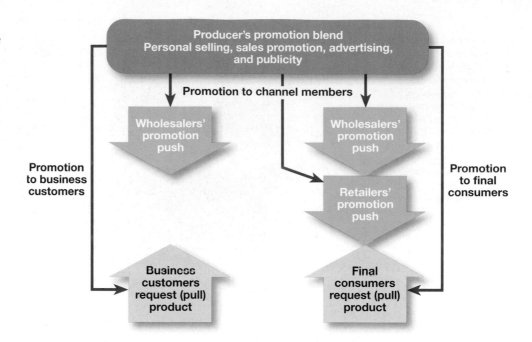

middlemen are forced to carry the product to satisfy customer requests. However, this approach is risky. Customers may lose interest before reluctant middlemen make the product available. At minimum, middlemen should be told about the planned pulling effort—so they can be ready if the promotion succeeds.

Who handles promotion to final customers at the end of the channel varies in different channel systems, depending on the mix of pushing and pulling. Further, the promotion blend typically varies depending on whether customers are final consumers or business users.[14]

Promotion to final consumers

The large number of consumers almost forces producers of consumer products and retailers to emphasize advertising and sales promotion. Sales promotion—such as coupons, contests, or free samples—builds consumer interest and short-term sales of a product. Effective mass selling may build enough brand familiarity so that little personal selling is needed, as in self-service and discount operations.[15]

Personal selling can be effective too. But aggressive personal selling to final consumers usually is found in expensive channel systems, such as those for financial services, furniture, consumer electronics, designer clothing, and automobiles.

Promotion to business customers

Producers and wholesalers that target business customers often emphasize personal selling. This is practical because there are fewer of these customers and their purchases are typically larger. Sales reps can be more flexible in adjusting their companies' appeals to suit each customer—and personal contact is usually required to close a sale. A salesperson is also able to call back later to follow up, resolve any problems, and nurture the relationship with the customer.

While personal selling dominates in business markets, mass selling is necessary too. A typical sales call on a business customer costs about $200.[16] That's because salespeople spend less than half their time actually selling. The rest is consumed by such tasks as traveling, paperwork, sales meetings, and strictly service calls. So it's seldom practical for salespeople to carry the whole promotion load.

Ads in trade magazines or at a B2B e-commerce website, for instance, can inform potential customers that a product is available. Most trade ads give a toll-free telephone number, fax number, or website address to stimulate direct inquiries. Domestic and international trade shows also help identify prospects. Even so, most sellers

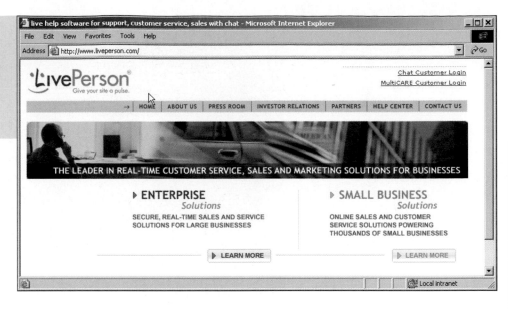

LivePerson helps firms identify the best prospects who visit the firm's website so that a salesperson can then immediately reach out and move them through the sales process.

who target business customers spend only a small percentage of their promotion budget on mass selling and sales promotion.

Each market segment may need a unique blend

Knowing what type of promotion is typically emphasized with different targets is useful in planning the promotion blend. But each unique market segment may need a separate marketing mix and a different promotion blend. You should be careful not to slip into a shotgun approach when what you really need is a rifle approach—with a more careful aim.

ADOPTION PROCESSES CAN GUIDE PROMOTION PLANNING

The AIDA and adoption processes look at individuals. This emphasis on individuals helps us understand how promotion affects the way that people behave. But it's also useful to look at markets as a whole. Different segments of customers within a market may behave differently—with some taking the lead in trying new products and, in turn, influencing others.

Promotion must vary for different adopter groups

Research on how markets accept new ideas has led to the adoption curve model. The **adoption curve** shows when different groups accept ideas. It emphasizes the relations among groups and shows that individuals in some groups act as leaders in accepting a new idea. Promotion efforts usually need to change over time to adjust to differences among the adopter groups.

Exhibit 14-9 shows the adoption curve for a typical successful product. Some of the important characteristics of each of these customer groups are discussed below. Which one are you?

Innovators don't mind taking some risks

The **innovators** are the first to adopt. They are eager to try a new idea and willing to take risks. Innovators tend to be young and well educated. They are likely to be mobile and have many contacts outside their local social group and community. Business firms in the innovator group are often specialized and willing to take the risk of doing something new.

Innovators tend to rely on impersonal and scientific information sources, or other innovators, rather than salespeople. They often search for information on the Internet, read articles in technical publications, or look for informative ads in special-interest magazines.

Exhibit 14-9
The Adoption Curve

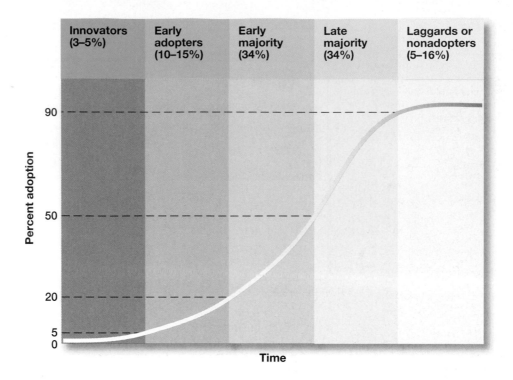

Innovators (3–5%)	Early adopters (10–15%)	Early majority (34%)	Late majority (34%)	Laggards or nonadopters (5–16%)

Percent adoption

90
50
20
5
0

Time

Early adopters are often opinion leaders

Early adopters are well respected by their peers and often are opinion leaders. They tend to be younger, more mobile, and more creative than later adopters. But unlike innovators, they have fewer contacts outside their own social group or community. Business firms in this category also tend to be specialized.

Of all the groups, this one tends to have the greatest contact with salespeople. Mass media are important information sources too. Marketers should be very concerned with attracting and selling the early adopter group. Their acceptance is crucial. The next group, the early majority, look to the early adopters for guidance. The early adopters can help the promotion effort by spreading *word-of-mouth* information and advice among other consumers.

The new "smart" LG refrigerator, which features a digital display on the door and an Internet connection, is likely to appeal to innovators who want to be among the first to adopt new products.

Opinion leaders help spread the word

Marketers know the importance of personal recommendations by opinion leaders. For example, some movie fans like to be the first to see new flicks. If they like a movie, they quickly tell their friends and word-of-mouth publicity does the real selling job. However, consumers are even more likely to talk about a negative experience than a positive experience. So if early groups reject the product, it may never get off the ground.

Some companies target promotion to encourage opinion leadership and word-of-mouth publicity. The Internet is one easy way to do this. For example, a retail shop called Hot Hot Hot, which carries a wide variety of hot sauces for food, established a website. It urged customers to click a link and e-mail the web address to their friends. Very quickly, largely because of word-of-mouth, 1,500 people were visiting the website each day.[17]

DO YOU HEAR THAT BUZZ, AND WHERE IS IT COMING FROM?

Computer viruses can spread like wildfire. Some marketers are trying to get attention for their products by promoting the same kind of "viral" spread of word-of-mouth promotion from a small set of opinion leaders to other consumers. For example, BMW commissions short-action films that show BMWs in high-performance chases because it couldn't show all of the dangerous stunts in TV ads. One of its recent films, *The Hostage,* created by famous director John Woo, highlights the new z4 roadster. The films are available for online viewing at www.bmwfilms.com. Car enthusiasts who hear about the site love the action and tell their friends to check it out. It's all a well-planned effort to create more buzz about BMW as the ultimate driving machine.

When Gillette introduced its three-bladed Venus razor for women, it wanted more buzz among college students. A fancy tractor-trailer truck, painted to look like a Venus billboard, parked beside spring break beach spots in Florida. A crew of young people invited coeds to come in and learn about Venus, enter a sweepstakes, and make a digital greeting card with a picture of the coeds enjoying the beach. When coeds e-mailed the pictures to friends, the message automatically included an invitation to enter the "Celebrate the Venus Goddess in You" sweepstakes. Recipients of the e-mail who entered the contest saw an online pitch for the Venus razor.

It's clear why a marketer might want target consumers to hear the buzz about a new product from their coolest friends—so they won't just dismiss it as some commercial pitch. But often the intent is to mislead consumers about where the buzz starts. Some say that makes it unethical; others say that the marketer is only planting a few seeds and that it really is consumers who spread the word. Of course, this can backfire. Sony Ericsson Mobile Communication, for instance, got bad publicity after Ralph Nader threatened legal action over its "fake tourist" gambit. Pairs of trained actors asked real tourists at attractions like Seattle's Space Needle to use the Sony Ericsson phone to take their picture. While taking the picture (or is that doing the product demo?), the good Samaritan got a sales pitch on the phone's features.[18]

| Early majority group is deliberate | The **early majority** avoid risk and wait to consider a new idea after many early adopters have tried it—and liked it. Average-sized business firms that are less specialized often fit in this category. If successful companies in their industry adopt the new idea, they will too. |

The early majority have a great deal of contact with mass media, salespeople, and early adopter opinion leaders. Members usually aren't opinion leaders themselves.

| Late majority is cautious | The **late majority** are cautious about new ideas. Often they are older and more set in their ways, so they are less likely to follow early adopters. In fact, strong social pressure from their own peer group may be needed before they adopt a new product. Business firms in this group tend to be conservative, smaller-sized firms with little specialization. |

The late majority make little use of marketing sources of information—mass media and salespeople. They tend to be oriented more toward other late adopters rather than outside sources they don't trust.

| Laggards or nonadopters hang on to tradition | **Laggards** or **nonadopters** prefer to do things the way they've been done in the past and are very suspicious of new ideas. They tend to be older and less well educated. The smallest businesses with the least specialization often fit this category. They cling to the status quo and think it's the safe way. |

The main source of information for laggards is other laggards. This certainly is bad news for marketers. In fact, it may not pay to bother with this group.[19]

PROMOTION BLENDS VARY OVER THE LIFE CYCLE

Stage of product in its life cycle

The adoption curve helps explain why a new product goes through the product life-cycle stages described in Chapter 10. Promotion blends usually have to change to achieve different promotion objectives at different life-cycle stages.

Market introduction stage—"this new idea is good"

During market introduction, the basic promotion objective is informing. If the product is a really new idea, the promotion must build **primary demand**—demand for the general product idea—not just for the company's own brand. Video phone service and "smart" appliances (that connect to the Internet) are good examples of product concepts where primary demand is just beginning to grow. There may be few potential innovators during the introduction stage, and personal selling can help find them. Firms also need salespeople to find good channel members and persuade them to carry the new product. Sales promotion may be targeted at salespeople or channel members to get them interested in selling the new product. And sales promotion may also encourage customers to try it.

Market growth stage—"our brand is best"

In the market growth stage, more competitors enter the market, and promotion emphasis shifts from building primary demand to stimulating **selective demand**—demand for a company's own brand. The main job is to persuade customers to buy, and keep buying, the company's product.

Now that there are more potential customers, mass selling becomes more economical. But salespeople and personal selling must still work in the channels, expanding the number of outlets and cementing relationships with channel members.

Banquet Homestyle Bakes illustrate this stage. When ConAgra Foods introduced Homestyle Bakes, it was the first shelf-stable meal kit with the meat already in the package. ConAgra, also the producer of Armour processed meats, had the expertise to create a tasty product that a consumer could prepare in a few minutes and then just stick in the oven. When Homestyle Bakes came out there was no direct competition. The sales force used market research data to convince retailers to give the product shelf space, and ads used humor to highlight that the package was so heavy because it already included meat. However, over time promotion shifted to emphasize that Homestyle Bakes was adding a variety of new flavors and 10 percent more meat. Similarly, the sales force shifted its efforts to get retailers to participate in

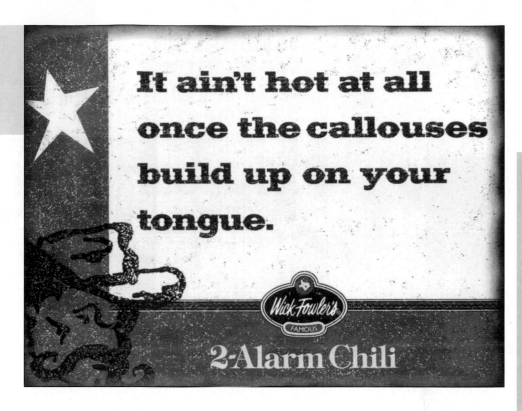

Homestyle Bakes' "Super Meals/Super Moms" contests, which offered harried moms prizes such as a visit to a spa, to keep them interested in the Homestyle brand.[20]

Market maturity stage—"our brand is better, really"

In the market maturity stage, mass selling and sales promotion may dominate the promotion blends of consumer products firms. Business products may require more aggressive personal selling—perhaps supplemented by more advertising. The total dollars allocated to promotion may rise as competition increases.

If a firm already has high sales—relative to competitors—it may have a real advantage in promotion at this stage. For example, sales of Tylenol tablets are about four times the sales of Motrin's competing tablets. If both Tylenol and Motrin spend the same percentage of sales (say 35 percent) on promotion, Tylenol will spend four times as much as its smaller competitor and will probably communicate to more people.

Firms that have differentiated their marketing mixes may favor mass selling because they have something to talk about. For instance, a firm with a strong brand may use reminder-type advertising or target frequent-buyer promotions at current customers to strengthen the relationship and keep customers loyal. This may be more effective than costly efforts to win customers away from competitors.

However, as a market drifts toward pure competition, some companies resort to price-cutting. This may temporarily increase the number of units sold, but it is also likely to reduce total revenue and the money available for promotion. The temporary sales gains disappear and prices are dragged down even lower when competitors retaliate with their own short-term sales promotions, like price-off coupons. As cash flowing into the business declines, spending may have to be cut back.[21]

Sales decline stage—"let's tell those who still want our product"

During the sales decline stage, the total amount spent on promotion usually decreases as firms try to cut costs to remain profitable. Since some people may still want the product, firms need more targeted promotion to reach these customers.

On the other hand, some firms may increase promotion to try to slow the cycle, at least temporarily. Crayola had almost all of the market for children's crayons, but sales were slowly declining as new kinds of markers came along. Crayola increased ad spending to urge parents to buy their kids a "fresh box."

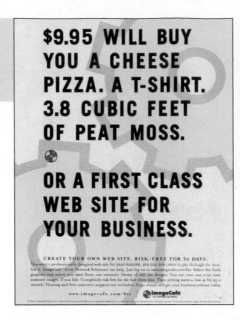

SETTING THE PROMOTION BUDGET

Size of budget affects promotion efficiency and blend

There are some economies of scale in promotion. An ad on national TV might cost less *per person* reached than an ad on local TV. Similarly, citywide radio, TV, and newspapers may be cheaper than neighborhood newspapers or direct personal contact. But the *total cost* for some mass media may force small firms, or those with small promotion budgets, to use promotion alternatives that are more expensive per contact. For example, a small retailer might want to use local television but find that there is only enough money for a web page, an ad in the Yellow Pages, and an occasional newspaper ad.

Find the task, budget for it

The most common method of budgeting for promotion expenditures is to compute a percentage of either past sales or sales expected in the future. The virtue of this method is its simplicity. However, just because this mechanical approach is common doesn't mean that it's smart. It leads to expanding marketing expenditures when business is good and cutting back when business is poor. When business is poor, this approach may just make the problem worse—if weak promotion is the reason for declining sales.

Other common methods of budgeting for marketing expenditures are

1. Match expenditures with competitors.
2. Set the budget as a certain number of cents or dollars per sales unit (by case, by thousand, or by ton) using the past year or estimated year ahead as a base.
3. Base the budget on any uncommitted revenue, perhaps including budgeted profits. Companies with limited resources may use this approach. Or a firm may be willing to sacrifice some or all of its current profits for future sales— that is, it looks at promotion spending as an *investment* in future growth.
4. Base the budget on the job to be done. For example, the spending level might be based on the number of new customers desired and the percentage of current customers that the firm must retain to leverage investments in already established relationships. This is called the **task method**—basing the budget on the job to be done.

400

Task method can lead to budgeting without agony

In the light of our continuing focus on planning marketing strategies to reach objectives, the most sensible approach to budgeting promotion expenditures is the task method. It helps you to set priorities so that the money you spend produces specific results. In fact, this approach makes sense for *any* marketing expenditure, but here we'll focus on promotion.

A practical approach is to determine which promotion objectives are most important and which promotion methods are most economical and effective for the communication tasks relevant to each objective. The costs of these tasks are then totaled—to determine how much should be budgeted for promotion (just as money is allocated for other marketing activities required by the strategy). In other words, the firm can assemble its total promotion budget directly from detailed plans rather than by simply relying on historical patterns or ratios.

This method also helps to eliminate budget fights between managers responsible for different promotion methods who see themselves as pitted against each other for limited budget dollars. The specialists may still make their own suggestions about how to perform tasks. But then the budget allocations are based on the most effective ways of getting things done, not on what the firm did last year, what some competitor does, or even on internal politics. With this approach, different promotion specialists are also more likely to recognize that they must all work together to achieve truly integrated marketing communications.[22]

CONCLUSION

Promotion is an important part of any marketing mix. Most consumers and intermediate customers can choose from among many products. To be successful, a producer must not only offer a good product at a reasonable price but also inform potential customers about the product and where they can buy it. Further, producers must tell wholesalers and retailers in the channel about their product and their marketing mix. These middlemen, in turn, must use promotion to reach their customers.

The promotion blend should fit logically into the strategy being developed to satisfy a particular target market. Strategy planning needs to state *what* should be communicated to the target market and *how*. The overall promotion objective is to affect buying behavior, but the basic promotion objectives are informing, persuading, and reminding.

Three basic promotion methods can be used to reach these objectives. Behavioral science findings can help firms combine various promotion methods for effective communication. In particular, what we know about the communication process and how individuals and groups adopt new products is important in planning promotion blends.

An action-oriented framework called AIDA can help marketing managers plan promotion blends. But the marketing manager has the final responsibility for combining the promotion methods into one integrated promotion blend for each marketing mix.

In this chapter, we considered some basic concepts that apply to all areas of promotion. In the next two chapters, we'll discuss personal selling, advertising, and sales promotion in more detail.

KEY TERMS

promotion, 378
personal selling, 379
mass selling, 379
advertising, 379
publicity, 379
sales promotion, 380

sales managers, 381
advertising managers, 382
public relations, 382
sales promotion managers, 382
integrated marketing communications, 382

AIDA model, 385
communication process, 386
source, 386
receiver, 386
noise, 386
encoding, 386

QUESTIONS AND PROBLEMS

1. Briefly explain the nature of the three basic promotion methods available to a marketing manager. What are the main strengths and limitations of each?

2. In your own words, discuss the integrated marketing communications concept. Explain what its emphasis on "consistent" and "complete" messages implies with respect to promotion blends.

3. Relate the three basic promotion objectives to the four jobs (AIDA) of promotion using a specific example.

4. Discuss the communication process in relation to a producer's promotion of an accessory product—say, a new electronic security system businesses use to limit access to areas where they store confidential records.

5. If a company wants its promotion to appeal to a new group of target customers in a foreign country, how can it protect against its communications being misinterpreted?

6. Promotion has been the target of considerable criticism. What specific types of promotion are probably the object of this criticism? Give a specific example that illustrates your thinking.

7. With direct-response promotion, customers provide feedback to marketing communications. How can a marketing manager use this feedback to improve the effectiveness of the overall promotion blend?

8. How can a promotion manager target a message to a certain target market with electronic media (like the Internet) when the customer initiates the communication? Give an example.

9. What promotion blend would be most appropriate for producers of the following established products? Assume average- to large-sized firms in each case and support your answer.
   a. Chocolate candy bar.
   b. Car batteries.
   c. Panty hose.
   d. Castings for truck engines.
   e. A special computer used by manufacturers for control of production equipment.
   f. Inexpensive plastic rainhats.
   g. A digital tape recorder that has achieved specialty-product status.

10. A small company has developed an innovative new spray-on glass cleaner that prevents the buildup of electrostatic dust on computer screens and TVs. Give examples of some low-cost ways the firm might effectively promote its product. Be certain to consider both push and pull approaches.

11. Would promotion be successful in expanding the general demand for: (a) almonds, (b) air travel, (c) golf clubs, (d) walking shoes, (e) high-octane unleaded gasoline, (f) single-serving, frozen gourmet dinners, and (g) bricks? Explain why or why not in each case.

12. Explain how an understanding of the adoption process would help you develop a promotion blend for digital tape recorders, a new consumer electronics product that produces high-quality recordings. Explain why you might change the promotion blend during the course of the adoption process.

13. Explain how opinion leaders affect a firm's promotion planning.

14. Discuss how the adoption curve should be used to plan the promotion blend(s) for a new automobile accessory—an electronic radar system that alerts a driver if he or she is about to change lanes into the path of a car that is passing through a blind spot in the driver's mirrors.

15. If a marketing manager uses the task method to budget for marketing promotions, are competitors' promotion spending levels ignored? Explain your thinking and give an example that supports your point of view.

16. Discuss the potential conflict among the various promotion managers. How could this be reduced?

SUGGESTED CASES

18. Village Bank

19. myWedding.com

COMPUTER-AIDED PROBLEM

14. Selecting a Communications Channel

RESOURCE REMINDER

Helen Troy, owner of three Sound Haus stereo equipment stores, is deciding what message channel (advertising medium) to use to promote her newest store. Her current promotion blend includes direct-mail ads that are effective for reaching her current customers. She also has knowledgeable salespeople who work well with consumers once they're in the store. However, a key objective in opening a new store is to attract new customers. Her best prospects are professionals in the 25–44 age range with incomes over $38,000 a year. But only some of the people in this group are audiophiles who want the top-of-the-line brands she carries. Troy has decided to use local advertising to reach new customers.

Troy narrowed her choice to two advertising media: an FM radio station and a biweekly magazine that focuses on entertainment in her city. Many of the magazine's readers are out-of-town visitors interested in concerts, plays, and restaurants. They usually buy stereo equipment at home. But the magazine's audience research shows that many local professionals do subscribe to the magazine. Troy doesn't think that the objective can be achieved with a single ad. However, she believes that ads in six issues will generate good local awareness with her target market. In addition, the magazine's color format will let her present the prestige image she wants to convey in an ad. She thinks that will help convert aware prospects to buyers. Specialists at a local advertising agency will prepare a high-impact ad for $2,000, and then Troy will pay for the magazine space.

The FM radio station targets an audience similar to Troy's own target market. She knows repeated ads will be needed to be sure that most of her target audience is exposed to her ads. Troy thinks it will take daily ads for

several months to create adequate awareness among her target market. The FM station will provide an announcer and prepare a tape of Troy's ad for a one-time fee of $200. All she has to do is tell the station what the message content for the ad should say.

Both the radio station and the magazine gave Troy reports summarizing recent audience research. She decides that comparing the two media in a spreadsheet will help her make a better decision.

a. Based on the data displayed on the initial spreadsheet, which message channel (advertising medium) would you recommend to Troy? Why?

b. The agency that offered to prepare Troy's magazine ad will prepare a fully produced radio ad—including a musical jingle—for $2,500. The agency claims that its musical ad will have much more impact than the ad the radio station will create. The agency says its ad should produce the same results as the station ad with 20 percent fewer insertions. If the agency claim is correct, would it be wise for Troy to pay the agency to produce the ad?

c. The agency will not guarantee that its custom-produced radio ad will reach Troy's objective—making 80 percent of the prospects aware of the new store. Troy wants to see how lower levels of awareness—between 50 percent and 70 percent—would affect the advertising cost per buyer and the cost per aware prospect. Use the analysis feature to vary the percent of prospects who become aware. Prepare a table showing the effect on the two kinds of costs. What are the implications of your analysis?

For additional questions related to this problem, see Exercise 14-3 in the *Learning Aid for Use with Basic Marketing*, 15th edition.

1. Understand the importance and nature of personal selling.

2. Know the three basic sales tasks and what the various kinds of salespeople can be expected to do.

3. Know how sales technology affects the way sales are performed.

4. Know what the sales manager must do—including selecting, training, and organizing salespeople—to carry out the personal selling job.

5. Understand how the right compensation plan can help motivate and control salespeople.

6. Understand when and where to use the three types of sales presentations.

7. Understand the important new terms (shown in red).

CHAPTER FIFTEEN

Personal Selling

In the go-go economy during the development of the Internet, flashy TV ads declared that Cisco Systems, Inc., was "empowering the Internet generation." Indeed, Cisco enjoyed breakneck growth by meeting the demand for all the backroom gear and systems that businesses, government agencies, schools, and other organizations needed to support their computer networks, websites, and e-commerce applications. Cisco's website (www.cisco.com) turbocharged the pace of e-commerce sales, and sales reps had their hands full just taking orders. But by 2001 that economy slumped and so did Cisco's growth. Some critics said that it was the end of Cisco. By 2004, however, Cisco was back in the groove with a profitable new strategy. Personal selling, by Cisco's own salespeople and by its distributors, played a crucial role in that strategy. Cisco's CEO made that clear when he explained the new strategy to the firm's huge sales force that had gathered for its annual sales meeting. After his motivating speech, he came out from behind the podium, moved to the front of the stage, and sincerely said "I think we're ready to grow again. I'm asking you to help me."

sionals specialize by industry and type of application, so they understand the problems these executives face and are able to sell them business solutions rather than "gear." Of course, the customers' IT departments may also get in the act—and they want to know about technical details ("Will Cisco's router work with our systems security software?"). Technical specialists from Cisco's local sales office handle some of these concerns as part of the sales team effort. And when a rep identifies a prospect that has the potential to become one of Cisco's premier accounts, Cisco's top brass, including experts like Sue Bostrom (shown here)

And help is what they've done. Cisco's salespeople handle the critical job of getting and keeping major accounts. They're working to get new orders from established customers that delayed major upgrades during the weak economy. They're also focusing on specific new target customers, including big telecom firms, that offer renewed opportunities for growth. Cisco's sales force is as central to that strategy as is Cisco's new technology for the telecom market. Decisions by customer firms to invest millions of dollars in information technology involve top management. Most of Cisco's sales profes-

who heads the Internet Business Solutions Group, helps cement a close relationship. Then when a relationship is established, Cisco provides top-notch after-the-sale support whenever a customer has a problem that can't be quickly handled online.

To be certain that these challenging jobs are done well, Cisco's sales managers recruit talented people using a wide variety of methods. For example, the careers@Cisco section of its website collects job applicant profiles on an ongoing basis. When a position opens up, qualified candidates—which often means those with knowledge of target customers' industries and not just IT skills—are notified. After the best people are selected, Cisco provides the sales training to make them even better. New people may need training to build professional problem-solving skills as well as technical knowledge. Even experienced sales reps need ongoing training. For example, Cisco gives its salespeople training in everything from the firm's new policies about entering customers into Cisco's database to the latest strategies for working with Cisco's specialized distributors—with training approaches ranging from traditional instructor-led workshops to cutting-edge e-learning opportunities.

Cisco's salespeople have an array of different skills and experience. And Cisco has customers and sales offices all over the world. So Cisco must carefully match each salesperson to particular territories, industries, customers, and product lines. And to be sure that each salesperson is highly motivated, Cisco's sales managers must make certain that sales compensation arrangements and benefits reward salespeople for producing needed results. For example, the new strategy includes bonus incentives for sales teams who earn high customer satisfaction ratings from the distributors in Cisco's channel.[1]

THE IMPORTANCE AND ROLE OF PERSONAL SELLING

Salespeople are communicators who build relationships

Promotion is communicating with potential customers. As the Cisco case suggests, personal selling is often the best way to do it. While face-to-face with prospects, salespeople can get more attention than an advertisement or a display. They can adjust what they say or do to the prospect's interests, needs, questions, and feedback. If, and when, the prospect is ready to buy, the salesperson is there to ask for the order. And afterward, the salesperson works to be certain that the customer is satisfied and will buy again in the future.

Personal selling requires strategy decisions

In this chapter, we'll discuss the importance and nature of personal selling so you'll understand the strategy decisions sales and marketing managers face. These strategy decisions are shown in Exhibit 15-1.

We'll also discuss a number of frameworks and how-to approaches that guide these strategy decisions. Because these approaches apply equally to domestic and international markets, we won't emphasize that distinction in this chapter. This does not mean, however, that personal selling techniques don't vary from one country to another. To the contrary, in dealing with *any* customer, the salesperson must adjust for cultural influences and other factors that might affect communication. For example, a Japanese customer and an Arab customer might respond differently

Exhibit 15-1   Strategy Planning for Personal Selling

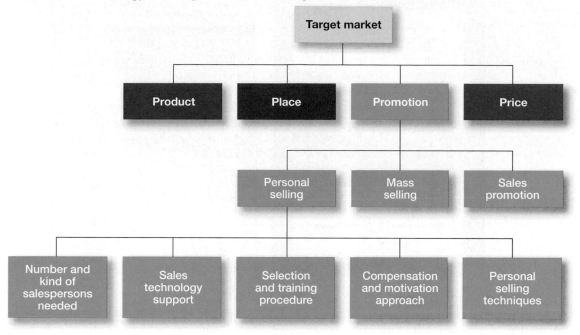

to subtle aspects of a salesperson's behavior. The Arab customer might expect to be very close to a salesperson, perhaps only two feet away, while they talk. The Japanese customer might consider that distance rude. Similarly, what topics of discussion are considered sensitive, how messages are interpreted, and which negotiating styles are used vary from one country to another. A salesperson must know how to communicate effectively with each customer—wherever and whoever that customer is.[2]

Personal selling is important

Personal selling is absolutely essential in the promotion blends of some firms. Consider how you would feel if you regularly had to meet payrolls and somehow, almost miraculously, your salespeople kept coming in with orders just in time to keep the business profitable.

Personal selling is often a company's largest single operating expense. This is another reason why it is important to understand sales management decisions. Bad ones are costly in both lost sales and in actual out-of-pocket expenses.

Every economy needs and uses many salespeople. In the United States, one person out of every ten in the total labor force is involved in sales work. By comparison, that's about 20 times more people than are employed in advertising. Any activity that employs so many people and is so important to the economy deserves study. Looking at what salespeople do is a good way to start.

Helping to buy is good selling

Good salespeople don't just try to *sell* the customer. Rather, they try to *help the customer buy*—by understanding the customer's needs and presenting the advantages and disadvantages of their products. Such helpfulness results in satisfied customers and long-term relationships. And strong relationships often form the basis for a competitive advantage, especially in business markets.

You may think in terms of an old-time stereotype of a salesperson: a bag of wind with no more to offer than a funny story, a big expense account, and an engaging grin. But that isn't true any more. Old-time salespeople are being replaced by real professionals—problem solvers—who have something definite to contribute to their employers *and* their customers.

Good salespeople try to help the customer solve problems and meet needs—and often that requires both careful listening to really understand the customer and then effective service after the sale.

IT'S OUR BUSINESS
TO KNOW YOUR SMALL BUSINESS.
WE LIVE WHERE YOU LIVE.™

LIKE A GOOD NEIGHBOR STATE FARM IS THERE.®

Some service and marketing types keep a low profile between orders.

SAUDER woodworking

Salespeople represent the whole company—and customers too

The salesperson is often a representative of the whole company—responsible for explaining its total effort to customers rather than just pushing products. The salesperson may provide information about products, explain company policies, and even negotiate prices or diagnose technical problems.

The sales rep is often the only link between the firm and its customers, especially if customers are far away. When a number of people from the firm work with the customer organization—which is common when suppliers and customers form close relationships—it is usually the sales rep who coordinates the relationship for his or her firm. See Exhibit 7-6.

The salesperson also represents the *customer* back inside the selling firm. Recall that feedback is an essential part of both the communication process *and* the basic management process of planning, implementing, and control. For example, it's likely to be the sales rep who explains to the production manager why a customer is unhappy with product quality or to the e-commerce specialist how better order status information available on the website could cut the customer's costs.

As evidence of these changing responsibilities, some companies give their salespeople such titles as account representative, field manager, sales consultant, market specialist, or sales engineer.

Sales force aids in market information function as well

The sales force can aid in the marketing information function too. The sales rep may be the first to hear about a new competitor or a competitor's new strategy. And sales reps who are well attuned to customers' needs can be a key source of ideas for new products or new uses for existing products.

Material Sciences Corporation developed a product called Quiet Steel, two thin layers of steel bonded together to absorb vibration so that it doesn't rattle. A sales rep who worked with the Ford team developing the new F-150 truck probed to understand where Ford was trying to reduce noise and recommended how Quiet Steel could help. Feedback to the company about the most promising applications helps Quiet Steel reps who call on other car makers pursue similar applications. And the R&D department for Quiet Steel benefits from hearing from the sales reps about applications where the current product isn't quite right, but where there might be an opportunity for a new product.[3]

Salespeople can be strategy planners too

Some salespeople are expected to be marketing managers in their own territories. And some become marketing managers by default because top management hasn't provided detailed strategy guidelines. Either way, the salesperson may have choices about (1) what target customers to aim at, (2) which particular products to emphasize, (3) which middlemen to rely on or help, (4) how to use promotion money, and (5) how to adjust prices. A salesperson who can put together profitable strategies and implement them well can rise very rapidly. The opportunity is there for those prepared and willing to work.[4]

WHAT KINDS OF PERSONAL SELLING ARE NEEDED?

If a firm has too few salespeople, or the wrong kind, some important personal selling tasks may not be completed. And having too many salespeople wastes money. In addition, the balance that is right may change over time with other changes in strategy or the market environment. That's why many firms have to restructure their sales forces.

One of the difficulties of determining the right number and kind of salespeople is that every sales job is different. While an engineer or accountant can look forward to fairly specific duties, the salesperson's job changes constantly. However, there are three basic types of sales tasks. This gives us a starting point for understanding what selling tasks need to be done and how many people are needed to do them.

Personal selling is divided into three tasks

The three **basic sales tasks** are order-getting, order-taking, and supporting. For convenience, we'll describe salespeople by these terms—referring to their primary task—*although one person may do all three tasks in some situations*.

ORDER GETTERS DEVELOP NEW BUSINESS RELATIONSHIPS

Order getters are concerned with establishing relationships with new customers and developing new business. **Order-getting** means seeking possible buyers with a well-organized sales presentation designed to sell a good, service, or idea.

Order getters must know what they're talking about, not just be personal contacts. Order-getting salespeople normally are well paid—many earn more than $80,000 a year.

Producers' order getters—find new opportunities

Producers of all kinds of products, especially business products, have a great need for order getters. They use order getters to locate new prospects, open new accounts, see new opportunities, and help establish and build channel relationships.

Top-level customers are more interested in ways to save or make more money than in technical details. Good order getters cater to this interest. They help the customer identify ways to solve problems; then they sell concepts and ideas, not just physical products. The goods and services they supply are merely the means of achieving the customer's end.

To be effective at this sort of "solutions selling," an order getter often needs to understand a customer's whole business as well as technical details about the product and its applications. For example, a salesperson for automated manufacturing equipment must understand a prospect's production process as well as the technical details of converting to computer-controlled equipment.

Order getters for professional services—and other products where service is a crucial element of the marketing mix—face a special challenge. The customer usually can't inspect a service before deciding to buy. The order getter's communication and

Customers who are making an important purchase want relationships with salespeople whose advice they can trust.

relationship with the customer may be the only basis on which to evaluate the quality of the supplier.

Wholesalers' order getters—almost hand it to the customer

Agent middlemen often are order getters—particularly the more aggressive manufacturers' agents and brokers. They face the same tasks as producers' order getters. But, unfortunately for them, once the order-getting is done and the customers become established and loyal, producers may try to eliminate the agents and save money with their own order takers.

Producers sometimes aid in the personal selling effort by providing innovative displays that communicate not only the features but also the benefits of their products. To help salespeople explain the benefits of its new Profile washer and dryer, GE places this interactive display in dealers' stores.

Progressive merchant wholesaler sales reps should be consultants and store advisors rather than just order takers. Such order getters become retailers' partners in the job of moving goods from the wholesale warehouse through the retail store to consumers. These order getters almost become a part of the retailer's staff—helping to solve consumers' problems, train employees, conduct demonstrations, and plan advertising, special promotions, and other retailing activities.

Retail order getters influence consumer behavior

Convincing consumers about the value of products they haven't seriously considered takes a high level of personal selling ability. Order getters for unsought consumer products must help customers see how a new product can satisfy needs now being filled by something else. Without order getters, many common products—ranging from mutual funds to air conditioners—might have died in the market introduction stage. The order getter helps bring products out of the introduction stage into the market growth stage.

Order getters are also helpful for selling *heterogeneous* shopping products. Consumers shop for many of these items on the basis of suitability and value. They welcome useful information.

ORDER TAKERS NURTURE RELATIONSHIPS TO KEEP THE BUSINESS COMING

Order takers sell to the regular or established customers, complete most sales transactions, and maintain relationships with their customers. After a customer becomes interested in a firm's products through an order getter or supporting salesperson or through advertising or sales promotion, an order taker usually answers any final questions and completes the sale. **Order-taking** is the routine completion of sales made regularly to target customers. It usually requires ongoing follow-up to make certain that the customer is totally satisfied.

Friendly and capable retail order takers can play an important role in building good relations with customers.

Producers' order takers—train, explain, and collaborate	Order takers work on improving the whole relationship with their accounts, not just on completing a single sale. Even in e-commerce, where customers place routine orders with computerized order systems and EDI, order takers do a variety of important jobs that are essential to the business relationship. Someone has to explain details, make adjustments, handle complaints, explain new prices or terms, place sales promotion materials, and keep customers informed of new developments. An order taker who fails to meet a customer's expectations on any of these activities might jeopardize the relationship and future sales.

Producers' order takers often have a regular route with many calls. To handle these calls well, they must have energy, persistence, and a friendly personality that wears well over time. They sometimes have to take the heat when something goes wrong with some other element of the marketing mix.

Firms sometimes use order-taking jobs to train potential order getters and managers. Such jobs give them an opportunity to meet customers and better understand their needs. And frequently, they run into some order-getting opportunities.

Order takers who are alert to order-getting possibilities can make the big difference in generating new sales. Some firms lose sales just because no one ever asks for the order. Banks try to avoid this problem. For example, when a customer walks into a Bank of America branch to make a deposit, the teller's computer screen shows information about the customer's accounts. If the balance in a checking account is high but the customer does not use any of the bank's other investment services, the teller is trained to ask if the customer would be interested in learning about the bank's certificates of deposit. Some firms use more sophisticated customer relationship management (CRM) database systems that figure out which specific financial service would be best for the teller to recommend.[5]

Wholesalers' order takers—not getting orders but keeping them

While producers' order takers usually handle relatively few items, wholesalers' order takers often sell thousands of items. Sales reps who handle that many items may single out a few of the newer or more profitable items for special attention, but it's not possible to give aggressive sales effort to many. So the main job of wholesalers' order takers is to maintain close contact with customers, place orders, and check to be sure the company fills orders promptly. Order takers also handle any adjustments or complaints and generally act as liaisons between the company and its customers.

Retail order takers—often they are poor salesclerks

Order-taking may be almost mechanical at the retail level—for example, at the supermarket checkout counter. Some retail clerks perform poorly because they aren't paid much—often only the minimum wage. Even so, retail order takers play a vital role in a retailer's marketing mix. Customers expect prompt and friendly service. They will find a new place to shop, or to do their banking or have their car serviced, rather than deal with a salesclerk who is rude or acts annoyed by having to complete a sale.

SUPPORTING SALES FORCE INFORMS AND PROMOTES IN THE CHANNEL

Supporting salespeople help the order-oriented salespeople—but they don't try to get orders themselves. Their activities are aimed at enhancing the relationship with the customer and getting sales in the long run. For the short run, however, they are ambassadors of goodwill who may provide specialized services and information. Almost all supporting salespeople work for producers or middlemen who do this supporting work for producers. There are two types of supporting salespeople: missionary salespeople and technical specialists.

Missionary salespeople can increase sales

Missionary salespeople are supporting salespeople who work for producers—calling on their middlemen and their customers. They try to develop goodwill and stimulate demand, help the middlemen train their salespeople, and often take orders for delivery by the middlemen. Missionary salespeople are sometimes called *merchandisers* or *detailers*.

Producers who rely on merchant wholesalers or e-commerce to obtain widespread distribution often use missionary salespeople. The sales rep can give a promotion boost to a product that otherwise wouldn't get much attention because it's just one of many. A missionary salesperson for Vicks' cold remedy products, for example, might visit druggists during the cold season and encourage them to use a special end-of-aisle display for Vicks' cough syrup—and then help set it up. The wholesaler that supplies the drugstore would benefit from any increased sales, but might not take the time to urge use of the special display.

An imaginative missionary salesperson can double or triple sales. Naturally, this doesn't go unnoticed. Missionary sales jobs are often a route to order-oriented jobs.

Technical specialists are experts who know product applications

Technical specialists are supporting salespeople who provide technical assistance to order-oriented salespeople. Technical specialists are often science or engineering graduates with the know-how to understand the customer's applications and explain the advantages of the company's product. They are usually more skilled in showing the technical details of their product than in trying to persuade customers to buy it. Before the specialist's visit, an order getter probably has stimulated interest. The technical specialist provides the details.

Three tasks may have to be blended

We have described three sales tasks—order-getting, order-taking, and supporting. However, a particular salesperson might be given two, or all three, of these tasks. Ten percent of a particular job may be order-getting, 80 percent order-taking, and the additional 10 percent supporting. Another company might have many different people handling the different sales tasks. This can lead to **team selling**—when different people work together on a specific account. Sometimes members of a sales

The Clorox sales team responsible for the launch of liquid bleach in the Brazilian market drew on people from R&D, marketing, and sales.

team are not from the sales department at all. If improving the relationship with the customer calls for inputs from the quality control manager, then that person becomes a part of the team, at least temporarily.

Producers of high-ticket items often use team selling. AT&T uses team selling to sell office communications systems for a whole business. Different specialists handle different parts of the job—but the whole team coordinates its efforts to achieve the desired result.[6]

THE RIGHT STRUCTURE HELPS ASSIGN RESPONSIBILITY

A sales manager must organize the sales force so that all the necessary tasks are done well. A large organization might have different salespeople specializing by different selling tasks *and* by the target markets they serve.

Different target markets need different selling tasks

Sales managers often divide sales force responsibilities based on the type of customer involved. For example, Bigelow—a company that makes quality carpet for homes and office buildings—divided its sales force into two groups of specialists. Some Bigelow salespeople call only on architects to help them choose the best type of carpet for new office buildings. These reps know all the technical details, such as how well a certain carpet fiber will wear or its effectiveness in reducing noise from office equipment. Often no selling is involved because the architect only suggests specifications and doesn't actually buy the carpet.

Other Bigelow salespeople call on retail carpet stores. These reps encourage the store manager to keep a variety of Bigelow carpets in stock. They also introduce new products, help train the store's salespeople, and try to solve any problems that occur.

Big accounts get special treatment

Very large customers often require special selling effort—and relationships with them are treated differently. Moen, a maker of plumbing fixtures, has a regular sales force to call on building material wholesalers and an elite **major accounts sales force** that sells directly to large accounts—like Lowe's or other major retail chains that carry plumbing fixtures.

You can see why this sort of special attention is justified when you consider Procter & Gamble's relationship with Wal-Mart. Wal-Mart accounts for one-fourth or more of the total national sales in many of the product categories in which P&G competes. For instance, Wal-Mart sells about one-third of the toothpaste in the U.S. If P&G wants to grow its 23 percent share of the toothpaste market, it has to make certain that it stimulates an effective sales effort with Wal-Mart. It's understandable why the P&G sales team that calls on Wal-Mart lives in Bentonville, Arkansas, where Wal-Mart is based.[7]

Some salespeople specialize in telephone selling

Some firms have a group of salespeople who specialize in **telemarketing**—using the telephone to "call" on customers or prospects. In Chapter 14, we highlighted the consumer backlash to the use of "cold call" telemarketing for prospecting. However, the reception to telemarketing in business markets is often quite different.

In business markets, a telemarketing sales force can often build profitable relationships with small or hard-to-reach customers the firm might otherwise have to ignore. Telemarketing is also used to extend personal selling efforts to new target markets or increase the frequency of contact with current customers. The big advantage of telemarketing in these situations is that it saves time and money for the seller, and it gives customers a fast and easy way to solve a purchasing problem. For example, many firms use toll-free telephone lines to make it convenient for customers to call the telemarketing sales force for assistance or to place an order. Firms also rely heavily on telemarketing to provide support a customer may need in an e-commerce situation.[8]

Telemarketing is an economical way to contact consumers that are small. Allegheny Power uses telemarketing to identify prospects and reach small customers.

Sales tasks are done in sales territories

Often companies organize selling tasks on the basis of a **sales territory**—a geographic area that is the responsibility of one salesperson or several working together. A territory might be a region of a country, a state, or part of a city, depending on the market potential. An airplane manufacturer like Boeing might consider a whole country as *part* of a sales territory for one salesperson.

Carefully set territories can reduce travel time and the cost of sales calls. Assigning territories can also help reduce confusion about who has responsibility for a set of selling tasks. Consider the Hyatt Hotel chain. A few years ago, each hotel had its own salespeople to get bookings for big conferences and business meetings. That meant that people who had responsibility for selecting meeting locations might be called on by sales reps from 20 or 30 different Hyatt hotels. Now, the Hyatt central office divides up responsibility for working with specific accounts; one rep calls on an account and then tries to sell space in the Hyatt facility that best meets the customer's needs.

Sometimes simple geographic division isn't easy. A company may have different products that require very different knowledge or selling skills—even if products sell in the same territory or to the same customer. For example, Du Pont makes special films for hospital X-ray departments as well as chemicals used in laboratory blood tests.

Size of sales force depends on workload

Once the important selling tasks are specified and the responsibilities divided, the sales manager must decide how many salespeople are needed. The first step is estimating how much work can be done by one person in some time period. Then the sales manager can make an educated guess about how many people are required in total, as the following example shows.

For many years, the Parker Jewelry Company was very successful selling its silver jewelry to department and jewelry stores in the southwestern region of the United States. But top managers wanted to expand into the big urban markets in the northeastern states. They realized that most of the work for the first few years would require order getters. They felt that a salesperson would need to call on each account at least once a month to get a share of this competitive business. They estimated that a salesperson could make only five calls a day on prospective buyers and still allow time for travel, waiting, and follow-up on orders that came in. This meant that a sales rep who made calls 20 days a month could handle about 100 stores (5 a day × 20 days).

Exhibit 15-2
Examples of Possible
Personal Selling Emphasis in
Some Different Business-
Market Selling Situations

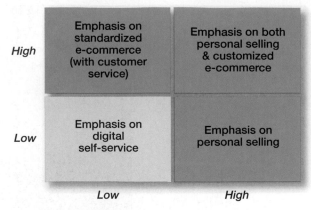

Standardized information
exchanged on a recurring basis
(orders, invoices, delivery status,
product information, prices)

Relationship building required
(problem solving, coordination, support, cooperation)

The managers used a CD-ROM database that included all of the telephone Yellow Pages listings for the country. Then they simply divided the total number of stores by 100 to estimate the number of salespeople needed. This also helped them set up territories—by defining areas that included about 100 stores for each salesperson. Obviously, managers might want to fine tune this estimate for differences in territories—such as travel time. But the basic approach can be adapted to many different situations.[9]

Some managers forget that over time the right number of salespeople may change as selling tasks change. Then when a problem becomes obvious, they try to change everything in a hurry—a big mistake. Consideration of what type of salespeople and how many should be ongoing. If the sales force needs to be reduced, it doesn't make sense to let a lot of people go all at once, especially when that could be avoided with some planning.

E-commerce sometimes substitutes for personal selling

Some tasks that have traditionally been handled by a salesperson can now be handled effectively and at lower cost by e-commerce systems. The nature of the selling situation that the firm faces may influence which approach makes the most sense and how many salespeople are really needed. See Exhibit 15-2.

A salesperson is required in important selling situations where there is a need to create and build relationships. Here the salesperson focuses on tasks like creative problem solving, persuading, coordinating among people who do different jobs, and finding ways to support the customer. On the other hand, information technology is cost effective for handling needs related to the recurring exchange of standardized information (such as inventory, orders, and delivery status). Similarly, details of product specifications and prices can be organized at a website. Of course, there should be some way to provide good customer service when needs arise. In a complex relationship, using technology for standard information frees the sales rep to spend time on value-added communication.

When relationship building by a sales rep is not required and there is not a recurring need for routine information, a firm may be able to meet customer needs best by providing digital self-service. This is basically the role of ATMs for banks—to service customers who don't want to wait until a teller is available. Similarly, Amazon's virtual shopping carts play this role. But digital self-service can be more sophisticated. Some firms provide "intelligent agents" at their websites. An intelligent agent is a computer program that helps customers solve their own problems. At the CompUSA website, a customer who wants to buy a notebook computer can respond to a series of structured questions about how the computer will be used, and the intelligent agent recommends which features are most important and what brands have those features.

SALESPEOPLE WORK SMARTER —WITH THEIR FINGERTIPS

Tablet PCs, PDAs, and laptops help more salespeople work smarter, not just harder. Salespeople use computers in many different ways.

Without a laptop, it was impossible for a wholesaler's salespeople to master Cincinnati Milacron's product line. Now a computer asks a series of questions and then helps the salesperson figure out which of 65,000 grinding wheels and hundreds of cutting fluids to sell to each metal shop. After adding this system, Milacron doubled its market share—without adding any new salespeople.

Sales reps for Crown Beer Distributors found that laptops were too bulky to take with them when they called on accounts along their routes. However, a handheld tablet PC was just right for the task. The sales reps enter inventory data and orders right into the tablet. The screen is small, but they can instantly pull up whatever information a customer may want to see. With everything at their fingertips, some salespeople save an hour each day—and in the process handle required administrative reporting without it becoming tedious. As the president of the firm noted, "When you start to multiply that out for distributors with 20 or 30 salespeople, that's a significant amount of savings."

Salespeople for Metropolitan Life Insurance company use laptops to help customers analyze the financial implications of different investments. For example, when the manager of a pension fund wanted to see what would happen if she switched money from one investment to another, the salesperson used spreadsheet software on the laptop to do the analysis—on the spot. The customer was convinced, and the sales rep closed a $633,000 sale.

Herman Miller, the office equipment company, provides dealers who sell its furniture with software that allows their sales reps to do a better job in a variety of tasks ranging from competitor analysis to preparation of realistic three-dimensional graphics that show an arrangement of furniture in a customer's office space. The competitor database provides very useful information about the limitations of office furniture available from many other firms. For instance, a sales rep learned that a prospect was leaning toward buying a competitor's office cubicles. She got back on track when the database revealed that the cubicles had no electrical outlets.

Results like these explain why the number of companies equipping salespeople with computers is growing so rapidly. New computers that feature built-in DVD drives (to handle massive amounts of information, including full-motion video for demonstrations and presentations), wireless Internet access, and the power to handle e-commerce applications are attracting even more attention. Further, web-enabled PDAs and cell phones now offer capabilities once reserved only for computers, providing a link to company databases and all the resources of the Internet.[10]

Similarly, a wholesaler's website might provide an agent to help retailers forecast demand for a new product based on information about their local market areas.

The total amount of personal selling effort justified in any of these situations may depend on other factors, including how important the customer is. Further, we've focused on technology that substitutes for personal contact by a salesperson. But marketing managers also need to make decisions about providing sales technology support to help salespeople communicate more effectively.

INFORMATION TECHNOLOGY PROVIDES TOOLS TO DO THE JOB

Changes in how sales tasks are handled

How sales tasks and responsibilities are planned and handled is changing in many companies because of the new sales technology tools that are available. It is usually the sales manager's job—perhaps with help from specialists in technology—to decide what types of tools are needed and how they will be used.

To get a sense of what is involved, consider a day in the life of a sales rep for a large consumer packaged goods firm. Over a hasty breakfast, she plans the day's sales

Information technology is making the modern sales force more efficient and giving salespeople new ways to meet the needs of their customers while achieving the objectives of their jobs.

calls on her laptop's organizer, logs onto the company network, and sorts through a dozen e-mail messages she finds there. One is from a buyer for a supermarket chain. Sales in the chain's paper towel category are off 10 percent, and he wants to know if the rep can help. The rep downloads sales trend data for the chain and its competitors from her firm's intranet. A spreadsheet analysis of the data reveals that the sales decline is due to new competition from warehouse clubs. After a conference call with a brand manager and a company sales promotion specialist to seek advice, she prepares a PowerPoint presentation, complete with a proposed shelf-space plan, that recommends that the buyer promote larger size packages of both her company's and competitors' brands. Before leaving home, the rep e-mails an advance copy of the report to the buyer and her manager. In her car, she calls the buyer to schedule an appointment.

New software and hardware provide a competitive advantage

As in the example given above, sales reps today rely on support from an array of software and hardware that was hardly imaginable even a decade ago. Software for spreadsheet sales analysis, digital presentations, time management, sales forecasting, customer contact, and shelf-space management is at the salesperson's fingertips. Commonplace hardware includes everything from PDAs with wireless Internet access to personal videoconferencing systems. In many situations, these technologies give sales reps new ways to meet customers' needs while achieving the objectives of their jobs.

The basic sales tasks are not different, but the tools change how well the job is done. Yet this is not simply a matter that is best left to individual sales reps. Use of these tools may be necessary just to compete effectively. For example, if a customer expects a sales rep to access data on past sales and provide an updated sales forecast, a sales organization that does not have this capability will be at a real disadvantage in keeping that customer's business.

On the other hand, these tools have costs. There is an obvious expense of buying the technology. But there is also the training cost of keeping everyone up-to-date. Often that is not a simple matter. Some salespeople who have done the sales job well for a long time "the old-fashioned way" resent being told that they have to change what they are doing, even if it's what customers expect. So if a firm expects salespeople to be able to use these technologies, that requirement needs to be included in selecting and training people for the job.[11]

Customers who rent heavy construction equipment want to deal with a knowledgeable salesperson. So Cat selects salespeople who have experience with the applications for which the equipment will be used and gives them training on Cat products and new developments in the market.

SOUND SELECTION AND TRAINING TO BUILD A SALES FORCE

Selecting good salespeople takes judgment, plus

It is important to hire *well-qualified* salespeople who will do a good job. But selection in many companies is done without serious thought about exactly what kind of person the firm needs. Managers may hire friends and relations, or whoever is available, because they feel that the only qualifications for sales jobs are a friendly personality. This approach leads to poor sales and costly sales force turnover.

Progressive companies are more careful. They constantly update a list of possible job candidates. They invite applications at the company's website. They schedule candidates for multiple interviews with various executives and do thorough background checks. Unfortunately, such techniques don't guarantee success. But a systematic approach based on several different inputs results in a better sales force.

One problem in selecting salespeople is that two different sales jobs with identical titles may involve very different selling tasks and require different skills. A carefully prepared job description helps avoid this problem.

Job descriptions should be in writing and specific

A **job description** is a written statement of what a salesperson is expected to do. It might list 10 to 20 specific tasks—as well as routine prospecting and sales report writing. Each company must write its own job specifications. And it should provide clear guidelines about what selling tasks the job involves. This is critical to determine the kind of salespeople who should be selected—and later it provides a basis for seeing how they should be trained, how well they are performing, and how they should be paid.

Good salespeople are trained, not born

The idea that good salespeople are born may have some truth—but it isn't the whole story. A salesperson needs to be taught about the company and its products, about giving effective sales presentations, and about building relationships with customers. But this isn't always done. Many salespeople do a poor job because they haven't had good training. Firms often hire new salespeople and immediately send them out on the road, or the retail selling floor, with no grounding in the basic selling steps and no information about the product or the customer. They just get a price list and a pat on the back. This isn't enough!

All salespeople need some training

It's up to sales and marketing management to be sure that salespeople know what they're supposed to do and how to do it. Hewlett-Packard Co. recently faced this problem. For years the company was organized into divisions based on different product lines—printers, networks servers, and the like. However, sales reps who specialized in the products of one division often couldn't compete well against firms that could offer customers total solutions to computing problems. When a new top executive came in and reorganized the company, all sales reps needed training in their new responsibilities, how they would be organized, and what they should say to their customers about the benefits of the reorganization.[12]

Sales training should be modified based on the experience and skills of the group involved. But the company's sales training program should cover at least the following areas: (1) company policies and practices, (2) product information, (3) building relationships with customer firms, and (4) professional selling skills.

Selling skills can be learned

Many companies spend the bulk of their training time on product information and company policy. They neglect training in selling techniques because they think selling is something anyone can do. But training in selling skills can pay off. Estée Lauder, for example, has selling skills for the "beauty advisors" who sell its cosmetics down to a fine art—and its training manual and seminars cover every detail. Its advisors who take the training seriously immediately double their sales.[13] Training can also help salespeople learn how to be more effective in cold calls on new prospects, in listening carefully to identify a customer's real objections, and in closing the sale.

INTERNET EXERCISE

The Motivating Tape Company sells various sales training videos. Go to the firm's website (www.achievement.com) and then scroll down and select *Sales Training Videos*. Review the list of sales training videos offered. If a sales manager were going to rely on some of these tapes for training people just moving into a sales career, what key areas of sales training would he have to cover by some other approach?

Training on selling techniques often starts in the classroom with lectures, case studies, and videotaped trial presentations and demonstrations. But a complete training program adds on-the-job observation of effective salespeople and coaching from sales supervisors. Many companies also use web-based training, weekly sales meetings or work sessions, annual conventions, and regular e-mail messages and newsletters, as well as ongoing training sessions, to keep salespeople up-to-date.[14]

COMPENSATING AND MOTIVATING SALESPEOPLE

To recruit, motivate, and keep good salespeople, a firm has to develop an effective compensation plan. Ideally, sales reps should be paid in such a way that what they want to do—for personal interest and gain—is in the company's interest too. Most companies focus on financial motivation—but public recognition, sales contests, and simple personal recognition for a job well done can be highly effective in encouraging greater sales effort.[15] Our main emphasis here, however, will be on financial motivation.[16]

Two basic decisions must be made in developing a compensation plan: (1) the level of compensation and (2) the method of payment.

Compensation varies with job and needed skills

To build a competitive sales force, a company must pay at least the going market wage for different kinds of salespeople. To be sure it can afford a specific type of salesperson, the company should estimate—when the job description is written—how valuable such a salesperson will be. A good order getter may be worth $50,000 to $100,000 to one company but only $15,000 to $25,000 to another—just because the second firm doesn't have enough to sell! In such a case, the second company should rethink its job specifications, or completely change its promotion plans, because the going rate for order getters is much higher than $15,000 a year.

If a job requires extensive travel, aggressive pioneering, or contacts with difficult customers, the pay may have to be higher. But the salesperson's compensation level should compare, at least roughly, with the pay scale of the rest of the firm. Normally, salespeople earn more than the office or production force but less than top management.

Payment methods vary

Given some competitive level of compensation, there are three basic methods of payment: (1) *straight salary,* (2) *straight commission,* or (3) a *combination plan.* Straight salary normally supplies the most security for the salesperson—and straight commission, the most incentive. Most companies want to offer their salespeople some balance between incentive and security, so the most popular method is a combination plan that includes some salary and some commission. Bonuses, profit sharing, pensions, stock plans, insurance, and other fringe benefits may be included too.

Salary gives control—if there is close supervision

A salesperson on straight salary earns the same amount regardless of how he or she spends time. So the salaried salesperson is expected to do what the sales manager asks—whether it is order-taking, supporting sales activities, solving customer problems, or completing sales call reports. However, the sales manager maintains control *only* by close supervision. As a result, straight salary or a large salary element in the compensation plan increases the amount of sales supervision needed.

Commissions can both motivate and direct

If personal supervision would be difficult, a firm may get better control with a compensation plan that includes some commission, or even a straight commission plan, with built-in direction. One trucking company, for example, has a sales incentive plan that pays higher commissions on business needed to balance freight shipments—depending on how heavily traffic has been moving in one direction or another. Another company that wants to motivate its salespeople to devote more time to developing new accounts could pay higher commissions on shipments to a new customer. However, a salesperson on a straight commission tends to be his or her own boss. The sales manager is less likely to get help on sales activities that won't increase the salesperson's earnings.

An incentive compensation plan can help motivate salespeople, but incentives must be carefully aligned with the firm's objectives. For example, IBM at one time had a sales commission plan that resulted in IBM salespeople pushing customers to buy expensive computers that were more powerful than they needed. The sales reps got sales and increased their income, but later many customers were dissatisfied and switched to other suppliers. Now most IBM sales reps receive incentive pay that is in part based on satisfaction ratings they earn from their customers. Many firms use variations of this approach—because incentives that just focus on short-term sales objectives may not motivate sales reps to develop long-term, need-satisfying relationships with their customers.

Incentives should link efforts to results

The incentive portion of a sales rep's compensation should be large only if there is a direct relationship between the salesperson's effort and results. Otherwise, a salesperson in a growing territory might have rapidly increasing earnings, while the

Exhibit 15-3
Relation between Personal
Selling Expenses and Sales
Volume—for Three Basic
Personal Selling
Compensation Alternatives

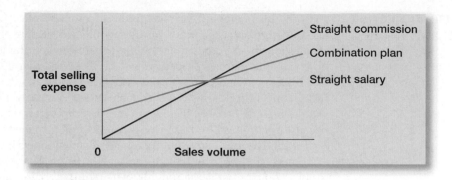

sales rep in a poor area will have little to show for the same amount of work. Such a situation isn't fair, and it can lead to high turnover and much dissatisfaction. A sales manager can take such differences into consideration when setting a salesperson's **sales quota**—the specific sales or profit objective a salesperson is expected to achieve.

Sometimes it is difficult to make such adjustments. For example, the relationship between a salesperson's efforts and sales results is less direct if a number of other people—engineers, top management, or supporting salespeople—are involved in the sale. In this case, each one's contribution is less obvious, and greater emphasis on salary may make more sense.

Commissions reduce need for working capital

Small companies that have limited working capital or uncertain markets often prefer straight commission, or combination plans with a large commission element. When sales drop off, costs do too. Such flexibility is similar to using manufacturers' agents who get paid only if they deliver sales. This advantage often dominates in selecting a sales compensation method. Exhibit 15-3 shows the general relation between personal selling expense and sales volume for each of the basic compensation alternatives.

Compensation plans should be clear

Salespeople are likely to be dissatisfied if they can't see the relationship between the results they produce and their pay. A compensation plan that includes different commissions for different products or types of customers can become quite complicated. Simplicity is best achieved with straight salary. But in practice, it's usually better to sacrifice some simplicity to gain some incentive, flexibility, and control. The best combination of these factors depends on the job description and the company's objectives.

To make it easier for a sales rep to see the relationship between effort and compensation, some firms provide the rep with that information online. For example, Oracle, a company that sells database systems, developed a system that allows sales reps, at any point, to check a website and see how they are doing. As new sales results come in, the report at the website is updated. Sales managers can also make changes quickly—for example, by putting a higher commission on a product or more weight on customer satisfaction scores. Other firms use the same idea but just give their sales reps a spreadsheet so that they can keep their own information up-to-date.[17]

Sales managers must plan, implement, and control

Managers must regularly evaluate each salesperson's performance and be certain that all the needed tasks are being done well. The compensation plan may have to be changed if the pay and work are out of line. And by evaluating performance, firms can also identify areas that need more attention—by the salesperson or management.[18] In Chapter 19, we'll talk more about controlling marketing activities.

Exhibit 15-4
Key Steps in the Personal
Selling Process

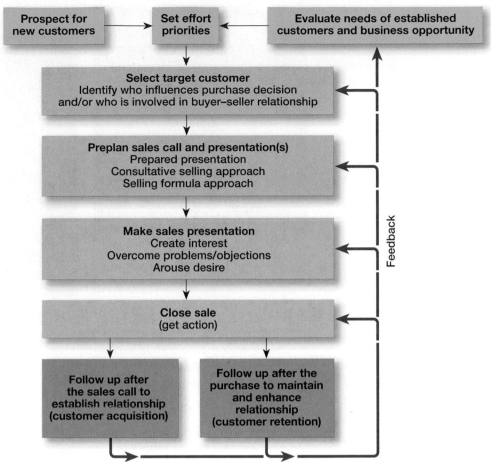

PERSONAL SELLING TECHNIQUES—PROSPECTING AND PRESENTING

We've stressed the importance of training in selling techniques. Now let's discuss these ideas in more detail so you understand the basic steps each salesperson should follow—including prospecting and selecting target customers, planning sales presentations, making sales presentations, and following up after the sale. Exhibit 15-4 shows the steps we'll consider. You can see that the salesperson is just carrying out a planned communication process, as we discussed in Chapter 14.[19]

**Prospecting—
narrowing down to
the right target**

Narrowing the personal selling effort down to the right target requires constant, detailed analysis of markets and much prospecting. Basically, **prospecting** involves following all the leads in the target market to identify potential customers.

Finding live prospects who will help make the buying decision isn't as easy as it sounds. In business markets, for example, the salesperson may need to do some hard detective work to find the real purchase decision makers.

Some companies provide prospect lists or a customer relationship management (CRM) database to make this part of the selling job easier. Inquiries that come in at the firm's website, for example, can be passed along to a sales rep for follow up. A more indirect approach may be required. For example, one insurance company checks the local newspaper for marriage announcements—then a salesperson calls to see if the new couple is interested in finding out more about life insurance.

All customers are not equal

While prospecting focuses on identifying new customers, established customers require attention too. It's often time-consuming and expensive to establish a relationship with a customer, so once established it makes sense to keep the relationship healthy. That requires the rep to routinely review active accounts, rethink customers' needs, and reevaluate each customer's long-term business potential. Some small accounts may have the potential to become big accounts, and some accounts that previously required a lot of costly attention may no longer warrant it. So a sales rep may need to set priorities both for new prospects and existing customers.

INTERNET EXERCISE

Best Software sells various software products, including ACT! personal management software that is used by many salespeople to organize information about their customers, sales calls, and tasks they need to do. Visit the ACT! website (www.act.com) for information about this product. Give a few specific examples of ways that a salesperson could use ACT! to build better relationships with customers.

How long to spend with whom?

Once a set of prospects and customers who need attention have been identified, the salesperson must decide how much time to spend with each one. A sales rep must qualify customers—to see if they deserve more effort. The salesperson usually makes these decisions by weighing the potential sales volume as well as the likelihood of a sale. This requires judgment. But well-organized salespeople usually develop some system because they have too many demands on their time.[20]

Many firms provide their reps with computer programs to help with this process. Most of them use some grading scheme. A sales rep might estimate how much each prospect is likely to purchase and the probability of getting and keeping the business given the competition. The computer then combines this information and grades each prospect. Attractive accounts may be labeled A—and the salesperson may plan to call on them weekly until the sale is made, the relationship is in good shape, or the customer is moved into a lower category. B customers might offer somewhat lower potential and be called on monthly. C accounts might be called on only once a year—unless they happen to contact the salesperson. And D accounts might be transferred to a telemarketing group.[21]

Three kinds of sales presentations may be useful

Once the salesperson selects a target customer, it's necessary to make a **sales presentation**—a salesperson's effort to make a sale or address a customer's problem. But someone has to plan what kind of sales presentation to make. This is a strategy decision. The kind of presentation should be set before the sales rep goes calling. And in situations where the customer comes to the salesperson—in a retail store, for instance—planners have to make sure that prospects are brought together with salespeople.

A marketing manager can choose two basically different approaches to making sales presentations: the prepared approach or the consultative selling approach. Another approach, the selling formula approach, is a combination of the two. Each of these has its place.

The prepared sales presentation

The **prepared sales presentation** approach uses a memorized presentation that is not adapted to each individual customer. This approach says that a customer faced with a particular stimulus will give the desired response—in this case, a yes answer to the salesperson's prepared statement, which includes a **close,** the salesperson's request for an order.

If one trial close doesn't work, the sales rep tries another prepared presentation and attempts another closing. This can go on for some time—until the salesperson runs out of material or the customer either buys or decides to leave. Exhibit 15-5 shows the relative participation of the salesperson and customer in the prepared approach. Note that the salesperson does most of the talking.

Firms may rely on this canned approach when only a short presentation is practical. It's also sensible when salespeople aren't very skilled. The company can control what they say and in what order. For example, Novartis uses missionary salespeople to tell doctors about new drugs when they're introduced. Doctors are busy, so they only give the rep a minute or two. That's just enough time to give a short, prepared pitch and leave some samples. To get the most out of the presentation, Novartis refines it based on feedback from doctors whom it pays to participate in focus groups.[22]

But a canned approach has a weakness. It treats all potential customers alike. It may work for some and not for others. A prepared approach may be suitable for simple order-taking—but it is no longer considered good selling for complicated situations.

Consultative selling—builds on the marketing concept

The **consultative selling approach** involves developing a good understanding of the individual customer's needs before trying to close the sale. This name is used because the salesperson is almost acting as a consultant to help identify and solve the customer's problem. With this approach, the sales rep makes some general benefit statements to get the customer's attention and interest. Then the salesperson asks questions and *listens carefully* to understand the customer's needs. Once they agree on needs, the seller tries to show the customer how the product fills those needs and to close the sale. This is a problem-solving approach—in which the customer and salesperson work together to satisfy the customer's needs. That's why it's sometimes called the need-satisfaction approach. Exhibit 15-6 shows the participation of the customer and the salesperson during such a sales presentation.

The consultative selling approach takes skill and time. The salesperson must be able to analyze what motivates a particular customer and show how the company's offering would help the customer satisfy those needs. The sales rep may even conclude that the customer's problem is really better solved with someone else's product. That might result in one lost sale, but it also is likely to build real trust and more sales opportunities over the life of the relationship with the customer. That's why this kind of selling is typical in business markets when a salesperson already has established a close relationship with a customer.

Exhibit 15-5
Prepared Approach to Sales
Presentation

Exhibit 15-6
Consultative Selling
Approach to Sales
Presentation

Exhibit 15-7
Selling Formula Approach to
Sales Presentation

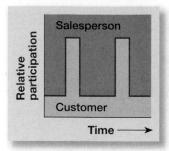

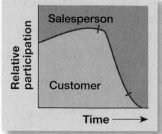

Selling formula approach—some of both

The **selling formula approach** starts with a prepared presentation outline—much like the prepared approach—and leads the customer through some logical steps to a final close. The prepared steps are logical because we assume that we know something about the target customer's needs and attitudes.

Exhibit 15-7 shows the selling formula approach. The salesperson does most of the talking at the beginning of the presentation—to communicate key points early. This part of the presentation may even have been prepared as part of the marketing strategy. As the sales presentation moves along, however, the salesperson brings the customer into the discussion to help clarify just what needs this customer has. The salesperson's job is to discover the needs of a particular customer to know how to proceed. Once it is clear what kind of customer this is, the salesperson comes back to show how the product satisfies this specific customer's needs and to close the sale.

AIDA helps plan sales presentations

AIDA—Attention, Interest, Desire, Action: Most sales presentations follow this AIDA sequence. The time a sales rep spends on each of the steps varies depending on the situation and the selling approach being used. But it is still necessary to begin a presentation by getting the prospect's *attention* and, hopefully, to move the customer to *action*.[23]

Each sales manager and salesperson needs to think about this sequence in deciding what sales approach to use and in evaluating a possible presentation. Does the presentation get the prospect's attention quickly? Will it be interesting? Will the benefits be clear? Does the presentation consider likely objections so the sales rep can close the sale when the time is right? These may seem like simple things. But too frequently they aren't done at all—and a sale is lost.

Ethical issues may arise

As in every other area of marketing communications, ethical issues arise in the personal selling area. The most basic issue, plain and simple, is whether a salesperson's presentation is honest and truthful. But addressing that issue is a no-brainer. No company is served well by a salesperson who lies or manipulates customers to get their business.

On the other hand, most sales reps sooner or later face a sales situation in which they must make more difficult ethical decisions about how to balance company interests, customer interests, and personal interests. Conflicts are less likely to arise if the firm's marketing mix really meets the needs of its target market. Similarly, they are less likely to arise when the firm sees the value of developing a longer-term relationship with the customer. Then the salesperson is arranging a happy marriage. By contrast, ethical conflicts are more likely when the sales rep's personal outcomes (such as commission income) or the selling firm's profits hinge on making sales to customers whose needs are only partially met by the firm's offering. A number of financial services firms, for example, have garnered bad publicity—and even legal problems—from situations like this.

Keebler salespeople use an interactive tool called Instant Data Evaluation Access ("IDEA") Wizard on their laptop computers. It provides research data related to the marketing of cookies and crackers on topics such as shelf space management and consumer purchase patterns. The sales rep can use the Wizard to support a consultative selling approach in working to develop closer relationships with retailers.

Ideally, companies can avoid the whole problem by supporting their salespeople with a marketing mix that really offers target customers unique benefits. Moreover, top executives, marketing managers, and sales managers set the tone for the ethical climate in which a salesperson operates. If they set impossible goals or project a "do-what-you-need-to-do" attitude, a desperate salesperson may yield to the pressure of the moment. When a firm clearly advocates ethical selling behavior and makes it clear that manipulative selling techniques are not acceptable, the salesperson is not left trying to swim "against the flow."[24]

CONCLUSION

In this chapter, we discussed the importance and nature of personal selling. Selling is much more than just getting rid of the product. In fact, a salesperson who is not given strategy guidelines may have to become the strategy planner for the market he or she serves. Ideally, however, the sales manager and marketing manager work together to set some strategy guidelines: the kind and number of salespersons needed, what sales technology support will be provided, the kind of sales presentation desired, and selection, training, and motivation approaches.

We discussed the three basic sales tasks: (1) order-getting, (2) order-taking, and (3) supporting. Most sales jobs combine at least two of these three tasks. Once a firm specifies the important tasks, it can decide on the structure of its sales organization and the number of salespeople it needs. The nature of the job and the level

and method of compensation also depend on the blend of these tasks. Firms should develop a job description for each sales job. This, in turn, provides guidelines for selecting, training, and compensating salespeople.

Once the marketing manager agrees to the basic plan and sets the budget, the sales manager must implement the plan, including directing and controlling the sales force. This includes assigning sales territories and controlling performance. You can see that the sales manager has more to do than jet around the country sipping martinis and entertaining customers. A sales manager is deeply involved with the basic management tasks of planning and control—as well as ongoing implementation of the personal selling effort.

We also reviewed some basic selling techniques and identified three kinds of sales presentations. Each has its place—but the consultative selling approach seems best for higher-level sales jobs. In these kinds of jobs, personal selling is achieving a new, professional status because of the competence and level of personal responsibility required of the salesperson. The day of the old-time glad-hander is passing in favor of the spe-cialist who is creative, industrious, persuasive, knowl-edgeable, highly trained, and therefore able to help the buyer. This type of salesperson always has been, and probably always will be, in short supply. And the demand for high-level salespeople is growing.

KEY TERMS

basic sales tasks, 409	technical specialists, 413	prospecting, 423
order getters, 409	team selling, 413	sales presentation, 425
order-getting, 409	major accounts sales force, 414	prepared sales presentation, 425
order takers, 411	telemarketing, 414	close, 425
order-taking, 411	sales territory, 415	consultative selling approach, 425
supporting salespeople, 412	job description, 419	selling formula approach, 426
missionary salespeople, 413	sales quota, 422	

QUESTIONS AND PROBLEMS

1. What strategy decisions are needed in the personal selling area? Why should the marketing manager make these strategy decisions?

2. What kind of salesperson (or what blend of the basic sales tasks) is required to sell the following products? If there are several selling jobs in the channel for each product, indicate the kinds of salespeople re-quired. Specify any assumptions necessary to give definite answers.
   a. Laundry detergent.
   b. Costume jewelry.
   c. Office furniture.
   d. Men's underwear.
   e. Mattresses.
   f. Corn.
   g. Life insurance.

3. Distinguish among the jobs of producers', whole-salers', and retailers' order-getting salespeople. If one order getter is needed, must all the salespeople in a channel be order getters? Illustrate.

4. Discuss the role of the manufacturers' agent in a marketing manager's promotion plans. What kind of salesperson is a manufacturers' agent? What type of compensation plan is used for a manufacturers' agent?

5. Discuss the future of the specialty shop if producers place greater emphasis on mass selling because of the inadequacy of retail order-taking.

6. Compare and contrast missionary salespeople and technical specialists.

7. Explain how a compensation plan could be devel-oped to provide incentives for experienced salespeo-ple and yet make some provision for trainees who have not yet learned the job.

8. Cite an actual local example of each of the three kinds of sales presentations discussed in the chapter. Explain for each situation whether a different type of presentation would have been better.

9. Are the benefits and limitations of a canned presen-tation any different if it is supported with a slide show or videotape than if it is just a person talking? Why or why not?

10. Describe a consultative selling sales presentation that you experienced recently. How could it have been improved by fuller use of the AIDA framework?

11. How would our economy operate if personal sales-people were outlawed? Could the economy work? If so, how? If not, what is the minimum personal sell-ing effort necessary? Could this minimum personal selling effort be controlled by law?

SUGGESTED CASES

COMPUTER-AIDED PROBLEM

15. Sales Compensation

RESOURCE REMINDER

Franco Welles, sales manager for Nanek, Inc., is trying to decide whether to pay a sales rep for a new territory with straight commission or a combination plan. He wants to evaluate possible plans—to compare the compensation costs and profitability of each. Welles knows that sales reps in similar jobs at other firms make about $36,000 a year.

The sales rep will sell two products. Welles is planning a higher commission for Product B—because he wants it to get extra effort. From experience with similar products, he has some rough estimates of expected sales volume under the different plans and various ideas about commission rates. The details are found in the spreadsheet. The program computes compensation and how much the sales rep will contribute to profit. "Profit contribution" is equal to the total revenue generated by the sales rep minus sales compensation costs and the costs of producing the units.

a. For the initial values shown in the spreadsheet, which plan—commission or combination—would give the rep the highest compensation, and which plan would give the greatest profit contribution to Nanek, Inc.?

b. Welles thinks a sales rep might be motivated to work harder and sell 1,100 units of Product B if the commission rate (under the commission plan) were increased to 10 percent. If Welles is right (and everything else stays the same), would the higher commission rate be a good deal for Nanek? Explain your thinking.

c. A sales rep interested in the job is worried about making payments on her new car. She asks if Welles would consider paying her with a combination plan but with more guaranteed income (an $18,000 base salary) in return for taking a 3 percent commission on Products B and A. If this arrangement results in the same unit sales as Welles originally estimated for the combination plan, would Nanek, Inc., be better off or worse off under this arrangement?

d. Do you think the rep's proposal will meet Welles' goals for Product B? Explain your thinking.

For additional questions related to this problem, see Exercise 15-3 in the *Learning Aid for Use with Basic Marketing,* 15th edition.

CHAPTER SIXTEEN

Advertising and Sales Promotion

In the summer of 1965, 17-year-old Fred DeLuca was trying to figure out how to pay for college. A family friend suggested that Fred open a sandwich shop—and then the friend invested $1,000 to help get it started. Within a month, they opened their first sandwich shop. From that humble start grew the Subway franchise chain with over 20,000 outlets in 70 countries.

Targeted advertising and sales promotion have been important to Subway's growth. Some memorable Subway ads featured Jared Fogle, a college student who was overweight but lost 245 pounds by only eating Subway's low-fat sandwiches, like the "Veggie Delite." Jared says it was a fluke that he ended up in Subway's ads. After all, he was recruited to do the ads because of good publicity that Subway got after national media picked up a story that Jared's friend wrote about him in a college newspaper. On the other hand, Subway's strategy at that time focused on its line of seven different sandwiches with under 6 grams of fat. The objective was to set Subway apart from other fast food in a way that would appeal to health-conscious eaters and spark new sales growth. Jared walked past a nearby Subway every day, but what pulled him in the first time was Subway's point-of-purchase promotion for the "7 under 6" menu. So maybe it wasn't as random as it seems to Jared.

As soon as Jared's ads began to run, word of his inspiring story spread and consumer awareness of Subway and its healthy fare increased. It's always hard to isolate the exact impact of ads on sales, but sales grew more than 18 percent that year. Another benefit was that the ads attracted attention from potential franchisees. Many of them followed up by requesting the franchise brochure, which explains how Subway's strategy works and why it is profitable for franchisees. For instance, it describes how franchisees elect a group to help manage advertising and media buying decisions—so that Subway outlets get the most return from their advertising

dollars. Subway headquarters also supports franchisees by providing materials and guidance for the local advertising and sales promotion they do to reach their own target customers.

Recently, Subway has been squeezed at the high end by rival sandwich shops like Quiznos' Sub and Panera Bread. So Subway has to balance its menu and promotion. Balance is needed to appeal to the segment of customers who are most interested in taste as well as the low-fat segment. Subway balances the menu with a line of "Subway Selects" sandwiches made with zesty sauces and special breads. It turned to a new ad agency, Fallon Worldwide, to create new ads that would balance the copy thrust. Fallon in turn calls on specialized agencies, like one in Miami that focuses on advertising to Hispanics, to help with specific parts of Subway's campaign. Subway can also expect cooperative promotional support from Coca-Cola now that it is taking over as the exclusive supplier for all Subway outlets.

Subway includes many other elements in its promotion blend. For example, it is a national sponsor of the American Heart Walk. It also has contests and games to keep its customers interested. One is a trivia contest in which customers can win a boxed set of recordings. The contest ties in with a section of Subway's website that keeps customers coming back by providing handy reviews of current movies and music. The website also provides tips on dieting and exercise as well as nutritional details about its sandwiches. These details help consumers who want all the health-related facts. They also make sense given the scrutiny that the Federal Trade Commission is giving to firms that make promotional claims related to weight loss and health.

Subway is in a very competitive, dynamic market. More change is sure to come. But so far, Subway has achieved profitable growth with a targeted strategy that includes effective use of promotion.[1]

ADVERTISING, SALES PROMOTION, AND MARKETING STRATEGY DECISIONS

The Subway case shows that carefully planned advertising and sales promotion are often critical elements in the success or failure of a strategy. They can provide an inexpensive way—on a per-contact or per-sale basis—to inform, persuade, and activate customers. Advertising and sales promotion often play a central role in efforts to position a firm's marketing mix as the one that meets customers' needs. They can help motivate channel members or a firm's own employees, as well as final customers.

Unfortunately, the results that marketers *actually achieve* with advertising and sales promotion are very uneven. It's often said that half of the money spent on these activities is wasted—but that too few managers know which half. Mass selling can be exciting and involving, or it can be downright obnoxious. Sometimes it's based on careful research, yet much of it is just based on someone's pet idea. A creative idea may produce great results or be a colossal waste of money. Ads can stir deep emotions or go unnoticed.

Many managers do a poor job with advertising and sales promotion. So just copying how lots of other firms handle these important strategy decisions is not "good enough." There's no sense in imitating bad practices. Instead, it makes sense to understand the important strategy decisions involved in each of these areas.

As the Subway case illustrates, marketing managers and the advertising agencies that work with them have important advertising decisions to make, including (1) who their target audience is, (2) what kind of advertising to use, (3) how to reach customers (via which types of media), (4) what to say to them (the copy thrust), and (5) who will do the work—the firm's own advertising department or outside agencies. See Exhibit 16-1.

International dimensions are important

The basic strategy planning decisions for advertising and sales promotion are the same regardless of where in the world the target market is located. However, the look and feel of advertising and sales promotion vary a lot in different countries. The choices available to a marketing manager within each of the decision areas may also vary dramatically from one country to another.

Commercial television may not be available. If it is, government rules may limit the type of advertising permitted or when ads can be shown. Radio broadcasts in a

Exhibit 16-1   Strategy Planning for Advertising

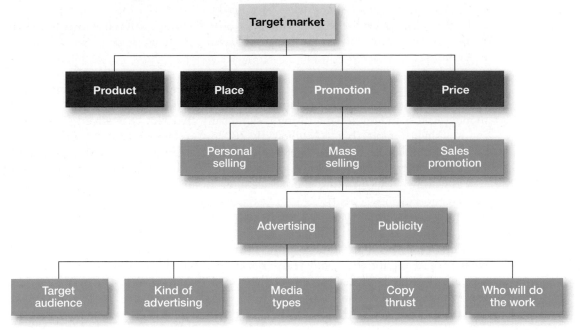

```
                          Target market
                              │
        ┌──────────────┬──────┴──────┬──────────────┐
    Product         Place        Promotion        Price
                                     │
                      ┌──────────────┼──────────────┐
                  Personal         Mass           Sales
                  selling         selling       promotion
                                     │
                              ┌──────┴──────┐
                         Advertising     Publicity
                              │
     ┌──────────────┬─────────┼─────────┬──────────────┐
  Target          Kind of    Media     Copy        Who will do
  audience       advertising types    thrust        the work
```

market area may not be in the target market's language. The target audience may not be able to read. Access to interactive media like the Internet may be nonexistent. Cultural influences may limit ad messages. Ad agencies who already know a nation's unique advertising environment may not be available.

International dimensions also impact sales promotion. Trade promotion may be difficult, or even impossible, to manage. A typical Japanese grocery retailer with only 250 square feet of space, for example, doesn't have room for *any* special end-of-aisle displays. Consumer promotions may be affected too. Many Polish consumers, for example, are skeptical about product samples; they figure that if it's free something's amiss. In some developing nations, samples can't be distributed through the

Traditional media choices are more limited in some international markets, so marketers must be creative to communicate their messages. In North Africa and the Middle East, Coke uses hot-air balloons. The 12-stories-tall Ariel shirt was mounted on a building in China.

mail, because they're routinely stolen before they get to target customers. And some countries ban consumer sweepstakes because they see it as a form of gambling.

In this chapter we'll consider a number of these international issues, but we'll focus on the array of choices available in the U.S. and other advanced economies.[2]

Total spending is big—and growing internationally

As an economy grows, advertising becomes more important—because more consumers have income and advertising can get results. But good advertising results cost money. And spending on advertising is significant. In 1946, U.S. advertising spending was slightly more than $3 billion. By 2002, it was about $236 billion.

During the last decade, the rate of advertising spending has increased even more rapidly in other countries. However, advertising in the U.S. accounts for roughly half of worldwide ad spending. Europe accounts for about 23 percent, and Asia about 22 percent. For most countries in other regions, advertising spending has traditionally been quite low.[3]

Most advertisers aren't really spending that much

While total spending on advertising seems high, it represents a small portion of what people pay for the goods and services they buy. U.S. corporations spend an average of only about 2.5 percent of their sales dollar on advertising. Worldwide, the percentage is even smaller.

Exhibit 16-2 shows, however, that advertising spending as a percent of sales dollars varies significantly across product categories. Producers of consumer products generally spend a larger percent than firms that produce business products. For example, U.S. companies that make soap and detergent spend a whopping 11.3 percent. However, companies that sell plastics to manufacturers spend only about 2.6 percent on advertising. Some business products companies—those that depend on e-commerce or personal selling—may spend less than $1/10$ of 1 percent.

In general, the percent is smaller for retailers and wholesalers than for producers. Large chains like JCPenney spend about 3 percent, but many retailers and wholesalers spend 1 percent or less. Individual firms may spend more or less than others in the industry, depending on the role of advertising in their promotion blend.

Of course, percentages don't tell the whole story. Nissan, which spends less than 1 percent of sales on advertising, is among the top 20 advertisers worldwide. The really big spenders are very important to the advertising industry because they account for a large share of total advertising spending. For example, in the United States, the top 100 advertisers (many of which are based in other countries) account for about 35 percent of all advertising spending. Worldwide, the top 100 global advertisers spend about $65 billion a year. At, or near, the top of that list in most years are the three biggest consumer packaged goods companies (P&G, Unilever, and Nestlé) and major car companies, including GM, Toyota, and Ford.[4]

Advertising spending is very important in certain markets, especially final consumer markets. Nevertheless, in total, advertising costs much less than personal selling and sales promotion.

Advertising doesn't employ that many people

While total advertising expenditures are large, the advertising industry itself employs relatively few people. The major expense is for media time and space. In the United States, the largest share of this—28 percent—goes for television (including cable). Newspapers take about 22 percent of the total and direct mail about 23 percent. The shares for radio (9 percent), the Yellow Pages (7 percent), magazines (6 percent), outdoor (3 percent), and the Internet (2 percent) are much smaller.[5]

Many students hope for a glamorous job in advertising, but there are fewer jobs in advertising than you might think. In the United States, only about 500,000

Exhibit 16-2 Advertising Spending as Percent of Sales for Illustrative Product Categories

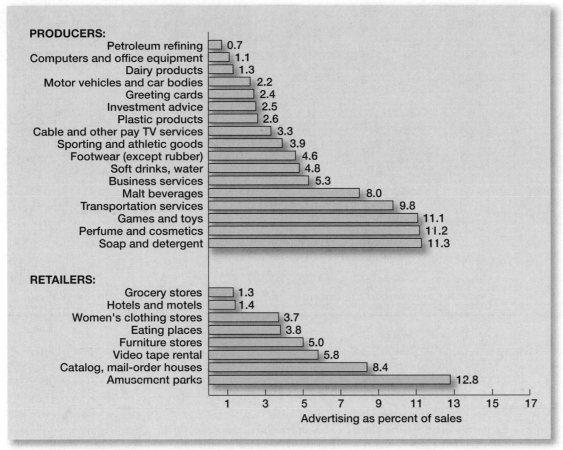

people work directly in the advertising industry. Advertising agencies employ only about half of all these people.[6]

ADVERTISING OBJECTIVES ARE A STRATEGY DECISION

Advertising objectives must be specific

Every ad and every advertising campaign should have clearly defined objectives. These should grow out of the firm's overall marketing strategy and the promotion jobs assigned to advertising. It isn't enough for the marketing manager to say "Promote the product." The marketing manager must decide exactly what advertising should do.

Advertising objectives should be more specific than personal selling objectives. One of the advantages of personal selling is that a salesperson can shift the presentation for a specific customer. Each ad, however, must be effective not just for one customer but for thousands, or millions, of them.

The marketing manager sets the overall direction

The marketing manager might give the advertising manager one or more of the following specific objectives, along with the budget to accomplish them:

1. Help position the firm's brand or marketing mix by informing and persuading target customers or middlemen about its benefits.
2. Help introduce new products to specific target markets.
3. Help obtain desirable outlets and tell customers where they can buy a product.

Awareness	Interest	Evaluation and trial	Decision	Confirmation

Teaser campaigns
Pioneering ads
Jingles/slogans
Internet banners
Announcements
	Informative or
	  descriptive ads
	Image/celebrity ads
	Flash ads
	Demonstration of
	  benefits
		Competitive ads
		Persuasive copy
		Comparative ads
		Testimonials
			Direct-action retail
			  ads
			Point-of-purchase
			  ads
			Price deal offers
				Reminder ads
				Informative "why"
				  ads

4. Provide ongoing contact with target customers, even when a salesperson isn't available.

5. Prepare the way for salespeople by presenting the company's name and the merits of its products.

6. Get immediate buying action.

7. Help to maintain relationships with satisfied customers and encourage more purchases.

If you want half the market, say so!

The objectives listed above highlight that a balancing act may be required. The first objective is quite broad and relates to the basic decisions about how the marketing manager wants to differentiate and position the whole marketing mix. That should guide decisions about what other specific objectives are most important. In fact, some of the objectives listed are not as specific as they could be. If a marketing manager really wants specific results, they should be clearly stated. A general objective is "To help expand market share." This could be rephrased more specifically: "To increase shelf space in our cooperating retail outlets by 25 percent during the next three months."

Objectives guide implementation too

The specific objectives obviously affect what type of advertising is best. Exhibit 16-3 shows that the type of advertising that achieves objectives for one stage of the adoption process may be off target for another. For example, most advertising for cameras in the United States, Germany, and Japan focuses on foolproof pictures or state-of-the-art digital designs because most consumers in these countries already own *some* camera. In Africa, where only about 20 percent of the population owns a camera, ads must sell the whole concept of picture-taking.

OBJECTIVES DETERMINE THE KINDS OF ADVERTISING NEEDED

The advertising objectives largely determine which of two basic types of advertising to use—product or institutional.

Product advertising tries to sell a product. It may be aimed at final users or channel members.

Institutional advertising tries to promote an organization's image, reputation, or ideas rather than a specific product. Its basic objective is to develop goodwill or improve an organization's relations with various groups—not only customers but also current and prospective channel members, suppliers, shareholders, employees, and the general public. The British government, for instance, uses institutional advertising to promote England as a place to do business.

Hoechst's attention-getting institutional ad is effective in promoting the company's name and image, rather than trying to sell just one of its many specific product lines.

Product advertising—know us, like us, remember us

Product advertising falls into three categories: pioneering, competitive, and reminder advertising.

Pioneering advertising builds primary demand

Pioneering advertising tries to develop primary demand for a product category rather than demand for a specific brand. Pioneering advertising is usually done in the early stages of the product life cycle; it informs potential customers about the new product and helps turn them into adopters. When digital cameras first came out, consumers didn't know their benefits or why they might want one—and at the same time they worried about how they could get printed pictures. So advertising for the early products in the market had to explain these basics and build primary demand. Now that there are a hundred brands of digital cameras, each brand's ads try to highlight its own advantages—like the number of megapixels, amount of memory, or ease of use.

Comparative ads make direct comparisons with other brands using actual product names. For example, the ad for Clorox Disinfecting Wipes notes that a competing wipe by Windex doesn't disinfect. The Baby Orajel ad touts its fast relief compared to Children's Tylenol.

Competitive advertising—emphasizes selective demand

Competitive advertising tries to develop selective demand for a specific brand. A firm is forced into competitive advertising as the product life cycle moves along—to hold its own against competitors.

Competitive advertising may be either direct or indirect. The **direct type** aims for immediate buying action. The **indirect type** points out product advantages to affect future buying decisions.

Most of Delta Airlines' advertising is of the competitive variety. Much of it tries for immediate sales—so the ads are the direct type with prices, timetables, and phone numbers to call for reservations. Some of its ads are the indirect type. They focus on the quality of service and suggest you mention Delta's name the next time you talk to your travel agent.

Comparative advertising is even rougher. **Comparative advertising** means making specific brand comparisons—using actual product names. A recent comparative ad for Clorox Disinfecting Wipes, for example, claimed that a competing wipe from Windex didn't disinfect as well.

Many countries forbid comparative advertising, but that situation is changing. For example, Japan banned comparative advertising until about 15 years ago, when the restrictions were relaxed. Japan's move followed an earlier change in the United States. The Federal Trade Commission decided to encourage comparative ads, after banning them for years—because it thought they would increase competition and provide consumers with more useful information.

In the United States, superiority claims are supposed to be supported by research evidence—but the guidelines aren't clear. When P&G's Dryel did not fare well in independent test comparisons with stain removal by professional dry cleaners, P&G changed its ad claims. However, some firms just keep running tests until they get the results they want. Others talk about minor differences that don't reflect a product's overall benefits. Comparative ads can also backfire by calling attention to competing products that consumers had not previously considered.[7]

Reminder advertising—reinforces a favorable relationship

Reminder advertising tries to keep the product's name before the public. It may be useful when the product has achieved brand preference or insistence, perhaps in the market maturity or sales decline stages. It is used primarily to reinforce previous promotion. Here the advertiser may use soft-sell ads that just mention or show

Buster Brown is a well-known brand with a 100-year history, but at back-to-school, shoe-buying time it ran print and outdoor ads to remind parents of their positive feelings about Buster Brown shoes. Ads featured a toll-free number to call or website address so consumers could learn the location of the closest retailer. The ad for V8 Juice shows an image that looks like a vegetable blender, to remind customers that V8 is 100 percent vegetable juice.

the name—as a reminder. Hallmark, for example, often relies on reminder ads because most consumers already know the brand name and, after years of promotion, associate it with high product quality.

<table>
<tr><td>

Institutional advertising— remember our name

</td><td>

Institutional advertising usually focuses on the name and prestige of an organization or industry. It may seek to inform, persuade, or remind. Many Japanese firms, like Hitachi, emphasize institutional advertising, in part because they often use the company name as a brand name.

Companies sometimes rely on institutional advertising to present the company in a favorable light, perhaps to overcome image problems. General Electric recently launched a $100 million institutional ad campaign, along with the new tagline "innovation at work." A new team of executives at GE felt that many of the people who influence big purchase decisions in the varied business markets where GE competes associated GE with products like light bulbs and refrigerators and that the familiar "we bring good things to life" tagline just reinforced an old-fashioned image. The purpose of the new TV spots—which feature jet engines, high-tech plastics, and medical systems—is to reposition GE as a company that produces revolutionary innovations.[8]

Some organizations use institutional advertising to advocate a specific cause or idea. Insurance companies and organizations like Mothers Against Drunk Driving, for example, use these advocacy ads to encourage people not to drink and drive.[9]

</td></tr>
</table>

COORDINATING ADVERTISING EFFORTS WITH COOPERATIVE RELATIONSHIPS

<table>
<tr><td>

Vertical cooperation— advertising allowances, cooperative advertising

</td><td>

Sometimes a producer knows that an advertising job can be done more effectively or more economically by someone further along in the channel. Alternatively, a retail chain like Best Buy may approach a manufacturer like Panasonic with an ad program and tell them how much it will cost to participate. In either case, the producer may offer **advertising allowances**—price reductions to firms further along in the channel to encourage them to advertise or otherwise promote the firm's products locally.

Cooperative advertising involves middlemen and producers sharing in the cost of ads. This helps wholesalers and retailers compete in their local markets. It also helps the producer get more promotion for the advertising dollar because media usually give local advertisers lower rates than national or international firms. In addition, a retailer or wholesaler who is paying a share of the cost is more likely to follow through.

</td></tr>
<tr><td>

Integrated communications from cooperative relationships

</td><td>

Coordination and integration of ad messages in the channel is another reason for cooperative advertising. One big, well-planned, integrated advertising effort is often better than many different, perhaps inconsistent, local efforts. Many franchise operations like the idea of communicating with one voice. KFC, for example, encourages its franchises to use a common advertising program. Before, many developed their own local ads—with themes like "Eight clucks for four bucks"—that didn't fit with the company's overall marketing strategy.

To get this coordination, producers often provide a master of an ad on a DVD, CD, website, or printed sheets. The middlemen add their identification before turning the ad over to local media.

However, allowances and support materials alone don't ensure cooperation. When channel members don't agree with the advertising strategy, it can be a serious source of conflict. For example, Wendy's strategy includes an objective to be the late-night, quick-serve restaurant of choice for its target market. This requires staying open late at night and advertising the longer hours. However, some Wendy's restaurants are franchise operations rather than company-owned. A franchise operator who does not think that late-night hours will be profitable in his or her local

</td></tr>
</table>

market may not want to stay open for the longer hours or pay franchise fees to support the national ad campaign. If a situation like this affected only a few restaurants, it might not be a big problem. However, if concerns about the campaign are widespread, it might require that the whole strategy be revisited.[10]

Ethical concerns may arise

Ethical issues sometimes arise concerning advertising allowance programs. For example, a retailer may run one producer's ad to draw customers to the store but then sell them another brand. Is this unethical? Some producers think it is. A different view is that retailers are obligated to the producer to run the ad but obligated to consumers to sell them what they want, no matter whose brand it may be. A producer can often avoid the problem by setting the allowance amount as a percent of the retailer's *actual purchases*. Smart producers also insist on proof that the advertising was really done. That way, a retailer who doesn't produce sales—or even run the ads—doesn't get the allowance.[11]

CHOOSING THE "BEST" MEDIUM—HOW TO DELIVER THE MESSAGE

What is the best advertising medium? There is no simple answer to this question. Effectiveness depends on how well the medium fits with the rest of a marketing strategy—that is, it depends on (1) your promotion objectives, (2) what target markets you want to reach, (3) the funds available for advertising, and (4) the nature of the media, including who they *reach*, with what *frequency*, with what *impact*, and at what *cost*.

Exhibit 16-4 shows some pros and cons of major kinds of media and some examples of costs. However, some of the advantages noted in this table may not apply in all markets. For example, direct mail may not be a flexible choice in a country with a weak postal system. Internet ads might be worthless if few target customers have access to the Internet. Similarly, TV audiences are often less selective and targeted, but a special-interest cable TV show may reach a very specific audience.[12]

Specific promotion objectives

The medium should support the promotion objectives. If the objective requires demonstrating product benefits, TV may be the best alternative. If the objective is to inform, telling a detailed story and using precise pictures, then Internet advertising might be right. Alternatively, with a broad target market, print media like magazines and newspapers may be better. For example, Jockey switched its advertising to magazines from television when it decided to show the variety of styles of its men's briefs. Jockey worried that there were problems with modeling men's underwear on television. However, Jockey might have stayed with TV if it had been targeting consumers in France or Brazil, where nudity in TV ads is common.[13]

Match your market with the media

To guarantee good media selection, the advertiser first must *clearly* specify its target market. Then the advertiser can choose media that reaches those target customers.

The media available in a country may limit the choices. In less-developed nations, for example, radio is often the only way to reach a broad-based market of poor consumers who can't read or afford television.

In most cases, however, the major problem is to match media with the target audience. Most media firms use marketing research to develop profiles of their audiences. Generally, this research focuses on demographic characteristics rather than the segmenting dimensions specific to the planning needs of *each* different advertiser. The problem is even worse in some countries because available media don't provide any information.

Kinds of Media	Sales Volume, 2002 ($ billions)	Typical Costs, 2002	Advantages	Disadvantages
Television and cable	$54.1	$4,500 for a 30-second spot, prime time, Phoenix	Demonstrations, good attention, wide reach	Expensive in total, "clutter," less-selective audience
Newspaper	44.0	$42,570 for one-page (black/white) weekday, *Arizona Republic*	Flexible, timely, local market	May be expensive, short life, no "pass-along"
Direct mail	44.7	$215 per 1,000 for listing of 114,000 Human Resource executives by industry or employee size	Selected audience, flexible, can personalize	Relatively expensive per contact, "junk mail"—hard to retain attention
Radio	17.9	$350–$400 for one-minute drive time, Phoenix	Wide reach, segmented audience, inexpensive	Weak attention, many different rates, short exposure
Yellow Pages	13.8	$2,760 a year for a ⅛-page display ad in directory for a city with .5 million population	Reaches local customers seeking purchase information	Many other competitors listed in same place, hard to differentiate
Magazine	11.0	$192,000 for one-page, four-color in *Time* (national)	Very targeted, good detail, good "pass-along"	Inflexible, long lead times
Outdoor	5.2	$5,000 (painted) for prime billboard, 30- to 60-day showings, Phoenix	Flexible, repeat exposure, inexpensive	"Mass market," very short exposure
Internet	4.9	Banner ads average about $30 for every 1,000 ad impressions on a site	Ads link to more detailed website, some "pay for results"	Hard to compare costs with other media

Advertisers pay for the whole audience

Another problem is that the audience for media that *do* reach your target market may also include people who are *not* in the target group. But *you pay for the whole audience the media delivers*, including those who aren't potential customers. For example, Delta Faucet, a faucet manufacturer that wanted its ads to reach plumbers, placed ads on ESPN's Saturday college football telecasts. Research showed that many plumbers watched the ESPN games. Yet plumbers are only a very small portion of the total college football audience—and the size of the total audience determined the cost of the advertising time.[14]

The cost of reaching the real target market goes up fastest when the irrelevant audience is very large. For example, the last episode of the wildly popular *Seinfeld* sitcom drew about 75 million viewers and NBC charged $1.5 million or more for a 30-second ad slot. It may have been worth that for Visa to reach such a large, mainly adult, audience.[15] On the other hand, tiny Gardenburger, Inc., bought an ad slot in a shoot-for-the-moon effort to turn the audience on to its veggie patties. Yet only about 8 percent of consumers have ever tasted a veggie burger. A 30-second ad, even a memorable one, isn't likely to change a basic mind-set for most people. So in betting the farm on its *Seinfeld* ad, Gardenburger had to pay to reach a very large audience, most of whom were not interested in what the company had to offer.[16]

Because it's hard to pick the best media, media analysts often focus on cost per thousand of audience size or circulation. This may seem an objective approach, but

Spot TV is an ad medium that can help a firm zero in on a specific target audience. The Yellow Pages reaches a broader audience, but for many firms it is a "must buy" element in an integrated marketing communications plan.

advertisers preoccupied with keeping these costs down may ignore the relevant segmenting dimensions and slip into mass marketing.

Some media help zero in on specific target markets

Today, the major media direct more attention to reaching smaller, more defined target markets. The most obvious evidence of this is in the growth of spending on direct-mail advertising to consumers in databases. However, other media, even traditional ones, are becoming more targeted as well.

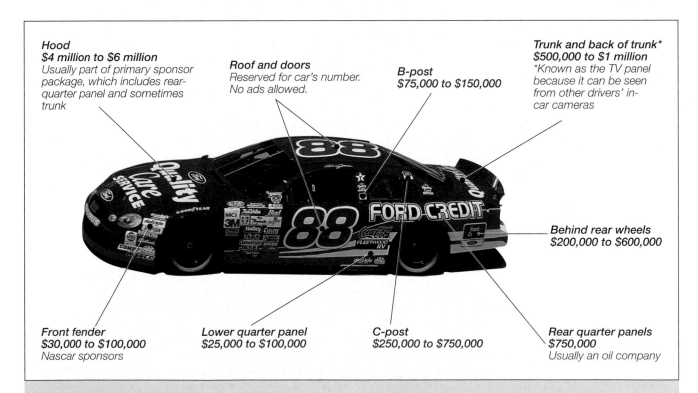

Hood
$4 million to $6 million
Usually part of primary sponsor package, which includes rear-quarter panel and sometimes trunk

Roof and doors
Reserved for car's number.
No ads allowed.

B-post
$75,000 to $150,000

Trunk and back of trunk*
$500,000 to $1 million
*Known as the TV panel because it can be seen from other drivers' in-car cameras

Behind rear wheels
$200,000 to $600,000

Front fender
$30,000 to $100,000
Nascar sponsors

Lower quarter panel
$25,000 to $100,000

C-post
$250,000 to $750,000

Rear quarter panels
$750,000
Usually an oil company

Advertising space on a race car reaches racing fans and often benefits from extended TV coverage. But the cost for primary sponsors can be millions of dollars.

DOES ADVERTISING THAT'S EVERYWHERE GET US ANYWHERE?

It's everywhere. You get to the beach, look down, and huge versions of the Skippy peanut butter logo are embossed in the sand. You roll your eyes in dismay and catch a view of a plane pulling a 100-foot-long banner ad with Catherine Zeta-Jones urging you to "Sign up for T-Mobile's free Friday minutes." You go in the bathroom to change into your swimsuit, but the walls are adorned with posters for Good Humor ice cream bars. Forget that. Maybe you should just eat your picnic lunch. Oops, the whole back of the bench you're going to sit on is an ad for a check-cashing service—and just for good measure the banana you pull out of your lunch bag has a sticker advertising Florida oranges. You look up just as a baby carriage rolls by with ads on its side. So you jump in your car to escape the onslaught. But when you stop to pump gas a miniature video screen by the credit card slot urges you to get a Visa debit card from a local bank (first in English and then in Spanish). The billboards you ignore along the way seem pretty civilized compared to the towering trucks whose trailers are rolling billboards. Back at the ranch, at last, you know you can watch the Grammy Awards show in peace because you have TiVo—so you can zap past the ads. But no, you can't see the celebrities arrive without staring at virtual logos digitally superimposed on the entry canopy and sidewalk by the front door. So there's no alternative but to pull the plug on the TV and check for e-mail from your sweetie. Wrong move. A pop-up ad for a video cam covers half of the screen—and why can't you make it go away? You can drag it to the side, but then there's so much spam in your mailbox that you've run out of disk space.

There are certainly many cases where promotion benefits both the consumer and the firm, and after all it is revenues from advertising that cover the cost of lots of great stuff consumers get for free. Yet sometimes you can't help but wish that you were not the target that somebody else is aiming at![17]

TV is a good example. Cable TV channels—like CNN, Nickelodeon, ESPN, and MTV—are taking advertisers away from the networks because they target specific audiences. ESPN, for example, has an audience heavily weighted toward affluent, male viewers. Moreover, being specialized doesn't necessarily mean that the target market is small. MTV appeals most strongly to young viewers, but its programming is seen in nearly 400 million homes worldwide—more than any other programmer.

Infomercials—long commercials that are broadcast with a TV show format—are a reminder of how targeted cable TV has become now that many consumers have access to hundreds of TV channels. With many channels competing for attention, most will succeed only if they offer programs and commercials specific to the interests of smaller, more homogeneous target markets.

Radio has also become a more specialized medium. Some stations cater to particular ethnic and racial groups, such as Hispanics, African Americans, or French Canadians. Others aim at specific target markets with rock, country, or classical music. Now that radio stations can get their programming to a larger number of consumers over the Internet and via satellite broadcast systems, expect even more targeting.

Many magazines serve only special-interest groups, such as fishermen, new parents, and personal computer users. In fact, the most profitable magazines seem to be the ones aimed at clearly defined markets. Many specialty magazines also have international editions that help marketers reach consumers with similar interests in different parts of the world. PC Magazine, for example, offers European, Japanese, and other editions.

There are also trade magazines in many fields, such as chemical engineering, furniture retailing, electrical wholesaling, farming, and the aerospace market. Standard Rate and Data provides a guide to the thousands of magazines now available in the United States. Similar guides exist in most other countries.

Many of the national print media offer specialized editions. Time magazine, for example, offers not only several regional and metropolitan editions but also special editions for college students, educators, doctors, and business managers. Magazines like *Newsweek,* France's *Paris Match International,* and Germany's *Wirtschaftwoche* provide international editions.

Specialized media are small, but gaining

The advertising media listed in Exhibit 16-4 are attracting the vast majority of advertising media budgets. But advertising specialists always look for cost-effective new media that will help advertisers reach their target markets. For example, one company successfully sells space for signs on bike racks that it places in front of 7-Eleven stores. In Eastern Europe, where major media are still limited, companies like Campbell's pay to put ads on bus shelters. A new generation of ATMs show video ads while customers wait to get their money. Some gas station pumps have similar displays.[18] And, of course, the Internet is a medium that can be highly targeted.

"Must buys" may use up available funds

Selecting which media to use is still pretty much an art. The media buyer starts with a budgeted amount and tries to buy the best blend to reach the target audience.

Some media are obvious "must buys," like *the* local newspaper for a retailer in a small town. Most firms serving local markets view a Yellow Pages listing as a must buy. Website advertising is increasingly seen as a must buy. It may be the only medium for firms trying to reach business buyers in overseas markets. Must buy ads may even use up the available funds.

For many firms, even national advertisers, the high cost of television may eliminate it from the media blend. The average cost just to produce a national TV ad is now about $250,000—and a big impact ad can easily cost twice that. In the United States, a 30-second commercial on a popular prime-time show like *Will and Grace* is well over $400,000. The price goes up rapidly for "big event" shows that attract the largest audiences. Thirty seconds of advertising on the 2004 Super Bowl cost sponsors about $2.3 million.[19]

ADVERTISING ON THE INTERNET—NEW OPPORTUNITIES AND NEW CHALLENGES

Internet advertising is taking hold

Even though Internet advertising accounts for a small proportion of total ad spending, many firms are experimenting to figure out what works and does not work. Spending on Internet advertising shot up during the 1990s until it peaked at around $8 million in 2000. However, much of that early Internet advertising was to promote dot-com firms. When technology stocks plummeted, so did spending on Internet ads.

Advertising managers are always looking for cost-effective new media that will help them reach their specific target markets.

However, in 2003, Internet advertising started to come back as mainstream advertisers increased both their spending and the percentage of it going to the Internet.

Most Internet ads seek a direct response

Advertising on the Internet takes a variety of forms—like buttons, banners, animations, and pop-ups—but the purpose of an ad is usually just to attract the interest of people in the advertiser's target market so that they'll click through to the firm's website. It is the website that does the heavy lifting, not the ads. But ads are the path to the site.

Website advertising tends to be more interactive than traditional advertising. Increasingly, the content moves beyond the text and pictures typical of print ads and instead includes videos, sound, a product database, and order-entry shopping carts. The website advertiser can also offer a great deal more information and allow customers to self-direct to pages that interest them the most. In addition, the website can provide links to other outside sources of information. Or it can invite the viewer to e-mail or start a chat session for more detailed information. Further, it can offer a sign-up for e-mail updates when there is some sort of news.

But many consumers don't want to respond

We talked about the benefits of this sort of interactive communication in Chapter 14. However, it can also have a downside if it interferes with what the customer wants to do on the Internet. Pop-ups that won't go away, loud music that starts unexpectedly, and animations that take over the computer while they load often just create aggravation rather than interest. It's no wonder that some of the most popular free downloads on the Internet are programs to block pop-ups, turn off interactive features at a website, and prevent advertisers' "cookies" from tracking customers. Internet advertisers face the challenge of figuring out how to stimulate customer interest in ways that are acceptable to the customer.

Some websites generate more exposure

Some advertisers are primarily interested in placing ads on websites that will give their ads more exposure, almost without regard to the content of the website or who visits it. Although there are millions of websites on the Internet, a small subset accounts for a large percentage of the potential audience. For example, many people start at the AOL, MSN, or Yahoo portal each time they use the Internet.

These websites are becoming for the Internet what the networks once were for television: *the* place where an advertiser is willing to pay high rates because they are uniquely able to reach a very large, broad market. For example, Dell might want its computer ads on the AOL or Yahoo home page so they will be viewed by the large number of computer user visitors. But what makes sense for Dell in that situation might not make sense for a firm with a different strategy. As with traditional media, getting lots of exposure for an Internet ad doesn't help if viewers are not in the firm's target market. At many websites, rates are set based on number of exposures, and you pay for an exposure regardless of who it is.

Some websites are better for reaching target customers

Bristol-Myers Squibb's experiment with web advertising is typical of what many other firms do—place ads on websites that attract the desired target market. In the middle of income tax season, Bristol-Myers Squibb ran ads on financial websites extolling Excedrin as "the tax headache medicine." The ads offered a free sample of Excedrin. Within a month, more than 30,000 people clicked on the ad and typed their names into the firm's customer database. The cost of obtaining those names was half that of traditional methods. Now the firm can follow up the Excedrin samples with other database-directed promotions, either by e-mail or other methods.

Context advertising links ad to content being viewed

Targeting on the Internet can be even more precise. For example, ads for PerfumeOutlet.net pop up when an Internet user does a search on a term such as perfume or Estée Lauder. This approach is called *context advertising*—monitoring the content a net surfer is viewing and then serving up related ads. For example, if a consumer visits a website with information about cars, an ad for Amazon.com might appear and note that it carries books on buying a car. If the consumer clicks on the Amazon ad, a list of links to relevant books appears on screen.

Pointcasting determines which customers see an ad

Another approach that offers more precise targeting is pointcasting. Pointcasting means displaying an ad *only* to an individual who meets certain qualifications, perhaps a person who has previously expressed direct interest in the topic of the advertising. A pointcasting ad is usually included with other information that the customer wants and that a pointcasting service provides for free. An example shows how this works. A woman who is interested in financial planning might sign up with Time-Warner Cable's Road Runner service and request that it routinely send her newly published articles on independent retirement accounts. When the service sends her that information over the Internet, it might include an ad from a mutual fund company. Many advertisers like this concept but worry that pointcasting overwhelms the recipient with too much clutter.

Sending ads directly to the target customer via e-mail is a simpler approach. A limitation of e-mail is that a person's e-mail software may reformat messages in different ways. That is changing with increased use of e-mail in HTML format and high-speed connections. However, a different problem will continue: Most people resent being "spammed" with a lot of unsolicited e-mail, and spam can become a big problem. Many firms send e-mail only to people who have given the firm permission to send it.

INTERNET EXERCISE

ValueClick is a firm that provides services for firms that want to advertise on the Internet and also for website publishers that host Internet advertising. Go to its website (www.valueclick.com) and click on *ValueClick Media*. Briefly describe the main benefits it provides for advertisers and the main benefits it provides for publishers.

Some viewers get benefits if they agree to look at ads

Some websites offer people a benefit—like free e-mail or a chance to enter a contest—if they provide information about themselves and agree to view ads selected to match their interests. Juno offers free Internet and e-mail service when people sign up and provide detailed information about themselves. The information might include demographics as well as interests, what products they use, where they shop, and where they live. Then when a person checks for e-mail messages, ads are displayed. Each ad is selected specifically for that person based on his or her characteristics. For example, a cosmetics firm might specify that its ads be shown only to females who are 16 or older and who routinely wear nail polish.

While some consumers are willing to be targeted with advertising in exchange for free services, it is an ethical concern when many firms capture personal information about consumers without their knowledge. Even a brand new computer may come with "spyware" already installed. Stealth tracking programs can be installed just by visiting a website or opening an e-mail. The intent of these advertisers may be to target more effectively, but in the process they impose costs on consumers. Invasion of privacy is one cost. Another is that a computer bogged down by a number of tracking programs slows to a crawl. Some stealth systems even divert consumers to websites they did not want to visit. The consumer backlash against these abuses is growing, and marketers who do not exercise judgment are likely to suffer the consequences.

At some websites, ads are free if they don't get results

Many websites charge advertisers a fee based on how frequently or how long an ad is shown. However, competition for advertisers has prompted some websites to display an ad for free and charge a fee only if the ad gets results. The fee the advertiser pays is sometimes based on "clickthrough"—the number of people who actually click on the ad and link to the advertiser's website. Some websites set fees based on actual sales that result from the clickthrough. This is a big shift from traditional

The right copy thrust helps an ad clearly communicate to its target market.

media where firms have to pay for their ads whether they work or not. A lot more firms will put ads on websites if there is a direct relationship between costs and results. Moreover, this arrangement gives a website more incentive to attract an audience that some specific advertiser wants to reach.[20]

PLANNING THE "BEST" MESSAGE—WHAT TO COMMUNICATE

Specifying the copy thrust

Once you decide *how* the messages will reach the target audience, you have to decide on the **copy thrust**—what the words and illustrations should communicate.

Carrying out the copy thrust is the job of advertising specialists. But the advertising manager and the marketing manager need to understand the process to be sure that the job is done well.

Let AIDA help guide message planning

Basically, the overall marketing strategy should determine *what* the message should say. Then management judgment, perhaps aided by marketing research, can help decide how to encode this content so it will be decoded as intended.

As a guide to message planning, we can use the AIDA concept: getting Attention, holding Interest, arousing Desire, and obtaining Action.

Getting attention

Getting attention is an ad's first job. Many readers leaf through magazines without paying attention to any of the ads, and viewers get snacks during TV commercials. When watching a program on TiVo, they may zap past the commercial with a flick of a button. On the Internet, they may use a pop-up blocker or click on the next website before the ad message finishes loading onto the screen.

Many attention-getting devices are available. A large headline, computer animations, shocking statements, attractive models, animals, special effects—anything

Billboards are good for getting attention with a simple copy thrust.

different or eye-catching—may do the trick. However, the attention-getting device can't detract from, and hopefully should lead to, the next step, holding interest.

Holding interest

Holding interest is more difficult. A humorous ad, an unusual video effect, or a clever photo may get your attention—but once you've seen it, then what? If there is no relation between what got your attention and the marketing mix, you'll move on. To hold interest, the tone and language of the ad must fit with the experiences and attitudes of the target customers and their reference groups. As a result, many advertisers develop ads that relate to specific emotions. They hope that the good feeling about the ad will stick, even if its details are forgotten.

To hold interest, informative ads need to speak the target customer's language. Persuasive ads must provide evidence that convinces the customer. For example, TV ads often demonstrate a product's benefits.

Layouts for print ads should be arranged to encourage the eye to move smoothly through the ad—perhaps from a headline that starts in the upper left-hand corner to the illustration or body copy in the middle and finally to the lower right corner where the ad's "signature" usually gives the company or brand name, toll-free number, and website address. If all of the elements of the ad work together as a whole, they will help to hold interest and build recall.[21]

Arousing desire

Arousing desire to buy a particular product is one of an ad's most difficult jobs. The ad must convince customers that the product can meet their needs. Testimonials may persuade a consumer that other people with similar needs like the product. Product comparisons may highlight the advantages of a particular brand.

Although products may satisfy certain emotional needs, many consumers find it necessary to justify their purchases on some logical basis. Snickers candy bar ads helped ease the guilt of calorie-conscious snackers by assuring them that "Snickers satisfies you when you need an afternoon energy break."

An ad should usually focus on a *unique selling proposition* that aims at an important unsatisfied need. This can help differentiate the firm's marketing mix and position its brand as offering superior value to the target market. For example, Altoids has used humor in its ads to highlight the "curiously strong" flavor of its mints. Too

Ads that feature a unique selling proposition help consumers focus on what is different and better about a firm's marketing mix. This ad highlights the fact that Adobe's Acrobat 5.0 allows users to create electronic documents that can't be altered.

many advertisers ignore the idea of a unique selling proposition. Rather than using an integrated blend of communications to tell the whole story, they cram too much into each ad—and then none of it has any impact.

Obtaining action

Getting action is the final requirement—and not an easy one. From communication research, we now know that prospective customers must be led beyond considering how the product *might* fit into their lives to actually trying it.

Direct-response ads can sometimes help promote action by encouraging interested consumers to do *something* even if they are not ready to make a purchase. For example, an ad that includes a toll-free telephone number or website address might prompt some consumers to at least follow up for more information. Then follow-up brochures or a telephone salesperson can attempt to prompt another action—perhaps a visit to a store or a "satisfaction guaranteed" trial period. This approach seeks to get action one step at a time, where the first step provides a "foot in the door" for subsequent communication efforts.

Careful research on attitudes in the target market may help uncover strongly felt *unsatisfied* needs. Appealing to important needs can get more action and also provide the kind of information buyers need to confirm the correctness of their decisions. Some customers seem to read more advertising *after* a purchase than before.

Can global messages work?

Many international consumer products firms try to use one global advertising message all around the world. Of course, they translate the message or make other minor adjustments—but the focus is one global copy thrust. Some do it to cut the cost of developing different ads for each country. Others feel their customers' basic needs are the same, even in different countries. Some just do it because it's fashionable to "go global."

This approach works for some firms. Coca-Cola and IBM, for example, feel that the needs their products serve are very similar for customers around the world. They focus on the similarities among customers who make up their target market rather than the differences. However, most firms who use this approach experience terrible results. They may save money by developing fewer ads, but they lose sales because they don't develop advertising messages, and whole marketing mixes, aimed at specific target markets. They just try to appeal to a global "mass market."

Combining smaller market segments into a single, large target market makes sense if the different segments can be served with a single marketing mix. But when that is not the case, the marketing manager should treat them as different target markets and develop different marketing mixes for each target.[22]

ADVERTISING AGENCIES OFTEN DO THE WORK

An advertising manager manages a company's advertising effort. Many advertising managers, especially those working for large retailers, have their own advertising departments that plan specific advertising campaigns and carry out the details. Others turn over much of the advertising work to specialists—the advertising agencies.

Ad agencies are specialists

Advertising agencies are specialists in planning and handling mass-selling details for advertisers. Agencies play a useful role. They are independent of the advertiser and have an outside viewpoint. They bring experience to an individual client's problems because they work for many other clients. They can often do the job more economically than a company's own department. And if an agency isn't doing a good job, the client can select another. However, ending a relationship with an agency is a serious decision. Too many marketing managers just use their advertising agency as a scapegoat. Whenever anything goes wrong, they blame the agency.

Exhibit 16-5 Top Nine Advertising Agency Supergroups and Examples of Products They Advertise

Organization	Headquarters	Worldwide Gross Income, 2002 ($ millions)	Products
Omnicom Group	New York	$7,536.3	Visa, Pepsi, Gillette, FedEx, DaimlerChrysler
Interpublic Group of Cos.	New York	6,203.6	John Deere, Circuit City, Samsung, Dockers, Hewlett-Packard
WPP Group	London	5,781.5	Ford, IBM, Motorola, Mattel, American Express
Publicis Groupe	Paris	2,711.9	BMW, Citibank, L'Oréal, Hallmark, Timberland
Dentsu	Tokyo	2,060.9	Sega Enterprises, Toshiba, Dreamcast, Matsushita, Hitachi
Havas	Suresnes, France	1,841.6	Peugeot, Royal Caribbean, Intel, Evian, Air France
Grey Global Group	New York	1,199.7	Hasbro, Mars, Oracle, Procter & Gamble, Nokia
Hakuhodo	Tokyo	860.8	Sapporo, Sony, Honda, Citizen, Panasonic
Cordiant Communications Group	London	788.5	Wendy's, Pfizer, CDW, Kellogg's, Nestlé

Some full-service agencies handle any activities related to advertising, publicity, or sales promotion. They may even handle overall marketing strategy planning as well as marketing research, product and package development, and sales promotion. Other agencies are more specialized. For example, in recent years there has been rapid growth of firms that specialize in developing websites and Internet ads. Similarly, creative specialists just handle the artistic elements of advertising but leave media scheduling and buying, research, and related services to other specialists or full-service agencies.

The biggest agencies handle much of the advertising

The vast majority of advertising agencies are small, with 10 or fewer employees. But the largest agencies account for most of the billings. Over the past decade many of the big agencies merged, creating mega-agencies with worldwide networks. Exhibit 16-5 shows a list of nine of the largest agency networks and examples of some of the products they advertise. Although their headquarters are located in different nations, they have offices worldwide. The move toward international marketing is a key reason behind the mergers.

The mega-agency can offer varied services, wherever in the world a marketing manager needs them. This may be especially important for managers in large corporations—like Toyota, Renault, Unilever, NEC, and PepsiCo—that advertise worldwide.[23]

The really big agencies are less interested in smaller accounts. Smaller agencies will continue to appeal to customers who want more personal attention and a close relationship that is more attuned to their marketing needs.

Are they paid too much?

Traditionally, U.S. advertising agencies have been paid a commission of about 15 percent on media and production costs. This arrangement evolved because media usually have two prices: one for national advertisers and a lower rate for local advertisers, such as local retailers. The advertising agency gets a 15 percent commission on national rates but not on local rates. This makes it worthwhile for producers and national middlemen to use agencies. National advertisers have to pay the full media rate anyway, so it makes sense to let the agency experts do the work and earn their commission. Local retailers—allowed the lower media rate—seldom use agencies.

Many firms—especially big producers of consumer packaged goods—resist the idea of paying agencies the same way regardless of the work performed or *the results achieved*. The commission approach also makes it hard for agencies to be completely objective about inexpensive media. But agencies don't always like a commission arrangement, either. Some try to charge additional fees when advertisers spend relatively little on media or need extra services, like preparation of materials to support a website or the personal selling effort. About half of all advertisers now pay agencies some sort of labor-based fee.

Firms that spend huge amounts for help from advertising agencies are increasingly involving their purchasing departments in the process of negotiating agency compensation and other terms of the agency-client relationship. Procurement specialists may also set up procedures to audit agency charges for "billable hours" or other expenses. Auditing may become even more common in the future because of a few highly publicized cases in which agency executives have been accused of padding their time sheets.

Some firms pay the agency based on results

A number of advertisers now grade the work done by their agencies—and the agencies' pay depends on the grade. General Foods was the first to do this. It lowered its basic commission to about 13 percent. However, it paid the agency a bonus of about 3 percent on campaigns that earned an A rating. If the agency only earned a B, it lost the bonus. If it earned a C, it had to improve fast or GF removed the account.

Variations on this approach are becoming common. For example, Carnation directly links its agency's compensation with how well its ads score in market research tests. Gillette uses a sliding scale, and the percentage of compensation declines with increased advertising volume. And some agencies develop their own plans in which they guarantee to achieve the results expected or give the advertiser a partial refund. This approach forces the advertiser and agency to agree on very specific objectives for their ads and what they expect to achieve. It also reduces the likelihood of the creative people in an agency focusing on ads that will win artistic approval in their industry rather than ads that do what the firm needs done.[24]

Ethical conflicts may arise

Ad agencies usually work closely with their clients, and they often have access to confidential information. This can create ethical conflicts if an agency is working with two or more competing clients. Most agencies are sensitive to the potential problems and keep people and information from competing accounts separated. Even so, that doesn't always happen. For example, PepsiCo got a restraining order to stop an ad agency from assigning four people who had worked on advertising for its Aquafina bottled water to the account for Coca-Cola's competing brand, Dasani. Coca-Cola, in turn, yanked the account away from the agency. In another case, the part of General Motors' ad agency that handles ads for archrival Toyota hired an employee away from GM to work on the Toyota account. GM's marketing managers were outraged by the agency's lack of loyalty. Because of situations like these, many advertisers refuse to work with any agency that handles any competing accounts, even if they are handled in different offices.[25]

MEASURING ADVERTISING EFFECTIVENESS IS NOT EASY

Success depends on the total marketing mix

It would be convenient if we could measure the results of advertising by looking at sales. Some breakthrough ads do have a very direct effect on a company's sales—and the advertising literature is filled with success stories that "prove" advertising increases sales. Similarly, market research firms like Information Resources can

The new Mercedes-Benz A-Class. A dream come true.

Will your copy pass the test?

Mercedes used the ad (above) to help introduce its new model and attract younger customers in Latin America. A bad economy dampened sales, but the ad did pull the target market into showrooms. This increased names in the dealers' customer database, used to target other promotions, by 50 percent. Firms like QuickTake.com do research to help advertisers determine if a creative ad is also effective.

sometimes compare sales levels before and after the period of an ad campaign. Yet we usually can't measure advertising success just by looking at sales. The total marketing mix—not just advertising—is responsible for the sales result. Sales results are also affected by what competitors do and by other changes in the external marketing environment. Only with direct-response advertising can a company make a direct link between advertising and sales results.

Research and testing can improve the odds

Ideally, advertisers should pretest advertising before it runs rather than relying solely on their own guesses about how good an ad will be. The judgment of creative people or advertising experts may not help much. They often judge only on the basis of originality or cleverness of the copy and illustrations.

Many progressive advertisers now demand laboratory or market tests to evaluate an ad's effectiveness. For example, split runs on cable TV systems in test markets are an important approach for testing ads in a normal viewing environment. Scanner sales data from retailers in those test markets can provide an estimate of how an ad is likely to affect sales. This approach will become even more powerful in the future as more cable systems allow viewers to provide immediate feedback to an ad as it appears on TV or on the Internet.

Hindsight may lead to foresight

After ads run, researchers may try to measure how much consumers recall about specific products or ads. The response to radio or television commercials or magazine readership can be estimated using various survey methods to check the size and composition of audiences (the Nielsen and Starch reports are examples). Similarly, most Internet advertisers keep track of how many "hits" on the firm's website come from ads placed at other websites.[26]

HOW TO AVOID UNFAIR ADVERTISING

Government agencies may say what is fair

In most countries, the government takes an active role in deciding what kinds of advertising are allowable, fair, and appropriate. For example, France and Japan limit the use of cartoon characters in advertising to children, and Canada bans *any* advertising targeted directly at children. Greece and Sweden have similar policies and want the rest of the European Union to adopt them. In Switzerland, an advertiser cannot use an actor to represent a consumer. New Zealand and Switzerland limit political ads on TV. In the United States, print ads must be identified so they aren't confused with editorial matter; in other countries ads and editorial copy can be intermixed. Most countries limit the number and length of commercials on broadcast media.

What is seen as positioning in one country may be viewed as unfair or deceptive in another. For example, when Pepsi was advertising its cola as "the choice of the new generation" in most countries, Japan's Fair Trade Committee didn't allow it—because in Japan Pepsi was not "the choice." Similarly, Hungary's Economic Competition Council fined Unilever $25,000 for running an ad that claimed that its OMO detergent removed stains better than ordinary detergent. The Council said the ad was unfair because Hungarian consumers would interpret the phrase "ordinary detergent" as a reference to a locally produced detergent.[27]

Differences in rules mean that a marketing manager may face very specific limits in different countries, and local experts may be required to ensure that a firm doesn't waste money developing ads that will never be shown or which consumers will think are deceptive.

FTC controls unfair practices in the United States

In the United States, the Federal Trade Commission (FTC) has the power to control unfair or deceptive business practices, including deceptive advertising. The FTC has been policing deceptive advertising for many years. And it may be getting results now that advertising agencies as well as advertisers must share equal responsibility for false, misleading, or unfair ads.

This is a serious matter. If the FTC decides that a particular practice is unfair or deceptive, it has the power to require affirmative disclosures—such as the health warnings on cigarettes—or **corrective advertising**—ads to correct deceptive advertising. Years ago the FTC forced Listerine to spend millions of dollars on advertising to "correct" earlier ads that claimed the mouthwash helped prevent colds. Advertisers still remember that lesson. The possibility of large financial penalties or the need to pay for corrective ads has caused more agencies and advertisers to stay well within the law.

However, sometimes ad claims seem to get out of hand anyway. For example, there have been many ads and infomercials that tout various gadgets and dietary supplements as effective for weight loss. For most of these products there is no evidence that they work (unless used while training to compete in a marathon). Given the heightened concerns about obesity, the FTC has started to crack down on claims related to weight loss and health. For example, KFC quickly stopped running several of its TV ads after the FTC objected to the ads and opened an investigation. KFC's ads positioned fried chicken as a healthy choice in fast food, but there was also lots of small print at the bottom of the screen to qualify the claims.[28]

What is unfair or deceptive is changing

What constitutes unfair and deceptive advertising is a difficult question. The law provides some guidelines, but the marketing manager must make personal judgments as well. The social and political environment is changing worldwide. Practices considered acceptable some years ago are now questioned or considered deceptive. Saying or even implying that your product is best may be viewed as deceptive. And a 1988 revision of the Lanham Act protects firms whose brand names are unfairly tarnished in comparative ads.

Supporting ad claims is a fuzzy area

It's really not hard to figure out how to avoid criticisms of being unfair and deceptive. A little puffing is acceptable, and probably always will be. But marketing managers need to put a stop to the typical production-oriented approach of trying to use advertising to differentiate me-too products that are not different and don't offer customers better value.[29]

SALES PROMOTION—DO SOMETHING DIFFERENT TO STIMULATE CHANGE

The nature of sales promotion

Sales promotion refers to those promotion activities—other than advertising, publicity, and personal selling—that stimulate interest, trial, or purchase by final customers or others in the channel. Exhibit 14-2 shows examples of typical sales promotions targeted at final customers, channel members, or a firm's own employees.

Sales promotion is generally used to complement the other promotion methods. While advertising campaigns and sales force strategy decisions tend to have longer-term effects, a particular sales promotion activity usually lasts for only a limited time period. But sales promotion can often be implemented quickly and get sales results sooner than advertising. Further, sales promotion objectives usually focus on prompting some short-term action. For a middleman, such an action might be a decision to stock a product, provide a special display space, or give the product extra sales emphasis. For a consumer, the desired action might be to try a new product, switch from another brand, or buy more of a product. The desired action by an employee might be a special effort to satisfy customers.

Sales promotion objectives and situation should influence decision

There are many different types of sales promotion, but what type is appropriate depends on the situation and objectives. For example, Exhibit 16-6 shows some possible ways that a short-term promotion might affect sales. The sales pattern in the graph on the left might occur if Hellmann's issues coupons to help clear its excess mayonnaise inventory. Some consumers might buy earlier to take advantage of the coupon, but unless they use extra mayonnaise their next purchase will be delayed. In the center graph, kids might convince parents to eat more Big Macs while McDonald's has a *Lord of the Rings* promotion, but when it ends things go back to normal. The graph on the right shows a Burger King marketer's dream come true: Free samples of a new style of french fries quickly pull in new customers who like what they try and keep coming back after the promotion ends. This is also the kind of long-term result that is the aim of effective advertising. From these examples, you can see that the situation and the objective of the promotion should determine what specific type is best.

Exhibit 16-6 Some Possible Effects of a Sales Promotion on Sales

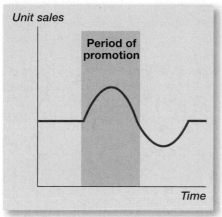

Sales temporarily increase, then decrease, then return to regular level

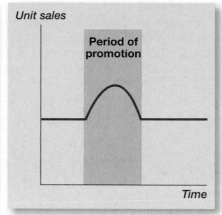

Sales temporarily increase and then return to regular level

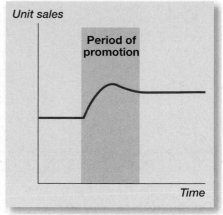

Sales increase and then remain at higher level

Sales promotion spending has grown in mature markets

Sales promotion involves so many different types of activities that it is difficult to estimate accurately how much is spent in total. There is general consensus, however, that the total spending on sales promotion exceeds spending on advertising. Companies that sell frequently purchased consumer products shifted their promotion blends to put more emphasis on sales promotion during the 1990s.[30]

One reason for increased use of sales promotion by many consumer products firms is that they are generally competing in mature markets. There's only so much soap that consumers want to buy, regardless of how many brands there are vying for their dollars. There's also only so much shelf space that retailers will allocate to a particular product category.

The competitive situation is intensified by the growth of large, powerful retail chains. They have put more emphasis on their own dealer brands and also demanded more sales promotion support for the manufacturer brands they do carry.

Perhaps in part because of this competition, many consumers have become more price sensitive. Many sales promotions, like coupons, have the effect of lowering the prices consumers pay. So sales promotion has been used as a tool to overcome consumer price resistance.

A number of firms that specialize in different aspects of consumer promotion, ranging from in-store ideas to games, are available to create solutions for marketing managers.

Changes in technology have also made sales promotion more efficient. For example, scanners at retail checkout counters instantly pinpoint a customer who is the target for a particular coupon. If a customer buys a bottle of Kraft salad dressing, Kraft can have the retailer's cash register print out a coupon, on the spot, to encourage the customer to buy Kraft again the next time.

The growth of sales promotion has also been fostered by the availability of more ad agencies and specialists who plan and implement sales promotion programs. Of course, the most basic reason for the growth of spending on sales promotion is that it can be very effective if it is done properly. But there are problems in the sales promotion area.

PROBLEMS IN MANAGING SALES PROMOTION

Does sales promotion erode brand loyalty?

Some experts think that marketing managers—especially those who deal with consumer packaged goods—put too much emphasis on sales promotion. They argue that the effect of most sales promotion is temporary and that money spent on advertising and personal selling helps the firm more over the long term. Their view is that most sales promotion doesn't help develop close relationships with consumers and instead erodes brand loyalty.

There is heavy use of sales promotion in mature markets where competition for customers and attention from middlemen is fierce. When the market is not growing, sales promotion may just encourage "deal-prone" customers (and middlemen)

Some successful sales promotion ideas at first seem pretty wild. Marketers for Charmin toilet tissue outfitted trucks with fancy bathrooms and sent the portable potties to big events, like the Super Bowl, where public restrooms would be in short supply. Two million curious consumers tried out these facilities. The payoff? Research shows a 14 percent increase in Charmin sales among those people.

to switch back and forth among brands. Here, all the expense of the sales promotion simply contributes to lower profits. It also increases the prices that consumers pay because it increases selling costs.

However, once a marketing manager is in this situation there may be little choice other than to continue. In mature markets, frequent sales promotions may be needed just to offset the effects of competitors' promotions. One escape from this competitive rat race is for the marketing manager to seek new opportunities—with a strategy that doesn't rely solely on short-term sales promotions for competitive advantage.

There are alternatives

Procter & Gamble is a company that changed its strategy, and promotion blend, to decrease its reliance on sales promotion targeted at middlemen. It is offering middlemen lower prices on many of its products and supporting those products with more advertising and promotion to final consumers. P&G believes that this approach builds its brand equity, serves consumers better, and leads to smoother-running relationships in its channels. Not all retailers are happy with P&G's changes. However, many other producers are following P&G's lead.[31]

Sales promotion is hard to manage

Another problem in the sales promotion area is that it is easy to make big, costly mistakes. Because sales promotion includes such a wide variety of activities, it's difficult for the typical company to develop skill in managing all of them. Even large firms and agencies that specialize in sales promotion run into difficulties because each promotion is typically custom-designed and then used only once. Yet mistakes caused by lack of experience can be costly or hurt relationships with customers.

In a promotion for Pampers diapers that was designed to reward loyal buyers and steal customers away from competing Huggies, marketing managers offered parents Fisher-Price toys if they collected points printed on Pampers' packages. At first the promotion seemed to be a big success because so many parents were collecting points. But that turned into a problem when Fisher-Price couldn't produce enough toys to redeem all the points. Pampers had to add 50 toll-free phone lines to handle all the complaints, and a lot of mad parents stopped buying Pampers for good. Burger King has also had problems with toys. Several times in recent years it has had to issue recalls because toys included in its Kid's Meal promotions were not safe. McDonald's had a different problem. An employee of an outside firm hired to run McDonald's Monopoly game promotion was accused of rigging the top prizes. McDonald's sued the outside firm, but in the meantime it had to offer an additional $10 million game to fulfill its promises to customers. These are not isolated examples. Such problems are common.[32]

Not a sideline for amateurs

Sales promotion mistakes are likely to be worse when a company has no sales promotion manager. If the personal selling or advertising managers are responsible for sales promotion, they often treat it as a "stepchild." They allocate money to sales promotion if there is any "left over" or if a crisis develops.

Making sales promotion work is a learned skill, not a sideline for amateurs. That's why specialists in sales promotion have developed, both inside larger firms and as outside consultants. Some of these people are real experts. But it's the marketing manager's responsibility to set sales promotion objectives and policies that will fit in with the rest of each marketing strategy.[33]

DIFFERENT TYPES OF SALES PROMOTION FOR DIFFERENT TARGETS

Sales promotion for final consumers or users

Much of the sales promotion aimed at final consumers or users tries to increase demand, perhaps temporarily, or speed up the time of purchase. Such promotion might involve developing materials to be displayed in retailers' stores, including banners, sample packages, calendars, and various point-of-purchase materials. It might include sweepstakes contests as well as coupons designed to get customers to buy a product by a certain date. Coupon distribution has dropped off some in recent years but still averages about 3,000 coupons per household in America! However, only about 1 percent of all coupons are redeemed.[34]

All of these sales promotion efforts are aimed at specific objectives. For example, if customers already have a favorite brand, it may be hard to get them to try anything new. A free trial-sized bottle of mouthwash might be just what it takes to get cautious consumers to try the new product. Samples might be distributed house to house, by mail, at stores, or attached to other products sold by the firm. In this type of situation, sales of the product might start to pick up as soon as customers try the product and find out that they like it. And sales will continue at the higher level after the promotion is over if satisfied customers make repeat purchases. Thus, the cost of the sales promotion in this situation might be viewed as a long-term investment.

Once a product is established, consumer sales promotion usually focuses on short-term sales increases. For example, after a price-off coupon for a soft drink is distributed, sales might temporarily pick up as customers take advantage of buying at a lower price. When the objective of the promotion is focused primarily on producing a short-term increase in sales, it's sensible for the marketing manager to evaluate the cost of the promotion relative to the extra sales expected. If the increase in sales won't at least cover the cost of the promotion, it probably doesn't make sense to do it. Otherwise, the firm is "buying sales" at the cost of reduced profit.

Sales promotion directed at industrial customers might use the same kinds of ideas. In addition, the sales promotion people might set up and staff trade show exhibits. Here, attractive models are often used to encourage buyers to look at a firm's product, especially when it is displayed near other similar products in a circuslike atmosphere. Trade shows are a cost-effective way to reach target customers and generate a list of "live" prospects for sales rep follow-up. However, many firms handle these leads badly. One study indicated that 85 percent of leads never got followed up by anybody.

Some sellers give promotion items—pen sets, watches, or clothing (perhaps with the firm's brand name on them)—to remind business customers of their products. This is common, but it can be a problem. Some companies do not allow buyers to take any gifts.[35]

Sales promotion for middlemen

Sales promotion aimed at middlemen—sometimes called *trade promotion*—emphasizes price-related matters. The objective may be to encourage middlemen to stock new items, buy in larger quantity, buy early, or stress a product in their own promotion efforts.

The tools used here include merchandise allowances, promotion allowances, and perhaps sales contests to encourage retailers or wholesalers to sell specific items or the company's whole line. Offering to send contest winners to Hawaii, for example, may increase sales.

About half of the sales promotion spending targeted at middlemen has the effect of reducing the price that they pay for merchandise. So we'll go into more detail on different types of trade discounts and allowances in the next chapter.[36]

Sales promotion for own employees

Sales promotion aimed at the company's own sales force might try to encourage providing better service, getting new customers, selling a new product, or selling the company's whole line. Depending on the objectives, the tools might be contests, bonuses on sales or number of new accounts, and holding sales meetings at fancy resorts to raise everyone's spirits.

Ongoing sales promotion work might also be aimed at the sales force—to help sales management. Sales promotion might be responsible for preparing sales portfolios, digital videos or PowerPoint presentations on new products, displays, and other sales aids, as well as sales training material.

Service-oriented firms such as hotels and restaurants use sales promotions targeted at their employees. Some, for example, give a monthly cash prize for the employee who provides the "best service." And the employee's picture is displayed to give recognition.[37]

CONCLUSION

It may seem simple to develop an advertising campaign. Just pick the medium and develop a message. But it's not that easy. Effectiveness depends on using the "best" available medium and the "best" message considering (1) promotion objectives, (2) the target markets, and (3) the funds available for advertising.

Specific advertising objectives determine what kind of advertising to use—product or institutional. If product advertising is needed, then the particular type must be decided—pioneering, competitive (direct or indirect), or reminder. And advertising allowances and cooperative advertising may be helpful.

Many technical details are involved in mass selling, and specialists—advertising agencies—handle some of these jobs. But specific objectives must be set for them, or their advertising may have little direction and be almost impossible to evaluate.

Effective advertising should affect sales. But the whole marketing mix affects sales—and the results of advertising usually can't be measured by sales changes alone. By contrast, sales promotion tends to be more action-oriented.

Sales promotion spending is big and growing. This approach is especially important in prompting action—by customers, middlemen, or salespeople. There are many different types of sales promotion, and it is a problem area in many firms because it is difficult for a firm to develop expertise with all of the possibilities.

Advertising and sales promotion are often important parts of a promotion blend—but in most blends personal selling also plays an important role. Further, promotion is only a part of the total marketing mix a marketing manager must develop to satisfy target customers. So to broaden your understanding of the four Ps and how they fit together, in the next two chapters we'll go into more detail on the role of Price in strategy decisions.

KEY TERMS

product advertising, 436

institutional advertising, 436

pioneering advertising, 437

competitive advertising, 438

direct type advertising, 438

indirect type advertising, 438

comparative advertising, 438

reminder advertising, 438

advertising allowances, 439

cooperative advertising, 439

copy thrust, 447

advertising agencies, 449

corrective advertising, 453

QUESTIONS AND PROBLEMS

1. Identify the strategy decisions a marketing manager must make in the advertising area.

2. Discuss the relation of advertising objectives to marketing strategy planning and the kinds of advertising actually needed. Illustrate.

3. List several media that might be effective for reaching consumers in a developing nation with low per capita income and a high level of illiteracy. Briefly discuss the limitations and advantages of each medium you suggest.

4. Give three examples where advertising to middlemen might be necessary. What are the objective(s) of such advertising?

5. What does it mean to say that "money is invested in advertising"? Is all advertising an investment? Illustrate.

6. Find advertisements to final consumers that illustrate the following types of advertising: (a) institutional, (b) pioneering, (c) competitive, and (d) reminder. What objective(s) does each of these ads have? List the needs each ad appeals to.

7. Describe the type of media that might be most suitable for promoting: (a) tomato soup, (b) greeting cards, (c) a business component material, and (d) playground equipment. Specify any assumptions necessary to obtain a definite answer.

8. Briefly discuss some of the pros and cons an advertising manager for a producer of sports equipment might want to think about in deciding whether to advertise on the Internet.

9. Discuss the use of testimonials in advertising. Which of the four AIDA steps might testimonials accomplish? Are they suitable for all types of products? If not, for which types are they most suitable?

10. Find a magazine ad that you think does a particularly good job of communicating to the target audience. Would the ad communicate well to an audience in another country? Explain your thinking.

11. Johnson & Johnson sells its baby shampoo in many different countries. Do you think baby shampoo would be a good product for Johnson & Johnson to advertise with a single global message? Explain your thinking.

12. Discuss the future of smaller advertising agencies now that many of the largest are merging to form mega-agencies.

13. Does advertising cost too much? How can this be measured?

14. How would your local newspaper be affected if local supermarkets switched their weekly advertising and instead used a service that delivered weekly, free-standing ads directly to each home?

15. Is it unfair to criticize a competitor's product in an ad? Explain your thinking.

16. Explain why P&G and other consumer packaged goods firms are trying to cut back on some types of sales promotion like coupons for consumers and short-term trade promotions such as "buy a case and get a case free."

17. Discuss some ways that a firm can link its sales promotion activities to its advertising and personal selling efforts—so that all of its promotion efforts result in an integrated effort.

18. Indicate the type of sales promotion that a producer might use in each of the following situations and briefly explain your reasons:

    a. A firm has developed an improved razor blade and obtained distribution, but customers are not motivated to buy it.
    b. A competitor is about to do a test market for a new brand and wants to track sales in test market areas to fine tune its marketing mix.
    c. A big grocery chain won't stock a firm's new popcorn-based snack product because it doesn't think there will be much consumer demand.

19. Why wouldn't a producer of toothpaste just lower the price of its product rather than offer consumers a price-off coupon?

20. If sales promotion spending continues to grow—often at the expense of media advertising—how do you think this might affect the rates charged by mass media for advertising time or space? How do you think it might affect advertising agencies?

SUGGESTED CASES

18. Village Bank

20. Leisure World, Inc.

COMPUTER-AIDED PROBLEM

16. Sales Promotion

RESOURCE REMINDER

As a community service, disc jockeys from radio station WMKT formed a basketball team to help raise money for local nonprofit organizations. The host organization finds or fields a competing team and charges $5 admission to the game. Money from ticket sales goes to the nonprofit organization.

Ticket sales were disappointing at recent games, averaging only about 300 people per game. When WMKT's marketing manager, Bruce Miller, heard about the problem, he suggested using sales promotion to improve ticket sales. The PTA for the local high school—the sponsor for the next game—is interested in the idea but is concerned that its budget doesn't include any promotion money. Miller tries to help them by reviewing his idea in more detail.

Specifically, he proposes that the PTA give a free T-shirt (printed with the school name and date of the game) to the first 500 ticket buyers. He thinks the T-shirt giveaway will create a lot of interest. In fact, he says he is almost certain the promotion would help the PTA sell 600 tickets, double the usual number. He speculates that the PTA might even have a sellout of all 900 seats in the school gym. Further, he notes that the T-shirts will more than pay for themselves if the PTA sells 600 tickets.

A local firm that specializes in sales promotion items agrees to supply the shirts and do the printing for $2.40

a shirt if the PTA places an order for at least 400 shirts. The PTA thinks the idea is interesting but wants to look at it more closely to see what will happen if the promotion doesn't increase ticket sales. To help the PTA evaluate the alternatives, Miller sets up a spreadsheet with the relevant information.

a. Based on the data from the initial spreadsheet, does the T-shirt promotion look like a good idea? Explain your thinking.

b. The PTA treasurer worries about the up-front cost of printing the T-shirts and wants to know where they would stand if they ordered the T-shirts and still sold only 300 tickets. He suggests it might be safer to order the minimum number of T-shirts (400). Evaluate his suggestion.

c. The president of the PTA thinks the T-shirt promotion will increase sales but wonders if it wouldn't be better just to lower the price. She suggests $2.60 a ticket, which she arrives at by subtracting the $2.40 T-shirt cost from the usual $5.00 ticket price. How many tickets would the PTA have to sell at the lower price to match the money it would make if it used the T-shirt promotion and actually sold 600 tickets? (Hint: Change the selling price in the spreadsheet and then vary the quantity using the analysis feature.)

For additional questions related to this problem, see Exercise 16-3 in the *Learning Aid for Use with Basic Marketing,* 15th edition.

CHAPTER SEVENTEEN

Pricing Objectives and Policies

In the early 1960s, the electric toothbrush was a new idea. A number of brands were on the market, and the American Dental Association declared that electric brushes were better at cleaning teeth. Yet when Consumers' Union found that the available models created an electric shock hazard, demand fizzled. In the 1990s, SonicCare introduced a safe, rechargeable unit at a premium price. Braun and other competitors followed its lead. But demand was limited. Few consumers saw an electric brush priced at more than $50 as a good value.

In 1998, John Osher and his three business partners had an idea for a battery-powered toothbrush that has changed the market. Even before 1998, Osher had been successful developing new-product ideas and then selling them to big companies. One hit was the Spin Pop, a spinning lollipop attached to a battery-powered plastic handle. After selling Spin Top to Hasbro, Osher and his partners searched for their next big idea. While looking at the toothbrush display at a Wal-Mart store, they realized that they could adapt the Spin Pop idea to create an electric toothbrush. They reasoned that many consumers would trade up to their product if it was more effective than the premium manual brushes—and not much more expensive. So they spent the next year and a half researching, designing, and sourcing a high-quality brush that could sell for $5, including the batteries.

Their next challenge was to prove that the brush would sell. Large firms typically support new-product introductions with a hefty advertising budget and by giving retailers introductory deals or allowances. Then, to cover all the costs, they charge a premium price—at least until competition heats up. But Osher's small firm wanted to penetrate the market at a low initial price, where demand would be the greatest. And at a low price it couldn't afford all of the promotion. Instead, they decided to build interest at the point of purchase with packaging that said "Try me" and that left the button exposed so consumers could see the brush work. With the help of a salesperson who had experience working with big discount chains, they set up a test market. In the test, their new SpinBrush outsold the leading manual brush nearly 3 to 1. Using that sales data as evidence of the profit a retailer could make selling SpinBrush, they persuaded Walgreens

Drugstores and then other retailers to carry it. Within a year, by the end of 2000, their new SpinBrush had expanded sales in the electric toothbrush market by 300 percent.

With that track record, Osher approached Procter & Gamble about buying SpinBrush. The timing was good. Price competition was making it tough for P&G's Crest oral care line to meet its profit objectives. Worse, Colgate had just launched its $19.95 ActiBrush electric toothbrush and it was off to a fast start. So P&G quickly struck a deal and soon was selling the SpinBrush with the Crest brand name. P&G kept the suggested retail price of the SpinBrush at $5.99, and relied on its sales reps to expand distribution. Even without TV ads, sales took off like a rocket.

ActiBrush suffered in comparison, so by 2002 Colgate cut its price to $12 and also introduced a brush like the SpinBrush at the same $5.99 price. However, by then marketing managers for SpinBrush had introduced new models, including new colors and designs to appeal to kids. They also offered an improved $7.99 SpinBrush Pro with dual action heads and replaceable brushes. The higher price on the Pro model gave P&G a better profit margin and gave retailers greater incentive to give it more shelf space. Consumers saw SpinBrush as a good value, and that was confirmed when *Consumer's Digest* declared it a best buy.

Oral-B didn't want to sit by while SpinBrush took customers from its regular brushes and high-end electrics, so it added a battery brush in the middle of its line. To help fend off the increasing competition, P&G came out with testimonial ads for SpinBrush that also included a toll-free number for a $1-off coupon. The price-off coupons didn't leave much profit margin, but they attracted customers who will bolster profits each time they buy replacement brushes, in a package of two for $5.95. Penetration of battery-powered brushes is now about 12 percent of U.S. households, but here and in overseas markets—where SpinBrush is already building strong distribution—there appears to be room for more profitable growth.[1]

PRICE HAS MANY STRATEGY DIMENSIONS

Price is one of the four major strategy decision variables a marketing manager controls. Price decisions affect both the number of sales a firm makes and how much money it earns. Price is what a customer must give up to get the benefits offered by the rest of a firm's marketing mix, so it plays a direct role in shaping customer value.

Guided by the company's objectives, marketing managers must develop a set of pricing objectives and policies. They must spell out what price situations the firm will face and how it will handle them. These policies should explain (1) how flexible prices will be, (2) at what level they will be set over the product life cycle, (3) to whom and when discounts and allowances will be given, and

Ragged Mountain wants its customers to know that its price is a good value compared to what they get at other ski resorts.

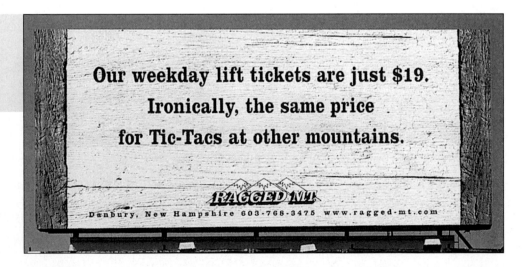

Our weekday lift tickets are just $19. Ironically, the same price for Tic-Tacs at other mountains.

RAGGED MT

Danbury, New Hampshire 603-768-3475 www.ragged-mt.com

Exhibit 17-1
Strategy Planning for Price

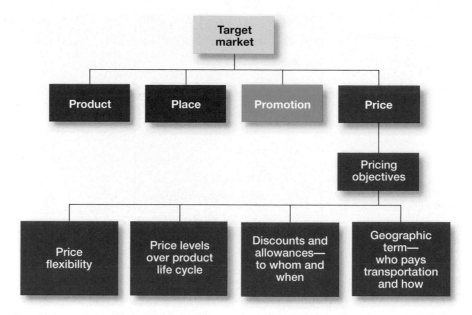

(4) how transportation costs will be handled. See Exhibit 17-1. These Price-related strategy decision areas are the focus of this chapter. After we've looked at specific decision areas, we will discuss how they combine to impact customer value as well as laws that are relevant. In the next chapter, we will discuss how specific prices are set.

It's not easy to define price in real-life situations because price reflects many dimensions. People who don't realize this can make big mistakes.

Suppose you've been saving to buy a new car and you see in an ad that, after a $1,000 rebate, the base price for the new-year model is $16,494—5 percent lower than the previous year. At first this might seem like a real bargain. However, your view of this deal might change if you found out you also had to pay a $400 transportation charge and an extra $480 for an extended service warranty. The price might look even less attractive if you discovered that the fancy stereo, side air bags, and moonroof that were standard the previous year are now options that cost $1,400. The cost of the higher interest rate on the car loan and the sales tax on all of this might come as an unpleasant surprise too. Further, how would you feel if you bought the car anyway and then learned that a friend who just bought the exact same model got a much lower price from the dealer by using a broker he found on the Internet?[2]

The price equation: Price equals something of value

This example emphasizes that when a seller quotes a price, it is related to *some* assortment of goods and services. So **Price** is the amount of money that is charged for "something" of value. Of course, price may be called different things in different settings. Colleges charge tuition. Landlords collect rent. Motels post a room rate. Country clubs get dues. Banks ask for interest when they loan money. Airlines have fares. Doctors set fees. Employees want a wage. People may call it different things, but *almost every business transaction in our modern economy involves an exchange of money—the Price—for something.*

The something can be a physical product in various stages of completion, with or without supporting services, with or without quality guarantees, and so on. Or it could be a pure service—dry cleaning, a lawyer's advice, or insurance on your car.

The nature and extent of this something determines the amount of money exchanged. Some customers pay list price. Others obtain large discounts or

Exhibit 17-2
Price as Seen by Consumers
or Users

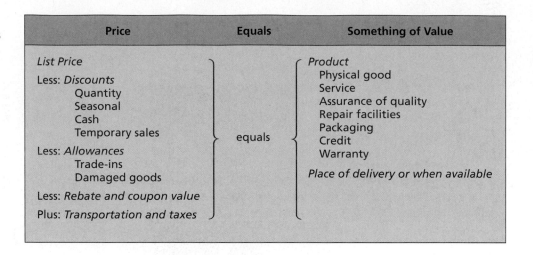

Price	Equals	Something of Value

List Price
 	
Less: *Discounts*
    Quantity
    Seasonal
    Cash
    Temporary sales
 	
Less: *Allowances*
    Trade-ins
    Damaged goods
 	
Less: *Rebate and coupon value*
 	
Plus: *Transportation and taxes*
	equals	*Product*
		    Physical good
		    Service
		    Assurance of quality
		    Repair facilities
		    Packaging
		    Credit
		    Warranty
		
		Place of delivery or when available

allowances because something is *not* provided. Exhibit 17-2 summarizes some possible variations for consumers or users, and Exhibit 17-3 does the same for channel members. These variations are discussed more fully below, and then we'll consider the customer value concept more fully—in terms of competitive advantage. But here it should be clear that Price has many dimensions. How each of these dimensions is handled affects customer value. If a customer sees greater value in spending money in some other way, no exchange will occur.

OBJECTIVES SHOULD GUIDE STRATEGY PLANNING FOR PRICE

Pricing objectives should flow from, and fit in with, company-level and marketing objectives. Pricing objectives should be *explicitly stated* because they have a direct effect on pricing policies as well as the methods used to set prices. Exhibit 17-4 shows the various types of pricing objectives we'll discuss.

Exhibit 17-3
Price as Seen by Channel
Members

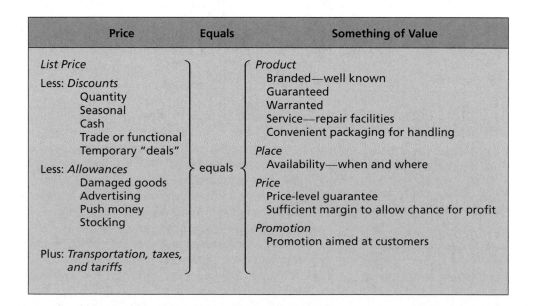

Price	Equals	Something of Value

List Price
 	
Less: *Discounts*
    Quantity
    Seasonal
    Cash
    Trade or functional
    Temporary "deals"
 	
Less: *Allowances*
    Damaged goods
    Advertising
    Push money
    Stocking
 	
Plus: *Transportation, taxes, and tariffs*
	equals	*Product*
		    Branded—well known
		    Guaranteed
		    Warranted
		    Service—repair facilities
		    Convenient packaging for handling
		
		Place
		    Availability—when and where
		
		Price
		    Price-level guarantee
		    Sufficient margin to allow chance for profit
		
		Promotion
		    Promotion aimed at customers

Exhibit 17-4
Possible Pricing Objectives

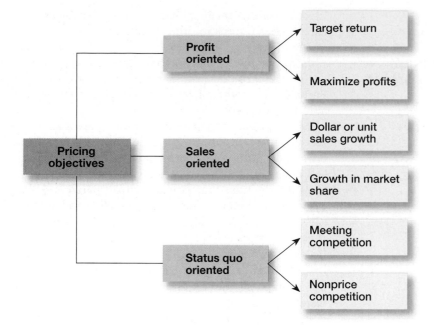

PROFIT-ORIENTED OBJECTIVES

Target returns provide specific guidelines

A **target return objective** sets a specific level of profit as an objective. Often this amount is stated as a percentage of sales or of capital investment. A large manufacturer like Motorola might aim for a 15 percent return on investment. The target for Safeway and other supermarket chains might be a 1 percent return on sales.

A target return objective has administrative advantages in a large company. Performance can be compared against the target. Some companies eliminate divisions, or drop products, that aren't yielding the target rate of return. For example, General

Some politicians want to control the prices of drugs, but that may not be in the public interest if it reduces the incentive for firms to make the big investment required to develop innovative new medicines that people need. That, in turn, would reduce consumer choices.

Electric sold its small appliance division to Black & Decker because it felt it could earn higher returns in other product-markets.

Some just want satisfactory profits

Some managers aim for only satisfactory returns. They just want returns that ensure the firm's survival and convince stockholders they're doing a good job. Similarly, some small family-run businesses aim for a profit that will provide a comfortable lifestyle.[3]

Many private and public nonprofit organizations set a price level that will just recover costs. In other words, their target return figure is zero. For example, a government agency may charge motorists a toll for using a bridge but then drop the toll when the cost of the bridge is paid.

Similarly, firms that provide critical public services—including many utility and insurance companies, transportation firms, and defense contractors—sometimes pursue only satisfactory long-run targets. They are well aware that the public expects them to set prices that are in the public interest. They may also have to face public or government agencies that review and approve prices.[4]

This kind of situation can lead to decisions that are not in the public interest. For example, some critics argue that some power companies that serve California were not motivated to keep costs low or expand capacity. After deregulation, there were big shortages, and even price gouging by some firms, because it takes a long time to add new power systems.

Profit maximization can be socially responsible

A **profit maximization objective** seeks to get as much profit as possible. It might be stated as a desire to earn a rapid return on investment—or, more bluntly, to charge all the traffic will bear.

Pricing to achieve profit maximization doesn't always lead to high prices. Low prices may expand the size of the market and result in greater sales and profits. For example, when prices of cell phones were very high, only businesses and wealthy people bought them. When producers lowered prices, nearly everyone bought one.

If a firm is earning a very large profit, other firms will try to copy or improve on what the company offers. Frequently, this leads to lower prices. In 1981, IBM unveiled the first 1-gigabyte disk drive. It was the size of a school locker, weighed 500 pounds, and cost $40,000. It was very profitable. Twenty years later, IBM offered a 1-gigabyte drive the size of a matchbox. It weighed 1 ounce and cost about $350. Now customers can buy a tiny flash memory card with that much memory for about half that price, and the prices continue to drop.[5]

SALES-ORIENTED OBJECTIVES

A **sales-oriented objective** seeks some level of unit sales, dollar sales, or share of market—*without referring to profit.*

Sales growth doesn't necessarily mean big profits

Some managers are more concerned about sales growth than profits. They think sales growth always leads to more profits. This kind of thinking causes problems when a firm's costs are growing faster than sales. Some major corporations have had declining profits in spite of growth in sales. At the extreme, many dot-coms kept lowering prices to increase market share but never earned any profits. Pets.com had growing sales until it burned through investors' money and went bankrupt. Generally, however, business managers now pay more attention to profits, not just sales.[6]

Some nonprofit organizations set prices to increase market share—precisely because they are *not* trying to earn a profit. For example, many cities set low fares

When the price of a barrel of crude oil suddenly doubled, gasoline prices at the pump jumped 50 cents a gallon almost overnight. In this situation, a customer may have no choice but to pay the "arm and leg" price. However, if prices stayed high for a longer period of time many consumers might switch to more energy efficient vehicles or perhaps to public transportation.

to fill up their buses. Buses cost the same to run empty or full, and there's more benefit when they're full even if the total revenue is no greater.

Market share objectives are popular

Many firms seek to gain a specified share (percent) of a market. If a company has a large market share, it may have better economies of scale than its competitors. In addition, it's usually easier to measure a firm's market share than to determine if profits are being maximized.

A company with a longer-run view may aim for increased market share when the market is growing. The hope is that future volume will justify sacrificing some profit in the short run. Companies as diverse as 3M and Coca-Cola look at opportunities in Eastern Europe this way.

Of course, market share objectives have the same limitations as straight sales growth objectives. A larger market share, if gained at too low a price, may lead to profitless "success." This is a too-common symptom of death-wish marketing.

Unfortunately, profitless market share is exactly what the Ford Taurus achieved. In the late 1990s, it was the family sedan with the highest market share in the U.S. When competitors started to take away customers, Ford kept its market share high by selling thousands of cars at highly discounted rates to rental car companies and corporate fleets. That made things look better for a while, but profits were poor. Worse, when all of those cars flooded into the used-car market, the resale value of the Taurus went down the tubes. Consumers who had bought a new Taurus expecting the value of their investment to hold up felt betrayed, and many said they'd never buy another Ford.[7]

STATUS QUO PRICING OBJECTIVES

Don't-rock-the-boat objectives

Managers satisfied with their current market share and profits sometimes adopt **status quo objectives**—don't-rock-the-*pricing*-boat objectives. Managers may say that they want to stabilize prices, or meet competition, or even avoid competition. This don't-rock-the-boat thinking is most common when the total market is not growing.

Or stress nonprice competition instead

A status quo pricing objective may be part of an aggressive overall marketing strategy focusing on **nonprice competition**—aggressive action on one or more of the Ps other than Price. Fast-food chains like McDonald's, Wendy's, and Burger King experienced very profitable growth by sticking to nonprice competition for many years. However, when Taco Bell and others started to take away customers with price-cutting, the other chains also turned to price competition.

Some Internet firms originally thought that they'd compete with low prices and still earn high profits from volume. However, when they didn't get the sales volume they hoped for, they realized that there were also some nonprice ways to compete. For example, Zappos.com offers free shipping and guarantees that it will meet local shoe store prices. But it wins customers with its enormous selection of shoes, a website that makes it easy for customers to find what they want, and excellent customer service before and after the sale.[8]

MOST FIRMS SET SPECIFIC PRICING POLICIES—TO REACH OBJECTIVES

Administered prices help achieve objectives

Price policies usually lead to **administered prices**—consciously set prices. In other words, instead of letting daily market forces (or auctions) decide their prices, most firms set their own prices. They may hold prices steady for long periods of time or change them more frequently if that's what's required to meet objectives.

If a firm doesn't sell directly to final customers, it usually wants to administer both the price it receives from middlemen and the price final customers pay. After all, the price final customers pay will ultimately affect the quantity it sells.

Yet it is often difficult to administer prices throughout the channel. Other channel members may also wish to administer prices to achieve their own objectives. This is what happened to Alcoa, one of the largest aluminum producers. To reduce

Marketing managers for Hydra Pools and HTH consciously set prices so that consumers receive a good value at a price that will yield attractive profits for both the producer and the retailer.

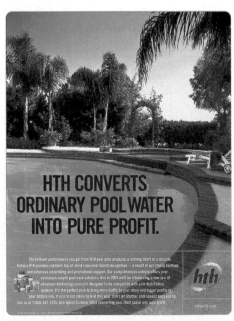

470

its excess inventory, Alcoa offered its wholesalers a 30 percent discount off its normal price. Alcoa expected the wholesalers to pass most of the discount along to their customers to stimulate sales throughout the channel. Instead, wholesalers bought *their* aluminum at the lower price but passed on only a small discount to customers. As a result, the quantity Alcoa sold didn't increase much, and it still had excess inventories, while the wholesalers made much more profit on the aluminum they did sell.[9]

Some firms don't even try to administer prices. They just meet competition—or worse, mark up their costs with little thought to demand. They act as if they have no choice in selecting a price policy.

Remember that Price has many dimensions. Managers usually *do* have many choices. They *should* administer their prices. And they should do it carefully because, ultimately, customers must be willing to pay these prices before a whole marketing mix succeeds. In the rest of this chapter, we'll talk about policies a marketing manager must set to do an effective job of administering Price.[10]

PRICE FLEXIBILITY POLICIES

One-price policy— the same price for everyone

One of the first decisions a marketing manager has to make is whether to use a one-price or a flexible-price policy. A **one-price policy** means offering the same price to all customers who purchase products under essentially the same conditions and in the same quantities. The majority of U.S. firms use a one-price policy—mainly for administrative convenience and to maintain goodwill among customers.

A one-price policy makes pricing easier. But a marketing manager must be careful to avoid a rigid one-price policy. This can amount to broadcasting a price that competitors can undercut, especially if the price is somewhat high. One reason for the growth of mass merchandisers is that conventional retailers rigidly applied traditional margins and stuck to them.

Flexible-price policy—different prices for different customers

A **flexible-price policy** means offering the same product and quantities to different customers at different prices. When computers are used to implement flexible pricing, the decisions focus more on what type of customer will get a price break.

Pricing databases make flexible pricing easier

Various forms of flexible pricing are more common now that most prices are maintained in a central computer database. Frequent changes are easier. You see this when supermarket chains give frequent-shopper club members reduced prices on weekly specials. The checkout scanner reads the code on the package, then the computer looks up the club price or the regular price depending on whether a club card has been scanned.

Some marketing managers have set up relationships with Internet companies whose ads invite customers to "set your own price." For example, Priceline operates a website at www.priceline.com. Visitors to the website specify the desired schedule for an airline flight and what price they're willing to pay. Priceline electronically forwards the information to airlines and if one accepts the offer the consumer is notified.

It may appear that these marketing managers have given up on administering prices. Just the opposite is true. They are carefully administering a flexible price. Most airlines, for example, set a very high list price. Not many people pay it. Travelers who plan ahead or who accept nonpeak flights get a discount. Business travelers who want high demand flights on short notice pay the higher prices. However, it doesn't make sense to stick to a high price and fly the plane half empty. So the

airline continuously adjusts the price on the basis of how many seats are left to fill. If seats are still empty at the last minute, the website offers a rock-bottom fare. Other firms, especially service businesses, use this approach when they have excess capacity.[11]

Salespeople can adjust prices to the situation

Flexible pricing is most common in the channels, in direct sales of business products, and at retail for expensive shopping products. Retail shopkeepers in less-developed economies typically use flexible pricing. These situations usually involve personal selling, not mass selling. The advantage of flexible pricing is that the salesperson can adjust price—considering prices charged by competitors, the relationship with the customer, and the customer's bargaining ability. Flexible-price policies often specify a *range* in which the actual price charged must fall.[12]

Too much price-cutting erodes profits

Some sales reps let price-cutting become a habit. This can lead to a lower price level and lower profit. A small price cut may not seem like much; but keep in mind that all of the revenue that is lost would go to profit. If salespeople for a producer that usually earns profits equal to 15 percent of its sales cut prices by an average of about 5 percent, profits would drop by a third!

Disadvantages of flexible pricing

Flexible pricing does have disadvantages. A customer who finds that others paid lower prices for the same marketing mix will be unhappy. This can cause real conflict in channels. For example, the Winn-Dixie supermarket chain stopped carrying products of some suppliers who refused to give Winn-Dixie the same prices available to chains in other regions of the country. Similarly, companies that post different prices for different segments on a website that all can see often get complaints.

If buyers learn that negotiating is in their interest, the time needed for bargaining will increase. This can increase selling costs and reduce profits. It can also frustrate customers. For example, most auto dealers use flexible pricing and bargain for what they can get. Inexperienced consumers, reluctant to bargain, often pay hundreds of dollars more than the dealer is willing to accept. By contrast, CarMax has earned high customer-satisfaction ratings by offering haggle-weary consumers a one-price policy.[13]

PRICE-LEVEL POLICIES—OVER THE PRODUCT LIFE CYCLE

Marketing managers who administer prices must consciously set a price-level policy. As they enter the market, they have to set introductory prices that may have long-run effects. They must consider where the product life cycle is and how fast it's moving. And they must decide if their prices should be above, below, or somewhere in between relative to the market.

Let's look for a moment at a new product in the market introduction stage of its product life cycle. There are few (or no) direct substitute marketing mixes. So the price-level decision should focus first on the nature of market demand. A high price may lead to higher profit from each sale but also to fewer units sold. A lower price might appeal to more potential customers. With this in mind, should the firm set a high or low price?

Skimming pricing— feeling out demand at a high price

A **skimming price policy** tries to sell the top (skim the cream) of a market—the top of the demand curve—at a high price before aiming at more price-sensitive customers. Skimming may maximize profits in the market introduction stage for an innovation, especially if there are few substitutes or if some customers are not price sensitive. Skimming is also useful when you don't know very much about the shape of the demand curve. It's sometimes safer to start with a high price that customers can refuse and then reduce it if necessary.

Skimming has critics

Some critics argue that firms should not try to maximize profits by using a skimming policy on new products that have important social consequences—a patent-protected, life-saving drug or a technique that increases crop yields, for example. Many of those who need the product may not have the money to buy it. This is a serious concern. However, it's also a serious problem if firms don't have any incentive to take risks and develop new products.[14]

Price moves down the demand curve

A skimming policy usually involves a slow reduction in price over time. See Exhibit 17-5. Note that as price is reduced, new target markets are probably being sought. So as the price level steps down the demand curve, new Place, Product, and Promotion policies may be needed too.

This is happening with hang-on-the-wall, flat-panel TVs. In 2000, the average selling price for a plasma TV was $12,000. Most of these units were sold by dealers who sell commercial lines to business customers who are less price sensitive. For instance, a firm that wanted a plasma TV to display product demo videos at a trade show was more likely to focus on picture quality, saving space, and the "wow factor." Yet by 2001, about 16,000 of these pricey plasma TVs had been sold to early-adopter consumers. When Sony, Mitsushita (Panasonic), and other firms saw that trend, they came out with consumer models and distributed them through electronics superstores, like Best Buy. These retailers used a lower markup (about 30 percent) than the commercial dealers. Their lower prices stimulated consumer demand, so producers built more factories. Then, with more production capacity than demand, price competition increased— and producers came out with new models to appeal to different market segments. As the demand for flat-panel TVs surged, manufacturers of computer LCD displays added TV tuners and improved the picture quality on their large screens. By 2004, general-merchandise retailers like Sears and Wal-Mart were selling flat-panel TVs, and firms like Dell and HP had added them to their lines. At that point, prices were only about 60 percent of where they had started—and they continue to fall as demand grows and more firms switch from producing traditional TVs to flat-panel ones.[15]

Penetration pricing— get volume at a low price

A **penetration pricing policy** tries to sell the whole market at one low price. This approach might be wise when the elite market—those willing to pay a high price—is small. This is the case when the whole demand curve is fairly elastic.

DuPont Corian, a solid countertop material, was costly to develop. When Corian was introduced, there was little direct competition and a premium price helped to recover development costs. Now that there is more competition, discounted prices are sometimes available. Marketing managers for PalmPilot used a different approach. With penetration pricing they sold a million units of the innovative PalmPilot within 24 months of its introduction. Now Palm has introduced an even lower-priced Zire model that is targeted at parents.

See Exhibit 17-5. A penetration policy is even more attractive if selling larger quantities results in lower costs because of economies of scale. Penetration pricing may be wise if the firm expects strong competition very soon after introduction.

When the first version of the PalmPilot was introduced, competitors were close behind. In addition, Apple had failed when it tried to introduce the Newton personal information manager at a skimming price of $1,000. So the focus for Palm was on a combination of features and price that would be a good value and help penetrate the market quickly. The initial price of about $250 resulted in sales of a million units in 24 months. A $250 retail price may not seem that low now that the PDA market is maturing and the Palm Zire, for example, is priced at about $70 to appeal to first-time PDA buyers. However, Palm's initial price was low enough to discourage some competitors from quickly entering the market.

Even a very low penetration price usually won't keep competitors out of a growth market permanently—and product life cycles do march on. For instance, competition is now intense among firms that sell PDAs, and different models appeal to different segments. Higher-priced PDAs that combine a cell phone, digital camera, and Internet access as well as MP3 and video players compete with single-use products in other product categories.[16]

Exhibit 17-5 Alternative Introductory Pricing Policies

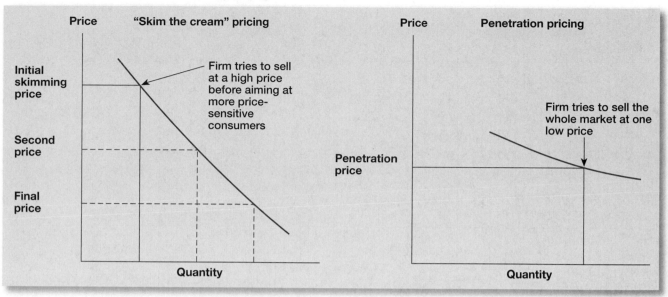

"Skim the cream" pricing — Firm tries to sell at a high price before aiming at more price-sensitive consumers. (Price axis: Initial skimming price, Second price, Final price; Quantity axis)

Penetration pricing — Firm tries to sell the whole market at one low price. (Price axis: Penetration price; Quantity axis)

Introductory price dealing—temporary price cuts

Low prices do attract customers. Therefore, marketers often use **introductory price dealing**—temporary price cuts—to speed new products into a market and get customers to try them. However, don't confuse these *temporary* price cuts with low penetration prices. The plan here is to raise prices as soon as the introductory offer is over. By then, hopefully, target customers will have decided it is worth buying again at the regular price.

Established competitors often choose not to meet introductory price dealing—as long as the introductory period is not too long or too successful. However, some competitors match introductory price deals with their own short-term sale prices to discourage customers from shopping around.

Marketers often use introductory price dealing—in the form of temporary price cuts or introductory coupons—to speed new products into a market.

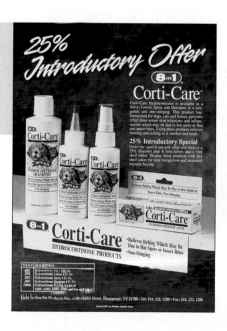

Exhibit 17-6 Exchange Rates for Various Currencies against the U.S. Dollar over Time

Base Currency	Number of Units of Base Currency per U.S. Dollar*							
	1989	1991	1993	1995	1997	1999	2001	2003
British pound	0.62	0.57	0.67	0.67	0.61	0.62	0.70	0.64
Thai baht	25.72	25.53	25.33	24.92	31.07	37.40	45.65	42.89
Japanese yen	138.07	134.59	111.08	94.11	121.09	117.86	124.58	120.04
Australian dollar	1.26	1.32	1.47	1.35	1.34	1.55	1.96	1.64
Canadian dollar	1.18	1.15	1.29	1.37	1.38	1.49	1.56	1.46
German mark	1.88	1.66	1.65	1.43	1.73			
Euro						1.07	1.13	0.92

*Units shown are the average for each year 1989–1997. For 1999, 2001, and 2003 units shown are for April 16, 1999, April 16, 2001, and April 16, 2003.

Different price-level policies through the channel

The price of a product sold to channel members should be set so that channel members can cover their costs and make a profit. For example, a producer of a slightly better product might set a price level that is low relative to competitors when selling to retailers but suggest an above-the-market retail price. This encourages retailers to emphasize the product because it yields higher profits.

The price of money may affect the price level

We've been talking about the price level of a firm's product. But a nation's money also has a price level—what it is worth in some other currency. For example, on January 1, 2004, one U.S. dollar was worth 0.56 British pounds. In other words, the exchange rate for the British pound against the U.S. dollar was 0.56. Exhibit 17-6

PayPal is an online financial service that makes it easier and less risky for firms or individuals who sell over the Internet to receive payment from a distant buyer.

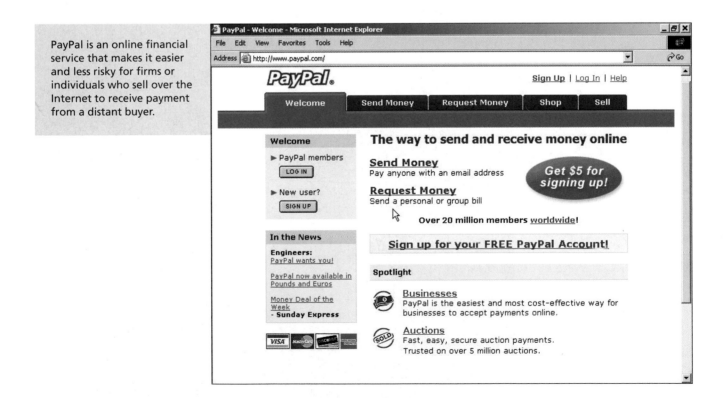

lists exchange rates for money from several countries over a number of years. From this exhibit you can see that exchange rates change over time—and sometimes the changes are significant. For example, on April 16, 2001, a U.S. dollar was worth 1.13 Euros; in April 2003 it was worth only 0.92 Euros.

Exchange rate changes can have a significant effect on international trade. From a manager's viewpoint, they also affect whether or not a price level has the expected result. As the following example shows, this can be an important factor even for a small firm that sells only in its own local market.

In 2001, the marketing manager for EControl, Inc.—a small firm that produces electronic controllers for producers of satellite TV receiving dishes—set a meeting competition wholesale price of about $100 for a carton of the controllers. The profit margin on the controllers at that price was about $10 per carton. The wholesalers who distribute the controllers also carried a product by a British firm. Its wholesale price was also $100, which means that the British firm got about 70 British pounds ($100 × 0.70 pounds per dollar) per carton. Prices were stable for some time. However, when the exchange rate for the pound against the dollar fell from 0.70 to 0.64, the British producer got 6 fewer pounds for each $100 carton of controllers (70 pounds − 64 pounds = 6 pounds).

Because EControl's marketing manager was only selling controllers in the domestic market, she didn't pay any attention to the drop in the exchange rate at first. However, she did pay attention when the British producer decided to raise its wholesale price to $110 a carton. At the $110 price, the British firm got about 70.4 pounds per carton ($110 × 0.64 pounds per dollar)—about the same as it was getting before the exchange rate change. EControl's market share and sales increased substantially—at the British competitor's expense—because EControl's price was $10 lower than its British competitor. EControl's marketing manager concluded that it would probably take a while for the British firm to lower its price, even if the exchange rate went up again. So she decided that she could safely raise her price level by 5 percent—up to $105—and still have a solid price advantage over the British supplier. At a price of $105 per carton, EControl's profit per carton jumped from $10 to $15, a 50 percent increase in profit.

Things turned out well for EControl even though the manager initially ignored exchange rates. Note, however, that during the 1999–2001 period the exchange rate for the British pound against the U.S. dollar *increased*. So in the 1999–2001 period EControl's situation might have been reversed![17]

INTERNET EXERCISE

There is a website (www.x-rates.com) that converts one country's currency to another. Go to the website, click on *Currency Calculator*, and determine how much $100 U.S. is worth in Thai bahts, British pounds, and euros. How do those numbers compare with April 2003 (see Exhibit 17-6)?

MOST PRICE STRUCTURES ARE BUILT AROUND LIST PRICES

Prices start with a list price

Most price structures are built around a base price schedule or list price. **Basic list prices** are the prices final customers or users are normally asked to pay for products. In this book, unless noted otherwise, list price refers to basic list price.

In the next chapter, we discuss how firms set these list prices. For now, however, we'll consider variations from list price and why they are made.

DISCOUNT POLICIES—REDUCTIONS FROM LIST PRICES

Discounts are reductions from list price given by a seller to buyers who either give up some marketing function or provide the function themselves. Discounts can be useful in marketing strategy planning. In the following discussion, think about what function the buyers are giving up, or providing, when they get each of these discounts.

Quantity discounts encourage volume buying

Quantity discounts are discounts offered to encourage customers to buy in larger amounts. This lets a seller get more of a buyer's business, or shifts some of the storing function to the buyer, or reduces shipping and selling costs—or all of these. There are two kinds of quantity discounts: cumulative and noncumulative.

Cumulative quantity discounts apply to purchases over a given period—such as a year—and the discount usually increases as the amount purchased increases. Cumulative discounts encourage *repeat* buying by reducing the customer's cost for additional purchases. This is a way to develop loyalty and ongoing relationships with customers. For example, a Lowe's lumberyard might give a cumulative quantity discount to a building contractor who is not able to buy all of the needed materials at once. Lowe's wants to reward the contractor's patronage and discourage shopping around.

A cumulative quantity discount is often attractive to business customers who don't want to run up their inventory costs. They are rewarded for buying large quantities, even though individual orders may be smaller.

Noncumulative quantity discounts apply only to individual orders. Such discounts encourage larger orders but do not tie a buyer to the seller after that one purchase. Lowe's lumberyard may resell insulation products made by several competing producers. Owens-Corning might try to encourage Lowe's to stock larger quantities of its pink insulation by offering a noncumulative quantity discount.

While quantity discounts are usually given as price cuts, sometimes they are given as free or bonus products. Southwest Airline's frequent flier program uses this approach.

Quantity discounts can be a very useful tool for the marketing manager. Some customers are eager to get them. But marketing managers must use quantity discounts carefully. In business markets, they must offer such discounts to all customers on equal terms—to avoid price discrimination.

Noncumulative discounts sometimes produce unexpected results. If the discount is too big, wholesalers or retailers may buy more than they can possibly sell to their own customers—to get the low price. Then they sell the excess at a low price to whoever will buy it—as long as the buyer doesn't compete in the same market area. These gray-market channels often take customers away from regular channel members, perhaps with a selling price even lower than what most channel members pay.

HOW MUCH DOES IT REALLY COST TO RENT A VIDEO?

The price a customer actually pays to rent a video at Blockbuster isn't always easy to figure out. At first glance, it seems that everyone pays one price for a New Release and a lower price for Favorites. But that's not the whole story. Members of the $10-a-year Blockbuster Rewards program get a free movie each month—and another one free when they rent five during a month. They also get a free Favorite when they rent a movie Monday to Wednesday—and there are other special offers, like three-for-one deals some weekends. The Blockbuster Rewards website (www.Blockbuster.com) provides a special online calculator so movie buffs can plug in their own rental numbers and figure out how many free movies they would get with the Rewards program. But, oops, the calculator does not include a way to plug in how often a customer is late in returning movies. A late fee can apply even if the rental was free. Some cynics think that Blockbuster offers its Rewards Gold membership—and even more free movies—to customers who return a lot of movies late. Those late fees add up to more than 10 percent of Blockbuster revenues.

Netflix (www.netflix.com) and Wal-Mart (www.walmart.com) both compete with Blockbuster by offering a subscription service that has no late fees. Subscribers pay a fixed fee of about $20 a month and can request as many DVDs as they want (with prepaid postage both ways) but with a limit of three out at a time. Given a fixed fee, the most profitable customers are the ones who don't view many movies. Netflix and Wal-Mart have both offered free trial periods to pull in subscribers. Prompted by this competition, Blockbuster has experimented with its own subscription approach. However, Netflix hopes that its customers will be loyal because many of them like Netflix's free online movie reviews.

Some experts think that video-on-demand movies—distributed over the Internet or from cable services—will be tough competition for all these firms. Yet current rental firms will probably also offer video-on-demand if that is what their customers want. Either way, if things continue on the current path, customers still won't know what it actually costs to see a movie.[18]

This problem plagues channels for products ranging from electronic components to toilet paper. To avoid these problems, a marketing manager must consider the effect of discounts on the whole strategy, not just the effect on sales to a given middleman.

Seasonal discounts— buy sooner

Seasonal discounts are discounts offered to encourage buyers to buy earlier than present demand requires. If used by a manufacturer, this discount tends to shift the storing function further along in the channel. It also tends to even out sales over the year. For example, Kyota offers wholesalers a lower price on its garden tillers if they buy in the fall, when sales are slow.

Service firms that face irregular demand or excess capacity often use seasonal discounts. For example, some tourist attractions, like ski resorts, offer lower weekday rates when attendance would otherwise be down.

Payment terms and cash discounts set payment dates

Most sales to businesses are made on credit. The seller sends a bill (invoice) by mail or electronically, and the buyer's accounting department processes it for payment. Some firms depend on their suppliers for temporary working capital (credit). Therefore, it is very important for both sides to clearly state the terms of payment—including the availability of cash discounts—and to understand the commonly used payment terms.

Net means that payment for the face value of the invoice is due immediately. These terms are sometimes changed to net 10 or net 30, which means payment is due within 10 or 30 days of the date on the invoice.

Cash discounts are reductions in price to encourage buyers to pay their bills quickly. The terms for a cash discount usually modify the net terms.

2/10, net 30 means the buyer can take a 2 percent discount off the face value of the invoice if the invoice is paid within 10 days. Otherwise, the full face value is due within 30 days. And it usually is stated or understood that an interest charge will be added after the 30-day free-credit period.

INVOICE NO.			4838
ORDER NO.		INVOICE DATE	
179642		1/8/200x	
DATE SHIPPED		SHIPPED VIA	
1/1/200x		Truck	
NO. PCS	WT.	FOB	TERMS
5	300	Lansing, MI	2/10 net 30

479

Why cash discounts are given and should be evaluated

Smart buyers carefully evaluate cash discounts. A discount of 2/10, net 30 may not look like much at first. But the buyer earns a 2 percent discount for paying the invoice just 20 days sooner than it should be paid anyway. By not taking the discount, the company in effect is borrowing at an annual rate of 36 percent. That is, assuming a 360-day year and dividing by 20 days, there are 18 periods during which the company could earn 2 percent—and 18 times 2 equals 36 percent a year.

Consumers say "charge it"

Credit sales are also important to retailers. Most retailers use credit card services, such as Visa or MasterCard, and pay a percent of the revenue from each credit sale for this service. For this reason, some retailers offer discounts to consumers who pay cash.

Many consumers like the convenience of credit card buying. But some critics argue that the cards make it too easy for consumers to buy things they really can't afford. Credit card interest rates can increase the total costs to consumers.

Trade discounts often are set by tradition

A **trade (functional) discount** is a list price reduction given to channel members for the job they are going to do.

A manufacturer, for example, might allow retailers a 30 percent trade discount from the suggested retail list price to cover the cost of the retailing function and their profit. Similarly, the manufacturer might allow wholesalers a *chain* discount of 30 percent and 10 percent off the suggested retail price. In this case, the wholesalers would be expected to pass the 30 percent discount on to retailers.[19]

Special sales reduce list prices—temporarily

A **sale price** is a temporary discount from the list price. Sale price discounts encourage immediate buying. In other words, to get the sale price, customers give up the convenience of buying when they want to buy and instead buy when the seller wants to sell.

Special sales provide a marketing manager with a quick way to respond to changing market conditions without changing the basic marketing strategy. For example, a retailer might use a sale to help clear extra inventory or to meet a competing store's price.

In recent years, sale prices and deals have become much more common. Some retailers have sales so often that consumers just wait to purchase when there's a sale. Others check out a website like www.fatwallet.com to figure out where the product

Many stores guarantee that they have the lowest price and promise a refund if a customer finds an item lower somewhere else. Sun Television and Appliances woos customers to its stores with automatic refunds. Sun hires an outside firm to do daily price checks. When a customer is due a refund, it is sent automatically.

they want is already on sale. At first it may seem that consumers benefit from all this. But prices that change constantly erode brand loyalty.

To avoid these problems, some firms that sell consumer convenience products offer **everyday low pricing**—setting a low list price rather than relying on frequent sales, discounts, or allowances. Many supermarkets use this approach.

Sale prices should be used carefully, consistent with well-thought-out pricing objectives and policies. A marketing manager who constantly uses temporary sales to adjust the price level probably has not done a good job setting the normal price.[20]

ALLOWANCE POLICIES—OFF LIST PRICES

Allowances, like discounts, are given to final consumers, customers, or channel members for doing something or accepting less of something.

Advertising allowances—something for something

Advertising allowances are price reductions given to firms in the channel to encourage them to advertise or otherwise promote the supplier's products locally. For example, Sony might give an allowance (3 percent of sales) to its retailers. They, in turn, are expected to spend the allowance on local advertising.

Stocking allowances—get attention and shelf space

Stocking allowances—sometimes called *slotting allowances* —are given to a middleman to get shelf space for a product. For example, a producer might offer a retailer cash or free merchandise to stock a new item. Stocking allowances are used mainly to get supermarket chains to handle new products. Supermarkets are more willing to give space to a new product if the supplier will offset their handling costs and risks. With a big stocking allowance, the middleman makes extra profit—even if a new product fails and the producer loses money.

Most firms don't release information about how much they pay in stocking allowances. However, a change in U.S. accounting rules in 2001 provided a one-time glimpse—and the dollar amount was startling. For example, Campbell Soup, Kellogg, Coca-Cola, Pepsi, and Kraft all made payments that were between 13 and 15 percent of sales.

Are stocking allowances ethical?

Critics say that retailer demands for big stocking allowances slow new product introductions and make it hard for small producers to compete. Some producers feel that retailers' demands are unethical—just a different form of extortion. Retailers, on the other hand, point out that the fees protect them from producers that simply want to push more and more me-too products onto their shelves. Perhaps the best way for a producer to cope with the problem is to develop new products that really do offer consumers superior value. Then it benefits everyone in the channel, including retailers, to get the products to the target market.[21]

PMs—push for cash

Push money (or prize money) allowances—sometimes called *PMs* or *spiffs*—are given to retailers by manufacturers or wholesalers to pass on to the retailers' salesclerks for aggressively selling certain items. PM allowances are used for new items, slower-moving items, or higher-margin items. They are often used for pushing furniture, clothing, consumer electronics, and cosmetics. A salesclerk, for example, might earn an additional $5 for each new model Panasonic DVD player sold.

Bring in the old, ring up the new—with trade-ins

A **trade-in allowance** is a price reduction given for used products when similar new products are bought. Trade-ins give the marketing manager an easy way to lower the effective price without reducing list price. Proper handling of trade-ins is important when selling durable products.

SOME CUSTOMERS GET SOMETHING EXTRA

Clipping coupons— more for less

Many producers and retailers offer discounts (or free items) through coupons distributed in packages, mailings, print ads, or at the store. By presenting a coupon to a retailer, the consumer is given a discount off list price. This is especially common in the consumer packaged goods business—but the use of price-off coupons is growing in other lines of business too.

Retailers are willing to redeem producers' coupons because it increases their sales—and they usually are paid for the trouble of handling the coupons. For example, a retailer that redeems a 50 cents off coupon might be repaid 75 cents.

Couponing is so common that firms have been set up to help repay retailers for redeeming manufacturers' coupons. The total dollar amounts involved are so large that crime has become a big problem. Some dishonest retailers have gone to jail for collecting on coupons they redeemed without requiring customers to buy the products.

INTERNET EXERCISE

Catalina, a firm that specializes in targeted sales promotions, set up an online system called "ValuPage." Consumers can print out a sheet with a list of discounts that sponsoring supermarkets redeem with "web bucks"—which the consumer can then use for any future purchase at the store. Go to the website (www.supermarkets.com), type in your *Zip Code* only, and press *Enter* to review the system. Do you think this system will be more or less susceptible to fraud than regular coupons? Explain your thinking.

Cash rebates when you buy

Some firms offer **rebates**—refunds paid to consumers after a purchase. Sometimes the rebate is very large. Some automakers offer rebates of $500 to $6,000 to promote sales of slow-moving models. Rebates are also used on lower-priced items, ranging from Duracell batteries and Memorex CD-Rs to Logitech webcams and Paul Masson wines. Rebates give a producer a way to be certain that final consumers actually get the price reduction. If the rebate amount were just taken off the price charged middlemen, they might not pass the savings along to consumers.

However, what explains the big increase in the use of rebates is that many consumers buy because of the rebate but then don't request the refund. That's why some retailers lure consumers with their own mail-in rebates rather than just lowering prices at checkout. However, many consumers resent sellers who make it an unnecessary hassle to claim a rebate. So don't be surprised if there is a consumer backlash against some of the current rebate practices.[22]

LIST PRICE MAY DEPEND ON GEOGRAPHIC PRICING POLICIES

Retail list prices sometimes include free delivery. Or free delivery may be offered to some customers as an aid to closing the sale. But deciding who pays the freight charge is more important on sales to business customers than to final consumers because more money is involved. Purchase orders usually specify place, time, method of delivery, freight costs, insurance, handling, and other charges. There are many possible variations for an imaginative marketing manager, and some specialized terms have developed.

F.O.B. pricing is easy

A commonly used transportation term is **F.O.B.**—which means free on board some vehicle at some place. Typically, F.O.B. pricing names the place—often the location of the seller's factory or warehouse—as in F.O.B. Taiwan or F.O.B. mill. This means that the seller pays the cost of loading the products onto some vehicle, then title to the products passes to the buyer. The buyer pays the freight and takes responsibility for damage in transit.

If a firm wants to pay the freight for the convenience of customers, it can use F.O.B. delivered or F.O.B. buyer's factory. In this case, title does not pass until the products are delivered. If the seller wants title to pass immediately but is willing to prepay freight (and then include it in the invoice), F.O.B. seller's factory-freight prepaid can be used.

F.O.B. shipping point pricing simplifies the seller's pricing—but it may narrow the market. Since the delivered cost varies depending on the buyer's location, a customer located farther from the seller must pay more and might buy from closer suppliers.

Zone pricing smooths delivered prices

Zone pricing means making an average freight charge to all buyers within specific geographic areas. The seller pays the actual freight charges and bills each customer for an average charge. For example, a company in Canada might divide the United States into seven zones, then bill all customers in the same zone the same amount for freight even though actual shipping costs might vary.

Zone pricing reduces the wide variation in delivered prices that results from an F.O.B. shipping point pricing policy. It also simplifies transportation charges.

Uniform delivered pricing—one price to all

Uniform delivered pricing means making an average freight charge to all buyers. It is a kind of zone pricing—an entire country may be considered as one zone—that includes the average cost of delivery in the price. Uniform delivered pricing is most often used when (1) transportation costs are relatively low and (2) the seller wishes to sell in all geographic areas at one price, perhaps a nationally advertised price.

Freight-absorption pricing—competing on equal grounds in another territory	When all firms in an industry use F.O.B. shipping point pricing, a firm usually competes well near its shipping point but not farther away. As sales reps look for business farther away, delivered prices rise and the firm finds itself priced out of the market.

This problem can be reduced with **freight-absorption pricing**—which means absorbing freight cost so that a firm's delivered price meets the nearest competitor's. This amounts to cutting list price to appeal to new market segments. Some firms look at international markets this way; they just figure that any profit from export sales is a bonus.

PRICING POLICIES COMBINE TO IMPACT CUSTOMER VALUE

Look at Price from the customer's viewpoint

We've discussed pricing policies separately so far, but from the customer's view they all combine to impact customer value. So when we talk about Price we are really talking about the whole set of price policies that define the real price level. On the other hand, superior value isn't just based on having a lower price than some competitor but rather on the whole marketing mix.

Value pricing leads to superior customer value

Smart marketers look for the combination of Price decisions that result in value pricing. **Value pricing** means setting a fair price level for a marketing mix that really gives the target market superior customer value.

Value pricing doesn't necessarily mean cheap if cheap means bare-bones or low-grade. It doesn't mean high prestige either if the prestige is not accompanied by the right quality goods and services. Rather, the focus is on the customer's requirements and how the whole marketing mix meets those needs.

Toyota is a firm that has been effective with value pricing. It has different marketing mixes for different target markets. But from the $10,000 Echo to the $55,000 Land Cruiser, the Japanese automaker consistently offers better quality and lower prices than its competitors. Among fast-food restaurants, Wendy's has a good reputation for value pricing.

Companies that use value pricing deliver on their promises. They try to give the consumer pleasant surprises—like an unexpected service—because it increases value and builds customer loyalty. They return the price if the customer isn't completely satisfied. They avoid unrealistic price levels—prices that are high only

When a customer rents a car, both the rental fee and the quality of the car influence the customer value. Thrifty wants customers to know that it offers both great rates and great cars.

Marketers for Luvs diapers want consumers to know that Luvs' value price, compared to the pricey brands, is equivalent to getting 275 diapers a year for free. The ad for Dawn detergent uses a similar approach. It emphasizes that "Dawn does 20% more greasy dishes while suds last."

because consumers already know the brand name. They build relationships so customers will come back time and again.

There are Price choices in most markets

Some marketing managers miss the advantages of value pricing. They've heard economists say that in perfect competition it's foolish to offer products above or below the market price. But most firms *don't* operate in perfect competition where what firms offer is exactly the same.

Most operate in monopolistic competition, where products and whole marketing mixes are *not* exactly the same. This means that there are pricing options. At one extreme, some firms are clearly above the market—they may even brag about it. Tiffany's is well known as one of the most expensive jewelry stores in the world.

Epeda sells high-quality mattresses. It wants customers to know that its higher price is worth it. This ad says, "Lots of mattresses are cheap to buy. The reason is to make you forget how much sleeping on them is going to cost you."

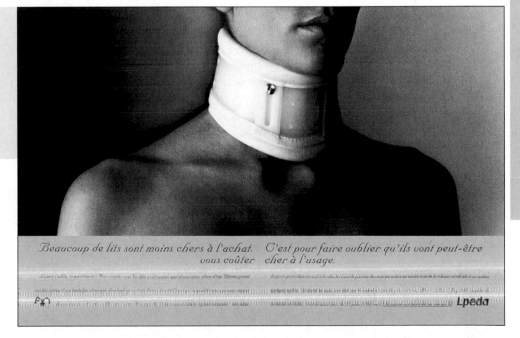

Other firms emphasize below-the-market prices in their marketing mixes. Prices offered by discounters and mass-merchandisers, such as Wal-Mart and Tesco, illustrate this approach. They may even promote their pricing policy with catchy slogans like "guaranteed lowest prices."

Value pricers define the target market and the competition

In making price decisions and using value pricing, it is important to clearly define the *relevant target market* and *competitors* when making price comparisons.

Consider Wal-Mart prices again from this view. Wal-Mart may have lower camera prices than conventional camera retailers, but it offers less help in the store, less selection, and it won't take old cameras in trade. Wal-Mart may be appealing to budget-oriented shoppers who compare prices *and* value among different mass-merchandisers. But a specialty camera store may be trying to appeal to different customers and not even be a direct competitor!

A camera producer with this point of view might offer the specialty store models that are not available to Wal-Mart—to ensure that customers don't view price as the only difference between the two stores.

Further, the specialty store needs to communicate clearly to its target market *how* it offers superior value. Wal-Mart is certainly going to communicate that it offers low prices. If that's all customers hear, it's no wonder that they just focus on price. The specialty retailer has to be certain that consumers understand that price is not the only thing of value that is different. This same logic applies to comparisons between Internet sellers and brick-and-mortar competitors. Each may have advantages or disadvantages that relate to value.

Meeting competitors' prices may be necessary

In a mature market there is downward pressure on both prices and profit margins. Moreover, differentiating the value a firm offers may not be easy when competitors can quickly copy new ideas. Extending our camera example, if our speciality store is in a city with a number of similar stores with the same products, there may not be a way to convince consumers that one beats all of the others. In such circumstances there may be no real pricing choice other than to "meet the competition." With profit margins already thin, they would quickly disappear or turn into losses at a lower price. And a higher price would simply prompt competitors to promote their price advantage.[23]

Similarly, a B2B supplier may have a better marketing mix than competitors; but if buyers have decided to use a procurement hub and reverse auction as the only way to buy, the supplier may not have any choice but to decide what the lowest price is that it will bid to get the business. Winning the bid at a profit-losing price doesn't help.

Even though competition can be intense, too many marketers give up too easily. They often can find a way to differentiate, even if it's something that competitors dismiss as less important. For example, Kellogg was facing soggy sales and tough competition in the dry cereal category. Dealer brands made price competition even tougher. However, when Kellogg added freeze-dried fruit to create Special K Red Berries, it attracted many customers away from competing brands. The berries did increase costs, but Kellogg's profits still improved. In Europe, where price sensitivity was greatest, Kellogg kept the price the same but reduced the size of the Red Berries box. In the U.S., the size of the box is standard but the price was increased enough to provide profit margins. Even though General Mills later copied the idea, Kellogg had a head start and quickly came out with other fruit-added cereals. And both producers benefited by having a way to differentiate from the low-price store brands in their category.[24]

There may be little choice about Price in oligopoly situations. Pricing at the market—that is, meeting competition—may be the only sensible policy. To raise prices might lead to a large loss in sales, unless competitors adopt the higher price too. And cutting prices would probably lead to similar reductions by competitors—downward along an inelastic industry demand curve. This can only lead to a decrease in total revenue for the industry and probably for each firm. The major airlines faced these problems recently.

To avoid these problems, each oligopolist may choose a status quo pricing objective and set its price at the competitive level. Some critics call this pricing behavior conscious parallel action, implying it is unethical and the same as intentional conspiracy among firms. As a practical matter, however, that criticism seems overly harsh. It obviously isn't sensible for firms to ignore their competitors.

Value pricing fits with market-oriented strategy planning

There are times when the marketing manager's hands are tied and there is little that can be done to differentiate the marketing mix. However, most marketing managers do have choices—many choices. They can vary strategy decisions with respect to all of the marketing mix variables, not just Price, to offer target customers superior value. And when a marketer's hands are really tied, it's time to look for new opportunities that offer more promise.

LEGALITY OF PRICING POLICIES

This chapter discusses the many pricing decisions that must be made. However, some pricing decisions are limited by government legislation. The first step to understanding pricing legislation is to know the thinking of legislators and the courts. To get a better idea of the "why" of legislation, we'll focus on U.S. legislation here, but many other countries have similar pricing laws.[25]

Minimum prices are sometimes controlled

Unfair trade practice acts put a lower limit on prices, especially at the wholesale and retail levels. They have been passed in more than half the states in the United States. Selling below cost in these states is illegal. Wholesalers and retailers are usually required to take a certain minimum percentage markup over their merchandise-plus-transportation costs. The practical effect of these laws is to protect certain limited-line food retailers—such as dairy stores—from the kind of "ruinous" competition supermarkets might offer if they sold milk as a leader, offering it below cost for a long time.

The United States and most other countries control the minimum price of imported products with antidumping laws. **Dumping** is pricing a product sold in a foreign

Local media in China claimed that both Fuji from Japan and Kodak from the U.S. were dumping their products in China, even though China's Lucky brand of film and paper had a price that was 50 percent lower.

market below the cost of producing it or at a price lower than in its domestic market. These laws are usually designed to protect the country's domestic producers and jobs. But there is debate about how well they work.

Consider what happened in 2002 when U.S. steel producers pushed for tariffs because overseas steel mills, many of which are subsidized by their own governments, were selling at a lower price in the U.S. than at home. Most U.S. steel producers suffered losses and were forced to cut jobs. After the tariffs went into place, U.S. steel producers increased their profits by raising prices. But, as a result, other U.S. firms that needed to buy steel faced higher costs. Yet these firms couldn't raise *their* prices because they still had global competitors in their own product-markets. Some critics argued that U.S. steel companies were inefficient and that the tariffs protected them by sacrificing their customers. Late in 2003, the U.S. dropped the steel tariffs. However, by then other countries seized the excuse to impose tariffs of their own, which made it harder for U.S. companies to get export business. Dumping can have big macro-marketing effects, but it is a difficult problem to fix.[26]

Even very high prices may be OK

Generally speaking, firms can charge high prices—even outrageously high prices as long as they don't conspire with their competitors to fix prices, discriminate against some of their customers, or lie.

Of course, there are exceptions. Firms in regulated businesses may need to seek approval for their prices. For example, in the United States, most states regulate automobile insurance rates. Some countries impose more general price controls—to reduce inflation or try to control markets. However, most countries have followed the move toward a market-directed economy. That doesn't mean, however, that there aren't important regulations in the pricing area.

You can't lie about prices

Phony list prices are prices customers are shown to suggest that the price has been discounted from list. Some customers seem more interested in the supposed discount than in the actual price. Most businesses, trade associations, and government agencies consider the use of phony list prices unethical. In the United States, the FTC tries to stop such pricing—using the **Wheeler Lea Amendment,** which bans "unfair or deceptive acts in commerce."[27]

In recent years some electronics retailers, like Best Buy, have been criticized on these grounds. They'd advertise a $300 discount on a computer when the customer signed up for an Internet service provider, but it might not be clear to the consumer that a three-year commitment—costing over $700—was required.

Price fixing is illegal—you can go to jail

Difficulties with pricing—and violations of pricing legislation—usually occur when competing marketing mixes are quite similar. When the success of an entire marketing strategy depends on price, there is pressure (and temptation) to make agreements with competitors (conspire). And **price fixing**—competitors getting together to raise, lower, or stabilize prices—is common and relatively easy. *But it is also completely illegal in the United States.* It is considered "conspiracy" under the Sherman Act and the Federal Trade Commission Act. To discourage price fixing, both companies and individual managers are held responsible. In a recent case, an executive at Archer Daniels Midland (ADM) Company was sentenced to three years in jail and the company was fined $100 million.

Federal price-fixing laws in the United States focus on protecting customers who purchase directly from a supplier. For example, a wholesaler could bring action against a producer-supplier for fixing prices. However, retailers or consumers who bought the producer's products from the wholesaler could not bring action. In contrast, many state laws now allow "indirect customers" in the channel to sue the price fixer.[28]

Different countries have different rules concerning price fixing, and this has created problems in international trade. Japan, for example, allows price fixing, especially if it strengthens the position of Japanese producers in world markets.

U.S. antimonopoly laws ban price discrimination unless . . .

Price level and price flexibility policies can lead to price discrimination. The **Robinson-Patman Act** (of 1936) makes illegal any **price discrimination**—selling the same products to different buyers at different prices—*if it injures competition*. The law does permit some price differences—but they must be based on (1) cost differences or (2) the need to meet competition. Both buyers and sellers are considered guilty if they know they're entering into discriminatory agreements.

What does "like grade and quality" mean?

Firms in businesses as varied as transportation services, book publishing, and auto parts have been charged with violations of the Robinson-Patman Act in recent, nationally publicized cases. Competitors who have been injured by a violation of the law have incentive to go to court because they can receive a settlement that is three times larger than the damage suffered.

The Robinson-Patman Act allows a marketing manager to charge different prices for similar products if they are *not* of "like grade and quality." But the FTC says that if the physical characteristics of a product are similar, then they are of like grade and quality. A landmark U.S. Supreme Court ruling against the Borden Company upheld the FTC's view that a well-known label *alone* does not make a product different from one with an unknown label. The company agreed that the canned milk it sold at different prices under different labels was basically the same.

But the FTC's victory in the Borden case was not complete. The U.S. Court of Appeals found no evidence of injury to competition and further noted that there could be no injury unless Borden's price differential exceeded the "recognized consumer appeal of the Borden label." How to measure "consumer appeal" was not spelled out, so producers who want to sell several brands—or dealer brands at lower prices than their main brand—probably should offer physical differences, and differences that are really useful.[29]

Can cost analysis justify price differences?

The Robinson-Patman Act allows price differences if there are cost differences—say, for larger quantity shipments or because middlemen take over some of the physical distribution functions. But justifying cost differences is a difficult job. And the justification must be developed *before* different prices are set. The seller can't wait until a competitor, disgruntled customer, or the FTC brings a charge. At that point, it's too late.[30]

Can you legally meet price cuts?

Under the Robinson-Patman Act, meeting a competitor's price is permitted as a defense in price discrimination cases. A major objective of antimonopoly laws is to protect competition, not competitors. And "meeting competition in good faith" still seems to be legal.

Special promotion allowances might not be allowed

Some firms violate the Robinson-Patman Act by providing push money, advertising allowances, and other promotion aids to some customers and not others. The act prohibits such special allowances, *unless they are made available to all customers on "proportionately equal" terms.*[31]

How to avoid discriminating

Because price discrimination laws are complicated and penalties for violations heavy, many business managers follow the safest course by offering few or no quantity discounts and the same cost-based prices to *all* customers. This is *too* conservative a reaction. But when firms consider price differences, they may need a lawyer involved in the discussion!

CONCLUSION

The Price variable offers an alert marketing manager many possibilities for varying marketing mixes. What pricing policies should be used depends on the pricing objectives. We looked at profit-oriented, sales-oriented, and status quo-oriented objectives.

A marketing manager must set policies about price flexibility, price levels over the product life cycle, who will pay the freight, and who will get discounts and allowances. While doing this, the manager should be aware of legislation that affects pricing policies.

In most cases, a marketing manager must set prices—that is, administer prices. Starting with a list price, a variety of discounts and allowances may be offered to adjust for the something of value being offered in the marketing mix.

Throughout this chapter, we talk about what may be included or excluded in the something of value and what objectives a firm might set to guide its pricing policies. We discuss how pricing policies combine to impact customer value. Price setting itself is not discussed. It will be covered in the next chapter, where we show ways to carry out the various pricing objectives and policies.

KEY TERMS

price, 465

target return objective, 467

profit maximization objective, 468

sales-oriented objective, 468

status quo objectives, 469

nonprice competition, 470

administered prices, 470

one-price policy, 471

flexible-price policy, 471

skimming price policy, 473

penetration pricing policy, 473

introductory price dealing, 475

basic list prices, 477

discounts, 478

quantity discounts, 478

cumulative quantity discounts, 478

noncumulative quantity discounts, 478

seasonal discounts, 479

net, 479

cash discounts, 479

2/10, net 30, 479

trade (functional) discount, 480

sale price, 480

everyday low pricing, 481

allowances, 481

advertising allowances, 481

stocking allowances, 481

push money (or prize money) allowances, 481

trade-in allowance, 481

rebates, 482

F.O.B, 483

zone pricing, 483

uniform delivered pricing, 483

freight-absorption pricing, 484

value pricing, 484

unfair trade practice acts, 487

dumping, 487

phony list prices, 488

Wheeler Lea Amendment, 488

price fixing, 488

Robinson-Patman Act, 489

price discrimination, 489

QUESTIONS AND PROBLEMS

1. Identify the strategy decisions a marketing manager must make in the Price area. Illustrate your answer for a local retailer.

2. How should the acceptance of a profit-oriented, a sales-oriented, or a status quo-oriented pricing objective affect the development of a company's marketing strategy? Illustrate for each.

3. Distinguish between one-price and flexible-price policies. Which is most appropriate for a hardware store? Why?

4. What pricing objective(s) is a skimming pricing policy most likely implementing? Is the same true for a penetration pricing policy? Which policy is probably most appropriate for each of the following products: (a) a new type of home lawn-sprinkling system, (b) a

skin patch drug to help smokers quit, (c) a DVD of a best-selling movie, and (d) a new children's toy?

5. How would differences in exchange rates between different countries affect a firm's decisions concerning the use of flexible-price policies in different foreign markets?

6. Are seasonal discounts appropriate in agricultural businesses (which are certainly seasonal)?

7. What are the effective annual interest rates for the following cash discount terms: (a) 1/10, net 20; (b) 1/5, net 10; and (c) net 25?

8. Do stocking allowances increase or reduce conflict in a channel of distribution? Explain your thinking.

9. Why would a manufacturer offer a rebate instead of lowering the suggested list price?

10. How can a marketing manager change a firm's F.O.B. terms to make an otherwise competitive marketing mix more attractive?

11. What type of geographic pricing policy is most appropriate for the following products (specify any assumptions necessary to obtain a definite answer): (*a*) a chemical by-product, (*b*) nationally advertised candy bars, (*c*) rebuilt auto parts, and (*d*) tricycles?

12. How would a ban on freight absorption (that is, requiring F.O.B. factory pricing) affect a producer with substantial economies of scale in production?

13. Give an example of a marketing mix that has a high price level but that you see as a good value. Briefly explain what makes it a good value.

14. Think about a business from which you regularly make purchases even though there are competing firms with similar prices. Explain what the firm offers that improves value and keeps you coming back.

15. Cite two examples of continuously selling above the market price. Describe the situations.

16. Explain the types of competitive situations that might lead to a meeting-competition pricing policy.

17. Would consumers be better off if all nations dropped their antidumping laws? Explain your thinking.

18. How would our marketing system change if manufacturers were required to set fixed prices on *all* products sold at retail and *all* retailers were required to use these prices? Would a manufacturer's marketing mix be easier to develop? What kind of an operation would retailing be in this situation? Would consumers receive more or less service?

19. Is price discrimination involved if a large oil company sells gasoline to taxicab associations for resale to individual taxicab operators for 2½ cents a gallon less than the price charged to retail service stations? What happens if the cab associations resell gasoline not only to taxicab operators but to the general public as well?

SUGGESTED CASES

13. Paper Products, Inc.

25. PlastiForm Mfg., Inc.

COMPUTER-AIDED PROBLEM

17. Cash Discounts

RESOURCE REMINDER

Joe Tulkin owns Tulkin Wholesale Co. He sells paper, tape, file folders, and other office supplies to about 120 retailers in nearby cities. His average retailer customer spends about $900 a month.

When Tulkin started business in 1991, competing wholesalers were giving retailers invoice terms of 3/10, net 30. Tulkin never gave the issue much thought—he just used the same invoice terms when he billed customers. At that time, about half of his customers took the discount. Recently, he noticed a change in the way his customers were paying their bills. Checking his records, he found that 90 percent of the retailers were taking the cash discount. With so many retailers taking the cash discount, it seems to have become a price reduction. In addition, Tulkin learned that other wholesalers were changing their invoice terms.

Tulkin decides he should rethink his invoice terms. He knows he could change the percent rate on the cash discount, the number of days the discount is offered, or the number of days before the face amount is due. Changing any of these, or any combination, will change the interest rate at which a buyer is, in effect, borrowing money if he does not take the discount. Tulkin decides that it will be easier to evaluate the effect of different invoice terms if he sets up a spreadsheet to let him change the terms and quickly see the effective interest rate for each change.

a. With 90 percent of Tulkin's customers now taking the discount, what is the total monthly cash discount amount?

b. If Tulkin changes his invoice terms to 1/5, net 20, what interest rate is each buyer paying by not taking the cash discount? With these terms, would fewer buyers be likely to take the discount? Why?

c. Tulkin thinks 10 customers will switch to other wholesalers if he changes his invoice terms to 2/10, net 30, while 60 percent of the remaining customers will take the discount. What interest rate does a buyer pay by not taking this cash discount? For this situation, what will the total gross sales (total invoice) amount be? The total cash discount? The total net sales receipts after the total cash discount? Compare Tulkin's current situation with what will happen if he changes his invoice terms to 2/10, net 30.

For additional questions related to this problem, see Exercise 17-3 in the *Learning Aid for Use with Basic Marketing*, 15th edition.

CHAPTER EIGHTEEN

Price Setting in the Business World

Wal-Mart is the largest retailer in the world. It sells more food than any supermarket chain and more toys than Toys "R" Us. Procter & Gamble and Kimberly-Clark are giants in consumer packaged goods, but more than 10 percent of their sales are at Wal-Mart; for many major producers, it's more than 20 percent of sales. In the winter of 2004, Wal-Mart announced that its sales revenue for the previous year was $244 billion, about 10 times what it was in 1990. Back then, Wal-Mart and Kmart had equal sales. However, Wal-Mart made about twice as much profit for each dollar of revenue. Trying to compete with Wal-Mart over the decade of the 90s ultimately pushed Kmart into bankruptcy. Now, out of bankruptcy and trying to streamline operations, Kmart is back trying to compete with Wal-Mart again. That's a tough fight. By taking a longer-term look at how

Wal-Mart has grown so fast in the past, you'll get a pretty good idea how this wrestling match is likely to turn out.

What explains the big difference in growth and profits when the two chains are in many ways similar? Part of the answer is that Wal-Mart has more sales volume in each store. Even after Kmart closed about 25 percent of its poorer stores, Wal-Mart's sales revenue per square foot is about twice that at Kmart. Wal-Mart's lower prices on similar products increases demand in its stores. But that also reduces its fixed operating costs as a percentage of sales. That means it can add a

smaller markup, still cover its operating expenses, and make a larger profit. And as ongoing price rollbacks pull in more and more customers, its percentage of overhead costs to sales revenue continues to drop— from about 20.2 percent in 1980 to about 17 percent now.

Wal-Mart has become even more efficient in cutting unnecessary inventory. In one sweeping set of improvements a few years ago, Wal-Mart cut more than $2 billion in average inventory, thereby saving $150 million in carrying costs and reducing the need for markdowns. Now Wal-Mart gets close to 10 stockturns on its inventory each year, while most other mass-merchandisers average about 7. Wal-Mart also has lower costs for the goods it sells. Its buyers are tough in negotiating the best prices from suppliers—to be able to offer Wal-Mart customers the brands they want at low prices. But Wal-Mart also works closely with producers to reduce costs in the channel. For example, Wal-Mart was one of the first major retailers to insist that all orders be placed by computer and more recently has been one of the first to use radio frequency ID "smart tags" to precisely track the flow of goods from vendors through its distribution centers to stores. That reduces stock-outs on store shelves and lost sales at the checkout counter. Wal-Mart also works with vendors to create quality private-label brands, like Sam's Choice Cola. Its low price—about 15 percent below what consumers expect to pay for well-known colas—doesn't leave a big profit margin. Yet when customers come in to buy it, they also pick up other, more profitable, products.

Even with its lower costs, Wal-Mart isn't content to take the convenient route to price setting by just adding a standard percentage markup on different items. The company was one of the first retailers to give managers in every department in every store frequent, detailed information about what is selling and what isn't. Managers drop items that are collecting dust and roll back prices on the ones with the fastest turnover and highest margins. That not only increases stockturns but also puts the effort behind products with the most potential. For instance, Wal-Mart's analysis of checkout-scanner sales data revealed that parents often pick up more than one kid's video at a time. So now managers make certain that special displays feature several videos and that the rest of the selection is close by. And while many stores carry DVDs instead of video-tapes, Wal-Mart carries both because it knows that its parent-customers often prefer VHS for kids' movies.

Wal-Mart was the first major retailer to move to online selling (www.walmart.com). Its online sales still account for only a small percentage of its total sales, so there's lots of room to grow there too. Further, Wal-Mart is aggressively taking its low-price approach to other countries, ranging from Mexico to Japan.

To return to where we started, as Kmart comes out of bankruptcy it is trying to copy many of Wal-Mart's innovations. However, Wal-Mart has such advantages on sales volume, unit costs, and margins that it will be difficult for Kmart to win in any price war—unless Wal-Mart somehow stumbles because of its enormous size. But don't bet on that anytime soon.[1]

Exhibit 18-1
Key Factors That Influence
Price Setting

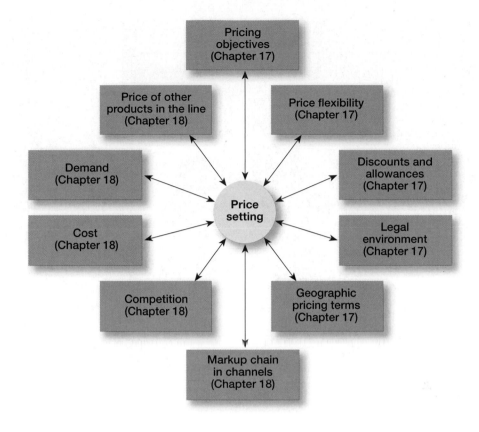

PRICE SETTING IS A KEY STRATEGY DECISION

In the previous chapter, we discussed the idea that pricing objectives and policies should guide pricing decisions. We accepted the idea of a list price and went on to discuss variations from list and how they combine to impact customer value. Now we'll see how the basic list price is set in the first place—based on information about costs, demand, and profit margins. See Exhibit 18-1.

There are many ways to set list prices. But for simplicity they can be reduced to two basic approaches: *cost-oriented* and *demand-oriented* price setting. We will discuss cost-oriented approaches first because they are most common. Also, understanding the problems of relying only on a cost-oriented approach shows why a marketing manager must also consider demand to make good Price decisions. Let's begin by looking at how most retailers and wholesalers set cost-oriented prices.

SOME FIRMS JUST USE MARKUPS

Markups guide pricing by middlemen

Some firms, including most retailers and wholesalers, set prices by using a **markup**—a dollar amount added to the cost of products to get the selling price. For example, suppose that a CVS drugstore buys a bottle of Pert Plus shampoo and conditioner for $2. To make a profit, the drugstore obviously must sell Pert Plus for more than $2. If it adds $1 to cover operating expenses and provide a profit, we say that the store is marking up the item $1.

Markups, however, usually are stated as percentages rather than dollar amounts. And this is where confusion sometimes arises. Is a markup of $1 on a cost of $2 a

Kohler is an example of a specialized product that relies on selective distribution and sells in smaller volumes usually offering retailers higher markups, in part to offset the retailer's higher carrying costs and marketing expenses. Bic is an example of a product that relies on intensive distribution and sells in larger volumes offering retailers smaller markups.

markup of 50 percent? Or should the markup be figured as a percentage of the selling price—$3.00—and therefore be 33⅓ percent? A clear definition is necessary.

Markup percent is based on selling price—a convenient rule

Unless otherwise stated, **markup (percent)** means percentage of selling price that is added to the cost to get the selling price. So the $1 markup on the $3.00 selling price is a markup of 33⅓ percent. Markups are related to selling price for convenience.

There's nothing wrong with the idea of markup on cost. However, to avoid confusion, it's important to state clearly which markup percent you're using.

A manager may want to change a markup on selling price to one based on cost, or vice versa. The calculations used to do this are simple. (See the section on markup conversion in Appendix B on marketing arithmetic. The appendixes follow Chapter 22.)[2]

Many use a standard markup percent

Many middlemen select a standard markup percent and then apply it to all their products. This makes pricing easier. When you think of the large number of items the average retailer and wholesaler carry—and the small sales volume of any one item—this approach may make sense. Spending the time to find the best price to charge on every item in stock (day to day or week to week) might not pay.

Moreover, different companies in the same line of business often use the same markup percent. There is a reason for this: Their operating expenses are usually similar. So they see a standard markup as acceptable as long as it's large enough to cover the firm's operating expenses and provide a reasonable profit.

Markups are related to gross margins

How does a manager decide on a standard markup in the first place? A standard markup is often set close to the firm's *gross margin*. Managers regularly see gross margins on their operating (profit and loss) statements. The gross margin is the amount left—after subtracting the cost of sales (cost of goods sold) from net sales—to cover the expenses of selling products and operating the business. (See Appendix B on marketing arithmetic if you are unfamiliar with these ideas.) Our CVS manager knows that there won't be any profit if the gross margin is not large enough. For this reason, CVS might accept a markup percent on Pert Plus that is close to the store's usual gross margin percent.

Smart producers pay attention to the gross margins and standard markups of middlemen in their channel. They usually allow trade (functional) discounts similar to the standard markups these middlemen expect.

Markup chain may be used in channel pricing

Different firms in a channel often use different markups. A **markup chain**—the sequence of markups firms use at different levels in a channel—determines the price structure in the whole channel. The markup is figured on the *selling price* at each level of the channel.

For example, Black & Decker's selling price for an electric drill becomes the cost the Ace Hardware wholesaler pays. The wholesaler's selling price becomes the hardware retailer's cost. And this cost plus a retail markup becomes the retail selling price. Each markup should cover the costs of running the business and leave a profit.

Exhibit 18-2 illustrates the markup chain for an electric drill at each level of the channel system. The production (factory) cost of the drill is $21.60. In this case, the producer takes a 10 percent markup and sells the product for $24. The markup is 10 percent of $24 or $2.40. The producer's selling price now becomes the wholesaler's cost—$24. If the wholesaler is used to taking a 20 percent markup on selling price, the markup is $6—and the wholesaler's selling price becomes $30. The $30 now becomes the cost for the hardware retailer. And a retailer who is used to a 40 percent markup adds $20, and the retail selling price becomes $50.

High markups don't always mean big profits

Some people, including many conventional retailers, think high markups mean big profits. Often this isn't true. A high markup may result in a price that's too high—a price at which few customers will buy. You can't earn much if you don't sell much, no matter how high your markup on a single item. So high markups may lead to low profits.

Lower markups can speed turnover and the stockturn rate

Some retailers and wholesalers, however, try to speed turnover to increase profit—even if this means reducing their markups. They realize that a business runs up costs over time. If they can sell a much greater amount in the same time period,

Exhibit 18-2 Example of a Markup Chain and Channel Pricing

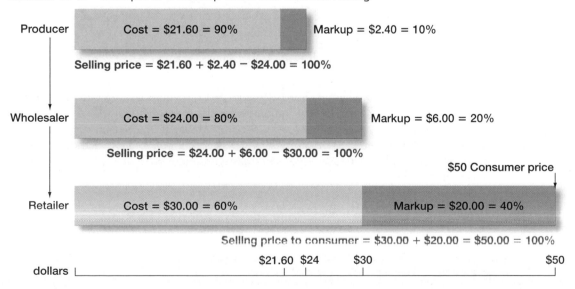

Items with a high stockturn rate may have a lower markup.

they may be able to take a lower markup and still earn higher profits at the end of the period.

An important idea here is the **stockturn rate**—the number of times the average inventory is sold in a year. Various methods of figuring stockturn rates can be used (see the section "Computing the Stockturn Rate" in Appendix B). A low stockturn rate may be bad for profits.

At the very least, a low stockturn increases inventory carrying cost and ties up working capital. If a firm with a stockturn of 1 (once per year) sells products that cost it $100,000, it has that much tied up in inventory all the time. But a stockturn of 5 requires only $20,000 worth of inventory ($100,000 cost ÷ 5 turnovers a year). If annual inventory carrying cost is about 20 percent of the inventory value, that reduces costs by $16,000 a year. That's a big difference on $100,000 in sales!

Whether a stockturn rate is high or low depends on the industry and the product involved. An electrical parts wholesaler may expect an annual rate of 2—while a supermarket might expect 8 stockturns on average but 20 stockturns for soaps and 70 stockturns for fresh fruits and vegetables.

Mass-merchandisers run in fast company

Although some middlemen use the same standard markup percent on all their products, this policy ignores the importance of fast turnover. Mass-merchandisers know this. They put low markups on fast-selling items and higher markups on items that sell less frequently. For example, Wal-Mart may put a small markup on fast-selling health and beauty aids (like toothpaste or shampoo) but higher markups on appliances and clothing.

Where does the markup chain start?

Some markups eventually become standard in a trade. Most channel members tend to follow a similar process—adding a certain percentage to the previous price. But who sets price in the first place? The firm that brands a product is usually the one that sets its basic list price. It may be a large retailer, a large wholesaler, or most often, the producer.

Some producers just start with a cost per unit figure and add a markup—perhaps a standard markup—to obtain their selling price. Or they may use some rule-of-thumb formula such as:

$$\text{Selling price} = \text{Average production cost per unit} \times 3$$

A producer who uses this approach might develop rules and markups related to its own costs and objectives. Yet even the first step—selecting the appropriate cost per unit to build on—isn't easy. Let's discuss several approaches to see how cost-oriented price setting really works.

AVERAGE-COST PRICING IS COMMON AND CAN BE DANGEROUS

Average-cost pricing means adding a reasonable markup to the average cost of a product. A manager usually finds the average cost per unit by studying past records. Dividing the total cost for the last year by all the units produced and sold in that period gives an estimate of the average cost per unit for the next year. If the cost was $32,000 for all labor and materials and $30,000 for fixed overhead expenses—such as selling expenses, rent, and manager salaries—then the total cost is $62,000. If the company produced 40,000 items in that time period, the average cost is $62,000 divided by 40,000 units, or $1.55 per unit. To get the price, the producer decides how much profit per unit to add to the average cost per unit. If the company considers 45 cents a reasonable profit for each unit, it sets the new price at $2.00. Exhibit 18-3A shows that this approach produces the desired profit if the company sells 40,000 units.

It does not make allowances for cost variations as output changes

It's always a useful input to pricing decisions to understand how costs operate at different levels of output. Further, average cost pricing is simple. But it can also be dangerous. It's easy to lose money with average-cost pricing. To see why, let's follow this example further.

Exhibit 18-3 Results of Average-Cost Pricing

A. Calculation of Planned Profit if 40,000 Items Are Sold		B. Calculation of Actual Profit if Only 20,000 Items Are Sold	
Calculation of Costs:		**Calculation of Costs:**	
Fixed overhead expenses	$30,000	Fixed overhead expenses	$30,000
Labor and materials ($.80 a unit)	32,000	Labor and materials ($.80 a unit)	16,000
Total costs	$62,000	Total costs	$46,000
"Planned" profit	18,000		
Total costs and planned profit	$80,000		
Calculation of Profit (or Loss):		**Calculation of Profit (or Loss):**	
Actual unit sales × price ($2.00*)	$80,000	Actual unit sales × price ($2.00*)	$40,000
Minus: total costs	62,000	Minus: total costs	46,000
Profit (loss)	$18,000	Profit (loss)	($6,000)
Result:		**Result:**	
Planned profit of $18,000 is earned if 40,000 items are sold at $2.00 each.		Planned profit of $18,000 is not earned. Instead, $6,000 loss results if 20,000 items are sold at $2.00 each.	

*Calculation of "reasonable" price: $\dfrac{\text{Expected total costs and planned profit}}{\text{Planned number of items to be sold}} = \dfrac{\$80,000}{40,000} = \$2.00$

First, remember that the average cost of $2.00 per unit was based on output of 40,000 units. But if the firm is only able to produce and sell 20,000 units in the next year, it may be in trouble. Twenty thousand units sold at $2.00 each ($1.55 cost plus 45 cents for expected profit) yield a total revenue of only $40,000. The overhead is still fixed at $30,000, and the variable material and labor cost drops by half to $16,000—for a total cost of $46,000. This means a loss of $6,000, or 30 cents a unit. The method that was supposed to allow a profit of 45 cents a unit actually causes a loss of 30 cents a unit! See Exhibit 18-3B.

The basic problem with the average-cost approach is that it doesn't consider cost variations at different levels of output. In a typical situation, costs are high with low output, and then economies of scale set in—the average cost per unit drops as the quantity produced increases. This is why mass production and mass distribution often make sense. It's also why it's important to develop a better understanding of the different types of costs a marketing manager should consider when setting a price.

MARKETING MANAGERS MUST CONSIDER VARIOUS KINDS OF COSTS

Average-cost pricing may lead to losses because there are a variety of costs—and each changes in a *different* way as output changes. Any pricing method that uses cost must consider these changes. To understand why, we need to define six types of costs.

There are three kinds of total cost

1. **Total fixed cost** is the sum of those costs that are fixed in total—no matter how much is produced. Among these fixed costs are rent, depreciation, managers' salaries, property taxes, and insurance. Such costs stay the same even if production stops temporarily.
2. **Total variable cost,** on the other hand, is the sum of those changing expenses that are closely related to output—expenses for parts, wages, packaging materials, outgoing freight, and sales commissions.

At zero output, total variable cost is zero. As output increases, so do variable costs. If Levi's doubles its output of jeans in a year, its total cost for denim cloth also (roughly) doubles.

Average fixed costs are lower when a larger quantity is produced.

JetBlue Airways just got its start in 2000, but it has achieved profitable growth while major airlines have been fighting just to survive. JetBlue offers a low-cost, high-quality flying experience—so it's not exactly an "economy" carrier. JetBlue offers each passenger seat-back DirectTV and high-touch service. Its sleek look—on everything from fashionable blue uniforms to comfortable leather seats—sends the signal that low fares don't preclude high style. Its strategy is to excel at the things that can really distinguish the airline but cost relatively little—such as comfort, punctuality, and courtesy—while dispensing with things that can't, like airline grub. For example, when delays do occur, JetBlue goes out of its way to keep passengers fully informed.

JetBlue's quality service and low fares explain why it attracts customers. Yet its small fleet limits the quantity of customers it can serve. So how can JetBlue make higher profits when it has lower prices and lower quantity? The answer is that JetBlue earns an above-average 16 percent profit margin on the revenue it takes in. For that to happen, its costs must be, on a relative basis, even lower than its fares. And that's the case. For example, JetBlue's operating cost per "seat mile" is just over 5 cents. American and Delta are close to 9 cents per seat mile. JetBlue's new planes are fuel efficient, and with fewer types of planes, its costs for training and maintenance are lower. The planes are also the right size to match demand on the routes that JetBlue picks; empty seats would mean missed revenue. JetBlue picks routes where competing airlines have high fares, but it ignores expensive-to-serve "feeder routes." Some of JetBlue's advantages accrue because it is small and new. As JetBlue grows and others copy or improve its approach, it may need to modify its strategy. But for now it is flying high.[3]

3. **Total cost** is the sum of total fixed and total variable costs. Changes in total cost depend on variations in total variable cost, since total fixed cost stays the same.

There are three kinds of average cost

The pricing manager usually is more interested in cost per unit than total cost because prices are usually quoted per unit.

1. **Average cost (per unit)** is obtained by dividing total cost by the related quantity (that is, the total quantity that causes the total cost).
2. **Average fixed cost (per unit)** is obtained by dividing total fixed cost by the related quantity.
3. **Average variable cost (per unit)** is obtained by dividing total variable cost by the related quantity.

An example shows cost relations

A good way to get a feel for these different types of costs is to extend our average-cost pricing example (Exhibit 18-3A). Exhibit 18-4 shows the six types of cost and how they vary at different levels of output. The line for 40,000 units is highlighted because that was the expected level of sales in our average-cost pricing example. For simplicity, we assume that average variable cost is the same for each unit. Notice, however, that total variable cost increases when quantity increases.

Exhibit 18-5 shows the three average cost curves from Exhibit 18-4. Notice that average fixed cost goes down steadily as the quantity increases. Although the average variable cost remains the same, average cost decreases continually too. This is because average fixed cost is decreasing. With these relations in mind, let's reconsider the problem with average-cost pricing.

Exhibit 18-4   Cost Structure of a Firm

Quantity (Q)	Total Fixed Costs (TFC)	Average Fixed Costs (AFC)	Average Variable Costs (AVC)	Total Variable Costs (TVC)	Total Cost (TC)	Average Cost (AC)
0	$30,000	—	—	—	$ 30,000	—
10,000	30,000	$3.00	$0.80	$ 8,000	38,000	$3.80
20,000	30,000	1.50	0.80	16,000	46,000	2.30
30,000	30,000	1.00	0.80	24,000	54,000	1.80
40,000	30,000	0.75	0.80	32,000	62,000	1.55
50,000	30,000	0.60	0.80	40,000	70,000	1.40
60,000	30,000	0.50	0.80	48,000	78,000	1.30
70,000	30,000	0.43	0.80	56,000	86,000	1.23
80,000	30,000	0.38	0.80	64,000	94,000	1.18
90,000	30,000	0.33	0.80	72,000	102,000	1.13
100,000	30,000	0.30	0.80	80,000	110,000	1.10

$$\begin{bmatrix} 110,000\ \text{(TC)} \\ -80,000\ \text{(TVC)} \\ 30,000\ \text{(TFC)} \end{bmatrix}$$

$$\text{(Q) } 100,000 \overline{\big)\, 30,000\ \text{(TFC)}}\quad 0.30\ \text{(AFC)}$$

$$\begin{bmatrix} 100,000\ \text{(Q)} \\ \times 0.80\ \text{(AVC)} \\ 80,000\ \text{(TVC)} \end{bmatrix}\quad \begin{bmatrix} 30,000\ \text{(TFC)} \\ +80,000\ \text{(TVC)} \\ 110,000\ \text{(TC)} \end{bmatrix}$$

$$\text{(Q) } 100,000 \overline{\big)\, 110,000\ \text{(TC)}}\quad 1.10\ \text{(AC)}$$

Ignoring demand is the major weakness of average-cost pricing

Average-cost pricing works well if the firm actually sells the quantity it used to set the average-cost price. Losses may result, however, if actual sales are much lower than expected. On the other hand, if sales are much higher than expected, then profits may be very good. But this will only happen by luck—because the firm's demand is much larger than expected.

To use average-cost pricing, a marketing manager must make *some* estimate of the quantity to be sold in the coming period. Without a quantity estimate, it isn't possible to compute average cost. But unless this quantity is related to price—that is, unless the firm's demand curve is considered—the marketing manager may set a price

Exhibit 18-5
Typical Shape of Cost (per unit) Curves When Average Variable Cost per Unit Is Constant

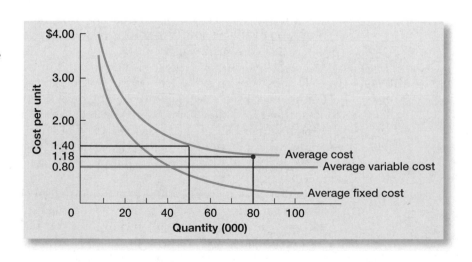

Exhibit 18-6
Evaluation of Various Prices along a Firm's Demand Curve

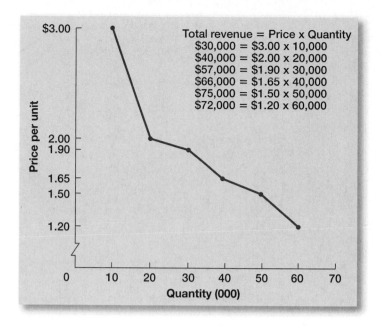

Total revenue = Price x Quantity
$30,000 = $3.00 x 10,000
$40,000 = $2.00 x 20,000
$57,000 = $1.90 x 30,000
$66,000 = $1.65 x 40,000
$75,000 = $1.50 x 50,000
$72,000 = $1.20 x 60,000

that doesn't even cover a firm's total cost! You saw this happen in Exhibit 18-3B, when the firm's price of $2.00 resulted in demand for only 20,000 units and a loss of $6,000.

The demand curve is still important even if a manager doesn't take time to think about it. For example, Exhibit 18-6 shows the demand curve for the firm we're discussing. This demand curve shows *why* the firm lost money when it tried to use average-cost pricing. At the $2.00 price, quantity demanded is only 20,000. With this demand curve and the costs in Exhibit 18-4, the firm will incur a loss whether management sets the price at a high $3 or a low $1.20. At $3, the firm will sell only 10,000 units for a total revenue of $30,000. But total cost will be $38,000—for a loss of $8,000. At the $1.20 price, it will sell 60,000 units—at a loss of $6,000. However, the curve suggests that at a price of $1.65 consumers will demand about 40,000 units, producing a profit of about $4,000.

In short, average-cost pricing is simple in theory but often fails in practice. In stable situations, prices set by this method may yield profits but not necessarily *maximum* profits. And note that such cost-based prices may be higher than a price that would be more profitable for the firm, as shown in Exhibit 18-6. When demand conditions are changing, average-cost pricing is even more risky.

Exhibit 18-7 summarizes the relationships discussed above. Cost-oriented pricing requires an estimate of the total number of units to be sold. That estimate determines the *average* fixed cost per unit and thus the average total cost. Then the firm adds the desired profit per unit to the average total cost to get the cost-oriented selling price. How customers react to that price determines the actual quantity the firm will be able to sell. But that quantity may not be the quantity used to compute the average cost![4]

Experience curve pricing is even riskier

Some aggressive firms use a variation of average-cost pricing called experience curve pricing. **Experience curve pricing** is average-cost pricing using an estimate of *future* average costs. This approach is based on the observation that over time—as an industry gains experience in certain kinds of production—managers learn new ways to reduce costs. In some industries, costs decrease about 15 to 20 percent each time cumulative production volume (experience) doubles. So a firm might

Exhibit 18-7
Summary of Relationships
among Quantity, Cost, and
Price Using Cost-Oriented
Pricing

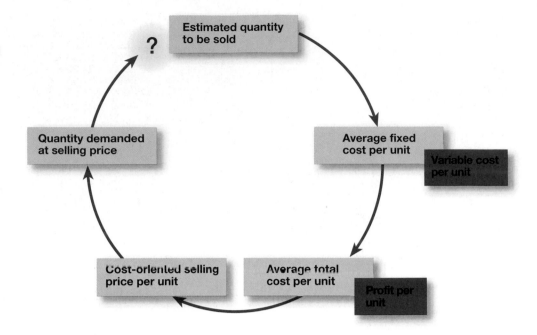

set average-cost prices based on where it expects costs to be when products are sold in the future—not where costs actually are when the strategy is set. This approach is more common in rapidly growing markets because cumulative production volume (experience) grows faster.

If costs drop as expected, this approach works. But it has the same risks as regular average-cost pricing. The price setter has to estimate what quantity will be sold to be able to read the right price from the experience-based average-cost curve.[5]

Don't ignore competitors' costs

Another danger of average-cost pricing is that it ignores competitors' costs and prices. Just as the price of a firm's own product influences demand, the price of available substitutes may impact demand. We saw this operate in our Wal-Mart case at the start of this chapter. By finding ways to cut costs, Wal-Mart was able to offer prices lower than competitors and still make an attractive profit.

SOME FIRMS ADD A TARGET RETURN TO COST

Target return pricing scores sometimes

Target return pricing—adding a target return to the cost of a product—has become popular in recent years. With this approach, the price setter seeks to earn (1) a percentage return (say, 10 percent per year) on the investment or (2) a specific total dollar return.

This method is a variation of the average-cost method since the desired target return is added into total cost. As a simple example, if a company had $180,000 invested and wanted to make a 10 percent return on investment, it would add $18,000 to its annual total costs in setting prices.

This approach has the same weakness as other average-cost pricing methods. If the quantity actually sold is less than the quantity used to set the price, then the company doesn't earn its target return, even though the target return seems to be part of the price structure. In fact, we already saw this in Exhibit 18-3. Remember that we added $18,000 as an expected profit, or target return. But the return was much lower when the expected quantity was not sold. (It could be higher too—but only if the quantity sold is much larger than expected.) Target return pricing clearly does not guarantee that a firm will hit the target.

Hitting the target in the long run

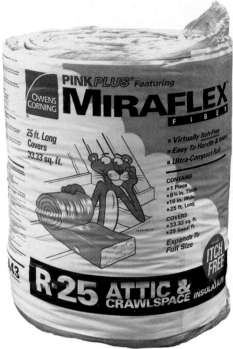

Managers in some larger firms who want to achieve a long-run target return objective use another cost-oriented pricing approach—**long-run target return pricing**—adding a long-run average target return to the cost of a product. Instead of estimating the quantity they expect to produce in any one year, they assume that during several years' time their plants will produce at, say, 80 percent of capacity. They use this quantity when setting their prices.

Companies that take this longer-run view assume that there will be recession years when sales drop below 80 percent of capacity. For example, Owens-Corning Fiberglas sells insulation. In years when there is little construction, output is low, and the firm does not earn the target return. But the company also has good years when it sells more insulation and exceeds the target return. Over the long run, Owens-Corning managers expect to achieve the target return. And sometimes they're right—depending on how accurately they estimate demand!

BREAK-EVEN ANALYSIS CAN EVALUATE POSSIBLE PRICES

Some price setters use break-even analysis in their pricing. **Break-even analysis** evaluates whether the firm will be able to break even—that is, cover all its costs—with a particular price. This is important because a firm must cover all costs in the long run or there is not much point being in business. This method focuses on the **break-even point (BEP)**—the quantity where the firm's total cost will just equal its total revenue.

Break-even charts help find the BEP

To help understand how break-even analysis works, look at Exhibit 18-8, an example of the typical break-even chart. *The chart is based on a particular selling price*—in this case $1.20 a unit. The chart has lines that show total costs (total variable plus total fixed costs) and total revenues at different levels of production. The break-even point on the chart is at 75,000 units, where the total cost and total revenue lines intersect. At that production level, total cost and total revenue are the same—$90,000.

The difference between the total revenue and total cost at a given quantity is the profit—or loss! The chart shows that below the break-even point, total cost is higher than total revenue and the firm incurs a loss. The firm would make a profit above the break-even point. However, the firm would only reach the break-even point, or get beyond it into the profit area, *if* it could sell at least 75,000 units at the $1.20 price.

Break-even analysis can be helpful if used properly, so let's look at this approach more closely.

Exhibit 18-8
Break-Even Chart for a
Particular Situation

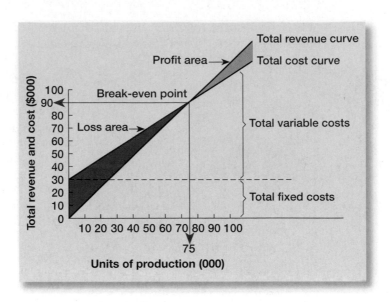

How to compute a
break-even point

A break-even chart is an easy-to-understand visual aid, but it's also useful to be able to compute the break-even point.

The BEP, in units, can be found by dividing total fixed costs (TFC) by the **fixed-cost (FC) contribution per unit**—the assumed selling price per unit minus the variable cost per unit. This can be stated as a simple formula:

$$\text{BEP (in units)} = \frac{\text{Total fixed cost}}{\text{Fixed cost contribution per unit}}$$

This formula makes sense when we think about it. To break even, we must cover total fixed costs. Therefore, we must figure the contribution each unit will make to covering the total fixed costs (after paying for the variable costs to produce the item). When we divide this per-unit contribution into the total fixed costs that must be covered, we have the BEP (in units).

To illustrate the formula, let's use the cost and price information in Exhibit 18-8. The price per unit is $1.20. The average variable cost per unit is 80 cents. So the FC contribution per unit is 40 cents ($1.20 − 80 cents). The total fixed cost is $30,000 (see Exhibit 18-8). Substituting in the formula:

$$\text{BEP} = \frac{\$30,000}{.40} = 75,000 \text{ units}$$

From this you can see that if this firm sells 75,000 units, it will exactly cover all its fixed and variable costs. If it sells even one more unit, it will begin to show a profit—in this case, 40 cents per unit. Note that once the fixed costs are covered, the part of revenue formerly going to cover fixed costs is now *all profit*.

BEP can be stated in
dollars too

The BEP can also be figured in dollars. The easiest way is to compute the BEP in units and then multiply by the assumed per-unit price. If you multiply the selling price ($1.20) by the BEP in units (75,000) you get $90,000—the BEP in dollars.

Each possible price
has its own break-even point

Often it's useful to compute the break-even point for each of several possible prices and then compare the BEP for each price to likely demand at that price. The marketing manager can quickly reject some price possibilities when the expected quantity demanded at a given price is way below the break-even point for that price.

The money that a firm spends on marketing and other expenses must be at least covered by a firm's price if it is to make a profit. That's why Gillette enjoys big economies of scale by selling the same razors in many markets around the world.

A target profit can be included

So far in our discussion of BEP we've focused on the quantity at which total revenue equals total cost—where profit is zero. We can also vary this approach to see what quantity is required to earn a certain level of profit. The analysis is the same as described above for the break-even point in units, but the amount of target profit is added to the total fixed cost. Then when we divide the total fixed cost plus profit figure by the contribution from each unit, we get the quantity that will earn the target profit.

Break-even analysis shows the effect of cutting costs

Break-even analysis makes it clear why managers must constantly look for effective new ways to get jobs done at lower costs. For example, if a manager can reduce the firm's total fixed costs—perhaps by using computer systems to cut out excess inventory carrying costs—the break-even point will be lower and profits will start to build sooner. Similarly, if the variable cost to produce and sell an item can be reduced, the fixed-cost contribution per unit increases; that too lowers the break-even point and profit accumulates faster for each product sold beyond the break-even point.

Break-even analysis is helpful—but not a pricing solution

Break-even analysis is helpful for evaluating alternatives. It is also popular because it's easy to use. Yet break-even analysis is too often misunderstood. Beyond the BEP, profits seem to be growing continually. And the graph—with its straight-line total revenue curve—makes it seem that any quantity can be sold at the assumed price. But this usually isn't true. It is the same as assuming a perfectly horizontal demand curve at that price. In fact, most managers face down-sloping demand situations. And their total revenue curves do *not* keep going up.

The firm and costs we discussed in the average-cost pricing example earlier in this chapter illustrate this point. You can confirm from Exhibit 18-4 that the total fixed cost ($30,000) and average variable cost (80 cents) for that firm are the same ones shown in the break-even chart (Exhibit 18-8). So this break-even chart is the one we would draw for that firm assuming a price of $1.20 a unit. But the demand curve for that case showed that the firm could only sell 60,000 units at a price of $1.20. So that firm would never reach the 75,000 unit break-even point at a $1.20 price. It would only sell 60,000 units, and it would lose $6,000! A firm with a different demand curve—say, one where the firm could sell 80,000 units at a price of $1.20—would in fact break even at 75,000 units.

Break-even analysis is a useful tool for analyzing costs and evaluating what might happen to profits in different market environments. But it is a cost-oriented approach. Like other cost-oriented approaches, it does not consider the effect of price on the quantity that consumers will want—that is, the demand curve.

So to really zero in on the most profitable price, marketers are better off estimating the demand curve itself and then using marginal analysis, which we'll discuss next.[6]

MARGINAL ANALYSIS CONSIDERS BOTH COSTS AND DEMAND

Marginal analysis helps find the right price

The best pricing tool marketers have for looking at costs and revenue (demand) at the same time is marginal analysis. **Marginal analysis** focuses on the changes in total revenue and total cost from selling one more unit to find the most profitable price and quantity. Marginal analysis shows how costs, revenue, and profit change at different prices. The price that maximizes profit is the one that results in the greatest difference between total revenue and total cost.[7]

Demand estimates involve "if-then" thinking

Since the price determines what quantity will be sold, a manager needs an estimate of the demand curve to compute total revenue. A practical approach here is for managers to think about a price that appears to be too high and one that is too low. Then, for a number of prices between these two extremes, the manager estimates what quantity it might be possible to sell. You can think of this as a summary of the answers to a series of what-if questions—*What* quantity will be sold *if* a particular price is selected?

Profit is the difference between total revenue and total cost

The first two columns in Exhibit 18-9 give quantity and price combinations (demand) for an example firm. Total revenue in column 3 of Exhibit 18-9 is equal to a price multiplied by its related quantity. Costs at the different quantities are also shown. The profit at each quantity and price is the difference between total revenue and total cost. In this example, the best price is $79 (and a quantity of six units sold) because that combination results in the highest profit ($106). Now let's look at this example in more detail.

Exhibit 18-9   Revenue, Cost, and Profit at Different Prices for a Firm

(1) Quantity (Q)	(2) Price (P)	(3) Total Revenue (TR)	(4) Total Variable Cost (TVC)	(5) Total Cost (TC)	(6) Profit (TR − TC)	(7) Marginal Revenue (MR)	(8) Marginal Cost (MC)	(9) Marginal Profit (MR − MC)
0	$150	$ 0	$ 0	$200	$−200			
1	140	140	96	296	−156	$140	$96	$ + 44
2	130	260	116	316	− 56	120	20	+100
3	117	351	131	331	+ 20	91	15	+ 76
4	105	420	144	344	+ 76	69	13	+ 56
5	92	460	155	355	+105	40	11	+ 29
6	79	474	168	368	+106	14	13	+ 1
7	66	462	183	383	+ 79	−12	15	− 27
8	53	424	223	423	+ 1	−38	40	− 78
9	42	378	307	507	−129	−46	84	−130
10	31	310	510	710	−400	−68	203	−271

Marginal revenue can be negative

This firm faces a demand curve that slopes down. That means that the marketer can expect to increase sales volume by lowering the price. Yet the lower price required to sell the larger quantity may reduce total revenue. Therefore, it's important to evaluate the likely effect of alternative prices on total revenue and profit. The way to do this is to look at marginal revenue.

Marginal revenue is the change in total revenue that results from the sale of one more unit of a product. At a price of $105, the firm in this example can sell four units for total revenue of $420. By cutting the price to $92, it can sell five units for total revenue of $460. Thus, the marginal revenue for the fifth unit is $460 − $420, or $40. But will total revenue continue to rise if the firm sells more units at lower prices? Exhibit 18-9 shows that total revenue goes down at price levels lower than $79. Note in the table that marginal revenue is negative when total revenue decreases. Profit depends on both revenue and costs, so let's look at costs next.

The marginal cost of just one more can be important

Column 5 in Exhibit 18-9 shows the total cost increasing as quantity increases. Remember that total cost is the sum of fixed cost (in this example, $200) and total variable cost. The fixed cost does not change over the entire range of output. However, total variable costs increase as more units are produced. So it's the increases in variable cost that explain the increase in total cost.

There is another kind of cost that is vital to marginal analysis. **Marginal cost** is the change in total cost that results from producing one more unit. In Exhibit 18-9, you can see that it costs $355 to produce five units of a product but only $344 to produce four units. Thus, the marginal cost for the fifth unit is $11. In other words, marginal cost is the additional cost of producing one more specific unit. By contrast, average cost is the average for *all* units (total cost divided by the number of units).

Profit is largest when marginal revenue = marginal cost

To maximize profit, a manager generally wants to lower the price and sell more units as long as the marginal revenue from selling them is at least equal to the marginal cost of the extra units. From this we get the following **rule for maximizing profit:** The highest profit is earned at the price where marginal cost is just less than or equal to marginal revenue.*

You can see this rule operating in Exhibit 18-9. As the price is cut from $140 down to $79, the quantity sold increases to six units and the profit increases to its maximum level, $106. At that point, marginal revenue and marginal cost are about equal. However, beyond that point further price cuts result in lower profits (or losses).

At the point where marginal revenue (MR) equals marginal cost (MC), **marginal profit**—the extra profit on the last unit—is near zero. So when the firm is looking for the best price to charge, it should lower the price—to increase the quantity it will sell—as long as the last unit it sells will yield extra profit.

Profit maximization with total revenue and total cost curves

Exhibit 18-10 graphs the total revenue, total cost, and total profit relationships for the numbers we've been working with in Exhibit 18-9. The highest point on the total profit curve is at a quantity of six units. This is also the quantity where we find the greatest vertical distance between the total revenue curve and the total cost curve. Exhibit 18-9 shows that it is the $79 price that results in selling six units, so $79 is the price that leads to the highest profit. A price lower than $79 would result in a higher sales volume. But you can see that the total profit curve declines beyond a quantity of six units. So a profit-maximizing marketing manager would not be interested in setting a lower price.

A profit range is reassuring

Marginal analysis focuses on the price that earns the *highest* profit. But a slight miss doesn't mean failure because demand estimates don't have to be exact. There

---

*This rule applies in typical situations where the curves are shaped similarly to those discussed here. As a technical matter, however, we should add the following to the rule for maximizing profit: The marginal cost must be increasing, or decreasing, at a lesser rate than marginal revenue.

Exhibit 18-10
Graphic Determination of
the Price Giving the Greatest
Total Profit for a Firm

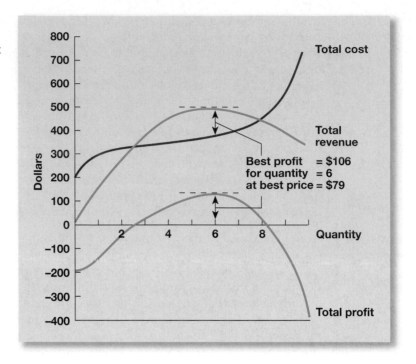

is usually a range of profitable prices. You can see this in Exhibit 18-9 and in the section of Exhibit 18-10 shown in yellow. Although the price that would result in the highest profit is $79, the firm's strategy would be profitable all the way from a price of $53 to $117. So the effort of trying to estimate demand will probably lead to being some place in the profitable range. In contrast, mechanical use of average-cost pricing could lead to a price that is much too high—or much too low.

How to lose less, if you must

In a weak market, demand may fall off and there may be no way to operate at a profit. If this is a permanent situation—as might occur in the decline stage of the product life cycle—there may be no choice other than to go out of business or do something totally different. However, if it appears that the situation is temporary, it may be best to sell at a low price, even if it's not profitable.

Why would you sell at a price that is unprofitable? Marginal analysis provides the answer. Most fixed costs will continue even if the firm doesn't sell anything. So if the firm can charge a price that at least recovers the marginal cost of the last unit (or more generally, the variable cost of the units being considered), the extra income would help pay the fixed costs and reduce the firm's losses.

Marginal analysis applies in oligopoly too

Exhibit 18-11
Marginal Revenue Drops
Fast in an Oligopoly

In Chapter 17 we noted that marketing managers who compete in oligopoly situations often just set a price that meets what competitors charge. Marginal analysis also helps to explain why they do this.

Exhibit 18-11 shows a demand curve and marginal revenue curve typical of what a marketing manager in an oligopoly situation faces. The demand curve is kinked, and the current market price is at the kink. The dashed part of the marginal revenue line in Exhibit 18-11 shows that marginal revenue drops sharply at the kinked point.

Even if costs change somewhat, the marginal revenue curve drops so fast that the marginal cost curve is still likely to cross the marginal revenue curve (that is, marginal cost will be equal to marginal revenue) someplace along the drop in the marginal revenue curve. In other words, marginal costs and marginal revenue will continue to be equal to each other at a price and quantity combination that is close to where the kink occurs already. So even though the change in costs seems to be a reason for changing the price, prices are relatively "sticky" at the kinked point. Setting the price at the level of the kink maximizes profit.

A price leader usually sets the price

Most managers who compete in oligopoly markets (or markets headed toward oligopoly) are aware of the economics of their situation, at least intuitively. As a result, a **price leader** usually sets a price for all to follow, perhaps to maximize profits or to get a certain target return on investment. Without any collusion, other members of the industry follow. The price leader is usually the firm with the lowest costs. That may give it more flexibility than competitors. This price may be maintained for a long time.

Sometimes, however, a price leader tries to lower the price, and a competitor lowers it even further. This can lead to price wars. You sometimes see this in competition between major computer companies. But price wars usually pass quickly because they are unprofitable for each firm and the whole industry.

A rough demand estimate is better than none

Some managers don't take advantage of marginal analysis because they think they can't determine the exact shape of the demand curve. But that view misses the point of marginal analysis. Marginal analysis encourages managers to think carefully about what they *do know* about costs and demand. Only rarely is either type of information exact. So in practice, the focus of marginal analysis is not on finding the precise price that will maximize profit. Rather, the focus is on getting an estimate of how profit might vary across a *range of relevant prices*. Further, a number of practical demand-oriented approaches can help a marketing manager do a better job of understanding the likely shape of the demand curve for a target market. We'll discuss these approaches next.

DEMAND-ORIENTED APPROACHES FOR SETTING PRICES

Evaluating the customer's price sensitivity

A manager who knows what influences target customers' price sensitivity can do a better job estimating the demand curve that the firm faces. Marketing researchers have identified a number of factors that influence price sensitivity across many different market situations.

The first is the most basic. When customers have *substitute ways* of meeting a need, they are likely to be more price sensitive. A cook who wants a cappuccino maker to be able to serve something distinctive to guests at a dinner party may be

Hallmark's ad prompts consumers to think of the reference price for a greeting card in terms of the value it creates for the person who receives the card. Abbey National ads highlight its low monthly insurance rates. The total expenditure might seem larger—and consumers might be even more price sensitive—if rates were for a whole year instead of just a month.

Think small. Car insurance from only £18 a month.
0800 90 90 90   Abbey National

willing to pay a high price. However, if different machines are available and our cook sees them as pretty similar, price sensitivity will be greater. It's important not to ignore dissimilar alternatives if the customer sees them as substitutes. If a machine for espresso were much less expensive than one for cappuccino, our cook might decide that an espresso machine would meet her needs just as well.

The impact of substitutes on price sensitivity is greatest when it is easy for customers to *compare prices*. For example, unit prices make it easier for our cook to compare the prices of espresso and cappuccino grinds on the grocery store shelf. Many people believe that the ease of comparing prices on the Internet increases price sensitivity and brings down prices. If nothing else, it may make sellers more aware of competing prices.

INTERNET EXERCISE

Bizrate.com is a website that makes it easy to find different brands of products from different sellers and compare prices. Go to www.bizrate.com and search for *popcorn poppers*. Review the products and prices listed and check a few of the links to related information. How useful is this sort of service? Is there more variety in features and prices than you expected? Do you think that this sort of comparison makes people more price sensitive? Why or why not?

People tend to be less price sensitive when someone else pays the bill or *shares the cost*. Perhaps this is just human nature. Insurance companies think that consumers would reject high medical fees if they were paying all of their own bills. And executives might plan longer in advance to get better discounts on airline flights if their companies weren't footing the bills.

Customers tend to be more price sensitive the greater the *total expenditure*. Sometimes a big expenditure can be broken into smaller pieces. Mercedes knows this. When its ads focused on the cost of a monthly lease rather than the total price of the car, more consumers got interested in biting the bullet.

Customers are less price sensitive the greater the *significance of the end benefit* of the purchase. Computer makers will pay more to get Intel processors if they believe that having an "Intel inside" sells more machines. Positioning efforts often focus on emotional benefits of a purchase to increase the significance of a benefit. Ads for L'Oréal hair color, for example, show closeups of beautiful hair while popular celebrities like Heather Locklear tell women to buy it "because you're worth it." A consumer who cares about the price of a bottle of hair color might still have no question that she's worth the difference in price.

Customers are sometimes less price sensitive if they already have a *sunk investment* that is related to the purchase. This is especially relevant with business customers. For example, once managers of a firm have invested to train employees to use Microsoft Excel, they are less likely to resist the high price of a new version of that software.

These factors apply in many different purchase situations, so it makes sense for a marketing manager to consider each of them in refining estimates of how customers might respond at different prices.[8]

Value in use pricing—how much will the customer save?

Organizational buyers think about how a purchase will affect their total costs. Many marketers who aim at business markets keep this in mind when estimating demand and setting prices. They use **value in use pricing**—which means setting prices that will capture some of what customers will save by substituting the firm's product for the one currently being used.

For example, a producer of computer-controlled machines used to assemble cars knows that the machine doesn't just replace a standard machine. It also reduces

Value in use pricing considers what a customer will save by buying a product. Axilok's ad reminds its business customers that its wheel bearing nut system can cut labor costs by 50 percent. Similarly, Emerson Electric invites prospective customers to use computer models available on the PlantWeb Internet site to calculate project savings for their plants.

labor costs, quality control costs, and—after the car is sold—costs of warranty repairs. The marketer can estimate what each auto producer will save by using the machine—and then set a price that makes it less expensive for the auto producer to buy the computerized machine than to stick with the old methods. The number of customers who have different levels of potential savings also provides some idea about the shape of the demand curve.

Creating a superior product that could save customers money doesn't guarantee that customers will be willing to pay a higher price. To capture the value created, the seller must convince buyers of the savings—and buyers are likely to be skeptical. A salesperson needs to be able to show proof of the claims.[9]

Auctions show what a customer will pay

Auctions have always been a way to determine exactly what some group of potential customers would pay, or not pay, for a product. However, the use of online auctions has dramatically broadened the use of this approach for both consumer and business products. About 5 million auctions are on eBay each day. And some firms are setting up their own auctions, especially for products in short supply. The U.S. government is using online auctions as well. It recently auctioned off airwave rights for cell phone services. Count on more growth in online auctions.[10]

Some sellers use sequential price reductions

Some sellers are taking the auction approach and adapting it by using sequential price reductions over time. The basic idea is that the seller starts with a relatively high price and sells as much of the product as possible at that price, but plans from the start on a series of step-by-step price reductions until the product is sold out. This approach is most commonly used with products that have a short life or are in short supply, but which would just run up inventory costs if they are not sold. Retailers like TJ Maxx use this approach with women's fashions, and grocery stores use it with perishable food like fruits and vegetables. Cruise lines sell space this way; they don't want the ship to sail with empty cabins. Some people may think of this as a "clearance" sale. But the difference here is that the plan from the outset is to work down the demand curve in steps—appealing to segments who are least price sensitive first—until all of a product is sold. However, sellers hope that if they offer the right products they'll never get to price reductions (which earn lower margins). Rather, they prefer to be bringing in the next round of products to start the process over again.

Customers may have reference prices

Some people don't devote much thought to what they pay for the products they buy, including some frequently purchased goods and services. But consumers often have a **reference price**—the price they expect to pay—for many of the products they purchase. And different customers may have different reference prices for the same basic type of purchase. For example, a person who really enjoys reading might have a higher reference price for a popular paperback book than another person who is only an occasional reader.[11]

If a firm's price is lower than a customer's reference price, customers may view the product as a better value and demand may increase. See Exhibit 18-12. Sometimes a firm will try to position the benefits of its product in such a way that consumers compare it with a product that has a higher reference price. Public Broadcasting System TV stations do this when they ask viewers to make donations that match what they pay for "just one month of cable service." Insurance companies frame the price of premiums for homeowners' coverage in terms of the price to repair flood damage—and advertising makes the damage very vivid. Some retailers just want consumers to use the manufacturer's list price as the reference price, even if no one anywhere actually pays that list price.

Exhibit 18-12 How Customer's Reference Price Influences Perceived Value (for a marketing mix with a given set of benefits and costs)

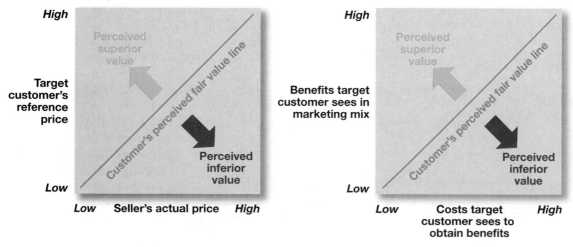

Leader pricing—make it low to attract customers

Leader pricing means setting some very low prices—real bargains—to get customers into retail stores. The idea is not only to sell large quantities of the leader items but also to get customers into the store to buy other products. Certain products are picked for their promotion value and priced low but above cost. In food stores, the leader prices are the "specials" that are advertised regularly to give an image of low prices. Leader pricing is normally used with products for which consumers do have a specific reference price.

Leader pricing can backfire if customers buy only the low-priced leaders. To avoid hurting profits, managers often select leader items that aren't directly competitive with major lines—as when bargain-priced blank CDs are a leader for an electronics store.[12]

Bait pricing—offer a steal, but sell under protest

Bait pricing is setting some very low prices to attract customers but trying to sell more expensive models or brands once the customer is in the store. For example, a furniture store may advertise a color TV for $199. But once bargain hunters come to the store, salespeople point out the disadvantages of the low-priced TV and try to convince them to trade up to a better, and more expensive, set. Bait pricing is something like leader pricing. But here the seller *doesn't* plan to sell many at the low price.

If bait pricing is successful, the demand for higher-quality products expands. This approach may be a sensible part of a strategy to trade up customers. And customers may be well served if—once in the store—they find a higher-priced product offers features better suited to their needs. But bait pricing is also criticized as unethical.

Is bait pricing ethical?

Extremely aggressive and sometimes dishonest bait-pricing advertising has given this method a bad reputation. Some stores make it very difficult to buy the bait item. The Federal Trade Commission considers this type of bait pricing a deceptive act and has banned its use in interstate commerce. Even well-known chains like Sears have been criticized for bait-and-switch pricing.

Psychological pricing—some prices just seem right

Psychological pricing means setting prices that have special appeal to target customers. Some people think there are whole ranges of prices that potential customers see as the same. So price cuts in these ranges do not increase the quantity sold. But just below this range, customers may buy more. Then, at even lower prices, the quantity demanded stays the same again—and so on. Exhibit 18-13 shows the kind of demand curve that leads to psychological pricing. Vertical drops mark the price ranges that customers see as the same. Pricing research shows that there *are* such demand curves.[13]

Exhibit 18-13
Demand Curve When Psychological Pricing Is Appropriate

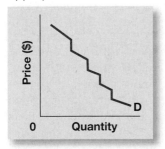

Odd-even pricing is setting prices that end in certain numbers. For example, products selling below $50 often end in the number 5 or the number 9—such as 49 cents or $24.95. Prices for higher-priced products are often $1 or $2 below the next even dollar figure—such as $99 rather than $100.

Some marketers use odd-even pricing because they think consumers react better to these prices—perhaps seeing them as "substantially" lower than the next highest even price. Marketers using these prices seem to assume that they have a rather jagged demand curve—that slightly higher prices will substantially reduce the quantity demanded. Long ago, some retailers used odd-even prices to force their clerks to make change. Then the clerks had to record the sale and could not pocket the money.[14]

Price lining—a few prices cover the field

Price lining is setting a few price levels for a product line and then marking all items at these prices. This approach assumes that customers have a certain reference price in mind that they expect to pay for a product. For example, many neckties are priced between $20 and $50. In price lining, there are only a few prices within this range. Ties will not be priced at $20, $21, $22, $23, and so on. They might be priced at four levels—$20, $30, $40, and $50.

Price lining has advantages other than just matching prices to what consumers expect to pay. The main advantage is simplicity—for both salespeople and customers.

It is less confusing than having many prices. Some customers may consider items in only one price class. Their big decision, then, is which item(s) to choose at that price.

For retailers, price lining has several advantages. Sales may increase because (1) they can offer a bigger variety in each price class and (2) it's easier to get customers to make decisions within one price class. Stock planning is simpler because demand is larger at the relatively few prices. Price lining can also reduce costs because inventory needs are lower.

Demand-backward pricing and prestige pricing

Demand-backward pricing is setting an acceptable final consumer price and working backward to what a producer can charge. It is commonly used by producers of consumer products, especially shopping products such as women's clothing and appliances. It is also used with gift items for which customers will spend a specific amount—because they are seeking a $10 or a $15 gift. Here a reverse cost-plus pricing process is used. This method has been called market-minus pricing.

The producer starts with the retail (reference) price for a particular item and then works backward—subtracting the typical margins that channel members expect. This gives the approximate price the producer can charge. Then the average or planned marketing expenses can be subtracted from this price to find how much can be spent producing the item. Candy companies do this. They alter the size of the candy bar to keep the bar at the expected price.

Prestige pricing is setting a rather high price to suggest high quality or high status. Some target customers want the best, so they will buy at a high price. But if the price seems cheap, they worry about quality and don't buy. Prestige pricing is most common for luxury products such as furs, jewelry, and perfume.

It is also common in service industries, where the customer can't see the product in advance and relies on price to judge its quality. Target customers who respond to prestige pricing give the marketing manager an unusual demand curve. Instead

Exhibit 18-14
Demand Curve Showing a Prestige Pricing Situation

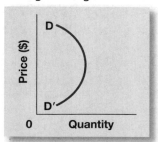

Prestige pricing is often used with luxury products like diamonds and high-end consumer electronics to suggest high quality. But Paradigm wants consumers to view its low price as a sign of good quality and good value, not as a signal of low quality.

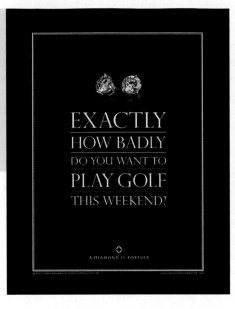

of a normal down-sloping curve, the curve goes down for a while and then bends back to the left again.[15] See Exhibit 18-14.

INTERNET EXERCISE

Tiffany & Co. is widely recognized as one of the world's premiere jewelers. It commands high prices for what it offers. Go to the Tiffany website (www.tiffany.com) and review the different sections. Do you think that the website communicates superior customer value to the Tiffany target market? Explain your opinion and which specific aspects of the website support your view.

PRICING A FULL LINE

Our emphasis has been, and will continue to be, on the problem of pricing an individual product mainly because this makes our discussion clearer. But most marketing managers are responsible for more than one product. In fact, their "product" may be the whole company line! So we'll discuss this matter briefly.

Full-line pricing— market- or firm- oriented

Full-line pricing is setting prices for a whole line of products. How to do this depends on which of two basic situations a firm is facing.

In one case, all products in the company's line are aimed at the same general target market, which makes it important for all prices and value to be logically related. This is a common approach with shopping products. A producer of TV sets might offer several models with different features at different prices to give its target customers some choice. The difference among the prices and benefits should appear reasonable when the target customers are evaluating them. Customer perceptions can be important here. A low-priced item, even one that is a good value at that price, may drag down the image of the higher end of the line. Alternatively, one item that consumers do not see as a good value may spill over to how they judge other products in the line.

In other cases, the different products in the line are aimed at entirely different target markets so there doesn't have to be any relation between the various prices. A chemical producer of a wide variety of products with several target markets, for example, probably should price each product separately.

| Costs are complicated in full-line pricing | The marketing manager must try to recover all costs on the whole line—perhaps by pricing quite low on more competitive items and much higher on ones with unique benefits. However, estimating costs for each product is a challenge because there is no single right way to assign a company's fixed costs to each of the products; we'll address this topic in more detail in Chapter 21. Regardless of how costs are allocated, any cost-oriented pricing method that doesn't consider demand can lead to very unrealistic prices. To avoid mistakes, the marketing manager should judge demand for the whole line as well as demand for each individual product in each target market. |

| Complementary product pricing | **Complementary product pricing** is setting prices on several products as a group. This may lead to one product being priced very low so that the profits from another product will increase, thus increasing the product group's total profits. When Gillette introduced the M3Power battery-powered wet-shaving system, the shaver, two blade cartridges, and a Duracell battery had a relatively low suggested retail price of $14.99. However, the blade refill cartridges, which must be replaced frequently, come in a package of four at a hefty price of $10.99. |

Complementary product pricing differs from full-line pricing because different production facilities may be involved—so there's no cost allocation problem. Instead, the problem is really understanding the target market and the demand curves for each of the complementary products. Then various combinations of prices can be tried to see what set will be best for reaching the company's pricing objectives.

| Product-bundle pricing—one price for several products | A firm that offers its target market several different products may use **product-bundle pricing**—setting one price for a set of products. Firms that use product-bundle pricing usually set the overall price so that it's cheaper for the customer to buy the products at the same time than separately. Drugstores sometimes bundle the cost of a roll of film and the cost of the processing. A bank may offer a product-bundle price for a safe-deposit box, traveler's checks, and a savings account. Sprint bundles wireless minutes and long distance. Bundling encourages customers to spend more and buy products that they might not otherwise buy—because the added cost of the extras is not as high as it would normally be, so the value is better. |

Most firms that use product-bundle pricing also set individual prices for the unbundled products. This may increase demand by attracting customers who want one item in a product assortment but don't want the extras. Many firms treat services this way. A software company may have a product-bundle price for its software and access to a toll-free telephone assistance service. However, customers who don't need help can pay a lower price and get just the software.[16]

BID PRICING AND NEGOTIATED PRICING DEPEND HEAVILY ON COSTS

| A new price for every job | We introduced the issue of competitive bidding and reverse auctions in Chapter 7. But now let's take a closer look at bid pricing. **Bid pricing** means offering a specific price for each possible job rather than setting a price that applies for all customers. In an e-commerce reverse auction for a standardized product, this may just require that the manager decide the firm's lowest acceptable selling price. But in many situations bid pricing is more complicated. For example, building contractors usually must bid on possible projects. And many companies selling services (like cleaning or data processing) must submit bids for jobs they would like to have. |

A big problem in bid pricing on a complicated job is estimating all the costs that will apply. This may sound easy, but a complicated bid may involve thousands of cost components. Further, management must include an overhead charge and a charge for profit.

Because many firms use an e-mail distribution list or website to solicit bids, the process is fast and easy for the buyer. But a seller has to be geared up to set a price and respond quickly. However, this system does allow the seller to set a price based on the precise situation and what marginal costs and marginal revenue are involved.

Bids are usually based on purchase specifications provided by the customer. The specs may be sent as an attachment to an e-mail message, or increasingly, they are posted on a website. Sometimes the seller can win the business, even with a higher bid price, by suggesting changes in the specs that save the customer money.

At times it isn't possible to figure out specs or costs in advance. This may lead to a negotiated contract where the customer agrees to pay the supplier's total cost plus an agreed-on profit figure (say, 10 percent of costs or a dollar amount)—after the job is finished.

Ethical issues in cost-plus bid pricing

Some unethical sellers give bid prices based on cost-plus contracts a bad reputation by faking their records to make costs seem higher than they really are. In other cases, there may be honest debate about what costs should be allowed. We've already considered, for instance, the difficulties in allocating fixed costs.

Demand must be considered too

Competition must be considered when adding in overhead and profit for a bid price. Usually, the customer will get several bids and accept the lowest one. So unthinking addition of typical overhead and profit rates should be avoided. Some bidders use the same overhead and profit rates on all jobs, regardless of competition, and then are surprised when they don't get some jobs.[17]

Negotiated prices— what will a specific customer pay?

Sometimes the customer asks for bids and then singles out the company that submits the *most attractive* bid, not necessarily the lowest, for further bargaining. What a customer will buy—if the customer buys at all—depends on the **negotiated price,** a price set based on bargaining between the buyer and seller. As with simple bid pricing, negotiated pricing is most common in situations where the marketing mix is adjusted for each customer—so bargaining may involve the whole marketing mix, not just the price level. Through the bargaining process, the seller tries to determine what aspects of the marketing mix are most important—and worth the most—to the customer.

Sellers must know their costs to negotiate prices effectively. However, negotiated pricing is a demand-oriented approach. Here the seller analyzes very carefully a particular customer's position on a demand curve, or on different possible demand curves based on different offerings, rather than the overall demand curve for a group of customers.

CONCLUSION

In this chapter, we discussed various approaches to price setting. Generally, retailers and wholesalers use markups. Some just use the same markups for all their items. Others find that varying the markups increases turnover and profit. In other words, they consider demand and competition.

Many firms use average-cost pricing to help set their prices. But this approach sometimes ignores demand completely.

Break-even analysis is useful for evaluating possible prices. But management must estimate demand to evaluate the chance of reaching these possible break-even points.

The major difficulty with demand-oriented pricing is estimating the demand curve. But experienced managers, aided perhaps by marketing research, can estimate the nature of demand for their products. Such estimates are useful even if they aren't exact. They get you thinking in the right ballpark. Sometimes, when all you need is a decision about raising or lowering price, even rough demand estimates can be very revealing. Further, a firm's demand curve does not cease to exist simply because it's ignored. Some information is better than none at all. And marketers should consider demand in their pricing. We see this with value in use pricing, online auctions, leader pricing, bait pricing, psychological pricing, odd-even pricing, full-line pricing, and even bid pricing. Understanding the factors that influence price sensitivity can make these approaches more effective.

Throughout the book, we stress that firms must consider the customer before they do anything. This certainly applies to pricing. It means that when managers are setting a price, they have to consider what customers will be willing to pay. This isn't always easy. But it's nice to know that there is usually a profit range around the best price. Therefore, even rough estimates about what potential customers will buy at various prices will probably lead to a better price than mechanical use of traditional markups or cost-oriented formulas.

While our focus in this chapter is on price setting, it's clear that pricing decisions must consider the cost of offering the whole marketing mix. Smart marketers don't just accept costs as a given. Target marketers always look for ways to be more efficient—to reduce costs while improving the value that they offer customers.

KEY TERMS

markup, 495

markup (percent), 496

markup chain, 497

stockturn rate, 498

average-cost pricing, 499

total fixed cost, 500

total variable cost, 500

total cost, 501

average cost (per unit), 501

average fixed cost (per unit), 501

average variable cost (per unit), 501

experience curve pricing, 503

target return pricing, 504

long-run target return pricing, 505

break-even analysis, 505

break-even point (BEP), 505

fixed-cost (FC) contribution per unit, 506

marginal analysis, 508

marginal revenue, 509

marginal cost, 509

rule for maximizing profit, 509

marginal profit, 509

price leader, 511

value in use pricing, 512

reference price, 514

leader pricing, 515

bait pricing, 515

psychological pricing, 515

odd-even pricing, 515

price lining, 515

demand-backward pricing, 516

prestige pricing, 516

full-line pricing, 517

complementary product pricing, 518

product-bundle pricing, 518

bid pricing, 518

negotiated price, 519

QUESTIONS AND PROBLEMS

1. Why do many department stores seek a markup of about 30 percent when some discount houses operate on a 20 percent markup?

2. A producer distributed its riding lawn mowers through wholesalers and retailers. The retail selling price was $800, and the manufacturing cost to the

company was $312. The retail markup was 35 percent and the wholesale markup 20 percent. (*a*) What was the cost to the wholesaler? To the retailer? (*b*) What percentage markup did the producer take?

3. Relate the concept of stock turnover to the growth of mass-merchandising. Use a simple example in your answer.

4. If total fixed costs are $200,000 and total variable costs are $100,000 at the output of 20,000 units, what are the probable total fixed costs and total variable costs at an output of 10,000 units? What are the average fixed costs, average variable costs, and average costs at these two output levels? Explain what additional information you would want to determine what price should be charged.

5. Explain how experience curve pricing differs from average-cost pricing.

6. Construct an example showing that mechanical use of a very large or a very small markup might still lead to unprofitable operation while some intermediate price would be profitable. Draw a graph and show the break-even point(s).

7. The Davis Company's fixed costs for the year are estimated at $200,000. Its product sells for $250. The variable cost per unit is $200. Sales for the coming year are expected to reach $1,250,000. What is the break-even point? Expected profit? If sales are forecast at only $875,000, should the Davis Company shut down operations? Why?

8. Discuss the idea of drawing separate demand curves for different market segments. It seems logical because each target market should have its own marketing mix. But won't this lead to many demand curves and possible prices? And what will this mean with respect to functional discounts and varying prices in the marketplace? Will it be legal? Will it be practical?

9. Distinguish between leader pricing and bait pricing. What do they have in common? How can their use affect a marketing mix?

10. Cite a local example of psychological pricing and evaluate whether it makes sense.

11. Cite a local example of odd-even pricing and evaluate whether it makes sense.

12. How does a prestige pricing policy fit into a marketing mix? Would exclusive distribution be necessary?

13. Is a full-line pricing policy available only to producers? Cite local examples of full-line pricing. Why is full-line pricing important?

SUGGESTED CASES

17. Eco Water, Inc.
24. Metal Solutions, Inc.

27. Injection Molding, Inc.

COMPUTER-AIDED PROBLEM

18. Break-Even/Profit Analysis

RESOURCE REMINDER

This problem lets you see the dynamics of break-even analysis. The starting values (costs, revenues, etc.) for this problem are from the break-even analysis example in this chapter (see Exhibit 18-8).

The first column computes a break-even point. You can change costs and prices to figure new break-even points (in units and dollars). The second column goes further. There you can specify target profit level, and the unit and dollar sales needed to achieve your target profit level will be computed. You can also estimate possible sales quantities, and the program will compute costs, sales, and profits. Use this spreadsheet to address the following issues.

a. Vary the selling price between $1.00 and $1.40. Prepare a table showing how the break-even point (in units and dollars) changes at the different price levels.

b. If you hope to earn a target profit of $15,000, how many units would you have to sell? What would total cost be? Total sales dollars? (Note: Use the right-hand ["profit analysis"] column in the spreadsheet.)

c. Using the "profit analysis" column (column 2), allow your estimate of the sales quantity to vary between 64,000 and 96,000. Prepare a table that shows, for each quantity level, what happens to average cost per unit and profit. Explain why average cost changes as it does over the different quantity values.

For additional questions related to this problem, see Exercise 18-5 in the *Learning Aid for Use with Basic Marketing*, 15th edition.

1. Understand how information technology speeds up feedback for better implementation and control.

2. Know why effective implementation is critical to customer satisfaction and profits.

3. Know how total quality management can improve implementation, including implementation of service quality.

4. Understand how sales analysis can aid marketing strategy planning.

5. Understand the differences in sales analysis, performance analysis, and performance analysis using performance indexes.

6. Understand the difference between the full-cost approach and the contribution-margin approach.

7. Understand how planning and control can be combined to improve the marketing management process.

8. Understand what a marketing audit is and when and where it should be used.

9. Understand the important new terms (shown in red).

CHAPTER NINETEEN

Implementing and Controlling Marketing Plans: Evolution and Revolution

BEN & JERRY'S BRINGS ITS SWEET-TOOTH FANS A LOT OF PLEASURE WITH UNIQUE ICE CREAM CONCOCTIONS LIKE UNCANNY CASHEW. THERE MAY BE A FEW MOMENTS OF PAIN IF YOUR FAVORITE FLAVOR DISAPPEARS FROM STORE SHELVES TO JOIN A FEW HUNDRED OTHERS ON BEN & JERRY'S

"dearly departed flavors list." But the odds are that the flavor that replaces it will be even more popular. In fact, that doesn't happen by chance. And the proof of that is the growth in sales that Ben & Jerry's has achieved over the years.

Ben & Jerry's produces and distributes only about 30 different flavors at a time. Its down-home image might make you think that's all it can handle. But that image belies the fact that massive pipes in the Ben & Jerry's factory pump out 190,000 pints of ice cream each day. Tractor-trailer loads of pints continuously flow into depots and from there are shipped to hundreds of scoop shops as well 50,000 grocery stores in the U.S. and in 12 other countries.

Ben and Jerry's marketing managers use an information system that tracks every pint—from what ingredients went into it to where it sells. They constantly study sales to see if Cherry Garcia is still in the number 1 sales spot or if Chunky Monkey is moving up or down the top 10 sellers list. And if sales of a flavor are not doing as well in Oregon as in Georgia, they alter the mix that goes to that region. If sales of a flavor start to slip in one channel of distribution, they watch to see if it's a onetime blip or if it's the start of a trend that spreads. And if it is a trend, they replace that flavor with a new one before the drop in sales turns into a problem.

Everyone at Ben & Jerry's is obsessed with the quality they offer customers. It's the key to their customers' loyalty. Each time a call or an e-mail with a comment or complaint comes into the customer service people, they follow up and match it to the particular pint that's a problem to determine when it was produced and where it was sold. They receive more than 200 calls and e-mails each week, so they sort all the inputs to see if they bring to light undetected problems—whether it's the milk from a particular supplier, a specific production batch in the factory, or how the product is stored in the channel. All this scrutiny sometimes reveals an implementation problem rather than a problem with product quality. In one such case, the customer service people were getting a lot of complaints from customers that their Cherry Garcia ice cream pops didn't have enough cherries. After the service people matched the complaints with sales records, they concluded it wasn't a regional problem—complaints pointed to pints that were sold all over the country. There wasn't a quality problem with just certain production batches either. Finally they discovered that the photo on the box was not of ice cream but of frozen yogurt treats—a product with more cherries. The difference wasn't great, but customers expected more cherries than they were getting. When Ben & Jerry's fixed the image on the box, the complaints melted away.

Ben & Jerry's faces a lot of competition from other premium brands. Some consumers have increased concern about fat in their diets, and that impacts the market too. But in this dynamic market, marketing managers at Ben & Jerry's have access to the data they need to get fast feedback that helps them constantly improve their strategy and how it is implemented.[1]

GOOD PLANS SET THE FRAMEWORK FOR IMPLEMENTATION AND CONTROL

Our primary emphasis in this book is on the strategy planning part of the marketing manager's job. There's a good reason for this focus. Effective strategy planning decisions set the firm on a course toward profitable opportunities. And when good strategies and plans are developed, everyone in the organization knows *what* needs to be done. Thus, good marketing plans set the framework for effective implementation and control.

Implementation puts plans into operation—and control provides feedback

Even so, successful marketing requires effective implementation and control. See Exhibit 2-1. In fact, in today's competitive markets customer satisfaction often hinges on skillful implementation. Further, ongoing success usually depends on **control**—the feedback process that helps the marketing manager learn (1) how ongoing plans and implementation are working and (2) how to plan for the future.

In this chapter, we'll go into more depth on concepts and how-to approaches for making implementation and control more effective. We'll start with a discussion of

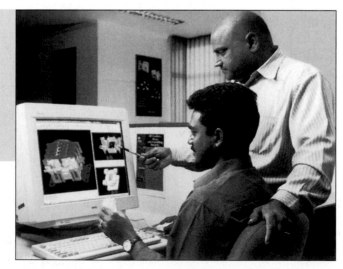

GE developed a software system so that its design engineers in different parts of the world could collaborate over the Internet in real time—which helps GE implement new strategies more quickly and effectively.

Lotus software allows managers in different locations, including different countries, to quickly share information, which helps to make implementation and control faster and more effective.

how improvements in information technology and e-commerce have changed implementation and control. Next we'll highlight some approaches, including total quality management, for improving implementation. Then we'll explain how marketing managers use control-related tools such as sales and performance analysis. We'll conclude with a discussion of what a marketing audit is, and why it is sometimes necessary.

SPEED UP INFORMATION FOR BETTER IMPLEMENTATION AND CONTROL

Feedback improves the marketing management process

Not long ago, marketing managers planned their strategies and put them into action—but then it usually took a long time to know if the strategy and implementation were really working as intended. For example, a marketing manager might not have much feedback on what was happening with sales, expenses, and profits until financial summaries were available—and that sometimes took months or even longer. Further, summary data often wasn't very useful in pinpointing which specific aspects of the plan were working and which weren't.

That situation is dramatically different today. In Chapter 8, we discussed how firms are using intranets, databases, and marketing information systems to track sales and cost details day by day. For example, checkout scanner data can provide a retailer with immediate feedback on how well a new product is selling in each specific store. Similarly, e-commerce order systems can feed into real-time sales reports for each product.

Fast feedback can be a competitive advantage

Marketing managers can often use faster feedback to develop a competitive advantage. They can quickly fine-tune a smooth-running implementation to make it even better. If there are problems, they can spot them early and fix them.

For example, a manager who gets detailed daily reports that compare actual sales results in different cities with sales forecasts in the plan is able to see very quickly if there is a problem in a specific city. Then the manager can track down the cause of the problem. If sales are going slowly because the new salesperson in that city is inexperienced, then the sales manager might immediately spend more time working with that rep. Or if the problem is that a retail chain in that city isn't allocating shelf space for the firm's product, then the salesperson might need to show buyers for that chain how the product could improve the chain's profit.

The marketing manager must take charge

Fast feedback is not possible unless data is in a form that can be quickly sorted and analyzed by computer. Here the creative marketing manager plays a crucial role by insisting that necessary data be captured as it comes in. It will be difficult, if not impossible, to get the information later.

A marketing manager may need to compile different types of information to improve implementation efforts or develop new strategies. This can cause delays. In a large company, for example, a marketing manager may need to track down information from other departments or from sales offices in other countries.

New information technologies offer speed and detail

Digital communication and e-commerce help solve these problems. Many companies use the Internet, fiber-optic telephone lines, or satellite transmission systems to *immediately* share data among locations. A sales manager with a notebook computer can pull data off the firm's intranet from anywhere in the world. Database applications that run on a website give similar access. Marketing managers working on different aspects of a strategy can use e-mail, messaging, or online video conferencing to communicate.

With the electronic pipeline a report summarizing sales by product, salesperson, or type of customer now can be available whenever an online user wants it. Software can be programmed to flag results that indicate a problem or create graphs that are easy to interpret. Then the manager can allocate time to resolve whatever problems show up.

These approaches are becoming common. So marketing managers who don't adopt them are losing out to more nimble competitors who get information more quickly and adjust their implementation and strategies more often.[2]

EFFECTIVE IMPLEMENTATION MEANS THAT PLANS WORK AS INTENDED

A good marketing plan often involves the challenge of implementing hundreds of operational decisions and activities. In a small company, these may all be handled by a single person. In a large corporation, thousands of people may be involved in implementation, requiring careful coordination and communication. Either way,

The marketing strategy for the kid's book *Harry Potter and the Goblet of Fire* called for it to be released everywhere on the same day. It was an implementation challenge for Amazon.com to get copies to 250,000 eager kids all at once, but FedEx helped solve the delivery problem.

even a great plan can leave customers unhappy, and switching to someone else's offering, if implementation is poor.

Good implementation builds relationships with customers

Implementation is especially critical in mature and highly competitive markets. When several firms all follow basically the same strategy—quickly imitating competitors' ideas—customers are often won or lost based on the quality of implementation. Consider the rental car business. Hertz has a strategy that targets business travelers with a choice of quality cars, convenient online reservations, fast pick-up and drop-off, accessories like cell phones and GPS, availability at most major airports, and a premium price. Hertz is successful with this strategy even though other companies can try the same approach. Hertz's success is due to implementation. Customers keep coming back because Hertz's service is reliable and pain-free.

When a Hertz #1 Club Gold customer calls to make a reservation, the company already has the standard information about that customer in a customer database. At the airport, the customer skips the line at the Hertz counter and instead just picks up an already-completed rental contract and goes straight to the Hertz bus. The driver gets the customer's name and radios ahead to have someone start the car that customer will drive. That way the air conditioner or heater is already doing its job when the bus driver delivers the customer right to the car. Customers are certain they're at the right place because there's an electronic sign beside each car with the customer's name on it. When the customer returns the car, an agent comes to the car, scans the customer's contract with a hand-held computer, and prints the receipt.

It's all very smooth. Making this work—day in and day out, customer after customer—isn't easy. But Hertz has set up systems to make it all easier because that's what it takes to implement its plan and to keep customers loyal.[3]

Implementation deals with internal or external matters

As the Hertz example illustrates, marketing implementation usually involves decisions and activities related to both internal and external matters. Figuring out how to get the correct car to the right parking slot, how the bus driver will contact the office, and who will get the message to the person who starts the car are all internal matters. They are *invisible to the customer if they work as planned*. On the other hand, some implementation issues are external and involve the customer. For example, the contract must be correct and in the right spot when the customer picks it up, and someone needs to fill the car with gas and clean it.

Implementation has its own objectives

Whether implementation decisions and activities are internal or external, they all must be consistent with the objectives of the overall strategy and with the other details of the plan. However, there are also three general objectives that apply to all implementation efforts. Other things equal, the manager wants to get each implementation job done:

Better, so customers really get superior value as planned.
Faster, to avoid delays that cause customers problems.
At lower cost, without wasting money on things that don't add value for the customer.

The ideal of doing things better, faster, and at lower cost is easy to accept. But in practice implementation is often complicated by trade-offs among the three objectives. For example, doing a job better may take longer or cost more.

So just as a marketing manager should constantly look for new strategy opportunities, it's important to be creative in looking for better solutions to implementation problems. That may require finding ways to better coordinate the efforts of the different people involved, setting up standard operating procedures to deal with recurring problems, or juggling priorities to deal with the unexpected. When the Hertz bus driver is sick, someone still has to be there to pick up the customers and deliver them to their cars.

Customer complaints bring implementation problems to light

There are thousands of ways that a plan or its implementation can go astray. A consumer's box of laundry detergent may be missing the measuring scoop. A digital camera's instructions may be very clear about how to take a picture but not explain how to hook the camera to a computer. Left unresolved, implementation glitches like these often result in dissatisfied customers. Smart marketers encourage customers to complain and make suggestions when there's a problem. Then it's possible to do something to correct it. In business markets complaints are usually handled by salespeople. But most firms that deal with large numbers of consumers have to rely on toll-free telephone lines, websites, and e-mail customer service support to help customers with questions and complaints.

Pillsbury's toll-free telephone line is typical. Some calls involve a question or praise, but about a third are complaints. For example, soon after Pillsbury introduced Funfetti cake mix with bits of edible confetti, callers began complaining that the confetti packet was missing from their box. A check of the manufacturing line showed the confetti packets were too light to alert weight scales when they were missing from the boxes. After the firm changed to a foil package, the complaints stopped.

But complaints need a response

Toll-free customer service lines and e-mail features built into websites probably don't win many new customers. But they do help a firm keep its current customers—if complaints are handled well. Yet too many firms drop the ball in this area of implementation as well. The customer may be shuffled from one person to another with no one taking responsibility to solve the problem; cell phone companies have a bad reputation for this.

Firms that get feedback by e-mail need to have a system that ensures that there is follow-up on each complaint. Many firms handle the first step smoothly. There is

Exhibit 19-1 Examples of Approaches to Overcome Specific Marketing Implementation Problems

Marketing Mix Decision Area	Operational Problem	Implementation Approach
Product	Develop design of a new product as rapidly as possible without errors.	Use 3-D computer-aided design software.
	Pretest consumer response to different versions of a label.	Prepare sample labels with graphics software and test them on the Internet.
Place	Coordinate inventory levels with middlemen to avoid stock-outs.	Use bar code scanners, RFID (smart) tags, EDI, and inventory reorder software.
	Get franchisee's inputs and cooperation on a new program.	Set up a televideo conference.
Promotion	Quickly distribute TV ad to local stations in many different markets.	Distribute digital video version of the ad via satellite link.
	Answer final consumers' questions about how to use a product.	Put a toll-free telephone number and website address on product label.
Price	Identify frequent customers for a quantity discount.	Create a "favored customer" club with an ID card.
	Figure out if price sensitivity impacts demand for a product; make it easier for customers to compare prices.	Show unit prices (for example, per oz.) on shelf markers; set different prices in similar markets and track sales, including sales of competing products.

someone who reads each message and forwards it to the department or person who seems right to handle the problem. However, there also should be a tracking system to be certain that the customer gets a response. This follow-up can be very important. One study found that callers who had their complaints resolved on average told five people about the help they got. The flip side is that those who weren't satisfied told twice as many people.[4]

Implementation requires innovation too

Sometimes implementation can be improved by approaching the task in a new way. Exhibit 19-1 shows some of the ways that firms are using information technology to improve specific implementation jobs. Note that some of the examples in Exhibit 19-1 focus on internal matters and some on external, customer-oriented matters.

While finding new approaches can help, better implementation often depends on being vigilant in improving what people are already doing. So let's take a closer look at some important ways that managers can improve the quality of their implementation efforts.[5]

BUILDING QUALITY INTO THE IMPLEMENTATION EFFORT

Total quality management meets customer requirements

There are many ways to improve implementation in each of the four Ps decision areas, but here we will focus on total quality management, which you can use to improve *any* implementation effort. With **total quality management (TQM)**, everyone in the organization is concerned about quality, throughout all of the firm's activities, to better serve customer needs.

In Chapter 9 we explained that product quality means the ability of a product to satisfy a customer's needs or requirements. Now we'll expand that idea and think about the quality of the whole marketing mix and how it is implemented—to meet customer requirements.

Customers want the paint on their new Toyota Tundra to be free from any scratches and that requires attention to implementation details. Factory workers take off their jewelry, wear shirts with rubber buttons, and use belts with special buckles that leave no metal exposed.

The cost of poor quality is lost customers

Most of the early attention in quality management focused on reducing defects in goods produced in factories. At one time most firms assumed defects were an inevitable part of mass production. They saw the cost of replacing defective parts or goods as just a cost of doing business—an insignificant one compared to the advantages of mass production. However, many firms were forced to rethink this assumption when Japanese producers of cars, electronics, and cameras showed that defects weren't inevitable. Much to the surprise of some production-oriented managers, the Japanese experience showed that it is less expensive to do something right the first time than to pay to do it poorly and *then* pay again to fix problems. And their success in taking customers away from established competitors made it clear that the cost of defects wasn't just the cost of replacement!

From the customer's point of view, getting a defective product and having to complain about it is a big headache. The customer can't use the defective product and suffers the inconvenience of waiting for someone to fix the problem—if *someone* gets around to it. It certainly doesn't deliver superior value. Rather, it erodes goodwill and leaves customers dissatisfied. The big cost of poor quality is the cost of lost customers.

Firms that adopted TQM methods to reduce manufacturing defects soon used the same approaches to overcome many other implementation problems. Their success brought attention to what is possible with TQM—whether the implementation problem concerns unreliable delivery schedules, poor customer service, advertising that appears on the wrong TV show, or salespeople who can't answer customers' questions.

Getting a handle on doing things right the first time

The idea of doing things right the first time seems obvious, but it's easier said than done. Problems always come up, and it's not always clear what isn't being done as well as it could be. People tend to ignore problems that don't pose an immediate crisis. But firms that adopt TQM always look for ways to improve implementation with **continuous improvement**—a commitment to constantly make things better one step at a time. Once you accept the idea that there *may* be a better way to do something and you look for it, you may just find it! The place to start is to clearly define "defects" in the implementation *process*, from the customer's point of view.

Things gone right and things gone wrong

Managers who use the TQM approach think of quality improvement as a sorting process—a sorting out of things gone right and things gone wrong. The sorting process calls for detailed measurements related to a problem. Then managers use a set of statistical tools to analyze the measurements and identify the problem areas that are the best candidates for fixing. The statistical details are beyond our focus here, but it's useful to get a feel for how managers use the tools.

Starting with customer needs

Let's consider the case of a restaurant that does well during the evening hours but wants to improve its lunch business. The restaurant develops a strategy that targets local businesspeople with an attractive luncheon buffet. The restaurant decides on a buffet because research shows that target customers want a choice of good healthy food and are willing to pay reasonable prices for it—as long as they can eat quickly and get back to work on time.

As the restaurant implements its new strategy, the manager wants a measure of how things are going. So she encourages customers to fill out comment cards that ask "How did we do today?" After several months of operation, things seem to be going reasonably well—although business is not as brisk as it was at first. The manager reads the comment cards and divides the ones with complaints into categories—to count up different reasons why customers weren't satisfied.

Slay the dragons first

Then the manager creates a graph showing a frequency distribution for the different types of complaints. Quality people call this a **Pareto chart**—a graph that shows the number of times a problem cause occurs, with problem causes ordered from most frequent to least frequent. The manager's Pareto chart, shown in Exhibit 19-2, reveals that customers complain most frequently that they have to wait for a seat. There were other common complaints—the buffet was not well organized, the table was not clean, and so on. However, the first complaint is much more common than the next most frequent.

This type of pattern is typical. The worst problems often occur over and over again. This focuses the manager's attention on which implementation problem to fix first. A rule of quality management is to slay the dragons first—which simply means start with the biggest problem. After removing that problem, the battle moves on to the next most frequent problem. If you do this *continuously*, you solve a lot of problems—and you don't just satisfy customers, you delight them.

Exhibit 19-2
Pareto Chart Showing Frequency of Different Complaints

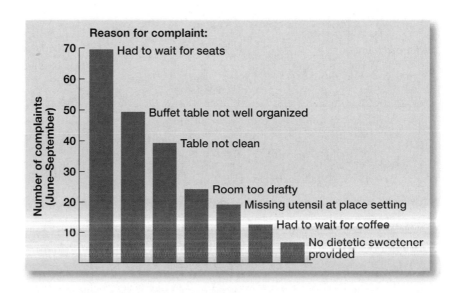

Figure out why things go wrong

So far, our manager has only identified the problem. To solve it, she creates a **fishbone diagram**—a visual aid that helps organize cause-and-effect relationships for "things gone wrong."

Our restaurant manager, for example, discovers that customers wait to be seated because tables aren't cleared soon enough. In fact, the Pareto chart (Exhibit 19-2) shows that customers also complain frequently about tables not being clean. So the two implementation problems may be related.

The manager's fishbone diagram (Exhibit 19-3) summarizes the various causes for tables not being cleaned quickly. There are different basic categories of causes—restaurant policy, procedures, people problems, and the physical environment. With this overview of different ways the service operation is going wrong, the manager can decide what to fix. She establishes different formal measures. For example, she counts how frequently different causes delay customers from being seated. She finds that the cashier's faulty credit card scanning machine holds up check processing. About half the time the cashier has to stop and enter the credit card information by hand. The fishbone diagram shows that restaurant policy is to clear the table after the entire party leaves. But customers have to wait at their tables while the staff deals with the faulty credit card machine, and cleaning is delayed. With the credit card machine replaced, the staff can clear the tables sooner—and because they're not so hurried they do a better cleaning job. Two dragons are on the way to being slayed!

Exhibit 19-3 Fishbone Diagram Showing Cause and Effect for "Why Tables Are Not Cleared Quickly"

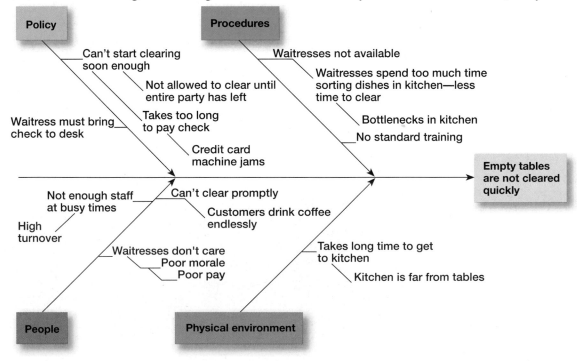

Our case shows that people in different areas of the restaurant affect customer satisfaction. The waitperson couldn't do what was needed to satisfy customers because the cashier had trouble with the credit card machine. The TQM approach helps everyone see and understand how their job affects what others do and the customer's satisfaction.[6]

Building quality into services

The restaurant case illustrates how a firm can improve implementation with TQM approaches. We used a service example because providing customer service is often a difficult area of implementation whether a firm's product is primarily a service, primarily a physical good, or a blend of both. For example, a manufacturer of ball bearings isn't just providing wholesalers or producers with round pieces of steel. Customers need information about deliveries, they need orders filled properly, and they may have questions to ask the firm's accountant, receptionist, or engineers. Because almost every firm must manage the service it provides customers, let's focus on some of the special concerns of implementing quality service.

Train people and empower them to serve

It's difficult to maintain consistent quality in services because the server is inseparable from the service. A person doing a specific service job may perform one specific task correctly but still annoy the customer in a host of other ways. So two keys to improving how people implement quality service are: (1) training and (2) empowerment.

All employees who have any contact with customers need training—many firms see 40 hours a year of training as a minimum. Simply showing customer-contact employees around the rest of the business—so that they learn how their contribution fits in the total effort—can be very effective. Good training usually includes role-playing on handling different types of customer requests and problems. A rental car attendant who is rude when a customer is trying to turn in a car may leave the customer dissatisfied—even if the rental car was perfect. How employees treat a customer is as important as whether they perform the task correctly.

Companies can't afford an army of managers to inspect how each employee implements a strategy—and such a system usually doesn't work anyway. Quality cannot be "inspected in." It must come from the people who do the service jobs. So firms that commit to service quality empower employees to satisfy customers' needs. **Empowerment** means giving employees the authority to correct a problem without first checking with management. At a hotel, for instance, an empowered room-service employee knows it's OK to run across the street to buy the specific brand of bottled water a guest requests.

Manage expectations—with good communication

The implementation effort sometimes leaves customers dissatisfied because they expect much more than it is possible for the firm to deliver. Some firms react to this by shrugging their shoulders and faulting customers for being unreasonable. However, customers are satisfied when the service matches their expectations, and careful communication leads to reasonable expectations. At Disney World, for example, waiting in line for a popular ride can be very tiring. Disney found, however, that by posting signs that show how long the wait will likely be, it reduced customer frustration. And it allowed people to know how to pick another ride with less waiting time.

Separate the routine and plan for the special

Implementation usually involves some routine services and some that require special attention. Customer satisfaction increases when the two types of service encounters are separated. For example, banks set up special windows for commercial deposits and supermarkets have cash-only lines.

Most firms try to use computers and other equipment to handle routine services whenever they can. ATMs are quick and convenient for dispensing cash. Airlines use touchscreen displays so travelers can check themselves in at airports. The UPS website (www.ups.com) makes it easy for customers to track a delivery.

Firms can study special service requests they get and then use training so that even unusual customer requests become routine to the staff. Every day, hotel guests lose their keys, bank customers run out of checks, and supermarket shoppers leave their wallets at home. A well-run service operation anticipates these special events so service providers can respond in a way that satisfies customers' needs.

Managers lead the quality effort

Quality implementation doesn't just happen by itself. Managers must show that they are committed to doing things right to satisfy customers and that quality is everyone's job. Without top-level support, some people won't get beyond their business-as-usual attitude—and TQM won't work. The top executive at American Express had his board of directors give him the title Chief Quality Officer so that everyone in the company would know he was personally involved in the TQM effort.

Specify jobs and benchmark performance

Managers who develop successful quality programs clearly specify and write out exactly what tasks need to be done, how, and by whom. This may seem unnecessary. After all, most people know, in general, what they're supposed to do. However, if the tasks are clearly specified, it's easier to see what criteria should be used to measure performance.

Once criteria are established, there needs to be some basis on which to evaluate the job being done. In our restaurant example, one part of the job specification for the cashier is to process credit card payments. In that case, relevant criteria might include the amount of time that it takes and the number of people waiting in line to pay. If the restaurant manager had seen a record of how long it was taking to process credit cards, she would have known that for many customers it was taking too long. Without the measure, the precise nature of the problem was hidden.

That takes us to the issue of **benchmarking**—picking a basis of comparison for evaluating how well a job is being done. For example, consider a case in which a firm asks each of its customers to rate their satisfaction with the sales rep with whom they work. Then the company might benchmark each sales rep against other sales reps on the basis of average customer satisfaction. But if the firm's sales reps as a group are weak, that isn't a sensible approach. The ones that stink the least would

As a multinational corporation, Timken has earned high marks in implementing its marketing plans so that its customers get the quality they want—wherever they may be around the globe.

WHAT DO PRODUCTS, PLANTS, AND PEOPLE IN 29 COUNTRIES ULTIMATELY MEAN?
WE'LL BE RIGHT THERE.

TIMKEN
WORLDWIDE LEADER IN BEARINGS AND STEEL

look good on a relative basis. Many firms try to benchmark against some external standard. For example, a sales manager might want to benchmark against a competitor's sales reps. Or better, the manager might identify firms in which sales reps earn superlative customer satisfaction ratings, regardless of their industry, and benchmark against them. That approach can also reveal job specifications—things that should be done—that the sales manager had not considered or measured in the first place.

Getting a return on quality is important

While the cost of poor quality is lost customers, keep in mind that the type of quality efforts we've been discussing also result in costs. It's easy to fall into the trap of running up *unnecessary costs* trying to improve some facet of implementation that really isn't that important to customer satisfaction or customer retention. When that happens, customers may still be satisfied, but the firm can't make a profit because of the extra costs. In other words, there isn't a financial return on the money spent to improve quality. Remember that getting everyone to work together to satisfy customers should be the route to profits. A manager should focus on quality efforts that really provide the customer with superior value—quality that costs no more to provide than customers will ultimately be willing to pay.[7]

CONTROL PROVIDES FEEDBACK TO IMPROVE PLANS AND IMPLEMENTATION

Keeping a firmer hand on the controls

Although information technology speeds up the flow of feedback and allows managers to improve plans and implementation continuously, the basic control questions that a marketing manager wants to answer are pretty similar to what they've always been.

A good manager wants to know which products' sales are highest and why, which products are profitable, what is selling where, and how much the marketing process is costing. Managers need to know what's happening, in detail, to improve the bottom line.

Unfortunately, traditional accounting reports are usually too general to be much help in answering these questions. A company may be showing a profit, while 80 percent of its business comes from only 20 percent of its products—or customers. The other 80 percent may be unprofitable. But without special analyses, managers won't know it. This 80/20 relationship is fairly common—and it is often referred to as the *80/20 rule*.

What happened at Allegiance Healthcare Corporation (AHC), which recently became part of CardinalHealth, is a good example. As a major distributor of hospital supplies, AHC carried over 100,000 products—everything a hospital might need from scalpels and skin markers to gowns and bandages. The huge array of products was complicated, but AHC was doing well with its strategy of being a "single source" for hospitals. However, careful analysis of sales and costs by region and product line revealed that AHC's profitable level of sales was masking a problem: 57 percent of its products accounted for just 2 percent of sales. Further, these same products had larger than average costs. While waiting to be ordered, these products were sitting in warehouses all over the country, running up inventory costs. By analyzing sales within product categories, marketing managers were able to see where there was duplication and what they could drop. After all, they probably didn't need to give hospitals a choice among dozens of bedpans. Then they worked to make distribution of the products they kept more efficient. Products that hospitals order frequently—like needles and sutures—are stocked in the 68 regional distribution centers close to customers. Items that hospitals order infrequently—like odd sizes of surgical gloves—are shipped from a single distribution center. The changes allowed AHC to cut out 30 local warehouses and still offer hospitals just-in-time delivery by using its own trucks.[8]

As this example shows, it *is* possible for marketing managers to get detailed information about how marketing plans are working—but only if they ask for and analyze the necessary data. In this section, we'll discuss the kinds of information that can be available and how to use it. The techniques are not really complicated. They basically require only simple arithmetic—and of course computers easily take care of that when a large volume of sorting, adding, and subtracting is required.

SALES ANALYSIS SHOWS WHAT'S HAPPENING

Sales analysis looks at the details

Marketers are always interested in what sort of sales results they're achieving, but it's usually not enough to just know totals or summary information. Marketing executives need more detailed sales data to keep in touch with what's happening in the market. They get this detail by turning to **sales analysis**—a detailed breakdown of a company's sales records.

There is no one best way to break down or analyze sales data. Several breakdowns may be useful, depending on the nature of the company and product and what dimensions are relevant. Typical breakdowns include

1. Product category, brand, package size, grade, or color.
2. Geographic region—country, state, city, or sales rep's territory.
3. Customer characteristics (new or existing account, frequency of purchases, etc.).
4. Channel of distribution (type of middlemen involved, target markets served, etc.).
5. Price or discount class.
6. Method of sale—online, telephone, or sales rep.
7. Financial arrangement—cash or charge.
8. Order size.

Sales analysis is easy to do, and usually it's inexpensive because the data for the analysis can easily be obtained as a by-product of basic billing and accounts receivable

Information Resources, Inc., developed the DataServer Analyzer Software, illustrated here, to make it easy to do sales analysis and produce graphs that make it easy to see patterns that might otherwise be hidden in a table of numbers.

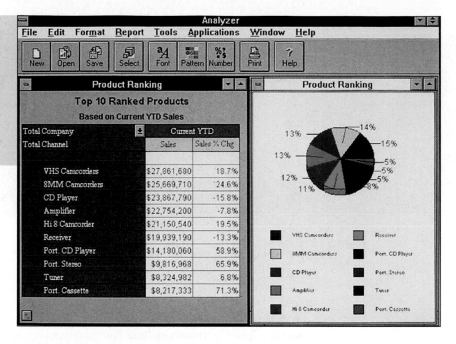

procedures. However, the manager must make sure the company captures identifying information on important dimensions such as territory, sales reps, product model, customer, and so forth in a database. Then the marketing information system can easily provide detailed sales analyses broken down by any variable (or combination of variables) in the database.

Sales analyses over time highlight trends

When sales analyses are routinely prepared over time (every day, week, month, or quarter), they show trends and help managers develop more accurate sales forecasts. A manager who ignores trends may not be able to spot shifts in the market that point to new opportunities or alternatively, problems. This is critical because today's profit is no guarantee that you'll make money tomorrow.

A graph is worth a thousand numbers

While detailed and timely sales analysis can be very useful, information that is too detailed or complex can drown a manager. Information systems can spew out more data than a manager can absorb. Well-designed information systems provide managers with color graphs and charts that make it easy to see patterns that otherwise might be hidden scrolling through online tables with a browser. For example, a sales analysis breakdown of sales by product might show a bar graph for each product, where the height of the bar reflects the level of sales and where increases from the previous period are in green and decreases are in red.

While graphs can help a manager sort through raw sales data, another way to identify what data is most relevant and really needs attention is *performance analysis*.

PERFORMANCE ANALYSIS LOOKS FOR DIFFERENCES

Numbers are compared

Performance analysis looks for exceptions or variations from planned performance. In simple sales analysis, the figures are merely listed or graphed—they aren't compared against standards. In performance analysis, managers make comparisons. They might compare one territory against another, against the same territory's performance last year, or against expected performance.

Exhibit 19-4 Comparative Performance of Sales Reps

Sales Area	Total Calls	Total Orders	Order-Call Ratio	Sales by Sales Rep	Average Sales Rep Order	Total Consumers
A	1,900	1,140	60.0%	$ 912,000	$800	195
B	1,500	1,000	66.7	720,000	720	160
C	1,400	700	50.0	560,000	800	140
D	1,030	279	27.1	132,000	478	60
E	820	165	20.1	62,000	374	50
Total	6,650	3,284	49.3%	$2,386,000	$634	605

The purpose of performance analysis is to improve operations. The salesperson, territory, or other factors showing poor performance can be identified and singled out for detailed analysis and corrective action. Or outstanding performances can be analyzed to see if the successes can be explained and made the general rule.

Performance analysis doesn't have to be limited to sales. Other data can be analyzed too. This data may include the frequency of stock-outs, the number of sales calls made, the number of orders, customer satisfaction ratings, or the cost of various tasks.

A performance analysis can be quite revealing, as shown in the following example.

Straight performance analysis—an illustration

A manufacturer of business products sells to wholesalers through five sales reps, each serving a separate territory. Total net sales for the year amount to $2,386,000. Sales force compensation and expenses come to $198,000, yielding a direct-selling expense ratio of 8.3 percent—that is, $198,000 ÷ $2,386,000 × 100.

This information—taken from a profit and loss statement—is interesting, but it doesn't explain what's happening from one territory to another. To get a clearer picture, the manager compares the sales results with other data *from each territory*. See Exhibits 19-4 and 19-5. Keep in mind that exhibits like these and others that follow in this chapter are easy to generate with programs like Microsoft Office. Larger companies make such analysis available at a website so the manager can sort out whatever is needed.

The reps in sales areas D and E aren't doing well. Sales are low and marketing costs are high. Perhaps more aggressive sales reps could do a better job, but the number of customers suggests that sales potential might be low. Perhaps the whole plan needs revision.

Exhibit 19-5 Comparative Cost of Sales Reps

Sales Area	Annual Compensation	Expense Payments	Total Sales Rep Cost	Sales Produced	Cost-Sales Ratio
A	$ 22,800	$11,200	$ 34,000	$ 912,000	3.7%
B	21,600	14,400	36,000	720,000	5.0
C	20,400	11,600	32,000	560,000	5.7
D	19,200	24,800	44,000	132,000	33.3
E	20,000	32,000	52,000	62,000	83.8
Total	$104,000	$94,000	$198,000	$2,386,000	8.3%

The figures themselves, of course, don't provide the answers. But they do reveal the areas that need improvement. This is the main value of performance analysis. It's up to management to find the remedy, either by revising or changing the marketing plan.

PERFORMANCE INDEXES SIMPLIFY HUMAN ANALYSIS

Comparing against "what ought to have happened"

With a straight performance analysis, the marketing manager can evaluate the variations among sales reps to try to explain the "why." But this takes time. And poor performances are sometimes due to problems that bare sales figures don't reveal. Some uncontrollable factors in a particular territory—tougher competitors or ineffective middlemen—may lower the sales potential. Or a territory just may not have much potential.

To get a better check on performance effectiveness, the marketing manager compares what did happen with what ought to have happened. This involves the use of performance indexes.

A performance index is like a batting average

When a manager sets standards—that is, quantitative measures of what ought to happen—it's relatively simple to compute a **performance index**—a number like a baseball batting average that shows the relation of one value to another.

Baseball batting averages are computed by dividing the actual number of hits by the number of times at bat (the possible number of times the batter could have had a hit) and then multiplying the result by 100 to get rid of decimal points. A sales performance index is computed the same way—by dividing actual sales by expected sales for the area (or sales rep, product, etc.) and then multiplying by 100. If a sales rep is batting 82 percent, the index is 82.

A simple example shows where the problem is

We show how to compute a performance index in the following example, which assumes that population is an effective measure of sales potential.

In Exhibit 19-6, the population of the United States is broken down by region as a percent of the total population. The regions are Northeastern, Southern, Midwestern, and Western.

A firm already has $1 million in sales and now wants to evaluate performance in each region. Column 2 shows the actual sales of $1 million broken down in proportion to the population in the four regions. This is what sales *should* be if population were a good measure of future performance. Column 3 in Exhibit 19-6 shows the actual sales for the year for each region. Column 4 shows measures of performance (performance indexes)—Column 3 ÷ Column 2 × 100.

Exhibit 19-6 Development of a Measure of Sales Performances (by region)

Regions	(1) Population as Percent of United States	(2) Expected Distribution of Sales Based on Population	(3) Actual Sales	(4) Performance Index
Northeastern	20	$ 200,000	$ 210,000	105
Southern	25	250,000	250,000	100
Midwestern	35	350,000	420,000	120
Western	20	200,000	120,000	60
Total	100	$1,000,000	$1,000,000	

The Western region isn't doing as well as expected. It has 20 percent of the total population—and expected sales (based on population) are $200,000. Actual sales, however, are only $120,000. This means that the Western region's performance index is only 60—$(120,000 \div 200,000) \times 100$—because actual sales are much lower than expected on the basis of population. If population is a good basis for measuring expected sales (an important *if*), the poor sales performance should be analyzed further. Perhaps sales reps in the Western region aren't working as hard as they should. Perhaps promotion there isn't as effective as elsewhere. Or competitive products may have entered the market.

Whatever the cause, it's clear that performance analysis does not solve problems. Managers do that. But performance analysis does point out potential problems—and it does this well.

INTERNET EXERCISE

SPSS sells software that can be used for a variety of purposes, including analyses of sales, cost, and customer data. Browse the SPSS website (www.spss.com) and identify three ways that SPSS could make it easier for a manager to do a performance analysis.

A SERIES OF PERFORMANCE ANALYSES MAY FIND THE REAL PROBLEM

Performance analysis helps a marketing manager see if the firm's marketing plans are working properly—and, if they aren't, it can lead to problem solving. But a marketing manager may need a series of performance analyses, as shown in the following example.

To get a feel for how performance analysis can be part of a problem-solving process, follow this example carefully—one exhibit at a time. Try to anticipate the marketing manager's decision.

The case of CarAudio, Inc.

CarAudio's sales manager finds that sales for the Pacific Coast region are $130,000 below the quota of $14,500,000 (that is, actual sales are $14,370,000) for the January through June period. The quota is based on forecast sales of the various types of replacement car audio equipment the company sells. Specifically, the quota is based on forecasts for each product type in each store in each sales rep's territory.

Pam Dexter, the sales manager, thinks this difference isn't too large (1.52 percent) and is inclined to forget the matter—especially since forecasts usually err to some extent. But she thinks about sending an e-mail message to all sales reps and district supervisors in the region—a message aimed at stimulating sales effort.

Exhibit 19-7 shows the overall picture of CarAudio's sales on the Pacific Coast. What do you think the manager should do?

The Portland district has the poorest performance—but it isn't too bad. Before writing a "let's get with it" letter to Portland and then relaxing, the sales manager decides to analyze the performance of the four sales reps in the Portland district. Exhibit 19-8 shows a breakdown of the Portland figures by sales rep. What conclusion or action do you suggest now?

Since Shanna Smith previously was the top sales rep, the sales manager wonders if Smith is having trouble with some of her larger customers. Before making a drastic move, she does an analysis of Smith's sales to the five largest customers. See Exhibit 19-9. What action could the sales manager take now? Should Smith be fired?

Smith's sales in all the large stores are down significantly, although her sales in many small stores are holding up well. Smith's problem seems to be general. Perhaps

Exhibit 19-7
Sales Performance—Pacific
Coast Region, January–June
($000)

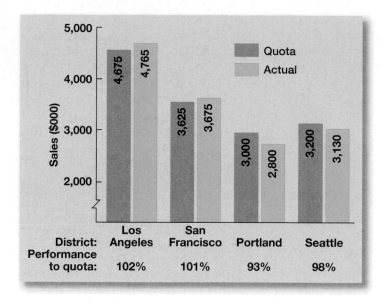

she just isn't working. Before calling her, the sales manager decides to look at Smith's sales of the four major products. Exhibit 19-10 shows Smith's sales. What action is indicated now?

Smith is having real trouble with radio receivers. Was the problem Smith or the radios?

Further analysis by product for the whole region shows that everyone on the Pacific Coast is having trouble with radio receivers because customers there are buying new satellite radios that come from another company. But higher sales on other products hid this fact. Since radio sales are doing all right nationally, the problem is only now showing up. You can see that this is the *major* problem. If CarAudio doesn't offer a satellite radio, it will just slowly lose sales as more customers shift to satellite.

Since overall company sales are fairly good, many sales managers wouldn't bother with this analysis. Some might trace the problem to Smith. But without detailed sales records and performance analysis, they might assume that Smith—rather than

Exhibit 19-8
Sales Performance—
Portland District,
January–June ($000)

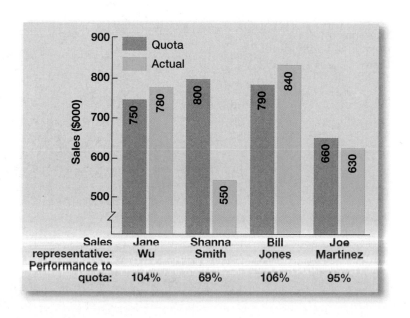

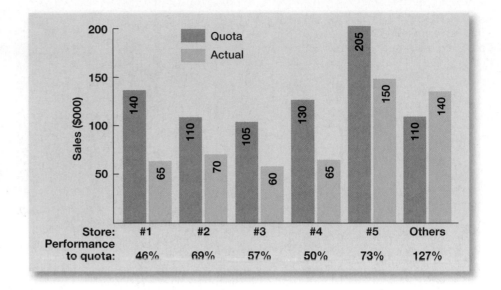

Store:	#1	#2	#3	#4	#5	Others
Performance to quota:	46%	69%	57%	50%	73%	127%

the missed opportunity to add a new product—is at fault. And Smith herself might not be able to pinpoint what's happening.

The iceberg principle—90 percent is below the surface

The CarAudio case illustrates the **iceberg principle**—much good information is hidden in summary data. Icebergs show only about 10 percent of their mass above water level. The other 90 percent is below water level, and not directly below either. The submerged portion almost seems to search out ships that come too near.

The same is true of much business and marketing data. Since total sales may be large and company activities varied, problems in one area may hide below the surface. Everything looks calm and peaceful. But closer analysis may reveal jagged edges that can severely damage or even sink the business. The 90:10 ratio—or the 80/20 rule we mentioned earlier—must not be ignored. Averaging and summarizing data are helpful, but be sure summaries don't hide more than they reveal. Marketing managers need facts to avoid rash judgments based on incomplete information. Some students want to fire Smith after they see the store-by-store data (Exhibit 19-9).

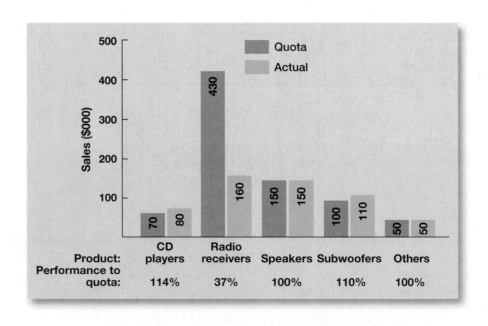

Product:	CD players	Radio receivers	Speakers	Subwoofers	Others
Performance to quota:	114%	37%	100%	110%	100%

For a restaurant to be profitable, the manager needs to worry not only about satisfying customers but also about how much each item contributes to overall costs.

MARKETING COST ANALYSIS—CONTROLLING COSTS TOO

So far we've emphasized sales analysis. But sales come at a cost. And costs can and should be analyzed and controlled too. You can see why in the case of Watanake Packaging, Ltd. (WPL). WPL developed a new strategy to target the packaging needs of producers of high-tech electronic equipment. WPL designed unique Styrofoam inserts to protect electronic equipment during shipping. It assigned order getters to develop new accounts and recruited agent middlemen to develop overseas markets. WPL's marketing mix was well received and led to good profits. But over time as marketing managers at WPL analyzed costs, they realized their once-successful strategy was slipping. Personal selling expense as a percent of sales had doubled because it took longer to find and sell new accounts. It was costly to design special products for the many customers who purchased only small quantities. Profit margins were falling too because of increased price competition. In contrast, the analysis showed that online sales of ordinary cardboard shipping boxes for agricultural products were very profitable. So WPL stopped calling on *small* electronics firms and developed a new plan to improve its website and build the firm's share of the less glamorous, but more profitable, cardboard box business.

Marketing costs have a purpose

Detailed cost analysis is very useful in understanding production costs—but much less is done with *marketing cost analysis*.[9] One reason is that many accountants show little interest in their firm's marketing process—or they don't understand the different marketing activities. They just treat marketing as overhead and forget about it.

In the next chapter, when we discuss the relationship between marketing and accounting in more detail, we'll explain how some accountants and marketing managers are working together to address this problem. For now, however, you should see that careful analysis of most marketing costs shows that the money is spent for a specific purpose—for example, to develop or promote a particular product or to serve particular customers.

Let's reconsider Exhibit 19-5 from this perspective. It shows that the company's spending on sales compensation and sales expenses varies by salesperson and market area. By breaking out and comparing the costs of different sales reps, the marketing manager has a much better idea of what it costs to implement the strategy in each sales area. In this example, it's clear that the sales reps in sales areas D and especially E are not only falling short in sales, but also that their costs are high relative to other reps who are getting more results. The table shows that the difference isn't due to annual compensation; that's lower. Rather, these reps have expenses that are two or three times the average. The smaller number of total customers in these sales areas (Exhibit 19-4) might explain the lower levels of sales, but it probably doesn't explain the higher expenses. Perhaps the customers are more spread out and require more travel to reach. Here again, the cost analysis doesn't explain *why* the results are as they are—but it does direct the manager's attention to a specific area that needs improvement. A more detailed breakdown of costs may help pinpoint the specific cause.

Allocate costs to specific customers and products

Because marketing costs have a purpose, it usually makes sense to allocate costs to specific market segments, or customers, or to specific products. In some situations, companies allocate costs directly to the various geographical market segments they serve. This may let managers directly analyze the profitability of the firm's target markets. In other cases, companies allocate costs to specific customers or specific products and then add these costs for market segments depending on how much of which products each customer buys.

Should all costs be allocated?

So far we've discussed general principles. But allocating costs is tricky. Some costs are likely to be fixed for the near future, regardless of what decision is made. And some costs are likely to be *common* to several products or customers, making allocation difficult.

There are two basic approaches to handling this allocating problem: the full-cost approach and the contribution-margin approach.

Full-cost approach— everything costs something

In the **full-cost approach,** all costs are allocated to products, customers, or other categories. Even fixed costs and common costs are allocated in some way. Because all costs are allocated, we can subtract costs from sales and find the profitability of various customers, products, and so on. This *is* of interest to some managers.

The full-cost approach requires that difficult-to-allocate costs be split on some basis. Here the managers assume that the work done for those costs is equally beneficial to customers, to products, or to whatever group they are allocated. Sometimes this allocation is done mechanically. But often logic can support the allocation—if we accept the idea that marketing costs are incurred for a purpose. For example, advertising costs not directly related to specific customers or products might be allocated to *all* customers based on their purchases—on the theory that advertising helps bring in the sales. We'll go into more detail on allocating costs in the next chapter.

Contribution-margin—ignores some costs to get results

When we use the **contribution-margin approach,** all costs are not allocated in *all* situations. Why?

When we compare various alternatives, it may be more meaningful to consider only the costs directly related to specific alternatives. Variable costs are relevant here.

The contribution-margin approach focuses attention on variable costs rather than on total costs. Total costs may include some fixed costs that do not change in the short run and can safely be ignored or some common costs that are more difficult to allocate.[10]

The two approaches can lead to different decisions

The difference between the full-cost approach and the contribution-margin approach is important. The two approaches may suggest different decisions, as we'll see in the following example.

OFFICE SUPPLIES CHAIN REFINES IMPLEMENTATION TO HIGHLIGHT PROFITS

Managers for Staples, the big office supplies chain, rely heavily on detailed data about each product and store to make better decisions on everything from where new stores will be located to how display space is organized.

One analysis, which considered sales and costs in detail, led to the conclusion that the chain's basic emphasis on furniture lines (like desks and file cabinets) was a mistake. These high-ticket furniture lines offer better gross margins than everyday office supplies (like Bic pens and Scotch tape), but at the same time they take up a lot more floor space. Moreover, managers at Staples found that when they allocated costs of storage, distribution, handling, damage, labor, rent, and the like to the bulky furniture products, the overall profitability of

the category was much less than other less space-intensive categories. Selling furniture also took up more time from salespeople, so they weren't available to handle as many questions with fast-and-easy answers—like where a customer could find the Post-it note pads.

After Staples shrunk the furniture department in some stores and eliminated it in stores where sales had been lowest, more room was available for Avery labels and Accent highlighters. This shift increased sales and profits and ultimately prompted another round of cutbacks in the floor space allocated to computer inventory and displays. Most stores shifted to build-to-order options for computers. In combination, these changes contributed to a 12 percent rate of growth in profits over a five-year period.[11]

Full-cost example

Exhibit 19-11 shows a profit and loss statement, using the full-cost approach, for a department store with three operating departments. (These could be market segments or customers or products.)

The administrative expenses, which are the only fixed costs in this case, have been allocated to departments based on the sales volume of each department. This is a typical method of allocation. In this case, some managers argued that Department 1 was clearly unprofitable and should be eliminated because it showed a net loss of $500. Were they right?

To find out, see Exhibit 19-12, which shows what would happen if Department 1 were eliminated.

Several facts become clear right away. The overall profit of the store would be reduced if Department 1 were dropped. Fixed costs of $3,000, now being charged to Department 1, would have to be allocated to the other departments. This would reduce net profit by $2,500, since Department 1 previously covered $2,500 of the

Exhibit 19-11 Profit and Loss Statement by Department

	Totals	Dept. 1	Dept. 2	Dept. 3
Sales	$100,000	$50,000	$30,000	$20,000
Cost of sales	80,000	45,000	25,000	10,000
Gross margin	20,000	5,000	5,000	10,000
Other expenses:				
Selling expenses	5,000	2,500	1,500	1,000
Administrative expenses	6,000	3,000	1,800	1,200
Total other expenses	11,000	5,500	3,300	2,200
Net profit or (loss)	$ 9,000	$ (500)	$ 1,700	$ 7,800

Exhibit 19-12   Profit and Loss Statement by Department if Department 1 Were Eliminated

	Totals	Dept. 2	Dept. 3
Sales	$50,000	$30,000	$20,000
Cost of sales	35,000	25,000	10,000
Gross margin	15,000	5,000	10,000
Other expenses:			
Selling expenses	2,500	1,500	1,000
Administrative expenses	6,000	3,600	2,400
Total other expenses	8,500	5,100	3,400
Net profit or (loss)	$ 6,500	$ (100)	$ 6,600

$3,000 in fixed costs. Such shifting of costs would then make Department 2 look unprofitable!

Contribution-margin example

Exhibit 19-13 shows a contribution-margin income statement for the same department store. Note that each department has a positive contribution margin. Here the Department 1 contribution of $2,500 stands out better. This actually is the amount that would be lost if Department 1 were dropped. (Our simple example assumes that the fixed administrative expenses are *truly* fixed—that none of them would be eliminated if this department were dropped.)

A contribution-margin income statement shows the contribution of each department more clearly, including its contribution to both fixed costs and profit. As long as a department has some contribution-margin, and as long as there is no better use for the resources it uses, the department should be retained.

Contribution-margin versus full-cost— choose your side

Using the full-cost approach often leads to arguments within a company. Any method of allocation can make some products or customers appear less profitable.

For example, it seems logical to assign all common advertising costs to customers based on their purchases. But this approach can be criticized on the grounds that it may make large-volume customers appear less profitable than they really are. Those in the company who want the smaller customers to look more profitable usually argue *for* this allocation method.

Exhibit 19-13   Contribution-Margin Statement by Departments

	Totals	Dept. 1	Dept. 2	Dept. 3
Sales	$100,000	$50,000	$30,000	$20,000
Variable costs:				
Cost of sales	80,000	45,000	25,000	10,000
Selling expenses	5,000	2,500	1,500	1,000
Total variable costs	85,000	47,500	26,500	11,000
Contribution margin	15,000	$ 2,500	$ 3,500	$ 9,000
Fixed costs				
Administrative expenses	6,000			
Net profit	$ 9,000			

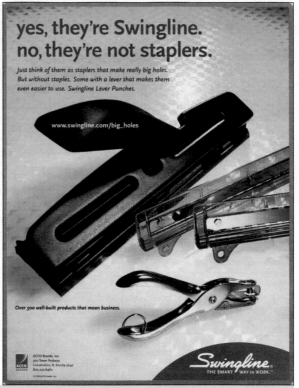

An ad for a single product, like Bawls Guarana high caffeine beverage, involves a cost that can be allocated directly to the product. In contrast, if an ad (like this one from Swingline) promotes several products or product lines at the same time, it may be more difficult to allocate the correct portion of the cost to individual products.

Arguments over allocation methods can be deadly serious. The method used may reflect on the performance of various managers—and it may affect their salaries and bonuses. Product managers, for example, are especially interested in how the various fixed and common costs are allocated to their products. Each, in turn, might like to have costs shifted to others' products.

Arbitrary allocation of costs also may have a direct impact on sales reps' morale. If they see their variable costs loaded with additional common or fixed costs over which they have no control, they may ask, "What's the use?"

To avoid these problems, firms often use the contribution-margin approach. It's especially useful for evaluating alternatives and for showing operating managers and salespeople how they're doing. The contribution-margin approach shows what they've actually contributed to covering general overhead and profit.

Top management, on the other hand, often finds full-cost analysis more useful. In the long run, some products, departments, or customers must pay for the fixed costs. Full-cost analysis has its place too.

PLANNING AND CONTROL COMBINED

We've been treating sales and cost analyses separately up to this point. But management often combines them to keep a running check on its activities—to be sure the plans are working—and to see when and where new strategies are needed.

Sales + Costs +
Everybody helps =
$163,000

Let's see how this works at Cindy's Fashions, a small-town apparel retailer. This firm netted $155,000 last year. Cindy Reve, the owner, expects no basic change in competition and slightly better local business conditions. So she sets this year's profit objective at $163,000—an increase of about 5 percent.

Next she develops tentative plans to show how she can make this higher profit. She estimates the sales volumes, gross margins, and expenses—broken down by months and by departments in her store—that she would need to net $163,000.

Exhibit 19-14 is a planning and control chart Reve developed to show the contribution each department should make each month. At the bottom of Exhibit 19-14, the plan for the year is summarized. Note that space is provided to insert the actual performance and a measure of variation. So this chart can be used to do both planning and control.

Exhibit 19-14 shows that Reve is focusing on the monthly contribution to overhead and profit by each department. The purpose of monthly estimates is to get more frequent feedback and allow faster adjustment of plans. Generally, the shorter the planning and control period, the easier it is to correct problems before they become emergencies.

In this example, Reve uses a modified contribution-margin approach—some of the fixed costs can be allocated logically to particular departments. On this chart, the balance left after direct fixed and variable costs are charged to departments is called Contribution to Store. The idea is that each department will contribute to covering *general* store expenses—such as top-management salaries and holiday decorations—and to net profits.

In Exhibit 19-14, we see that the whole operation is brought together when Reve computes the monthly operating profit. She totals the contribution from each of the

Exhibit 19-14 Planning and Control Chart for Cindy's Fashions

	Contribution to Store					Store Expense	Operating Profit	Cumulative Operating Profit
	Dept. A	Dept. B	Dept. C	Dept. D[*]	Total			
January								
Planned	27,000	9,000	4,000	−1,000	39,000	24,000	15,000	15,000
Actual								
Variation								
February								
Planned	20,000	6,500	2,500	−1,000	28,000	24,000	4,000	19,000
Actual								
Variation								
November								
Planned	32,000	7,500	2,500	0	42,000	24,000	18,000	106,500
Actual								
Variation								
December								
Planned	63,000	12,500	4,000	9,000	88,500	32,000	56,500	163,000
Actual								
Variation								
Total								
Planned	316,000	70,000	69,000	−4,000	453,000	288,000	163,000	163,000
Actual								
Variation								

[*]The objective of minus $4,000 for this department was established on the same basis as the objectives for the other departments—that is, it represents the same percentage gain over last year when Department D's loss was $4,200. Plans call for discontinuance of the department unless it shows marked improvement by the end of the year.

four departments, then subtracts general store expenses to obtain the operating profit for each month.

As time passes, Reve can compare actual sales with what's projected. If actual sales were less than projected, corrective action could take either of two courses: improving implementation efforts or developing new, more realistic strategies.

THE MARKETING AUDIT

While crises pop up, planning and control must go on

The analyses we've discussed so far are designed to help a firm plan and control its operations. They can help a marketing manager do a better job. Often, however, the control process focuses on short-run problems and adjustments.

To make sure that the whole marketing program is evaluated *regularly*, marketing specialists developed the marketing audit. A marketing audit is similar to an accounting audit or a personnel audit, which businesses have used for some time.

The **marketing audit** is a systematic, critical, and unbiased review and appraisal of the basic objectives and policies of the marketing function and of the organization, methods, procedures, and people employed to implement the policies.[12]

A marketing audit requires a detailed look at the company's current marketing plans to see if they are still the best plans the firm can offer. Customers' needs and attitudes change—and competitors continually develop new and better plans. Plans more than a year or two old may be out-of-date or even obsolete. Sometimes marketing managers are so close to the trees that they can't see the forest. An outsider can help the firm see whether it really focuses on some unsatisfied needs and offers appropriate marketing mixes. Basically, the auditor uses our strategy planning framework. But instead of developing plans, the auditor works backward and evaluates the plans being implemented. The consultant-auditor also evaluates the quality of the effort, looking at who is doing what and how well. This means interviewing customers, competitors, channel members, and employees. A marketing audit can be a big job. But if it helps ensure that the company's strategies are on the right track and being implemented properly, it can be well worth the effort.

An audit shouldn't be necessary—but often it is

A marketing audit takes a big view of the business—and it evaluates the whole marketing program. It might be done by a separate department within the company, perhaps by a marketing controller. But to get both expert and objective evaluation, it's probably better to use an outside organization such as a marketing consulting firm.

Ideally, a marketing audit should not be necessary. Good managers do their best in planning, implementing, and controlling—and they should continually evaluate the effectiveness of the operation. In practice, however, managers often become identified with certain strategies, and pursue them blindly, when other strategies might be more effective. Since an outside view can give needed perspective, marketing audits may be more common in the future.

CONCLUSION

In this chapter, we've focused on the important role of implementation and control in satisfying customers and ensuring the firm's ongoing success. We explained how improvements in information technology are playing a critical role in revolutionizing these areas. Managers should seek new and creative ways to improve implementation, which can often give a firm a competitive advantage in building stronger relationships with customers, even in highly competitive mature markets.

We also went into some detail on how total quality management can help the firm get the type of implementation it needs—implementation that continuously improves and does a better job of meeting customers' needs and at lower cost.

A marketing program must also be controlled. Good control helps the marketing manager locate and correct weak spots and at the same time find strengths that may be applied throughout the marketing program. Control works hand in hand with planning.

Simple sales analysis just gives a picture of what happened. But when sales forecasts or other data showing expected results are brought into the analysis, we can evaluate performance—using performance indexes.

Cost analysis also can be useful. There are two basic approaches to cost analysis—full-cost and contribution-margin. Using the full-cost approach, all costs are allocated in some way. Using the contribution-margin approach, only the variable costs are allocated. Both methods have their advantages and special uses.

Ideally, the marketing manager should arrange for a constant flow of data that can be analyzed routinely, preferably by computer, to help control present plans and plan new strategies. A marketing audit can help this ongoing effort. Either a separate department within the company or an outside organization may conduct this audit.

KEY TERMS

control, 524

total quality management (TQM), 529

continuous improvement, 530

Pareto chart, 531

fishbone diagram, 532

empowerment, 534

benchmarking, 534

sales analysis, 536

performance analysis, 537

performance index, 539

iceberg principle, 542

full-cost approach, 544

contribution-margin approach, 544

marketing audit, 549

QUESTIONS AND PROBLEMS

1. Give an example of how a firm has used information technology to improve its marketing implementation and do a better job of meeting your needs.

2. Should marketing managers leave it to the accountants to develop reports that the marketing manager will use to improve implementation and control? Why or why not?

3. Give an example of a firm that has a competitive advantage because of the excellent job it does with implementation activities that directly impact customer satisfaction. Explain why you think your example is a good one.

4. What are the major advantages of total quality management as an approach for improving implementation of marketing plans? What limitations can you think of?

5. If you were asked to recommend a firm (with which you have dealt) as a benchmark for good customer service after the sale, what firm would you recommend? What does this firm do that other firms do not do as well?

6. Various breakdowns can be used for sales analysis depending on the nature of the company and its products. Describe a situation (one for each) where each of the following breakdowns would yield useful information. Explain why.

    a. By geographic region.
    b. By product.
    c. By customer.
    d. By size of order.
    e. By size of sales rep commission on each product or product group.

7. Distinguish between a sales analysis and a performance analysis.

8. Carefully explain what the iceberg principle should mean to the marketing manager.

9. Explain the meaning of the comparative performance and comparative cost data in Exhibits 19-4 and 19-5. Why does it appear that eliminating sales areas D and E would be profitable?

10. Most sales forecasting is subject to some error (perhaps 5 to 10 percent). Should we then expect variations in sales performance of 5 to 10 percent above or below quota? If so, how should we treat such variations in evaluating performance?

11. Why is there controversy between the advocates of the full-cost and the contribution-margin approaches to cost analysis?

12. The June profit and loss statement for the Browning Company is shown. If competitive conditions make price increases impossible and management has cut costs as much as possible, should the Browning Company stop selling to hospitals and schools? Why?

Browning Company Statement

	Retailers	Hospitals and Schools	Total
Sales:			
80,000 units at $0.70	$56,000		$56,000
20,000 units at $0.60		$12,000	12,000
Total	56,000	12,000	68,000
Cost of sales	40,000	10,000	50,000
Gross margin	16,000	2,000	18,000
Sales and administrative expenses:			
Variable	6,000	1,500	7,500
Fixed	5,600	900	6,500
Total	11,600	2,400	14,000
Net profit (loss)	$ 4,400	$ (400)	$ 4,000

SUGGESTED CASES

33. Bushman & Associates

35. Sal's

COMPUTER-AIDED PROBLEM

19. Marketing Cost Analysis

RESOURCE REMINDER

This problem emphasizes the differences between the full-cost approach and contribution-margin approach to marketing cost analysis.

Tapco, Inc., currently sells two products. Sales commissions and unit costs vary with the quantity of each product sold. With the full-cost approach, Tapco's administrative and advertising costs are allocated to each product based on its share of total sales dollars. Details of Tapco's costs and other data are given in the spreadsheet. The first column shows a cost analysis based on the full-cost approach. The second column shows an analysis based on the contribution-margin approach.

a. If the number of Product A units sold were to increase by 1,000 units, what would happen to the allocated administrative expense for Product A? How would the change in sales of Product A affect the allocated administrative expense for Product B? Briefly discuss why the changes you observe might cause conflict between the product managers of the two different products.

b. What would happen to total profits if Tapco stopped selling Product A but continued to sell 4,000 units of Product B? What happens to total profits if the firm stops selling Product B but continues to sell 5,000 units of Product A? (Hint: To stop selling a product means that the quantity sold would be zero.)

c. If the firm dropped Product B and increased the price of Product A by $2.00, what quantity of Product A would it have to sell to earn a total profit as large as it was originally earning with both products? (Hint: Change values in the spreadsheet to reflect the changes the firm is considering, and then use the What If analysis to vary the quantity of Product A sold and display what happens to total profit.)

For additional questions related to this problem, see Exercise 19-3 in the *Learning Aid for Use with Basic Marketing,* 15th edition.

13. Explain why a marketing audit might be desirable, even in a well-run company. Who or what kind of an organization would be best to conduct a marketing audit? Would a marketing research firm be good? Would the present CPA firms be most suitable? Why?

1. Understand why turning a marketing plan into a profitable business requires money, information, people, and a way to get or produce goods and services.

2. Understand the ways that marketing strategy decisions may need to be adjusted in light of available financing.

3. Understand how a firm can implement and expand a marketing plan using internally generated cash flow.

4. Understand how different aspects of production capacity and flexibility should be coordinated with marketing strategy planning.

5. Understand the ways that the location and cost of production affect marketing strategy planning.

6. Know how marketing managers and accountants can work together to improve analysis of the costs and profitability of specific products and customers.

7. Know some of the human resource issues that a marketer should consider when planning a strategy and implementing a plan.

8. Understand the important new terms (shown in red).

CHAPTER TWENTY

Managing Marketing's Link with Other Functional Areas

Going to one of the new blue and yellow U.S. IKEA stores is as much an adventure as a shopping trip. Perhaps any furniture store the size of a football field would be an adventure. But let's face it, wandering through four or five complete model homes filled with stylish IKEA furnishings—all under one roof—is a bit different. For a store that size, there are relatively few salespeople; instead, there are information kiosks to provide advice on home décor. It is also different that IKEA furniture is inexpensive. To keep costs low, it all breaks down into flat cartons that consumers can take home in a hatchback and assemble themselves. But IKEA does offer some special services, like child care facilities and food service with (could you guess?) tasty Swedish meatballs.

These differences in strategy help to explain how IKEA (of Swedish origin) has opened an average of about one store a year in the U.S. since 1985, has become one of the top furniture retailers in the U.S. An important part of IKEA's success is the care with which it coordinates its marketing strategy with production capabilities, human resources, and financial data.

Most of IKEA's growth has been financed from the cash flow generated by its profitable strategy. It is still a privately held company. One reason that IKEA has been able to grow so rapidly—without greater capital investments—is that most of its production is outsourced to other firms. Many factories are in developing countries, like China and Vietnam, where costs are very low. IKEA's marketing managers often use demand-backward pricing to help select a specific factory. For example, they develop a plan for a stylish Pöang armchair for $79, but then they work to find the most cost-effective materials and production facilities before finalizing the design.

IKEA learned long ago that if it was going to ship its products from overseas factories that it would need to pay attention to shipping costs. Because the furniture is designed to break down flat, shipping cartons are packed solid and that saves IKEA the expense of paying to ship "air." You can get a better idea of just how careful IKEA is in analyzing costs by considering how it has redesigned its popular fired-clay coffee mugs. With the original design, 864 mugs would fit on a shipping pallet. After IKEA refined the design to make the mug shorter and gave it a new handle, 2,024 will fit on a pallet. The mug's selling price has remained at $.50, but shipping costs have been reduced 60 percent. Production costs are also lower because more mugs will fit in the kiln at the factory. Given that IKEA sells 25 million of these mugs each year, this attention to detail adds up!

Pernille Spiers-Lopez, the president of IKEA North America, believes that addressing employees' concerns isn't just a nice thing to do; it's the best way to build a workforce committed to IKEA and its customers. On her watch, IKEA has given full benefits to the part-time employees who are crucial to IKEA's retail operations. Employees can also work flexible part-time hours and job-share to fill one full-time slot; this has been especially helpful in recruiting women. The changes helped reduce annual sales-staff turnover by about 25 percent. Being able to attract and retain good employees will help Spiers-Lopez implement her plans to open 41 more IKEA stores in the U.S. and Canada by 2010.[1]

MARKETING IN THE BROADER CONTEXT

Cross-functional links affect strategy planning

Throughout the text we've emphasized that a marketing manager should try to develop a marketing strategy that will give the firm a competitive advantage in delivering value to target customers. Yet a strategy that would be the basis for competitive advantage by one firm might not fit well with another firm's resources. So in this chapter we'll take a closer look at how marketing strategy decisions are influenced by financial factors, the people available to implement a plan, and what the firm can effectively produce. In other words, we'll consider some of the important ways that marketing links to other functional areas. Our emphasis is not on the technical details of other functional areas but rather on the most important ways that cross-functional links impact your ability to develop marketing strategies and plans that really work. See Exhibit 20-1.

Implementing a marketing plan usually requires a financial investment—so we'll consider money required both to start up a new plan and to meet ongoing expenses. Then we'll look at production and operations and review how available production capacity, production flexibility, and operating issues impact marketing planning. We'll also take a closer look at how accounting people and marketing managers work together to get a better handle on marketing costs. We'll conclude

Which opportunities a firm decides to pursue may depend on resources and capabilities in functional areas other than marketing. For example, to introduce the wireless Pocket PC Phone (shown in this ad) requires financial resources, people with technical know-how to develop the design, and an efficient way to produce the final product.

with a discussion of human resource issues—because it's people who put plans into action.

How important the linkages with production, finance, accounting, and human resources are for the marketing manager depends on the situation. In an entrepreneurial start-up, the same person may be making all of the decisions. In a big company, managing the linkages among many specialists may be much more complicated.

Cross-functional challenges are greatest with new efforts

Our emphasis will be on new efforts. When a new strategy involves only minor changes to a plan that the firm is already implementing, the specialists usually have a pretty good idea of how their activities link to other areas. However, when a potential strategy involves a more significant change—like the introduction of a totally new product idea—understanding the links between the different functional areas is usually much more critical.

Exhibit 20-1
Some Important Links between Marketing and Other Functional Areas

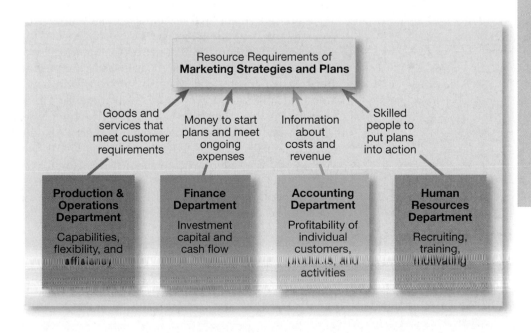

When evaluating new opportunities, Unilever brings together a team of managers with experience around the world to be certain that marketing plans that the firm implements will give it a competitive advantage and earn a return that will be attractive to investors.

THE FINANCE FUNCTION: MONEY TO IMPLEMENT MARKETING PLANS

Chief financial officer handles money matters

Bright marketing ideas for new ways to satisfy customer needs don't go very far if there isn't enough money to put a plan into operation. Finding and allocating **capital**—the money invested in a firm—is usually handled by a firm's chief financial officer. Entrepreneurs and others who own their own companies may handle this job themselves. In most firms, however, there is a separate financial manager who works with the chief executive to make major finance decisions.

A firm's marketing manager and financial manager must work together to ensure that the firm can successfully implement its marketing plans with the money that is or will be available. Further, a successful strategy should ultimately generate profit. And the financial manager needs to know how much money to expect and when to expect it to be able to plan for how it will be used.

Opportunities compete for capital and budgets

In most firms, different possible opportunities compete for capital. There's usually not enough money to do everything, so strategies that are inconsistent with the firm's financial objectives and resources are not likely to be funded. That's why marketing managers use relevant financial measures as quantitative screening criteria when evaluating various alternatives in the first place.

Marketing plans that *are* funded usually must work within a budget constraint. Ideally, the marketing manager should have some inputs on what that budget is—to get the marketing tasks done. Further, strategy decisions may need to be adjusted to work within the available budget. For example, a marketing manager might prefer to have control over the selling effort for a new product by hiring new people for a separate sales force. However, if there isn't enough money available for salesperson salaries, then the best alternative might be to start with manufacturers' agents. They work for a commission and aren't paid until after they generate a sale and some sales revenue. Then after the market develops and the plan becomes profitable, the firm might expand its own sales force.

Working capital pays for short-term expenses

Financial managers usually think about two different uses of capital. First, capital may be required to pay for investments in facilities, equipment, computer networks, and other "fixed assets." These installations are usually purchased and then used, and depreciated, over a number of years. In addition, a firm needs **working capital**—money to pay for short-term expenses such as employee salaries, advertising, marketing research, inventory storing costs, and what the firm owes suppliers. A firm usually must pay for these ongoing expenses as they occur. As a result there is usually a continuing need for working capital.

A firm that has a promising marketing plan will usually have more success In obtaining financial resources from external lenders or investors. For example, KeyBank can help a firm with a capacity constraint evaluate a full range of financial options. And when a big home furnishings business needed financing to expand, it cozied up to CIT, source of lending and leasing for everything from retail to rail.

Capital is usually a critical resource when a marketing plan calls for rapid growth, especially if the growth calls for expensive new facilities. Clearly, a plan to build a chain of 15 hotels requires more money for buildings and equipment, as well as more money for salaries, food, and supplies, than a plan for a single hotel. Such a plan might require that the firm borrow money from a commercial lender. In contrast, a plan that simply calls for improving the service in an existing hotel, perhaps by adding several people to handle room service, would require much less money. In fact, increased food sales from room service might quickly generate more than enough earnings to pay for the added people.

Capital comes from internal and external sources

As these examples imply, there are a number of different possible sources of capital. However, it's useful to boil them down to two categories: *external sources*, such as loans or sales of stocks or bonds, and *internal sources*, such as cash accumulated from the firm's profits. A firm usually seeks outside funding before it is needed to invest in a new strategy. Internally generated profits may be accumulated and used in the same way, but often internal money is used as it becomes available. In other words, with internally generated funding a firm's marketing program may be expected to "pay its own way."

The timing of when financing is available has an important effect on marketing strategy planning, so we'll look at this topic in more detail. We'll start by looking at external sources of funds.

External funding—investors expect a return

While a firm might like to fund its marketing program from rapid growth in its own profits, that is not always possible. New companies often don't have enough money to start that way. An established company may not have enough capital to make long-term investments and still pay for routine expenses. Getting started may also involve losses, perhaps for several years, before earnings come in. In these circumstances, the firm may need to turn to one of several sources of external capital.

A firm may be able to raise money by selling **stock**—a share in the ownership of a company. Stock sales may be public or private, and the buyers may be individuals, including a firm's own employees, or institutional investors (such as a pension fund or venture capital firm).

People who own stock in a firm want a good return on their investment. That can happen if the company pays owners of its stock a regular dividend. It also happens if the value of the stock goes up over time. Neither is likely if the firm isn't consistently earning profits. Further, the value of a firm's stock typically doesn't increase unless its profits are *growing*. This is one reason that marketing managers are always looking for profitable new growth opportunities. Profits can also improve by being more efficient—getting the marketing jobs done at lower cost, doing a better job of holding on to customers, and the like. Ultimately, a firm that doesn't have a successful or at least promising marketing strategy can't attract and keep investors.

On the other hand, it's a sad reality that a firm with a great strategy can't always attract investors. In a weak economy, many investors just have a wait-and-see attitude and won't invest in anything until overall business conditions seem more favorable. And in a good economy, investors sometimes get caught up in the current fad—and then it seems that the only thing that will get their attention is a company in the "what's new" line of business.

Investors' time horizon is important

How quickly investors expect profit and growth can be very important to the marketing manager. If investors are patient, a marketing manager may have the luxury of developing a plan that will be very profitable in the long run even if it racks up short-term losses. Many Japanese firms take this approach. However, most marketing managers face intense pressure to develop plans that will generate profits quickly; there's more risk for investors if potential profits are off in the future.

It is sometimes a challenge to develop a plan that produces profit in the short term and also positions the firm for long-run success. For example, a low penetration price for a new product may help to prevent competition and to attract repeat purchasers long into the future. Yet a skimming price may be better for profits in the short term. Even so, the marketing manager's plans must take the investors' time horizon into consideration. Unhappy investors can demand new management or put their money somewhere else.

Forecasts may become an ethical issue

Investors usually want detailed information about a firm's plans before they invest. The firm's financial people usually provide this information, but financial estimates don't mean much unless they're based on realistic estimates of demand, revenue, and marketing expenses from the marketing manager. An optimistic marketing manager may be hesitant to lay out the potential limitations of a plan or its forecasts, especially if the full story might scare off needed investors. However, this is an important ethical issue. While investors know that there is always some uncertainty in forecasts, they have a right to information that is as accurate as possible. Put another way, just as a marketing manager shouldn't mislead a buyer of the firm's products, it's not appropriate to mislead investors who are buying into the firm's marketing plan.

Debt financing involves an interest cost

Rather than sell stock, some firms prefer **debt financing**—borrowing money based on a promise to repay the loan, usually within a fixed time period and with a specific interest charge. This might involve a loan from a commercial bank or the use of corporate bonds. People or institutions that loan the money typically do not get an ownership share in the company, and they are usually even less willing to take a risk than are investors who buy stock.

Most commercial banks are conservative. They usually won't loan money to a firm that doesn't have some valuable asset to put up as a guarantee that the lender will get its money. Investors who buy a firm's bonds are also very concerned about security—but they often don't have a legal right to some specific assets if the firm can't repay the borrowed money when it's due. In general, the greater the risk that the lender takes on to provide the loan, the greater the interest rate charge will be.

Interest expense may impact prices

The cost of borrowing money can be a real financial burden. Just as a firm's selling price must cover all of the marketing expenses and the other costs of doing business before profits begin to accumulate, it must also cover the interest charge on borrowed money. The impact of interest charges on prices can be significant. For example, the spread between the prices charged by fast-growing, efficient supermarket chains and individual grocery stores would be even greater if the chains weren't paying interest on loans to fund new facilities.

While the cost of borrowing money can be high, it may still make sense if the money is used to implement a marketing plan that earns an even greater return. In that way, the firm leverages the borrowed money to make a profit. Even so, there are often advantages if a firm can pay for its plans with internally generated capital.[2]

Winning strategies generate capital

A company with a successful marketing strategy has its own internal source of funds—profits that become cash in the bank! For example, Starbucks reported a profit of about $281 million in 2001. The company didn't pay out any of that money to stockholders. Instead, Starbucks reinvested the money to open new stores and do other things to support the growth of the business. During the next year it opened about 1,172 new stores, which helped earnings for 2002 grow to about $319 million. With the growth in stores and earnings, the value of the stock went from about $22 a share at the start of 2001 to $35 a share at the start of 2004, and investors also got two shares of stock for each one they owned along the way.[3]

Reinvesting cash generated from operations is usually less expensive than borrowing money because no interest expense is involved. So internal financing often helps a firm earn more profit than a competitor that is operating on borrowed money—even if the internally financed company is selling at a lower price.

Expanding profits may support expanded plan

Firms that can't get a loan or that don't want the expense of borrowed money often start with a less costly strategy and a plan to expand it as quickly as is allowed by earnings. Consider the case of Sorrell Ridge, a small brand that wanted to compete with the jams and jellies of big competitors like Welch's and Smucker's. Sorrell Ridge started small with a strategy that focused on a better product—"spreadable fruit" with no sugar added—that was targeted at health-conscious consumers. After paying to update its production facilities, Sorrell Ridge didn't have much working capital to pay for promotion and other marketing expenses. So it turned to health-food wholesalers and retailers to give the product a promotion push in the channel. As profits from the health-food channel started to grow, Sorrell Ridge used some of the money for local TV and print ads in big cities in the Northeast. The ads increased consumer demand for Sorrell Ridge's spreads and helped get shelf space from supermarkets in that region. Success from selling through supermarkets in the Northeast generated more volume and profit, which provided Sorrell Ridge with the financial base to enter the big California market. The big supermarket chains there wouldn't consider carrying a new fruit

Alien Workshop, which markets skateboarding and snowboarding equipment and apparel, was growing rapidly and needed to move into larger facilities. Key Corp, a provider of financial services, helped the firm develop a plan that made its growth objectives achievable.

spread without a lot of trade promotion, including hefty stocking allowances. Sorrell Ridge had the money to pay for a coupon program to stimulate consumer trial, but that didn't leave enough money for the stocking allowance. However, the marketing manager had a creative idea that involved giving retailers the stocking allowance in the form of a credit against future purchases rather than cash up front. With a plan for that blend of trade and consumer promotion in place, one of the best food brokers in California agreed to take on the line. And expanding into the new market resulted in profitable growth.[4]

A company with a mature product that has limited growth potential can invest the earnings from that product to develop a new opportunity that is more profitable. Kodak is a good example. It milks profits from its 35 mm film, which faces tough competition from Fuji and store brands, to fund development of digital cameras and other digital photography products.[5]

Cash flow looks at when money will be available

A marketing manager who wants to plan strategies based on the expected flow of internal funding needs a good idea of how much cash will be available. A **cash flow statement** is a financial report that forecasts how much cash will be available after paying expenses. The amount that's available isn't always just the bottom line or net profit figure shown on the firm's operating statement. Some expenses, like depreciation of facilities, are subtracted from revenue for tax and accounting purposes but do not actually involve writing a check. So in determining cash flow, managers often look at a company's earnings *before* subtracting out these noncash expenses.[6]

Improve return of current investment

When finances are tight, it's sensible to look for strategy alternatives that help get a better return on money that's already invested. A firm that sells diagnostic equipment to hospitals might look for another related product for its current salespeople to sell while calling on the same customers. Similarly, a firm that has a successful domestic product might look for new international markets. Any increase in profit contribution that the strategy generates—without increasing capital invested—increases the firm's return on investment.

Market mix decisions affect capital needed

Strategy decisions within each of the marketing mix areas often have different capital requirements. For example, offering more models of a product usually increases front-end capital needs.

Indirect distribution usually requires less investment capital than direct approaches. Middlemen who pay for products when they purchase them and pay the costs of carrying inventory help a producer's cash flow. Public warehousers and transportation firms may reduce the capital needed for logistics facilities. Similarly, less capital is needed when intermediaries take on the responsibility for promotion.

PRODUCTION MUST BE COORDINATED WITH THE MARKETING PLAN

Production capacity takes many forms

If a firm is going to pursue an opportunity, there needs to be effective coordination between marketing planning and **production capacity**—the ability to produce a certain quantity and quality of specific goods or services.

Different aspects of production capacity have different impacts on marketing planning, so we'll consider this topic in more depth.[7]

Use excess capacity to improve profits

If a firm has unused capacity, a marketing manager can try to identify new markets or new products that make more effective use of that investment. For example, a company that produces rubber floor mats for automobiles might be able to add a similar line of cargo-area mats for SUVs. Expanded production might result in lower costs because of economies of scale. Profit contribution from the new products could improve the return on investment the firm had already made. If a firm's production capacity is flexible, many different marketing opportunities might be possible. For example, there might be better growth and profits in static-electricity-free mats for Internet server equipment than for auto accessories.

Excess capacity may be a safety net, or a signal of problems

Excess capacity can be a safety net if demand suddenly picks up. For example, many firms that make products for the construction industry faced costly excess capacity in 2001. However, many of those firms were glad that they had that capacity when construction demand picked up again in 2003.

Excess capacity may exist because there is little demand for what a firm can produce or there's too much competition. In these situations, rather than struggling to improve capacity use, it might be better for the marketing manager to lead the firm toward other, more profitable alternatives.

When Kellogg's introduced Rice Krispies Treats Squares, production couldn't keep up with the unexpectedly high demand. So Kellogg's used advertising to tell consumers and retailers about the shortages and to ask them to be patient. When the squares were back in stock, Kellogg's again used advertising to communicate with consumers.

Scarce supply wastes marketing effort

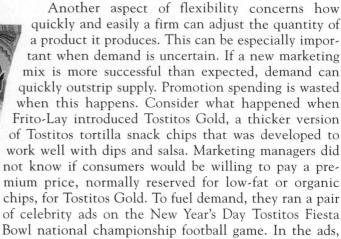

Another aspect of flexibility concerns how quickly and easily a firm can adjust the quantity of a product it produces. This can be especially important when demand is uncertain. If a new marketing mix is more successful than expected, demand can quickly outstrip supply. Promotion spending is wasted when this happens. Consider what happened when Frito-Lay introduced Tostitos Gold, a thicker version of Tostitos tortilla snack chips that was developed to work well with dips and salsa. Marketing managers did not know if consumers would be willing to pay a premium price, normally reserved for low-fat or organic chips, for Tostitos Gold. To fuel demand, they ran a pair of celebrity ads on the New Year's Day Tostitos Fiesta Bowl national championship football game. In the ads, Jay Leno and Little Richard liven up parties with Tostitos Gold. The ads show how serving the chip "that's extra thick for hearty dips" can inject life into otherwise boring situations. The ads did a better job than expected in stirring interest, and chip lovers were so enthusiastic about Tostitos Gold that the chips were quickly out-of-stock at most supermarkets because the factory couldn't keep up with incoming orders. The stock-outs resulted in lost sales of about $500,000 a week.[8]

As this suggests, shortages can be a costly problem. Stock-outs also frustrate both channel members and their customers. This can have a serious impact on relationships in business markets. Intel faced that problem when it came out with its Xeon processor. After promising its computer-maker customers that the chip would be available for their new lines of network servers, Intel couldn't keep up with demand and lost over $1 billion when it couldn't fill orders. A big problem like that gives nimble competitors the opportunity to introduce imitation products and steal customers.[9]

Staged distribution may match capacity

Problems of matching supply and demand often occur when a marketing plan calls for expansion into many market areas all at once. That's one reason a marketing manager may plan a regional rollout of a new product. Similarly, initial distribution may focus on certain channels—say, drugstores alone rather than drugstores and supermarkets. Experience with the initial distribution efforts can help the marketing manager determine how much promotion effort is required to keep distribution channels full and avoid stock-outs.

Virtual corporations may not make anything at all

Many firms are finding that they can satisfy customers and build profits without doing any production in house. Instead, they look for capable suppliers to produce a product that meets the specs laid out in the firm's marketing plan. This is the approach that Sara Lee took. It sold off the factories that made its apparel products—brands like Champion, Hanes, and Playtex. Now, Sara Lee just buys the goods that it wants from independent manufacturers that produce to its specs.

Sara Lee is not alone in this shift. Many firms now outsource manufacturing and basically act like a **virtual corporation,** where the firm is primarily a coordinator, with a good marketing concept.[10]

Outsourcing production can reduce costs and increase flexibility. However, it sometimes introduces problems. The reputation of a firm's brand often depends on the quality of the manufacturing behind it. Some firms are finding it difficult to control quality with outsourcing, especially if several firms are involved in different parts of production. That can also increase coordination and logistics problems.

A company with a line of accessories for bicycle riders faced this problem when it decided to introduce a water bottle. Its other products were metal, so it turned

One reason that Bertolli Pasta sauce tastes so fresh is because it has a production process that makes it possible for the tomatoes used in the sauce to go from the vine to the jar in just one day. Oral-B is able to satisfy the needs of a large number of different market segments because it has the production flexibility to produce brushes in many different sizes, shapes, and styles.

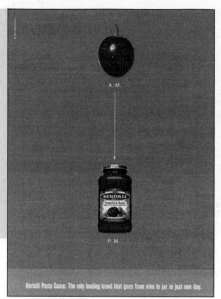

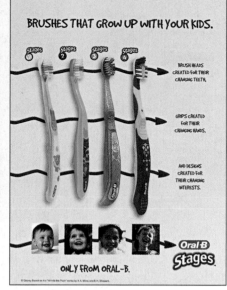

to outside suppliers to produce the plastic bottles. However, getting the job done required three suppliers. One made the bottle, another printed the colorful designs on it, and the third attached a clip to hold the bottle to a bike. Moving the product from one specialist to another added costs, and whenever one supplier hit a snag, all of the others were affected. The firm was constantly struggling to fill orders on time, and too often it was losing the battle. To avoid these problems, the firm invested in its own production facilities.[11]

Where products are produced matters

It may make sense for a firm to produce where it can produce most economically, if the cost of transporting and storing products to match demand doesn't offset the savings. On the other hand, production in areas distant from customers can make the distribution job much more complicated. Consider the marketing implications of Sara Lee's decision to turn to offshore producers for many of its Hanes men's underwear products. Mass-merchandiser chains put pressure on Hanes to find ways to cut prices—because they wanted to offer consumers low prices. So Hanes moved much of the sewing work to the Caribbean Islands where labor costs are low. However, the only practical way to transport the bulky and inexpensive finished products back to the U.S. market is by boat. Boats are slow, and clearing customs adds further delays. At the port, the bulky cases of underwear must be handled again and broken down into quantities and assortments for shipping to the retailers' distribution centers. And at the distribution centers, the cases need to be grouped with other products going to a specific store. All of these steps are necessary, but they also make it difficult to quickly adjust supply.[12]

Moving production to low-cost countries

Many products—ranging from furniture and fashions to machinery and electronics—that in the recent past were manufactured in U.S. factories are now being produced on a contract basis in huge factories in China, Mexico, India, and other countries where wages and manufacturing costs are low.

Service firms are also finding ways to reduce the cost of some of their production work with **task transfer**—using telecommunications to move service operations to places where there are pools of skilled workers. For example, Bank of America puts its automatic teller machines and branch offices where they're convenient for customers, but many of the programmers who do its backroom computer work are in India.

Overseas production has critics

The trend toward outsourcing to where labor costs are low is resulting in the loss of thousands of manufacturing jobs in the U.S. It's also sparking economic growth in some of the less-developed areas of the world and changing the balance of trade among nations. Some people think that workers in the U.S. will ultimately be able to shift to better jobs—where U.S. firms have a competitive advantage that doesn't rely on low-cost labor. But others worry that these shifts hurt the U.S. economy. Marketing managers must be aware of and sensitive to criticisms that may arise concerning overseas production.

Some of these concerns relate to nationalism. But other issues are sometimes at stake. Although overseas production may reduce prices for domestic consumers, some critics argue that the costs are only lower because the work is handled in countries with lower workplace safety standards and fewer employee protections. At the extreme, some firms have been boycotted for relying on Chinese suppliers who were accused of using political prisoners as slave labor.

Marketing managers can't ignore such concerns. Just as a firm has a social responsibility in the country where it sells products, it also has a social responsibility to the people who produce its products. However, pay or safety standards that seem low in developed nations may make it possible for workers in an undeveloped nation to have a better, healthier life.[13]

Design flexibility into operations

Production flexibility can give a firm a competitive advantage in meeting a target market's needs better or faster. Without flexible operations, it can be difficult to provide business customers with just-in-time delivery or rapid response to orders placed by EDI or some other type of e-commerce reorder system.

Producing to order requires flexibility too

A flexible manufacturing system makes Dell's Internet order approach possible. Early on, most other computer firms produced large quantities of standardized computers and then shipped them to dealers for resale. If the dealer didn't have the right model in stock, it often took weeks to get it. Dell's approach allowed customers to order whatever computer configuration they wanted—then the parts were assembled to match the order. This reduced the cost of finished goods inventories, precisely matched output to customer needs, and kept everyone focused on satisfying each customer. It's been hard for firms like HP to directly copy this approach without alienating the dealers that it relies on.[14]

Mass customization— serves individual needs

Automobile companies, producers of specialized machine tools, and other types of manufacturers, as well as many service firms, have been creating products based on specific orders from individual customers for a long time. However, a wide variety of companies are now looking for innovative ways to serve smaller segments of

BALDOR ELECTRIC GETS WIRED FOR WORLDWIDE PROFITS

Baldor Electric Company produces and markets electric motors, drives, and generators. While sales in recent times have been depressed by a weak economy, Baldor has weathered bad markets in the past. One of the worst times was in the 1980s. Back then, demand for electric motors was in a slump. Worse, producers in Asia were pumping out low-cost commodity-type motors from automated factories. The market was so tough that Westinghouse, the original developer of the electric motor, got out of the business altogether. Yet Baldor's sales have increased five times over since that time, and its profits have been on an upward trend. So how has Baldor, an old company in a mature market, achieved profitable growth?

Rather than trying to compete with motors like those available from many suppliers, Baldor focused on specific target markets. It came out with special motors, like the one to run heart pumps in hospitals or the 500-horsepower unit for rolling steel. The R&D group also added computer controllers to motors to improve their value to the customer and to work with factory automation systems that are replacing old approaches. In fact, Baldor's innovations earned a "Product of the Year" Gold Award from a major trade magazine. That kind of publicity brings in inquiries and gives Baldor's knowledgeable sales reps the chance to work with individual customers to help

them increase their productivity. For example, in a recent sale Baldor's drive doubled the output from the equipment in a customer's factory. Individually, these specialized motors are not big sellers. Rather, Baldor's strategy takes advantage of flexible production to focus on getting higher margins on each motor.

Even more important is Baldor's push to develop energy-efficient motors. They not only help the environment but also cut the customer's operating costs. The energy savings are in some cases enough to justify changing to a new drive even if an old motor still works well. Baldor has also developed a new line of generators for use when electricity is not available at any cost. If you remember the blackout in August 2003 when 50 million people in the U.S. lost power altogether, you can understand why there's demand for Baldor's generators.

Baldor has also expanded distribution into 50 countries. And to make it easy for customers worldwide to get information, Baldor supplements its website (www.baldor.com) with an electronic catalog on a CD. Its CD includes CAD drawings, performance data, and installation manuals for over 2,500 Baldor motors. Product designers in customer-firms use it to pick the right motor, and it also helps the customer-firm train its employees. All of these innovations mean that Baldor can command a premium price.[15]

customers by using **mass customization**—tailoring the principles of mass production to meet the unique needs of individual customers.

Note that using the principles of mass production is not the same thing as trying to appeal to everyone in some mass market. With the mass-customization approach, a firm may still focus on certain market segments within a broad product-market. However, in serving individuals within those target segments it tries to get a competitive advantage by finding a low-cost way to give each customer more or better choices.

A few years ago, there were predictions that thousands of companies would quickly begin to offer consumers better product choices based on mass customization. The widespread shift to mass customization has not occurred, mainly because many firms that experimented with it found that production costs were still high even if the Internet offered a low-cost way to get a lot of orders.

Some of the biggest successes in mass customization have been in business markets. For example, Andersen gives builders and architects software that they use to design custom windows by combining different types of glass, different sizes of frames, and a variety of hardware styles that Andersen already manufactures. Similarly, sales reps for ChemStation, a firm that produces industrial detergents, work closely with customers to understand their special cleaning needs—a car wash wants something very different from a metal-working plant. Then scientists at ChemStation develop

Lear Corp. has designed modular, interchangeable components that make it possible for car buyers to customize their car interiors. This sort of mass customization could become available in the near future.

just the right product, with the correct amount of foam, grease cutting, grit, and the like. After starting this program, ChemStation's profit margins doubled.[16]

There have also been interesting offerings based on mass customization in consumer markets. For example, Lands' End offers shoppers custom pants. At the company's website (www.landsend.com), a shopper can enter his or her measurements, specify the style and fit desired, and then place the order. Software then processes the measurements and prepares a pattern that is transmitted to the manufacturer in Mexico. A few weeks later, the customer receives the pants. A custom pair of jeans or chinos that fit precisely costs about $20 more than a pair of pants off-the rack.

INTERNET EXERCISE Nike offers an online service in which customers can design their own shoes. Go to the Nike website (www.nike.com), select *North America*, then select *USA*, then select *Nike iD*, and check out this feature. What do you think are the major strengths and weaknesses of Nike's service?

Batched production requires inventories

If it is expensive for a firm to switch from producing one product (or product line) to another, there may be no alternative but to produce in large batches and maintain large inventories. Then it can supply demand from inventory while it is producing some other product. However, a firm that must pay the costs of carrying extra inventory to avoid stock-outs may not be able to compete with a firm that has more flexible production.

Excess inventory that a firm can't sell with its normal strategy can be a problem. In some industries there are middlemen whose primary role is to buy and liquidate excess inventories. There has been an increase in the buying and selling of surplus inventory during the past few years, mainly because the Internet makes it possible for buyers to locate sellers. Excess inventory is often sold with an online auction.

Cut production costs that don't add value for customers

Production costs are usually an important part of the overall costs that must be considered in pricing, so a marketing manager needs to understand the costs associated with production, especially when product features called for in the marketing plan drive costs.

A well-informed marketing manager can play an important role in working with production people to decide which costs are necessary to add value that meets customer needs and which are just added expense with little real benefit. For example, a software firm was providing a very detailed instruction book along with a CD in its distribution package. The book was running up costs and causing delays because it needed to be changed and reprinted every time the firm came out with a new

version of its software. The marketing manager realized that when users of the software had a problem, they didn't want to search for the book but instead wanted the information on the computer screen. Providing the updated information on a CD was faster and cheaper, packaging costs were lower without the book, and customers were more satisfied with the online help.

In a situation like this, it is easy to identify specific costs associated with the production job. However, often it's difficult to get a good handle on all of the costs associated with a product without help from the firm's accountants.

ACCOUNTING DATA CAN HELP IN UNDERSTANDING COSTS AND PROFIT

Accounting data that helps managers track where costs and profit are coming from is an important aid for strategy decisions. Unfortunately, summary accounting statements that are prepared for tax purposes and for outside investors often aren't helpful for managers who need to make decisions about marketing strategy.

Understanding profitability depends on being able to identify the specific costs of different goods and services. You saw this in the last chapter when the full-cost approach and the contribution-margin approach to handling costs resulted in different views of profitability. Now let's look at how marketing managers and accountants can work together to allocate costs to products or customers. In recent years, accountants have devoted more attention to this problem and given it the name "activity-based accounting." In spite of the new name, the basic ideas behind marketing cost analysis were developed years ago by a marketing specialist.[17]

Marketing cost analysis usually requires a new way of classifying accounting data. Instead of using the type of accounts typically used for financial analysis, we have to use functional accounts.

Natural versus functional accounts—what is the purpose?

Natural accounts are the categories to which various costs are charged in the normal financial accounting cycle. These accounts include salaries, wages, supplies, raw materials, advertising, and others. These accounts are called natural because they have the names of their expense categories.

However, factories don't use this approach to cost analysis—and it's not the one we will use. In the factory, **functional accounts** show the *purpose* for which

Marketing managers often need to assign costs to specific products or customers to be able to understand the profitability of different possible strategies.

expenditures are made. Factory functional accounts include milling, grinding, maintenance, and so on. Factory cost accounting records are organized so that managers can determine the cost of particular products or jobs.

Marketing jobs are done for specific purposes too. With some planning, the costs of marketing can also be assigned to specific categories, such as customers and products. Then their profitability can be calculated.

INTERNET EXERCISE

Illinois Tool Works (ITW) has a variety of different businesses that produce different products. ITW mainly targets business markets, but its ITW Brands division sells through home improvement retailers. Go to the ITW website (www.itwinc.com) and review the company information at *About ITW*. Next, select *Business Units* and click on several of the links to the websites of ITW's business units. Briefly review the descriptions of the business units, considering the markets they serve. Finally, visit the ITW Brands website (www.itwbrands.com) and study it in more detail. From a cost standpoint, does it make sense to have a unit like ITW Brands? Why or why not?

First, get costs into functional accounts

The first step in marketing cost analysis is to reclassify all the dollar cost entries in the natural accounts into functional cost accounts. For example, the many cost items in the natural *salary* account may be allocated to functional accounts with the following names: storing, inventory control, order assembly, packing and shipping, transporting, selling, advertising, order entry, billing, credit extension, and accounts receivable. The same is true for rent, power, and other natural accounts.

The way natural account amounts are shifted to functional accounts depends on the firm's method of operation. It may require time studies, space measurements, actual counts, and managers' estimates.

Then reallocate to evaluate profitability of profit centers

The costs allocated to the functional accounts equal, in total, those in the natural accounts. But instead of being used only to show *total* company profits, the costs can now be used to calculate the profitability of territories, products, customers, salespeople, price classes, order sizes, distribution methods, sales methods, or any other breakdown desired. Each unit can be treated as a profit center.

Exhibit 20-2
Profit and Loss Statement,
One Month

Sales		$17,000
Cost of sales		11,900
Gross margin		5,100
Expenses:		
Salaries	$2,500	
Rent	500	
Wrapping supplies	1,012	
Stationery and stamps	50	
Office equipment	100	
		4,162
Net profit		$ 938

Cost analysis helps track down the loser

The following example illustrates these ideas. This case is simplified, and the numbers are small, so you can follow each step. However, you can use the same basic approach in more complicated situations.

In this case, the usual financial accounting approach, with natural accounts, shows that the company made a profit of $938 last month (Exhibit 20-2). But this profit and loss statement doesn't show the profitability of the company's three customers. So the managers decide to use marketing cost analysis because they want to know whether a change in the marketing mix will improve profit.

First, we distribute the costs in the five natural accounts to four functional accounts—sales, packaging, advertising, and billing and collection (see Exhibit 20-3)—according to the functional reason for the expenses. Specifically, $1,000 of the total salary cost is for sales reps who seldom even come into the office since their job is to call on customers; $900 of the salary cost is for packaging labor; and $600 is for office help. Assume that the office staff split their time about evenly between addressing advertising material and billing and collection. So we split the $600 evenly into these two functional accounts.

The $500 for rent is for the entire building. But the company uses 80 percent of its floor space for packaging and 20 percent for the office. Thus, $400 is allocated to the packaging account. We divide the remaining $100 evenly between the advertising and billing accounts because these functions use the office space about equally. Stationery, stamps, and office equipment charges are allocated equally to the latter two accounts for the same reason. Charges for wrapping supplies are allocated to the packaging account because these supplies are used in packaging. In another situation, different allocations and even different accounts may be sensible—but these work here.

Exhibit 20-3 Spreading Natural Accounts to Functional Accounts

		Functional Accounts			
Natural Accounts		Sales	Packaging	Advertising	Billing and Collection
Salaries	$2,500	$1,000	$ 900	$300	$300
Rent	500		400	50	50
Wrapping supplies	1,012		1,012		
Stationery and stamps	50			25	25
Office equipment	100			50	50
Total	$4,162	$1,000	$2,312	$425	$425

Exhibit 20-4 Basic Data for Cost and Profit Analysis Example

Products	Cost/Unit	Selling Price/Unit	Number of Units Sold in Period	Sales Volume in Period	Relative "Bulk" per Unit	Packaging "Units"
A	$ 7	$ 10	1,000	$10,000	1	1,000
B	35	50	100	5,000	3	300
C	140	200	10	2,000	6	60
			1,110	$17,000		1,360

Customers	Number of Sales Calls in Period	Number of Orders Placed in Period	Number of Each Product Ordered in Period		
			A	B	C
Rao	30	30	900	30	0
Mack	40	3	90	30	3
Davis	30	1	10	40	7
Total	100	34	1,000	100	10

Allocating functional cost to customers

Now we can calculate the profitability of the company's three customers. But we need more information before we can allocate these functional accounts to customers or products. It is presented in Exhibit 20-4.

Exhibit 20-4 shows that the company's three products vary in cost, selling price, and sales volume. The products also have different sizes, and the packaging costs aren't related to the selling price. So when packaging costs are allocated to products, size must be considered. We can do this by computing a new measure—a packaging unit—which is used to allocate the costs in the packaging account. Packaging units adjust for relative size and the number of each type of product sold. For example, Product C is six times larger than A. While the company sells only 10 units of Product C, it is bulky and requires 10 times 6, or 60 packaging units. So we must allocate more of the costs in the packaging account to each unit of Product C.

Exhibit 20-4 also shows that the three customers require different amounts of sales effort, place different numbers of orders, and buy different product combinations.

Mack seems to require more sales calls. Rao places many orders that must be processed in the office, with increased billing expense. Davis placed only one order—for 70 percent of the sales of highly valued Product C.

Exhibit 20-5 shows the calculations for allocating the functional amounts to the three customers. There were 100 sales calls in the period. Assuming that all calls took the same amount of time, we can figure the average cost per call by dividing the $1,000

Exhibit 20-5
Functional Cost Account
Allocations

Sales calls	$1,000/100 calls	=	$10/call
Billing	$425/34 orders	=	$12.50/order
Packaging units costs	$2,312/1,360 packaging units	=	$1.70/packaging unit or $1.70 for Product A $5.10 for Product B $10.20 for Product C
Advertising	$425/10 units of C	=	$42.50/unit of C

sales cost by 100 calls—giving an average cost of $10. We use similar reasoning to break down the billing and packaging account totals. Advertising during this period was for the benefit of Product C only—so we split this cost among the units of C sold.

Calculating profit and loss for each customer

Now we can compute a profit and loss statement for each customer. Exhibit 20-6 shows how each customer's purchases and costs are combined to prepare a statement for each customer. The sum of each of the four major components (sales, cost of sales, expenses, and profit) is the same as on the original statement (Exhibit 20-2)—all we've done is rearrange and rename the data.

For example, Rao bought 900 units of A at $10 each and 30 units of B at $50 each—for the respective sales totals ($9,000 and $1,500) shown in Exhibit 20-6. We compute cost of sales in the same way. Expenses require various calculations. Thirty sales calls cost $300—30 × $10 each. Rao placed 30 orders at an average cost of $12.50 each for a total ordering cost of $375. Total packaging costs amounted to $1,530 for A (900 units purchased × $1.70 per unit) and $153 for B (30 units purchased × $5.10 per unit). There were no packaging costs for C because Rao didn't buy any of Product C. Neither were any advertising costs charged to Rao—all advertising costs were spent promoting Product C, which Rao didn't buy.

Analyzing the results

We now see that Rao was the most profitable customer, yielding over 75 percent of the net profit.

Exhibit 20-6   Profitability of Individual Customers and Whole Company

	Rao	Mack	Davis	Whole Company
Sales				
Product A	$9,000	$ 900	$ 100	
Product B	1,500	1,500	2,000	
Product C		600	1,400	
Total sales	$10,500	$ 3,000	$ 3,500	$17,000
Cost of Sales				
Product A	6,300	630	70	
Product B	1,050	1,050	1,400	
Product C		420	980	
Total cost of sales	7,350	2,100	2,450	11,900
Gross margin	3,150	900	1,050	5,100
Expenses				
Sales calls ($10 each)	300	400.00	300.00	
Order costs ($12.50 each)	375	37.50	12.50	
Packaging costs				
Product A	1,530	153.00	17.00	
Product B	153	153.00	204.00	
Product C		30.60	71.40	
Advertising		127.50	297.50	
	2,358	901.60	902.40	4,162
Net profit (or loss)	$ 792	$ (1.60)	$147.60	$ 938

This analysis shows that Davis was profitable too—but not as profitable as Rao because Rao bought three times as much. Mack was unprofitable. Mack didn't buy very much and received one-third more sales calls.

The iceberg principle is operating here. Although the company as a whole is profitable, customer Mack is not. But before dropping Mack, the marketing manager should study the figures and the marketing plan very carefully. Perhaps Mack should be called on less frequently. Or maybe Mack will grow into a profitable account. Now the firm is at least covering some fixed costs by selling to Mack. Dropping this customer may only shift those fixed costs to the other two customers, making them look less attractive. (See the discussion on contribution margin in Chapter 19.)

The marketing manager may also want to analyze the advertising costs against results—since a heavy advertising expense is charged against each unit of Product C. Perhaps the whole marketing plan should be revised.

PEOPLE PUT PLANS INTO ACTION

People are an important resource

A great marketing plan may fail if the right people aren't available to implement it. Large firms usually have a separate human resources department staffed by specialists who work with others in the firm to ensure that good people are available to do jobs that need to be done. A small firm may not have a separate department—but somebody (perhaps the owner or other managers) must deal with people-management matters, like recruiting and hiring new employees, deciding how people will be compensated, and what to do when a job is not being performed well or is no longer necessary. Human resource issues can be important both in a marketing manager's choice among different possible marketing opportunities and in the actual implementation of marketing plans—especially new plans that involve major change.

New strategies usually require people changes

New strategies often require changes that upset the status quo and vested interests. A production manager who has spent a career becoming an expert in fine wood furniture may not like the idea of switching to an assemble-it-yourself line—even if that's what customers want. And when the market maturity stage of the product life cycle hits, a financial manager who looked like a hero during the profitable

572

growth stage may not see that the picnic is over, or that profit growth will resume only if the firm takes some risk and invests in a new product concept.

People affected by a new strategy may not be under the control of the marketing manager. And the marketing manager may not be able to change everyone into enthusiastic supporters of the plan. However, the marketing manager should think about how a new strategy will affect people—and how they will affect its success.

Communication helps promote change

Good communication is crucial. The marketing manager must find ways to explain the new strategy, what needs to happen, and why. You can't expect people to pull together in a companywide effort if they don't know what's going on. Communication might be handled in meetings, memos, casual discussions, newsletters, or any number of other ways. However, at a minimum, the marketing manager needs to have clear communication with other managers who will participate in preparing the firm's personnel for a change.

Rapid growth strains human resources

The success of a marketing plan often depends on how quickly the firm's personnel can get geared up for what needs to be done. Firms that grow rapidly may face challenges finding enough qualified people. A fast-growing retail chain like Lowe's that is opening many new stores needs new store managers, salespeople, customer service people, computer operators, and maintenance people. New employees have to learn about the company, its customers, and its products at the same time they are learning how to do their jobs well.

Allow time for training and other changes

Training takes time. A marketing manager who wants to reorganize the firm's sales force so that salespeople are assigned to specific customers rather than by product line may have a great idea, but it can't be implemented overnight. A salesperson who is supposed to be a specialist in meeting the needs of a certain customer won't be able to do a good job if all he or she knows about is the product that was the previously speciality.

Each change may result in several others

A change in sales assignments is also likely to require changes in compensation. Someone needs to figure out the specifics of the new compensation system, and accountants need time to adjust their computer programs to make certain that the

Siemens has a competitive advantage in pursuing many market opportunities because it has a large pool of creative employees with diverse skills.

salespeople actually get paid. Similarly, the changes in the sales force are likely to require changes in who they report to and the structure of sales management assignments. Our point with this example is that each change may require several others and that each change may take time.

Plan time for changes from the outset

A marketing manager who ignores the ripple effects of a change in strategy may later expect everyone to meet a schedule that won't work. Certainly there are cases of heroic efforts by people in organizations to turn someone's vision into a reality. Yet it's more typical for such a plan to fall behind schedule, to run up unnecessary costs, or to just plain fail.

Cutbacks need human resources plans too

Decisions to drop products, channels of distribution, or customers can be traumatic, especially if jobs will be cut. To the extent possible, it's important to plan a phase-out period so that people can make other plans. In fact, a carefully planned phase-out can sometimes work hand-in-hand with development of new strategies that will create exciting jobs for those who would otherwise be displaced.[18]

Marketing pumps life into an organization

Marketing managers who create profitable marketing strategies and implement them well create a need for a firm's production workers, accountants, financial managers, and human resources people. In this chapter we've talked about marketing links with those other functions; but when you get down to brass tacks, organizations and the various departments within them consist of *individuals*. When the marketing manager makes good strategy decisions—ones that lead to satisfied customers and profits—each individual in the organization has a chance to prosper and grow.

CONCLUSION

Even when everyone in an entire company embraces the marketing concept, coordinating marketing strategies and plans with other functional areas is a challenge. Yet it's a challenge that marketing managers must address. It doesn't make sense to select a strategy that the firm can't implement. And implementing new plans usually requires money, people, and a way to produce goods or services the firm will sell.

Cooperation between the marketing manager and the finance people helps to ensure that there's enough money available for initial investments and to implement the marketing plan. If money comes from outside investors, the marketing manager may need to develop a strategy that satisfies them as well as customers. If funding is limited, the strategy may need to be scaled back, or the strategy may need to be phased in over time so that it generates enough cash flow to "pay its own way."

There also needs to be close coordination between a firm's production specialists and its marketing planners. The marketing manager needs to consider the firm's production capacity when evaluating alternative strategies. And flexibility in production may allow the firm to pursue different strategies at the same time or to switch strategies more easily when new opportunities develop.

Figuring out the profitability of a strategy, product, or customer often requires a real understanding of costs—production costs, marketing costs, and other costs that may accumulate. Traditional accounting reports are often not very useful in pinpointing these costs. However, marketing managers and accountants are now working together to get more accurate cost information—by developing functional accounts rather than just relying on natural accounts typically used for financial analysis.

Money, facilities, and information are all important in developing a successful strategy, but most strategies are implemented by people. So a marketing manager must also be concerned with the availability and skills of the firm's people—its human resources. New marketing strategies may upset established ways of doing things. Plans need to be clearly communicated so that everyone knows what to expect. Further, plans need to take into consideration the time and effort that will be required to get people up to speed on the new jobs they will be expected to do.

Making the strategic planning decisions that concern how a firm is going to use its overall resources—from marketing, production, finance, and other areas—is the responsibility of the chief executive officer, not the marketing manager. Further, the marketing manager usually can't dictate what a manager in some other department should do. However, it is sensible for the marketing manager to make recommendations on these matters. And marketing strategies and plans that the marketing manager recommends are more likely to be accepted, and then successfully implemented, if the links between marketing and other functional areas have been carefully considered from the outset.

KEY TERMS

capital, 556

working capital, 556

stock, 558

debt financing, 558

cash flow statement, 560

production capacity, 561

virtual corporation, 562

task transfer, 563

mass customization, 565

natural accounts, 567

functional accounts, 567

QUESTIONS AND PROBLEMS

1. Identify some of the ways that a firm can raise money to support a new marketing plan. Give the advantages and limitations—from a marketing manager's perspective—of each approach.

2. An entrepreneur who started a chain of auto service centers to do fast oil changes wants to quickly expand by building new facilities in new markets but doesn't have enough capital. His financial advisor suggested that he might be able to get around the financial constraint and still grow rapidly if he franchised his idea. That way the franchisees would invest to build their own centers, but fees from the franchise agreement would also provide cash flow to build more company-owned outlets. Do you think this is a good idea? Why or why not?

3. Explain, in your own words, why investors in a firm's stock might be interested in a firm's marketing manager developing a new growth-oriented strategy. Would it be just as good, from the investors' standpoint, for the manager to just maintain the same level of profits? Why or why not?

4. A woman with extensive experience in home health care and a good marketing plan has approached a bank for a loan, most of which she has explained she intends to "invest in advertising designed to recruit part-time nurses and to attract home-care patients for her firm's services." Other than the furniture in her leased office space, she has few assets. Is the bank likely to loan her the money? Why?

5. Could the idea of mass customization be used by a publisher of college textbooks to allow different

instructors to order customized teaching materials—perhaps even unique books made up of chapters from a number of different existing books? What do you think would be the major advantages and disadvantages of this approach?

6. Give examples of two different ways that a firm's production capacity might influence a marketing manager's choice of a marketing strategy.

7. Is a small company's flexibility increased or decreased by turning to outside suppliers to produce the products it sells? Explain your thinking.

8. Explain how a marketing manager's sales forecast for a new marketing plan might be used by

   a. A financial manager.
   b. An accountant.
   c. A production manager.
   d. A human resources manager.

9. Explain the difference between natural accounts and functional accounts.

10. Could the approaches to cost allocation that we discussed in this chapter apply to a firm, like a travel agency, that produces only services? Explain your thinking.

11. What types of human resource issues does a marketing manager face when planning to expand sales operations from a branch office in a new overseas market? Are the problems any different than they would be in a new domestic market?

SUGGESTED CASES

17. Eco Water, Inc.

35. Sal's

1. Know the content of
and differences
among strategies,
marketing plans, and
a marketing program.

2. Understand all the
elements of the
marketing strategy
planning process and
the strategy decisions
for the four Ps.

3. Understand why
product classes and
typical mixes should
be considered when
developing a
marketing plan.

4. Understand ways the
marketing strategy
and plan is likely to
need to change at
different stages of
the product life cycle.

5. Understand the basic
forecasting
approaches and why
they are used to
evaluate the
profitability of
potential strategies.

6. Know what is
involved in preparing
a marketing plan,
including estimates of
costs and revenue and
specification of other
time-related details.

7. Understand ways
firms can become
involved in interna-
tional marketing.

8. Understand the
important new terms
(shown in red).

CHAPTER TWENTY-ONE

Developing Innovative Marketing Plans

If asked what you know about Maytag's marketing program, the first thing to come to mind would probably be its "lonely repairman" ad campaigns. For 35 years, those ads have helped position Maytag as a reliable brand for major appliances. Gordon Jump, an actor who really was a former Maytag repairman, played the lonely repairman role in ads for 14 years. In 2004, another veteran character actor, Hardy Rawls, took on that job. Although Maytag's basic positioning has been consistent over many years, marketing managers at Maytag are constantly developing new marketing strategies. So let's take a closer look at what they did in one innovative strategy planning process that resulted in profitable growth for Maytag by offering target customers superior value. This case is longer than others we've covered—to help you review what is in a marketing plan and the process of creating one. As you read the case, relate it to the ideas you've studied throughout the text.

Changes in the external environment called for a new strategy. The U.S. Department of Energy (DOE) was considering new regulations to require that clothes washers use less water and energy. The U.S. uses three times as much water a day—1,300 gallons per person—as the average European country. One reason is that front-loading clothes washers have long been standard in Europe. This is in part an economic issue. Front-loaders heat less water so less energy is used, and Europeans face steeper energy costs. There is also a cultural difference. North Americans are more convenience-oriented, but front-loaders make you stoop, they spill water on the floor, and you can't throw in a stray sock during the wash cycle.

Maytag's R&D people thought that they could use technology to improve the design of a front-loading washer to make it more convenient and to conserve water and energy as well. With inputs from marketers about broader needs in the clothes care product-market they looked at needs beyond just cleaning. It appeared that a consumer-oriented design could improve basic benefits like easier loading and gentler care of fabrics.

Competitors were also on the move. Frigidaire came out with a front-load unit just in time to be the only one tested for a *Consumer Reports* article. It tested well on cleaning, but Maytag thought it fell short in improving other customer benefits. GE was further behind in working on a front-loader. But these were strong competitors, so if Maytag didn't move quickly they could get a lead.

Maytag formed a cross-functional new-product development team to quickly focus the effort. It screened various product ideas and strategies on criteria such as potential for superior customer value, initial costs, long-term growth, social responsibility, and profitability. Using nearly 40 pieces of consumer research, the team refined what the strategy might be and what it would cost.

S.W.O.T. analysis showed that Maytag's advantages included a strong dealer network, the technical skills to develop the product, and the financial resources to do it. Major threats were mainly related to competitors' efforts and consumers' prior attitudes about front-loading machines. Addressing those threats would take informing and real persuading.

Market segmentation helped to narrow down to a target market. Various segments could be identified. For example, there was a homogeneous business market. It consisted of owners of coin-operated laundries who were mainly interested in operating costs and attracting customers. Consumer segments were more varied. Relevant needs focused on cleaning, removing stains, caring for fabrics, and saving water or energy. Some people just wanted less hassle on wash days and a care-free washer.

Maytag decided not to target just the segment that conserved energy; that was not a qualifying dimension. Instead they combined several segments into a larger target market. The main qualifying dimension was the ability to pay for a dependable washer that provided superior cleaning. Determining dimensions were interests in saving time, hassle, and expense while getting better results.

The design of the washing machine evolved from target consumers' needs, so it is different from most washers. The stainless steel tub tilts at a 15-degree angle, which improves visibility and reach. Cutting out the normal agitator increases load capacity by about a third while decreasing damage to clothes. It also increases access space for bulky items and makes loading and unloading easier. Fins inside lift the clothes and then plop them back in the shallow basin of water. This eliminates spills because the water level is below the door. In fact, it uses half the water and energy of regular machines but removes tough stains better.

As Maytag's design progressed, consumer tests showed that consumers liked the unique benefits and were willing to pay for them. Financial analysis of the marketing plan for this new product indicated that it could meet Maytag's objectives, so Maytag invested the money to put the plan into action.

The new product needed a memorable brand name—Neptune. The existing marketing program positioned Maytag as "the dependability people," so the plan called for a strategy that would build on that base but also position the new product as really new and superior—as "the washer for the new millennium."

The plan specified a warranty that would signal real dependability to consumers. It called for a 10-year warranty on the drive motor or rust damage and for lifetime coverage on the stainless steel wash basket. Coverage of other parts was two years, and a year on labor. The plan also specified a way to further differentiate Neptune with an unprecedented level of after-sale support. Neptune buyers would get Priority One Service that offers dedicated toll-free assistance and priority scheduling should any in-home calls be required. The plan also got down to details: The easy-to-remember toll-free number is 888-4-MAYTAG.

In stores, the washer is displayed out of the carton, so the plan focused on a package designed to protect the product during handling and, by using bar codes and clear model labels, make logistics in the channel more efficient. But the thrust of the packaging was to protect, not promote.

While our focus here is on the washer, the plan also considered product-line issues. It called for a matching dryer designed so that the length of wash and dry cycles would be virtually the same. This means that a user can move load after load from washer to dryer without the waiting that's typical with conventional laundry pairs. What's more, the dryer handles Neptune's extra large loads with ease and uses the same angled styling—so transferring a load to the dryer is easier than ever.

To reduce start-up costs and keep the effort focused, the initial plan called for only one model of the Neptune washer. However, a full-sized stacked version of a combination washer/dryer was planned for later.

The plan called for a national rollout using Maytag's established dealers. Making a product available in so many places at once added difficulties, but it was consistent with the plan of using national promotion to give the product a big introduction.

To help coordinate efforts in the channel, Maytag released stories in *Merchandiser*, a magazine it publishes for dealers. As channel captain, Maytag kept dealers informed about the specific timing of the program, including when stock would be available. Maytag salespeople got dealers' orders and helped them to plan their own strategies.

The plan anticipated that product availability could be a constraint if the introduction went extremely well. So dealers could participate in a program that allowed consumers to reserve one of the early units off the production line. This preselling activity improved inventory management, reduced stock-outs, and got sales early in the program.

Even with these efforts at coordination, the promotion portion of the plan was developed recognizing that some independent dealers were skeptical about carrying and promoting a premium-price front-loader. So the plan called for a mix of push and pull promotion.

Details of promotion planning were handled as a team effort by Maytag and Leo Burnett, its Chicago agency. The plan called for integrated marketing communications. To make it easy for the sales force, dealers, customers, and potential customers to remember all of Neptune's benefits, the promotion effort consistently focused on Neptune's four Cs—Cleaning, Convenience, Clothes Care, and Conservation. (You can probably figure out where a group of marketing folks got the idea of using a catchy acronym like that.)

The plan relied on different promotion methods to emphasize different benefits and objectives. For example, much of the prerelease publicity focused on conservation of water, energy, and related costs. Then initial advertising focused on availability and cleaning benefits. The marketing plan also specified tests by independent laboratories so that there would be evidence to support claims of superiority.

The distinctive advantages of the Neptune offered a particularly good opportunity to use publicity to create broad awareness and generate interest. Thus, the plan detailed an extensive set of public relations events, including a glitzy media launch at New York's Lincoln Center. It featured famous TV moms talking about the Maytag washer they used—followed by the introduction of the Neptune, "the washer for the next millennium." This garnered widespread media attention just a few weeks before the product launch.

The plan also laid out an attention-getting venture with the Department of Energy that involved benchmarking the water and energy usage of all of the washers in a small, water-starved town in Kansas and then replacing half of them with Neptune washers. The test showed that the Neptune produced savings of 39 percent in water usage and 58 percent in energy usage. Media coverage ranged from *NBC Nightly News* to the front page of *USA Today*.

An unknown new product calls for attention-getting advertising, and that is exactly what the plan specified. A big-budget TV commercial debuted at precisely the same moment on both CBS and NBC and then was scheduled for frequent repetitions over the next three months. The ad features Maytag's lonely repairman out for a late-night walk with his dog. Ol' Lonely spills a cupful of coffee down his front when the pooch starts racing in circles. You see why when a spaceship appears overhead, beaming down a Neptune washer and three happy little aliens. In a flash, they strip the coffee-stained uniform off Ol' Lonely and throw it in the washer. Following a demo of the washer's tumbling action, the now-spotless uniform reappears on the famous repairman. As the Neptunians depart in their spaceship, Ol' Lonely says, "They're never gonna believe this. A washer that removes stains."

The plan also called for promotion support for dealers. For example, to attract attention Maytag dealers received 20-foot-high balloons that looked like Ol' Lonely to put on top of their stores, as well as in-store banners, posters, and brochures.

Maytag didn't miss the opportunity to plan interactive marketing communications. At the website (www.maytag.com) consumers could see pictures and read about the benefits of the Neptune. A website visitor who was ready to buy could even reserve a Neptune that would be delivered by the local dealer or use an interactive dealer locator to find a store.

The plan didn't ignore the coin-laundry segment. The website featured a special section on how the Neptune could help improve profits for those firms. It went into detail about savings on energy, water, and sewer costs, as well as technical matters related to maintenance.

Of course, the plan called for dealers to pitch in with some promotion efforts of their own, such as setting up displays to demo the Neptune in action. Dealers were required to correctly and attractively display point-of-purchase materials. And salespeople were brought up-to-speed about Neptune's four Cs so they could explain its benefits and help customers determine if it met their needs.

The plan called for an initial suggested list price of $1,099, which was high relative to most washers. The washer-dryer combination was about $1,700. Some dealers, however, cut that price because the plan allowed dealers a higher than normal dollar profit.

The plan anticipated that Frigidaire and GE might cut prices when faced with competition (and in fact that later happened). However, Maytag stuck with its planned higher price because many consumers viewed its design as offering a better value. Further, the plan provided information to help salespeople reduce price sensitivity by reminding consumers that water and energy savings from the Neptune are about $100 a year, so it pays for itself in 10 years.

The plan did not include use of rebates, but some utility companies offered rebates to customers who purchased a Neptune. For example, one water company handed out 1,500 rebates of $50 each. It figures that those Neptunes save 18,000 gallons of water a day.

With the plan finally in operation, Neptunes flew off the dealers' floors and truckload orders began rolling in. This caused some implementation problems, but Maytag production workers went into overdrive and moved Neptunes off the loading docks around the clock. Swiftly, new tooling was installed to raise plant production rates.

In this case, our focus has been on the launch of a new product. Of course, a successful launch doesn't guarantee ongoing success—nor does it mark the end of a strategy. Rather, as a product-market grows and matures, a strategy usually needs to be continually adjusted to deal with changes in competition, in target markets, and in the marketing environment. For example, after the launch of the Neptune, Maytag faced an economic downturn that reduced consumer spending for high-end appliances. During this period, Maytag worked to improve profits by cutting costs and improving quality in its factories. Then, as the economy started to recover, Maytag introduced an improved Neptune Drying Center; it includes a drying cabinet, above the traditional dryer, that serves as a wrinkle reducer, odor eliminator, and clothes freshener. Place changes are underway as well. The opening of new Maytag Stores will allow consumers to try out appliances so they can see for themselves how well they work. And, going full circle back to our lonely repairman, Maytag expanded its at-home appliance repair service to fix other major brands rather than just Maytag.[1]

Bali Blinds come in a large variety of colors to give consumers nearly unlimited choices for interior design. There's usually nothing very interesting about a photo of even the nicest blinds. But this ad builds interest in the firm's positioning by matching the color of the blinds to the color of the fish in the bowl. Similarly, when Mr. Clean brand managers wanted to differentiate their cleaner with a new line of scents, this clever picture of a lemon slice, adorned with Mr. Clean's earring, helps to convey the message.

MARKETING PLANNING PROCESS IS MORE THAN ASSEMBLING THE FOUR Ps

The Maytag case shows that developing a successful marketing plan is a creative process. But it is also a logical process. And the logic that leads to a sound strategy may need to change as the marketing environment and target customers change.

Even so, the strategy planning process is guided by basic principles. The marketing concept emphasizes that all of a firm's activities should focus on its target markets. Further, a firm should try to find a competitive advantage in meeting the needs of some target market(s) that it can satisfy very well. If it can do that, it provides target customers with superior value. The target market(s) should be large enough to support the firm's efforts and yield a profit. And ideally, the strategy should take advantage of trends in the external market, not buck them.

As we explained in Chapter 2, the marketing strategy planning process involves narrowing down from a broad set of possible marketing opportunities to a specific strategy the firm will pursue. A marketing *strategy* consists of a target market and a marketing mix; it specifies what a firm will do in some target market. A marketing *plan* includes the time-related details—including expected costs and revenues—for that strategy. In most firms, the marketing manager must ultimately combine the different marketing plans into an overall marketing *program*.

We'll start with a review of the many variables that must be considered in the marketing strategy planning process. You'll recognize that most of these are highlighted in the Maytag case. Next we'll look at some of the key ways a marketing manager can identify the right blend of the marketing mix for an innovative strategy. Then we'll discuss how these ideas come together in a marketing plan.

We'll also discuss ways to forecast target market potential and sales, which is important not only in evaluating opportunities but also in developing the time-related details for a plan. Of course, plans must ultimately be blended into an overall program—and we'll suggest ways to approach that task. Planning strategies for international markets presents some special challenges, so we'll conclude the chapter by describing the different ways a marketer can address these challenges.

Marketing strategy planning process brings focus to efforts

Developing a good marketing strategy and turning the strategy into a marketing plan requires blending the ideas we've discussed throughout this text. Exhibit 21-1 provides a broad overview of the major areas we've been talking about. You saw this before in Chapter 2—before you learned what's really involved in each idea. Now we must integrate ideas about these different areas to narrow down to logical marketing mixes, marketing strategies, marketing plans—and a marketing program.

As suggested in Exhibit 21-1, developing an effective marketing strategy involves a process of narrowing down to a specific target market and marketing mix that represents a real opportunity. This narrowing-down process requires a thorough understanding of the market. That understanding is enhanced by careful analysis of customers' needs, current or prospective competitors, and the firm's own objectives and resources. Similarly, favorable or unfavorable factors and trends in the external marketing environment may make a potential opportunity more or less attractive.

There are often more different strategy possibilities than a firm can pursue. Each possible strategy usually has a number of different potential advantages and disadvantages. This can make it difficult to zero in on the best target market and marketing mix. However, as we discussed in Chapter 4, developing a set of specific qualitative and quantitative screening criteria—to define what business and markets the firm wants to compete in—can help eliminate potential strategies that are not well suited for the firm.

Another useful aid for zeroing in on a feasible strategy is **S.W.O.T. analysis**—which identifies and lists the firm's strengths and weaknesses and its opportunities and threats. A good S.W.O.T. analysis helps the manager focus on a strategy that takes advantage of the firm's opportunities and strengths while avoiding its weaknesses and threats to its success. These can be compared with the pros and cons of strategies that are considered. For example, if a firm is considering a strategy that focuses on a target market that is already being served by several strong competitors, success will usually hinge on some sort of competitive advantage. Such a competitive advantage might be based on a better marketing mix—perhaps an innovative new product, improved distribution, more effective promotion, or a better price. Just offering a marketing mix that is like what is available from competitors usually

Exhibit 21-1
Overview of Marketing Strategy Planning Process

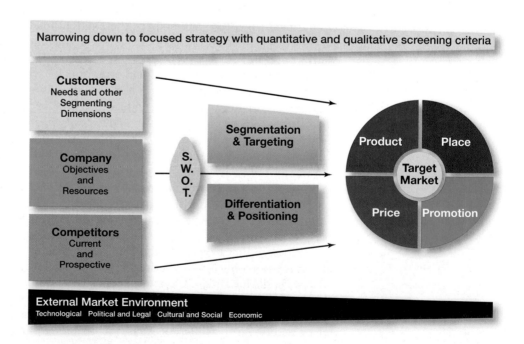

Narrowing down to focused strategy with quantitative and qualitative screening criteria

Customers
Needs and other Segmenting Dimensions

Company
Objectives and Resources

Competitors
Current and Prospective

S. W. O. T.

Segmentation & Targeting

Differentiation & Positioning

Product · Place · Price · Promotion
Target Market

External Market Environment
Technological   Political and Legal   Cultural and Social   Economic

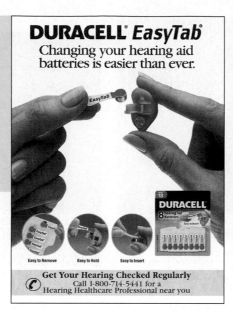

Other firms offer hearing-aid batteries, but Duracell's new EasyTab makes it easier for hearing-aid users to handle the small batteries. Time Warner Cable competes with satellite TV services, but one of its advantages is that its signal is not affected by the weather.

doesn't provide superior value—or any real basis for the firm to position or differentiate its marketing mix as better for customers.

Marketing mix flows from target market dimensions

Ideally, the ingredients of a good marketing mix flow logically from all the relevant dimensions of a target market. The market definition and segmenting approaches we discussed in Chapter 3 help the marketing manager identify which dimensions are qualifying and which are determining in customers' choices.

Product benefits must match needs. If and how customers search for information helps to define the promotion blend. Demographic dimensions reveal where customers are located and if they have the income to buy. Where customers shop for or buy products helps define channel alternatives. The value of the whole marketing mix and the urgency of customer needs, combined with an understanding of what customers see as substitute ways of meeting needs, help companies estimate price sensitivity.

It would seem that if we fully understand the needs and attitudes of a target market, then combining the four Ps should be easy. Yet there are three important gaps in this line of reasoning. (1) We don't always know as much as we would like to about the needs and attitudes of our target markets. (2) Competitors are also trying to satisfy these or similar needs—and their efforts may force a firm to shift its marketing mix. (3) The other dimensions of the marketing environment may be changing, which may require more changes in marketing mixes. These points warrant further consideration.

Product classes suggest typical marketing mixes

Even if you don't or can't know all you would like to about a potential target market, you usually know enough to decide whether the product is a consumer product or a business product and which product class is most relevant (Exhibit 9-3 summarizes the consumer product classes, and Exhibit 9-4 summarizes the business product classes).

Identifying the proper product class helps because it suggests how a typical product should be distributed and promoted. So if you don't know as much as you'd like about potential customers' needs and attitudes, at least knowing how *they* would view the company's product can give you a head start on developing a marketing mix. A convenience product, for example, usually needs more intensive distribution, and the producer usually takes on more responsibility for promotion. A specialty product needs a clear brand identity, which may require a more extensive positioning effort. A new unsought product will need a mix that leads customers through the adoption process.

It's reassuring to see that product classes do summarize some of what you would like to know about target markets and what marketing mixes are relevant. After all,

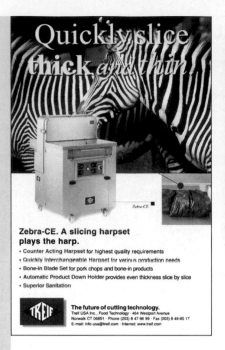

knowing what others have done in similar situations can serve as a guide to get started. From that base you may see a better way to meet needs that is *not* typical and that provides a competitive advantage.

Typical is not necessarily right

The typical marketing mix for a given product class is not necessarily right for all situations. To the contrary, some marketing mixes are profitable because they depart from the typical—to satisfy some target markets better. In fact, it is often through differentiation of the firm's product or other elements of the marketing mix that the marketing manager can offer target customers unique value.

Superior mixes may be breakthrough opportunities

When marketing managers fully understand their target markets, they may be able to develop marketing mixes that are superior to competitors' mixes. Such understanding may provide breakthrough opportunities. Taking advantage of these opportunities can lead to large sales and profitable growth. This is why we stress the importance of looking for breakthrough opportunities rather than just trying to imitate competitors' offerings.

Inferior mixes are easy to reject

Just as some mixes are superior, some mixes are clearly inferior—or unsuitable. For example, a national TV advertising campaign might make sense for a large company like Maytag—but it could quickly be screened out by a small firm that only has the resources to put a web page on the Internet and perhaps get some help from manufacturers' agents.

Marketing manager must blend the four Ps

Exhibit 21-2 reviews the major marketing strategy decision areas organized by the four Ps. Each of these requires careful decision making. Yet marketing planning involves much more than just independent decisions and assembling the parts into a marketing mix. The four Ps must be creatively *blended*—so the firm develops the best mix for its target market. In other words, each decision must work well with all of the others to make a logical whole.

584

WHY THE WIRELESS PHONE SERVICE FOR CAB DRIVERS HAS BEEN A WINNER

For years, Nextel has been out of step with other firms that offer wireless service. But recently its atypical strategy has earned better profits and had the highest revenue per customer of any firm in the business. In the wake of a new rule that allowed customers to switch their cell phone numbers to a new carrier, most firms were scrambling to hang on to subscribers, but Nextel increased subscribers by 20 percent. And while people often view wireless as a commodity and shop on price, many of Nextel's 10 million subscribers see its Direct Connect service as essential. Direct Connect is a walkie-talkie-like feature that allows a cell phone user to push a button and instantly talk with someone else who has the same service carrier. Nextel has had this service since the early 1990s, and it has set Nextel apart. It has been especially popular with construction workers, delivery drivers, firefighters, and others accustomed to working with two-way radios. Ninety percent of Nextel customers use Direct Connect.

However, freed by a change in regulations, other cell phone firms that once derided Nextel as the service for "cab drivers" are now imitating its proprietary technology. What they offer doesn't work as well so far. For example, conversations with Verizon's service are punctuated with pauses because there is a five-second delay between when a message is spoken and when it is heard. However, within a few years competitors will catch up. And Sprint PCS is planning to sell push-to-talk service as part of a comprehensive set of business services, including high-speed wireless Internet access for laptops.

Until recently, Nextel's push-to-talk worked only within a local service area. To broaden the appeal of its service, Nextel has made it available nationwide, which makes it more attractive to professionals. Nextel is also testing strategies to reach other target markets, including government agencies, with homeland security applications. At the same time it is expanding its profitable wireless data service. For example, its @Road service helps truck fleet operators locate vehicles with a global positioning system. Nextel will feel the impact of competitors nipping at its heels, but with new strategy planning it may be able to keep its edge over rivals.[2]

Throughout the text, we've given the job of integrating the four Ps strategy decisions to the marketing manager. The title of that person might vary, but now you should see the need for this integrating role. It is easy for specialists to focus on their own areas and expect the rest of the company to work for or around them. This is especially true in larger firms like Maytag—where specialists are needed—just because the size of the whole marketing job is too big for one person. Yet the

Exhibit 21-2
Strategy Decision Areas
Organized by the Four Ps

Product	Place	Promotion	Price
Physical good	Objectives	Objectives	Objectives
Service	Channel type	Promotion blend	Flexibility
Features	Market exposure	Salespeople	Level over
Benefits	Kinds of	Kind	product life
Quality level	middlemen	Number	cycle
Accessories	Kinds and	Selection	Geographic terms
Installation	locations of	Training	Discounts
Instructions	stores	Motivation	Allowances
Warranty	How to handle	Advertising	
Product lines	transporting	Targets	
Packaging	and storing	Kinds of ads	
Branding	Service levels	Media type	
	Recruiting	Copy thrust	
	middlemen	Prepared by	
	Managing	whom	
	channels	Sales promotion	
		Publicity	

ideas of the product manager, the advertising manager, the sales manager, the logistics manager, and whoever makes pricing decisions may have to be adjusted to improve the whole mix. It's critical that each marketing mix decision work well with all of the others. A breakdown in any one decision area may doom the whole strategy to failure.

Product life cycle guides planning

Careful consideration of where a firm's offering fits in the product life cycle can also be a big help in evaluating the best marketing mix. We introduced Exhibit 21-3 in Chapter 10 to summarize how marketing mix variables typically change over the product life cycle. Now you can see that this exhibit is a good review of many topics we've discussed throughout the text. Certainly, the pioneering effort required for a really new product concept is different from the job of taking market share away from an established competitor late in the market growth stage.

Further, when you're thinking about the product life cycle don't forget that markets change continually. This means you must plan strategies that can adjust to changing conditions. The original marketing plan for a new marketing strategy may even include details about what adjustments in the marketing mix or target market will be required as the nature of competition and the adoption process evolve.[3]

FORECASTING TARGET MARKET POTENTIAL AND SALES

Effective strategy planning and developing a marketing plan require estimates of future sales, costs, and profits. Without such information, it's hard to know if a strategy is potentially profitable.

The marketing manager's estimates of sales, costs, and profits are usually based on a forecast (estimate) of target **market potential**—what a whole market segment might buy—and a **sales forecast**—an estimate of how much an industry or firm hopes to sell to a market segment. Usually we must first try to judge market potential before we can estimate what share a particular firm may be able to win with its particular marketing mix.

Exhibit 21-3
Typical Changes in
Marketing Variables over
the Product Life Cycle

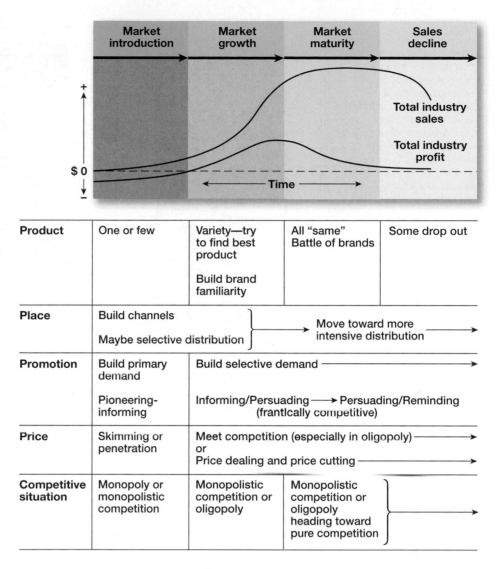

	Market introduction	Market growth	Market maturity	Sales decline
Product	One or few	Variety—try to find best product Build brand familiarity	All "same" Battle of brands	Some drop out
Place	Build channels Maybe selective distribution	Move toward more intensive distribution		
Promotion	Build primary demand Pioneering-informing	Build selective demand Informing/Persuading → Persuading/Reminding (frantically competitive)		
Price	Skimming or penetration	Meet competition (especially in oligopoly) → or Price dealing and price cutting →		
Competitive situation	Monopoly or monopolistic competition	Monopolistic competition or oligopoly	Monopolistic competition or oligopoly heading toward pure competition	

Three levels of forecasts are useful

We're interested in forecasting the potential in specific market segments. To do this, it helps to make three levels of forecasts.

Some economic conditions affect the entire global economy. Others may influence only one country or a particular industry. And some may affect only one company or one product's sales potential. For this reason, a common top-down approach to forecasting is to

1. Develop a *national income forecast* (for each country in which the firm operates) and use this to
2. Develop an *industry sales forecast*, which then is used to
3. Develop forecasts for a *specific company*, its *specific products*, and the *segments* it targets.

Generally, a marketing manager doesn't have to make forecasts for a national economy or the broad industry. This kind of forecasting—basically trend projecting—is a specialty in itself. Such forecasts are available in business and government publications, and large companies often have their own technical specialists. Managers can use just one source's forecast or combine several. Unfortunately, however, the more targeted the marketing manager's earlier segmenting efforts have been, the less likely that industry forecasts will match the firm's product-markets. So managers have to

move directly to estimating potential for their own companies and for their specific products.

Two approaches to forecasting

Many methods are used to forecast market potential and sales, but they can all be grouped into two basic approaches: (1) extending past behavior and (2) predicting future behavior. The large number of methods may seem confusing at first, but this variety has an advantage. Forecasts are so important that managers often develop forecasts in two or three different ways and then compare the differences before preparing a final forecast.

Extending past behavior can miss important turning points

When we forecast for existing products, we usually have some past data to go on. The basic approach, called **trend extension,** extends past experience into the future. With existing products, for example, the past trend of actual sales may be extended into the future. See Exhibit 21-4.

Ideally, when extending past sales behavior, we should decide why sales vary. This is the difficult and time-consuming part of sales forecasting. Usually we can gather a lot of data about the product or market or about changes in the marketing environment. But unless we know the *reason* for past sales variations, it's hard to predict in what direction, and by how much, sales will move. Graphing the data and statistical techniques—including correlation and regression analysis—can be useful

Exhibit 21-4
Straight-Line Trend Projection—Extends Past Sales into the Future

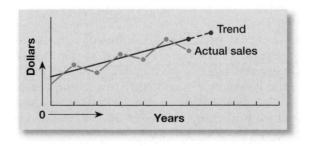

here. (These techniques, which are beyond our scope, are discussed in beginning statistics courses.)

Once we know why sales vary, we can usually develop a specific forecast. Sales may be moving directly up as population grows in a specific market segment, for example. So we can just estimate how population is expected to grow and project the impact on sales.

The weakness of the trend extension method is that it assumes past conditions will continue unchanged into the future. In fact, the future isn't always like the past. An agent wholesaler's business may have been on a steady path, but the development of the Internet added a totally new factor. The past trend for the agent's sales changed because now the agent can quickly reach a broader market.

As another example, for years the trend in sales of disposable diapers moved closely with the number of new births. However, as the number of women in the workforce increased and as more women returned to jobs after babies were born, use of disposable diapers increased, and the trend changed. As in these examples, trend extension estimates will be wrong whenever big changes occur. For this reason—although they may extend past behavior for one estimate—most managers look for another way to help them forecast sharp market changes.

Predicting future behavior takes judgment

When we try to predict what will happen in the future, instead of just extending the past, we have to use other methods and add more judgment. Some of these methods (to be discussed later) include juries of executive opinion, salespeople's estimates, surveys, panels, and market tests.

FORECASTING COMPANY AND PRODUCT SALES BY EXTENDING PAST BEHAVIOR

Past sales can be extended

At the very least, a marketing manager ought to know what the firm's present markets look like and what it has sold to them in the past. A detailed sales analysis for products and geographic areas helps to project future results.

Just extending past sales into the future may not seem like much of a forecasting method. But it's better than just assuming that next year's total sales will be the same as this year's.

Factor method includes more than time

A simple extension of past sales gives one forecast. But it's usually desirable to tie future sales to something more than the passage of time.

The factor method tries to do this. The **factor method** tries to forecast sales by finding a relation between the company's sales and some other factor (or factors). The basic formula is: something (past sales, industry sales, etc.) *times* some factor *equals* sales forecast. A **factor** is a variable that shows the relation of some other variable to the item being forecast. For instance, in our example above, both the birthrate and the number of working mothers are factors related to sales of disposable diapers.

A bread producer example

The following example, about a bread producer, shows how firms can make forecasts for many geographic market segments using the factor method and available data. This general approach can be useful for any firm—producer, wholesaler, or retailer.

Analysis of past sales relationships showed that the bread manufacturer regularly sold one-tenth of 1 percent (0.001) of the total retail food sales in its various target markets. This is a single factor. By using this single factor, a manager could estimate the producer's sales in a new market for the coming period by multiplying a forecast of expected retail food sales by 0.001.

Sales & Marketing Management magazine makes retail food sales estimates each year. Exhibit 21-5 shows the kind of geographically detailed data available.

Let's carry this bread example further—using the data in Exhibit 21-5 for the Denver, Colorado, metro area. Denver's food sales were $4,700,116,000 for the previous year. By simply accepting last year's food sales as an estimate of next year's sales and multiplying the food sales estimate for Denver by the 0.001 factor (the firm's usual share of food purchases in such markets), the manager would have an estimate of next year's bread sales in Denver. That is, last year's food sales estimate ($4,700,116,000) times 0.001 equals this year's bread sales estimate of $4,700,116.

Factor method can use several factors

The factor method is not limited to just one factor; several factors can be used together. For example, *Sales & Marketing Management* regularly gives a "buying power index" (BPI) as a measure of the potential in different geographic areas. See Exhibit 21-5. This index considers (1) the population in a market, (2) the retail sales in that market, and (3) income in that market. The BPI for the Denver, Colorado, metro area, for example, is 0.9282—that is, Denver accounts for 0.9282 percent of the total U.S. buying power. This means that consumers who live in Denver have higher than average buying power. We know this because Denver accounts for about 0.7723 percent of the U.S. population. We can calculate this figure by using Denver's total population of 2,199,500 (in Exhibit 21-5) and dividing it by the total population of the U.S.—284,797,000 (in Exhibit 5-2). So the people in Denver have buying power that is about 20 percent higher than average.

Using several factors rather than only one uses more information. And in the case of the BPI, it gives a single measure of a market's potential. Rather than falling back on using population only, or income only, or trying to develop a special index, the BPI can be used in the same way that we used the 0.001 factor in the bread example.

INTERNET EXERCISE

The Survey of Buying Power has an online site that is available on a pay-for-use basis. However, background information and some top-10 listings are available without charge. Go to the website (cluster2.claritas.com/MySBP), select *Learn More.* How would the information from the Survey of Buying Power be helpful to a retail chain that is considering a new facility for this sample market?

Producers of business products can use several factors too

Exhibit 21-6 shows how a marketing manager for a firm that makes corrugated fiber boxes used several factors to estimate the sales potential in a particular geographic area. The manager started with trade association data on the value of shipments (sales) by all fiber box suppliers to firms in particular industries (column 1). The trade association estimates were for the *national* market. Note, however, that they were grouped by North American Industry Classification System (NAICS) industry groups. As we discussed in Chapter 7, data on business markets is often organized by NAICS codes. That makes it possible to combine different types of data, which is what the manager did here.

Specifically, the manager divided the trade association estimates by government data on the number of people employed in each industry NAICS group (column 2). The result, shown in column 3, is simply an estimate of the value of boxes used per employee in each industry group. For example, furniture and fixture manufacturers buy an average of $245 worth of boxes per employee.

Then the manager multiplied the value per employee number by the number of people employed in each industry group in the target county (column 4). This results in an estimate of the market potential for each industry group (column 5) in that county. For example, since there are 616 people in this county who work in

Exhibit 21-5 Sample of Pages from *Sales & Marketing Management's* Survey of Buying Power: Metro and County Totals

COLORADO

METRO AREA County City	Total Population (000s)	% of Population by Age Group				House-holds (000s)	Total Retail Sales	Food & Beverage Stores	Food Service & Drinking Establish-ments	General Merchan-dise	Furniture & Home Furnish. & Electron. & Appliances	Motor Vehicle & Parts Dealers	Total EBI ($000)	Median Hsld. EBI	Effective Buying Income % of Hslds: by EBI Group			Buying Power Index
		18-24	25-34	35-49	50+										A $20,000–$34,999	B $35,000–$49,999	C $50,000 & Over	
BOULDER-LONGMONT	303.7	13.6	15.5	25.6	22.4	119.6	5,081,227	1,001,555	556,377	448,453	247,484	1,220,087	7,716,546	51,714	17.8	17.1	51.6	0.1360
BOULDER	303.7	13.6	15.5	25.6	22.4	119.6	5,081,227	1,001,555	556,377	448,453	247,484	1,220,087	7,716,546	51,714	17.8	17.1	51.6	0.1360
•Boulder	97.1	26.4	18.8	20.0	20.1	40.7	2,147,663	439,133	267,970	121,357	117,520	447,464	2,480,204	43,427	21.5	15.8	43.1	0.0479
•Longmont	74.6	8.7	14.6	25.3	23.6	28.0	1,126,804	250,483	122,965	125,103	40,068	272,449	1,531,271	47,526	19.4	20.1	46.8	0.0290
COLORADO SPRINGS	537.3	10.7	14.4	24.7	22.6	200.1	7,883,675	819,826	647,101	984,753	465,488	2,031,112	10,259,019	42,082	24.7	21.0	38.7	0.1994
EL PASO	537.3	10.7	14.4	24.7	22.6	200.1	7,883,675	819,826	647,101	984,753	465,488	2,031,112	10,259,019	42,082	24.7	21.0	38.7	0.1994
•Colorado Springs	373.1	10.5	14.8	24.5	23.7	146.5	6,786,693	628,690	549,107	858,048	443,063	1,848,219	7,353,670	41,212	24.9	20.9	37.5	0.1515
DENVER	2,199.5	9.2	16.2	25.0	23.8	858.0	33,750,880	4,700,116	3,232,590	3,615,646	2,518,616	9,368,057	52,585,220	49,109	18.8	19.0	48.9	0.9282
ADAMS	382.9	10.5	16.7	23.3	21.1	134.3	4,558,882	670,017	371,810	416,956	385,657	1,466,781	6,459,840	42,802	22.5	22.4	38.7	0.1253
Thornton	87.3	9.7	17.5	24.9	18.0	30.6	707,386	152,812	68,679	122,478	40,099	150,769	1,594,293	48,053	19.4	22.4	46.8	0.0270
Westminster	105.4	9.9	17.1	26.0	20.3	40.1	1,052,771	153,993	114,177	292,678	100,304	88,416	2,368,971	51,512	17.0	21.6	51.9	0.0384
ARAPAHOE	505.4	8.8	15.1	25.7	23.9	197.5	9,846,119	1,160,676	872,314	963,885	595,477	4,049,257	13,314,002	52,887	18.2	18.6	53.1	0.2422
Aurora	286.8	10.4	17.2	24.0	21.0	109.0	3,889,713	531,245	378,269	566,166	225,882	1,236,463	5,874,943	47,398	20.7	21.5	46.0	0.1076
DENVER	568.5	11.1	19.9	22.1	25.1	243.7	9,287,630	1,235,129	1,270,413	730,810	755,362	1,701,220	13,899,851	42,540	21.6	18.4	41.0	0.2474
•Denver	568.5	11.1	19.9	22.1	25.1	243.7	9,275,551	1,224,988	1,269,426	730,810	755,362	1,700,815	13,899,851	42,540	21.6	18.4	41.0	0.2474
DOUGLAS	203.7	4.9	15.9	29.6	18.0	69.6	2,725,601	517,182	250,871	294,714	289,389	355,394	5,147,699	59,715	10.9	18.2	64.7	0.0851
JEFFERSON	542.0	8.3	13.2	26.8	26.5	212.9	7,332,648	1,117,112	467,182	1,209,281	492,731	1,795,405	13,763,828	54,470	16.4	18.6	55.1	0.2282
Arvada	104.0	8.0	11.9	25.9	28.1	40.0	1,007,245	224,707	79,597	133,524	60,181	74,965	2,332,241	51,557	18.1	19.3	51.8	0.0376
Lakewood	148.0	9.9	15.2	24.1	28.8	62.3	2,065,827	297,529	149,068	292,832	124,879	567,796	3,451,207	46,782	20.8	21.1	45.2	0.0599
DENVER-BOULDER-GREELEY CONSOLIDATED AREA	2,695.8	10.0	15.9	24.9	23.6	1,044.7	40,882,936	5,939,206	3,929,774	4,267,775	2,809,610	11,246,398	63,170,157	48,397	19.2	19.0	47.9	1.1216

Exhibit 21-6 Estimated Market for Corrugated and Solid Fiber Boxes for Industry Groups, Phoenix, Arizona, Metropolitan Statistical Area

		National Data			Maricopa County	
		(1)	**(2)**	**(3)**	**(4)**	**(5)**
NAICS Code	Major Industry Group	Value of Box Shipments by End Use ($000)*	Employment by Industry Group	Value of Shipments per Employee by Industry Group (1 ÷ 2) ($)	Employment by Industry Group	Estimated Sales in This Market (3 × 4) ($000)
311	Food and kindred products	$586,164	1,578,305	$371	4,973	$1,845
337	Furniture and fixtures	89,341	364,166	245	616	151
327	Stone, clay, and glass products	226,621	548,058	413	1,612	666
331	Primary metal industries	19,611	1,168,110	16	2,889	46
332	Fabricated metal products	130,743	1,062,096	123	2,422	298
333	Machinery (except electrical)	58,834	1,445,558	40	5,568	228
335	Electrical machinery, equipment, and supplies	119,848	1,405,382	85	6,502	553
					Total	$3,787

*Based on data reported in *Fiber Box Industry Statistics,* Fiber Box Association.

furniture and fixture companies, the sales potential in that industry is only about $151,000 (616 employees × $245 per employee). The sum of the estimates for specific industries is the total market potential in that county.

A firm thinking of going into that market would have to estimate the share it could get with its own marketing mix in order to determine its sales forecast. This approach could be used county by county to estimate the potential in many geographic target markets. It could also aid management's control job. If the firm is already in this industry, it can compare its actual sales (by NAICS code) with the potential to see how it's doing. If its typical market share is 10 percent of the market—and it has only 2 to 5 percent of the market in various NAICS submarkets—then it may need to change its marketing mix to get better penetration.

Times series and leading series may help estimate a fluctuating future

Not all past economic or sales behavior can be neatly extended with a straight line or some manipulation. Economic activity has ups and downs, and other uncontrollable factors change. To cope with such variation, statisticians have developed time series analysis techniques. **Time series** are historical records of the fluctuations in economic variables. We can't give a detailed discussion of these techniques here, but note that there are techniques to handle daily, weekly, monthly, seasonal, and annual variations.[4]

All forecasters dream of finding an accurate **leading series**—a time series that changes in the same direction *but ahead of* the series to be forecast. For example, car producers watch trends in the Index of Consumer Sentiment, which is based on regular surveys of consumers' attitudes about their likely future financial security. People are less likely to buy a car or other big-ticket item if they are worried about their future income. As this suggests, a drop in the index usually "leads" a drop in car sales. It is important that there be some logical relation between the leading series and what is being forecast.

No single series has yet been found that leads GDP or other national figures. Lacking such a series, forecasters develop **indices**—statistical combinations of several time series—in an effort to find some time series that will lead the series they're trying to forecast. Government agencies publish some indices of this type. And business publications, like *Business Week* and *The London Financial Times,* publish their own indices.

Kellogg's used market testing to develop a sales forecast and provide evidence to retailers that its new Snack 'Ums would be profitable. Online surveys and concept tests are a faster and less expensive way to develop an initial forecast; however, they are also likely to be less accurate.

PREDICTING FUTURE BEHAVIOR CALLS FOR MORE JUDGMENT AND SOME OPINIONS

These past-extending methods use quantitative data—projecting past experience into the future and assuming that the future will be like the past. But this is risky in competitive markets. Usually, it's desirable to add some judgment to other forecasts before making the final forecast yourself.

Jury of executive opinion adds judgment

One of the oldest and simplest methods of forecasting—the **jury of executive opinion**—combines the opinions of experienced executives, perhaps from marketing, production, finance, purchasing, and top management. Each executive estimates market potential and sales for the *coming years*. Then they try to work out a consensus.

The main advantage of the jury approach is that it can be done quickly and easily. On the other hand, the results may not be very good. There may be too much extending of the past. Some of the executives may have little contact with outside market influences. But their estimates could point to major shifts in customer demand or competition.

Estimates from salespeople can help too

Using salespeople's estimates to forecast is like the jury approach. But salespeople are more likely than home office managers to be familiar with customer reactions and what competitors are doing. Their estimates are especially useful in some business markets where the few customers may be well known to the salespeople. But this approach may be useful in any type of market.

However, managers who use estimates from salespeople should be aware of the limitations. For example, new salespeople may not know much about their markets. Even experienced salespeople may not be aware of possible changes in the economic climate or the firm's other environments. And if salespeople think the manager is going to use the estimates to set sales quotas, the estimates may be low!

Surveys, panels, and market tests

Special surveys of final buyers, retailers, or wholesalers can show what's happening in different market segments. Some firms use panels of stores—or final consumers—to keep track of buying behavior and to decide when just extending past behavior isn't enough.

Surveys are sometimes combined with market tests when the company wants to estimate customers' reactions to possible changes in its marketing mix. A market test might show that a product increased its share of the market by 10 percent when its price was dropped 1 cent below competition. But this extra business might be quickly lost if the price were increased 1 cent above competition. Such market experiments help the marketing manager make good estimates of future sales when one or more of the four Ps is changed.

Accuracy depends on the marketing mix

Forecasting can help a marketing manager estimate the size of possible market opportunities. But the accuracy of any sales forecast depends on whether the firm selects and implements a marketing mix that turns these opportunities into sales and profits.[5]

ANALYSIS OF COSTS AND SALES CAN GUIDE PLANNING

Once a manager has narrowed down to a few reasonable marketing mixes and the relevant forecasts, comparing the sales, costs, and profitability of the different alternatives helps in selecting the marketing mix the firm will implement.

Estimate the cost of each activity

Estimating the costs of the marketing activities for a strategy may be easy or hard depending on the situation. Sometimes the accounting department can help with information about what average costs for similar activities have been in the past. Or sometimes estimates of competitors' costs—perhaps pulled out of annual reports or investor information posted on the Internet—can provide some guidance. However, in general the best approach for estimating costs is to use the task method. We recommended this approach in Chapter 14 when we focused on promotion costs and budgets. However, the same ideas apply to any area of marketing activity. The estimated cost and budget for each activity is based on the job to be done—perhaps the number of salespeople needed to call on new customers or the amount of inventory required to provide some distribution customer service level. The costs of these individual tasks are then totaled—to determine how much should be budgeted for the

A marketing plan spells out the detailed costs of different marketing activities in the strategy. For example, Hershey used print ads and free coupons to help introduce its Reese's FastBreak candy bar. The plan would include an estimate of the cost of the ads and the cost of the coupon program, including the cost of the free products. Similarly, strategy for Coke that included a price-off coupon for use in Eckerd/Genovese stores might include an estimate of any discount offered to the drugstore chain as an incentive to handle the coupon promotion.

Exhibit 21-7 A Spreadsheet Comparing the Estimated Sales, Costs, and Profits of
Four "Reasonable" Alternative Marketing Mixes

Marketing Mix	Price	Selling Cost	Advertising Cost	Total Units	Sales Revenue	Total Cost	Total Profit
A	$15	$20,000	$5,000	5,000	$75,000	$70,000	$5,000
B	$15	$20,000	$20,000	7,000	$105,000	$95,000	$10,000
C	$20	$30,000	$30,000	7,000	$140,000	$115,000	$25,000
D	$20	$40,000	$40,000	5,000	$125,000	$125,000	$0

overall plan. With this detailed approach, the firm can subsequently assemble its overall marketing budget directly from individual plans rather than just relying on historical patterns or ratios.

Compare the profitability of alternative strategies

Once costs and revenue for possible strategies are estimated, it makes sense to compare them with respect to overall profitability. Exhibit 21-7 shows such a comparison for a small appliance currently selling for $15—Mix A in the example. Here the marketing manager simply estimates the costs and likely results of four reasonable alternatives. And assuming profit is the objective *and* there are adequate resources to consider each of the alternatives, Marketing Mix C is obviously the best alternative.

Spreadsheet analysis speeds through calculations

Comparing the alternatives in Exhibit 21-7 is quite simple. But sometimes marketing managers need much more detail to evaluate a plan. Hundreds of calculations may be required to see how specific marketing resources relate to expected outcomes—like total costs, expected sales, and profit. To make that part of the planning job simpler and faster, marketing managers often use spreadsheet analysis. With **spreadsheet analysis,** costs, sales, and other information related to a problem are organized into a data table—a spreadsheet—to show how changing the value of one or more of the numbers affects the other numbers. This is possible because the relationships among the variables are programmed into the computer software. The table in Exhibit 21-7 was prepared using Excel, Microsoft's widely used spreadsheet program.

A spreadsheet helps answer what–if questions

Spreadsheet analysis allows the marketing manager to evaluate what-if type questions. For example, a marketing manager might be interested in the question, "What if I charge a higher price and the number of units sold stays the same? What will happen to profit?" To look at how a spreadsheet program might be used to help answer this what-if question, let's take a closer look at Mix C in Exhibit 21-7. The table involves a number of relationships. For example, price times total units equals sales revenue; and sales revenue minus total cost equals total profit. If these relationships are programmed into the spreadsheet, a marketing manager can ask questions like: "What if I raise the price to $20.20 and still sell 7,000

Exhibit 21-8   A Spreadsheet Analysis Showing How a Change in Price Affects Sales Revenue and Profit (based on Marketing Mix C from Exhibit 21-7)

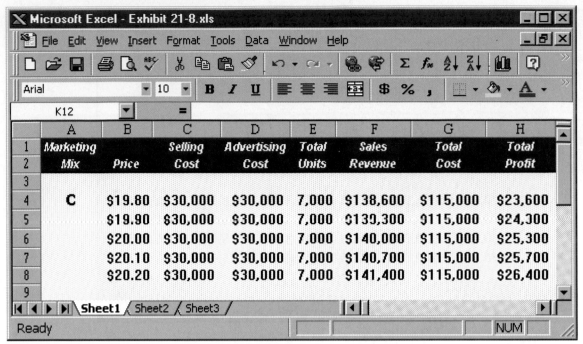

Marketing Mix	Price	Selling Cost	Advertising Cost	Total Units	Sales Revenue	Total Cost	Total Profit
C	$19.80	$30,000	$30,000	7,000	$138,600	$115,000	$23,600
	$19.90	$30,000	$30,000	7,000	$139,300	$115,000	$24,300
	$20.00	$30,000	$30,000	7,000	$140,000	$115,000	$25,300
	$20.10	$30,000	$30,000	7,000	$140,700	$115,000	$25,700
	$20.20	$30,000	$30,000	7,000	$141,400	$115,000	$26,400

units? What will happen to profit?" To get the answer, all the manager needs to do is type the new price in the spreadsheet and the program computes the new profit—$26,400.

In addition, the manager may also want to do many what-if analyses—for example, to see how sales and profit change over a range of prices. Computerized spreadsheet analysis does this quickly and easily. If the manager wants to see what happens to total revenue as the price varies between some minimum (say, $19.80) and a maximum (say, $20.20), the program can show the sales revenue and total profit for a number of price levels in the range from $19.80 to $20.20. The results are shown in the Excel spreadsheet table in Exhibit 21-8.

In a problem like this, the marketing manager might be able to do the same calculations quickly by hand. But with more complicated problems, the spreadsheet program can be a big help, making it very convenient to more carefully analyze different alternatives.

THE MARKETING PLAN BRINGS ALL THE DETAILS TOGETHER

Marketing plan provides a blueprint for implementation

Once the manager has selected the target market, decided on the (integrated) marketing mix to meet that target market's needs, and developed estimates of the costs and revenue for that strategy, it's time to put it all together in the marketing plan. The plan basically serves as a blueprint for what the firm will do.

Exhibit 21-9 provides a summary outline of the different sections of a complete marketing plan. You can see that this outline is basically an abridged overview of the topics we've covered throughout the text and highlighted in this chapter. Thus, you can flesh out your thinking for any portion of a marketing plan by reviewing the section of the book where that topic is discussed in more detail. Further, the Maytag case at the beginning of this chapter also gives you a real example of the types of thinking and detail that are included.

Marketing plan spells out the timing of the strategy

Some time schedule is implicit in any strategy. A marketing plan simply spells out this time period and the time-related details. Usually, we think in terms of some reasonable length of time—such as six months, a year, or a few years. But it might be only a month or two in some cases, especially when rapid changes in fashion or technology are important. Or a strategy might be implemented over several years, perhaps the length of a product life cycle or at least the early stages of the product's life.

Although the outline in Exhibit 21-9 does not explicitly show a place for the time frame for the plan or the specific costs for each decision area, these should be included in the plan—along with expected estimates of sales and profit—so that the plan can be compared with *actual performance* in the future. In other words, the plan not only makes it clear to everyone what is to be accomplished and how—it also provides a basis for the control process after the plan is implemented.

Tools help set time-related details for the plan

Figuring out and planning the time-related details and schedules for all of the activities in the marketing plan can be a challenge, especially if the plan involves a big start-from-scratch effort. To do a better job in this area, many managers have turned to flowcharting techniques such as CPM (critical path method) or PERT (program evaluation and review technique). These methods were originally developed as part of the U.S. space program (NASA) to ensure that the various contractors and subcontractors stayed on schedule and reached their goals as planned. PERT, CPM, and other similar project management approaches are even more popular now since inexpensive programs for personal computers make them easier and faster to use. Updating is easier too.

The computer programs develop detailed flowcharts to show which marketing activities must be done in sequence and which can be done concurrently. These charts also show the time needed for various activities. Totaling the time allotments along the various chart paths shows the most critical (the longest) path—as well as the best starting and ending dates for the various activities.

Flowcharting is not complicated. Basically, it requires that all the activities—which have to be performed anyway—be identified ahead of time and their probable duration and sequence shown on one diagram. (It uses nothing more than addition and subtraction.) Working with such information should be part of the planning function anyway. Then the chart can be used later to guide implementation and control.[6]

A complete plan spells out the reasons for decisions

The plan outline shown in Exhibit 21-9 is quite complete. It doesn't just provide information about marketing mix decisions—it also includes information about customers (including segmenting dimensions), competitors' strategies, other aspects of the marketing environment, and the company's objectives and resources. This material provides important background information relevant to the "why" of the marketing mix and target market decisions.

Too often, managers do not include this information; their plans just lay out the details of the target market and the marketing mix strategy decisions. This shortcut approach is more common when the plan is really just an update of a strategy that has been in place for some time. However, that approach can be risky.

Managers too often make the mistake of casually updating plans in minor ways—perhaps just changing some costs or sales forecasts—but otherwise sticking with what was done in the past. A big problem with this approach is that it's easy to lose sight of why those strategy decisions were made in the first place. When the market situation changes, the original reasons may no longer apply. Yet if the logic for those strategy decisions is not retained, it's easy to miss changes taking place that should result in a plan being reconsidered. For example, a plan that was established in the growth stage of the product life cycle may have been very successful for a number of years. But a marketing manager can't be complacent and assume that success will continue forever. When market maturity hits, the firm may be in for

Exhibit 21-9 Summary Outline of Different Sections of Marketing Plan

Name of Product-Market

Major screening criteria relevant to product-market opportunity selected
    Quantitative (ROI, profitability, risk level, etc.)
    Qualitative (nature of business preferred, social responsibility, etc.)
    Major constraints

Analysis of Other Aspects of External Market Environment (favorable and unfavorable factors and trends)

Economic environment
Technological environment
Political and legal environment
Cultural and social environment

Customer Analysis (organizational and/or final consumer)

Possible segmenting dimensions (customer needs, other characteristics)
    Identification of qualifying dimensions and determining dimensions
Identification of target market(s) (one or more specific segments)
    Operational characteristics (demographics, geographic locations, etc.)
    Potential size (number of people, dollar purchase potential, etc.) and likely growth
Key psychological and social influences on buying
Type of buying situation
Nature of relationship with customers

Competitor Analysis

Nature of current/likely competition
Current and prospective competitors (or rivals)
    Current strategies and likely responses to plan
Competitive barriers to overcome and sources of potential competitive advantage

Company Analysis

Company objectives and overall marketing objectives
Company resources
S.W.O.T.: Identification of major *s*trengths, *w*eaknesses, *o*pportunities, and *t*hreats (based on above analyses of company resources, customers, competitors, and other aspects of external market environment)

Marketing Information Requirements

Marketing research needs (with respect to customers, marketing mix effectiveness, external environment, etc.)
Secondary data and primary data needs
Marketing information system needs, models to be used, etc.

Product

Product class (type of consumer or business product)
Current product life cycle stage
New-product development requirements (people, dollars, time, etc.)
    Product liability, safety and social responsibility considerations
Specification of core physical good or service
    Features, quality, etc.
Supporting customer service(s) needed
Warranty (what is covered, timing, who will support, etc.)
Branding (manufacturer versus dealer, family brand versus individual brand, etc.)
Packaging
    Promotion and labeling needs
    Protection needs
Cultural sensitivity of product
Fit with product line

Place

Objectives
    Degree of market exposure required
    Distribution customer service level required
Type of channel (direct, indirect)
    Other channel members or facilitators required
    Type/number of wholesalers (agent, merchant, etc.)
    Type/number of retailers

(continued)

Exhibit 21-9 Summary Outline of Different Sections of Marketing Plan

Place (continued)

How discrepancies and separations will be handled

How marketing functions will be shared

Coordination needed in company, channel, and supply chain

Information requirements (EDI, the Internet, e-mail, etc.)

Transportation requirements

Inventory product-handling requirements

Facilities required (warehousing, distribution centers, etc.)

Reverse channels (for returns, recalls, etc.)

Promotion

Objectives

Major message theme(s) for integrated marketing communications (desired "positioning")

Promotion blend

Advertising (type, media, copy thrust, etc.)

Personal selling (type and number of salespeople, how compensated, how effort will be allocated, etc.)

Sales promotion (for channel members, customers, employees)

Publicity

Interactive media

Mix of push and pull required

Who will do the work

Price

Nature of demand (price sensitivity, price of substitutes)

Demand and cost analyses (marginal analysis)

Markup chain in channel

Price flexibility

Price level(s) (under what conditions) and impact on customer value

Adjustments to list price (geographic terms, discounts, allowances, etc.)

Special Implementation Problems to Be Overcome

People required

Manufacturing, financial, and other resources needed

Control

Marketing information system needs

Criterion measures comparison with objectives (customer satisfaction, sales, cost, performance analysis, etc.)

Forecasts and Estimates

Costs (all elements in plan, over time)

Sales (by market, over time, etc.)

Estimated operating statement (pro forma)

Timing

Specific sequence of activities and events, etc.

Likely changes over the product life cycle

big trouble—unless the basic strategy and plan are modified. If a plan spells out the details of the market analysis and logic for the marketing mix and target market selected, then it is a simple matter to routinely check and update it. Remember: The idea is for all of the analysis and strategy decisions to fit together as an integrated whole. Thus, as some of the elements of the plan or marketing environment change, the whole plan may need a fresh approach.

INTERNET EXERCISE

Go to the Maytag website (www.maytag.com) and review the information about the Neptune line. Do you see any indication that the strategy for Neptune is changing from what is described in the case that introduces this chapter? Explain your point of view.

Land Rover's billboard ad is only one element of a comprehensive market plan, but it cleverly reinforces Land Rover's positioning as a go-anywhere, off-road vehicle that drives like a car.

COMPANIES PLAN AND IMPLEMENT WHOLE MARKETING PROGRAMS

Several plans make a program

Most companies implement more than one marketing plan at the same time. A *marketing program* blends all a firm's marketing plans into one big plan.

When the various plans in the company's program are different, managers may be less concerned with how well the plans fit together—except as they compete for the firm's usually limited financial resources.

When the plans are more similar, however, the same sales force may be expected to carry out several plans. Or the firm's advertising department may develop the publicity and advertising for several plans. In these cases, product managers try to get enough of the common resources, say, salespeople's time, for their own plans.

Since a company's resources are usually limited, the marketing manager must make hard choices. You can't launch plans to pursue every promising opportunity. Instead, limited resources force you to choose among alternative plans while you develop the program.

Finding the best program requires judgment

How do you find the best program? There is no one best way to compare various plans. Managers usually rely on evaluation tools like those discussed in Chapter 4. Even so, much management judgment is usually required. Some calculations are helpful too. If a five-year planning horizon seems realistic for the firm's markets, managers can compare expected profits over the five-year period for each plan.

Assuming the company has a profit-oriented objective, managers can evaluate the more profitable plans first—in terms of both potential profit and resources required. They also need to evaluate a plan's impact on the entire program. One profitable-looking alternative might be a poor first choice if it eats up all the company's resources and sidetracks several plans that together would be more profitable and spread the risks.

Some juggling among the various plans—comparing profitability versus resources needed and available—moves the company toward the most profitable program.

A marketing plan often includes the time-related details for each strategy in the plan. But most companies plan and implement whole marketing programs that are comprised of many different marketing plans. So all of a firm's products and strategies need to work together as part of the overall marketing program.

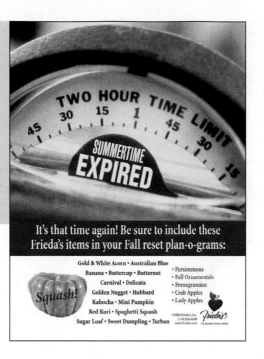

This is another area where spreadsheet analysis can help the manager evaluate a large number of alternatives.[7]

PLANNING FOR INVOLVEMENT IN INTERNATIONAL MARKETING

When developing a plan for international markets, marketing managers must decide how involved the firm will be. We will discuss six basic kinds of involvement: exporting, licensing, contract manufacturing, management contracting, joint venturing, and wholly owned subsidiaries.

Exporting often comes first

Some companies get into international marketing just by **exporting**—selling some of what the firm produces to foreign markets. Some firms start exporting just to get rid of surplus output. For others, exporting comes from a real effort to look for new opportunities.

Some firms try exporting without doing much planning. They don't change the product or even the service or instruction manuals! As a result, some early efforts are not very satisfying—to buyers or sellers.[8]

Specialists can help develop the plan

Exporting does require knowledge about the foreign market. But managers who don't have enough knowledge to plan the details of a program can often get expert help from middlemen specialists. As we discussed in Chapter 13, export agents can handle the arrangements as products are shipped outside the country. Then agents or merchant wholesalers can handle the importing details. Even large producers with many foreign operations turn to international middlemen for some products or markets. Such middlemen know how to handle the sometimes confusing formalities and specialized functions. A manager trying to develop a plan alone can make a small mistake that ties products up at national borders for days or months.[9]

Exporting doesn't have to involve permanent relationships. Of course, channel relationships take time to build and shouldn't be treated lightly—sales reps' contacts

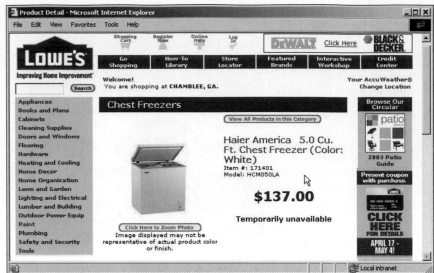

To establish a presence more quickly in the United States, Haier of China has entered joint ventures with several American retailers, including Wal-Mart, Home Depot, Lowe's, Target, and Best Buy.

in foreign countries are investments. But it's relatively easy to cut back on these relationships, or even drop them, if the plan doesn't work.

Some firms, on the other hand, plan more formal and permanent relationships with nationals in foreign countries. The relationships might involve licensing, contract manufacturing, management contracting, and joint venturing.

Licensing is an easy way

Licensing is a relatively easy way to enter foreign markets. **Licensing** means selling the right to use some process, trademark, patent, or other right for a fee or royalty. The licensee takes most of the risk because it must invest some capital to use the right. Further, the licensee usually does most of the planning for the markets it is licensed to serve. If good partners are available, this can be an effective way to enter a market. Gerber entered the Japanese baby food market this way but exports to other countries.[10]

Contract manufacturing takes care of the production problems

Contract manufacturing means turning over production to others while retaining the marketing process. Sears used this approach when it opened stores in Latin America and Spain. This approach doesn't make it any easier to plan the marketing program, but it may make it a lot easier to implement.

For example, this approach can be especially desirable where labor relations are difficult or where there are problems obtaining supplies or government cooperation. Growing nationalistic feelings may make this approach more attractive in the future.

Management contracting sells know-how

Management contracting means the seller provides only management skills—others own the production and distribution facilities. Some mines and oil refineries are operated this way—and Hilton operates hotels all over the world for local owners. This is a relatively low-risk approach to international marketing. The company makes no commitment to fixed facilities, which can be taken over or damaged in riots or wars. If conditions get too bad, key management people can fly off on the next plane and leave the nationals to manage the operation.

Joint venturing is more involved

Joint venturing means a domestic firm entering into a partnership with a foreign firm. As with any partnership, there can be honest disagreements over objectives—for example, how much profit is desired and how fast it should be paid out—as well as operating policies. Where a close working relationship can be developed—perhaps based on one firm's technical and marketing know-how and the foreign partner's knowledge of the market and political connections—this approach can be very attractive to both parties.

In some situations, a joint venture is the only type of involvement possible. For example, financial services firms like J.P. Morgan Chase and ING Investment Management are interested in opportunities in China because it is likely to become Asia's largest market for financial services. However, the Chinese government has said that starting in 2004 a Western bank may own no more than 49 percent of an investment bank or a money management firm in China. A big firm like J.P. Morgan Chase might prefer to have complete control, but it also doesn't want to stand by and watch competitors take the market. So for now, the logical way to enter the market is with a minority share in a joint venture with a Chinese firm.[11]

A joint venture usually requires a big commitment from both parties—and they both must agree on a joint plan. When the relationship doesn't work out well, the ensuing nightmare can make the manager wish that the venture had been planned as a wholly owned operation. But the terms of the joint venture may block this for years.[12]

Wholly owned subsidiaries give more control

When a firm thinks a foreign market looks really promising, it may want to take the final step. A **wholly owned subsidiary** is a separate firm—owned by a parent company. This gives the firm complete control of the marketing plan and operations, and also helps a foreign branch work more easily with the rest of the company. If a firm has too much capacity in a country with low production costs, for example, it can move some production there from other plants and then export to countries with higher production costs.

Multinational corporations evolve to meet the challenge

As firms become more involved in international marketing, some begin to see themselves as worldwide businesses that transcend national boundaries. These **multinational corporations** have a direct investment in several countries and run their businesses depending on the choices available anywhere in the world. Well-known U.S.-based multinational firms include Coca-Cola, Eastman Kodak, Ford, and IBM. They regularly earn over a third of their total sales or profits abroad. And well-known foreign-based multinationals—such as Nestlé, Unilever, Sony, and Honda—have well-accepted brands all around the world.

Internet websites that specialize by product-market and that bring together producers, intermediaries, and customers are quickly creating new types of international relationships and opportunities.

These multinational operations no longer just export or import. They hire local workers and build local plants. They have relationships with local businesses and politicians. These powerful organizations learn to plan marketing strategies that deal with nationalistic feelings and typical border barriers, treating them simply as part of the marketing environment. We don't yet have one world politically, but business is moving in that direction. We may have to develop new kinds of corporations and laws to govern multinational operations. In the future, it will make less and less sense for business and politics to be limited by national boundaries.

Planning for international markets

Usually marketing managers must plan the firm's overall marketing program so it's flexible enough to be adapted for differences in various countries. When the differences are significant, top management should delegate a great deal of responsibility for strategy planning to local managers (or even middlemen). In many cases, it's not possible to develop a detailed plan without a local feel. In extreme cases, local managers may not even be able to fully explain some parts of their plans because they're based on subtle cultural differences. Then plans must be judged only by their results. The organizational setup should give these managers a great deal of freedom in their planning but ensure tight control against the plans they develop. Top management can simply insist that managers stick to their budgets and meet the plans that they themselves create. When a firm reaches this stage, it is being managed like a well-organized domestic corporation—which insists that its managers (of divisions and territories) meet their own plans so that the whole company's program works as intended.[13]

CONCLUSION

In this chapter, we stressed the importance of developing whole marketing mixes—not just developing policies for the individual four Ps and hoping they will fit together into some logical whole. The marketing manager is responsible for developing a workable blend—integrating all of a firm's efforts into a coordinated whole that makes effective use of the firm's resources and guides it toward its objectives.

As a starting place for developing new marketing mixes, a marketing manager can use the product classes that have served as a thread through this text. Even if the manager can't fully describe the needs and attitudes of target markets, it is usually possible to select the appropriate product class for a particular product. This, in turn, will help set Place and Promotion policies. It may also clarify what type of marketing mix is typical for the product. However, just doing what is typical may not give a firm any competitive advantage. Creative strategies are often the ones that identify new and better ways of uniquely giving target customers what they want or need. Similarly, seeing where a firm's offering fits in the product life cycle helps to clarify how current marketing mixes are likely to change in the future.

Developing and evaluating marketing strategies and plans usually requires that the manager use some approach to forecasting. We talked about two basic approaches to forecasting market potential and sales: (1) extending past behavior and (2) predicting future behavior. The most common approach is to extend past behavior into the future. This gives reasonably good results if market conditions are fairly stable. Methods here include extension of past sales data and the factor method. We saw that projecting the past into the future is risky when big market changes are likely. To make up for this possible weakness, marketers predict future behavior using their own experience and judgment. They also bring in the judgment of others, using the jury of executive opinion method and salespeople's estimates. And they may use surveys, panels, and market tests. Of course, any sales forecast depends on the marketing mix the firm actually selects.

Once forecasts of the expected sales and estimates of the associated costs for possible strategies are available, alternatives can be compared on potential profitability. Spreadsheet analysis software is an important tool for such comparisons. In the same vein, project planning approaches, such as CPM and PERT, can help the marketing manager do a better job in planning the time-related details for the strategy that is selected.

Throughout the text, we've emphasized the importance of marketing strategy planning. In this chapter, we went on to show that the marketing manager must develop a marketing plan for carrying out each strategy and then merge a set of plans into a marketing program.

Finally, we discussed different approaches that are helpful in planning strategies to enter international markets. The different approaches have different strengths and weaknesses.

KEY TERMS

QUESTIONS AND PROBLEMS

1. Distinguish clearly between a marketing strategy, a marketing plan, and a marketing program.

2. Discuss how a marketing manager could go about choosing among several possible marketing plans, given that choices must be made because of limited resources. Would the job be easier in the consumer product or in the business product area? Why?

3. Explain how understanding the product classes can help a marketing manager develop a marketing strategy for a really new product that is unlike anything currently available.

4. Distinguish between competitive marketing mixes and superior mixes that lead to breakthrough opportunities.

5. Explain the difference between a forecast of market potential and a sales forecast.

6. Suggest a plausible explanation for sales fluctuations for (a) computers, (b) ice cream, (c) washing machines, (d) tennis rackets, (e) oats, (f) disposable diapers, and (g) latex for rubber-based paint.

7. Explain the factor method of forecasting. Illustrate your answer.

8. Based on data in Exhibit 21-5, discuss the relative market potential of the city of Boulder, Colorado, and the city of Lakewood, Colorado, for (a) prepared cereals, (b) automobiles, and (c) furniture.

9. Why is spreadsheet analysis a popular tool for marketing strategy planning?

10. In your own words, explain how a project management technique such as PERT or CPM can help a marketing manager develop a better marketing plan.

11. Why should a complete marketing plan include details concerning the reasons for the marketing strategy decisions and not just the marketing activities central to the four Ps?

12. Consider how the marketing manager's job becomes more complex when it's necessary to develop and plan *several* strategies as part of a marketing program. Be sure to discuss how the manager might have to handle different strategies at different stages in the product life cycle. To make your discussion more concrete, consider the job of a marketing manager for a sporting goods manufacturer.

13. How would marketing planning be different for a firm that has entered foreign marketing with a joint venture and a firm that has set up a wholly owned subsidiary?

14. How can a firm set the details of its marketing plan when it has little information about a foreign market it wants to enter?

15. Review the Maytag case at the beginning of this chapter and the outline of a marketing plan in Exhibit 21-9. Indicate which sections of the plan would probably require the most change as the competition among high-efficiency, front-load washing machines significantly increases. Briefly explain your thinking.

SUGGESTED CASES

WHEN YOU FINISH THIS
CHAPTER, YOU SHOULD

1. Understand why marketing must be evaluated differently at the micro and macro levels.

2. Understand why the text argues that micro-marketing costs too much.

3. Understand why the text argues that macro-marketing does not cost too much.

4. Know some of the challenges marketers face as they work to develop ethical marketing strategies that serve consumers' needs.

CHAPTER TWENTY-TWO

Ethical Marketing in a Consumer-Oriented World: Appraisal and Challenges

More than ever, the macro-marketing systems of the world are interconnected. The worldwide drive toward market-directed economies is dramatic evidence that consumer-citizens want freedom and choices not only in politics but in markets. Centrally planned economies simply weren't able to meet needs. Even in China, government officials have been gradually softening their hard line on central planning and allowing Western firms to sell products that will improve the life of Chinese consumers.

Although there's much talk about the world as a global village, we're not there yet. Someone in a real village on the plains of Kenya may be able to try a cell phone or watch a TV and get a glimpse of the quality of life that consumers in the advanced Western

economies enjoy, but for that person it doesn't seem real. What is real is the struggle to meet the basic physical needs of life—to survive starvation, malnutrition, and epidemic-carrying water. The plight of consumers doesn't seem quite as severe in the emerging democracies, like those in Eastern Europe. But the vast majority of citizen-consumers in those societies can still only wonder if they'll ever have choices among a wide variety of goods and services—and the income to buy them—that most consumers take for granted in the United States, Canada, England, most countries in Western Europe, Australia, and a few other advanced economies.

The challenges faced by consumers, and marketing managers, in the advanced economies seem minor by contrast. In England, for example, some consumers who live in villages that are off the beaten path may need to worry that they are not included in the 96 percent of the British population served by Tesco delivery vans. Tesco, the largest supermarket chain in England, created its online shopping service for groceries (and hundreds of other products) just a few years ago, but now its fleet of vans make over 100,000 deliveries a week.

If online shopping for groceries has had a slower start in the U.S., it just may be because many Americans are more interested in instant gratification. We expect the corner convenience store to have a nice selection of frozen gourmet dinners that we can prepare in minutes in a microwave oven. Or perhaps that's too much hassle. After all, Domino's will deliver a hot pizza in less than 30 minutes. And McDonald's has our McGriddles ready when we pull up at the drive-thru at 7 in the morning. In a relative sense, few of the world's consumers can expect so much, and get so much of what they expect.

But is it a good thing that firms give us what we want? For example, there is national attention to problems of obesity. Many nutritionists and public-health officials point the finger of blame at food processors and fast food. When a group of obese teenagers sued McDonald's, claiming that it made them fat, the widely publicized case was fodder for jokes on late-night TV shows. But fast-food companies are not laughing. The judge threw out the case but left open the door for future suits. Some legal experts say that this is just the beginning of legal actions—and they draw the parallel with suits against tobacco companies 30 years ago. Many fast-food companies are scrambling to add salads and other low-fat fare to their menus. But should consumers have the right to chose high-fat foods if that is what they want?

When you think about the contrast between problems of starvation and too much fast food, it's not hard to decide which consumers are better off. But is that just a straw man comparison? Is the situation in the less-developed nations one extreme, with the system in the United States and similar societies just as extreme—only in a different way? Would we be better off if we didn't put quite so much emphasis on marketing? Do we need so many brands of products? Does all the money spent on advertising really help consumers? Should we expect to be able to get fast food any hour of the day—or order groceries over the Internet and have a van deliver them to the front door? Or, conversely, do all of these choices just increase the prices consumers pay without really adding anything of value? More generally, does marketing serve society well?

That question is what this chapter is about. Now that you have a better understanding of what marketing is all about, and how the marketing manager contributes to the macro-marketing process, you should be able to decide whether marketing costs too much.[1]

HOW SHOULD MARKETING BE EVALUATED?

We must evaluate at two levels

As we saw in Chapter 1, it's useful to distinguish between two levels of marketing: the *micro* level (how individual firms run) and the *macro* level (how the whole system works). Some complaints against marketing are aimed at only one of these levels at a time. In other cases, the criticism *seems* to be directed to one level but actually is aimed at the other. Some critics of specific ads, for example, probably wouldn't be satisfied with *any* advertising. When evaluating marketing, we must treat each of these levels separately.

Nation's objectives affect evaluation

Different nations have different social and economic objectives. Dictatorships, for example, may be mainly concerned with satisfying the needs of society as seen by the political elite. In a socialist state, the objective might be to satisfy society's needs as defined by government planners. In a society that has recently broken the chains of communism, the objective may be to make the transition to a market-directed economy as quickly as possible—before there are more revolts.

Consumer satisfaction is the objective in the United States

In the United States, *the basic objective of our market-directed economic system has been to satisfy consumer needs as they, the consumers, see them.* This objective implies that political freedom and economic freedom go hand in hand and that citizens in a free society have the right to live as they choose. The majority of American consumers would be unwilling to give up the freedom of choice they now enjoy. The same can be said for Canada, Great Britain, and most other countries in the European Union. However, for focus we will concentrate on marketing as it exists in American society.

Therefore, let's try to evaluate the operation of marketing in the American economy—where the present objective is to satisfy consumer needs *as consumers see them.* This is the essence of our system.

1. *Video:* An office. People at work.

2. *Audio* (MVO): "If you are now waiting for something amusing to happen, ..."

3. "... you'll be disappointed. A bank is not a theater."

4. *Video* (cut): Under one of the desks a cat is napping.
Audio (MVO): "Rikk Bank. The most boring bank in the world."

5. *Video:* Cut to view of the whole office.
Audio (MVO): "The people are working. The money is working."

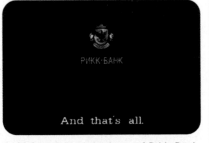

6. *Video:* Cut to the logo of Rikk Bank.
Audio (MVO): "And that's all."

In the U.S., banks provide all kinds of special services to meet customer expectations. In Russia, consumer expectations about banks are different, so Rikk uses TV ads to emphasize that it's not going to do anything unusual, it's just going to be a solid bank.

CAN CONSUMER SATISFACTION BE MEASURED?

Since consumer satisfaction is our objective, marketing's effectiveness must be measured by *how well* it satisfies consumers. There have been various efforts to measure overall consumer satisfaction not only in the United States but also in other countries. For example, a team of researchers at the University of Michigan has created the American Customer Satisfaction Index based on regular interviews with thousands of customers of about 200 companies and 39 industries. Similar studies are available for member countries of the European Union.

Satisfaction depends on individual aspirations

This sort of index makes it possible to track changes in consumer satisfaction measures over time and even allows comparison among countries. That's potentially useful. Yet there are limits to interpreting any measure of consumer satisfaction when we try to evaluate macro-marketing effectiveness in any absolute sense. One basic issue is that satisfaction depends on and is *relative to* your level of aspiration or expectation. Less prosperous consumers begin to expect more out of an economy as they see the higher living standards of others. Also, aspiration levels tend to rise with repeated successes and fall with failures. Products considered satisfactory one day may not be satisfactory the next day, or vice versa. A decade ago, most people were satisfied with a 21-inch color TV that pulled in three or four channels. But once you become accustomed to a large-screen model and enjoy all the options possible with a digital satellite receiver or a DVD, that old TV is never the same again. And when high-definition digital TVs and interactive broadcast systems become more widespread, today's most satisfying units won't seem quite so acceptable.

In addition, consumer satisfaction is a highly personal concept—and looking at the "average" satisfaction of a whole society does not provide a complete picture for evaluating macro-marketing effectiveness. At a minimum, some consumers are more

Planetfeedback.com is a website that makes it easy for consumers to give feedback to companies. Of course, some feedback is clear from customers' choices in the marketplace. For example, Country Inns & Suites by Carlson has gained positive feedback by providing customers with a satisfying experience at an affordable price. J. D. Power and Associates ranked it "Highest in Guest Satisfaction among Mid-Price Hotel Chains with Limited Service."

satisfied than others. So although efforts to measure satisfaction are useful, any evaluation of macro-marketing effectiveness has to be largely subjective.

Probably the supreme test is whether the macro-marketing system satisfies enough individual consumer-citizens so that they vote—at the ballot box—to keep it running. So far, we've done so in the United States.[2]

There are many measures of micro-marketing effectiveness

Measuring micro-marketing effectiveness is also difficult, but it can be done. Expectations may change just as other aspects of the marketing environment change—so firms have to do a good job of coping with the change. Individual business firms can and should try to measure how well their marketing mixes satisfy their customers (or why they fail). In fact, most large firms now have some type of ongoing effort to determine whether they're satisfying their target markets. For example, the J. D. Power marketing research firm is well known for its studies of consumer satisfaction with different makes of automobiles and computers. And the American Customer Satisfaction Index is also used to rate individual companies.

Many large and small firms measure customer satisfaction with attitude research studies. Other widely used methods include comment cards, e-mail response features on websites, unsolicited consumer responses (usually complaints), opinions of middlemen and salespeople, market test results, and profits. Of course, customers may be very satisfied about some aspects of what a firm is doing but dissatisfied about other dimensions of performance.[3]

In our market-directed system, it's up to each customer to decide how effectively individual firms satisfy his or her needs. Usually, customers will buy more of the products that satisfy them—and they'll do it repeatedly. That's why firms that develop really satisfying marketing mixes are able to develop profitable long-term relationships with the customers that they serve. Because efficient marketing plans can increase profits, profits can be used as a rough measure of a firm's efficiency in satisfying customers. Nonprofit organizations have a different bottom line, but they too will fail if they don't satisfy supporters and get the resources they need to continue to operate.

Evaluating marketing effectiveness is difficult, but not impossible

It's easy to see why opinions differ concerning the effectiveness of micro- and macro-marketing. If the objective of the economy is clearly defined, however—and the argument is stripped of emotion—the big questions about marketing effectiveness probably *can* be answered.

In this chapter, we argue that micro-marketing (how individual firms and channels operate) frequently *does* cost too much but that macro-marketing (how the whole marketing system operates) *does not* cost too much, *given the present objective of the American economy—consumer satisfaction.* Don't accept this position as *the* answer but rather as a point of view. In the end, you'll have to make your own judgment.[4]

MICRO-MARKETING OFTEN DOES COST TOO MUCH

Throughout the text, we've explored what marketing managers could or should do to help their firms do a better job of satisfying customers—while achieving company objectives. Many firms implement highly successful marketing programs, but others are still too production-oriented and inefficient. For customers of these latter firms, micro-marketing often does cost too much.

Research shows that many consumers are not satisfied. But you know that already. All of us have had experiences when we weren't satisfied—when some firm didn't deliver on its promises. And the problem is much bigger than some marketers want to believe. Research suggests that the majority of consumer complaints are never reported. Worse, many complaints that are reported never get fully resolved.

The failure rate is high

Further evidence that too many firms are too production-oriented—and not nearly as efficient as they could be—is the fact that so many new products fail. New and old businesses—even ones that in the past were leaders in their markets—fail regularly too.

Generally speaking, marketing inefficiencies are due to one or more of three reasons:

1. Lack of interest in or understanding of the sometimes fickle customer.
2. Improper blending of the four Ps—caused in part by overemphasis on internal problems as contrasted with a customer orientation.
3. Lack of understanding of or adjustment to the marketing environment, especially what competitors do.

Any of these problems can easily be a fatal flaw—the sort of thing that leads to business failures. A firm can't create value if it doesn't have a clue what customers think or say. Even if a firm listens to the "voice of the customer," there's no incentive for the customer to buy if the benefits of the marketing mix don't exceed the costs. And if the firm succeeds in coming up with a marketing mix with benefits greater than costs, it still won't be a superior value unless it's better than what competitors offer.

The high cost of missed opportunities

Another sign of failure is the inability of firms to identify new target markets and new opportunities. A new marketing mix that isn't offered doesn't fail—but the lost opportunity can be significant for both a firm and society. Too many

Maxwell House ready-to-drink coffee came in a package that looked like a milk carton, but it had an inner foil liner that caused problems when consumers heated the carton in a microwave. There was no mention on the package that it might make good iced coffee. Fixing these problems might not have made the product a success, but they certainly contributed to its failure.

managers seize on whatever strategy seems easiest rather than seeking really new ways to satisfy customers. Too many companies stifle really innovative thinking. Layers of bureaucracy and a "that's not the way we do things" mentality just snuff it out.

On the other hand, not every new idea is a good idea for every company. For example, there is no doubt that e-commerce is having a dramatic effect in improving how many firms serve their customers. But hundreds of firms have lost millions of dollars with failed efforts to capitalize on the Internet or some "hot" website idea. Just jumping on the "what's new" bandwagon—without stopping to figure out how it is going to really satisfy the customer and result in profit for the firm—is as much a ticket for failure as being too slow or bureaucratic.

Micro-marketing does cost too much, but things are changing

For reasons like these, marketing does cost too much in many firms. Despite much publicity, the marketing concept is not applied in many places.

But not all firms and marketers deserve criticism. More of them *are* becoming customer-oriented. And many are paying more attention to market-oriented planning to carry out the marketing concept more effectively. Throughout the text, we've highlighted firms and strategies that are making a difference. The successes of innovative firms—like Wal-Mart, 3M, IKEA, JetBlue, Dell, Tesco, UPS, and Schwab—do not go unnoticed. Yes, they make some mistakes. That's human—and marketing is a human enterprise. But they have also showed the results that market-oriented strategy planning can produce.

Another encouraging sign is that more companies are recognizing that they need a diverse set of backgrounds and talents to meet the increasingly varied needs of their increasingly global customers. They're shedding "not-invented-here" biases and embracing new technologies, comparing what they do with the best practices of firms in totally different industries, and teaming up with outside specialists who can bring a fresh perspective.

Managers who adopt the marketing concept as a way of business life do a better job. They look for target market opportunities and carefully blend the elements of the marketing mix to meet their customers' needs. As more of these managers rise in business, we can look forward to much lower micro-marketing costs and strategies that do a better job of satisfying customer needs.

INTERNET EXERCISE

IKEA is an innovative furniture company that is using its website to refine its strategy. It has always relied on information technology to keep costs low by tracking sales at individual stores and using the information to control inventory and reduce shipping costs between the factory, distribution centers, and its massive retail stores. Go to the IKEA website (www.ikea.com). What else does the website tell you about IKEA's strategy? Does the website help IKEA offer superior value? Explain your answer.

MACRO-MARKETING DOES NOT COST TOO MUCH

Some critics of marketing take aim at the macro-marketing system. They typically argue that the macro-marketing system causes a poor use of resources and leads to an unfair distribution of income. Most of these complaints imply that some micro-marketing activities should not be permitted—and because they are, our macro-marketing system does a less-than-satisfactory job. Let's look at some of these positions to help you form your own opinion.

Marketing stimulates innovation and the development of new ways to meet customers' needs. But marketing is also important in a mature product market. For example, firms may continue to improve product quality or promote advantages that already exist to help attract customers away from other brands and satisfy and retain customers the firm already serves.

Micro-efforts help the economy grow

Some critics feel that marketing helps create a monopoly or at least monopolistic competition. Further, they think this leads to higher prices, restricted output, and reduction in national income and employment.

It's true that firms in a market-directed economy try to carve out separate monopolistic markets for themselves with new products. But consumers do have a choice. They don't *have* to buy the new product unless they think it's a better value. The old products are still available. In fact, to meet the new competition, prices of the old products usually drop. And that makes them even more available.

Over several years, the innovator's profits may rise—but rising profits also encourage further innovation by competitors. This leads to new investments, which contribute to economic growth and higher levels of national income and employment. Around the world, many countries failed to achieve their potential for economic growth under centrally planned systems because this type of profit incentive didn't exist. Even now, many of the regulations that are imposed by the developed countries are left over from old ways of thinking and get in the way of progress.

Increased profits also attract competition. Profits then begin to drop as new competitors enter the market and begin producing somewhat similar products. (Recall the rise and fall of industry profit during the product life cycle.)

Is advertising a waste of resources?

Advertising is the most criticized of all micro-marketing activities. Indeed, many ads *are* annoying, insulting, misleading, and downright ineffective. This is one reason why micro-marketing often does cost too much. However, advertising can also make both the micro- and macro-marketing processes work better.

Advertising is an economical way to inform large numbers of potential customers about a firm's products. Provided that a product satisfies customer needs, advertising can increase demand for the product—resulting in economies of scale in manufacturing, distribution, and sales. Because these economies may more than offset advertising costs, advertising can actually *lower* prices to the consumer.[5]

Consumers are not puppets

The idea that firms can manipulate consumers to buy anything the company chooses to produce simply isn't true. A consumer who buys a soft drink that tastes

Some critics argue that people are bombarded with too much advertising. The Cow Placard Company in Switzerland, for example, paints logos and slogans on cows—and then releases them to graze in pastures along Swiss highways. Swiss apparel company Alprausch used this approach and it attracted a lot of attention. Some people thought it was interesting—but there was also negative publicity by animal rights groups.

terrible won't buy another can of that brand, regardless of how much it's advertised. In fact, many new products fail the test of the market. Not even large corporations are assured of success every time they launch a new product. Consider, for example, the dismal fate of Pets.com and eToys.com, Ford's Edsel, Sony's beta format VCRs, Xerox's personal computers, and half of the TV programs put on the air in recent years by CBS. And if powerful corporations know some way to get people to buy products against their will, would companies like Lucent, General Motors, and Eastern Airlines have ever gone through long periods losing hundreds of millions of dollars?

Needs and wants change

Consumer needs and wants change constantly. Few of us would care to live the way our grandparents lived when they were our age. Marketing's job is not just to satisfy consumer wants as they exist at any particular point in time. Rather, marketing must keep looking for new and better ways to create value and serve consumers.[6]

Does marketing make people materialistic?

There is no doubt that marketing caters to materialistic values. However, people disagree as to whether marketing creates these values or simply appeals to values already there.

Even in the most primitive societies, people want to accumulate possessions. Further, the tendency for ancient pharaohs to surround themselves with wealth and treasures can hardly be attributed to the persuasive powers of advertising agencies!

Marketing reflects our own values

Critics say that advertising elevates the wrong values—for example, by relying on sex appeal to get attention and generally sending the signal that what really matters most is self-gratification. Experts who study values seem to agree that, in the short run, marketing reflects social values, while in the long run it enhances and reinforces them. Further, many companies work hard to figure out their customers' beliefs and values. Then they refuse to use ads that would be offensive to their target customers.[7]

Products do improve the quality of life

Clearly, the quality of life can't be measured just in terms of quantities of material goods. But when we view products as the means to an end rather than the end itself, they *do* make it possible to satisfy higher-level needs. Microwave ovens, for example, greatly reduced the amount of time and effort people must spend preparing meals, leaving them free to pursue other interests. The Internet empowers people with information in ways that few could have even imagined a decade ago.

Not all needs are met

Some critics argue that our macro-marketing system is flawed because it does not provide solutions to important problems, such as questions about how to help the homeless, the uneducated, dependent children, minorities who have suffered discrimination, the elderly poor, and the sick. Many of these people do live in dire circumstances. But is that the result of a market-directed system?

There is no doubt that many firms focus their effort on people who can pay for what they have to offer. But as the forces of competition drive down prices, more people are able to afford more of what they need. And the matching of supply and demand stimulates economic growth, creates jobs, and spreads income among more people. In other words, a market-directed economy makes efficient use of resources. However, it can't guarantee that government aid programs are effective. It doesn't ensure that all voters and politicians agree on which problems should be solved first—or how taxes should be set and allocated. It can't eliminate the possibility of a child being ignored.

These are important societal issues. Citizen-consumers in a democratic society assign some responsibilities to business and some to government. Ultimately, consumer-citizens vote in the ballot box for how they want governments to deal with these concerns—just as they vote with their dollars for which firms to support. As more managers in the public sector understand and apply marketing concepts, we should be able to do a better job meeting the needs of all people.

CHALLENGES FACING MARKETERS

We've said that our macro-marketing system does *not* cost too much, given the present objective of our economy. But we admit that the performance of many business firms leaves a lot to be desired. This presents a challenge to serious-minded students and marketers. What needs to be done—if anything?

Change is the only thing that's constant

We need better marketing performance at the micro level. Progressive firms pay attention to changes in the market—including trends in the marketing environment—and how marketing strategies need to be improved to consider these changes. Exhibit 22-1 lists some of the important trends and changes we've discussed throughout this text.

Most of the changes and trends summarized in Exhibit 22–1 are having a positive effect on how marketers serve society. And this ongoing improvement is self-directing. As consumers shift their support to firms that do meet their needs, laggard businesses are forced to either improve or get out of the way.

If it ain't broke, improve it

Marketing managers must constantly evaluate their strategies to be sure they're not being left in the dust by competitors who see new and better ways of doing things. It's crazy for a marketing manager to constantly change a strategy that's working well. But too many managers fail to see or plan for needed changes. They're afraid to do anything different and adhere to the idea that "if it ain't broke, don't fix it." But a firm can't always wait until a problem becomes completely obvious to do something about it. When customers move on and profits disappear, it may be too late to fix the problem. Marketing managers who take the lead in finding innovative new markets and approaches get a competitive advantage.

Communication Technologies
The Internet and intranets
Satellite communications
HTML e-mail and instant messaging
Videoconferencing and Internet telephone
Cell telephones

Role of Computerization
E-commerce, websites
Computers and PDAs
Spreadsheet analysis
Wireless networks
Scanners and bar codes for tracking
Multimedia integration

Marketing Research
Search engines
Growth of marketing information systems
Decision support systems
XML data exchange
Single source data (and scanner panels)
Data warehouses and data mining
Multimedia data and questionnaires
Customer relationship management (CRM) systems

Demographic Patterns
"Wired" households
Explosion in teen and ethnic submarkets
Aging of the baby boomers
Population growth slowdown in U.S.
Geographic shifts in population
Slower real income growth in U.S.

Business and Organizational Customers
Closer relationships and single sourcing
Just-in-time inventory systems/EDI
Web portals and Internet sourcing
Interactive bidding and proposal requests
Shift to NAICS
ISO 9000
E-commerce and supply chain management

Product Area
More attention to "really new" products
Faster new-product development
Computer-aided design (CAD)
R&D teams with market-driven focus
More attention to quality
More attention to service technologies
More attention to design, including packages
Category management

Channels and Logistics
Internet selling (wholesale and retail)
More vertical marketing systems
Clicks and bricks (multichannel)
Larger, more powerful retail chains
More attention to distribution service
Real-time inventory replenishment
Rapid response, JIT, and ECR
Automated warehousing and handling
Cross-docking at distribution centers
Logistics outsourcing
Cross-channel logistics coordination
Growth of mass-merchandising

Sales Promotion
Database-directed promotion
Point-of-purchase promotion
Trade promotion becoming more sensible
Event sponsorships
Product placement
Better support from agencies
Customer loyalty programs
Customer acquisition cost analysis

Personal Selling
Sales technology
Automated order-taking
Use of laptop computers
Major accounts specialization
More telemarketing and team selling
Use of e-mail, fax, and voice mail

Mass Selling
Interactive media (websites, etc.)
Integrated marketing communication
More targeted media
   Pointcasting
   Specialty publications
   Specialty radio and TV (cable, satellite)
   Point-of-purchase
Growth of interactive agencies
Consolidation of global agencies
Consolidation of media companies
Changing agency compensation
Direct-response advertising
Shrinking media budgets

Pricing
Electronic bid pricing and auctions
Value pricing
Overuse of sales and deals
Bigger differences in functional discounts
More attention to exchange rate effects
Lower markups on higher stockturn items
Spreadsheets for marginal analysis

International Marketing
More international market development
Global competitors—at home and abroad
Global communication over Internet
New trade rules (NAFTA, WTO, EU, etc.)
More attention to exporting by small firms
International expansion by retailers
Impact of "pop" culture on traditional cultures
Tensions between "have" and "have-not" cultures
Growing role of airfreight

General
Explicit mission statements
S.W.O.T. analysis
Privacy issues
Benchmarking and total quality management
More attention to positioning and differentiation
Less regulation of business
Increased use of alliances
Shift away from diversification
More attention to profitability, not just sales
Greater attention to superior value
Addressing environmental concerns

We need to welcome international competition

Marketers can't afford to bury their heads in the sand and hope that international competition will go away. Rather, they must realize that it is part of today's marketing environment. It creates even more pressure on marketing managers to figure out what it takes to gain a competitive advantage—both at home and in foreign markets. But with the challenge comes opportunities. The forces of competition in and among market-directed economies will help speed the diffusion of marketing advances to consumers everywhere. As macro-marketing systems improve worldwide, more consumers will have income to buy products—from wherever in the world those products come.

We need to use technology wisely

We live in a time of dramatic new technologies. Many marketers hate the idea that what they've learned from years of on-the-job experience may no longer apply when a technology like the Internet comes along. Or they feel that it's the job of the technical specialist to figure out how a new technology can help the firm serve its customers. But marketers can't just pawn that responsibility off on "somebody else." If that means learning about new technologies, then that is just part of the marketing job.

At a broader level, firms face the challenge of determining what technologies are acceptable and which are not. For example, gene research has opened the door to life-saving medicines, genetically altered crops that resist drought or disease, and even cloning of human beings. Yet in all of these arenas there is intense conflict among different groups about what is appropriate. How should these decisions be made? There is no simple answer to this question, but it's clear that old production-oriented views are *not* the answer. Perhaps we will move toward developing answers if some of the marketing ideas that have been applied to understanding individual needs can be extended to better understand the needs of society as a whole.

May need more social responsibility

Good business managers put themselves in the consumer's position. A useful rule to follow might be: Do unto others as you would have others do unto you. In practice, this means developing satisfying marketing mixes for specific target markets. It may mean building in more quality or more safety. The consumer's long-run satisfaction should be considered too. How will the product hold up in use? What about service guarantees? While trying to serve the needs of some target market, does the marketing strategy disregard the rights and needs of other consumers or create problems that will be left for future generations?[8]

The environment is everyone's need

Marketers need to work harder and smarter at finding ways to satisfy consumer needs without sacrificing the environment. All consumers need the environment, whether they realize it yet or not. We are only beginning to understand the consequences of the environmental damage that's already been done. Acid rain, depletion of the ozone layer, global warming, and toxic waste in water supplies—to mention but a few current environmental problems—have catastrophic effects.

In the past, most firms didn't pass the cost of environmental damage on to consumers in the prices that they paid. Pollution was a hidden and unmeasured cost for most companies. That is changing rapidly. Firms are already paying billions of dollars to correct problems, including problems created years ago. The government isn't accepting the excuse that "nobody knew it was a big problem."[9]

May need attention to consumer privacy

Marketers must also be sensitive to consumers' rights and privacy. Today, sophisticated marketing research methods, the Internet, and other technologies make it easier to abuse these rights. For example, credit card records—which reveal much about consumers' purchases and private lives—are routinely computerized and sold to anybody who pays for the list.

PROMOTION MANAGERS GO BACK TO SCHOOL

Schools are a targeted place for youth-oriented marketers to promote their products to the U.S.'s 45 million elementary and secondary students. Coke and Pepsi are eager to contribute scoreboards (or is that billboards?) for high school sports fields. In school cafeterias, which serve 30 million meals a day, Kellogg's cereal and Dannon's yogurt sponsor programs to motivate learning (and increase consumption). A school district in Colorado got national attention for selling advertising space on the sides of its school buses. This is not a new idea. The National Dairy Council has promoted dairy products in the schools since 1915.

Even so, the launch of the Channel One television network with ads and programming for schools brought new attention, and controversy, to the issue. Many critics saw it as a crass attempt to exploit captive students. Some schools even hand out coupons tied in with the ads. Channel One notes that schools get benefits. Besides the excellent news programs, they get video equipment and chances to win support for Internet access. Even Internet access is a mixed blessing. It's a great research tool, but there are virtually no limits on Internet advertising banners or websites. A teacher who does an in-class search on an innocent topic like "Asian teens" may click on one of the websites listed and instantly face a screen full of explicit pictures from a Japanese website that sells porno videos. To prevent this sort of thing, many schools use a web-filtering program from N2H2, Inc. But critics are troubled that N2H2 sells information about student surfing habits collected by the program.

To find more targeted ways of reaching students, some consumer products firms turn to promotion specialists, like Sampling Corporation of America (SCA). About 70 percent of all schools participate in SCA programs. For example, every Halloween SCA provides schools with safety literature wrapped around product samples or coupons provided by sponsor companies. Other firms create teaching materials or sponsor programs for school assemblies. Dole Foods, for example, created a multimedia CD featuring 30 animated fruits and vegetables. Recently, it sponsored a series of staged performances by the National Theatre for Children (NTC). The NTC performances highlight nutrition issues (and brand recognition for Dole's line of fruits and salads). For a fee, NTC has developed programs for other companies.

There is no question that in-school promotion efforts do provide budget-strapped educators with added resources, including useful teaching materials. Yet promotions targeted at students also raise sensitive issues of educational standards, ethics, and taste. Because of that, Coke has new guidelines for its bottlers that limit cola sales in some schools or make juice and water available at the same price. Kraft has gone further and stopped all promotions in schools. Other marketers who are not responsive to these concerns may provoke a hostile public backlash, including a host of new regulations.[10]

Most consumers don't realize how much data about their personal lives—some of it incorrect but treated as fact—is collected and available. A simple computer billing error may land consumers on a bad-credit list without their knowledge. Marketing managers should use technology responsibly to improve the quality of life, not disrupt it. If you don't think privacy is a serious matter, enter your social security number in an Internet search engine and see what pops up. You may be surprised.[11]

May need to change laws and how they are enforced

One of the advantages of a market-directed economic system is that it operates automatically. But in our version of this system, consumer-citizens provide certain constraints (laws), which can be modified at any time. Managers who ignore consumer attitudes must realize that their actions may cause new restraints.

Before piling on too many new rules, however, some of the ones we have may need to be revised—and others may need to be enforced more carefully. Antitrust laws, for example, are often applied to protect competitors from each other—but they were really intended to encourage competition.

On the other hand, U.S. antitrust laws were originally developed so that all firms in a market would compete on a level playing field. That is no longer always

The Utah Transit Authority (UTA) thought that more university students would ride the bus long-term if they were motivated by personal benefit rather than environmental or social conscience. For most people, the pros and cons of riding the bus, like other product choices, are more a personal matter. So UTA decided it should offer an answer to the question, "What's in it for me?" The answer in this particular UTA ad is "social opportunities." Although public transit is not exactly a sexy product, the ad employs a "sex sells" approach. What do you think? Is this a good idea? Why?

Chemistry 101

You can learn a lot on the bus.

University of Utah students ride free with student I.D. **U T A**

true. In many markets, individual U.S. firms compete with foreign firms whose governments urge them to cooperate with each other. Such foreign firms don't see each other as competitors; rather they see U.S. firms, as a group, as the competitors.

Laws should affect top managers

Strict enforcement of present laws could have far-reaching results if more price fixers, fraudulent or deceptive advertisers, and others who violate existing laws—thus affecting the performance of the macro-marketing system—were sent to jail or given heavy fines. A quick change in attitudes might occur if unethical top managers—those who plan strategy—were prosecuted, instead of the salespeople or advertisers expected to deliver on weak or undifferentiated strategies.

Laws merely define minimal ethical standards

Whether a marketer is operating in his or her own country or in a foreign nation, the legal environment sets the *minimal* standards of ethical behavior as defined by a society. In addition, the American Marketing Association's code of ethics (Exhibit 1-8) provides a checklist of basic guidelines that a marketing manager should observe. But marketing managers constantly face ethical issues where there are no clearly defined answers. Every marketing manager should make a personal commitment to carefully evaluate the ethical consequences of marketing strategy decisions.

Both consumers and businesses have social responsibilities.

On the other hand, innovative new marketing strategies *do* sometimes cause problems for those who have a vested interest in the old ways. Some people try to portray anything that disrupts their own personal interest as unethical. But that is not an appropriate ethical standard. The basic ethical charge to marketers is to find new and better ways to serve society's needs.

Need socially responsible consumers

We've stressed that marketers should act responsibly—but consumers have responsibilities too. Some consumers abuse policies about returning goods, change price tags in self-service stores, and are downright abusive to salespeople. Others think nothing of ripping off businesses because "they're rich." Shoplifting is a major problem for most traditional retailers, averaging almost 2 percent of sales nationally. In supermarkets, losses to shoplifters are on average greater than profits. Online retailers, in turn, must fight the use of stolen or fraudulent credit cards. Honest consumers pay for the cost of this theft in higher prices.[12]

Americans tend to perform their dual role of consumer-citizens with a split personality. We often behave one way as consumers and then take the opposite position at the ballot box. For example, we cover our beaches and parks with garbage and litter while urging our legislators to take stiff action to curb pollution. We protest sex and violence in the media, but some of the most profitable websites on the Internet are purveyors of pornography. Parents complain about advertising aimed at children but use TV as a Saturday morning babysitter.

Unethical or illegal behavior is widespread. In a major survey of workers, managers, and executives from a wide range of industries, 48 percent admitted to taking unethical or illegal actions in the past year. Offenses included things like cheating on expense accounts, paying or accepting kickbacks, trading sex for sales, lying to customers, leaking company secrets, and looking the other way when environmental laws are violated. Think about it—we're talking about half of the workforce.[13]

As consumer-citizens, each of us shares the responsibility for preserving an effective macro-marketing system. And we should take this responsibility seriously. That even includes the responsibility to be smarter customers. Let's face it, a majority of consumers ignore most of the available information that could help them spend money (and guide the marketing process) more wisely. Consumerism has encouraged nutritional labeling, open dating, unit pricing, truth-in-lending, plain-language

The Domino's logo shown here behind home plate does not actually exist on the playing field of this major league baseball game but rather is created electronically. The advertiser pays the TV broadcaster to get the exposure. As new imaging technologies emerge, companies will have to decide what is fair and appropriate.

contracts and warranties, and so on. Many companies provide extensive information at their websites or in brochures. Government agencies publish many consumer buying guides on everything from tires to appliances, as do organizations such as Consumers Union. Most of this information is available from home, over the Internet. It makes sense to use it.

HOW FAR SHOULD THE MARKETING CONCEPT GO?

Should marketing managers limit consumers' freedom of choice?

Achieving a better macro-marketing system is certainly a desirable objective. But what part should a marketer play in deciding what products to offer?

This is extremely important, because some marketing managers, especially those in large corporations, can have an impact far larger than they do in their roles as consumer-citizens. For example, should they refuse to produce hazardous products, like skis or motorcycles, even though such products are in strong demand? Should they install safety devices that increase costs but that customers don't want?

These are difficult questions to answer. Some things marketing managers do clearly benefit both the firm and consumers because they lower costs or improve consumers' options. But other decisions may actually reduce consumer choice and conflict with a desire to improve the effectiveness of our macro-marketing system.

Consumer-citizens should vote on the changes

It seems fair to suggest, therefore, that marketing managers should be expected to improve and expand the range of goods and services they make available—always trying to add value and better satisfy consumers' needs and preferences. This is the job we've assigned to business.

If pursuing this objective makes excessive demands on scarce resources or has an unacceptable ecological effect, then consumer-citizens have the responsibility to vote for laws restricting individual firms that are trying to satisfy consumers' needs. This is the role that we, as consumers, have assigned to the government—to ensure that the macro-marketing system works effectively.

It is important to recognize that some *seemingly minor* modifications in our present system *might* result in very big, unintended problems. Allowing some government agency to prohibit the sale of products for seemingly good reasons could lead to major changes we never expected and could seriously reduce consumers' present rights to freedom of choice, including "bad" choices.

CONCLUSION

Macro-marketing does *not* cost too much. Consumers have assigned business the role of satisfying their needs. Customers find it satisfactory and even desirable to permit businesses to cater to them and even to stimulate wants. As long as consumers are satisfied, macro-marketing will not cost too much—and business firms will be permitted to continue as profit-making entities.

But business exists at the consumer's discretion. It's mainly by satisfying the consumer that a particular firm—and *our* economic system—can justify its existence and hope to keep operating.

In carrying out this role—granted by consumers—business firms are not always as effective as they could be. Many business managers don't understand the marketing concept or the role that marketing plays in our way of life. They seem to feel that business has a God-given right to operate as it chooses. And they proceed in their typical production-oriented ways. Further, many managers have had little or no training in business management and are not as competent as they should be. Others fail to adjust to the changes taking place around them. And a few dishonest or unethical managers can do a great deal of damage before consumer-citizens take steps to stop them. As a result, micro-marketing often *does* cost too much. But the situation is improv-ing. More business training is now available, and more competent people are being attracted to marketing and business generally. Clearly, *you* have a role to play in improving marketing activities in the future.

Marketing has new challenges to face in the future. *Our* consumers may have to settle for a lower standard of living. Resource shortages, slower population growth, and a larger number of elderly—with a smaller proportion of the population in the workforce—may all combine to reduce our income growth. This may force consumers to shift their consumption patterns and politicians to change some of the rules governing business. Even our present market-directed system may be threatened.

To keep our system working effectively, individual firms should implement the marketing concept in a more efficient, ethical, and socially responsible way. At the same time, we—as consumers—should consume goods and services in an intelligent and socially responsible way. Further, we have the responsibility to vote and ensure that we get the kind of macro-marketing system we want. What kind do you want? What should you do to ensure that fellow consumer-citizens will vote for your system? Is your system likely to satisfy you as well as another macro-marketing system? You don't have to answer these questions right now—but your answers will affect the future you'll live in and how satisfied you'll be.

QUESTIONS AND PROBLEMS

1. Explain why marketing must be evaluated at two levels. What criteria should be used to evaluate each level of marketing? Defend your answer. Explain why your criteria are better than alternative criteria.

2. Discuss the merits of various economic system objectives. Is the objective of the American economic system sensible? Could it achieve more consumer satisfaction if sociologists or public officials determined how to satisfy the needs of lower-income or less-educated consumers? If so, what education or income level should be required before an individual is granted free choice?

3. Should the objective of our economy be maximum efficiency? If your answer is yes, efficiency in what? If not, what should the objective be?

4. Discuss the conflict of interests among production, finance, accounting, and marketing executives. How does this conflict affect the operation of an individual firm? The economic system? Why does this conflict exist?

5. Why does adoption of the marketing concept encourage a firm to operate more efficiently? Be specific about the impact of the marketing concept on the various departments of a firm.

6. In the short run, competition sometimes leads to inefficiency in the operation of our economic system. Many people argue for monopoly in order to eliminate this inefficiency. Discuss this solution.

7. How would officially granted monopolies affect the operation of our economic system? Consider the effect on allocation of resources, the level of income and employment, and the distribution of income. Is the effect any different if a firm obtains a monopoly by winning out in a competitive market?

8. Comment on the following statement: "Ultimately, the high cost of marketing is due only to consumers."

9. How far should the marketing concept go? How should we decide this issue?

10. Should marketing managers, or business managers in general, refrain from producing profitable products that some target customers want but that may not be in their long-run interest? Should firms be expected to produce "good" but less profitable products? What if such products break even? What if they are unprofitable but the company makes other profitable products—so on balance it still makes some profit? What criteria are you using for each of your answers?

11. Should a marketing manager or a business refuse to produce an "energy-gobbling" appliance that some consumers are demanding? Should a firm install an expensive safety device that will increase costs but that customers don't want? Are the same principles involved in both these questions? Explain.

12. Discuss how one or more of the trends or changes shown in Exhibit 22-1 is affecting marketing strategy planning for a specific firm that serves the market where you live.

13. Discuss how slower economic growth or no economic growth would affect your college community—in particular, its marketing institutions.

SUGGESTED CASES

27. Injection Molding, Inc.
28. QCT, Inc.
29. Custom Castings, Inc.

30. DeLuxe Foods, Ltd.
32. Lever, Ltd.

Economics Fundamentals

WHEN YOU FINISH THIS APPENDIX, YOU SHOULD

1. Understand the "law of diminishing demand."

2. Understand demand and supply curves and how they set the size of a market and its price level.

3. Know about elasticity of demand and supply.

4. Know why demand elasticity can be affected by availability of substitutes.

5. Know the different kinds of competitive situations and understand why they are important to marketing managers.

6. Recognize the important new terms (shown in red).

The economist's traditional analysis of demand and supply is a useful tool for analyzing markets. In particular, you should master the concepts of a demand curve and demand elasticity. A firm's demand curve shows how the target customers view the firm's Product—really its whole marketing mix. And the interaction of demand and supply curves helps set the size of a market and the market price. The interaction of supply and demand also determines the nature of the competitive environment, which has an important effect on strategy planning. These ideas are discussed more fully in the following sections.

PRODUCTS AND MARKETS AS SEEN BY CUSTOMERS AND POTENTIAL CUSTOMERS

Economists see individual customers choosing among alternatives

A basic idea from economics is that most customers have a limited income and simply cannot buy everything they want. They must balance their needs and the prices of various products. Economists usually assume that customers have a fairly definite set of preferences and that they evaluate alternatives in terms of whether the alternatives will make them feel better or in some way improve their situation.

But what exactly is the nature of a customer's desire for a particular product?

Usually economists answer this question in terms of the extra utility the customer can obtain by buying more of a particular product—or how much utility would be lost if the customer had less of the product. It is easier to understand the idea of utility if we look at what happens when the price of one of the customer's usual purchases changes.

The law of diminishing demand

Suppose that consumers buy potatoes in 10-pound bags at the same time they buy other foods such as bread and rice. If the consumers are mainly interested in buying a certain amount of food and the price of the potatoes drops, it seems reasonable to expect that they will switch some of their food money to potatoes and away from some other foods. But if the price of potatoes rises, you expect our consumers to buy fewer potatoes and more of other foods.

The general relationship between price and quantity demanded illustrated by this food example is called the **law of diminishing demand**—which says that if the price of a product is raised, a smaller quantity will be demanded and if the price of a product is lowered, a greater quantity will be demanded. Experience supports this relationship between price and total demand in a market, especially for broad product categories or commodities such as potatoes.

The relationship between price and quantity demanded in a market is what economists call a "demand schedule." An example is shown in Exhibit A-1. For each

Exhibit A-1
Demand Schedule for Potatoes (10-pound bags)

Point	(1) Price of Potatoes per Bag (P)	(2) Quantity Demanded (bags per month) (Q)	(3) Total Revenue per Month (P × Q = TR)
A	$1.60	8,000,000	$12,800,000
B	1.30	9,000,000	_____
C	1.00	11,000,000	11,000,000
D	0.70	14,000,000	_____
E	0.40	19,000,000	_____

Exhibit A-2
Demand Curve for Potatoes
(10-pound bags)

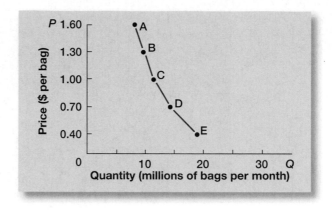

row in the table, column 2 shows the quantity consumers will want (demand) if they have to pay the price given in column 1. The third column shows that the total revenue (sales) in the potato market is equal to the quantity demanded at a given price times that price. Note that as prices drop, the total *unit* quantity increases, yet the total *revenue* decreases. Fill in the blank lines in the third column and observe the behavior of total revenue, an important number for the marketing manager. We will explain what you should have noticed, and why, a little later.

The demand curve—usually down-sloping

If your only interest is seeing at which price the company will earn the greatest total revenue, the demand schedule may be adequate. But a demand curve shows more. A **demand curve** is a graph of the relationship between price and quantity demanded in a market, assuming that all other things stay the same. Exhibit A-2 shows the demand curve for potatoes—really just a plotting of the demand schedule in Exhibit A-1. It shows how many potatoes potential customers will demand at various possible prices. This is a "down-sloping demand curve."

Most demand curves are down-sloping. This just means that if prices are decreased, the quantity customers demand will increase.

Demand curves always show the price on the vertical axis and the quantity demanded on the horizontal axis. In Exhibit A-2, we have shown the price in dollars. For consistency, we will use dollars in other examples. However, keep in mind that these same ideas hold regardless of what money unit (dollars, yen, francs, pounds, etc.) is used to represent price. Even at this early point, you should keep in mind that markets are not necessarily limited by national boundaries—or by one type of money.

Note that the demand curve only shows how customers will react to various possible prices. In a market, we see only one price at a time, not all of these prices. The curve, however, shows what quantities will be demanded, depending on what price is set.

Microwave oven demand curve looks different

To get a more complete picture of demand-curve analysis, let's consider another product that has a different demand schedule and curve. A demand schedule for standard 1-cubic-foot microwave ovens is shown in Exhibit A-3. Column (3) shows the total revenue that will be obtained at various possible prices and quantities. Again, as the price goes down, the quantity demanded goes up. But here, unlike the potato example, total revenue increases as prices go down—at least until the price drops to $150.

Every market has a demand curve, for some time period

These general demand relationships are typical for all products. Each product has its own demand schedule and curve in each potential market, no matter how small the market. In other words, a particular demand curve has meaning only

Point	(1) Price per Microwave Oven (P)	(2) Quantity Demanded per Year (Q)	(3) Total Revenue (TR) per Year (P × Q = TR)
A	$300	20,000	$6,000,000
B	250	70,000	15,500,000
C	200	130,000	26,000,000
D	150	210,000	31,500,000
E	100	310,000	31,000,000

for a particular market. We can think of demand curves for individuals, groups of individuals who form a target market, regions, and even countries. And the time period covered really should be specified, although this is often neglected because we usually think of monthly or yearly periods.

The difference between elastic and inelastic

The demand curve for microwave ovens (see Exhibit A-4) is down-sloping—but note that it is flatter than the curve for potatoes. It is important to understand what this flatness means.

We will consider the flatness in terms of total revenue, since this is what interests business managers.*

When you filled in the total revenue column for potatoes, you should have noticed that total revenue drops continually if the price is reduced. This looks undesirable for sellers and illustrates inelastic demand. **Inelastic demand** means that although the quantity demanded increases if the price is decreased, the quantity demanded will not "stretch" enough—that is, it is not elastic enough—to avoid a decrease in total revenue.

In contrast, **elastic demand** means that if prices are dropped, the quantity demanded will stretch (increase) enough to increase total revenue. The upper part of the microwave oven demand curve is an example of elastic demand.

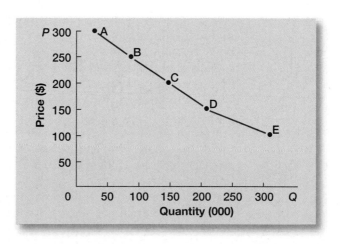

---

*Strictly speaking, two curves should not be compared for flatness if the graph scales are different, but for our purposes now we will do so to illustrate the idea of "elasticity of demand." Actually, it would be more accurate to compare two curves for one product on the same graph. Then both the shape of the demand curve and its position on the graph would be important.

But note that if the microwave oven price is dropped from $150 to $100, total revenue will decrease. We can say, therefore, that between $150 and $100, demand is inelastic—that is, total revenue will decrease if price is lowered from $150 to $100.

Thus, elasticity can be defined in terms of changes in total revenue. *If total revenue will increase if price is lowered, then demand is elastic. If total revenue will decrease if price is lowered, then demand is inelastic.* (Note: A special case known as "unitary elasticity of demand" occurs if total revenue stays the same when prices change.)

Total revenue may increase if price is raised

A point often missed in discussions of demand is what happens when prices are raised instead of lowered. With elastic demand, total revenue will *decrease* if the price is *raised*. With inelastic demand, however, total revenue will *increase* if the price is *raised*.

The possibility of raising price and increasing dollar sales (total revenue) at the same time is attractive to managers. This only occurs if the demand curve is inelastic. Here total revenue will increase if price is raised, but total costs probably will not increase—and may actually go down—with smaller quantities. Keep in mind that profit is equal to total revenue minus total costs. So when demand is inelastic, profit will increase as price is increased!

The ways total revenue changes as prices are raised are shown in Exhibit A-5. Here total revenue is the rectangular area formed by a price and its related quantity. The larger the rectangular area, the greater the total revenue.

P_1 is the original price here, and the total potential revenue with this original price is shown by the area with blue shading. The area with red shading shows the total revenue with the new price, P_2. There is some overlap in the total revenue areas, so the important areas are those with only one color. Note that in the left-hand figure—where demand is elastic—the revenue added (the red-only area) when the price is increased is less than the revenue lost (the blue-only area). Now let's contrast this to the right-hand figure, when demand is inelastic. Only a small blue revenue area is given up for a much larger (red) one when price is raised.

Exhibit A-5
Changes in Total Revenue as Prices Increase

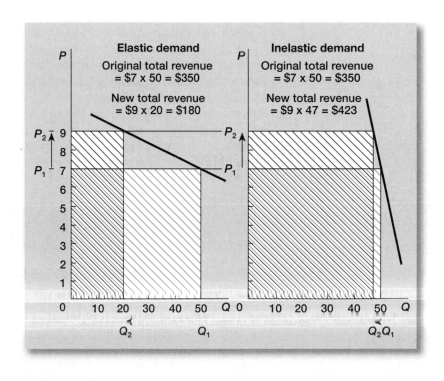

An entire curve is not elastic or inelastic

It is important to see that it is *wrong to refer to a whole demand curve as elastic or inelastic*. Rather, elasticity for a particular demand curve refers to the change in total revenue between two points on the curve, not along the whole curve. You saw the change from elastic to inelastic in the microwave oven example. Generally, however, nearby points are either elastic or inelastic—so it is common to refer to a whole curve by the degree of elasticity in the price range that normally is of interest—the *relevant range*.

Demand elasticities affected by availability of substitutes and urgency of need

At first, it may be difficult to see why one product has an elastic demand and another an inelastic demand. Many factors affect elasticity, such as the availability of substitutes, the importance of the item in the customer's budget, and the urgency of the customer's need and its relation to other needs. By looking more closely at one of these factors—the availability of substitutes—you will better understand why demand elasticities vary.

Substitutes are products that offer the buyer a choice. For example, many consumers see grapefruit as a substitute for oranges and hot dogs as a substitute for hamburgers. The greater the number of "good" substitutes available, the greater will be the elasticity of demand. From the consumer's perspective, products are "good" substitutes if they are very similar (homogeneous). If consumers see products as extremely different, or heterogeneous, then a particular need cannot easily be satisfied by substitutes. And the demand for the most satisfactory product may be quite inelastic.

As an example, if the price of hamburger is lowered (and other prices stay the same), the quantity demanded will increase a lot, as will total revenue. The reason is that not only will regular hamburger users buy more hamburger, but some consumers who formerly bought hot dogs or steaks probably will buy hamburger too. But if the price of hamburger is raised, the quantity demanded will decrease, perhaps sharply. Still, consumers will buy some hamburger, depending on how much the price has risen, their individual tastes, and what their guests expect (see Exhibit A-6).

In contrast to a product with many "substitutes"—such as hamburger—consider a product with few or no substitutes. Its demand curve will tend to be inelastic. Motor oil is a good example. Motor oil is needed to keep cars running. Yet no one person or family uses great quantities of motor oil. So it is not likely that the quantity of motor oil purchased will change much as long as price changes are *within a reasonable range*. Of course, if the price is raised to a staggering figure, many people will buy less oil (change their oil less frequently). If the price is dropped to an extremely low level, manufacturers may buy more—say, as a lower-cost substitute for other chemicals typically used in making plastic (Exhibit A-7). But these extremes are outside the relevant range.

Demand curves are introduced here because the degree of elasticity of demand shows how potential customers feel about a product—and especially whether they see substitutes for the product. But to get a better understanding of markets, we must extend this economic analysis.

Exhibit A-6
Demand Curve for Hamburger (a product with many substitutes)

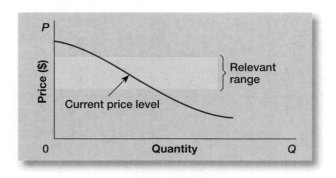

Exhibit A-7
Demand Curve for Motor
Oil (a product with few
substitutes)

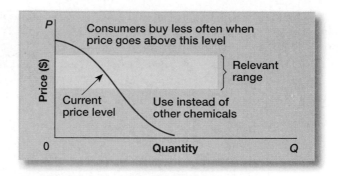

MARKETS AS SEEN BY SUPPLIERS

Customers may want some product—but if suppliers are not willing to supply it, then there is no market. So we'll study the economist's analysis of supply. And then we'll bring supply and demand together for a more complete understanding of markets.

Economists often use the kind of analysis we are discussing here to explain pricing in the marketplace. But that is not our intention. Here we are interested in how and why markets work and the interaction of customers and potential suppliers. Later in this appendix we will review how competition affects prices, but how individual firms set prices, or should set prices, is discussed fully in Chapters 17 and 18.

Supply curves reflect supplier thinking

Generally speaking, suppliers' costs affect the quantity of products they are willing to offer in a market during any period. In other words, their costs affect their supply schedules and supply curves. While a demand curve shows the quantity of products customers will be willing to buy at various prices, a **supply curve** shows the quantity of products that will be supplied at various possible prices. Eventually, only one quantity will be offered and purchased. So a supply curve is really a hypothetical (what-if) description of what will be offered at various prices. It is, however, a very important curve. Together with a demand curve, it summarizes the attitudes and probable behavior of buyers and sellers about a particular product in a particular market—that is, in a product-market.

Some supply curves are vertical

We usually assume that supply curves tend to slope upward—that is, suppliers will be willing to offer greater quantities at higher prices. If a product's market price is very high, it seems only reasonable that producers will be anxious to produce more of the product and even put workers on overtime or perhaps hire more workers to increase the quantity they can offer. Going further, it seems likely that producers of other products will switch their resources (farms, factories, labor, or retail facilities) to the product that is in great demand.

On the other hand, if consumers are only willing to pay a very low price for a particular product, it's reasonable to expect that producers will switch to other products, thus reducing supply. A supply schedule (Exhibit A-8) and a supply curve (Exhibit A-9) for potatoes illustrate these ideas. This supply curve shows how many potatoes would be produced and offered for sale at each possible market price in a given month.

In the very short run (say, over a few hours, a day, or a week), a supplier may not be able to change the supply at all. In this situation, we would see a vertical supply curve. This situation is often relevant in the market for fresh produce. Fresh strawberries, for example, continue to ripen, and a supplier wants to sell them quickly—preferably at a higher price—but in any case, they must be sold.

Point	Possible Market Price per 10-lb. Bag	Number of Bags Sellers Will Supply per Month at Each Possible Market Price
A	$1.60	17,000,000
B	1.30	14,000,000
C	1.00	11,000,000
D	0.70	8,000,000
E	0.40	3,000,000

Note: This supply curve is for a month to emphasize that farmers might have some control over when they deliver their potatoes. There would be a different curve for each month.

If the product is a service, It may not be easy to expand the supply in the short run. Additional barbers or medical doctors are not quickly trained and licensed, and they only have so much time to give each day. Further, the prospect of much higher prices in the near future cannot easily expand the supply of many services. For example, a hit play or an "in" restaurant or nightclub is limited in the amount of product it can offer at a particular time.

Elasticity of supply

The term *elasticity* also is used to describe supply curves. An extremely steep or almost vertical supply curve, often found in the short run, is called **inelastic supply** because the quantity supplied does not stretch much (if at all) if the price is raised. A flatter curve is called **elastic supply** because the quantity supplied does stretch more if the price is raised. A slightly up-sloping supply curve is typical in longer-run market situations. Given more time, suppliers have a chance to adjust their offerings, and competitors may enter or leave the market.

DEMAND AND SUPPLY INTERACT TO DETERMINE THE SIZE OF THE MARKET AND PRICE LEVEL

We have treated market demand and supply forces separately. Now we must bring them together to show their interaction. The *intersection* of these two forces determines the size of the market and the market price—at which point (price and quantity) the market is said to be in *equilibrium*.

Exhibit A-9
Supply Curve for Potatoes
(10-pound bags)

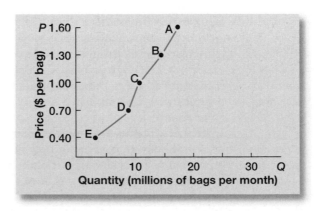

Exhibit A-10
Equilibrium of Supply and
Demand for Potatoes
(10-pound bags)

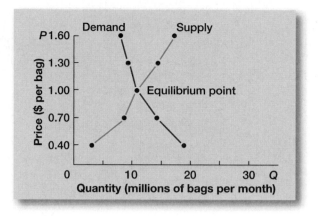

The intersection of demand and supply is shown for the potato data discussed above. In Exhibit A-10, the demand curve for potatoes is now graphed against the supply curve in Exhibit A-9.

In this potato market, demand is inelastic—the total revenue of all the potato producers would be greater at higher prices. But the market price is at the **equilibrium point**—where the quantity and the price sellers are willing to offer are equal to the quantity and price that buyers are willing to accept. The $1.00 equilibrium price for potatoes yields a smaller *total revenue* to potato producers than a higher price would. This lower equilibrium price comes about because the many producers are willing to supply enough potatoes at the lower price. *Demand is not the only determiner of price level. Cost also must be considered—via the supply curve.*

Some consumers get a surplus

Presumably, a sale takes place only if both buyer and seller feel they will be better off after the sale. But sometimes the price a consumer pays in a sales transaction is less than what he or she would be willing to pay.

The reason for this is that demand curves are typically down-sloping, and some of the demand curve is above the equilibrium price. This is simply another way of showing that some customers would have been willing to pay more than the equilibrium price—if they had to. In effect, some of them are getting a bargain by being able to buy at the equilibrium price. Economists have traditionally called these bargains the **consumer surplus**—that is, the difference to consumers between the value of a purchase and the price they pay.

Some business critics assume that consumers do badly in any business transaction. In fact, sales take place only if consumers feel they are at least getting their money's worth. As we can see here, some are willing to pay much more than the market price.

DEMAND AND SUPPLY HELP US UNDERSTAND THE NATURE OF COMPETITION

The elasticity of demand and supply curves and their interaction help predict the nature of competition a marketing manager is likely to face. For example, an extremely inelastic demand curve means that the manager will have much choice in strategy planning, especially price setting. Apparently customers like the product and see few substitutes. They are willing to pay higher prices before cutting back much on their purchases.

	Types of Situations			
Important Dimensions	**Pure Competition**	**Oligopoly**	**Monopolistic Competition**	**Monopoly**
Uniqueness of each firm's product	None	None	Some	Unique
Number of competitors	Many	Few	Few to many	None
Size of competitors (compared to size of market)	Small	Large	Large to small	None
Elasticity of demand facing firm	Completely elastic	Kinked demand curve (elastic and inelastic)	Either	Either
Elasticity of industry demand	Either	Inelastic	Either	Either
Control of price by firm	None	Some (with care)	Some	Complete

The elasticity of a firm's demand curve is not the only factor that affects the nature of competition. Other factors are the number and size of competitors and the uniqueness of each firm's marketing mix. Understanding these market situations is important because the freedom of a marketing manager, especially control over price, is greatly reduced in some situations.

A marketing manager operates in one of four kinds of market situations. We'll discuss three kinds: pure competition, oligopoly, and monopolistic competition. The fourth kind, monopoly, isn't found very often and is like monopolistic competition. The important dimensions of these situations are shown in Exhibit A-11.

When competition is pure

Many competitors offer about the same thing

Pure competition is a market situation that develops when a market has

1. Homogeneous (similar) products.
2. Many buyers and sellers who have full knowledge of the market.
3. Ease of entry for buyers and sellers; that is, new firms have little difficulty starting in business—and new customers can easily come into the market.

More or less pure competition is found in many agricultural markets. In the potato market, for example, there are thousands of small producers—and they are in pure competition. Let's look more closely at these producers.

Although the potato market as a whole has a down-sloping demand curve, each of the many small producers in the industry is in pure competition, and each of them faces a flat demand curve at the equilibrium price. This is shown in Exhibit A-12.

As shown at the right of Exhibit A-12, an individual producer can sell as many bags of potatoes as he chooses at $1—the market equilibrium price. The equilibrium price is determined by the quantity that all producers choose to sell given the demand curve they face.

But a small producer has little effect on overall supply (or on the equilibrium price). If this individual farmer raises 1/10,000th of the quantity offered in the market, for example, you can see that there will be little effect if the farmer goes out of business—or doubles production.

Interaction of Demand and Supply in the Potato Industry and the Resulting Demand Curve
Facing Individual Potato Producers

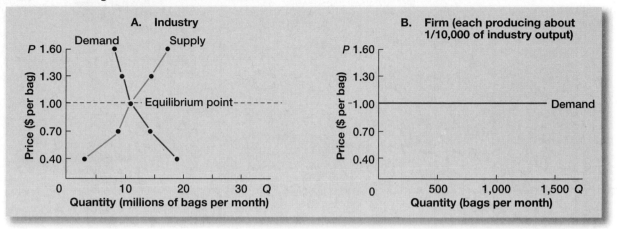

The reason an individual producer's demand curve is flat is that the farmer probably couldn't sell any potatoes above the market price. And there is no point in selling below the market price! So in effect, the individual producer has no control over price.

Markets tend to become more competitive

Not many markets are *purely* competitive. But many are close enough so we can talk about "almost" pure competition situations—those in which the marketing manager has to accept the going price.

Such highly competitive situations aren't limited to agriculture. Wherever *many* competitors sell *homogeneous* products—such as textiles, lumber, coal, printing, and laundry services—the demand curve seen by *each producer* tends to be flat.

Markets tend to become more competitive, moving toward pure competition (except in oligopolies—see below). On the way to pure competition, prices and profits are pushed down until some competitors are forced out of business. Eventually, in long-run equilibrium, the price level is only high enough to keep the survivors in business. No one makes any profit—they just cover costs. It's tough to be a marketing manager in this situation!

When competition is oligopolistic

A few competitors offer similar things

Not all markets move toward pure competition. Some become oligopolies. **Oligopoly** situations are special market situations that develop when a market has

1. Essentially homogeneous products—such as basic industrial chemicals or gasoline.
2. Relatively few sellers—or a few large firms and many smaller ones who follow the lead of the larger ones.
3. Fairly inelastic industry demand curves.

The demand curve facing each firm is unusual in an oligopoly situation. Although the industry demand curve is inelastic throughout the relevant range, the demand curve facing each competitor looks "kinked." See Exhibit A-13. The current market price is at the kink.

There is a market price because the competing firms watch each other carefully—and they know it's wise to be at the kink. Each firm must expect that raising its own price above the market price will cause a big loss in sales. Few, if any, competitors will follow the price increase. So the firm's demand curve is relatively flat

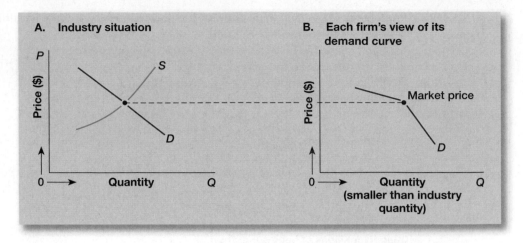

above the market price. If the firm lowers its price, it must expect competitors to follow. Given inelastic industry demand, the firm's own demand curve is inelastic at lower prices, assuming it keeps its share of this market at lower prices. Since lowering prices along such a curve will drop total revenue, the firm should leave its price at the kink—the market price.

Sometimes there are price fluctuations in oligopolistic markets. This can be caused by firms that don't understand the market situation and cut their prices to try to get business. In other cases, big increases in demand or supply change the basic nature of the situation and lead to price cutting. Price cuts can be drastic, such as Du Pont's price cut of 25 percent for Dacron. This happened when Du Pont decided that industry production capacity already exceeded demand, and more plants were due to start production.

It's important to keep in mind that oligopoly situations don't just apply to whole industries and national markets. Competitors who are focusing on the same local target market often face oligopoly situations. A suburban community might have several gas stations, all of which provide essentially the same product. In this case, the "industry" consists of the gas stations competing with each other in the local product-market.

As in pure competition, oligopolists face a long-run trend toward an equilibrium level, with profits driven toward zero. This may not happen immediately—and a marketing manager may try to delay price competition by relying more on other elements in the marketing mix.

When competition is monopolistic

A price must be set

You can see why marketing managers want to avoid pure competition or oligopoly situations. They prefer a market in which they have more control. **Monopolistic competition** is a market situation that develops when a market has

1. Different (heterogeneous) products—in the eyes of some customers.
2. Sellers who feel they do have some competition in this market.

The word *monopolistic* means that each firm is trying to get control in its own little market. But the word *competition* means that there are still substitutes. The vigorous competition of a purely competitive market is reduced. Each firm has its own down-sloping demand curve. But the shape of the curve depends on the similarity of competitors' products and marketing mixes. Each monopolistic competitor has freedom—but not complete freedom—in its own market.

Judging elasticity will help set the price

Since a firm in monopolistic competition has its own down-sloping demand curve, it must make a decision about price level as part of its marketing strategy planning. Here, estimating the elasticity of the firm's own demand curve is helpful. If it is highly inelastic, the firm may decide to raise prices to increase total revenue. But if demand is highly elastic, this may mean there are many competitors with acceptable substitutes. Then the price may have to be set near that of the competition. And the marketing manager probably should try to develop a better marketing mix.

CONCLUSION

The economist's traditional demand and supply analysis provides a useful tool for analyzing the nature of demand and competition. It is especially important that you master the concepts of a demand curve and demand elasticity. How demand and supply interact helps determine the size of a market and its price level. The interaction of supply and demand also helps explain the nature of competition in different market situations. We discuss three competitive situations: pure competition, oligopoly, and monopolistic competition. The fourth kind, monopoly, isn't found very often and is like monopolistic competition.

The nature of supply and demand—and competition—is very important in marketing strategy planning. We discuss these topics more fully in Chapters 3 and 4 and then build on them throughout the text. This appendix provides a good foundation on these topics.

KEY TERMS

law of diminishing demand, 626

demand curve, 627

inelastic demand, 628

elastic demand, 628

substitutes, 630

supply curve, 631

inelastic supply, 632

elastic supply, 632

equilibrium point, 633

consumer surplus, 633

pure competition, 634

oligopoly, 635

monopolistic competition, 636

QUESTIONS AND PROBLEMS

1. Explain in your own words how economists look at markets and arrive at the "law of diminishing demand."

2. Explain what a demand curve is and why it is usually down-sloping. Then give an example of a product for which the demand curve might not be down-sloping over some possible price ranges. Explain the reason for your choice.

3. What is the length of life of the typical demand curve? Illustrate your answer.

4. If the general market demand for men's shoes is fairly elastic, how does the demand for men's dress shoes compare to it? How does the demand curve for women's shoes compare to the demand curve for men's shoes?

5. If the demand for perfume is inelastic above and below the present price, should the price be raised? Why or why not?

6. If the demand for shrimp is highly elastic below the present price, should the price be lowered?

7. Discuss what factors lead to inelastic demand and supply curves. Are they likely to be found together in the same situation?

8. Why would a marketing manager prefer to sell a product that has no close substitutes? Are high profits almost guaranteed?

9. If a manufacturer's well-known product is sold at the same price by many retailers in the same community, is this an example of pure competition? When a community has many small grocery stores, are they in pure competition? What characteristics are needed to have a purely competitive market?

10. List three products that are sold in purely competitive markets and three that are sold in monopolistically competitive markets. Do any of these products have anything in common? Can any generalizations be made about competitive situations and marketing mix planning?

11. Cite a local example of an oligopoly, explaining why it is an oligopoly.

Marketing Arithmetic

1. Understand the components of an operating statement (profit and loss statement).

2. Know how to compute the stockturn rate.

3. Understand how operating ratios can help analyze a business.

4. Understand how to calculate markups and markdowns.

5. Understand how to calculate return on investment (ROI) and return on assets (ROA).

6. Understand the important new terms (shown in red).

Marketing students must become familiar with the essentials of the language of business. Businesspeople commonly use accounting terms when talking about costs, prices, and profit. And using accounting data is a practical tool in analyzing marketing problems.

THE OPERATING STATEMENT

An **operating statement** is a simple summary of the financial results of a company's operations over a specified period of time. Some beginning students may feel that the operating statement is complex, but as we'll soon see, this really isn't true. *The main purpose of the operating statement is determining the net profit figure and presenting data to support that figure.* This is why the operating statement is often referred to as the *profit and loss statement.*

Exhibit B 1 shows an operating statement for a wholesale or retail business. The statement is complete and detailed so you will see the framework throughout the discussion, but the amount of detail on an operating statement is *not* standardized. Many companies use financial statements with much less detail than this one. They emphasize clarity and readability rather than detail. To really understand an operating statement, however, you must know about its components.

Only three basic components

The basic components of an operating statement are *sales*—which come from the sale of goods and services; *costs*—which come from the producing and selling process; and the balance—called *profit or loss*—which is just the difference between sales and costs. So there are only three basic components in the statement: sales, costs, and profit (or loss). Other items on an operating statement are there only to provide supporting details.

Time period covered may vary

There is no one time period an operating statement covers. Rather, statements are prepared to satisfy the needs of a particular business. This may be at the end of each day or at the end of each week. Usually, however, an operating statement summarizes results for one month, three months, six months, or a full year. Since the time period does vary, this information is included in the heading of the statement as follows:

> **Perry Company**
> Operating Statement
> For the (Period) Ended (Date)

Also see Exhibit B-1.

Management uses of operating statements

Before going on to a more detailed discussion of the components of our operating statement, let's think about some of the uses for such a statement. Exhibit B-1 shows that a lot of information is presented in a clear and concise manner. With this information, a manager can easily find the relation of net sales to the cost of sales, the gross margin, expenses, and net profit. Opening and closing inventory figures are available—as is the amount spent during the period for the purchase of goods for resale. Total expenses are listed to make it easier to compare them with previous statements and to help control these expenses.

All this information is important to a company's managers. Assume that a particular company prepares monthly operating statements. A series of these statements is a valuable tool for directing and controlling the business. By comparing results from one month to the next, managers can uncover unfavorable trends in the sales, costs, or profit areas of the business and take any needed action.

Perry Company
Operating Statement
For the Year Ended December 31, 200X

Gross sales			$540,000
Less: Returns and allowances			40,000
Net sales			$500,000
Cost of sales:			
Beginning inventory at cost		$ 80,000	
Purchases at billed cost	$310,000		
Less: Purchase discounts	40,000		
Purchases at net cost	270,000		
Plus: freight-in	20,000		
Net cost of delivered purchases		290,000	
Cost of goods available for sale		370,000	
Less: Ending inventory at cost		70,000	
Cost of sales			300,000
Gross margin (gross profit)			200,000
Expenses:			
Selling expenses:			
Sales salaries	60,000		
Advertising expense	20,000		
Website updates	10,000		
Delivery expense	10,000		
Total selling expense		100,000	
Administrative expense:			
Office salaries	30,000		
Office supplies	10,000		
Miscellaneous administrative expense	5,000		
Total administrative expense		45,000	
General expense:			
Rent expense	10,000		
Miscellaneous general expenses	5,000		
Total general expense		15,000	
Total expenses			160,000
Net profit from operation			$ 40,000

A skeleton statement gets down to essential details

Let's refer to Exhibit B-1 and begin to analyze this seemingly detailed statement to get first-hand knowledge of the components of the operating statement.

As a first step, suppose we take all the items that have dollar amounts extended to the third, or right-hand, column. Using these items only, the operating statement looks like this:

Gross sales	$540,000
Less: Returns and allowances	40,000
Net sales	500,000
Less: Cost of sales	300,000
Gross margin	200,000
Less: Total expenses	100,000
Net profit (loss)	$ 40,000

Is this a complete operating statement? The answer is *yes*. This skeleton statement differs from Exhibit B-1 only in supporting detail. All the basic components are included. In fact, the only items we must list to have a complete operating statement are

Net sales	$500,000
Less: Costs	460,000
Net profit (loss)	$ 40,000

These three items are the essentials of an operating statement. All other subdivisions or details are just useful additions.

Meaning of sales

Now let's define the meaning of the terms in the skeleton statement.

The first item is sales. What do we mean by sales? The term **gross sales** is the total amount charged to all customers during some time period. However, there is always some customer dissatisfaction or just plain errors in ordering and shipping goods. This results in returns and allowances, which reduce gross sales.

A **return** occurs when a customer sends back purchased products. The company either refunds the purchase price or allows the customer dollar credit on other purchases.

An **allowance** usually occurs when a customer is not satisfied with a purchase for some reason. The company gives a price reduction on the original invoice (bill), but the customer keeps the goods and services.

These refunds and price reductions must be considered when the firm computes its net sales figure for the period. Really, we're only interested in the revenue the company manages to keep. This is **net sales**—the actual sales dollars the company receives. Therefore, all reductions, refunds, cancellations, and so forth made because of returns and allowances are deducted from the original total (gross sales) to get net sales. This is shown below.

Gross sales	$540,000
Less: Returns and allowances	40,000
Net sales	$500,000

Meaning of cost of sales

The next item in the operating statement—**cost of sales**—is the total value (at cost) of the sales during the period. We'll discuss this computation later. Meanwhile, note that after we obtain the cost of sales figure, we subtract it from the net sales figure to get the gross margin.

Meaning of gross margin and expenses

Gross margin (gross profit) is the money left to cover the expenses of selling the products and operating the business. Firms hope that a profit will be left after subtracting these expenses.

Selling expense is commonly the major expense below the gross margin. Note that in Exhibit B-1, **expenses** are all the remaining costs subtracted from the gross margin to get the net profit. The expenses in this case are the selling, administrative, and general expenses. (Note that the cost of purchases and cost of sales are not included in this total expense figure—they were subtracted from net sales earlier to get the gross margin. Note, also, that some accountants refer to cost of sales as cost of goods sold.)

Net profit—at the bottom of the statement—is what the company earned from its operations during a particular period. It is the amount left after the cost of sales and the expenses are subtracted from net sales. *Net sales and net profit are not the same.* Many firms have large sales and no profits—they may even have losses! That's why understanding costs, and controlling them, is important.

DETAILED ANALYSIS OF SECTIONS OF THE OPERATING STATEMENT

Cost of sales for a wholesale or retail company

The cost of sales section includes details that are used to find the cost of sales ($300,000 in our example).

In Exhibit B-1, you can see that beginning and ending inventory, purchases, purchase discounts, and freight-in are all necessary to calculate cost of sales. If we pull the cost of sales section from the operating statement, it looks like this:

Cost of sales:		
Beginning inventory at cost		$ 80,000
Purchases at billed cost	$310,000	
Less: Purchase discounts	40,000	
Purchases at net cost	270,000	
Plus: Freight-in	20,000	
Net cost of delivered purchases		290,000
Cost of goods available for sale		370,000
Less: Ending inventory at cost		70,000
Cost of sales		$300,000

Cost of sales is the cost value of what is *sold,* not the cost of goods on hand at any given time.

Inventory figures merely show the cost of goods on hand at the beginning and end of the period the statement covers. These figures may be obtained by physically counting goods on hand on these dates or estimated from perpetual inventory records that show the inventory balance at any given time. The methods used to determine the inventory should be as accurate as possible because these figures affect the cost of sales during the period and net profit.

The net cost of delivered purchases must include freight charges and purchase discounts received since these items affect the money actually spent to buy goods and bring them to the place of business. A **purchase discount** is a reduction of the original invoice amount for some business reason. For example, a cash discount may be given for prompt payment of the amount due. We subtract the total of such discounts from the original invoice cost of purchases to get the *net* cost of purchases. To this figure we add the freight charges for bringing the goods to the place of business. This gives the net cost of *delivered* purchases. When we add the net cost of delivered purchases to the beginning inventory at cost, we have the total cost of goods available for sale during the period. If we now subtract the ending inventory at cost from the cost of the goods available for sale, we get the cost of sales.

One important point should be noted about cost of sales. The way the value of inventory is calculated varies from one company to another—and it can cause big differences in the cost of sales and the operating statement. (See any basic accounting textbook for how the various inventory valuation methods work.)

Cost of sales for a manufacturing company

Exhibit B-1 shows the way the manager of a wholesale or retail business arrives at his cost of sales. Such a business *purchases* finished products and resells them. In a manufacturing company, the purchases section of this operating statement is

Exhibit B-2
Cost of Sales Section of an
Operating Statement for a
Manufacturing Firm

Cost of sales:		
Finished products inventory (beginning)	$ 20,000	
Cost of production (Schedule 1)	100,000	
Total cost of finished products available for sale	120,000	
Less: Finished products inventory (ending) ...	30,000	
Cost of sales		$ 90,000

Schedule 1, Schedule of cost of production			
Beginning work in process inventory			15,000
Raw materials:			
Beginning raw materials inventory		10,000	
Net cost of delivered purchases		80,000	
Total cost of materials available for use		90,000	
Less: Ending raw materials inventory		15,000	
Cost of materials placed in production		75,000	
Direct labor		20,000	
Manufacturing expenses:			
Indirect labor	$4,000		
Maintenance and repairs	3,000		
Factory supplies	1,000		
Heat, light, and power	2,000		
Total manufacturing expenses		10,000	
Total manufacturing costs....................			105,000
Total work in process during period			120,000
Less: Ending work in process inventory			20,000
Cost of production			$100,000

replaced by a section called cost of production. This section includes purchases of raw materials and parts, direct and indirect labor costs, and factory overhead charges (such as heat, light, and power) that are necessary to produce finished products. The cost of production is added to the beginning finished products inventory to arrive at the cost of products available for sale. Often, a separate cost of production statement is prepared, and only the total cost of production is shown in the operating statement. See Exhibit B-2 for an illustration of the cost of sales section of an operating statement for a manufacturing company.

Expenses

Expenses go below the gross margin. They usually include the costs of selling and the costs of administering the business. They do not include the cost of sales, either purchased or produced.

There is no right method for classifying the expense accounts or arranging them on the operating statement. They can just as easily be arranged alphabetically or according to amount, with the largest placed at the top and so on down the line. In a business of any size, though, it is clearer to group the expenses in some way and use subtotals by groups for analysis and control purposes. This was done in Exhibit B-1.

Summary on operating statements

The statement presented in Exhibit B-1 contains all the major categories in an operating statement—together with a normal amount of supporting detail. Further detail can be added to the statement under any of the major categories without changing the nature of the statement. The amount of detail normally is determined by how the statement will be used. A stockholder may be given a sketchy operating statement—while the one prepared for internal company use may have a lot of detail.

COMPUTING THE STOCKTURN RATE

A detailed operating statement can provide the data needed to compute the **stockturn rate**—a measure of the number of times the average inventory is sold during a year. Note that the stockturn rate is related to the *turnover during a year*, not the length of time covered by a particular operating statement.

The stockturn rate is a very important measure because it shows how rapidly the firm's inventory is moving. Some businesses typically have slower turnover than others. But a drop in turnover in a particular business can be very alarming. It may mean that the firm's assortment of products is no longer as attractive as it was. Also, it may mean that the firm will need more working capital to handle the same volume of sales. Most businesses pay a lot of attention to the stockturn rate, trying to get faster turnover (and lower inventory costs).

Three methods, all basically similar, can be used to compute the stockturn rate. Which method is used depends on the data available. These three methods, which usually give approximately the same results, are shown below.*

$$(1) \qquad \frac{\text{Cost of sales}}{\text{Average inventory at cost}}$$

$$(2) \qquad \frac{\text{Net sales}}{\text{Average inventory at selling price}}$$

$$(3) \qquad \frac{\text{Sales in units}}{\text{Average inventory in units}}$$

Computing the stockturn rate will be illustrated only for Formula 1, since all are similar. The only difference is that the cost figures used in Formula 1 are changed to a selling price or numerical count basis in Formulas 2 and 3. Note: Regardless of the method used, you must have both the numerator and denominator of the formula in the same terms.

If the inventory level varies a lot during the year, you may need detailed information about the inventory level at different times to compute the average inventory. If it stays at about the same level during the year, however, it's easy to get an estimate. For example, using Formula 1, the average inventory at cost is computed by adding the beginning and ending inventories at cost and dividing by 2. This average inventory figure is then divided into the cost of sales (in cost terms) to get the stockturn rate.

For example, suppose that the cost of sales for one year was $1,000,000. Beginning inventory was $250,000 and ending inventory $150,000. Adding the two inventory figures and dividing by 2, we get an average inventory of $200,000. We next divide the cost of sales by the average inventory ($1,000,000 ÷ $200,000) and get a stockturn rate of 5. The stockturn rate is covered further in Chapter 18.

OPERATING RATIOS HELP ANALYZE THE BUSINESS

Many businesspeople use the operating statement to calculate **operating ratios**—the ratio of items on the operating statement to net sales—and to compare these ratios from one time period to another. They can also compare their own operating ratios with those of competitors. Such competitive data is often available

*Differences occur because of varied markups and nonhomogeneous product assortments. In an assortment of tires, for example, those with low markups might have sold much better than those with high markups. But with Formula 3, all tires would be treated equally.

Appendix B 645 Marketing Arithmetic

through trade associations. Each firm may report its results to a trade association, which then distributes summary results to its members. These ratios help managers control their operations. If some expense ratios are rising, for example, those particular costs are singled out for special attention.

Operating ratios are computed by dividing net sales into the various operating statement items that appear below the net sales level in the operating statement. The net sales is used as the denominator in the operating ratio because it shows the sales the firm actually won.

We can see the relation of operating ratios to the operating statement if we think of there being another column to the right of the dollar figures in an operating statement. This column contains percentage figures, using net sales as 100 percent. This approach can be seen below.

Gross sales	$540,000	
Less: Returns and allowances	40,000	
Net sales	500,000	100%
Less: Cost of sales	300,000	60
Gross margin	200,000	40
Less: Total expenses	160,000	32
Net profit	$ 40,000	8%

The 40 percent ratio of gross margin to net sales in the above example shows that 40 percent of the net sales dollar is available to cover sales expenses and administering the business and provide a profit. Note that the ratio of expenses to sales added to the ratio of profit to sales equals the 40 percent gross margin ratio. The net profit ratio of 8 percent shows that 8 percent of the net sales dollar is left for profit.

The value of percentage ratios should be obvious. The percentages are easily figured and much easier to compare than large dollar figures.

Note that because these operating statement categories are interrelated, only a few pieces of information are needed to figure the others. In this case, for example, knowing the gross margin percent and net profit percent makes it possible to figure the expenses and cost of sales percentages. Further, knowing just one dollar amount and the percentages lets you figure all the other dollar amounts.

MARKUPS

A **markup** is the dollar amount added to the cost of sales to get the selling price. The markup usually is similar to the firm's gross margin because the markup amount added onto the unit cost of a product by a retailer or wholesaler is expected to cover the selling and administrative expenses and to provide a profit.

The markup approach to pricing is discussed in Chapter 18, so it will not be discussed at length here. But a simple example illustrates the idea. If a retailer buys an article that costs $1 when delivered to his store, he must sell it for more than this cost if he hopes to make a profit. So he might add 50 cents onto the cost of the article to cover his selling and other costs and, hopefully, to provide a profit. The 50 cents is the markup.

The 50 cents is also the gross margin or gross profit from that item *if* it is sold. But note that it is *not* the net profit. Selling expenses may amount to 35 cents, 45 cents, or even 55 cents. In other words, there is no guarantee the markup will cover costs. Further, there is no guarantee customers will buy at the marked-up price. This may require markdowns, which are discussed later in this appendix.

Markup conversions

Often it is convenient to use markups as percentages rather than focusing on the actual dollar amounts. But markups can be figured as a percent of cost or selling price. To have some agreement, *markup (percent)* will mean percentage of selling price unless stated otherwise. So the 50-cent markup on the $1.50 selling price is a markup of 33 ⅓ percent. On the other hand, the 50-cent markup is a 50 percent markup on cost.

Some retailers and wholesalers use markup conversion tables or spreadsheets to easily convert from cost to selling price, depending on the markup on selling price they want. To see the interrelation, look at the two formulas below. They can be used to convert either type of markup to the other.

(4) $$\text{Percent markup on selling price} = \frac{\text{Percent markup on cost}}{100\% + \text{Percent markup on cost}}$$

(5) $$\text{Percent markup on cost} = \frac{\text{Percent markup on selling price}}{100\% - \text{Percent markup on selling price}}$$

In the previous example, we had a cost of $1, a markup of 50 cents, and a selling price of $1.50. We saw that the markup on selling price was 33 ⅓ percent—and on cost, it was 50 percent. Let's substitute these percentage figures—in Formulas 4 and 5—to see how to convert from one basis to the other. Assume first of all that we only know the markup on selling price and want to convert to markup on cost. Using Formula 5, we get

$$\text{Percent markup on cost} = \frac{33\tfrac{1}{3}\%}{100\% - 33\tfrac{1}{3}\%} = \frac{33\tfrac{1}{3}\%}{66\tfrac{2}{3}\%} = 50\%$$

On the other hand, if we know only the percent markup on cost, we can convert to markup on selling price as follows:

$$\text{Percent markup on selling price} = \frac{50\%}{100\% + 50\%} = \frac{50\%}{150\%} = 33\tfrac{1}{3}\%$$

These results can be proved and summarized as follows:

Markup $0.50 = 50% of cost, or 33 ⅓% of selling price

+ Cost $1.00 = 100% of cost, or 66 ⅔% of selling price

Selling price $1.50 = 150% of cost, or 100% of selling price

Note that when the selling price ($1.50) is the base for a markup calculation, the markup percent (33 ⅓ percent = $.50/$1.50) must be less than 100 percent. As you can see, that's because the markup percent and the cost percent (66 ⅔ percent = $1.00/$1.50) sums to exactly 100 percent. So if you see a reference to a markup percent that is greater than 100 percent, it could not be based on the selling price and instead must be based on cost.

MARKDOWN RATIOS HELP CONTROL RETAIL OPERATIONS

The ratios we discussed above were concerned with figures on the operating statement. Another important ratio, the **markdown ratio,** is a tool many retailers use to measure the efficiency of various departments and their whole business. But note that it is *not directly related to the operating statement.* It requires special calculations.

A **markdown** is a retail price reduction required because customers won't buy some item at the originally marked-up price. This refusal to buy may be due to a variety of reasons—soiling, style changes, fading, damage caused by handling, or an original price that was too high. To get rid of these products, the retailer offers them at a lower price.

Markdowns are generally considered to be due to business errors, perhaps because of poor buying, original markups that are too high, and other reasons. (Note, however, that some retailers use markdowns as a way of doing business rather than a way to correct errors. For example, a store that buys out overstocked fashions from other retailers may start by marking each item with a high price and then reduce the price each week until it sells.) Regardless of the reason, however, markdowns are reductions in the original price—and they are important to managers who want to measure the effectiveness of their operations.

Markdowns are similar to allowances because price reductions are made. Thus, in computing a markdown ratio, markdowns and allowances are usually added together and then divided by net sales. The markdown ratio is computed as follows:

$$\text{Markdown \%} = \frac{\$ \text{ Markdowns} + \$ \text{ Allowances}}{\$ \text{ Net sales}} \times 100$$

The 100 is multiplied by the fraction to get rid of decimal points.

Returns are *not* included when figuring the markdown ratio. Returns are treated as consumer errors, not business errors, and therefore are not included in this measure of business efficiency.

Retailers who use markdown ratios usually keep a record of the amount of markdowns and allowances in each department and then divide the total by the net sales in each department. Over a period of time, these ratios give management one measure of the efficiency of buyers and salespeople in various departments.

It should be stressed again that the markdown ratio is not calculated directly from data on the operating statement since the markdowns take place before the products are sold. In fact, some products may be marked down and still not sold. Even if the marked-down items are not sold, the markdowns—that is, the reevaluations of their value—are included in the calculations in the time period when they are taken.

The markdown ratio is calculated for a whole department (or profit center), *not* individual items. What we are seeking is a measure of the effectiveness of a whole department, not how well the department did on individual items.

RETURN ON INVESTMENT (ROI) REFLECTS ASSET USE

Another off-the-operating-statement ratio is **return on investment (ROI)**—the ratio of net profit (after taxes) to the investment used to make the net profit, multiplied by 100 to get rid of decimals. Investment is not shown on the operating statement. But it is on the **balance sheet** (statement of financial condition), another accounting statement, which shows a company's assets, liabilities, and net worth. It may take some digging or special analysis, however, to find the right investment number.

Investment means the dollar resources the firm has invested in a project or business. For example, a new product may require $4 million in new money—for inventory, accounts receivable, promotion, and so on—and its attractiveness may be judged by its likely ROI. If the net profit (after taxes) for this new product is expected to be $1 million in the first year, then the ROI is 25 percent—that is, ($1 million ÷ $4 million) × 100.

There are two ways to figure ROI. The *direct* way is

$$\text{ROI (in \%)} = \frac{\text{Net profit (after taxes)}}{\text{Investment}} \times 100$$

The *indirect* way is

$$\text{ROI (in \%)} = \frac{\text{Net profit (after taxes)}}{\text{Sales}} = \frac{\text{Sales}}{\text{Investment}} \times 100$$

This way is concerned with net profit margin and turnover—that is,

$$\text{ROI (in \%)} = \text{Net profit margin} \times \text{Turnover} \times 100$$

This indirect way makes it clearer how to *increase* ROI. There are three ways:

1. Increase profit margin (with lower costs or a higher price).
2. Increase sales.
3. Decrease investment.

Effective marketing strategy planning and implementation can increase profit margins or sales, or both. And careful asset management can decrease investment.

ROI is a revealing measure of how well managers are doing. Most companies have alternative uses for their funds. If the returns in a business aren't at least as high as outside uses, then the money probably should be shifted to the more profitable uses.

Some firms borrow more than others to make investments. In other words, they invest less of their own money to acquire assets—what we called *investments*. If ROI calculations use only the firm's own investment, this gives higher ROI figures to those who borrow a lot—which is called *leveraging*. To adjust for different borrowing proportions—to make comparisons among projects, departments, divisions, and companies easier—another ratio has come into use. **Return on assets (ROA)** is the ratio of net profit (after taxes) to the assets used to make the net profit—times 100. Both ROI and ROA measures are trying to get at the same thing—how effectively the company is using resources. These measures became increasingly popular as profit rates dropped and it became more obvious that increasing sales volume doesn't necessarily lead to higher profits—or ROI or ROA. Inflation and higher costs for borrowed funds also force more concern for ROI and ROA. Marketers must include these measures in their thinking or top managers are likely to ignore their plans and requests for financial resources.

KEY TERMS

operating statement, 640

gross sales, 642

return, 642

allowance, 642

net sales, 642

cost of sales, 642

gross margin (gross profit), 642

expenses, 642

net profit, 642

purchase discount, 643

stockturn rate, 645

operating ratios, 645

markup, 646

markdown ratio, 647

markdown, 647

return on investment (ROI), 648

balance sheet, 648

return on assets (ROA), 649

QUESTIONS AND PROBLEMS

1. Distinguish between the following pairs of items that appear on operating statements: (*a*) gross sales and net sales, and (*b*) purchases at billed cost and purchases at net cost.

2. How does gross margin differ from gross profit? From net profit?

3. Explain the similarity between markups and gross margin. What connection do markdowns have with the operating statement?

4. Compute the net profit for a company with the following data:

Beginning inventory (cost)	$ 150,000
Purchases at billed cost	330,000
Sales returns and allowances	250,000
Rent	60,000
Salaries	400,000
Heat and light	180,000
Ending inventory (cost)	250,000
Freight cost (inbound)	80,000
Gross sales	1,300,000

5. Construct an operating statement from the following data:

Returns and allowances	$150,000
Expenses	20%
Closing inventory at cost	600,000
Markdowns	2%
Inward transportation	30,000
Purchases	1,000,000
Net profit (5%)	300,000

6. Compute net sales and percent of markdowns for the data given below:

Markdowns	$ 40,000
Gross sales	400,000
Returns	32,000
Allowances	48,000

7. (a) What percentage markups on cost are equivalent to the following percentage markups on selling price: 20, 37½, 50, and 66⅔? (b) What percentage markups on selling price are equivalent to the following percentage markups on cost: 33⅓, 20, 40, and 50?

8. What net sales volume is required to obtain a stock-turn rate of 20 times a year on an average inventory at cost of $100,000 with a gross margin of 25 percent?

9. Explain how the general manager of a department store might use the markdown ratios computed for her various departments. Is this a fair measure? Of what?

10. Compare and contrast return on investment (ROI) and return on assets (ROA) measures. Which would be best for a retailer with no bank borrowing or other outside sources of funds (that is, the retailer has put up all the money that the business needs)?

APPENDIX C

Career Planning in Marketing

WHEN YOU FINISH THIS APPENDIX, YOU SHOULD

1. Know that there is a job or a career for you in marketing.

2. Know that marketing jobs can be rewarding, pay well, and offer opportunities for growth.

3. Understand the difference between "people-oriented" and "thing-oriented" jobs.

4. Know about the many marketing jobs you can choose from.

5. Know some ways to use the Internet to help with career planning.

One of the hardest decisions facing most college students is the choice of a career. Of course, you are the best judge of your own objectives, interests, and abilities. Only you can decide what career *you* should pursue. However, you owe it to yourself to at least consider the possibility of a career in marketing.

THERE'S A PLACE IN MARKETING FOR YOU

We're happy to tell you that many opportunities are available in marketing. There's a place in marketing for everyone, from a service provider in a fast-food restaurant to a vice president of marketing in a large company such as Microsoft or Procter & Gamble. The opportunities range widely, so it will help to be more specific. In the following pages, we'll discuss (1) the typical pay for different marketing jobs, (2) setting your own objectives and evaluating your interests and abilities, and (3) the kinds of jobs available in marketing. We'll also provide some ideas about how to use the Internet to get more information and perhaps even to apply for a job or post your own information; this material is in the special box with the title "Getting Wired for a Career in Marketing."

THERE ARE MANY MARKETING JOBS, AND THEY CAN PAY WELL

There are many interesting and challenging jobs for those with marketing training. You may not know it, but 60 percent of graduating college students take their initial job in a sales, marketing, or customer service position regardless of their stated major. So you'll have a head start because you've been studying marketing, and companies are always looking for people who already have skills in place. In terms of upward mobility, more CEOs have come from the sales and marketing side than all other fields combined. The sky is the limit for those who enter the sales and marketing profession prepared for the future!

Further, marketing jobs open to college-level students do pay well. At the time this went to press, marketing undergraduates were being offered starting salaries around $30,000, with a range from about $18,000 to $45,000 a year. Students with a master's in marketing averaged about $50,000; those with an MBA averaged about $60,000. Starting salaries can vary considerably, depending on your background, experience, and location.

Starting salaries in marketing compare favorably with many other fields. They are lower than those in such fields as computer science and electrical engineering where college graduates are currently in demand. But there is even better opportunity for personal growth, variety, and income in many marketing positions. The *American Almanac of Jobs and Salaries* ranks the median income of marketers number 10 in a list of 125 professions. Marketing also supplies about 50 percent of the people who achieve senior management ranks.

How far and fast your career and income rise above the starting level, however, depends on many factors, including your willingness to work, how well you get along with people, and your individual abilities. But most of all, it depends on *getting results*—individually and through other people. And this is where many marketing jobs offer the newcomer great opportunities. It is possible to show initiative, ability, creativity, and judgment in marketing jobs. And some young people move up very rapidly in marketing. Some even end up at the top in large companies or as owners of their own businesses.

Marketing is often the route to the top

Marketing is where the action is! In the final analysis, a firm's success or failure depends on the effectiveness of its marketing program. This doesn't mean the other

Exhibit C-1
Organizing Your Own
Personal Marketing Strategy
Planning

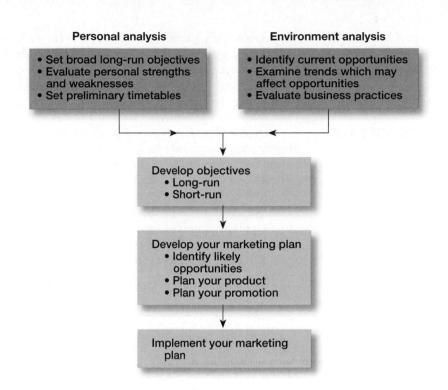

Personal analysis
- Set broad long-run objectives
- Evaluate personal strengths and weaknesses
- Set preliminary timetables

Environment analysis
- Identify current opportunities
- Examine trends which may affect opportunities
- Evaluate business practices

Develop objectives
- Long-run
- Short-run

Develop your marketing plan
- Identify likely opportunities
- Plan your product
- Plan your promotion

Implement your marketing plan

functional areas aren't important. It merely reflects the fact that a firm won't have much need for accountants, finance people, production managers, and so on if it can't successfully meet customers' needs and sell its products.

Because marketing is so vital to a firm's survival, many companies look for people with training and experience in marketing when filling key executive positions. In general, chief executive officers for the nation's largest corporations are more likely to have backgrounds in marketing and distribution than in other fields such as production, finance, and engineering.

DEVELOP YOUR OWN PERSONAL MARKETING STRATEGY

Now that you know there are many opportunities in marketing, your problem is matching the opportunities to your own personal objectives and strengths. Basically the problem is a marketing problem: developing a marketing strategy to sell a product—yourself—to potential employers. Just as in planning strategies for products, developing your own strategy takes careful thought. Exhibit C-1 shows how you can organize your own strategy planning. This exhibit shows that you should evaluate yourself first—a personal analysis—and then analyze the environment for opportunities. This will help you sharpen your own long- and short-run objectives, which will lead to developing a strategy. Finally, you should start implementing your own personal marketing strategy. These ideas are explained more fully below.

CONDUCT YOUR OWN PERSONAL ANALYSIS

You are the Product you are going to include in your own marketing plan. So first you have to decide what your long-run objectives are—what you want to do, how hard you want to work, and how quickly you want to reach your objectives.

Be honest with yourself—or you will eventually face frustration. Evaluate your own personal strengths and weaknesses—and decide what factors may become the key to your success. Finally, as part of your personal analysis, set some preliminary timetables to guide your strategy planning and implementation efforts. Let's spell this out in detail.

Set broad long-run objectives

Strategy planning requires much trial-and-error decision making. But at the very beginning, you should make some tentative decisions about your own objectives—what you want out of a job and out of life. At the very least, you should decide whether you are just looking for a job or whether you want to build a career. Beyond this, do you want the position to be personally satisfying—or is the financial return enough? And just how much financial return do you need? Some people work only to support themselves (and their families) and their leisure-time activities. These people try to find job opportunities that provide adequate financial returns but aren't too demanding of their time or effort.

Other people look first for satisfaction in their job—and they seek opportunities for career advancement. Financial rewards may be important too, but these are used mainly as measures of success. In the extreme, the career-oriented individual may be willing to sacrifice a lot, including leisure and social activities, to achieve success in a career.

Once you've tentatively decided these matters, then you can get more serious about whether you should seek a job or a career in marketing. If you decide to pursue a career, you should set your broad long-run objectives to achieve it. For example, one long-run objective might be to pursue a career in marketing management (or marketing research). This might require more academic training than you planned, as well as a different kind of training. If your objective is to get a job that pays well, on the other hand, then this calls for a different kind of training and different kinds of job experiences before completing your academic work.

Evaluate personal strengths and weaknesses

What kind of a job is right for you?

Because of the great variety of marketing jobs, it's hard to generalize about what aptitudes you should have to pursue a career in marketing. Different jobs attract people with various interests and abilities. We'll give you some guidelines about what kinds of interests and abilities marketers should have. However, if you're completely lost about your own interests and abilities, see your campus career counselor and take some vocational aptitude and interest tests. These tests will help you to compare yourself with people who are now working in various career positions. They will *not* tell you what you should do, but they can help, especially in eliminating possibilities you are less interested in or less able to do well in.

Are you people-oriented or thing-oriented?

One useful approach is to decide whether you are basically "people-oriented" or "thing-oriented." This is a very important decision. A people-oriented person might be very unhappy in an inventory management job, for example, whereas a thing-oriented person might be miserable in a personal selling or retail management job that involves a lot of customer contact.

Marketing has both people-oriented and thing-oriented jobs. People-oriented jobs are primarily in the promotion area—where company representatives must make contact with potential customers. This may be direct personal selling or customer service activities—for example, in technical service or installation and repair. Thing-oriented jobs focus more on creative activities and analyzing data—as in advertising and marketing research—or on organizing and scheduling work—as in operating warehouses, transportation agencies, or the back-end of retailers.

People-oriented jobs tend to pay more, in part because such jobs are more likely to affect sales, the lifeblood of any business. Thing-oriented jobs, on the other hand, are often seen as cost generators rather than sales generators. Taking a big view of

The Internet is a great resource at every stage of career planning and job hunting. It can help you learn: how to do a self-assessment, the outlook for different industries and jobs, what firms have jobs open, how to improve a résumé and post it online for free, and just about anything else you can imagine. Here we'll highlight just a few ideas and websites that can help you get started. However, if you start with some of these suggestions, each website you visit will provide links to other relevant sites that will give you new ideas to think about.

One good place to start is at Yahoo (www.yahoo.com). Select *jobs* under the business and economy heading, and then click on *Yahoo HotJobs*. Take a look at all of the information and services that are available when you select the *Career Tools* link. For example, you can browse résumé tools and salary information, look at job listings, and much more. You may also want to study the similar information at www.monster.com.

Another website to check is at www.marketingjobs.com. It has listings of marketing jobs, links to a number of companies with openings, a résumé center with ideas for preparing a résumé and posting it on the Internet, and lists of helpful periodicals. You might also go to www.careerjournal.com. There are job listings, job-hunting advice, career articles from *The Wall Street Journal,* and more. You can create and post a résumé here as well. Professional associations are another great resource. For example, the American Marketing Association website is at www.marketingpower.com, and the Sales and Marketing Executives International website is at www.smei.org. The Council of Logistics Management website is at www.clm1.org.

Another potentially useful website address is www.collegegrad.com. It has links for posting a résumé, information on writing cover letters and getting references, and ideas about how to find a company with job openings. To get a sample of what's possible in tracking down jobs, visit the website at www.thejobresource.com and experiment with its search engine, which lets you look at what's available by state. For example, you might want to search through job listings that mention terms such as *entry level, marketing, advertising,* and *sales.*

This should get you started. Remember, however, that in Chapter 8 we gave addresses for a number of websites with search engines. You can use one of them to help find more detail on any topic that interests you. For example, you might go to www.altavista.com and do a search on terms such as *marketing jobs, salary surveys, post a résumé,* or *entry level position.*

---

the whole company's operations, the thing-oriented jobs are certainly necessary—but without sales, no one is needed to do them.

Thing-oriented jobs are usually done at a company's facilities. Further, especially in lower-level jobs, the amount of work to be done and even the nature of the work may be spelled out quite clearly. The time it takes to design questionnaires and tabulate results, for example, can be estimated with reasonable accuracy. Similarly, running a warehouse, analyzing inventory reports, scheduling outgoing shipments, and so on are more like production operations. It's fairly easy to measure an employee's effectiveness and productivity in a thing-oriented job. At the least, time spent can be used to measure an employee's contribution.

A sales rep, on the other hand, might spend all weekend thinking and planning how to make a half-hour sales presentation on Monday. For what should the sales rep be compensated—the half-hour presentation, all of the planning and thinking that went into it, or the results? Typically, sales reps are rewarded for results—and this helps account for the sometimes extremely high salaries paid to effective order getters. At the same time, some people-oriented jobs can be routinized and are lower paid. For example, salespeople in some retail stores are paid at or near the minimum wage.

Managers needed for both kinds of jobs

Here we have oversimplified deliberately to emphasize the differences among types of jobs. Actually, of course, there are many variations between the two extremes. Some sales reps must do a great deal of analytical work before they make a presentation. Similarly, some marketing researchers must be extremely people-sensitive to get potential customers to reveal their true feelings. But the division is still useful because it focuses on the primary emphasis in different kinds of jobs.

Managers are needed for the people in both kinds of jobs. Managing others requires a blend of both people and analytical skills—but people skills may be the more important of the two. Therefore, people-oriented individuals are often promoted into managerial positions more quickly.

What will differentiate your Product?

After deciding whether you're generally people-oriented or thing-oriented, you're ready for the next step—trying to identify your specific strengths (to be built on) and weaknesses (to be avoided or remedied). It is important to be as specific as possible so you can develop a better marketing plan. For example, if you decide you are more people-oriented, are you more skilled in verbal or written communication? Or if you are more thing-oriented, what specific analytical or technical skills do you have? Are you good at working with numbers, using a computer, solving complex problems, or coming to the root of a problem? Other possible strengths include past experience (career-related or otherwise), academic performance, an outgoing personality, enthusiasm, drive, motivation, and so on.

It is important to see that your plan should build on your strengths. An employer will be hiring you to do something—so promote yourself as someone who is able to do something *well*. In other words, find your competitive advantage in your unique strengths—and then communicate these unique things about *you* and what you can do. Give an employer a reason to pick you over other candidates by showing that you'll add superior value to the company.

While trying to identify strengths, you also must realize that you may have some important weaknesses, depending on your objectives. If you are seeking a career that requires technical skills, for example, then you need to get those skills. Or if you are seeking a career that requires independence and self-confidence, then you should try to develop those characteristics in yourself—or change your objectives.

Set some timetables

At this point in your strategy planning process, set some timetables to organize your thinking and the rest of your planning. You need to make some decisions at this point to be sure you see where you're going. You might simply focus on getting your first job, or you might decide to work on two marketing plans: (1) a short-run plan to get your first job and (2) a longer-run plan—perhaps a five-year plan—to show how you're going to accomplish your long-run objectives. People who are basically job-oriented may get away with only a short-run plan, just drifting from one opportunity to another as their own objectives and opportunities change. But those interested in careers need a longer-run plan. Otherwise, they may find themselves pursuing attractive first-job opportunities that satisfy short-run objectives but quickly leave them frustrated when they realize that they can't achieve their long-run objectives without additional training or other experiences that require starting over again on a new career path.

ENVIRONMENT ANALYSIS

Strategy planning is a matching process. For your own strategy planning, this means matching yourself to career opportunities. So let's look at opportunities available in the marketing environment. (The same approach applies, of course, in the whole business area.) Exhibit C-2 shows some of the possibilities and salary ranges.

Keep in mind that the salary ranges in Exhibit C-2 are rough estimates. Salaries for a particular job often vary depending on a variety of factors, including company

Exhibit C-2   Some Career Paths and Salary Ranges

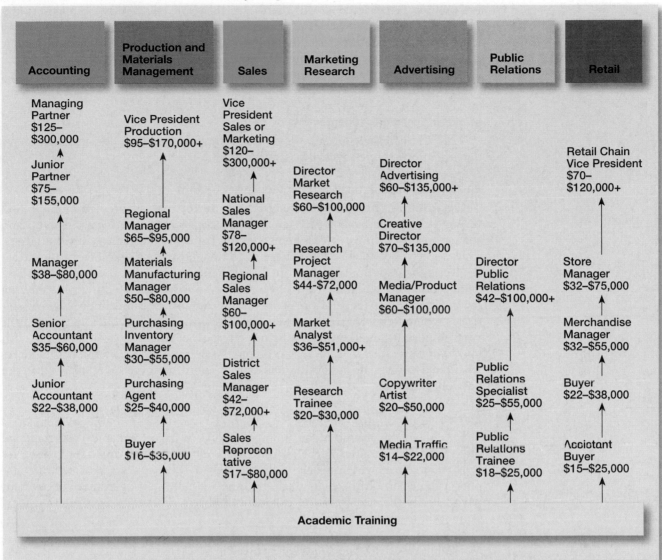

size, industry, and geographic area. People in some firms also get big bonuses that are not counted in salary. In recent years, *Advertising Age* has been publishing an annual survey of salary levels for different marketing and advertising jobs, with breakdowns by company size and other factors. Many trade associations, across a variety of different industries, also publish surveys. If you use the Internet search engine at www.google.com and do a search on *salary survey,* you will find that there are hundreds of such surveys available on the Internet for a number of different industries. There is also a useful "salary wizard" at www.salary.com that provides salary ranges for specific jobs and geographic areas.

Identifying current opportunities in marketing

Because of the wide range of opportunities in marketing, it's helpful to narrow your possibilities. After deciding on your own objectives, strengths, and weaknesses, think about where in the marketing system you might like to work. Would you like to work for manufacturers, or wholesalers, or retailers? Or does it really matter? Do you want to be involved with consumer products or business products? By analyzing your feelings about these possibilities, you can begin to zero in on the kind of job and the functional area that might interest you most.

One simple way to get a better idea of the kinds of jobs available in marketing is to review the chapters of this text—this time with an eye for job opportunities rather than new concepts. The following paragraphs contain brief descriptions of job areas that marketing graduates are often interested in with references to specific chapters in the text. Some, as noted below, offer good starting opportunities, while others do not. While reading these paragraphs, keep your own objectives, interests, and strengths in mind.

Marketing manager (Chapter 2)

This is usually not an entry-level job, although aggressive students may move quickly into this role in smaller companies.

Customer or market analyst (Chapters 3, 4, 5, and 6)

Opportunities as consumer analysts and market analysts are commonly found in large companies, marketing research organizations, advertising agencies, and some consulting firms. Investment banking firms also hire entry-level analysts; they want to know what the market for a new business is like before investing. Beginning market analysts start in thing-oriented jobs until their judgment and people-oriented skills are tested. The job may involve collecting or analyzing secondary data or preparation of reports and plans. Because knowledge of statistics, computer software, Internet search techniques, or behavioral sciences is very important, marketing graduates often find themselves competing with majors from statistics, sociology, computer science, and economics. Graduates who have courses in marketing *and* one or more of these areas may have the best opportunities.

Purchasing agent/buyer (Chapter 7)

Entry-level opportunities are commonly found in large companies, and there are often good opportunities in the procurement area. Many companies are looking for bright newcomers who can help them find new and better ways to work with suppliers. To get off on the right track, beginners usually start as trainees or assistant buyers under the supervision of experienced buyers. That's good preparation for a promotion to more responsibility.

Marketing research opportunities (Chapter 8)

There are entry-level opportunities at all levels in the channel (but especially in large firms where more formal marketing research is done in-house), in advertising agencies, and in marketing research firms. Some general management consulting firms also have marketing research groups. Quantitative and behavioral science skills are extremely important in marketing research, so some firms are more interested in business graduates who have studied statistics or psychology as electives. But there still are many opportunities in marketing research for marketing graduates, especially if they have some experience in working with computers and statistical software. A recent graduate might begin in a training program—conducting interviews or summarizing open-ended answers from questionnaires and helping to prepare electronic slide presentations for clients—before being promoted to a position as an analyst, assistant project manager, account representative, and subsequent management positions.

Packaging specialists (Chapter 9)

Packaging manufacturers tend to hire and train interested people from various backgrounds—there is little formal academic training in packaging. There are many sales opportunities in this field—and with training, interested people can become specialists fairly quickly in this growing area.

Product/brand manager (Chapters 9 and 10)

Many multiproduct firms have brand or product managers handling individual products—in effect, managing each product as a separate business. Some firms hire marketing graduates as assistant brand or product managers, although larger firms typically recruit MBAs for these jobs. Many firms prefer that recent college graduates spend some time in the field doing sales work or working with an ad agency or sales promotion agency before moving into brand or product management positions.

Product planner (Chapter 10)

This is usually not an entry-level position. Instead, people with experience on the technical side of the business or in sales might be moved onto a new-product development team as they demonstrate judgment and analytical skills. However, new employees with winning ideas for new products don't go unnoticed—and they sometimes have the opportunity to grow fast with ideas they spearhead. Having a job that puts you in contact with customers is often a good way to spot new needs.

Distribution channel management (Chapter 11)

This work is typically handled or directed by sales managers and therefore is not an entry-level position. However, many firms form teams of specialists who work closely with their counterparts in other firms in the channel to strengthen coordination and relationships. Such a team often includes new people in sales or purchasing because it gives them exposure to a different part of the firm's activities. It's also not unusual for people to start working in a particular industry and then take a different job at a different level in the channel. For example, a graduate who has trained to be a store manager for a chain of sporting goods stores might go to work for a manufacturers' representative that handles a variety of sports equipment.

Logistics opportunities (Chapter 12)

There are many sales opportunities with physical distribution specialists—but there are also many thing-oriented jobs involving traffic management, warehousing, and materials handling. Here training in accounting, finance, and computer methods could be very useful. These kinds of jobs are available at all levels in channels of distribution.

Retailing opportunities (Chapter 13)

Not long ago, most entry-level marketing positions in retailing involved some kind of sales work. That has changed rapidly in recent years because the number of large retail chains is expanding and they often recruit graduates for their management training programs. Retailing positions tend to offer lower-than-average starting salaries—but they often provide opportunities for very rapid advancement. In a fast-growing chain, results-oriented people can move up very quickly. Most retailers require new employees to have some selling experience before managing others—or buying. A typical marketing graduate can expect to work as an assistant manager or do some sales work and manage one or several departments before advancing to a store management position—or to a staff position that might involve buying, advertising, location analysis, and so on.

Wholesaling opportunities (Chapter 13)

Entry-level jobs with merchant wholesalers typically fall into one of two categories. The first is in the logistics area—working with transportation management, inventory control, distribution customer service, and related activities. The other category usually involves personal selling and customer support. Agent wholesalers typically focus on selling, and entry-level jobs often start out with order-taking responsibilities that grow into order-getting responsibilities. Many wholesalers are moving much of their information to the Internet, so marketing students with skills and knowledge in this arena may find especially interesting opportunities.

Personal selling opportunities (Chapter 15)

Because there are so many different types of sales jobs and so many people are employed in sales, there are many good entry-level opportunities in personal selling. This might be order-getting, order-taking, or missionary selling. Many sales jobs now rely on sales technology, so some of the most challenging opportunities will go to students who know how to prepare spreadsheets and presentation materials using software programs like Microsoft Office. Many students are reluctant to get into personal selling—but this field offers benefits that are hard to match in any other field. These include the opportunity to earn extremely high salaries and commissions quickly, a chance to develop your self-confidence and resourcefulness, an opportunity to work with minimal supervision—almost to the point of being your own boss—and a chance to acquire product and customer knowledge that many firms consider necessary for a successful career in product/brand management, sales management, and marketing management. On the other hand, many salespeople prefer to spend their entire careers in selling. They like the freedom and earning potential that go with a sales job over the headaches and sometimes lower salaries of sales management positions.

Advertising opportunities (Chapters 14 and 16)

Job opportunities in this area are varied and highly competitive. And because the ability to communicate and a knowledge of the behavioral sciences are important, marketing graduates often find themselves competing with majors from fields such as English, communication, psychology, and sociology. There are thing-oriented jobs such as copywriting, media buying, art, computer graphics, and so on. Competition for these jobs is very competitive—and they go to people with a track record. So the entry-level positions are as assistant to a copywriter, media buyer, or art director. There are also people-oriented positions involving work with clients, which are probably of more interest to marketing graduates. This is a glamorous but small and extremely competitive industry where young people can rise very rapidly—but they can also be as easily displaced by new bright young people. Entry-level salaries in advertising are typically low. There are sometimes good opportunities to get started in advertising with a retail chain that prepares its advertising internally. Another way to get more experience with advertising is to take a job with one of the media, perhaps in sales or as a customer consultant. Selling advertising space on a website or cable TV station or newspaper may not seem as glamorous as developing TV ads, but media salespeople help their customers solve promotion problems and get experience dealing with both the business and creative side of advertising.

Sales promotion opportunities (Chapters 14 and 16)

The number of entry-level positions in the sales promotion area is growing because the number of specialists in this area is growing. For example, specialists might help a company plan a special event for employees, figure out procedures to distribute free samples, or perhaps set up a database to send customers a newsletter. Because clients' needs are often different, creativity and judgment are required. It is usually difficult for an inexperienced person to show evidence of these skills right out of school, so entry-level people often work with a project manager until they learn the ropes. In companies that handle their own sales promotion work, a beginner usually starts by getting some experience in sales or advertising.

Pricing opportunities (Chapters 17 and 18)

Pricing decisions are usually handled by experienced executives. However, in some large companies and consulting firms there are opportunities as pricing analysts for marketing graduates who have quantitative skills. These people work as assistants to higher-level executives and collect and analyze information about competitors' prices and costs, as well as the firm's own costs. Thus, being able to work with accounting numbers and computer spreadsheets is often important in these jobs. However, sometimes the route to these jobs is through experience in marketing research or product management.

Credit management opportunities

Specialists in credit have a continuing need for employees who are interested in evaluating customers' credit ratings and ensuring that money gets collected. Both people skills and thing skills can be useful here. Entry-level positions normally involve a training program and then working under the supervision of others until your judgment and abilities are tested.

International marketing opportunities

Many marketing students are intrigued with the adventure and foreign travel promised by careers in international marketing. Some firms hire recent college graduates for positions in international marketing, but more often these positions go to MBA graduates. However, that is changing as more and more firms are pursuing international markets. It's an advantage in seeking an international marketing job to know a second language and to know about the culture of countries where you would like to work. Your college may have courses or international exchange programs that would help in these areas. Graduates aiming for a career in international marketing usually must spend time mastering the firm's domestic marketing operations before being sent abroad. So a good way to start is to focus on firms that are already involved in international marketing, or who are planning to move in that direction soon. On the other hand, there are many websites with listings of international jobs. For example, you might want to visit www.overseasjobs.com.

Customer relations/consumer affairs opportunities (Chapters 14 and 22)

Most firms are becoming more concerned about their relations with customers and the general public. Employees in this kind of work, however, usually have held various positions with the firm before doing customer relations.

Study trends that may affect your opportunities

A strategy planner should always be evaluating the future because it's easier to go along with trends than to buck them. This means you should watch for political, technical, or economic changes that might open, or close, career opportunities.

If you can spot a trend early, you may be able to prepare yourself to take advantage of it as part of your long-run strategy planning. Other trends might mean you should avoid certain career options. For example, technological changes in computers and communications, including the Internet, are leading to major changes in retailing and advertising, as well as in personal selling. Cable television, telephone selling, and direct-mail selling may reduce the need for routine order takers, while increasing the need for higher-level order getters. More targeted and imaginative sales presentations for delivery by mail, e-mail, phone, or Internet websites may be needed. The retailers that prosper will have a better understanding of their target markets. And they may need to be supported by wholesalers and manufacturers that can plan targeted promotions that make economic sense. This will require a better understanding of the production and physical distribution side of business, as well as the financial side. And this means better training in accounting, finance, inventory control, and so on. So plan your personal strategy with such trends in mind.

One good way to get more detailed analysis is to go to the U.S. Bureau of Labor Statistics website at http://stats.bls.gov and use the search procedure to look for the term *occupational outlook*. The Bureau provides detailed comments about the outlook for employment and growth in different types of jobs, industries, and regions.

Evaluate business practices

Finally, you need to know how businesses really operate and the kind of training required for various jobs. We've already seen that there are many opportunities in marketing—but not all jobs are open to everyone, and not all jobs are entry-level jobs. Positions such as marketing manager, brand manager, and sales manager are higher rungs on the marketing career ladder. They become available only when you have a few years of experience and have shown leadership and judgment. Some positions require more education than others. So take a hard look at your long-run objectives—and then see what degree you may need for the kinds of opportunities you might like.

DEVELOP OBJECTIVES

Once you've done a personal analysis and environment analysis—identifying your personal interests, your strengths and weaknesses, and the opportunities in the environment—define your short-run and long-run objectives more specifically.

Develop long-run objectives

Your long-run objectives should clearly state what you want to do and what you will do for potential employers. You might be as specific as indicating the exact career area you want to pursue over the next 5 to 10 years. For example, your long-run objective might be to apply a set of marketing research and marketing management tools to the food manufacturing industry, with the objective of becoming director of marketing research in a small food manufacturing company.

Your long-run objectives should be realistic and attainable. They should be objectives you have thought about and for which you think you have the necessary skills (or the capabilities to develop those skills) as well as the motivation to reach the objectives.

Develop short-run objectives

To achieve your long-run objective(s), you should develop one or more short-run objectives. These should spell out what is needed to reach your long-run objective(s). For example, you might need to develop a variety of marketing research skills *and* marketing management skills—because both are needed to reach the longer-run objective. Or you might need an entry-level position in marketing

research for a large food manufacturer to gain experience and background. An even shorter-run objective might be to take the academic courses that are necessary to get that desired entry-level job. In this example, you would probably need a minimum of an undergraduate degree in marketing, with an emphasis on marketing research. (Note that, given the longer-run objective of managerial responsibility, a business degree would probably be better than a degree in statistics or psychology.)

DEVELOPING YOUR MARKETING PLAN

Now that you've developed your objectives, move on to developing your own personal marketing plan. This means zeroing in on likely opportunities and developing a specific marketing strategy for these opportunities. Let's talk about that now.

Identify likely opportunities

An important step in strategy planning is identifying potentially attractive opportunities. Depending on where you are in your academic training, this can vary all the way from preliminary exploration to making detailed lists of companies that offer the kinds of jobs that interest you. If you're just getting started, talk to your school's career counselors and placement officers about the kinds of jobs being offered to your school's graduates. Your marketing instructors can help you be realistic about ways you can match your training, abilities, and interests to job opportunities. Also, it helps to read business publications such as *BusinessWeek*, *Fortune*, *The Wall Street Journal*, and *Advertising Age*. *Applications in Basic Marketing*, which comes shrinkwrapped with this text, provides reprints of recent articles from these publications. If you are interested in opportunities in a particular industry, check at your library or on the Internet to see if there are trade publications or websites that can bring you up to speed on the marketing issues in that area. Your library or college may also have an online service to make it easier to search for articles about specific companies or industries. And many companies have their own websites that can be a very useful source of information.

Don't overlook the business sections of your local newspapers to keep in touch with marketing developments in your area. And take advantage of any opportunity to talk with marketers directly. Ask them what they're doing and what satisfactions they find in their jobs. Also, if your college has a marketing club, join it and participate actively in the club's programs. It will help you meet marketers and students with serious interest in the field. Some may have had interesting job experiences and can provide you with leads on part-time jobs or exciting career opportunities.

If you're far along in your present academic training, list companies that you know something about or are willing to investigate, trying to match your skills and interests with possible opportunities. Narrow your list to a few companies you might like to work for.

If you have trouble narrowing down to specific companies, make a list of your personal interest areas—sports, travel, reading, music, or whatever. Think about the companies that compete in markets related to these interests. Often your own knowledge about these areas and interest in them can give you a competitive advantage in getting a job. This helps you focus on companies that serve needs you think are important or interesting. A related approach is to do a search on the Internet for websites related to your areas of interest. Websites often display ads or links to firms that are involved in that specific interest area. Further, many companies post job openings on their own websites or at websites that specialize in promoting job searches by many companies.

Then do some research on these companies. Find out how they are organized, their product lines, and their overall strategies. Try to get clear job descriptions for the kinds of positions you're seeking. Match these job descriptions against your understanding of these jobs and your objectives. Jobs with similar titles may offer very different opportunities. By researching job positions and companies in depth, you should begin to have a feel for where you would be comfortable as an employee. This will help you narrow your target market of possible employers to perhaps five firms. For example, you may decide that your target market for an entry-level position consists of large corporations with (1) in-depth training programs, (2) a wide product line, and (3) a wide variety of marketing jobs that will enable you to get a range of experiences and responsibilities within the same company.

Planning your Product

Just like any strategy planner, you must decide what Product features are necessary to appeal to your target market. Identify which credentials are mandatory and which are optional. For example, is your present academic program enough, or will you need more training? Also, identify what technical skills are needed, such as computer programming or accounting. Further, are there any business experiences or extracurricular activities that might help make your Product more attractive to employers? This might involve active participation in college organizations or work experience, either on the job or in internships.

Planning your Promotion

Once you identify target companies and develop a Product you hope will be attractive to them, you have to tell these potential customers about your Product. You can write directly to prospective employers, sending a carefully developed résumé that reflects your strategy planning. Or you can visit them in person (with your résumé). Many colleges run well-organized interviewing services. Seek their advice early in your strategy planning effort.

IMPLEMENTING YOUR MARKETING PLAN

When you complete your personal marketing plan, you have to implement it, starting with working to accomplish your short-run objectives. If, as part of your plan, you decide that you need specific outside experience, then arrange to get it. This may mean taking a low-paying job or even volunteering to work in political organizations or volunteer organizations where you can get that kind of experience. If you decide that you need skills you can learn in academic courses, plan to take these courses. Similarly, if you don't have a good understanding of your opportunities, then learn as much as you can about possible jobs by talking to professors, taking advanced courses, and talking to businesspeople. Of course, trends and opportunities can change—so continue to read business publications, talk with professionals in your areas of interest, and be sure that the planning you've done still makes sense.

Strategy planning must adapt to the environment. If the environment changes or your personal objectives change, you have to develop a new plan. This is an ongoing process—and you may never be completely satisfied with your strategy planning. But even trying will make you look much more impressive when you begin your job interviews. Remember, while all employers would like to hire a Superman or a Wonder Woman, they are also impressed with candidates who know what they want to do and are looking for a place where they can fit in and make a contribution. So planning a personal strategy and implementing it almost guarantee you'll do a better job of career planning, and this will help ensure that you reach your own objectives, whatever they are.

Whether or not you decide to pursue a marketing career, the authors wish you the best of luck in your search for a challenging and rewarding career, wherever your interests and abilities may take you.

Video Cases

Basic Marketing includes two different types of marketing cases: the 7 special video cases in this section and the 35 traditional cases in the next section. All of the cases offer you the opportunity to evaluate marketing concepts at work in a variety of real-world situations. However, the video cases add a multimedia dimension because we have produced a special video to accompany each of the written cases. An abbreviated version of the video for each case is available on the *Student CD-ROM to Accompany Basic Marketing*. The full-length videos are available to professors who adopt *Basic Marketing* for use in their course. (These case-based videos are in addition to the teaching videos we have custom produced and made available to instructors for possible use with other parts of the text.)

The videos bring to life many of the issues considered in each case. However, you can read and analyze the written case descriptions even if there is no time or opportunity to view the video. Either way, you'll find the case interesting and closely tied to the important concepts you've studied in the text.

The set of questions at the end of each case will get you started in thinking about the marketing issues in the case. Further, we provide instructors with a number of suggestions on using the video cases—both for group discussion in class or individual assignments. Thus, as is also true with the traditional cases in the next section, the video cases can be used in many different ways and sequences. You can analyze all of the cases, or only a subset. In fact, the same case can be analyzed several times for different purposes. As your understanding of marketing deepens throughout the course, you'll "see" many more of the marketing issues considered in each case.

1. Suburban Regional Shopping Malls: Can the Magic Be Restored?*

The suburban regional shopping mall is regarded by many as the "crown jewel" of shopping experiences. In a single location, shoppers can visit over a hundred stores, go to a movie, eat, walk, and lounge for an entire day in a secure, pleasant atmosphere sheltered from undesirable weather and the demands of everyday life. Most Americans at one time or another have escaped for the day to such a mall and felt "uplifted" in spirit by the experience. So pervasive is the suburban regional shopping mall that William Kowinski in the *The Malling of America* (1985) claims that in the United States alone there are more enclosed malls than cities, four-year colleges, or television stations! Indeed, few of us can remember a time when shopping was a trip to "downtown," or the central business district (CBD) of a large city.

Many suburban regional shopping malls are over one million square feet in size, contain over a hundred stores, and offer shoppers free parking, restaurants, play facilities, lounge facilities, restrooms, and movie theaters. Some centers even provide amusement rides and other entertainment opportunities. One of the dominant features of these large shopping complexes is the presence of multiple department stores that "anchor" the extreme points of the mall's layout and "pull" shoppers to the mall from surrounding suburban areas. Department stores also encourage shoppers to walk through the mall. In fact, department stores were the driving force behind the original development of suburban regional shopping malls and have played a critical role in their continuing success.

The movement of traditional department stores from CBD locations to the suburbs, complete with large "full-line" departments, contributed greatly to the explosive growth of suburban regional shopping malls during the post–World War II era. At its inception, the suburban regional shopping mall was designed to be a substitute, or even a replacement, for a city's CBD, but without the usual congestion or parking difficulties. This strategy was particularly attractive after the opening of Southdale Center in suburban Minneapolis in 1956 (www.southdale.com), which demonstrated the viability of a regional shopping mall with multiple anchors.

In 2002 there were a total of 46,336 shopping centers in the United States, of which about 1,200 could be considered regional or superregional malls (www.icsc.org). In addition to regional and superregional malls, numerous types of shopping centers have evolved since the 1950s. The International Council of Shopping Centers has defined eight principal shopping center types: neighborhood, community, regional, superregional, fashion/specialty, power, theme/festival, and outlet.

The suburban regional shopping malls and their department store anchors enjoyed great success for almost 50 years and seemed virtually invincible to threats until the final decade of the twentieth century. During that era, several chinks developed in the competitive armor of this type of retail institution, and the problems seem to be getting worse. Shopper activity is declining; the number of tenant vacancies is increasing; and the delinquency rate on mall mortgages is disturbing. Increasingly larger percentages of consumer discretionary income are being spent elsewhere. To make matters worse, many of the older malls need renovating to remain attractive to shoppers. Renovation of an older mall can cost tens of millions of dollars.

Changes in consumers and in their wants and needs appear to be the major factor that underlies the woes of suburban regional shopping malls. Since the first multi-anchor center opened in 1956, the lifestyles of American families have changed significantly. In 1950, for instance, only 24 percent of wives worked outside the home; today, that percentage exceeds 60 percent. Women between the ages of 18 and 45, the mainstay of mall shoppers, simply do not have the time to shop like they once had. As a result, shopping has become much more purpose-driven. Shopping statistics bear this out. Shoppers are visiting suburban regional shopping malls less frequently, visiting fewer stores when they do shop, and also spending less time at the mall when they do shop. Shoppers, however, are more likely to make a purchase when they do visit a mall. Yet the typical suburban regional shopping mall was designed for a "shop-all-day" or a "shop-'til-you drop" philosophy.

Another consumer trend that spells trouble for suburban regional shopping malls is increased shopper price sensitivity. A wider selection of shopping alternatives from which to choose and the desire to make the family income go farther (which, in essence, is equal to a pay increase) have proven to be strong forces pushing shoppers to comparison shop between retail establishments—something that most malls are not designed to facilitate. Despite the large number of stores contained within a regional suburban shopping mall, comparison shopping between stores is not an easy task. Most malls are laid out to cater to a leisure-oriented shopper. Similar stores are located in different wings of the shopping mall to encourage shoppers to walk through the entire center. Shoppers may walk upwards to a quarter-mile in their quest to compare products! This is not consistent with the desire for shopping convenience and efficiency on the part of most consumers.

Competition also has played a role in the problems that plague suburban regional shopping malls. High levels of competition characterize most mature industries, and the shopping center industry is no exception. Regional malls have both direct and indirect competitors. Direct competitors are nearby shopping centers with either similar or dissimilar formats. Indirect competitors comprise other types of retail store sites like freestanding or clustered sites and nonstore retailing sites. Nonstore retailing includes online shopping, catalog shopping, home TV shopping, telemarketing, and other forms of direct marketing, all of which have made considerable inroads into retail store sales. Suburban regional shopping malls have been especially vulnerable to both forms of competition.

Many of the more successful retailers (e.g., Kohl's, Home Depot) are located on freestanding sites or in large open-air centers—locations that have greater appeal to time-pressed, purpose-driven shoppers than mall locations. Similarly, many outlet malls, which cater to price-sensitive shoppers, are typically open-air centers to facilitate store access. In addition,

*This case and the script for the accompanying video were prepared by Dr. J. B. Wilkinson, Youngstown State University, and Dr. David J. Burns, Xavier University.

some of the newer small shopping centers cater to a focused lifestyle (teen or professional woman) or have an organizing theme (home decor, hobby) that satisfies the specific needs of a market niche by offering a more focused product assortment than what can be found in a suburban regional shopping mall.

Oversupply of retail space has posed considerable problems to all shopping centers. The United States has 20 square feet for every man, woman, and child, compared to 1.4 square feet per person in Great Britain. Sales per square foot of retail space is declining in the United States. In fact, revenue from retail sales is contracting. It grew an average of 2.5 percent in the 1970s; 1.3 percent in the 1980s; and only 0.8 percent in the 1990s, adjusted for inflation. The result has been retail consolidation, store closings, and bankruptcies, leaving shopping centers fighting for a shrinking base of retail tenants.

Finally, department stores, the primary traffic generators for suburban regional shopping malls, are experiencing serious competitive problems. Over the past two decades, department stores have lost half of their market share to discounters and specialty stores. They also have suffered a significant sales revenue decline, causing store closings and consolidation. Given the role department stores have played as traffic generators for shopping malls, the problems of department stores have added to the problems of suburban regional shopping malls. Quite simply, fewer department store shoppers have meant fewer shoppers in the mall. To make matters worse, an empty department store space in a mall gives shoppers less reason to visit that portion of the mall and often leads to the closure of nearby stores. Besides being unproductive, the resulting empty retail space is unsightly, projecting the same image that empty storefronts in the CBDs of cities do—decay and decline.

The predictable outcome of all these changes is that construction of new suburban regional shopping malls has virtually come to a halt. Furthermore, a significant number of existing centers are being "decommissioned"—converted into alternative uses such as office space, learning centers, and telemarketing call centers, or torn down to be replaced by other forms of retail centers. Over 300 malls have been decommissioned since the mid-1990s, a trend which is expected to continue.

The dim outlook for suburban regional shopping malls has stimulated much creative thought about turnaround strategies for those still in operation. One turnaround strategy that has been suggested deals with the way suburban regional shopping malls are traditionally configured and involves changing the way stores in the center are arranged with respect to one another. The traditional layout locates similar stores in different wings or corridors of the center to encourage shoppers to travel through the entire center in their quest to locate and compare products. This type of layout maximizes customer interchange between stores but does not address shopping efficiency. Zonal merchandising represents a different approach to a center's layout. Under zonal merchandising, similar tenants are located in close proximity to one another. This reduces shopping time for shoppers who come to the mall to purchase a specific product. It also creates opportunities for differentiating mall areas in terms of decor, music, amenities, and special events to suit the tastes of shoppers who are most likely to be visiting stores in those areas.

Zonal merchandising has been used most commonly for fast food. Called "food courts," these clusters of fast-food providers have been very successful. Food court tenants have experienced higher levels of sales than under traditional layouts. Food courts also have shown that they are able to draw shoppers from other locations in the mall, similar to the traffic-generating role of a traditional anchor store.

Based on the success of the food court, several attempts to implement zonal merchandising on a wider scale have been made. Beginning with Bridgewater Commons in New Jersey (www.bridgewatercommons.com), several new projects have incorporated zonal merchandising principles, including Rivertown Crossings in Grand Rapids, Michigan (www.rivertowncrossings. com), which has grouped some categories of stores by product line carried, and Park Meadows in Denver, Colorado (www.parkmeadows.com), which has grouped stores by customer lifestyle. The results of these endeavors have been promising, and General Growth (www.generalgrowth.com), the developer of Rivertown Crossings, plans to implement some form of clustering at all of its future projects. Attempts to reconfigure existing centers around zonal merchandising ideas, such as the changes at Glendale Galleria in Glendale, California (www.glendalegalleria.com), seem to be successful as well.

An alternative strategy, which has been proposed for turning around traditional suburban regional shopping malls, is the incorporation of entertainment within the center. The idea behind this strategy is quite simple: add value to the shopper's visit to a mall and give shoppers additional reasons to shop in the mall rather than at home. Entertainment can run the gamut from simple play areas or a carousel for children to video arcades and virtual golf courses to a full-scale amusement park, such as the Mall of America (www.mallofamerica. com). However, adding entertainment offerings to suburban regional shopping malls does not guarantee success. The entertainment must be something that will attract shoppers and keep their interest for a lengthy period of time—not something which shoppers tire of easily. Also the effect of the entertainment activities on a center's retailing activities must be considered. Entertainment centers in suburban regional malls often attract people with social goals instead of shopping goals, which does not benefit a center's merchandise-based stores.

Some industry analysts suggest that the key to revitalizing the suburban regional shopping mall is to make the shopping experience itself more exciting. Even at Mall of America, the home of the largest mall-based entertainment facility in the United States, the primary attraction of the center is the entertainment and excitement provided by the shopping experience itself; shoppers find stores and products which they cannot find elsewhere in the region.

Most suburban regional shopping malls are unexciting. They offer shoppers a relatively nondescript homogeneous shopping experience. They look alike, possess the same stores, and sell the same products. What has been forgotten by mall managers is that entertainment, in a mall sense, is not necessarily what activities can be added to the center, but what entertainment is provided by the shopping experience. Shoppers are searching for shopping experiences that are fresh, different, and fun. To provide this experience, suburban regional shopping malls need to attract stores and sell products that are unique, interesting, and ever-changing. The recent addition of the Build-a-Bear Workshop to the offerings of several suburban regional shopping malls is one such example. The Build-a-Bear Workshop (www.buildabear.com) is a novel retail concept that provides a playful, creative environment. The challenge for mall managers is to find new and exciting retailing concepts like Build-a-Bear Workshop on a continual basis.

The Easton Town Center in Columbus, Ohio (www.eastontowncenter.com) is an example of a suburban regional shopping center that was explicitly designed to provide shoppers with a fun, exciting, entertaining place to shop. Easton Town Center was designed as an open-air center that mimics small-town America over 50 years ago. The center possesses an entertainment-oriented product mix with numerous restaurants, 30 movie theaters, spas, a comedy club, a cabaret, specialty stores, and Nordstrom and Lazarus as anchor department stores. The center has a "town square" and special event areas. It is considered to be one of the most successful retail centers in the region.

The challenge to mall developers and managers is clear. Since the opening of Southdale Center in 1956, changes in competition, retailing, and consumer shopping behavior have resulted in significant threats and opportunities. If suburban regional shopping malls are to enjoy continued success, they must creatively adapt to the new industry and shopping environment. Managers and owners of suburban regional shopping malls must determine the change strategy that is best for them. A number of considerations should guide their thinking—the competition, the needs of shoppers in their area, the opportunities available, and the center's resources. Just as one size does not fit all, the same turnaround strategy will not suit all suburban regional shopping malls.

1. Imagine yourself as the manager of a struggling local suburban regional shopping mall. What do you think the mall should do to improve its performance?

2. What shopping trends do you foresee over the next 10 years? How might these trends affect suburban regional shopping malls?

3. What new retail concepts can you identify? How might you learn about more? What strategies do you suggest for learning about new retail concepts?

2. Celestial Seasonings*

In the late 1960s, the era of Woodstock and Summer of Love music festivals, Mo and Peggy Siegel and two friends began picking herbs in the mountains around Aspen, Colorado. They decided to start a company that they named after one of their friends—Lucinda Ziesing, whose nickname was Celestial. The next year, 10,000 muslin bags of Mo's 36 Herb Tea were sewn, filled, and sold to a health-food store in Boulder, Colorado. A year later, Sleepytime Herb Tea was created, and the business was moved to a barn in Boulder. But that didn't last long. Mo and his friends were onto something hot! Soon

*This case and the script for the accompanying video were prepared by Professor Davis Folsom of USC Beaufort.

they were purchasing herbs around the world and learning how to mass produce their product in a factory. Loose-pack tea was eventually replaced with single-serve tea bags, and additional flavors were created—all of which fueled sales. Today, Celestial Seasonings is recognized as a leader in herbal products, accounting for half the herbal tea market in the United States and expanding worldwide.

Celestial Seasonings' core business is herbal teas. Along with Mo's 36 Herb, Red Zinger, and their best-selling product, Sleepytime, the company has created over 60 different herbal teas.

The tea market is comprised of black teas, herbal and medicinal teas, diet teas, iced teas, and Chai, a sweet Indian spiced blend. The U.S. tea market has an annual growth rate of about 10 percent in recent years. Herbal and medicinal teas represent two-thirds of the total tea market and are growing at about 12 percent a year. Celestial Seasonings is the leading competitor in the herbal tea category, holding 50 percent market share. Other herbal tea competitors include Republic of Tea, Tazo (Starbucks), Yogi Tea, and Oregon Chai.

Herbal teas compete with traditional black teas, dominated by Lipton Tea Company. In the 70s, Celestial revolutionized the tea industry when it introduced the idea of herbal teas as flavorful, healthy beverages for everyday consumption. At that time, herbal teas were perceived as foul-tasting medicinal brews. Few retail stores carried a complete line of herbal teas, so creating awareness, favorable image, and distribution posed a daunting challenge to the company. Initially, Celestial Seasonings promoted and distributed its products through health-food stores.

In 1984, food industry giant Kraft Foods bought Celestial Seasonings. With its marketing muscle and channel power, Kraft expanded distribution of Celestial Seasonings and added a line of gourmet black teas under the Celestial brand name. Shortly after the Kraft buyout, Mo Siegel retired from the company, and Barney Feinblum was named successor. However, the Kraft way of doing business sometimes conflicted with Celestial's culture, which from the beginning was influenced by "hippie-style" entrepreneurship, employee involvement, and earth-friendly community initiatives.

The values of the company are epitomized in its belief statement:

> We believe in marketing and selling healthful and naturally oriented products that nurture people's bodies and uplift their souls. Our products must be superior in quality, of good value, beautifully artistic, and philosophically inspiring.

In 1988, Celestial Seasonings management along with a venture capital firm bought the company back from Kraft. A new board of directors was created, and new headquarters were constructed outside of Boulder, Colorado. In 1991, Mo Siegel returned as CEO and chairman of the board and agreed to stay until 1997.

During Mo's second period of leadership, Celestial Seasonings went public and attempted a variety of product diversifications. A partnership with Perrier was formed to license and produce a line of ready-to-drink bottled teas under the Celestial Seasonings brand. A line of After Dinner Teas was launched, targeting more upscale consumers than Celestial's original back-to-the-earth customers and promoting tea as an after-dinner beverage. Iced Delight teas were created and marketed as "Brews in Your Fridge." A licensing agreement with Warner-Lambert produced Celestial Seasonings Soothers, herbal throat drops. In 1995, with HP Hood Company, Celestial created iced tea flavored frozen popsicles, but they were not a market success. That same year, Celestial developed its first medicinal herb tea—Herbal Comfort. In 1997, based on the success of Herbal Comfort, Celestial Seasonings expanded the line of medicinal teas to include Echinacea, Green Tea, GinkoSharp, Diet Partner, GingerEase, Detox A.M., LaxaTea, and Melatonin P.M. Celestial Seasonings now has 46 percent (up from 24 percent in June 1998) of the fast-growing medicinal tea category.

In 1998, Celestial acquired Mountain Chai, a Boulder-based manufacturer of concentrated Indian-style tea. Six varieties of Mountain Chai were reformulated and introduced under the Celestial logo. That same year, a line of six green teas was launched. Green teas have been used in Asian cultures for hundreds of years and are known for their curative qualities. Green teas were introduced to the American market in the 60s but were not widely successful due to their bland taste.

In 1997, Mo Siegel's commitment to manage the company ended, and Steve Hughes, known in the industry for growing the Healthy Choice line of food products, became Celestial's CEO. With Hughes at the helm, Celestial Seasonings entered a new phase. Saying that Celestial was "a $500 million brand trapped in a $100 million business," Hughes initiated a series of efforts to leverage the Celestial brand name, including the creation of herbal supplements. According to Hughes,

> For 25 years we've cared about one thing—creating healthy, natural products that make our customers feel good. Our herbal supplement line is a natural extension of that mission. We know the power of herbs and the simple solutions they provide for good health. We want to share that.

Launched in April 1998 in capsule form, the herbal supplements line included nine single-herb extracts and eight advanced-formula blend products. The timing seemed perfect. Herbal supplements were rapidly gaining consumer acceptance as alternatives and additions to traditional health and wellness products. A 1998 Market Facts survey showed the percentage of Americans who reported using herbal supplements had grown from just 3 percent in 1990 to 37 percent in 1998, and almost 80 percent of respondents felt herbal supplements were safe to take. Herbal supplements also have a number of logical synergies with Celestial's existing products. Many of the same ingredients are used, and herbal supplements can be sold through the same distribution channels.

Herbal supplements are promoted on the company's Natural Wellness website (www.celestialseasonings.com):

> We do our best to eat right, get enough rest, and exercise, and the benefits are undeniable. But our health can be affected by things we can't control. Environmental toxins, emotional and physical stress and simply getting older create concerns that show up in many ways—as wrinkles, low energy, a flagging mood, and more. We're not defenseless, though. Nature, as usual, provides what we need.

Clearly, Celestial Seasonings is appealing to specific target market segments, like aging baby boomers and health conscious consumers of all ages. In fact, whenever a new Celestial product or service is proposed, the first question asked is "What will Tracy think?" Tracy Jones is the company's nickname for their primary target market: a 35- to 54-year-old, college-educated, socially involved woman with a focus on healthy lifestyle and household income greater than $50,000. Tracy also is not a major viewer of television. Herbal supplements are primarily targeted to Tracy and secondarily targeted to other health-conscious consumers. With labels that talk about "Tummy Mint" and "Tension Tamer," these new herbal supplements are designed to strike an emotional chord in Tracy.

Launched with a $4 million campaign and priced at a premium, the herbal supplements line brought in 21 percent of Celestial's revenues in 1998. But just as things looked as bright as a summer day in the Rockies, Celestial learned a classic marketing lesson. The market for herbal supplements peaked at the same time two major competitors, One a Day and Centrum, entered the market. Also, 1999 SPINS and ACNielsen market research data indicated a variety of changes in the herbal market. Green teas, medicinal blend teas, and Chai were gaining sales, but previously popular single-herb supplements, including St. John's Wort and Ginseng, showed sharp declines.

In response, Celestial restaged the herbal supplements line in 1999 by dropping six products, reducing the advertising budget, and doubling the number of capsules per bottle. Celestial's herbal supplements line still represents a major part of company sales, but initial enthusiasm has mellowed, and the marketing team has begun to look for new opportunities. Also, companies specializing in herbal supplements face several ethical and legal issues.

Almost 80 percent of American consumers believe that herbal supplements are *safe*. However, as one FDA director has stated, "Realize that the label term 'natural' doesn't guarantee that a product is safe. Think of poisonous mushrooms. They're natural." Herbal supplements companies must abide by FDA rules regarding claims of effectiveness of their products; they cannot represent their products as medicines. Mike Gross, Celestial's regulatory expert, explains, "What it all boils down to is that you cannot make any claim to cure, treat, prevent, mitigate, or diagnose any disease state—or even mention a disease! For example, you cannot say 'for the treatment of prostate enlargement' but you can say 'to keep your prostate healthy.'"

One new direction under consideration at most consumer goods companies is the Internet. The Internet initiative at Celestial started in the Information Technology division of the organization. Celestial started a modest web storefront designed to educate consumers and sell seasonal items and gifts from its mail-order catalog. Then the catalog manager got onboard and the marketing group joined in to build this alternative channel.

Part of the success of Celestial's catalog and Internet sales is attributable to the company kitchen! Started in 1973 as a free lunch program for employees, outsiders began to drift in, wanting to buy products. As more and more customers visited the factory, the idea of a factory tour gained favor. Between 1994 and 1999, over 350,000 people took Celestial's factory tour, creating a huge database for catalog and Internet marketing strategies.

1. What kinds of synergies do herbal supplements have with herbal teas?

2. What environmental trends seem to be fueling sales growth for herbal supplements? What environmental trends pose threats to the sales and profits of herbal supplements?

3. What kinds of new products should Celestial Seasonings develop? What criteria would you use to evaluate new product ideas for Celestial Seasonings? Why?

3. Briggs & Stratton Corporation*

Briggs & Stratton is the world's largest producer of air-cooled gasoline engines for outdoor power equipment, mainly for lawn mowers. The company designs, manufactures, markets, and services these products—which are sold as components to original equipment manufacturers (OEMs) in 85 countries.

Steve Briggs and Harry Stratton started the company in 1909 to produce a six-cylinder, two-cycle engine similar to one Briggs had developed a few years earlier as an engineering student in college. The engine turned out to be too expensive to mass produce, so the partners turned their attention to designing and producing electrical parts for automobiles, including switches, starters, and regulators.

Later B&S acquired the patent for the Motor Wheel—a gasoline engine designed to fit on a bicycle. It was a market success and ultimately proved to be a good way to power several other types of vehicles. In some parts of Asia it was even used on rickshas.

To build on the success of the Motor Wheel, B&S looked for new markets for engines. Its search led to the development of a stationary utility engine for use on such products as garden cultivators and reel-type mowers. Before utility companies brought electricity to rural parts of the U.S., these B&S engines even powered refrigerators, milking machines, and elevators.

After World War II, the booming U.S. economy, the shift of population to the suburbs, and the growth of leisure time prompted new consumer interest in lawn and garden equipment. B&S saw this growth opportunity and shifted its focus to producing motors for the lawn mower manufacturers who served that market. But B&S didn't just try to push engines it was already producing.

At that time, most power mowers used two-cycle engines; their light weight made mowers easy to push. However, two-cycles weren't reliable and needed a mix of gas and oil, which was inconvenient for consumers. Four-cycle engines like the ones B&S produced were very reliable, but they were made from cast iron and very heavy. Marketing people at B&S realized that consumers wanted *both* reliability and light weight, so the firm designed a new lawn mower engine from aluminum alloy.

---

*This case and the script for the accompanying video were prepared by Roger C. Shoenfeldt.

Over time, the Briggs & Stratton name has become almost synonymous with the lawn mower. Top producers such as Toro, Snapper, and John Deere proudly proclaim in their ads that their mowers are powered by a Briggs & Stratton engine. In fact, Briggs & Stratton is often the most prominent brand name on the mower, even though the engine is just a component. The Briggs & Stratton name helps sell the mowers because it means quality, reliability, and performance to consumers. Because of this reputation—and consumer demand—many retailers won't sell a mower unless it uses a Briggs & Stratton motor.

Early in the 1980s B&S faced a serious competitive threat. A shift in international exchange rates made Japanese products less expensive in the U.S. and other parts of the world. This gave Japanese motorcycle producers a pricing edge to expand into the market for small engines. Because B&S was the leading producer of small engines, any competitive inroads would be at its expense.

Marketers at B&S realized that to keep competitors from carving up its market they would need to fine-tune the firm's offerings for specific market segments. A starting point for that effort was to develop new product lines—actually, whole marketing strategies—for each type of need rather than just trying to get economies of scale by serving bigger, but heterogeneous, product-markets. B&S invested $250 million to develop carefully targeted new products, build new plants, and develop new processes to improve quality and reduce costs.

B&S' new-product development effort for specific segments cut short the Japanese invasion and increased customer satisfaction and brand loyalty. That put B&S in a better position to deal with another change—a big shift in the channel of distribution for lawn mowers. In the past, most consumers bought lawn mowers from independent lawn and garden equipment dealers. However, over time mass-merchandisers have taken away almost all of that business. In fact, five of the largest retail chains now account for half of all the lawn mowers sold in the U.S.—and about 80 percent of B&S' lawn and garden equipment sales are through mass-merchandisers.

This concentration of purchasing power has given the big retail chains new clout in the channel of distribution. Retail buyers pressure lawn mower producers to keep costs and prices low; and the producers in turn expect B&S to keep its prices in check. While this has probably reduced the price premium that the B&S brand commands, it hasn't eliminated it. Retailers know that consumers want lawn mowers with B&S engines. So brand loyalty by final consumers gives B&S an advantage in negotiations with its producer-customers. Even so, the squeeze on profit margins throughout the channel—and intense competition—means that B&S must continue to find better ways to meet customers' needs if it is to maximize market share and earn attractive profits. And for B&S, developing innovative new products has long been the key to meeting needs better. Its skill in this arena is illustrated by its success in developing a 4-horsepower motor to fill a gap in its product line.

In 1993 B&S had four main lines of lawn mower engines. B&S' Classic 3.5-horsepower (HP) engine was at the low end of the price range and it was found on mowers priced at about $99. As the name implies, this reliable model has been popular for many years. If a customer wanted a bit more power and a mower that took less pulling effort to start, B&S' 3.75-HP Sprint engine was available on mowers that sell for about $119. For consumers who wanted an easy-starting engine that quietly conquered even the thickest grass, the Quantum 5.0-HP Plus line was the choice—on a mower that cost from $160 up to $500. Finally, B&S offered a top-of-the-line Diamond Plus model with about 6.0 HP, unique European styling, and all the bells and whistles. A customer who had to ask how much it cost probably couldn't afford it.

In spite of multiple models in each of these lines, B&S did not have a good 4-HP mower engine. Yet there was a clear market for one. B&S' main competitor, Tecumseh, proved that. Its 4-HP engine was a market leader. And B&S needed to develop a new engine if it wanted to compete for the segment of customers who wanted a 4-HP engine. To take customers away from Tecumseh, B&S marketers knew they needed to develop a cost-effective engine that was better than the Tecumseh model on all operating and performance criteria. Research also showed that styling was becoming an important purchase criterion for many customers—perhaps because that was the one difference in engines that consumers could see while shopping.

Although they had a clear idea of what the market wanted, marketing managers at B&S faced a real challenge. Creating a superior new engine wouldn't do much good if lawn mower producers and retailers didn't know about it, and the time and place to introduce an important new lawn and garden product was at a big, national trade show that was less than a year away. If they missed that date, they'd effectively lose a year. So getting the new product to market fast—without making costly mistakes—was critical.

To speed up development and also reduce costs, B&S designers created a contemporary, aerodynamic look with a computer-aided design (CAD) system; the tooling of the parts—direct from the computer drawings—was very fast. Further, B&S engineers used standard parts from other B&S engines when they could. This helped to control costs, reduce development time, cut inventory requirements, and later would make after-the-sale service easier and faster. As a result of efforts like these, the new product went from the concept stage to production in about nine months—in time for the trade show deadline.

While the new product team was developing the engine, B&S marketing people had other work to do. To emphasize the new engine's distinct identity, they used an individual brand name, Quattro, which means four in Spanish. They also developed promotional materials to use at the trade show, and started work on ads and other cooperative promotional materials so they would be ready for producers and retailers to use when the Quattro started to appear on lawn mowers in retail stores.

The B&S salespeople also started to call on their top OEM customers. Besides explaining the advantages of the new Quattro motor and answering questions, they provided hundreds of sample motors. That made it possible for the producers to get a head start in creating prototypes of new mowers to show their retailer-customers. And since the retailers have a big influence on the producer's purchase decisions, B&S salespeople also promoted the features of the new motor—and the pull appeal of the Briggs & Stratton name—to retail buyers.

The salespeople also explained the benefits of the B&S cooperative advertising arrangements and how they work. B&S provides cooperative advertising allowances and materials to all of its OEM customers and to the retailers who sell their products.

As a result of all this front-end planning, the Quattro got off to a very successful start. In fact, customer reaction to the new engine's sleek appearance, power, and reliability was so strong that demand was double what B&S had forecast. By mid-1995, the company was hard-pressed to keep up with demand.

That's one reason that during the first year B&S decided to focus the marketing effort for the Quattro primarily on the U.S. market. It didn't make sense to spend money promoting the product in foreign markets if supply would be limited. However, exports account for 21 percent of all B&S engine and parts sales, and the Quattro isn't likely to be an exception to that pattern. When the time comes for the Quattro's international rollout some changes in the domestic marketing strategies may be required. For example, while lawn and garden equipment is important in nations with developed economies, in less-developed countries the Quattro is likely to be used for other types of applications—in agricultural, marine, and other commercial markets.

1. Are there any disadvantages to Briggs & Stratton's decision to hold off introducing its new Quattro engine in international markets? Explain your thinking.

2. What are the marketing implications for Briggs & Stratton of the fact that the U.S. market for lawn mowers is in the market maturity stage?

3. Given that engines are such an important component in manufacturing lawn mowers, would it make sense for Briggs & Stratton to develop and market its own line of mowers? Explain your thinking.

4. Given B&S' ability to compete well with Japanese motorcycle producers when they tried to take market share away from Briggs & Stratton's small engines, would it make sense for Briggs & Stratton to produce a small motorcycle—or perhaps a motorscooter—to market in India and other countries where incomes are low but demand for personal transportation is increasing? Explain your thinking.

4. Frog's Leap Winery*

In order to save a $2.00 camping fee, John Williams rode his motorcycle into a field in the Napa Valley, pitched his tent, and was enjoying a good night's sleep until he was rudely awakened early the next morning by the owner of the property, Larry Turley, a local doctor. In order to make amends,

*This case and the script for the accompanying video were prepared by Peter Rainsford. He would like to thank John Williams, founder and owner of Frog's Leap Winery, for providing information in the case and for his constructive suggestions during its preparation.

John offered to share a bottle of wine with the doctor, and by the time the bottle was empty, the two had discovered they both shared a strong desire to make wine.

Having grown up on a dairy farm in western New York, John originally went to Cornell University to extend his studies as a dairyman. However, a fortuitous work-study program at Taylor Wine Company—and a few bottles of wine later—made John realize he was more interested in making wine than in returning to the family dairy farm. His newfound interest led him to enroll in the Enology and Viticulture Masters Program at the University of California, Davis. After concluding his studies at Davis, John returned to the Finger Lakes area of New York as the start-up winemaker at Glenora Wine Cellars. But having been exposed to the superior climate and soils of the Napa Valley, John eventually headed back to the Napa Valley to assume winemaking duties at Spring Mountain Vineyards.

Back in the Napa Valley, John reacquainted himself with the good doctor whose land he had poached on several years before, Larry Turley. Larry was now living on a small parcel of land called The Frog Farm, so named because an old ledger revealed that around the turn of the century frogs were raised there and sold for $.33 per dozen, destined no doubt for the tables of Victorian San Francisco restaurants. As a lark, they gathered some grapes and made a small quantity of wine. They called the Wine "Frog's Leap," a combination of a good-natured dig at Stag's Leap, the classy Napa Valley winery, and a tribute to The Frog Farm where Larry lived.

Because of their love of winemaking, they continued to make small quantities of the wine for several years and managed to sell a few cases each year to help defray expenses. John and Larry continued to produce the wine as a hobby—they both were still working full-time in their real jobs—and probably wouldn't have changed except for the fact that a wine writer from *The New York Times* picked up a bottle and wrote a column entitled "Frog's Leap: A Prince of a Wine." The free publicity resulted in hundreds of telephone calls and the sale of their entire year's production.

The opportunity to attempt to grow the winery was too hard to resist, and, according to John, the hobby became a real business when "We made the ultimate male sacrifice and decided to sell our motorcycles in order to raise the capital necessary to start the winery as a commercial venture."

Production grew from 700 cases of wine at its inception in 1982, to 2,900 cases in 1983, to 4,400 cases in 1984. By 1985, the winery was doing well enough for John to quit his paid employment at Spring Mountain Winery and make Frog's Leap his full-time job. Frog's Leap has continued to grow and produced more than 50,000 cases in 2000. There are a variety of reasons for its success, but the overriding theme is best summed up by the following paragraph from the company's mission statement:

> We will strive to produce wines of excellent value that are fresh, delicious, and natural using the best of Napa Valley's organically grown grapes. Our professional presentation will be juxtaposed with our image of irreverent humor, fun, genuine hospitality, openness, and honest caring.

The winery has always been committed to quality and has refused to compromise with respect to quality. As John says, "Our goal is to have fun making elegant wines with superb balance."

While the contents of the bottle may be award-winning quality, the exterior of the bottle reflects the fun and humor of the company. The company's motto is "Time's Fun When You're Having Flies." Each bottle's label—which won a prestigious wine label award at the time it was designed—features an elongated frog in mid leap; it also contains the instructions, "Open Other End," at the base of the label. The humor continues when the bottle is opened as the word "ribbit" is clearly marked on every cork. But make no mistake, their first objective is to produce world-class wines, and if awards are any indication, they are clearly meeting this objective.

Dan Berger described the quality of the wines in the holiday 1995 issue of *Wine Enthusiast*. In an article about the 10 most underrated wineries on the West Coast, Berger states,

> I don't know why people don't see the utter greatness in the wines John Williams makes. His Cabernets are packed with fruit and elegance, his Zinfandel is among the best made anywhere, and his Sauvignon Blanc is a world-beater. This is simply one of the best producers in California and it never seems to get the acclaim it deserves. Maybe John's label note "Open Other End" is too subtle for the number of reviewers. (For that matter, his cork says it all!)

Speaking of the label, John looked for an unknown artist who would be willing to design a label for $100 and several cases of wine. Charles House agreed to do the job and was specifically told not to put a frog on the label. But that's exactly what House created—a captivating, eye-catching rendition of a frog in full leap—a frog "going for it" all out! The label went on to win one of the nation's top graphic design awards, House became famous, and Frog's Leap wine labels became part of the Smithsonian's permanent collection.

By 1994, the winery was not only successful but was bursting at the seams. The company was still located at The Frog Farm, but the business had "succeeded far beyond our expectations." According to John, "Frog's Leap was faced with a lack of production space, a lack of office space, and the need to make the winery accessible to the public." There was also a sense that John and Larry had different goals for both the winery and their personal lives. Larry wanted to spend less time being a doctor and more time involved in the day-to-day aspects of making wine—but on a much smaller scale. They decided, in a very amicable agreement, to split the winery in half. Larry, who owned the property where Frog's Leap had been located, kept the winery, all the winemaking equipment, and the one acre of sauvignon blanc vines located at the site. John retained the Frog's Leap brand, the wine inventory, and the marketing program.

The only problem with the split was the fact that John needed a place to put his winery—it was a winery in name only. He quickly found the ideal spot, a 38-acre parcel on the Rutherford Crossroad with a 8,000-square-foot barn, The Red Barn, which had been built in 1884 as a winery. Although the barn needed a great deal of renovation, it was restorable for use as a winery. The site also provided John with the land he needed to grow some of his own grapes and to practice sustainable agriculture and organic farming.

In the six years since John moved the winery to The Red Barn location, Frog's Leap has continued to improve both its reputation and the quality of its wines. And it has been able to succeed even though more and more wineries have been built in the Napa Valley and as more and more big corporate wineries (e.g., Sutter Home, Robert Mondavi, and Kendall-Jackson, just to name a few) have dominated the Napa and Sonoma Valleys.

1. How would you describe the position strategy for Frog's Leap? How do you think it differs from a large, corporate winery such as Sutter Home?

2. How has Frog's Leap grown over the years? What are the growth strategies that John Williams plans to follow in the future?

3. Do you think the first half of the twenty-first century will be a hospitable environment for winemakers in the U.S.? Why or why not?

5. Girl Scouts*

Girl Scouting is dedicated to and available to all girls age 5 to 17. Today there are approximately 3.6 million Girl Scouts in the U.S., including over 2.7 million girls and nearly 900,000 adult members, most of whom are volunteers. Membership categories for the girls are

Category	Age	Grade
Daisy	5–6	K, 1
Brownie	6, 7, 8	1, 2, 3
Junior Girl Scout	8, 9, 10, 11	3, 4, 5, 6
Cadette Girl Scout	11, 12, 13, 14	6, 7, 8, 9
Senior Girl Scout	14–17	9–12

Membership is at an all-time high. In 1999, as a result of specific target market initiatives, growth was especially strong among Hispanic (a 6.3 percent increase) and African American (5.9 percent increase) girls. And membership is not just limited to the United States. Through its membership in the World Association of Girl Guides and Girl Scouts, Girl Scouts of the U.S.A. (GSUSA) is part of a larger entity of over 10 million girls in 140 countries. Although some programs for overseas travel and adventure exist, the international link is still being developed and is not nearly as strong as the link between GSUSA and the local councils.

As is true for many nonprofit organizations, the Girl Scouts organization operates on two levels. At the corporate or headquarters level is Girl Scouts of the U.S.A., located in New York. A board of directors, a national president, and a national executive director run GSUSA. From these offices, plans are made for the national parent and for the local councils. These local councils may be thought of as strategic business units (SBUs) for the Girl Scouts. Over 300 local councils serve to direct the activities of the more than 226,000 troops in the United States and overseas. A local board of directors and an executive director manages each of these local councils. To become a part of GSUSA, each of these local councils must go

*This case and accompanying video script were prepared by Dr. George Prough, the University of Akron, with assistance from Lori Arguelles, Communications Director, GSUSA, and Mary Kintz, Director of Member Services, Western Reserve Girl Scouts Council.

through a type of accreditation review by the national organization. Every four years each council is reviewed, and if it continues to meet the established criteria, it will be rechartered. This chartering process provides GSUSA with a strong weapon to maintain some level of consistency for the strategies and actions of the member Girl Scout councils.

Strategic marketing planning clearly is necessary to run such a large organization. GSUSA does extensive corporate-level planning and also provides the local councils with assistance for their own formulation and execution of plans. Strategic marketing planning at the corporate level is the responsibility of the president and the board, with input from board committees, board task groups, community leaders, and community groups. Four steps are involved. The first step is a S.W.O.T. analysis, a review of internal strengths and external trends. This includes using the database maintained by GSUSA that details membership, program attendance, financial and development data, and similar benchmarks. The study of external trends results in the *Environmental Scanning Report*, which uses social, economic, political, and technological data from a variety of sources. This document is then made available to corporate- and council-level planners. One result of this S.W.O.T. analysis is the identification of a set of critical issues facing GSUSA. These issues are then used in the second step: to develop corporate goals covering a six-year period. These goals are reviewed at the midpoint of the planning period. In the third step, the group develops strategic guidelines, strategies, and long-range projects. Finally, the group develops long-range resource strategies that are needed to support the projects identified in the third step.

Staff and volunteers involved in implementing the strategic plans are responsible for the development of one-year plans (tactical planning). At this fourth step, priorities are established; specific operational goals are set; action plans are developed, including decisions about who, how, what, and when; and the operational budget is determined.

The completed corporate plan shapes all efforts and programs at the national level. However, local planners can exercise some discretion in planning for their markets. To accomplish local planning, some councils hold planning retreats with local board and community experts; some hold planning sessions for just staff; and some limit the efforts to a committee of the board. Whatever the process, the council board develops a set of five-year goals that it reviews annually. While these usually mirror national goals, each local council has the opportunity to change priorities or to add other goals peculiar to their local efforts. Using these goals, the staff develops proposals for specific objectives and action steps for board approval. These approved objectives and action steps form the basis for the local council's annual operating plan.

During the year, results are measured, compared to objectives, and subjected to corrective actions. Also during the year, the staff has the opportunity to reevaluate the goals that have been set by the board for the coming year and may provide suggestions to the board. The board then meets again early in the following year to plan for that year and to add goals for the fifth year in the current plan. Thus, the local council board always has a plan that looks five years ahead.

Marketing plans and efforts must be directed at three distinct groups. First, plans must be developed for recruiting and marketing efforts directed to the target market for Scouting: girls and their families. In addition, marketing plans also must target volunteers. Scouting could not function nearly as effectively without its giant network of volunteers, both at the local and national levels. There are over 880,000 adult members of Girl Scouting and most of them are volunteers. Many of these volunteers were involved in scouting when they were young. Others are parents of current scouts.

Finally, the community at large represents an important stakeholder group. This group includes donors, both corporate and individual, who provide financial and other resources; schools and school counselors; church organizations and the like. During the S.W.O.T. analysis, all three groups are studied, and this provides input for recruitment plans and for the ongoing marketing efforts.

Quite clearly, young girls in the target demographic are the first and most important marketing target. Marketing efforts aimed at this group include recruitment efforts as well as retention efforts (keeping existing Scouts delighted with their experiences).

Plans of both types must consider the competition faced by Girl Scouting. All organizations face competition of various sorts, but Girl Scouts planners face an unusual situation. Essentially, the competition for Scouting is other activities that compete for a girl's time. This includes school clubs and other school-related activities; sports; private lessons such as piano, ballet, and music; church; and other social activities, including dating boys. However, the thinking about competition at Girl Scouts is different. Girl Scouting does not attempt to defeat the competition. Instead, Scouting embraces many of these competing activities and offers them as part of their product mix. If it finds that a certain activity is becoming more important to young girls, then Scouting looks at the possibility of incorporating that activity into its product mix of activities.

As girls mature, this kind of competition grows more intense. Older girls have more choices, making retention in these categories more difficult. As a result, there has been a growing concern that the programs and offerings of Girl Scouting, especially in the older age categories, is not sufficiently contemporary. Retention of these older girls is a problem. For instance, analysis of the U.S. membership shows the following data regarding the number of girls served by the Girl Scouts in each membership category:

Category	Girls Served in the Category
Daisy	1 of every 8
Brownie	1 of every 4
Junior Girl Scout	1 of every 7
Cadette Girl Scout	1 of every 25
Senior Girl Scout	1 of every 73

To better understand customers and the competing demands on their lives, Girl Scouts USA is beginning to do extensive market and customer research among young girls. During the fall of 2000, GSUSA launched the Girl Scout Research Institute, a research and public policy information center focusing on the healthy development of girls. Through this Institute, the GSUSA hopes to develop a large database of information on girls, with the additional goal of positioning itself as an information resource and expert on girls.

Within this competitive market, the GSUSA uses a variety of plans and strategies in order to attract new girls. The national website offers an overview for interested girls; however, it is not very interactive and has limited recruiting value. Nationally prepared brochures and literature are also available. Often these can be useful as stuffers in store, mall, and other point-of-sale display units. But many councils choose to localize and personalize these efforts. For these councils, most of the recruitment and marketing efforts are planned and developed at the local level. Local websites, school visits, locally prepared fliers, recruiting efforts at malls, churches, and other similar local activities lend a more personal touch to their recruiting.

Specific to certain types of competition, GSUSA has responded with a changing product mix. Each year, Girl Scouts adds to its diversity of activities and merit badges, all awarded for participation and mastery of particular tasks. With the increase in girls participating in sporting activities, Girl Scouts developed GirlSports, a program offering senior Girl Scouts from around the country a chance to spend a week during the summer developing certain sporting skills. During the 2000 version, 26 girls met in Oakland, California, with local athletes and trainers, learned 13 extreme sports, and met with and studied with ESPN fitness experts and Olympic athletes. An expanded version of GirlSports is being developed to include over 100,000 girls competing in nearly 2,300 different sporting events in over 300 councils.

Another trend identified was the increasing interest of girls in the sciences. As a result, the Girl at the Center program was developed. This is a science and technology program in which local councils can take advantage of partnerships between the Girl Scouts and over 31 science museums, encouraging families and girls to explore and to learn more about the sciences. Girl at the Center and the GirlSports program are examples of how the Girl Scouts organization is forming partnerships with others to make its programs relevant and successful.

Girl Scouting uses several methods to appeal to its second target, its volunteers—both to attract them and to keep them motivated and involved. To attract volunteers at the national level, the website offers valuable insight as do the nationally prepared brochures highlighting the benefits of volunteering and the many ways of doing so. But again, the local councils often develop their own marketing efforts. Parents are targeted by maintaining a parents' network and involving parents in meetings and events. When the local council has events at malls or churches, the council staff involved makes every attempt to sell volunteering to adults as much as they do scouting to young girls. Additionally, many local councils work with area organizations in an attempt to generate volunteers. Universities, schools, the local housing authority, and other volunteer-based organizations have proven to be excellent sources of interns or other types of volunteers.

To keep volunteers motivated and involved, GSUSA national offers a variety of adult development and training opportunities. These include programs at the corporate training center, a number of online training offerings, and certification programs that support and enable the volunteers to improve their abilities to perform their functions.

Girl Scouting's third target, its stakeholder group, consists of the community at large. Efforts to interact with this stakeholder group can be planned, and suggestions are made at the national level; however, many of these efforts involve personal contacts and one-on-one relationships with donors or other partnership targets. As a result, many of these efforts are developed and conducted by people at the local council level.

1. Compare strategic marketing planning by the Girl Scouts with planning by for-profit organizations. What are the similarities? What are the differences?

2. What changes would you suggest to improve the planning process in the Girl Scouts?

6. Volkswagen's New Beetle*

Volkswagen management was very surprised at the reaction to their latest design study, the Concept 1. Unveiled in Detroit at the North American International Auto Show in January 1994, the car was an instant hit with the public. Throngs of people crowded around the viewing stand to get a close look at what VW designers had created, a 90s version of the much-loved Beetle. The original Beetle had been sold in the U.S. from 1948 to 1981, and (until recently) was still sold in some countries such as Mexico and Brazil.

Automotive design studies are used to gauge public reaction to styling and design ideas. The overwhelming response to the Concept 1, which closely resembled the looks of the original Beetle, prompted VW to study what was behind the strong consumer response. They wanted to know if the favorable response was because of the uniquely identifiable profile of the Beetle, the fond memories of the millions of U.S. Beetle owners, or simple nostalgia—a desire to be carried back to a "different" time.

It was clear that the Concept 1 touched the buying public at the auto show. The number of phone calls and letters to U.S. Volkswagen headquarters was so overwhelming that VW management promptly put a product-development team into action. The charge was to create a thoroughly modern version of the beloved Beetle, a car that would utilize the latest cutting-edge technologies housed in the uniquely identifiable shape of the most widely produced car in history.

Twenty-one million original Beetles have been built since the original idea for the car was shown to the German government in 1934 by Dr. Ferdinand Porsche. Porsche's dream was to build a simple, high-quality car for the masses, a car that even the average owner could learn to care for and maintain with minimal expense. That was the formula that had worked so well in the United States when Henry Ford introduced the Model T and put America on wheels.

Porsche's dream for the "people's car" (or Volkswagen) would not become a commercial reality until after World War II, though some prototypes and early production units had reached the public prior to the war's outbreak. By 1948, the war-damaged factory was rebuilt and the Beetle was being produced in full scale in Europe. It was also in that year that the Beetle was shown to the U.S. public at the N.Y. Auto Show. By the late 1950s the Beetle was the leading imported car in America, and

* This case and the script for the accompanying video were prepared by Professor Jim Burley.

hundreds of thousands of Americans were driving the small cars with air-cooled engines. Many people loved the simplicity and economy of the car, and the quality was very high. The car represented a very good value for the consumer's money.

Japanese auto manufacturers took notice of Volkswagen's success in the United States and designed their own competing models of small, economical cars. But they were different in character than the Beetle. The Japanese-produced small cars were more like shrunken versions of full-sized cars. They had big car styling and incorporated many features that U.S. car buyers of the 60s wanted, including power-assisted steering, power windows, and automatic transmissions. The small cars introduced by Toyota, Nissan, and Honda quickly cut into Volkswagen's sales volume. Although sales in the small-car category grew rapidly, increased competition left smaller sales volume for the previously dominant Beetle.

VW management held steadfastly to the "simple is beautiful" positioning that was carefully reinforced in the Beetle's advertising campaign. Advertisements with headlines such as "Ugly is only skin deep" reminded customers that the real beauty of the VW was its simplicity, reliability, and the economical ownership experience it produced. Despite this message, many people in the market were attracted to the larger choice of options and features found on the Japanese entries. After the Beetle's U.S. sales peaked at 423,000 units in 1968, sales began to decline.

Volkswagen responded to the market changes that were taking place by introducing the Rabbit, a small European hatchback that was refined to incorporate many of the features Americans wanted. The Rabbit was an immediate hit. Even though it did not have the instant recognizability of the Beetle, it benefited from the Beetle's reputation.

The decline of the Beetle in the U.S. was complete in 1981 when VW management removed it from sale in the U.S. market. However, VW continued to produce and sell the car in Mexico and South America. These were strong markets for the car because the Beetle was ideally suited to developing economies where simple and reliable transportation was more important than a long list of fancy accessories.

Although the original Beetle was a simple car, the New Beetle is not. As VW marketers began to develop the concept for the "New Beetle" they realized that the affluent American consumer expected features such as air conditioning, stereo systems, and security features—as well as government-mandated safety items such as airbags and 5-MPH bumpers. The New Beetle would clearly require a degree of complexity and sophistication that Dr. Porsche could never have imagined.

The product development process incorporated customers' reactions from auto shows around the world. The reaction to the Concept 1 was nearly uniform worldwide, so VW management knew they would have a winner if they could build a street vehicle that incorporated the looks of the Concept 1 with an affordable platform. They found that platform in the one they were developing for the Golf, Europe's most popular car. With a few modifications, a New Beetle body could be built over a Golf chassis. This eliminated much of the time and expense of developing a completely new automobile. The use of the Golf platform also made it possible for VW to bring the New Beetle to market more quickly.

Just four years after first showing the Concept 1, VW management unveiled the New Beetle at the 1998 North

American International Auto Show. The response to the "real" car was overwhelming. During much of the show it wasn't even possible to get near the car because of the crowds.

Executives from competing auto producers were astonished at consumers' reaction to the car, and were even more concerned when they learned more about VW's marketing strategy. Preintroduction guesses by the automotive media had suggested a price of $18,000 for the base car, but VW management priced the New Beetle at a low $15,200. This price included airbags, air-conditioning, power door locks, a multispeaker stereo system, tilt and telescoping steering, and many other attractive features. The automotive press in attendance at the unveiling applauded loudly when the price was announced.

Volkswagen marketers had crafted a very desirable new product that their dealers and customers were anxious to have. A promotional strategy was created to build enthusiasm for the car's official arrival in showrooms in spring 1998. Dealers were shown the car at a special party at Disney World in Orlando, Florida. There they not only got to drive the car but also to participate in Disney-style clinics on the attitudes and expectations of the New Beetle target market. Nostalgia was an important component of the target customers' feelings toward the car, but testing also revealed a broad demographic and psychographic appeal that included many young buyers who had never owned an older-style Beetle.

The dealers thought that the 50,000 units scheduled for production the first year would not be enough to satisfy the demand, but they were hopeful that some of the visitors to their showrooms could be switched to other VW products. VW's product line included cars that were either more economical or more spacious depending on the customers' needs. Jeff Williams, a VW dealer, explained the problems and the excitement associated with the new car:

> I'm sure we'll have trouble meeting the demand that seems to be in the market. The car is really exciting customers. I have one customer who's ordered one for his 19-year-old daughter. He hopes she can have as much fun with her car as he did with his Beetle 30 years ago.

1. Why didn't VW managers more accurately forecast the sales potential for the New Beetle?
2. Is styling really what sells cars or is it other factors?

7. Royal Appliance Manufacturing Company: Dirt Devil*

You've just arrived on campus for the fall semester at college. Whether you're in a dorm room, apartment, or a rented home, in no time at all the place is sure to be a mess. And, looking at your current roommate situation, you probably won't get much help with the cleaning. You can either live with the disorder or get a new roommate—the Dirt Devil RoomMate. This new, lightweight upright vacuum may very well be the best companion a college student could ever have.

---

*This case and the script for the accompanying video were prepared by Professor Douglas Hausknecht. He expresses appreciation to Thomas F. Sherer, who assisted in developing the case.

So begins an August 1997 press release from Dirt Devil, a subsidiary of Royal Appliance Manufacturing Company. The once staid and boring vacuum cleaner industry now sees college students as an interesting, vital target market.

The Dirt Devil brand has been responsible, in large part, for this new-found excitement. New product introductions and a groundbreaking advertising campaign are the latest chapters in the story of arguably the oldest vacuum cleaner manufacturing company in the world.

The first Royal vacuum cleaners were made by the P. A. Geier Company of Cleveland, Ohio, in 1905. As was the case with home computer companies in the 1970s and 1980s, Royal has its roots in a backyard garage. The company grew quickly and moved from the garage to a large, four-story structure where it produced vacuum cleaners, mixers, hair dryers, and washing machine units.

The core business of the P. A. Geier Company, however, continued to be vacuum cleaners. The industry's first hand-held vacuum, the Royal Prince, was introduced in 1937. The Geier company maintained its position in the vacuum cleaner industry until the firm was acquired in 1953 and renamed the Royal Appliance Manufacturing Company. The newly named organization was purchased by a group of employees in 1954 and moved to Highland Heights, Ohio, in 1969.

In 1984 Royal Appliance introduced another innovative product, the Dirt Devil Hand Vac, which was touted as a cleaner for couch cushions, stairs, and other hard-to-reach places. Between 1984 and 1997, its light weight, low price, and attractive red plastic body combined to create total sales of over 17 million units, making it the largest selling hand vac in the world. Royal now claims over 95 percent brand name awareness of the Dirt Devil name (up from 4 percent in 1990 and 21 percent in 1992), and it now commands 42 percent of the U.S. market for hand-held vacuums.

Of course, there have been some stumbles along the way. In 1990, Royal began to market Dirt Devil products throughout Europe and Great Britain. However, the European market did not take to the new products as well as Royal had hoped. And, on the domestic front, expensive promotion did not deliver a focused, unified message to American consumers. For example, dispersed promotion efforts in the U.S. in 1991 included advertising on Paul Harvey's radio program and sponsorship of race cars on the Indy Car and Nascar circuits. Because of problems such as these, performance began to dip. By 1995 mounting financial losses necessitated a change in company management and the sale of Royal's European operations. Royal's stock price at the end of 1995 was $2.50 per share, but it rebounded to $9 per share by the end of 1996—a year that saw $286 million in sales and $9.4 million in profit.

A revitalized Royal states its mission on its website:

> The company's mission is to bring innovative household products to the marketplace and thrill customers. It strives to recognize the needs of its customers and supply them with quality products that solve their cleaning problems. . . . The success of the company depends upon the continued introduction and promotion of new, innovative, high-quality products (www.dirtdevil.com).

This mission is associated with the Dirt Devil name—now used on virtually all of the company's consumer goods. The

Royal brand name is reserved for high-end, heavy-duty, mostly industrial products. Most manufacturing is contracted out, leaving only some assembly to be done at corporate-owned facilities. This structure allows for the versatility and flexibility needed for the introduction and management of innovative products.

One of these new, innovative products is the Broom Vac. Launched in 1996, the Broom Vac was seen to be as creative as the original Royal Prince was at its debut. It also represented the type of newsworthy breakthrough that the Dirt Devil group needed. The Dirt Devil Broom Vac is a cordless, rechargeable broom that has a vacuum in the center of the unit's bristles to suck up dirt and dust in seconds. It does a better job of sweeping, and the user needs only to empty the filter and dirt compartment when full instead of bending over a dustpan.

Traditionally, the vacuum industry's products are classified as canister, upright, stick, or extractor cleaners. Hoover is recognized as the industry leader, emphasizing middle- and upper-end canisters, uprights, and sticks for an overall U.S. market share of 27 percent, followed by Eureka at 22 percent. Royal's strategy of innovative designs and distribution through mass-merchandisers has earned the company third place in the market and an 18 percent share.

But the industry doesn't know how to classify the Broom Vac. It is usually categorized as a stick vacuum by retailers and in industry sales figures, but it does not really fit in that market sector.

The development team at Dirt Devil was also concerned about how consumers would view the product. Would they perceive sufficient advantage over the usual broom and dustpan to pay a premium price? How much of a premium would they be willing to pay? Where would they want to purchase the product? How should the product be promoted? What should be the message?

In the past, Royal has distributed its products through independent vacuum cleaner dealers, regional retail chains, mass-merchants, and electronic and discount stores. However, none of these was considered to be completely adequate for introducing a high-volume product that would require demonstration of its advantages.

The decision was made to introduce the Broom Vac using direct-response television advertising. This enabled Dirt Devil to control the demonstrations that were seen by prospective purchasers and to experiment with marketing variables. In test markets, variables such as price, shipping cost, and payment options were manipulated. A $50 price point was selected for the direct-response introduction. As the product moved into regular retail channels, this price was expected to be retained throughout the first year of sales.

In order to demonstrate the product fully, a two-minute infomercial was developed. The longer format allowed for a more complete explanation of the features and advantages. Dirt Devil and its advertising agency took pains to produce a high-quality infomercial to counter consumers' possible negative stereotypes of this advertising form. The infomercials concluded with toll-free telephone numbers and shipping information.

Most of the infomercials aired during lower-cost daytime and late-night hours. This provided added cost efficiency in the media purchase. Later, 15-second lifts (excerpts) from the infomercial were aired during prime time for the retail launch of the product.

At first, retailers were concerned that direct-response TV ads would just compete for their customers, but that did not happen. Dirt Devil's retailers found that customers came in looking for the product that they had seen on television. This exposed consumers to the Dirt Devil displays, which featured bright, colorful packaging and plenty of product information. Retailers found that sales volumes were enhanced and that customers required less "selling effort."

Retailers were also encouraged to use special shelf or floor displays of the product. Additionally, some retailers used newspaper inserts or other retail advertising in which Dirt Devil participated on a cooperative advertising basis. Eventually, as the original Broom Vac diffused throughout the market, retailers discounted the product from its original $50 price point.

As 1996 drew to a close, Dirt Devil was poised to once again agitate the industry. This time the shock would come not from a product innovation but rather from attention-getting communication. The grungy, boring, mature vacuum cleaner industry was to be represented in the showcase of American advertising—the Super Bowl.

On January 26, 1997, Dirt Devil aired three 15-second spots during the Super Bowl. Each spot highlighted a different product: the Broom Vac, the Ultra Hand Vac, and the Ultra MVP upright vacuum. This was the first Super Bowl exposure not only for Royal but for any vacuum cleaner.

The commercials featured these products acting as "dance partners" with the late Fred Astaire. The ad campaign, designed by Cleveland advertising agency Meldrum and Fewsmith, achieved several technical breakthroughs in its execution.

Although requested many times in the past, Fred Astaire's image had never been licensed to market any product. An agreement was reached with Astaire's widow based, in part, on the fact that actual dance footage would be used and that Mr. Astaire would not be seen as verbally endorsing any product. In fact, he does not speak in any of the commercials.

Why use Fred Astaire? In his films, Astaire often danced with props. Atomic Films SME of Los Angeles created the movie magic that substituted Dirt Devil products for the props originally used in the films *Royal Wedding* (1951) and *Easter Parade* (1948). The message to be communicated was that using Dirt Devil products could make cleaning appear to be effortless, even fun!

Royal Appliance and its ad agency felt that the campaign needed to be both attention getting and entertaining in order to be successful. Happily, it was both! Independent tests immediately following the Super Bowl credited the Dirt Devil commercials with achieving good brand name recall (fifth overall among Super Bowl advertisers) and excellent recall of celebrity/brand name pairing (second among the advertisers using this technique). Separate research found the Astaire commercials finishing number one for correct sponsor identification and celebrity association with the brand. The performance was particularly notable since the Dirt Devil brand had relatively little exposure time (45 total seconds) compared to the other advertisers (ranging from one- to four-minute on-air times). Yet Dirt Devil had higher-ranked recall scores. The Bruzzone Research Company, which has extensively studied Super Bowl advertising since 1992, concluded that the Dirt Devil spots were "noticed by more people per dollar investment in airtime than anything we've seen in the past six years."

The commercials were also well received by the broadcasting and advertising industries. *Advertising Age* and other trade outlets gave favorable exposure and reviews. In addition to the 130 million plus Super Bowl viewers, the commercials were shown and/or described on *Entertainment Tonight, CBS Evening News, NBC Today Show, Good Morning America* (ABC), and *Dateline NBC*, and in over 200 additional television stories and 1,100 newspaper and magazine articles.

Concurrently, retail insert advertising was increased. Mr. Astaire was featured in the print advertising as well as in retail display material and on product packaging. Retailers were given advance notice of the campaign so that they could be prepared with adequate stock and have the option to participate in cooperative advertising. In most states, a Dirt Devil free standing insert (FSI) also promoted a sweepstakes with a $1 million grand prize. Finally, positive publicity was generated when Mrs. Astaire announced that the campaign was the first outcome of a joint effort by the Astaire estate and Dirt Devil to sponsor the Arthritis Foundation. The "ease of use" benefit delivered by Dirt Devil's products was a natural linkage to the arthritis cause. Royal executives, for their part, promised a redoubled effort to be responsive to the needs of consumers with arthritis in the design of new and modified products.

During 1997, some of these new products were tested and launched. The Mop Vac was introduced in April as a natural extension of the Broom Vac. With the Mop Vac, consumers could clean up by releasing a cleaning solution where needed from a container on the mop handle, scrubbing, then vacuuming the fluid through a squeegee to leave a clean, dry, streak-free floor. This new household tool was also introduced using direct-response advertising, at a $100 price point. The retail rollout was to follow in time for Christmas shopping in the fall.

Other products flesh out the Dirt Devil line, ranging from two old-fashioned carpet sweepers (using only rollers and brushes, no electricity required) to a new Broom Vac Extra (more suction and more dirt capacity than the original). Two wet/dry vacuums also are available, both featuring a detachable leaf blower (when the suction motor detaches from the storage "tank"). This foray into the outdoors was followed late in 1997 with the Dirt Devil Pick-up. This is a plastic wheelbarrow that was test-marketed via direct-response television. Its unique feature is the lift-and-load wheel mechanism, which allows the container to be flush to the ground for loading and unloading, then lift up to 400 pounds. The pick-up also includes a front trap door that makes the wheelbarrow easy to empty. Another nonvacuum product that was tested, this time without advertising, was a rug cleaner spray. Dirt Devil Carpet Stain Remover was marketed in Wal-Mart stores without manufacturer advertising beyond point of sale.

With all of these products and more on the way, it is no wonder that the Royal Appliance Manufacturing Company's well-known tagline boasts, "Nothing escapes the power of a Dirt Devil!"

1. Describe Dirt Devil's pricing strategy for its recent product introductions.
2. Explain how Dirt Devil integrated its marketing mix in the introduction of the Broom Vac.
3. Was the use of Fred Astaire in television commercials a good idea?
4. What kinds of products might Dirt Devil introduce next?
5. What problems might arise with retailers if Dirt Devil continues to expand its product line beyond basic floor care?

Cases

Guide to the Use of These Cases

Cases can be used in many ways. And the same case can be analyzed several times for different purposes.

"Suggested cases" are listed at the end of most chapters, but these cases can also be used later in the text. The main criterion for the order of these cases is the amount of technical vocabulary—or text principles—that are needed to read the case meaningfully. The first cases are "easiest" in this regard. This is why an early case can easily be used two or three times—with different emphasis. Some early cases might require some consideration of Product and Price, for example, and might be used twice, perhaps regarding product planning and later pricing. In contrast, later cases, which focus more on Price, might be treated more effectively *after* the Price chapters are covered.

In some of the cases, we have disguised certain information—such as names or proprietary financial data—at the request of the people or firms involved in the case. However, such changes do not alter the basic substantive problems you will be analyzing in a case.

1. McDonald's "Seniors" Restaurant

Suzanne Drolet is manager of a McDonald's restaurant in a city with many "seniors." She has noticed that some senior citizens have become not just regular patrons—but patrons who come for breakfast and stay on until about 3 PM. Many of these older customers were attracted initially by a monthly breakfast special for people aged 55 and older. The meal costs $1.99, and refills of coffee are free. Every fourth Monday, between 100 and 150 seniors jam Suzanne's McDonald's for the special offer. But now almost as many of them are coming every day—turning the fast-food restaurant into a meeting place. They sit for hours with a cup of coffee, chatting with friends. On most days, as many as 100 will stay from one to four hours.

Suzanne's employees have been very friendly to the seniors, calling them by their first names and visiting with them each day. In fact, Suzanne's McDonald's is a happy place—with her employees developing close relationships with the seniors. Some employees have even visited customers who have been hospitalized. "You know," Suzanne says, "I really get attached to the customers. They're like my family. I really care about these people." They are all "friends" and it is part of McDonald's corporate philosophy (as reflected in its website, www.mcdonalds.com) to be friendly with its customers and to give back to the communities it serves.

These older customers are an orderly group and very friendly to anyone who comes in. Further, they are neater than most customers and carefully clean up their tables before they leave. Nevertheless, Suzanne is beginning to wonder if anything should be done about her growing "non-fast-food" clientele. There's no crowding problem yet, during the time when the seniors like to come. But if the size of the senior citizen group continues to grow, crowding could become a problem. Further, Suzanne is concerned that her restaurant might come to be known as an "old people's" restaurant—which might discourage some younger customers. And if customers felt the restaurant was crowded, some might feel that they wouldn't get fast service. On the other hand, a place that seems busy might be seen as "a good place to go" and a "friendly place."

Suzanne also worries about the image she is projecting. McDonald's is a fast-food restaurant (there are over 30,000 of them in 119 countries), and normally customers are expected to eat and run. Will allowing people to stay and visit change the whole concept? In the extreme, Suzanne's McDonald's might become more like a European-style restaurant where the customers are never rushed and feel very comfortable about lingering over coffee for an hour or two! Suzanne knows that the amount her senior customers spend is similar to the average customer's purchase—but the seniors do use the facilities for a much longer time. However, most of the older customers leave McDonald's by 11:30, before the noon crowd comes in.

Suzanne is also concerned about another possibility. If catering to seniors is OK, then should she do even more with this age group? In particular, she is considering offering bingo games during the slow morning hours—9 AM to 11 AM. Bingo is popular with some seniors, and this could be a new revenue source—beyond the extra food and drink purchases that probably would result. She figures she could charge $5 per person for the two-hour period and run it with two underutilized employees. The prizes would be coupons for purchases at her store (to keep it legal) and would amount to about two-thirds of the bingo receipts (at retail prices). The party room area of her McDonald's would be perfect for this use and could hold up to 150 persons.

Evaluate Suzanne Drolet's current strategy regarding senior citizens. Does this strategy improve this McDonald's image? What should she do about the senior citizen market—that is, should she encourage, ignore, or discourage her seniors? What should she do about the bingo idea? Explain.

2. Healthy Foods, Inc.

It is 2004, and Don Warren, newly elected president of Healthy Foods, Inc., faces a severe decline in profits. Healthy Foods, Inc., is a 127-year-old California-based food processor. Its multiproduct lines are widely accepted under the Healthy Foods brand. The company and its subsidiaries prepare, package, and sell canned and frozen foods, including fruits, vegetables, pickles, and condiments. Healthy Foods, which operates more than 30 processing plants in the United States, is one of the larger U.S. food processors—with annual sales of about $650 million.

Until 2002, Healthy Foods was a subsidiary of a major midwestern food processor, and many of the present managers came from the parent company. Healthy Foods' last president recently said:

> The influence of our old parent company is still with us. As long as new products look like they will increase the company's sales volume, they are introduced. Traditionally, there has been little, if any, attention paid to margins. We are well aware that profits will come through good products produced in large volume.

Frederico Montegro, a 25-year employee and now production manager, agrees with the multiproduct-line policy. As he puts it: "Volume comes from satisfying needs. We will can or freeze any vegetable or fruit we think consumers might want." Frederico Montegro also admits that much of the expansion in product lines was encouraged by economics. The typical plants in the industry are not fully used. By adding new products to use this excess capacity, costs are spread over greater volume. So the production department is always looking for new ways to make more effective use of its present facilities.

Healthy Foods has a line-forcing policy, which requires that any store wanting to carry its brand name must be willing to carry most of the 65 items in the Healthy Foods line. This policy, coupled with its wide expansion of product lines, has resulted in 88 percent of the firm's sales coming from major supermarket chain stores, such as Safeway, Kroger, and A&P. Smaller stores are generally not willing to accept the Healthy Foods policy. Frederico Montegro explains, "We know that only large stores can afford to stock all our products. But the large stores are the volume! We give consumers the choice of any Healthy Foods product they want, and the result is maximum sales." Many small retailers have complained about Healthy Foods' policy, but they have been ignored because they are considered too small in potential sales volume per store to be of any significance.

In late 2004, a stockholders' revolt over low profits (in 2004, they were only $500,000) resulted in Healthy Foods' president and two of its five directors being removed. Don Warren, an accountant from the company's outside auditing firm, was brought in as president. One of the first things he focused on was the variable and low levels of profits in the past several years. A comparison of Healthy Foods' results with comparable operations of some large competitors supported his concern. In the past 13 years, Healthy Foods' closest competitors had an average profit return on shareholders' investment of 5 to 9 percent, while Healthy Foods averaged only 1.5 percent. Further, Healthy Foods' sales volume has not increased much from the 1987 level (after adjusting for inflation)—while operating costs have soared upward. Profits for the firm were about $8 million in 1987. The closest Healthy Foods has come since then is about $6 million—in 1995. The outgoing president blamed his failure on an inefficient sales department. He said, "Our sales department has deteriorated. I can't exactly put my finger on it, but the overall quality of salespeople has dropped, and morale is bad. The team just didn't perform." When Don Warren e-mailed Lars Svensson, the vice president of sales, with this charge, his reply was,

It's not our fault. I think the company made a key mistake in the early 80s. It expanded horizontally—by increasing its number of product offerings—while major competitors were expanding vertically, growing their own raw materials and making all of their packing materials. They can control quality and make profits in manufacturing that can be used in promotion. I lost some of my best people from frustration. We just aren't competitive enough to reach the market the way we should with a comparable product and price.

In a lengthy e-mail from Lars Svensson, Don Warren learned more about the nature of Healthy Foods' market. Although all the firms in the food-processing industry advertise heavily, the size of the market for most processed foods hasn't grown much for many years. Further, most consumers are pressed for time and aren't very selective. If they can't find the brand of food they are looking for, they'll pick up another brand rather than go to some other store. No company in the industry has much effect on the price at which its products are sold. Chain store buyers are very knowledgeable about prices and special promotions available from all the competing suppliers, and they are quick to play one supplier against another to keep the price low. Basically, they have a price they are willing to pay—and they won't exceed it. However, the chains will charge any price they wish on a given brand sold at retail. (That is, a 48-can case of beans might be purchased from any supplier for $23.10, no matter whose product it is. Generally, the shelf price for each is no more than a few pennies different, but chain stores occasionally attract customers by placing a well-known brand on sale.)

Besides insisting that processors meet price points, like for the canned beans, some chains require price allowances if special locations or displays are desired. They also carry nonadvertised brands and/or their own brands at lower price—to offer better value to their customers. And most will willingly accept producers' cents-off coupons, which are offered by Healthy Foods as well as most of the other major producers of full lines.

At this point, Don Warren is trying to decide why Healthy Foods, Inc., isn't as profitable as it once was. And he is puzzled about why some competitors are putting products on the market with low potential sales volume. (For example, one major competitor recently introduced a line of exotic foreign vegetables with gourmet sauces.) And others have been offering frozen dinners or entrees with vegetables for several years. Apparently, Healthy Foods' managers considered trying such products several years ago but decided against it because of the small potential sales volumes and the likely high costs of new-product development and promotion.

Evaluate Healthy Foods' present situation. What would you advise Don Warren to do to improve Healthy Foods' profits? Explain why.

3. Pillsbury's Häagen-Dazs

Jan Phillips is the newly hired ice cream product-market manager for the United States for Häagen-Dazs—the world's leading brand of super premium ice cream (now available in 55 countries) and the market leader in the U.S. Pillsbury says Häagen-Dazs (www.pillsbury.com/main/brands/haagen) is profitable globally, with total sales of more than $900 million. The company saw its sales grow rapidly during the 1990s, but now its markets are facing significant change and very aggressive competition. Phillips is responsible for Häagen-Dazs' ice cream strategy planning for the United States.

Other product-market managers are responsible for Europe, Japan, and other global markets. Therefore, Phillips will be expected to focus only on the United States while knowing that "everyone" will be watching her (and the United States) for clues about what may happen elsewhere.

Overall, ice cream sales in the U.S. have been off 1 to 2 percent in recent years. Still, some new entries have made a big splash. Starbucks, the coffee king, is one such brand. In its first year in grocery-store freezer sections, its Frappuccino bars—in several flavors—were a big hit. Coldstone Creamery is a fast-growing franchise, increasing from 1 store in 1988 to about 1,000 now. Häagen-Dazs, along with a few other super premium producers, are continuing to grow at rates of 2 to 3 percent. But most other U.S. super premium producers are reporting flat sales, and some are going out of business. The easy availability of super premium ice cream in supermarkets has hurt some of these producers who sell through ice cream stores, which specialize in take-out cones, sundaes, and small containers of ice cream. It is also thought that, at least in part, the decline in sales growth of super premium ice cream in the U.S. since the early 1990s is due to competition from other products such as lower-calorie yogurts and low-fat ice cream.

Despite a real concern about healthy diets, Americans seem to swing back and forth in their yearnings for low fat and rich taste. There is some evidence that "dessert junkies" who want to indulge without too much guilt are turning to low-fat frozen yogurt and low-fat ice cream. This has encouraged a number of super premium ice cream competitors to offer these products too. Pillsbury's Häagen-Dazs, International Dairy Queen, and Baskin Robbins are selling frozen yogurt. And Kraft—which makes Frusen Glädjè, Edy's, and Dreyer's Grand Ice Cream—is among many other ice cream makers that are promoting gourmet versions of low-fat ice cream.

Because of the competition from low-fat products, Häagen-Dazs introduced a line of low-fat super premium ice cream. The low-fat line contains no more than three grams of fat per serving. That compares with six times more grams of fat in a half-cup serving of its full-fat versions. Häagen-Dazs believes that its low-fat super premium ice cream is better tasting than other alternatives. Its belief is that "people like to make every calorie count." Having worked on the low-fat item for more than two years, it developed a process whereby a concentration of dairy proteins from lactose-reduced skim milk give a mouth-feel that approximates that of a higher-fat product. Häagen-Dazs sells its low-fat products in a variety of flavors.

Most ice cream products are considered economy and regular brands—priced at $2 to $5 a half gallon. Super premium ice cream retails for $2.50 to $3.50 a *pint*, or $8 to $10 a half gallon. The retail price for a pint of Häagen-Dazs is usually over $3.00. The low-fat version is comparably priced to the full-fat product.

Many other U.S. ice cream producers have turned to frozen yogurt for growth. Frozen yogurt sales were in a slump for a long time because many people didn't like the tart taste. But after the product was reformulated it started to win customers. The difference is that today's frozen yogurt tastes more like ice cream.

The yogurt market leader, TCBY (www.tcby.com), which had sales of only about $2 million in 1983, has risen to over $100 million in sales. It numbers over 2,500 shops worldwide and is franchised in over 67 countries. In the U.S., yogurt makers are using aggressive promotion against ice cream. TCBY ads have preached: "Say goodbye to high calories—say goodbye to ice cream" and "All the pleasure, none of the guilt." And the ads for its nonfat frozen yogurt emphasize: "Say goodbye to fat and high calories with the great taste of TCBY Nonfat Frozen Yogurt."

Baskin Robbins has introduced yogurt in many of its U.S. stores and has even changed its name to Baskin Robbins Ice Cream and Yogurt. Häagen-Dazs also offers yogurt in most of its stores.

Although the flurry of consumer interest in low-fat yogurt and low-fat ice cream certainly created some new market opportunities, it is not clear how consumers will react to these products over the longer term. One reason is that many consumers who were initially excited about being able to buy a good tasting, low-fat frozen dessert have realized that low fat does not necessarily mean low calorie. In fact, Jan Phillips has been trying to identify a product that Häagen-Dazs could produce that would offer consumers great taste, low fat, and low calories all at the same time. One possibility she is seriously considering is to introduce a line of sorbets based on exotic fruits like kiwi and mango and that use low-calorie sweeteners.

A sorbet is basically the same as sherbet, but European sorbets usually have an icy texture and include less milk. This is the sort of product that Jan Phillips has in mind. She thinks that it might have an upscale appeal and also be different from what is already in the premium ice cream case.

On the other hand, calling a product by a different name doesn't make it really new and different, and basic sherbet has been around for a long time and never been a big seller. Further, consumers don't think of sorbet in the same way that they think about a rich-tasting bowl of ice cream. You don't have to convince people that they might like premium ice cream. Sorbet, on the other hand, isn't something that consumers crave and make a special trip to buy.

Further, Phillips is very conscious that the Häagen-Dazs brand should stand for high quality and the best ingredients. Yet, it's not clear that consumers will think of sorbet as a premium product. Rather, they might just see it as ground-up ice with some flavoring thrown in. But if sorbet isn't the right way to go with new-product development, how should Häagen-Dazs counter the competition from other low-fat ice cream brands like Ben & Jerry's and other new entries to the super premium category like Coldstone Creamery?

Evaluate what is happening in the ice cream market, especially regarding the apparent leveling off of super premium ice cream sales and the possibilities for growth of the sorbet market. Is Jan Phillips' idea about rolling out a low-cal fruit sorbet a good idea? Would it be better to use the Häagen-Dazs brand name or a different brand name? What else, if anything, would need to be different about the strategy? Why?

4. Computer Support Services

Sharon Bidwell is getting desperate about her new business. She's not sure she can make a go of it—and she really wants to stay in her hometown of Petoskey, Michigan, a beautiful summer resort area along the eastern shore of Lake Michigan. The area's permanent population of 10,000 more than triples in the summer months and doubles at times during the winter skiing and snowmobiling season.

Sharon spent four years in the Navy after college graduation, returning home in June 2003. When she couldn't find a good job in the Petoskey area, she decided to go into business for herself and set up Computer Support Services. Sharon's plan was to work by herself and basically serve as a "for hire" computer consultant and troubleshooter for her customers. She knew that many of the upscale summer residents relied on a home computer to keep in touch with business dealings and friends at home, and it seemed that someone was always asking her for computer advice. She was optimistic that she could keep busy with a variety of "on-site" services—setting up a customer's new computer, repairing hardware problems, installing software or upgrades, creating a wireless network, correcting problems created by viruses, and the like.

Sharon thought that her savings would allow her to start the business without borrowing any money. Her estimates of required expenditures were: $7,000 for a used SUV; $1,125 for tools, diagnostic equipment, and reference books; $1,700 for a laptop computer, software, and accessories; $350 for an initial supply of fittings and cables; and $500 for insurance and other incidental expenses. This total of $10,675 still left Sharon with about $5,000 in savings to cover living expenses while getting started.

Sharon chose the computer services business because of her previous work experience. She worked at a computer "help desk" in college and spent her last year in the Navy troubleshooting computer network problems. In addition, from the time Sharon was 16 until she finished college, she had also worked during the summer for Peter Kittany. Kittany operates the only successful computer services company in Petoskey. (There was one other local computer store that also did some "on location" service work when the customer bought equipment at the store, but that store recently went out of business.)

Kittany prides himself on quality work and has been able to build up a good business with repeat customers. Specializing in services to residential, small business, and professional offices, Kittany has built a strong customer franchise. For 20 years, Kittany's major source of new business has been satisfied customers who tell friends or coworkers about his quality service. He is highly regarded as a capable person who always treats clients fairly and honestly. For example, seasonal residents often give Kittany the keys to their vacation homes so that he can do upgrades or maintenance while they are away for months at a time. Kittany's customers are so loyal, in fact, that Fix-A-Bug—a national computer service franchise—found it impossible to compete with him. Even price-cutting was not an effective weapon against Kittany.

From having worked with Kittany, Sharon Bidwell thought that she knew the computer service business as well as he did; in fact, she had sometimes been able to solve technical problems that left him stumped. Sharon was anxious to reach her $60,000-per-year sales objective because she thought this would provide her with a comfortable living in Petoskey. While aware of opportunities to do computer consulting for larger businesses, Sharon felt that the sales volume available there was limited because many firms had their own computer specialists or even IT departments. As Sharon saw it, her only attractive opportunity was direct competition with Kittany.

To get started, Sharon spent $1,400 to advertise her business in the local newspaper and on an Internet website. With this money she bought two large announcement ads and 52 weeks of daily ads in the classified section, listed under Miscellaneous Residential and Business Services. The website simply listed businesses in the Petoskey area and gave a telephone number, e-mail address, and brief description. She put magnetic sign boards on her SUV and waited for business to take off.

Sharon had a few customers, but much of the time she wasn't busy and she was able to gross only about $200 a week. Of course, she had expected much more. Many of the people who did call were regular Kittany customers who had some sort of crisis when he was already busy. While these people agreed that Sharon's work was of the same quality as Kittany's, they preferred Kittany's "quality-care" image and they liked the fact that they had an ongoing relationship with him.

Sometimes Sharon did get more work than she could handle. This happened during April and May, when seasonal businesses were preparing for summer openings and owners of summer homes and condos were ready to "open the cottage."

The same rush occurred in September and October, as many of these places were being closed for the winter; those customers often wanted help backing up computer files or packing up computer equipment so they could take it with them. During these months, Sharon was able to gross about $150 to $200 a day.

Toward the end of her discouraging first year in business, Sharon Bidwell is thinking about quitting. While she hates to think about leaving Petoskey, she can't see any way of making a living there with her independent computer services business. Kittany seems to dominate the market, except in the rush seasons and for people who need emergency help. And the resort market is not growing very rapidly, so there is little hope of a big influx of new businesses and homeowners to spur demand.

Evaluate Sharon Bidwell's strategy planning for her new business. Why isn't she able to reach her objective of $60,000? What should Sharon do now? Explain.

5. ResinTech

Sally Walden, a chemist in ResinTech's polymer resins laboratory, is trying to decide how hard to fight for the new product she has developed. Walden's job is to find new, more profitable applications for the company's present resin products—and her current efforts are running into unexpected problems.

During the last four years, Walden has been under heavy pressure from her managers to come up with an idea that will open up new markets for the company's foamed polystyrene.

Two years ago, Walden developed the "foamed-dome concept"—a method of using foamed polystyrene to make dome-shaped roofs and other structures. She described the procedure for making domes as follows: The construction of a foamed dome involves the use of a specially designed machine that bends, places, and bonds pieces of plastic foam together into a predetermined dome shape. In forming a dome, the machine head is mounted on a boom, which swings around a pivot like the hands of a clock, laying and bonding layer upon layer of foam board in a rising spherical form.

According to Walden, polystyrene foamed boards have several advantages:

1. Foam board is stiff—but can be formed or bonded to itself by heat alone.

2. Foam board is extremely lightweight and easy to handle. It has good structural rigidity.

3. Foam board has excellent and permanent insulating characteristics. (In fact, the major use for foam board is as an insulator.)

4. Foam board provides an excellent base on which to apply a variety of surface finishes, such as a readily available concrete-based stucco that is durable and inexpensive.

Using her good selling abilities, Walden easily convinced her managers that her idea has potential.

According to a preliminary study by the marketing research department, the following were areas of construction that could be served by the domes:

1. Bulk storage.
2. Cold storage.
3. Educational construction.
4. Covers for industrial tanks.
5. Light commercial construction.
6. Planetariums.
7. Recreational construction (such as a golf-course starter house).

The marketing research study focused on uses for existing dome structures. Most of the existing domes are made of cement-based materials. The study showed that large savings would result from using foam boards, due to the reduction of construction time.

Because of the new technology involved, the company decided to do its own contracting (at least for the first four to five years). Walden thought this was necessary to make sure that no mistakes were made by inexperienced contractor crews. (For example, if not applied properly, the plastic may burn.)

After building a few domes in the United States to demonstrate the concept, Walden contacted some leading U.S. architects. Reactions were as follows:

"It's very interesting, but we're not sure the fire marshal of Chicago would ever give his OK."

"Your tests show that foamed domes can be protected against fires, but there are no *good* tests for unconventional building materials as far as I am concerned."

"I like the idea, but foam board does not have the impact resistance of cement."

"We design a lot of recreational facilities, and kids will find a way to poke holes in the foam."

"Building codes in our area are written for wood and cement structures. Maybe we'd be interested if the codes change."

After this unexpected reaction, management didn't know what to do. Walden still thinks they should go ahead with the project. She wants to build several more demonstration projects in the United States and at least three each in Europe and Japan to expose the concept in the global market. She thinks architects outside the United States may be more receptive to really new ideas. Further, she says, it takes time for potential users to "see" and accept new ideas. She is sure that more exposure to more people will speed acceptance. And she is convinced that a few reports of well-constructed domes in leading trade papers and magazines will go a long way toward selling the idea. She is working on getting such reports right now. But her managers aren't sure they want to OK spending more money on "her" project. Her immediate boss is supportive, but the rest of the review board is less sure about more demonstration projects or going ahead at all—just in the United States or in global markets.

Evaluate how ResinTech got into the present situation. What should Sally Walden do? What should Walden's managers do? Explain.

6. Valley Steel Company

Valley Steel Company is one of two major producers of wide-flange beams in the United States. The other producer is United Steel Corporation (now USX). A number of small firms also compete, but they tend to compete mainly on price in nearby markets where they can keep transport costs low. Typically, all interested competitors charge the same delivered price, which varies some depending on how far the customer is from either of the two major producers. In other words, local prices are higher in more remote geographic markets.

Wide-flange beams are one of the principal steel products used in construction. They are the modern version of what are commonly known as I-beams. USX rolls a full range of wide flanges from 6 to 36 inches. Valley entered the field about 30 years ago, when it converted an existing mill to produce this product. Valley's mill is limited to flanges up to 24 inches, however. At the time of the conversion, Valley felt that customer usage of sizes over 24 inches was likely to be small. In recent years, however, there has been a definite trend toward the larger and heavier sections.

The beams produced by the various competitors are almost identical—since customers buy according to standard dimensional and physical-property specifications. In the smaller size range, there are a number of competitors. But above 14 inches, only USX and Valley compete. Above 24 inches, USX has no competition.

All the steel companies sell these beams through their own sales forces. The customer for these beams is called a structural fabricator. This fabricator typically buys unshaped beams and other steel products from the mills and shapes them according to the specifications of each customer. The fabricator sells to the contractor or owner of the structure being built.

The structural fabricator usually must sell on a competitive-bid basis. The bidding is done on the plans and specifications prepared by an architectural or structural engineering firm and forwarded to the fabricator by the contractor who wants the bid. Although thousands of structural fabricators compete in the U.S., relatively few account for the majority of wide-flange tonnage in the various geographical regions. Since the price is the same from all producers, they typically buy beams on the basis of availability (i.e., availability to meet production schedules) and performance (i.e., reliability in meeting the promised delivery schedule).

Several years ago, Valley's production schedulers saw that they were going to have an excess of hot-rolled plate capacity in the near future. At the same time, development of a new production technology allowed Valley to weld three plates together into a section with the same dimensional and physical properties and almost the same cross section as a rolled wide-flange beam. This development appeared to offer two key advantages to Valley: (1) It would enable Valley to use some of the excess plate capacity, and (2) larger sizes of wide-flange beams could be offered. Cost analysts showed that by using a fully depreciated plate mill and the new welding process it would be possible to produce and sell larger wide-flange beams at competitive prices—that is, at the same price charged by USX.

Valley's managers were excited about the possibilities, because customers usually appreciate having a second source of supply. Also, the new approach would allow the production of up to a 60-inch flange. With a little imagination, these larger sizes might offer a significant breakthrough for the construction industry.

Valley decided to go ahead with the new project. As the production capacity was converted, the salespeople were kept well informed of the progress. They, in turn, promoted this new capability to their customers, emphasizing that soon they would be able to offer a full range of beam products. Valley sent several general information letters to a broad mailing list but did not advertise. The market development section of the sales department was very busy explaining the new possibilities of the process to fabricators at engineering trade associations and shows.

When the new production line was finally ready to go, the market reaction was disappointing. No orders came in and none were expected. In general, customers were wary of the new product. The structural fabricators felt they couldn't use it without the approval of their customers, because it would involve deviating from the specified rolled sections. And as long as they could still get the rolled section, why make the extra effort for something unfamiliar, especially with no price advantage. The salespeople were also bothered with a very common question: How can you take plate that you sell for about $460 per ton and make a product that you can sell for $470? This question came up frequently and tended to divert the whole discussion to the cost of production rather than to the way the new product might be used or its value in the construction process.

Evaluate Valley's situation. What should Valley do?

7. Lilybank Lodge

Nestled in the high country of New Zealand's South Island is a getaway adventure playground aimed unashamedly at the world's very wealthy. Presidents, playboys, and other such globe-trotters are the prime targets of this fledgling tourism business developed by Lilybank Lodge. The lodge offers this exclusive niche the opportunity of a secluded holiday in a little-known paradise. Guests, commonly under public scrutiny in their everyday lives, can escape such pressures at a hunting retreat designed specifically with their needs in mind.

A chance meeting between a New Zealand Department of Conservation investigator and the son of the former Indonesian president marked the beginning of this specialty tourist operation. Recognizing that "filthy rich" public figures are constantly surrounded by security and seldom have the luxury of going anywhere incognito, the New Zealander, Gerard Olde-Olthof, suggested that he and his new friend purchase a high-country station and hunting guide company that was for sale. Olde-Olthof believed that the facilities, and their secluded and peaceful environment, would make an ideal holiday haven for this elite group. His Indonesian partner concurred.

Olde-Olthof, who was by now the company's managing director, developed a carefully tailored package of goods and services for the property. Architecturally designed accommodations, including a game trophy room and eight guest rooms, were constructed using high-quality South Island furniture and fittings, to create the ambience necessary to attract and satisfy the demands of their special clientele.

Although New Zealand had an international reputation for being sparsely populated and green, Olde-Olthof knew that rich travelers frequently complained that local accommodations were below overseas standards. Since the price (NZ$700 a night) was not a significant variable for this target market, sumptuous guest facilities were built. These were designed to be twice the normal size of most hotel rooms, with double-glazed windows that revealed breathtaking views. Ten full-time staff and two seasonal guides were recruited to ensure that visitors received superior customized service, in fitting with the restrained opulence of the lodge.

The 28,000 hectares of original farmland that made up the retreat and backed onto the South Island's Mount Cook National Park were converted into a big-game reserve. All merino sheep on the land were sold, and deer, elk, chamois, and wapiti were brought in and released. This was a carefully considered plan. Olde-Olthof, the former conservationist, believed that financially and environmentally this was the correct decision. Not only do tourists, each staying for one week and taking part in safari shooting, inject as much cash into the business as the station's annual wool clip used to fetch, but the game does less harm to the environment than sheep. Cattle, however, once part of the original station, were left to graze on lower riverflat areas.

For those high-flying customers seeking less bloodthirsty leisure activities, Lilybank developed photographic "safaris" and other product-line extensions. Horse-trekking, golfing on a nearby rural course (with no need for hordes of security forces), helicopter trips around nearby Lake Tekapo, nature walks, and other such activities formed part of the exclusive package.

While still in the early stages of operation, this retreat has already attracted a steady stream of visitors. To date, the manager has relied solely on positive word of mouth, publicity, and public relations to draw in new customers. Given the social and business circles in which his potential target market moves, Olde-Olthof considers these to be the most appropriate forms of marketing communication. The only real concern for Lilybank Lodge has been the criticism of at least one New Zealand lobby group that the company is yet another example of local land passing into "foreign" hands, and that New Zealanders are prevented from using the retreat and excluded from its financial returns. However, this unwelcome attention has been fairly short-lived.

Identify the likely characteristics of the market segment being targeted by the company. Why are most target customers likely to be foreign nationals rather than New Zealanders? What expectations target customers are likely to have regarding the quality, reliability, and range of services. What are the implications for Lilybank Lodge? How difficult is it for Lilybank Lodge to undertake market research? Elaborate.

8. Marie's Ristorante

Marie Trevia, the owner and manager of Marie's Ristorante, is reviewing the slow growth of her restaurant. She's also thinking about the future and wondering if she should change her strategy. In particular, she is wondering if she should join a fast-food or family restaurant franchise chain. Several are located near her, but there are many franchisors without local restaurants. After doing some research on the Internet, she has learned that with help from the franchisors, some of these places gross $500,000 to $1 million a year. Of course, she would have to follow someone else's strategy and thereby lose her independence, which she doesn't like to think about. But those sales figures do sound good, and she has also heard that the return to the owner-manager (including salary) can be over $150,000 per year. She has also considered putting a web page for Marie's Ristorante on the Internet but is not sure how that will help.

Marie's Ristorante is a fairly large restaurant—about 3,000 square feet—located in the center of a small shopping center completed early in 2002. Marie's sells mainly full-course "home-cooked" Italian-style dinners (no bar) at moderate prices. In addition to Marie's restaurant, other businesses in the shopping center include a supermarket, a hair salon, a liquor store, a video rental store, and a vacant space that used to be a hardware store. The hardware store failed when a Home Depot located nearby. Marie has learned that a pizzeria is considering locating there soon. She wonders how that competition will affect her. Ample parking space is available at the shopping center, which is located in a residential section of a growing suburb in the East, along a heavily traveled major traffic route.

Marie graduated from a local high school and a nearby university and has lived in this town with her husband and two children for many years. She has been self-employed in the restaurant business since her graduation from college in 1985. Her most recent venture before opening Marie's was a large restaurant that she operated successfully with her brother from 1993 to 1999. In 1999, Marie sold out her share because of illness. Following her recovery, she was anxious for something to do and opened the present restaurant in April 2002. Marie feels her plans for the business and her opening were well thought out. When she was ready to start her new restaurant, she looked at several possible locations before finally deciding on the present one. Marie explained: "I looked everywhere, but here I particularly noticed the heavy traffic when I first looked at it. This is the crossroads for three major interstate highways. So obviously the potential is here."

Having decided on the location, Marie signed a 10-year lease with option to renew for 10 more years, and then eagerly attacked the problem of outfitting the almost empty store space in the newly constructed building. She tiled the floor, put in walls of surfwood, installed plumbing and electrical fixtures and an extra washroom, and purchased the necessary restaurant equipment. All this cost $120,000—which came from her own cash savings. She then spent an additional $1,500 for glassware, $2,000 for an initial food stock, and $2,125 to advertise Marie's Ristorante's opening in the local newspaper. The paper serves the whole metro area, so the $2,125 bought only three quarter-page ads. These expenditures also came from her own personal savings. Next she hired five waitresses at $275 a week and one chef at $550 a week. Then, with $24,000 cash reserve for the business, she was ready to open. Reflecting her sound business sense, Marie knew she would need a substantial cash reserve to fall back on until the business got on its feet. She expected this to take about one year. She had no expectations of getting rich overnight. (Her husband, a high school teacher, was willing to support the family until the restaurant caught on.)

The restaurant opened in April and by August had a weekly gross revenue of only $2,400. Marie was a little discouraged with this, but she was still able to meet all her operating expenses without investing any new money in the business. By September business was still slow, and Marie had to invest an additional $3,000 in the business just to survive.

Business had not improved in November, and Marie stepped up her advertising—hoping this would help. In December, she spent $1,200 of her cash reserve for radio advertising—10 late-evening spots on a news program at a station that aims at middle-income America. Marie also spent $1,600 more during the next several weeks for some metro newspaper ads.

By April 2003, the situation had begun to improve, and by June her weekly gross was up to between $3,100 and $3,300. By March 2004, the weekly gross had risen to about $4,200. Marie increased the working hours of her staff six to seven hours a week and added another cook to handle the increasing number of customers. Marie was more optimistic for the future because she was finally doing a little better than breaking even. Her full-time involvement seemed to be paying off. She had not put any new money into the business since summer 2003 and expected business to continue to rise. She had not yet taken any salary for herself, even though she had built up a small surplus of about $9,000. Instead, she planned to put in a bigger air-conditioning system at a cost of $5,000 and was also planning to use what salary she might have taken for herself to hire two new waitresses to handle the growing volume of business. And she saw that if business increased much more she would have to add another cook.

Evaluate Marie's past and present marketing strategy. What should she do now? Should she seriously consider joining some franchise chain?

9. SleepEasy Motel

Eng Huang is trying to decide whether he should make some minor changes in the way he operates his SleepEasy Motel or if he should join either the Days Inn or Holiday Inn motel chains. Some decision must be made soon because his present operation is losing money. But joining either of the chains will require fairly substantial changes, including new capital investment if he goes with Holiday Inn.

Huang bought the recently completed 60-room motel two years ago after leaving a successful career as a production manager for a large producer of industrial machinery. He was looking for an interesting opportunity that would be less demanding than the production manager job. The SleepEasy is located at the edge of a very small town near a rapidly expanding resort area and about one-half mile off an interstate highway. It is 10 miles from the tourist area, with several nationally franchised full-service resort motels suitable for "destination" vacations. There is a Best Western, a Ramada Inn, and a Hilton Inn, as well as many mom and pop and limited-service, lower-priced motels—and some quaint bed and breakfast facilities—in the tourist area. The interstate highway near the SleepEasy carries a great deal of traffic, since the resort area is between several major metropolitan areas. No development has taken place around the turnoff from the interstate highway. The only promotion for the tourist area along the interstate highway is two large signs near the turnoffs. They show the popular name for the area and that the area is only 10 miles to the west. These signs are maintained by the tourist area's Tourist Bureau. In addition, the state transportation department maintains several small signs showing (by symbols) that near this turnoff one can find gas, food, and lodging. Huang does not have any signs advertising SleepEasy except the two on his property. He has been relying on people finding his motel as they go toward the resort area.

Initially, Huang was very pleased with his purchase. He had traveled a lot himself and stayed in many different hotels and motels—so he had some definite ideas about what travelers wanted. He felt that a relatively plain but modern room with a comfortable bed, standard bath facilities, and free cable TV would appeal to most customers. Further, Huang thought a swimming pool or any other nonrevenue-producing additions were not necessary. And he felt a restaurant would be a greater management problem than the benefits it would offer. However, after many customers commented about the lack of convenient breakfast facilities, Huang served a free continental breakfast of coffee, juice, and rolls in a room next to the registration desk.

Day-to-day operations went fairly smoothly in the first two years, in part because Huang and his wife handled registration and office duties as well as general management. During the first year of operation, occupancy began to stabilize around 55 percent of capacity. But according to industry figures, this was far below the average of 68 percent for his classification—motels without restaurants.

After two years of operation, Huang was concerned because his occupancy rates continued to be below average. He decided to look for ways to increase both occupancy rate and profitability and still maintain his independence.

Huang wanted to avoid direct competition with the full-service resort motels. He stressed a price appeal in his signs and brochures and was quite proud of the fact that he had been able to avoid all the "unnecessary expenses" of the full-service resort motels. As a result, Huang was able to offer lodging at a very modest price—about 40 percent below the full-service hotels and comparable to the lowest-priced resort area motels. The customers who stayed at SleepEasy said they found it quite acceptable. But he was troubled by what seemed to be a large number of people driving into his parking lot, looking around, and not coming in to register.

Huang was particularly interested in the results of a recent study by the regional tourist bureau. This study revealed the following information about area vacationers:

1. 68 percent of the visitors to the area are young couples and older couples without children.
2. 40 percent of the visitors plan their vacations and reserve rooms more than 60 days in advance.
3. 66 percent of the visitors stay more than three days in the area and at the same location.
4. 78 percent of the visitors indicated that recreational facilities were important in their choice of accommodations.
5. 13 percent of the visitors had family incomes of less than $27,000 per year.
6. 38 percent of the visitors indicated that it was their first visit to the area.

After much thought, Huang began to seriously consider affiliating with a national motel chain in hopes of attracting more customers and maybe protecting his motel from the increasing competition. There were constant rumors that more motels were being planned for the area. After some investigating, he focused on two national chain possibilities: Days Inn and Holiday Inn. Neither had affiliates in the area even though they each have about 2,000 units nationwide.

Days Inn of America, Inc., is an Atlanta-based chain of economy lodgings. It has been growing rapidly and is willing to take on new franchisees. A major advantage of Days Inn is that it would not require a major capital investment by Huang. The firm is targeting people interested in lower-priced motels, in particular, senior citizens, the military, school sports teams, educators, and business travelers. In contrast, Holiday Inn would probably require Huang to upgrade some of his facilities, including adding a swimming pool. The total new capital investment would be between $300,000 and $500,000, depending on how fancy he got. But then Huang would be able to charge higher prices, perhaps $75 per day on the average rather than the $45 per day per room he's charging now.

The major advantages of going with either of these national chains would be their central reservation systems and their national names. Both companies offer nationwide, toll-free reservation lines, which produce about 40 percent of all bookings in affiliated motels. Both companies also offer websites (www.daysinn.com and www.holiday-inn.com) that help find a specific hotel by destination, rate, amenities, quality rating, and availability.

A major difference between the two national chains is their method of promotion. Days Inn uses little TV advertising and less print advertising than Holiday Inn. Instead, Days Inn emphasizes sales promotions. In one campaign, for example, Blue Bonnet margarine users could exchange proof-of-purchase seals for a free night at a Days Inn. This tie-in led to the Days Inn system *selling* an additional 10,000 rooms. Further, Days Inn operates a September Days Club for travelers 50 and over who receive such benefits as discount rates and a quarterly travel magazine.

Days Inn also has other membership programs, including its InnCentives loyalty club for frequent business and leisure travelers. Other programs targeted to business travelers include two Corporate Rate programs and its new Days Business Place hotels. Not to be outdone, Holiday Inn has a membership program called Priority Club Worldwide.

Both firms charge 8 percent of gross room revenues for belonging to their chain—to cover the costs of the reservation service and national promotion. This amount is payable monthly. In addition, franchise members must agree to maintain their facilities and make repairs and improvements as required. Failure to maintain facilities can result in losing the franchise. Periodic inspections are conducted as part of supervising the whole chain and helping the members operate more effectively.

Evaluate Eng Huang's present strategy. What should he do? Explain.

10. Murphy's Ice Land

Eduardo Black, the manager of Murphy's Ice Land, is trying to decide what strategies to use to increase profits.

Murphy's Ice Land is an ice-skating rink with a conventional hockey rink surface (85 feet × 200 feet). It is the only indoor ice rink in a northern U.S. city of about 450,000. The city's recreation department operates some outdoor rinks in the winter, but they don't offer regular ice skating programs because of weather variability.

Eduardo runs a successful hockey program that is more than breaking even—but this is about all he can expect if he only offers hockey. To try to increase his profits, Eduardo is trying to expand and improve his public skating program. With such a program, he could have as many as 700 people in a public session at one time, instead of limiting the use of the ice to 12 to 24 hockey players per hour. While the receipts from hockey can be as high as $200 an hour (plus concession sales), the receipts from a two-hour public skating session—charging $5 per person—could yield up to $3,500 for a two-hour period (plus much higher concession sales). The potential revenue from such large public skating sessions could make Murphy's Ice Land a really profitable operation. But, unfortunately, just scheduling public sessions doesn't mean that a large number will come. In fact, only a few prime times seem likely: Friday and Saturday evenings and Saturday and Sunday afternoons.

Eduardo has included 14 public skating sessions in his ice schedule, but so far they haven't attracted as many people as he hoped. In total, they only generate a little more revenue than if the times were sold for hockey use. Offsetting this extra revenue are extra costs. More staff people are needed to handle a public skating session—guards, a ticket seller, skate rental, and more concession help. So the net revenue from either use is about the same. He could cancel some of the less attractive public sessions—like the noon-time daily sessions, which have very low attendance—and make the average attendance figures look a lot better. But he feels that if he is going to offer public skating he must have a reasonable selection of times. He does recognize, however, that the different public skating sessions do seem to attract different people and, really different kinds of people.

The Saturday and Sunday afternoon public skating sessions have been the most successful, with an average of 200 people attending during the winter season. Typically, this is a "kid-sitting" session. More than half of the patrons are young children who have been dropped off by their parents for several hours, but there are also some family groups.

In general, the kids and the families have a good time—and a fairly loyal group comes every Saturday and/or Sunday during the winter season. In the spring and fall, however, attendance drops about in half, depending on how nice the weather is. (Eduardo schedules no public sessions in the summer, focusing instead on hockey clinics and figure skating.)

The Friday and Saturday evening public sessions are a big disappointment. The sessions run from 8 until 10, a time when he had hoped to attract teenagers and young adult couples. At $5 per person, plus $1.50 for skate rental, this would be an economical date. In fact, Eduardo has seen quite a few young couples—and some keep coming back. But he also sees a surprising number of 8- to 14-year-olds who have been dropped off by their parents. The younger kids tend to race around the rink playing tag. This affects the whole atmosphere, making it less appealing for dating couples and older patrons.

Eduardo has been hoping to develop a teenage and young-adult market for a "social activity," adapting the format used by roller-skating rinks. Their public skating sessions feature a variety of couples-only and group games as well as individual skating to dance music. Turning ice skating sessions into such social activities is not common, however, although industry newletters suggest that a few ice-rink operators have had success with the roller-skating format. Seemingly, the ice skating sessions are viewed as active recreation, offering exercise or a sports experience.

Eduardo installed some soft lights to try to change the evening atmosphere. The music was selected to encourage people to skate to the beat and couples to skate together. Some people complained about the "old" music; but it was "danceable," and some skaters really liked it. For a few sessions, Eduardo even tried to have some couples-only skates. The couples liked it, but this format was strongly resisted by the young boys who felt that they had paid their money and there was no reason why they should be kicked off the ice. Eduardo also tried to attract more young people and especially couples by bringing in a local rock radio station disk jockey to broadcast from Murphy's Ice Land—playing music and advertising the Friday and Saturday evening public sessions. But this had no effect on attendance, which varies from 50 to 100 per two-hour session during the winter.

Eduardo seriously considered the possibility of limiting the Friday and Saturday evening sessions to people age 14 and over—to try to change the environment. He knew it would take time to change people's attitudes. But when he counted the customers, he realized this would be risky. More than a quarter of his customers on an average weekend night appear to be 13 or under. This means that he would have to make a serious commitment to building the teen and young-adult market. And, so far, his efforts haven't been successful. He has already invested over $3,000 in lighting changes and over $9,000 promoting the sessions over the rock music radio station, with very disappointing results. Although the station's sales rep said they reached teenagers all over town, an on-air offer for a free skating session did not get a single response!

Some days, Eduardo feels it's hopeless. Maybe he should accept that most public ice skating sessions are a mixed bag. Or maybe he should just sell the time to hockey groups. Still he keeps hoping that something can be done to improve weekend evening public skating attendance, because the upside potential is so good. And the Saturday and Sunday afternoon sessions are pretty good money-makers.

Evaluate Murphy's Ice Land's situation. What should Eduardo Black do? Why?

11. Joggers Universe

Sue Koenig, owner of Joggers Universe, is trying to decide what she should do with her retail business and how committed she should be to her current target market.

Sue is 42 years old, and she started her Joggers Universe retail store in 1987 when she was only 24 years old. She was a nationally ranked runner herself and felt that the growing interest in jogging offered real potential for a store that provided serious runners with the shoes and advice they needed. The jogging boom quickly turned Joggers Universe into a profitable business selling high-end running shoes—and Sue made a very good return on her investment for the first 10 years. From 1987 until 1997, Sue emphasized Nike shoes, which were well accepted and seen as top quality. Nike's aggressive promotion and quality shoes resulted in a positive image that made it possible to get a $5 to $7 per pair premium for Nike shoes. Good volume and good margins resulted in attractive profits for Sue Koenig.

Committing so heavily to Nike seemed like a good idea when its marketing and engineering was the best available. In addition to running shoes, Nike had other athletic shoes Sue could sell. So even though they were not her primary focus, Sue did stock other Nike shoes including walking shoes, shoes for aerobic exercise, basketball shoes, tennis shoes, and cross-trainers. She also added more sportswear to her store and put more emphasis on fashion rather than just function.

Even with this broadened product line, Sue's sales flattened out—and she wasn't sure what to do to get her business back in growth mode. She realized that she was growing older and so were many of her longer-term customers. Many of them were finding that jogging isn't just hard work—it's hard on the body, especially the knees. So many of her previously loyal runner-customers were switching to other, less demanding exercise programs. However, when she tried to orient her store and product line more toward these people she wasn't as effective in serving the needs of serious runners—still an important source of sales for the store.

She was also facing more competition on all fronts. Many consumers who don't really do any serious exercise buy running shoes as their day-to-day casual shoes. As a result, many department stores, discount stores, and regular shoe stores have put more and more emphasis on athletic shoes in their product assortment. When Sue added other brands and put more emphasis on fashion she found that she was in direct competition with a number of other stores, which put more pressure on her to lower prices and cut her profit margins. For example, in Sue's area there are a number of local and online retail chains offering lower-cost and lower-quality versions of similar shoes as well as related fashion apparel. Wal-Mart also expanded its assortment of athletic shoes—and it offers rock-bottom prices. Other chains, like Foot Locker, have focused their promotion and product lines on specific target markets. Still, all of them (including Sue's Joggers Universe, the local chains, Wal-Mart, and Foot Locker) are scrambling to catch up with rival category killers whose selections are immense.

In the spring of 2003 Sue tried an experiment. She took on a line of high-performance athletic shoes that were made to order. The distinctive feature of these shoes was that the sole was molded to precisely fit the customer's foot. A pair of these custom-made shoes cost about $170, so the market was not large. Further, Sue didn't put much promotional emphasis on this line. However, when a customer came in the store with a serious interest in high-performance shoes, Sue's sales clerks would tell them about the custom shoe alternative and show a sample. When a customer was interested, a mold of the customer's bare foot was made at the store, using an innovative material that hardened in just a few minutes without leaving a sticky mess. Sue sent the mold off to the manufacturer by UPS, and about two weeks later the finished shoes arrived. Customers who tried these shoes were delighted with the result. However, the company that offered them ran into financial trouble and went out of business.

Sue recently learned about another company that is offering a very similar custom shoe program. However, that company requires more promotion investment by retailers and in return provides exclusive sales territories. Another requirement is that the store establish a website promoting the shoes and providing more detail on how the order process works. All of a retailer's sales-clerks are also required to go through a special two-day training program so that they know how to present the benefits of the shoe and do the best job creating the molds. The training program is free, but Sue would have to pay travel, hotel, and food expenses for her salespeople. So before even getting started, the new program would cost her several thousand dollars.

Sue is uncertain about what to do. Although sales have dropped, she is still making a reasonable profit and has a relatively good base of repeat customers, with the serious runners still more than half of her sales and profits. She thinks that the custom shoe alternative is a way to differentiate her store from the mass-merchandisers and to sharpen her focus on the target market of serious runners. On the other hand, that doesn't really solve the problem that the "runners" market seems to be shrinking. It also doesn't address the question of how best to keep a lot of the aging customers she already serves who seem to be shifting away from an emphasis on running. She also worries that she'll lose the loyalty of her repeat customers if she shifts the store further away from her running niche and more toward fashionable athletic shoes or fashionable casual wear. Yet athletic wear—women's, in particular—has come a long way in recent years. Designers like Donna Karan, Calvin Klein, Georgio Armani, and Ralph Lauren are part of the fast-growing women's wear business.

So Sue is trying to decide if there is anything else she can do to better promote her current store and product line, or if she should think about changing her strategy in a more dramatic way. Any change from her current focus would involve retraining her current salespeople and perhaps hiring new salespeople. Adding and maintaining a website isn't an insurmountable challenge, but it is not an area where she has either previous experience or skill.

Clearly, a real shift in emphasis would require that Sue make some hard decisions about her target market and her whole marketing mix. She's got some flexibility—it's not like she's a manufacturer of shoes with a big investment in a factory that can't be changed. On the other hand, she's not certain she's ready for a big change, especially a change that would mean starting over again from scratch. She started Joggers Universe because she was interested in running and felt she had something special to offer. Now she worries that she's just clutching at straws without a real focus or any obvious competitive advantage. She also knows that she is already much more successful than she ever dreamed when she started her business—and in her heart she wonders if she wasn't just spoiled by growth that came fast and easy at the start.

Evaluate Sue Koenig's present strategy. Evaluate the alternative strategies she is considering. Is her primary problem her emphasis on running shoes, her emphasis on trying to hang on to her current customers, or is it something else? What should she do? Why?

12. Applied Chemistry Corporation

Jeannie Trenton, a new product manager for Applied Chemistry Corporation (ACC), must decide what to do with a new engine cooling system product that is not doing well compared to the company's other cooling system products. ACC is one of the large chemical companies in the United States, making a wide line of organic and inorganic chemicals and plastics. Technical research has played a vital role in the company's growth.

Recently, one of ACC's researchers developed a new engine cooling system product—EC-301. Much time and money was spent on the technical phase, involving various experiments concerned with the quality of the new product. Then Jeannie Trenton took over and has been trying to develop a strategy for the product.

The engine coolant commonly used now is ethylene glycol. If it leaks into the crankcase oil, it forms a thick, pasty sludge that can cause bearing damage, cylinder scoring, or a dozen other costly and time-consuming troubles for both the operator and the owner of heavy-duty engines.

ACC researchers believed that the new product—EC-301—would be very valuable to the owners of heavy-duty diesel and gasoline trucks, as well as other heavy-equipment owners. Chemically, EC-301 uses a propanol base instead of the conventional glycol and alcohol bases. It cannot prevent leakage, but if it does get into the crankcase, it won't cause serious problems.

The suggested list price of EC-301 is $22 per gallon, more than twice the price of regular coolants. The higher price was set because of higher production costs and to obtain a "premium" for making a better engine coolant.

At first, Trenton thought she had two attractive markets for EC-301: (1) the manufacturers of heavy-duty trucks and (2) the users of heavy-duty trucks. ACC sales reps have made numerous calls. So far neither type of customer has shown much interest, and the sales manager is discouraging any more calls for EC-301. He feels there are more profitable uses for the sales reps' time. The truck manufacturer prospects are reluctant to show interest in the product until it has been proven in actual use. The maintenance managers for truck fleets, construction companies, and other users of heavy-duty trucks have also been hesitant. Some say the suggested price is far too high for the advantages offered. Others don't understand what is wrong with the present coolants and refuse to talk any more about paying extra for just another me-too product.

Explain what has happened so far. What should Jeannie Trenton do? Why?

13. Paper Products, Inc.*

Diane Chin, marketing manager for Paper Products, Inc. (PPI) must decide whether she should permit her largest customer to buy some of PPI's commonly used file folders under the customer's brand rather than PPI's own FILEX brand. She is afraid that if she refuses, this customer—Office Center, Inc.—will go to another file folder producer and PPI will lose this business.

Office Center, Inc., is a major distributor of office supplies and has already managed to put its own brand on more than 45 high-sales-volume office supply products. It distributes these products—as well as the branded products of many manufacturers—through its nationwide distribution network, which includes 150 retail stores. Now Ken Sawyer, vice president of marketing for Office Center, is seeking a line of file folders similar in quality to PPI's FILEX brand, which now has over 60 percent of the market.

This is not the first time that Office Center has asked PPI to produce a file folder line for Office Center. On both previous occasions, Diane Chin turned down the requests and Office Center continued to buy. In fact, Office Center not only continued to buy the file folders but also the rest of PPI's lines. And total sales continued to grow as Office Center built new stores. Office Center accounts for about 30 percent of Diane Chin's business. And FILEX brand file folders account for about 35 percent of this volume.

In the past PPI consistently refused such dealer-branding requests as a matter of corporate policy. This policy was set some years ago because of a desire (1) to avoid excessive dependence on any one customer and (2) to sell its own brands so that its success is dependent on the quality of its products rather than just a low price. The policy developed from a concern that if it started making products under other customers' brands, those customers could shop around for a low price and

---

*Adapted from a case written by Professor Hardy, University of Western Ontario, Canada.

the business would be very fickle. At the time the policy was set, Diane Chin realized that it might cost PPI some business. But it was felt wise nevertheless, to be better able to control the firm's future.

PPI has been in business 28 years and now has a sales volume of $40 million. Its primary products are file folders, file markers and labels, and a variety of indexing systems. PPI offers such a wide range of size, color, and type that no competition can match it in its part of the market. About 40 percent of PPI's file folder business is in specialized lines such as files for oversized blueprint and engineer drawings; see-through files for medical markets; and greaseproof and waterproof files for marine, oil field, and other hazardous environmental markets. PPI's competitors are mostly small paper converters. But excess capacity in the industry is substantial, and these converters are always hungry for orders and willing to cut price. Further, the raw materials for the FILEX line of file folders are readily available.

PPI's distribution system consists of 10 regional stationery suppliers (40 percent of total sales), Office Center, Inc. (30 percent), and more than 40 local stationers who have wholesale and retail operations (30 percent). The 10 regional stationers each have about six branches, while the local stationers each have one wholesale and three or four retail locations. The regional suppliers sell directly to large corporations and to some retailers. In contrast, Office Center's main volume comes from sales to local businesses and walk-in customers at its 150 retail stores.

Diane Chin has a real concern about the future of the local stationers' business. Some are seriously discussing the formation of buying groups to obtain volume discounts from vendors and thus compete more effectively with Office Center's 150 retail stores, the large regionals, and the superstore chains, which are spreading rapidly. These chains—for example, Staples, Office World, Office Max, and Office Depot—operate stores of 16,000 to 20,000 square feet (i.e., large stores compared to the usual office supply stores) and let customers wheel through high-stacked shelves to supermarket-like checkout counters. These chains stress convenience, wide selection, and much lower prices than the typical office supply retailers. They buy directly from manufacturers, such as PPI, bypassing wholesalers like Office Center. It is likely that the growing pressure from these chains is causing Office Center to renew its proposal to buy a file line with its own name. For example, Staples offers its own dealer brand of files and many other types of products.

None of Diane's other accounts is nearly as effective in retailing as Office Center, which has developed a good reputation in every major city in the country. Office Center's profits have been the highest in the industry. Further, its brands are almost as well known as those of some key producers—and its expansion plans are aggressive. And now, these plans are being pressured by the fast-growing superstores, which are already knocking out many local stationers.

Diane is sure that PPI's brands are well entrenched in the market, despite the fact that most available money has been devoted to new-product development rather than promotion of existing brands. But Diane is concerned that if Office Center brands its own file folders it will sell them at a discount and may even bring the whole market price level down. Across all the lines of file folders, Diane is averaging a 35 percent gross margin, but the commonly used file folders sought by Office Center are averaging only a 20 percent gross margin. And cutting this margin further does not look very attractive to Diane.

Diane is not sure whether Office Center will continue to sell PPI's FILEX brand of folders along with Office Center's own file folders if Office Center is able to find a source of supply. Office Center's history has been to sell its own brand and a major brand side by side, especially if the major brand offers high quality and has strong brand recognition.

Diane is having a really hard time deciding what to do about the existing branding policy. PPI has excess capacity and could easily handle the Office Center business. And she fears that if she turns down this business, Office Center will just go elsewhere and its own brand will cut into PPI's existing sales at Office Center stores. Further, what makes Office Center's offer especially attractive is that PPI's variable manufacturing costs would be quite low in relation to any price charged to Office Center—that is, there are substantial economies of scale, so the extra business could be very profitable—if Diane doesn't consider the possible impact on the FILEX line. This Office Center business will be easy to get, but it will require a major change in policy, which Diane will have to sell to Paul Jennings, PPI's president. This may not be easy. Paul is primarily interested in developing new and better products so the company can avoid the "commodity end of the business."

Evaluate PPI's current strategy. What should Diane Chin do about Office Center's offer? Explain.

14. Multimedia Corral

Josh Sullivan, manager of Multimedia Corral, is looking for ways to increase profits. But he's turning cautious after the poor results of his last effort, during the previous Christmas season. Multimedia Corral (MC), is located along a busy crosstown street about two miles from the downtown of a metropolitan area of 1 million and near a large university. It sells a wide variety of products used for its different types of multimedia presentations. Its lines include high-quality video and digital cameras, color scanners for use with computers, teleprompters and projection equipment, including video-beam overhead projectors and electronic projectors that produce large-screen versions of computer output. Most of the sales of this specialized equipment are made to area school boards for classroom use, to industry for use in research and sales, and to the university for use in research and instruction.

Multimedia Corral also offers a good selection of production-quality video media (including hard-to-get multilayer recordable DVDs), specialized supplies (such as the large-format acetates used with backlit signs), video and audio editing equipment, and a specialized video editing service. Instead of just duplicating videos on a mass production basis, Multimedia Corral gives each video editing job individual attention—to add an audio track or incorporate computer graphics as requested by a customer. This service is really appreciated by local firms that need help producing high-quality DVDs—for example, for training or sales applications.

To encourage the school and industrial trade, Multimedia Corral offers a graphics consultation service. If a customer wants to create a video or computerized presentation, professional advice is readily available. In support of this free service, Multimedia Corral carries a full line of computer software for multimedia presentations and graphics work.

Multimedia Corral has four full-time store clerks and two outside sales reps. The sales reps call on business firms, attend trade shows, make presentations for schools, and help both present and potential customers in their use and choice of multimedia materials. Most purchases are delivered by the sales reps or the store's delivery truck. Many repeat orders come in by phone or mail, but e-mail and electronic file exchange has become common.

The people who make most of the over-the-counter purchases are (1) serious amateurs and (2) some professionals who prepare videos or computerized presentation materials on a fee basis. Multimedia Corral gives price discounts of up to 25 percent of the suggested retail price to customers who buy more than $2,000 worth of goods per year. Most regular customers qualify for the discount.

In recent years, many amateur photo buffs have purchased digital cameras to capture family pictures. Frequently, the buyer is a computer user who wants to use the computer as a digital darkroom—and the cameras now available make this easy. Multimedia Corral has not previously offered the lower-priced and lower-quality digital models such buyers commonly want. But Josh Sullivan knew that lots of such digital cameras were bought and felt that there ought to be a good opportunity to expand sales during the Christmas gift-giving season. Therefore, he planned a special pre-Christmas sale of two of the most popular brands of digital cameras and discounted the prices to competitive discount store levels—about $169 for one and $229 for the other. To promote the sale, he posted large signs in the store windows and ran ads in a Christmas gift-suggestion edition of the local newspaper. This edition appeared each Wednesday during the four weeks before Christmas. At these prices and with this promotion, Josh hoped to sell at least 100 cameras. However, when the Christmas returns were in, total sales were five cameras. Josh was extremely disappointed with these results—especially because trade experts suggested that sales of digital cameras in these price and quality ranges were up 200 percent over last year—during the Christmas selling season.

Evaluate what Multimedia Corral is doing and what happened with the special promotion. What should Josh Sullivan do to increase sales and profits?

15. Growth Enterprises

Melita Sanchez, owner of Growth Enterprises is deciding whether to take on a new line. She is very concerned, however, because although she wants more lines she feels that something is wrong with her latest possibility.

Melita Sanchez graduated from a large midwestern university in 2001 with a B.S. in business. She worked selling cell phones for a year. Then Melita decided to go into business for herself and formed Growth Enterprises. Looking for opportunities, Melita placed several ads in her local newspaper in Columbus, Ohio, announcing that she was interested in becoming a sales representative in the area. She was quite pleased to receive a number of responses. Eventually, she became the sales representative in the Columbus area for three local computer software producers: Accto Company, which produces accounting-related software; Saleco, Inc., a producer of sales management software; and Invo, Inc., a producer of inventory control software. All of these companies were relatively small and were represented in other areas by other sales representatives like Melita Sanchez.

Melita's main job was to call on possible customers. Once she made a sale, she would fax the signed license agreement to the respective producer, who would then UPS the programs directly to the customer or provide a key code for a website download. The producer would bill the customer, and Sanchez would receive a commission varying from 5 to 10 percent of the dollar value of the sale. Sanchez was expected to pay her own expenses. And the producers would handle any user questions, either by using 800 numbers for out-of-town calls or by e-mail queries to a technical support group.

Sanchez called on anyone in the Columbus area who might use the products she sold. At first, her job was relatively easy, and sales came quickly because she had little competition. Many national companies offer similar products, but at that time they were not well represented in the Columbus area. Most small businesses needed someone to demonstrate what the software could do.

In 2003, Sanchez sold $250,000 worth of Accto software, earning a 10 percent commission; $100,000 worth of Saleco software, also earning a 10 percent commission; and $200,000 worth of Invo software, earning a 5 percent commission. She was encouraged with her progress and looked forward to expanding sales in the future. She was especially optimistic because she had achieved these sales volumes without overtaxing herself. In fact, she felt she was operating at about 60 percent of her capacity and could easily take on new lines. So she began looking for other products she could sell in the Columbus area. A local software company has recently approached Melita about selling its newly developed software, which is basically a network security product. It is designed to secretly track all of the keystrokes and mouse clicks of each employee as he or she uses the computer—so that an employer can identify inappropriate uses of its computers or confidential data. Melita isn't too enthusiastic about this offer because the commission is only 2 percent on potential annual sales of about $150,000—and she also doesn't like the idea of selling a product that might undermine the privacy of employees who are not doing anything wrong.

Now Melita Sanchez is faced with another decision. The owner of the Metclean Company, also in Columbus, has made what looks like an attractive offer. She called on Metclean to see if the firm might be interested in buying her accounting software. The owner didn't want the software, but he was very impressed with Melita. After two long discussions, he asked if she would like to help Metclean solve its current problem. Metclean is having trouble with marketing and the owner would like Melita Sanchez to take over the whole marketing effort.

Metclean produces solvents used to make coatings for metal products. It sells mainly to industrial customers in the mid-Ohio area and faces many competitors selling essentially the same products and charging the same low prices. Metclean is a small manufacturer. Last year's sales were $500,000. It could handle at least four times this sales volume with ease, and is willing to expand to increase sales—its main objective in the short run. Metclean's owner is offering Melita a 12 percent commission on all sales if she will take charge of their pricing, advertising, and sales efforts. Melita is flattered by the offer, but she is a little worried because it is a different type of product and she would have to learn a lot about it. The job also might require a great deal more traveling than she is doing now. For one thing, she would have to call on new potential customers in mid-Ohio, and she might have to travel up to 200 miles around Columbus to expand the solvent business. Further, she realizes that she is being asked to do more than just sell. But she did have marketing courses in college, and thinks the new opportunity might be challenging.

Evaluate Melita Sanchez's current strategy and how the proposed solvent line fits in with what she is doing now. What should she do? Why?

16. Matisse Company

Timothy Matisse, owner of Matisse Company, feels his business is threatened by a tough new competitor. And now Timothy must decide quickly about an offer that may save his business.

Timothy Matisse has been a sales rep for lumber mills for about 20 years. He started selling in a clothing store but gave it up after two years to work in a lumberyard because the future looked much better in the building materials industry. After drifting from one job to another, Timothy finally settled down and worked his way up to manager of a large wholesale building materials distribution warehouse in Buffalo, New York. In 1985, he formed Matisse Company and went into business for himself, selling carload lots of lumber to lumberyards in western New York and Pennsylvania.

Timothy works with five large lumber mills on the West Coast. They notify him when a carload of lumber is available to be shipped, specifying the grade, condition, and number of each size board in the shipment. Timothy isn't the only person selling for these mills—but he is the only one in his area. He isn't required to take any particular number of carloads per month—but once he tells a mill he wants a particular shipment, title passes to him and he has to sell it to someone. Timothy's main function is to find a buyer, buy the lumber from the mill as it's being shipped, and have the railroad divert the car to the buyer.

Having been in this business for 20 years, Timothy knows all of the lumberyard buyers in his area very well and is on good working terms with them. He does most of his business over the telephone or by e-mail from his small office, but he tries to see each of the buyers about once a month. He has been marking up the lumber between 4 and 6 percent—the standard markup, depending on the grades and mix in each car—and has been able to make a good living for himself and his family. The going prices are widely publicized in trade publications and are listed on the Internet, so the buyers can easily check to be sure Timothy's prices are competitive.

In the last few years, a number of Timothy's lumberyard customers have gone out of business—and others have lost sales. The main problem is competition from several national home-improvement chains that have moved into Timothy's market area. These chains buy lumber in large quantities direct from a mill, and their low prices, available inventory, and one-stop shopping are taking some customers away from the traditional lumberyards. Some customers think the quality of the lumber is not quite as good at the big chains, and some contractors stick with the lumberyards out of loyalty or because they get better service, including rush deliveries when they're needed. However, if it weren't for low interest rates and a boom in the construction market—helping to make up for lost market share—Timothy's profits would have taken an even bigger hit.

Six months ago, things got worse. An aggressive young salesman set up in the same business, covering about the same area but representing different lumber mills. This new salesman charges about the same prices as Timothy but undersells him once or twice a week in order to get the sale. On several occasions he even set up what was basically an e-mail-based auction to quickly sell excess wood that was not moving fast enough. Many lumber buyers—feeling the price competition from the big chains and realizing that they are dealing with a homogeneous product—seem to be willing to buy from the lowest-cost source. This has hurt Timothy financially and personally—because even some of his old friends are willing to buy from the new competitor if the price is lower. The near-term outlook seems dark, since Timothy doubts that there is enough business to support two firms like his, especially if the markup gets shaved any closer. Now they seem to be splitting the shrinking business about equally, as the newcomer keeps shaving his markup.

A week ago, Timothy was called on by Mr. DeBeer of Good Timber Mfg. Co., a large manufacturer of windows, raised-panel doors, and accessories. Good Timber doesn't sell to the big chains and instead distributes its quality line only through independent lumberyards. DeBeer knows that Timothy is well acquainted with the local lumberyards and wants him to become Good Timber's exclusive distributor (sales rep) of residential windows and accessories in his area. DeBeer gave Timothy several brochures on the Good Timber product lines. He also explained Good Timber's new support program, which will help train and support Timothy and interested lumberyards on how to sell the higher markup accessories. Later, in a lengthy e-mail, DeBeer explained how this program will help Timothy and interested lumberyards differentiate themselves in this very competitive market.

Most residential windows of specified grades are basically "commodities" that are sold on the basis of price and availability, although some premium and very low end windows are sold also. The national home-improvement chains usually stock and sell only the standard sizes. Most independent lumberyards do not stock windows because there are so many possible sizes. Instead, the lumberyards custom order from the stock sizes each factory offers. Stock sizes are not set by industry standards; they vary from factory to factory, and some offer more sizes. Most factories can deliver these custom orders in two to six weeks, which is usually adequate to satisfy contractors who buy and install them according to architectural plans. This part of the residential window business is well established, and most lumberyards buy from several different window manufacturers—to ensure sources of supply in case of strikes, plant fires, and so on. How the business is split depends on price and the personality and persuasiveness of the sales reps. And given that prices are usually similar, the sales rep–customer relationship can be quite important.

Good Timber Mfg. Co. gives more choice than just about any other supplier. It offers many variations in $\frac{1}{8}$-inch increments—to cater to remodelers who must adjust to many situations. Good Timber has even set up a special system on an Internet website. The lumberyard can connect to the website, enter the specs for a window online, and within seconds get a price quote and estimated delivery time.

One reason DeBeer has approached Timothy Matisse is because of Timothy's many years in the business. But the other reason is that Good Timber is aggressively trying to expand—relying on its made-to-order windows, a full line of accessories, and a newly developed factory support system to help differentiate it from the many other window manufacturers.

To give Timothy a quick big picture of the opportunity he is offering, DeBeer explained the window market as follows:

1. For commercial construction, the usual building code ventilation requirements are satisfied with mechanical ventilation. So the windows do not have to operate to permit natural ventilation. They are usually made with heavy-grade aluminum framing. Typically, a distributor furnishes and installs the windows. As part of its service, the distributor provides considerable technical support, including engineered drawings and diagrams to the owners, architects, and/or contractors.

2. For residential construction, on the other hand, windows must be operable to provide ventilation. Residential windows are usually made of wood, frequently with light-gauge aluminum or vinyl on the exterior. The national chains get some volume with standard size windows, but lumberyards are the most common source of supply for contractors in Timothy's area. These lumberyards do not provide any technical support or engineered drawings. A few residential window manufacturers do have their own sales centers in selected geographic areas, which provide a full range of support and engineering services, but none are anywhere near Timothy's area.

Good Timber Mfg. Co. feels a big opportunity exists in the commercial building repair and rehabilitation market (sometimes called the retrofit market) for a crossover of residential windows to commercial applications—and it has designed some accessories and a factory support program to help lumberyards get this "commercial" business. For applications such as nursing homes and dormitories (which must meet commercial codes), the wood interior of a residential window is desired, but the owners and architects are accustomed to commercial grades and building systems. And in some older

facilities, the windows may have to provide supplemental ventilation for a deficient mechanical system. So what is needed is a combination of the residential *operable* window with a heavy-gauge commercial exterior frame that is easy to specify and install. And this is what Good Timber Mfg. Co. is offering with a combination of its basic windows and easily adjustable accessory frames. Two other residential window manufacturers offer a similar solution, but neither has pushed its products aggressively and neither offers technical support to lumberyards or trains sales reps like Timothy to do the necessary job. DeBeer feels this could be a unique opportunity for Timothy.

The sales commission on residential windows would be about 5 percent of sales. Good Timber Mfg. Co. would do the billing and collecting. By getting just 20 to 30 percent of his lumberyards' residential window business, Timothy could earn about half of his current income. But the real upside would come from increasing his residential window share. To do this, Timothy would have to help the lumberyards get a lot more (and more profitable) business by invading the commercial market with residential windows and the bigger markup accessories needed for this market. Timothy would also earn a 20 percent commission on the accessories, adding to his profit potential.

Timothy is somewhat excited about the opportunity because the retrofit market is growing. And owners and architects are seeking ways of reducing costs (which Good Timber's approach does—over usual commercial approaches). But he is also concerned that a lot of sales effort will be needed to introduce this new idea. He is not afraid of work, but he is concerned about his financial survival.

Timothy thinks he has three choices:

1. Take DeBeer's offer and sell both window and lumber products.
2. Take the offer and drop lumber sales.
3. Stay strictly with lumber and forget the offer.

DeBeer is expecting an answer within one week, so Timothy has to decide soon.

Evaluate Timothy Matisse's current strategy and how the present offer fits in. What should he do now? Why?

17. Eco Water, Inc.

Manish (Manny) Krishna established his company, Eco Water, Inc. (Eco), to market a product designed to purify drinking water. The product, branded as the PURITY II Naturalizer Water Unit, is produced by Environmental Control, Inc., a corporation that focuses primarily on water purification and filtering products for industrial markets.

Eco Water is a small but growing business. Manny started the business with initial capital of only $20,000, which came from his savings and loans from several relatives. Manny manages the company himself. He has a secretary and six full-time salespeople. In addition, he employs two college students part-time; they make telephone calls to prospect for customers and set up appointments for a salesperson to demonstrate the unit in the consumer's home. By holding spending to a minimum, Manny has kept the firm's monthly operating budget at only $4,500—and most of that goes for rent, his secretary's salary, and other necessities like computer supplies and telephone bills.

The PURITY II system uses a reverse osmosis purification process. Reverse osmosis is the most effective technology known for improving drinking water. The device is certified by the Environmental Protection Agency to reduce levels of most foreign substances, including mercury, rust, sediment, arsenic, lead, phosphate, bacteria, and most insecticides.

Each PURITY II unit consists of a high-quality 1-micron sediment removal cartridge, a carbon filter, a sediment filter, a housing, a faucet, and mounting hardware. The compact system fits under a kitchen sink or a wet bar sink. An Eco salesperson can typically install the PURITY II in about a half hour. Installation involves attaching the unit to the cold-water supply line, drilling a hole in the sink, and fastening the special faucet. It works equally well with water from a municipal system or well water and it can purify up to 15 gallons daily. Eco sells the PURITY II to consumers for $395, which includes installation.

The system has no movable parts or electrical connections and it has no internal metal parts that will corrode or rust. However, the system does use a set of filters that must be replaced after about two years. Eco sells the replacement filters for $80. Taking into consideration the cost of the filters, the system provides water at a cost of approximately $.05 per gallon for the average family.

There are two major benefits from using the PURITY II system. First, water treated by this system tastes better. Blind taste tests confirm that most consumers can tell the difference between water treated with the PURITY II and ordinary tapwater. Consequently, the unit improves the taste of coffee, tea, frozen juices, ice cubes, mixed drinks, soup, and vegetables cooked in water. Perhaps more important, the PURITY II's ability to remove potentially harmful foreign matter makes the product of special interest to people who are concerned about health and the safety of the water they consume.

The number of people with those concerns is growing. In spite of increased efforts to protect the environment and water supplies, there are many problems. Hundreds of new chemical compounds—ranging from insecticides to industrial chemicals to commercial cleaning agents—are put into use each year. Some of the residue from chemicals and toxic waste eventually enters water supply sources. Further, floods and hurricanes have damaged or completely shut down water treatment facilities in some cities. Problems like these have led to rumors of possible epidemics of such dread diseases as cholera and typhoid—and more than one city has recently experienced near-panic buying of bottled water.

Given these problems and the need for pure water, Manny believes that the market potential for the PURITY II system is very large. Residences, both single-family and apartment, are one obvious target. The unit is also suitable for use in boats and recreational vehicles; in fact, the PURITY II is standard equipment on several upscale RVs. And it can be used in taverns and restaurants, in institutions such as schools and hospitals, and in commercial and industrial buildings.

There are several competing ways for customers to solve the problem of getting pure water. Some purchase bottled water. Companies such as Ozarka deliver water monthly for an average price of $.60 per gallon. The best type of bottled water is distilled water; it is absolutely pure because it is produced by the process of evaporation. However, it may be *too pure*. The distilling process removes needed elements such as calcium and phosphate—and there is some evidence that removing these trace elements contributes to heart disease. In fact, some health-action groups recommend that consumers not drink distilled water.

A second way to obtain pure water is to use some system to treat tapwater. PURITY II is one such system. Another system uses an ion exchange process that replaces ions of harmful substances like iron and mercury with ions that are not harmful. Ion exchange is somewhat less expensive than the PURITY II process, but it is not well suited for residential use because bacteria can build up before the water is used. In addition, there are a number of other filtering and softening systems. In general, these are less expensive and less reliable than the PURITY II. For example, water softeners remove minerals but do not remove bacteria or germs.

Manny's first year with his young company has gone quite well. Customers who have purchased the system like it, and there appear to be several ways to expand the business and increase profits. For example, so far he has had little time to make sales calls on potential commercial and institutional users or residential builders. He also sees other possibilities such as expanding his promotion effort or targeting consumers in a broader geographic area.

At present, Eco distributes the PURITY II in the 13-county gulf coast region of Texas. Because of the Robinson-Patman Act, the manufacturer cannot grant an exclusive distributorship. However, Eco is currently the only PURITY II distributor in this region. In addition, Eco has the right of first refusal to set up distributorships in other areas of Texas. The manufacturer has indicated that it might even give Eco distribution rights in a large section of northern Mexico.

The agreement with the manufacturer allows Eco to distribute the product to retailers, including hardware stores, plumbing supply dealers, and the like. Manny has not yet pursued this channel, but a PURITY II distributor in Florida reported some limited success selling the system to retailers at a wholesale price of $275. Retailers for this type of product typically expect a markup of about 33 percent of their selling price.

Environmental Control, Inc., ships the PURITY II units directly from its warehouse to the Eco office via UPS. The manufacturer's $200 per unit selling price includes the cost of shipping. Eco only needs to keep a few units on hand because the manufacturer accepts faxed orders and then ships immediately—so delivery never takes more than a few days. Further, the units are small enough to inventory in the back room of the Eco sales office. Several of the easy-to-handle units will fit in the trunk of a salesperson's car.

Manny is thinking about recruiting additional salespeople. Finding capable people has not been a problem so far. However, there has already been some turnover, and one of the current salespeople is complaining that the compensation is not high enough. Manny pays salespeople on a straight commission basis. A salesperson who develops his or her own prospects gets $100 per sale; the commission is $80 per unit on sales leads generated by the company's telemarketing people. For most salespeople, the mix of sales is about half and half. Eco pays the students who make the telephone contacts $4 per appointment set up and $10 per unit sold from an appointment.

An average Eco salesperson easily sells 20 units per month. However, Manny believes that a really effective and well-prepared salesperson can sell much more, perhaps 40 units per month.

Eco and its salespeople get good promotion support from Environmental Control, Inc. For example, Environmental Control supplies sales training manuals and sales presentation flip charts. The materials are also well done, in part because Environment Control's promotion manager previously worked for Electrolux vacuum cleaners, which are sold in a similar way. The company also supplies print copy for magazine and newspaper advertising and tapes of commercials for radio and television. Thus, all Eco has to do is buy media space or time. In addition, Environmental Control furnishes each salesperson with a portable demonstration unit, and the company recently gave Eco three units to be placed in models of condominium apartments.

Manny has worked long hours to get his company going, but he realizes that he has to find time to think about how his strategy is working and to plan for the future.

Evaluate Manish Krishna's current marketing strategy for Eco Water. How do you think he's doing so far, and what should he do next? Why?

18. Village Bank

Phil McNeill isn't having much luck convincing his father that their bank needs the new look and image he is proposing.

Phil McNeill was recently appointed director of marketing by his father, Mack McNeill, long-time president of Village Bank. Phil is a recent marketing graduate of the nearby state college. He worked in the bank during summer vacations, but this is his first full-time job.

Village Bank is a profitable, family-run business located in Hillsborough, the county seat. The town itself has a population of only 15,000, but it serves suburbanites and farmers as far away as 20 miles. About 10 miles east is a metropolitan area of 350,000, to which many in the Hillsborough area commute. Banking competition is quite strong there. But Hillsborough has only one other downtown full-service bank—of about the same size—and two small limited-service branches of two metro banks on the main highway going east. Village Bank has been quite profitable, last year earning about $400,000— or 1 percent of assets—a profit margin that would look very attractive to big-city bankers.

Village Bank has prospered over the years by emphasizing its friendly, small-town atmosphere. The employees are all local residents and are trained to be friendly with all customers, greeting them on a first-name basis. Even Phil's father tries to know all the customers personally and often comes out of his office to talk with them. The bank has followed a conservative policy—for example, insisting on 25 percent down payments on homes and relatively short maturities on loans. The interest rates charged are competitive or slightly higher than in the nearby city, but they are similar to those charged by the other full-service bank in town. In fact, the two local banks seem to be following more or less the same approach—friendly, small-town service. Since they both have fairly convenient downtown locations, Phil feels that the two banks will continue to share the business equally unless some change is made.

Phil has an idea that he thinks will attract a greater share of the local business. At a recent luncheon meeting with his father, he floated his idea and was disappointed when it wasn't enthusiastically received. Nevertheless, he has continued to push the idea—even going to the trouble to prepare an elaborate PowerPoint presentation with a detailed plan.

Phil has tried to explain that he wants to differentiate the bank by promoting a new look and image. His proposal is to try to get all the people in town to think of the bank as "The Friendly Bank." He believes that this positioning would differentiate Village Bank from the other local bank and make it much harder for one of the really big banks to come into town with a new branch office. The big banks can offer diverse financial services, but Phil figures that their size would make it hard for any of them to position themselves as friendly or personal. And Phil wants to paint the inside and outside of the bank in residential-like designers' colors (e.g., pastels) and have all the bank's advertising and printed materials refer to "The Friendly Bank" campaign. The bank would give away pastel shopping bags, offer pastel deposit slips, mail out pastel interest checks, advertise on pastel billboards, and have pastel stationery for the bank's correspondence. The friendly bank message would be printed on all of these items. And all the employees will be trained to be even more friendly to everyone.

Phil knows that his proposal is different for a conservative bank. But that's exactly why he thinks it will work. He wants people to notice his bank instead of just assuming that both banks are alike. He is sure that after the initial surprise, the local people will think even more positively about Village Bank. Its reputation is very good now, but he would like it to be recognized as different. Phil feels that this will help attract a larger share of new residents and businesses. Further, he hopes that his "The Friendly Bank" campaign will cause people to talk about Village Bank—and given that word-of-mouth comments are likely to be positive, the bank might win a bigger share of the present business.

Mack McNeill is less than excited about his son's proposal. He thinks the bank has done very well under his direction— and he is concerned about changing a good thing. He worries that some of the older townspeople and farmers who are loyal customers will question the sincerity of the bank. His initial request to Phil was to come up with some way of differentiating the bank without offending present customers. Further, Mack McNeill thinks that Phil is talking about an important change that will be expensive and difficult to undo once the decision is made. On the plus side, Mack agrees that the proposal will make the bank appear quite different from its local competitor. Further, people are continuing to move into the

Hillsborough area, and he wants an increasing share of this business—and he doesn't want one of the big banks to come in and make a strong competitive push.

Evaluate Village Bank's situation and Phil's proposal. What should the bank do to increase its market share?

19. myWedding.com

Gray Hunter is happy with her life but disappointed that the idea she had for starting her own business hasn't taken off as expected. Within a few weeks she either has to renew the contract for her Internet website or decide not to put any more time and money into her idea. She knows that it doesn't make sense to renew the contract if she doesn't come up with a plan to make her website-based business profitable—and she doesn't like to plan. She's a "doer," not a planner.

Gray's business, myWedding.com, started as an idea 18 months ago as she was planning her own wedding. She attended a bridal fair at the convention center in Raleigh, North Carolina, to get ideas for a wedding dress, check out catering companies and florists, and in general learn more about the various services available to newlyweds. While there she and her fiancé went from one retailer's booth to another to sign up for their wedding gift registries. Almost every major retailer in the city—ranging from the Home Depot warehouse to the Belk's department store to the specialty shops that handle imported crystal glassware—offered a gift registry. Some had computers set up to provide access to their online registries. Being listed in all of the registries improved the odds that her wedding gifts would be items she wanted and could use—and it saved time and hassle for gift-givers. On the way back from the fair, Gray and her fiancé discussed the idea that it would be a lot easier to register gift preferences once on a central Internet site than to provide lots of different stores with bits and pieces of information. A list at a website would also make it easier for gift-givers, at least those who were computer users.

When Gray got back home, she did an Internet search and found several sites that focused on weddings. The biggest seemed to be www.weddingchannel.com. It had features for couples who were getting married, including a national gift registry. The site featured products from a number of companies, especially large national retail chains; however, there was a search feature to locate people who provide wedding-related services in a local ZIP code area. Gray thought that the sites she found looked quite good, but that they were not as helpful as a site could be with a more local focus.

The more Gray and her fiancé discussed the idea of a website offering local wedding-related services, the more it looked like an interesting opportunity. Except for the annual bridal fair, there was no other obvious local place for consumers to get information about planning a wedding and buying wedding-related services. And for local retailers, florists, catering companies, immitten renting limits builders, and many other types of firms, there was no other central place to target promotion at newlyweds. Further, the amount of money spent on weddings and wedding gifts is very substantial, and right before and after getting married many young couples make many important purchase decisions for everything from life insurance to pots and pans. Spending on the wedding itself can easily exceed the cost of a year of college.

Gray was no stranger to the Internet. She worked as a website designer for a small firm whose one and only client was IBM. That IBM was the only client was intentional rather than accidental. A year earlier IBM had decided that it wanted to outsource certain aspects of its website development work and have it handled by an outside contractor. After negotiating a three-year contract to do IBM's work, several IBM employees quit their jobs and started the business. IBM was a good client, and all indications were that IBM could give the firm as much work as it could handle as it hired new people and prospected for additional accounts over the next few years. Gray especially liked the creative aspects of designing the "look" of a website, and technical specialists handled a lot of the subtle details.

Before joining this new company, Gray had several marketing-related jobs—but none had been the glamorous ad agency job she dreamed of in college as an advertising major. Her first job as a college graduate was with an ad agency, but she was in a backroom operation handling a lot of the arrangements for printing and mailing large-scale direct-mail promotions. In spite of promises that it was a path to other jobs at the agency, the pay was bad, the work was always pressured, and every aspect of what she had to do was boring. After six punishing months, she quit and went looking for something else.

When a number of job applications didn't turn up something quickly, she took a part-time job doing telemarketing calls for a mortgage refinance company. Gray's boss told her that she was doing a great job reeling in prospects but she hated disturbing people at night and just didn't like making sales pitches. Fortunately for her, that pain didn't last long. A neighbor in Gray's apartment complex got Gray an interview for a receptionist position at an ad agency. That, at least, got her foot in the door. Her job description wasn't very interesting, but in a small agency she had the opportunity to learn a lot about all aspects of the business—ranging from working on client proposals and media plans to creative sessions for new campaigns. In fact, it was from a technician at that agency that she learned to work with the graphics software used to create ad layouts and website pages. When the website design job came open at the new firm, her boss gave her a glowing recommendation, and in two days she was off on her new career.

Although Gray's jobs had not been high-profile positions, they did give her some experience in sales promotion, personal selling, and advertising. Those skills were complemented by the technical computer skills of her fiancé (now husband), who made a living as a database programmer for a large software consulting firm. Taking everything as a whole, they thought that they could get a wedding-related website up and running and make it profitable.

There were a number of different facets to the original plan for myWedding.com. One part focused on recruiting local advertisers and "sponsors" who would pay to be listed at the website and be allocated a web page (which Gray would design) describing their services, giving contact information, and links to their own websites. Another facet focused on services for people who were planning to be married. In addition to an online wedding gift registry, sections of the website provided information about typical wedding costs, planning checklists, details about how to get a required marriage license, and other helpful information (including a discussion forum with comments about the strengths and weaknesses of various local suppliers). A man and woman could sign up for the service online and could pay the modest $20 "membership" fee for a year by credit card. Friends, family, and invited guests could visit the website at no charge and get information about wedding preferences, local hotels, discounts on local car rentals, and even printable maps to all of the churches and synagogues in the area.

When Gray told friends about her plan they all thought it sounded like a great idea. In fact, each time she discussed it someone came up with another idea for a locally oriented feature to add to the website. Several friends said that they had tried national websites but that the information was often too general. But generating more new ideas was not the problem. The problem was generating revenue. Gray had already contracted for space from an Internet service provider and created some of the initial content for the website, but she only had four paying sponsors, two of whom happened to be family friends.

Gray started by creating a colorful flyer describing the website and sent it to most of the firms that had participated in the bridal fair. When no one sent back the reply coupon for more information, Gray started to make calls (mainly during her lunch hour at her full-time job). Some stores seemed intrigued by the concept, but no one seemed ready to sign up. One reason was that they all seemed surprised at the cost to participate and get ad space at the website—$2,400 a year (about the same as a $\frac{1}{16}$-page display ad in the Raleigh Yellow Pages). Another problem was that no one wanted to be the first to sign up. As one florist shop owner put it, "If you pull this off and other florists sign up, then come back and I will too."

Getting couples to sign up went slowly too. Gray paid for four display ads in local Sunday newspapers in the society section, sent information sheets about the website to clergy in the area, listed the website with about 25 Internet search engines, and sent carefully crafted press releases announcing the service to almost every publication in the area. One article that resulted from a press release got some attention, and for a few weeks there was a flurry of e-mail inquiries about her web page. But after that it slowed to a trickle again.

Gray's diagnosis of the problem was simple. Most people thought it was a great idea, but few couples knew to look on the Internet for such a service. Similarly, potential advertisers—many of them small local businesses—were not accustomed to the idea of paying for Internet advertising. They didn't know if the cost was reasonable or if her site would be effective in generating business.

Gray's life as a married person was going great and her job as a web page designer kept her very busy. Her free time outside of work was always in short supply because the young crowd at her office always had some scheme for how to keep entertained. So she wasn't about to quit her job to devote full time to her business idea. Further, she thought that once it got rolling she would only have to devote 10 hours a week to it to earn an extra $30,000 a year. She didn't have delusions of becoming a "dot-com millionaire." She just wanted a good locally oriented business.

However, it still wasn't clear how to get it rolling. After a year of trying on and off, she only had four paying ad sponsors, and one of them had already notified her that he didn't plan to sign up again because it wasn't clear that the website had generated any direct leads or sales. Further, it looked like anything she could do to attract more "members" would end up being expensive and inefficient.

Gray thinks the idea has real potential, and she's willing to do the work. But she's not certain if she can make it pay off. She has to decide soon, however, because the bill for the Internet service provider is sitting on her desk.

What is Gray's strategy? What should she do? If she were to move forward, what strategy would you recommend? Does her financial goal seem realistic? Why?

20. Leisure World, Inc.

Jamie McCullough, owner of Leisure World, Inc., is worried about his business' future. He has tried various strategies for two years now, and he's still barely breaking even.

Two years ago, Jamie McCullough bought the inventory, supplies, equipment, and business of Leisure World, located on the edge of Minneapolis, Minnesota. The business is in an older building along a major highway leading out of town, several miles from any body of water. The previous owner had sales of about $500,000 a year but was just breaking even. For this reason—plus the desire to retire to Arizona—the owner sold to Jamie for roughly the value of the inventory.

Leisure World had been selling two well-known brands of small pleasure boats, a leading outboard motor, two brands of snowmobiles and jet-skis, and a line of trailer and pickup-truck campers. The total inventory was valued at $250,000—and Jamie used all of his own savings and borrowed some from two friends to buy the inventory and the business. At the same time, he took over the lease on the building—so he was able to begin operations immediately.

Jamie had never operated a business of his own before, but he was sure that he would be able to do well. He had worked in a variety of jobs—as a used-car salesman, an auto repairman, and a jack-of-all-trades in the maintenance departments of several local businesses.

Soon after starting his business, Jamie hired his friend, Omar, who had a similar background. Together, they handle all selling and setup work on new sales and do maintenance work as needed. Sometimes the two are extremely busy—at the peaks of each sport season. Then both sales and maintenance keep them going up to 16 hours a day. At these times it's difficult to have both new and repaired equipment available as soon as customers want it. At other times, however, Jamie and Omar have almost nothing to do.

Jamie usually charges the prices suggested by the various manufacturers, except at the end of a weather season when he is willing to make deals to clear the inventory. He is annoyed that some of his competitors sell mainly on a price basis—offering 10 to 30 percent off a manufacturer's suggested list prices—even at the beginning of a season! Jamie doesn't want to get into that kind of business, however. He hopes to build a loyal following based on friendship and personal service. Further, he doesn't think he really has to cut price because all of his lines are exclusive for his store. No stores within a five-mile radius carry any of his brands, although nearby retailers offer many brands of similar products.

To try to build a favorable image for his company, Jamie occasionally places ads in local papers and buys some radio spots. The basic theme of this advertising is that Leisure World is a friendly, service-oriented place to buy the equipment needed for the current season. Sometimes he mentions the brand names he carries, but generally Jamie tries to build an image for concerned, friendly service—both in new sales and repairs—stressing "We do it right the first time." He chose this approach because, although he has exclusives on the brands he carries, there generally are 10 to 15 different manufacturers' products being sold in the area in each product category—and most of the products are quite similar. Jamie feels that this similarity among competing products almost forces him to try to differentiate himself on the basis of his own store's services.

The first year's operation wasn't profitable. In fact, after paying minimal salaries to Omar and himself, the business just about broke even. Jamie made no return on his $250,000 investment.

In hopes of improving profitability, Jamie jumped at a chance to add a line of lawn mowers, tractors, and trimmers as he was starting into his second year of business. This line was offered by a well-known equipment manufacturer who wanted to expand into the Minneapolis area. The equipment is similar to that offered by other lawn equipment manufacturers. The manufacturer's willingness to do some local advertising and to provide some point-of-purchase displays appealed to Jamie. And he also liked the idea that customers probably would want this equipment sometime earlier than boats and other summer items. So he thought he could handle this business without interfering with his other peak selling seasons.

It's two years since Jamie bought Leisure World—and he's still only breaking even. Sales have increased a little, but costs have gone up too because he had to hire some part-time help. The lawn equipment helped to expand sales—as he had expected—but unfortunately, it did not increase profits as he had hoped. Jamie needed part-time helpers to handle this business—in part because the manufacturer's advertising had generated a lot of sales inquiries. Relatively few inquiries resulted in sales, however, because many people seemed to be shopping for deals. So Jamie may have even lost money handling the new line. But he hesitates to give it up because he doesn't want to lose that sales volume, and the manufacturer's sales rep has been most encouraging, assuring Jamie that things will get better and that his company will be glad to continue its promotion support during the coming year.

Jamie is now considering the offer of a mountain bike producer that has not been represented in the area. The bikes have become very popular with students and serious bikers in the last several years. The manufacturer's sales rep says industry sales are still growing (but not as fast as in the past) and probably will grow for many more years. The sales rep has praised Jamie's service orientation and says this could help him sell lots of bikes because many mountain bikers are serious about buying a quality bike and then keeping it serviced. He says Jamie's business approach would be a natural fit with bike customers' needs and attitudes. As a special inducement to get Jamie to take on the line, the sales rep says Jamie will not have to pay for the initial inventory of bikes, accessories, and repair parts for 90 days. And, of course, the company will supply the usual promotion aids and a special advertising allowance of $10,000 to help introduce the line to Minneapolis. Jamie kind of likes the idea of carrying mountain bikes because he has one himself and knows that they do require some service year-round. But he also knows that the proposed bikes are very similar in price and quality to the ones now being offered by the bike shops in town. These bike shops are service- rather than price-oriented, and Jamie feels that they are doing a good job on service—so he is concerned with how he could be "different."

Evaluate Jamie McCullough's overall strategy(ies) and the mountain bike proposal. What should he do now?

21. Lextron International, Inc.

Lextron International, Inc., is a multinational producer of various chemicals and plastics with plants in the United States, England, France, and Germany. It is run from its headquarters in New Jersey.

Kevin Duryea is marketing manager of Lextron International's plastics business. Kevin is reconsidering his promotion approach. He is evaluating what kind of promotion—and how much—should be directed to car producers and to other major plastics customers worldwide. Currently, Kevin has one salesperson who devotes most of his time to the car industry. This man is based in the Detroit area and focuses on GM, Ford, and DaimlerChrysler—as well as the various firms that mold plastics to produce parts to supply the car industry. This approach worked well when relatively little plastic was used in each car *and* the auto producers did all of the designing themselves and then sent out specifications for very price-oriented competitive bidding. But now the whole product planning and buying system is changing—and of course foreign producers with facilities in the U.S. are much more important.

How the present system works can be illustrated in terms of the approach DaimlerChrysler used on its project to design the Crossfire.

Instead of the old five-year process of creating a new automobile in sequential steps, the new system is a team approach. Under the old system, product planners would come up with a general concept and then expect the design team to give it artistic form. Next engineering would develop the specifications and pass them on to manufacturing and suppliers. There was little communication between the groups and no overall project responsibility.

Under the new approach, representatives from all the various functions—planning, design, engineering, purchasing, marketing, and manufacturing—work together. In fact, representatives from key suppliers are usually involved from the outset. The whole team takes final responsibility for a car. Because all of the departments are involved from the start, problems are resolved as the project moves on—before they cause a crisis. Manufacturing, for example, can suggest changes in design that will result in higher productivity or better quality.

In the Crossfire project, DaimlerChrysler engineers followed the Japanese lead and did some reverse engineering of their own. They dismantled several competitors' cars, piece by piece, looking for ideas they could copy or improve. This helped them learn how the parts were assembled and how they were designed. Eventually, DaimlerChrysler incorporated almost all of the best features into its design of the Crossfire. For example, the Crossfire platform is even more rigid than that of the Porsche 911.

In addition to reverse engineering, DaimlerChrysler researchers conducted a series of market studies. This led to the inclusion of additional features, such as 18-inch wheels, a six-speed transmission, and its finely tuned exhaust system that gives a sports car tone.

DaimlerChrysler also asked assembly-line workers for suggestions before the car was redesigned and then incorporated their ideas into the new car. Most bolts had the same-size head, for example, so workers didn't have to switch from one wrench to another.

Finally, DaimlerChrysler included its best suppliers as part of the planning effort. Instead of turning to a supplier after the car's design was completed, DaimlerChrysler invited them to participate in product planning.

Most other vehicles are now developed with an approach similar to this, and DaimlerChrysler is not alone in the effort. Ford, for example, used a very similar team approach to redesign its new Mustang. And major firms in most other industries are using similar approaches. A major outgrowth of this effort has been a trend by these producers to develop closer working relationships with a smaller number of suppliers.

For example, the suppliers selected for the Crossfire project were major suppliers who had already demonstrated a serious commitment to the car industry. They had not only the facilities, but also the technical and professional managerial staff who could understand—and become part of—the program management approach. DaimlerChrysler expected these major suppliers to join in its total quality management push and to be able to provide just-in-time delivery systems. DaimlerChrysler dropped suppliers whose primary sales technique was to entertain buyers and then submit bids on standard specifications.

Because many firms have moved to these team-oriented approaches and developed closer working relationships with a subset of their previous suppliers, Kevin Duryea is trying to determine if Lextron International's present effort is still appropriate. Kevin's strategy has focused primarily on responding to inquiries and bringing in Lextron International technical people as the situation seems to require. Potential customers with technical questions are sometimes referred to other noncompeting customers already using the materials or to a Lextron International plant—to be sure that all questions are answered. But basically, all producer-customers are treated more or less alike. The sales reps make calls and try to find good business wherever they can.

Each Lextron International sales rep usually has a geographic area. If an area like Detroit needs more than one rep, each may specialize in one or several similar industries. But Lextron International uses the same basic approach—call on present users of plastic products and try to find opportunities for getting a share (or bigger share) of existing purchases or new applications. The sales reps are supposed to be primarily order getters rather than technical specialists. Technical help can be brought in when the customer wants it or sometimes the sales rep simply sets up a conference call between Lextron International's technical experts, the buyer, and the users at the buyer's facility.

Kevin sees that some of his major competitors—including General Electric and Dow Chemical—are becoming more aggressive. They are seeking to affect specifications and product design from the start rather than after a product design is completed. This takes a lot more effort and resources, but Kevin thinks it may get better results. A major problem he sees, however, is that he may have to drastically change the nature of Lextron International's promotion. Instead of focusing primarily on buyers and responding to questions, it may be necessary to try to contact *all* the multiple buying influences and not only answer their questions but help them understand what questions to raise—and help answer them. Such a process may even require more technically trained sales reps. In fact, it may require that people from Lextron International's other departments—engineering, manufacturing, R&D, and distribution—get actively involved in discussions with their counterparts in customer firms. Further, use of e-mail and an Internet website might make ongoing contacts faster and easier.

While Kevin doesn't want to miss the boat if changes are needed, he also doesn't want to go off the deep end. After all, many of the firm's customers don't seem to want Lextron International to do anything very different from what it's been doing. In fact, some say that they're very satisfied with their current supply arrangements and really have no interest in investing in a close relationship with a single supplier.

Contrast the previous approach to designing and producing cars to Crossfire's program management approach, especially as it might affect suppliers' promotion efforts. Given that many other major producers have moved in the program management direction, what promotion effort should Kevin Duryea develop for Lextron International? Should every producer in every geographic area be treated alike, regardless of size? Explain.

22. Structural Wire Corporation

Steve Russell, vice president of marketing for Structural Wire Corporation, is deciding how to organize and train his sales force—and what to do about Ron Pittman.

At its plant in Pittsburgh, Pennsylvania, Structural Wire Corporation, produces wire cable, ranging from ½ inch to 4 inches in diameter. Structural Wire sells across the United States and Canada. Customers include firms that use cranes and various other overhead lifts in their own operations—ski resorts and amusement parks, for example. The company's main customers, however, are cement plants, railroad and boat yards, heavy-equipment manufacturers, mining operations, construction companies, and steel manufacturers.

Structural Wire employs its own sales specialists to call on and try to sell the buyers of potential users. All of Structural Wire's sales reps are engineers who go through an extensive training program covering the different applications, product strengths, and other technical details concerning wire rope and cable. Then they are assigned their own district, the size depending on the number of potential customers. They are paid a good salary plus generous travel expenses, with small bonuses and prizes to reward special efforts.

Ron Pittman went to work for Structural Wire in 1985, immediately after receiving an engineering degree from the University of Wisconsin. After going through the training program, he took over as the only company rep in the Illinois district. His job was to call on and give technical help to present customers of wire cable. He was also expected to call on new customers, especially when inquiries came in. But his main activities were to (1) service present customers and supply the technical assistance needed to use cable in the most efficient and safe manner, (2) handle complaints, and (3) provide evaluation reports to customers' management regarding their use of cabling.

Ron Pittman soon became Structural Wire's outstanding representative. His exceptional ability to handle customer complaints and provide technical assistance was noted by many of the firm's customers. This helped Ron bring in more sales dollars per customer and more in total from present customers than any other rep. He also brought in many new customers, mostly heavy equipment manufacturers and commercial construction companies in northern Illinois. Over the years, his sales have been about twice the sales rep average, and always at least 20 percent higher than the next best rep—even though each district is supposed to have about the same sales potential.

Ron's success established Illinois as Structural Wire's largest-volume district. Although the company's sales in Illinois have not continued to grow as fast in the last few years because Ron seems to have found most of the possible applications and won a good share for Structural Wire, the replacement market has been steady and profitable. This fact is mainly due to Ron Pittman. As one of the supply managers for a large machinery manufacturer mentioned,

> When Ron makes a recommendation regarding use of our equipment and cabling, even if it is a competitor's cable we are using, we are sure it's for the best of our company. Last week, for example, a cable of one of his competitors broke, and we were going to give him a contract. He told us it was not a defective cable that caused the break, but rather the way we were using it. He told us how it should be used and what we needed to do to correct our operation. We took his advice and gave him the contract as well!

Four years ago, Structural Wire introduced a unique and newly patented wire sling device for holding cable groupings together. The sling makes operations around the cable much safer—and its use could reduce both injuries and lost-time costs due to accidents. The slings are expensive—and the profit margin is high. Structural Wire urged all its representatives to push the sling, but the only sales rep to sell the sling with any success was Ron Pittman. Eighty percent of his customers are currently using the wire sling. In other areas, sling sales are disappointing.

As a result of Ron's success, Steve Russell is now considering forming a separate department for sling sales and putting Ron Pittman in charge. His duties would include traveling to the various sales districts and training other representatives to sell the sling. The Illinois district would be handled by a new rep.

Evaluate Steve Russell's strategy(ies). What should he do about Ron Pittman and his sales force? Explain.

23. Heritage Furniture

Susan Kurczak, owner of Heritage Furniture, is discouraged with her salespeople and is even thinking about hiring some new blood. Kurczak has been running Heritage Furniture for 10 years and has slowly built the sales to $3.5 million a year. Her store is located on the outskirts of a growing city of 275,000 population. This is basically a factory city, and she has deliberately selected blue-collar workers as her target market. She carries some higher-priced furniture lines but emphasizes budget combinations and easy credit terms.

Kurczak is concerned that she may have reached the limit of her sales growth—her sales have not been increasing during the last two years even though total furniture sales have been increasing in the city as new people move in. Her local cable-TV spots and newspaper advertising seem to attract her target customers, but many of these people come in, shop around, and leave. Some of them come back—but most do not. She thinks her product selections are very suitable for her target market and is concerned that her salespeople don't close more sales with potential customers. Several times, she has discussed this matter with her 10 salespeople. Her staff feels they should treat customers the way they personally want to be treated. They argue that their role is to answer questions and be helpful when asked—not to make suggestions or help customers make decisions. They think this would be too "hard sell."

Kurczak says their behavior is interpreted as indifference by the customers attracted to the store by her advertising. She has tried to convince her salespeople that customers must be treated on an individual basis and that some customers need more help in looking and deciding than others. Moreover, Kurczak is convinced that some customers would appreciate more help and suggestions than the salespeople themselves might want. To support her views, she showed her staff the data from a study of furniture store customers (see Tables 1 and 2 on next page) that she found on the Internet website for a furniture trade association. She tried to explain the differences in demographic groups and pointed out that her store was definitely trying to aim at specific people. She argued that they (the salespeople) should cater to the needs and attitudes of their customers and think less about how they would like to be treated themselves. Further, Kurczak announced that she is considering changing the sales compensation plan or hiring new blood if the present employees can't do a better job. Currently, the sales reps are paid $26,000 per year plus a 5 percent commission on sales.

Contrast Kurczak's strategy and thoughts about her salespeople with their apparent view of her strategy and especially their role in it. What should she do now? Explain.

Table 1

In Shopping for Furniture I Found (Find) That	Demographic Groups			
	Group A	Group B	Group C	Group D
I looked at furniture in many stores before I made a purchase.	78%	72%	52%	50%
I went (am going) to only one store and bought (buy) what I found (find) there.	2	5	10	11
To make my purchase I went (am going) back to one of the stores I shopped in previously.	63	59	27	20
I looked (am looking) at furniture in no more than three stores and made (will make) my purchase in one of these.	20	25	40	45
I like a lot of help in selecting the right furniture.	27	33	62	69
I like a very friendly salesperson.	23	28	69	67

Table 2   The Sample Design

Demographic Status
Upper class (Group A); 13% of sample
This group consists of managers, proprietors, or executives of large businesses; professionals, including doctors, lawyers, engineers, college professors, and school administrators; and research personnel and sales personnel, including managers, executives, and upper-income salespeople above level of clerks. *Family income over $60,000*
Middle class (Group B); 37% of sample
Group B consists of white-collar workers, including clerical, secretarial, salesclerks, bookkeepers, etc. It also includes school teachers, social workers, semiprofessionals, proprietors or managers of small businesses, industrial foremen, and other supervisory personnel. *Family income between $35,000 and $70,000*
Lower middle class (Group C); 36% of sample
Skilled workers and semiskilled technicians are in this category, along with custodians, elevator operators, telephone linemen, factory operatives, construction workers, and some domestic and personal service employees. *Family income between $20,000 and $45,000. No one in this group has above a high school education.*
Lower class (Group D); 14% of sample
Nonskilled employees, day laborers. It also includes some factory operatives and domestic and service people. *Family income under $28,000. None has completed high school; some have only grade school education.*

24. Metal Solutions, Inc.

Myra Martinez, marketing manager of consumer products for Metal Solutions, Inc., is trying to set a price for her most promising new product—a space-saving shoe rack suitable for small homes or apartments.

Metal Solutions, Inc.—located in Ft. Worth, Texas—is a custom producer of industrial wire products. The company has a lot of experience bending wire into many shapes and also can chrome- or gold-plate finished products. The company was started 16 years ago and has slowly built its sales volume to $3.6 million a year. Just one year ago, Myra Martinez was appointed marketing manager of the consumer products division. It is her responsibility to develop this division as a producer and marketer of the company's own branded products—as distinguished from custom orders, which the industrial division produces for others.

Martinez has been working on a number of different product ideas for almost a year now and has developed several designs for DVD holders, racks for soft-drink cans, plate holders, doll stands, collapsible book ends, and other such products. Her most promising product is a shoe rack for crowded homes and apartments. The wire rack attaches to the inside of a closet door and holds eight pairs of shoes.

The rack is very similar to one the industrial division produced for a number of years for another company. That company sold the shoe rack and hundreds of other related items out of its "products for organizing and storing" mail-order catalog. Managers at Metal Solutions were surprised by the high sales volume the catalog company achieved with the rack. In fact, that is what interested Metal Solutions in the consumer market and led to the development of the separate consumer products division.

Martinez has sold hundreds of the shoe racks to various local hardware, grocery, and general merchandise stores, and wholesalers on a trial basis, but each time she has negotiated a price—and no firm policy has been set. Now she must determine what price to set on the shoe rack, which she plans to push aggressively wherever she can. Actually, she hasn't decided on exactly which channels of distribution to use. But trials in the local area have been encouraging, and as noted above, the experience in the industrial division suggests that there is a large market for this type of product. Further, she noticed that a Wal-Mart store in her local area was selling a similar rack made of plastic. When she talked casually about her product with the store manager, he suggested that she contact the chain's houseware buyers in the home office in Arkansas. The manufacturing cost on this product—when made in reasonable quantities—is approximately $2.80 if it is painted black and $3.60 if it is chromed. Similar products have been selling at retail in the $9.95 to $19.95 range. The sales and administrative overhead to be charged to the division will amount to $95,000 a year. This will include Martinez's salary and some travel and office expenses. She expects that a number of other products will be developed in the near future. But for the coming year, she hopes the shoe rack will account for about half the consumer products division's sales volume.

Evaluate Myra Martinez's strategy planning so far. What should she do now? What price should she set for the shoe rack? Explain.

25. PlastiForm Mfg., Inc.

David Houston, the marketing manager of PlastiForm Mfg., Inc., wants to increase sales by adding sales reps rather than "playing with price." That's how David describes what Will Houston, his father and PlastiForm's president, is suggesting. Will is not sure what to do either. But he does want to increase sales, so something new is needed.

PlastiForm Mfg., Inc.—of Long Beach, California—is a leading producer in the plastic forming machinery industry. It has patents covering over 200 variations, but PlastiForm's customers seldom buy more than 30 different types in a year. The machines are sold to plastic forming manufacturers to increase production capacity or replace old equipment.

Established in 1970, the company has enjoyed a steady growth to its present position with annual sales of $50 million.

Twelve U.S. firms compete in the U.S. plastic forming machinery market. Several Japanese, German, and Swedish firms compete in the global market, but the Houstons have not seen much of them on the West Coast. Apparently the foreign firms rely on manufacturers' agents who have not provided an ongoing presence. They are not good about following up on inquiries, and their record for service on the few sales they have made on the East Coast is not satisfactory. So the Houstons are not worried about them right now.

Each of the 12 U.S. competitors is about the same size and manufactures basically similar machinery. Each has tended to specialize in its own geographic region. Six of the competitors are located in the East, four in the Midwest, and two—including PlastiForm—on the West Coast. The other West Coast firm is in Tacoma, Washington. All of the competitors offer similar prices and sell F.O.B. their factories. Demand has been fairly strong in recent years. As a result, all of the competitors

have been satisfied to sell in their geographic areas and avoid price-cutting. In fact, price-cutting is not a popular idea in this industry. About 15 years ago, one firm tried to win more business and found that others immediately met the price cut—but industry sales (in units) did not increase at all. Within a few years, prices returned to their earlier level, and since then competition has tended to focus on promotion and avoid price.

PlastiForm's promotion depends mainly on six company sales reps, who cover the West Coast. In total, these reps cost about $880,000 per year including salary, bonuses, supervision, travel, and entertaining. When the sales reps are close to making a sale, they are supported by two sales engineers—at a cost of about $130,000 per year per engineer. PlastiForm does some advertising in trade journals—less than $100,000—and occasionally uses direct mailings and trade show exhibits. It also has a simple website on the Internet. But the main promotion emphasis is on personal selling. Any personal contact outside the West Coast market is handled by manufacturers' agents who are paid 4 percent on sales—but sales are very infrequent.

Will Houston is not satisfied with the present situation. Industry sales have leveled off and so have PlastiForm's sales—although the firm continues to hold its share of the market. Will would like to find a way to compete more effectively in the other regions because he sees great potential outside the West Coast.

Competitors and buyers agree that PlastiForm is the top-quality producer in the industry. Its machines have generally been somewhat superior to others in terms of reliability, durability, and productive capacity. The difference, however, usually has not been great enough to justify a higher price—because the others are able to do the necessary job—unless a PlastiForm sales rep convinces the customer that the extra quality will improve the customer's product and lead to fewer production line breakdowns. The sales rep also tries to sell the advantages of PlastiForm's better sales engineers and technical service people—and sometimes is successful. But if a buyer is mainly interested in comparing delivered prices for basic machines—the usual case—PlastiForm's price must be competitive to get the business. In short, if such a buyer has a choice between PlastiForm's and another machine *at the same price*, PlastiForm will usually win the business in its part of the West Coast market. But it's clear that PlastiForm's price has to be at least competitive in such cases.

The average plastic forming machine sells for about $220,000, F.O.B. shipping point. Shipping costs within any of the three major regions average about $4,000—but another $3,000 must be added on shipments between the West Coast and the Midwest (either way) and another $3,000 between the Midwest and the East.

Will Houston is thinking about expanding sales by absorbing the extra $3,000 to $6,000 in freight cost that occurs if a midwestern or eastern customer buys from his West Coast location. By doing this, he would not actually be cutting price in those markets but rather reducing his net return. He thinks that his competitors would not see this as price competition and therefore would not resort to cutting prices themselves.

David Houston, the marketing manager, disagrees. David thinks that the proposed freight absorption plan would stimulate price competition in the Midwest and East and perhaps on the West Coast. He proposes instead that PlastiForm hire some sales reps to work the Midwest and Eastern regions—selling quality—rather than relying on the manufacturers' agents. He argues that two additional sales reps in each of these regions would not increase costs too much and might greatly increase the sales from these markets over that brought in by the agents. With this plan, there would be no need to absorb the freight and risk disrupting the status quo. Adding more of PlastiForm's own sales reps is especially important, he argues, because competition in the Midwest and East is somewhat hotter than on the West Coast—due to the number of competitors (including foreign competitors) in those regions. A lot of expensive entertaining, for example, seems to be required just to be considered as a potential supplier. In contrast, the situation has been rather quiet in the West—because only two firms are sharing this market and each is working harder near its home base. The eastern and midwestern competitors don't send any sales reps to the West Coast—and if they have any manufacturers' agents, they haven't gotten any business in recent years.

Will Houston agrees that his son has a point, but industry sales are leveling off and Will wants to increase sales. Further, he thinks the competitive situation may change drastically in the near future anyway, as global competitors get more aggressive and some possible new production methods and machines become more competitive with existing ones. He would rather be a leader in anything that is likely to happen rather than a follower. But he is impressed with David's comments about the greater competitiveness in the other markets and therefore is unsure about what to do.

Evaluate PlastiForm's current strategies. Given Will Houston's sales objective, what should PlastiForm Mfg. do? Explain.

26. Riverside Packers, Inc.

Hans Fleming, president of Riverside Packers, Inc., is not sure what he should propose to the board of directors. His recent strategy change isn't working. And Niels Sondergaard, Riverside's only sales rep (and a board member), is so frustrated that he refuses to continue his discouraging sales efforts. Sondergaard wants Hans Fleming to hire a sales force or do *something.*

Riverside Packers, Inc., is a long-time processor in the highly seasonal vegetable canning industry. Riverside packs and sells canned beans, peas, carrots, corn, peas and carrots mixed, and kidney beans. It sells mainly through food brokers to merchant wholesalers, supermarket chains (such as Kroger, Safeway, A&P, and Jewel), cooperatives, and other outlets, mostly in the Midwest. Of less importance, by volume, are sales to local institutions, grocery stores, and supermarkets—and sales of dented canned goods at low prices to walk-in customers.

Riverside is located in Wisconsin's Devil's River Valley. The company has more than $28 million in sales annually (exact sales data is not published by the closely held corporation). Plants are located in strategic places along the valley, with

main offices in Riverside. The Riverside brand is used only on canned goods sold in the local market. Most of the goods are sold and shipped under a retailer's label or a broker's/wholesaler's label.

Riverside is well known for the consistent quality of its product offerings. And it's always willing to offer competitive prices. Strong channel relations were built by Riverside's former chairman of the board and chief executive officer Dane Christian. Christian—who owns controlling interest in the firm—worked the Chicago area as the company's sales rep in its earlier years, before he took over from his father as president in 1972. Christian was an ambitious and hardworking top manager—the firm prospered under his direction. He became well known within the canned food processing industry for technical/product innovations.

During the off-canning season, Christian traveled widely. In the course of his travels, he arranged several important business deals. His 1986 and 1997 trips resulted in the following two events: (1) inexpensive pineapple was imported from Taiwan and sold by Riverside, primarily to expand the product line, and (2) a technically advanced continuous process cooker (65 feet high) was imported from England and installed at one of the Riverside plants. It was the first of its kind in the United States and cut processing time sharply while improving quality.

Christian retired in 2004 and named his son-in-law, 35-year-old Hans Fleming, as his successor. Fleming is intelligent and hardworking. He was concerned primarily with the company's financial matters and only recently with marketing problems. During his seven years as financial director, the firm received its highest credit rating and was able to borrow working capital ($5 million to meet seasonal can and wage requirements) at the lowest rate ever.

The fact that the firm isn't unionized allows some competitive advantage. However, changes in minimum wage laws have increased costs. And these and other rising costs have squeezed profit margins. This led to the recent closing of two plants as they became less efficient to operate. Riverside expanded capacity of the remaining two plants (especially warehouse facilities) so they could operate more profitably with maximum use of existing processing equipment.

Shortly after Christian's retirement, Hans Fleming reviewed the company's situation with his managers. He pointed to narrowing profit margins, debts contracted for new plants and equipment, and an increasingly competitive environment. Even considering the temporary labor-saving competitive advantage of the new cooker system, there seemed to be no way to improve the status quo unless the firm could sell direct—as they do in the local market—thereby eliminating the food brokers' 5 percent commission on sales. This was the plan decided on, and Niels Sondergaard was given the new sales job. An inside salesperson was retained to handle incoming orders and do some telemarketing to smaller accounts.

Niels Sondergaard, the only full-time outside sales rep for the firm, lives in Riverside. Other top managers do some selling but not much. Being a nephew of Christian, Niels Sondergaard is also a member of the board of directors. He is well qualified in technical matters and has a college degree in food chemistry. Although Niels Sondergaard formerly did call on some important customers with the brokers' sales reps, he is not well-known in the industry or even by Riverside's usual customers.

It is now five months later. Niels Sondergaard is not doing very well. He has made several selling trips, placed hundreds of telephone calls, and maintained constant e-mail contacts with prospective customers—all with discouraging results. He is unwilling to continue sales efforts on his own. There seem to be too many potential customers for one person to reach. And much negotiating, wining, and dining seems to be needed—certainly more than he can or wants to do.

Sondergaard insists that Riverside hire a sales force to continue the present way of operating. Sales are down in comparison both to expectations and to the previous year's results. Some regular supermarket chain customers have stopped buying—though basic consumer demand has not changed. Further, buyers for some supermarket chains that might be potential new customers have demanded quantity guarantees much larger than Riverside Packers can supply. Expanding supply would be difficult in the short run—because the firm typically must contract with growers to ensure supplies of the type and quality they normally offer.

Christian, still the controlling stockholder, has asked for a special meeting of the board in two weeks to discuss the present situation.

Evaluate Riverside's past and current strategy planning. What should Hans Fleming tell Mr. Christian? What should Riverside do now?

27. Injection Molding, Inc.

Nora Hall is trying to decide whether to leave her present job to buy into another business and be part of top management.

Hall is now a sales rep for a plastics components manufacturer. She calls mostly on large industrial accounts—such as refrigerator manufacturers—who might need large quantities of custom-made products like door liners. She is on a straight salary of $45,000 per year, plus expenses and a company car. She expects some salary increases but doesn't see much long-run opportunity with this company.

As a result, she is seriously considering changing jobs and investing $60,000 in Injection Molding, Inc., an established Chicago (Illinois) thermoplastic molder (manufacturer). Mr. Hanson, the present owner, is nearing retirement and has not trained anyone to take over the business. He has agreed to sell the business to Steve Burton, a lawyer, who has invited Nora Hall to invest and become the sales manager. Steve Burton has agreed to match Hall's current salary plus expenses, plus a bonus of 2 percent of profits. However, she must invest to become part of the new company. She will get a 5 percent interest in the business for the necessary $60,000 investment—all of her savings.

Injection Molding, Inc., is well established and last year had sales of $3.2 million but zero profits (after paying Hanson a salary of $80,000). In terms of sales, cost of materials was 46 percent; direct labor, 13 percent; indirect factory labor, 15 percent; factory overhead, 13 percent; and sales overhead and general expenses, 13 percent. The company has not been making any profit for several years—but it has been continually adding new computer-controlled machines to replace those made obsolete by technological developments. The machinery is well maintained and modern, but most of it is similar to that used by its many competitors. Most of the machines in the industry are standard. Special products are made by using specially made dies with these machines.

Sales have been split about two-thirds custom-molded products (that is, made to the specification of other producers or merchandising concerns) and the balance proprietary items (such as housewares and game items, like poker chips). The housewares are copies of articles developed by others and indicate neither originality nor style. Hanson is in charge of selling the proprietary items, which are distributed through any available wholesale channels. The custom-molded products are sold through two full-time sales reps—who receive a 10 percent commission on individual orders up to $30,000 and then 3 percent above that level—and also by three manufacturers' reps who get the same commissions.

The company seems to be in fairly good financial condition, at least as far as book value is concerned. The $60,000 investment will buy almost $88,000 in assets—and ongoing operations should pay off the seven-year note (see Table 1). Steve Burton thinks that with new management the company

Cases

705

Table 1 Injection Molding, Inc., Statement of Financial Conditions, December 31, 200x

Assets			Liabilities and Net Worth		
Cash		$ 19,500	Liabilities:		
Accounts receivable		82,500	Accounts payable		$ 105,000
Building	$337,500		Notes payable—7 years (machinery)		291,000
Less: depreciation	112,500				
		225,000			
Machinery	2,100,000		Net worth:		
Less: depreciation	675,000		Capital stock		1,350,000
		1,425,000	Retained earnings		6,000
Total assets		$1,752,000	Total liabilities and net worth		$1,752,000

has a good chance to make big profits. He expects to make some economies in the production process—because he feels most production operations can be improved. He plans to keep custom-molding sales at approximately the present $2 million level. His new strategy will try to increase the proprietary sales volume from $1.2 million to $3 million a year. Nora Hall is expected to be a big help here because of her sales experience. This will bring the firm up to about capacity level—but it will mean adding additional employees and costs. The major advantage of expanding sales will be spreading overhead.

Some of the products proposed by Steve Burton for expanding proprietary sales are listed below.

New products for consideration:
Safety helmets for cyclists.
Water bottles for cyclists and in-line skaters.
Waterproof cases for digital cameras.
Toolboxes.
Closet organizer/storage boxes for toys.
Short legs for furniture.
Step-on garbage cans without liners.
Outside house shutters and siding.
Importing and distributing foreign housewares.

Injection Molding faces heavy competition from many other similar companies including firms that have outsourced production to China and Eastern Europe where labor costs are much lower. Further, most retailers expect a wide margin, sometimes 50 to 60 percent of retail selling price. Even so, manufacturing costs are low enough so Injection Molding can spend some money for promotion while still keeping the price competitive. Apparently, many customers are willing to pay for novel new products—if they see them in stores. And Hall isn't worried too much by tough competition. She sees plenty of that in her present job. And she does like the idea of being an "owner and sales manager."

Evaluate Injection Molding's situation and Steve Burton's strategy. What should Nora Hall do? Why?

28. QCT, Inc.

Ben Colavito, president and marketing manager of Quality Cutting Tools, Inc., is deciding what strategy, or strategies, to pursue.

Quality Cutting Tools (QCT) is a manufacturer of industrial cutting tools. These tools include such items as lathe blades, drill press bits, and various other cutting edges used in the operation of large metal cutting, boring, or stamping machines. Ben Colavito takes great pride in the fact that his company—whose $5,700,000 sales in 2004 is small by industry standards—is recognized as a producer of a top-quality line of cutting tools.

Competition in the cutting-tool industry is intense. QCT competes not only with the original machine manufacturers, but also with many other larger domestic and foreign manufacturers offering cutting tools as one of their many different product lines. This has had the effect, over the years, of standardizing the price, specifications, and, in turn, the quality of the competing products of all manufacturers. It has also led to fairly low prices on standard items.

About a year ago, Ben was tiring of the financial pressure of competing with larger companies enjoying economies of scale. At the same time, he noted that more and more potential cutting-tool customers were turning to small tool-and-die shops that used computer-controlled equipment to meet specialized needs that could not be met by the mass production firms. Ben thought perhaps he should consider some basic strategy changes. Although he was unwilling to become strictly a custom producer, he thought that the recent trend toward buying customized cutting edges suggested new markets might be developing—markets too small for the large, multiproduct-line companies to serve profitably but large enough to earn a good profit for a flexible company of QCT's size.

Ben hired a marketing research company, Fennell Associates, to study the feasibility of serving these markets. The initial results were encouraging. It was estimated that QCT might increase sales by 65 percent and profits by 90 percent by serving the emerging markets. This research showed that there are many large users of standard cutting tools who buy directly from large cutting-tool manufacturers (domestic or foreign) or wholesalers who represent these manufacturers. This is the bulk of the cutting-tool business (in terms of units sold and sales dollars). But there are also many smaller users all over the United States who buy in small but regular quantities. And some of these needs are becoming more specialized. That is, a special cutting tool may make a machine and/or worker much more productive, perhaps eliminating several steps with time-consuming setups. This is the area that the research company sees as potentially attractive.

Next, Ben had the sales manager hire two technically oriented market researchers (at a total cost of $65,000 each per year, including travel expenses) to maintain continuous contact with potential cutting-tool customers. The researchers were supposed to identify any present or future needs that might exist in enough cases to make it possible to profitably produce a specialized product. The researchers were not to take orders or sell QCT's products to the potential customers. Ben felt that only through this policy could these researchers talk to the right people.

The initial feedback from the market researchers was most encouraging. Many firms (large and small) had special needs—although it often was necessary to talk to the shop foreman or individual machine operators to find these needs. Most operators were making do with the tools available. Either they didn't know customizing was possible or doubted that their supervisors would do anything about it if they suggested that a more specialized tool would increase productivity. But these operators were encouraging because they said that it would be easier to persuade supervisors to order specialized tools if the tools were already produced and in stock than if they had to be custom made. So Ben decided to continually add high-quality products to meet the ever-changing, specialized needs of users of cutting tools and edges.

QCT's potential customers for specialized tools are located all over the United States. The average sale per customer is likely to be less than $500, but the sale will be repeated several times within a year. Because of the widespread market and the small order size, Ben doesn't think that selling direct—as is done by small custom shops—is practical. At the present time, QCT sells 90 percent of its regular output through a large industrial wholesaler—National Mill Supplies, Inc.—which serves the area east of the Mississippi River and carries a very complete line of industrial supplies (to "meet every industrial need"). National Mill Supplies carries over 10,000 items. Some sales come from customers who know exactly what they want and just place orders directly by fax or at the firm's Internet website. But most of the selling is by National's sales reps, who work from an electronic catalog on a laptop computer. National Mill Supplies, although very large and well-known, is having trouble moving cutting tools. National is losing sales of cutting tools in some cities to newer wholesalers specializing in the cutting-tool industry. The new wholesalers are able to give more technical help to potential customers and therefore better service. National's president is convinced that the newer, less-experienced concerns will either realize that a substantial profit margin can't be maintained along with their aggressive strategies, or they will eventually go broke trying to overspecialize.

From Ben's standpoint, the present wholesaler has a good reputation and has served QCT well in the past. National Mill Supplies has been of great help in holding down Ben's inventory costs—by increasing the inventory in National's 35 branch locations. Although Ben has received several complaints about the lack of technical assistance given by National's sales reps—as well as their lack of knowledge about QCT's new special products—he feels that the present wholesaler is providing the best service it can. All its sales reps have been told about the new products at a special training session, and new pages have been added to the electronic catalog on their laptops. So regarding the complaints, Ben says, "The usual things you hear when you're in business."

Ben thinks there are more urgent problems than a few complaints. Profits are declining, and sales of the new cutting tools are not nearly as high as forecast—even though all research reports indicate that the company's new products meet the intended markets' needs perfectly. The high costs involved in producing small quantities of special products and in adding the market research team—together with lower-than-expected sales—have significantly reduced QCT's profits. Ben is wondering whether it is wise to continue to try to cater to the needs of many specific target markets when the results are this discouraging. He also is considering increasing advertising expenditures in the hope that customers will pull the new products through the channel.

Evaluate QCT's situation and Ben Colavito's present strategy. What should he do now?

29. Custom Castings, Inc.

Victor Carrington, marketing manager for Custom Castings, Inc., is trying to figure out how to explain to his boss why a proposed new product line doesn't make sense for them. Victor is sure it's wrong for Custom Castings, but isn't able to explain why.

Custom Castings, Inc., is a producer of malleable iron castings for automobile and aircraft manufacturers and a variety of other users of castings. Last year's sales of castings amounted to over $70 million.

Custom Castings also produces about 30 percent of all the original equipment bumper jacks installed in new U.S.-made automobiles each year. This is a very price-competitive business, but Custom Castings has been able to obtain its large market share with frequent personal contact between the company's executives and its customers—supported by very close cooperation between the company's engineering department and its customers' buyers. This has been extremely important because the wide variety of models and model changes frequently requires alterations in the specifications of the bumper jacks. All of Custom Castings' bumper jacks are sold directly to the automobile manufacturers. No attempt has been made to sell bumper jacks to final consumers through hardware and automotive channels—although they are available through the manufacturers' automobile dealers.

Tom Gaines, Custom Castings' production manager, now wants to begin producing hydraulic garage jacks for sale through automobile-parts wholesalers to retail auto parts stores. Gaines saw a variety of hydraulic garage jacks at a recent automotive show and knew immediately that his plant could produce these products. This especially interested him because of the possibility of using excess capacity. Further, he says "jacks are jacks," and the company would merely be broadening its product line by introducing hydraulic garage jacks. (Note: Hydraulic garage jacks are larger than bumper jacks and are intended for use in or around a garage. They are too big to carry in a car's trunk.)

As Tom Gaines became more enthusiastic about the idea, he found that Custom Castings' engineering department already had a patented design that appeared to be at least comparable to the products now offered on the market. Further, Gaines says that the company would be able to produce a product that is better made than the competitive products (i.e., smoother castings)—although he agrees that most customers probably wouldn't notice the difference. The production department estimates that the cost of producing a hydraulic garage jack comparable to those currently offered by competitors would be about $48 per unit.

Victor Carrington, the marketing manager, has just received an e-mail from George Daggett, the company president, explaining the production department's enthusiasm for broadening Custom Castings' present jack line into hydraulic jacks. George Daggett seems enthusiastic about the idea too, noting that it would be a way to make fuller use of the company's resources and increase its sales. Daggett's e-mail asks for Victor's reaction, but George Daggett already seems sold on the idea.

Given Daggett's enthusiasm, Victor Carrington isn't sure how to respond. He's trying to develop a good explanation of why he isn't excited about the proposal. The firm's six sales reps are already overworked with their current accounts. And Victor couldn't possibly promote this new line himself—he's already helping other reps make calls and serving as sales manager. So it would be necessary to hire someone to promote the line. And this sales manager would probably have to recruit manufacturers' agents (who probably will want 10 to 15 percent commission on sales) to sell to automotive wholesalers who would stock the jack and sell to the auto parts retailers. The wholesalers will probably expect trade discounts of about 20 percent, trade show exhibits, some national advertising, and sales promotion help (catalog sheets, mailers, and point-of-purchase displays). Further, Victor Carrington sees that Custom Castings' billing and collection system will have to be expanded because many more customers will be involved. It will also be necessary to keep track of agent commissions and accounts receivable.

Auto parts retailers are currently selling similar hydraulic garage jacks for about $99. Victor Carrington has learned that such retailers typically expect a trade discount of about 35 percent off of the suggested list price for their auto parts.

All things considered, Victor Carrington feels that the proposed hydraulic jack line is not very closely related to the company's present emphasis. He has already indicated his lack of enthusiasm to Tom Gaines, but this made little difference in Tom's thinking. Now it's clear that Victor will have to convince the president or he will soon be responsible for selling hydraulic jacks.

Contrast Custom Castings, Inc.'s current strategy and the proposed strategy. What should Victor Carrington say to George Daggett to persuade him to change his mind? Or should he just plan to sell hydraulic jacks? Explain.

30. Deluxe Foods, Ltd.*

Jessica Walters, marketing manager of Deluxe Foods, Ltd.—a Canadian company—is being urged to approve the creation of a separate marketing plan for Quebec. This would be a major policy change because Deluxe Foods' international parent is trying to move toward a global strategy for the whole firm and Jessica has been supporting Canada-wide planning.

Jessica Walters has been the marketing manager of Deluxe Foods, Ltd., for the last four years—since she arrived from international headquarters in Minneapolis. Deluxe Foods, Ltd., headquartered in Toronto, is a subsidiary of a large U.S.-based consumer packaged-food company with worldwide sales of more than $2.8 billion in 2003. Its Canadian sales are just over $450 million, with the Quebec and Ontario markets accounting for 69 percent of the company's Canadian sales.

The company's product line includes such items as cake mixes, puddings, pie fillings, pancakes, prepared foods, and frozen dinners. The company has successfully introduced at least six new products every year for the last five years. Products from Deluxe Foods are known for their high quality and enjoy much brand preference throughout Canada, including the Province of Quebec.

The company's sales have risen every year since Jessica Walters took over as marketing manager. In fact, the com-

pany's market share has increased steadily in each of the product categories in which it competes. The Quebec market has closely followed the national trend except that, in the past two years, total sales growth in that market began to lag.

According to Walters, a big advantage of Deluxe Foods over its competitors is the ability to coordinate all phases of the food business from Toronto. For this reason, Walters meets at least once a month with her product managers—to discuss developments in local markets that might affect marketing plans. While each manager is free to make suggestions and even to suggest major changes, Jessica Walters has the responsiblity of giving final approval for all plans.

One of the product managers, Marie LeMans, expressed great concern at the last monthly meeting about the poor performance of some of the company's products in the Quebec market. While a broad range of possible reasons—ranging from inflation and the threat of job losses to politics—were reviewed to try to explain the situation, LeMans insisted that it was due to a basic lack of understanding of that market. She felt not enough managerial time and money had been spent on the Quebec market—in part because of the current emphasis on developing all-Canada plans on the way to having one global strategy.

Marie LeMans felt the current marketing approach to the Quebec market should be reevaluated because an inappropriate marketing plan may be responsible for the sales slowdown. After all, she said, "80 percent of the market is French-speaking. It's in the best interest of the company to treat that market as being separate and distinct from the rest of Canada."

Marie LeMans supported her position by showing that Quebec's per capita consumption of many product categories (in which the firm competes) is above the national average (see Table 1). Research projects conducted by Deluxe Foods also support the "separate and distinct" argument. Over the years, the firm has found many French–English differences in brand attitudes, lifestyles, usage rates, and so on.

LeMans argued that the company should develop a unique Quebec marketing plan for some or all of its brands. She specifically suggested that the French-language advertising plan for a particular brand be developed independently of the plan for English Canada. Currently, the Toronto agency assigned to the brand just translates its English-language ads for the French market. Jessica Walters pointed out that the present advertising approach assured Deluxe Foods of a uniform brand image across Canada. Marie LeMans said she knew what the agency is doing, and that straight translation into Canadian-French may not communicate the same brand image. The discussion that followed suggested that a different brand image

Table 1   Per Capita Consumption Index, Province of Quebec (Canada = 100)

Cake mixes	107	Soft drinks	126
Pancakes	87	Pie fillings	118
Puddings	114	Frozen dinners	79
Salad dressings	85	Prepared packaged foods	83
Molasses	132	Cookies	123

*This case was adapted from one written by Professor Roberta Tamilia, University of Windsor, Canada.

might be needed in the French market if the company wanted to stop the brand's decline in sales.

The managers also discussed the food distribution system in Quebec. The major supermarket chains have their lowest market share in that province. Independents are strongest there—the "mom-and-pop" food stores fast disappearing outside Quebec remain alive and well in the province. Traditionally, these stores have stocked a higher proportion (than supermarkets) of their shelf space with national brands, an advantage for Deluxe Foods.

Finally, various issues related to discount policies, pricing structure, sales promotion, and cooperative advertising were discussed. All of this suggested that things were different in Quebec and that future marketing plans should reflect these differences to a greater extent than they do now.

After the meeting, Jessica Walters stayed in her office to think about the situation. Although she agreed with the basic idea that the Quebec market was in many ways different, she wasn't sure how far the company should go in recognizing this fact. She knew that regional differences in food tastes and brand purchases existed not only in Quebec but in other parts of Canada as well. But people are people, after all, with far more similarities than differences, so a Canadian and eventually a global strategy makes some sense too.

Jessica Walters was afraid that giving special status to one region might conflict with top management's objective of achieving standardization whenever possible—one global strategy for Canada, on the way to one worldwide global strategy. She was also worried about the long-term effect of such a policy change on costs, organizational structure, and brand image. Still, enough product managers had expressed their concern over the years about the Quebec market to make her wonder if she shouldn't modify the current approach. Perhaps they could experiment with a few brands—and just in Quebec. She could cite the language difference as the reason for trying Quebec rather than any of the other provinces. But Walters realizes that any change of policy could be seen as the beginning of more change, and what would Minneapolis think? Could she explain it successfully there?

Evaluate Deluxe Foods, Ltd.'s present strategy. What should Jessica Walters do now? Explain.

31. Home Nursing Services, Inc.

Carol Crane, executive director of Home Nursing Services, Inc., is trying to clarify her strategies. She's sure some changes are needed, but she's less sure about how *much* change is needed and/or whether it can be handled by her people.

Home Nursing Services, Inc. (HNS), is a nonprofit organization that has been operating—with varying degrees of success—for 25 years, offering nursing services in clients' homes. Some of its funding comes from the local United Way—to provide emergency nursing services for those who can't afford to pay. The balance of the revenues—about 90 percent of the $2.2 million annual budget—comes from charges made directly to the client or to third-party payers,

including insurance companies, health maintenance organizations (HMOs), and the federal government, for Medicare or Medicaid services.

Carol Crane has been executive director of HNS for two years. She has developed a well-functioning organization able to meet most requests for service that come from some local doctors and from the discharge officers at local hospitals. Some business also comes by self-referral—the client finds the HNS name in the Yellow Pages of the local phone directory.

The last two years have been a rebuilding time—because the previous director had personnel problems. This led to a weakening of the agency's image with the local referring agencies. Now the image is more positive. But Carol is not completely satisfied with the situation. By definition, Home Nursing Services is a nonprofit organization. But it still must cover all its costs: payroll, rent payments, phone expenses, and so on, including Carol's own salary. She can see that while HNS is growing slightly and is now breaking even, it doesn't have much of a cash cushion to fall back on if (1) the demand for HNS nursing services declines, (2) the government changes its rules about paying for HNS' kind of nursing services, either cutting back what it will pay for or reducing the amount it will pay for specific services, or (3) new competitors enter the market. In fact, the last possibility concerns Carol greatly. Some hospitals, squeezed for revenue, are expanding into home health care—especially nursing services as patients are being released earlier from hospitals because of payment limits set by government guidelines. For-profit organizations (e.g., Kelly Home Care Services) are expanding around the country to provide a complete line of home health care services, including nursing services of the kind offered by HNS. These for-profit organizations appear to be efficiently run, offering good service at competitive and sometimes even lower prices than some nonprofit organizations. And they seem to be doing this at a profit, which suggests that it would be possible for these for-profit companies to lower their prices if nonprofit organizations try to compete on price.

Carol is considering whether she should ask her board of directors to let her offer a complete line of home health care services—that is, move beyond just nursing services into what she calls "care and comfort" services.

Currently, HNS is primarily concerned with providing professional nursing care in the home. But HNS nurses are much too expensive for routine home health care activities—helping fix meals, bathing and dressing patients, and other care and comfort activities. The full cost of a nurse to HNS, including benefits and overhead, is about $65 per hour. But a registered nurse is not needed for care and comfort services. All that is required is someone who is honest, can get along with all kinds of people, and is willing to do this kind of work. Generally, any mature person can be trained fairly quickly to do the job—following the instructions and under the general supervision of a physician, a nurse, or family members. The full cost of aides is $9 to $16 per hour for short visits and as low as $75 per 24 hours for a live-in aide who has room and board supplied by the client.

The demand for all kinds of home health care services seems to be growing. With more dual-career families and more single-parent households, there isn't anyone in the family to take over home health care when the need arises—due to emergencies or long-term disabilities. Further, hospitals send patients home earlier than in the past. And with people living longer, there are more single-survivor family situations where there is no one nearby to take care of the needs of these older people. But often some family members—or third-party payers such as the government or insurers—are willing to pay for some home health care services. Carol now occasionally recommends other agencies or suggests one or another of three women who have been doing care and comfort work on their own, part-time. But with growing demand, Carol wonders if HNS should get into this business, hiring aides as needed.

Carol is concerned that a new, full-service home health care organization may come into her market and be a single source for both nursing services *and* less-skilled home care and comfort services. This has happened already in two nearby but somewhat larger cities. Carol fears that this might be more appealing than HNS to the local hospitals and other referrers. In other words, she can see the possibility of losing nursing service business if HNS does not begin to offer a complete home health care service. This would cause real problems for HNS—because overhead costs are more or less fixed. A loss in revenue of as little as 10 percent would require some cutbacks—perhaps laying off some nurses or secretaries, giving up part of the office, and so on.

Another reason for expanding beyond nursing services—using paraprofessionals and relatively unskilled personnel—is to offer a better service to present customers *and* make more effective use of the computer systems and organization structure that she has developed over the last two years. Carol estimates that the administrative and office capabilities could handle twice as many clients without straining the system. It would be necessary to add some clerical help—if the expansion were quite large. But this increase in overhead would be minor compared to the present proportion of total revenue that goes to covering overhead. In other words, additional clients or more work for some clients could increase revenue and ensure the survival of HNS, provide a cushion to cover the normal fluctuations in demand, and ensure more job security for the administrative personnel.

Further, Carol thinks that if HNS were successful in expanding its services—and therefore could generate some surplus—it could extend services to those who aren't now able to pay. Carol says one of the worst parts of her job is refusing service to clients whose third-party benefits have run out or for whatever reason can no longer afford to pay. She is uncomfortable about having to cut off service, but she must schedule her nurses to provide revenue-producing services if she's going to meet the payroll every two weeks. By expanding to provide more services, she might be able to keep serving more of these nonpaying clients. This possibility excites Carol because her nurse's training has instilled a deep desire to serve people in need, whether they can pay or not. This continual pressure to cut off service because people can't pay has been at the root of many disagreements and even arguments between the nurses serving the clients and Carol, as executive director and representative of the board of directors.

Carol knows that expanding into care and comfort services won't be easy. Some decisions would be needed about relative pay levels for nurses, paraprofessionals, and aides. HNS would also have to set prices for these different services and tell the present customers and referral agencies about the expanded services.

These problems aren't bothering Carol too much, however—she thinks she can handle them. She is sure that care and comfort services are in demand and could be supplied at competitive prices.

Her primary concern is whether this is the right thing for Home Nursing Services—basically a nursing organization—to do. HNS' whole history has been oriented to supplying *nurses' services.* Nurses are dedicated professionals who bring high standards to any job they undertake. The question is whether HNS should offer less-professional services. Inevitably, some of the aides will not be as dedicated as the nurses might like them to be. And this could reflect unfavorably on the nurse image. At a minimum, she would need to set up some sort of training program for the aides. As Carol worries about the future of HNS, and her own future, it seems that there are no easy answers.

Evaluate HNS' present strategy. What should Carol Crane do? Explain.

32. Lever, Ltd.*

Alan Cooke is product manager for Guard Deodorant Soap. He was just transferred to Lever, Ltd., a Canadian subsidiary of Lever Group, Inc., from world headquarters in New York. Alan is anxious to make a good impression because he is hoping to transfer to Lever's London office. He is working on developing and securing management approval of next year's marketing plan for Guard. His first job is submitting a draft marketing plan to Wendy Lee, his recently appointed group product manager, who is responsible for several such plans from product managers like Alan.

Alan's marketing plan is the single most important document he will produce on this assignment. This annual marketing plan does three main things:

1. It reviews the brand's performance in the past year, assesses the competitive situation, and highlights problems and opportunities for the brand.

2. It spells out marketing strategies and the plan for the coming year.

3. Finally, and most importantly, the marketing plan sets out the brand's sales objectives and advertising/promotion budget requirements.

In preparing this marketing plan, Alan gathered the information in Table 1.

Alan was somewhat surprised at the significant regional differences in the bar soap market:

1. The underdevelopment of the deodorant bar segment in Quebec, with a corresponding overdevelopment of the

---

*Adapted from a case prepared by Daniel Aronchick, who at the time of its preparation was marketing manager at Thomas J. Lipton, Limited.

Table 1 Past 12-Month Share of Bar Soap Market (percent)

	Maritimes	Quebec	Ontario	Manitoba/Saskatchewan	Alberta	British Columbia
Deodorant segment						
Zest	21.3%	14.2%	24.5%	31.2%	30.4%	25.5%
Dial	10.4	5.1	12.8	16.1	17.2	14.3
Lifebuoy	4.2	3.1	1.2	6.4	5.8	4.2
Guard	2.1	5.6	1.0	4.2	4.2	2.1
Beauty bar segment						
Camay	6.2	12.3	7.0	4.1	4.0	5.1
Lux	6.1	11.2	7.7	5.0	6.9	5.0
Dove	5.5	8.0	6.6	6.3	6.2	4.2
Lower-priced bars						
Ivory	11.2	6.5	12.4	5.3	5.2	9.0
Sunlight	6.1	3.2	8.2	4.2	4.1	8.0
All others (including stores' own brands)	26.9	30.8	18.6	17.2	16.0	22.6
Total bar soap market	100.0%	100.0%	100.0%	100.0%	100.0%	100.0%

beauty bar segment. But some past research suggested that this is due to cultural factors—English-speaking people have been more interested than others in cleaning, deodorizing, and disinfecting. A similar pattern is seen in most European countries, where the adoption of deodorant soaps has been slower than in North America. For similar reasons, the perfumed soap share is highest in French-speaking Quebec.

2. The overdevelopment of synthetic bars in the Prairies. These bars, primarily in the deodorant segment, lather better in the hard water of the Prairies. Nonsynthetic bars lather very poorly in hard-water areas and leave a soap film.

3. The overdevelopment of the "all-other" segment in Quebec. This segment, consisting of smaller brands, fares better in Quebec, where 43 percent of the grocery trade is done by independent stores. Conversely, large chain grocery stores dominate in Ontario and the Prairies.

Alan's brand, Guard, is a highly perfumed deodorant bar. His business is relatively weak in the key Ontario market. To confirm this share data, Alan calculated consumption of Guard per thousand people in each region (see Table 2).

These differences are especially interesting since per capita sales of all bar soap products are roughly equal in all provinces.

A consumer attitude and usage research study was conducted approximately a year ago. This study revealed that con-

sumer "top-of-mind" awareness of the Guard brand differed greatly across Canada. This was true despite the even—by population—expenditure of advertising funds in past years. Also, trial of Guard was low in the Maritimes, Ontario, and British Columbia (see Table 3 on next page).

The attitude portion of the research revealed that consumers who had heard of Guard were aware that its deodorant protection came mainly from a high fragrance level. This was the main selling point in the copy, and it was well communicated by Guard's advertising. The other important finding was that consumers who had tried Guard were satisfied with the product. About 70 percent of those trying Guard had repurchased the product at least twice.

Alan has also discovered that bar soap competition is especially intense in Ontario. It is Canada's largest market, and many competitors want a share of it. The chain stores are also quite aggressive in promotion and pricing—offering specials, in-store coupons, and so on. They want to move goods. And because of this, two key Ontario chains have put Guard on their pending delisting sheets. These chains, which control about half the grocery volume in Ontario, are dissatisfied with how slowly Guard is moving off the shelves.

Now Alan feels he is ready to set a key part of the brand's marketing plan for next year: how to allocate the advertising/sales promotion budget by region.

Table 2 Standard Cases of 3-Ounce Bars Consumed per 1,000 People in 12 Months

	Maritimes	Quebec	Ontario	Manitoba/Saskatchewan	Alberta	British Columbia
Guard	4.1	10.9	1.9	8.1	4.1	6.2
Sales index	66	175	31	131	131	100

Table 3 Usage Results (in percent)

	Maritimes	Quebec	Ontario	Manitoba/ Saskatchewan	Alberta	British Columbia
Respondents aware of Guard	20%	58%	28%	30%	32%	16%
Respondents ever trying Guard	3	18	2	8	6	4

Guard's present advertising/sales promotion budget is 20 percent of sales. With forecast sales of $4 million, this would amount to an $800,000 expenditure. Traditionally such funds have been allocated in proportion to population (see Table 4).

Alan feels he should spend more heavily in Ontario where the grocery chain delisting problem exists. Last year, 36 percent of Guard's budget was allocated to Ontario, which accounted for only 12 percent of Guard's sales. Alan wants to increase Ontario spending to 48 percent of the total budget by taking funds evenly from all other areas. Alan expects this will increase business in the key Ontario market, which has over a third of Canada's population, because it is a big increase and will help Guard "outshout" the many other competitors who are promoting heavily.

Alan presented this idea to Wendy, his newly appointed group product manager. Wendy strongly disagrees. She has also been reviewing Guard's business and feels that promotion funds have historically been misallocated. It is her strong belief that, to use her words, "A brand should spend where its business is." Wendy believes that the first priority in allocating funds regionally is to support the areas of strength. She suggested to Alan that there may be more business to be had in the brand's strong areas, Quebec and the Prairies, than in chasing sales in Ontario. The needs and attitudes toward Guard, as well as competitive pressures, may vary a lot among the provinces. Therefore, Wendy suggested that spending for Guard in the coming year be proportional to the brand's sales by region rather than to regional population.

Alan is convinced this is wrong, particularly in light of the Ontario situation. He asked Wendy how the Ontario market should be handled. Wendy said that the conservative way to build business in Ontario is to invest incremental promotion funds. However, before these incremental funds are invested, a test of this Ontario investment proposition should be conducted. Wendy recommended that some of the Ontario money should be used to conduct an investment-spending

market test in a small area or town in Ontario for 12 months. This will enable Alan to see if the incremental spending results in higher sales and profits—profits large enough to justify higher spending. In other words, an investment payout should be assured before spending any extra money in Ontario. Similarly, Wendy would do the same kind of test in Quebec—to see if more money should go there.

After several e-mails back and forth, Alan feels this approach would be a waste of time and unduly cautious, given the importance of the Ontario market and the likely delistings in two key chains.

Evaluate the present strategy for Guard and Alan's and Wendy's proposed strategies How should the promotion money be allocated? Should investment-spending market tests be run first? Why? Explain.

33. Bushman & Associates

The partners of Bushman & Associates are having a serious discussion about what the firm should do in the near future.

Bushman & Associates (BA) is a medium-size regional certified public accounting firm based in Grand Rapids, Michigan, with branch offices in Lansing and Detroit. Bushman & Associates has nine partners and a professional staff of approximately 105 accountants. Gross service billings for the fiscal year ending June 30, 2003, were $6.9 million. Financial data for 2003, 2002, and 2001 are presented in Table 1.

BA's professional services include auditing, tax preparation, bookkeeping, and some general management consulting. Its client base includes municipal governments (cities, villages, and townships), manufacturing companies, professional organizations (attorneys, doctors, and dentists), and various

Table 4 Allocation of Advertising/Sales Promotion Budget, by Population

	Maritimes	Quebec	Ontario	Manitoba/ Saskatchewan	Alberta	British Columbia	Canada
Percent of population	10%	27%	36%	8%	8%	11%	100%
Possible allocation of budget based on population (in 000s)	$80	$216	$288	$64	$64	$88	$800
Percent of Guard business at present	7%	51%	12%	11%	11%	8%	100%

Table 1 Fiscal Year Ending June 30

	2003	2002	2001
Gross billings	$6,900,000	$6,400,000	$5,800,000
Gross billings by service area:			
Auditing	3,100,000	3,200,000	2,750,000
Tax preparation	1,990,000	1,830,000	1,780,000
Bookkeeping	1,090,000	745,000	660,000
Other	720,000	625,000	610,000
Gross billings by client industry:			
Municipal	3,214,000	3,300,000	2,908,000
Manufacturing	2,089,000	1,880,000	1,706,000
Professional	1,355,000	1,140,000	1,108,000
Other	242,000	80,000	78,000

other small businesses. A good share of revenue comes from the firm's municipal practice. Table 1 gives BA's gross revenue by service area and client industry for 2003, 2002, and 2001.

At the monthly partners' meeting held in July 2003, Pat Hogan, the firm's managing partner (CEO), expressed concern about the future of the firm's municipal practice. Hogan's presentation to his partners appears below:

> Although our firm is considered to be a leader in municipal auditing in our geographic area, I am concerned that as municipals attempt to cut their operating costs, they will solicit competitive bids from other public accounting firms to perform their annual audits. Three of the four largest accounting firms in the world have local offices in our area. Because they concentrate their practice in the manufacturing industry—which typically has December 31 fiscal year-ends—they have "available" staff during the summer months.
>
> Therefore, they can afford to low-ball competitive bids to keep their staffs busy and benefit from on-the-job training provided by municipal clientele. I am concerned that we may begin to lose clients in our most established and profitable practice area.*

Ann Yost, a senior partner in the firm and the partner in charge of the firm's municipal practice, was the first to respond to Pat Hogan's concern.

> Pat, we all recognize the potential threat of being underbid for our municipal work by our large accounting competitors. However, BA is a leader in municipal auditing in Michigan, and we have much more local experience than our competitors. Furthermore, it is a fact that we offer a superior level of service to our clients—which goes beyond the services normally expected during an audit to include consulting on financial and other operating issues. Many of our less sophisticated clients depend on our nonaudit consulting assistance. Therefore, I believe, we have been successful in differentiating our services

*Organizations with December fiscal year-ends require audit work to be performed during the fall and in January and February. Those with June 30 fiscal year-ends require auditing during the summer months.

from our competitors. In many recent situations, BA was selected over a field of as many as 10 competitors even though our proposed prices were much higher than those of our competitors.

The partners at the meeting agreed with Ann Yost's comments. However, even though BA had many success stories regarding their ability to retain their municipal clients—despite being underbid—they had lost three large municipal clients during the past year. Ann Yost was asked to comment on the loss of those clients. She explained that the lost clients are larger municipalities with a lot of in-house financial expertise and therefore less dependent on BA's consulting assistance. As a result, BA's service differentiation went largely unnoticed. Ann explained that the larger, more sophisticated municipals regard audits as a necessary evil and usually select the low-cost reputable bidder.

Pat Hogan then requested ideas and discussion from the other partners at the meeting. One partner, Joe Reid, suggested that BA should protect itself by diversifying. Specifically, he felt a substantial practice development effort should be directed toward manufacturing. He reasoned that since manufacturing work would occur during BA's off-season, BA could afford to price very low to gain new manufacturing clients. This strategy would also help to counter (and possibly discourage) low-ball pricing for municipals by the three large accounting firms mentioned earlier.

Another partner, Bob LaMott, suggested that "if we have consulting skills, we ought to promote them more, instead of hoping that the clients will notice and come to appreciate us. Further, maybe we ought to be more aggressive in calling on smaller potential clients."

Another partner, John Smith, agreed with LaMott, but wanted to go further. He suggested that they recognize that there are at least two types of municipal customers and that two (at least) different strategies be implemented, including lower prices for auditing only for larger municipal customers and/or higher prices for smaller customers who are buying consulting too. This caused a big uproar from some who said this would lead to price-cutting of professional services and BA didn't want to be price cutters: "One price for all is the professional way."

However, another partner, Megan Cullen, agreed with John Smith and suggested they go even further—pricing consulting services separately. In fact, she suggested that the partners consider setting up a separate department for consulting—like the large accounting firms have done. This can be very profitable business. But it is a different kind of business and eventually may require different kinds of people and a different organization. For now, however, it may be desirable to appoint a manager for consulting services—with a budget—to be sure it gets proper attention. This suggestion too caused serious disagreement. Partners pointed out that having a separate consulting arm had led to major conflicts, especially in some larger accounting firms. The initial problems were internal. The consultants often brought in more profit than the auditors, but the auditors controlled the partnership and the successful consultants didn't always feel that they got their share of the rewards. But there had also been serious external problems and charges of unethical behavior based on the concern that big accounting firms had a conflict of interest when they did audits on publicly traded companies that they in turn relied on for consulting income. Because of problems in this area, the Securities Exchange Commission created new guidelines that have changed how the big four accounting firms handle consulting. On the other hand, several partners argued that this was really an opportunity for BA because their firm handled very few companies listed with the SEC, and the conflict of interest issues didn't even apply with municipal clients.

Pat Hogan thanked everyone for their comments and encouraged them to debate these issues in smaller groups and to share ideas by e-mail before coming to a one-day retreat (in two weeks) to continue this discussion and come to some conclusions.

Evaluate BA's situation. What strategy(ies) should the partners select? Why?

34. Alumco International*

Mark Parcells, newly hired VP of marketing for Alumco International, is reviewing the firm's international distribution arrangements because they don't seem to be very well thought out. He is not sure if anything is wrong, but he feels that the company should follow a global strategy rather than continuing its current policies.

Alumco based in Atlanta, Georgia, produces finished aluminum products, such as aluminum ladders, umbrella-type clothes racks, scaffolding, and patio tables and chairs that fold flat. Sales in 2004 reached $25 million, primarily to U.S. customers.

In 2000, Alumco decided to try foreign markets. The sales manager, Bonnie Pope, believed the growing affluence of European workers would help the company's products gain market acceptance quickly.

Bonnie's first step in investigating foreign markets was to join a trade mission to Europe, a tour organized by the U.S. Department of Commerce. This trade mission visited Italy, Germany, Denmark, Holland, France, and England. During this trip, Bonnie was officially introduced to leading buyers for department store chains, import houses, wholesalers, and buying groups. The two-week trip convinced Bonnie that there was ample buying power to make exporting a profitable opportunity.

On her return to Atlanta, Bonnie's next step was to obtain credit references for the firms she considered potential distributors. To those who were judged creditworthy, she sent letters expressing interest and samples, brochures, prices, and other relevant information.

The first orders were from a French wholesaler. Sales in this market totaled $70,000 in 2001. Similar success was achieved in Germany and England. Italy, on the other hand, did not produce any sales. Bonnie felt the semiluxury nature of the company's products and the lower incomes in Italy encouraged

a "making do" attitude rather than purchase of goods and services that would make life easier.

In the United States, Alumco distributes through fairly aggressive and well-organized merchant hardware distributors and buying groups, such as cooperative and voluntary hardware chains, which have taken over much of the strategy planning for cooperating producers and retailers. In its foreign markets, however, there is no recognizable pattern. Channel systems vary from country to country. To avoid mixing channels of distribution, Alumco has only one account in each country. The chosen distributor is the exclusive distributor.

In France, Alumco distributes through a wholesaler based in Paris. This wholesaler has five salespeople covering the country. The firm specializes in small housewares and has contacts with leading buying groups, wholesalers, and department stores. Bonnie is impressed with the firm's aggressiveness and knowledge of merchandising techniques.

In Germany, Alumco sells to a Hamburg-based buying group for hardware wholesalers throughout the country. Bonnie felt this group would provide excellent coverage of the market because of its extensive distribution network.

In Denmark, Alumco's line is sold to a buying group representing a chain of hardware retailers. This group recently expanded to include retailers in Sweden, Finland, and Norway. Together this group purchases goods for about 500 hardware retailers. The buying power of Scandinavians is quite high, and it is expected that Alumco's products will prove very successful there.

In the United Kingdom, Alumco uses an importer-distributor, who both buys on his own account and acts as a sales agent. This firm sells to department stores and hardware wholesalers. This firm has not done very well overall, but it has done very well with Alumco's line of patio tables and chairs.

Australia is handled by an importer who operates a chain of discount houses. It heard about Alumco from a United Kingdom contact. After extensive e-mailing, this firm discovered it could land aluminum patio furniture in Melbourne at prices competitive with Chinese imports. So it started ordering because it wanted to cut prices in a high-priced garden furniture market.

The Argentina market is handled by an American who came to the United States from Buenos Aires in search of new lines. Alumco attributes success in Argentina to the efforts of this aggressive and capable agent. He has built a sizable trade in aluminum ladders.

In Trinidad and Jamaica, Alumco's products are handled by traders who carry such diversified lines as insurance, apples, plums, and fish. They have been successful in selling aluminum ladders. This business grew out of inquiries sent to the U.S. Department of Commerce and in researching its website (www.commerce.gov), which Bonnie Pope followed up by phone.

Bonnie Pope's export policies for Alumco are as follows:

1. Product: No product modifications will be made in selling to foreign customers. This may be considered later after a substantial sales volume develops.

2. Price: The company does not publish suggested list prices. Distributors add their own markup to their landed costs. Supply prices will be kept as low as possible. This is

*Adapted from a case written by Professor Peter Banting, McMaster University, Canada.

accomplished by (a) removing advertising expenses and other strictly domestic overhead charges from price calculations, (b) finding the most economical packages for shipping (smallest volume per unit), and (c) bargaining with carriers to obtain the lowest shipping rates possible.

3. Promotion: The firm does no advertising in foreign markets. Brochures and sales literature already being used in the United States are supplied to foreign distributors, who are encouraged to adapt them or create new materials as required. Alumco will continue to promote its products by participating in overseas trade shows. These are handled by the sales manager. All inquiries are forwarded to the firm's distributor in that country.

4. Distribution: New distributors will be contacted through foreign trade shows. Bonnie Pope considers large distributors desirable. She feels, however, that they are not as receptive as smaller distributors to a new, unestablished product line. Therefore, she prefers to appoint small distributors. Larger distributors may be appointed after the company has gained a strong consumer franchise in a country.

5. Financing: Alumco sees no need to provide financial help to distributors. The company views its major contribution as providing good products at the lowest possible prices.

6. Marketing and planning assistance: Bonnie Pope feels that foreign distributors know their own markets best. Therefore, they are best equipped to plan for themselves.

7. Selection of foreign markets: The evaluation of foreign market opportunities for the company's products is based primarily on disposable income and lifestyle patterns. For example, Bonnie fails to see any market in North Africa for Alumco's products, which she thinks are of a semiluxury nature. She thinks that cheaper products such as wood ladders (often homemade) are preferred to prefabricated aluminum ladders in regions such as North Africa and Southern Europe. Argentina, on the other hand, she thinks is a more highly industrialized market with luxury tastes. Thus, Bonnie sees Alumco's products as better suited for more highly industrialized and affluent societies.

Evaluate Alumco's present foreign markets strategies Should it develop a global strategy? What strategy or strategies should Mark Parcells (the new VP of marketing) develop? Explain.

35. Sal's

Angelina Cello, manager of the Sal's store in Flint, Michigan, is trying to develop a plan for the "sick" store she just took over.

Sal's is an owner-managed pizza take-out and delivery business with three stores located in Ann Arbor, Southfield, and Flint, Michigan. Sal's business comes from telephone, fax, or walk-in orders. Each Sal's store prepares its own pizzas. In ad-

dition to pizzas, Sal's also sells and delivers a limited selection of soft drinks.

Sal's Ann Arbor store has been very successful. Much of the store's success may be due to being close to the University of Michigan campus. Most of these students live within five miles of Sal's Ann Arbor store.

The Southfield store has been moderately successful. It serves mostly residential customers in the Southfield area, a largely residential suburb of Detroit. Recently, the store advertised—using direct-mail flyers—to several office buildings within three miles of the store. The flyers described Sal's willingness and ability to cater large orders for office parties, business luncheons, and so on. The promotion was quite successful. With this new program and Sal's solid residential base of customers in Southfield, improved profitability at the Southfield location seems assured.

Sal's Flint location has had mixed results during the last three years. The Flint store has been obtaining only about half of its orders from residential delivery requests. The Flint store's new manager, Angelina Cello, believes the problem with residential pizza delivery in Flint is due to the location of residential neighborhoods in the area. Flint has several large industrial plants (mostly auto industry related) located throughout the city. Small, mostly factory-worker neighborhoods are distributed in between the various plant sites. As a result, Sal's store location can serve only two or three of these neighborhoods on one delivery run. Competition is also relevant. Sal's has several aggressive competitors who advertise heavily, distribute cents-off coupons, and offer 2-for-1 deals. This aggressive competition is probably why Sal's residential sales leveled off in the last year or so. And this competitive pressure seems likely to continue as some of this competition comes from aggressive national chains that are fighting for market share and squeezing little firms like Sal's. For now, anyway, Angelina feels she knows how to meet this competition and hold on to the present sales level.

Most of the Flint store's upside potential seems to be in serving the large industrial plants. Many of these plants work two or three shifts, five days a week. During each work shift, workers are allowed one half-hour lunch break—which usually occurs at 11 AM, 8 PM, or 2:30 AM, depending on the shift.

Generally, a customer will phone or fax from a plant about 30 minutes before a scheduled lunch break and order several (5 to 10) pizzas for a work group. Sal's may receive many orders of this size from the same plant (i.e., from different groups of workers). The plant business is very profitable for several reasons. First, a large number of pizzas can be delivered at the same time to the same location, saving transportation costs. Second, plant orders usually involve many different toppings (double cheese, pepperoni, mushrooms, hamburger) on each pizza. This results in $11 to $14 revenue per pizza. The delivery drivers also like delivering plant orders because the tips are usually $1 to $2 per pizza.

Despite the profitability of the plant orders, several factors make it difficult to serve the plant market. Sal's store is located 5 to 8 minutes from most of the plant sites, so Sal's staff must prepare the orders within 20 to 25 minutes after it receives the telephone order. Often, inadequate staff and/or oven capacity means it is impossible to get all the orders heated at the same time.

Table 1 Practical Capacities and Sales Potential of Current Equipment and Personnel

	11 AM Break	8 PM Break	2:30 AM Break	Daily Totals
Current capacity (pizzas)	48	48	48	144
Average selling price per unit	$ 12.50	$ 12.50	$ 12.50	$ 12.50
Sales potential	$600	$600	$600	$1,800
Variable cost (approximately 40 percent of selling price)*	240	240	240	720
Contribution margin of pizzas	360	360	360	1,080
Beverage sales (2 medium-sized beverages per pizza ordered at 75¢ a piece)[†]	72	72	72	216
Cost of beverages (30% per beverage)	22	22	22	66
Contribution margin of beverages	50	50	50	150
Total contribution of pizza and beverages	$410	$410	$410	$1,230

*The variable cost estimate of 40% of sales includes variable costs of delivery to plant locations.
[†]Amounts shown are not physical capacities (there is almost unlimited physical capacity), but potential sales volume is constrained by number of pizzas that can be sold.

Generally, plant workers will wait as long as 10 minutes past the start of their lunch break before ordering from various vending trucks that arrive at the plant sites during lunch breaks. (Currently, no other pizza delivery stores are in good positions to serve most plant locations and/or have chosen to compete.) But there have been a few instances when workers refused to pay for pizzas that were only five minutes late! Worse yet, if the same work group gets a couple of late orders, they are lost as future customers. Angelina Cello believes that the inconsistent profitability of the Flint store is partly the result of such lost customers.

In an effort to rebuild the plant delivery business, Angelina is considering various methods to ensure prompt customer delivery. She thinks that potential demand during lunch breaks is significantly above Sal's present capacity. Angelina also knows that if she tries to satisfy all phone or fax orders on some peak days, she won't be able to provide prompt service and may lose more plant customers.

Angelina has outlined three alternatives that may win back some of the plant business for the Flint store. She has developed these alternatives to discuss with Sal's owner. Each alternative is briefly described below:

Alternative 1: Determine practical capacities during peak volume periods using existing equipment and personnel. Accept orders only up to that capacity and politely decline orders beyond. This approach will ensure prompt customer service

and high product quality. It will also minimize losses resulting from customers' rejection of late deliveries. Financial analysis of this alternative—shown in Table 1—indicates that a potential daily contribution to profit of $1,230 could result if this alternative is implemented successfully. This would be profit before promotion costs, overhead, and net profit (or loss). Note: Any alternative will require several thousand dollars to reinform potential plant customers that Sal's has improved its service and "wants your business."

Alternative 2: Add additional equipment (one oven and one delivery car) and hire additional staff to handle peak loads. This approach would ensure timely customer delivery and high product quality as well as provide additional capacity to handle unmet demand. Table 2 is a conservative estimate of

Table 2 Capacity and Demand for Plant Customer Market

	Estimated Daily Demand	Current Daily Capacity	Proposed Daily Capacity
Pizza units (1 pizza)	320	144	300

Table 3 Cost of Required Additional Assets

	Cost	Estimated Useful Life	Salvage Value	Annual Depreciation*	Daily Depreciation[†]
Delivery car (equipped with pizza warmer)	$11,000	5 years	$1,000	$2,000	$5.71
Pizza oven	$20,000	8 years	$2,000	$2,250	$6.43

*Annual depreciation is calculated on a straight-line basis.
[†]Daily depreciation assumes a 350-day (plant production) year. All variable expenses related to each piece of equipment (e.g., utilities, gas, oil) are included in the variable cost of a pizza.

potential daily demand for plant orders compared to current capacity and proposed increased capacity. Table 3 gives the cost of acquiring the additional equipment and relevant information related to depreciation and fixed costs.

Using this alternative, the following additional pizza preparation and delivery personnel costs would be required:

	Hours Required	Cost per Hour	Total Additional Daily Cost
Delivery personnel	6	6	$36.00
Preparation personnel	8	6	48.00
			$84.00

The addition of even more equipment and personnel to handle all unmet demand was not considered in this alternative because the current store is not large enough.

Alternative 3: Add additional equipment and personnel as described in alternative 2, but move to a new location that would reduce delivery lead times to two to five minutes. This move would probably allow Sal's to handle all unmet demand— because the reduction in delivery time will provide for additional oven time. In fact, Sal's might have excess capacity using this approach.

A suitable store is available near about the same number of residential customers (including many of the store's current residential customers). The available store is slightly larger than needed. And the rent is higher. Relevant cost information on the proposed store appears next:

Additional rental expense of proposed store over current store	$ 1,600 per year
Cost of moving to new store (one-time cost)	$16,000

Angelina Cello presented the three alternatives to Sal's owner, Sal Marino. Sal was pleased that Angelina had done her homework. He decided that Angelina should make the final decision on what to do (in part because she had a profit-sharing agreement with Sal) and offered the following comments and concerns:

1. Sal agreed that the plant market was extremely sensitive to delivery timing. Product quality and pricing, although important, were of less importance.

2. He agreed that plant demand estimates were conservative. "In fact, they may be 10 to 30 percent low."

3. Sal expressed concern that under alternative 2, and especially under alternative 3, much of the store's capacity would go unused over 80 percent of the time.

4. He was also concerned that Sal's store had a bad reputation with plant customers because the prior store manager was not sensitive to timely plant delivery. So Sal suggested that Angelina develop a promotion plan to improve Sal's reputation in the plants and be sure that everyone knows that Sal's has improved its delivery service.

Evaluate Angelina's possible strategies for the Flint store's plant market. What should Angelina do? Why? Suggest possible promotion plans for your preferred strategy.

Computer-Aided Problems

GUIDE TO THE USE OF THE COMPUTER-AIDED PROBLEMS

Computer-Aided Problem Solving

Marketing managers are problem solvers who must make many decisions. Solving problems and making good decisions usually involves analysis of marketing information. Such information is often expressed in numbers—like costs, revenues, prices, and number of customers or salespeople. Most marketing managers use a computer to keep track of the numbers and speed through calculations. The computer can also make it easier to look at a problem from many different angles—for example, to see how a change in the sales forecast might impact expected sales revenue, costs, and profit.

The computer can only take a manager so far. The manager is the one who puts it all together—and it still takes skill to decide what the information means. The computer-aided problems at the end of the chapters in this text were developed by the authors to help you develop this skill. To work on the problems, you use the computer-aided problem (CAP) software that is included on the *Student CD-ROM to Accompany Basic Marketing* shrinkwrapped with this text.

The problems are short descriptions of decisions faced by marketing managers. Each description includes information to help make the decision. With each problem there are several questions for you to answer. Further, the *Learning Aid for Use with Basic Marketing* includes additional questions related to each problem.

Although you will use the computer program to do an analysis, most problems ask you to indicate what decision you would make and why. Thus, in these problems—as in the marketing manager's job—the computer is just a tool to help you make better decisions.

Each problem focuses on one or more of the marketing decision areas discussed in the corresponding chapter. The earlier problems require less marketing knowledge and are simpler in terms of the analysis involved. The later problems build on the principles already covered in the text. The problems can be used in many ways. And the same problem can be analyzed several times for different purposes. Although it is not necessary to do all of the problems or to do them in a particular order, you will probably want to start with the first problem. This practice problem is simpler than the others. In fact, you could do the calculations quite easily without a computer. But this problem will help you see how the program works and how it can help you solve the more complicated problems that come later.

Spreadsheet Analysis of Marketing Problems

Marketing managers often use spreadsheet analysis to evaluate their alternatives—and the program for the computer-aided problems does computerized spreadsheet analysis. In spreadsheet analysis, costs, revenue, and other data related to a marketing problem are organized into a data table—a spreadsheet. The spreadsheet analysis allows you to change the value of one or more of the variables in the data table—to see how each change affects the value of other variables. This is possible because the relationships among the variables are already programmed into the computer. You do not need to do any programming. Let's look at an overly simple example.

You are a marketing manager interested in the total revenue that will result from a particular marketing strategy. You are considering selling your product at $10.00 per unit. You expect to sell 100 units. In our CAP analysis, this problem might be shown in a (very simple) spreadsheet that looks like this:

Variable	Value
Selling price	$10.00
Units sold	100
Total revenue	$1,000.00

There is only one basic relationship in this spreadsheet: Total revenue is equal to the selling price multiplied by the number of units sold. If that relationship has been programmed into the computer (as it is in these problems), you can change the selling price or the number of units you expect to sell, and the program will automatically compute the new value for total revenue.

But now you can ask questions like: What if I raise the price to $10.40 and still sell 100 units? What will happen to total revenue? To get the answer, all you have to do is enter the new price in the spreadsheet, and the program will compute the total revenue for you.

You may also want to do many "what-if" analyses—for example, to see how total revenue changes over a range of prices. Spreadsheet analysis allows you to do this quickly and easily. For instance, if you want to see what happens to total revenue

as you vary the price between some minimum value (say, $8.00) and a maximum value (say, $12.00), the program will provide the results table for a what-if analysis showing total revenue for 11 different prices in the range from $8.00 to $12.00.

In a problem like this—with easy numbers and a simple relationship between the variables—the spreadsheet does not do that much work for you. You could do it in your head. But with more complicated problems, the spreadsheet makes it very convenient to more carefully analyze different alternatives or situations.

Using the Program

You don't have to know about computers or using a spreadsheet to use the computer-aided problems program. It was designed to be easy to learn and use. The Help button will give you more detailed information if you need it. But it's best to just try things out to see how it works. A mistake won't hurt anything.

You're likely to find that it's quicker and easier to just use the program than it is to read the instructions. So you may want to go ahead and install the CD-ROM on your own computer and try the practice problem now. Check the label on the CD-ROM for instructions about how to install the software. It takes just a few minutes and there's nothing to it.

The Spreadsheet Is Easy to Use

The spreadsheet software is very easy to use and specifically designed for the computer-aided problems. Like the other software on the Student CD-ROM, it follows conventions that are standard to browser programs (like Microsoft Internet Explorer or Netscape Navigator). If you have used a browser to surf the Internet, using this will be the same. Even if you have not used a browser before, using this program will make it easy for you to learn. However, if you want more general information about using Microsoft Windows software, you can review the Help file or tutorial that comes with the Windows operating system.

As with other browser-based programs, you typically use a mouse to move around in the program and select options. When you move the mouse, the cursor (which appears on your screen as an arrow) also moves. If you move the mouse so that the cursor is over one of the options on the screen and quickly press and release the left button on the mouse, the program will perform the action associated with that option. This process of using the mouse to position the cursor and then quickly pressing and releasing the left button is called "clicking" or "selecting." In these instructions, we'll refer to this often. For example, we'll say things like "click the Results button" or "select a problem from the list."

Let's use the first problem to illustrate how the program works.

Start by Selecting a Problem

When you start the *Basic Marketing* CD-ROM software, the first screen displayed is a home page with the title of the book and various options. Click on the label that says CAPs (short for computer-aided problems).

The computer-aided problem page will appear, and you will see a small window in the upper-left corner with the phrase "Choose a problem by clicking on the arrow." When you click the small arrow to the right of that label, a drop-down list of problems will appear. Select the problem you want to work (in this case, select the first one, "Revenue, Cost, and Profit Relationships").

Note: When you first select a problem, be patient while the program loads. It may take a minute or so. Once the program has loaded, calculations are immediate.

Once you select a problem, the problem description window appears. This is simply a convenient reminder of the problem description found in this text. (The assignment questions for each problem are in this book, so it's useful to have your book with you at the computer when you're working on a problem.)

Across the top of the box in which the problem description appears you will see buttons labeled Description, Spreadsheet, Results, Graph, and Calculator. After you've reviewed the problem description, click the Spreadsheet button.

Each spreadsheet consists of one or two columns of numbers. Each column and row is labeled. Look at the row and column labels carefully to see what variable is represented by the value (number) in the spreadsheet. Study the layout of the spreadsheet, and get a feel for how it organizes the information from the problem description. The spreadsheet displays the starting values for the problem. Keep in mind that sometimes the problem description does not provide as much detail about the starting values as is provided in the spreadsheet.

You will see that some of the values in the spreadsheet appear in a highlighted edit box. These are usually values related to the decision variables in the problem you are solving. You can change any value (number) that appears in one of these boxes. When you make a change, the rest of the values (numbers) in that column are recalculated to show how a change in the value of that one variable affects the others. Think about how the numbers relate to each other.

Making changes in values is easy. When the spreadsheet first appears your cursor appears as a free-floating arrow; however, when you pass the cursor over the box for the value that you want to change the cursor changes to the shape of an I-beam. When you click on the value in that box you can change it. Or to move the cursor to a value in a different box, just click on that box.

When you have selected the box with the value (number) you want to change, there are different ways to type in your new number. A good approach is to position the I-beam cursor before the first digit, and while depressing the mouse button drag the cursor across all of the digits in the number. This will highlight the entire number. Then simply type in the new number and the old one will be replaced. Alternatively, you can use other keys to edit the number. For example, you can use the backspace key to erase digits to the left of the I-beam cursor; similarly, you can use the Del key to erase digits to the right of the cursor. Or you can use the arrow keys to move the cursor to the point where you want to change part of a number. Then you just type in your change. You may want to experiment to see which of these editing approaches you like the best.

When you are finished typing the new number, press the Enter key and the other values in the spreadsheet will be recalculated to show the effect of your new value. Similarly, the other numbers will recalculate if you click on a different box after you have entered a number.

When you are typing numbers into the edit boxes, you'll probably find it most convenient to type the numbers and the decimal point with the keys on the main part of the keyboard (rather than those on the cursor control pad). For example, a price of one thousand dollars and 50 cents would be typed as 1000.50 or just 1000.5—using the number keys on the top row of the keyboard and the period key for the decimal point. *Do not type in the dollar sign or the commas to indicate thousands.* Be careful not to type the letters o or l (lowercase L) instead of the numbers 0 or 1.

Typing percent values is a possible point of confusion, since there are different ways to think about a percent. For example, "ten and a half" percent might be represented by 10.5 or .105. To avoid confusion, the program always expects you to enter percents using the first approach, which is the way percents are discussed in the problems. Thus, if you want to enter the value for ten and a half percent you would type 10.5.

To help prevent errors, each problem is programmed with a set of permitted values for each boxed field. After you click on a specific edit box, the range of permitted values is shown in the line at the bottom left corner of the spreadsheet window. It may be useful to explain what we mean by "permitted values." For example, if you accidentally type a letter when the computer program expects a number, the entry will turn red and what you typed will not be accepted. Further, the program won't allow you to enter a new value for a variable that is outside of a permitted range of values.

For example, if you try to type −10.00 as the price of a product, the entry will turn red. (It doesn't make sense to set the price as a negative number!) If you make an error, check what range of values is permitted—and then retype a new number that is in the permitted range, and press the Enter key to recompute the spreadsheet. When you have entered a permitted value, the value will no longer appear in red.

Remember that a value on the spreadsheet stays changed until you change it again. Some of the questions that accompany the problems ask you to evaluate results associated with different sets of values. It's good practice to check that you have entered all the correct values on a spreadsheet before interpreting the results.

In addition to changing values (numbers) on the spreadsheet itself, there are other options on the spreadsheet menu bar. Click the Description button to go back and review the problem description—or you can use the drop-down list again to select another problem. If you click the Results button, a new window will appear that shows the results table for a what-if analysis. We'll discuss what-if analysis after we cover printing.

Adding Your Comments and Printing

After you have done an analysis, you may want to print a copy of your results (especially if you are expected to hand in your answers to the questions that accompany the computer-aided problem). In fact, the print feature gives you the opportunity to type your name and answers right on the sheet that is printed. To use this feature, just click the printer icon while the spreadsheet is displayed with the results you want to print. A new window will open with a printable version of your analysis. You will also see an edit box area where you can type in your comments. Each comment can be up to 500 characters, and that should be plenty of space for you to type your answers to a question. Sometimes you will want to print more than one spreadsheet (each with its own comments) to answer the different questions.

Once you are satisfied with any comments you have added, you are ready to print your results. Of course, to be able to print you will need to have a printer properly hooked up to your computer and configured for Windows. *Before you select the Print button, make sure that the printer is turned on and loaded with paper!*

Results of a What-if Analysis

The Results button makes it easy for you to study in more detail the effect of changing the value of a particular variable. It systematically changes the value of one variable (which you select) and displays the effect that variable has on two other variables. You could do the same thing manually at the spreadsheet—by entering a value for a variable, checking the effect on other variables, and then repeating the process over and over again. But the manual approach is time-consuming and requires you to keep track of the results after each change. A what-if analysis does all this very quickly and presents the results table summary; you can also print or graph the results table if you wish.

Now let's take a step-by-step look at how you can get the exact what-if analysis that you want. The first step is to decide what variable (value) you want to vary and what result values you want to see in the results table.

You select the variables for your analysis by simply clicking the circle ("radio button") beside the number of interest. Click the radio button beside the value of the variable in an edit box that you want to vary. The radio button for the selected value is filled in. You can only select one variable to vary at a time. So if you want to vary some other variable, simply click on your new selection.

When you select a value to vary, the program computes a default "suggested" minimum value and maximum value for the range over which that variable may vary. The minimum value is usually 20 percent smaller than the value shown on the spreadsheet, and the maximum value is 20 percent larger. These default values are used as the minimum and maximum values to compute the results table for a what-if analysis (when you click the Results button).

You can also select the two variables that you want to display in the results table of the what-if analysis. Typically, you will want to display the results (computed values) for variables that will be affected by the variable you select to vary. Remember the example we used earlier. If you had specified that price was going to vary, you might want to display total revenue—to see how it changes at different price levels.

You select a variable to display in the same way that you select the variable you are going to vary. Simply click on the radio button beside a number on the spreadsheet that is not in an edit box. Then use this approach to select a second variable

to be displayed in the results table. If you change your mind, you can click on the radio button for another variable. When you have completed this step, you will see a solid radio button next to the variable you chose to vary and solid radio buttons next to the two variables that you want to display.

Now you can let the computer take over. On the button bar at the top of the spreadsheet window, click the Results button and the results table for the what-if analysis will appear. Each row in the first column of the results table will show a different value for the variable you wanted to vary. The minimum value will be in the first row. The maximum value will be in the bottom row. Evenly spaced values between the minimum and maximum will be in the middle rows. The other columns show the calculated results for the values you selected to display. Each column of values is labeled at the top to identify the column and row from the spreadsheet. The row portion of the label is a short version of the label from the spreadsheet. The results are based on the values that were in the spreadsheet when you selected the Results button, except for the value you selected to vary.

After the results table is displayed, you have the option to type in your own minimum value and maximum value in the edit boxes below the results table. To do that, just use the same approach you used to enter new values in the spreadsheet. When you enter a new minimum or maximum, the results table will be updated based on the new range of values between the minimum and maximum you entered.

At this point you will want to study the results of your analysis. You can also print a copy of the results table by clicking the Print button. The button bar also shows other possibilities. For example, if you select the Spreadsheet button, the spreadsheet will reappear. The radio buttons will still show the values you selected in the previous analysis. From there you can make additional changes in the values in the spreadsheet, check the results table for a new what-if analysis, or select another problem to work. Or you can look at (and print) a graph of values in the results table for the what-if analysis.

Viewing a Graph of Your Results

You can create a graph of values in the results table by clicking the Graph button. The horizontal axis for the graph will be the variable in the first column of the display. The vertical axis on the left side is based on the first variable you selected to display in the results table. The vertical axis on the right side of the graph is for the second variable. There will be a line on the graph that corresponds to each axis.

What to Do Next

The next section gives additional tips on the program. You will probably want to look through it after you have done some work with the practice problem. For now, however, you're probably tired of reading instructions. So work a problem or two. It's easier and faster to use the program than to read about it. Give it a try, and don't be afraid to experiment. If you have problems, remember that the Help button is available when you need it.

Some Tips on Using the CAP Program

Resetting the Spreadsheet to the Initial Values

The initial spreadsheet for each problem gives the "starting values" for the problem. While working a problem, you will often change one or more of the starting values to a new number. A changed value stays in effect, unless you change it again. This is a handy feature. But after you make several changes, you may not be able to remember the starting values. There is a simple solution—you can click the button to return to the home page, then click the CAPs label again, and reselect the problem you want. The spreadsheet will appear with the original set of starting values.

Checking the Computer's Calculations

Some values appear in the spreadsheet as whole numbers, and others appear with one or more digits to the right of a decimal point. For example, dollar values usually have two digits to the right of the decimal point, indicating how many cents are involved. A value indicating, say, number of customers, however, will appear as a whole number.

When you are doing arithmetic by hand, or with a calculator, you sometimes have to make decisions about how much detail is necessary. For example, if you divide 13 by 3 the answer is 4.33, 4.333, 4.3333, or perhaps 4.33333, depending on how important it is to be precise. Usually we round off the number to keep things manageable. Similarly, computers usually display results after rounding off the numbers. This has the potential to create confusion and seeming inaccuracy when many calculations are involved. If the computer uses a lot of detail in its calculations and then displays intermediate results after rounding off, the numbers may appear to be inconsistent.

To illustrate this, let's extend the example. If you multiply 4.33 times 2640, you get 11431.20. But if you multiply 4.333 by 2640, you get 11439.12. To make it easier for you to check relationships between the values on a spreadsheet, the CAP software does not use a lot of hidden detail in calculations. If it rounds off a number to display it in the spreadsheet, the rounded number is used in subsequent calculations. It would be easy for the computer to keep track of all of the detail in its calculations—but that would make it harder for you to check the results yourself. If you check the results on a spreadsheet (perhaps with the calculator provided) and find that your numbers are close but do not match exactly, it is probably because you are making different decisions about rounding than were programmed into the spreadsheet.

The software was designed and tested to be easy to use and error free. In fact, it is programmed to help prevent the user from making typing errors. But it is impossible to anticipate every possible combination of numbers you might enter—and some combinations of numbers can cause problems. For example, a certain combination of numbers might result in an instruction for the computer to divide a number by zero, which is a mathematical impossibility. When a problem of this sort occurs, the word ERROR will appear in the spreadsheet (or in the results table for the what-if analysis) instead of a number. If this happens, you should recheck the numbers in the spreadsheet and redo the analysis—to make certain that the numbers you typed in were what you intended. That should straighten out the problem in almost every case. Yet with any computer program there can be a hidden bug that only surfaces in unusual situations or on certain computers. Thus, if you think you have found a bug, we would like to know so that we can track down the source of the difficulty.

Notes

CHAPTER 1

1. For more on Starbucks, see "The Virtually Cashless Society," *Business Week*, November 17, 2003, p. 125; "Starbucks Unwired," *Business Week*, November 10, 2003, pp. A20–A21; "Starbucks Brews Up New Prepaid Card," *USA Today*, October 13, 2003, p. 2B; "Not a Johnny-Come-Latte," *USA Today*, September 9, 2003, p. 3B; "Starbucks Gives Chile a Chance to Wake Up and Smell the Coffee," *The Wall Street Journal*, August 27, 2003, p. B3A; "At Starbucks, the Future Is in Plastic," *Business 2.0*, August 2003, p. 56; "Tea, Coffee Energizing Multiple Retail Segments," *Food Retailing Today*, July 21, 2003, p. 10; "Starbucks' Road to China," *The Wall Street Journal*, July 14, 2003, p. B1; "In Japan, Adding Beer, Wine to Latte List," *The Wall Street Journal*, July 14, 2003, p. B1; "Another Overpriced Coffee Option," *The Wall Street Journal*, June 17, 2003, p. D1; "We've Jumped the Shark," *Brandweek*, June 2, 2003, p. 28; "Starbucks Adds Buzz to DoubleShot, Frappuccino Drinks with New Push," *Brandweek*, May 12, 2003, p. 9; "Mr. Coffee," *Fortune*, April 14, 2003, p. 139; "Marketers of the Next Generation," *Brandweek*, April 7, 2003, p. 40; "Chain Brewing Rewards for Latte Lovers," *Investor's Business Daily*, April 2, 2003, p. A6; "America's Most Admired Companies," *Fortune*, March 3, 2003, p. 87; "Starbucks Plans to Offer Its Own Credit Card in Fall," *The New York Times*, February 21, 2003, p. C6; "Wi-Fi Connects as a Marketing Tool," *Advertising Age (Special Report Technology Marketing)*, January 27, 2003, p. S2; "Counting Beans: Despite the Jitters, Most Coffeehouses Survive Starbucks," *The Wall Street Journal*, September 24, 2002, p. A1; "Starbucks' Asian Tea Party," *Business Week*, September 23, 2002, p. 14; "Planet Starbucks," *Business Week*, September 9, 2002, p. 100; "Starbucks May Indeed Be a Robust Staple," *The Wall Street Journal*, July 26, 2002, p. B4; "Starbucks Corp. Overseas Growth Plan Should Have Its Perks," *Investor's Business Daily*, June 14, 2002, p. A7; "Starbucks Goes to Europe . . . with Humility and Respect," *The Wall Street Journal*, April 9, 2002, p. B16; "The Best Global Brands," *Business Week*, August 6, 2001, p. 56; "Starbucks Fills Asia's Cup," *USA Today*, June 7, 2000, p. 10B; "Now, Starbucks Uses Its Bean," *Business Week*, February 14, 2000, p. 92; "Trouble Brewing," *Newsweek*, July 19, 1999, p. 40; "Battle Grounds," *Inc.*, July 1999, p. 52; "Still Perking after All These Years," *Fortune*, May 24, 1999, p. 203; "Starbucks.com Will Let Coffee Drinkers Get Wired," *Brandweek*, April 27, 1998, p. 33; "Starbucks: Making Values Pay," *Fortune*, September 29, 1997, p. 261; "Restaurant Brands Fill Supermarkets," *USA Today*, August 26, 1997, p. 1B.

2. Eric H. Shaw, "A Review of Empirical Studies of Aggregate Marketing Costs and Productivity in the United States," *Journal of the Academy of Marketing Science*, Fall, 1990, p. 285; Christopher H. Lovelock and Charles B. Weinberg, *Marketing for Public and Nonprofit Managers* (New York: John Wiley & Sons, 1984).

3. Gregory D. Upah and Richard E. Wokutch, "Assessing Social Impacts of New Products: An Attempt to Operationalize the Macromarketing Concept," *Journal of Public Policy and Marketing* 4 (1985), p. 166.

4. An American Marketing Association committee developed a similar—but more complicated—definition of marketing: "Marketing is the process of planning and executing conception, pricing, promotion, and distribution of ideas, goods, and services to create exchanges that satisfy individual and organizational objectives." See *Marketing News*, March 1, 1985, p. 1. See also Ernest F. Cooke, C. L. Abercrombie, and J. Michael Rayburn, "Problems With the AMA's New Definition of Marketing Offer

Opportunity to Develop an Even Better Definition," *Marketing Educator*, Spring 1986, p. 1.

5. George Fisk, "Editor's Working Definition of Macromarketing," *Journal of Macromarketing* 2, no. 1 (1982), p. 3; Shelby D. Hunt and John J. Burnett, "The Macromarketing/ Micromarketing Dichotomy: A Taxonomical Model," *Journal of Marketing*, Summer 1982, p. 11.

6. William McInnes, "A Conceptual Approach to Marketing," in *Theory in Marketing*, second series, ed. Reavis Cox, Wroe Alderson, and Stanley J. Shapiro (Homewood, IL: Richard D. Irwin, 1964), p. 51.

7. Fang Wu, Vijay Mahajan, and Sridhar Balasubramanian, "An Analysis of E-Business Adoption and its Impact on Business Performance," *Journal of the Academy of Marketing Science*, Fall 2003, p. 425; Peter R. Dickson, "Understanding the Trade Winds: the Global Evolution of Production, Consumption, and the Internet," *Journal of Consumer Research*, June 2000, p. 115; Hans H. Bauer, Mark Grether, and Mark Leach, "Building Customer Relations over the Internet," *Industrial Marketing Management*, February 2002, p. 155; Roger A. Layton, "Measures of Structural Change in Macromarketing Systems," *Journal of Macromarketing*, Spring 1989, p. 5.

8. Graham Hooley, Tony Cox, John Fahy, David Shipley et al. "Market Orientation in the Transition Economies of Central Europe: Tests of the Narver and Slater Market Orientation Scales," *Journal of Business Research*, December 2000, p. 273; Saeed Samiee, "Globalization, Privatization, and Free Market Economy," *Journal of the Academy of Marketing Science*, Summer 2001, p. 319; Robert A. Peterson and Ashutosh Prasad, "A General Theory of Competition: Resources, Competencies, Productivity, Economic Growth," *Journal of the Academy of Marketing Science*, Fall 2001, p. 422; Robert W. Nason and Phillip D. White, "The Visions of Charles C. Slater: Social Consequences of Marketing," *Journal of Macromarketing* 1, no. 2 (1981), p. 4.

9. Victor V. Cordell, "Effects of Public Policy on Marketing," *Journal of Macromarketing*, Spring 1993, p. 20; James M. Carman and Robert G. Harris, "Public Regulation of Marketing Activity, Part III: A Typology of Regulatory Failures and Implications for Marketing and Public Policy," *Journal of Macromarketing*, Spring 1986, p. 51.

10. "Making Sense of India," *Newsweek*, August 4, 1997, p. 41; "In Rural India, Video Vans Sell Toothpaste, and Shampoo," *The Wall Street Journal*, January 10, 1996, p. B1. See also "Good Reason for Smiles: Colgate Brings Dental Care to Brazilian Indian Tribes, Ravages of Tobacco and Rice," *The Wall Street Journal*, July 23, 2003, p. B1.

11. Dave Webb, Cynthia Webster, and Areti Krepapa, "An Exploration of the Meaning and Outcomes of a Customer-Defined Market Orientation," *Journal of Business Research*, May 2000, p. 101; Jagdish N. Sheth, Rajendra S. Sisodia, and Arun Sharma, "The Antecedents and Consequences of Customer-Centric Marketing," *Journal of the Academy of Marketing Science*, Winter 2000, p. 55; Ken Matsuno, John T. Mentzer, and Aysegul Ozsomer, "The Effects of Entrepreneurial Proclivity and Market Orientation on Business Performance," *Journal of Marketing*, July 2002, p. 18; Karen Norman Kennedy, Jerry R. Goolsby, and Eric J. Arnould, "Implementing a Customer Orientation: Extension of Theory and Application," *Journal of Marketing*, October 2003, p. 67; Karen Norman Kennedy, Felicia G. Lassk, and Jerry R. Goolsby, "Customer Mind-Set of Employees Throughout the Organization," *Journal of the Academy of Marketing Science*, Spring 2002, p. 159. See also Charles R. Weiser,

"Championing the Customer," *Harvard Business Review*, November–December 1995, p. 113; Stanley F. Slater and John C. Narver, "Market Orientation and the Learning Organization," *Journal of Marketing*, July 1995, p. 63; Regina F. Maruca, "Getting Marketing's Voice Heard," *Harvard Business Review*, January–February 1998, p. 10; Christine Steinman, "Beyond Market Orientation: When Customers and Suppliers Disagree," *Journal of the Academy of Marketing Science*, Winter 2000, p. 109; R.W. Ruekert, "Developing a Market Orientation: An Organizational Strategy Perspective," *International Journal of Research in Marketing*, August 1992, p. 225; George J. Avlonitis and Spiros P. Gounaris, "Marketing Orientation and Company Performance: Industrial Vs. Consumer Goods Companies," *Industrial Marketing Management*, September 1997, p. 385; Bernard J. Jaworski and Ajay K. Kohli, "Market Orientation: Antecedents and Consequences," *Journal of Marketing*, July 1993, p. 53; Franklin S. Houston, "The Marketing Concept: What It Is and What It Is Not," *Journal of Marketing*, April 1986, p. 81.

12. For more on the marketing concept in the banking industry, see "Service Charge: As Banks Elbow for Consumers, Washington Mutual Thrives," *The Wall Street Journal*, November 6, 2003, p. A1; "Is This Any Way to Run a Bank?" *Business Week*, October 13, 2003, p. 44; "The Hot News in Banking: Bricks and Mortar," *Business Week*, April 21, 2003, p. 83; "Bank of the Americas," *Fortune*, April 14, 2003, p. 144; "A New Banking Model," *Fortune*, March 31, 2003, p. 102; "Doral Financial: Bank Grows New York Business by Luring One Client at a Time," *Investor's Business Daily*, March 27, 2003, p. A6; "Putting Banks in Touch with Their Retailer Side," *The New York Times*, March 9, 2003, Sect. 3, p. 4; "Buy a Toaster, Open a Bank Account," *Business Week*, January 13, 2003, p. 54; "Welcome to the Un-Bank," *Brandweek*, November 4, 2002, p. 28; "Do You Really Need a Bank?" *The Wall Street Journal*, July 10, 2002, p. D1; "Why Banks Are Getting Nicer," *The Wall Street Journal*, May 29, 2002, p. D1; "A Mini-Mall in Your ATM," *Time*, April 8, 2002, p. 61; "Commerce Bancorp: It's a Bank, It's a Retail Firm, It's . . . Both?" *Investor's Business Daily*, February 4, 2002, p. A10; "Branching Out," *Business 2.0*, November 2001, p. 137; "Altering Course, Banks Welcome Check Cashers," *The Wall Street Journal*, July 6, 2001, p. B1; "Banks Cozy Up to Customers," *The Wall Street Journal*, April 26, 2001, p. B1. For more on the marketing concept and churches, see "The Glorious Rise of Christian Pop," *Newsweek*, July 16, 2001, p. 38; "God, Mammon and 'Bibleman,'" *Newsweek*, July 16, 2001, pp. 44–48: "Religious Advertising Converts, Moving Toward a Tougher Sell," *The Wall Street Journal*, February 24, 1998, p. B2. For more on the marketing concept and the academic community, see "Cash-Cow Universities," *Business Week*, November 17, 2003, p. 70; "The New U: A Tough Market Is Reshaping Colleges," *Business Week*, December 22, 1997, p. 96; "Some Small Colleges Hire Recruiters to Get Bigger Freshman Class," *The Wall Street Journal*, September 5, 1995, p. A1. For more on the marketing concept and the dental and medical professions, see "Massaging More than Your Gums," *The Wall Street Journal*, September 11, 2002, p. D1; "Hospitals Use TV Spots to Boost Business," *The Wall Street Journal*, September 26, 1996, p. B10; "Rx: Thirty Minutes on the StairMaster Twice Weekly," *Newsweek*, March 17, 1997, p. 46; "Offering Aerobics, Karate, Aquatics, Hospitals Stress Business of 'Wellness,'" *The Wall Street Journal*, August 9, 1993, p. B1. See also Gary D. Hailey, "The Federal Trade Commission, the Supreme Court and Restrictions on Professional Advertising," *International Journal of Advertising* 8, no. 1 (1989), p. 1.

13. "Remedies for an Economic Hangover," *Fortune*, June 25, 2001, p. 130; "The Best Little Grocery Store in America," *Inc.*, June 2001, p. 54; "Fanatics!" *Inc.*, April 2001, p. 36; "Internet Nirvana," *Ecompany*, December 2000, p. 99; "Why Women Find Lauder Mesmerizing," *Fortune*, May 25, 1998, p. 96; "Smart Managing: The Power of Reflection," *Fortune*, November 24, 1997, p. 291; "Why Some Customers Are More Equal than Others," *Fortune*, September 19, 1994, p. 215. See also Youn-Kyung Kim, "Consumer Value: an Application to Mall and Internet Shopping," *International Journal of Retail & Distribution Management*, (11) 2002, p. 595; Jillian C. Sweeney and Geoffrey N. Soutar,

"Consumer Perceived Value: the Development of a Multiple Item Scale," *Journal of Retailing*, Summer 2001, p. 203; Ronald L. Hess, Jr. Shankar Ganesan, and Noreen M. Klein, "Service Failure and Recovery: the Impact of Relationship Factors on Customer Satisfaction," *Journal of the Academy of Marketing Science*, Spring 2003, p. 127; Ziv Carmon and Dan Ariely, "Focusing on the Forgone: How Value Can Appear So Different to Buyers and Sellers," *Journal of Consumer Research*, December 2000, p. 360; Mihaly Csikszentmihalyi, "The Costs and Benefits of Consuming," *Journal of Consumer Research*, September 2000, p. 267; Jaishankar Ganesh, Mark J. Arnold, and Kristy E. Reynolds, "Understanding the Customer Base of Service Providers: an Examination of the Differences Between Switchers and Stayers," *Journal of Marketing*, July 2000, p. 65; Wolfgang Ulaga and Samir Chacour, "Measuring Customer-Perceived Value in Business Markets: a Prerequisite for Marketing Strategy Development and Implementation," *Industrial Marketing Management*, August 2001, p. 525; Maria Jose Sanzo, Maria Leticia Santos, Rodolfo Vazquez and Luis Ignacio Alvarez, "The Effect of Market Orientation on Buyer-Seller Relationship Satisfaction," *Industrial Marketing Management*, May 2003, p. 327; C. B. Bhattacharya and Sankar Sen, "Consumer-Company Identification: a Framework for Understanding Consumers' Relationships with Companies," *Journal of Marketing*, April 2003, p. 76; George S. Day, "Managing Market Relationships," *Journal of the Academy of Marketing Science*, Winter 2000, p. 24; Deepak Sirdeshmukh, Jagdip Singh and Barry Sabol, "Consumer Trust, Value, and Loyalty in Relational Exchanges," *Journal of Marketing*, January 2002, p. 15; Denise D. Schoenbachler and Geoffrey L. Gordon, "Trust and Customer Willingness to Provide Information in Database-Driven Relationship Marketing," *Journal of Interactive Marketing*, Summer 2002, p. 2; Stanley F. Slater and John C. Narver, "Market Orientation, Customer Value, and Superior Performance," *Business Horizons*, March–April 1994, p. 22; Sharon E. Beatty, "Keeping Customers," *Journal of Marketing*, April 1994, p. 124; Thomas W. Gruen, "Relationship Marketing: The Route to Marketing Efficiency and Effectiveness," *Business Horizons*, November–December 1997, p. 32; Diana L. Deadrick, R. B. McAfee, and Myron Glassman, "'Customers for Life': Does It Fit Your Culture?" *Business Horizons*, July–August 1997, p. 11.

14. Available from World Wide Web: <http://www.llbean. com>; "Entrepreneur L.L. Bean Never Sold Out," *Investor's Business Daily*, October 8, 2001, p. A6; "L.L. Bean Scales Back Expansion Goals to Ensure Pride in Its Service Is Valid," *The Wall Street Journal*, July 31, 1989, p. B3.

15. "Dot-Com Decline Turns into Lift for the Dot-Orgs," *The Wall Street Journal*, March 12, 2001, p. B1; "With Recruiting Slow, the Air Force Seeks a New Ad Campaign," *The Wall Street Journal*, February 14, 2001, p. A1; "Big Retailers Cutting into Nonprofits' Tree Sales," *The Wall Street Journal*, December 19, 2000, p. B1; "When Nonprofits Go After Profits," *Business Week*, June 26, 2000, p. 173; "Army Enlists Net to Be All It Can Be," *USA Today*, April 19, 2000, p. 10B; "Modern Marketing Helps Sell Life as a Nun," *The Wall Street Journal*, May 11, 1999, p. B1; "Charities Draw Younger Donors with Hip Events and Door Prizes," *The Wall Street Journal*, April 25, 1994, p. B1. See also Thomas W. Gruen, John O. Summers, and Frank Acito, "Relationship Marketing Activities, Commitment, and Membership Behaviors in Professional Associations," *Journal of Marketing*, July 2000, p. 34; Glenn B. Voss and Zannie Giraud Voss, "Strategic Orientation and Firm Performance in an Artistic Environment," *Journal of Marketing*, January 2000, p. 67; Dennis B. Arnett, Steve D. German and Shelby D. Hunt, "The Identity Salience Model of Relationship Marketing Success: the Case of Nonprofit Marketing," *Journal of Marketing*, April 2003, p. 89; William A. Sutton, "Sports Marketing: Competitive Business Strategies for Sports," *Journal of the Academy of Marketing Science*, Spring 1996, p. 176; Russell W. Jones, Carolyn Marshall, and Thomas P. Bergman, "Can a Marketing Campaign Be Used to Achieve Public Policy Goals?" *Journal of Public Policy & Marketing*, Spring 1996, p. 98; C. Scott Greene and Paul Miesing, "Public Policy, Technology, and Ethics: Marketing Decisions for NASA's Space Shuttle," *Journal of*

Marketing, Summer 1984, p. 56; Alan R. Andreasen, "Nonprofits: Check Your Attention to Customers," *Harvard Business Review*, May–June 1982, p. 105.

16. "The Black Market Vs. the Ozone," *Business Week*, July 7, 1997, p. 128; "CFC-Span: Refrigerant's Reign Nears an End," *USA Today*, August 22, 1994, p. 5B; "Air-Conditioner Firms Put Chill on Plans to Phase Out Use of Chlorofluorocarbons," *The Wall Street Journal*, May 10, 1993, p. B1. See also Alan R. Andreasen, "Social Marketing: Its Definition and Domain," *Journal of Public Policy & Marketing*, Spring 1994, p. 108.

17. For more on Wal-Mart's efforts, see "Wrestling with Your Conscience," *Time*, November 15, 1999, p. 72; "Wal-Mart Provides Many an Introduction to Sport Shooting," *The Wall Street Journal*, April 15, 1999, p. A1. For more on Kmart's efforts, see "Kmart Sells Out: Ammo Sales End, under Pressure from PC Prankster," *Investor's Business Daily*, July 10, 2001, p. A18. For more on Green Mountain, see "GreenMountain.com Makes Pitch for Clean Energy," *The Wall Street Journal*, May 1, 2000, p. A36; "Energy: Green Fees," *The Wall Street Journal Reports*, September 13, 1999, p. R12. For more on overseas sweatshops, see "Sweatshops: Finally, Airing the Dirty Linen," *Business Week*, June 23, 2003, p. 100. See also Maria Piacentini, Lynn MacFadyen and Douglas Eadie, "Corporate Social Responsibility in Food Retailing," *International Journal of Retail & Distribution Management*, (11) 2000, p. 459.

18. Edward J. O'Boyle and Lyndon E. Dawson, Jr., "The American Marketing Association Code of Ethics: Instructions for Marketers," *Journal of Business Ethics*, December 1992, p. 921; Ellen J. Kennedy and Leigh Lawton, "Ethics and Services Marketing," *Journal of Business Ethics*, October 1993, p. 785; Michael R. Hyman, Robert Skipper, and Richard Tansey, "Ethical Codes Are Not Enough," *Business Horizons*, March/April, 1990, p. 15.

19. Lawrence B. Chonko and Shelby D. Hunt, "Ethics and Marketing Management: a Retrospective and Prospective Commentary," *Journal of Business Research*, December 2000, p. 235; Barry J. Babin, James S. Boles, and Donald P. Robin, "Representing the Perceived Ethical Work Climate among Marketing Employees," *Journal of the Academy of Marketing Science*, Summer 2000, p. 345; Peter J. Vander Nat and William W. Keep, "Marketing Fraud: an Approach for Differentiating Multilevel Marketing from Pyramid Schemes," *Journal of Public Policy & Marketing*, Spring 2002, p. 139; Jeffrey G. Blodgett, Long-Chuan Lu, Gregory M. Rose, and Scott J. Vitell, "Ethical Sensitivity to Stakeholder Interests: a Cross-Cultural Comparison," *Journal of the Academy of Marketing Science*, Spring 2001, p. 190; George G. Brenkert, "Ethical Challenges of Social Marketing," *Journal of Public Policy & Marketing*, Spring 2002, p. 14; Stanley J. Shapiro, "Ethical Decision Making in Marketing," *Journal of Public Policy & Marketing*, Fall 1996, p. 321; Oswald A. Mascarenhas, "Exonerating Unethical Marketing Executive Behaviors: A Diagnostic Framework," *Journal of Marketing*, April 1995, p. 43. For a discussion of some criticisms of advertising, see Banwari Mittal, "Public Assessment of TV Advertising: Faint Praise and Harsh Criticism," *Journal of Advertising Research*, January/February 1994, p. 35.

20. "Too Much Corporate Power?" *Business Week*, September 11, 2000, p. 144; "Ad Nauseam," *Advertising Age*, July 10, 2000, p. 1; Stephen J. Arnold and Monika Narang Luthra, "Market Entry Effects of Large Format Retailers: a Stakeholder Analysis," *International Journal of Retail & Distribution Management*, (4) 2000, p. 139.

CHAPTER 2

1. Available from World Wide Web: <http://www.dell.com>; *2003 Annual Report*, Dell; "New Products, Markets Boost Dell's Profit," *USA Today*, November 14, 2003, p. 3B; "Dell Pins Hopes on Services to Boost Profit," *The Wall Street Journal*, November 11, 2003, p. B1; "What You Don't Know about Dell," *Business Week*, November 3, 2003, p. 76; "Slowing PC Sales Drive Computer Firms' Push to Consumer Gadgets," *Investor's Business Daily*, October 8, 2003, p. A1; "Dell Wants Your

Home," *Time*, October 6, 2003, p. 48; "Dell to Dive into Consumer Electronics Market," *USA Today*, September 25, 2003, p. 1B; "Dell Blitz Surprises Printer Market," *Investor's Business Daily*, May 30, 2003, p. A4; "How IBM, Dell Managed to Build Crushing Tech Dominance," *USA Today*, May 21, 2003, p. 3B; "Dell Gets Greener," *Business Week*, May 5, 2002, p. 97; "Taking Dell's Limelight HP Unveils Printers and New Web Site," *Investor's Business Daily*, April 2, 2003, p. A4; "After the Sale," *Brandweek*, March 31, 2003, p. 20; "The Dell Way," *Business 2.0*, February 2003, p. 61; "Dell Plans to Peddle PCs Inside Sears, Other Large Chains," *The Wall Street Journal*, January 30, 2003, p. B1; "Dell Business Model Turns to Muscle as Rivals Struggle," *USA Today*, January 20, 2003, p. 1B; "How to Thrive in a Sick Economy," *Business 2.0*, January 2003, p. 88; "The Upper Hand in Handhelds?" *Business Week*, December 23, 2002, p. 20; "The 'Dude' You May Not Know," *Brandweek*, October 14, 2002, pp. M6–M11; "Dell Takes Time to Build," *USA Today*, October 10, 2002, p. 6B; "Dell Slashes Prices and Still Turns a Profit; Credit It to Planning," *Investor's Business Daily*, September 30, 2002, p. A4; "Integrated Marketing Success Stories" (Special Report), *BtoB*, June 10, 2002, p. 25; "Dell Does Domination," *Fortune*, January 21, 2002, p. 70; "The Net as a Lifeline," *Business Week E.Biz*, October 29, 2001, pp. EB16–EB23; "Dell, the Conqueror," *Business Week*, September 24, 2001, p. 92; "The Mother of All Price Wars," *Business Week*, July 20, 2001, p. 32; "How Dell Fine-Tunes Its PC Pricing to Gain Edge in a Slow Market," *The Wall Street Journal*, June 8, 2001, p. A1; "Price War Squeezes PC Makers," *The Wall Street Journal*, March 26, 2001, p. B1; "How a Low-Cost Provider like Dell also Delivers Best Customer Service," *Investor's Business Daily*, November 13, 2000, p. A1; "Going Digital? Think First," *Fortune*, November 13, 2000, p. 190; "Dell Looks for Ways to Rekindle the Fire It Had as an Upstart," *The Wall Street Journal*, August 31, 2000, p. A1; "Dell to Offer Hosting of Small-Business Web Sites," *The Wall Street Journal*, February 22, 2000, p. B23; "Dell Cracks China," *Fortune*, June 21, 1999, p. 120; "Dell Builds an Electronics Superstore on the Web," *The Wall Street Journal*, March 3, 1999, p. B1; Joan Magretta, "The Power of Virtual Integration: An Interview With Dell Computer's Michael Dell," *Harvard Business Review*, March–April 1998, p. 72; "And Give Me an Extra-Fast Modem with That, Please," *Business Week*, September 29, 1997, p. 38; "Now Everyone in PCs Wants to Be like Mike," *Fortune*, September 8, 1997, p. 91; "Dell Fights PC Wars by Emphasizing Customer Service," *The Wall Street Journal*, August 15, 1997, p. B4.

2. Charles H. Noble, Rajiv K. Sinha, and Ajith Kumar, "Market Orientation and Alternative Strategic Orientations: a Longitudinal Assessment of Performance Implications," *Journal of Marketing*, October 2002, p. 25; Mary Anne Raymond and Hiram C. Barksdale, "Corporate Strategic Planning and Corporate Marketing: Toward an Interface," *Business Horizons*, September/ October, 1989, p. 41; George S. Day, "Marketing's Contribution to the Strategy Dialogue," *Journal of the Academy of Marketing Science*, Fall 1992, p. 323; P. Rajan Varadarajan and Terry Clark, "Delineating the Scope of Corporate, Business, and Marketing Strategy," *Journal of Business Research*, October–November 1994, p. 93.

3. Available from World Wide Web: <http://www.learningco. com>; "Broderbund: Identify a Need, Turn a Profit," *Fortune*, November 30, 1992, p. 78.

4. "What Customers Want," *Fortune*, July 7, 2003, p. 122; "The Unprofitable Customers," *The Wall Street Journal Reports*, October 28, 2002, p. R7; "Will This Customer Sink Your Stock," *Fortune*, September 30, 2002, p. 126; "With the Telecom Industry on Hold, Nextel Sends Out a Different Signal," *Investor's Business Daily*, March 2, 2001, p. A1; "Keep 'Em Coming Back," *Business Week E. Biz*, May 15, 2000, p. EB20; "Marketers Put a Price on Your Life," *USA Today*, July 7, 1999, p. 3B. See also Heinz K. Stahl, Kurt Matzler, and Hans H. Hinterhuber, "Linking Customer Lifetime Value with Shareholder Value," *Industrial Marketing Management*, May 2003, p. 267; Valarie A. Zeithaml, "Service Quality, Profitability, and the Economic Worth of Customers: What We Know and What We Need to Learn," *Journal of the Academy of Marketing Science*,

727

Notes

Winter 2000, p. 67; Dipak Jain and Siddhartha S. Singh, "Customer Life-time Value Research in Marketing: a Review and Future Directions," *Journal of Interactive Marketing*, Spring 2002, p. 34; Charlotte H. Mason, "Tuscan Lifestyles: Assessing Customer Lifetime Value," *Journal of Interactive Marketing*, Autumn 2003, p. 54; Vikas Mittal, "Driving Customer Equity: How Customer Lifetime Value Is Reshaping Corporate Strategy," *Journal of Marketing*, April 2001, p. 107; Werner J. Reinartz and V. Kumar, "The Impact of Customer Relationship Characteristics on Profitable Lifetime Duration," *Journal of Marketing*, January 2003, p. 77.

5. "Genesco Names New Executive of Children's Footwear Division," *Press Release*, Genesco, July 15, 1994; "Toddler University Ends Up in Westport," *Westport News*, March 8, 1991, p. A13; "Whiz Kid," *Connecticut*, August 1989, p. 56; "The Young and the Restless," *Children's Business*, May 1989, p. 29.

6. Orville C. Walker, Jr., and Robert W. Ruekert, "Marketing's Role in the Implementation of Business Strategies: A Critical Review and Conceptual Framework," *Journal of Marketing*, July 1987, p. 15; Thomas V. Bonoma, "A Model of Marketing Implementation," *1984 AMA Educators' Proceedings* (Chicago: American Marketing Association, 1984), p. 185; Kevin Romer and Doris C. Van Doren, "Implementing Marketing in a High-Tech Business," *Industrial Marketing Management*, August 1993, p. 177.

7. *2003 Annual Report*, Gillette Company.

8. "What Was Dick Tracy's Monthly Fee," *Business Week*, October 13, 2003, p. 14; "Now, Even Your Watch Can Help You Carry Your Computer Files," *The Wall Street Journal*, September 25, 2003, p. B1; "Good Timing," *Brandweek*, September 8, 2003, p. 28; "Fossil's New Watch Has Awkward PDA, but Cool Style Feature," *The Wall Street Journal*, July 17, 2003, p. B1; "Research a Bigger Part of Microsoft Mix," *Investor's Business Daily*, June 11, 2003, p. A6; "Bill Has Designs on Your Wrist," *Business Week*, January 20, 2003, p. 68; "Are Profits in Gadgets for Sickness, or for Health?" *The Wall Street Journal*, August 10, 2001, p. B1; "For the Wrist that Has Everything," *Newsweek*, June 25, 2001, p. 80; "Now That's Good Timing," *Business Week Small Biz*, April 23, 2001, p. 14; "Movado Winds Up Lifestyle Effort, Expanded Line, with $15M in Print," *Brandweek*, April 2, 2001, p. 4; "Timex Pursues Hip, Younger Set in Ads for Its New iControl Watch," *The Wall Street Journal*, May 19, 2000, p. B2; "Swatch: Ready for Net Time," *Business Week*, February 14, 2000, p. 61; "Timex Puts 'Iron' into TV with $5M," *Brandweek*, September 22, 1997, p. 6; "Timex Back to Basics to Retro-fit Gen X," *Brandweek*, August 5, 1996, p. 3; "Swatch Adds Metal Watch," *Advertising Age*, November 7, 1994, p. 60; Benetton Readies Watch Campaign," *Brandweek*, August 8, 1994, p. 5; "Indiglo Watch Lights Up Better Times for Timex," *Brandweek*, April 25, 1994, p. 30.

9. Mark B. Houston, "Competing for the Future: Breakthrough Strategies for Seizing Control of Your Industry and Creating the Markets of Tomorrow," *Journal of the Academy of Marketing Science*, Winter 1996, p. 77; George S. Day and Robin Wensley, "Assessing Advantage: A Framework for Diagnosing Competitive Superiority," *Journal of Marketing*, April 1988, p. 1; Kevin P. Coyne, "Sustainable Competitive Advantage—What It Is, What It Isn't," *Business Horizons*, January/February 1986, p. 54; Michael E. Porter, *Competitive Advantage—Creating and Sustaining Superior Performance* (New York: Free Press, MacMillan, 1986).

10. "GM Warms Up Its Branding Iron," *Business Week*, April 16, 2001, p. 56; "GM Still Pushing Lame-Duck Oldsmobiles," *USA Today*, February 19, 2001, p. 4B; "One Last Look at Oldsmobile," *Brandweek*, January 8, 2001, p. 28; "GM: 'Out with the Olds' Is Just the Start," *Business Week*, December 25, 2000, p. 57; "After Decades of Brand Bodywork, GM Parks Oldsmobile—for Good," *The Wall Street Journal*, December 13, 2000, p. B1.

11. Available from World Wide Web: <http://www.soapworks.com>; "Taking On Procter & Gamble," *Inc.*, October 2000, p. 66.

12. Stephen J. Arnold, "Lessons Learned from the World's Best Retailers," *International Journal of Retail & Distribution Management*, (11) 2002, p. 562; Ashesh Mukherjee and Wayne D. Hoyer, "The Effect of Novel Attributes on Product Evaluation," *Journal of Consumer Research*, December 2001, p. 462; Jin K. Han, Namwoon Kim and Hong-Bumm Kim, "Entry Barriers: a Dull-, One-, or Two-Edged Sword for Incumbents? Unraveling the Paradox from a Contingency Perspective," *Journal of Marketing*, January 2001, p. 1; Douglas W. Vorhies and Neil A. Morgan, "A Configuration Theory Assessment of Marketing Organization Fit with Business Strategy and its Relationship with Marketing Performance," *Journal of Marketing*, January 2003, p. 100; Jean L. Johnson, Ruby Pui-Wan Lee, Amit Saini, and Bianca Grohmann, "Market-Focused Strategic Flexibility: Conceptual Advances and an Integrative Model," *Journal of the Academy of Marketing Science*, Winter 2003, p. 74; Ian C. MacMillan and Rita G. McGrath, "Discovering New Points of Differentiation," *Harvard Business Review*, July–August 1997, p. 133; Des Thwaites, Keith Walley, and Steve Foots, "Systematic Management of Differential Advantage," *Industrial Marketing Management*, May 1996, p. 209.

13. For more on Coleman, see "The Grill of Their Dreams," *Business 2.0*, February 2002, p. 96; "Growing to Match Its Brand Name," *Fortune*, June 13, 1994, p. 114. See also Peter C. Verhoef, "Understanding the Effect of Customer Relationship Management Efforts on Customer Retention and Customer Share Development," *Journal of Marketing*, October 2003, p. 30; Youjae Yi and Hoseong Jeon, "Effects of Loyalty Programs on Value Perception, Program Loyalty, and Brand Loyalty," *Journal of the Academy of Marketing Science*, Summer 2003, p. 229.

14. For more on E-Z-Go, see "Off-Roading, Golf-Cart Style," *The Wall Street Journal*, June 14, 2001, p. B1. For more on McDonald's, see World Wide Web: <http://www.mcdonalds.com>; *2003 Annual Report*, McDonald's; "You Want Ambiance with That?" *USA Today*, October 30, 2003, p. 3B; "Will Ratatouille Bring Japanese to McDonald's?" *The Wall Street Journal*, August 14, 2003, p. B1; "100 Innovations: McD's Tests Wi-Fi, Self-Service and 'China,'" *Advertising Age*, August 11, 2003, p. 4; "McDonald's Salads Lure Women," *USA Today*, June 16, 2003, p. 7B; "It's Back to Basics for McDonald's," *USA Today*, May 21, 2003, p. 1B; "What's This? The French Love McDonald's?" *Business Week*, January 13, 2003, p. 50; "McHaute Cuisine: Armchairs, TVs, and Espresso—Is It McDonald's?" *The Wall Street Journal*, August 30, 2002, p. A1; "How Mr. Bambang Markets Big Macs in Muslim Indonesia," *The Wall Street Journal*, October 26, 2001, p. A1; "Why You Won't Find Any Egg McMuffins for Breakfast in Brazil," *The Wall Street Journal*, October 23, 1997, p. A1; "Burger Wars Sizzle as McDonald's Clones the Whopper," *The Wall Street Journal*, September 17, 1997, p. B1. See also Michael S. Garver, "Best Practices in Identifying Customer-Driven Improvement Opportunities," *Industrial Marketing Management*, August 2003, p. 455; John H. Roberts, "Developing New Rules for New Markets," *Journal of the Academy of Marketing Science*, Winter 2000, p. 31.

15. For more on Heinz EZ Squirt, see *2003 Annual Report*, Heinz; "Heinz Picks Purple as New EZ Squirt Color," *Brandweek*, June 25, 2001, p. 7; "Kids Salivate for New, Yucky, Weirdly Colored Food," *USA Today*, April 23, 2001, p. 7B; "Do E-Ads Have a Future?" *Business Week E.Biz*, January 22, 2001, pp. EB46–EB50; "Squeezing New from Old," *USA Today*, January 4, 2001, p. 1B. For more on ski resorts, see "Bikers Give Ski Resorts Summer Time Lift," *The Wall Street Journal*, July 7, 1994, p. B1. For more on Nike, see *2003 Annual Report*, Nike; "Nike Puts Its Swoosh on MP3 Players, Walkie-Talkies, Heart Monitors," *The Wall Street Journal*, May 10, 2000, p. B1. See also Sarah J. Marsh and Gregory N. Stock, "Building Dynamic Capabilities in New Product Development Through Intertemporal Integration," *The Journal of Product Innovation Management*, March 2003, p. 136; George C. Kingston and Beebe Nelson, "Leading Product Innovation: Accelerating Growth in a Product-Based Business," *The Journal of Product Innovation Management*, November 2001, p. 414.

16. For more on McDonald's and its hotel diversification effort, see World Wide Web: <http://www.goldenarcheshotel.com>; "Would You

Like a Bed with Your Burger?" *Ad Age Global*, February 2001, p. 12; "The Golden Arches: Burgers, Fries and 4-Star Rooms," *The Wall Street Journal*, November 17, 2000, p. B1.

17. For more on Purafil, see "Small Businesses Find International Success," *USA Today*, June 30, 2000, p. 1B.

18. For more on JLG, see "The Secret of U.S. Exports: Great Products," *Fortune*, January 10, 2000, pp. 154C–J.

19. Peter N. Golder, "Insights from Senior Executives about Innovation in International Markets," *The Journal of Product Innovation Management*, September 2000, p. 326; Shaoming Zou and S. Tamer Cavusgil, "The GMS: a Broad Conceptualization of Global Marketing Strategy and its Effect on Firm Performance," *Journal of Marketing*, October 2002, p. 40; Susan P. Douglas, "Exploring New Worlds: the Challenge of Global Marketing," *Journal of Marketing*, January 2001, p. 103; Catharine M. Curran, "Selling to Newly Emerging Markets," *Journal of the Academy of Marketing Science*, Summer 2001, p. 324; "Key Ingredient in Going Global Is Acquiring Local Tastes," *USA Today*, December 2, 1997, p. 15A; Judith Clair, "International Marketing: Your Company's Next Stage of Growth," *Journal of the Academy of Marketing Science*, Summer 1997, p. 257.

CHAPTER 3

1. "Run, Carly, Run," *Business 2.0*, October 2003, p. 42; "HP Bidding to Be Key Software Provider," *Investor's Business Daily*, September 29, 2003, p. A4; "H-P Introduces Over 100 Devices, in Biggest Rollout," *The Wall Street Journal*, August 12, 2003, p. D2; "H-P Blitz Simplifies, Upgrades," *USA Today*, August 11, 2003, p. 1B; "Fiorina: Homes Are Going Digital," *USA Today*, August 11, 2003, p. 3B; "HP Buddies Up with Uncle Sam, Seeks Growth in Public Sector," *Investor's Business Daily*, July 31, 2003, p. A4; "Hewlett-Packard Looks Overseas for Ways to Spur Sales Growth," *Investor's Business Daily*, July 22, 2003, p. A6; "Can HP's Printer Biz Keep Printing Money?" *Business Week*, July 14, 2003, p. 68; "Taking Dell's Limelight HP Unveils Printers and New Web Site," *Investor's Business Daily*, April 2, 2003, p. A4; "What's Wrong with This Printer?" *Fortune*, February 17, 2003, pp. 120C–120H; "Cannibalize Your Own Products? If You Don't, Someone Else Will," *Investor's Business Daily*, January 16, 2002, p. A1.

2. Available from World Wide Web: <http://www.hallmark. com>; *2003 Annual Report*, Hallmark; "Hallmark Cards' Joyce C. Hall," *Investor's Business Daily*, October 14, 2003, p. A3; "Hallmark Hits the Mark," *USA Today*, June 14, 2001, p. 1D; "American Greetings Thinks Time for 'Anytime' Is Now," *The Wall Street Journal*, March 24, 1998, p. B9; "Old-Fashioned Sentiments Go High-Tech," *The Wall Street Journal*, November 9, 1992, p. B1.

3. Terri C. Albert, "Need-Based Segmentation and Customized Communication Strategies in a Complex-Commodity Industry: a Supply Chain Study," *Industrial Marketing Management*, May 2003, p. 281; Shelby D. Hunt and Robert M. Morgan, "Resource-Advantage Theory: A Snake Swallowing Its Tail or a General Theory of Competition?" *Journal of Marketing*, October 1997, p. 74; Stavros P. Kalafatis and Vicki Cheston, "Normative Models and Practical Applications of Segmentation in Business Markets," *Industrial Marketing Management*, November 1997, p. 519; Lisa R. Adam, "Nichecraft: Using Your Specialness to Focus Your Business, Corner Your Market, and Make Customers Seek You Out," *Journal of the Academy of Marketing Science*, Summer 1997, p. 259; George S. Day, A. D. Shocker, and R. K. Srivastava, "Customer-Oriented Approaches to Identifying Product-Markets," *Journal of Marketing*, Fall 1979, p. 8; Rajendra K. Srivastava, Mark I. Alpert, and Allan D. Shocker, "A Customer-Oriented Approach for Determining Market Structures," *Journal of Marketing*, Spring 1984, p. 32.

4. For more on Nvidia, see "Nvidia Kicks in Its 3-D Skills on TV Show," *Investor's Business Daily*, December 1, 2003, p. A5; "ATI Is Enlisted to Design Chips for Xbox Console," *The Wall Street Journal*, August 15, 2003, p. B5; "Nvidia Envisions Future beyond the 3D Computer-Games Market," *The Wall Street Journal*, April 23, 2003, p. A19; "Seven Secrets of Success," *Business 2.0*, October 2002, p. 87; "Little Niches that Grew," *Business Week*, June 18, 2001, p. 100. For more on Herman Miller, see World Wide Web: <http://www.hermanmillerred.com>; *2003 Annual Report*, Herman Miller; "A Cult Chair Gets a Makeover," *The Wall Street Journal*, September 17, 2002, p. D1; "The Net as a Lifeline," *Business Week E.Biz*, October 29, 2001, pp. EB16–EB23; "Reinventing Herman Miller," *Business Week E.Biz*, April 3, 2000, pp. EB89–EB96. See also "The Riches in Market Niches," *Fortune*, April 27, 1987, p. 227; Robert E. Linneman and John L. Stanton, Jr., "Mining for Niches," *Business Horizons*, May–June 1992, p. 43.

5. Sally Dibb and Lyndon Simkin, "Market Segmentation: Diagnosing and Treating the Barriers," *Industrial Marketing Management*, November 2001, p. 609; Terry Elrod and Russell S. Winer, "An Empirical Evaluation of Aggregation Approaches for Developing Market Segments," *Journal of Marketing*, Fall 1982, p. 32; Frederick W. Winter, "A Cost-Benefit Approach to Market Segmentation," *Journal of Marketing*, Fall 1979, p. 103.

6. Available from World Wide Web: <http://www.kaepa.com>; "Tapping into Cheerleading," *Adweek's Marketing Week*, March 2, 1992, p. 17.

7. C. Samuel Craig and Susan P Douglas, "Configural Advantage in Global Markets," *Journal of International Marketing*, (1) 2000, p. 6; Ruth N. Bolton and Matthew B. Myers, "Price-Based Global Market Segmentation for Services," *Journal of Marketing*, July 2003, p. 108; Philip A. Dover, "Segmentation and Positioning for Strategic Marketing Decisions," *Journal of the Academy of Marketing Science*, Summer 2000, p. 438; John Hogan, "Defining Your Market: Winning Strategies for High-Tech, Industrial, and Service Firms," *Journal of the Academy of Marketing Science*, Summer 2000, p. 442; Alex Chernev, "The Effect of Common Features on Brand Choice: Moderating Role of Attribute Importance," *Journal of Consumer Research*, March 1997, p. 304; Robert L. Armacost and Jamshid C. Hosseini, "Identification of Determinant Attributes Using the Analytic Hierarchy Process," *Journal of the Academy of Marketing Science*, Fall 1994, p. 383; Joel S. Dubow, "Occasion-based vs. User-based Benefit Segmentation, A Case Study," *Journal of Advertising Research*, March/April 1992, p. 11; Peter R. Dickson and James L. Ginter, "Market Segmentation, Product Differentiation, and Marketing Strategy," *Journal of Marketing*, April 1987, p. 1; Russell I. Haley, "Benefit Segmentation— 20 Years Later," *Journal of Consumer Marketing* 1, no. 2 (1984), p. 5.

8. For more on General Mills, see "General Mills Intends to Reshape Doughboy in Its Own Image," *The Wall Street Journal*, July 18, 2000, p. A1. See also "Food Marketing," *Brandweek*, April 30, 2001, p. 20.

9. "Marketers Find 'Tweens' Too Hot to Ignore," *USA Today*, July 10, 2001, p. 13A; "Yamada Card Gives Credit to Struggling Brazilians," *The Wall Street Journal*, March 27, 2001, p. B1; "Grown-Up Drinks for Tender Taste Buds," *Business Week*, March 5, 2001, p. 96; "Boosting Diageo's Spirits," *The Wall Street Journal*, February 12, 2001, p. B1; "Soda Pop That Packs a Punch," *Newsweek*, February 19, 2001, p. 45; Suzanne Benet, Robert E. Pitts, and Michael LaTour, "The Appropriateness of Fear Appeal Use for Health Care Marketing to the Elderly: Is It OK to Scare Granny?" *Journal of Business Ethics*, January 1993, p. 45; "New Converse Shoe Named Run 'N Gun Is Angering Critics," *The Wall Street Journal*, February 8, 1993, p. B5; "Malt Liquor Makers Find Lucrative Market in the Urban Young," *The Wall Street Journal*, March 9, 1992, p. A1; Richard W. Pollay, S. Siddarth, Michael Siegel, Anne Haddix et al., "The Last Straw? Cigarette Advertising and Realized Market Shares Among Youths and Adults, 1979–1993," *Journal of Marketing*, April 1996, p. 1; N. C. Smith and Elizabeth Cooper-Martin, "Ethics and Target Marketing: The Role of Product Harm and Consumer Vulnerability," *Journal of Marketing*, July 1997, p. 1.

10. For more on new hotel features, see "Hotels Pump Up Their Gyms to Lure Execs Seeking Pecs," *The Wall Street Journal*, November 13, 2003, p. D1; "New Concepts in Lodging," *The Wall Street Journal*,

October 8, 2003, p. B1; "New at the Inn: Remote-Control Curtains," *The Wall Street Journal*, April 27, 2001, p. W9; "Hotels Target Generation X," *USA Today*, February 10, 2000, p. 1B; "Sweet Dreams Are Made of This," *USA Today*, August 31, 1999, p. 1B. See also Per Vagn Freytag and Ann Hojbjerg Clarke, "Business to Business Market Segmentation," *Industrial Marketing Management*, August 2001, p. 473.

11. Girish Punj and David W. Stewart, "Cluster Analysis in Marketing Research: Review and Suggestions for Application," *Journal of Marketing Research*, May 1983, p. 134; Fernando Robles and Ravi Sarathy, "Segmenting the Computer Aircraft Market with Cluster Analysis," *Industrial Marketing Management*, February 1986, p. 1.

12. For more on CRM, see Chapter 8, footnote #6. For more on Amazon, see "Reprogramming Amazon: Sure, It Still Sells Loads of Books and CDs, but . . . ," *Business Week*, December 22, 2003, p. 82; "Amazon Moves to Front Line of Shaping Web Services," *USA Today*, September 30, 2003, p. 1B; "Amazon Plans a Search Service to Drive Sales," *The Wall Street Journal*, September 25, 2003, p. B1; "New Chapter: A Web Giant Tries to Boost Profits by Taking on Tenants," *The Wall Street Journal*, September 24, 2003, p. A1; "Mighty Amazon," *Fortune*, May 26, 2003, p. 60; "Amazon: Creative Coddling, Great Word of Mouth," *Business Week E. Biz*, September 16, 2000; "Secrets of the New Brand Builders," *Fortune*, June 22, 1998, p. 167. See also Katherine N. Lemon, Tiffany Barnett White, and Russell S. Winer, "Dynamic Customer Relationship Management: Incorporating Future Considerations into the Service Retention Decision," *Journal of Marketing*, January 2002, p. 1; Richard A. Feinberg, Rajesh Kadam, Leigh Hokama, and Iksuk Kim, "The State of Electronic Customer Relationship Management in Retailing," *International Journal of Retail & Distribution Management*, (10) 2002, p. 470; Jonghyeok Kim, Euiho Suh, and Hyunseok Hwang, "A Model for Evaluating the Effectiveness of CRM Using the Balanced Scorecard," *Journal of Interactive Marketing*, Spring 2003, p. 5. For more on privacy, see Chapter 14, footnote #12 and Chapter 22, footnote #11.

13. "Return of the Middleman," *Business 2.0*, March 2003, p. 52.

14. Girish Punj and Junyean Moon, "Positioning Options for Achieving Brand Association: a Psychological Categorization Framework," *Journal of Business Research*, April 2002, p. 275; Kalpesh Kaushik Desai and S. Ratneshwar, "Consumer Perceptions of Product Variants Positioned on Atypical Attributes," *Journal of the Academy of Marketing Science*, Winter 2003, p. 22; Hans Muhlbacher, Angelika Dreher, and Angelika Gabriel-Ritter, "MIPS—Managing Industrial Positioning Strategies," *Industrial Marketing Management*, October 1994, p. 287; David A. Aaker and J. Gary Shansby, "Positioning Your Product," *Business Horizons*, May/June, 1982, p. 56; Al Ries and Jack Trout, *Positioning: The Battle for Your Mind* (New York: McGraw-Hill, 1981), p. 53. For some examples of positioning, see "Getting Corian Out of the Kitchen," *The Wall Street Journal*, December 12, 2000, p. B1; "Pie in the Sky," *Brandweek*, December 16, 1996, p. 23; "From the Horse's Mouth: Try a Little Hoof Fix on Your Nails," *The Wall Street Journal*, July 29, 1994, p. B1.

CHAPTER 4

1. Available from World Wide Web: <http://www.ups.com>; *2003 Annual Report*, UPS; "New UPS Delivery Service Sends Packages through the Post Office," *The Wall Street Journal*, November 6, 2003, p. A1; "UPS Cuts Ground-Delivery Time," *The Wall Street Journal*, October 6, 2003, p. A3; "Deutsche Post Girds for Battle," *The Wall Street Journal*, October 6, 2003, p. A14; "Shippers Deliver Hidden Fee Increases," *The Wall Street Journal*, August 12, 2003, p. D1; "FedEx and Brown Are Going Green," *Business Week*, August 11, 2003, p. 60; "What Can Brown Do, if Anything, to Mass?" *DSN Retailing Today*, June 23, 2003, p. 20; "UPS, FedEx Wage Handheld Combat," *Investor's Business Daily*, May 19, 2003, p. A6; "Squeezing Out Seconds," *Newsweek*, April 28, 2003, p. 48; "UPS Delivers New Brand Campaign," *BtoB*, April 14, 2003, p. 3; "UPS to Roll Out New Logo for Fleet," *The Wall Street Journal*, March 25, 2003, p. B4; "Brand Builders: Up with Brown," *Brandweek*, January 27, 2003, p. 16; "Ground Wars," *Business Week*, May 21, 2001, p. 64; "UPS Targets Logistics Business in Asia," *The Wall Street Journal*, April 26, 2001, p. A17; "Outside the Box," *The Wall Street Journal* (Special Report: E-Commerce), February 12, 2001, p. R20; "Shippers Brace for E-Commerce," *Investor's Business Daily*, November 24, 2000, p. A5; "UPS Logistics: Delivering Solutions, Not Packages," *Fortune*, October 30, 2000, pp. T208L–R; "Big Brown's Big Coup," *Business Week E.Biz*, September 18, 2000, pp. EB76–EB77; "UPS Is in Talks to Buy 2 Logistics Firms," *The Wall Street Journal*, June 12, 2000, p. A3; "Ford Is Hiring UPS to Track Vehicles as They Move from Factories to Dealers," *The Wall Street Journal*, February 2, 2000, p. A6; "Men in Brown," *Forbes*, January 10, 2000; *2000 Annual Report*, UPS.

2. See Peter F. Drucker, *Management: Tasks, Responsibilities, Practices, and Plans* (New York: Harper and Row, 1973); Sev K. Keil, "The Impact of Business Objectives and the Time Horizon of Performance Evaluation on Pricing Behavior," *International Journal of Research in Marketing*, June 2001, p. 67; Kenneth E. Clow, "Marketing Strategy: The Challenge of the External Environment," *Journal of the Academy of Marketing Science*, Summer 2000, p. 437.

3. This point of view is discussed at much greater length in a classic article by T. Levitt, "Marketing Myopia," *Harvard Business Review*, September–October 1975, p. 1. See also David J. Morris, Jr., "The Railroad and Movie Industries: Were They Myopic?" *Journal of the Academy of Marketing Science*, Fall, 1990, p. 279.

4. Lance Leuthesser and Chiranjeev Kohli, "Corporate Identity: The Role of Mission Statements," *Business Horizons*, May–June 1997, p. 59; Christopher K. Bart, "Sex, Lies, and Mission Statements," *Business Horizons*, November–December 1997, p. 9; Christopher K. Bart, "Industrial Firms and the Power of Mission," *Industrial Marketing Management*, July 1997, p. 371.

5. "Why Inflation Is Not Inevitable," *Fortune*, September 12, 1988, p. 117.

6. Available from World Wide Web: <http://www. harley-davidson. com>; *2003 Annual Report*, Harley-Davidson; "Hurdles on the Road to Hog Heaven," *Business Week*, November 10, 2003, p. 96; "Harley-Davidson Merchandising Goes Full Throttle," *USA Today*, August 25, 2003, p. 1B; "Where Hundreds Failed, Harley-Davidson Succeeded," *USA Today*, August 25, 2003, p. 3B; "Harley-Davidson Sees Decrease in Registrations," *The Wall Street Journal*, May 14, 2003, p. B5A; "How Harley Revved Online Sales," *Business 2.0*, December 2002, p. 44; "Richer, Older Harley Riders 'Like Everyone Else,'" *USA Today*, March 8, 2002, p. 1A; "Gearing Up for the Cruiser Wars," *Fortune*, August 3, 1998, pp. 128B–L; "Motorcycle Maker Caters to the Continent," *USA Today*, April 22, 1998, p. 8B; "Killer Strategies that Make Shareholders Rich," *Fortune*, June 23, 1997, p. 70; "Aided by Research, Harley Goes Whole Hog," *Marketing News*, December 2, 1996, p. 16; "Tune-Up Time for Harley," *Business Week*, April 8, 1996, p. 90; "The Rumble Heard Round the World," *Business Week*, May 24, 1993, p. 58; "How Harley Beat Back the Japanese," *Fortune*, September 25, 1989, p. 155.

7. For more on Starbucks, see Chapter 1, endnote 1.

8. For more on patents, see "Would You Buy a Patent License from This Man?" *Ecompany*, April 2001, p. 104; "Eli Lilly Loses Prozac Patent-Protection Battle," *The Wall Street Journal*, August 10, 2000, p. A3; "Businesses Battle over Intellectual Property," *USA Today*, August 2, 2000, p. 1B; "Qualcomm Hits the Big Time," *Fortune*, May 15, 2000, p. 213; "New Teeth for Old Patents," *Business Week*, November 30, 1998, p. 92; "What's Next—A Patent for the 401(K)?" *Business Week*, October 26, 1998, p. 104; "Drug Pirates," *Fortune*, October 12, 1998, p. 146.

9. "PlayStation 2 to Rivals: Game On!" *Brandweek*, November 17, 2003, p. 1; "Microsoft's Xbox to Use IBM Chips," *The Wall Street Journal*, November 4, 2003, p. B4; "Fear Not, Hardcore Violence Fans: Game

Maker's Not Going Soft," *Investor's Business Daily*, October 23, 2003, p. A10; "The Biggest Game in Town," *Fortune*, September 15, 2003, p. 132; "New Sony Videogame Camera Sells Well," *The Wall Street Journal*, August 29, 2003, p. B6; "Is Nintendo Playing the Wrong Game?" *Business 2.0*, August 2003, p. 110; "Pay and Play," *The Wall Street Journal Reports*, June 16, 2003, p. R6; "Xbox Problems? Microsoft's Not Singing the Blues," *Business Week*, May 19, 2003, p. 64; "Hackers Use Xbox for More than Games," *USA Today*, May 15, 2003, p. 3B; "Choosing Sides: Videogame Giant Links with Sony, Snubbing Microsoft," *The Wall Street Journal*, May 12, 2003, p. A1; "On the Web, Word-of-Mouth Marketing Can Become Viral," *Investor's Business Daily*, January 30, 2003, p. A4; "Sony's Big Bazooka," *Fortune*, December 30, 2002, p. 111; "Marketer of the Year: Xbox, We Know What Guys Want," *Brandweek*, October 14, 2002, p. M48; "Why Videogame Makers Are Taking Aim at You," *The Wall Street Journal*, May 16, 2002, p. D1; "Sony to Cut Price of PlayStation 2 by a Third in U.S.," *The Wall Street Journal*, May 14, 2002, p. D8; "Showdown in Mario Land," *The Wall Street Journal*, April 19, 2002, p. A14; "Game Wars," *Time*, March 20, 2000, p. 44; "How Four Renegades Persuaded Microsoft to Make a Game Machine," *The Wall Street Journal*, March 10, 2000, p. B1.

10. Peter J. Williamson, "Asia's New Competitive Game," *Harvard Business Review*, September–October 1997, p. 55; David J. Collis and Cynthia A. Montgomery, "Competing on Resources: Strategy in the 1990s," *Harvard Business Review*, July–August 1995, p. 118; "Firms Analyze Rivals to Help Fix Themselves," *The Wall Street Journal*, May 3, 1994, p. B1; Thomas S. Gruca and D. Sudharshan, "A Framework for Entry Deterrence Strategy: The Competitive Environment, Choices, and Consequences," *Journal of Marketing*, July 1995, p. 44; Venkatram Ramaswamy, Hubert Gatignon, and David J. Reibstein, "Competitive Marketing Behavior in Industrial Markets," *Journal of Marketing*, April 1994, p. 45; Z. S. Deligonul and S. T. Cavusgil, "Does the Comparative Advantage Theory of Competition Really Replace the Neoclassical Theory of Perfect Competition?" *Journal of Marketing*, October 1997, p. 65; J. S. Armstrong, "Co-Opetition," *Journal of Marketing*, April 1997, p. 92; John L. Haverty and Myroslaw J. Kyj, "What Happens when New Competitors Enter an Industry," *Industrial Marketing Management* 20, no. 1 (1991), p. 73; William W. Keep, Glenn S. Omura, and Roger J. Calantone, "What Managers Should Know about Their Competitors' Patented Technologies," *Industrial Marketing Management*, July 1994, p. 257.

11. Timothy B. Heath, Gangseog Ryu, Subimal Chatterjee, Michael S. McCarthy et al. "Asymmetric Competition in Choice and the Leveraging of Competitive Disadvantages," *Journal of Consumer Research*, December 2000, p. 291; *Kao* (Cambridge, MA: Harvard Business School Press, 1984); Bruce R. Klemz, "Managerial Assessment of Potential Entrants: Processes and Pitfalls," *International Journal of Research in Marketing*, June 2001, p. 37. For more on P&G's diaper competition in U.S., see "Opportunity Knocks: In Lean Times, Big Companies Make a Grab for Market Share," *The Wall Street Journal*, September 5, 2003, p. A1; "Rivals Take P&G to Court to Challenge Ads," *The Wall Street Journal*, June 17, 2003, p. B1; "Dueling Diapers," *Fortune*, February 17, 2003, p. 115. For a different competitor analysis in the cosmetics market, see "Face-Off: An Unlikely Rival Challenges L'Oreal in Beauty Market," *The Wall Street Journal*, January 9, 2003, p. A1; "L'Oreal's Global Makeover," *Fortune*, September 30, 2002, p. 141.

12. "P&G Wins Lawsuit, Loses Market," *Advertising Age*, September 18, 1989, p. 72. For more on corporate spying and competitive intelligence, see "Snooping on a Shoestring," *Business 2.0*, May 2003, p. 64; "More U.S. Trade Secrets Walk Out Door with Foreign Spies," *USA Today*, February 13, 2003, p. 1B; "This Paparazzo Stalks the Auto World's Next Big Thing," *The Wall Street Journal*, May 22, 2002, p. B1; "Corporate Intelligence: I-Spy," *The Wall Street Journal*, January 14, 2002, p. R14; "The Case of the Corporate Spy," *Business Week*, November 26, 2001, p. 56; "More Firms Hire Sleuths to Avoid Nasty Surprises," *USA Today*, June 26, 2001, p. 1B; "Spooked: Is That Salesman Really a Spy?"

Fortune, January 8, 2001, p. 192; "Call It Mission Impossible *Inc.*—Corporate-Spying Firms Thrive," *The Wall Street Journal*, July 3, 2000, p. B1; "Eyeing the Competition," *Time*, March 22, 1999, p. 58; "How Safe Are Your Secrets?" *Fortune*, September 8, 1997, p. 114. For more on the Oracle/Microsoft case, see "Oracle Case Shines Light on Corporate Spying," *Investor's Business Daily*, June 30, 2000, p. A7; "Oracle-Style Investigations Common, Experts Say," *USA Today*, June 29, 2000, p. 3B; "How Piles of Trash Became Latest Focus in Bitter Software Feud," *The Wall Street Journal*, June 29, 2000, p. A1. See also Shaker A. Zahra, "Unethical Practices in Competitive Analysis: Patterns, Causes and Effects," *Journal of Business Ethics*, January 1994, p. 53.

13. "A Whole New Wave of Japanese Exports Is Headed Westward," *The Wall Street Journal*, November 14, 1997, p. A1.

14. "Chinese Economic Engine Revs as Worldwide Low-Cost Leader," *Investor's Business Daily*, August 12, 2003, p. A1; "Follow the Leader: As U.S. Shows Signs of Strength, Global Economies Look Up, Too," *The Wall Street Journal*, August 12, 2003, p. A1; Rajdeep Grewal, "Building Organizational Capabilities for Managing Economic Crisis: The Role of Market Orientation and Strategic Flexibility," *Journal of Marketing*, April 2001, p. 67; "Daimler Thinks Small: With Gas Prices Soaring, Will Americans Get 'Smart'?" *Newsweek*, May 21, 2001, p. 48; "Europeans Unmoved by USA's Energy Plight," *USA Today*, May 17, 2001, p. 8A; "Wary Consumers Watch as Inflation Nudges Prices Up," *USA Today*, April 30, 2001, p. 1B; "Time for a Reality Check," *Business Week*, December 2, 1996, p. 58.

15. "Technology: Emerging Technologies," *USA Today (Bonus Section E)*, November 17, 2003; "What's Next," *Time*, September 8, 2003, p. 46; "The Future of Tech," *Business Week*, August 25, 2003, p. 62; "Special Report: Digital Homes," *Business Week*, July 21, 2003, p. 58; "Technology: There Goes the Status Quo," *The Wall Street Journal Reports*, May 19, 2003; "Six Technologies that Will Change the World," *Business 2.0*, May 2003, p. 116; "Special Report: Next Frontiers, Moving into the Future," *Newsweek*, April 29, 2002, p. 40; "Technology: What's Ahead," *The Wall Street Journal Reports*, June 25, 2001; "Technology: How Technology Has Changed the Way We . . . ," *The Wall Street Journal Reports*, November 13, 2000; "The Internet Age," *Business Week*, October 4, 1999, p. 69. See also Gary S. Lynn, Sharon M. Lipp, Ali E. Akgun, and Alexander Cortex Jr, "Factors Impacting the Adoption and Effectiveness of the World Wide Web in Marketing," *Industrial Marketing Management*, January 2002, p. 35; P. Rajan Varadarajan and Manjit S Yadav, "Marketing Strategy and the Internet: an Organizing Framework," *Journal of the Academy of Marketing Science*, Fall 2002, p. 296; A. Parasuraman and George M Zinkhan, "Marketing to and Serving Customers Through the Internet: an Overview and Research Agenda," *Journal of the Academy of Marketing Science*, Fall 2002, p. 286; Guilherme D. Pires and Janet Aisbett, "The Relationship Between Technology Adoption and Strategy in Business-to-Business Markets: the Case of E-Commerce," *Industrial Marketing Management*, May 2003, p. 291; Edward U. Bond III and Mark B. Houston, "Barriers to Matching New Technologies and Market Opportunities in Established Firms," *The Journal of Product Innovation Management*, March 2003, p. 120; Paul Whysall, "Retailing and the Internet: a Review of Ethical Issues," *International Journal of Retail & Distribution Management*, (11) 2000, p. 481; Robert A. Peterson, Sridhar Balasubramanian, and Bart J. Bronnenberg, "Exploring the Implications of the Internet for Consumer Marketing," *Journal of the Academy of Marketing Science*, Fall 1997, p. 329; Karen A. Graziano, "The Innovator's Dilemma: When New Technologies Cause Great Firms to Fail," *Journal of Product Innovation Management*, January 1998, p. 95; Edward McDonough, "Strategic Management of Technology and Innovation," *Journal of Product Innovation Management*, November 1997, p. 533.

16. "Technology: A Tech To-Do List," *The Wall Street Journal Reports*, November 17, 2003; "Advances in Car Technology Bring Higher-class Headaches," *USA Today*, November 12, 2003, p. 1B; "Epidemic: Crippling Computer Viruses and Spam Attacks Threaten the Information

Economy," *Business Week*, September 8, 2003, p. 28; "Technology: Just Make It Simpler," *Business Week*, September 8, 2003, p. 38; "Getting Unplugged Sheds Light on What Is Wired These Days," *The Wall Street Journal*, August 18, 2003, p. A1; "Innovation on Hold," *The Wall Street Journal*, May 29, 2003, p. B1; "Chips: Breaking the Light Barrier," *Business Week*, April 16, 2001, p. 74; "Handhelds That Do It All," *Business Week*, February 12, 2001, p. 98; "Will Light Bulbs Go the Way of the Victrola?" *Business Week*, January 22, 2001, p. 94H; "High-Tech Applications Transform Old Economy," *USA Today*, September 7, 2000, p. 3B; "In Japan, the World Goes Flat," *The Wall Street Journal*, June 29, 2000, p. B1; "The World Is Your Office," *Fortune*, June 12, 2000, p. 227; "Wireless Gets Easier and Faster," *Business Week*, May 29, 2000, p. 34; "Wireless Option Opens Door to a New E-World," *USA Today*, February 18, 2000, p. 1A; "This Frame Fetches Photos from the Net, Staging a Slide Show," *The Wall Street Journal*, February 3, 2000, p. B1; "The Soul of a New Refrigerator," *Business Week*, January 17, 2000, p. 42; Noel Capon and Rashi Glazer, "Marketing and Technology: A Strategic Coalignment," *Journal of Marketing*, July 1987, p. 1. For more on privacy, see Chapter 14, footnote #12 and Chapter 22, footnote #11.

17. "Lessons of a Crisis," *Business Week*, April 23, 2001, p. 56; "Made in Japan? Not for Home Team," *The Wall Street Journal*, February 18, 1998, p. A6; "U.S. Backpedals on Law that Hung 'Made in China' Tag on European Goods," *The Wall Street Journal*, August 8, 1997, p. A2. See also George Balabanis and Adamantios Diamantopoulos, "Domestic Country Bias, Country-of-Origin Effects, and Consumer Ethnocentrism: a Multidimensional Unfolding Approach," *Journal of the Academy of Marketing Science*, Winter 2004, p. 80; Zeynep Gurhan-Canli and Durairaj Maheswaran, "Determinants of Country-of-Origin Evaluations," *Journal of Consumer Research*, Jun 2000, p. 96; Kent L. Granzin and John J. Painter, "Motivational Influences on 'Buy Domestic' Purchasing: Marketing Management Implications from a Study of Two Nations," *Journal of International Marketing*, (2) 2001, p. 73; Gopalkrishnan R. Iyer, "Anticompetitive Practices in Japan: Their Impact on the Performance of Foreign Firms," *Journal of Marketing*, October 1997, p. 97; Michael G. Harvey, 'Buy American': Economic Concept or Political Slogan?" *Business Horizons*, May–June 1993, p. 40; Terry Clark, "National Boundaries, Border Zones, and Marketing Strategy: A Conceptual Framework and Theoretical Model of Secondary Boundary Effects," *Journal of Marketing*, July 1994, p. 67.

18. For more on Lands' End example, see "German Shoppers May Get Sale Freedom," *The Wall Street Journal*, January 23, 2002, p. B7A; "Border Crossings," *The Wall Street Journal* (Special Report: E-Commerce), November 22, 1999, p. R41. For more on EU, see "The Euro: How Damaging a Hit?" *Business Week*, September 29, 2003, p. 63; "Expanded EU Will Be an Uneven One," *The Wall Street Journal*, September 22, 2003, p. A16; "Mega Europe," *Business Week*, November 25, 2002, p. 62; "EU's New Car-Sales Rules Leave Much Up in Air," *The Wall Street Journal*, July 17, 2002, p. A14; "Future of Euro Sparks a Marketing Contest," *Ad Age Global*, March 2001, p. 21; "The End of a Free Ride for Carmakers?" *Business Week*, June 26, 2000, p. 70; "A Tale of Two Nations Shows Europe's Union Has Differing Sides," *The Wall Street Journal*, July 28, 1997, p. A1; "Europe's Borders Fade and People and Goods Can Move More Freely," *The Wall Street Journal*, May 18, 1993, p. A1. See also Andrew Paddison, "Retailing in the European Union: Structures, Competition and Performance," *International Journal of Retail & Distribution Management*, (6) 2003, p. 379; Valerie L. Vaccaro, "European Retailing's Vanishing Borders," *Journal of the Academy of Marketing Science*, Fall 1996, p. 386.

19. Available from World Wide Web: <http://www.nafta.org>. For more on NAFTA, see "After NAFTA's Thaw, a New Chill," *The Wall Street Journal*, October 7, 2003, p. A18; "Border Crossing? No Problema," *Business Week Small Biz*, July 16, 2001, p. 10; "NAFTA Scorecard: So Far, So Good," *Business Week*, July 9, 2001, p. 54; "Mexican Trucks Won't Fill the U.S. Soon," *The Wall Street Journal*, February 16, 2001, p. C4; "Mexico Thrives under NAFTA, Seeks More," *USA Today*, August 28,

2000, p. 1B; "Mexico Pulls Off Another Trade Coup," *Business Week*, February 7, 2000, p. 56; "In the Wake of NAFTA, a Family Firm Sees Business Go South," *The Wall Street Journal*, February 23, 1999, p. A1; "Mexican Makeover," *Business Week*, December 21, 1998, p. 50; Kent Jones, "NAFTA Chapter 19: Is There Hope for Bilateral Dispute Resolution of Unfair Trade Law Decisions?" *Journal of Public Policy & Marketing*, Fall 1994, p. 300.

20. Thomas L. Osterhus, "Pro-Social Consumer Influence Strategies: When and How Do They Work?" *Journal of Marketing*, October 1997, p. 16; Roger Swagler, "Evolution and Applications of the Term Consumerism: Theme and Variations," *Journal of Consumer Affairs*, Winter 1994, p. 347; Alan Morrison, "The Role of Litigation in Consumer Protection," *Journal of Consumer Affairs*, Winter, 1991, p. 209; William K. Darley and Denise M. Johnson, "Cross-National Comparison of Consumer Attitudes Toward Consumerism in Four Developing Countries," *Journal of Consumer Affairs*, Summer 1993, p. 37.

21. For more on Beech-Nut, see "What Led Beech-Nut Down the Road to Disgrace," *Business Week*, February 22, 1988, p. 124. See also "Stock Now, Pay Later," *Forbes*, October 27, 2003, p. 60; "EU Court Sends a Tough Antitrust Message," *The Wall Street Journal*, October 24, 2003, p. A12; "Big Drug Wholesaler Fights Charges of Fakes, Price Fixing," *The Wall Street Journal*, October 7, 2003, p. B1; "A Brazilian Challenge for Microsoft," *The Wall Street Journal*, September 8, 2003, p. A14; "The EU vs. Microsoft: A Rugged Endgame," *Business Week*, August 25, 2003, p. 40; "Europe Decides to Fine Nintendo," *The Wall Street Journal*, October 25, 2002, p. B5; "Patent Disputes Get a Fast Fix at Trade Agency," *The Wall Street Journal*, June 20, 2002, p. B1; "Sotheby's Taubman Is Sentenced to Jail Time, Fined $7.5 Million," *The Wall Street Journal*, April 23, 2002, p. B4; "Hard Profits: A Cement Titan in Mexico Thrives by Selling to Poor," *The Wall Street Journal*, April 22, 2002, p. A1; David A. Balto, "Emerging Antitrust Issues in Electronic Commerce," *Journal of Public Policy & Marketing*, Fall 2000, p. 277; Shelby D. Hunt, "Competition as an Evolutionary Process and Antitrust Policy," *Journal of Public Policy & Marketing*, Spring 2001, Vol. 20, 1, p. 15; "Europe: A Different Take on Antitrust," *Business Week*, June 25, 2001, p. 40; "Antitrust: Laying the Tracks a Bit to the Right," *Business Week*, February 12, 2001, p. 36; "How a Whistle-Blower Spurred Pricing Case Involving Drug Makers," *The Wall Street Journal*, May 12, 2000, p. A1; "A Little Internet Firm Got a Big Monopoly; Is That Such a Bad Thing?" *The Wall Street Journal*, October 8, 1998, p. A1; "In Archer-Daniels Saga, Now the Executives Face Trial," *The Wall Street Journal*, July 9, 1998, p. B10. See also Donna L. Hoffman, Thomas P. Novak, and Ann E. Schlosser, "Locus of Control, Web Use, and Consumer Attitudes Toward Internet Regulation," *Journal of Public Policy & Marketing*, Spring 2003, p. 41; Jeff Langenderfer and Steven W. Kopp, "Which Way to the Revolution? The Consequences of Database Protection as a New Form of Intellectual Property," *Journal of Public Policy & Marketing*, Spring 2003, p. 83; Mary W. Sullivan, "The Role of Marketing in Antitrust," *Journal of Public Policy & Marketing*, Fall 2002, p. 247; David E. M. Sappington and Donald K. Stockdale Jr, "The Federal Communications Commission's Competition Policy and Marketing's Information Technology Revolution," *Journal of Public Policy & Marketing*, Spring 2003, p. 26; Gregory T. Gundlach, "Exchange Relationships and the Efficiency Interests of the Law," *Journal of Public Policy & Marketing*, Fall 1996, p. 185; Ann C. Morales, "Corporate Officer Liability: FTC Expands Its Remedial Reach Over Deceptive Marketing Practices," *Journal of the Academy of Marketing Science*, Spring 1998, p. 163; Jef I. Richards, "Legal Potholes on the Information Superhighway," *Journal of Public Policy & Marketing*, Fall 1997, p. 319; Dan A. Fuller and Debra L. Scammon, "Newly Evolving Organizational Structures in the Health Care Industry: Principles of Antitrust Enforcement and Implications for Marketing," *Journal of Public Policy & Marketing*, Spring 1996, p. 128; G. S. Erickson, "Export Controls: Marketing Implications of Public Policy Choices," *Journal of Public Policy & Marketing*, Spring 1997, p. 83; Charles S. Gulas, "Marketing Strategies for Services: Globalization, Client-Orientation, Deregulation,"

Journal of the Academy of Marketing Science, Spring 1996, p. 178; Joan T. A. Gabel, "Lanham Act Not Limited to Advertisements Aimed at the Ultimate Consumer," *Journal of the Academy of Marketing Science*, Spring 1997, p.178. See also Louis W. Stern and Thomas L. Eovaldi, *Legal Aspects of Marketing Strategy: Antitrust and Consumer Protection Issues* (Englewood Cliffs, N.J.: Prentice-Hall, 1984).

22. For more on auto safety, see "U.S. Pushes for Wider Seat Belt Use," *USA Today*, May 20, 2003, p. 1A; "Shopping for Safety," *Business Week*, April 14, 2003, p. 84; "Smash, Bang, Crunch, Screech—Wow, What a Car!" *The Wall Street Journal*, April 13, 2001, p. B1; "Safety First," *Newsweek*, October 30, 2000, p. 56; "Formula Predicts Rollover Risk," *USA Today*, July 17, 2000, p. 1B. For more on food and drug safety, see "The Big Gap at the FDA," *Fortune*, July 22, 2002, p. 113; "Product Recalls Are Rising Amid Concern the Public Ignores Them" *The Wall Street Journal*, March 22, 2002, p. B1; "Pills on a Pedestal," *USA Today*, February 6, 2001, p. 1D; "Complex Drug Labels Bury Safety Messages," *USA Today*, May 3, 2000, p. 1A.

23. "Microsoft: New Rules of the Road," *Business Week*, July 16, 2001, p. 34; "No Split but Microsoft's a Monopolist," *Time*, July 9, 2001, p. 36; "A Cloud Lifted," *Newsweek*, July 9, 2001, p. 38; "Living in Microsoft's Shadow," *The Wall Street Journal*, July 2, 2001, p. B1; "They're Here, They're Feared, So Get Used to It," *The Wall Street Journal*, July 2, 2001, p. B1; "Microsoft Scores a Big Legal Victory," *The Wall Street Journal*, June 29, 2001, p. B1; "Microsoft: Let the Negotiations Begin," *USA Today*, June 29, 2001, p. 1B; "Are Antitrust Laws Obsolete in the New Economy?" *Investor's Business Daily*, April 16, 2001, p. A6; "The Great Antitrust Debate," *Business Week*, June 26, 2000, p. 40; "For Policy Makers, Microsoft Suggests Need to Recast Models," *The Wall Street Journal*, June 9, 2000, p. A1; "Antitrust for the Digital Age," *Business Week*, May 15, 2000, p. 46. See also Peter R. Dickson and Philippa K. Wells, "The Dubious Origins of the Sherman Antitrust Act: the Mouse That Roared," *Journal of Public Policy & Marketing*, Spring 2001, p. 3; Venkatesh Shankur, "Winners, Losers & Microsoft. Competition and Antitrust in High Technology," *The Journal of Product Innovation Management*, November 2000, p. 484; Rudolph J. R. Peritz, "Antitrust Policy and Aggressive Business Strategy: a Historical Perspective on Understanding Commercial Purposes and Effects," *Journal of Public Policy & Marketing*, Fall 2002, p. 237.

24. "Marketing Law: A Marketer's Guide to Alphabet Soup," *Business Marketing*, January 1990, p. 56; Ray O. Werner, "Marketing and the Supreme Court in Transition, 1982–1984," *Journal of Marketing*, Summer 1985, p. 97; Ray O. Werner, "Marketing and the United States Supreme Court, 1975–1981," *Journal of Marketing*, Spring 1982, p. 73; Dorothy Cohen, "Trademark Strategy," *Journal of Marketing*, January 1986, p. 61.

25. "Green—and Red-Hot, Too," *Business Week*, December 1, 2003, p. 116; "It's Easy Being Green," *Business 2.0*, December 2003, p. 132; "Can Anything Stop Toyota?" *Business Week*, November 17, 2003, p. 114; "Automakers Think Outside the Hybrid," *USA Today*, November 17, 2003, p. 5E; "Japan's Power Play," *Business Week*, October 13, 2003, p. 90; "GM'S Race to the Future," *Business 2.0*, October 2003, p. 86; "Ford Delays Hybrid and Faces Race with Toyota," *The Wall Street Journal*, September 24, 2003, p. D4; "It's Easy Being Green," *Time*, September 22, 2003, p. 81; "Toyota's Prius: No Plug Required," *The Wall Street Journal*, September 11, 2003, p. D6; "Pump Lets Natural Gas Civics Go to Market," *USA Today*, August 27, 2003, p. 2B; "Hybrid Autos May Proliferate but at a Price," *The Wall Street Journal*, August 22, 2003, p. B1; "Dude, Where's My Hybrid?" *Fortune*, April 28, 2003, p. 112; "$2.50 a Gallon Gas? Not a Problem," *Advertising Age*, April 14, 2003, p. S6; "Hybrid Cars Attract More Buyers," *The Wall Street Journal*, March 13, 2003, p. D3; "Hybrids: How Detroit Can Gun the Engines," *Business Week*, February 17, 2003, p. 80; "When Hybrid Cars Collide," *The Wall Street Journal*, February 6, 2003, p. B1; "Police Vehicles Go Green and Help Save Green," *The Wall Street Journal*, February 6, 2003, p. B1; "The Hybrid Car Moves beyond Curiosity Stage," *The New York Times*, January 28, 2003, p. A1.

26. "Where the Girls Are," *The Wall Street Journal*, October 28, 2003, p. B1; "If You Build It, Will She Come?" *Brandweek*, September 29, 2003, p. 28; "Fisher-Price Courts Gen-X Mothers," *The Wall Street Journal*, September 19, 2003, p. B3; "Tractor Supply: Retail Chain Uses Horse Sense to Plow New Growth Avenues," *Investor's Business Daily*, September 4, 2003, p. A9; "Tech Companies Try Wooing Women with Girlie Marketing," *The Wall Street Journal*, August 26, 2003, p. B1; "Ads Remind Women They Have Two Hands," *The Wall Street Journal*, August 14, 2003, p. B1; "Lowe's: Retailer Improves Your Home, Its Financials," *Investor's Business Daily*, May 16, 2003, p. A5; "A Slim Gym's Fat Success," *Time (Inside Business Bonus Section)*, May 2003; "Lowe's Is Sprucing Up Its House. . . by Appealing to Women," *Business Week*, June 3, 2002, p. 56; "Tapping Girl Power," *Brandweek*, April 22, 2002, p. 26; "Tool Sellers Tap Their Feminine Side," *The Wall Street Journal*, March 29, 2002, p. B1; "The NFL Tackles Mom," *The Wall Street Journal*, February 1, 2002, p. W1; "Aiming to Please Women," *USA Today*, June 10, 1999, p. 1B; Patricia Braus, "The Mother Market," *American Demographics*, October 1996, p. 37. See also Kathleen Brewer Doran, "Lessons Learned in Cross-Cultural Research of Chinese and North American Consumers," *Journal of Business Research*, October 2002, p. 823; Craig J. Thompson and Maura Troester, "Consumer Value Systems in the Age of Postmodern Fragmentation: the Case of the Natural Health Microculture," *Journal of Consumer Research*, March 2002, p. 550; Inger L. Stole, "Stronger than Dirt: a Cultural History of Advertising: Personal Hygiene in America, 1875–1940," *Journal of Advertising*, Summer 2002, p. 93; Bert Rosenbloom and Trina Larsen, "Communication in International Business-to-business Marketing Channels: Does Culture Matter?," *Industrial Marketing Management*, May 2003, p. 309.

27. For more on the changing nature of families, see "Power: Do Women Really Want It," *Fortune*, October 13, 2003, p. 80; "She Works, He Doesn't," *Newsweek*, May 12, 2003, p. 44; "Gen X Moms Have It Their Way," *USA Today*, May 7, 2003, p. 1D; "Mommy Is Really Home from Work," *Business Week*, November 25, 2002, p. 101; "How to Shrink the Pay Gap," *Business Week*, June 24, 2002, p. 151; "Career Matters," *American Demographics*, April 2002, p. 18; "In 24-Hour Workplace, Day Care Is Moving to the Night Shift," *The Wall Street Journal*, July 6, 2001, p. A1; "Net Lets Japanese Women Join Work Force at Home," *The Wall Street Journal*, February 29, 2000, p. B1; "Ads that Portray Women," *USA Today*, September 9, 1996, p. 4B. For more on changing food habits, see "The Fine Art of Finding the Fat," *Business Week*, October 13, 2003, p. 134; "Are They Safe? The Skinny on Fat and Sugar Substitutes," *The Wall Street Journal*, August 12, 2003, p. D1; "The End of Nesting," *The Wall Street Journal*, May 16, 2003, p. W1; "The New Kitchen—Your Car," *The Wall Street Journal*, April 11, 2003, p. W10; "America Adds Salsa to Its Burgers and Fries," *The Wall Street Journal*, January 2, 2003, p. A9; "Fleeing from Fast Food," *The Wall Street Journal*, November 11, 2002, p. B1; "Fast-Growing Casual Restaurants Have the Burger Joints Drooling," *Investor's Business Daily*, June 20, 2002, p. A1; "Upper Crust: Fast-Food Chains Vie to Carve Out Empire in Pricey Sandwiches," *The Wall Street Journal*, February 5, 2002, p. A1; "Can Tyson Fight 'Chicken Fatigue' with Pork, Beef?" *The Wall Street Journal*, January 10, 2001, p. B1. For more on poverty of time, see "America Untettered," *American Demographics*, March 2003, p. 34; "How Much Is Your Time Worth?" *The Wall Street Journal*, February 26, 2003, p. D1; "Can Workplace Stress Get Worse?" *The Wall Street Journal*, January 16, 2001, p. B1; "Telecommuters' Lament," *The Wall Street Journal*, October 31, 2000, p. B1; "The Price of Speed," *USA Today*, August 3, 2000, p. 10D; "The End of Leisure," *American Demographics*, July 2000, p. 50. See also Laura M. Milner and James M. Collins, "Sex-Role Portrayals and the Gender of Nations," *Journal of Advertising*, Spring 2000, p. 67; Eric Panitz, "Marketing in a Multicultural World: Ethnicity, Nationalism and Cultural Identity," *Journal of the Academy of Marketing Science*, Spring 1997, p. 169; Victoria D. Bush and Thomas Ingram, "Adapting to Diverse Customers: A Training Matrix for International Marketers," *Industrial Marketing Management*, September 1996, p. 373.

28. Frank R. Bacon, Jr., and Thomas W. Butler, Jr., *Planned Innovation*, rev. ed. (Ann Arbor: Institute of Science and Technology, University of Michigan, 1980).

29. Paul F. Anderson, "Marketing, Strategic Planning and the Theory of the Firm," *Journal of Marketing*, Spring 1982, p. 15; George S. Day, "Analytical Approaches to Strategic Market Planning," in *Review of Marketing 1981*, ed. Ben M. Enis and Kenneth J. Roering (Chicago: American Marketing Association, 1981), p. 89; Ronnie Silverblatt and Pradeep Korgaonkar, "Strategic Market Planning in a Turbulent Business Environment," *Journal of Business Research*, August 1987, p. 339.

30. Jimme A. Keizer, Johannes I. M. Halman, and Michael Song, "From Experience: Applying the Risk Diagnosing Methodology," *The Journal of Product Innovation Management*, May 2002, p. 213; Richard N. Cardozo and David K. Smith, Jr., "Applying Financial Portfolio Theory to Product Portfolio Decisions: An Empirical Study," *Journal of Marketing*, Spring 1983, p. 110; Yoram Wind, Vijay Mahajan, and Donald J. Swire, "An Empirical Comparison of Standardized Portfolio Models," *Journal of Marketing*, Spring 1983, p. 89; Philippe Haspeslagh, "Portfolio Planning: Uses and Limits," *Harvard Business Review*, January–February 1982, p. 58.

31. Keith B. Murray and Edward T. Popper, "Competing under Regulatory Uncertainty: A U.S. Perspective on Advertising in the Emerging European Market," *Journal of Macromarketing*, Fall 1992, p. 38; "Inside Russia—Business Most Unusual," *UPS International Update*, Spring 1994, p. 1; "Freighted with Difficulties," *The Wall Street Journal*, December 10, 1993, p. R4; "Russia Snickers after Mars Invades," *The Wall Street Journal*, July 13, 1993, p. B1; Michael G. Harvey and James T. Rothe, "The Foreign Corrupt Practices Act: The Good, the Bad and the Future," in *1983 American Marketing Association Educators' Proceedings*, ed. P. E. Murphy et al. (Chicago: American Marketing Association, 1983), p. 374.

32. "Sensitive Export: Seeking New Markets for Tampons, P&G Faces Cultural Barriers," *The Wall Street Journal*, December 8, 2000, p. A1; "Pizza Queen of Japan Turns Web Auctioneer," *The Wall Street Journal*, March 6, 2000, p. B1; "What Makes Italy Easier?" *Going Global—Italy* (supplement to *Inc.*), 1994; "Jean Cloning," *Brandweek*, May 30, 1994, p. 15; "Double Entendre: The Life and the Life of Pepsi Max," *Brandweek*, April 18, 1994, p. 40; "Global Ad Campaigns, After Many Missteps, Finally Pay Dividends," *The Wall Street Journal*, August 27, 1992, p. A1; Kamran Kashani, "Beware the Pitfalls of Global Marketing," *Harvard Business Review*, September–October 1989, p. 91.

CHAPTER 5

1. Available from World Wide Web: <http://www.schwab. com>; *Schwab Resources: An Overview of Schwab's Products and Services* (Charles Schwab & Co, 2003); *The Schwab Way: Built for the Individual Investor* (Charles Schwab & Co, 2003); "Advertisers Are Cautious as Household Makeup Shifts," *The Wall Street Journal*, May 15, 2001, p. B1; "Schwab, Going Upscale, Steps on Some Toes," *Business Week*, December 11, 2000, p. 112; "Brokers Are from Mars, Women Are from Venus," *Business Week*, December 4, 2000, p. 158; "Multicultural Marketing," *Advertising Age* (Special Report), November 30, 2000, p. S1; "The Best Way to Trade Stocks," *The Wall Street Journal* (Special Report: The Internet), November 27, 2000, p. R6; "Online Brokerages Go from Clicks to Bricks," *USA Today*, November 1, 2000, p. 1B; "The World's Most Admired Companies," *Fortune*, October 2, 2000, p. 183; "Charles Schwab," *Business Week E.Biz* (Special Report: Web Smart 50), September 18, 2000, p. EB88; "Reinvent Your Company," *Fortune*, June 12, 2000, p. 99; "How Schwab Grabbed the Lion's Share," *Business Week*, June 28, 1999, p. 88; "Schwab Puts It All Online," *Fortune*, December 7, 1998, p. 94.

2. Based on U.S. Census data, including *Global Population Profile: 2000* and *World Population Profile: 1998* and *World Population at a Glance: 1998 and Beyond, IB/98-4* (Washington, DC: Government Printing Office); and other Census data available from World Wide Web: <http://www.census.gov/ipc>.

3. Based on U.S. Census "International Data Base" available from World Wide Web: <http://www.census.gov/cgi-bin/ipc/idbsum? cty=??> and other U.S. Census data, including *An Aging World: 2001, P95/01-1* and World Bank data including, *World Development Indicators: 2003* (Washington, DC: International Bank for Reconstruction and Development/The World Bank, 2003) and available from World Wide Web: <http://devdata.worldbank. org/data-query>; Central Intelligence Agency data and available from World Wide Web: <http://www.odci. gov/cia/publications/ factbook>; Population Reference Bureau data, including *2002 World Population Data Sheet* (Washington, DC: Population Reference Bureau, 2002) and available from World Wide Web: http://www.prb.org/pubs/ wpds2002 and *World Population: More Than Just Numbers* (Washington, DC: Population Reference Bureau, 1999); and CountryWatch, available from World Wide Web: <http://www. countrywatch.com>; "To Put It in Perspective," *American Demographics*, June 2003, p. 9; "When Globalization Suffers, the Poor Take the Heat," *Business Week*, April 21, 2003, p. 28; "Leveraging the Age Gap: Nations that Skew Young Have Small Window to Try to Catch Up with the Wealthy," *The Wall Street Journal*, February 27, 2003, p. B1; "Time for Marketers to Grow Up?" *The Wall Street Journal*, February 27, 2003, p. B1; "Going Gray: For Ailing Japan, Longevity Begins to Take a Toll," *The Wall Street Journal*, February 11, 2003, p. A1; "Global Baby Bust: Economic, Social Implications Are Profound as Birthrates Drop in Almost Every Nation," *The Wall Street Journal*, January 24, 2003, p. B1; "The Middle East Baby Boom," *American Demographics*, September 2002, p. 55; "Arrested Development: Botswana Watches Economic Success Destroyed by AIDS," *The Wall Street Journal*, August 29, 2002, p. A1; Tarun Khanna and Krishna Palepu, "Why Focused Strategies May Be Wrong for Emerging Markets," *Harvard Business Review*, July–August 1997, p. 41; Tamer S. Cavusgil, "Measuring the Potential of Emerging Markets: An Indexing Approach," *Business Horizons*, January–February 1997, p. 87; E. B. Keehn, "A Yen to Spend," *Harvard Business Review*, March–April 1996, p. 154.

4. Based on World Bank GNI and GDP data and available from World Wide Web: <http://devdata.worldbank.org>.

5. "Two Ways to Help the Third World," *Fortune*, October 27, 2003, p. 187; "Good Reasons for Smiles: Colgate Brings Dental Care to Brazilian Indian Tribes, Ravages of Tobacco and Rice," *The Wall Street Journal*, July 23, 2003, p. B1; "A Way to Help Africa Help Itself," *Business Week*, July 21, 2003, p. 40; "Companies Market to India's Have-Littles," *The Wall Street Journal*, June 5, 2003, p. B1; "Tech Where It's Needed," *Business 2.0*, July 2003, p. 124; "With Little Loans, Mexican Women Overcome," *The New York Times*, March 19, 2003, p. A8; "CelPay Puts Africa on Wireless Map," *The Wall Street Journal*, December 2, 2002, p. B4; "Digital Divide: The Hunt for Globalization that Works," *Fortune*, October 28, 2002, pp. 163–176, "Special Report: Global Poverty," *Business Week*, October 14, 2002, p. 108; "World Poverty Rates," *Investor's Business Daily*, June 12, 2002, p. A15; "Small Change: Bank that Pioneered Loans for the Poor Hits Repayment Snag," *The Wall Street Journal*, November 27, 2001, p. A1; "America's Future: Smart Globalization," *Business Week*, August 27, 2001, p. 130; "Global Capitalism: Can It Be Made to Work Better?" *Business Week*, November 6, 2000, p. 72; "The Fight Against Latin Poverty," *Business Week*, May 1, 2000, p. 72; and World Bank statistical data available from World Wide Web: <http://devdata. worldbank.org>. See also Chapter 1, endnote 10.

6. "Pfizer Makes Aid Pledge, Breaks Aid Pact," *The Wall Street Journal*, November 12, 2003, p. B1; "African Gold Giant Finds History Impeded a Fight Against AIDS," *The Wall Street Journal*," June 26, 2001, p. A1; "Bottled Up: As UNICEF Battles Baby-Formula Makers, African Infants Sicken," *The Wall Street Journal*, December 5, 2000, p. A1; "Death of a Continent," *Fortune*, November 13, 2000, p. 258; "World Bank Is Targeting AIDS in Africa," *The Wall Street Journal*, September 12, 2000,

p. A3; "American Home Infant-Formula Giveaway to End," *The Wall Street Journal*, February 4, 1991, p. B1.

7. Based on World Bank statistical data available from World Wide Web: <http://devdata.worldbank.org/data-query>; "The Lowdown on Literacy," *American Demographics*, June 1994, p. 6.

8. Based on U.S. Census data, including U.S. Bureau of the Census, *Statistical Abstract of the United States 2002* (Washington, DC: U.S. Government Printing Office, 2001), pp. 22–23 and available from World Wide Web: <http://www.census.gov/ statab> and *Census 2000 Special Reports: Demographic Trends in the 20th Century CENSR-4* and "The Next 25 Years," *American Demographics* (Marketing Tools Sourcebook 2004), pp. D26–D29; "Moving West Is No Longer the Norm," *USA Today*, August 6, 2003, p. 1A; "Decade of Change for USA," *USA Today*, June 5, 2002, p. 3B; "The Census Report," *American Demographics*, January 2002, pp. S3–S6; "Snapshot of America 2000," *The Wall Street Journal*, August 6, 2001, p. B1; "Exploring a Nation of Extremes," *The Wall Street Journal*, May 25, 2001, p. B1; "Census Tracks Geographical Generation Gap," *USA Today*, May 25, 2001, p. 3A; "Lust for Statistics," *American Demographics*, March 2001, p. 68. Also based on data from Population Reference Bureau and Ameristat, available from World Wide Web: <http://www.prb.org> and <http://www.ameristat.org>.

9. Based on U.S. Census data, including U.S. Bureau of the Census, *Statistical Abstract of the United States 2002* (Washington, DC: U.S. Government Printing Office, 2001), p. 9 and p. 59 and available from World Wide Web: <http://www.census.gov/ statab>.

10. Based on U.S. Census data, including U.S. Bureau of the Census, *Statistical Abstract of the United States 2002* (Washington, DC: U.S. Government Printing Office, 2001), p. 18, p. 20, and p. 25 and available from World Wide Web: http://www.ccnsus.gov/statab and *Census 2000 Special Reports: Demographic Trends in the 20th Century CENSR-4* and "The Next 25 Years," *American Demographics*, April 2003, p. 24; "Gadgets Help Baby Boomers Navigate Old Age," *USA Today*, November 17, 2003, p. 1A; "The Dream Vacation: Go Home Younger," *The Wall Street Journal*, August 13, 2003, p. D1; Michael J. Weiss, "Great Expectations," *American Demographics*, May 2003, p. 26; "Boomers: A Forgotten Generation," *Brandweek*, October 7, 2002, p. 1; Carol M. Morgan and Doran J. Levy, "The Boomer Attitude," *American Demographics*, October 2002, p. 42; Michael Weiss, "Chasing Youth," *American Demographics*, October 2002, p. 34; Rebecca Gardyn, "Retirement Redefined," *American Demographics*, November 2000, p. 52. See also Linda L. Price, Eric J. Arnould and Carolyn Folkman Curasi, "Older Consumers' Disposition of Special Possessions," *Journal of Consumer Research*, September 2000, p. 179; William R. Swinyard and Heikki J. Rinne, "The Six Shopping Worlds of Baby Boomers," *Business Horizons*, September–October 1994, p. 64.

11. "Hooking Up with Gen Y," *Business 2.0*, October 2003, p. 49; "Degree of Challenge," *American Demographics*, May 2003, p. 20.

12. Based on U.S. Census data and "New Baby Boom Swamps Colleges," *USA Today*, January 2, 2003, p. 1A; Pamela Paul, "Echo-boomerang," *American Demographics*, June 2001, p. 44; *Teen Fact Book* (Channel One Network, 2000) and available from World Wide Web: <http://www.TeenFactBook.com>; Susan Mitchell, "The Next Baby Boom," *American Demographics*, October 1995, p. 22; "Teens, the Most Global Market of All," *Fortune*, May 16, 1994, p. 90.

13. Based on U.S. Census data, including U.S. Bureau of the Census, *Statistical Abstract of the United States 2002* (Washington, DC: U.S. Government Printing Office, 2001), p. 47, p. 48, and p. 53 and *Census 2000 Special Reports: Demographic Trends in the 20th Century CENSR-4*; "Unmarried America," *Business Week*, October 20, 2003, p. 106; "Married with Children," *American Demographics*, March 2003, p. 17; "The American Family in the 21st Century," *American Demographics*, August 2001, p. 20; "Living Alone in America: Singleness Not the Same as Untitled," *USA Today*, October 23, 2001, p. 1D; "Unmarried with Children,"

Newsweek, May 28, 2001, p. 46; "Census 2000: The New Demographics," *The Wall Street Journal*, May 15, 2001, p. B1; "Advertisers Are Cautious as Household Makeup Shifts," *The Wall Street Journal*, May 15, 2001, p. B1; Rebecca Gardyn, "Unmarried Bliss," *American Demographics*, December 2000, p. 56.

14. Based on U.S. Census data and "Population of Rural America Is Swelling," *The Wall Street Journal*, July 21, 1996, p. B1; "The Rural Rebound," *American Demographics*, May 1994, p. 24. See also Hugh M. Cannon and Attila Yaprak, "Will the Real-World Citizen Please Stand Up! The Many Faces of Cosmopolitan Consumer Behavior," *Journal of International Marketing*, (4) 2002, p. 30.

15. Based on U.S. Census data, including U.S. Bureau of the Census, *Statistical Abstract of the United States 2002* (Washington, DC: U.S. Government Printing Office, 2001), p. 30 and *Census 2000 Special Reports: Demographic Trends in the 20th Century CENSR-4* and "Minorities Reshape Suburbs," *USA Today*, July 9, 2001, p. 1A; "Counting Change," *Advertising Age*, May 14, 2001, p. 16; "U.S. Cities Buck Trend with Boom Downtown," *USA Today*, May 7, 2001, p. 1A; "Downtowns Make Cities Winners," *USA Today*, May 7, 2001, p. 3A; "Immigration Helped Restore Cities," *USA Today*, March 19, 2001, p. 3A.

16. Based on U.S. Census data, including U.S. Bureau of the Census, *Statistical Abstract of the United States 2002* (Washington, DC: U.S. Government Printing Office, 2001), p. 29 and "Geographical Mobility: March 1998 to March 1999 (Update), p. 20 531" and available from World Wide Web: <http://www.census.gov/population/www/socdemo/migrate>; Roberto Suro, "Movement at Warp Speed," *American Demographics*, August 2000, p. 61.

17. Based on U.S. Census data, including U.S. Bureau of the Census, *Statistical Abstract of the United States 2002* (Washington, DC: U.S. Government Printing Office, 2001), pp. 41–42 and pp. 441–442 and "Table F-1. Income Limits for Each Fifth and Top 5 Percent of Families (All Races): 1947 to 2001" and "Table F-2. Share of Aggregate Income Received by Each Fifth and Top 5 Percent of Families (All Races): 1947 to 2001" and "Table F-6. Regions—Families (All Races) by Median and Mean Income: 1953 to 2001" and all 3 tables available from World Wide Web: <http://www.census.gov/hhes/income/hitinc> and "Table 1. People and Families in Poverty by Selected Characteristics: 2000 and 2001" and available from World Wide Web: <http://www.census.gov/hhes/poverty>. For more on income, see "Waking Up from the American Dream," *Business Week*, December 1, 2003, p. 54; "Middle Class Barely Treads Water," *USA Today*, September 15, 2003, p. 1B; "Economic Inequality Grew in 90's Boom, Fed Reports," *The New York Times*, January 23, 2003, p. C1; "Defining the Rich in the World's Wealthiest Nation," *The New York Times*, January 12, 2003, Sect. 4, p. 1; "The Income Report," *American Demographics*, January 2003, p. 35; Peter Francese, "Older and Wealthier," *American Demographics*, November 2002, p. 40. For more on poverty, see "Is Poverty Rate Rise as Bad as It Looks?" *Investor's Business Daily*, September 29, 2003, p. A1; "Income Gap Steady, Poverty Spreads," *The Wall Street Journal*, September 29, 2003, p. A14; "Poverty Rate Rise Greater for Whites," *The Wall Street Journal*, September 25, 2002, p. D2; "Down and Out in the Midst of a Boom," *Business Week*, May 28, 2001, p. 24; "Poverty in America," *Business Week*, October 18, 1999, p. 156; "Income Gap between Rich and Poor Grows Nationwide," *The Wall Street Journal*, December 17, 1997, p. B2.

18. Ronald W. Hasty, Joseph A. Bellizzi, and Fernando R. Diaz, "A Cross-Cultural Study of Ethical Perceptions of Whites and Hispanics Toward 14 Questionable Retail Practices," *Journal of Marketing Theory & Practice*, Winter 1997, p. 135; "Nutrament, Debunked as a 'Fitness' Drink, Is Reborn in the Slums," *The Wall Street Journal*, November 2, 1994, p. B1; "Some Mortgage Firms Neglect Black Areas More Than Banks Do," *The Wall Street Journal*, August 9, 1994, p. A1; "A Marketing Giant Uses Its Sales Prowess to Profit on Poverty," *The Wall Street Journal*, September 22, 1993, p. A1.

19. "Chasing Viking," *Brandweek*, August 18, 2003, p. 20; Michael J. Weiss, "Inconspicuous Consumption," *American Demographics*, April 2002, p. 31; "Marketing to the New Millionaire," *The Wall Street Journal*, October 11, 2000, p. B1; "The Lure of the Entrepreneur," *American Demographics*, February 1998, p. 41; "Spending at Our Discretion," *American Demographics*, August 1997, p. 2; Peter K. Francese, "Big Spenders," *American Demographics*, August 1997, p. 51; "Disposable Dollars Determine Spending," *American Demographics*, June 1997, p. 18.

20. Pamela Paul, "Make Room for Granddaddy," *American Demographics*, April 2002, p. 40; "The Grandparent Industry," *The Wall Street Journal*, November 2, 2001, p. W1; Jan Larson, "The New Face of Homemakers," *American Demographics*, September 1997, p. 45; "Work & Family" (Special Section), *The Wall Street Journal*, March 31, 1997, p. 1; "A Snapshot of Younger Lifestage Group Purchases," *American Demographics*, November 9, 1992, p. 28. See also Richard G. Netemeyer, Thomas Brashear-Alejandro and James S. Boles, "A Cross-National Model of Job-Related Outcomes of Work Role and Family Role Variables: a Retail Sales Context," *Journal of the Academy of Marketing Science*, Winter 2004, p. 49; Patrick E. Murphy and William A. Staples, "A Modernized Family Life Cycle," *Journal of Consumer Research*, June 1979, p. 12.

21. Based on U.S. Census data and "Do Us Part," *American Demographics*, September 2002, p. 9; Joan Raymond, "The Ex-Files," *American Demographics*, February 2001, p. 60; "The Ties that Bind," *Time*, August 18, 1997, p. 48; Frank F. Fustenberg, Jr., "The Future of Marriage," *American Demographics*, June 1996, p. 34. See also James A. Roberts, Chris Manolis, and John F. Tanner Jr, "Family Structure, Materialism, and Compulsive Buying: a Reinquiry and Extension," *Journal of the Academy of Marketing Science*, Summer 2003, p. 300.

22. Based on U.S. Census data and "More Parents Are Leaving School Shopping to the Kids," *USA Today*, August 11, 2003, p. 1A; "Special Report: Kids, Tweens & Teens," *Advertising Age*, February 17, 2003, pp. S1–S6; "Just How Deep Are Those Teen Pockets?" *Business Week*, July 30, 2001, p. 39; "Special Report: Teen Marketing," *Advertising Age*, June 25, 2001, p. S1; "To Reach the Unreachable Teen," *Business Week*, September 18, 2000, p. 78; "Rushing to Cash In on the New Baby Boom," *The Wall Street Journal*, August 9, 2000, p. B1; "The Six Value Segments of Global Youth," *Brandweek*, May 22, 2000, p. 38; Elissa Moses, *The $100 Billion Allowance: Accessing the Global Teen Market* (John Wiley & Sons, 2000); "Generation Y," *Business Week*, February 15, 1999, p. 80; Soyeon Shim, "Adolescent Consumer Decision-Making Styles: The Consumer Socialization Perspective," *Psychology & Marketing*, September 1996, p. 547.

23. Based on U.S. Census data and "Mom and Dad, I'm Home— Again," *Business Week*, November 3, 2003, p. 110; "Free at Last!" *Newsweek*, October 13, 2003, p. 62; "Bringing Up Adultolescents," *Newsweek*, March 25, 2002, p. 38; Joan Raymond, "The Joy of Empty Nesting," *American Demographics*, May 2000, p. 48; "Take My Stuff, Please!" *The Wall Street Journal*, March 31, 2000, p.W1; "Extreme Nesting," *The Wall Street Journal*, January 7, 2000, p. W1.

24. Based on Census data, including "The Older Population in the United States: March 1999, P20–532"; "Your New Neighbor: Mom," *The Wall Street Journal*, December 20, 2002, p. W1; "Take My Mother— Please!" *The Wall Street Journal*, October 4, 2002, p. W1; "The Exotic Travel Boom," *American Demographics*, June 2002, p. 48; "Senior Theses," *Brandweek*, August 4, 1997, p. 22; "The Ungraying of America," *American Demographics*, July 1997, p. 12; Linda J. Barton, "A Shoulder to Lean On: Assisted Living in the U.S.," *American Demographics*, July 1997, p. 45; "Brave Old World," *Newsweek*, June 30, 1997, p. 63; George P. Moschis, "Life Stages of the Mature Market," *American Demographics*, September 1996, p. 44.

25. Based on U.S. Census data, including *Census 2000 Special Reports: Demographic Trends in the 20th Century CENSR-4*. For an overview of ethnic populations in the U.S., see *Racial and Ethnic Diversity* (Ithaca, NY:

New Strategist, 2000); "Ads for Ethnic Hair Care Show a New Face" *The Wall Street Journal*, July 21, 2003, p. B1; "Multicultural Marketing," *Advertising Age* (Special Report), July 7, 2003, p. S1; "Ethnic Marketing," *DSN Retailing Today* (Special Report), March 24, 2003, p. 13; Sean Kelly, "Race, Ethnicity, and the Way We Shop," *American Demographics*, February 2003, p. 30; Alison Stein Wellner, "Diversity in America," *American Demographics* (Supplement), November 2002, p. S1; "Ethnic Marketing," *DSN Retailing Today* (Special Report), May 6, 2002, p. 17; Geng Cui, "Marketing to Ethnic Minority Consumers: An Historical Journey (1932–1997)," *Journal of Macromarketing*, June 2001, Vol. 21, 1, p. 23; Marilyn Halter, *Shopping for Identity: The Marketing of Ethnicity* (Schocken Books, 2000); William H. Frey, "Micro Melting Pots," *American Demographics*, June 2001, p. 20; "Color Them Beautiful—and Visible," *USA Today*, May 2, 2001, p. 1B; "The New Age of Ethnic Marketing," *Brandweek*, March 19, 2001, p. 24; "The New America: The New Face of Race," *Newsweek*, September 18, 2000, p. 38; "Our New Look: The Colors of Race," *Newsweek*, January 1, 2000, p. 28. For more on the white population, see U.S. Census data, including "The White Population: August 2001, C2KBR/01-4." For more on the African-American market, see U.S. Census data, including "The Black Population in the United States: April 2003, P20–541" and available from World Wide Web: <http://www.census.gov/population/www/socdemo/race>; William H. Frey, "Revival," *American Demographics*, October 2003, p. 26; Sandra Yin, "Color Bind," *American Demographics*, September 2003, p. 22; "Card Crafter Uses Creativity to Carve Out Niche," *USA Today*, March 19, 2003, p. 7B; "The Black Gender Gap," *Newsweek*, March 3, 2003, p. 46; "Black Boom in the 'Burbs," *American Demographics*, July 2001, p. 20; "The New Demographics of Black Americans," *Business Week*, December 4, 2000, p. 14; Carol M. Motley, "Aunt Jemima, Uncle Ben, and Rastus: Blacks in Advertising, Yesterday, Today, and Tomorrow," *Journal of Marketing*, April 1995, p. 111. For more on the Hispanic market, see U.S. Census data, including "The Hispanic Population: May 2001, C2KBR/01-3" and available from World Wide Web: <http://www.census.gov/population/www/socdemo/race>; "Once-Spurned Clamato Juice Is Big with Latinos, and Not Just for Its Taste," *The Wall Street Journal*, October 21, 2003, p. A17; "Marketing to Hispanics," *Advertising Age* (Special Report), September 15, 2003, p. S1; "39 Million Make Hispanics Largest Minority Group," *USA Today*, June 19, 2003, p. 1A; "New Brooklyns Replace White Suburbs," *USA Today*, May 19, 2003, p. 1A; "Buying Power of Hispanics Is Set to Soar," *The Wall Street Journal*, April 18, 2003, p. B1; "Advertisers Point and Click to Find Hispanic Audiences," *Adweek*, April 7, 2003, p. 8; "Fresh from the Border," *Time* (Inside Business Supplement), April 2003; "Advertisers Tap into Hispanic Gold Mine," *USA Today*, February 21, 2003, p. 1B; "Prospecting: As Latinos Fan Out across America, Businesses Follow," *The Wall Street Journal*, November 26, 2002, p. A1; "Marketing to Hispanics," *Advertising Age* (Special Report), September 16, 2002, p. S1; "Goya Foods Leads an Ethnic Sales Trend," *The Wall Street Journal*, July 9, 2002, p. B4; "Big Advertising Firms Scoop Up Hispanic-Focused Agencies," *USA Today*, July 5, 2002, p. 2B; "Hispanic-Targeted Advertising Outpaces Overall Ad Growth," *The Wall Street Journal*, April 19, 2002, p. A17; Rebecca Gardyn, "Habla English?" *American Demographics*, April 2001, p. 54; M. Isabel Valdes, *Marketing to American Latinos* (Ithaca, NY: Paramount, 2000); "P&G Reaches Out to Hispanics," *The Wall Street Journal*, October 13, 2000, p. B1; "Why the Latino Market Is So Hard to Count," *The Wall Street Journal*, October 13, 2000, p. B1. For more on the Asian-American market, see U.S. Census data, including "The Asian Population: February 2002, C2KBR/01-16" and available from World Wide Web: <http://www.census.gov/population/www/socdemo/race>; "More Firms Reach Out to Asian Americans," *Investor's Business Daily*, September 29, 2003, p. A6; "Chinese at Home," *American Demographics*, February 2003, p. 12; "The Asian American Blind Spot," *American Demographics*, July 2001, p. 16; "U.S. Asian Population Grew and Diversified, Census Shows," *The Wall Street Journal*, May 15, 2001, p. B4; "Ford, Penney's Targeting Calif.'s Asian Populations," *Advertising Age*, January 4, 1999, p. 28; Charles R. Taylor and Barbara B. Stern,

"Asian-Americans: Television Advertising and the 'Model Minority' Stereotype," *Journal of Advertising*, Summer 1997, p. 47; Charles R. Taylor and Ju Yung Lee, "Not in *Vogue*: Portrayals of Asian Americans in Magazine Advertising," *Journal of Public Policy & Marketing*, Fall 1994, p. 239. See also Lucette B. Comer and J. A. F. Nicholls, "Communication Between Hispanic Salespeople and Their Customers: A First Look," *The Journal of Personal Selling & Sales Management*, Summer 2000, p. 121; Scott D. Roberts and H. S. Hart, "A Comparison of Cultural Value Orientations As Reflected by Advertisements Directed at the General U.S. Market, the U.S. Hispanic Market, and the Mexican Market," *Journal of Marketing Theory & Practice*, Winter 1997, p. 91; Geng Cui, "Marketing Strategies in a Multi-Ethnic Environment," *Journal of Marketing Theory & Practice*, Winter 1997, p. 122; Michael Laroche, Chung K. Kim, and Madeleine Clarke, "The Effects of Ethnicity Factors on Consumer Deal Interests: An Empirical Study of French- and English-Canadians," *Journal of Marketing Theory & Practice*, Winter 1997, p. 100.

CHAPTER 6

1. Available from World Wide Web: <http://www.yoplait. com>; "Wacky Colors, Unconventional Flavors Appeal to the Savvy Younger Set," *DSN Retailing Today*, May 19, 2003, p. 18; "Down with Tubes?" *Brandweek*, March 3, 2003, p. 1; "Spread 'Em," *Brandweek*, June 3, 2002, p. 1; "'To Go' Becoming the Way to Go," *Advertising Age*, May 13, 2002, p. 73; "Marketers Get Creative to Fit Needs of Retailers, Time-Pressed Consumers," *Brandweek*, May 13, 2002, p. 13; "You've Got Surveys," *American Demographics*, November 2000, p. 42; "Marketers of the Year: Groove Tube," *Brandweek* (SuperBrands Issue), October 16, 2000, pp. M111–M116; "Yoplait's Revenge Is Portable Yogurt that Kids Slurp Up," *Advertising Age*, September 11, 2000, p. 28; "Dannon Struggles against Go-Gurt's Market Incursions," *Advertising Age*, September 11, 2000, p. 28; "Squeezable Yogurt? Eggs on a Stick? You Got It!" *USA Today*, March 31, 2000, p. 1D; *Annual Report 2000*, General Mills; "Yogurt Goes Tubular," *Newsweek*, October 11, 1999, p. 63.

2. Kristina D. Frankenberger, "Consumer Psychology for Marketing," *Journal of the Academy of Marketing Science*, Summer 1996, p. 279; K. H. Chung, *Motivational Theories and Practices* (Columbus, Ohio: Grid, 1977), p. 40; A. H. Maslow, *Motivation and Personality* (New York: Harper & Row, 1970).

3. "Features Drive Kitchen Gadget Evolution," *DSN Retailing Today*, May 19, 2003, p. 20; "What Works for One Works for All," *Business Week*, April 20, 1992, p. 112.

4. "Who Said That? Buyers Don't Recognize Some Slogans," *USA Today*, October 1, 2003, p. 1B; "Super Tags, Still Believers," *Brandweek*, February 3, 2003, p. 16; "Big Ideas for Ducks and Their Keepers," *Brandweek*, October 13, 2003, p. 24; "Advertising that Keeps Going and Going . . . ," *Adweek*, February 3, 2003, p. 38.

5. For more on Ben & Jerry's, see Chapter 19, endnote 1. See also Les Carlson, Russell N. Laczniak, and Ann Walsh, "Socializing Children about Television: an Intergenerational Study," *Journal of the Academy of Marketing Science*, Summer 2001, p. 276; Elizabeth Cowley and Andrew A. Mitchell, "The Moderating Effect of Product Knowledge on the Learning and Organization of Product Information," *Journal of Consumer Research*, December 2003, p. 443; Stacy L. Wood and John G. Lynch Jr, "Prior Knowledge and Complacency in New Product Learning," *Journal of Consumer Research*, December 2002, p. 416; Naomi Mandel and Eric J. Johnson, "When Web Pages Influence Choice: Effects of Visual Primes on Experts and Novices," *Journal of Consumer Research*, September 2002, p. 235; Elizabeth S. Moore and Richard J. Lutz, "Children, Advertising, and Product Experiences: a Multimethod Inquiry," *Journal of Consumer Research*, Jun 2000, p. 31; Julie Ann Ruth, Frederic F. Brunel, and Cele C. Otnes, "Linking Thoughts to Feelings: Investigating Cognitive Appraisals and Consumption Emotions in a Mixed Emotions Context," *Journal of the Academy of Marketing Science*, Winter 2002, p. 44; Stijn M.

J. Van Osselaer and Chris Janiszewski, "Two Ways of Learning Brand Associations," *Journal of Consumer Research*, September 2001, p. 202; William E. Baker, "When Can Affective Conditioning and Mere Exposure Directly Influence Brand Choice?," *Journal of Advertising*, Winter 1999, p. 31; Jaideep Sengupta and Gita Venkataramani Johar, "Effects of Inconsistent Attribute Information on the Predictive Value of Product Attitudes: Toward a Resolution of Opposing Perspectives," *Journal of Consumer Research*, Jun 2002, p. 39; J. Jeffrey Inman, "The Role of Sensory-Specific Satiety in Attribute-Level Variety Seeking," *Journal of Consumer Research*, Jun 2001, p. 105; Jennifer Gregan-Paxton and Deborah R. John, "Consumer Learning by Analogy: A Model of Internal Knowledge Transfer," *Journal of Consumer Research*, December 1997, p. 266; M. C. Macklin, "Preschoolers' Learning of Brand Names From Visual Cues," *Journal of Consumer Research*, December 1996, p. 251; Jaideep Sengupta, Ronald C. Goodstein, and David S. Boninger, "All Cues Are Not Created Equal: Obtaining Attitude Persistence Under Low-Involvement Conditions," *Journal of Consumer Research*, March 1997, p. 351; John Kim, Jeen-Su Lim, and Mukesh Bhargava, "The Role of Affect in Attitude Formation: A Classical Conditioning Approach," *Journal of the Academy of Marketing Science*, Spring 1998, p. 143; Paul S. Speck and Michael T. Elliott, "Predictors of Advertising Avoidance in Print and Broadcast Media," *Journal of Advertising*, Fall 1997, p. 61; Frances K. McSweeney and Calvin Bierley, "Recent Developments in Classical Conditioning," *Journal of Consumer Research*, September 1984, p. 619; Scott A. Hawkins and Stephen J. Hoch, "Low-Involvement Learning: Memory without Evaluation," *Journal of Consumer Research*, September 1992, p. 212.

6. "Secrets of That New-Car Smell," *Car and Driver*, November 2003, p. 141; "Battling the Inferior-Interior Complex," *The Wall Street Journal*, December 3, 2001, p. B1. See also Anna S. Mattila and Jochen Wirtz, "Congruency of Scent and Music as a Driver of In-Store Evaluations and Behavior," *Journal of Retailing*, Summer 2001, p. 273.

7. "Sweet Success," *Brandweek*, May 12, 2003, p. 22.

8. "Purina Dog Chow: Grand Effie Winner, Pet Care/Gold Winner," *Brandweek*, (Special Effies Winner Supplement), 1997. See also Edward Rosbergen, Rik Pieters, and Michel Wedel, "Visual Attention to Advertising: A Segment-Level Analysis," *Journal of Consumer Research*, December 1997, p. 305; Gavan J. Fitzsimons and Vicki G. Morwitz, "The Effect of Measuring Intent on Brand-Level Purchase Behavior," *Journal of Consumer Research*, June 1996, p. 1; Ellen C. Garbarino and Julie A. Edell, "Cognitive Effort, Affect, and Choice," *Journal of Consumer Research*, September 1997, p. 147.

9. "A New Oxymoron: Hip Minivan," *Business Week*, October 20, 2003, p. 156; "Automakers Lavish Attention on Van Market," *USA Today*, August 6, 2003, p. 12B; "Nissan Attempts to Sex Up Quest," *Advertising Age*, August 4, 2003, p. 7; "Operation: Minivan," *The Wall Street Journal*, August 1, 2003, p. W1. See also Rohini Ahluwalia, "Examination of Psychological Processes Underlying Resistance to Persuasion," *Journal of Consumer Research*, September 2000, p. 217; Dena Cox and Anthony D. Cox, "Beyond First Impressions: the Effects of Repeated Exposure on Consumer Liking of Visually Complex and Simple Product Designs," *Journal of the Academy of Marketing Science*, Spring 2002, p. 119; J. Joseph Cronin Jr, Michael K Brady end G Tomas M Hult, "Assessing the Effects of Quality, Value, and Customer Satisfaction on Consumer Behavioral Intentions in Service Environments," *Journal of Retailing*, Summer 2000, p. 193; Yih Hwai Lee, "Manipulating Ad Message Involvement Through Information Expectancy: Effects on Attitude Evaluation and Confidence," *Journal of Advertising*, Summer 2000, p. 29; Vikas Mittal, William T. Ross, and Patrick M. Baldasare, "The Asymmetric Impact of Negative and Positive Attribute-Level Performance on Overall Satisfaction and Repurchase Intentions," *Journal of Marketing*, January 1998, p. 33; Mary F. Luce, "Choosing to Avoid: Coping With Negatively Emotion-Laden Consumer Decisions," *Journal of Consumer Research*, March 1998, p. 409; Calvin P. Duncan and Richard W. Olshavsky, "External Search: The Role of Consumer Beliefs," *Journal of Marketing*

Research, February 1982, p. 32; M. Joseph Sirgy, "Self-Concept in Consumer Behavior: A Critical Review," Journal of Consumer Research, December 1982, p. 287.

10. "Chock Full of Peanuts," American Demographics, April 1997, p. 60.

11. "For Asian Women, Weight-Loss Rule 1 Is Skip the Gym," The Wall Street Journal, October 9, 2003, p. A1; "Unilever Expands Slim-Fast to Create a Diet Megabrand," Advertising Age, June 23, 2003, p. 8; "Living Larger," USA Today, March 16, 1998, p. 4D; "If Fat-Free Pork Is Your Idea of Savory, It's a Bright Future," The Wall Street Journal, January 29, 1998, p. A1.

12. "The Dirt on At-Home Dry Cleaning," The Wall Street Journal, September 15, 2000, p. W14; "P&G Shifts Strategy for Dryel," Advertising Age, January 24, 2000, p. 4; "Novel P&G Product Brings Dry Cleaning Home," The Wall Street Journal, November 19, 1997, p. B1.

13. For more on wrinkle-free clothing, see "Botox for Broadcloth," The Wall Street Journal, October 7, 2002, p. A19; "'Wrinkle-Free' Shirts Don't Live Up to the Name," The Wall Street Journal, May 11, 1994, p. B1. For more on stain-resistant clothing, see "A Tie You Can Wipe Your Mouth With," The Wall Street Journal, October 14, 2003, p. D1; "Look, Ma, No Stains," Time, December 9, 2002, p. 64. For more on service quality, see Chapter 9, footnote #3. For more on service expectations, see "Can I Get a Smile with My Burger and Fries?" The Wall Street Journal, September 23, 2003, p. D6; "After the Sale," Brandweek, March 31, 2003, p. 20; "Service—with a Side of Sales," The Wall Street Journal Reports, October 29, 2001, p. R13; "Why Service Stinks," Business Week, October 23, 2000, p. 118; "Customer Service: Rewriting the Rules of the Road," Business Week E.Biz, September 18, 2000, p. EB86; "It's the Service, Stupid," Business Week E.Biz, April 3, 2000, p. EB118. See also A. Parasuraman, Valarie A. Zeithaml, and Leonard L. Berry, "Reassessment of Expectations As a Comparison Standard in Measuring Service Quality: Implications for Further Research," Journal of Marketing, January 1994, p. 111; Alain Genestre and Paul Herbig, "Service Expectations and Perceptions Revisited: Adding Product Quality to SERVQUAL," Journal of Marketing Theory & Practice, Fall 1996, p. 72; Valarie A. Zeithaml, Leonard L. Berry, and A. Parasuraman, "The Nature and Determinants of Customer Expectations of Service," Journal of the Academy of Marketing Science, Winter 1993, p. 1.

14. Harold H. Kassarjian and Mary Jane Sheffet, "Personality and Consumer Behavior: An Update," in H. Kassarjian and T. Robertson, Perspectives in Consumer Behavior (Glenview, IL: Scott, Foresman, 1981), p. 160; Todd A. Mooradian and James M. Olver, "'I Can't Get No Satisfaction:' The Impact of Personality and Emotion on Postpurchase Processes," Psychology & Marketing, July 1997, p. 379.

15. "It's Mind Vending . . . in the World of Psychographics," Time (Inside Business Bonus Section), October 2003; "Lifestyles Help Shape Innovation," DSN Retailing Today, August 4, 2003, p. 20; "Generation Next," Advertising Age, January 15, 2001, p. 14; "Head Trips," American Demographics, October 2000, p. 38; "Join the Club," Brandweek, February 15, 1999, p. 26; Rebecca Piirto Heath, "The Frontier of Psychographics," American Demographics, July 1996, p. 38; Robert A. Mittelstaedt, "Economics, Psychology, and the Literature of the Subdiscipline of Consumer Behavior," Journal of the Academy of Marketing Science, Fall 1990, p. 303; W. D. Wells, "Psychographics: A Critical Review," Journal of Marketing Research, May 1975, p. 196.

16. Available from World Wide Web: <www.sric-bi.com>; Judith Waldrop, "Markets with Attitude," American Demographics, July 1994, p. 22; "New VALS 2 Takes Psychological Route," Advertising Age, February 13, 1989, p. 24; Lynn R. Kahle, Sharon E. Beatty, and Pamela Homer, "Alternative Measurement Approaches to Consumer Values: The List of Values (LOV) and Values and Life Styles (VALS)," Journal of Consumer Research, December 1986, p. 405.

17. For more on kids' influence in purchase decisions, see "My Two Front Teeth—and a Handheld," Business Week, December 15, 2003,

p. 42; "My First Handheld," Business Week, September 1, 2003, p. 98; "Spending It All on the Kids," Time, July 14, 2003, p. 42; "Ads Put Kids in Minivan Spotlight," USA Today, June 30, 2003, p. 6B; "Targeting the Family's Chief Tech Officer," Adweek, June 16, 2003, p. 8; "Special Report: Kids, Tweens & Teens," Advertising Age, February 17, 2003, pp. S1–S6; "Deconstructing Cute," Business 2.0, December 2002, p. 47; "Family Secret: The Concierge Floor," The Wall Street Journal, September 27, 2002, p. W1; "Child's Play for Furniture Retailers," The Wall Street Journal, September 25, 2002, p. B1; "Catering to Kids," The Wall Street Journal, May 3, 2002, p. W1; "Peek-a-Boo, I See You—Clearly," The Wall Street Journal, January 25, 2002, p. W1; "Marketers Find 'Tweens' Too Hot to Ignore," USA Today, July 10, 2001, p. 13A; "Marketers Call on Kids to Help Design Web Sites," USA Today, June 5, 2001, p. 1B; "Kid-Fluence," USA Today, December 29, 2000, p. 1E; "Young Girls Targeted by Makeup Companies," Advertising Age, November 27, 2000, p. 15; "Retailers Reaching Out to Capture Kids' Clout," Advertising Age, October 9, 2000, p. 16; Alison Stein Wellner, "Generation Z," American Demographics, September 2000, p. 60; "Foods Targeting Children Aren't Just Child Play," Advertising Age, March 1, 1999, p. 16; James U. McNeal, "Tapping the Three Kids' Markets," American Demographics, April 1998, p. 37; "Hey Kid, Buy This!" Business Week, June 30, 1997, p. 62; Sharon E. Beatty and Salil Talpade, "Adolescent Influence in Family Decision Making: A Replication with Extension," Journal of Consumer Research, September 1994, p. 332. See also Ugur Yavas, Emin Babakus, and Nejdet Delener, "Family Purchasing Roles in Saudi Arabia: Perspectives from Saudi Wives," Journal of Business Research, September 1994, p. 75; Eric H. Shaw and Stephen F. I. Pirog, "A Systems Model of Household Behavior," Journal of Marketing Theory & Practice, Summer 1997, p. 17; Kay M. Palan and Robert E. Wilkes, "Adolescent-Parent Interaction in Family Decision Making," Journal of Consumer Research, September 1997, p. 159; Conway L. Lackman, David P. Hanson, and John M. Lanasa, "Social Relations in Culture and Marketing," Journal of Marketing Theory & Practice, Winter 1997, p. 144; Ellen R. Foxman, Patriya S. Tansuhaj, and Karin M. Ekstrom, "Adolescents' Influence in Family Purchase Decisions: A Socialization Perspective," Journal of Business Research, March 1989, p. 159; C. Lackman and J.M. Lanasa, "Family Decision-Making Theory: An Overview and Assessment," Psychology & Marketing, March/April 1993, p. 81. For more on women's influence in purchase decisions, see U.S. Census data, including "Women in the United States: A Profile, March 2000," and available from World Wide Web: <http://www.census.gov/population/www/ socdemo/women>; "A Guide to Who Holds the Purse Strings," The Wall Street Journal, June 22, 2000, p. A14; "How to Market to Women," Advertising Age, June 12, 2000, p. 24.

18. "Consumers Enjoy Lap of Luxury," Investor's Business Daily, October 27, 2003, p. A7; "Downsized Luxury," The Wall Street Journal, October 14, 2003, p. B1; "The Japanese Paradox," The Wall Street Journal, September 23, 2003, p. B1; "Luxury for the Masses," Brandweek, June 25, 2001, p. 16; "Special Report: Luxury Marketing," Advertising Age, June 11, 2001, p. S1; "Which Is Luxury?" USA Today, May 4, 2001, p. 1B; Hassan Fattah, "The Rising Tide," American Demographics, April 2001, p. 48; "Despite Downturn, Japanese Are Still Having Fits for Luxury Goods," The Wall Street Journal, April 24, 2001, p. B1; "The Rise of the Comfortable," Advertising Age, October 16, 2000, p. 60; "Class in America," Fortune, February 7, 1994, p. 114. See also Cornelia Pechmann and Susan J. Knight, "An Experimental Investigation of the Joint Effects of Advertising and Peers on Adolescents' Beliefs and Intentions about Cigarette Consumption," Journal of Consumer Research, Jun 2002, p. 5; Albert M. Muniz Jr and Thomas C. O'Guinn, "Brand Community," Journal of Consumer Research, March 2001, p. 412; Gary Cross, "Valves of Desire: a Historian's Perspective on Parents, Children, and Marketing," Journal of Consumer Research, December 2002, p. 441; Basil G. Englis and Michael R. Solomon, "To Be and Not to Be: Lifestyle Imagery, Reference Groups, and the Clustering of America," Journal of Advertising, Spring 1995, p. 13; Greg J. Duncan, Timothy M. Smeeding, and Willard Rodgers, "The Incredible Shrinking Middle Class," *American Demographics*, May 1992, p. 34; Dennis L. Rosen and Richard W. Olshavsky, "The Dual Role of Informational Social Influence: Implications for Marketing Management," *Journal of Business Research*, April 1987, p. 123; Terry L. Childers and Akshay R. Rao, "The Influence of Familial and Peer-based Reference Groups on Consumer Decisions," *Journal of Consumer Research*, September 1992, p. 198; Basil G. Englis and Michael R. Solomon, "To Be and Not to Be: Lifestyle Imagery, Reference Groups, and The Clustering of America," *Journal of Advertising*, Spring 1995, p. 13.

19. For more on opinion leaders and word-of-mouth publicity, see Chapter 14, endnote 17. See also "Auto Makers Find They Don't Want to Avoid Collisions in Movies," *The Wall Street Journal*, July 5, 2001, p. B1; "Small Wonder," *The Wall Street Journal*, June 25, 2001, p. R1; Rebecca Gardyn, "Granddaughters of Feminism," *American Demographics*, April 2001, p. 43; "A Wide Web of Advice," *Business Week E.Biz*, January 22, 2001, pp. EB18–EB20; "How to Generate Buzz to Sell Your Product," *Investor's Business Daily*, October 3, 2000, p. A1; "Word of Mouth in the Digital Age: Marketers Win when Friends Hit 'Send,'" *Brandweek*, October 2, 2000, p. 24. See also Barbara Bickart and Robert M. Schindler, "Internet Forums as Influential Sources of Consumer Information," *Journal of Interactive Marketing*, Summer 2001, p. 31; Robert Madrigal, "The Influence of Social Alliances with Sports Teams on Intentions to Purchase Corporate Sponsors' Products," *Journal of Advertising*, Winter 2000, p. 13; Peter C. Verhoef, Philip Hans Franses and Janny C. Hoekstra, "The Effect of Relational Constructs on Customer Referrals and Number of Services Purchased from a Multiservice Provider: Does Age of Relationship Matter?" *Journal of the Academy of Marketing Science*, Summer 2002, p. 202.

20. "Art of Noise," *Brandweek*, November 1, 1999, p. 78.

21. "Overcoming the Stigma of Dishwashers in Japan," *The Wall Street Journal*, May 19, 2000, p. B1; Sydney Roslow, "International Consumer Behavior: Its Impact on Marketing Strategy Development," *Journal of the Academy of Marketing Science*, Summer 1996, p. 278; R. Mead, "Where is the Culture of Thailand?" *International Journal of Research in Marketing*, September 1994, p. 401.

22. "Does Class Count in Today's Land of Opportunity?" *The New York Times*, January 18, 2003, p. A17; John L. Graham, "How Culture Works," *Journal of Marketing*, April 1996, p. 134; Gary D. Gregory and James M. Munch, "Cultural Values in International Advertising: An Examination of Familial Norms and Roles in Mexico," *Psychology & Marketing*, March 1997, p. 99; Shiretta F. Ownbey and Patricia E. Horridge, "Acculturation Levels and Shopping Orientations of Asian-American Consumers," *Psychology & Marketing*, January 1997, p. 1; Jennifer L. Aaker and Durairaj Maheswaran, "The Effect of Cultural Orientation on Persuasion," *Journal of Consumer Research*, December 1997, p. 315; Grant McCracken, "Culture and Consumption: A Theoretical Account of the Structure and Movement of the Cultural Meaning of Consumer Goods," *Journal of Consumer Research*, June 1986, p. 71.

23. "Will the British Warm Up to Iced Tea? Some Big Marketers Are Counting on It," *The Wall Street Journal*, August 22, 1994, p. B1. See also "Starbucks Hits a Humorous Note in Pitching Iced Coffee to Brits," *The Wall Street Journal*, September 1, 1999, p. B7.

24. "No More Shoppus Interruptus," *American Demographics*, May 2001, p. 39; "No Buy? Then Bye-Bye," *Business Week E.Biz*, April 16, 2001, p. EB6; "Ok, Forget the Whole Damn Thing," *Ecompany*, December 2000, p. 185; "Special Report: E-Tailing," *Business Week E.Biz*, May 15, 2000, pp. EB103–EB118; "Many Web Shoppers Abandon Virtual Carts," *Investor's Business Daily*, May 11, 2000, p. A8. See also Rajneesh Suri and Kent B. Monroe, "The Effects of Time Constraints on Consumers' Judgments of Prices and Products," *Journal of Consumer Research*, Jun 2003, p. 92; Pratibha A. Dabholkar and Richard P. Bagozzi, "An Attitudinal Model of Technology-Based Self-Service: Moderating Effects of

Consumer Traits and Situational Factors," *Journal of the Academy of Marketing Science*, Summer 2002, p. 184; Darren W. Dahl, Rajesh V. Manchanda and Jennifer J. Argo, "Embarrassment in Consumer Purchase: the Roles of Social Presence and Purchase Familiarity," *Journal of Consumer Research*, December 2001, p. 473; Charles S. Areni, Pamela Kiecker, and Kay M. Palan, "Is It Better to Give Than to Receive? Exploring Gender Differences in the Meaning of Memorable Gifts," *Psychology & Marketing*, January 1998, p. 81; Russell W. Belk, "Situational Variables and Consumer Behavior," *Journal of Consumer Research* 2, 1975, p. 157; John F. Sherry, Jr., "Gift Giving in Anthropological Perspective," *Journal of Consumer Research*, September 1983, p. 157.

25. Adapted and updated from James H. Myers and William H. Reynolds, *Consumer Behavior and Marketing Management* (Boston: Houghton Mifflin, 1967), p. 49. See also Ronald E. Goldsmith, "A Theory of Shopping," *Journal of the Academy of Marketing Science*, Fall 2000, p. 541; Judith Lynne Zaichkowsky, "Consumer Behavior: Yesterday, Today, and Tomorrow," *Business Horizons*, May/June 1991, p. 51.

26. Dawn Iacobucci, Phipps Arabie and Anand Bodapati, "Recommendation Agents on the Internet," *Journal of Interactive Marketing*, Summer 2000, p. 2; Dan Ariely, "Controlling the Information Flow: Effects on Consumers' Decision Making and Preferences," *Journal of Consumer Research*, September 2000, p. 233; Amitav Chakravarti and Chris Janiszewski, "The Influence of Macro-Level Motives on Consideration Set Composition in Novel Purchase Situations," *Journal of Consumer Research*, September 2003, p. 244; Mary Frances Luce, Jianmin Jia, and Gregory W. Fischer, "How Much Do You like It? Within-Alternative Conflict and Subjective Confidence in Consumer Judgments," *Journal of Consumer Research*, December 2003, p. 464; Ravi Dhar and Steven J. Sherman, "The Effect of Common and Unique Features in Consumer Choice," *Journal of Consumer Research*, December 1996, p. 193; Victor V. Cordell, "Consumer Knowledge Measures As Predictors in Product Evaluation," *Psychology & Marketing*, May 1997, p. 241; John V. Petrof and Naoufel Daghfous, "Evoked Set: Myth or Reality?" *Business Horizons*, May–June 1996, p. 72; Wayne D. Hoyer, "An Examination of Consumer Decision Making for a Common Repeat Purchase Product," *Journal of Consumer Research*, December 1984, p. 822; James R. Bettman, *An Information Processing Theory of Consumer Choice* (Reading, MA.: Addison-Wesley Publishing, 1979); Richard W. Olshavsky and Donald H. Granbois, "Consumer Decision Making: Fact or Fiction?" *Journal of Consumer Research*, September 1979, p. 93.

27. Fuan Li, Paul W. Miniard, and Michael J. Barone, "The Facilitating Influence of Consumer Knowledge on the Effectiveness of Daily Value Reference Information," *Journal of the Academy of Marketing Science*, Summer 2000, p. 424; Robin A. Coulter, Linda L. Price, and Lawrence Feick, "Rethinking the Origins of Involvement and Brand Commitment: Insights from Postsocialist Central Europe," *Journal of Consumer Research*, September 2003, p. 151; Gal Zauberman, "The Intertemporal Dynamics of Consumer Lock-In," *Journal of Consumer Research*, December 2003, p. 405; Brian T. Ratchford, "The Economics of Consumer Knowledge," *Journal of Consumer Research*, March 2001, p. 397; Cele Otnes, Tina M. Lowrey, and L J. Shrum, "Toward an Understanding of Consumer Ambivalence," *Journal of Consumer Research*, June 1997, p. 80; Ronald E. Goldsmith, "Consumer Involvement: Concepts and Research," *Journal of the Academy of Marketing Science*, Summer 1996, p. 281; Jeffrey B. Schmidt and Richard A. Spreng, "A Proposed Model of External Consumer Information Search," *Journal of the Academy of Marketing Science*, Summer 1996, p. 246; Raj Arora, "Consumer Involvement—What It Offers to Advertising Strategy," *International Journal of Advertising* 4, no. 2 (1985), p. 119; J. Brock Smith and Julia M. Bristor, "Uncertainty Orientation: Explaining Differences in Purchase Involvement and External Search," *Psychology & Marketing*, November/December 1994, p. 587.

28. Adapted from E. M. Rogers, *Diffusion of Innovation* (New York: Free Press, 2003). For an excellent example of sampling, see Krispy Kreme example in Chapter 19, endnote 2. For other sampling examples, see "Mr.,

Mrs., Meet Mr. Clean," *The Wall Street Journal*, January 30, 2003, p. B1; "J&J Supports Marathon Runners at Point of Pain," *Brandweek*, December 2, 2002, p. 32; "Taking the Free Out of Free Samples," *The Wall Street Journal*, September 25, 2002, p. D1; "Marketers Revel with Spring Breakers," *USA Today*, March 12, 2002, p. 3B; "When Free Samples Become Saviors," *The Wall Street Journal*, August 14, 2001, p. B1; "Small Wonder," *The Wall Street Journal*, June 25, 2001, p. R1; "Use of Samples in Drug Industry Raises Concern," *The Wall Street Journal*, July 19, 2000, p. B1; "Try It. You'll Like It," *The Wall Street Journal*, September 27, 1999, p. 15. See also Michael A. Jones, David L. Mothersbaugh, and Sharon E. Beatty, "Switching Barriers and Repurchase Intentions in Services," *Journal of Retailing*, Summer 2000, p. 259; Kevin Mason, Thomas Jensen, Scot Burton, and Dave Roach, "The Accuracy of Brand and Attribute Judgments: the Role of Information Relevancy, Product Experience, and Attribute-Relationship Schemata," *Journal of the Academy of Marketing Science*, Summer 2001, p. 307; Jan-Benedict E. M. Steenkamp and Katrijn Gielens, "Consumer and Market Drivers of the Trial Probability of New Consumer Packaged Goods," *Journal of Consumer Research*, December 2003, p. 368; Stephen J. Hoch, "Product Experience Is Seductive," *Journal of Consumer Research*, December 2002, p. 448.

29. "PepsiCo Tries to Clarify Pepsi One's Image," *The Wall Street Journal*, February 25, 2000, p. B7.

30. J. Jeffrey Inman and Marcel Zeelenberg, "Regret in Repeat Purchase Versus Switching Decisions: the Attenuating Role of Decision Justifiability," *Journal of Consumer Research*, Jun 2002, p. 116; Michael Tsiros and Vikas Mittal, "Regret: A Model of its Antecedents and Consequences in Consumer Decision Making," *Journal of Consumer Research*, March 2000, p. 401; Thomas A. Burnham, Judy K. Frels, and Vijay Mahajan, "Consumer Switching Costs: a Typology, Antecedents, and Consequences," *Journal of the Academy of Marketing Science*, Spring 2003, p. 109; Ziv Carmon, Klaus Wertenbroch, and Marcel Zeelenberg, "Option Attachment: When Deliberating Makes Choosing Feel like Losing," *Journal of Consumer Research*, Jun 2003, p. 15; Alan D. J. Cooke, Tom Meyvis, and Alan Schwartz, "Avoiding Future Regret in Purchase-Timing Decisions," *Journal of Consumer Research*, March 2001, p. 447; Anna S. Mattila, "The Impact of Cognitive Intertia on Postconsumption Evaluation Processes," *Journal of the Academy of Marketing Science*, Summer 2003, p. 287; William Cunnings and Mark Venkatesan, "Cognitive Dissonance and Consumer Behavior: A Review of the Evidence," *Journal of Marketing Research*, August 1976, p. 303; Sarah Fisher Gardial et al., "Comparing Consumers' Recall of Prepurchase and Postpurchase Product Evaluation Experience," *Journal of Consumer Research*, March 1994, p. 548.

31. Robert M. March, *The Honourable Customer: Marketing and Selling to the Japanese in the 1990s* (Melbourne, Vic.: Longman Professional, 1990); Robert Gottliebsen, "Japan's Stark Choices," *Business Review Weekly*, October 16, 1992. See also Annamma Joy, "Gift Giving in Hong Kong and the Continuum of Social Ties," *Journal of Consumer Research*, September 2001, p. 239.

32. "Fuel and Freebies," *The Wall Street Journal*, June 10, 2002, p. B1.

CHAPTER 7

1. Available from World Wide Web: <http://www.johndeere. com> and <http://www.jdparts.com> and <http://www. metokote.com>. See also "Outsourcing Is More than Cost Cutting," *Fortune*, October 26, 1998, p. 238C; *2003 Annual Report*, Deere & Company; *1999 Annual Report*, Deere & Company.

2. "Detroit to Suppliers: Quality or Else," *Fortune*, September 30, 1996, p. 134C. See also Thomas H. Stevenson and Frank C. Barnes, "What Industrial Marketers Need to Know Now about ISO 9000 Certification: a Review, Update, and Integration with Marketing," *Industrial Marketing Management*, November 2002, p. 695; Roger Calantone and Gary Knight, "The Critical Role of Product Quality in the International Performance of Industrial Firms," *Industrial Marketing Management*, November 2000, p. 493; Stanley E. Fawcett, Roger J. Calantone, and Anthony Roath, "Meeting Quality and Cost Imperatives in a Global Market," *International Journal of Physical Distribution & Logistics Management*, (6) 2000, p. 472; G. M. Naidu, V. K. Prasad, and Arno Kleimenhagen, "Purchasing's Preparedness for ISO 9000 International Quality Standards," *International Journal of Purchasing & Materials Management*, Fall 1996, p. 46; Wade Ferguson, "Impact of the ISO 9000 Series Standards on Industrial Marketing," *Industrial Marketing Management*, July 1996, p. 305.

3. "The Push to Streamline Supply Chains," *Fortune*, March 3, 1997, pp. 108C–R; P. F. Johnson, Michiel R. Leenders, and Harold E. Fearon, "Evolving Roles and Responsibilities of Purchasing Organizations," *International Journal of Purchasing & Materials Management*, Winter 1998, p. 2; Scott Elliott, "Collaborative Advantage: Winning Through Extended Enterprise Supplier Networks," *The Journal of Product Innovation Management*, September 2001, p. 352; Chris Howgego, "Maximizing Competitiveness Through the Supply Chain," *International Journal of Retail & Distribution Management*, (11) 2002, p. 603; Robert J. Trent and Robert M. Monczka, "Understanding Integrated Global Sourcing," *International Journal of Physical Distribution & Logistics Management*, (7) 2003, p. 607; Harry R. Page, "Revolution in Purchasing: Building Competitive Power Through Proactive Purchasing," *International Journal of Purchasing & Materials Management*, Fall 1996, p. 56; Joseph R. Carter and Ram Narasimhan, "A Comparison of North American and European Future Purchasing Trends," *International Journal of Purchasing & Materials Management*, Spring 1996, p. 12.

4. Jae H. Pae, Namwoon Kim, Jim K. Han, and Leslie Yip, "Managing Intraorganizational Diffusion of Innovations: Impact of Buying Center Dynamics and Environments," *Industrial Marketing Management*, November 2002, p. 719; Jeffrey E. Lewin, "The Effects of Downsizing on Organizational Buying Behavior: An Empirical Investigation," *Journal of the Academy of Marketing Science*, Spring 2001, p. 151; Larry C. Giunipero and Judith F. Vogt, "Empowering the Purchasing Function: Moving to Team Decisions," *International Journal of Purchasing & Materials Management*, Winter 1997, p. 8; Jerome M. Katrichis, "Exploring Departmental Level Interaction Patterns in Organizational Purchasing Decisions," *Industrial Marketing Management*, March 1998, p. 135; Robert D. McWilliams, Earl Naumann, and Stan Scott, "Determining Buying Center Size," *Industrial Marketing Management*, February 1992, p. 43; Ajay Kohli, "Determinants of Influence in Organizational Buying: A Contingency Approach," *Journal of Marketing*, July 1989, p. 50; Melvin R. Mattson, "How to Determine the Composition and Influence of a Buying Center," *Industrial Marketing Management*, August 1988, p. 205; Barbara C. Perdue, "The Size and Composition of the Buying Firm's Negotiation Team in Rebuys of Component Parts," *Journal of the Academy of Marketing Science*, Spring 1989, p. 121; R. Venkatesh, Ajay K. Kohli, and Gerald Zaltman, "Influence Strategies in Buying Centers," *Journal of Marketing*, October 1995, p. 71.

5. Daniel J. Flint, Robert B. Woodruff, and Sarah Fisher Gardial, "Exploring the Phenomenon of Customers' Desired Value Change in a Business-to-Business Context," *Journal of Marketing*, October 2002, p. 102; E. Stephen Grant, "Buyer-Approved Selling: Sales Strategies from the Buyers Side of the Desk," *Journal of the Academy of Marketing Science*, Winter 2004, p. 99; W. E. I. Patton, "Use of Human Judgment Models in Industrial Buyers' Vendor Selection Decisions," *Industrial Marketing Management*, March 1996, p. 135; Minette E. Drumwright, "Socially Responsible Organizational Buying: Environmental Concern As a Noneconomic Buying Criterion," *Journal of Marketing*, July 1994, p. 1; Lisa M. Ellram, "A Structured Method for Applying Purchasing Cost Management Tools," *International Journal of Purchasing & Materials Management*, Winter 1996, p. 11; Morgan P. Miles, Linda S. Munilla, and Gregory R. Russell, "Marketing and Environmental Registration/Certification: What Industrial Marketers Should Understand About ISO 14000," *Industrial*

Marketing Management, July 1997, p. 363; Sime Curkovic and Robert Handfield, "Use of ISO 9000 and Baldrige Award Criteria in Supplier Quality Evaluation," *International Journal of Purchasing & Materials Management,* Spring 1996, p. 2; M. Bixby Cooper, Cornelia Droge, and Patricia J. Daugherty, "How Buyers and Operations Personnel Evaluate Service," *Industrial Marketing Management* 20, no. 1 (1991), p. 81.

6. Richard F. Beltramini, "Exploring the Effectiveness of Business Gifts: Replication and Extension," *Journal of Advertising,* Summer 2000, p. 75; Dong-Jin Lee, M. Joseph Sirgy, James R. Brown and Monroe Murphy Bird, "Importers' Benevolence Toward Their Foreign Export Suppliers," *Journal of the Academy of Marketing Science,* Winter 2004, p. 32; Jeanette J. Arbuthnot, "Identifying Ethical Problems Confronting Small Retail Buyers During the Merchandise Buying Process," *Journal of Business Ethics,* May 1997, p. 745; Gail K. McCracken and Thomas J. Callahan, "Is There Such a Thing As a Free Lunch?" *International Journal of Purchasing & Materials Management,* Winter 1996, p. 44; Robert W. Cooper, Garry L. Frank, and Robert A. Kemp, "The Ethical Environment Facing the Profession of Purchasing and Materials Management," *International Journal of Purchasing & Materials Management,* Spring 1997, p. 2; I. Fredrick Trawick, John E. Swan, Gail W. McGee, and David R. Rink, "Influence of Buyer Ethics and Salesperson Behavior on Intention to Choose a Supplier," *Journal of the Academy of Marketing Science,* Winter 1991, p. 17; J. A. Badenhorst, "Unethical Behaviour in Procurement: A Perspective on Causes and Solutions," *Journal of Business Ethics,* September 1994, p. 739.

7. Michael D. Smith, "The Impact of Shopbots on Electronic Markets," *Journal of the Academy of Marketing Science,* Fall 2002, p. 446; Carol C. Bienstock, "Understanding Buyer Information Acquisition for the Purchase of Logistics Services," *International Journal of Physical Distribution & Logistics Management,* (8) 2002, p. 636; David Tucker and Laurie Jones, "Leveraging the Power of the Internet for Optimal Supplier Sourcing," *International Journal of Physical Distribution & Logistics Management,* (3) 2000, p. 255; H. L. Brossard, "Information Sources Used by an Organization During a Complex Decision Process: An Exploratory Study," *Industrial Marketing Management,* January 1998, p. 41; Michele D. Bunn, "Taxonomy of Buying Decision Approaches," *Journal of Marketing,* January 1993, p. 38; Patricia M. Doney and Gary M. Armstrong, "Effects of Accountability on Symbolic Information Search and Information Analysis by Organizational Buyers," *Journal of the Academy of Marketing Science,* Winter 1996, p. 57; Thomas G. Ponzurick, "International Buyers Perspective Toward Trade Shows and Other Promotional Methods," *Journal of Marketing Theory & Practice,* Winter 1996, p. 9; Mark A. Farrell and Bill Schroder, "Influence Strategies in Organizational Buying Decisions," *Industrial Marketing Management,* July 1996, p. 293; Richard G. Newman, "Monitoring Price Increases With Economic Data: A Practical Approach," *International Journal of Purchasing & Materials Management,* Fall 1997, p. 35; Barbara Kline and Janet Wagner, "Information Sources and Retailer Buyer Decision-Making: The Effect of Product-Specific Buying Experience," *Journal of Retailing,* Spring 1994, p. 75; Ellen Day and Hiram C. Barksdale, Jr., "How Firms Select Professional Services," *Industrial Marketing Management,* May 1992, p. 85; Edward F. Fern and James R. Brown, "The Industrial/Consumer Marketing Dichotomy: A Case of Insufficient Justification," *Journal of Marketing,* Spring 1984, p. 68; Rowland T. Moriarty, Jr. and Robert E. Spekman, "An Empirical Investigation of the Information Sources Used During the Industrial Buying Process," *Journal of Marketing Research,* May 1984, p. 137.

8. "With Promise of Big Savings, Net Bill Paying Could Soon Win Fans among U.S. Businesses," *Investor's Business Daily,* February 26, 2001, p. A7; "How Baxter, PNC, Pratt & Whitney Make the Internet Work for Them," *Investor's Business Daily,* February 12, 2001, p. A1; "Look, Ma, No Humans," *Business Week E-Biz,* November 20, 2000, p. EB122; "Hewlett-Packard's Slick Procurement System," *Ecompany,* November 2000, p. 236; "Setting Standards for Corporate Purchasing on the Internet," *Fortune,* September 8, 1997, p. 156; "Invoice? What's an Invoice?"

Business Week, June 10, 1996, p. 110. See also Werner Delfmann, Sascha Albers and Martin Gehring, "The Impact of Electronic Commerce on Logistics Service Providers," *International Journal of Physical Distribution & Logistics Management,* (3) 2002, p. 203; Daniel Knudsen, "Aligning Corporate Strategy and E-procurement Tools," *International Journal of Physical Distribution & Logistics Management,* (8) 2003, p. 720; Earl D. Honeycutt, Theresa B. Flaherty, and Ken Benassi, "Marketing Industrial Products on the Internet," *Industrial Marketing Management,* January 1998, p. 63.

9. "The New Golden Rule of Business," *Fortune,* February 21, 1994, p. 60; Janet L. Hartley and Thomas Y. Choi, "Supplier Development: Customers As a Catalyst of Process Change," *Business Horizons,* July–August 1996, p. 37; Theodore P. Stank, Margaret A. Emmelhainz, and Patricia J. Daugherty, "The Impact of Information on Supplier Performance," *Journal of Marketing Theory & Practice,* Fall 1996, p. 94.

10. "The Push to Streamline Supply Chains," *Fortune,* March 3, 1997, p. 108C; "Push from Above," *The Wall Street Journal,* May 23, 1996, p. R24; "The New Golden Rule of Business," *Fortune,* February 21, 1994, p. 60.

11. Much of the discussion in this section is based on research reported in Joseph P. Cannon and William D. Perreault, Jr., "Buyer-Seller Relationships in Business Markets," *Journal of Marketing Research,* November 1999. See also Joseph P. Cannon, "Buyer-Supplier Relationships and Customer Firm Costs," *Journal of Marketing,* January 2001, p. 29; Kelly Hewett, R. Bruce Money, and Subhash Sharma, "An Exploration of the Moderating Role of Buyer Corporate Culture in Industrial Buyer-Seller Relationships," *Journal of the Academy of Marketing Science,* Summer 2002, p. 229; Christian Homburg, Harley Krohmer, Joseph P. Cannon and Ingo Kiedaisch, "Customer Satisfaction in Transnational Buyer-Supplier Relationships," *Journal of International Marketing,* (4) 2002, p. 1; Christopher R. Moberg, Bob D. Cutler, Andrew Gross and Thomas W. Speh, "Identifying Antecedents of Information Exchange Within Supply Chains," *International Journal of Physical Distribution & Logistics Management,* (9) 2002, p. 755; Fred Lemke, Keith Goffin and Marek Szwejczewski, "Investigating the Meaning of Supplier-Manufacturer Partnerships: an Exploratory Study," *International Journal of Physical Distribution & Logistics Management,* (1) 2003, p. 12; Arnt Buvik and George John, "When Does Vertical Coordination Improve Industrial Purchasing Relationships?" *Journal of Marketing,* October 2000, p. 52; Alexandra J. Campbell, "What Affects Expectations of Mutuality in Business Relationships?" *Journal of Marketing Theory & Practice,* Fall 1997, p. 1; James C. Anderson, Hakan Hakansson, and Jan Johanson, "Dyadic Business Relationships Within a Business Network Context," *Journal of Marketing,* October 1994, p. 1; William W. Keep, Stanley C. Hollander, and Roger Dickinson, "Forces Impinging on Long-Term Business-to-Business Relationships in the United States: An Historical Perspective," *Journal of Marketing,* April 1998, p. 31.

12. "Purchasing's New Muscle," *Fortune,* February 20, 1995, p. 75; "Can Chrysler Get Blood from a Supplier?" *Business Week,* December 25, 2000, p. 56; "Chrysler's Checks to Suppliers, Shoppers to Shrink," *The Wall Street Journal,* December 8, 2000, p. B4; Christine Steinman, Rohit Deshpande, and John U. Farley, "Beyond Market Orientation: When Customers and Suppliers Disagree," *Journal of the Academy of Marketing Science,* Winter 2000, p. 109; Rosemary P. Ramsey and Ravipreet S. Sohi, "Listening to Your Customers: The Impact of Perceived Salesperson Listening Behavior on Relationship Outcomes," *Journal of the Academy of Marketing Science,* Spring 1997, p. 127.

13. "Jeep Builds a New Kind of Plant," *Fortune,* November 11, 2002, pp. T168B–L.

14. For more on outsourcing, see Chapter 20, endnote 12. See also "Why Some Sony Gear Is Made in Japan — by Another Company," *The Wall Street Journal,* June 14, 2001, p. A1; "Inside Out-Sourcing," *Fortune*/CNET Technology Review, Summer 2001, p. 85; "Outsourcing as a

Strategic Option: It's about More than Saving Money," *Investor's Business Daily*, May 7, 2001, p. A1; "You Order It, They'll Make It," *Business Week*, May 29, 2000, pp. 218D–J. For more on supplier speeds and costs, see "When Cool Heads Prevail," *Business Week*, June 11, 2001, p. 114; "Should Suppliers Be Partners?" *Business Week*, June 4, 2001, pp. 30B–D; "Machete Time," *Business Week*, April 9, 2001, p. 42; "Firms Boost Suppliers' Speeds, Win Investors' Hearts," *The Wall Street Journal*, April 6, 1998, p. A20; "Stores' Demands Squeeze Apparel Companies," *The Wall Street Journal*, July 15, 1997, p. B1. For more on JIT, see "Parts Shortages Hamper Electronics Makers," *The Wall Street Journal*, July 7, 2000, p. B5; "The Web at Work: Clorox Co." *The Wall Street Journal*, October 9, 2000, p. B21; "Kimberly-Clark Keeps Costco in Diapers, Absorbing Costs Itself," *The Wall Street Journal*, September 7, 2000, p. A1; "At Ford, E-Commerce Is Job 1," *Business Week*, February 28, 2000, p. 74; "Where 'Build to Order' Works Best," *Fortune*, April 26, 1999, pp. 160C–V. See also Leonard V. Coote, Edward J. Forrest and Terence W. Tam, "An Investigation into Commitment in Non-Western Industrial Marketing Relationships," *Industrial Marketing Management*, October 2003, p. 595; Teresa M. McCarthy and Susan L. Golicic, "Implementing Collaborative Forecasting to Improve Supply Chain Performance," *International Journal of Physical Distribution & Logistics Management*, (6) 2002, p. 431; James Hoyt and Faizul Huq, "From Arms-Length to Collaborative Relationships in the Supply Chain, an Evolutionary Process," *International Journal of Physical Distribution & Logistics Management*, (9) 2000, p. 750; Susan L. Golicic, Donna F. Davis, Teresa M. McCarthy and John T. Mentzer, "The Impact of E-Commerce on Supply Chain Relationships," *International Journal of Physical Distribution & Logistics Management*, (9) 2002, p. 851; Jan B. Heide, "Plural Governance in Industrial Purchasing," *Journal of Marketing*, October 2003, p. 18; John Ramsay, "The Case Against Purchasing Partnerships," *International Journal of Purchasing & Materials Management*, Fall 1996, p. 13.

15. For another example of a Toyota partnership, see "Why Toyota Wins Such High Marks on Quality Surveys," *The Wall Street Journal*, March 15, 2001, p. A1. See also "Japanese Auto Makers Help U.S. Suppliers Become More Efficient," *The Wall Street Journal*, September 9, 1991, p. A1.

16. For other examples of big/small partnerships, see "A Fruitful Relationship," *Business Week E.Biz*, November 20, 2000, pp. EB94–EB96; "Automating an Automaker," *Inc. Tech 2000*, No. 4, p. 86. See also "Polaroid Corp. Is Selling Its Technique for Limiting Supplier Price Increases," *The Wall Street Journal*, February 13, 1985, p. 36; "Making Honda Parts, Ohio Company Finds, Can Be Road to Ruin," *The Wall Street Journal*, October 5, 1990, p. A1. See also Paul N. Bloom and Vanessa G. Perry, "Retailer Power and Supplier Welfare: the Case of Wal-Mart," *Journal of Retailing*, Fall 2001, p. 379.

17. "A Blaze in Albuquerque Sets Off Major Crisis for Cell-Phone Giants," *The Wall Street Journal*, January 29, 2001, p. A1; "Toyota's Fast Rebound after Fire at Supplier Shows Why It Is Tough," *The Wall Street Journal*, May 8, 1997, p. A1; Larry R. Smeltzer and Sue P. Siferd, "Proactive Supply Management: The Management of Risk," *International Journal of Purchasing & Materials Management*, Winter 1998, p. 38; Paul D. Larson and Jack D. Kulchitsky, "Single Sourcing and Supplier Certification: Performance and Relationship Implications," *Industrial Marketing Management*, January 1998, p. 73; Cathy Owens Swift, "Preferences for Single Sourcing and Supplier Selection," *Journal of Business Research*, February 1995, p. 105.

18. "You Buy My Widgets, I'll Buy Your Debt," *Business Week*, August 1, 1988, p. 85; Robert E. Weigand, "The Problems of Managing Reciprocity," *California Management Review*, Fall 1973, p. 40.

19. Norman Anthony Johnson and Hershey H. Friedman, *The National Public Acountant*, June 2002, p. 6.

20. "Net Marketing 100 Best B-to-B Websites," *BtoB*, August 11, 2003, p. 1; "A Bazaar World Continues Online with Business Exchanges Thriv-

ing," *Investor's Business Daily*, December 18, 2002, p. A4; "Building a Market," *The Wall Street Journal Reports*, April 15, 2002, p. R14; "Exchanges: Making It Work," *The Wall Street Journal*, February 11, 2002, p. R16; "B2B: Doing What You Know Best," *ZDNet*, January 17, 2002; "Collaboration Replaces B2B," *Investor's Business Daily*, October 11, 2001, p. A6; "America's Future: The Tech Challenge," *Business Week*, August 27, 2001, p. 140; "Collaboration Software: Bic Finds Right Stuff for Cutting Costs in E-Rooms," *Investor's Business Daily*, August 9, 2001, p. A6; "B2B Tomorrow: Beyond Exchanges," *AME Info*, March 24, 2001; "B2B Exchanges Promise Click Fix," *Natural Foods Merchandiser*, November 2000, p. 20; "Industries, from Steel to Chemicals, Say One Internet Site May Not Meet Needs," *The Wall Street Journal*, February 28, 2000, p. A16; "Manufacturers Turning to B2B," *Investor's Business Daily*, March 20, 2001, p. A6. See also Goutam Chakraborty, Vishal Lala and David Warren, "An Empirical Investigation of Antecedents of B2B Websites' Effectiveness," *Journal of Interactive Marketing*, Autumn 2002, p. 51; C. M. Sashi and Bay O' Leary, "The Role of Internet Auctions in the Expansion of B2B Markets," *Industrial Marketing Management*, February 2002, p. 103; Geoff Easton and Luis Araujo, "Evaluating the Impact of B2B E-commerce: a Contingent Approach," *Industrial Marketing Management*, July 2003, p. 431; Irvine Clarke III and Theresa B. Flaherty, "Web-based B2B Portals," *Industrial Marketing Management*, January 2003, p. 15; Rajdeep Grewal, "An Investigation into the Antecedents of Organizational Participation in Business-to-Business Electronic Markets," *Journal of Marketing*, July 2001, p. 17; Li-Peng Khoo, Shu B. Tor, and Stephen S. G. Lee, "The Potential of Intelligent Software Agents in the World Wide Web in Automating Part Procurement," *International Journal of Purchasing & Materials Management*, Winter 1998, p. 46; Rodney L. Stump and Ven Sriram, "Employing Information Technology in Purchasing: Buyer-Supplier Relationships and Size of the Supplier Base," *Industrial Marketing Management*, March 1997, p. 127; Joel Herche, "Innovations in Procurement Management," *Journal of the Academy of Marketing Science*, Summer 2000, p. 450.

21. Available from World Wide Web: <http://www.getradeweb.com> and <http://www.gegxs.com>. See also "Why EDI Won't Die," *Business 2.0*, August 2003, p. 68; "Sales Are Clicking on Manufacturing's Internet Mart," *Fortune*, July 7, 1997, pp. 136C–T.

22. Available from World Wide Web: <http://www.national.com>. See also "Web Masters," *Sales & Marketing Management*, 2000 and 2001.

23. "Making It in the USA," *Business 2.0*, December 2003, p. 33; "Will 'Made in USA' Fade Away?" *Fortune*, November 24, 2003, p. 98; "Heroes of U.S. Manufacturing," *Fortune*, March 19, 2001, pp. 178C–HH. See also U.S. Bureau of the Census, *Statistical Abstract of the United States 2002* (Washington, DC: U.S. Government Printing Office, 2001); U.S. Bureau of the Census, *County Business Patterns 1998, United States* (Washington, DC: U.S. Government Printing Office, 2000); U.S. Bureau of the Census, *1997 Census of Manufacturers, Subject Series, General Summary* (Washington, DC: U.S. Government Printing Office, 2001).

24. Available from World Wide Web: <http://www.naics.com>. See also "Classified Information," *American Demographics*, July 1999, p. 16; "SIC: The System Explained," *Sales and Marketing Management*, April 22, 1985, p. 52; "Enhancement of SIC System Being Developed," *Marketing News Collegiate Edition*, May 1988, p. 4.

25. U.S. Bureau of the Census, *Statistical Abstract of the United States 2002* (Washington, DC: U.S. Government Printing Office, 2001); U.S. Bureau of the Census, *County Business Patterns 1998, United States* (Washington, DC: U.S. Government Printing Office, 2000). For more on targeting small business, see "Small Firms Enjoy Courtship of Big Suppliers," *The Wall Street Journal*, June 24, 2003, p. B9. For more on Canon, see "Perfecting the Pitch," *The Wall Street Journal*, May 23, 1996, p. R26; *1996 Annual Report*, Canon; "Can Anyone Duplicate Canon's Personal Copiers' Success?" *Marketing and Media Decisions*, Special Issue, Spring 1985, p. 97.

26. *2003 Annual Report*, Super Valu; *1996 Annual Report*, Super Valu.

27. *2003 Annual Report*, Safeway; *2003 Annual Report*, Food Lion; *2003 Annual Report*, Winn-Dixie; *2003 Annual Report*, A&P; Daulatram B. Lund, "Retail Scanner Checkout System: How Buying Committees Functioned," *Industrial Marketing Management* 18, no. 3 (1989), p. 179; Janet Wagner, Richard Ettenson, and Jean Parrish, "Vendor Selection Among Retail Buyers: An Analysis by Merchandise Division," *Journal of Retailing*, Spring 1989, p. 58.

28. "Create Open-to-Buy Plans the Easy Way," *Retail Control*, December 1984, p. 21.

29. Based on U.S. Census data and "Uncle Sam Is a Tough Customer," *Investor's Business Daily*, October 20, 2003, p. A8; "Hand-Helds' New Frontier," *The Wall Street Journal*, August 8, 2003, p. B1; "Super Soldiers," *Business Week*, July 28, 2003, p. 62; "For G.I. Joe, Smart Uniforms via Nanotech," *Business Week*, June 9, 2003, p. 125; "Supplier's Armor Plates Find a Ready Market," *Investor's Business Daily*, May 8, 2003, p. A7; "The Humvee of Laptops," *Business Week*, April 21, 2003, p. 74; "Invented to Save Gas, Kevlar Now Saves Lives," *USA Today*, April 16, 2003, p. 1B; "Raytheon on Target," *Business 2.0*, February 2003, p. 79; "Mickey Mouse, Nike Give Advice on Air Security," *The Wall Street Journal*, January 24, 2002, p. B1; "The Marines Learn New Tactics—from Wal-Mart," *Business Week*, December 24, 2001, p. 74; Sheryl B. Ball and Catherine C. Eckel, "Buying Status: Experimental Evidence on Status in Negotiation," *Psychology & Marketing*, July 1996, p. 381; Robert Gulbro and Paul Herbig, "Negotiating Successfully in Cross-Cultural Situations," *Industrial Marketing Management*, May 1996, p. 235; William C. Perkins, James C. Hershauer, Abbas Foroughi, and Michael M. Delaney, "Can a Negotiation Support System Help a Purchasing Manager?" *International Journal of Purchasing & Materials Management*, Spring 1996, p. 37.

30. For a detailed discussion of business ethics in a number of countries, see *Journal of Business Ethics*, (Special Issue) October 1997. See also John B. Ford, Michael S. LaTour, and Tony L. Henthorne, "Cognitive Moral Development and Japanese Procurement Executives: Implications for Industrial Marketers," *Industrial Marketing Management*, November 2000, p. 589; "How Can a U.S. Company Go International, Avoid the Economic Disaster of a Thai Baht. . . and Pay No Bribes?" *USA Today*, November 17, 1997, p. 5B; Larry R. Smeltzer and Marianne M. Jennings, "Why an International Code of Business Ethics Would Be Good for Business," *Journal of Business Ethics*, January 1998, p. 57; James J. Kellaris, Robert F. Dahlstrom, and Brett A. Boyle, "Contextual Bias in Ethical Judgment of Marketing Practices," *Psychology & Marketing*, October 1996, p. 677.

CHAPTER 8

1. Available from World Wide Web: <http://www.whitestrips. com>; "The New and Improved P&G," *Brandweek*, November 17, 2003, p. 44; "Crest Biting Back with Whiter Strips," *Brandweek*, September 8, 2003, p. 6; "P&G: New and Improved," *Business Week*, July 7, 2003, p. 52; "P&G Seeks Rejuvenating Effect for New Crest Line," *Brandweek*, June 16, 2003, p. 7; "The Cranky Consumer Works on Its Smile," *The Wall Street Journal*, January 14, 2003, p. D1; "Information, Please," *The Wall Street Journal Reports*, October 29, 2001, p. R6; "How Do You Feel about a $44 Tooth-Bleaching Kit?" *Business 2.0*, October 2001, p. 126.

2. "Winging into Wireless," *Business Week E. Biz*, February 18, 2002, pp. EB8–EB9; "How an Intranet Opened Up the Door to Profits," *Business Week E. Biz*, July 26, 1999, pp. EB32–EB38; "Here Comes the Intranet," *Business Week*, February 26, 1996, p. 76. See also Dale D. Achabal, Shelby H. McIntyre, Stephen A. Smith and Kirthi Kalyanam, "A Decision Support System for Vendor Managed Inventory," *Journal of Retailing*, Winter 2000, p. 430.

3. Gary L. Lilien, Arvind Rangaswamy, Gerrit H. van Bruggen, and Detlind Wierenga, "Bridging the Marketing Theory-Practice Gap with Marketing Engineering," *Journal of Business Research*, February 2002, p. 111; "Virtual Management," *Business Week*, September 21, 1998, p. 80; John T. Mentzer and Nimish Gandhi, "Expert Systems in Marketing: Guidelines for Development," *Journal of the Academy of Marketing Science*, Winter, 1992, p. 73; William D. Perreault, Jr., "The Shifting Paradigm in Marketing Research," *Journal of the Academy of Marketing Science*, Fall 1992, p. 367; J.M. McCann, W.G. Lahti, and J. Hill, "The Brand Manager's Assistant: A Knowledge-Based System Approach to Brand Management," *International Journal of Research in Marketing*, April 1991, p. 51.

4. Available from World Wide Web: <http://www.lenscrafters. com>; "LensCrafters Hits One Billion in Sales," *Business Wire*, February 3, 1998; "LensCrafters Polishes Image with Style," *Chain Store Age Executive*, October 1996, p. 144; "'SuperOpticals' Edge out the Corner Optician," *Adweek's Marketing Week*, October 1, 1990, p. 36; "LensCrafters Takes the High Road," *Adweek's Marketing Week*, April 30, 1990, p. 26.

5. Ram Narasimhan and Soo Wook Kim, "Information System Utilization Strategy for Supply Chain Integration," *Journal of Business Logistics*, (2) 2001, p. 51; Stanley F. Slater and John C. Narver, "Intelligence Generation and Superior Customer Value," *Journal of the Academy of Marketing Science*, Winter 2000, p. 120; Mark Peyrot, Nancy Childs, Doris Van Doren, and Kathleen Allen, "An Empirically Based Model of Competitor Intelligence Use," *Journal of Business Research*, September 2002, p. 747; Bruce H. Clark, "Business Intelligence Using Smart Techniques," *Journal of the Academy of Marketing Science*, Fall 2003, p. 488; Philip B. Evans and Thomas S. Wurster, "Strategy and the New Economics of Information," *Harvard Business Review*, September–October 1997, p. 70; Deborah Utter, "Information-Driven Marketing Decisions: Development of Strategic Information Systems," *Journal of the Academy of Marketing Science*, Spring 1998, p. 157; James M. Sinkula, "Market Information Processing and Organizational Learning," *Journal of Marketing*, January 1994, p. 35; Lawrence B. Chonko, John F. Tanner, Jr., and Ellen Reid Smith, "The Sales Force's Role in International Marketing Research and Marketing Information Systems," *Journal of Personal Selling and Sales Management*, Winter, 1991, p. 69; James C. Bondra and Tim R. V. Davis, "Marketing's Role in Cross-Functional Information Management," *Industrial Marketing Management*, May 1996, p. 187.

6. For more on CRM, see Chapter 3, endnote 12. See also "Study Finds High CRM Success Rate," *BtoB*, December 9, 2002, p. 19; "Data Mining: Welcome to Harrah's," *Business 2.0*, April 2002, p. 48; "The Net as a Lifeline," *Business Week E.Biz*, October 29, 2001, pp. EB16–EB23; "Moving Up to CRM," *Business 2.0*, August/September 2001, p. 149; "Marketers Hone Targeting," *Advertising Age*, June 18, 2001, p. T16; "Data Miners Reel after Wal-Mart Snub," *Brandweek*, May 21, 2001, p. 9; "Closer Than Ever," *Business Week Small Biz*, May 21, 2001, p. 14; "CRM: Shooting Holes in the Hype," *Advertising Age*, April 16, 2001, p. 1; "Firms See Value of CRM Software, but Adoption Can Be Costly," *Investor's Business Daily*, April 4, 2001, p. A7; "A Singular Sensation," *Brandweek*, February 28, 2001, p. 32; "The New Software Whizzes," *Business Week E.Biz*, December 11, 2000, pp. EB30–EB42; "Looking for Patterns," *The Wall Street Journal*, June 21, 1999, p. R16; "Know Your Customer," *The Wall Street Journal*, June 21, 1999, p. R18. See also Kim Bartel Sheehan and Mariea Grubbs Hoy, "Dimensions of Privacy Concern among Online Consumers," *Journal of Public Policy & Marketing*, Spring 2000, p. 62; Siva K. Balasubramanian, "The New Marketing Research Systems—How to Use Strategic Database Information for Better Marketing Decisions," *Journal of the Academy of Marketing Science*, Spring 1996, p. 179; "What's the Best Source of Market Research?" *Inc.*, June 1992, p. 108. For more on privacy, see Chapter 14, footnote #12 and Chapter 22, footnote #11.

7. For a discussion of ethical issues in marketing research, see "Name, Please: Surveyor Quietly Sells Student Information to Youth Marketer," *The Wall Street Journal*, December 13, 2001, p. A1; "How 'Tactical Research' Muddied Diaper Debate: a Case," *The Wall Street Journal*, May 17,

1994, p. B1. See also Rita Marie Cain, "Supreme Court Expands Federal Power to Regulate the Availability and Use of Data," *Journal of the Academy of Marketing Science*, Fall 2001, p. 425; Malcolm Kirkup and Marylyn Carrigan, "Video Surveillance Research in Retailing: Ethical Issues," *International Journal of Retail & Distribution Management*, (11) 2000, p. 470; Brian Carroll, "Price of Privacy: Selling Consumer Databases in Bankruptcy," *Journal of Interactive Marketing*, Summer 2002, p. 47; Eve M. Caudill and Patrick E. Murphy, "Consumer Online Privacy: Legal and Ethical Issues," *Journal of Public Policy & Marketing*, Spring 2000, p. 7; John R. Sparks and Shelby D. Hunt, "Marketing Researcher Ethical Sensitivity: Conceptualization, Measurement, and Exploratory Investigation," *Journal of Marketing*, April 1998, p. 92; Naresh K. Malhotra and Gina L. Miller, "An Integrated Model for Ethical Decisions in Marketing Research," *Journal of Business Ethics*, February 1998, p. 263; Stephen B. Castleberry, Warren French and Barbara A. Carlin, "The Ethical Framework of Advertising and Marketing Research Practitioners: A Moral Development Perspective," *Journal of Advertising*, June 1993, p. 39.

8. Linda I. Nowak, Paul D. Boughton, and Arun J. A. Pereira, "Relationships Between Businesses and Marketing Research Firms," *Industrial Marketing Management*, November 1997, p. 487; Peter M. Chisnall, "The Effective Use of Market Research: A Guide for Management to Grow the Business," *International Journal of Market Research*, Summer 2000, Vol. 42, 3, p. 359; Seymour Sudman and Edward Blair, *Marketing Research: A Problem Solving Approach* (Burr Ridge, IL: Irwin/McGraw-Hill, 1998). See also Christine Moorman, Rohit Deshpande, and Gerald Zaltman, "Factors Affecting Trust in Market Research Relationships," *Journal of Marketing*, January 1993, p. 81.

9. "Special Report: 2001 David Ogilvy Research Awards," *American Demographics*, March 2001, p. S1; "Special Report: 2000 David Ogilvy Research Awards," *American Demographics*, March 2000, p. S1; "What Consumer Research Won't Tell You," *Brandweek*, November 1, 1999, p. 40; "Intelligence Agents," *American Demographics*, March 1999, p. 52; "Grandma Got Run Over by Bad Research," *Inc.*, January 1998, p. 27.

10. For more on Google, see "Can Google Grow Up?" *Fortune*, December 8, 2003, p. 102; "Seeking Growth, Search Engine Google Acts like Ad Agency," *The Wall Street Journal*, October 18, 2003, p. B1; "Google: The Search Engine that Could," *USA Today*, August 26, 2003, p. 1D; "Search Star: Rising Clout of Google Prompts Rush by Internet Rivals to Adapt," *The Wall Street Journal*, July 16, 2003, p. A1; "The World According to Google," *Newsweek*, December 16, 2002, p. 46. For more on search engines, see World Wide Web: <http://www.windweaver.com/searchtools> and <http://www.windweaver.com/ searchengines>; "Sharpen Your Internet Search," *Business Week*, November 3, 2003, p. 106; "Web Searches: The Fix Is In," *Business Week*, October 6, 2003, p. 89; "No Excuse for Rigging Searches," *Business Week*, October 6, 2003, p. 168; "Ask Jeeves Gets 'Intuitive' in Ads, without Butler's Help," *Adweek*, August 11, 2003, p. 12; "Battle of the Search Bots," *BtoB*, August 11, 2003, p. 1; "Technical Adviser: Making the Most of Searches," *The Wall Street Journal Reports*, June 16, 2003, p. R10.

11. For more on Census data, see "The National Headcount," *American Demographics*, March 2001, p. S12; "Counting on the Census," *The Wall Street Journal*, February 14, 2001, p. B1. See also "Library Sites Can Be Useful when Doing Online Research," *Investor's Business Daily*, April 5, 2001, p. A13.

12. Available from World Wide Web: <http://www.burke.com/ ice/online>; "A Face Any Business Can Trust," *Business 2.0*, December 2003, p. 58; "No Focus Groups Here," *Investor's Business Daily*, November 19, 2003, p. A4; "Is Viagra Vulnerable?" *Business Week*, October 27, 2003, p. 70; "How the Roomba Was Realized," *Business Week*, October 6, 2003, pp. IM10–IM12; "Borders Sets Out to Make the Book Business Businesslike," *The Wall Street Journal*, May 20, 2002, p. B1; "Quite Contrary: How Gingham and Polyester Rescued a Retailer," *The Wall Street Journal*, May 9, 2003, p. A1; "The New Science of Focus Groups," *American*

Demographics, March 2003, p. 29; "Selling Cellphone with Mixed Messages," *The Wall Street Journal*, February 27, 2003, p. B5; "Botox for Broadcloth," *The Wall Street Journal*, October 7, 2002, p. A19; "Heinz Picks Purple as New EZ Squirt Color," *Brandweek*, June 25, 2001, p. 7; "Web Enhances Market Research," *Advertising Age*, June 18, 2001, p. T18. See also William J. McDonald, "Focus Group Research Dynamics and Reporting: An Examination of Research Objectives and Moderator Influences," *Journal of the Academy of Marketing Science*, Spring 1993, p. 161; Thomas Kiely, "Wired Focus Groups," *Harvard Business Review*, January–February 1998, p. 12.

13. "How Big Blue Is Turning Geeks into Gold," Fortune, June 9, 2003, p. 133.

14. "Japan's High-School Girls Excel in Art of Setting Trends," *The Wall Street Journal*, April 24, 1998, p. B1.

15. "Selling Sibelius Isn't Easy," *American Demographics*, The 1994 Directory, p. 24; "Symphony Strikes a Note for Research as It Prepares to Launch a New Season," *Marketing News*, August 29, 1988, p. 12.

16. Available from World Wide Web: <http://www.sawtooth.com/pages/glossary>; "A New Style: QB Net. . . Japanese Consumers," *The Wall Street Journal Reports*, September 22, 2003, p. R3; "Marketers Re-Evaluate Research," *BtoB*, February 10, 2003, p. 1; "Today, Brawny Men Help with the Kids and the Housework," *The Wall Street Journal*, October 4, 2002, p. B2; "Educated Guesses: Sampling Is Taboo, but the Census Does Plenty of Imputing," *The Wall Street Journal*, August 30, 2001, p. A1; "You've Got Surveys," *American Demographics*, November 2000, p. 42; "A Matter of Opinion," *The Wall Street Journal Reports*, October 23, 2000, p. R46; "Online Testing Rated," *Advertising Age*, May 8, 2000, p. 64; "The Surfer in the Family," *American Demographics*, April 2000, p. 34; "Market Research for the Internet Has Its Drawbacks," *The Wall Street Journal*, March 2, 2000, p. B4; "High Level of Comfort Leads to Truthful Research Worth a Mint," *USA Today*, May 17, 1999, p. 1A. See also Stanley E. Griffis, Thomas J. Goldsby, and Martha Cooper, "Web-Based and Mail Surveys: a Comparison of Response, Data, and Cost," *Journal of Business Logistics*, (2) 2003, p. 237; Christine M. Fox, K. L. Robinson, and Debra Boardley, "Cost-Effectiveness of Follow-Up Strategies in Improving the Response Rate of Mail Surveys," *Industrial Marketing Management*, March 1998, p. 127; Kathy E. Green, "Sociodemographic Factors and Mail Survey Response," *Psychology & Marketing*, March 1996, p. 171; Terry L. Childers and Steven J. Skinner, "Toward a Conceptualization of Mail Survey Response Behavior," *Psychology & Marketing*, March 1996, p. 185.

17. Available from World Wide Web: <http://www.whirlpool.com> and <http://acsi.asqc.org>; " Like, What's a Spin Cycle?" The Wall Street Journal, June 4, 2002, p. B1; "Firms Hope to Clean Up Taking Housework High-Tech," *The Wall Street Journal*, March 16, 2001, p. B4; "As I Was Saying to My Refrigerator. . .," *Business Week E.Biz*, September 18, 2000, p. EB40; "Now Are You Satisfied?" *Fortune*, February 16, 1998, p.161; "Product Pampering," *Brandweek*, June 16, 1997, p. 29; Deborah Duarte and Nancy Snyder, "From Experience: Facilitating Global Organizational Learning in Product Development at Whirlpool Corporation," *Journal of Product Innovation Management*, January 1997, p. 48.

18. "Red, White, and Blue," *Beverage Industry*, February 2002, p. 20.

19. For more on types of observation, see "Sharpening the Focus," *Brandweek*, November 3, 2003, p. 28; "Rear Window," *Business 2.0*, August 2003, p. 72; "U.S. Satellite May Play 'I Spy' with Brazil Citrus Industry," *The Wall Street Journal*, January 28, 2003, p. B1; "Shop, You're on Candid Camera," *USA Today*, November 6, 2002, p. 1B; "Special Report Ethnographic Research: Watch Me Now," *American Demographics*, October 2002, pp. S1–S8; "McDonald's Asks Mysetery Shoppers What Ails Sales," *The Wall Street Journal*, December 17, 2001, p. B1; "P&G Checks Out Real Life," *The Wall Street Journal*, May 17, 2001, p. B1; "Research on a Shoestring," *American Demographics*, April 2001, p. 38; "Attention

Shoppers: This Man Is Watching You," *Fortune*, July 19, 1999, p. 131; "The New Market Research," *Inc.*, July 1998, p. 87. See also Stephen J. Grove and Raymond P. Fisk, "Observational Data Collection Methods for Services Marketing: An Overview," *Journal of the Academy of Marketing Science*, Summer 1992, p. 217; Magid M. Abraham and Leonard M. Lodish, "An Implemented System for Improving Promotion Productivity Using Store Scanner Data," *Marketing Science*, Summer 1993, p. 248.

20. "Will Your Web Business Work? Take It for a Test Drive," *Ecompany*, May 2001, p. 101; "Ads Awaken to Fathers' New Role in Family Life," *Advertising Age*, January 10, 1994, p. S8; "AT&T's Secret Multi-Media Trials Offer Clues to Capturing Interactive Audiences," *The Wall Street Journal*, July 28, 1993, p. B1; "Experimenting in the U.K.: Phone, Cable Deals Let U.S. Test Future," *USA Today*, June 28, 1993, p. 1B. See also Raymond R. Burke, "Virtual Shopping: Breakthrough in Marketing Research," *Harvard Business Review*, March–April 1996, p. 120; Glen L. Urban, Bruce D. Weinberg, and John R. Hauser, "Premarket Forecasting of Really-New Products," *Journal of Marketing*, January 1996, p. 47.

21. For more on Nielsen's people meters, see "Nielsen's Feud with TV Networks Shows Scarcity of Marketing Data," *The Wall Street Journal*, October 29, 2003, p. A1; "Nielsen Adapts Its Methods as TV Evolves," *The Wall Street Journal*, September 29, 2003, p. B1; "People Meters Push Right Button," *Advertising Age*, May 12, 2003, p. S22; "Confessions of a Nielsen Household," *American Demographics*, May 2001. See also "Trying to Clean Up Sweeps," *American Demographics*, May 2001, p. 42; "The Metrics System," *Brandweek*, November 13, 2000, p. 106; "Special Report: Top 25 Global Research Organizations," *Advertising Age*, August 24, 2000; "We're Being Watched," *American Demographics*, October 1998, p. 52; "Special Report: 100 Leading Research Companies," *Advertising Age*, May 19, 1997; Peter J. Danaher and Terence W. Beed, "A Coincidental Survey of People Meter Panelists: Comparing What People Say with What They Do," *Journal of Advertising Research*, January/February 1993, p. 86.

22. For more detail on data analysis techniques, see Joe Hair, Rolph Anderson, Ron Tatham, and William Black, *Multivariate Data Analysis* (New York: Prentice-Hall, 1998) or other marketing research texts. See also "Merry Maids Clean Up Territories with MapInfo System," *Investor's Business Daily*, February 20, 2001, p. A8; Michael D. Johnson and Elania J. Hudson, "On the Perceived Usefulness of Scaling Techniques in Market Analysis," *Psychology & Marketing*, October 1996, p. 653; Milton D. Rosenau, "Graphing Statistics and Data: Creating Better Charts," *Journal of Product Innovation Management*, March 1997, p. 144.

23. "Careful What You Ask For," *American Demographics*, July 1998, p. 8; See also John G. Keane, "Questionable Statistics," *American Demographics*, June 1985, p. 18. Detailed treatment of confidence intervals is beyond the scope of this text, but it is covered in most marketing research texts, such as Donald R. Lehmann and Russ Winer, *Analysis for Marketing Planning* (Burr Ridge, IL: Irwin/McGraw-Hill, 2001).

24. "Chinese Puzzle: Spotty Consumer Data," *The Wall Street Journal*, October 15, 2003, p. B1. See also Thomas Tsu Wee Tan and Tan Jee Lui, "Globalization and Trends in International Marketing Research in Asia," *Journal of Business Research*, October 2002, p. 799; Masaaki Kotabe, "Using Euromonitor Database in International Marketing Research," *Journal of the Academy of Marketing Science*, Spring 2002, p. 172.

25. Alan R. Andreasen, "Cost-Conscious Marketing Research," *Harvard Business Review*, July–August, 1983, p. 74; A. Parasuraman, "Research's Place in the Marketing Budget," *Business Horizons*, March/April 1983, p. 25; Jack J. Honomichl, "Point of View: Why Marketing Information Should Have Top Executive Status," *Journal of Advertising Research*, November/December 1994, p. 61; Jim Bessen, "Riding the Marketing Information Wave," *Harvard Business Review*, September–October 1993, p. 150.

CHAPTER 9

1. "Segway Conference in Chicago Lures Device's Die-Hard Fans," *Investor's Business Daily*, September 2, 2003, p. A6; "President's Tumble Off a Segway Seems a Tiny Bit Suspicious," *USA Today*, June 18, 2003, p. 3B; "Watch Your Step: Segways Ahead," *USA Today*, June 17, 2003, p. 1A; "A Costly Segway," *Fortune*, April 28, 2003, p. 42; "Segway Gives an Easy Ride, but It's Best on City Sidewalks," *The Wall Street Journal*, April 10, 2003, p. B1; "A Glint in Detroit's Eyes," *Business 2.0*, February 2003, p. 44; "Is Segway Going Anywhere?" *Business Week*, January 27, 2003, p. 42; "On the Pavement, a New Contender," *The New York Times*, January 23, 2003, p. E1; "Zippy Transport for City and Surf," *Business Week*, July 8, 2002, p. 86; "Smoothing the Way for Segway," *Business Week*, April 15, 2002, p. 10; "Can Segway Deliver for Postal Service?" *Investor's Business Daily*, January 15, 2002, p. A6.

2. R. Kenneth Teas and Sanjeev Agarwal, "The Effects of Extrinsic Product Cues on Consumers' Perceptions of Quality, Sacrifice, and Value," *Journal of the Academy of Marketing Science*, Spring 2000, p. 278; Amna Kirmani and Akshay R. Rao, "No Pain, No Gain: a Critical Review of the Literature on Signaling Unobservable Product Quality," *Journal of Marketing*, April 2000, p. 66; Neil A. Morgan and Douglas W. Vorhies, "Product Quality Alignment and Business Unit Performance," *The Journal of Product Innovation Management*, November 2001, p. 396; Joseph M. Juran, "Made In U.S.A.: A Renaissance in Quality," *Harvard Business Review*, July–August 1993, p. 47; "Measuring Quality Perception of America's Top Brands," *Brandweek*, April 4, 1994, p. 24; Neil A. Morgan and Nigel F. Piercy, "Market-Led Quality," *Industrial Marketing Management*, May 1992, p. 111.

3. For more on service expectations, see Chapter 6, footnote #13. For more on service quality, see *2003 Annual Report*, MCI; *2003 Annual Report*, Merrill Lynch. For an excellent example on Avis, see "The Payoff for Trying Harder," *Business 2.0*, July 2002, p. 84; "Avis to Try Even Harder with Ads Touting High Quality of Service," *The Wall Street Journal*, February 18, 2000, p. B9. For more on air service, see "Paved Paradise: The New Airport Parking Lots," *The Wall Street Journal*, November 12, 2003, p. D1; "Flat-Out Winners," *Business Week*, October 27, 2003, p. 132. See also "The Demise of Free Pizza Delivery," *The Wall Street Journal*, August 19, 2003, p. D1; "Pizza Chains Deliver . . . Fees," *USA Today*, September 4, 2002, p. 3B. See also Neeli Bendapudi and Robert P. Leone, "Psychological Implications of Customer Participation in Co-Production," *Journal of Marketing*, January 2003, p. 14; Leonard L. Berry, Kathleen Seiders and Dhruv Grewal, "Understanding Service Convenience," *Journal of Marketing*, July 2002, p. 1; Matthew L. Meuter, Amy L. Ostrom, Robert I. Roundtree, and Mary Jo Bitner, "Self-Service Technologies: Understanding Customer Satisfaction with Technology-Based Service Encounters," *Journal of Marketing*, July 2000, p. 50; Valarie A. Zeithaml, A. Parasuraman and Arvind Malhotra, "Service Quality Delivery Through Web Sites: a Critical Review of Extant Knowledge," *Journal of the Academy of Marketing Science*, Fall 2002, p. 362; James L. Thomas, Scott J. Vitell, Faye W. Gilbert, and Gregory M. Rose, "The Impact of Ethical Cues on Customer Satisfaction with Service," *Journal of Retailing*, Fall 2002, p. 167; Mary Jo Bitner, Stephen W. Brown and Matthew L. Meuter, "Technology Infusion in Service Encounters," *Journal of the Academy of Marketing Science*, Winter 2000, p. 138; Valerie S. Folkes and Vanessa M. Patrick, "The Positivity Effect in Perceptions of Services: Seen One, Seen Them All?," *Journal of Consumer Research*, June 2003, p. 125; Dwayne D. Gremler, "Discovering the Soul of Service: The Nine Drivers of Sustainable Business Success," *Journal of the Academy of Marketing Science*, Spring 2000, p. 311; James Golleher, "Value-Added Customer Service," *Journal of Personal Selling & Sales Management*, Spring 1997, p. 71; James Reardon, Chip Miller, Ronald Hasty, and Blaise J. Waguespack, "A Comparison of Alternative Theories of Services Marketing," *Journal of Marketing Theory & Practice*, Fall 1996, p. 61; James C. Anderson and James A. Narus, "Capturing the Value of Supplementary Services," *Harvard Business Review*, January–February 1995, p. 75;

Mary Jo Bitner, Bernard H. Booms, and Lois A. Mohr, "Critical Service Encounters: The Employee's Viewpoint," *Journal of Marketing*, October 1994, p. 95.

4. Edward M. Tauber, "Why Do People Shop?" *Journal of Marketing*, October 1972, p. 46; Christopher H. Lovelock, "Classifying Services to Gain Strategic Marketing Insights," *Journal of Marketing*, Summer 1983, p. 9. Tom Boyt and Michael Harvey, "Classification of Industrial Services," *Industrial Marketing Management*, July 1997, p. 291.

5. Dennis W. Rook, "The Buying Impulse," *Journal of Consumer Research*, September 1987, p. 189; Cathy J. Cobb and Wayne D. Hoyer, "Planned Versus Impulse Purchase Behavior," *Journal of Retailing*, Winter 1986, p. 384.

6. For example, see "Russian Maneuvers Are Making Palladium Ever More Precious," *The Wall Street Journal*, March 6, 2000, p. A1. See also William S. Bishop, John L. Graham, and Michael H. Jones, "Volatility of Derived Demand in Industrial Markets and Its Management Implications," *Journal of Marketing*, Fall 1984, p. 95.

7. William B. Wagner and Patricia K. Hall, "Equipment Lease Accounting in Industrial Marketing Strategy," *Industrial Marketing Management 20*, no. 4 (1991), p. 305; Robert S. Eckley, "Caterpillar's Ordeal: Foreign Competition in Capital Goods," *Business Horizons*, March/April 1989, p. 80; M. Manley, "To Buy or Not to Buy," *Inc.*, November 1987, p. 189.

8. P. Matthyssens and W. Faes, "OEM Buying Process for New Components: Purchasing and Marketing Implications," *Industrial Marketing Management*, August 1985, p. 145; Paul A. Herbig and Frederick Palumbo, "Serving the Aftermarket in Japan and the United States," *Industrial Marketing Management*, November 1993, p. 339; Timothy L. Wilson and Frank E. Smith, "Business Services 1982–1992: Growth, Industry Characteristics, Financial Performance," *Industrial Marketing Management*, March 1996, p. 162.

9. Ruth H. Krieger and Jack R. Meredith, "Emergency and Routine MRO Part Buying," *Industrial Marketing Management*, November 1985, p. 277; Warren A. French et al., "MRO Parts Service in the Machine Tool Industry," *Industrial Marketing Management*, November 1985, p. 283. See also "The Web's New Plumbers," *Ecompany*, March 2001, p. 126.

10. For more on Listerine PocketPaks, see "The Strip Club," *Business 2.0*, June 2003, p. 36; "Marketer of the Year: PocketPaks, a Breath of Minty Fresh Air," *Brandweek*, October 14, 2002, pp. M42–M46. For more on brand extensions, see "Hershey Has a Taste for Line Extensions," *Brandweek*, October 27, 2003, p. 4; Kellogg Milks Vanilla Trend for Special K," *Brandweek*, September 15, 2003, p. 4; "Mr. Clean Gets $50M Push," *Advertising Age*, August 18, 2003, p. 3; "Great for Combat and Camping," *Business Week*, May 12, 2003, p. 12. For more on brand equity and brand value, see "Hard Lesson Learned: Premium and No-Frills Don't Mix," *The Wall Street Journal*, November 3, 2003, p. B1; "Nonprofits Can Provide a Brand Name that Sells," *The Wall Street Journal*, September 23, 2003, p. B11; "Rip Van Brands," *Brandweek*, July 14, 2003, p. 24; "Tyson: Is There Life Outside the Chicken Coop?" *Business Week*, March 10, 2003, p. 77; "Can GE Make Lexan as Famous as Teflon?" *The Wall Street Journal*, March 7, 2003, p. B1; "The Art of Brand Revival," *Business 2.0*, September 2002, p. 45; "New ABCs of Branding," *The Wall Street Journal*, August 26, 2002, p. B1; "Cookware Heavyweights," *The Wall Street Journal*, June 21, 2002, p. B1; "Big Brands (Small Companies)," *Business Week Small Biz*, August 13, 2001, p. 12; "When Designers Attack!" *Ecompany*, June 2001, p. 45. See also Arjun Chaudhuri and Morris B. Holbrook, "The Chain of Effects from Brand Trust and Brand Affect to Brand Performance: the Role of Brand Loyalty," *Journal of Marketing*, April 2001, p. 81; Boonghee Yoo, Naveen Donthu and Sungho Lee, "An Examination of Selected Marketing Mix Elements and Brand Equity," *Journal of the Academy of Marketing Science*, Spring 2000, p. 195; Zeynep Gurhan-Canli, "The Effect of Expected Variability of Product Quality and Attribute Uniqueness on Family Brand Evaluations," *Journal*

of Consumer Research, June 2003, p. 105; Russell Casey, "Designing Brand Identity: A Complete Guide to Creating, Building, and Maintaining Strong Brands," *Journal of the Academy of Marketing Science*, Winter 2004, p. 100; Subramanian Balachander and Sanjoy Ghose, "Reciprocal Spillover Effects: a Strategic Benefit of Brand Extensions," *Journal of Marketing*, January 2003, p. 1; Rashmi Adaval, "How Good Gets Better and Bad Gets Worse: Understanding the Impact of Affect on Evaluations of Known Brands," *Journal of Consumer Research*, December 2003, p. 352; Stijn M. J. Van Osselaer and Joseph W. Alba, "Consumer Learning and Brand Equity," *Journal of Consumer Research*, June 2000, p. 1; Sheri Bridges, Kevin Lane Keller and Sanjay Sood, "Communication Strategies for Brand Extensions: Enhancing Perceived Fit by Establishing Explanatory Links," *Journal of Advertising*, Winter 2000, p. 1; Elizabeth S. Moore, William L. Wilkie, and Richard J. Lutz, "Passing the Torch: Intergenerational Influences as a Source of Brand Equity," *Journal of Marketing*, April 2002, p. 17; Rohini Ahluwalia and Zeynep Gurhan-Canli, "The Effects of Extensions on the Family Brand Name: An Accessibility-Diagnosticity Perspective," *Journal of Consumer Research*, December 2000, p. 371; Kevin P. Gwinner and John Eaton, "Building Brand Image Through Event Sponsorship: the Role of Image Transfer," *Journal of Advertising*, Winter 1999, p. 47; Susan Mudambi, "Branding Importance in Business-To-Business Markets: Three Buyer Clusters," *Industrial Marketing Management*, September 2002, p. 525; James H. McAlexander, John W. Schouten, and Harold F. Koening, "Building Brand Community," *Journal of Marketing*, January 2002, p. 38; Richard C. Leventhal, "Branding Strategy," *Business Horizons*, September–October 1996, p. 17; Deborah R. John, Barbara Loken, and Christopher Joiner, "The Negative Impact of Extensions: Can Flagship Products Be Diluted?" *Journal of Marketing*, January 1998, p. 19; Cathy J. Cobb-Walgren, Cynthia A. Ruble, and Naveen Donthu, "Brand Equity, Brand Preference, and Purchase Intent," *Journal of Advertising*, Fall 1995, p. 25; Vijay Vishwanath and Jonathan Mark, "Your Brand's Best Strategy," *Harvard Business Review*, May–June 1997, p. 123; John A. Quelch and David Kenny, "Extend Profits, Not Product Lines," *Harvard Business Review*, September 1994–October 1994, p. 153; Linda B. Samuels and Samuels Jeffery M, "Famous Marks Now Federally Protected Against Dilution," *Journal of Public Policy & Marketing*, Fall 1996, p. 307; Pamela W. Henderson and Joseph A. Cote, "Guidelines for Selecting or Modifying Logos," *Journal of Marketing*, April 1998, p. 14; Erich Joachimsthaler and David A. Aaker, "Building Brands Without Mass Media," *Harvard Business Review*, January–February 1997, p. 39.

11. "Long Live the Dudes," *Adweek*, June 2, 2003, p. 32; "Pepsi Is Planning Promotions to Put Some Fizz into Summer," *The Wall Street Journal*, May 1, 2003, p. B5; "Pepsi Plans New Mountain Dew Flavor," *The Wall Street Journal*, March 12, 2003, p. B9A; "Call It the Pepsi Blue Generation," *Business Week*, February 3, 2003, p. 96; "On the Web, Word-of-Mouth Marketing Can Become Viral," *Investor's Business Daily*, January 30, 2002, p. A4; "Cracking the Code for Pepsi," *Brandweek*, October 14, 2002, p. M13; "Beat Is On for Pepsi," *USA Today*, August 28, 2002, p. 3B" Pepsi Adds Blue-Hued Beverage to Spectrum of Colored Sodas," *The Wall Street Journal*, May 8, 2002. p. B2; "Code Red: PepsiCo's Guerrilla Conquest," *The Wall Street Journal*, August 17, 2001, p. B5.

12. "Global Products Require Name-Finders," *The Wall Street Journal*, April 11, 1996, p. B8; Martin S. Roth, "Effects of Global Market Conditions on Brand Image Customization and Brand Performance," *Journal of Advertising*, Winter 1995, p. 55.

13. Available from World Wide Web: <http://www.yahoo. com>. See also "Coterie of Early Hires Made Yahoo! A Hit but an Insular Place," *The Wall Street Journal*, March 9, 2001, p. A1; "Voulez-vous Yahoo Avec Moi?" *Fortune*, October 16, 2000, p. 245; "The Two Grown-Ups behind Yahoo!'s Surge," *The Wall Street Journal*, April 10, 1998, p. B1.

14. "Road to Foreign Franchises Is Paved with New Problems," *The Wall Street Journal*, May 14, 2001, p. B10; "Tiger Fight Sees Kellogg, ExxonMobil Clash in Court," *Ad Age Global*, November 2000;

"Wrestling, Wildlife Fund Battle over WWF Site," *USA Today*, October 25, 2000, p. 1A; "More Firms Flash New Badge," *USA Today*, October 4, 2000, p. 3B; "Name Lawsuit Prompts AppleSoup to Become Flycode," *USA Today*, September 11, 2000, p. 6B. See also Karen Gantt, "Revisiting the Scope of Lanham Act Protection," *Journal of the Academy of Marketing Science*, Winter 2004, p. 102; Maureen Morrin and Jacob Jacoby, "Trademark Dilution: Empirical Measures for an Elusive Concept," *Journal of Public Policy & Marketing*, Fall 2000, p. 265; Chris Janiszewski and Tom Meyvis, "Effects of Brand Logo Complexity, Repetition, and Spacing on Processing Fluency and Judgment," *Journal of Consumer Research*, June 2001, p. 18; F. C. Hong, Anthony Pecotich and Clifford J. Schultz II, "Brand Name Translation: Language Constraints, Product Attributes, and Consumer Perceptions in East and Southeast Asia," *Journal of International Marketing*, (2) 2002, p. 29; Daniel J. Howard, Roger A. Kerin, and Charles Gengler, "The Effects of Brand Name Similarity on Brand Source Confusion: Implications for Trademark Infringement," *Journal of Public Policy & Marketing*, Fall 2000, p. 250; Charles H. Schwepker, "Trademark Problems and How to Avoid Them," *Journal of the Academy of Marketing Science*, Winter 1997, p. 89; Lee B. Burgunder, "Trademark Protection of Product Characteristics: A Predictive Model," *Journal of Public Policy & Marketing*, Fall 1997, p. 277; Itamar Simonson, "Trademark Infringement from the Buyer Perspective: Conceptual Analysis and Measurement Implications," *Journal of Public Policy & Marketing*, Fall 1994, p. 181; "Asian Trademark Litigation Continues," *The Wall Street Journal*, February 16, 1994, p. B8.

15. "From Betamax to Kazaa: The Real War over Piracy," *Fortune*, October 27, 2003, p. 148; "Debate Heats Up as Student Spots Hole in CD Protection," *USA Today*, October 27, 2003, p. 1A; "Can Copyright Be Saved?" *The Wall Street Journal Reports*, October 20, 2003, p. R1; "Striking Back," *Business Week*, September 29, 2003, p. 94; "Hollywood's Burning Issue," *The Wall Street Journal*, September 18, 2003, p. B1; "Hammering Away at Piracy," *USA Today*, September 11, 2003, p. 1D; "Music Industry Doesn't Know What Else to Do as It Lashes Out at File-Sharing," *USA Today*, September 10, 2003, p. 3B; "Indonesia Turns to Trademark Piracy," *The Wall Street Journal*, September 9, 2003, p. A20; "Increase in Software Piracy Could Blight Financial Future," *USA Today*, August 1, 2002, p. 1B; "Road Warriors: Motorcycle Makers from Japan Discover Piracy Made in China," *The Wall Street Journal*, July 25, 2001, p. A1; "Beijing's Phony War on Fakes," *Fortune*, October 30, 2000, p. 188; "Knocking Out the Knockoffs," *Fortune*, October 2, 2000, p. 213. See also Laurence Jacobs, A. Coskun Samli and Tom Jedlik, "The Nightmare of International Product Piracy: Exploring Defensive Strategies," *Industrial Marketing Management*, August 2001, p. 499; Janeen E. Olsen and Kent L. Granzin, "Using Channels Constructs to Explain Dealers' Willingness to Help Manufacturers Combat Counterfeiting," *Journal of Business Research*, June 1993, p. 147; Ronald F. Bush, Peter H. Bloch, and Scott Dawson, "Remedies for Product Counterfeiting," *Business Horizons*, January–February 1989, p. 59; Alexander Nill and Clifford J. Schultz II, "The Scourge of Global Counterfeiting," *Business Horizons*, November–December 1996, p. 37.

16. For more on licensing, see "Testing Limits of Licensing: SpongeBob-Motif Holiday Inn," *The Wall Street Journal*, October 9, 2003, p. B1ff,; "Making Tracks beyond Tires," *Brandweek*, September 15, 2003, p. 16; "Candy Cosmetics: Licensing's Sweet Spot," *DSN Retailing Today*, August 4, 2003, p. 24; "The Creative License," *Brandweek*, June 9, 2003, p. 36; "Procter & Gamble Deals License Several Brand Names," *USA Today*, April 18, 2003, p. 3B; "Whoa, Cool Shirt. Yeah, It's a Pepsi," *Business Week*, September 10, 2001, p. 84; "In Europe, Hot New Fashion for Urban Hipsters Comes from Peoria," *The Wall Street Journal*, August 8, 2001, p. B1; "Washed Up at Warnaco?" *Time*, June 25, 2001, p. 36; "Brand New Goods," *Time*, November 1, 1999; "Brand Builders: Licensing the Color of Money," *Brandweek*, September 15, 1997, p. 22.

17. For more on branding organic foods, see "Health Food Maker Ham Faces Rivals," *The Wall Street Journal*, August 13, 2003, p. B5B; "Big Brand Logos Pop Up in Organic Aisle," *The Wall Street Journal*, July 29, 2003, p. B1; "USDA Enters Debate on Organic Label Law," *The New York Times*, February 26, 2003, p. D1; "Food Industry Gags at Proposed Label Rule for Trans Fat," *The Wall Street Journal*, December 27, 2002, p. B1; "Curbs Are Eased on Food Makers' Health Claims," *The Wall Street Journal*, December 19, 2002, p. D4; "Organic Rules!" *Brandweek*, October 21, 2002, p. 3; "In Natural Foods, a Big Name's No Big Help," *The Wall Street Journal*, June 7, 2002, p. B1. See also Amitabh Mungale, "Managing Product Families," *Journal of Product Innovation Management*, January 1998, p. 102; Gloria Barczak, "Product Management," *Journal of Product Innovation Management*, September 1997, p. 425.

18. "Ten Years May Be Generic Lifetime," *Advertising Age*, March 23, 1987, p. 76; Brian F. Harris and Roger A. Strang, "Marketing Strategies in the Age of Generics," *Journal of Marketing*, Fall 1985, p. 70.

19. "Brand Killers, *Fortune*, August 11, 2003, p. 88; "Going Private (Label), *The Wall Street Journal*, June 12, 2003, p. B1; "7-Eleven Cracks Open a Private-Label Brew," *The Wall Street Journal*, May 2, 2003, p. B1; "Retailers Create Own-Label PCs as Brand Names Dwindle," *The Wall Street Journal*, May 3, 2002, p. B1; "White Clouds Could Bring Rain on P&G," *Advertising Age*, July 2, 2001, p. 4; "National Tool Brands Vie for Maximum Exposure," *DSN Retailing Today*, March 5, 2001, p. 26; "New Private-Label Alternatives Bring Changes to Supercenters, Clubs," *DSN Retailing Today*, February 5, 2001, p. 66; "Popularity of PL Toys Stems from Benefits in Cost, Exclusivity," *DSN Retailing Today*, November 20, 2000, p. 4; "Wal-Mart Stores Go Private (Label)," *Advertising Age*, November 29, 1999, p. 1. See also Rajeev Batra and Indrajit Sinha, "Consumer-Level Factors Moderating the Success of Private Label Brands," *Journal of Retailing*, Summer 2000, p. 175; John Low and Keith Blois, "The Evolution of Generic Brands in Industrial Markets: the Challenges to Owners of Brand Equity," *Industrial Marketing Management*, August 2002, p. 385; Judith A. Garretson, Dan Fisher, and Scot Burton, "Antecedents of Private Label Attitude and National Brand Promotion Attitude: Similarities and Differences," *Journal of Retailing*, Summer 2002, p. 91; Kusum L. Ailawadi, Scott A. Neslin and Karen Gedenk, "Pursuing the Value-Conscious Consumer: Store Brands Versus National Brand Promotions," *Journal of Marketing*, January 2001, p. 71; R. Sethuraman and J. Mittelstaedt, "Coupons and Private Labels: A Cross-Category Analysis of Grocery Products," *Psychology & Marketing*, November/ December 1992, p. 487; John A. Quelch and David Harding, "Brands Versus Private Labels: Fighting to Win," *Harvard Business Review*, January– February 1996, p. 99.

20. For more on SoupatHand, see "Demand for Convenient Foods Continues to Rise," *Brandweek*, November 18, 2002, p. 8. For another example, milk packaging, see "Dean Foods: Dairy Processor Looks to Milk Other Products," *Investor's Business Daily*, March 28, 2003, p. A6; "Dean Foods: Dairy Firm Milks New Products for Growth, though Cows Still Account for Most Sales," *Investor's Business Daily*, September 18, 2002, p. A8; "Milk Chug Sweetens Double Chocolate Push," *Brandweek*, February 25, 2002, p. 9; "Many-Flavored Milk Competes with Sodas," *USA Today*, January 26, 2001, p. 1D.

21. "Thinking Outside the Can," *Brandweek*, October 13, 2003, p. 13; "Are Your Competitors Packing?" *Business 2.0*, July 2003, p. 52; "Packaging Is the Capper," *Advertising Age*, May 5, 2003, p. 22; "Here's the Beef. So, Where's the Butcher?" *The New York Times*, February 15, 2003, p. B1; "Salad in Sealed Bags Isn't So Simple, It Seems," *The New York Times*, January 14, 2003, p. A1; "Finger Food: Marketers Push Individual Portions and Families Bite," *The Wall Street Journal*, July 23, 2002, p. A1; "Getting a Grip on Consumer Tastes," *Business Week*, July 16, 2001, p. 12; "Color Me Popular: Marketers Shape Up Packaging," *USA Today*, February 8, 2001, p. 7B; "Heinz Puts Squeeze on Places Refilling Its Ketchup Bottles," *The Wall Street Journal*, June 22, 2000, p. A1; "Who's Foiling the Aluminum Can," *Business Week*, October 6, 1997, p. 106; "Breakthrough Bottles," *Brandweek*, May 20, 1996, p. 32. See also Brian Wansink and Koert van Ittersum, "Bottoms Up! The Influence of

Elongation on Pouring and Consumption Volume," *Journal of Consumer Research*, December 2003, p. 455; Brian Wansink, "Can Package Size Accelerate Usage Volume?" *Journal of Marketing*, July 1996, p. 1.

22. "Bar Codes: Beyond the Checkout Counter," *Business Week*, April 8, 1985, p. 90; Ronald C. Goodstein, "UPC Scanner Pricing Systems: Are They Accurate?" *Journal of Marketing*, April 1994, p. 20.

23. For more on transfat labeling, see "A 'Fat-Free' Product that's 100% Fat: How Food Labels Legally Mislead," *The Wall Street Journal*, July 15, 2003, p. D1; "The Truth about Trans Fats: Coming to a Label near You," *The Wall Street Journal*, July 10, 2003, p. D1. For more on nutrition labeling, see "Carbohydrate Confusion," *The Wall Street Journal*, November 24, 2003, p. B1; "FDA ReExamines 'Serving Sizes,' May Change Misleading Labels," *The Wall Street Journal*, November 20, 2003, p. A1; "FDA Considers Nutrition Labels in Restaurants," *The Wall Street Journal*, October 23, 2003, p. B1. See also Siva K. Balasubramanian and Catherine Cole, "Consumers' Search and Use of Nutrition Information: the Challenge and Promise of the Nutrition Labeling and Education Act," *Journal of Marketing*, July 2002, p. 112; Bruce A. Silverglade, "The Nutrition Labeling and Education Act—Progress to Date and Challenges for the Future," *Journal of Public Policy & Marketing*, Spring 1996, p. 148; Sandra J. Burke, Sandra J. Milberg, and Wendy W. Moe, "Displaying Common but Previously Neglected Health Claims on Product Labels: Understanding Competitive Advantages, Deception, and Education," *Journal of Public Policy & Marketing*, Fall 1997, p. 242; Scott B. Keller, Mike Landry, Jeanne Olson, Anne M. Velliquette et al., "The Effects of Nutrition Package Claims, Nutrition Facts Panels, and Motivation to Process Nutrition Information on Consumer Product Evaluations," *Journal of Public Policy & Marketing*, Fall 1997, p. 256; Christine Moorman, "A Quasi Experiment to Assess the Consumer and Informational Determinants of Nutrition Information Processing Activities: The Case of the Nutrition Labeling and Education Act," *Journal of Public Policy & Marketing*, Spring 1996, p. 28.

24. "Open at Your Own Risk," *USA Today*, July 13, 2001, p. 1A; "Pushing Paper in a Plastic World," *The Wall Street Journal*, February 24, 1998, p. B1; "Record Makers Giving Retailers the Blues," *The Wall Street Journal*, March 16, 1992, p. B1; "New Packaging That's Thriftier! Niftier! and Cooks Your Food!" *Fortune*, September 5, 1994, p. 109.

25. Paula Fitzgerald, Bone Corey, and Robert J. Corey, "Ethical Dilemmas in Packaging: Beliefs of Packaging Professionals," *Journal of Macromarketing*, Spring 1992, p. 45. For more on package volume, see "Pay the Same, Get Less as Package Volume Falls," *USA Today*, March 17, 2003, p. 3B; "Taking the Value Out of Value-Sized," *The Wall Street Journal*, August 14, 2002, p. D1; "Critics Call Cuts in Package Size Deceptive Move," *The Wall Street Journal*, February 5, 1991, p. B1; "Disposing of the Green Myth," *Adweek's Marketing Week*, April 13, 1992, p. 20; "The Waste Land," *Adweek*, November 11, 1991, p. 26.

26. Anthony D. Miyazaki, David E. Sprott, and Kenneth C. Manning, "Unit Prices on Retail Shelf Labels: an Assessment of Information Prominence," *Journal of Retailing*, Spring 2000, p. 93; J. E. Russo, "The Value of Unit Price Information," *Journal of Marketing Research*, May 1977, p. 193; David A. Aaker and Gary T. Ford, "Unit Pricing Ten Years Later: A Replication," *Journal of Marketing*, Winter 1983, p. 118.

27. For more on Hyundai warranty, see "Hyundai's Reliability Rankings Now Tie Honda's," *USA Today*, March 11, 2003, p. 2B; "Hyundai's Reputation Is Rising, as It's Proving in India and U.S.," *The Wall Street Journal*, November 12, 2002, p. D3; "Garfield's Ad Review: Hyundai Brand Work Ahead of Its Time," *Advertising Age*, October 14, 2002, p. 57. For more on warranties and service guarantees, see "The Best Car Deal Around: Never Paying for Repairs," *The Wall Street Journal*, November 12, 2002, p. D1; "Forbes.com Offers Brand Guarantee," *BtoB*, October 14, 2002, p. 14; "Sheraton Plans to Pay Guests for Bad Service," *The Wall Street Journal*, September 6, 2002, p. B1; "Guaranteed to Last a Whole 90 Days," *The Wall Street Journal*, July 16, 2002, p. D1; "Best Buy Co.:

Retailer's 'Guaranteed' Strategy for Growth," *Investor's Business Daily*, May 21, 2002, p. A10; "Amtrak Rolls Out Service Guarantee, New Logo," *Investor's Business Daily*, July 7, 2000, p. A7. See also Jennifer Hamilton and Ross D. Petty, "The European Union's Consumer Guarantees Directive," *Journal of Public Policy & Marketing*, Fall 2001, p. 289; M. E. Blair and Daniel E. Innis, "The Effects of Product Knowledge on the Evaluation of Warranteed Brands," *Psychology & Marketing*, August 1996, p. 445; Ellen M. Moore and F. Kelly Shuptrine, "Warranties: Continued Readability Problems After the 1975 Magnuson-Moss Warranty Act," *Journal of Consumer Affairs*, Summer 1993, p. 23; M.A.J. Menezes and I.S. Currim, "An Approach for Determination of Warranty Length," *International Journal of Research in Marketing*, May 1992, p. 177.

CHAPTER 10

1. "America Zooms In on Camera Phones," *Business Week*, December 22, 2003, p. 44; "Windows on a Phone: Not Bad for a First Foray," *Business Week*, December 1, 2003, p. 26; "Plantronics Hears Sound of New Opportunities as Core Sales Slow," *Investor's Business Daily*, November 17, 2003, p. A8; "Motorola Makes Good," *Business Week*, October 27, 2003, p. 52; "A Motorola Spin-Off," *Business Week*, October 20, 2003, p. 56; "Cordless—and Hands-Free, Too," *Business Week*, October 20, 2003, p. 157; "Motorola Needs a Revolutionary," *Business Week*, October 6, 2003, p. 52; "Cell Phone Motorists Driving Headset Sales," *Investor's Business Daily*, August 8, 2003, p. A4; "Box Makers Putting Their Stamp on Looks," *Investor's Business Daily*, August 4, 2003, p. A4; "Can Mike Z Work More Magic at Motorola?" *Business Week*, April 14, 2003, p. 58; "Tech Companies Scramble to Fill Military Orders," *The Wall Street Journal*, March 24, 2003, p. B1; "Cutting the Cell Phone Cord," *Business Week*, February 10, 2003, p. 84; "Can You Hear Me?" *Time*, December 30, 2002, p. 156; "Great-Looking Product (Too Bad Nobody Wants It)," *Business 2.0*, April 2002, p. 120.

2. Alina B. Sorescu, Rajesh K. Chandy, and Jaideep C. Prabhu, "Sources and Financial Consequences of Radical Innovation: Insights from Pharmaceuticals," *Journal of Marketing*, October 2003, p. 82; Ulrike de Brentani, "Innovative Versus Incremental New Business Services: Different Keys for Achieving Success," *The Journal of Product Innovation Management*, May 2001, p. 169; Erik Jan Hultink and Fred Langerak, "Launch Decisions and Competitive Reactions: an Exploratory Market Signaling Study," *The Journal of Product Innovation Management*, May 2002, p. 199; Barry L. Bayus, "The Languages of Edison's Light," *The Journal of Product Innovation Management*, May 2000, p. 254; Marion Debruyne, Rudy Moenaert, Abbie Griffin, Susan Hart et al. "The Impact of New Product Launch Strategies on Competitive Reaction in Industrial Markets," *The Journal of Product Innovation Management*, March 2002, p. 159; X. Michael Song, C. Anthony Di Benedetto and Lisa Z. Song, "Pioneering Advantage in New Service Development: a Multi-Country Study of Managerial Perceptions," *The Journal of Product Innovation Management*, September 2000, p. 378; Beverly B. Tyler and Devi R. Gnyawali, "Mapping Managers' Market Orientations Regarding New Product Success," *The Journal of Product Innovation Management*, July 2002, p. 259; Christopher M. McDermott and Gina Colarelli O'Connor, "Managing Radical Innovation: an Overview of Emergent Strategy Issues," *The Journal of Product Innovation Management*, November 2002, p. 424; George J. Avlonitis, Paulina G. Papastathopoulou and Spiros P. Gounaris, "An Empirically-Based Typology of Product Innovativeness for New Financial Services: Success and Failure Scenarios," *The Journal of Product Innovation Management*, September 2001, p. 324; Ronald W. Niedrich and Scott D. Swain, "The Influence of Pioneer Status and Experience Order on Consumer Brand Preference: a Mediated-Effects Model," *Journal of the Academy of Marketing Science*, Fall 2003, p. 468; Rajesh K. Chandy and Gerard J. Tellis, "The Incumbent's Curse? Incumbency, Size, and Radical Product Innovation," *Journal of Marketing*, July 2000, p. 1; Robert W. Veryzer, "Key Factors Affecting Customer Evaluation of Discontinuous New Products," *Journal of Product Innovation Management*, March 1998,

p. 136; Frank H. Alpert and Michael A. Kamins, "An Empirical Investigation of Consumer Memory, Attitude and Perceptions Toward Pioneer and Follower Brands," *Journal of Marketing*, October 1995, p. 34; Neil A. Morgan, "Managing Imitation Strategies: How Later Entrants Seize Market Share From Pioneers," *Journal of Marketing*, October 1995, p. 104; David M. Szymanski, Lisa C. Troy, and Sundar G. Bharadwaj, "Order of Entry and Business Performance: An Empirical Synthesis and Reexamination," *Journal of Marketing*, October 1995, p. 17; George Day, "The Product Life Cycle: Analysis and Applications Issues," *Journal of Marketing*, Fall 1981, p. 60; Igal Ayal, "International Product Life Cycle: A Reassessment and Product Policy Implications," *Journal of Marketing*, Fall 1981, p. 91; Mary Lambkin and George S. Day, "Evolutionary Processes in Competitive Markets: Beyond the Product Life Cycle," *Journal of Marketing*, July 1989, p. 4.

3. Jorge Alberto Sousa De Vasconcellos, "Key Success Factors in Marketing Mature Products," *Industrial Marketing Management* 20, no. 4 (1991), p. 263; Paul C.N. Michell, Peter Quinn, and Edward Percival, "Marketing Strategies for Mature Industrial Products," *Industrial Marketing Management* 20, no. 3 (1991), p. 201; Peter N. Golder and Gerard J. Tellis, "Pioneer Advantage: Marketing Logic or Marketing Legend?" *Journal of Marketing Research*, May 1993, p. 158.

4. For more on Xbox, see Chapter 4, endnote 9.

5. U.S. Bureau of the Census, *Statistical Abstract of the United States 2002* (Washington, DC: U.S. Government Printing Office, 2001), p. 605; U.S. Bureau of the Census, *Statistical Abstract of the United States 2000* (Washington, DC: U.S. Government Printing Office, 2000), p. 726.

6. "DVD: It Pays to Spend a Little More," *USA Today*, December 3, 2003, p. 10D; "Backseat Movies: Car DVD Entertainment Systems . . . ," *Business Week*, May 26, 2003, p. 108; "High-Definition Discs Aim to Outshine DVDs," *Investor's Business Daily*, May 6, 2003, p. A6; "Safe at Home and All Plugged In," *USA Today*, January 8, 2002, p. 1D; "Pioneer, Panasonic Drive toward Recordable DVD," *Investor's Business Daily*, June 26, 2001, p. A7; "Blockbuster Tests Postvideo Future," *The Wall Street Journal*, June 18, 2001, p. B1; "DVDs' Popularity Gives Studio Earnings Much-Needed Spin," *USA Today*, April 30, 2001, p. 4B; "Sales of DVD Players Boom, but Makers Record Little Profit," *Investor's Business Daily*, January 22, 2001, p. A6; "DVD Makers Battle over Recording Standard," *The Wall Street Journal*, November 9, 2000, p. B6; "To DVD—or Not to DVD?" *The Wall Street Journal*, November 3, 2000, p. W1.

7. For more on Cisco, see "Cisco: In Hot Pursuit of a Chinese Rival," *Business Week*, May 19, 2003, p. 62; "Cisco: Making a Federal Case of it," *Business Week*, February 10, 2003, p. 36. See also "Would You Buy a Patent License from This Man?" *Ecompany*, April 2001, p. 104; "Rivals Square Off Toe to Toe," *USA Today*, August 24, 1993, p. 1B; "Is It Time to Reinvent the Patent System?" *Business Week*, December 2, 1991, p. 110; C. C. Baughn, Michael Bixby, and L. S. Woods, "Patent Laws and the Public Good: IPR Protection in Japan and the United States," *Business Horizons*, July–August 1997, p. 59.

8. For more on EV1, see "An Electric Car Propelled by Star Power?" *Business Week*, December 9, 1996, p. 40; "GM Energizes EV1 Launch with $8 Mil Ad Blitz," *Advertising Age*, December 2, 1996, p. 12; "A Big Charge for Electric Vehicles," *Business Week*, November 18, 1996, p. 102; "Batteries Not Included," *Business Week*, September 23, 1996, p. 78. For more on Toyota and Honda hybrids, see Chapter 4, endnote 25. See also Sigvald J. Harryson, "How Canon and Sony Drive Product Innovation Through Networking and Application-Focused R&D," *Journal of Product Innovation Management*, July 1997, p. 288; M. Lambkin, "Pioneering New Markets: A Comparison of Market Share Winners and Losers," *International Journal of Research in Marketing*, March 1992, p. 5.

9. For more on Zara, see "Fashion Fast Forward," *Business 2.0*, May 2002, p. 61; "Just in Time Fashion," *The Wall Street Journal*, May 18, 2001, p. B1; "The Fashion Cycle Hits High Gear," *Business Week E.Biz*,

September 18, 2000, p. EB66; "Zara Has a Made-to-Order Plan for Success," *Fortune*, September 4, 2000, p. 80; "The Mark of Zara," *Business Week*, May 29, 2000, p. 98.

10. "UGG Boots a Fashion Kick," *USA Today*, December 11, 2003, p. 3B; "Fashion Tip: Get Online," *The Wall Street Journal*, October 31, 2003, p. B1; "Denim Gets Daring in Asia," *The Wall Street Journal*, July 7, 2003, p. A9; "Care Bears' Second Act," *The Wall Street Journal*, June 11, 2003, p. B1; "Fashion Emergency: Duct Tape Makes a Fine Prom Dress," *The Wall Street Journal*, February 28, 2003, p. A1; "The Skinny on the Mini," *The Wall Street Journal*, February 4, 2003, p. B1; "Nothing Comes Between Teens and Their Jeans—Not Even Cost," *USA Today*, September 5, 2002, p. 1D; "Fashion Flip-Flop: Lowly Sandal Leaves the Shower Behind," *The Wall Street Journal*, August 8, 2002, p. A1; "Too Trendy for You?" *The Wall Street Journal*, May 17, 2002, p. W1; "Recipe for a Fashion Brand?" *The Wall Street Journal*, June 25, 2001, p. B1; "Dusting Off Fashion's Old Bags," *Time* (Special Issue: Your Business), June 2001, pp. Y2–Y4; "Designers Howl for Fur," *The Wall Street Journal*, September 22, 2000, p. B1. See also Martin G. Letscher, "How to Tell Fads from Trends," *American Demographics*, December 1994, p. 38; R.E. Goldsmith, J.B. Freiden, and J.C. Kilsheimer, "Social Values and Female Fashion Leadership: A Cross-Cultural Study," *Psychology & Marketing*, September/October 1993, p. 399; "Special Report: Fashion Marketing," *Advertising Age*, August 22, 1994, p. 23; Craig J. Thompson and Diana L. Haytko, "Speaking of Fashion: Consumers' Uses of Fashion Discourses and the Appropriation of Countervailing Cultural Meanings," *Journal of Consumer Research*, June 1997, p. 15.

11. "DVD Acceptance Picks Up Pace," *Discount Store News*, August 9, 1999, p. 29; "DVD and Conquer: Why One Technology Prevailed," *Business Week*, July 5, 1999, p. 34; "Divx: The Video Technology That Geeks Love to Hate," *Fortune*, June 21, 1999, p. 177; "Circuit City Pulls the Plug on Its Divx Videodisk Venture," *The Wall Street Journal*, June 17, 1999, p. B10; "8-Tracks, Betamax—and Divx?" *Business Week*, November 9, 1998, p. 108.

12. "Big Brands (Small Companies)," *Business Week Small Biz*, August 13, 2001, p. 13.

13. *2003 Annual Report*, RJR Nabisco; "Oreo, Ritz Join Nabisco's Low-Fat Feast," *Advertising Age*, April 4, 1994, p. 3; "They're Not Crying in Their Crackers at Nabisco," *Business Week*, August 30, 1993, p. 61; "Nabisco Unleashes a New Batch of Teddies," *Adweek's Marketing Week*, September 24, 1990, p. 18.

14. For more on Tide, see *2003 Annual Report*, Procter & Gamble; "Detergent Tablets of the '70s Make a Comeback," *USA Today*, July 27, 2000, p. 9B; "Boom in Liquid Detergents Has P&G Scrambling," *The Wall Street Journal*, September 25, 1997, p. B1; "Ultra-Clean—Retail Cheers Still More P&G Concentrates," *Advertising Age*, August 22, 1994, p. 1; "Detergent Industry Spins into New Cycle," *The Wall Street Journal*, January 5, 1993, p. B1; "P&G Unleashes Flood of New Tide Products," *Advertising Age*, June 16, 1986, p. 3. See also "The Hard Life of Orphan Brands," *The Wall Street Journal*, April 13, 2001, p. B1; "Orphan Relief," *Advertising Age*, March 19, 2001, p. 3.

15. Brian Wansink, "Making Old Brands New," *American Demographics*, December 1997, p. 53; "Classic Roller Skates Return as Safety Fears Dull Blades," *The Wall Street Journal*, October 24, 1997, p. B1; "Dusting Off the *Britannica*," *Business Week*, October 20, 1997, p. 143; "At Du Pont, Time to Both Sow and Reap," *Business Week*, September 29, 1997, p. 107; "A Boring Brand Can Be Beautiful," *Fortune*, November 18, 1991, p. 169; "Teflon Is 50 Years Old, but Du Pont Is Still Finding New Uses for Invention," *The Wall Street Journal*, April 7, 1988, p. 34; Stephen W. Miller, "Managing Imitation Strategies: How Later Entrants Seize Markets From Pioneers," *Journal of the Academy of Marketing Science*, Summer 1996, p. 277; Regina Fazio Maruca and Amy L. Halliday, "When New Products and Customer Loyalty Collide," *Harvard Business Review*, November–December 1993, p. 22.

16. For more on Logitech, see "The Fastest-Growing Technology Companies," *Business 2.0*, October 2002, p. 81. For more on Gatorade, see "Gatorade Gallon Goes Rectangular," *Packaging Digest*, June 2003, p. 2; "Latest Gatorade Bottle Edges toward Ergonomics," *Packaging Digest*, November 1999, p. 15.

17. "Reposition: Simplifying the Customer's Brandscape," *Brandweek*, October 2, 2000, p. 36; "Consumers to GM: You Talking to Me?" *Business Week*, June 19, 2000, p. 213; "How Growth Destroys Differentiation," *Brandweek*, April 24, 2000, p. 42; "P&G, Seeing Shoppers Were Being Confused, Overhauls Marketing," *The Wall Street Journal*, January 15, 1997, p. A1; "Make It Simple," *Business Week*, September 9, 1996, p. 96; "Diaper Firms Fight to Stay on the Bottom," *The Wall Street Journal*, March 23, 1993, p. B1.

18. "Too Many Choices," *The Wall Street Journal*, April 20, 2001, p. B1; "Special Report: New Products," *Ad Age International*, April 13, 1998, p. 17; "The Ghastliest Product Launches," *Fortune*, March 16, 1998, p. 44; "New and Improved," *American Demographics*, March 1998, p. 32; "Flops: Too Many New Products Fail. Here's Why—and How to Do Better," *Business Week*, August 16, 1993, p. 76; Brian D. Ottum and William L. Moore, "The Role of Market Information in New Product Success/Failure," *Journal of Product Innovation Management*, July 1997, p. 258.

19. "Makers of Chicken Tonight Find Many Cooks Say, 'Not Tonight,'" *The Wall Street Journal*, May 17, 1994, p. B1; "Failure of Its Oven Lovin' Cookie Dough Shows Pillsbury Pitfalls of New Products," *The Wall Street Journal*, June 17, 1993, p. B1; Sharad Sarin and Gour M. Kapur, "Lessons From New Product Failures: Five Case Studies," *Industrial Marketing Management*, November 1990, p. 301.

20. "Design Tools Move into the Fast Lane," *Business Week*, June 2, 2003, pp. 84B–84C; "How Top Software Firms Dominate," *Investor's Business Daily*, June 12, 2001, p. A1; "Opening the Spigot," *Business Week E.Biz*, June 4, 2001, pp. EB16–Eb20; "Digital Workflow Speeds Time to Shelf," *Brand Packaging*, March/April 2001, p. 24; "How Fast Can This Baby Go?" *Business Week*, April 10, 2000, p. 38. See also Muammer Ozer, "Process Implications of the Use of the Internet in New Product Development: a Conceptual Analysis," *Industrial Marketing Management*, August 2003, p. 517; J. Daniel Sherman, William E. Souder, and Svenn A. Jenssen, "Differential Effects of the Primary Forms of Cross Functional Integration on Product Development Cycle Time," *The Journal of Product Innovation Management*, July 2000, p. 257; Greg Githens, "Successful Product Development: Speeding from Opportunity to Profit," *The Journal of Product Innovation Management*, May 2000, p. 250; Daniel J. Flint, "Compressing New Product Success-to-Success Cycle Time: Deep Customer Value Understanding and Idea Generation," *Industrial Marketing Management*, July 2002, p. 305; Cornelia Droge, Jayanth Jayaram, and Shawnee K. Vickery, "The Ability to Minimize the Timing of New Product Development and Introduction: an Examination of Antecedent Factors in the North American Automobile Supplier Industry," *The Journal of Product Innovation Management*, January 2000, p. 24; Ajay Menon, Jhinuk Chowdhury and Bryan A. Lukas, "Antecedents and Outcomes of New Product Development Speed: an Interdisciplinary Conceptual Framework," *Industrial Marketing Management*, July 2002, p. 317; Kathleen M. Eisenhardt and Shona L. Brown, "Time Pacing: Competing in Markets That Won't Stand Still," *Harvard Business Review*, March–April 1998, p. 59; Richard Bauhaus, "Developing Products in Half the Time," *Journal of Product Innovation Management*, January 1997, p. 68. For more on P&G's efforts to bring products to market faster, see "Brands in a Bind," *Business Week*, August 28, 2000, p. 234; "Warm and Fuzzy Won't Save Procter & Gamble," *Business Week*, June 26, 2000, p. 48.

21. "Building a Better R&D Mousetrap," *Business 2.0*, September 2003, p. 50; "Critical Curds: At Kraft, Making Cheese Fun Is Serious Business," *The Wall Street Journal*, May 31, 2002, p. A1; "Stuck on You: P&G's New Outlast Lipstick Is Nothing to Pout About," *The Wall Street*

Journal, May 9, 2002, p. B1; "Bleeding Cash: Pfizer Youth Pill Ate Up $71 Million before It Flopped," *The Wall Street Journal*, May 2, 2002, p. A1; "How Burger King Got Burned in Quest to Make the Perfect Fry," *The Wall Street Journal*, January 16, 2001, p. A1; "Tailoring World's Cars to U.S. Tastes," *The Wall Street Journal*, January 15, 2001, p. B1; "From Research Dollars to Riches," *Investor's Business Daily*, December 5, 2000, p. A1; "Why Dow Chemical Finds Slime Sublime," *The Wall Street Journal*, November 15, 1999, p. B1. See also Lisa C. Troy, David M. Szymanski and P. Rajan Varadarajan, "Generating New Product Ideas: an Initial Investigation of the Role of Market Information and Organizational Characteristics," *Journal of the Academy of Marketing Science*, Winter 2001, p. 89; Rajesh Sethi, "New Product Quality and Product Development Teams," *Journal of Marketing*, April 2000, p. 1; Mark A. A. M. Leenders and Berend Wierenga, "The Effectiveness of Different Mechanisms for Integrating Marketing and R&D," *The Journal of Product Innovation Management*, July 2002, p. 305; George J. Avlonitis, Susan J. Hart, and Nikolaos X. Tzokas, "An Analysis of Product Deletion Scenarios," *The Journal of Product Innovation Management*, January 2000, p. 41; Elliot Maltz, William E. Souder, and Ajith Kumar, "Influencing R&D/Marketing Integration and the Use of Market Information by R&D Managers: Intended and Unintended Effects of Managerial Actions," *Journal of Business Research*, April 2001, p. 69; Angel Martinez Sanchez and Manuela Perez Perez, "Cooperation and the Ability to Minimize the Time and Cost of New Product Development Within the Spanish Automotive Supplier Industry," *The Journal of Product Innovation Management*, January 2003, p. 57; Robert Polk, Richard E. Plank, and David A. Reid, "Technical Risk and New Product Success: An Empirical Test in High Technology Business Markets," *Industrial Marketing Management*, November 1996, p. 531; X. M. Song and Mark E. Parry, "A Cross-National Comparative Study of New Product Development Processes: Japan and the United States," *Journal of Marketing*, April 1997, p. 1; Robert G. Cooper, "Overhauling the New Product Process," *Industrial Marketing Management*, November 1996, p. 465; Jeffrey B. Schmidt and Roger J. Calantone, "Are Really New Product Development Projects Harder to Shut Down?" *Journal of Product Innovation Management*, March 1998, p. 111; Cheryl Nakata and K. Sivakumar, "National Culture and New Product Development: An Integrative Review," *Journal of Marketing*, January 1996, p. 61; Gary S. Lynn, Joseph G. Morone, and Albert S. Paulson, "Marketing and Discontinuous Innovation: The Probe and Learn Process," *California Management Review*, Spring 1996, p. 8; Gary L. Ragatz, Robert B. Handfield, and Thomas V. Scannell, "Success Factors for Integrating Suppliers into New Product Development," *Journal of Product Innovation Management*, May 1997, p. 190; X. M. Song and Mitzi M. Montoya-Weiss, "Critical Development Activities for Really New Versus Incremental Products," *Journal of Product Innovation Management*, March 1998, p. 124.

22. "Pickups Get Women's Touch," *USA Today*, June 13, 2001 p. 1B; "Windstar's Designing Women," *USA Today*, July 19, 1999, p. 3B; "Where Great Ideas Come From," *Inc.*, April 1998, p. 76; "Seeing the Future First," *Fortune*, September 5, 1994, p. 64. See also Edward F. McDonough III, Kenneth B. Kahn and Gloria Barczak, "An Investigation of the Use of Global, Virtual, and Colocated New Product Development Teams," *The Journal of Product Innovation Management*, March 2001, p. 110; Ari-Pekka Hameri and Jukka Nihtila, "Distributed New Product Development Project Based on Internet and World-Wide Web: A Case Study," *Journal of Product Innovation Management*, March 1997, p. 77.

23. "It Was a Hit in Buenos Aires—So Why Not Boise?" *Business Week*, September 7, 1998, p. 56. See also Rudy K. Moenaert, Filip Caeldries, Annouk Lievens and Elke Wauters, "Communication Flows in International Product Innovation Teams," *The Journal of Product Innovation Management*, September 2000, p. 360; Vittorio Chiesa, "Global R&D Project Management and Organization: a Taxonomy," *The Journal of Product Innovation Management*, September 2000, p. 341; Jinhong Xie, Michael Song and Anne Stringfellow, "Antecedents and Consequences of Goal Incongruity on New Product Development in Five Countries: a

Marketing View," *The Journal of Product Innovation Management*, May 2003, p. 233; John J. Cristiano, Jeffrey K. Liker, and Chelsea C. White III, "Customer-Driven Product Development Through Quality Function Deployment in the U.S. and Japan," *The Journal of Product Innovation Management*, July 2000, p. 286; Don R. Graber, "How to Manage a Global Product Development Process," *Industrial Marketing Management*, November 1996, p. 483; "U.S. Companies Shop Abroad for Product Ideas," *The Wall Street Journal*, March 14, 1990, p. B1.

24. Erik L. Olson and Geir Bakke, "Implementing the Lead User Method in a High Technology Firm: a Longitudinal Study of Intentions Versus Actions," *The Journal of Product Innovation Management*, November 2001, p. 388; Eric von Hippel, *The Sources of Innovation* (New York: Oxford University Press, 1988).

25. "Shielding the Shield Makers," *The Wall Street Journal*, November 26, 2003, p. B1; "Gun Makers to Push Use of Gun Locks," *The Wall Street Journal*, May 9, 2001, p. B12; "U.S. Recalls Millions of Evenflo 'Joyride' Infant Seats, Carriers," *The Wall Street Journal*, May 2, 2001, p. B6; "Stand Up and Fight," *Business Week*, September 11, 2000, p. 54; "Why One Jury Dealt a Big Blow to Chrysler in Minivan-Latch Case," *The Wall Street Journal*, November 19, 1997, p. A1; "Chinese Discover Product-Liability Suits," *The Wall Street Journal*, November 13, 1997, p. B1; Paula Mergenhagen, "Product Liability: Who Sues?" *American Demographics*, June 1995, p. 48; "How a Jury Decided that a Coffee Spill Is Worth $2.9 Million," *The Wall Street Journal*, September 1, 1994, p. A1; Paul A. Herbig and James E. Golden, "Innovation and Product Liability," *Industrial Marketing Management*, July 1994, p. 245; Robert N. Mayer and Debra L. Scammon, "Caution: Weak Product Warnings May Be Hazardous to Corporate Health," *Journal of Business Research*, June 1992, p. 347.

26. "Want Shelf Space at the Supermarket? Ante Up," *Business Week*, August 7, 1989, p. 60; "Grocer 'Fee' Hampers New-Product Launches," *Advertising Age*, August 3, 1987, p. 1.

27. "This Bright Idea Could Make GE a Billion," *Business Week*, December 4, 1989, p. 120.

28. Joseph M. Bonner, Robert W. Ruekert, and Orville C. Walker, Jr. "Upper Management Control of New Product Development Projects and Project Performance," *The Journal of Product Innovation Management*, May 2002, p. 233; Madeleine E. Pullman, William L. Moore, and Don G. Wardell, "A Comparison of Quality Function Deployment and Conjoint Analysis in New Product Design," *The Journal of Product Innovation Management*, September 2002, p. 354; Harold Z. Daniel, Donald J. Hempel and Narasimhan Srinivasan, "A Model of Value Assessment in Collaborative R&D Programs," *Industrial Marketing Management*, November 2002, p. 653; Sundar Bharadwaj and Anil Menon, "Making Innovations Happen in Organizations: Individual Creativity Mechanisms, Organizational Creativity Mechanisms or Both?" *The Journal of Product Innovation Management*, November 2000, p. 424; Kwaku Atuahene-Gima and Haiyang Li, "Marketing's Influence Tactics in New Product Development: a Study of High Technology Firms in China," *The Journal of Product Innovation Management*, November 2000, p. 451; Preston G. Smith, "Mastering Virtual Teams: Strategies, Tools, and Techniques That Succeed," *The Journal of Product Innovation Management*, March 2001, p. 127; Eugene Sivadas and F. Robert Dwyer, "An Examination of Organizational Factors Influencing New Product Success in Internal and Alliance-Based Processes," *Journal of Marketing*, January 2000, p. 31; Gregory D. Githens, "Customer Centered Products: Creating Successful Products Through Smart Requirements Management," *The Journal of Product Innovation Management*, September 2001, p. 350; Fred Langerak, Ed Peelen, and Harry Commandeur, "Organizing for Effective New Product Development," *Industrial Marketing Management*, May 1997, p. 281; Kenti Goffin, "Evaluating Customer Support During New Product Development—An Exploratory Study," *Journal of Product Innovation Management*, January 1998, p. 42; Paul S. Adler, Avi Mandelbaum, Vien Nguyen, and Elizabeth Schwerer, "Getting the Most

Out of Your Product Development Process," *Harvard Business Review*, March–April 1996, p. 134; Frank R. Bacon, Jr., and Thomas W. Butler, Jr., *Planned Innovation*, rev. ed. (Ann Arbor: Institute of Science and Technology, University of Michigan, 1980).

29. "Torture Testing," *Fortune*, October 2, 2000, pp. 244B–X; "Industry's Amazing New Instant Prototypes," *Fortune*, January 12, 1998, pp. 120E–L; "Secrets of Product Testing," *Fortune*, November 28, 1994, p. 166; "A Smarter Way to Manufacture," *Business Week*, April 30, 1990, p. 110.

30. For more on Gillette's razor costs, see "Cutting Edge," *Brandweek*, February 4, 2002, p. 16; "Gillette's Edge," *Brandweek*, May 28, 2001, p. 5; "No New CEO, but Gillette Does Have a New Product," *Advertising Age*, November 6, 2000, p. 25; "Brands in a Bind," *Business Week*, August 28, 2000, p. 234; "How Gillette Brought Its MACH3 to Market," *The Wall Street Journal*, April 15, 1998, p. B1.

31. "Oops! Marketers Blunder Their Way Through the 'Herb Decade,'" *Advertising Age*, February 13, 1989, p. 3.

32. "An Rx for Drug Trials," *Business Week E.Biz*, December 11, 2000, p. EB66; "Web Sites Give Retailers Better Way to Test-Market Products," *USA Today*, August 29, 2000, p. 3B; "Can Procter & Gamble Change Its Culture, Protect Its Market Share, and Find the Next Tide?" *Fortune*, April 26, 1999, p. 146; "To Test or Not to Test . . . ," *American Demographics*, June 1998, p. 64; John R. Dickinson and Carolyn P. Wilby, "Concept Testing With and Without Product Trial," *Journal of Product Innovation Management*, March 1997, p. 117; "Born to Be a Little Too Wild," *Business Week*, December 18, 2000, p. 69.

33. Jeffrey B. Schmidt and Roger J. Calantone, "Escalation of Commitment During New Product Development," *Journal of the Academy of Marketing Science*, Spring 2002, p. 103; Ely Dahan and V. Srinivasan, "The Predictive Power of Internet-Based Product Concept Testing Using Visual Depiction and Animation," *The Journal of Product Innovation Management*, March 2000, p. 99; Erwin Danneels and Elko J. Kleinschmidt, "Product Innovativeness from the Firm's Perspective: Its Dimensions and Their Relation with Project Selection and Performance," *The Journal of Product Innovation Management*, November 2001, p. 357; R. Jeffrey Thieme, Michael Song and Geon-Cheol Shin, "Project Management Characteristics and New Product Survival," *The Journal of Product Innovation Management*, March 2003, p. 104; William E. Souder, David Buisson, and Tony Garrett, "Success Through Customer-Driven New Product Development: A Comparison of U.S. and New Zealand Small Entrepreneurial High Technology Firms," *Journal of Product Innovation Management*, November 1997, p. 459; Artemis March, "Usability: The New Dimension of Product Design," *Harvard Business Review*, September–October 1994, p. 144; Peter H. Bloch, "Seeking the Ideal Form: Product Design and Consumer Response," *Journal of Marketing*, July 1995, p. 16; Alan Flaschner, "Technology Fountainheads: The Management Challenge of R&D Consortia," *Journal of Product Innovation Management*, July 1997, p. 309; William Q. Judge, Gerald E. Fryxell, and Robert S. Dooley, "The New Task of R&D Management: Creating Goal-Directed Communities for Innovation," *California Management Review*, Spring 1997, p. 72; John P. Workman, Jr., "Marketing's Limited Role in New Product Development in One Computer Systems Firm," *Journal of Marketing Research*, November 1993, p. 405.

34. Available from World Wide Web: <http://www.3m.com>; *2003 Annual Report*, 3M; "How Leader at 3M Got His Employees to Back Big Changes," *The Wall Street Journal*, April 23, 2002, p. B1; "3M: A Lab for Growth?" *Business Week*, January 21, 2002, p. 50; "How to Get the Most Out of R&D: Balance Funds against Risk, Timing" *Investor's Business Daily*, May 11, 2001, p. A1; "The Changing MACH: Business Week E.Biz*, November 20, 2000, p. EB65; "Steel Wool Dino Roars a Powerful Message," *Advertising Age*, September 16, 1996, p. 55; "How 3M, by Tiptoeing into Foreign Markets, Became a Big Exporter," *The Wall Street Journal*, March 29, 1991, p. A1.

35. "Brands at Work," *Brandweek*, April 13, 1998, p. 27; "Special Report: Auto Marketing & Brand Management," *Advertising Age*, April 6, 1998, p. S1; "P&G Redefines the Brand Manager," *Advertising Age*, October 13, 1997, p. 1. See also Sanjay K. Dhar, Stephen J. Hoch, and Nanda Kumar, "Effective Category Management Depends on the Role of the Category," *Journal of Retailing*, Summer 2001, p. 165; Don Frey, "Learning the Ropes: My Life as a Product Champion," *Harvard Business Review*, September/October 1991, p. 46; Stephen K. Markham, "New Products Management," *Journal of Product Innovation Management*, July 1997, p. 312; Manfred F. Maute and William B. Locander, "Innovation as a Socio-Political Process: An Empirical Analysis of Influence Behavior among New Product Managers," *Journal of Business Research*, June 1994, p. 161.

CHAPTER 11

1. Available from World Wide Web: <http://www.gamestop. com> and <http://www.bn.com> and <http://www.amazon. com>; "Barnes & Noble Buys Out Interest of Online Partner," *The Wall Street Journal*, July 30, 2003, p. B3; "Title Role: Barnes & Noble Pushes Books from Ambitious Publisher, Itself," *The Wall Street Journal*, June 18, 2003, p. A1; "Selling Books like Bacon," *Business Week*, June 16, 2003, p. 80; "Ingram Book Group and Valley Media Partner," *Nashville Business Journal*, May 29, 2001; "Virtual Bookstores Start to Get Real," *Business Week*, October 27, 1997, p. 146; "Why the Bookstore Wars Are Good," *Fortune*, October 27, 1997, p. 50; "Why Barnes & Noble May Crush Amazon," *Fortune*, September 29, 1997, p. 248; "A Haven for the Intellect," *USA Today*, July 10, 1997, p. 1D; "Bookstore Survival Stunts Have Scant Literary Merit," *The Wall Street Journal*, June 3, 1997, p. B1; "Book Superstores Bring Hollywood-Like Risks to Publishing Business," *The Wall Street Journal*, May 29, 1997, p. A1; "Superstores, Megabooks—and Humongous Headaches," *Business Week*, April 14, 1997, p. 92.

2. *2003 Annual Report*, Colgate-Palmolive; *2003 Annual Report*, Procter & Gamble; "For Petco, Success Is a Bitch," *Business 2.0*, November 2003, p. 54; "Petsmart: Why Dogs Don't Worry about a Soft Economy," *Investor's Business Daily*, October 30, 2003, p. A12; "P&G Is Set to Unleash Dental Adult-Pet Food," *The Wall Street Journal*, December 12, 2002, p. B4; "Petco: Pet Supplies Retailer Marks Its Territory in a Dog-Eat-Dog World," *Investor's Business Daily*, December 5, 2002, p. A7; "The Money in Creature Comforts," *Business Week*, September 23, 2002, p. 128; "Well, Doggone! Pet Suppliers Survived the Dot-Bombs," *Investor's Business Daily*, September 9, 2002, p. A5; "For Online Pet Stores, It's Dog-Eat-Dog," *Business Week*, March 6, 2000, p. 78; "P&G Is Out to Fetch Distribution Gains for Iams Pet Food," *The Wall Street Journal*, January 6, 2000, p. A6; "Big Pet-Supply Retailers Try to Tame the Competition," *The Wall Street Journal*, August 20, 1999, p. B4; "Pet Superstores Collar Customers from Supermarkets, Small Shops," *The Wall Street Journal*, November 18, 1993, p. B12.

3. For more on Apple, see "Retail Outlets Help Apple Register Growth," *Investor's Business Daily*, July 15, 2003, p. A6; "A Bigger Retail Bite for Apple," *Investor's Business Daily*, October 31, 2001, p. A6; "Apple Gambles with Retail Plan," *Advertising Age*, June 4, 2001, p. 45; "Sorry, Steve: Here's Why It Won't Work," *Business Week*, May 21, 2001, p. 44. For more on SoBe, see "New Age Dawns as Soda Giants Go Alternative," *Advertising Age*, November 6, 2000, p. 96; "Pepsi Edges Coke in Deal to Buy New Age SoBe," *The Wall Street Journal*, October 30, 2000, p. B1; "Snapple vs. SoBe," *Brandweek*, July 10, 2000, p. 1; "A Fruity Kind of Cola War," *USA Today*, August 3, 1999, p. 1B.

4. S. Chan Choi, "Expanding to Direct Channel: Market Coverages as Entry Barrier," *Journal of Interactive Marketing*, Winter 2003, p. 25; David Shipley, Colin Egan, and Scott Edgett, "Meeting Source Selection Criteria: Direct versus Distributor Channels," *Industrial Marketing Management* 20, no. 4 (1991), p. 297; Thomas L. Powers, "Industrial Distribution Options: Trade-Offs to Consider," *Industrial Marketing Management* 18, no. 3 (1989), p. 155.

5. For more on Avon, see "Avon's Makeover," *Time (Inside Business Bonus Section)*, December 2003; "Avon Calling—Lots of New Reps," *Business Week*, June 2, 2003, p. 53; "Avon Tries Knocking on Dorm Doors," *The Wall Street Journal*, March 28, 2003, p. B2; "Avon Is Set to Call on Teens," *The Wall Street Journal*, October 17, 2002, p. B1; "Sears Says Stores Won't Sell Makeup, a Setback for Avon's New Line," *The Wall Street Journal*, July 11, 2001, p. B1; "Avon Thinks Younger, Wealthier," *Advertising Age*, October 2, 2000, p. 69; "Ding-Dong, Avon Calling (on the Web, Not Your Door)," *The Wall Street Journal*, December 28, 1999, p. B4; "Deck the Mall with Kiosks," *Business Week*, December 13, 1999, p. 86; "Is the Bell Tolling for Door-to-Door Selling?" *Business Week E.Biz*, November 1, 1999, pp. EB58–EB60; "Avon's New Calling: Sell Barbie in China," *The Wall Street Journal*, May 1, 1997, p. B1. For other examples of direct channels, see "Catwalk to Coffee Table," *The Wall Street Journal*, November 7, 2003, p. B1; "India's Retailing Makeover," *The Wall Street Journal*, October 28, 2003, p. A14; "Amway in China: Once Barred, Now Booming," *The Wall Street Journal*, March 12, 2003, p. B1; "Knock, Knock: In Brazil, an Army of Underemployed Goes Door-to-Door," *The Wall Street Journal*, February 19, 2003, p. A1; "Skechers: Savvy Marketing Keeps Shoe Firm Hopping," *Investor's Business Daily*, August 27, 2002, p. A8. See also Mitzi M. Montoya-Weiss, Glenn B. Voss and Dhruv Grewal, "Determinants of Online Channel Use and Overall Satisfaction with a Relational, Multichannel Service Provider," *Journal of the Academy of Marketing Science*, Fall 2003, p. 448; Inge Geyskens, Katrijn Gielens and Marnik G. Dekimpe, "The Market Valuation of Internet Channel Additions," *Journal of Marketing*, April 2002, p. 102; Stewart Brodie, John Stanworth and Thomas R. Wotruba, "Comparisons of Salespeople in Multilevel Vs. Single Level Direct Selling Organizations," *The Journal of Personal Selling & Sales Management*, Spring 2002, p. 67.

6. Edward L. Nash, *Direct Marketing* (New York: McGraw-Hill, 1986).

7. For an example of a Levi Strauss' new indirect channels via discount stores, see "Lessons from a Faded Levi Strauss," *Business Week*, December 15, 2003, p. 44; "At Levi Strauss, Trouble Comes from All Angles," *The Wall Street Journal*, October 13, 2003, p. B1; "Levi's Adds Signature," *Advertising Age*, October 6, 2003, p. 24; "Wal-Mart Adds Touch of Hip to Fashion Choices," *USA Today*, July 22, 2003, p. 3B; "Levi's Won't Fly Signature Ads," *Brandweek*, June 16, 2003, p. 18; "Mass Levi's, Class Levi's," *The Wall Street Journal*, October 31, 2002, p. B1. For other examples of new indirect channels, see "Health-Food Maker Hain Faces Rivals," *The Wall Street Journal*, August 13, 2003, p. B5B; "TRU, Albertsons Launch Toy Box," *DSN Retailing Today*, June 23, 2003, p. 1. For a discussion of indirect channel systems, see Richard Parker and G. R. Funkhouser, "The Consumer As an Active Member of the Channel: Implications for Relationship Marketing," *Journal of Marketing Theory & Practice*, Spring 1997, p. 72; Lou E. Pelton, David Strutton, and James R. Lumpkin, *Marketing Channels: A Relationship Management Approach* (Burr Ridge, IL: Irwin/McGraw-Hill, 2002). See also Bert Rosenbloom and Trina L. Larsen, "How Foreign Firms View Their U.S. Distributors," *Industrial Marketing Management*, May 1992, p. 93; Frank Lynn, "The Changing Economics of Industrial Distribution," *Industrial Marketing Management*, November 1992, p. 355. For more on intermediaries and their functions, see Richard Greene, "Wholesaling," *Forbes*, January 2, 1984, p. 226; Elizabeth J. Wilson and Arch G. Woodside, "Marketing New Products with Distributors," *Industrial Marketing Management*, February 1992, p. 15; W. Benoy et al., "How Industrial Distributors View Distributor-Supplier Partnership Arrangements," *Industrial Marketing Management*, January 1995, p. 27.

8. For a classic discussion of the discrepancy concepts, see Wroe Alderson, "Factors Governing the Development of Marketing Channels," in *Marketing Channels for Manufactured Goods*, ed. Richard M. Clewett (Homewood, IL: Richard D. Irwin, 1954), p. 7.

9. "13,000 and Counting: Cell Stores Multiply Even as Sign-Ups Slow," *Investor's Business Daily*, June 4, 2002, p. A1; "Cellular Carriers Bypass Dealers, Creating Static," *The Wall Street Journal*, March 9, 1998,

p. B1; "Mobile Warfare," *Time*, May 26, 1997, p. 52; "Cell-Phone Service May Be Getting Cheaper," *The Wall Street Journal*, January 11, 1996, p. B1.

10. For some examples on how channels change to adjust discrepancies, see "Selling Literature like Dog Food Gives Club Buyer Real Bite," *The Wall Street Journal*, April 10, 2002, p. A1. See also Robert Tamilia, Sylvain Senecal, and Gilles Corriveau, "Conventional Channels of Distribution and Electronic Intermediaries: a Functional Analysis," *Journal of Marketing Channels*, (3,4) 2002, p. 27; Robert A. Mittelstaedt and Robert E. Stassen, "Structural Changes in the Phonograph Record Industry and Its Channels of Distribution, 1946–1966," *Journal of Macromarketing*, Spring 1994, p. 31; Arun Sharma and Luis V. Dominguez, "Channel Evolution: A Framework for Analysis," *Journal of the Academy of Marketing Science*, Winter 1992, p. 1.

11. Arne Nygaard and Robert Dahlstrom, "Role Stress and Effectiveness in Horizontal Alliances," *Journal of Marketing*, April 2002, p. 61; M. B. Sarkar, Raj Echambadi, S. Tamer Cavusgil and Preet S. Aulakh, "The Influence of Complementarity, Compatibility, and Relationship Capital on Alliance Performance," *Journal of the Academy of Marketing Science*, Fall 2001, p. 358; Jakki J. Mohr, Robert J. Fisher, and John R. Nevin, "Collaborative Communication in Interfirm Relationships: Moderating Effects of Integration and Control," *Journal of Marketing*, July 1996, p. 103; Joseph P. Cannon, "Contracts, Norms, and Plural Form Governance," *Journal of the Academy of Marketing Science*, Spring 2000, p. 180; Amy E. Cox and Orville C. Walker, "Reactions to Disappointing Performance in Manufacturer-Distributor Relationships: The Role of Escalation and Resource Commitments," *Psychology & Marketing*, December 1997, p. 791; Rajiv P. Dant and Patrick L. Schul, "Conflict Resolution Processes in Contractual Channels of Distribution," *Journal of Marketing*, January 1992, p. 38.

12. "What's Wrong with Selling Used CDs?" *Business Week*, July 26, 1993, p. 38.

13. "Get Great Results from Salespeople by Finding What Really Moves Them," *Investor's Business Daily*, July 2, 2001, p. A1.

14. "How Goodyear Blew Its Chance to Capitalize on a Rival's Woes," *The Wall Street Journal*, February 19, 2003, p. A1; "For Two Tire Makers, a Flat-Out Pitch for Safer Wheels," *The Wall Street Journal*, July 3, 1997, p. B4; "Goodyear Revs Image," *Brandweek*, February 10, 1997, p. 12; "Goodyear Wins Court Dispute with Dealers," *The Wall Street Journal*, July 2, 1996, p. B6; "Stan Gault's Designated Driver," *Business Week*, April 8, 1996, p. 128; "Goodyear Expands Just Tires by Converting Full Service Centers," *Discount Store News*, May 16, 1994, p. 6. See also David I. Gilliland, "Toward a Business-to-business Channel Incentives Classification Scheme," *Industrial Marketing Management*, January 2003, p. 55; Keysuk Kim and Changho Oh, "On Distributor Commitment in Marketing Channels for Industrial Products: Contrast Between the United States and Japan," *Journal of International Marketing*, (1) 2002, p. 72; Pierre Berthon, Leyland F. Pitt, Michael T. Ewing and Gunnar Bakkeland, "Norms and Power in Marketing Relationships: Alternative Theories and Empirical Evidence," *Journal of Business Research*, September 2003, p. 699; Rajiv Mehta, Alan J. Dubinsky, and Rolph E. Anderson, "Marketing Channel Management and the Sales Manager," *Industrial Marketing Management*, August 2002, p. 429; Wujin Chu and Paul R. Messinger, "Information and Channel Profits," *Journal of Retailing*, Winter 1997, p. 487; Donald V. Fites, "Make Your Dealers Your Partners," *Harvard Business Review*, March–April 1996, p. 84; John F. Tanner, Rick E. Ridnour, and Stephen B. Castleberry, "Types of Vertical Exchange Relationships: An Empirical Re-Examination of the Cadre/ Hired-Hand Distinction," *Journal of Marketing Theory & Practice*, Summer 1997, p. 109; Zhan G. Li and Rajiv P. Dant, "An Exploratory Study of Exclusive Dealing in Channel Relationships," *Journal of the Academy of Marketing Science*, Summer 1997, p. 201.

15. See G. Peter Dapiran and Sandra Hogarth-Scott, "Are Co-operation and Trust Being Confused with Power? An Analysis of Food Retailing in Australia and the UK," *International Journal of Retail & Distribution Management*, (4) 2003 p. 256; David I. Gilliland and Daniel C. Bello, "Two Sides to Attitudinal Commitment: the Effect of Calculative and Loyalty Commitment on Enforcement Mechanisms in Distribution Channels," *Journal of the Academy of Marketing Science*, Winter 2002, p. 24; Keysuk Kim, "On Interfirm Power, Channel Climate, and Solidarity in Industrial Distributor-Supplier Dyads," *Journal of the Academy of Marketing Science*, Summer 2000, p. 388; "Making the Middleman an Endangered Species," *Business Week*, June 6, 1994, p. 114; Jule B. Gassenheimer et al., "Models of Channel Maintenance: What Is the Weaker Party to Do?" *Journal of Business Research*, July 1994, p. 225; Gregory T. Gundlach, Ravi S. Achrol, and John T. Mentzer, "The Structure of Commitment in Exchange," *Journal of Marketing*, January 1995, p. 78; Jan B. Heide, "Interorganizational Governance in Marketing Channels," *Journal of Marketing*, January 1994, p. 71; Jean L. Johnson et al., "The Exercise of Interfirm Power and Its Repercussions in U.S.-Japanese Channel Relationships," *Journal of Marketing*, April 1993, p. 1.

16. "Crowded House: With the Web Shaking Up Music, a Free-for-All in Online Songs," *The Wall Street Journal*, November 19, 2003, p. A1; "Microsoft Plans to Sell Music over the Web," *The Wall Street Journal*, November 17, 2003, p. B1; "Ads Aim to Sell That Tune," *The Wall Street Journal*, November 10, 2003, p. B1; "Everybody Wants a Piece of the iPod," *Business Week*, October 27, 2003, p. 48; "Pumping Up the Volume," *Newsweek*, October 27, 2003, p. 52; "Walt Rocks: Rating the New Music Sites," *The Wall Street Journal*, October 22, 2003, p. D1; "Apple Opens Door of E-Music Store to Windows Users," *The Wall Street Journal*, October 17, 2003, p. B2; "Music Industry Presses 'Play' on Plan to Save Its Business," *The Wall Street Journal*, September 9, 2003, p. A1; "Best Buy Gets Jump on Retailers," *Investor's Business Daily*, August 27, 2003, p. A4; "Special Report: Music Marketing," *Advertising Age*, July 28, 2003, pp. S1–S8; "Lawsuits May Help Net Song Sellers," *USA Today*, June 30, 2003, p. 2B; "Taps for Music Retailers?" *Business Week*, June 23, 2003, p. 40; "Free Samples at the Record Store," *The Wall Street Journal*, June 12, 2003, p. D1; "Music Sites Launch Battle of the Brands," *Advertising Age*, May 12, 2003, p. 3; "Apple Brings Its Flair for Smart Designs to Digital Music Player," *The Wall Street Journal*, November 1, 2001, p. B1.

17. "Mothers Work: Oh Baby, Business at This Retailer Is Booming," *Investor's Business Daily*, December 2, 2002, p. A10; "Mothers Work: Giving the Lady What She Wants," *Fortune*, October 30, 2000, pp. T208BB–HH.

18. "Kimberly-Clark Keeps Costco in Diapers, Absorbing Costs Itself," *The Wall Street Journal*, September 7, 2000, p. A1. For another example, see "Made to Measure: Invisible Supplier Has Penney's Shirts All Buttoned Up," *The Wall Street Journal*, September 11, 2003, p. A1.

19. Kevin L. Webb, "Managing Channels of Distribution in the Age of Electronic Commerce," *Industrial Marketing Management*, February 2002, p. 95; Carolyn Y. Nicholson, Larry D. Compeau and Rajesh Sethi, "The Role of Interpersonal Liking in Building Trust in Long-Term Channel Relationships," *Journal of the Academy of Marketing Science*, Winter 2001, p. 3; Charles A. Ingene and Mark E. Parry, "Is Channel Coordination All it Is Cracked up to Be?," *Journal of Retailing*, Winter 2000, p. 511; Kenneth H. Wathne and Jan B. Heide, "Opportunism in Interfirm Relationships: Forms, Outcomes, and Solutions," *Journal of Marketing*, October 2000, p. 36; James R. Brown, Chekitan S. Dev, and Dong-Jin Lee, "Managing Marketing Channel Opportunism: the Efficacy of Alternative Governance Mechanisms," *Journal of Marketing*, April 2000, p. 51; Ashwin W. Joshi and Alexandra J. Campbell, "Effect of Environmental Dynamism on Relational Governance in Manufacturer-Supplier Relationships: a Contingency Framework and an Empirical Test," *Journal of the Academy of Marketing Science*, Spring 2003, p. 176; Kersi D. Antia and Gary L. Frazier, "The Severity of Contract Enforcement in Interfirm Channel Relationships," *Journal of Marketing*, October 2001, p. 67; Ravi S. Achrol, "Changes in the Theory of Interorganizational Relations in Marketing: Toward a Network Paradigm," *Journal of the Academy of

Marketing Science, Winter 1997, p. 56; Aric Rindfleisch and Jan B. Heide, "Transaction Cost Analysis: Past, Present, and Future Applications," *Journal of Marketing,* October 1997, p. 30; Robert F. Lusch and James R. Brown, "Interdependency, Contracting, and Relational Behavior in Marketing Channels," *Journal of Marketing,* October 1996, p. 19; Robert D. Buzzell, "Is Vertical Integration Profitable?" *Harvard Business Review,* January–February 1983, p. 92.

20. "Special Report: Partners," *Business Week,* October 25, 1999, p. 106.

21. "A Talk with the Man Who Got Rayovac All Charged Up," *Business Week,* February 21, 2000, p. 32F.

22. "Can Esprit Be Hip Again?" *The Wall Street Journal,* June 17, 2002, p. B1; "Esprit's Spirited Style Is Hot Seller," *USA Today,* March 25, 1986, p. B5. See also Carol J. Johnson, Robert E. Krapfel, Jr. and Curtis M. Grimm, "A Contingency Model of Supplier-Reseller Satisfaction Perceptions in Distribution Channels," *Journal of Marketing Channels,* (1,2) 2001, p. 65; Inge Geyskens and Jan-Benedict E. M. Steenkamp, "Economic and Social Satisfaction: Measurement and Relevance to Marketing Channel Relationships," *Journal of Retailing,* Spring 2000, p. 11; Gary L. Frazier and Walfried M. Lassar, "Determinants of Distribution Intensity," *Journal of Marketing,* October 1996, p. 39; Adam J. Fein and Erin Anderson, "Patterns of Credible Commitments: Territory and Brand Selectivity in Industrial Distribution Channels," *Journal of Marketing,* April 1997, p. 19.

23. "Antitrust Issues and Marketing Channel Strategy" and "Case 1— Continental T.V., Inc., et al. v. GTE Sylvania, Inc.," in Louis W. Stern and Thomas L. Eovaldi, *Legal Aspects of Marketing Strategy* (Englewood Cliffs, NJ: Prentice-Hall, 1984), p. 300. See also Debra M. Desrochers, Gregory T. Gundlach and Albert A. Foer, "Analysis of Antitrust Challenges to Category Captain Arrangements," *Journal of Public Policy & Marketing,* Fall 2003, p. 201.

24. For more on Reebok, see *2003 Annual Report,* Reebok; "Reebok's Direct Sales Spark a Retail Revolt," *Adweek's Marketing Week,* December 2, 1991, p. 7. See also Saul Sands and Robert J. Posch, Jr., "A Checklist of Questions for Firms Considering a Vertical Territorial Distribution Plan," *Journal of Marketing,* Summer 1982, p. 38; Debra L. Scammon and Mary Jane Sheffet, "Legal Issues in Channels Modification Decisions: The Question of Refusals to Deal," *Journal of Public Policy and Marketing* 5 (1986), p. 82.

25. Gregory T. Gundlach and Patrick E. Murphy, "Ethical and Legal Foundations of Relational Marketing Exchanges," *Journal of Marketing,* October 1993, p. 35; Craig B. Barkacs, "Multilevel Marketing and Antifraud Statutes: Legal Enterprises or Pyramid Schemes?" *Journal of the Academy of Marketing Science,* Spring 1997, p. 176; Robert A. Robicheaux and James E. Coleman, "The Structure of Marketing Channel Relationships," *Journal of the Academy of Marketing Science,* Winter 1994, p. 38; Brett A. Boyle and F. Robert Dwyer, "Power, Bureaucracy, Influence and Performance: Their Relationships in Industrial Distribution Channels," *Journal of Business Research,* March 1995, p. 189.

26. For more on online return policies, see "I Ordered That? Web Retailers Make It Easier to Return Goods," *The Wall Street Journal,* September 4, 2003, p. D1; "Gone Today, Here Tomorrow," *Business 2.0,* December 2001, p. 116; "Happy Returns," *Business Week Small Biz,* October 8, 2001, p. 12. For more on in-store return policies, see "I Take Thee . . . Back to the Store," *The Wall Street Journal,* May 30, 2002, p. D1; "The Point of No Return," *The Wall Street Journal,* May 14, 2002, p. D1. See also Andy A. Tsay, "Risk Sensitivity in Distribution Channel Partnerships: Implications for Manufacturer Return Policies," *Journal of Retailing,* Summer 2002, p. 147; Sara Lonn and Julie Ann Stuart, "Increasing Service Through Aggressive Dealer Inventory Return Policies," *International Journal of Physical Distribution & Logistics Management,* (6) 2003, p. 519.

27. See, for example, "P&G to Stores: Keep the Dented Crisco Cans," *The Wall Street Journal,* March 21, 1997, p. B1. See also "Cellphone

Makers Connect for Recycling Program," *USA Today,* October 22, 2003, p. 6B; "The Information Age's Toxic Garbage," *Business Week,* October 6, 2003, p. 54. See also Rene B. M. de Koster, Marisa P. de Brito and Masja A. van de Vendel, "Return Handling: an Exploratory Study with Nine Retailer Warehouses," *International Journal of Retail & Distribution Management,* (8) 2002, p. 407; Ronald S. Tibben-Lembke, "Life after Death: Reverse Logistics and the Product Life Cycle," *International Journal of Physical Distribution & Logistics Management,* (3) 2002, p. 223; A. Michael Knemeyer, Thomas G. Ponzurick, and Cyril M. Logar, "A Qualitative Examination of Factors Affecting Reverse Logistics Systems for End-of-Life Computers," *International Journal of Physical Distribution & Logistics Management,* (6) 2002, p. 455; Chad W. Autry, Patricia J. Daugherty, and R. Glenn Richey, "The Challenge of Reverse Logistics in Catalog Retailing," *International Journal of Physical Distribution & Logistics Management,* (1) 2001, p. 26; Dale S. Rogers and Ronald Tibben-Lembke, "An Examination of Reverse Logistics Practices," *Journal of Business Logistics,* (2) 2001, p. 129.

CHAPTER 12

1. "Dial-a-Coke Is Slaking Thirsts in Australia," *The Wall Street Journal Reports,* October 20, 2003, p. R3; "Coke Lures Japanese Customers with Cellphone Come-Ons," *The Wall Street Journal,* September 8, 2003, p. B1; "Executive at Coke Gives Up His Post in Scandal's Wake," *The Wall Street Journal,* August 26, 2003, p. B4; "Coke, Pepsi Still Face Issues in India," *The Wall Street Journal,* August 25, 2003, p. B4; "Into the Fryer: How Coke Officials Beefed Up Results of Marketing Tests," *The Wall Street Journal,* August 20, 2003, p. A1; "Coke, Pepsi Fight Product-Contamination Charges in India," *The Wall Street Journal,* August 15, 2003, p. B1; "Mooove Over, Milkman," *The Wall Street Journal,* June 9, 2003, p. B1; "Fountain Dispenses Problems," *USA Today,* May 28, 2003, p. 1B; "Things Go Better for Coke's New Ad Campaign," *USA Today,* March 17, 2003, p. 8B; "Soft-Drink Suppliers Bottle a New Strategy," *Investor's Business Daily,* March 11, 2003, p. A10; "Coke and Pepsi Keep Pushing the Boundaries," *Food Retailing Today,* February 24, 2003, p. 10; "Cracking China's Market," *The Wall Street Journal,* January 9, 2003, p. B1; "After Flat Sales, Cott Challenges Pepsi, Coca-Cola," *The Wall Street Journal,* January 8, 2003, p. B1; "No Bull: Coke Targets Clubs," *Advertising Age,* December 9, 2002, p. 3; "Coke Works Harder at Being the Real Thing in Hinterland," *The Wall Street Journal,* November 26, 2002, p. B1; "Coke v. Pepsi: Return to War," *Advertising Age,* November 25, 2002, p. 1; "Coke Pops Top on New Colas," *USA Today,* October 1, 2002, p. 6B; "Cola's Color War," *Brandweek,* May 13, 2002, p. 5; "In Demand: Software that Helps Firms Keep Selling," *Investor's Business Daily,* April 25, 2002, p. A11; "Coke Is B2B Success Story," *Investor's Business Daily,* February 21, 2002, p. A13; "Shaking Up the Coke Bottle," *Business Week,* December 3, 2001, p. 74; "Will Coke.net Be the Real Thing to Put Fizz into Fountain Sales?" *Investor's Business Daily,* May 4, 2001, p. A5; "Coke Hopes to Add Fizz to Future with New Structure, Management," *Investor's Business Daily,* April 18, 2001, p. A1; "Guess Who's Winning the Cola Wars," *Fortune,* April 2, 2001, p. 164; "Coca-Cola Readies Global Assault," *Advertising Age,* April 2, 2001, p. 1; "Repairing the Coke Machine," *Business Week,* March 19, 2001, p. 86; "Coke Retains Top Spot in U.S. Soda Sales," *The Wall Street Journal,* February 16, 2001, p. B8; "Pepsi, Coke Duke It Out in India, China," *Ad Age Global,* October 2000, p. 6; "For Coke, Local Is It," *Business Week,* July 3, 2000, p. 122; "To Fix Coca-Cola, Daft Sets Out to Get Relationships Right," *The Wall Street Journal,* June 23, 2000, p. A1; "The China Card," *Fortune,* May 25, 1998, p. 82; "For Pepsi, a Battle to Capture Coke's Fountain Sales," *The Wall Street Journal,* May 11, 1998, p. B1; "Pepsi Hits Coca-Cola with an Antitrust Lawsuit," *The Wall Street Journal,* May 8, 1998, p. A3; "I'd Like the World to Buy a Coke," *Business Week,* April 13, 1998, p. 70; "If You Can't Beat 'Em, Copy 'Em," *Business Week,* November 17, 1997, p. 50; "Where Coke Goes from Here," *Fortune,* October 13, 1997, p. 88; "Coke Recruits Paraplegics to Help Fight PepsiCo in Soda War in India," *The*

Wall Street Journal, June 10, 1997, p. B9; "A Coke and a Perm? Soda Giant Is Pushing into Unusual Locales," *The Wall Street Journal*, May 8, 1997, p. A1; "Coke Pours into Asia," *Business Week*, October 28, 1996, p. 72; "Coke's Soda Fountain for Offices Fizzles, Dashing High Hopes," *The Wall Street Journal*, June 14, 1993, p. A1.

2. Available from World Wide Web: <http://www.transora. com> and <http://www.fmi.org/media/bg/ecr1>; "How to Make a Frozen Lasagna (with Just $250 Million)," *Fortune*, April 30, 2001, p. 149; "Delivering the Goods," *Fortune*, November 28, 1994, p. 64; "Making the Middleman an Endangered Species," *Business Week*, June 6, 1994, p. 114; "The Nitty-Gritty of ECR Systems: How One Company Makes It Pay," *Advertising Age*, May 2, 1994, p. S1; "Behind the Tumult at P&G," *Fortune*, March 7, 1994, p. 74. See also Stefan Borchert, "Implementation Hurdles of ECR Partnerships—the German Food Sector as an ECR Case Study," *International Journal of Retail & Distribution Management*, (6) 2002, p. 354.

3. "Compaq Stumbles as PCs Weather New Blow," *The Wall Street Journal*, March 9, 1998, p. B1; "At What Profit Price?" *Brandweek*, June 23, 1997, p. 24; "Delivering the Goods," *Fortune*, November 28, 1994, p. 64. See also Theodore P. Stank, Thomas J. Goldsby, Shawnee K. Vickery, and Katrina Savitskie, "Logistics Service Performance: Estimating its Influence on Market Share," *Journal of Business Logistics*, (1) 2003, p. 27; Katia Campo, Els Gijsbrechts and Patricia Nisol, "Towards Understanding Consumer Response to Stock-Outs," *Journal of Retailing*, Summer 2000, p. 219; Chris Dubelaar, Garland Chow and Paul D. Larson, "Relationships Between Inventory, Sales and Service in a Retail Chain Store Operation," *International Journal of Physical Distribution & Logistics Management*, (2) 2001, p. 96; Walter Zinn and Peter C. Liu, "Consumer Response to Retail Stockouts," *Journal of Business Logistics*, (1) 2001, p. 49; Lloyd M. Rinehart, M. Bixby Cooper, and George D. Wagenheim, "Furthering the Integration of Marketing and Logistics Through Customer Service in the Channel," *Journal of the Academy of Marketing Science*, Winter 1989, p. 63; Edward A. Morash and John Ozment, "Toward Management of Transportation Service Quality," *The Logistics and Transportation Review*, June 1994, p. 115; Michael H. Morris and Duane L. Davis, "Measuring and Managing Customer Service in Industrial Firms," *Industrial Marketing Management*, November 1992, p. 343; Gary L. Frazier, Robert E. Spekman, and Charles R. O'Neal, "Just-In-Time Exchange Relationships in Industrial Markets," *Journal of Marketing*, October 1988, p. 52; William D. Perreault, Jr., and Frederick A. Russ, "Physical Distribution Service in Industrial Purchase Decisions," *Journal of Marketing*, April 1976, p. 3.

4. "Logistics Gets a Little Respect," *Business Week E.Biz*, November 20, 2000, p. EB112; "One Smart Cookie," *Business Week E.Biz*, November 20, 2000, p. EB120; "A Cereal Maker Hitches Its Wagons to the Web," *Business Week E.Biz*, September 18, 2000, p. EB80; "Costs Too High? Bring in the Logistics Experts," *Fortune*, November 10, 1997, p. 200C. See also Thierry Sauvage, "The Relationship Between Technology and Logistics Third-Party Providers," *International Journal of Physical Distribution & Logistics Management*, (3) 2003, p. 236; Donald J. Bowersox, David J. Closs, and Theodore P. Stank, "Ten Mega-Trends That Will Revolutionize Supply Chain Logistics," *Journal of Business Logistics*, (2) 2000, p. 1; James R. Stock, "Marketing Myopia Revisited: Lessons for Logistics," *International Journal of Physical Distribution & Logistics Management*, (1) 2002, p. 12; Mark Goh and Charlene Ling, "Logistics Development in China," *International Journal of Physical Distribution & Logistics Management*, (9) 2003, p. 886; James H. Bookbinder and Chris S. Tan, "Comparison of Asian and European Logistics Systems," *International Journal of Physical Distribution & Logistics Management*, (1) 2003, p. 36; Carol J. Emerson and Curtis M. Grimm, "The Relative Importance of Logistics and Marketing Customer Service: A Strategic Perspective," ,ﬔﬔﬔﬔﬔﬔ ﬔﬔﬔﬔﬔﬔ ﬔﬔﬔﬔﬔ, ﬔﬔﬔﬔ, ﬔ ﬔﬔ; ﬔﬔﬔﬔﬔﬔﬔ ﬔ ﬔﬔﬔﬔﬔﬔ, ﬔﬔﬔﬔﬔﬔ ﬔ. M. Droge, and Shawnee K. Vickery, "Strategic Logistics Capabilities for Competitive Advantage and Firm Success," *Journal of Business Logistics*, 1996, p. 1; Steven R. Clinton and David J. Closs, "Logistics Strategy:

Does It Exist?" *Journal of Business Logistics*, 1997, p. 19; Prabir K. Bagchi and Helge Virum, "Logistical Alliances: Trends and Prospects in Integrated Europe," *Journal of Business Logistics*, 1998, p. 191.

5. "Inside the Race to Get Hot Video Games on Shelves," *The Wall Street Journal*, December 20, 2000, p. B1.

6. For more on Clorox, see *2003 Annual Report*, Clorox; "The Web @ Work/Clorox Co.," *The Wall Street Journal*, October 9, 2000, p. B21; also available from World Wide Web: <http://www. clorox.com>. See also Forrest E. Harding, "Logistics Service Provider Quality: Private Measurement, Evaluation, and Improvement," *Journal of Business Logistics*, 1998, p. 103; Carol C. Bienstock, John T. Mentzer, and Monroe M. Bird, "Measuring Physical Distribution Service Quality," *Journal of the Academy of Marketing Science*, Winter 1997, p. 31; G. T. M. Hult, "Measuring Cycle Time of the Global Procurement Process," *Industrial Marketing Management*, September 1997, p. 403; R. Mohan Pisharodi, "Preference for Supplier When Supplier and Customer Perceptions of Customer Service Levels Differ," *The Logistics and Transportation Review*, March 1994, p. 31.

7. Mikko Karkkainen, Timo Ala-Risku and Jan Holmstrom, "Increasing Customer Value and Decreasing Distribution Costs with Merge-In-Transit," *International Journal of Physical Distribution & Logistics Management*, (1) 2003, p. 132; Marc J. Schniederjans and Qing Cao, "An Alternative Analysis of Inventory Costs of JIT and EOQ Purchasing," *International Journal of Physical Distribution & Logistics Management*, (2) 2001, p. 109; Amy Z. Zeng and Christian Rossetti, "Developing a Framework for Evaluating the Logistics Costs in Global Sourcing Processes: an Implementation and Insights," *International Journal of Physical Distribution & Logistics Management*, (9) 2003, p. 785; Lisa M. Ellram and Sue P. Siferd, "Total Cost of Ownership: A Key Concept in Strategic Cost Management Decisions," *Journal of Business Logistics*, 1998, p. 55; Scott R. Swenseth and Michael R. Godfrey, "Estimating Freight Rates for Logistics Decisions," *Journal of Business Logistics*, 1996, p. 213; Philip T. Evers, "The Impact of Transshipments on Safety Stock Requirements," *Journal of Business Logistics*, 1996, p. 109.

8. "Etoys to Close Up Shop This Spring," *DSN Retailing Today*, February 19, 2001, p. 6; "The eToys Saga: Costs Kept Rising But Sales Slowed," *The Wall Street Journal*, January 22, 2001, p. B1; "Etoys' Disappointing Holiday Spells Disaster for Pure-Players," *DSN Retailing Today*, January 1, 2001, p. 11; "Etoys' Disappointing Forecast Prompts Hard Look at Rest of E-Commerce Sector," *The Wall Street Journal*, December 18, 2000, p. A3; "Santa's Middleman Takes Stock," *The Wall Street Journal*, December 8, 2000, p. B1; "Etoys' Strategy to Stay in the Game," *The Wall Street Journal*, April 25, 2000, p. B1; "Amazon, Etoys Make Big, Opposing Bets; Which One Is Right?" *The Wall Street Journal*, November 2, 1999, p. A1; "On the Internet, Toys R Us Plays Catch-Up," *The Wall Street Journal*, August 19, 1999, p. B1.

9. *2003 Annual Report*, Tyson Foods; "Holly Farms' Marketing Error: The Chicken that Laid an Egg," *The Wall Street Journal*, February 9, 1988, p. 44.

10. For more on JIT, see "Uncertain Economy Hinders Highly Precise Supply System," *The New York Times*, March 15, 2003, p. B1; "Port Tie-Up Shows Vulnerability," *USA Today*, October 9, 2002, p. 1B; "Deadline Scramble: A New Hazard for Recovery, Last-Minute Pace of Orders," *The Wall Street Journal*, June 25, 2002, p. A1; "Parts Shortages Hamper Electronics Makers," *The Wall Street Journal*, July 7, 2000, p. B5. See also Leroy B. Schwarz and Z. Kevin Weng, "The Design of a JIT Supply Chain: the Effect of Leadtime Uncertainty on Safety Stock," *Journal of Business Logistics*, (2) 2000, p. 231; Richard E. White and John N. Pearson, "JIT, System Integration and Customer Service," *International Journal of Physical Distribution & Logistics Management*, (5) 2001, p. 313; Richard Germain, Cornelia Droge, and Nancy Spears, "The Implications of Just-in-Time for Logistics Organization Management and Performance," *Journal of Business Logistics*, 1996, p. 19; Faye W. Gilbert, Joyce A. Young, and Charles R. O'Neal, "Buyer-Seller Relationships in Just-in-Time

Purchasing Environments," *Journal of Business Research*, February 1994, p. 111.

11. Available from World Wide Web: <http://silmaril.smeal. psu.edu/misc/supply_chain>; Taylor R. Randall, Ruskin M. Morgan and Alysse R. Morton, "Efficient Versus Responsive Supply Chain Choice: an Empirical Examination of Influential Factors," *The Journal of Product Innovation Management*, November 2003, p. 430; Lisa R. Williams, Terry L. Esper and John Ozment, "The Electronic Supply Chain: its Impact on the Current and Future Structure of Strategic Alliances, Partnerships and Logistics Leadership," *International Journal of Physical Distribution & Logistics Management*, (8) 2002, p. 703; Christopher R. Moberg and Thomas W. Speh, "Evaluating the Relationship Between Questionable Business Practices and the Strength of Supply Chain Relationships," *Journal of Business Logistics*, (2) 2003, p. 1; John T. Mentzer, Soonhong Min and Zach G. Zacharia, "The Nature of Interfirm Partnering in Supply Chain Management," *Journal of Retailing*, Winter 2000, p. 549; John T. Mentzer, William DeWitt, James S. Keebler, Soonhong Min and et al, "Defining Supply Chain Management," *Journal of Business Logistics*, (2) 2001, p. 1, Subroto Roy, K. Sivakumar, and Ian F. Wilkinson, "Innovation Generation in Supply Chain Relationships: a Conceptual Model and Research Propositions," *Journal of the Academy of Marketing Science*, Winter 2004, p. 61; W. Lemoine and Lars Dagnaes, "Globalisation Strategies and Business of Organisation of a Network of Logistics Service Providers," *International Journal of Physical Distribution & Logistics Management*, (3) 2003, p. 209; Katarina Kempainen and Ari P. J. Vepsalainen, "Trends in Industrial Supply Chains and Networks," *International Journal of Physical Distribution & Logistics Management*, (8) 2003, p. 701; Rakesh Niraj, "Customer Profitability in a Supply Chain," *Journal of Marketing*, July 2001, p. 1; William F. Crittenden, "Business Success: A Way of Thinking about Strategy, Critical Supply Chain Assets and Operational Best Practices," *Journal of the Academy of Marketing Science*, Summer 2000, p. 446; "The Push to Streamline Supply Chains," *Fortune*, March 3, 1997, pp. 108C–R; Harry L. Sink and C. J. Langley, "A Managerial Framework for the Acquisition of Third-Party Logistics Services," *Journal of Business Logistics*, 1997, p. 163; Robert C. Lieb and Hugh L. Randall, "A Comparison of the Use of Third-Party Logistics Services by Large American Manufacturers, 1991, 1994, and 1995," *Journal of Business Logistics*, 1996, p. 305.

12. For an excellent example of EDI, see "To Sell Goods to Wal-Mart, Get on the Net," *The Wall Street Journal*, November 21, 2003, p. B1. See also Cornelia Droge and Richard Germain, "The Relationship of Electronic Data Interchange with Inventory and Financial Performance," *Journal of Business Logistics*, (2) 2000, p. 209; Lisa R. Williams, Avril Nibbs, Dimples Irby, and Terence Finley, "Logistics Integration: The Effect of Information Technology, Team Composition, and Corporate Competitve Positioning," *Journal of Business Logistics*, 1997, p. 31; Paul R. Murphy and James M. Daley, "International Freight Forwarder Perspectives on Electronic Data Interchange and Information Management Issues," *Journal of Business Logistics*, 1996, p. 63; Ira Lewis and Alexander Talalayevsky, "Logistics and Information Technology: A Coordination Perspective," *Journal of Business Logistics*, 1997, p. 141.

13. "A Smart Cookie at Pepperidge," *Fortune*, December 22, 1986, p. 67.

14. "Deadline Scramble: A New Hazard for Recovery, Last-Minute Pace of Orders," *The Wall Street Journal*, June 25, 2002, p. A1; "As Stores Scrimp More and Order Less, Suppliers Take on Greater Risks, Costs," *The Wall Street Journal*, December 10, 1991, p. B1.

15. Douglas Lambert, James R. Stock, and Lisa M. Ellram, *Fundamentals of Logistics* (Burr Ridge, IL: Irwin/McGraw-Hill, 1998).

16. For more on transportation security, see "Protecting America's Ports," *Fortune*, November 10, 2003, p. T198C; "FedEx Takes Direct Approach to Terrorism," *The Wall Street Journal*, October 9, 2003, p. A4; "Safe Harbors?" *The Wall Street Journal*, April 21, 2003, p. B1; "Companies Must Add Rising Security Costs to Bottom Line," *USA Today*,

March 28, 2003, p. 1B; "Shippers Get Caught in Customs' Net," *Business Week*, March 24, 2003, p. 76B; "The Friction Economy," *Fortune*, February 18, 2002, p. 104; "Difficult Passage: After Terror Attacks, Shipping Goods Takes Longer and Costs More," *The Wall Street Journal*, September 27, 2001, p. A1. For more on deregulation of transportation, see Paul D. Larson, "Transportation Deregulation, JIT, and Inventory Levels," *The Logistics and Transportation Review*, June 1991, p. 99; James C. Nelson, "Politics and Economics in Transport Regulation and Deregulation—A Century Perspective of the ICC's Role," *The Logistics and Transportation Review*, March, 1987, p. 5.

17. For a more detailed comparison of mode characteristics, see Robert Dahlstrom, Kevin M. McNeilly, and Thomas W. Speh, "Buyer-Seller Relationships in the Procurement of Logistical Services," *Journal of the Academy of Marketing Science*, Spring 1996, p. 110; Roger Dale Abshire and Shane R. Premeaux, "Motor Carriers' and Shippers' Perceptions of the Carrier Choice Decision," *The Logistics and Transportation Review*, December 1991, p. 351; Brian J. Gibson, Harry L. Sink, and Ray A. Mundy, "Shipper-Carrier Relationships and Carrier Selection Criteria," *The Logistics and Transportation Review*, December 1993, p. 371.

18. "Next Stop: The 21st Century," *Business 2.0*, September 2003, p. 152; "Back on Track: Left for Dead, Railroads Revive by Watching Clock," *The Wall Street Journal*, July 25, 2003, p. A1; "Trains: Industry Report," *Investor's Business Daily*, May 7, 2001, p. B6; "America's Railroads Struggle to Recapture Their Former Glory," *The Wall Street Journal*, December 5, 1997, p. A1; "The Rails: Trouble Behind, Trouble Ahead," *Business Week*, November 24, 1997, p. 40.

19. "Costs of Trucking Seen Rising under New Safety Rules," *The Wall Street Journal*, November 12, 2003, p. A1; "Trucker Rewards Customers for Good Behavior," *The Wall Street Journal*, September 9, 2003, p. B4; "Trucking: Rig and Roll," *The Wall Street Journal*, October 23, 2000, p. R51; "Trucking Gets Sophisticated," *Fortune*, July 24, 2000, p. T270B; "Forward Air Corp.: Hauler Gets Freight from Jets to Businesses," *Investor's Business Daily*, June 6, 2000, p. A14; "Making Sure Big Rigs Have Something to Carry," *Business Week*, June 12, 2000, p. 168F; "Trucking Finds the Internet," *Heavy Duty Trucking*, October 1999, p. 116; "Riding the Data Highway," *Newsweek*, March 21, 1994, p. 54; "E-Commerce's Newest Portals: Truck Drivers," *The Wall Street Journal*, January 3, 2000, p. A11; "Getting the Goods," *The Wall Street Journal*, November 22, 1999, p. R39.

20. For more on overnight carriers, see "Why FedEx Is Gaining Ground," *Business 2.0*, October 2003, p. 56; "FedEx Recasts Itself on the Ground," *The Wall Street Journal*, September 4, 2003, p. B7; "UPS, FedEx Wage Handheld Combat," *Investor's Business Daily*, May 19, 2003, p. A6; "Shipping Firms' Web Sites Help You Track Items," *Investor's Business Daily*, July 6, 2001, p. A6; "UPS Puts Its Back into It," *Business Week*, October 27, 1997, p. 50.

21. K. Raguraman and Claire Chan, "The Development of Sea-Air Intermodal Transportation: An Assessment of Global Trends," *The Logistics and Transportation Review*, December 1994, p. 379; "Monsters of the High Seas," *Business Week*, October 13, 2003, p. 58; "Cargo that Phones Home," *Fortune*, November 15, 1993, p. 143.

22. *2003 Annual Report*, Du Pont; *2003 Annual Report*, Matlack; *2003 Annual Report*, Shell; *2003 Annual Report*, FedEx; *2003 Annual Report*, UPS; "FedEx and Brown Are Going Green," *Business Week*, August 11, 2003, p. 60; "Conservation Power," *Business Week*, September 16, 1991, p. 86. See also Lawrence Christensen, "The Environment and its Impact on the Supply Chain," *International Journal of Retail & Distribution Management*, (11) 2002, p. 571.

23. "Freight Forwarder at Home in Global Village," *Investor's Business Daily*, April 7, 2003, p. A8; Paul R. Murphy, "Third-Party Logistics: Some User Versus Provider Perspectives," *Journal of Business Logistics*, 2000, Vol. 21, 1, p. 121; Kant Rao, Richard R. Young, and Judith A.

Novick, "Third Party Services in the Logistics of Global Firms," *The Logistics and Transportation Review*, December 1993, p. 363.

24. "You Make It, They Distribute It," *Nation's Business*, March 1994, p. 46; C. H. White and R. B. Felder, "Turn Your Truck Fleet into a Profit Center," *Harvard Business Review*, May–June 1983, p. 14.

25. "Hospital Cost Cutters Push Use of Scanners to Track Inventories," *The Wall Street Journal*, June 10, 1997, p. A1. See also Charu Chandra and Sameer Kumar, "Taxonomy of Inventory Policies for Supply-Chain Effectiveness," *International Journal of Retail & Distribution Management*, (4) 2001, p. 164; Walter Zinn, John T. Mentzer and Keely L. Croxton, "Customer-Based Measures of Inventory Availability," *Journal of Business Logistics*, (2) 2002, p. 19; Gavan J. Fitzsimons, "Consumer Response to Stockouts," *Journal of Consumer Research*, September 2000, p. 249; Timothy L. Urban, "The Interdependence of Inventory Management and Retail Shelf Management," *International Journal of Physical Distribution & Logistics Management*, (1) 2002, p. 41; Matthew B. Myers, Patricia J. Daugherty, and Chad W. Autry, "The Effectiveness of Automatic Inventory Replenishment in Supply Chain Operations: Antecedents and Outcomes," *Journal of Retailing*, Winter 2000, p. 455; Paul Zinszer, "Supply Chain Strategies for Managing Excess Inventories," *Journal of Marketing Theory & Practice*, Spring 1996, p. 55.

26. Anita Lahey, "Brand Revolution," from World Wide Web: <http://www.fmi.org>.

27. "New Warehouses Take On a Luxe Look," *The Wall Street Journal*, June 18, 2003, p. B6; Arnold B. Maltz, "Outsourcing the Warehousing Function: Economics and Strategic Considerations," *The Logistics and Transportation Review*, September 1994, p. 245; Patricia J. Daugherty, Dale S. Rogers, and Theodore P. Stank, "Benchmarking: Strategic Implications for Warehousing Firms," *The Logistics and Transportation Review*, March 1994, p. 55.

28. "Down, but Far from Out: RFID Technology Is Off to a Disappointing Start, but Retailers Are Convinced," *The Wall Street Journal Reports*, January 12, 2004, p. R5; "Wal-Mart Keeps the Change," *Fortune*, November 10, 2003, p. 46; "Sensor Revolution: Bugging the World," *Business Week*, August 25, 2003, p. 100; "Cutting Navy Hospital Paperwork," *Investor's Business Daily*, May 22, 2003, p. A7; "Bar Codes Better Watch Their Backs," *Business Week*, July 14, 2003, p. 42; "Radio ID Tags Take on Bar Codes," *Investor's Business Daily*, March 13, 2003, p. A7; "A Radio Chip in Every Consumer Product," *The New York Times*, February 25, 2003, p. C1.

29. Kum Khiong Yang, "Managing a Single Warehouse, Multiple Retailer Distribution Center," *Journal of Business Logistics*, (2) 2000, p. 161; Chin Chia Jane, "Storage Location Assignment in a Distribution Center," *International Journal of Physical Distribution & Logistics Management*, (1) 2000, p. 55; "Distribution Center Doubles Output with Paperless System," *Modern Materials Handling/Scan Tech News*, September 1994, p. S17.

CHAPTER 13

1. Available from World Wide Web: <http://www.friedas.com>; "How Lower-Tech Gear Beat Web 'Exchanges' at Their Own Game," *The Wall Street Journal*, March 16, 2001, p. A1; "Family Firms Confront Calamities of Transfer," *USA Today*, August 29, 2000, p. 1B; "Business, Too Close to Home," *Time*, July 17, 2000, pp. B24–B27; "The Kiwi to My Success," *Hemispheres*, July 1999; "Searching for the Next Kiwi: Frieda's Branded Produce," *Brandweek*, May 2, 1994, p. 46; "Strange Fruits," *Inc.*, November 1989, p. 80; "The Produce Marketer," *Savvy*, June 1988, p. 26.

2. Available from World Wide Web: <http://www.census.gov>; U.S. Bureau of the Census, *Statistical Abstract of the United States* (Washington, DC: U.S. Government Printing Office, 2001); U.S. Bureau of the Census, *County Business Patterns 1998, United States* (Washington, DC: U.S. Government Printing Office, 2000); "Annual Industry Report, Top

150," *DSN Retailing Today*, July 7, 2003, p. 15; "Just Take the Money!" *Time (Inside Business Bonus Section)*, July 2003; "Paying Less for Prada," *The Wall Street Journal*, April 29, 2003, p. D1; "When Is a Mall Not Just a Mall? When Sign Says Shoppingtown," *Investor's Business Daily*, April 28, 2003, p. A1; "Point-of-Sale Technology Is Changing the Retailing Industry," *Investor's Business Daily*, February 25, 2003, p. A4; "Islands in the Mall: Pushcarts as Revenue Streams," *The New York Times*, January 22, 2003, p. C6; "Hunter Gatherer: Rare Retailer Scores by Targeting Men Who Hate to Shop," *The Wall Street Journal*, December 17, 2002, p. A1; "The 40 People and Events That Have Shaped Mass Market Retailing," *DSN Retailing Today (Special Issue)*, August 2002; "Retail Reckoning," *Business Week*, December 10, 2001, p. 72; "Remedies for an Economic Hangover," *Fortune*, June 25, 2001, p. 130; "Outlet Centers Go Upmarket with Amenities," *The Wall Street Journal*, June 6, 2001, p. B12.

3. For more on discount (dollar) stores, see "Dollar Stores Cutting New Food Channel," *Food Retailing Today*, October 13, 2003, p. F4; "Fred's: This Discount Retailer Is Whistling Dixie All the Way to the Bank," *Investor's Business Daily*, September 16, 2003, p. A9; "Family Dollar Continues Record Pace, Will Surpass 5,000 Stores," *DSN Retailing Today*, July 21, 2003, p. 1; "99 Cents Only Stores: Discount Retailer Keeps Bucking Tradition," *Investor's Business Daily*, May 12, 2003, p. A5; "Deep Discount Garners Interest Outside of Dollar Store Realm," *DSN Retailing Today*, September 23, 2002, p. 5; "Wal-Mart: Lengthening Its Lead," *DSN Retailing Today*, June 10, 2002, p. 83; "Family Dollar Stores: Growth Means Respect for Discount Retailer," *Investor's Business Daily*, February 22, 2002, p. A8; "Cheap Thrills for Shoppers," *Newsweek*, April 16, 2001, p. 45; "Beyond the Database: Sales and Service on a First-Name Basis," *Colloquy*, No. 1, 1997, p. 8; "Neiman Marcus, Saks Wage Expensive Battle for Upscale Shoppers," *The Wall Street Journal*, November 21, 1996, p. A1. See also Kristy E. Reynolds and Mark J. Arnold, "Customer Loyalty to the Salesperson and the Store: Examining Relationship Customers in an Upscale Retail Context," *The Journal of Personal Selling & Sales Management*, Spring 2000, p. 89; Christian Homburg, Wayne D. Hoyer and Martin Fassnacht, "Service Orientation of a Retailer's Business Strategy: Dimensions, Antecedents, and Performance Outcomes," *Journal of Marketing*, October 2002, p. 86; Glenn B. Voss and Kathleen Seiders, "Exploring the Effect of Retail Sector and Firm Characteristics on Retail Price Promotion Strategy," *Journal of Retailing*, (1) 2003, p. 37; Alain d'Astous, "Irritating Aspects of the Shopping Environment," *Journal of Business Research*, August 2000, p. 149; Eric R. Spangenberg, Ayn E. Crowley, and Pamela W. Henderson, "Improving the Store Environment: Do Olfactory Cues Affect Evaluations and Behaviors?" *Journal of Marketing*, April 1996, p. 67; Jeffrey S. Conant, Denise T. Smart, and Roberto Solano-Mendez, "Generic Retailing Types, Distinctive Marketing Competencies, and Competitive Advantage," *Journal of Retailing*, Fall, 1993, p. 254; John P. Dickson and Douglas L. MacLachlan, "Social Distance and Shopping Behavior," *Journal of the Academy of Marketing Science*, Spring 1990, p. 153.

4. "Small Retailers Outfox Big Rivals," *Investor's Business Daily*, November 28, 2000, p. A1; "Urban Rarity: Stores Offering Spiffy Service," *The Wall Street Journal*, July 25, 1996, p. B1; "Airports: New Destination for Specialty Retailers," *USA Today*, January 11, 1996, p. 5B; Sharon E. Beatty, Morris Mayer, James E. Coleman, Kristy E. Reynolds, and Jungki Lee, "Customer-Sales Associate Retail Relationships," *Journal of Retailing*, Fall 1996, p. 223.

5. Available from World Wide Web: <http://www.census.gov>; U.S. Bureau of the Census, *County Business Patterns 1998, United States*; U.S. Bureau of the Census, *1997 Census of Retail Trade, Subject Series, Establishment and Firm Size* (Washington, DC: U.S. Government Printing Office, 2000). For more on department stores, see "It's Not Your Mom's Penney's or Sears: Formerly Dowdy, Conservative, Department Stores Embrace Toy Chains as Holiday Lure," *The Wall Street Journal*, October 8, 2003, p. B1; "Department Stores Ring Up Centralized Checkouts," *USA Today*, June 6, 2002, p. 5B; "Idle Aisles: Department

Stores Fight an Uphill Battle Just to Stay Relevant," *The Wall Street Journal*, March 12, 2002, p. A1; "Department Stores and Designer Tenants Jockey Over Real Estate," *The Wall Street Journal*, October 31, 2000, p. A1.

6. David Appel, "The Supermarket: Early Development of an Institutional Innovation," *Journal of Retailing*, Spring 1972, p. 39.

7. Available from World Wide Web: <http://www.census. gov> and <http://www.fmi.org/food/superfact>; "Inventory Management 2002: Data, Detail, & Discipline in Supermarkets," *Chain Store Age*, December 2002, p. 17; "Grocery Shoppers Can Be Own Cashiers," *USA Today*, March 9, 1998, p. 6B; "The Taste of the Nation," *USA Today*, March 9, 1998, p. 1D. See also Brian T. Ratchford, "Has the Productivity of Retail Food Stores Really Declined?," *Journal of Retailing*, Fall 2003, p. 171; Mohammed A. Al-Sudairy and N.K.H. Tang, "Information Technology in Saudi Arabia's Supermarket Chains," *International Journal of Retail & Distribution Management*, (8) 2000, p. 341; Nobukaza Azuma and John Fernie, "Retail Marketing Strategies and Logistical Operations at a Japanese Grocery Supermarket Chain—Case Study of Summit Inc.," *International Journal of Retail & Distribution Management*, (6) 2001, p. 284; Terence A. Brown and David M. Bukovinsky, "ECR and Grocery Retailing: an Exploratory Financial Statement Analysis," *Journal of Business Logistics*, (2) 2001, p. 77.

8. "How Growth Destroys Differentiation," *Brandweek*, April 24, 2000, p. 42.

9. For more on Wal-Mart's Neighborhood Markets, see "Neighborhood Market Caps Year with Round of New Market Entries," *DSN Retailing Today*, January 27, 2003, p. 1; "For America's Big Retailers, Small Is Beautiful, Sometimes," *The New York Times*, January 22, 2003, p. C1; "Wal-Mart: Lengthening Its Lead," *DSN Retailing Today*, June 10, 2002, p. 83; "Meet Your New Neighborhood Grocer," *Fortune*, May 13, 2002, p. 93; "Wal-Mart Is Eating Everyone's Lunch," *Business Week*, April 15, 2002, p. 43.

10. For more on Wal-Mart as mass-merchandiser, see Chapter 18, endnote 1. For more on Target as mass-merchandiser, see "Target Applies GM Merchandising to Food," *Food Retailing Today*, November 10, 2003, p. 1; "Winemakers To Open Floodgates," *USA Today*, October 22, 2003, p. 6D; "New Targets Tweak Signage, Selection," *DSN Retailing Today*, August 18, 2003, p. 4; "Target: The Challenges and Rewards of Being the No. 2 Discount Retailer," *DSN Retailing Today*, April 7, 2003, p. 28; "Is Target's Wardrobe in Wal-Mart's Sights?" *AM Apparel Merchandising*, April 7, 2003, p. 1; "Target: The Cool Factor Fizzles," *Business Week*, February 24, 2003, p. 42; "Special Report: Target," *DSN Retailing Today*, April 2, 2001, p. 43; "Marketer of the Year: On Target," *Advertising Age*, December 11, 2000, p. 1.

11. For more on superstores, see "Wal-Mart, the Category King," *DSN Retailing Today*, June 9, 2003, p. 65; "Price War in Aisle 3," *The Wall Street Journal*, May 27, 2003, p. B1; "Supershoppers," *American Demographics*, May 2003, p. 17; "Wal-Mart, Target Gain Supercenter Share," *Food Retailing Today*, February 24, 2003, p. 4; "Supercenters Take Lead in Food Retailing," *Food Retailing Today*, May 6, 2002, p.8. "How Grocers Are Fighting Giant Rivals," *The Wall Street Journal*, March 27, 1997, p. B1.

12. For more on warehouse clubs, see "The Only Company Wal-Mart Fears," *Fortune*, November 24, 2003, p. 158; "Clubs Expand Despite Each Other," *Food Retailing Today*, July 21, 2003, p. 6; "Warehouse Stores Aren't Just for Those Pinching Pennies," *USA Today*, June 20, 2003, p. 1B; "Wal-Mart, the Category King," *DSN Retailing Today*, June 9, 2003, p. 65; "Retailers Try New Venues to Boost Sales," *USA Today*, May 13, 2003, p. 3B; "Out of the Box Thinking," *Newsweek*, May 12, 2003, p. 40; "Sam's Club: Back to Business," *DSN Retailing Today (Special Issue)*, April 2003; "Costco Home Poised to Revolutionize High-End Furniture," *DSN Retailing Today*, January 6, 2003, p. 5.

13. For more on category killers, see "Toys 'R' Us: Taking the Family of Brands to New Heights," *DSN Retailing Today (Special Issue)*, October 2003; "Category Killers Go from Lethal to Lame in the Space of a Decade," *The Wall Street Journal*, March 9, 2000, p. A1; "U.S. Superstores Find Japanese Are a Hard Sell," *The Wall Street Journal*, February 14, 2000, p. B1; "Office-Supply Superstores Find Bounty in the Boonies," *The Wall Street Journal*, September 1, 1998, p. B1; "Health-Care Superstores Experience Growing Pains," *The Wall Street Journal*, May 12, 1997, p. B1; "New Sneaker Superstores Aim to Step on Their Competition," *The Wall Street Journal*, March 19, 1997, p. B1; "Bridal Superstores Woo Couples with Miles of Gowns and Tuxes," *The Wall Street Journal*, February 14, 1996, p. B1.

14. For more on 7-Eleven in the U.S., see "At 7-Eleven, Fresh-Food Fix Is Focus," *The Wall Street Journal*, August 21, 2002, p. B3B; "7-Eleven Cracks the Code on Elusive Sugar-Free Slurpee," *The Wall Street Journal*, October 29, 2001, p. B9; "New Banking Hours: From 7 a.m. to 11 p.m.," *Newsweek*, May 7, 2001, p. 79; "Mobile Phone with That Slurpee? Holiday Shoppers Buy on the Run," *USA Today*, December 15, 2000, p. 1B. For more on 7-Eleven in Japan, see "From Convenience Store to Online Behemoth." *Business Week*, April 10, 2000, p. 64; "Japan Goes Web Crazy," *Fortune*, February 7, 2000, p. 115; "In Japan, the Hub of E-Commerce Is a 7-Eleven," *The Wall Street Journal*, November 1, 1999, p. B1.

15. For more on vending and wireless, see "Want a Soda? Call the Machine," *Investor's Business Daily*, November 13, 2002, p. A4; "Speedpass Use Shows Demand for Wireless Payments," *Investor's Business Daily*, April 19, 2002, p. A6; "Thirsty? Soon You May Be Able to Charge and Chug," *USA Today*, December 21, 2001, p. 7B; "Kodak Rages in Favor of the Machines," *Brandweek*, February 26, 2001, p. 6.

16. "Major Retailers to Stuff Mailboxes with Catalogs," *USA Today*, November 11, 2003, p. 6B; "New Page in E-Retailing: Catalogs," *The Wall Street Journal*, November 30, 2000, p. B1; "Beyond Mail Order: Catalogs Now Sell Image, Advice," *The Wall Street Journal*, July 29, 1997, p. B1; "Catalogers Expand in Asia," *USA Today*, October 18, 1996, p. 4B; "U.S. Catalogers Test International Waters," *The Wall Street Journal*, April 19, 1994, p. B1. See also Charla Mathwick, Naresh K. Malhotra, and Edward Rigdon, "The Effect of Dynamic Retail Experiences on Experiential Perceptions of Value: an Internet and Catalog Comparison," *Journal of Retailing*, Spring 2002, p. 51; C.R. Jasper and P.N.R. Lan, "Apparel Catalog Patronage: Demographic, Lifestyle, and Motivational Factors," *Psychology & Marketing*, July/August 1992, p. 275.

17. "Getting Ready for Prime Time," *Inc.*, November 2003, p. 17; "Is There a Future for the TV Mall?" *Brandweek*, March 25, 1996, p. 24; "QVC Draws Wares from Everywhere," *USA Today*, November 1, 1994, p. 1D; "Battling for Buck$," *Profiles*, November 1994, p. 49.

18. "Making Bank on Small Change," *Business 2.0*, November 2003, p. 56; "PayPal Pushes for Business Use," *Investor's Business Daily*, October 24, 2003, p. A4; "Marketer of the Year: The EBay Way, Brand It Now," *Brandweek*, October 20, 2003, p. M20; "Hitching a Ride on eBay," *The Wall Street Journal Reports*, October 20, 2003, p. R4; "Despite Auto-Unit Caution Flag, EBay Remains in the Fast Lane," *Investor's Business Daily*, October 16, 2003, p. A1; "Chic at a Click: EBay Fashions a Deal with Designers," *The Wall Street Journal*, September 15, 2003, p. B1; "Buying in Bulk: EBay Recasts Itself as Wholesaler Source," *Investor's Business Daily*, September 4, 2003, p. A5; "Meg and the Machine," *Fortune*, September 1, 2003, p. 68; "The eBay Economy," *Business Week*, August 25, 2003, p. 124; "eBay's Worst Nightmare," *Fortune*, May 26, 2003, p. 89; "EBay Earnings More than Double," *The Wall Street Journal*, April 23, 2003, p. B7; "EBAY Rules," *Business Week* (The Business Week 50), Spring 2003, p. 172; "Clicking the Tires: EBay Is Emerging as Unlikely Giant in Used-Car Sales," *The Wall Street Journal*, February 7, 2003, p. A1; "Take a Lesson from EBay in Buying, Selling," *Investor's Business Daily*, February 3, 2003, p. A4; "How eBay Spurred Sellers to Grab Hot Toys," *The Wall Street Journal*, December 13, 2002, p. B1; "eBay Bids on

B-to-B Business," *BtoB*, December 9, 2002, p. 1; "Why EBay Keeps Growing," *Investor's Business Daily*, November 15, 2002, p. A3; "Are You Satisfied?" *The Wall Street Journal Reports*, September 16, 2002, p. R7; "What eBay Isn't Telling You," *Business 2.0*, August 2002, p. 56.

19. "Web Shopping Gains Popularity," *USA Today*, November 26, 2003, p. 3B; "Online Comparison Shopping's on a Spree," *Investor's Business Daily*, October 22, 2003, p. A4; "He Turned Website in the Rough into Online Jewel," *USA Today*, October 20, 2003, p. 5B; "Online Shoppers Still Fear Security Issues," *Investor's Business Daily*, June 3, 2003, p. A4; "Can You Really Buy a Couch Online?" *The Wall Street Journal Reports*, April 28, 2003, p. R9; "Cruising the Online Mall," *Time (Inside Edition Bonus Section)*, April 2003; "Net vs. Not: Which Offers Better Shopping?" *USA Today*, March 10, 2003, p. 3B; "Merlot by Mail: Ordering Wine Online Gets Easier," *The Wall Street Journal*, August 21, 2002, p. D1; "Sears Enhances Service for Customers in Stores and on Web," *Investor's Business Daily*, August 5, 2002, p. A4; "Click and... Drive?" *The Wall Street Journal Reports*, July 15, 2002, p. R11; "Internet Firms Fish for Revenue from Fees," *USA Today*, June 11, 2002, p. 1B; "Retailers Discover Leap to Web's a Doozy," *USA Today*, December 18, 2001, p. 3B; "Making the Sale," *The Wall Street Journal Reports*, September 24, 2001, p. R6; "An Internet Model That Works," *Inc.*, May 2001, p. 25; "Battle-Tested Rules of Online Retail," *Ecompany*, April 2001, p. 72; Matthew L. Meuter, "Self-Service Technologies: Understanding Customer Satisfaction with Technology-Based Service Encounters," *Journal of Marketing*, July 2000, p. 50; "Special Report: Rethinking the Internet," *Business Week*, March 26, 2001, p. 117; "Online America," *American Demographics* March 2001, p. 53; "Bricks vs. Clicks," *The Wall Street Journal*, December 11, 2000, p. R10; "Wooing the Newbies," *Business Week E.Biz*, May 15, 2000, p. 116; "The Lessons Learned," *The Wall Street Journal*, April 17, 2000, p. R6. See also Fang-Fang Tang and Xiaolin Xing, "Will the Growth of Multi-Channel Retailing Diminish the Pricing Efficiency of the Web?," *Journal of Retailing*, Fall 2001, p. 319; Gerald L. Lohse, Steven Bellman and Eric J. Johnson, "Consumer Buying Behavior on the Internet: Findings from Panel Data," *Journal of Interactive Marketing*, Winter 2000, p. 15; Jonathan Reynolds, "Charting the Multichannel Future: Retail Choices and Constraints," *International Journal of Retail & Distribution Management*, (11) 2002, p. 530; Jennifer Rowley, "Shopping Bots: Intelligent Shopper or Virtual Department Store?" *International Journal of Retail & Distribution Management*, (7) 2000, p. 297; Sung-Joon Yoon, "The Antecedents and Consequences of Trust in Online-Purchase Decisions," *Journal of Interactive Marketing*, Spring 2002, p. 47; David M. Szymanski and Richard T. Hise, "E-Satisfaction: an Initial Examination," *Journal of Retailing*, Fall 2000, p. 309; Charla Mathwick, "Understanding the Online Consumer: a Typology of Online Relational Norms and Behavior," *Journal of Interactive Marketing*, Winter 2002, p. 40; Satya Menon and Barbara Kahn, "Cross-Category Effects of Induced Arousal and Pleasure on the Internet Shopping Experience," *Journal of Retailing*, Spring 2002, p. 31; Vijay Mahajan, Raji Srinivasan, and Jerry Wind, "The Dot.com Retail Failures of 2000: Were There Any Winners?," *Journal of the Academy of Marketing Science*, Fall 2002, p. 474; Kirthi Kalyanam and Shelby McIntyre, "The E-Marketing Mix: A Contribution of the E-Tailing Wars," *Journal of the Academy of Marketing Science*, Fall 2002, p. 487; Terry L. Childers, Christopher L. Carr, Joann Peck, and Stephen Carson, "Hedonic and Utilitarian Motivations for Online Retail Shopping Behavior," *Journal of Retailing*, Winter 2001, p. 511; Brian T. Ratchford, Xing Pan and Venkatesh Shankar, "On the Efficiency of Internet Markets for Consumer Goods," *Journal of Public Policy & Marketing*, Spring 2003, p. 4; Raymond R. Burke, "Technology and the Customer Interface: What Consumers Want in the Physical and Virtual Store," *Journal of the Academy of Marketing Science*, Fall 2002, p. 411; Joseph Alba, John Lynch, Barton Weitz, Chris Janiszewski et al. "Interactive Home Shopping: Consumer, Retailer, and Manufacturer Incentives to Participate in Electronic Marketplaces," *Journal of Marketing*, July 1997, p. 38.

20. Chip E. Miller, "The Effects of Competition on Retail Structure: an Examination of Intratype, Intertype, and Intercategory Competition,"
Journal of Marketing, October 1999, p. 107; "A Quart of Milk, a Dozen Eggs, and a 2.6-GHz Laptop," *Business 2.0*, October 2003, p. 58; "Jordan's Puts Imax in Its Furniture Picture," *The Wall Street Journal*, October 4, 2002, p. B6; "Latest Supermarket Special—Gasoline," *The Wall Street Journal*, April 30, 2001, p. B1; "Levi's Doesn't Fancy Selling with Cukes," *The Wall Street Journal*, April 10, 2001, p. B10; "Barnes & Noble Finds Grinch Effect in Games Strategy," *The Wall Street Journal*, December 20, 2000, p. B4; "Savoring Chocolate," *Advertising Age*, September 4, 2000, p. 24; "In Aisle 10, Soup, Tea—and Bikinis?" *The Wall Street Journal*, June 28, 2000, p. B1; Jack M. Cadeaux, "Industry Product Volatility and Retailer Assortments," *Journal of Macromarketing*, Fall 1992, p. 28; Ronald Savitt, "The 'Wheel of Retailing' and Retail Product Management," *European Journal of Marketing* 18, no. 6/7 (1984), p. 43.

21. "How Did Sears Blow This Gasket?" *Business Week*, June 29, 1992, p. 38; "An Open Letter to Sears Customers," *USA Today*, June 25, 1992, p. 8A; see also John Paul Fraedrich, "The Ethical Behavior of Retail Managers," *Journal of Business Ethics*, March 1993, p. 207.

22. Available from World Wide Web: <http://www.census.gov>; *County Business Patterns 1998, United States*; U.S. Bureau of the Census, *1997 Census of Retail Trade, Subject Series, Establishment and Firm Size*; "Retailers Grab Power, Control Marketplace," *Marketing News*, January 16, 1989, p. 1. See also Kusum L. Ailawadi, "The Retail Power Performance Conundrum: What Have We Learned?" *Journal of Retailing*, Fall 2001, p. 299; Dale D. Achabal, John M. Heineke, and Shelby H. McIntyre, "Issues and Perspectives on Retail Productivity," *Journal of Retailing*, Fall 1984, p. 107; Charles A. Ingene, "Scale Economies in American Retailing: A Cross-Industry Comparison," *Journal of Macromarketing* 4, no. 2 (1984), p. 49.

23. For an excellent example of AutoZone as successful chain, see "An Auto-Parts Store Your Mother Could Love," *Fortune*, November 10, 2003, p. 163; "Auto Accessories Still in the Fast Lane," *DSN Retailing Today*, May 5, 2003, p. 32; "AutoZone: The Hottest Growth Concept in Retailing," *DSN Retailing Today (Special Report)*, November 11, 2002; "In Corporate America It's Clean Up Time," *Fortune*, September 16, 2002, p. 62. See also "European Inns Take the Hilton Route," *The Wall Street Journal*, April 23, 2001, p. B1; "Forging Ahead with Custom Contracts," *Foodservice Equipment & Supplies Specialist*, June 1994, p. 52; "CLOUT! More and More, Retail Giants Rule the Marketplace," *Business Week*, December 21, 1992, p. 66. See also Gary K. Rhoads, William R. Swinyard, Michael D. Geurts and William D. Price, "Retailing as a Career: A Comparative Study of Marketers," *Journal of Retailing*, Spring 2002, p. 71; Marilyn Lavin, ""Not in My Neighborhood": Resistance to Chain Drug-Stores," *International Journal of Retail & Distribution Management*, (6) 2003, p. 321.

24. "Why Subway Is 'The Biggest Problem in Franchising,'" *Fortune*, March 16, 1998, p. 126; "Fast-Food Fight," *Business Week*, June 2, 1997, p. 34; "Rattling the Chains," *Brandweek*, April 21, 1997, p. 28; "Chicken and Burgers Create Hot New Class: Powerful Franchisees," *The Wall Street Journal*, May 21, 1996, p. A1. See also Surinder Tikoo, "Franchiser Influence Strategy Use and Franchisee Experience and Dependence," *Journal of Retailing*, Fall 2002, p. 183; Mika Tuunanen, "An Ounce of Prevention Is Worth a Pound of Cure: Findings from National Franchisee (Dis-)Satisfaction Study," *Journal of Marketing Channels*, (2) 2002, p. 57; Patrick J. Kaufmann and Rajiv P. Dant, "The Pricing of Franchise Rights," *Journal of Retailing*, Winter 2001, p. 537; Ram C. Rao and Shuba Srinivasan, "An Analysis of Advertising Payments in Franchise Contracts," *Journal of Marketing Channels*, (3,4) 2001, p. 85; Madhav Pappu and David Strutton, "Toward an Understanding of Strategic Inter-Organizational Relationships in Franchise Channels," *Journal of Marketing Channels*, (1,2) 2001, p. 111; Rajiv P. Dant and Patrick J. Kaufmann, "Structural and Strategic Dynamics in Franchising," *Journal of Retailing*, (2) 2003, p. 63; Robert Dahlstrom, "Franchising: Contemporary Issues and Research," *Journal of Public Policy & Marketing*, Spring 1996, p. 159; Roger D. Blair and Jill B. Herndon, "Franchise Supply Agreements:

Quality Control or Illegal Tying?" *Journal of the Academy of Marketing Science*, Spring 1997, p. 177.

25. "China's Rush to Convenience," *The Wall Street Journal*, November 3, 2003, p. A13; "Making the Cuts," *The Wall Street Journal Reports*, September 22, 2003, p. R3; "Big German Retailer Metro AG Brings Superstores to Vietnam," *The Wall Street Journal*, August 13, 2002, p. B3B; "Germans Put Stock in Store of Future," *The Wall Street Journal*, June 19, 2003, p. A10; "Western Stores Woo Chinese Wallets," *The Wall Street Journal*, November 26, 2002, p. B1; "To Russia, with Love: The Multinationals' Song," *Business Week*, September 16, 2002, p. 44; "European Inns Take the Hilton Route," *The Wall Street Journal*, April 23, 2001, p. B1; "U.S. Superstores Find Japanese Are a Hard Sell," *The Wall Street Journal*, February 14, 2000, p. B1; "How's This for a Cultural Revolution? Chinese Are Getting Home Shopping," *The Wall Street Journal*, January 4, 1996, p. A6; "Retailers Go Global," *Fortune*, February 20, 1995, p. 102. See also T. Wing-Chun Lo, Ho-Fuk Lau, and Gong-Shi Lin, "Problems and Prospects of Supermarket Development in China," *International Journal of Retail & Distribution Management*, (2) 2001, p. 66; Paul T. McGurr, "The Largest Retail Firms: a Comparison of Asia-, Europe- and US-based Retailers," *International Journal of Retail & Distribution Management*, (2) 2002, p. 145; Barry Quinn and Nicholas Alexander, "International Retail Franchising: a Conceptual Framework," *International Journal of Retail & Distribution Management*, (5) 2002, p. 264; Marieke de Mooij and Geert Hofstede, "Convergence and Divergence in Consumer Behavior: Implications for International Retailing," *Journal of Retailing*, Spring 2002, p. 61; Valerie Severin, Jordan J. Louviere, and Adam Finn, "The Stability of Retail Shopping Choices over Time and Across Countries," *Journal of Retailing*, Summer 2001, p. 185; Jozefina Simova, Colin M. Clarke-Hill, and Terry Robinson, "A Longitudinal Study of Changes in Retail Formats and Merchandise Assortment in Clothing Retailing in the Czech Republic in the Period 1994–1999," *International Journal of Retail & Distribution Management*, (6) 2003, p. 352; Arieh Goldman, "The Transfer of Retail Formats into Developing Economies: the Example of China," *Journal of Retailing*, Summer 2001, p. 221; Herbert Kotzab and Maria Madlberger, "European Retailing in E-Transition? An Empirical Evaluation of Web-Based Retailing—Indications from Austria," *International Journal of Physical Distribution & Logistics Management*, (6) 2001, p. 440; Nicholas Alexander and Marcelo de Lira e Silva "Emerging Markets and the Internationalisation of Retailing: the Brazilian Experience," *International Journal of Retail & Distribution Management*, (6) 2002, p. 300.

26. "Why the Web Can't Kill the Middleman," *Ecompany*, April 2001, p. 75; "Not Dead Yet," *Inc. Tech*, No. 1, 2001, p. 58; "Electronics Distributors Are Reporting Record Profits," *The Wall Street Journal*, July 13, 2000, p. B4; "Chow (On)Line," *Business Week E.Biz*, June 5, 2000, p. EB84; "Why Online Distributors—Once Written Off—May Thrive," *Fortune*, September 6, 1999, p. 270; "Middlemen Find Ways to Survive Cyberspace Shopping," *The Wall Street Journal*, December 12, 1996, p. B6; "Invoice? What's an Invoice?" *Business Week*, June 10, 1996, p. 110. See also Susan Mudambi and Raj Aggarwal, "Industrial Distributors: Can They Survive in the New Economy?" *Industrial Marketing Management*, May 2003, p. 317; Das Narayandas, Mary Caravella, and John Deighton, "The Impact of Internet Exchanges on Business-to-Business Distribution," *Journal of the Academy of Marketing Science*, Fall 2002, p. 500; Amrik S. Sohal, Damien J. Power, and Mile Terziovski, "Integrated Supply Chain Management from the Wholesaler's Perspective: Two Australian Case Studies," *International Journal of Physical Distribution & Logistics Management*, (1) 2002, p. 96.

27. "Cold War: Amana Refrigeration Fights Tiny Distributor," *The Wall Street Journal*, February 26, 1992, p. B2. For another example, see "Quickie-Divorce Curbs Sought By Manufacturers' Distributors," *The Wall Street Journal*, July 13, 1987, p. 27; "Merger of Two Bakers Teaches Distributors a Costly Lesson (3 parts)," *The Wall Street Journal*, September 14, 1987, p. 29; October 19, 1987, p. 35; November 11, 1987, p. 33.

28. Available from World Wide Web: <http://www.census. gov>; U.S. Bureau of the Census, *County Business Patterns 1998, United States*; U.S. Bureau of the Census, *1997 Census of Wholesale Trade, Geographic Area Series, United States* (Washington, DC: U.S. Government Printing Office, 2000); "Why Manufacturers Are Doubling as Distributors," *Business Week*, January 17, 1983, p. 41. See also "Who Is Bob Kierlin—and Why Is He So Successful?" *Fortune*, December 8, 1997, p. 245; Robert F. Lusch, Deborah S. Coykendall, and James M. Kenderdine, *Wholesaling in Transition: An Executive Chart Book* (Norman, OK: Distribution Research Program, University of Oklahoma, 1990).

29. Available from World Wide Web: <http://www.fastenal. com>; "Fastenal: In This Sluggish Market, You Gotta Have Faith," *Investor's Business Daily*, August 13, 2001, p. A12.

30. "Revolution in Japanese Retailing," *Fortune*, February 7, 1994, p. 143; Arieh Goldman, "Evaluating the Performance of the Japanese Distribution System," *Journal of Retailing*, Spring 1992, p. 11; "Japan Begins to Open the Door to Foreigners, a Little," *Brandweek*, August 2, 1993, p. 14.

31. Available from World Wide Web: <http://www.rell.com>; "Richardson Electronics Ltd.: Maker of Ancient Tech Finds a Way to Prosper," *Investor's Business Daily*, June 27, 2000, p. A12; *2000 Annual Report*, Richardson Electronics.

32. Available from World Wide Web: <http://www.inmac. com> and <http://www.grainger.com>; "B2B: Yesterday's Darling," *The Wall Street Journal*, October 23, 2000, p. R8; "W.W. Grainger's Web Investments: Money Well Spent? Don't Ask Street," *Investor's Business Daily*, September 19, 2000, p. A1.

33. For more on manufacturers' agents being squeezed, see "Philips to End Long Relations with North American Reps—Will Build Internal Sales Force Instead," *EBN*, November 10, 2003, p. 8; "Wal-Mart Draws Fire: Reps, Brokers Protest Being Shut Out by New Policy," *Advertising Age*, January 13, 1992, p. 3; Daniel H. McQuiston, "A Conceptual Model for Building and Maintaining Relationships Between Manufacturers' Representatives and Their Principals," *Industrial Marketing Management*, February 2001, p. 165; Patrick R. Mehr, "Identifying Independent Reps," *Industrial Marketing Management*, November 1992, p. 319. For more discussion on wholesaling abroad, see "Japan Rises to P&G's No. 3 Market," *Advertising Age*, December 10, 1990, p. 42; "'Papa-Mama' Stores in Japan Wield Power to Hold Back Imports," *The Wall Street Journal*, November 14, 1988, p. 1. See also Yoo S. Yang, Robert P. Leone, and Dana L. Alden, "A Market Expansion Ability Approach to Identify Potential Exporters," *Journal of Marketing*, January 1992, p. 84; Daniel C. Bello and Ritu Lohtia, "The Export Channel Design: The Use of Foreign Distributors and Agents," *Journal of the Academy of Marketing Science*, Spring 1995, p. 83; D. Steven White, "Behind the Success and Failure of U.S. Export Intermediaries: Transactions, Agents and Resources," *Journal of the Academy of Marketing Science*, Summer 2001, p. 18.

34. "Keep the Excess Moving," *Business Week E.Biz*, November 20, 2000, p. EB78; "Good-Bye to Fixed Pricing?" *Business Week*, May 4, 1998, p. 71; "Sales Are Clicking on Manufacturing's Internet Mart," *Fortune*, July 7, 1997, p. 136C.

35. "Delivering the Goods," *The Wall Street Journal Reports*, February 11, 2002, p. R14; "Sick of Checkout Lines? These Guys Can Help," *Investor's Business Daily*, July 9, 2001, p. A7; "What's Ahead for Retailing," *The Wall Street Journal*, June 25, 2001, p. R16; "Digital ID Cards," *The Wall Street Journal*, June 25, 2001, p. R16; "Now, Harried Shoppers Can Take Control at Supermarkets," *USA Today*, June 7, 2001, p. 1A; "Leave It in the Box," *Business Week E.Biz*, December 11, 2000, p. EB82. See also Enrico Colla, "International Expansion and Strategies of Discount Grocery Retailers: The Winning Models," *International Journal of Retail & Distribution Management*, (1) 2003, p. 55; Robert A. Peterson and Sridhar Balasubramanian, "Retailing in the 21st Century: Reflections and Prologue to Research," *Journal of Retailing*, Spring 2002, p. 9; Elliot

Rabinovich and Philip T. Evers, "Product Fulfillment in Supply Chains Supporting Internet-Retailing Operations," *Journal of Business Logistics*, (2) 2003, p. 205; Alan C. McKinnon and Deepak Tallam, "Unattended Delivery to the Home: an Assessment of the Security Implications," *International Journal of Retail & Distribution Management*, (1) 2003, p. 30; Hannu Yrjola, "Physical Distribution Considerations for Electronic Grocery Shopping," *International Journal of Physical Distribution & Logistics Management*, (9) 2001, p. 746; Stacy L. Wood, "Future Fantasies: a Social Change Perspective of Retailing in the 21st Century," *Journal of Retailing*, Spring 2002, p. 77.

CHAPTER 14

1. Available from World Wide Web: <http://www.mini-cooper.com>; "Mags Put Pedal to Mini's Metal," *Brandweek*, September 22, 2003; "Hot Off the Lot," *The Wall Street Journal*, September 10, 2003, p. D4; "Mini Ads Throw Tradition Aside," *Advertising Age*, September 8, 2003, p. M7; "Crispin Porter + Bogusky," *Adweek*, June 23, 2003, pp. SR6–SR7; "Mini's Wild Ride," *Adweek*, June 2, 2003, p. 24; "Mini Fever Spawns Line of Accessories," *The New York Times*, March 6, 2003, p. D13; "What Went Right," *Fortune*, December 30, 2002, p. 164; "Giving a Small Car Big 'Tude," *Brandweek*, December 9, 2002, p. 31; "Creating Max Buzz for New BMW Mini," *Advertising Age*, June 17, 2002, p. 12; "Most Innovative Campaign," *Business 2.0*, May 2002, p. 98; "Big Enough to Turn Heads," *Business Week*, April 22, 2002, p. 100; "BMW's Mini Driven to Generate Maximum Impact for Sub-Compact," *Brandweek*, April 15, 2002; "BMW 'Mini' Campaign: Odd to the Max," *The Wall Street Journal*, March 1, 2002, p. B5; "High Style in a Tiny Package," *The Wall Street Journal*, October 17, 2001, p. B1.

2. "Potter Book Brews Up Sales Magic," *DSN Retailing Today*, July 7, 2003, p. 1; "That Old Black Magic," *Time*, June 30, 2003, p. 60; "Harry Potter and—What Else?" *Business Week*, June 20, 2003, p. 79; "Wizard's Return," *The Wall Street Journal*, June 27, 2003, p. W13; "The Real Magic of Harry Potter," *Time*, June 23, 2003, p. 60; "Harry Potter Casts a Record-Breaking Spell," *USA Today*, June 23, 2003, p. 1D; "Booksellers Get Ready for Harry," *USA Today*, June 19, 2003, p. 3B; "Transportation," *Business Week*, January 8, 2001, p. 130; "Buzzmeisters of the Year," *Brandweek* (Marketers of the Year Special Issue), October 16, 2000, pp. M8–M18; "Harry Potter, Meet 'Ha-li Bo-te,'" *The Wall Street Journal*, September 21, 2000, p. B1; "Creative Coddling, Great Word of Mouth," *Business Week E.Biz*, September 18, 2000; "Wizard of Marketing," *Business Week*, July 24, 2000, p. 84; "Web Booksellers Give Potter Fans Rush Delivery," *The Wall Street Journal*, June 22, 2000, p. B1.

3. "Old-Fashioned PR Gives General Mills Advertising Bargains," *The Wall Street Journal*, March 20, 1997, p. A1. See also "Name That Chintz! How Shelter Magazines Boost Brands," *The Wall Street Journal*, March 14, 1997, p. B1; "Rosie and 'Friends' Make Drake's Cakes a Star," *The Wall Street Journal*, February 10, 1997, p. B1; "Toy Story: How Shrewd Marketing Made Elmo a Hit," *The Wall Street Journal*, December 16, 1996, p. B1; "PR Shouldn't Mean 'Poor Relations,'" *Industry Week*, February 3, 1992, p. 51; Siva K. Balasubramanian, "Beyond Advertising and Publicity: Hybrid Messages and Public Policy Issues," *Journal of Advertising*, December 1994, p. 29; Thomas H. Bivins, "Ethical Implications of the Relationship of Purpose to Role and Function in Public Relations," *Journal of Business Ethics*, January 1989, p. 65.

4. "The Potatoes Were Smiling; the Fries Were Blue," *The New York Times*, March 13, 2003, p. C1; "Marketing Tactics: Ries' Thesis, Ads Don't Build Brands, PR Does," *Advertising Age*, July 15, 2002, p. 14; "Want Some Blue Fries with That Shake?" *USA Today*, March 21, 2002, p. 8D; "Edible Entertainment," *The Wall Street Journal*, October 24, 2001, p. B1; "Marketers of the Year: Grand Marketer, Heinz," *Brandweek*, October 15, 2001, p. M6.

5. "President's Tumble Off a Segway Seems a Tiny Bit Suspicious," *USA Today*, June 18, 2003, p. 3B; "Watch Your Step: Segways Ahead," *USA Today*, June 17, 2003, p. 1A; "Segway Book: Inventor No 'Deep Throat,'" *Investor's Business Daily*, June 13, 2003, p. A4.

6. For more on Reebok's Terrible Terry Tate campaign, see "Grabbing Market Share," *Adweek Interactive Quarterly*, November 24, 2003, pp. IQ1–IQ5. For more on Tylenol 8 Hour campaign, see "Tylenol Hits the Gym for Launch," *Advertising Age*, May 26, 2003, p. 30. See also "Small Wonder," *The Wall Street Journal*, June 25, 2001, p. R1; "Minute Maid Opens Juicy Site to Promote New Drink," *Brandweek*, April 30, 2001; "PMA Reggie Awards 2001," *Brandweek* (Supplement), March 12, 2001, p. R1; "Mystery Shoppers," *American Demographics*, December 2000, p. 41; "Sweet Deals," *Inc. Tech*, No. 4, 2000, p. 98; "Hot Wheels," *American Demographics*, August 2000, p. 48; "Calling All Car Worms," *Brandweek*, March 6, 2000, p. 22; "Sharp Curves Ahead for Car Marketers," *Brandweek*, January 3, 2000, p. 18; "Talbots Mounting Its Biggest Integrated Marketing Push," *Advertising Age*, August 11, 1997, p. 29; "Olds' Intrigue Stars in Web Game Based on NBC TV Show," *Advertising Age*, July 28, 1997, p. 16; "Promotion Marketing," *Brandweek*, March 4, 1996, p. 22. See also X. Michael Song, Jinhong Xile, and Barbara Dyer, "Antecedents and Consequences of Marketing Managers' Conflict-Handling Behaviors," *Journal of Marketing*, January 2000, p. 50; David A. Griffith, Aruna Chandra and John K. Ryans, Jr. "Examining the Intricacies of Promotion Standardization: Factors Influencing Advertising Message and Packaging," *Journal of International Marketing*, (3) 2003, p. 30; Kim Bartel Sheehan and Caitlin Doherty, "Re-Weaving the Web: Integrating Print and Online Communications," *Journal of Interactive Marketing*, Spring 2001, p. 47; J. R. Shannon, "The New Promotions Mix: A Proposed Paradigm, Process, and Application," *Journal of Marketing Theory & Practice*, Winter 1996, p. 56; Kathleen J. Kelly, "Integrated Marketing Communication: Putting It Together & Making It Work," *Journal of the Academy of Marketing Science*, Winter 1997, p. 83.

7. "High-Tech Branding: Pushing Digital PCS," *Brandweek*, August 4, 1997, p. 30; "Brand Builders: Delivery Guy Chic," *Brandweek*, June 30, 1997, p. 18; "Eye-Catching Logos All Too Often Leave Fuzzy Images in Minds of Consumers," *The Wall Street Journal*, December 5, 1991, p. B1. See also George S. Low and Jakki J. Mohr, "Factors Affecting the Use of Information in the Evaluation of Marketing Communications Productivity," *Journal of the Academy of Marketing Science*, Winter 2001, p. 70; David I. Gilliland and Wesley J. Johnston, "Toward a Model of Business-to-Business Marketing Communications Effects," *Industrial Marketing Management*, January 1997, p. 15; Michel T. Pham and Gita V. Johar, "Contingent Processes of Source Identification," *Journal of Consumer Research*, December 1997, p. 249; Louisa Ha and Barry R. Litman, "Does Advertising Clutter Have Diminishing and Negative Returns?" *Journal of Advertising*, Spring 1997, p. 31; Barbara B. Stern, "A Revised Communication Model for Advertising: Multiple Dimensions of the Source, the Message, and the Recipient," *Journal of Advertising*, June 1994, p. 5; Ronald E. Dulek, John S. Fielden, and John S. Hill, "International Communication: An Executive Primer," *Business Horizons*, January/February 1991, p. 20; Kaylene C. Williams, Rosann L. Spiro, and Leslie M. Fine, "The Customer-Salesperson Dyad: An Interaction/Communication Model and Review," *Journal of Personal Selling and Sales Management*, Summer 1990, p. 29; Richard F. Beltramini and Edwin R. Stafford, "Comprehension and Perceived Believability of Seals of Approval Information in Advertising," *Journal of Advertising*, September 1993, p. 3.

8. "Finally, Some Help at the Health-Food Store," *The Wall Street Journal*, July 10, 2002, p. D1; "Good Housekeeping Unveils Web Site Review Program," *Brandweek*, May 29, 2000, p. 52; "Good Housekeeping to Offer 'Seal' to Autos," *Advertising Age*, June 29, 1998, p. 18; "Marketing in Which We Bash a Baby Seal," *Fortune*, September 8, 1997, p. 36.

9. "Global Branding: Same, But Different," *Brandweek*, April 9, 2001, p. 25; "When You Translate 'Got Milk' for Latinos, What Do You Get?" *The Wall Street Journal*, June 3, 1999, p. A1; "Cash, Cache, Cachet: All 3 Seem to Matter When You Buy a PC," *The Wall Street Journal*, December 18, 1998, p. A1; "Hey, #!@*% Amigo, Can You Translate the Word

'Gaffe'?" *The Wall Street Journal*, July 8, 1996, p. B2; "Lost in Translation: How to 'Empower Women' in Chinese," *The Wall Street Journal*, September 13, 1994, p. A1; "In World Cup Games, Words Get Lost and Gained in Translation," *The Wall Street Journal*, July 14, 1994, p. B1; "Too Many Computer Names Confuse Too Many Buyers," *The Wall Street Journal*, June 29, 1994, p. B1; "Go Ask Alice," *Adweek*, January 17, 1994, p. 32.

10. For more on video publicity releases, see "The Corruption of TV Health News," *Business Week*, February 28, 2000, p. 66; "Collagen Corp.'s Video Uses News Format," *The Wall Street Journal*," March 29, 1994, p. B8; "'News' Videos That Pitch Drugs Provoke Outcry for Regulations," *The Wall Street Journal*, February 8, 1990, p. B6; Thomas H. Bivins, "Public Relations, Professionalism, and the Public Interest," *Journal of Business Ethics*, February 1993, p. 117; Siva K. Balasubramanian, "Beyond Advertising and Publicity: Hybrid Messages and Public Policy Issues," *Journal of Advertising*, December 1994, p. 47. For more on celebrity endorsements, see "Marketers Drool over a Jordan Return," *USA Today*, April 11, 2001, p. 1B; "The Jordan Effect," *Fortune*, June 22, 1998, p. 124; "Yao Ming's Super Deals," *USA Today*, January 23, 2003, p. 3B; "Full-Court Press for LeBron," *The Wall Street Journal*, May 21, 2003, p. B1; "Biking Champ Armstrong to Get $12M to Peddle Subaru," *USA Today*, February 3, 2003, p. 3B; "Brand It like Beckham," *Time*, June 30, 2003, p. 49; "Woods' Latest Trophy: $100 Million Nike Deal," *USA Today*, September 15, 2000, p. 1A; "Phat News: Rappers Choose Reebok Shoes," *The Wall Street Journal*, November 14, 2003, p. B1; "The CEO of Hip Hop," *Business Week*, October 27, 2003, p. 90; "In the NBA, Shoe Money Is No Longer a Slam-Dunk," *The Wall Street Journal*, May 14, 1998, p. B1. See also Therese A. Louie and Carl Obermiller, "Consumer Response to a Firm's Endorser (Dis)association Decisions," *Journal of Advertising*, Winter 2002, p. 41; Marla Royne Stafford, Thomas F. Stafford, and Ellen Day, "A Contingency Approach: the Effects of Spokesperson Type and Service Type on Service Advertising Perceptions," *Journal of Advertising*, Summer 2002, p. 17; Dwane Hal Dean and Abhijit Biswas, "Third-Party Organization Endorsement of Products: an Advertising Cue Affecting Consumer Prepurchase Evaluation of Goods and Services," *Journal of Advertising*, Winter 2001, p. 41; Ronald E. Goldsmith, Barbara A. Lafferty and Stephen J. Newell, "The Impact of Corporate Credibility and Celebrity Credibility on Consumer Reaction to Advertisements and Brands," *Journal of Advertising*, Fall 2000, p. 43; Ron Coulter, "High Visibility: The Making and Marketing of Professionals into Celebrities," *Journal of the Academy of Marketing Science*, Winter 2001, p. 105; Jagdish Agrawal and Wagner A. Kamakura, "The Economic Worth of Celebrity Endorsers: An Event Study Analysis," *Journal of Marketing*, July 1995, p. 56; David J. Moore, John C. Mowen, and Richard Reardon, "Multiple Sources in Advertising Appeals: When Product Endorsers Are Paid by the Advertising Sponsor," *Journal of the Academy of Marketing Science*, Summer 1994, p. 234.

11. "Direct Marketing Special Report," *BtoB*, October 13, 2003, p. 24; "DMA Benchmarks Response Rates," *BtoB*, July 14, 2003, p. 13; "Direct Marketing Gets Cannes Do Spirit," *USA Today*, June 17, 2002, p. 4B; "Escalade Got Game," *Advertising Age*, June 11, 2001, p. 42; "All Juiced Up," *American Demographics*, January 2001, p. 42. For an electronic direct mail example, see "Web Slice," *Brandweek*, May 26, 1997, p. 22. See also Sally J. McMillan and Jang-Sun Hwang, "Measures of Perceived Interactivity: an Exploration of the Role of Direction of Communication, User Control, and Time in Shaping Perceptions of Interactivity," *Journal of Advertising*, Fall 2002, p. 29; Carrie M. Heilman, Frederick Kaefer, and Samuel D. Ramenofsky, "Determining the Appropriate Amount of Data for Classifying Consumers for Direct Marketing Purposes," *Journal of Interactive Marketing*, Summer 2003, p. 5; Mark J. Arnold and Shelley R. Tapp, "The Effects of Direct Marketing Techniques on Performance: an Application to Arts Organizations," *Journal of Interactive Marketing*, Summer 2001, p. 41; Patrick Barwise and Colin Strong, "Permission-Based Mobile Advertising," *Journal of Interactive Marketing*, Winter 2002, p. 14; Tito Tezinde, Brett Smith, and Jamie Murphy, "Getting Permission: Exploring Factors Affecting Permission Marketing," *Journal of Interactive*

Marketing, Autumn 2002, p. 28; Charles R. Taylor, George R. Franke, and Michael L. Maynard, "Attitudes Toward Direct Marketing and its Regulation: a Comparison of the United States and Japan," *Journal of Public Policy & Marketing*, Fall 2000, p. 228; Jennifer Rowley and Frances Slack, "Kiosks in Retailing: the Quiet Revolution," *International Journal of Retail & Distribution Management*, (6) 2003, p. 329; David W. Stewart and Paul A. Pavlou, "From Consumer Response to Active Consumer: Measuring the Effectiveness of Interactive Media," *Journal of the Academy of Marketing Science*, Fall 2002, p. 376; Yuping Liu and L. J. Shrum, "What Is Interactivity and Is it Always Such a Good Thing? Implications of Definition, Person, and Situation for the Influence of Interactivity on Advertising Effectiveness," *Journal of Advertising*, Winter 2002, p. 53; Fusun F. Gonul, Byung-Do Kim, and Mengze Shi, "Mailing Smarter to Catalog Customers," *Journal of Interactive Marketing*, Spring 2000, p. 2; Judy F. Davis, "Maintaining Customer Relationships Through Effective Database Marketing: A Perspective for Small Retailers," *Journal of Marketing Theory & Practice*, Spring 1997, p. 31; Craig A. Conrad, "Response! The Complete Guide to Direct Marketing," *Journal of the Academy of Marketing Science*, Winter 1998, p. 70; Kapil Bawa, "Influences on Consumer Response to Direct Mail Coupons: An Integrative Review," *Psychology & Marketing*, March 1996, p. 129; William J. Carner, "Direct Marketing Through Broadcast Media: TV, Radio, Cable, Infomercials, Home Shopping, and More," *Journal of the Academy of Marketing Science*, Winter 1997, p. 86.

12. For more on privacy, see Chapter 22, endnote 11. For more on regulation of spam, junk mail, and telemarketing calls, see "The Taming of the Internet," *Business Week*, December 15, 2003, p. 78; "Telemarketing after Do Not Call," *Inc.*, November 2003, p. 32; "Silence of the Spams," *Brandweek*, October 20, 2003, p. 14; "Closing Lid on Spam May Cause Problems," *Investor's Business Daily*, October 13, 2003, p. A1; "The Bad News: Telemarketers Will Still Call," *The Wall Street Journal*, October 9, 2003, p. D1; "America Hangs Up on Telemarketers," *Fortune*, October 13, 2003, p. 58; "FTC Told to Enforce Do-Not-Call List," *USA Today*, October 8, 2003, p. 1B; "A Stab at Stemming Spam," *Business Week*, October 6, 2003, p. 115; "Most Big Companies Stop Calling," *USA Today*, October 2, 2003, p. 3B; "It's FCC to the Rescue of Do-Not-Call List," *USA Today*, September 30, 2003, p. 1B; "The Do-Not-Call Law Won't Stop the Calls," *Business Week*, September 29, 2003, p. 89; "When E-Mail Ads Aren't Spam," *Business Week*, October 16, 2000, p. 112; "Special Report: Direct and Database Marketing," *Advertising Age*, October 16, 2000, p. S1; "E-Mail Direct," *Brandweek*, April 10, 2000, p. 108; "You've Got Snail Mail!" *American Demographics*, March 2000, p. 54; George R. Milne and Mary Ellen Gordon, "Direct Mail Privacy-Efficiency Trade-Offs Within an Implied Social Contract Framework," *Journal of Public Policy & Marketing*, Fall 1993, p. 206.

13. Monica Perry and Charles D. Bodkin, "Fortune 500 Manufacturer Websites: Innovative Marketing Strategies or Cyberbrochures?" *Industrial Marketing Management*, February 2002, p. 133; Nicole Coviello, Roger Milley and Barbara Marcolin, "Understanding IT-Enabled Interactivity in Contemporary Marketing," *Journal of Interactive Marketing*, Autumn 2001, p. 18; Donna L. Hoffman and Thomas P. Novak, "Marketing in Hypermedia Computer-Mediated Environments: Conceptual Foundations," *Journal of Marketing*, July 1996, p. 50; Pierre Berthon, Leyland Pitt, and Richard T. Watson, "Marketing Communication and the World Wide Web," *Business Horizons*, September–October 1996, p. 24.

14. For more on direct-to-consumer drug advertising, see "Introducing the All-Purpose Pill," *Brandweek*, July 28, 2003, p. 24; "Net Grows as DTC Platform," *Advertising Age*, May 12, 2003, p. 60; "DTC Ads Influence Majority of Consumers, Say Doctors," *Advertising Age*, January 20, 2003, p. 6; "Patient Channel to Blast Ads at Bedridden," *The Wall Street Journal*, September 26, 2002, p. B1; "Drug Markers Find New Way to Push Pills," *The Wall Street Journal*, June 14, 2002, p. B1; "Special Report: DTC Marketing," *Advertising Age*, May 27, 2002, p. S1; "Wearing Off: Schering-Plough Faces a Future with Coffers Unfortified by

Claritin," *The Wall Street Journal*, March 22, 2002, p. A1; "Reining In Drug Advertising," *The Wall Street Journal*, March 13, 2002, p. B1; "Drug Makers Offer Coupons for Free Prescriptions," *The Wall Street Journal*, March 13, 2002, p. B1; "Spotlight Falls on Drug Ads," *USA Today*, December 11, 2001, p. 9D; "While Critics May Fret, Public Likes DTC Ads," *Advertising Age*, March 26, 2001, p. 24; "The Fine Print," *The Wall Street Journal*, October 19, 1998, p. R6. See also Steven W. Kopp and Mary J. Sheffet, "The Effect of Direct-to-Consumer Advertising of Prescription Drugs on Retail Gross Margins: Empirical Evidence and Public Policy Implications," *Journal of Public Policy & Marketing*, Fall 1997, p. 270; Mary C. Gilly and Mary Wolfinbarger, "Advertising's Internal Audience," *Journal of Marketing*, January 1998, p. 69; S. A. Erdem and L. J. Harrison-Walker, "Managing Channel Relationships: Toward an Identification of Effective Promotional Strategies in Vertical Marketing Systems," *Journal of Marketing Theory & Practice*, Spring 1997, p. 80.

15. "Decker Scores with Sweepstakes to Promote Days Inn," *USA Today*, November 6, 1997, p. B10; "Biore: The Nose Knew at Lilith Fair," *Brandweek*, September 15, 1997, p. 28; "Brand Builders: Progresso Warriors," *Brandweek*, June 23, 1997, p. 20; "Advertisers Often Cheer the Loudest," *USA Today*, March 27, 1997, p. 1A; "Crossing the Border," *Brandweek*, December 16, 1996, p. 17; "Brand Builders: Pie in the Sky," *Brandweek*, December 16, 1996, p. 23; "Tractor Dealers Get Down in the Dirt Promoting Machines," *The Wall Street Journal*, July 16, 1996, p. A1; "Pepsi Cancels an Ad Campaign as Customers Clamor for Stuff," *The Wall Street Journal*, June 27, 1996, p. B1.

16. "Compensation and Expenses," *Sales & Marketing Management*, June 28, 1993, p. 65; "The Cost of Selling Is Going Up," *Boardroom Reports*, December 15, 1991, p. 15; "An In-House Sales School," *Inc.*, May 1991, p. 85.

17. For an example of TiVo's targeting innovators and early adopters, see "TiVo Creating Program Glut for Some Users," *Investor's Business Daily*, November 12, 2003, p. A7; "PVRs to Hit 20% by '07," *Advertising Age*, September 29, 2003, p. 6; "Switching Channels: TiVo Revamps Strategy," *Investor's Business Daily*, July 23, 2003, p. A4; "PVRs: A Shift in Time," *The Wall Street Journal Reports*, March 31, 2003, p. R10; "Time to Jettison the Old VCR? Set-Top Recorder Battle Looms," *Investor's Business Daily*, March 13, 2003, p. A1; "Couch Potato Crisis: Is It Time to Get TiVo?" *The Wall Street Journal*, November 13, 2002, p. D1; "The Ad Zappers," *Time (Inside Business Bonus Section)*, June 2002. For more on opinion leaders and word-of-mouth publicity, see Chapter 6, endnote 19. See also "The Influentials: Movers and Shakers," *Brandweek*, February 3, 2003, p. 27; "How Does This Work?" *American Demographics*, December 2002, p. 18; "Companies Fawn over Reviewers of Hand-Helds," *The Wall Street Journal*, April 1, 2002, p. B1; "Can You Set Your VCR?" *American Demographics*, March 2002, p. 8; "Auto Makers Find They Don't Want to Avoid Collisions in Movies," *The Wall Street Journal*, July 5, 2001, p. B1, "Small Wonder," *The Wall Street Journal*, June 25, 2001, p. R1; "Word of Mouth Makes Nike Slip-On Sneakers Take Off," *The Wall Street Journal*, June 7, 2001, p. B1; "Bristol-Myers Builds Buzz for True Intense Color Line," *Advertising Age*, April 23, 2001, p. 18; "How an Idea Spreads Like Flu," *Advertising Age*, May 8, 2000, p. 42; "Street Marketing Hits the Internet," *Advertising Age*, May 1, 2000, p. 32; "Ad Budget: Zero. Buzz: Deafening," *The Wall Street Journal*, December 29, 1999, p. B1; "Word of Mouth Makes Kansas Store a Star," *The Wall Street Journal*, November 7, 1997, p. B1; "Why the Veterinarian Really Recommends that 'Designer' Chow," *The Wall Street Journal*, November 3, 1997, p. A1. See also Jyh-Shen Chiou and Cathy Cheng, "Should a Company Have Message Boards on its Web Sites?," *Journal of Interactive Marketing*, Summer 2003, p. 50; Raji Srinivasan, Gary L. Lilien, and Arvind Rangaswamy, "Technological Opportunism and Radical Technology Adoption: An Application to E-Business," *Journal of Marketing*, July 2002, p. 47; Suman Basuroy, Subimal Chatterjee, and S. Abraham Ravid, "How Critical Are Critical Reviews? The Box Office Effects of Film Critics, Star Power, and Budgets," *Journal of Marketing*, October 2003, p. 103;

Jeffrey G. Blodgett, Donald H. Granbois, and Rockney G. Walters, "The Effects of Perceived Justice on Complainants' Negative Word-of Mouth Behavior and Repatronage Intentions," *Journal of Retailing*, Winter 1993, p. 399; Paula Fitzgerald Bone, "Word-of-Mouth Effects on Short-term and Long-term Product Judgments," *Journal of Business Research*, March 1995, p. 213; Bruce MacEvoy, "Change Leaders and the New Media," *American Demographics*, January 1994, p. 42; Dale F. Duhan, Scott D. Johnson, James B. Wilcox, and Gilbert D. Harrell, "Influences on Consumer Use of Word-of-Mouth Recommendation Sources," *Journal of the Academy of Marketing Science*, Fall 1997, p. 283; Russell N. Laczniak, Thomas E. DeCarlo, and Carol M. Motley, "Retail Equity Perceptions and Consumers' Processing of Negative Word-of-Mouth Communication," *Journal of Marketing Theory & Practice*, Fall 1996, p. 37.

18. "The Age of Reason," *Brandweek*, October 27, 2003, p. 24; "Buzz Helps Cypher Stent Sales Rocket," *Advertising Age*, September 1, 2003, p. 9; "BMW Rolls 5 Series with Test Drive on TV," *Advertising Age*, August 25, 2003, p. 8; "For Buzz, Dunlop Goes Where Others Fear to Tread," *Brandweek*, July 28, 2003, p. 12; "You Can't Always Answer Your Phone," *The Wall Street Journal*, July 18, 2003, p. B1; "Word of Mouth Is Where It's At," *Brandweek*, June 2, 2003, p. 26; "Silver Bullet Brands," *Brandweek*, April 21, 2003, p. 30; "Wot R They Up 2?" *Adweek*, February 17, 2003, p. 26; "On the Web, Word-of-Mouth Marketing Can Become Viral," *Investor's Business Daily*, January 30, 2003, p. A4; "Guerrilla Marketers of the Year," *Brandweek*, December 9, 2002, p. 18; "Screen Test," *Adweek*, November 18, 2002, p. 20; "Take 2," *Business 2.0*, November 2002, p. 66; "That Guy Showing Off His Hot New Phone May Be a Shill," *The Wall Street Journal*, July 31, 2002, p. B1; "Sprint's Sprightly Marketing Push," *Business Week*, July 1, 2002, p. 14; "Puma Uses Sushi to Move Its Cleats," *The Wall Street Journal*, May 9, 2002, p. B8; "BMW Films in High Gear," *Brandweek (Reggie Awards Supplement)*, March 18, 2002, pp. R4–R6; "Pass It On," *The Wall Street Journal*, January 14, 2002, p. R6; "Get Your Buzz to Breed like Hobbits," *Business 2.0*, January 2002, p. 96; "The Cool Kids Are Doing It. Should You?" *Business 2.0*, November 2001, p. 140; "Marketer of the Year: Nike Presto, Magic Feet That Art," *Brandweek*, October 15, 2001, p. M26; "Special Report: Buzz Marketing," *Business Week*, July 30, 2001, p. 50; "Viral Marketing Breaks Through," *Advertising Age*, June 25, 2001, p. S10; Barbara Bickart, "Internet Forums as Influential Sources of Consumer Information," *Journal of Interactive Marketing*, Summer 2001, p. 31; "How a Viral Marketing E-Mail Campaign Delivered for Lee Apparel," *Advertising Age*, 2000, pp. A10–A11; "This Is One Virus You Want to Spread," *Fortune*, November 27, 2000, p. 297. For more on Toyota's marketing of the Scion, see "Toyota Goes Guerilla to Roll Scion," *Advertising Age*, August 11, 2003, p. 4; "Toyota Finds Attractive Effort to Push the Plug-Ugly Scion," *Advertising Age*, August 4, 2003, p. 29; "Toyota's Gen Y Gamble," *The Wall Street Journal*, July 30, 2003, p. B1; "Are Customized Cars, Cosmetics the Way to Woo Generation Y?" *Investor's Business Daily*, July 30, 2003, p. A1; "Baby, You Can Drive My Car," *Time*, June 30, 2003, p. 46; "Carmakers Design for Generation Y," *The New York Times*, January 16, 2003, p. C1; "Marketers of the Year: Setting the Tone at Toyota," *Brandweek*, October 14, 2002, pp. M59–M61; "This Is Not Your Father's Toyota," *The Wall Street Journal*, March 26, 2002, p. B1.

19. Hokey Min and William P. Galle, "E-Purchasing: Profiles of Adopters and Nonadopters," *Industrial Marketing Management*, April 2003, p. 227; Yikuan Lee and Gina Colarelli O'Connor, "The Impact of Communication Strategy on Launching New Products: the Moderating Role of Product Innovativeness," *The Journal of Product Innovation Management*, January 2003, p. 4; David R. Fell, Eric N. Hansen, and Boris W. Becker, "Measuring Innovativeness for the Adoption of Industrial Products," *Industrial Marketing Management*, May 2003, p. 347; Subin Im, Barry L. Bayus and Charlotte H. Mason, "An Empirical Study of Innate Consumer Innovativeness, Personal Characteristics, and New-Product Adoption Behavior," *Journal of the Academy of Marketing Science*, Winter 2003, p. 61; Eric Waarts, Yvonne M. van Everdingen, and Jos van Hillegersberg, "The Dynamics of Factors Affecting the Adoption of

Innovations," *The Journal of Product Innovation Management*, November 2002, p. 412; Meera P. Venkatraman, "Opinion Leaders, Adopters, and Communicative Adopters: A Role Analysis," *Psychology and Marketing*, Spring 1989, p. 51; S. Ram and Hyung-Shik Jung, "Innovativeness in Product Usage: A Comparison of Early Adopters and Early Majority," *Psychology & Marketing*, January/February 1994, p. 57; Robert J. Fisher and Linda L. Price, "An Investigation into the Social Context of Early Adoption Behavior," *Journal of Consumer Research*, December 1992, p. 477; Leisa R. Flynn, Ronald E. Goldsmith, and Jacqueline K. Eastman, "Opinion Leaders and Opinion Seekers: Two New Measurement Scales," *Journal of the Academy of Marketing Science*, Spring 1996, p. 137; Everett M. Rogers and F. Floyd Shoemaker, *Communication of Innovations: A Cross-Cultural Approach* (New York: Free Press, 1971), p. 203.

20. "All-in-One Dinner Kits Gain Popularity," *Food Retailing Today*, May 5, 2003, p. 12; "Marketers of the Year: This One's a Stove Topper," *Brandweek*, October 14, 2002, pp. M30–M34.

21. Kusum L. Ailawadi, Paul W. Farris and Mark E. Parry, "Share and Growth Are Not Good Predictors of the Advertising and Promotion/ Sales Ratio," *Journal of Marketing*, January 1994, p. 86.

22. Kissan Joseph and Vernon J. Richardson, "Free Cash Flow, Agency Costs, and the Affordability Method of Advertising Budgeting," *Journal of Marketing*, January 2002, p. 94; John A. Weber, "Managing the Marketing Budget in a Cost-Constrained Environment," *Industrial Marketing Management*, November 2002, p. 705; Deborah Utter, "Marketing on a Budget," *Journal of the Academy of Marketing Science*, Summer 2000, p. 441; Kim P. Corfman and Donald R. Lehmann, "The Prisoner's Dilemma and the Role of Information in Setting Advertising Budgets," *Journal of Advertising*, June 1994, p. 35; C.L. Hung and Douglas West, "Advertising Budgeting Methods in Canada, the UK and the USA," *International Journal of Advertising* 10, no. 3 (1991), p. 239; Pierre Filiatrault and Jean-Charles Chebat, "How Service Firms Set Their Marketing Budgets," *Industrial Marketing Management*, February 1990, p. 63; James E. Lynch and Graham J. Hooley, "Industrial Advertising Budget Approaches in the U.K.," *Industrial Marketing Management* 18, no. 4 (1989), p. 265; "Beat the Budgeting Blues," *Business Marketing*, July 1989, p. 48; Douglas J. Dalrymple and Hans B. Thorelli, "Sales Force Budgeting," *Business Horizons*, July/August 1984, p. 31; Peter J. Danaher and Roland T. Rust, "Determining the Optimal Level of Media Spending," *Journal of Advertising Research*, January/February 1994, p. 28.

CHAPTER 15

1. Available from World Wide Web: <http://www.cisco. com>; "Cisco Changes Sales Compensation," *CRN*, December 8, 2003, p. 5; "Cisco's Comeback," *Business Week*, November 24, 2003, p. 116; "The New Phone Company," *Business 2.0*, November 2003, p. 82; "After the Boom: A Go-Go Giant of Internet Age, Cisco Is Learning to Go Slow," *The Wall Street Journal*, May 7, 2003, p. A1; "In Bid for Consumer Networking Market, Cisco to Buy Linksys," *Investor's Business Daily*, March 21, 2003, p. A4; "Cisco Systems Drastically Paring Its Suppliers," *Investor's Business Daily*, March 6, 2003, p. A6; "Cisco Seeks Bigger Role in Phone Networks," *The New York Times*, March 3, 2002, p. C4; "Cisco's Ads Going Mainstream," *Investor's Business Daily*, February 28, 2003, p. A5; "Consumer-Oriented Firms Aren't Only Ones Worried about Brands," *Investor's Business Daily*, July 30, 2002, p. A4; "Productivity Growth Is Boosted by Moving to Web Technologies," *The Wall Street Journal*, December 4, 2001, p. B1; "Tech Consultants: You'll Need One Sooner or Later—So Get It Right," *Investor's Business Daily*, March 5, 2001, p. A1; "How Cisco Makes Takeovers Work with Rules, Focus on Client Needs," *Investor's Business Daily*, November 20, 2000, p. A1; "Sue Bostrom's Internet Road Rules," *Forbes*, November 13, 2000, p. 124; "Cisco Keeps Growing, But Exactly How Fast Is Becoming an Issue," *The Wall Street Journal*, November 3, 2000, p. A1; "Accelerating Natural Contagion," *Brandweek*, October 30, 2000, p. 31; "At Cisco, Executives Accumulate Stakes in Clients, Suppliers," *The Wall Street Journal*, October 3, 2000, p. A1; "The World's Most Admired Companies," *Fortune*, October 2, 2000, p. 183; "Cisco: A Web-Profit Prophet Spreads the Word," *Business Week E.Biz*, September 18, 2000, p. EB68; "There's Something About Cisco," *Fortune*, May 15, 2000, p. 114; "Customers Move Into the Driver's Seat," *Business Week*, October 4, 1999, p. 103; "The New Economy Is Still Being Driven by the Old Hard Sell," *The Wall Street Journal*, August 13, 1999, p. B1.

2. "The Seoul Answer to Selling," *Going Global* (supplement to *Inc.*), March 1994; "AIG Sells Insurance in Shanghai, Testing Service Firms' Role," *The Wall Street Journal*, July 21, 1993, p. A1; "Hungarians Seeking to Find a New Way Find Instead Amway," *The Wall Street Journal*, January 15, 1993, p. A1; "The Secret to Northern's Japanese Success: When in Tokyo . . . ," *Business Week*, July 27, 1992, p. 57; "U.S. Companies in China Find Patience, Persistence and Salesmanship Pay Off," *The Wall Street Journal*, April 3, 1992, p. B1; Paul A. Herbig and Hugh E. Kramer, "Do's and Don'ts of Cross-Cultural Negotiations," *Industrial Marketing Management*, November 1992, p. 287; Alan J. Dubinsky et al., "Differences in Motivational Perceptions among U.S., Japanese, and Korean Sales Personnel," *Journal of Business Research*, June 1994, p. 175; Carl R. Ruthstrom and Ken Matejka, "The Meanings of 'YES' in the Far East," *Industrial Marketing Management*, August 1990, p. 191.

3. "Shhh!" *Forbes*, November 24, 2003, p. 84; "Deliver More Value to Earn Loyalty," *Selling*, May 2003; "Hush: Improving NVH through Improved Material," *Automotive Design and Production*, July 2003, p. 42.

4. Julie T. Johnson, Hiram C. Barksdale, Jr., and James S. Boles, "The Strategic Role of the Salesperson in Reducing Customer Defection in Business Relationships," *The Journal of Personal Selling & Sales Management*, Spring 2001, p. 123; Artur Baldauf, David W. Cravens, and Nigel F. Piercy, "Examining Business Strategy, Sales Management, and Salesperson Antecedents of Sales Organization Effectiveness," *The Journal of Personal Selling & Sales Management*, Spring 2001, p. 109; Michael Beverland, "Contextual Influences, and the Adoption and Practice of Relationship Selling in a Business-to-Business Setting: an Exploratory Study," *The Journal of Personal Selling & Sales Management*, Summer 2001, p. 207; Sandy D. Jap, "The Strategic Role of the Salesforce in Developing Customer Satisfaction Across the Relationship Lifecycle," *The Journal of Personal Selling & Sales Management*, Spring 2001, p. 95; John E. Swan, Cathy Goodwin, Michael A. Mayo and Lynne D. Richardson, "Customer Identities: Customers as Commercial Friends, Customer Coworkers or Business Acquaintances," *The Journal of Personal Selling & Sales Management*, Winter 2001, p. 29; Neeli Bendapudi and Robert P. Leone, "Managing Business-to-Business Customer Relationships Following Key Contact Employee Turnover in a Vendor Firm," *Journal of Marketing*, April 2002, p. 83; Michael J. Dorsch, Les Carlson, Mary Anne Raymond and Robert Ranson, "Customer Equity Management and Strategic Choices for Sales Managers," *The Journal of Personal Selling & Sales Management*, Spring 2001, p. 157; Thomas W. Leigh, Ellen Bolman Pullins and Lucette B. Comer, "The Top Ten Sales Articles of the 20th Century," *The Journal of Personal Selling & Sales Management*, Summer 2001, p. 217; Thomas Tellefsen and Nermin Eyuboglu, "The Impact of a Salesperson's In-House Conflicts and Influence Attempts on Buyer Commitment," *The Journal of Personal Selling & Sales Management*, November 2002, p. 157; Charles H. Schwepker, Jr. "Customer-Oriented Selling: a Review, Extension, and Directions for Future Research," *The Journal of Personal Selling & Sales Management*, Spring 2003, p. 151; Thomas R. Wotruba, "The Transformation of Industrial Selling: Causes and Consequences," *Industrial Marketing Management*, September 1996, p. 327; William M. Strahle, Rosann L. Spiro, and Frank Acito, "Marketing and Sales: Strategic Alignment and Functional Implementation," *Journal of Personal Selling & Sales Management*, Winter 1996, p. 1; Paul Boughton, "Winning Customers, Building Accounts: Some Do It Better Than Others," *Journal of the Academy of Marketing Science*, Spring 1996, p. 175; Jerome A. Colletti and Lawrence B. Chonko, "Change Management

Initiatives: Moving Sales Organizations From Obsolescence to High Performance," *Journal of Personal Selling & Sales Management*, Spring 1997, p. 1; Douglas M. Lambert, Howard Marmorstein, and Arun Sharma, "Industrial Salespeople as a Source of Market Information," *Industrial Marketing Management*, May 1990, p. 141.

5. "Bank of (Middle) America," *Fast Company*, March 2003, p. 104; "A French Bank Hits the Road," *Business Week*, November 17, 2003, p. 20; "NationsBank Asks Tellers to Branch Out," *Raleigh News & Observer*, September 12, 1993, p. 1F. See also "Forget 'May I Help You?'" *The Wall Street Journal*, July 8, 2003, p. B1; "Service—with a Side of Sales," *The Wall Street Journal Reports*, October 29, 2001, p. R13.

6. "Specialized Training Can Improve Sales Force Focus," *Investor's Business Daily*, January 16, 2003, p. A7; "Joe Galli's Army," *Fortune*, December 30, 2002, p. 134; Mark A. Moon and Susan F. Gupta, "Examining the Formation of Selling Centers: A Conceptual Framework," *Journal of Personal Selling & Sales Management*, Spring 1997, p. 31; S. Joe Puri and Pradeep Korgaonkar, "Couple the Buying and Selling Teams," *Industrial Marketing Management* 20, no. 4 (1991), p. 311; "P&G Rolls Out Retailer Sales Teams," *Advertising Age*, May 21, 1990, p. 18.

7. Sanjit Sengupta, Robert E. Krapfel and Michael A. Pusateri, "An Empirical Investigation of Key Account Salesperson Effectiveness," *The Journal of Personal Selling & Sales Management*, Fall 2000, p. 253; Christian Homburg, John P. Workman, Jr. and Ove Jensen, "A Configurational Perspective on Key Account Management," *Journal of Marketing*, April 2002, p. 38; Andrea L. Dixon, Jule B. Gassenheimer and Terri Feldman Barr, "Bridging the Distance Between Us: How Initial Responses to Sales Team Conflict Help Shape Core Selling Team Outcomes," *The Journal of Personal Selling & Sales Management*, Fall 2002, p. 247; Jim Blythe, "Using Trade Fairs in Key Account Management," *Industrial Marketing Management*, October 2002, p. 627; Michael G. Harvey, Milorad M. Novicevic, Thomas Hench and Matthew Myers, "Global Account Management: a Supply-Side Managerial View," *Industrial Marketing Management*, October 2003, p. 563; Roberta J. Schultz and Kenneth R. Evans, "Strategic Collaborative Communication by Key Account Representatives," *The Journal of Personal Selling & Sales Management*, Winter 2002, p. 23; Dan C. Weilbaker and William A. Weeks, "The Evolution of National Account Management: A Literature Perspective," *Journal of Personal Selling & Sales Management*, Fall 1997, p. 49; C. J. Lambe and Robert E. Spekman, "National Account Management: Large Account Selling or Buyer-Supplier Alliance?" *Journal of Personal Selling & Sales Management*, Fall 1997, p. 61; Catherine Pardo, "Key Account Management in the Business to Business Field: The Key Account's Point of View," *Journal of Personal Selling & Sales Management*, Fall 1997, p. 17; Sanjit Sengupta, Robert E. Krapfel, and Michael A. Pusateri, "Switching Costs in Key Account Relationships," *Journal of Personal Selling & Sales Management*, Fall 1997, p. 9; Paul Dishman and Philip S. Nitse, "National Accounts Revisited: New Lessons From Recent Investigations," *Industrial Marketing Management*, January 1998, p. 1.

8. For more on telemarketing and attempts to regulate it, see Chapter 14, endnote 12. See also "Telephone Sales Reps Do Unrewarding Jobs that Few Can Abide," *The Wall Street Journal*, September 9, 1993, p. A1; Brett A. Boyle, "The Importance of the Industrial Inside Sales Force: A Case Study," *Industrial Marketing Management*, September 1996, p. 339; "How to Unite Field and Phone Sales," *Inc.*, July 1992, p. 115.

9. "How to Remake Your Sales Force," *Fortune*, May 4, 1992, p. 98; "Apparel Makers Play Bigger Part on Sales Floor," *The Wall Street Journal*, March 2, 1988, p. 31. See also Charles D. Stevens and Gerrard Macintosh, "Personality and Attractiveness of Activities within Sales Jobs," *The Journal of Personal Selling & Sales Management*, Winter 2002–2003, p. 23; Ravipreet S. Sohi, Daniel C. Smith, and Neil M. Ford, "How Does Sharing a Sales Force Between Multiple Divisions Affect Salespeople?" *Journal of the Academy of Marketing Science*, Summer 1996, p. 195; David W. Cravens and Raymond W. LaForge, "Salesforce Deployment Analy-

sis," *Industrial Marketing Management*, July 1983, p. 179; Michael S. Herschel, "Effective Sales Territory Development," *Journal of Marketing*, April 1977, p. 39.

10. "The Task at Hand," *Beverage World*, December 15, 2003, p. 46; "Sales Force Effectiveness through E-Learning," *Pharmaceutical Executive*, October 2003, p. 106; "The Biggest Mouth in Silicon Valley," *Business 2.0*, September 2003, p. 107; "Software that Actually Useful," *Sales & Marketing Management*, August 2003, p. 25; Scott M. Widmier, Donald W. Jackson, Jr., and Deborah Brown McCabe, "Infusing Technology into Personal Selling," *The Journal of Personal Selling & Sales Management*, November 2002, p. 189; "Salespeople Say Automation Software Still Lacking," *Investor's Business Daily*, January 18, 2001, p. A4; "MarketSoft Tailors Products to Solve Problems," *The Wall Street Journal*, November 30, 2000, p. B8; "New Software's Payoff? Happier Salespeople," *Investor's Business Daily*, May 23, 2000, p. A8; "Making the Sale," *The Wall Street Journal*, November 15, 1999, p. R16; "Offices Goin' Mobile," *USA Today*, May 17, 1999, p. 3B; "Bob Schmonsees Has a Tool for Better Sales and It Ignores Excuses," *The Wall Street Journal*, March 26, 1999, p. B1; "New Software Is Helping Reps Fill Custom Orders without Glitches," *The Wall Street Journal*, August 11, 1992, p. B6; "Salespeople on Road Use Laptops to Keep in Touch," *The Wall Street Journal*, April 25, 1991, p. B1.

11. Amy J. Morgan and Scott A. Inks, "Technology and the Sales Force: Increasing Acceptance of Sales Force Automation," *Industrial Marketing Management*, July 2001, p. 463; Mary E. Shoemaker, "A Framework for Examining IT Enabled Market Relationships," *The Journal of Personal Selling & Sales Management*, Spring 2001, p. 177; Robert C. Erffmeyer and Dale A. Johnson, "An Exploratory Study of Sales Force Automation Practices: Expectations and Realities," *The Journal of Personal Selling & Sales Management*, Spring 2001, p. 167; Cheri Speier and Viswanath Venkatesh, "The Hidden Minefields in the Adoption of Sales Force Automation Technologies," *Journal of Marketing*, July 2002, p. 98; Eli Jones, Suresh Sundaram and Wynne Chin, "Factors Leading to Sales Force Automation Use: a Longitudinal Analysis," *The Journal of Personal Selling & Sales Management*, November 2002, p. 145; Mary Jo Bitner, "Technology Infusion in Service Encounters," *Journal of the Academy of Marketing Science*, Winter 2000, p. 138; Michael J. Swenson and Adilson Parrella, "Sales Technology Applications: Cellular Telephones and the National Sales Force," *Journal of Personal Selling & Sales Management*, Fall 1992, p. 67; Paul Dishman and Kregg Aytes, "Exploring Group Support Systems in Sales Management Applications," *Journal of Personal Selling & Sales Management*, Winter 1996, p. 65.

12. "HP Adapting to a New," *CRN*, March 29, 2004, p. 18; "Fiorina Whips H-P into Fighting Shape," *USA Today*, June 5, 2001, p. 3B; "H-P Profit Drops 66% But Tops Forecast," *The Wall Street Journal*, May 17, 2000, p. A3; "H-P Woes Are Deeper Than the Downturn," *Business Week*, May 7, 2001, p. 48; "The Radical: Carly Fiorina's Bold Management Experiment at HP," *Business Week*, February 19, 2001, p. 68; "The Boss," *Business Week*, August 2, 1999, p. 76.

13. "Selling Salesmanship," *Business 2.0*, December 2002, p. 66; "The Art of the Sale," *The Wall Street Journal*, January 11, 2001, p. B1.

14. Available from World Wide Web: <http://www.achievement.com/sales>; Brian P. Matthews and Tom Redman, "Recruiting the Wrong Salespeople: Are the Job Ads to Blame?," *Industrial Marketing Management*, October 2001, p. 541; R. Edward Bashaw, Thomas N. Ingram and Bruce D. Keillor, "Improving Sales Training Cycle Times for New Trainees: an Exploratory Study," *Industrial Marketing Management*, July 2002, p. 329; Ellen Bolman Pullins and Leslie M. Fine, "How the Performance of Mentoring Activities Affects the Mentor's Job Outcomes," *The Journal of Personal Selling & Sales Management*, Fall 2002, p. 259; Greg W. Marshall, Thomas H. Stone, and I. M. Jawahar, "Selection Decision Making by Sales Managers and Human Resource Managers: Decision Impact, Decision Frame and Time of Valuation," *The Journal of Personal Selling & Sales Management*, Winter 2001, p. 19; Phillip H. Wilson,

David Strutton and, M. Theodore Farris II, "Investigating the Perceptual Aspect of Sales Training," *The Journal of Personal Selling & Sales Management*, Spring 2002, p. 77; Hiram C. Barksdale, Jr. Danny N. Bellenger, James S. Boles, and Thomas G. Brashear, "The Impact of Realistic Job Previews and Perceptions of Training on Sales Force Performance and Continuance Commitment: a Longitudinal Test," *The Journal of Personal Selling & Sales Management*, Spring 2003, p. 125; Ashraf M. Attia, Earl D. Honeycutt, Jr., and Magdy Mohamed Attia, "The Difficulties of Evaluating Sales Training," *Industrial Marketing Management*, April 2002, p. 253; Earl D. Honeycutt, Jr. Kiran Karande, Ashraf Attia, and Steven D. Maurer, "An Utility Based Framework for Evaluating the Financial Impact of Sales Force Training Programs," *The Journal of Personal Selling & Sales Management*, Summer 2001, p. 229; Ellen B. Pullins, Leslie M. Fine, and Wendy L. Warren, "Identifying Peer Mentors in the Sales Force: An Exploratory Investigation of Willingness and Ability," *Journal of the Academy of Marketing Science*, Spring 1996, p. 125; Alan J. Dubinsky, "Some Assumptions About the Effectiveness of Sales Training," *Journal of Personal Selling & Sales Management*, Summer 1996, p. 67; Patrick L. Schul and Brent M. Wren, "The Emerging Role of Women in Industrial Selling: A Decade of Change," *Journal of Marketing*, July 1992, p. 38; William A. Weeks and Carl G. Stevens, "National Account Management Sales Training and Directions for Improvement: A Focus on Skills/Abilities," *Industrial Marketing Management*, September 1997, p. 423; Earl D. Honeycutt, Jr., John B. Ford, and John F. Tanner, Jr., "Who Trains Salespeople? The Role of Sales Trainers and Sales Managers," *Industrial Marketing Management*, February 1994, p. 65.

15. Ken Grant, David W. Cravens, George S. Low, and William C. Moncrief, "The Role of Satisfaction with Territory Design on the Motivation, Attitudes, and Work Outcomes of Salespeople," *Journal of the Academy of Marketing Science*, Spring 2001, p. 165; Balaji C. Krishnan, Richard G. Netemeyer and James S. Boles, "Self-Efficacy, Competitiveness, and Efforts as Antecedents of Salesperson Performance," *The Journal of Personal Selling & Sales Management*, Fall 2002, p. 285; Guangping Wang and Richard G. Netemeyer, "The Effects of Job Autonomy, Customer Demandingness, and Trait Competitiveness on Salesperson Learning, Self-Efficacy, and Performance," *Journal of the Academy of Marketing Science*, Summer 2002, p. 217; Joseph O. Rentz, C. David Shepherd, Armen Tashchian, Pratibha A. Dabholkar and Robert T. Ladd, "A Measure of Selling Skill: Scale Development and Validation," *The Journal of Personal Selling & Sales Management*, Winter 2002, p. 13; Erin Anderson and Thomas S. Robertson, "Inducing Multiline Salespeople to Adopt House Brands," *Journal of Marketing*, April 1995, p. 16; Stephen B. Knouse and David Strutton, "Molding a Total Quality Salesforce Through Managing Empowerment, Evaluation, and Reward and Recognition Processes," *Journal of Marketing Theory & Practice*, Summer 1996, p. 24; Ajay K. Kolhi and Bernard J. Jaworksi, "The Influence of Coworker Feedback on Salespeople," *Journal of Marketing*, October 1994, p. 82; William L. Cron, Alan J. Dubinsky, and Ronald E. Michaels, "The Influence of Career Stages on Components of Salesperson Motivation," *Journal of Marketing*, January 1988, p. 78.

16. "The Sales Commission Dilemma," *Inc.*, May 2003, p. 49; "Creating Incentives Down in Ranks: Marriott Ties Pay to Guest Replies," *Investor's Business Daily*, July 6, 2001, p. A1; "Get Great Results from Salespeople by Finding What Really Moves Them," *Investor's Business Daily*, July 2, 2001, p. A1; "Medical Gear Sales Force Works on Commission," *Investor's Business Daily*, July 25, 2000, p. A14; R. Venkatesh, Goutam Challagalla and Ajay K. Kohli, "Heterogeneity in Sales Districts: Beyond Individual-Level Predictors of Satisfaction and Performance," *Journal of the Academy of Marketing Science*, Summer 2001, p. 238; Ellen Bolman Pullins, "An Exploratory Investigation of the Relationship of Sales Force Compensation and Intrinsic Motivation," *Industrial Marketing Management*, July 2001, p. 403; Sridhar N. Ramaswami and Jagdip Singh, "Antecedents and Consequences of Merit Pay Fairness for Industrial Salespeople," *Journal of Marketing*, October 2003, p. 46; Goutam Ghallagalla, "Supervisory Orientations and Salesperson Work Out-

comes: the Moderating Effect of Salesperson Location," *The Journal of Personal Selling & Sales Management*, Summer 2000, p. 161; Kissan Joseph and Manohar U. Kalwani, "The Role of Bonus Pay in Salesforce Compensation Plans," *Industrial Marketing Management*, March 1998, p. 147; Rene Y. Darmon, "Selecting Appropriate Sales Quota Plan Structures and Quota-Setting Procedures," *Journal of Personal Selling & Sales Management*, Winter 1997, p. 1; Thomas E. Tice, "Managing Compensation Caps in Key Accounts," *Journal of Personal Selling & Sales Management*, Fall 1997, p. 41; Arun Sharma, "Customer Satisfaction-Based Incentive Systems: Some Managerial and Salesperson Considerations," *Journal of Personal Selling & Sales Management*, Spring 1997, p. 61.

17. "New Software's Payoff? Happier Salespeople," *Investor's Business Daily*, May 23, 2000, p. A8.

18. Thomas G. Brashear, James S. Boles, Danny N. Bellenger, and Charles M. Brooks, "An Empirical Test of Trust-Building Processes and Outcomes in Sales Manager-Salesperson Relationships," *Journal of the Academy of Marketing Science*, Spring 2003, p. 189; Kwaku Atuahene-Gima and Haiyang Li, "When Does Trust Matter? Antecedents and Contingent Effects of Supervisee Trust on Performance in Selling New Products in China and the United States," *Journal of Marketing*, July 2002, p. 61; Andrea L. Dixon, Rosann L. Spiro and Lukas P. Forbes, "Attributions and Behavioral Intentions of Inexperienced Salespersons to Failure: an Empirical Investigation," *Journal of the Academy of Marketing Science*, Fall 2003, p. 459; Mark C. Johlke, Dale F. Duhan, Roy D. Howell and Robert W. Wilkes, "An Integrated Model of Sales Managers' Communication Practices," *Journal of the Academy of Marketing Science*, Spring 2000, p. 263; Dominique Rouzies and Anne Macquin, "An Exploratory Investigation of the Impact of Culture on Sales Force Management Control Systems in Europe," *The Journal of Personal Selling & Sales Management*, Winter 2002–2003, p. 61; Scott B. MacKenzie, Philip M. Podsakoff, and Gregory A. Rich, "Transformational and Transactional Leadership and Salesperson Performance," *Journal of the Academy of Marketing Science*, Spring 2001, p. 115; Cengiz Yilmaz and Shelby D. Hunt, "Salesperson Cooperation: the Influence of Relational, Task, Organizational, and Personal Factors," *Journal of the Academy of Marketing Science*, Fall 2001, p. 335; Richard L. Oliver and Erin Anderson, "An Empirical Test of the Consequences of Behavior- and Outcome-Based Sales Control Systems," *Journal of Marketing*, October 1994, p. 53; Susan K. DelVecchio, "The Salesperson's Operating Freedom: A Matter of Perception," *Industrial Marketing Management*, January 1998, p. 31; Vlasis Stathakopoulos, "Sales Force Control: A Synthesis of Three Theories," *Journal of Personal Selling & Sales Management*, Spring 1996, p. 1; Gregory A. Rich, "The Constructs of Sales Coaching: Supervisory Feedback, Role Modeling and Trust," *Journal of Personal Selling & Sales Management*, Winter 1998, p. 53; Steven P. Brown and Robert A. Peterson, "The Effect of Effort on Sales Performance and Job Satisfaction," *Journal of Marketing*, April 1994, p. 70; Frederick A. Russ, Kevin M. McNeilly, and James M. Comer, "Leadership, Decision Making and Performance of Sales Managers: A Multi-Level Approach," *Journal of Personal Selling & Sales Management*, Summer 1996, p. 1; Jhinuk Chowdhury, "The Motivational Impact of Sales Quotas on Effort," *Journal of Marketing Research*, February 1993, p. 28; Douglas N. Behrman and William D. Perreault, Jr., "A Role Stress Model of the Performance and Satisfaction of Industrial Salespersons," *Journal of Marketing*, Fall 1984, p. 9.

19. "Chief Executives Are Increasingly Chief Salesmen," *The Wall Street Journal*, August 6, 1991, p. B1; Joe F. Alexander, Patrick L. Schul, and Emin Babakus, "Analyzing Interpersonal Communications in Industrial Marketing Negotiations," *Journal of the Academy of Marketing Science*, Spring 1991, p. 129.

20. Kirk Smith, Eli Jones, and Edward Blair, "Managing Salesperson Motivation in a Territory Realignment," *The Journal of Personal Selling & Sales Management*, Fall 2000, p. 215; Andris A. Zoltners, "Sales Territory Alignment: An Overlooked Productivity Tool," *The Journal of Personal Selling & Sales Management*, Summer 2000, p. 139; Ken Grant, "The

Role of Satisfaction with Territory Design on the Motivation, Attitudes, and Work Outcomes of Salespeople," *Journal of the Academy of Marketing Science*, Spring 2001, p. 165; J. David Lichtenthal, Saameer Sikri, and Karl Folk, "Teleprospecting: An Approach for Qualifying Accounts," *Industrial Marketing Management*, February 1989, p. 11.

21. "How to Get Your Company Where You Want It," *The American Salesman*, December 2003, p. 12; "When Should I Give Up on a Sales Prospect?" *Inc.*, May 1998, p. 129; "Downloading Their Dream Cars," *Business Week*, March 9, 1998, p. 93; "The New Wave of Sales Automation," *Business Marketing*, June 1991, p. 12. See also Sean Dwyer, John Hill and Warren Martin, "An Empirical Investigation of Critical Success Factors in the Personal Selling Process for Homogenous Goods," *The Journal of Personal Selling & Sales Management*, Summer 2000, p. 151; L. Brent Manssen, "Using PCs to Automate and Innovate Marketing Activities," *Industrial Marketing Management*, August 1990, p. 209; Doris C. Van Doren and Thomas A. Stickney, "How to Develop a Database for Sales Leads," *Industrial Marketing Management*, August 1990, p. 201.

22. "Novartis' Marketing Doctor," *Business Week*, March 5, 2001, p. 56.

23. For more on sales presentation approaches, see "Trapped in the Sales Presentation from Hell," *Information Week*, November 10, 2003, p. 122; "Advise and Conquer," *Brandweek*, May 14, 2001, p. 1; "Rick Francolini, TV Guide," *Brandweek*, October 25, 1999, p. 22; "The 60-Second Sales Pitch," *Inc.*, October 1994, p. 87. See also Daniel M. Eveleth and Linda Morris, "Adaptive Selling in a Call Center Environment: a Qualitative Investigation," *Journal of Interactive Marketing*, Winter 2002, p. 25; Thomas W. Leigh and John O. Summers, "An Initial Evaluation of Industrial Buyers' Impressions of Salespersons' Nonverbal Cues," *The Journal of Personal Selling & Sales Management*, Winter 2002, p. 41; Kalyani Menon and Laurette Dube, "Ensuring Greater Satisfaction by Engineering Salesperson Response to Customer Emotions," *Journal of Retailing*, Fall 2000, p. 285; Susan K. DelVecchio, James E. Zemanek, Roger P. McIntyre and Reid P. Claxton, "Buyers' Perceptions of Salesperson Tactical Approaches," *The Journal of Personal Selling & Sales Management*, Winter 2002–2003, p. 39; Alfred M. Pelham, "An Exploratory Model and Initial Test of the Influence of Firm Level Consulting-Oriented Sales Force Programs on Sales Force Performance," *The Journal of Personal Selling & Sales Management*, Spring 2002, p. 97; Annie H. Liu and Mark P. Leach, "Developing Loyal Customers with a Value-Adding Sales Force: Examining Customer Satisfaction and the Perceived Credibility of Consultative Salespeople," *The Journal of Personal Selling & Sales Management*, Spring 2001, p. 147; Richard S. Jacobs, Kenneth R. Evans, Robert E. Kleine III and Timothy D. Landry, "Disclosure and its Reciprocity as Predictors of Key Outcomes of an Initial Sales Encounter," *The Journal of Personal Selling & Sales Management*, Winter 2001, p. 51; Gary L. Frankwick, Stephen S. Porter, and Lawrence A. Crosby, "Dynamics of Relationship Selling: a Longitudinal Examination of Changes in Salesperson-Customer Relationship Status," *The Journal of Personal Selling & Sales Management*, Spring 2001, p. 135; Willemijn van Dolen, Jos Lemmink, Ko de Ruyter and Ad de Jong, "Customer-Sales Employee Encounters: a Dyadic Perspective," *Journal of Retailing*, Winter 2002, p. 265; Willem Verbeke and Richard P. Bagozzi, "Sales Call Anxiety: Exploring What it Means When Fear Rules a Sales Encounter," *Journal of Marketing*, July 2000, p. 88; Michael D. Hartline, James G. Maxham III and Daryl O. McKee, "Corridors of Influence in the Dissemination of Customer-Oriented Strategy to Customer Contact Service Employees," *Journal of Marketing*, April 2000, p. 35; David M. Szymanski, "Modality and Offering Effects in Sales Presentations for a Good Versus a Service," *Journal of the Academy of Marketing Science*, Spring 2001, p. 179; Cathy Waters, "Customer Centered Selling: Eight Steps to Success from the World's Best Sales Force," *Journal of the Academy of Marketing Science*, Fall 2000, p. 546; Jon M. Hawes, James T. Strong, and Bernard S. Winick, "Do Closing Techniques Diminish Prospect Trust," *Industrial Marketing Management*, September 1996, p. 349; Morgan P. Miles, Danny R. Arnold, and Henry W. Nash "Adaptive Communication: The Adaption of the Seller's Interpersonal

Style to the Stage of the Dyad's Relationship and the Buyer's Communication Style," *Journal of Personal Selling & Sales Management*, Winter 1990, p. 21; Harish Sujan, Barton A. Weitz, & Nirmalya Kumar, "Learning Orientation, Working Smart, and Effective Selling," *Journal of Marketing*, July 1994, p. 39.

24. For more on pharmaceutical company selling tactics, see "Side Effects: As Drug-Sales Teams Multiply, Doctors Start to Tune Them Out," *The Wall Street Journal*, June 13, 2003, p. A1; "New Prescription: Its Rivals in Funk, Novartis Finds a Way to Thrive," *The Wall Street Journal*, August 23, 2002, p. A1; "Swallow This: How Drug Makers Use Pharmacies to Push Pricey Pills," *The Wall Street Journal*, May 1, 2002, p. A1; "Sorry, Doc, No Dinners-to-Go," *The Wall Street Journal*, April 23, 2002, p. D4; "More than Ads, Drug Makers Rely on Sales Reps," *The Wall Street Journal*, March 14, 2002, p. B1; "Pushing Pills: Drug Firms' Incentives to Pharmacists in India Fuel Mounting Abuse," *The Wall Street Journal*, August 16, 2001, p. A1; "Doctors Step Out; Drug Salesmen Step In," *USA Today*, July 5, 2001, p. 11A; "Sales Pitch: Drug Firms Use Perks to Push Pills," *USA Today*, May 16, 2001, p. 1B. For more on Oracle's selling tactics, see "Learning to Be a Great Host," *Business 2.0*, May 2003, p. 70; "Oracle Puts Priority on Customer Service," *The Wall Street Journal*, January 21, 2003, p. B5; "Out of Control," *Business 2.0*, August 2002, p. 38. See also Terry W. Loe and William A. Weeks, "An Experimental Investigation of Efforts to Improve Sales Students' Moral Reasoning," *The Journal of Personal Selling & Sales Management*, Fall 2000, p. 243; Lawrence B. Chonko, Thomas R. Wotruba, and Terry W. Loe, "Direct Selling Ethics at the Top: an Industry Audit and Status Report," *The Journal of Personal Selling & Sales Management*, Spring 2002, p. 87; Eugene Sivadas, Susan Bardi Kleiser, James Kellaris, and Robert Dahlstrom, "Moral Philosophy, Ethical Evaluations, and Sales Manager Hiring Intentions," *The Journal of Personal Selling & Sales Management*, Winter 2002–2003, p. 7; John Cherry and John Fraedrich, "Perceived Risk, Moral Philosophy and Marketing Ethics: Mediating Influences on Sales Managers' Ethical Decision-Making," *Journal of Business Research*, December 2002, p. 951; Bulent Menguc, "Organizational Consequences, Marketing Ethics and Salesforce Supervision: Further Empirical Evidence," *Journal of Business Ethics*, March 1998, p. 333; David Strutton, J. B. I. Hamilton, and James R. Lumpkin, "An Essay on When to Fully Disclose in Sales Relationships: Applying Two Practical Guidelines for Addressing Truth-Telling Problems," *Journal of Business Ethics*, April 1997, p. 545; Lawrence B. Chonko, John F. Tanner, and William A. Weeks, "Ethics in Salesperson Decision Making: A Synthesis of Research Approaches and an Extension of the Scenario Method," *Journal of Personal Selling & Sales Management*, Winter 1996, p. 35.

CHAPTER 16

1. "Subway to Sell Kids Pak Meal that Focuses on Health," *USA Today*, September 26, 2003, p. 1B; "Subway on Track to Bow a Pair of Healthy Efforts," *Brandweek*, September 22, 2003, p. 5; "Subway Orders Weightier Campaign," *The Wall Street Journal*, August 21, 2003, p. B6; "Creative: Ordinary People," *Adweek*, August 11, 2003, p. 24; "Fast-Food Firms' Big Budgets Don't Buy Consumer Loyalty," *The Wall Street Journal*, July 24, 2003, p. B4; "Why Subway Chose Fallon," *Advertising Age*, July 21, 2003, p. 4; "Fallon Takes Home Subway after All-Star Shootout," *Adweek*, July 21, 2003, p. 7; "Subway Seeing Double in Trio of New Spots," *Adweek*, July 7, 2003, p. 9; "Subway Seeks Better Creative," *Adweek*, May 19, 2003, p. 7; "Marketers of the Year: Subway, in Search of Fresh Ideas," *Brandweek*, October 15, 2001, pp. M54–M63.

2. "Special Report: U.S. Multinationals," *Ad Age International*, January 1998, p. 17; "Colgate-Palmolive Is Really Cleaning Up in Poland," *Business Week*, March 15, 1993, p. 54. See also Carolyn A. Lin, "Cultural Values Reflected in Chinese and American Television Advertising," *Journal of Advertising*, Winter 2001, p. 83; Christophe Collard, Michael Pustay, Christophe Roquilly and Asghar Zardkoohi, "Competitive Cross-

Couponing: a Comparison of French and U.S. Perspectives," *Journal of Public Policy & Marketing*, Spring 2001, p. 64; Charles R. Taylor, Gordon E. Miracle, and R. D. Wilson, "The Impact of Information Level on the Effectiveness of U.S. and Korean Television Commercials," *Journal of Advertising*, Spring 1997, p. 1; Ann M. Barry, "Advertising and Culture: Theoretical Perspectives," *Journal of the Academy of Marketing Science*, Winter 1998, p. 67; Siew M. Leong, Sween H. Ang, and Leng L. Tham, "Increasing Brand Name Recall in Print Advertising Among Asian Consumers," *Journal of Advertising*, Summer 1996, p. 65; Ronald E. Taylor, Mariea G. Hoy, and Eric Haley, "How French Advertising Professionals Develop Creative Strategy," *Journal of Advertising*, Spring 1996, p. 1; Nan Zhou and Mervin Y. T. Chen, "A Content Analysis of Men and Women in Canadian Consumer Magazine Advertising: Today's Portrayal, Yesterday's Image?" *Journal of Business Ethics*, April 1997, p. 485; Johny K. Johansson, "The Sense of 'Nonsense': Japanese TV Advertising," *Journal of Advertising*, March 1994, p. 17; Yong Zhang and Betsy D. Gelb, "Matching Advertising Appeals to Culture: The Influence of Products' Use Conditions," *Journal of Advertising*, Fall 1996, p. 29; John L. Graham, Michael A. Kamins and Djoko S. Oetomo, "Content Analysis of German and Japanese Advertising in Print Media from Indonesia, Spain, and the United States," *Journal of Advertising*, June 1993, p. 5; Bob D. Cutler, and Rajshekhar G. Javalgi, "A Cross-Cultural Analysis of the Visual Components of Print Advertising: The United States and the European Community," *Journal of Advertising Research*, January/February 1992, p.71.

3. Available from World Wide Web: <http://www.adage.com>; "Ad-Spending Soothsayers Optimistic on Year Ahead," *Advertising Age*, December 15, 2003, p. 8; "Forecaster Trims View, Sees Upturn," *The Wall Street Journal*, June 18, 2003, p. B9: "The Top 5 Rules of the Ad Game," *Business Week*, January 20, 2003, p. 72; "Analysts See a Rise in Ad Spending as Firms Look to Spread the Word," *Investor's Business Daily*, January 3, 2003, p. A6; "Advertisers Compete to Become Pride of Lions," *USA Today*, June 18, 2002, p. 1B.

4. Available from World Wide Web: <http://www.adage.com>; "AdAge Feature: Global Marketing," *Advertising Age*, November 10, 2003, p. 26; "Ad Spenders Loosen Purse Strings," *The Wall Street Journal*, October 15, 2003, p. B3; "AdAge Feature: Megabrands," *Advertising Age*, October 13, 2003, p. 23; "Special Report: Top Advertisers," *BtoB*, September 15, 2003, p. 19; "2003 Fact Pack," *Advertising Age (supplement)*, September 2003; "Ad Spending in U.S. Climbs 6.8%," *The Wall Street Journal*, August 29, 2003, p. B6; AdAge Special Report: Megabrands," *Advertising Age*, July 21, 2003, p. S1; "AdAge Special Report: 100 Leading National Advertisers," *Advertising Age*, June 23, 2003, p. S1; "2001 Advertising-to-Sales Ratios for the 200 Largest Ad Spending Industries," *Advertising Age*, June 2001.

5. Available from World Wide Web: <http://www.adage.com>; "Ad Spending in U.S. Climbs 6.8%," *The Wall Street Journal*, August 29, 2003, p. B6; "Online Ad Spending: Steady March Back to Top," *Advertising Age*, July 14, 2003, p. 19; "Online Advertising Begins to Rebound," *Investor's Business Daily*, July 9, 2003, p. A5; "AdAge Special Report: 100 Leading National Advertisers," *Advertising Age*, June 23, 2003, p. S1; "Special Report: The E-Biz Surprise," *Business Week*, May 12, 2003, p. 60; "TV Fuels 4.2% Increase in 2002 Ad Spending," *Advertising Age*, March 10, 2003; "Ad Industry Looks Ahead with Cautious Optimism," *Advertising Age*, December 16, 2002, p. 4.

6. Exact data on this industry are elusive, but see U.S. Bureau of the Census, *Statistical Abstract of the United States 2002* (Washington, DC: U.S. Government Printing Office, 2001), p. 385, 396. See also "My Job Search," *Adweek*, January 12, 2004, p. 34; "Despite Slump, Students Flock to Ad Schools," *The Wall Street Journal*, October 14, 2003, p. B1; "Ads Rebound, but Jobs Don't," *Advertising Age*, August 4, 2003, p. 1.

7. For more on Dryel, see "The Dirt on At-Home Dry Cleaning," *The Wall Street Journal*, September 15, 2000, p. W14. See also "Industry Wrestles with Comparative Ads," *Advertising Age*, October 27, 2003,

p. 10; "Sour Dough: Pizza Hut v. Papa John's," *Brandweek*, May 21, 2001, p. 26; "Irate Firms Take Comparisons to Court," *The Wall Street Journal*, December 22, 1999, p. B8; "Survey: Comparative Ads Can Dent Car's Credibility," *Advertising Age*, May 4, 1998, p. 26. For more on AT&T, MCI, and Sprint's comparative ads, see "Best Phone Discounts Go to Hardest Bargainers," *The Wall Street Journal*, February 13, 1997, p. B1; "Fighting for Customers Gets Louder," *USA Today*, January 9, 1995, p. 1B. For other examples of comparative advertising, see "Allergy Drugs Wage a Bitter War of the Noses," *The Wall Street Journal*, May 23, 1996, p. B1; "New Drug Ads Give Doctors Heartburn," *The Wall Street Journal*, April 25, 1996, p. B9. See also Kenneth C. Manning, Paul W. Miniard, Michael J. Barone, and Randall L. Rose, "Understanding the Mental Representations Created by Comparative Advertising," *Journal of Advertising*, Summer 2001, p. 27; Paschalina Ziamou and S. Ratneshwar, "Innovations in Product Functionality: When and Why Are Explicit Comparisons Effective?" *Journal of Marketing*, April 2003, p. 49; Patrick Meirick, "Cognitive Responses to Negative and Comparitive Political Advertising," *Journal of Advertising*, Spring 2002, p. 49; Bruce E. Pinkleton, Nam-Hyun Um and Erica Weintraub Austin, "An Exploration of the Effects of Negative Political Advertising on Political Decision Making," *Journal of Advertising*, Spring 2002, p. 13; Diana L. Haytko, "Great Advertising Campaigns: Goals and Accomplishments," *Journal of Marketing*, April 1995, p. 113; Carolyn Tripp, "Services Advertising: An Overview and Summary of Research, 1980–1995," *Journal of Advertising*, Winter 1997, p. 21; Dhruv Grewal, Sukumar Kavanoor, Edward F. Fern, Carolyn Costley, and James Barnes, "Comparative Versus Noncomparative Advertising: A Meta-Analysis," *Journal of Marketing*, October 1997, p. 1; Thomas E. Barry, "Comparative Advertising: What Have We Learned in Two Decades?" *Journal of Advertising Research*, March/April 1993, p. 19; Naveen Donthu, "Comparative Advertising Intensity," *Journal of Advertising Research*, November/December 1992, p. 53.

8. "G.E. to Spend $100 Million Promoting Itself as Innovative," *The New York Times*, January 16, 2003, p. C1.

9. "The Selling of Breast Cancer," *Business 2.0*, February 2003, p. 88; "Seeking Cause and Effect," *Brandweek*, November 11, 2002, p. 18; "Brands Step Up to Battle Breast Cancer," *USA Today*, September 5, 2001, p. 3B; "Spiffing up the Corporate Image," *Fortune*, July 21, 1986, p. 68. See also T. Bettina Cornwell, Donald P. Roy, and Edward A. Steinard II, "Exploring Managers' Perceptions of the Impact of Sponsorship on Brand Equity," *Journal of Advertising*, Summer 2001, p. 41; Michael J. Barone, Anthony D. Miyazaki, and Kimberly A. Taylor, "The Influence of Cause-Related Marketing on Consumer Choice: Does One Good Turn Deserve Another?" *Journal of the Academy of Marketing Science*, Spring 2000, p. 248; Minette E. Drumwright, "Company Advertising With a Social Dimension: The Role of Noneconomic Criteria," *Journal of Marketing*, October 1996, p. 71; Eric Haley, "Exploring the Construct of Organization As Source: Consumer's Understandings of Organizational Sponsorship of Advocacy Advertising," *Journal of Advertising*, Summer 1996, p. 19.

10. For more on Wendy's, see "The Year in 2003—Review," *Nation's Restaurant News*, December 22, 2003, p. 51. For more on Cadillac, see "Cadillac Steers Dealers toward Unified Messages," *Brandweek*, October 6, 2003, p. 77. For more on Benetton, see "Store Owners Rip into Benetton," *Advertising Age*, February 6, 1995, p. 1; "Benetton, German Retailers Squabble," *Advertising Age*, February 6, 1995, p. 46. For more on Intel, see "Intel Inside at 10," *Advertising Age*, April 30, 2001, p. 4; "Co-op Crossroads," *Advertising Age*, November 15, 1999, p. 1. For more on GM, see "Still Pulling the Strings, But Locally, Too," *Brandweek*, April 17, 2000, p. 34; "GM Dealers Rebel Against Local Ad Structure," *Advertising Age*, January 24, 2000, p. 3. See also Steffen Jorgensen, Simon Pierre Sigue, and Georges Zaccour, "Dynamic Cooperative Advertising in a Channel," *Journal of Retailing*, Spring 2000, p. 71.

11. For more on co-op ads, see "Appeals Court Rules against Pork Council," *Advertising Age*, October 27, 2003, p. 4; "Big Blue Offers Solutions with $60 Mil Co-op Effort," *Advertising Age*, April 30, 2001, p. 8; "Revlon Plans Another Makeover," *The Wall Street Journal*, November 21, 2000, p. B1; "Joint Marketing with Retailers Spreads," *The Wall Street Journal*, October 24, 1996, p. B6; "H&R Block, Excedrin Discover Joint Promotions Can Be Painless," *The Wall Street Journal*, February 28, 1991, p. B3; John P. Murry and Jan B. Heide, "Managing Promotion Program Participation Within Manufacturer-Retailer Relationships," *Journal of Marketing*, January 1998, p. 58.

12. *Standard Rate and Data*, 2003; "What Makes Them Buy?" *Brandweek*, November 3, 2003, p. 22; "Marketers Slap Network TV in Survey on ROI," *Advertising Age*, October 13, 2003, p. 1; "POP Sharpens Its Focus," *Brandweek*, June 16, 2003, p. 31; "Special Report: Media Outlook 2001," *Adweek*, September 25, 2000. For more on the Yellow Pages medium, see "Print Yellow Pages Are Still Profitable," *The Wall Street Journal*, May 22, 2000, p. B16; Gerald L. Lohse and Dennis L. Rosen, "Signaling Quality and Credibility in Yellow Pages Advertising: the Influence of Color and Graphics on Choice," *Journal of Advertising*, Summer 2001, p. 73; "The Truth About Yellow Pages: Making Them Work for You," *Journal of the Academy of Marketing Science*, Winter 1998, p. 71. For more on the outdoor medium, see "Adidas Introduces Human Billboards," *Advertising Age*, September 1, 2003, p. 11; "Adidas' Billboard Ads Give a Kick to Japanese Pedestrians," *The Wall Street Journal*, August 29, 2003, p. B1; "Special Section: Introduce Yourself to Outdoor Advertising," *Advertising Age*, June 9, 2003, pp. C1–C13; "Firms Pitch Stuff Outside," *USA Today*, July 19, 2001, p. 3B; "A Market on the Move," *Ad Age Global*, April 2001, p. 38; "New Technology, Improved Image Draw Companies to Billboard Ads," *The Wall Street Journal*, July 31, 2000, p. B10. See also Charles R. Taylor and John C. Taylor, "Regulatory Issues in Outdoor Advertising: A Content Analysis of Billboards," *Journal of Public Policy & Marketing*, Spring 1994, p. 97. For more on the radio medium, see "Old Media Get a Web Windfall," *The Wall Street Journal*, September 17, 1999, p. B1. See also Darryl W. Miller and Lawrence J. Marks, "Mental Imagery and Sound Effects in Radio Commercials," *Journal of Advertising*, December 1992, p. 83. For more on the newspaper medium, see "Special Report: Newspapers," *Advertising Age*, April 29, 2002, pp. S1–S7; "How Newspaper Overcame Loss of Big Advertisers," *The Wall Street Journal*, January 25, 2002, p. A13; "Special Report: Newspaper Industry," *Advertising Age*, April 30, 2001, p. S1; "Special Report: Newspapers," *Adweek*, April 30, 2001, p. SR1. See also Lawrence C. Soley and Robert L. Craig, "Advertising Pressures on Newspapers: A Survey," *Journal of Advertising*, December 1992, p. 1; Srini S. Srinivasan, Robert P. Leone, and Francis J. Mulhern, "The Advertising Exposure Effect of Free Standing Inserts," *Journal of Advertising*, Spring 1995, p. 29; Karen W. King, Leonard N. Reid, and Margaret Morrison, "Large-Agency Media Specialists' Opinions on Newspaper Advertising for National Accounts," *Journal of Advertising*, Summer 1997, p. 1. For more on the magazine medium, see "Special Report: Magazines, the A-List," *Advertising Age*, October 20, 2003, pp. S1–S14; "Adweek Magazines Special Report," *Adweek*, October 13, 2003, pp. SR1–SR22; "Special Report: Magazines 300," *Advertising Age*, September 22, 2003, pp. S1–S8; "Special Section: Magazines 2003," *Advertising Age*, September 8, 2003, pp. M1–M62; "Adweek Magazines Special Report," *Adweek*, June 9, 2003, pp. SR1–SR28; "Special Report: Magazines 300," *Advertising Age*, September 23, 2002, pp. S1–S11; "To Sell Ad Pages, Magazines Offer Extra Services," *The Wall Street Journal*, July 9, 2001, p. B1. For more on the television and cable medium, see "Special Report: Cable TV," *Advertising Age*, June 9, 2003, pp. S1–S14; "Special Report: TV's Upfront," *Advertising Age*, May 14, 2001, p. S1; "Special Report: Cable TV," *Ad Age Global*, May 1, 2001, p. 25; "Special Report: Cable TV," *Advertising Age*, April 16, 2001, p. S1. See also James R. Coyle and Esther Thorson, "The Effects of Progressive Levels of Interactivity and Vividness in Web Marketing Sites," *Journal of Advertising*, Fall 2001, p. 65; Mandeep Singh, Siva K. Balasubramanian and Goutam Chakraborty, "A Comparative Analysis of Three Communication Formats: Advertising, Infomercial, and Direct Experience," *Journal of Advertising*, Winter 2000,

p. 59; Jean L. Rogers, "Mail Advertising and Consumer Behavior," *Psychology & Marketing*, March 1996, p. 211; Elizabeth C. Hirschman and Craig J. Thompson, "Why Media Matter: Toward a Richer Understanding of Consumers' Relationships With Advertising and Mass Media," *Journal of Advertising*, Spring 1997, p. 43; Richard J. Fox and Gary L. Geissler, "Crisis in Advertising?" *Journal of Advertising*, December 1994, p. 79.

13. "Staid U.S. Marketers Try Racier Ads," *The Wall Street Journal*, July 31, 2003, p. B6; "A Leap for Advertising," *Adweek*, June 16, 2003, p. 28; "Sex-Themed Ads Often Don't Travel Well," *The Wall Street Journal*, March 31, 2000, p. B7; "U.S. Admakers Cover It Up; Others Don't Give a Fig Leaf," *USA Today*, June 27, 1997, p. 1B; "Mars Inc. Dips into Sex to Lure Consumers into Arms of M&M's," *The Wall Street Journal*, January 21, 1997, p. B9; "Underwear Ads Caught in Bind over Sex Appeal," *Advertising Age*, July 8, 1996, p. 27.

14. "Looking for Mr. Plumber," *MediaWeek*, June 27, 1994, p. 7; "Those Really Big Shows Are Often Disappointing to Those Who Advertise," *The Wall Street Journal*, June 14, 1994, p. B1.

15. "Yech and Yada in 'Seinfeld' Ads," *Advertising Age*, May 18, 1998, p. 63; "'Seinfeld' Finale Advertisers Put on Game Faces," *USA Today*, April 29, 1998, p. 1B; "NBC May Get Only $1.5 Million for Ad Spots on 'Seinfeld' Finale," *The Wall Street Journal*, March 4, 1998, p. B6.

16. "Gardenburger's Ad May Help Its Rival," *The Wall Street Journal*, May 20, 1998, p. B8; "Gardenburger Bets the (Soybean) Farm on the Last 'Seinfeld,'" *The Wall Street Journal*, April 13, 1998, p. A1.

17. "Hey, Shoppers: Ads on Aisle 7!" *Fortune*, November 24, 2003, p. 50; "Asics Sneaks Are 'Kill Bill' Sleeper Hit," *Advertising Age*, November 10, 2003, p. 4; "Gone in 30 Seconds," *Business 2.0*, November 2003, p. 68; "Your Ad Should Be in Pictures," *Fortune*, October 27, 2003, p. 60; "Turn on '24' and You'll Also Catch a 6-Min. Film-ercial," *USA Today*, October 27, 2003, p. 4B; "Instant Messaging Programs Are No Longer Just for Messages," *USA Today*, October 20, 2003, p. 5D; "Why the Great American Brands Are Doing Lunch," *Business 2.0*, September 2003, p. 146; "Cue the Stapler!" *Time (Inside Business Bonus Section)*, September 2003; "Getting a Piece of the 'Eye,'" *Advertising Age*, August 4, 2003, p. 4; "The Wider World of Advertising," *Adweek*, June 23, 2003, p. 24; "Captive Marketing: There's No Escape," *Time (Time Bonus Section)*, June 2003; "Ads Invade Videogames!" *Fortune*, May 26, 2003, p. 46; "Consumers Give Movie Ads a Thumbs Up," *Adweek*, May 19, 2003, p. 10; "Your Ad Could Be Here!" *Business 2.0*, May 2003, p. 76; "Advertising: Altered Reality," *The New York Times*, March 12, 2003, p. C7; "Growing Pains for Placements," *Advertising Age*, February 3, 2003, p. S2; "Lights, Camera, Commercial," *American Demographics*, February 2003, p. 34; "Ad Intrusion Up, Say Consumers," *Advertising Age*, January 6, 2003, p. 1; "Clear Channel to Take the 'V' Train," *The Wall Street Journal*, December 23, 2002, p. B3; "Guerrilla Marketers of the Year: Brand's Best Friend," *Brandweek*, December 9, 2002, p. 28; "Cities Plan to Put Ads on Police Cars," *USA Today*, October 31, 2002, p. 1A; "The New Billboards: Buggies," *Advertising Age*, August 19, 2002, p. 11; "Pitch at the Pump: Talking Audio Ads Run at Gas Stations," *Advertising Age*, August 5, 2002, p. 16; "Bank of America Puts Ads in ATMs," *The Wall Street Journal*, July 25, 2002, p. B8; "Roxy Builds TV, Book Series around Its Own Surf Wear," *The Wall Street Journal*, February 19, 2002, p. B1; "Outdoor Interactive," *American Demographics*, August 2001, p. 32; "Advertisers Pepper Reality Shows with Product Placements," *USA Today*, July 23, 2001, p. 5B; "Firms Pitch New Place to Park Ads," *The Wall Street Journal*, July 11, 2001, p. B10; "Look Up, Down, All Around—Ads Fill Airports, Planes," *USA Today*, July 10, 2001, p. 12B; "It's an Ad, Ad, Ad, Ad World," *Time*, July 9, 2001, p. 17; "Ads Are Here, There, Everywhere," *USA Today*, June 11, 2001, p. 1B; "Odd, the Ad, the Ads and Tons of Ads," *USA Today*, May 24, 2001, p. 3B; "Ads Show Up in Unexpected Places," *USA Today*, March 23, 2001, p. 1D; "From Elevators to Gas Stations, Ads Multiplying," *Advertising Age*, November 13,

2000, p. 40; "Moving Targets," *American Demographics*, October 2000, p. 32; "From Cell Phones to Sell Phones," *Business Week*, September 11, 2000, p. 88; "Advertisers Find One of the Last Clutter-Free Places," *The Wall Street Journal*, June 15, 2000, p. B1; "Virtual Ads Grab More Attention from Marketers," *Advertising Age*, May 29, 2000. See also Cristel Antonio Russell, "Investigating the Effectiveness of Product Placements in Television Shows: the Role of Modality and Plot Connection Congruence on Brand Memory and Attitude," *Journal of Consumer Research*, December 2002, p. 306.

18. For more on ATM ads, see "Ads on Automated Teller Machines Multiply as Technology Improves," *Investor's Business Daily*, October 5, 2000, p. A6; "ATMs Are Latest Place-Based Medium," *Advertising Age*, November 24, 1997, p. 1. For more on Nascar ads, see "Hotel Rides with Race Fans," *USA Today*, November 4, 2003, p. 3B; "Nextel Link Takes Nascar to New Level," *Advertising Age*, October 27, 2003, p. S7; "The Changing Face of Nascar," *USA Today (Bonus Section E)*, August 29, 2003; "Space for Rent," *Brandweek*, June 2, 2003, p. 30; "Nascar's Image May Be In for a Wild Ride," *USA Today*, November 15, 2002, p. 1A.

19. "Friends' Tops TV Price Chart," *Advertising Age*, September 15, 2003, p. 1; "P&G Snaps Up Super Bowl Ad at $2.4 Million," *Advertising Age*, June 30, 2003, p. 1; "Low CPM Can Spell Bargain for Buyers," *Advertising Age*, May 19, 2003, p. 10; "Ad Buyers Back Off Reality Programs," *USA Today*, May 12, 2003, p. 1B; "Ad Meter," *USA Today*, January 27, 2003, p. 5B; "Name Brands: Super Bowl Ads Cost Plenty, but the Message Lasts Forever," *The New York Times*, January 24, 2003, p. 6; "A Super Sunday for Football and for Madison Avenue," *The New York Times*, January 24, 2003, p. C1.

20. "Long-Derided Banner Web Ads Could Be Worthwhile after All," *Investor's Business Daily*, November 11, 2003, p. A6; "Online Ad Sales Continue Upswing," *The Wall Street Journal*, November 11, 2003, p. B8; "FTC Clamps Down on Stealth Pop-Ups Today," *USA Today*, November 6, 2003, p. 1B; "Pop-Up Ads Explode in Popularity," *The Wall Street Journal*, October 28, 2003, p. B7; "Pop-Ups Assail through Windows," *USA Today*, September 25, 2003, p. 3B; "Stalk Market: New Battleground in Web Privacy War, Ads that Snoop," *The Wall Street Journal*, August 27, 2003, p. A1; "Web Ads on the Rebound," *The Wall Street Journal*, August 25, 2003, p. B1; "Contextual Ads Gather Steam," *Advertising Age*, August 11, 2003, p. 34; "Net Marketing: Top 5 Rich-Media Mistakes Advertisers Should Avoid," *BtoB*, July 14, 2003, p. 14; "Beyond the Banner," *Adweek*, May 12, 2003, p. 30; "Advertising: As an Alternative to Pop-Up Ads, Marketers Are Trying to Create Useful Web Sites to Draw Viewers," *The New York Times*, February 11, 2003, p. C8; "Behind the Wheel Driving the Web," *Advertising Age*, July 23, 2001, p. 10; "Web Ads Getting in Your Way? Try Blocking Software," *Investor's Business Daily*, July 12, 2001, p. A6; "Do e-Ads Have a Future?" *Business Week E.Biz*, January 22, 2001, pp. EB46–EB50; "Beyond the Banner Ad," *Business Week E.Biz*, December 11, 2000, p. EB16; "As Ads Fail to Heat Up, Sites Turning to Paid Subscribers," *Investor's Business Daily*, December 11, 2000, p. A8; "Clicks for Free," *American Demographics*, February 1999, p. 54; "Ads Click for Net Retailers," *USA Today*, January 28, 1999, p. 3B; "Web Sites Say: Your Ad Sells or It's on Us," *The Wall Street Journal*, June 27, 1997, p. B9. See also Kim Bartel Sheehan, "Re-Weaving the Web: Integrating Print and Online Communications," *Journal of Interactive Marketing*, Spring 2001, p. 47; Lee Sherman, "Banner Advertising: Measuring Effectiveness and Optimizing Placement," *Journal of Interactive Marketing*, Spring 2001, p. 60; Satya Menon and Dilip Soman, "Managing the Power of Curiosity for Effective Web Advertising Strategies," *Journal of Advertising*, Fall 2002, p. 1; Steven M. Edwards, Hairong Li, and Joo-Hyun Lee, "Forced Exposure and Psychological Reactance: Antecedents and Consequences of the Perceived Intrusiveness of Pop-Up Ads," *Journal of Advertising*, Fall 2002, p. 83; Xavier Dreze and Francois-Xavier Hussherr, "Internet Advertising: Is Anybody Watching?" *Journal of Interactive Marketing*, Autumn 2003, p. 8; Erik L. Olson and Robert E. Widing II, "Are Interactive Decision Aids Better than Passive Decision Aids? A Comparison with Implications for Information Providers on the Internet," *Journal of Interactive Marketing*, Spring 2002, p. 22; Richard T. Watson, Sigmund Akselsen, and Leyland F. Pitt, "Attractors: Building Mountains in the Flat Landscape of the World Wide Web," *California Management Review*, Winter 1998, p. 36; W. W. Kassaye, "Global Advertising and the World Wide Web," *Business Horizons*, May–June 1997, p. 33.

21. For some creative and controversial ads, see "Special Report: Marketers of the Year," *Brandweek*, October 20, 2003; "How to Sell a Strange Idea," *Adweek*, July 14, 2003, p. 22; "Downloading the Future of TV Advertising," *Business 2.0*, July 2003, p. 46; "Cheers and Jeers," *Adweek*, June 30, 2003, p. 20; "Ikea's 'Lamp' Wins Cannes," *Advertising Age*, June 23, 2003, p. 1; "A Leap for Advertising," *Adweek*, June 16, 2003, p. 28; "The Lowest Moments in Advertising," *Adweek*, June 9, 2003, p. 38; "Special Report: Best Awards," *Advertising Age*, May 26, 2003, pp. S1–S6; "Man behind Nike Ads Wants Innovation Rewarded," *USA Today*, June 17, 2003, p. 7B; "Special Report: Marketers of the Year," *Brandweek*, October 14, 2002; "You-Are-There Advertising," *The Wall Street Journal*, August 5, 2002, p. B1; "Special Report: Marketers of the Year," *Brandweek*, October 15, 2001; "Dip Ad Stirs Church Ire," *Advertising Age*, July 2, 2001, p. 8; "Duck Ads Have New Customers," *USA Today*, September 18, 2000, p. 13B; "Cough Syrup Touts 'Awful' Taste in U.S.," *The Wall Street Journal*, December 15, 1999, p. B10. See also Barbara J. Phillips and Edward F. McQuarrie, "The Development, Change, and Transformation of Rhetorical Style in Magazine Advertisements 1954–1999," *Journal of Advertising*, Winter 2002, p. 1; Susan E. Morgan and Tom Reichert, "The Message Is in the Metaphor: Assessing the Comprehension of Metaphors in Advertisements," *Journal of Advertising*, Winter 1999, p. 1; Parthasarathy Krishnamurthy and Anuradha Sivaraman, "Counterfactual Thinking and Advertising Responses," *Journal of Consumer Research*, March 2002, p. 650; Kineta Hung, "Framing Meaning Perceptions with Music: the Case of Teaser Ads," *Journal of Advertising*, Fall 2001, p. 39; Jennifer Edson Escalas and Barbara B. Stern, "Sympathy and Empathy: Emotional Responsed to Advertising Dramas," *Journal of Consumer Research*, March 2003, p. 566; Amanda B. Bower, "Highly Attractive Models in Advertising and the Women Who Loathe Them: the Implications of Negative Affect for Spokesperson Effectiveness," *Journal of Advertising*, Fall 2001, p. 51; Tom Reichert, Susan E. Heckler and Sally Jackson, "The Effects of Sexual Social Marketing Appeals on Cognitive Processing and Persuasion," *Journal of Advertising*, Spring 2001, p. 13; Barbara J. Phillips, "The Impact of Verbal Anchoring on Consumer Response to Image Ads," *Journal of Advertising*, Spring 2000, p. 15; Anne M. Brumbaugh, "Source and Nonsource Cues in Advertising and Their Effects on the Activation of Cultural and Subcultural Knowledge on the Route to Persuasion," *Journal of Consumer Research*, September 2002, p. 258; David Luna and Laura A. Peracchio, "Moderators of Language Effects in Advertising to Bilinguals: a Psycholinguistic Approach," *Journal of Consumer Research*, September 2001, p. 284; Erik L. Olson, "How Magazine Articles Portrayed Advertising From 1900 to 1940," *Journal of Advertising*, Fall 1995, p. 41; Audhesh K. Paswan, "Marketing to the Mind: Right Brain Strategies for Advertising and Marketing," *Journal of the Academy of Marketing Science*, Winter 1998, p. 68; Avery M. Abernethy and George R. Franke, "The Information Content of Advertising: A Meta-Analysis," *Journal of Advertising*, Summer 1996, p. 1; James H. Leigh, "The Use of Figures of Speech in Print Ad Headlines," *Journal of Advertising*, June 1994, p. 17; Bruce A. Huhmann and Timothy P. Brotherton, "A Content Analysis of Guilt Appeals in Popular Magazine Advertisements," *Journal of Advertising*, Summer 1997, p. 35; Margaret F. Callcott and Wei-Na Lee, "A Content Analysis of Animation and Animated Spokes-Characters in Television Commercials," *Journal of Advertising*, December 1994, p. 1; Alan J. Bush and Victoria D. Bush, "The Narrative Paradigm As a Perspective for Improving Ethical Evaluations of Advertisements," *Journal of Advertising*, September 1994, p. 31; L. W. Turley and Scott W. Kelley, "A Comparison of Advertising Content: Business to Business Versus Consumer Services," *Journal of Advertising*,

Winter 1997, p. 39; Eleonora Curlo and Robert Chamblee, "Ad Processing and Persuasion: The Role of Brand Identification," *Psychology & Marketing*, May 1998, p. 279; Noel M. Murray and Sandra B. Murray, "Music and Lyrics in Commercials: A Cross-Cultural Comparison Between Commercials Run in the Dominican Republic and in the United States," *Journal of Advertising*, Summer 1996, p. 51; Barbara B. Stern, "Advertising Intimacy: Relationship Marketing and the Services Consumer," *Journal of Advertising*, Winter 1997, p. 7; Baba Shiv, Julie A. Edell, and John W. Payne, "Factors Affecting the Impact of Negatively and Positively Framed Ad Messages," *Journal of Consumer Research*, December 1997, p. 285; Harlan E. Spotts, Marc G. Weinberger, and Amy L. Parsons, "Assessing the Use and Impact of Humor on Advertising Effectiveness: A Contingency Approach," *Journal of Advertising*, Fall 1997, p. 17; Martha Rogers and Kirk H. Smith, "Public Perceptions of Subliminal Advertising: Why Practitioners Shouldn't Ignore This Issue," *Journal of Advertising Research*, March/April 1993, p. 10; Kathryn T. Theus, "Subliminal Advertising and the Psychology of Processing Unconscious Stimuli: A Review of Research," *Psychology & Marketing*, May/June 1994, p. 271; Carolyn A. Lin, "Cultural Differences in Message Strategies: A Comparison between American and Japanese TV Commercials," *Journal of Advertising Research*, July/August 1993, p. 40.

22. "One Size Doesn't Fit All," *The Wall Street Journal*, October 1, 2003, p. B1; "Exxon Centralizes New Global Campaign," *The Wall Street Journal*, July 11, 2001, p. B6; "McCann Finds Global a Tough Sell in Japan," *The Wall Street Journal*, June 19, 1997, p. B2. See also Fahad S. Al-Olayan, "A Content Analysis of Magazine Advertisements from the United States and the Arab World," *Journal of Advertising*, Fall 2000, p. 69; Bongjin Cho, Up Kwon, James W. Gentry, Sunkyu Jun and Fredric Kropp, "Cultural Values Reflected in Theme and Execution: a Comparative Study of U.S. and Korean Television Commercials," *Journal of Advertising*, Winter 1999, p. 59; Michael G. Harvey, "A Model to Determine Standardization of the Advertising Process in International Markets," *Journal of Advertising Research*, July/August 1993, p. 57; Barbara Mueller, "Standardization vs. Specialization: An Examination of Westernization in Japanese Advertising," *Journal of Advertising Research*, January/February 1992, p. 15; Dana L. Alden, Wayne D. Hoyer, and Chol Lee, "Identifying Global and Culture-Specific Dimensions of Humor in Advertising: A Multinational Analysis," *Journal of Marketing*, April 1993, p. 64; "International Special Report: Global Media," *Advertising Age International*, July 18, 1994, p. I11; Ali Kanso, "International Advertising Strategies: Global Commitment to Local Vision," *Journal of Advertising Research*, January/February 1992, p. 10; Theodore Levitt, "The Globalization of Markets," *Harvard Business Review*, May–June 1983, p. 92; Kamran Kashani, "Beware the Pitfalls of Global Marketing," *Harvard Business Review*, September/October 1989, p. 91; William L. Shanklin and David A. Griffith, "Crafting Strategies for Global Marketing in the New Millennium," *Business Horizons*, September–October 1996, p. 11.

23. "China's Edgy Advertising," *The Wall Street Journal*, October 27, 2003, p. B1; "How Tiny German Shop Landed McDonald's," *The Wall Street Journal*, August 6, 2003, p. B1; "Still in the Hunt," *Business Week*, July 7, 2003, p. 42; "WPP's Sorrell Bests Publicis in Cordiant Bid," *The Wall Street Journal*, June 18, 2003, p. B1; "Are Holding Companies Obsolete?" *Adweek*, June 9, 2003, p. 30; "Special Report: Integrated Agencies," *Advertising Age*, May 19, 2003, pp. S1–S5; "Agency Report: Top 100 National Agencies," *Adweek*, April 7, 2003; "The Rise of the Superagency," *Advertising Age*, January 28, 2002, p. 1; "Will Ad Agencies Survive Slowdown?" *Investor's Business Daily*, May 8, 2001, p. A1; "A Chill Hits Madison Avenue," *The Wall Street Journal*, March 19, 2001, p. B1; "Culture Shock," *Advertising Age*, January 8, 2001, p. 1. See also Gerard Prendergast, Yizheng Shi and Douglas West, "Organizational Buying and Advertising Agency-Client Relationships in China," *Journal of Advertising*, Summer 2001, p. 61; George C. Hozier, Jr. and John D. Schatzberg, "Advertising Agency Terminations and Reviews: Stock Returns and Firm Performance," *Journal of Business Research*, November 2000, p. 169; Douglas West and John Ford, "Advertising Agency Philosophies and Employee Risking Taking," *Journal of Advertising*, Spring 2001, p. 77; Mark Davies and Mel Prince, "Examining the Longevity of New Agency Accounts: a Comparative Study of U.S. and U.K. Advertising Experiences," *Journal of Advertising*, Winter 1999, p. 75; Louise Ripley, "Why Industrial Advertising is Often Done in House," *Industrial Marketing Management*, November 1992, p. 331; Murray Young and Charles Steilen, "Strategy-Based Advertising Agency Selection: An Alternative to 'Spec' Presentations," *Business Horizons*, November–December 1996, p. 77; Douglas C. West, "Purchasing Professional Services: The Case of Advertising Agencies," *International Journal of Purchasing & Materials Management*, Summer 1997, p. 2; Douglas W. LaBahn and Chiranjeev Kohli, "Maintaining Client Commitment in Advertising Agency-Client Relationships," *Industrial Marketing Management*, November 1997, p. 497.

24. "Agencies Face New Accountability," *The Wall Street Journal*, October 2, 2003, p. B4; "Interpublic May Become More Open," *The Wall Street Journal*, September 10, 2003, p. B4; "Kraft Rethinks Agency Pay, Brand Duties," *Adweek*, August 18, 2003, p. 6; "GM Overhauls Compensation," *Advertising Age*, March 17, 2003, p. 1; "Up Close and Personal," *Adweek*, March 17, 2003, p. 26; "Adweek Adspend Survey: What Clients Think," *Adweek*, December 16, 2002, p. 21; "Nestle Move on Fees Will Rattle Agencies," *The Wall Street Journal*, October 8, 2001, p. A21; "Feeling the Squeeze," *Advertising Age*, June 4, 2001, p.1; "Unilever Reviews the Way It Pays for Ads," *The Wall Street Journal*, April 27, 2001, p. B6; "Performance Pays," *Advertising Age*, February 28, 2000, pp. S14–S16; "Dot-Compensation: Ad Agencies Feel Net Effect," *Advertising Age*, February 7, 2000, p. 1; "P&G Expands Its Program to Tie Agency Pay to Brand Performance," *The Wall Street Journal*, September 16, 1999, p. B12. See also R. Susan Ellis and Lester W. Johnson, "Agency Theory as a Framework for Advertising Agency Compensation Decisions," *Journal of Advertising Research*, September/October 1993, p. 76; Thorolf Helgesen, "Advertising Awards and Advertising Agency Performance Criteria," *Journal of Advertising Research*, July/August 1994, p. 43.

25. "GM to Publicis: Loyalty Matters," *Advertising Age*, May 26, 2003, p. 16; "Foote Cone Loses Two Accounts from Coke in Wake of Pepsi Suit," *The Wall Street Journal*, November 12, 2001, p. B3; "The Rise of the Superagency," *Advertising Age*, January 28, 2002, p. 1; "Commercial Break: An Ad Mega-Agency Faces Harsh Realities of a Shaken Industry," *The Wall Street Journal*, October 31, 2001, p. A1; "Can An Agency Be Guilty of Malpractice?" *Advertising Age*, January 31, 2000, p. 24.

26. For Got Milk? campaign, see "Got Milk? A Decade of Lessons Pours In," *Brandweek*, June 2, 2003, p. 24; "Dairy's Queen," *Adweek*, April 14, 2003, p. 32; "Borrowed Time," *Adweek*, November 18, 2002, p. 24; "Got Milk? An Campaign to Take On a Tough Target: Hispanic Teens," *The Wall Street Journal*, December 28, 2001, p. A9. For Taco Bell campaign, see "Dog-Gone Days: FCB Creates Ads for Taco Bell Acc't," *Advertising Age*, July 24, 2000, p. 4; "Taco Bell Drops the Chihuahua in Management Shuffle," *USA Today*, July 19, 2000, p. 1B; "Taco Bell Ads to Focus on Food, Not Dog," *The Wall Street Journal*, October 11, 1999, p. B10. For U.S. government's anti-drug campaign, see "Drug Czar Says Ad Campaign Has Flopped," *The Wall Street Journal*, May 14, 2002, p. B1. See also "How Terrific Ads Propelled Colgate, Dethroned Longtime Leader P&G," *Investor's Business Daily*, April 20, 2001, p. A1. See also "Budweiser Spot Sheds Tradition of Family-Friendly Advertising," *The Wall Street Journal*, September 11, 2003, p. B7; "At Last a Way to Measure Ads," *The Wall Street Journal Reports*, June 16, 2003, p. R4; "The Top 5 Rules of the Ad Game," *Business Week*, January 20, 2003, p. 72; "Buyers Seek Hard-to-Find Tostitos Gold," *USA Today*, January 10, 2003, p. 5B; "Consumers May Notice the Ads, but Will They Buy the Product?" *Investor's Business Daily*, December 19, 2002, p. A4; "Marketer of the Year: Dove's Key Softening Agents," *Brandweek*, October 15, 2001, p. M32; "Cautious Used Car Buyers Trust Carfax," *USA Today*, August 20, 2001, p. 7B; "Does Creativity Count?" *Brandweek*, December 11, 2000, p. 32; "The Metrics System," *Brandweek*, November 13, 2000, p. 106. See also Subodh Bhat, Michael Bevans, and Sanjit Sengupta, "Measuring Users' Web Activity to Evaluate and Enhance Advertising Effectiveness," *Journal of Advertising*, Fall 2002, p. 97; Ann Marie Barry, "How Advertising Works: the Role of Research," *Journal of the Academy of Marketing Science*, Winter 2001, p. 103; Els Gijsbrechts, Katia Campo, and Tom Goossens, "The Impact of Store Flyers on Store Traffic and Store Sales: a Geo-Marketing Approach," *Journal of Retailing*, (1) 2003, p. 1; Fuyuan Shen, "Banner Advertisement Pricing, Measurement, and Pretesting Practices: Perspectives from Interactive Agencies," *Journal of Advertising*, Fall 2002, p. 59; DeAnna S. Kempf and Russell N. Laczniak, "Advertising's Influence on Subsequent Product Trial Processing," *Journal of Advertising*, Fall 2001, p. 27; Gerald J. Tellis and Doyle L. Weiss, "Does TV Advertising Really Affect Sales? The Role of Measures, Models, and Data Aggregation," *Journal of Advertising*, Fall 1995, p. 1; John H. Holmes, "When Ads Work," *Journal of the Academy of Marketing Science*, Winter 1997, p. 88; Karen Whitehill King, John D. Pehrson, and Leonard N. Reid, "Pretesting TV Commercials: Methods, Measures, and Changing Agency Roles," *Journal of Advertising*, September 1993, p. 85; Erik du Plessis, "Recognition versus Recall," *Journal of Advertising Research*, May/June 1994, p. 75.

27. "McDonald's Arches Outlawed in Beijing," *USA Today*, March 5, 2002, p. 7B; "In Asia, It's Not a Wide-Open Web," *The Wall Street Journal*, July 9, 2001, p. B1; "Chinese Officials Force Magazines to Go Without Famous Names," *The Wall Street Journal*, February 2, 2000, p. B1; "Sweden Presses EU for Further Ad Restrictions," *Advertising Age*, April 12, 1999, p. 2; "Vietnamese Police Raid Bates' Ho Chi Minh Office," *Advertising Age*, May 4, 1998, p. 6; "Pakistan Cracks Whip," *Ad Age International*, February 9, 1998, p. 26; "Indian Court Tells Lever to Clean Up Ad Claims," *Ad Age International*, January 1998, p. 32; "PepsiCo's Pitch in Japan Has New Twist," *The Wall Street Journal*, May 23, 1997, p. B10. See also Young Sook Moon and George R. Franke, "Cultural Influences on Agency Practitioners' Ethical Perceptions: a Comparison of Korea and the U.S.," *Journal of Advertising*, Spring 2000, p. 51; Kim Bartel Sheehan, "Balancing Acts: an Analysis of Food and Drug Administration Letters about Direct-to-Consumer Advertising Violations," *Journal of Public Policy & Marketing*, Fall 2003, p. 159; J. Howard Beales III, "The Federal Trade Commission's Use of Unfairness Authority: its Rise, Fall, and Resurrection," *Journal of Public Policy & Marketing*, Fall 2003, p. 192; Alexander Simonson, "The Impact of Advertising Law on Business and Public Policy," *Journal of Marketing*, October 1994, p. 123; Ross D. Petty, "Advertising Law in the United States and European Union," *Journal of Public Policy & Marketing*, Spring 1997, p. 2; Steve Lysonski and Michael F. Duffy, "The New Zealand Fair Trading Act of 1986: Deceptive Advertising," *Journal of Consumer Affairs*, Summer 1992, p. 177; "Drop That Remote! In Britain, Watching TV Can Be a Crime," *The Wall Street Journal*, September 27, 1993, p. A1; "East Europeans Adjust to Western Ads; Information after Years of Propaganda," *The Wall Street Journal*, July 17, 1993, p. A5B; Albert Schofield, "International Differences in Advertising Practices: Britain Compared with Other Countries," *International Journal of Advertising* 10, no. 4 (1991), p. 299.

28. For more on KFC, see "Hey, Fast Food: We Love You Just the Way You Are," *Brandweek*, November 24, 2003, p. 30; "FTC Examines Health Claims in KFC's Ads," *The Wall Street Journal*, November 19, 2003, p. B1; "Garfield's Ad Review: KFC Serves Big, Fat Bucket of Nonsense in 'Healthy' Spots," *Advertising Age*, November 3, 2003, p. 61. See also "P&G Is Settling Disputes on Ads as Suits Pile Up," *The Wall Street Journal*, November 26, 2003, p. B1; "Watchdog Group Hits TV Product Placement," *Advertising Age*, October 6, 2003, p. 12; "Taco Bell Loses Chihuahua Battle," *Advertising Age*, June 9, 2003, p. 10; "Great Minds Think Alike—or Do They?" *Adweek*, June 9, 2003, p. 13; "Last Call for Camel, Marlboro Ads in Bars," *The Wall Street Journal*, May 9, 2003, p. B1; "The Party's Over," *Adweek*, May 5, 2003, p. 22; "Fantasy Island? Bermuda Ad Shows Hawaii," *The Wall Street Journal*, March 6, 2003, p. B1; "Merck Ads for Arthritis Drug Attract Regulatory Scrutiny," *The Wall Street Journal*, November 19, 2002, p. B6; "Branding by the Book," *Brandweek*, April 15, 2002, p. 18; "Marketers Increasingly Dispute Health Claims of Rivals'

Products," *The Wall Street Journal*, April 4, 2002, p. B1; "Duracell's Duck Ad Will Carry Disclaimer," *The Wall Street Journal*, February 7, 2002, p. B7; "Papa John's International: Better Pizza Boast Still Doesn't Sway Street," *Investor's Business Daily*, July 27, 2001, p. A10; "FDA Faults 'Misleading' Drug-Ad Images," *The Wall Street Journal*, May 4, 2001, p. B8; "FDA Scrambles to Police Drug Ads' Truthfulness," *The Wall Street Journal*, January 2, 2001, p. A24; "Microsoft WebTV Settles False-Advertising Complaint," *The Wall Street Journal*, October 26, 2000, p. B16. See also Boris W. Becker, "The Tangled Web They Weave: Truth, Falsity, & Advertisers," *Journal of Advertising*, Summer 1996, p. 83; Elizabeth K. LaFleur, R. E. Reidenbach, Donald P. Robin, and P. J. Forrest, "An Exploration of Rule Configuration Effects on the Ethical Decision Processes of Advertising Professionals," *Journal of the Academy of Marketing Science*, Winter 1996, p. 66; Barbara B. Stern, "'Crafty Advertisers': Literary Versus Literal Deceptiveness," *Journal of Public Policy & Marketing*, Spring 1992, p. 72; Joel J. Davis, "Ethics in Advertising Decisionmaking: Implications for Reducing the Incidence of Deceptive Advertising," *Journal of Consumer Affairs*, Winter 1994, p. 380. For more on advertising to kids, see "Lawsuit Alleges Alcohol Industry Targets Underage Drinkers," *The Wall Street Journal*, November 28, 2003, p. B1; "Beer Ads on TV, College Sports: Explosive Mix?" *The Wall Street Journal*, November 12, 2003, p. B1; "Coors Slammed for Targeting Kids," *Advertising Age*, November 3, 2003, p. 1; "Alcohol Advertisers Agree to Raise Standards to Help Keep Their Messages Away from Kids," *USA Today*, September 10, 2003, p. 5B; "Study Slams Philip Morris Ads Telling Teens Not to Smoke," *The Wall Street Journal*, May 29, 2002, p. B1; "Studios Admit to Targeting Children," *USA Today*, September 28, 2000, p. 1A; "Selling to Kids Blurs Ethical Picture," *USA Today*, March 20, 2000, p. 7D; "25 Years of Self-Regulation," *Advertising Age*, December 2, 1996, p. C1; Mary C. Martin, "Children's Understanding of the Intent of Advertising: A Meta-Analysis," *Journal of Public Policy & Marketing*, Fall 1997, p. 205; Avery M. Abernethy, "Advertising Clearance Practices of Radio Stations: A Model of Advertising Self-Regulation," *Journal of Advertising*, September 1993, p. 15.

29. Ivan L. Preston, "Regulatory Positions Toward Advertising Puffery of the Uniform Commercial Code and the Federal Trade Commission," *Journal of Public Policy & Marketing*, Fall 1997, p. 336; Claude R. Martin, Jr., "Ethical Advertising Research Standards: Three Case Studies," *Journal of Advertising*, September 1994, p. 17; William K. Darley and Robert E. Smith, "Advertising Claim Objectivity: Antecedents and Effects," *Journal of Marketing*, October 1993, p. 100; George M. Zinkhan, "Advertising Ethics: Emerging Methods and Trends," *Journal of Advertising*, September 1994, p. 1.

30. "P&G Breaks Out of Its Slump," *USA Today*, October 14, 2003, p. 3B; "Ads Mmm, Junk Mail," *Newsweek*, August 18, 2003, p. 12; "Road Shows Take Brands to the People," *The Wall Street Journal*, May 14, 2003, p. A10; "Offbeat Marketing Sells," *Investor's Business Daily*, March 27, 2002, p. A4; "Events & Promotions," *Advertising Age*, March 17, 1997, p. S1; "Special Report: Promotional Marketing," *Advertising Age*, March 21, 1994, p. S1. See also D. C. Gilbert and N. Jackaria, "The Efficacy of Sales Promotions in UK Supermarkets: A Consumer View," *International Journal of Retail & Distribution Management*, (6) 2002, p. 315; Pierre Chandon, Brian Wansink, and Gilles Laurent, "A Benefit Congruency Framework of Sales Promotion Effectiveness," *Journal of Marketing*, October 2000, p. 65; Andrew G. Parsons, "Assessing the Effectiveness of Shopping Mall Promotions: Customer Analysis," *International Journal of Retail & Distribution Management*, (2) 2003, p. 74; Nancy Spears, "Time Pressure and Information in Sales Promotion Strategy: Conceptual Framework and Content Analysis," *Journal of Advertising*, Spring 2001, p. 67; K. Sivakumar, "Tradeoff Between Frequency and Depth of Price Promotions: Implications for High- and Low-Priced Brands," *Journal of Marketing Theory & Practice*, Winter 1996, p. 1.

31. "Too Many Choices," *The Wall Street Journal*, April 20, 2001, p. B1; "Reposition: Simplifying the Customer's Brandscape," *Brandweek*, October

2, 2000, p. 36; "Make It Simple," *Business Week*, September 9, 1996, p. 96; "Pay for Performance Picking Up Speed," *Advertising Age*, August 9, 1993, p. 19. See also Page Moreau, Aradhna Krishna and Bari Harlam, "The Manufacturer-Retailer-Consumer Triad: Differing Perceptions Regarding Price Promotions," *Journal of Retailing*, Winter 2001, p. 547; Donald R. Lichtenstein, Scot Burton, and Richard G. Netemeyer, "An Examination of Deal Proneness Across Sales Promotion Types: A Consumer Segmentation Perspective," *Journal of Retailing*, Summer 1997, p. 283; Donald R. Glover, "Distributor Attitudes Toward Manufacturer-Sponsored Promotions," *Industrial Marketing Management* 20, no. 3 (1991), p. 241.

32. For more on Pampers example, see "P&G Promotion Is Too Successful, Angering Buyers," *The Wall Street Journal*, April 2, 2002, p. B1. For another example, see "Shopper Turns Lots of Pudding into Free Miles," *The Wall Street Journal*, January 24, 2000, p. B1; "The Pudding Guy Flies Again (and Again) Over Latin America," *The Wall Street Journal*, March 16, 2000, p. B1.

33. George E. Belch and Michael E. Belch, *Advertising and Promotion, an Integrated Marketing Communication Perspective* (Burr Ridge, IL: McGraw-Hill, 2004).

34. "Designated Shopper," *Brandweek*, February 4, 2002, p. 34; "Cyber-coupons," *Discount Store News*, March 9, 1998, p. 18; "The Scoop on Coupons," *Brandweek*, March 17, 1997, p. 34; "Many Companies Are Starting to Wean Shoppers Off Coupons," *The Wall Street Journal*, January 22, 1997, p. B1; "Internet Coupons offer H.O.T! Deals," *USA Today*, December 13, 1996, p. 17D; "First, Green Stamps. Now, Coupons?" *Business Week*, April 22, 1996, p. 68; "P&G Ad Chief Plots Demise of the Coupon," *The Wall Street Journal*, April 17, 1996, p. B1; Judy F. Graham, "Increasing Repurchase Rates: A Reappraisal of Coupon Effects," *Psychology & Marketing*, November/December 1994, p. 533; A. Krishna and R.W. Shoemaker, "Estimating the Effects of Higher Coupon Face Values on the Timing of Redemptions, the Mix of Coupon Redeemers, and Purchase Quality," *Psychology & Marketing*, November/December 1992, p. 453; Venkatram Ramaswamy and Srini S. Srinivasan, "Coupon Characteristics and Redemption Intentions: A Segment Level Analysis," *Psychology & Marketing*, January 1998, p. 59.

35. "The Show Goes On: Online Trade Shows," *The Wall Street Journal Reports*, April 28, 2003, p. R4; "The Cyber-Show Must Go On," *Trade Media*, May 7, 2001, p. SR3; "Getting the Most from a Trade-Show Booth," *Investor's Business Daily*, April 25, 2000, p. 1. See also Marnik G. Dekimpe, Pierre Francois, Srinath Gopalakrishna, Gary L. Lilien, and Christophe Van den Bulte, "Generalizing About Trade Show Effectiveness: A Cross-National Comparison," *Journal of Marketing*, October 1997, p. 55; Scott Barlass, "How to Get the Most Out of Trade Shows," *Journal of Product Innovation Management*, September 1997, p. 423; Srinath Gopalakrishna, Gary L. Lilien, Jerome D. Williams, and Ian K. Sequeira, "Do Trade Shows Pay Off?" *Journal of Marketing*, July 1995, p. 75; "Trade Promotion Rises," *Advertising Age*, April 3, 2000, p. 24; "Getting Tough on Trade," *Adweek*, April 13, 1992, p. 20; "A Shift in Direction?" *Adweek's Marketing Week*, April 13, 1992, p. 26; Sunil Gupta, "Impact of Sales Promotions on When, What, and How Much to Buy," *Journal of Marketing Research*, November 1988, p. 342.

37. "Creating Incentives Down in Ranks: Marriott Ties Pay to Guest Replies," *Investor's Business Daily*, July 6, 2001, p. A1; "Get Great Results from Salespeople by Finding What Really Moves Them," *Investor's Business Daily*, July 2, 2001, p. A1.

CHAPTER 17

1. "If the Pros Use a Tool or a Toothbrush, It Will Sell," *USA Today*, December 17, 2003, p. 1A; "Power Brushes a Hit at Every Level," *Advertising Age*, May 26, 2003, p. 10; "Less Power to You," *Newsweek*, January 27, 2003, p. 73; "Toothbrush Wars: Group's Findings Spark Another Battle," *The Wall Street Journal*, January 14, 2003, p. D4; "Do You Really Need a Turbo Toothbrush?" *The Wall Street Journal*, October 1, 2002, p. D1; "New SpinBrush Line Backed by $30 Mil," *Advertising Age*, September 9, 2002, p. 3; "Why P&G's Smile Is So Bright," *Business Week*, August 12, 2002, p. 58; "SpinBrush Cost P&G a Hefty $475 Million," *Advertising Age*, May 13, 2002, p. 4; "Colgate Adds Motion to Brush Market," *Marketing Magazine*, April 8, 2002, p. 2; "All About Gadgets and Gizmosity," *Fortune*, February 19, 2002, p. 264; "Think Small: Procter & Gamble Takes a New Approach to Tackling the Competition," *Advertising Age*, January 21, 2002, p. 1; "D'Arcy Switches Sonicare Ads' Focus to Technology," *Adweek*, October 8, 2001, p. 4; "What's Hot: Powered-Up Toothbrushes," *DSN Retailing Today*, April 16, 2001, p. 35; "Retailers Are Brushing Up on the Latest Oral Care Advances," *DSN Retailing Today*, April 16, 2001, p. 35; "Gillette Lines Up Oral-B Ad Push," *Advertising Age*, December 4, 2000, p. 22; "Fashionable Mouths Bristle at the Ordinary," *USA Today*, May 10, 2000, p. 5D; "Colgate Challenges Gillette Dominance in Electric Brushes," *Advertising Age*, April 3, 2000, p. 10.

2. "Detroit's Latest Offer: Pay More, Get Less," *The Wall Street Journal*, July 24, 2002, p. D1; "Did You Overpay for Your Car? States Sue Dealers over Fees," *The Wall Street Journal*, June 20, 2002, p. D1; "Sticker Shock: Detroit's Hidden Price Hikes," *The Wall Street Journal*, April 10, 2002, p. D1; "Adding Options Helps Car Firms Increase Prices," *The Wall Street Journal*, December 27, 1993, p. 9; "Car Makers Seek to Mask Price Increases," *The Wall Street Journal*, August 16, 1989, p. B1.

3. Alfred Rappaport, "Executive Incentives versus Corporate Growth," *Harvard Business Review*, July–August 1978, p. 81; David M. Szymanski, Sundar G. Bharadwaj, and P. Rajan Varadarajan, "An Analysis of the Market Share-Profitability Relationship," *Journal of Marketing*, July 1993, p. 1.

4. "EU Court Backs Resale of Drugs," *The Wall Street Journal*, April 2, 2004, p. B3; "The Telecom Follies," *The Wall Street Journal*, March 26, 2004, p. A8; "It's Time to Look at Rx Pricing," *Modern Healthcare*, March 15, 2004, p. 18; "The New Drug War," *Fortune*, March 8, 2004, p. 144; "Rethinking Restructuring," *Public Utilities Fortnightly*, February 2004, p. 12; "The Economy: Steel Prices Jump, Spurring Protests from Customers," *The Wall Street Journal*, January 23, 2004, p. A2.

5. "Tiny Storage Makes Big Impact," *Investor's Business Daily*, October 4, 2001, p. A6.

6. For more on the dot-com bust, see "Applying Old Pricing Lessons to a New Investing World," *The Wall Street Journal*, May 21, 2001, p. C1; Stephen E. Frank, *Net Worth* (2001); "E-Assets for Sale," *Business Week E.Biz*, May 14, 2001, p. EB20; "Last Guys Finish First," *Ecompany*, May 2001, p. 93; "After the Wild Ride," *Business Week E.Biz*, April 16, 2001, p. EB29; "Study: Net Start-Ups Ignored Economics 101," *Investor's Business Daily*, March 2, 2001, p. A8; "12 Months When the Dot Turned into a Dark Period," *Investor's Business Daily*, January 2, 2001, p. A6; "We're Heading into Something Big—but What?" *USA Today*, December 29, 2000, p. 1B; "What Detonated Dot-Bombs?" *USA Today*, December 4, 2000, p. 1B; "Dot-Bombs," *Brandweek*, November 27, 2000, p. IQ16.

7. For more on Taurus, see "How Detroit Is Ruining Your Car's Value," *The Wall Street Journal*, October 8, 2002, p. D1. For more on GM's recent attempts to add market share, see "GM Revs Incentives: $3,000 or 0% on 5-year Loans," *USA Today*, April 1, 2003, p. 1B.; "Rick Wagoner's Game Plan," *Business Week*, February 10, 2003, p. 52; "Record Sales Incentives Drive GM's Market Share," *USA Today*, January 17, 2003, p. 1B; "GM Raises Market Share and Increases Sales by 36%," *The New York Times*, January 4, 2003, p. B1; "For GM, Sweet Deals Are Smarter than They Look," *Business Week*, August 26, 2002, p. 44; "Job Accelerator: GM's 0% Finance Plan Is Good for Economy, Risky for the Company," *The Wall Street Journal*, October 30, 2001, p. A1. See also Robert Jacobson and David A. Aaker, "Is Market Share All That It's Cracked Up to Be?" *Journal of Marketing*, Fall 1985, p. 11; Carolyn Y. Woo, "Market-Share Leadership—Not Always So Good," *Harvard Business Review*,

January–February 1984, p. 50; "Reichhold Chemicals: Now the Emphasis Is on Profits Rather than Volume," *Business Week*, June 20, 1983, p. 178.

8. "E-Tailing Comes of Age," *The Wall Street Journal*, December 8, 2003, p. B1; "Deck the Halls with High Speed Access," *Business Week*, December 8, 2003, p. 54; "What Are Price Wars Good For? Absolutely Nothing," *Fortune*, May 12, 1997, p. 156; "Price Wars," *Adweek's Marketing Week*, June 8, 1992, p. 18; "A Remarkable Gamble in an Industry Slump Pays Off Fast for Agco," *The Wall Street Journal*, August 19, 1997, p. A1; "Why the Price Wars Never End," *Fortune*, March 23, 1992, p. 68.

9. "Aluminum Firms Offer Wider Discounts but Price Cuts Stop at Some Distributors," *The Wall Street Journal*, November 16, 1984, p. 50.

10. Kissan Joseph, "On the Optimality of Delegating Pricing Authority to the Sales Force," *Journal of Marketing*, January 2001, p. 62; Michael V. Marn and Robert L. Rosiello, "Managing Price, Gaining Profit," *Harvard Business Review*, September–October 1992, p. 84; Subhash C. Jain and Michael B. Laric, "A Framework for Strategic Industrial Pricing," *Industrial Marketing Management* 8 (1979), p. 75; Peter R. Dickson and Joel E. Urbany, "Retailer Reactions to Competitive Price Changes," *Journal of Retailing*, Spring 1994, p. 1; Mary Karr, "The Case of the Pricing Predicament," *Harvard Business Review*, March–April, 1988, p. 10; Saeed Samiee, "Pricing in Marketing Strategies of U.S. and Foreign-Based Companies," *Journal of Business Research*, February 1987, p. 17; Gerard J. Tellis, "Beyond the Many Faces of Price: An Integration of Pricing Strategies," *Journal of Marketing*, October 1986, p. 146.

11. For more on Priceline, see "A Humbler, Happier Priceline," *Business Week*, August 11, 2003, p. 34; "Inside Jay Walker's House of Cards," *Fortune*, November 13, 2000, p. 127; "Letting the Masses Name Their Price," *Business Week E.Biz*, September 18, 2000, p. EB44; "Name Your Price—for Everything?" *Business Week*, April 17, 2000, p. 72. See also "The Discount Cards that Don't Save You Money," *The Wall Street Journal*, January 21, 2003, p. D1; "Beating Retailers at the Discount Game," *The Wall Street Journal*, November 27, 2002, p. D1; "Lessons from a Grocer," *Investor's Business Daily*, April 3, 2002, p. A4; "Ways to Boost Sales Right Now: Price Wisely, Do What You Know," *Investor's Business Daily*, October 15, 2001, p. A1. For more on other online travel sites, see "Scoring a Travel Discount Gets Easier," *The Wall Street Journal*, November 4, 2003, p. D1; "The Travel Agent Bosses Love," *Business Week*, October 27, 2003, p. 134; "Convention Hotels Hurt by Web Bookings," *Investor's Business Daily*, August 21, 2003, p. A4; "When Hotel Discounts Are No Bargain," *The Wall Street Journal*, August 6, 2003, p. D1; "Expedia: Changing Pilots in Mid-Climb," *Business Week*, February 24, 2003, p. 120; "How to Get a Four-Star Hotel at Two-Star Prices," *The Wall Street Journal*, January 30, 2003, p. D1.

12. For more on EBay and its flexible pricing, see Chapter 13, endnote 18. See also "Will Auction Frenzy Cool?" *Business Week E. Biz*, September 18, 2000, p. EB140; "Going, Going, Gone," *Business Week*, April 12, 1999, p. 30; "Good-Bye to Fixed Pricing," *Business Week*, May 4, 1998, p. 71; "One-Price Deals Save Time, Hassles, but Not Money," *USA Today*, March 11, 1998, p.1B. See also Eric Matson, "Customizing Prices," *Harvard Business Review*, November–December 1995, p. 13; Sanjay K. Dhar and Stephen J. Hoch, "Price Discrimination Using in-Store Merchandising," *Journal of Marketing*, January 1996, p. 17; Michael H. Morris, "Separate Prices as a Marketing Tool," *Industrial Marketing Management*, May 1987, p. 79; P. Ronald Stephenson, William L. Cron, and Gary L. Frazier, "Delegating Pricing Authority to the Sales Force: The Effects on Sales and Profit Performance," *Journal of Marketing*, Spring 1979, p. 21.

13. For more on Amazon offering different prices to different customers, see "Price? For You, $2; For the Rich Guy, $5," *Investor's Business Daily*, September 29, 2000, p. A8. For more on Winn-Dixie example, see "Squeezin' the Charmin," *Fortune*, January 16, 1989, p. 11; "Grocers Join Winn-Dixie," *Advertising Age*, November 7, 1988, p. 3; "Grocery Chains

Pressure Suppliers for Uniform Prices," *The Wall Street Journal*, October 21, 1988, p. B1. For more on car haggling, see "CarMax: Psst, Wanna Buy a Used Car, Hassle-Free?" *Investor's Business Daily*, January 30, 2002, p. A9; "Haggling in Cyberspace Transforms Car Sales," *The Wall Street Journal*, December 30, 1997, p. B1; "Car Hagglers May Still Drive Best Car Deals," *The Wall Street Journal*, October 12, 1994, p. B1. See also "Pay-as-You-Go M.D.: The Doctor Is In, but Insurance Is Out," *The Wall Street Journal*, November 6, 2003, p. A1; "Medical Care: Can We Talk Price?" *The Wall Street Journal*, February 8, 2002, p. W1.

14. "What's a Fair Price for Drugs?" *Business Week*, April 30, 2001, p. 105; "AIDS Gaffes in Africa Come Back to Haunt Drug Industry at Home," *The Wall Street Journal*, April 23, 2001, p. A1; "Vaccine's Price Drives a Debate about Its Use," *The Wall Street Journal*, February 16, 2000, p. B1; "Breakthrough in Birth Control May Elude Poor," *The Wall Street Journal*, March 4, 1991, p. B1; "Burroughs Wellcome Reaps Profits, Outrage from Its AIDS Drug," *The Wall Street Journal*, September 15, 1989, p. A1; Richard A. Spinello, "Ethics, Pricing and the Pharmaceutical Industry," *Journal of Business Ethics*, August 1992, p. 617.

15. "In a Sleek Flat Set, Plasma's Price Plunges," *The New York Times*, January 8, 2004, p. E3; "For Digital TVs, the Future Is Now," *USA Today*, December 3, 2003, p. 10D; "The Skinny on Flat Screens," *The Wall Street Journal*, November 26, 2003, p. D1; "Rise of Flat-Screen TVs Reshapes Industry," *The Wall Street Journal*, November 20, 2003, p. B8; "I Want My Big TV . . . ," *The Wall Street Journal*, November 13, 2003, p. B1; "Consumer Spending Gives Tech Extra Push," *USA Today*, September 8, 2003, p. 1B; "Maker of Flat Screens Rounds Out Its Lines," *Investor's Business Daily*, August 6, 2003, p. A8; "Mirror, Mirror, on the Wall, Which Big-Screen TV Is Fairest of All?" *Fortune*, July 7, 2003, p. 145; "Prices of Flat-Panel Monitors, TVs to Drop," *The Wall Street Journal*, April 3, 2003, p. B4; "Flat Screens: Looking Good," *The Wall Street Journal*, March 31, 2003, p. R9; "Hit Show of the Season: The Revival of Digital TV," *The Wall Street Journal*, August 1, 2002, p. D1; "It's the Screens, Not the Sales, That Are Flat for Digital TVs," *Investor's Business Daily*, September 27, 2002, p. A6.

16. Available from World Wide Web: <http://www.palm.com>; "Stiff Competition, New Technology Mean Great Gadget Deals," *USA Today*, November 10, 2003, p. 3B; "Palm Reaches Out for a Hand," *Business Week*, November 3, 2003, p. 74; "Palm Hopes Breaking in Two Will Juice Its Sluggish Sales," *The Wall Street Journal*, October 28, 2003, p. B1; "Hand-Helds' New Frontier," *The Wall Street Journal*, August 8, 2003, p. B1; "Fewer Buyers Giving the Big Thumbs-Up to Handheld PC Gear," *Investor's Business Daily*, November 27, 2002, p. A5; "New Palms Offer Something for Every Pocketbook," *USA Today*, November 13, 2002, p. 5D.; "An Address Book that Shoots Movies," *The Wall Street Journal*, October 2, 2002, p. D1; "Palm, Seeking Business Clients, Targets Corporate Executives," *The Wall Street Journal*, May 13, 2002, p. B6; "Start-Up Joins Hand-Held-Device Battle," *The Wall Street Journal*, May 9, 2002, p. B5; "Price Wars Hit PDAs: Is It Time to Buy One Yet?" *The Wall Street Journal*, May 9, 2002, p. D1; "Pilot Error: How Palm Tumbled from Star of Tech to Target of Microsoft," *The Wall Street Journal*, September 7, 2001, p. A1; "Palm Slips to No. 2 in Revenue as iPaq Grabs the Top Spot," *Investor's Business Daily*, June 19, 2001, p. A6; "Palm Shares Sink as One-Time Star Says Sales Fading," *Investor's Business Daily*, May 21, 2001, p. A6; "HandEra's Hand-Held Puts Some New Twists on the Usual Formula," *The Wall Street Journal*, May 10, 2001, p. B1; "Hand-Helds that Are Less of a Handful," *Business Week*, April 9, 2001, p. 18; "PDA Wars: Round 2," *Time*, April 2, 2001, p. 40; "New Devices Shrink Difference in Price for Palm, Pocket PC," *Investor's Business Daily*, March 21, 2001, p. A6; "Seeding Demand for Handspring," *Advertising Age*, November 6, 2000, p. S36; "Palm Hopes to Blaze a New Image in Major Campaign," *The Wall Street Journal*, November 1, 2000, p. B10; "Hard Cell," *Fortune*, October 30, 2000, p. 305; "If at First You Don't Succeed . . . ," *Business Week*, April 24, 2000, p. 120; "3Com Tries to Solve Its Palm Problem," *Fortune*, October 11, 1999, p. 167; "Palm Has the Whole World in Its Hand," *USA Today*, September 14, 1999, p. 1B; "The Palm Pilot Sequel Is a Hit," *Fortune*, April 13, 1998, p. 154; "3Com Again Changes Name of Hot-Selling PalmPilot," *Advertising Age*, March 9, 1998, p. 4; "Apple Drops Newton, an Idea Ahead of Its Time," *The Wall Street Journal*, March 2, 1998, p. B1; "Little Computers, Big New Marketing Battle," *The Wall Street Journal*, November 17, 1997, p. B1; "How Palm Computing Became an Architect," *Harvard Business Review*, September–October 1997, p. 89. "A Rocket in Its Pocket," *Business Week*, September 9, 1996, p. 111.

17. Check out foreign exchange rates on the World Wide Web: <http://www.imf.org> and <http://www.federal reserve.gov> and <http://www.x-rates.com>; "Trade Winds," *Inc.*, November 2003, p. 36; "Same Cars Can Cost Oodles Less in Canada," *USA Today*, May 6, 2003, p. 1B; "Ship Those Boxes; Check the Euro!" *The Wall Street Journal*, February 7, 2003, p. C1; "Revealing Price Disparities, the Euro Aids Bargain-Hunters," *The Wall Street Journal*, January 30, 2002, p. A15; "One Dollar Is Worth One Dollar, but That Wasn't Always So," *The Wall Street Journal*, January 13, 1998, p. A1. See also Priya Raghubir and Joydeep Srivastava, "Effect of Face Value on Product Valuation in Foreign Currencies," *Journal of Consumer Research*, December 2002, p. 335; Matthew B. Myers and Michael Harvey, "The Value of Pricing Control in Export Channels: a Governance Perspective," *Journal of International Marketing*, (4) 2001, p. 1; Timothy A. Luehrman, "Exchange Rate Changes and the Distribution of Industry Value," *Journal of International Business Studies*, Winter 1991, p. 619; James K. Weekly, "Pricing in Foreign Markets: Pitfalls and Opportunities," *Industrial Marketing Management*, May 1992, p. 173.

18. "Netflix Expects Fast Subscriber, Earnings Gain," *Investor's Business Daily*, January 5, 2004, p. A7; "DVD-Rental Firm May be Victim of Its Success," *The Wall Street Journal*, November 20, 2003, p. C1; "Cable Fights for Its Movie Rights," *Business Week*, October 27, 2003, p. 88; "Blockbuster's Poor Sales Results Cast Shadow over a Rise in Net," *The Wall Street Journal*, October 22, 2003, p. B3; "For Netflix, It's So Far, So Good," *USA Today*, October 15, 2003, p. 3B; "No Late Fees: Disney to 'Beam' Rental Movies to Homes," *The Wall Street Journal*, September 29, 2003, p. B1; "The Next DTC: DVD Explodes," *Advertising Age*, September 1, 2003, p. 1; "90,000 DVDs. No Shelves," *Fast Company*, September 2003, p. 38; "The Transition from Rental to Retail Bodes Well for Blockbuster Sales," *DSN Retailing Today*, July 21, 2003, p. 4; "Netflix Bets on DVD Rental Market," *The Wall Street Journal*, April 30, 2003, p. B6B; "Can Netflix Keep Spinning Gold?" *Business Week*, April 21, 2003, p. 112; "Online DVD Rental Service Netflix Eyes Starring Role with Consumers," *Investor's Business Daily*, March 18, 2003, p. A4; "Future Looks Less than Stellar for Video Rental Firms," *USA Today*, January 23, 2003, p. 6B; "DVD Is Killing the Video Star," *Fortune*, January 20, 2003, p. 181; "DVD Sales Surge Puts Crimp in Blockbuster's Profit," *USA Today*, December 19, 2002, p. 4B; "Getting the Video-Store Guy Out of Your Life," *The Wall Street Journal*, October 24, 2002, p. D1; "DVDs Conquer the Movie World," *USA Today*, October 18, 2002, p. 1E; "Blockbuster Borrows from Netflix's Playbook, but Stays Offline," *Investor's Business Daily*, August 12, 2002, p. A4; "Blockbuster Bolsters Games Section," *DSN Retailing Today*, June 10, 2002, p. 8; "DVD Take Wind Out of Sails for Video on Demand," *USA Today*, May 7, 2002, p. 3B; "The Meteoric Rise of the DVD," *Business 2.0*, May 2002, p. 34; "At $70 a Pop, Consumers Put Discount DVD Players on Holiday List," *The Wall Street Journal*, December 13, 2001, p. B1.

19. "Fliers' Dilemma: Save Now or Later?" *Business Week*, October 13, 2003, p. 138; "Pizza Hut Adds Videos, Loyalty Cards to Recipe," *Brandweek*, September 29, 2003, p. 9; "Plastic's New Pitch: Something for Nothing," *The Wall Street Journal*, July 31 2003, p. D1; "Frequent Flier to Rental Driver Has Its Price," *The New York Times*, January 14, 2003, p. C4; "The Holy Grail: Getting Miles for Your Mortgage," *The Wall Street Journal*, December 5, 2002, p. D1; "Road Warriors' Secret: Hotel Points Trump Miles," *The Wall Street Journal*, November 14, 2002, p. D1; "Discounts Follow Dip in Business Travel," *USA Today*, June 21, 2001, p. 1B;

"Sailing on Sale: Travelers Ride a Wave of Discounts on Cruise Ships," *The Wall Street Journal*, July 17, 2000, p. B1; "Competing Online, Drugstore Chains Virtually Undersell Themselves," *The Wall Street Journal*, January 10, 2000, p. B1; "Prescription: Cash Only, Some Doctors Offer Discounts," *USA Today*, December 22, 1999, p. 1B; "Owens Corning: Back from the Dead," *Fortune*, May 26, 1997, p. 118. See also Andy A. Tsay, "Managing Retail Channel Overstock: Markdown Money and Return Policies," *Journal of Retailing*, Winter 2001, p. 457; David E. Sprott, Kenneth C. Manning and Anthony D. Miyazaki, "Grocery Price Setting and Quantity Surcharges," *Journal of Marketing*, July 2003, p. 34; Douglas D. Davis and Charles A. Holt, "List Prices and Discounts: The Interrelationship Between Consumer Shopping Patterns and Profitable Marketing Strategies," *Psychology & Marketing*, July 1996, p. 341; David W. Arnesen, C. P. Fleenor, and Rex S. Toh, "The Ethical Dimensions of Airline Frequent Flier Programs," *Business Horizons*, January–February 1997, p. 47; K.J. Blois, "Discounts in Business Marketing Management," *Industrial Marketing Management*, April 1994, p. 93; James B. Wilcox et al., "Price Quantity Discounts: Some Implications for Buyers and Sellers," *Journal of Marketing*, July 1987, p. 60; Mark T. Spriggs and John R. Nevin, "The Legal Status of Trade and Functional Price Discounts," *Journal of Public Policy & Marketing*, Spring 1994, p. 61; "Cash Discounts," *Electrical Wholesaling*, May 1989, p. 90.

20. For more on P&G's everyday low pricing, see "P&G, Others Try New Uses for Coupon-Heavy Media," *Advertising Age*, September 22, 1997, p. 20; "Move to Drop Coupons Puts Procter & Gamble in Sticky PR Situation," *The Wall Street Journal*, April 17, 1997, p. A1; "Zeroing In on Zero Coupons," *Brandweek*, June 3, 1996, p. 30; "Company Makes Big Cuts to Stay Fit," *USA Today*, July 16, 1993, p. 1B; "P&G Plays Pied Piper on Pricing," *Advertising Age*, March 9, 1992, p. 6. See also Kusum L. Ailawadi, Donald R. Lehmann, and Scott A. Neslin, "Market Response to a Major Policy Change in the Marketing Mix: Learning from Procter & Gamble's Value Pricing Strategy," *Journal of Marketing*, January 2001, p. 44; Monika Kukar-Kinney and Rockney G. Walters, "Consumer Perceptions of Refund Depth and Competitive Scope in Price-Matching Guarantees: Effects on Store Patronage," *Journal of Retailing*, Fall 2003, p. 153; Stephen J. Hoch, Xavier Dreze, and Mary E. Purk, "EDLP, Hi-Lo, and Margin Arithmetic," *Journal of Marketing*, October 1994, p. 16; George S. Bobinski, Dena Cox, and Anthony Cox, "Retail 'Sale' Advertising, Perceived Retailer Credibility, and Price Rationale," *Journal of Retailing*, Fall 1996, p. 291; Francis J. Mulhern and Daniel T. Padgett, "The Relationship Between Retail Price Promotions and Regular Price Purchases," *Journal of Marketing*, October 1995, p. 83.

21. For more on slotting fees, see "Kraft Speeds New Product Launch Times," *Advertising Age*, November 18, 2002, p. 1; "The Hidden Cost of Shelf Space," *Business Week*, April 15, 2002, p. 103. See also Ramarao Desiraju, "New Product Introductions, Slotting Allowances, and Retailer Discretion," *Journal of Retailing*, Fall 2001, p. 335; David Balto, "Recent Legal and Regulatory Developments in Slotting Allowances and Category Management," *Journal of Public Policy & Marketing*, Fall 2002, p. 289; William L. Wilkie, Debra M. Desrochers and Gregory T. Gundlach, "Marketing Research and Public Policy: the Case of Slotting Fees," *Journal of Public Policy & Marketing*, Fall 2002, p. 275; Paul N. Bloom, Gregory T. Gundlach and Joseph P. Cannon, "Slotting Allowances and Fees: Schools of Thought and the Views of Practicing Managers," *Journal of Marketing*, April 2000, p. 92; J. Chris White, Lisa C. Troy and R. Nicholas Gerlich, "The Role of Slotting Fees and Introductory Allowances in Retail Buyers' New-Product Acceptance Decisions," *Journal of the Academy of Marketing Science*, Spring 2000, p. 291; Paul N. Bloom, "Slotting Allowances and Fees: Schools of Thought and the Views of Practicing Managers," *Journal of Marketing*, April 2000, p. 92.

22. For more on coupons, see "The Latest Craze in Coupon-Clipping: Free Trial Offers for Prescription Drugs," *The Wall Street Journal*, April 16, 2002, p. D1; "Penny-Pinchers' Paradise," *Business Week E-Biz*, January 22, 2001, p. EB12; "E-Tailers Missing the Mark with Flood of Web

Coupons," *Advertising Age*, September 25, 2000, p. 104; Gail Ayala Taylor, "Coupon Response in Services," *Journal of Retailing*, Spring 2001, p. 139. For more on rebates, see "Let's Make a (Tough) Deal," *Newsweek*, June 23, 2003, p. 48; "Ford Tames the Rebate Monster," *Business Week*, May 5, 2003, p. 38; "Rejected! Rebates Get Harder to Collect," *The Wall Street Journal*, June 11, 2002, p. D1; "Free-with-Rebate Costs Web Buyers Some Big Bucks," *The Wall Street Journal*, May 18, 2001, p. B1. See also William D. Diamond, "Just What Is a 'Dollar's Worth'? Consumer Reactions to Price Discounts vs. Extra Product Promotions," *Journal of Retailing*, Fall 1992, p. 254; Kenneth A. Hunt and Susan M. Keaveney, "A Process Model of the Effects of Price Promotions on Brand Image," *Psychology & Marketing*, November/December 1994, p. 511; "Rebates' Secret Appeal to Manufacturers: Few Consumers Actually Redeem Them," *The Wall Street Journal*, February 10, 1998, p. B1; Peter K. Tat, "Rebate Usage: A Motivational Perspective," *Psychology & Marketing*, January/February 1994, p. 15.

23. "America's Pricing Paradox," *The Wall Street Journal*, May 16, 2003, p. B1; "Ideas + Innovations: How to Thrive When Prices Fall," *Fortune*, May 12, 2003, p. 130; "Why Some Companies Can Levy Premium Prices and Others Not," *Investor's Business Daily*, April 15, 2003, p. A1; "Survival Strategies: After Cost Cutting, Companies Turn toward Price Rises," *The Wall Street Journal*, September 18, 2002, p. A1; "Stepping Up: Middle Market Shrinks as Americans Migrate toward the High End," *The Wall Street Journal*, March 29, 2002, p. A1; "Two-Tier Marketing," *Business Week*, March 17, 1997, p. 82; "Makeup Ads Downplay Glamour for Value," *The Wall Street Journal*, June 20, 1994, p. B5; "Value Pricing Kicks off Model Year," *USA Today*, October 1, 1993, p. 1B; "Value Pricing Comes to Funerals," *USA Today*, July 14, 1993, p. 5B; "Tide, Cheer Join P&G 'Value Pricing' Plan," *Advertising Age*, February 15, 1993, p. 3; "More Stores Switch from Sales to 'Everyday Low Prices,'" *The Wall Street Journal*, November 12, 1992, p. B1; "Value Marketing," *Business Week*, November 11, 1991, p. 132; Louis J. De Rose, "Meet Today's Buying Influences with Value Selling," *Industrial Marketing Management* 20, no. 2 (1991), p. 87.

24. "Freeze-Dried Berries Heat Up Cereal Duel," *The Wall Street Journal*, May 15, 2003, p. B2; "Garfield's AdReview: A Few Spoons of Truth Tossed into Special K Red Berries Spot," *Advertising Age*, May 12, 2003, p. 65.

25. For an excellent discussion of laws related to pricing, see Louis W. Stern and Thomas L. Eovaldi, *Legal Aspects of Marketing Strategy: Antitrust and Consumer Protection Issues* (Englewood Cliffs, NJ: Prentice-Hall, 1984); Joseph P. Guiltinan and Gregory T. Gundlach, "Aggressive and Predatory Pricing: A Framework for Analysis," *Journal of Marketing*, July 1996, p. 87.

26. For more on steel tariff, see "Administration Weighs New Protection for Steel," *The New York Times*, December 12, 2003, p. C7; "The Genie Is Out of the Bottle," *The Wall Street Journal*, December 8, 2003, p. A14; "US-China Trade Tensions Rise," *Christian Science Monitor*, December 2, 2003, p. 1; "The Steel Tariff's Costs," *The Wall Street Journal*, February 25, 2003, p. A14; "Steel's Tariff Addiction," *The Wall Street Journal*, August 20, 2002, p. A18; "Calming the Steel Spat," *The Washington Post*, May 1, 2002, p. A24; "U.S. Steel Posts 1st Quarter Loss but Expects Profit for Full Year," *The Wall Street Journal*, April 29, 2002, p. A2. For more on dumping, see "Anti-Dumping Ruling May Buy More Time; A Preliminary Decision Lends Credence to the Furniture Industry's Claim . . . ," *Greensboro News Record*, January 13, 2004, p. A6; "Plastic Bag Fight Pits U.S. Makers v. U.S. Importers," *The Wall Street Journal*, October 9, 2003, p. B1; "Fair Tradeoff: Host of Companies Pocket Windfalls from Tariff Law," *The Wall Street Journal*, December 5, 2002, p. A1; "Will Kodak Get Lucky in China?" *Business Week*, July 28, 1997, p. 48.

27. Patrick J. Kaufmann, N. Craig Smith, and Gwendolyn K. Ortmeyer, "Deception in Retailer High-Low Pricing: A 'Rule of Reason' Approach," *Journal of Retailing*, Summer 1994, p. 115.

28. For more on airline pricing, see "Is American-United Rivalry Too Friendly?" *USA Today*, June 27, 2001, p. 1B; "Predatory Pricing: Cleared for Takeoff," *Business Week*, May 14, 2001, p. 50; "American Airlines Secures Antitrust Win," *The Wall Street Journal*, April 30, 2001, p. A3; "Caveat Predator?" *Business Week*, May 22, 2000, p. 116. For more on credit card pricing, see "House of Cards?" *Time*, October 23, 2000, pp. B10–B11; "Breaking Up the Old Card Game," *Business Week*, June 12, 2000, p. 98; "Antitrust Suit Targeting MasterCard and Visa Puts the Pair at Odds," *The Wall Street Journal*, June 12, 2000, p. B1. For more on CD pricing, see "Prices of CDs Likely to Drop, Thanks to FTC," *The Wall Street Journal*, May 11, 2000, p. B1. See also "Online Booksellers Abound in Japan, But Legal Price Fixing Poses Challenge," *The Wall Street Journal*, July 31, 2000, p. B8; "P&G Calls the Cops as It Strives to Expand Sales in Latin America," *The Wall Street Journal*, March 20, 1998, p. A1; "Independent Bookstores Are Suing Borders Group and Barnes & Noble," *The Wall Street Journal*, March 19, 1998, p. B10; "Cargill Agrees to Pay $24 Million to Settle Price-Fixing Suit," *The Wall Street Journal*, March 11, 2004, p. 8; "The ADM Scandal: Betrayal," *Fortune*, February 3, 1997, p. 82. See also Alexander James Nicholls, "Strategic Options in Fair Trade Retailing," *International Journal of Retail & Distribution Management*, (1) 2002, p. 6; Larry L. Miller, Steven P. Schnaars, and Valerie L. Vaccaro, "The Provocative Practice of Price Signaling: Collusion Versus Cooperation," *Business Horizons*, July–August 1993, p. 59; Mary Jane Sheffet, "The Supreme Court and Predatory Pricing," *Journal of Public Policy & Marketing*, Spring 1994, p. 163; Michael L. Ursic and James G. Helgeson, "Using Price as a Weapon: An Economic and Legal Analysis of Predatory Pricing," *Industrial Marketing Management*, April 1994, p. 125; Robert L. Cutts, "Capitalism in Japan: Cartels and Keiretsu," *Harvard Business Review*, July–August 1992, p. 48; Daniel T. Ostas, "Ethics of Contract Pricing," *Journal of Business Ethics*, February 1992, p. 137; Mary Jane Sheffet and Debra L. Scammon, "Resale Price Maintenance: Is It Safe to Suggest Retail Prices?" *Journal of Marketing*, Fall 1985, p. 82.

29. Richard L. Pinkerton and Deborah J. Kemp, "The Industrial Buyer and the Robinson-Patman Act," *International Journal of Purchasing & Materials Management*, Winter 1996, p. 29.

30. "Firms Must Prove Injury from Price Bias to Qualify for Damages, High Court Says," *The Wall Street Journal*, May 19, 1981, p. 8.

31. "Booksellers Say Five Publishers Play Favorites," *The Wall Street Journal*, May 27, 1994, p. B1; Joseph P. Vaccaro and Derek W. F. Coward, "Managerial and Legal Implications of Price Haggling: A Sales Manager's Dilemma," *Journal of Personal Selling & Sales Management*, Summer 1993, p. 79; John R. Davidson, "FTC, Robinson-Patman and Cooperative Promotion Activities," *Journal of Marketing*, January 1968, p. 14; L. X. Tarpey, Sr., "Buyer Liability under the Robinson-Patman Act: A Current Appraisal," *Journal of Marketing*, January 1972, p. 38.

CHAPTER 18

1. For more on Wal-Mart in the U.S., see *2003 Annual Report*, Wal-Mart; "Wal-Mart Fires the First Shot in Holiday-Toy Pricing War," *The Wall Street Journal*, November 19, 2003, p. B1; "Retail Giant Wal-Mart Faces Challenges on Many Fronts," *USA Today*, November 11, 2003, p. 1B; "Running the Gauntlet at Wal-Mart," *Inc.*, November 2003, p. 92; "Wal-Mart Eating Away at Big Supermarkets' Already Wilting Sales," *Investor's Business Daily*, October 14, 2003, p. A1; "Wal-Mart Continues Unabated Expansion," *DSN Retailing Today*, October 13, 2003, p. 1; "Wal-Mart Gains on a Feast of Advantages," *Food Retailing*, October 13, 2003, p. 1; "Is Wal-Mart Too Powerful?" *Business Week*, October 6, 2003, p. 100; "Wal-Mart Report," *Advertising Age*, October 6, 2003, p. 1; "Minn. Small Town Just Says No to Starbucks Nation," *USA Today*, October 1, 2003, p. 4A; "Wal-Mart Uber Alles," *American Demographics*, October 2003, p. 38; "Wal-Mart Debuts a More Contemporary Design," *DSN Retailing Today*, July 21, 2003, p. 5; "Call It Mall-Wart," *Business Week*, July 14, 2003, p. 40; "Price War in Aisle 3," *The Wall Street Journal*, May 27, 2003, p. B1;

"One Nation under Wal-Mart," *Fortune*, March 3, 2003, p. 64; "Can Wal-Mart Get Any Bigger?" *Time*, January 13, 2003, p. 38; "The World's Largest Focus Group," *Business 2.0*, October 2002, p. 58; "Pinstripes and Motor Oil?" *The Wall Street Journal*, September 3, 2002, p. B1; "Like My Pants? Pssst, They're Wal-Mart," *The Wall Street Journal*, September 3, 2002, p. B1; "Wal-Mart Consolidates Home into Destination Department," *DSN Retailing Today*, August 26, 2002, p. 1; "Wal-Mart: Lengthening Its Lead," *DSN Retailing Today*, June 10, 2002, p. 83; "Wal-Mart's Move into Banking Sparks New Worry on Main Street," *Investor's Business Daily*, December 27, 2001, p. A1; "Kmart, Wal-Mart Face Off in Price-Cutting Fight," *USA Today*, June 8, 2001, p. 1B; "How Wal-Mart Transfers Power," *The Wall Street Journal*, March 27, 2001, p. B1; Sharon M. Davidson and Amy Rummel, "Retail Changes Associated with Wal-Mart's Entry into Maine," *International Journal of Retail & Distribution Management*, (4) 2000, p. 162; "Wal*Mart, Retailer of the Century," *Discount Store News* (Special Issue), October 1999; "Logistics Whiz Rises at Wal-Mart," *The Wall Street Journal*, March 11, 1999, p. B1. See also Norman W. Hawker, "Wal-Mart and the Divergence of State and Federal Predatory Pricing Law," *Journal of Public Policy & Marketing*, Spring 1996, p. 141. For more on Wal-Mart International, see "Pacific Aisles: Wal-Mart's Foray into Japan Spurs a Retail Upheaval," *The Wall Street Journal*, September 19, 2003, p. A1; "Wal-Mart Adds to Global Reach with Tokyo Supermarket Stake," *Investor's Business Daily*, March 15, 2002, p. A1; Angela da Rocha and Luis Antonio Dib, "The Entry of Wal-Mart in Brazil and the Competitive Responses of Multinational and Domestic Firms," *International Journal of Retail & Distribution Management*, (1) 2002, p. 61; John Fernie and Stephen J. Arnold, "Wal-Mart in Europe: Prospects for Germany, the UK and France," *International Journal of Retail & Distribution Management*, (2) 2002, p. 92; "How Well Does Wal-Mart Travel?" *Business Week*, September 3, 2001, p. 82; "Wal-Mart de Mexico to Grow Stores by 10%," *DSN Retailing Today*, March 19, 2001, p. 3; "Wal-Mart Fumes at Argentine Legislation," *The Wall Street Journal*, November 28, 2000, p. A23; "Stores Told to Lift Prices in Germany," *The Wall Street Journal*, September 11, 2000, p. A27; "The Wal-Mart Way Sometimes Gets Lost in Translation Overseas," *The Wall Street Journal*, October 8, 1997, p. A1.

2. Ritu Lohtia, Ramesh Subramaniam and Rati Lohtia, "Are Pricing Practices in Japanese Channels of Distribution Finally Changing?" *Journal of Marketing Channels*, (1,2) 2001, p. 5; Marvin A. Jolson, "A Diagrammatic Model for Merchandising Calculations," *Journal of Retailing*, Summer 1975, p. 3; C. Davis Fogg and Kent H. Kohnken, "Price-Cost Planning," *Journal of Marketing*, April 1978, p. 97.

3. "Look Who's Buzzing the Discounters," *Business Week*, November 24, 2003, p. 48; "Unlike Rivals, JetBlue Won't Do the Bump," *USA Today*, October 24, 2003, p. 1B; "Cheaper Flights, Better Service: JetBlue Flies against the Wind," *Investor's Business Daily*, October 15, 2003, p. A9; "Off We Go into the Wild (Jet)Blue Yonder," *Brandweek*, September 22, 2003, p. 36; "JetBlue Gains on Its Competition," *USA Today*, August 13, 2003, p. 3B; "Discount Airlines Go Shopping for Jetliners," *USA Today*, July 2, 2003, p. 1B; "Is This the Future of Air Travel?" *Time* (Inside Business Bonus Section), July 2003; "JetBlue's Focus on Customers Pushes Airline's Sales Skyward," *Investor's Business Daily*, June 20, 2003, p. A1; "Delta Hopes Fliers Think It's Playing Their Song," *USA Today*, April 14, 2003, p. 6B; "How to Shake Up a Calcified Industry," *Business 2.0*, December 2002, p. 92; "Special Report: Marketer of the Year, JetBlue," *Advertising Age*, December 9, 2002, pp. S1–S6; "Lofty Goals: JetBlue Is Taking Technology to New Heights," *The Wall Street Journal Reports*, December 9, 2002, p. R8; "JetBlue Soars on CEO's Creativity," *USA Today*, October 8, 2002, p. 1B; "Something Stylish, Something Blue," *Business 2.0*, February 2002, p. 94.

4. "The Little Extras That Count (Up)," *The Wall Street Journal*, July 12, 2001, p. B1; "Battle-Tested Rules of Online Retail," *Ecompany*, April 2001; "The Return of Pricing Power," *Business Week*, May 8, 2000, p. 50; "The Power of Smart Pricing," *Business Week*, April 10, 2000, p. 160. See also Mary L. Hatten, "Don't Get Caught with Your Prices Down: Pricing in Inflationary Times," *Business Horizons*, March 1982, p. 23; Douglas G. Brooks, "Cost Oriented Pricing: A Realistic Solution to a Complicated Problem," *Journal of Marketing*, April 1975, p. 72; Steven M. Shugan, "Retail Product-Line Pricing Strategy When Costs and Products Change," *Journal of Retailing*, Spring 2001, Vol. 77, 1, p. 17.

5. John C. Lere, "Your Product-Costing System Seems to Be Broken: Now What?" *Industrial Marketing Management*, October 2001, p. 586; William W. Alberts, "The Experience Curve Doctrine Reconsidered," *Journal of Marketing*, July 1989, p. 36; G. Dean Kortge et al., "Linking Experience, Product Life Cycle, and Learning Curves: Calculating the Perceived Value Price Range," *Industrial Marketing Management*, July 1994, p. 221.

6. G. Dean Kortge, "Inverted Breakeven Analysis for Profitable Marketing Decisions," *Industrial Marketing Management*, October 1984, p. 219; Thomas L. Powers, "Breakeven Analysis with Semifixed Costs," *Industrial Marketing Management*, February 1987, p. 35.

7. Approaches for estimating price-quantity relationships are reviewed in Kent B. Monroe, *Pricing: Making Profitable Decisions* (New York: McGraw-Hill, 2003). For specific examples see Gordon A. Wyner, Lois H. Benedetti, and Bart M. Trapp, "Measuring the Quantity and Mix of Product Demand," *Journal of Marketing*, Winter 1984, p. 101. See also Michael F. Smith and Indrajit Sinha, "The Impact of Price and Extra Product Promotions on Store Preference," *International Journal of Retail & Distribution Management*, (2) 2000, p. 83; Michael H. Morris and Mary L. Joyce, "How Marketers Evaluate Price Sensitivity," *Industrial Marketing Management*, May, 1988, p. 169. David E. Griffith and Roland T. Rust, "The Price of Competitiveness in Competitive Pricing," *Journal of the Academy of Marketing Science*, Spring 1997, p. 109; Frank D. Jones, "A Survey Technique to Measure Demand under Various Pricing Strategies," *Journal of Marketing*, July 1975, p. 75; Robert J. Dolan, "How Do You Know When the Price Is Right?" *Harvard Business Review*, September–October 1995, p. 174; S. C. Choi, "Price Competition in a Duopoly Common Retailer Channel," *Journal of Retailing*, Summer 1996, p. 117.

8. "Getting Skewered by Shrimp Prices," *The Wall Street Journal*, October 16, 2003, p. D1; "Secret in the Dairy Aisle: Milk Is a Cash Cow," *The Wall Street Journal*, July 28, 2003, p. B1; "New Status Symbol: Overpaying for Your Minivan," *The Wall Street Journal*, July 23, 2003, p. D1; "No More Free Lunch . . . Please?" *The Wall Street Journal Reports*, September 24, 2001, p. R13; "Who Really Needs a Pentium 4?" *Fortune*, January 8, 2001, p. 217; "Marriott International: A Hotel That Clicks with Guests," *Business Week E.Biz*, September 18, 2000, p. EB58; "The Paradox of Value," *Brandweek*, June 5, 2000, p. 40; Watts Wacker and Jim Taylor, *The Visionary's Handbook: Nine Paradoxes That Will Shape the Future of Your Business* (HarperCollins, 2000). See also Kristin Diehl, Laura J. Kornish, and John G. Lynch Jr, "Smart Agents: When Lower Search Costs for Quality Information Increase Price Sensitivity," *Journal of Consumer Research*, Jun 2003, p. 56; Amir Heiman, Bruce McWilliams, Jinhua Zhao and David Zilberman, "Valuation and Management of Money-Back Guarantee Options," *Journal of Retailing*, Fall 2002, p. 193; Dhruv Grewal, Kent B. Monroe, and R. Krishnan, "The Effects of Price-Comparison Advertising on Buyers' Perceptions of Acquisition Value, Transaction Value, and Behavioral Intentions," *Journal of Marketing*, April 1998, p. 46; John T. Gourville, "Pennies-a-Day: The Effect of Temporal Reframing on Transaction Evaluation," *Journal of Consumer Research*, March 1998, p. 395; Joel E. Urbany, Rosemary Kalapurakal, and Peter R. Dickson, "Price Search in the Retail Grocery Market," *Journal of Marketing*, April 1996, p. 91; Venkatesh Shankar and Lakshman Krishnamurthi, "Relating Price Sensitivity to Retailer Promotional Variables and Pricing Policy: An Empirical Analysis," *Journal of Retailing*, Fall 1996, p. 249; Chakravarthi Narasimhan, Scott A. Neslin, and Subrata K. Sen, "Promotional Elasticities and Category Characteristics," *Journal of Marketing*, April 1996, p. 17; K. Sivakumar and S. P. Raj, "Quality Tier Competition: How Price Change Influences Brand Choice and Category Choice," *Journal of Marketing*, July 1997, p. 71.

9. Thomas T. Nagle and Reed R. Holder, *The Strategy and Tactics of Pricing* (Englewood Cliffs, NJ: Prentice-Hall, 2002); "Fram Pays Up Now," *Brandweek*, July 20, 1998, p. 16; "New Long-Life Bulbs May Lose Brilliance in a Crowded Market," *The Wall Street Journal*, June 2, 1992, p. B4; Benson P. Shapiro and Barbara P. Jackson, "Industrial Pricing to Meet Customer Needs," *Harvard Business Review*, November–December 1978, p. 119; "The Race to the $10 Light Bulb," *Business Week*, May 19, 1980, p. 124; see also Michael H. Morris and Donald A. Fuller, "Pricing an Industrial Service," *Industrial Marketing Management*, May 1989, p. 139.

10. For more on eBay, see Chapter 13, endnote 18. See also "Renaissance in Cyberspace," *The Wall Street Journal*, November 20, 2003, p. B1; "Sold! to Save the Farm," *The Wall Street Journal*, August 29, 2003, p. B1; "Online Liquidators Help Firm Shed Unsold Goods," *Investor's Business Daily*, August 13, 2002, p. A5; "Good-Bye to Fixed Pricing?" *Business Week*, May 4, 1998, p. 71. See also Larry R. Smeltzer and Amelia S. Carr, "Electronic Reverse Auctions: Promises, Risks and Conditions for Success," *Industrial Marketing Management*, August 2003, p. 481; Sandy D. Jap, "An Exploratory Study of the Introduction of Online Reverse Auctions," *Journal of Marketing*, July 2003, p. 96.

11. "The Price Is Really Right," *Business Week*, March 31, 2003, p. 62; "New Software Manages Price Cuts," *Investor's Business Daily*, March 31, 2003, p. A4; "The Power of Optimal Pricing," *Business 2.0*, September 2002, p. 68; "Priced to Move: Retailers Try to Get Leg Up on Markdowns with New Software," *The Wall Street Journal*, August 7, 2001, p. A1; "The Price Is Right," *Inc.*, July 2001, p. 40. See also Marc Vanhuele and Xavier Dreze, "Measuring the Price Knowledge Shoppers Bring to the Store," *Journal of Marketing*, October 2002, p. 72; Rashmi Adaval and Kent B. Monroe, "Automatic Construction and Use of Contextual Information for Product and Price Evaluations," *Journal of Consumer Research*, March 2002, p. 572; Sangman Han, Sunil Gupta and Donald R. Lehmann, "Consumer Price Sensitivity and Price Thresholds," *Journal of Retailing*, Winter 2001, p. 435; David Ackerman and Gerard Tellis, "Can Culture Affect Prices? A Cross-Cultural Study of Shopping and Retail Prices," *Journal of Retailing*, Spring 2001, p. 57; David M. Hardesty and William O. Bearden, "Consumer Evaluations of Different Promotion Types and Price Presentations: the Moderating Role of Promotional Benefit Level," *Journal of Retailing*, (1) 2003, p. 17; Rajesh Chandrashekaran and Dhruv Grewal, "Assimilation of Advertised Reference Prices: the Moderating Role of Involvement," *Journal of Retailing*, (1) 2003, p. 53; Thomas Jensen, Jeremy Kees, Scot Burton and Fernanda Lucarelli Turnipseed, "Advertised Reference Prices in an Internet Environment: Effects on Consumer Price Perceptions and Channel Search Intentions," *Journal of Interactive Marketing*, Spring 2003, p. 20; Joel E. Urbany, Peter R. Dickson and Alan G. Sawyer, "Insights into Cross- and Within-Store Price Search: Retailer Estimates vs. Consumer Self-Reports," *Journal of Retailing*, Summer 2000, p. 243; Merrie Brucks, Valarie A. Zeithaml and Gillian Naylor, "Price and Brand Name as Indicators of Quality Dimensions for Consumer Durables," *Journal of the Academy of Marketing Science*, Summer 2000, p. 359; Joydeep Srivastava and Nicholas Lurie, "A Consumer Perspective on Price-Matching Refund Policies: Effect on Price Perceptions and Search Behavior," *Journal of Consumer Research*, September 2001, p. 296; Ronald W. Niedrich, Subhash Sharma and Douglas H. Wedell, "Reference Price and Price Perceptions: a Comparison of Alternative Models," *Journal of Consumer Research*, December 2001, p. 339; Erica Mina Okada, "Trade-Ins, Mental Accounting, and Product Replacement Decisions," *Journal of Consumer Research*, March 2001, p. 433; Aradhna Krishna, Richard Briesch, Donald R. Lehmann and Hong Yuan, "A Meta-Analysis of the Impact of Price Presentation on Perceived Savings," *Journal of Retailing*, Summer 2002, p. 101; Valerie A. Taylor and William O. Bearden, "The Effects of Price on Brand Extension Evaluations: the Moderating Role of Extension Similarity," *Journal of the Academy of Marketing Science*, Spring 2002, p. 131; James K. Binkley and John Bejnarowicz, "Consumer Price Awareness in Food Shopping: the Case of Quantity Surcharges," *Journal of Retailing*, (1) 2003,

p. 27; Lesa E. Bolton, Luk Warlop and Joseph W. Alba, "Consumer Perceptions of Price (Un)fairness," *Journal of Consumer Research*, March 2003, p. 474; Amir Heiman, Bruce McWilliams and David Zilberman, "Demonstrations and Money-Back Guarantees: Market Mechanisms to Reduce Uncertainty," *Journal of Business Research*, October 2001, p. 71; Edward A. Blair, Judy Harris and Kent B. Monroe, "Effects of Shopping Information on Consumers' Responses to Comparative Price Claims," *Journal of Retailing*, Fall 2002, p. 175; Hooman Estelami, "The Impact of Research Design on Consumer Price Recall Accuracy: An Integrative Review," *Journal of the Academy of Marketing Science*, Winter 2001, p. 36; Richard A. Briesch, Lakshman Krishnamurthi, Tridib Mazumdar, and S. P. Raj, "A Comparative Analysis of Reference Price Models," *Journal of Consumer Research*, September 1997, p. 202; Tracy A. Suter and Scot Burton, "Believability and Consumer Perceptions of Implausible Reference Prices in Retail Advertisements," *Psychology & Marketing*, January 1996, p. 37; K. N. Rajendran and Gerard J. Tellis, "Contextual and Temporal Components of Reference Price," *Journal of Marketing*, January 1994, p. 22; Abhijit Biswas, Elizabeth J. Wilson, and Jane W. Licata, "Reference Pricing Studies in Marketing: A Synthesis of Research Results," *Journal of Business Research*, July 1993, p. 239; Daniel S. Putler, "Incorporating Reference Price Effects into a Theory of Consumer Choice," *Marketing Science*, Summer 1992, p. 287; Kristina D. Frankenberger and Ruiming Liu, "Does Consumer Knowledge Affect Consumer Responses to Advertised Reference Price Claims?" *Psychology & Marketing*, May/June 1994, p. 235.

12. For a classic example applied to a high-price item, see "Sale of Mink Coats Strays a Fur Piece from the Expected," *The Wall Street Journal*, March 21, 1980, p. 30.

13. K. Douglas Hoffman, L. W. Turley and Scott W. Kelley, "Pricing Retail Services," *Journal of Business Research*, December 2002, p. 1015; Steven M. Shugan and Ramarao Desiraju, "Retail Product-Line Pricing Strategy When Costs and Products Change," *Journal of Retailing*, Spring 2001, p. 17; Noel M. Noel and Nessim Hanna, "Benchmarking Consumer Perceptions of Product Quality With Price: An Exploration," *Psychology & Marketing*, September 1996, p. 591; Niraj Dawar and Philip Parker, "Marketing Universals: Consumers' Use of Brand Name, Price, Physical Appearance, and Retailer Reputation As Signals of Product Quality," *Journal of Marketing*, April 1994, p. 81; Tung-Zong Chang and Albert R. Wildt, "Impact of Product Information on the Use of Price As a Quality Cue," *Psychology & Marketing*, January 1996, p. 55; B. P. Shapiro, "The Psychology of Pricing," *Harvard Business Review*, July–August 1968, p. 14; Lutz Hildebrandt, "The Analysis of Price Competition Between Corporate Brands," *International Journal of Research in Marketing*, June 2001, p. 139.

14. Lee C. Simmons and Robert M. Schindler, "Cultural Superstitions and the Price Endings Used in Chinese Advertising," *Journal of International Marketing*, (2) 2003, p. 101; Robert M. Schindler and Thomas M. Kibarian, "Image Communicated by the Use of 99 Endings in Advertised Prices," *Journal of Advertising*, Winter 2001, p. 95; Robert M. Schindler and Patrick N. Kirby, "Patterns of Rightmost Digits Used in Advertised Prices: Implications for Nine-Ending Effects," *Journal of Consumer Research*, September 1997, p. 192; Mark Stiving and Russell S. Winer, "An Empirical Analysis of Price Endings With Scanner Data," *Journal of Consumer Research*, June 1997, p. 57; Robert M. Schindler and Alan R. Wiman, "Effects of Odd Pricing on Price Recall," *Journal of Business Research*, November 1989, p. 165.

15. "Tiffany & Co. Branches Out under an Alias," *The Wall Street Journal*, July 23, 2003, p. B1; "The Cocoon Cracks Open," *Brandweek*, April 28, 2003, p. 32; "Goodbye, Mr. Goodbar: Chocolate Gets Snob Appeal," *The Wall Street Journal*, February 13, 2003, p. D1; "Special Report: Luxury Marketing," *Advertising Age*, March 11, 2002, pp. S1–S10; "Keeping the Cachet," *The Wall Street Journal*, April 23, 2001, p. R28; "Luxury Sites Get Scrappy," *The Wall Street Journal*, December 4, 2000, p. B1; "Online Luxury Has Limits," *Business Week E.Biz*, September 18, 2000,

p. EB24; "Special Report: Luxury Marketing," *Advertising Age*, August 14, 2000, p. S1; "The Galloping Gourmet Chocolate," *Brandweek*, July 31, 2000, p. 32. See also Xing Pan, Brian T. Ratchford and Venkatesh Shankar, "Can Price Dispersion in Online Markets Be Explained by Differences in E-Tailer Service Quality?" *Journal of the Academy of Marketing Science*, Fall 2002, p. 433; Kusum L. Ailawadi, Donald R. Lehmann and Scott A. Neslin, "Revenue Premium as an Outcome Measure of Brand Equity," *Journal of Marketing*, October 2003, p. 1; Rebecca Piirto Heath, "Life on Easy Street," *American Demographics*, April 1997, p. 33; G. Dean Kortge and Patrick A. Okonkwo, "Perceived Value Approach to Pricing," *Industrial Marketing Management*, May 1993, p. 133.

16. "Can Gillette Regain Its Edge?" *Business Week*, January 26, 2004, p. 46; "Adobe Turns Page with New Software Line," *Investor's Business Daily*, November 13, 2003, p. A4; "The Allure of Bundling," *The Wall Street Journal*, October 7, 2003, p. B1; "Computer Deals Hit New Lows," *The Wall Street Journal*, August 13, 2003, p. D1. For more on phone bundling, see "Internet Phone Calls Could Squeeze Prices," *Investor's Business Daily*, December 12, 2003, p. A1; "Circuit Breaker: Battered Telecoms Face New Challenge: Internet Calling," *The Wall Street Journal*, October 9, 2003, p. A1; "BellSouth Hooks Up with DirecTV," *The Wall Street Journal*, August 27, 2003, p. B7; "Honey, I Shrunk the Phone Bill," *Business Week*, June 9, 2003, p. 132; "Cellphone Giveaways Get an Upgrade," *The Wall Street Journal*, May 20, 2003, p. D1; "A Nickel Here, a Buck There Add Up to Big Local Bills," *USA Today*, February 28, 2003, p. 1B; "Phone, Cable Cos. Use Bundling to Keep Users from Switching," *Investor's Business Daily*, December 13, 2002, p. A1. For more on airline food unbundling, see "Dining Out at 32,000 Feet," *The Wall Street Journal*, June 3, 2003, p. D1; "Food Flights," *USA Today*, January 17, 2003, p. 1D. See also Andrea Ovans, "Make a Bundle Bundling," *Harvard Business Review*, November–December 1997, p. 18; Preyas S. Desai and Kannan Srinivasan, "Aggregate Versus Product-Specific Pricing: Implications for Franchise and Traditional Channels," *Journal of Retailing*, Winter 1996, p. 357; Manjit S. Yadav and Kent B. Monroe, "How Buyers Perceive Savings in a Bundle Price: An Examination of a Bundle's Transaction Value," *Journal of Marketing Research*, August 1993, p. 350; Dorothy Paun, "When to Bundle or Unbundle Products," *Industrial Marketing Management*, February 1993, p. 29.

17. Mary Anne Raymond, John F. Tanner, Jr. and Jonghoon Kim, "Cost Complexity of Pricing Decisions for Exporters in Developing and Emerging Markets," *Journal of International Marketing*, (3) 2001, p. 19; Peter E. Connor and Robert K. Hopkins, "Cost Plus What? The Importance of Accurate Profit Calculations in Cost-Plus Agreements," *International Journal of Purchasing & Materials Management*, Spring 1997, p. 35; Daniel T. Ostas, "Ethics of Contract Pricing," *Journal of Business Ethics*, February 1992, p. 137; J. Steve Davis, "Ethical Problems in Competitive Bidding: The Paradyne Case," *Business and Professional Ethics Journal*, 7, no. 2 (1988), p. 3; David T. Levy, "Guaranteed Pricing in Industrial Purchases: Making Use of Markets in Contractual Relations," *Industrial Marketing Management*, October 1994, p. 307; Akintola Akintoye and Martin Skitmore, "Pricing Approaches in the Construction Industry," *Industrial Marketing Management*, November 1992, p. 311.

CHAPTER 19

1. *2003 Annual Report*, Ben & Jerry's; "Economic Crunch," *Fortune*, December 8, 2003, p. 64; "Vermont's Latest," *Dairy Foods*, September 2003, p. 50; "Ice Cream Rivals Prepare to Wage a New Cold War," *The Wall Street Journal*, June 26, 2003, p. B1; "Summer of the Smush-In: 31 Flavors—in a Single Cone," *The Wall Street Journal*, May 8, 2003, p. D1; "Looking for Intelligence in Ice Cream," *Fortune*, March 17, 2003, p. 114; "Ice Cream Innovations," *Dairy Foods*, November 2001, p. 14; "Ben & Jerry's Keeps Its Folksy Focus," *Advertising Age*, February 12, 2001, p. 4; "Ben & Jerry's: Surviving the Big Squeeze," *Food Business*, May 6, 1991, p. 10; "The Peace Pop Puzzle," *Inc.*, March 1990, p. 25.

2. For excellent example on Krispy Kreme, see "Software Giants Think Small," *USA Today*, December 11, 2003, p. 1B; "How to Create a Spontaneous Media Event," *Business 2.0*, December 2003, p. 87; "Special Report: The Web Smart," *Business Week*, November 24, 2003, p. 82; "Krispy Kreme Holds Up at Wal-Mart," *USA Today*, September 16, 2003, p. 5B; "Krispy Kreme's Secret Ingredient," *Business 2.0*, September 2003, p. 36; "Krispy Kreme's Sweet on Britain," *USA Today*, August 12, 2003, p. 1B; "How Krispy Kreme Became America's Hottest Brand," *Fortune*, July 7, 2003, p. 52; "Hot Bytes, by the Dozen," *Newsweek*, April 28, 2003, p. 42; "No Holes in Krispy Kreme's Strategy for Marketing Its Brand," *Investor's Business Daily*, May 17, 2002, p. A3; "War of the Doughnuts," *The Wall Street Journal*, August 23, 2001, p. B1; "Marketers of the Next Generation: Krispy Kreme," *Brandweek*, March 26, 2001, p. 21. For more on Weyerhaeuser as an example, see "How Fast Can This Baby Go?" *Business Week*, April 10, 2000, p. 38; "Weblining," *Business Week E.Biz*, April 3, 2000, p. EB26; "How an Intranet Opened Up the Door to Profits," *Business Week E.Biz*, July 26, 1999, p. EB32. For more on Pillsbury as an example, see "Pillsbury: Saving Dough with NetStat," *Business Week E.Biz*, September 18, 2000, p. EB94; "A Digital Doughboy," *Business Week E.Biz*, April 3, 2000, p. EB78. For more on Utz as an example, see "Using the Net to Stay Crisp," *Business Week E.Biz*, April 16, 2001, p. EB34. For more on Nestle as an example, see "Nestle: An Elephant Dances," *Business Week E.Biz*, December 11, 2000, p. EB44. For more on Webcor as an example, see "Wired at Webcor," *Business Week E.Biz*, November 20, 2000, p. EB58. For more on Kaiser as an example, see "Kaiser Takes the Cyber Cure," *Business Week E.Biz*, February 7, 2000, p. EB80. For more on Office Depot as an example, see "Empire Builders: Office Depot," *Business Week E.Biz*, May 14, 2001, p. EB28; "Why Office Depot Loves the Net," *Business Week E.Biz*, September 27, 1999, p. EB66. For more on Cemex as an example, see "Cemex Unit to Form E-Commerce Portal for Latin America," *The Wall Street Journal*, December 12, 2000, p. A23; "Going Digital? Think First," *Fortune*, November 13, 2000, p. 190; "Cemex Loves Its 'Ants' but Wants More," *The Wall Street Journal*, October 2, 2000, p. A22. See also Garold Lantz, "Clockspeed Winning Industry Control in the Age of Temporary Advantage," *Journal of the Academy of Marketing Science*, Summer 2000, p. 443; Peter R. Dickson, "Dynamic Strategic Thinking," *Journal of the Academy of Marketing Science*, Summer 2001, p. 216; Daniel C. Bello, Talai Osmonbekov, Frank Tian Xie, and David I. Gilliand, "E-Business Technological Innovations: Impact on Channel Processes and Structure," *Journal of Marketing Channels*, (3,4) 2002, p. 3; Anthony Ross, "A Multi-Dimensional Empirical Exploration of Technology Investment, Coordination and Firm Performance," *International Journal of Physical Distribution & Logistics Management*, (7) 2002, p. 591; Kevin Rollins, "Using Information to Speed Execution," *Harvard Business Review*, March–April 1998, p.81; Clayton M. Christensen, "Making Strategy: Learning by Doing," *Harvard Business Review*, November–December 1997, p. 141; William J. Bruns, Jr., and W. Warren McFarlan, "Information Technology Puts Power in Control Systems," *Harvard Business Review*, September–October, 1987, p. 89.

3. Available from World Wide Web: <http://www.hertz.com>; *2000 Annual Report*, Hertz; "How Market Leaders Keep Their Edge," *Fortune*, February 6, 1995, p. 88.

4. "Where the Customer Service Rep Is King," *Business 2.0*, June 2003, p. 70; "The Annoying New Face of Customer Service," *The Wall Street Journal*, January 21, 2003, p. D1; "Best Call Centers Stress Training, Track Results to Gauge Success," *Investor's Business Daily*, October 17, 2001, p. A1; "Do Call Us: More Companies Install 1-800 Phone Lines," *The Wall Street Journal*, April 20, 1994, p. B1; "Your Pet Iguana Swallowed a Staple? Computerized Help Desk Will Try to Help," *The Wall Street Journal*, December 7, 1999, p. B1. For more on Pillsbury as an example, see World Wide Web: <http://www.pillsbury. com>; World Wide Web: <http://www.betsycrocker.com>; "Pillsbury's Telephones Ring with Peeves, Praise," *The Wall Street Journal*, April 20, 1994, p. B1. See also Lance A. Bettencourt and Stephen W. Brown, "Role Stressors and

Customer-Oriented Boundary-Spanning Behaviors in Service Organizations," *Journal of the Academy of Marketing Science*, Fall 2003, p. 394.

5. Hemant C. Sashittal and Avan R. Jassawalla, "Marketing Implementation in Smaller Organizations: Definition, Framework, and Propositional Inventory," *Journal of the Academy of Marketing Science*, Winter 2001, p. 50; Thomas W. Gruen and Reshma H. Shah, "Determinants and Outcomes of Plan Objectivity and Implementation in Category Management Relationships," *Journal of Retailing*, Winter 2000, p. 483; Jagdish N. Sheth and Rajendra S. Sisodia, "Marketing Productivity: Issues and Analysis," *Journal of Business Research*, May 2002, p. 349; Thomas M. Hout and John C. Carter, "Getting It Done: New Roles for Senior Executives," *Harvard Business Review*, November 1995–December 1995, p. 133; Hemant C. Sashittal and David Wilemon, "Marketing Implementation in Small and Midsized Industrial Firms: An Exploratory Study," *Industrial Marketing Management*, January 1996, p. 67; Hemant C. Sashittal and Clint Tankersley, "The Strategic Market Planning-Implementation Interface in Small and Midsized Industrial Firms: An Exploratory Study," *Journal of Marketing Theory & Practice*, Summer 1997, p. 77.

6. The restaurant case is adapted from Marie Gaudard, Roland Coates and Liz Freeman, "Accelerating Improvement," *Quality Progress*, October 1991, p. 81. For more on quality management and control, see "By Focusing on Customers, Firms Can Boost Shareholder Value," *Investor's Business Daily*, October 11, 2002, p. A3; "Quality Isn't Just for Widgets," *Business Week*, July 22, 2002, p. 72; "Nicknamed 'Nag,' She's Just Doing Her Job," *The Wall Street Journal*, May 14, 2002, p. B1; "The Net as a Lifeline," *Business Week E.Biz*, October 29, 2001, p. EB16; "The Lure of Six Sigma Quality: It Gets Everyone Thinking Alike," *Investor's Business Daily*, November 7, 2001, p. A1; "How to Bring Out Better Products Faster," *Fortune*, November 23, 1998, p. 238B; Roland T. Rust, Anthony J. Zahorik, and Timothy L. Keiningham, "Return on Quality (ROQ): Making Service Quality Financially Accountable," *Journal of Marketing*, April 1995, p. 58. See also Mark R. Colgate and Peter J. Danaher, "Implementing a Customer Relationship Strategy: the Asymetric Impact of Poor Versus Excellent Execution," *Journal of the Academy of Marketing Science*, Summer 2000, p. 374; Jagdip Singh, "Performance Productivity and Quality of Frontline Employees in Service Organizations," *Journal of Marketing*, April 2000, p. 15; Simon J. Bell and Bulent Menguc, "The Employee-Organization Relationship, Organizational Citizenship Behaviors, and Superior Service Quality," *Journal of Retailing*, Summer 2002, p. 131; Roland T. Rust, Christine Moorman and Peter R. Dickson, "Getting Return on Quality: Revenue Expansion, Cost Reduction, or Both?" *Journal of Marketing*, October 2002, p. 7; Pratibha A. Dabholkar, C. David Shepherd and Dayle I. Thorpe, "A Comprehensive Framework for Service Quality: an Investigation of Critical Conceptual and Measurement Issues Through a Longitudinal Study," *Journal of Retailing*, Summer 2000, p. 139; Scott S. Elliott, "Managing by Measuring: How to Improve Your Organization's Performance Through Effective Benchmarking," *The Journal of Product Innovation Management*, July 2000, p. 321; William B. Locander and Daniel J. Goebel, "The Quality Train Is Leaving and Marketers Are Nodding Off in the Club Car," *Journal of Marketing Theory & Practice*, Summer 1996, p. 1; William C. LaFief, "Total Quality Marketing: The Key to Regaining Market Shares," *Journal of the Academy of Marketing Science*, Fall 1996, p. 377; David W. Finn, Julie Baker, Greg W. Marshall, and Roy Anderson, "Total Quality Management and Internal Customers: Measuring Internal Service Quality," *Journal of Marketing Theory & Practice*, Summer 1996, p. 36; Robert F. Hurley, Melissa T. Gropper, and Gianpaolo Roma, "The Role of TQM in Advertising: A Conceptualization and a Framework for Application," *Journal of Marketing Theory & Practice*, Summer 1996, p. 11; Teresa A. Swartz, "Why TQM Fails and What to Do About It," *Journal of the Academy of Marketing Science*, Fall 1996, p. 380; Iris Mohr-Jackson, "Managing a Total Quality Orientation: Factors Affecting Customer Satisfaction," *Industrial Marketing Management*, March 1998, p. 109; Cengiz Haksever, "Total Quality Management in the Small Business Environment," *Business Horizons*, March–April 1996, p. 33; Michael P. Bigwood, "Total Quality

Management at Work: Development of an Effective Competitive Analysis Process," *Industrial Marketing Management*, September 1997, p. 459.

7. For Whole Foods example of empowerment, see "No Preservatives, No Unions, Lots of Dough," *Fortune*, September 15, 2003, p. 127; "Whole Foods Vs. Wild Oats Markets: A Study in Culture, Vision, Execution," *Investor's Business Daily*, June 29, 2001, p. A1. See also "Thinking Outside the Cereal Box," *Business Week*, July 28, 2003, p. 74; "Pentair Fixes Its Own Mess," *Fortune*, September 30, 2002, p. 156C; "Glass Act: How a Window Maker Rebuilt Itself," *Fortune*, November 13, 2000, p. 384B. See also Dawn R. Deeter-Schmelz and Rosemary P. Ramsey, "An Investigation of Team Information Processing in Service Teams: Exploring the Link Between Teams and Customers," *Journal of the Academy of Marketing Science*, Fall 2003, p. 409; Emin Babakus, Ugur Yavas, Osman M. Karatepe and Turgay Avci, "The Effect of Management Commitment to Service Quality on Employees' Affective and Performance Outcomes," *Journal of the Academy of Marketing Science*, Summer 2003, p. 272; Roland T. Rust, Anthony J. Zahorik, and Timothy L. Keiningham, *Return on Quality* (Chicago: Probus, 1994); Timothy L. Keiningham, Roland T. Rust, and M. Marshall Weems, "The Bottom Line on Quality," *Financial Executive*, September/October 1994, p. 50; Warren S. Martin and Wendy K. Martin, "The Application of Benchmarking to Marketing," *Journal of Marketing Theory & Practice*, Summer 1996, p. 52; J. J. Cronin and Steven A. Taylor, "SERVPERF Versus SERVQUAL: Reconciling Performance-Based and Perceptions-Minus-Expectations Measurement of Service Quality," *Journal of Marketing*, January 1994, p. 125; Timothy C. Johnston and Molly A. Hewa, "Fixing Service Failures," *Industrial Marketing Management*, September 1997, p. 467; Shirley Taylor, "Waiting for Service: The Relationship Between Delays and Evaluations of Service," *Journal of Marketing*, April 1994, p. 56; Mary J. Bitner, Bernard H. Booms, and Lois A. Mohr, "Critical Service Encounters: The Employee's Viewpoint," *Journal of Marketing*, October 1994, p. 95; G. T. M. Hult, "Service Quality: New Directions in Theory and Practice," *Journal of the Academy of Marketing Science*, Summer 1997, p. 264; Scott W. Kelley, Timothy Longfellow, and Jack Malehorn, "Organizational Determinants of Service Employees' Exercise of Routine, Creative, and Deviant Discretion," *Journal of Retailing*, Summer 1996, p. 135; Pierre Filiatrault, Jean Harvey, and Jean-Charles Chebat, "Service Quality and Service Productivity Management Practices," *Industrial Marketing Management*, May 1996, p. 243; Robert Simons, "Control in an Age of Empowerment," *Harvard Business Review*, March–April 1995, p. 80.

8. Available from World Wide Web: <http://www.cardinal.com/mps/>; "Baxter's Big Makeover in Logistics," *Fortune*, July 8, 1996, p. 106C. See also William C. Taylor, "Control in an Age of Chaos," *Harvard Business Review*, November–December 1994, p. 64; Bernard J. Jaworski, Vlasis Stathakopoulos, and H. Shanker Krishnan, "Control Combinations in Marketing: Conceptual Framework and Empirical Evidence," *Journal of Marketing*, January 1993, p. 57; Subhash Sharma and Dale D. Achabal, "STEMCOM: An Analytical Model for Marketing Control," *Journal of Marketing*, Spring 1982, p. 104.

9. "The Numbers Game," *Business Week*, May 14, 2001, p. 100; "Accounting Gets Radical," *Fortune*, April 16, 2001, p. 184; "Kmart's Bright Idea," *Business Week*, April 9, 2001, p. 50; "Manufacturing Masters Its ABCs," *Business Week*, August 7, 2000, p. 86J. See also Joseph P. Cannon and Christian Homburg, "Buyers-Supplier Relationships and Customer Firm Costs," *Journal of Marketing*, January 2001, p. 29; Robin Cooper and W. B. Chew, "Control Tomorrow's Costs Through Today's Designs," *Harvard Business Review*, January–February 1996, p. 88; Robin Cooper and Robert S. Kaplan, "Profit Priorities From Activity-Based Costing," *Harvard Business Review*, May/June 1991, p. 130; Douglas M. Lambert and Jay U. Sterling, "What Types of Profitability Reports Do Marketing Managers Receive?" *Industrial Marketing Management*, November 1987, p. 295; Nigel F. Piercy, "The Marketing Budgeting Process: Marketing Management Implications," *Journal of Marketing*, October 1987, p. 45;

Michael J. Sandretto, "What Kind of Cost System Do You Need?" *Harvard Business Review*, January–February 1985, p. 110; Patrick M. Dunne and Harry I. Wolk, "Marketing Cost Analysis: A Modularized Contribution Approach," *Journal of Marketing*, July 1977, p. 83.

10. Technically, a distinction should be made between variable and direct costs, but we will use these terms interchangeably. Similarly, not all costs that are common to several products are fixed costs, and vice versa. But the important point here is to recognize that some costs are fairly easy to allocate, and other costs are not. See Stewart A. Washburn, "Establishing Strategy and Determining Costs in the Pricing Decision," Business Marketing, July 1985, p. 64.

11. "Office Supply Special Report: Three-Way Competition Is Here to Stay," *DSN Retailing Today*, November 10, 2003, p. 13; "Fire Awards: Staples Finest in Office Supplies," *DSN Retailing Today*, September 8, 2003, p. 41; "Staples: Office-Supplies Chain Beats Economic Blues," *Investor's Business Daily*, September 2, 2003, p. A9; "Staples: Thinking Outside the Big Box," *Business Week*, August 11, 2002, p. 62; "When Worlds Collide," *The Wall Street Journal Reports*, April 28, 2003, p. R1; "Looking for Intelligence in Ice Cream," *Fortune*, March 17, 2003, p. 114; "Advertising: Staples Is Changing Its Slogan to Stress the Ease of Shopping for Office Supplies in Its Stores," *The New York Times*, February 27, 2003, p. C6; "Web Delivers Big Results for Staples," *BtoB*, November 11, 2002, p. 14; "The Architect of Happy Customers," *Business 2.0*, August 2002, p. 85; "How to Lower Marketing Costs—and Eliminate Guesswork," *Investor's Business Daily*, November 21, 2001, p. A1.

12. Neil A. Morgan, Bruce H. Clark and Rich Gooner, "Marketing Productivity, Marketing Audits, and Systems for Marketing Performance Assessment: Integrating Multiple Perspectives," *Journal of Business Research*, May 2002, p. 363; James T. Rothe, Michael G. Harvey, and Candice E. Jackson, "The Marketing Audit: Five Decades Later," *Journal of Marketing Theory & Practice*, Summer 1997, p. 1; Douglas Brownlie, "The Conduct of Marketing Audits," *Industrial Marketing Management*, January 1996, p. 11; Leonard L. Berry, Jeffrey S. Conant, and A. Parasuraman, "A Framework for Conducting a Services Marketing Audit," *Journal of the Academy of Marketing Science*, Summer 1991, p. 255; John F. Grashof, "Conducting and Using a Marketing Audit," in *Readings in Basic Marketing*, eds. E. J. McCarthy, J. J. Grashof, and A. A. Brogowicz (Homewood, IL: Richard D. Irwin, 1984).

CHAPTER 20

1. "Ikea Makes Vietnam a Big Supplier," *The Wall Street Journal*, September 24, 2003, p. B4B; "Ikea Promotes Kid Connections," *DSN Retailing Today*, August 4, 2003, p. 20; "Ikea Expands Style and Square Footage," *DSN Retailing Today*, June 23, 2003, p. 2; "Ikea Adds Third Unit to Metro New York Market," *DSN Retailing Today*, July 21, 2003, p. 6; "How Ikea Designs Its Sexy Price Tags," *Business 2.0*, October 2002, p. 106; "Ikea's New Game Plan," *Business Week*, October 6, 1997, p. 99.

2. See also Douglas Reid, "Marketing-Related Motives in Mergers & Acquisitions: the Perspective of the U.S. Food Industry," *Journal of the Academy of Marketing Science*, Winter 2004, p. 98; Natalie Mizik and Robert Jacobson, "Trading off Between Value Creation and Value Appropriation: the Financial Implications of Shifts in Strategic Emphasis," *Journal of Marketing*, January 2003, p. 63; Elliot Maltz and Ajay K. Kohli, "Reducing Marketing's Conflict with Other Functions: the Differential Effects of Integrating Mechanisms," *Journal of the Academy of Marketing Science*, Fall 2000, p. 479; George M. Zinkhan and James A. Verbrugge, "The Marketing/Finance Interface: Two Divergent and Complementary Views of the Firm," *Journal of Business Research*, December 2000, p. 143; W. Keith Schilit, "The Globalization of Venture Capital," *Business Horizons*, January–February 1992, p. 17; Nikolaos Tzokas, Michael Saren, and Douglas Brownlie, "Generating Marketing Resources by Means of

R&D Activities in High Technology Firms," *Industrial Marketing Management*, July 1997, p. 331; George S. Bobinski and Gabriel G. Ramirez, "Advertising to Investors: The Effect of Financial-Relations Advertising on Stock Volume and Price," *Journal of Advertising*, December 1994, p. 13; Rajendra K. Srivastava, Tasadduq A. Shervani, and Liam Fahey, "Market-Based Assets and Shareholder Value: A Framework for Analysis," *Journal of Marketing*, January 1998, p. 2; Gary Tighe, "From Experience: Securing Sponsors and Funding for New Product Development Projects—The Human Side of Enterprise," *Journal of Product Innovation Management*, January 1998, p. 75; Robert C. Pozen, "Institutional Investors: The Reluctant Activists," *Harvard Business Review*, January–February 1994, p. 140; Michael E. Porter, "Capital Disadvantage: America's Failing Capital Investment System," *Harvard Business Review*, September–October 1992, p. 65; Bill Parks, "Rate of Return—The Poison Apple?" *Business Horizons*, May–June 1993, p. 55.

3. For more on Starbucks, see Chapter 1, endnote 1.

4. *Sorrell Ridge: Slotting Allowances* (Cambridge, MA: Harvard Business School Press, 1988).

5. "Losing Focus: As Kodak Eyes Digital Future, A Big Partner Starts to Fade," *The Wall Street Journal*, January 23, 2004, p. A1; "Kodak to Cut Staff up to 21%, Amid Digital Push," *The Wall Street Journal*, January 22, 2004, p. A1; "Kodak Refocuses," *Money*, January 2004, p. 44.

6. Julie H. Hertenstein and Sharon M. McKinnon, "Solving the Puzzle of the Cash Flow Statement," *Business Horizons*, January–February 1997, p. 69; Amar Bhide, "Bootstrap Finance: The Art of Start-Ups," *Harvard Business Review*, November–December 1992, p. 109; Marv Rubinstein, "Effective Industrial Marketing with a Piggy Bank Budget," *Industrial Marketing Management*, August 1992, p. 203; Amar Bhide, "How Entrepreneurs Craft Strategies That Work," *Harvard Business Review*, March–April 1994, p. 150.

7. For more on production flexibility, see "Garmin Finds the Perfect Spot," *Business 2.0*, December 2003, p. 64; "The Flexible Factory," *Business Week*, May 5, 2003, p. 90; "A Big Maker of Tiny Batches," *Fortune*, May 27, 2002, p. 152C. See also Edward F. McDonough III, "Investigation of Factors Contributing to the Success of Cross-Functional Teams," *The Journal of Product Innovation Management*, May 2000, p. 221; Eric M. Olson, Orville C. Walker, Jr. Robert W. Ruekert and Joseph M. Bonner, "Patterns of Cooperation During New Product Development among Marketing, Operations and R&D: Implications for Project Performance," *The Journal of Product Innovation Management*, July 2001, p. 258; Ioannis S. Papadakis, "On the Sensitivity of Configure-to-Order Supply Chains for Personal Computers after Component Market Disruptions," *International Journal of Physical Distribution & Logistics Management*, (9) 2003, p. 934; David M. Upton, "What Really Makes Factories Flexible?" *Harvard Business Review*, July–August 1995, p. 74; John P. MacDuffie and Susan Helper, "Creating Lean Suppliers: Diffusing Lean Production Through the Supply Chain," *California Management Review*, Summer 1997, p. 118; Robert J. Fisher, Elliot Maltz, and Bernard J. Jaworski, "Enhancing Communication Between Marketing and Engineering: The Moderating Role of Relative Functional Identification," *Journal of Marketing*, July 1997, p. 54; X. M. Song, Mitzi M. Montoya-Weiss, and Jeffrey B. Schmidt, "Antecedents and Consequences of Cross-Functional Cooperation: A Comparison of R&D, Manufacturing, and Marketing Perspectives," *Journal of Product Innovation Management*, January 1997, p. 35; Roger G. Schroeder and Michael J. Pesch, "Focusing the Factory: Eight Lessons," *Business Horizons*, September–October 1994, p. 76; Andrew D. Bartmess, "The Plant Location Puzzle," *Harvard Business Review*, March–April 1994, p. 20; Robert H. Hayes and Gary P. Pisano, "Beyond World-Class: The New Manufacturing Strategy," *Harvard Business Review*, January–February 1994, p. 77; Victoria L. Crittenden, Lorraine R. Gardiner, and Antonie Stam, "Reducing Conflict between Marketing and Manufacturing," *Industrial Marketing Management*, November 1993, p. 299; Paul A. Konijnendijk, "Dependence and Conflict Between

Production and Sales," *Industrial Marketing Management*, August 1993, p. 161; Kenneth B. Kahn and John T. Mentzer, "Norms that Distinguish between Marketing and Manufacturing," *Journal of Business Research*, June 1994, p. 111; William B. Wagner, "Establishing Supply Service Strategy for Shortage Situations," *Industrial Marketing Management*, December 1994, p. 393.

8. For more on Tostitos Gold example, see "Buyers Seek Hard-to-Find Tostitos Gold," *USA Today*, February 9, 2003, p. 1B; "Relevance Is Operative Word in Catfight or Chip-Dip Ads," *Advertising Age*, January 27, 2003, p. 20; "Frito-Lay Leverages National Championship Game as Major Marketing Platform for New Tostitos Gold Tortilla Chips," *PR Newswire*, December 30, 2002. For more on Rice Krispies Treats example, see "Special Report: Brands in Demand," *Advertising Age*, February 7, 1994, p. S1; "Kellogg to Consumers: Please Bear with Us," *Advertising Age*, March 29, 1993, p. 44. See also J. Mahajan et al., "An Exploratory Investigation of the Interdependence Between Marketing and Operations Functions in Service Firms," *International Journal of Research in Marketing*, January 1994, p. 1.

9. For more on Intel Xeon example, see "Intel: Xeon Channel Sales Poised to Double," *CRN*, March 10, 2003, p. 6.

10. "FTD: Florist Delivers a Bouquet of Financial Gains," *Investor's Business Daily*, March 31, 2003, p. A7; "Factory Fight: A Sneaker Maker Says China Partner Became Its Rival," *The Wall Street Journal*, December 19, 2002, p. A1; "Sri Lanka Keeps Victoria's Secret," *The Wall Street Journal*, July 13, 1999, p. B1; "Remember When Companies Made Things?" *The Wall Street Journal*, September 18, 1997, p. C1; "Virtual Companies Leave the Manufacturing to Others," *The New York Times*, July 17, 1994, Sect. 3, p. 5; "Shaken by a Series of Business Setbacks, Calvin Klein is Redesigning Itself," *The Wall Street Journal*, March 21, 1994, p. B1; "Calvin Klein Inc.: Definitive Pact Is Reached on Sale of Jeans Division," *The Wall Street Journal*, July 15, 1994, p. B4. See also Ravi Venkatesan, "Strategic Sourcing: To Make or Not To Make," *Harvard Business Review*, November–December 1992, p. 98.

11. L. Scott Flaig, "The 'Virtual Enterprise': Your New Model for Success," *Electronic Business*, March 30, 1992, p. 153; William H. Davidow and Michael S. Malone, *The Virtual Corporation* (New York: HarperCollins, 1992).

12. For more on outsourcing, see Chapter 7, endnote 14. See also *Sara Lee: Rapid Response at Hanes Knitware* (Cambridge, MA: Harvard Business School Press, 1993); "Outsourcing Trend Puts Tech Firm in a Sea of Green," *Investor's Business Daily*, December 10, 2003, p. A8; "Where Your Job Is Going," *Fortune*, November 24, 2003, p. 84; "All the World's a Call Center," *Business Week*, October 27, 2003, p. 43; "Offshore Outsourcing: Where the Growth Is," *Investor's Business Daily*, October 27, 2003, p. A9; "At 2 AM in Manila, It's Time to Break for a Midday Snack," *The Wall Street Journal*, October 20, 2003, p. A1; "Outsourcing Jobs—and Workers—to India," *The Wall Street Journal*, October 13, 2003, p. B1; "Surviving the Onslaught: U.S. Companies Customize, Rethink Strategies to Compete with Products from Abroad," *The Wall Street Journal*, October 6, 2003, p. B1; "India, the Export Launching Pad," *The Wall Street Journal*, October 2, 2003, p. A11; "Ah, That Excellent German Engineering—Straight from Southern Austria," *The Wall Street Journal*, September 10, 2003, p. B1; "Outsourcing Jobs: Is It Bad?" *Business Week*, August 25, 2003, p. 36; "Move Over, India," *Business Week*, August 11, 2003, p. 42; "Is Your Job Next?" *Business Week*, February 3, 2003, p. 50; "U.S. Manufacturing Jobs Fading Away Fast," *USA Today*, December 13, 2002, p. 1B; "Calling Bangalore," *Business Week*, November 25, 2002, p. 52; "A Killing in the Caymans?" *Business Week*, May 11, 1998, p. 50. See also Mosad Zineldin and Torbjorn Bredenlow, "Strategic Alliance: Synergies and Challenges: a Case of Strategic Outsourcing Relationship (SOUR)," *International Journal of Physical Distribution & Logistics Management*, (5) 2003, p. 449; Scott J. Mason, Michael H. Cole, Brian T. Ulrey and Li Yan, "Improving Electronics Manufacturing Supply Chain Agility

Through Outsourcing," *International Journal of Physical Distribution & Logistics Management*, (7) 2002, p. 610; Richard Peisch, "When Outsourcing Goes Awry," *Harvard Business Review*, May–June 1995, p. 24; Stanley E. Fawcett, Linda L. Stanley, and Sheldon R. Smith, "Developing a Logistics Capability to Improve the Performance of International Operations," *Journal of Business Logistics*, 1997, p. 101; P. F. Johnson and Michiel R. Leenders, "Make-or-Buy Alternatives in Plant Disposition Strategies," *International Journal of Purchasing & Materials Management*, Spring 1997, p. 20; Thomas Kiely, "Business Processes: Consider Outsourcing," *Harvard Business Review*, May–June 1997, p. 11.

13. For more on Levi Strauss hiring foreign labor, see "Sweatshops: Finally, Airing the Dirty Linen," *Business Week*, June 23, 2003, p. 100; "Managing by Values," *Business Week*, August 1, 1994, p. 46; "Working for Mr. Clean Jeans," *U.S. News & World Report*, August 2, 1993, p. 49; Martha Nichols, "Third-World Families at Work: Child Labor or Child Care?" *Harvard Business Review*, January–February 1993, p. 12.

14. For more on Dell and the PC Wars, see Chapter 2, endnote 1.

15. Available from World Wide Web. <http://www.baldor.com>, 2003 *Annual Report*, Baldor; "The Flexible Factory," *Business Week*, May 5, 2003, p. 90; "Elite Factories," *Fortune*, September 2, 2002, p. 172C; "Baldor's Success: Made in the U.S.A.," *Fortune*, July 17, 1989, p. 101. See also Jeen-Su Lim and David A. Reid, "Vital Cross-Functional Linkages with Marketing," *Industrial Marketing Management*, May 1992, p. 159.

16. "Have It Your Way," *Time*, December 23, 2002, p. 42; "A Mass Market of One," *Business Week*, December 2, 2002, p. 68; "Have It Your Way: Thanks to Net," *USA Today*, October 30, 2002, p. 3B; "Sneakers' Savile Row: Custom Running Shoes Are Gaining a Footing," *The Wall Street Journal*, August 22, 2002, p. D1; "Customized Clothing Sites Aim for a Perfect Fit," *Investor's Business Daily*, March 6, 2002, p. A6; "Brand Me," *On Monthly* (suppl. to *Time*), June 2001, p. 39; "Customizing for the Masses," *Business Week*, March 20, 2000, p. 130B; "Nike Lets You Be a Shoemaker," *USA Today*, November 22, 1999, p. 14B; "P&G Gives Birth to a Web Baby," *Business Week*, September 27, 1999, p. 87; "Mass Customization," *Fortune*, September 28, 1998, p. 114; "Producing Unique Goods—and Headaches," *Inc.*, May 1998, p. 24; "Mass Production Gives Way to Mass Customization," *USA Today*, February 16, 1998, p. 3B. See also Jerry Wind and Arvid Rangaswamy, "Customerization: the NEXT Revolution in Mass Customization," *Journal of Interactive Marketing*, Winter 2001, p. 13; James H. Gilmore and B. Joseph Pine, "The Four Faces of Mass Customization," *Harvard Business Review*, January– February 1997, p. 91; B. Joseph Pine, Bart Victor, and Andrew C. Boynton, "Making Mass Customization Work," *Harvard Business Review*, September–October 1993, p. 108.

17. "The Numbers Game," *Business Week*, May 14, 2001, p. 100; "Accounting Gets Radical," *Fortune*, April 16, 2001, p. 184; "Manufacturing Masters Its ABCs," *Business Week*, August 7, 2000, p. 86J. See also Thomas H. Stevenson and David W. E. Cabell, "Integrating Transfer Pricing Policy and Activity-Based Costing," *Journal of International Marketing*, (4) 2002, p. 77; Fred A. Jacobs, Wesley Johnston and Natalia Kotchetova, "Customer Profitability: Prospective Vs. Retrospective Approaches in a Business-to-Business Setting," *Industrial Marketing Management*, May 2001, p. 353; Erik M. van Raaij, Maarten J. A. Vernooij and Sander van Triest, "The Implementation of Customer Profitability Analysis: a Case Study," *Industrial Marketing Management*, October 2003, p. 573; Victoria Dickinson and John C. Lere, "Problems Evaluating Sales Representative Performance? Try Activity-Based Costing," *Industrial Marketing Management*, May 2003, p. 301; Binshan Lin, James Collins and Robert K. Su, "Supply Chain Costing: an Activity-Based Perspective," *International Journal of Physical Distribution & Logistics Management*, (9) 2001, p. 702; Joseph A. Ness and Thomas G. Cucuzza, "Tapping the Full Potential of ABC," *Harvard Business Review*, July–August 1995, p. 130; Jae K. Shim and Joel G. Siegel, *Modern Cost Management and Analysis* (Hauppauge, NY: Barrons, 1992); John K. Shank and Vijay Govindarajan, *Strategic Cost Management: The New Tool for Competitive Advantage* (New York: The Free Press, 1993); Robin Cooper and Robert S. Kaplan, "Profit Priorities From Activity-Based Costing," *Harvard Business Review*, May/June 1991, p. 130.

18. "Defectors Provide Key Information," *Investor's Business Daily*, November 17, 2003, p. A8; "Having Any Fun?" *Time (Inside Business Bonus Section)*, November 2003; "Doing Good and Doing Well at Timberland," *The Wall Street Journal*, September 9, 2003, p. B1; "A Job Well Done," *Time (Inside Business Bonus Section)*, May 2003; "H-P Designs Workshops to Break Post-Merger Ice," *The Wall Street Journal*, July 11, 2002, p. B6; "How to Get the Geeks and the Suits to Play Nice," *Business 2.0*, May 2002, p. 92; "Container Store's Workers Huddle Up to Help You Out," *USA Today*, April 30, 2002, p. 1B; "Creating Incentives Down in Ranks: Marriott Ties Pay to Guest Replies," *Investor's Business Daily*, July 6, 2001, p. A1; "How the Truly Innovative Leaders Get Those (Creative) Sparks Flying," *Investor's Business Daily*, June 22, 2001, p. A1; "A Training Program Should Zero in on What Your Staffers Must Know," *Investor's Business Daily*, June 18, 2001, p. A1; "IBM Uses Education, Skills Training to Fill Gaps, Give Workers Options," *Investor's Business Daily*, May 14, 2001, p. A1; "Don't Let Economy Sap Staff Morale: Duke Energy, Southwest Air Tell How," *Investor's Business Daily*, April 16, 2001, p. A1; "As More Companies End Little Perks, Critics Call Moves Petty, Pointless," *The Wall Street Journal*, January 4, 2001, p. B1; "Want Smarter Employees? Get on the E-Train," *Ecompany*, January/February 2001, p. 140; "If Pat Sajak Were Your CEO," *Fortune*, December 18, 2000, p. 330; "Tapping the Last Big Labor Pool," *Fortune*, September 4, 2000, p. 326B. See also Christian Homburg, John P. Workman, Jr., and Ove Jensen, "Fundamental Changes in Marketing Organization: the Movement Toward a Customer-Focused Organizational Structure," *Journal of the Academy of Marketing Science*, Fall 2000, p. 459; Randy Englund, "Human Resource Skills for the Project Manager: The Human Aspects of Project Management, Volume Two," *Journal of Product Innovation Management*, January 1998, p. 99; Patricia W. Meyers, "Organizational Change and Redesign: Ideas and Insights for Improving Performance," *Journal of Product Innovation Management*, March 1997, p. 144; Dave Ulrich, "A New Mandate for Human Resources," *Harvard Business Review*, January–February 1998, p. 124; Vincent A. Mabert and Roger W. Schmenner, "Assessing the Roller Coaster of Downsizing," *Business Horizons*, July–August 1997, p. 45; Madhubalan Viswanathan and Eric M. Olson, "The Implementation of Business Strategies: Implications for the Sales Function," *Journal of Personal Selling & Sales Management*, Winter 1992, p. 45; Jeanie Daniel Duck, "Managing Change: The Art of Balancing," *Harvard Business Review*, November–December 1993, p. 109.

CHAPTER 21

1. Available from World Wide Web: <http://www.maytag. com>; "Surviving the Onslaught: Three Countries, One Dishwasher," *The Wall Street Journal*, October 6, 2003, p. B1; "Maytag Repairman Presents New Face," *Advertising Age*, August 4, 2003, p. 12; "Maytag Makes a Clean Break with Old Tagline," *Brandweek*, May 19, 2003, p. 9; "The Dell Myth: The Middleman Isn't Dead After All," *The Wall Street Journal Reports*, September 16, 2002, p. R12; "When Machines Chat," *Business Week*, July 23, 2001, p. 76; "Maytag Chairman Ward Resigns after Tenure Lasting 15 Months," *The Wall Street Journal*, November 10, 2000, p. B8; "Maytag Through the Wringer," *Business Week*, September 27, 1999, p. 54; "A New Spin on Clothes Washers," *Consumer Reports*, July 1998, p. 50; "Maytag's Top Officer, Expected to Do Little, Surprises His Board," *The Wall Street Journal*, June 23, 1998, p. A1; "New Spin on an Old Chore: New Front-Loader Is Water-Stingy," *USA Today*, March 25, 1998, p. 1A; "Maytag's Neptune Takes the Market by Storm," *Maytag Merchandiser*, No. 3, 1997; "Product Pampering," *Brandweek*, June 16, 1997, p. 29.

2. Available from World Wide Web: <http://www.nextel. com>; "That Loud Squawk May Come from a Walkie-Talkie Phone," *The Wall Street Journal*, November 21, 2003, p. B1; "Eyeing Nextel's Success, Sprint PCS to Offer Push-to-Talk Service," *Investor's Business Daily*, November 17, 2003, p. A5; "Sprint PCS Plans to Unveil a New Walkie-Talkie Service," *The Wall Street Journal*, November 17, 2003, p. B4; "Cellphones Go Walkie-Talkie," *USA Today*, October 27, 2003, p. 4B; "Push-to-Talk: Nextel Is Still the One to Beat," *Business Week*, October 13, 2003, p. 24; "Push to Talk: New Twist on Cellular Is Connecting," *USA Today*, October 13, 2003, p. 1D; "Guarding Nextel's Niche," *Fortune*, September 29, 2003, p. 133; "Nextel Execs Bullish on Growth Prospects," *Investor's Business Daily*, July 23, 2003, p. A6; "Nextel Wins the Race to Sponsor NASCAR," *BtoB*, July 14, 2003, p. 3; "Why Rivals Want Nextel's Number," *Business Week*, May 5, 2003, p. 74; "Nextel's Users Connect with Push to Talk," *Investor's Business Daily*, May 2, 2003, p. A6; "Business Customers Buoy Nextel," *Investor's Business Daily*, December 13, 2002, p. A6; "In Front: Barry West, the Great Communicator," *Business 2.0*, November 2002, p. 25; "Free-Spending Nextel Customers Help It Pull Away from the Rest," *Investor's Business Daily*, September 18, 2002, p. A1.

3. "Good Product. Sound Plans. No Sure Thing," *The New York Times*, January 18, 1998, Sect. 3, p. 1; John E. Smallwood, "The Product Life Cycle: A Key to Strategic Marketing Planning," *MSU Business Topics*, Winter 1973, p. 29; Richard F. Savach and Laurence A. Thompson, "Resource Allocation within the Product Life Cycle," *MSU Business Topics*, Autumn 1978, p. 35; Peter F. Kaminski and David R. Rink, "PLC: The Missing Link between Physical Distribution and Marketing Planning," *International Journal of Physical Distribution and Materials Management* 14, no. 6 (1984), p. 77.

4. See most basic statistics textbooks under time series analysis.

5. Checking the accuracy of forecasts is a difficult subject. See "Can This Weatherman See Your Future?" *Business 2.0*, August 2003, p. 96; Kenneth B. Kahn, "An Exploratory Investigation of New Product Forecasting Practices," *The Journal of Product Innovation Management*, March 2002, p. 133; Manoj K. Agarwal, "Developing Global Segments and Forecasting Market Shares: a Simultaneous Approach Using Survey Data," *Journal of International Marketing*, (4) 2003, p. 56; Jonathon T. Fite, G. Don Taylor, John S. Usher, John R. English, and John N. Roberts, "Forecasting Freight Demand Using Economic Indices," *International Journal of Physical Distribution & Logistics Management*, (3) 2002, p. 299; John B. Mahaffie, "Why Forecasts Fail," *American Demographics*, March 1995, p. 34; "Don't Be Trapped By Past Success," *Nation's Business*, March 1992, p. 52; Margaret K. Ambry, "States of the Future," *American Demographics*, October 1994, p. 36; Marcus O'Connor, William Remus, and Ken Griggs, "Going Up—Going Down: How Good Are People at Forecasting Trends and Changes in Trends?" *Journal of Forecasting*, May 1997, p. 165; Marshall L. Fisher, Janice H. Hammond, Walter R. Obermeyer, and Ananth Raman, "Making Supply Meet Demand in an Uncertain World," *Harvard Business Review*, May–June 1994, p. 83; Craig S. Galbraith and Gregory B. Merrill, "The Politics of Forecasting: Managing the Truth," *California Management Review*, Winter 1996, p. 29; Larry D. Compeau, "Forecasting and Market Analysis Techniques: A Practical Approach," *Journal of the Academy of Marketing Science*, Spring 1996, p. 181; Richard H. Evans, "Analyzing the Potential of a New Market," *Industrial Marketing Management*, February 1993, p. 35; Shelby H. McIntyre, Dale D. Achabal, and Christopher M. Miller, "Applying Case-Based Reasoning to Forecasting Retail Sales," *Journal of Retailing*, Winter 1993, p. 372; Paul A. Berbig, John Milewicz, and James E. Golden, "The Do's and Don'ts of Sales Forecasting," *Industrial Marketing Management*, February 1993, p. 49; David L. Kendall and Michael T. French, "Forecasting the Potential for New Industrial Products," *Industrial Marketing Management* 20, no. 3 (1991), p. 177; F. William Barrett, "Four Steps to Forecast Total Market Demand," *Harvard Business Review*, July–August 1988, p. 28; D. M. Georgoff and R. G. Murdick, "Manager's Guide to Forecasting," *Harvard Business Review*, January–February 1986, p. 110.

6. Peter R. Dickson, Paul W. Farris and Willem J. M. I. Verbeke, "Dynamic Strategic Thinking," *Journal of the Academy of Marketing Science,* Summer 2001, p. 216; Gloria Barczak, "Analysis for Marketing Planning," *Journal of Product Innovation Management,* September 1997, p. 424; William A. Sahlman, "How to Write a Great Business Plan," *Harvard Business Review,* July–August 1997, p. 98; Paul Boughton, "The 1-Day Marketing Plan: Organizing and Completing the Plan That Works," *Journal of the Academy of Marketing Science,* Summer 1996, p. 275; William Sandy, "Avoid the Breakdowns Between Planning and Implementation," *The Journal of Business Strategy,* September/ October 1991, p. 30; Michael MacInnis and Louise A. Heslop, "Market Planning in a High-Tech Environment," *Industrial Marketing Management,* May 1990, p. 107; David Strutton, "Marketing Strategies: New Approaches, New Techniques," *Journal of the Academy of Marketing Science,* Summer 1997, p. 261; Rita G. McGrath and Ian C. MacMillan, "Discovery-Driven Planning," *Harvard Business Review,* July 1995–August 1995, p. 44; Jeffrey Elton and Justin Roe, "Bringing Discipline to Project Management," *Harvard Business Review,* March– April 1998, p. 153; Andrew Campbell and Marcus Alexander, "What's Wrong With Strategy?" *Harvard Business Review,* November–December 1997, p. 42.

7. For further discussion on evaluating and selecting alternative plans, see Francis Buttle, "The Marketing Strategy Worksheet—A Practical Planning Tool," *Long Range Planning,* August 1985, p. 80; Douglas A. Schellinck, "Effect of Time on a Marketing Strategy," *Industrial Marketing Management,* April 1983, p. 83; George S. Day and Liam Fahey, "Valuing Market Strategies," *Journal of Marketing,* July 1988, p. 45.

8. Preet S. Aulakh and Esra F. Gencturk, "International Principal-Agent Relationships: Control, Governance and Performance," *Industrial Marketing Management,* November 2000, p. 521; Michael R. Czinkota and Masaaki Kotabe, "Entering the Japanese Market: a Reassessment of Foreign Firms' Entry and Distribution Strategies," *Industrial Marketing Management,* November 2000, p. 483; Huu-Phuong Ta and Hwee-Ling Choo and Chee-Chuong Sum, "Transportation Concerns of Foreign Firms in China," *International Journal of Physical Distribution & Logistics Management,* (1) 2000, p. 35; Oliver Burgel and Gordon C. Murray, "The International Market Entry Choices of Start-Up Companies in High-Technology Industries," *Journal of International Marketing,* (2) 2000, p. 33; Irini Dimou, Jean Chen, and Simon Archer, "The Choice Between Management Contracts and Franchise Agreements in the Corporate Development of International Hotel Firms," *Journal of Marketing Channels,* (3,4) 2003, p. 33; Naresh K. Malhotra, James Agarwal and Francis M. Ulgado, "Internationalization and Entry Modes: a Multitheoretical Framework and Research Propositions," *Journal of International Marketing,* (4) 2003, p. 1; George S. Yip, Javier Gomez Biscarri and Joseph A. Monti, "The Role of the Internationalization Process in the Performance of Newly Internationalizing Firms," *Journal of International Marketing,* (3) 2000, p. 10; Sam C. Okoroafo, "Modes of Entering Foreign Markets," *Industrial Marketing Management* 20, no. 4 (1991), p. 341; Mike Van Horn, "Market-Entry Approaches for the Pacific Rim," *The Journal of Business Strategy,* March/April 1990, p. 14; Refik Culpan, "Export Behavior of Firms: Relevance of Firm Size," *Journal of Business Research,* May, 1989, p. 207; Anthony C. Koh and Robert A. Robicheaux, "Variations in Export Performance Due to Differences in Export Marketing Strategy: Implications for Industrial Marketers," *Journal of Business Research,* November 1988, p. 249; S. Tamer Cavusgil, Shaoming Zou, and G.M. Naidu, "Product and Promotion Adaptation in Export Ventures: An Empirical Investigation," *Journal of International Business Studies,* Third Quarter 1993, p. 479.

9. S. Tamer Cavusgil, Kwong Chan, and Chun Zhang, "Strategic Orientations in Export Pricing: a Clustering Approach to Create Firm Taxonomies," *Journal of International Marketing,* (1) 2003, p. 47; Evangelia Katsikea and Robert E. Morgan, "Exploring Export Sales Management Practices in Small- and Medium-Sized Firms," *Industrial Marketing Management,* August 2003, p. 467; Constantine S. Katsikeas and Neil M.

Morgan, "Firm-Level Export Performance Assessment: Review, Evaluation, and Development," *Journal of the Academy of Marketing Science,* Fall 2000, p. 493; Jerry Haar and Marta Ortiz-Buonafina, "The Internationalization Process and Marketing Activities: The Case of Brazilian Export Firms," *Journal of Business Research,* February 1995, p. 175; Robert E. Morgan and Constantine S. Katsikeas, "Exporting Problems of Industrial Manufacturers," *Industrial Marketing Management,* March 1998, p. 161.

10. Masaaki Kotabe, Arvind Sahay, and Preet S. Aulakh, "Emerging Role of Technology Licensing in the Development of Global Product Strategy: Conceptual Framework and Research Propositions," *Journal of Marketing,* January 1996, p. 73; John A. Quelch, "How to Build a Product Licensing Program," *Harvard Business Review,* May–June 1985, p. 186.

11. "A Wild World for Funds," *Business Week,* February 10, 2004, p. 50.

12. For an excellent example of Haier joint ventures, see "When Your Customer Says Jump . . . ," *Business 2.0,* October 2003, p. 62; "Breaking into the Name Game," *Business Week,* April 7, 2003, p. 54; "China's Power Brands Eye Global Expansion," *Advertising Age,* January 13, 2003, p. 12; Roger J. Calantone and Yushan Sam Zhao, "Joint Ventures in China: a Comparative Study of Japanese, Korean, and U.S. Partners," *Journal of International Marketing,* (1) 2001, p. 1; Robert Porter Lynch, "Building Alliances to Penetrate European Markets," *The Journal of Business Strategy,* March/April 1990, p. 4; D. Robert Webster, "International Joint Ventures with Pacific Rim Partners," *Business Horizons,* March/ April 1989, p. 65; Kenichi Ohmae, "The Global Logic of Strategic Alliances," *Harvard Business Review,* March/April 1989, p. 143; Ashish Nanda and Peter J. Williamson, "Use Joint Ventures to Ease the Pain of Restructuring," *Harvard Business Review,* November–December 1995, p. 119.

13. "Barilla Cooks Up a Storm in U.S. Aisles," *USA Today,* November 10, 2003, p. 1B; "Saying 'Beamer' in Chinese," *The Wall Street Journal,* November 6, 2003, p. B1; "Borders Are So 20th Century," *Business Week,* September 22, 2003, p. 68; "A New Twist in Legend's Tale," *Business Week,* June 23, 2003, p. 50; "The Bold Struggle for China's Belly," *The New York Times,* March 6, 2003, p. C1; "North of Beijing, California Dreams Come True," *The New York Times,* February 3, 2003, p. A3; "Winning in China," *Business Week,* January 27, 2003, p. 98; "Cracking China's Market," *The Wall Street Journal,* January 9, 2003, p. B1; "Made in China, Bought in China," *The New York Times,* January 5, 2003, Sect. 3, p. 1; "Sony Finds It's a Small World," *The Wall Street Journal,* December 20, 2002, p. A10; "Peeling Out: World's Car Makers Race to Keep Up with China Boom," *The Wall Street Journal,* December 13, 2002, p. A1; "Greater China," *Business Week,* December 9, 2002, p. 50; "China's Low-Cost Labor Lures More Japanese Companies," *USA Today,* November 21, 2002, p. 1B; "As China's Women Change, Marketers Notice," *The Wall Street Journal,* May 30, 2002, p. A11; "How KFC, UT-Starcom Learned to Operate Profitably in China," *Investor's Business Daily,* February 13, 2002, p. A1; "The Export Bust," *Business Week Small Biz,* October 8, 2001, p. 15; "Place vs. Product: It's Tough to Choose a Management Model," *The Wall Street Journal,* June 27, 2001, p. A1; "Distractions Make Global Manager a Difficult Role," *The Wall Street Journal,* November 21, 2000, p. B1; "How to Project Power Around the World," *The Wall Street Journal,* November 13, 2000, p. A23; "New CEO Preaches Rebellion for P&G's Cult," *The Wall Street Journal,* December 11, 1998, p. B1. See also Cheryl Nakata and K. Sivakumar, "Instituting the Marketing Concept in a Multinational Setting: the Role of National Culture," *Journal of the Academy of Marketing Science,* Summer 2001, p. 255; Regina F. Maruca, "The Right Way to Go Global: An Interview With Whirlpool CEO David Whitwam," *Harvard Business Review,* March–April 1994, p. 134; Tevfik Dalgic, "Multinational Companies in United States International Trade: A Statistical and Analytical Sourcebook," *Journal of the Academy of Marketing Science,* Spring 1997, p. 172; Keith Cerny, "Making Local Knowledge Global," *Harvard Business Review,* May–June 1996, p. 22; Chi-fai Chan and Neil B. Holbert, "Whose

Empire Is This, Anyway? Reflections on the Empire State of Multi-National Corporations," *Business Horizons*, July–August 1994, p. 51; Syed H. Akhter and Yusuf A. Choudhry, "Forced Withdrawal from a Country Market: Managing Political Risk," *Business Horizons*, May–June 1993, p. 47; M. Krishna Erramilli and C.P. Rao, "Service Firms' International Entry-Mode Choice: A Modified Transaction-Cost Analysis Approach," *Journal of Marketing*, July 1993, p. 19.

CHAPTER 22

1. For more on consumer choice, see Ross D. Petty, "Limiting Product Choice: Innovation, Market Evolution, and Antitrust," *Journal of Public Policy & Marketing*, Fall 2002, p. 269; Mitch Griffin, Barry J. Babin, and Doan Modianos, "Shopping Values of Russian Consumers: The Impact of Habituation in a Developing Economy," *Journal of Retailing*, Spring 2000, p. 33; Suk-ching Ho, "The Emergence of Consumer Power in China," *Business Horizons*, September–October 1997, p. 15; Matthew B. Myers, "New and Improved: The Story of Mass Marketing in America," *Journal of the Academy of Marketing Science*, Summer 1997, p. 258; Terry Clark, "Moving Mountains to Market: Reflections on Restructuring the Russian Economy," *Business Horizons*, March–April 1994, p. 16. See also "From Sour Grapes to Online Whine," *USA Today*, April 7, 2000, p. 1B; "Service with a What?" *Business Week*, September 8, 1997, pp. 130F–H; "Oh, What a Feeling," *Newsweek*, July 28, 1997, p. 51; "Attention, Wal-Mart Shoppers: You Want Fries with That?" *The Wall Street Journal*, July 25, 1997, p. B6; "Buyers Get No Satisfaction," *USA Today*, July 22, 1997, p. 1B. For more on Tesco, see "British Supermarket Giant Cooks Up Plans to Go Global," *The Wall Street Journal*, July 5, 2001, p. A9; "British Grocer Tesco Thrives Filling Web Orders from Its Stores' Aisles," *The Wall Street Journal*, October 16, 2000, p. B1; "Tesco: A Fresh Approach to Online Groceries," *Business Week E.Biz*, September 18, 2000, p. EB79. For more on online shopping for groceries in the U.S., see "Virtual Bounty: Groceries to Go," *Brandweek*, November 24, 2003, p. 19; "Services: Online Grocers," *Newsweek*, August 4, 2003, p. 60; "Amazon, Mail-Order Retailers Reheat Online Food Sales," *The Wall Street Journal*, June 23, 2003, p. B1; "What's for Dinner?" *Time*, May 19, 2003, p. 85; "Online Grocers: Finally Delivering the Lettuce," *Business Week*, April 28, 2003, p. 67; "Back from the Dead: Buying Groceries Online," *The Wall Street Journal*, February 25, 2003, p. D1; "Webvan May Be Long Gone, but the Concept's Living On," *Investor's Business Daily*, November 5, 2001, p. A9. For more on Webvan's failed effort, see "Traditional Grocers Feel Vindicated by Webvan's Failure," *The Wall Street Journal*, July 11, 2001, p. B4. See also "Information Gridlock: Fate, Fortune Ride on Flow of Critical Data," *USA Today*, July 2, 1996, p. 1B; Michael B. Mazis, "Marketing and Public Policy: Prospects for the Future," *Journal of Public Policy & Marketing*, Spring 1997, p. 139; Cornelia Droge et al., "The Consumption Culture and Its Critiques: A Framework for Analysis," *Journal of Macromarketing*, Fall 1993, p. 32. For more on obesity concerns, see "Today's Kids Are Helping Themselves," *USA Today*, November 20, 2003, p. 1D; "Junk Food Super-Sizing Europeans," *USA Today*, November 18, 2003, p. 13A; "The Dining Hall Diet," *The Wall Street Journal*, November 7, 2003, p. W1; "Dieters' Taboo Foods Not So Bad, Ads Claim," *USA Today*, November 3, 2003, p. 4B; "Pizza Hut to Serve Up Slices of Healthier Pie," *USA Today*, October 15, 2003, p. 1B; "Americans Start to Shape Up, Eat Healthier," *The Wall Street Journal*, October 14, 2003, p. B1; "Obesity Predicted for 40% of America," *USA Today*, October 14, 2003, p. 7D; "A Real Food Fight Breaks Out in Schools," *Investor's Business Daily*, September 22, 2003, p. A8; "Guess What F Is For? Fat," *Time*, September 15, 2003, p. 68; "Obesity Suit against McDonald's Is Dismissed by Federal Judge," *The Wall Street Journal*, September 5, 2003, p. B4; "Fast Foods: Back in Court," *Time (Inside Edition Bonus Section)*, September 2003; "Saving Mickey D's Bacon," *Business Week*, August 25, 2003, p. 46; "Obesity Goes Global," *Time*, August 25, 2003, p. 53; "Frito-Lay Puts Smart-Snack Label on Baked Chips," *The Wall Street Journal*, August 6, 2003, p. D3; "Judge Drops Lawsuit against McDonald's," *USA Today*, January 23, 2003, p. 2B; "That Veggie Wrap You Just Chowed Down Is More Fattening than a Ham Sandwich," *The Wall Street Journal*, January 14, 2003, p. D1; "Advertising: As Waistlines Expand, So Does Advertising," *The New York Times*, January 13, 2003, p. C12; "Gerber Pushes Parents to Feed Healthier Diet to Their Babies," *The Wall Street Journal*, August 19, 2002, p. B5; "Obesity: A World-Wide Woe," *The Wall Street Journal*, July 1, 2002, p. B1; "Is Food the Next Tobacco?" *The Wall Street Journal*, June 13, 2002, p. B1.

2. *The American Customer Satisfaction Index*, 2000; "Now Are You Satisfied? The 1998 American Customer Satisfaction Index," *Fortune*, February 16, 1998, p. 161. See also Terrence H. Witkowski and Mary F. Wolfinbarger, "Comparative Service Quality: German and American Ratings Across Service Settings," *Journal of Business Research*, November 2002, p. 875; Eugene W. Anderson and Linda Court Salisbury, "The Formation of Market-Level Expectations and its Covariates," *Journal of Consumer Research*, Jun 2003, p. 115; Claes Fornell, Michael D. Johnson, Eugene W. Anderson, Jaesung Cha, and Barbara E. Bryant, "The American Customer Satisfaction Index: Nature, Purpose, and Findings," *Journal of Marketing*, October 1996, p. 7; Eugene W. Anderson, Claes Fornell, and Donald R. Lehmann, "Customer Satisfaction, Market Share, and Profitability: Findings From Sweden," *Journal of Marketing*, July 1994, p. 53; John F. Gaski and Michael J. Etzel, "The Index of Consumer Sentiment Toward Marketing," *Journal of Marketing*, July 1986, p. 71; "The Limits of Customer Satisfaction," *Brandweek*, March 3, 1997, p. 17; Hiram C. Barksdale et al., "A Cross-National Survey of Consumer Attitudes Toward Marketing Practices, Consumerism, and Government Regulations," *Columbia Journal of World Business*, Summer 1982, p. 71; Hiram C. Barksdale and William D. Perreault, Jr., "Can Consumers Be Satisfied?" *MSU Business Topics*, Spring 1980, p. 19.

3. "Consumer Complaints Soared in 2002," *The Wall Street Journal*, November 25, 2003, p. D2; "Will Jeff Immelt's New Push Pay Off for GE?" *Business Week*, October 13, 2003, p. 94; "Whatever Happened to Customer Service?" *USA Today*, September 26, 2003, p. 1A; "Ma'am, Please: Never Call Us Again," *Brandweek*, September 22, 2003, p. 38; "J.D. Power for the People," *USA Today*, August 28, 2003, p. 3B; "Web-Portal Satisfaction Rises," *The Wall Street Journal*, August 20, 2003, p. D2; "My Cookies Are Crumbled; the Art of Consumer Griping," *The Wall Street Journal*, August 27, 2002, p. D1. See also Judy Strauss and Donna J. Hill, "Consumer Complaints by E-Mail: an Exploratory Investigation of Corporate Responses and Customer Reactions," *Journal of Interactive Marketing*, Winter 2001, p. 63; James G. Maxham III and Richard G. Netemeyer, "Modeling Customer Perceptions of Complaint Handling over Time: the Effects of Perceived Justice on Satisfaction and Intent," *Journal of Retailing*, Winter 2002, p. 239; James G. Maxham III and Richard G. Netemeyer, "A Longitudinal Study of Complaining Customers' Evaluations of Multiple Service Failures and Recovery Efforts," *Journal of Marketing*, October 2002, p. 57; James G. Maxham III and Richard G. Netemyer, "Firms Reap What They Sow: the Effects of Shared Values and Perceived Organizational Justice on Customers' Evaluations of Complaint Handling," *Journal of Marketing*, January 2003, p. 46; Roger Bougie, Rik Pieters and Marcel Zeelenberg, "Angry Customers Don't Come Back, They Get Back: the Experience and Behavioral Implications of Anger and Dissatisfaction in Services," *Journal of the Academy of Marketing Science*, Fall 2003, p. 377; Amy K. Smith and Ruth N. Bolton, "The Effect of Customers' Emotional Responses to Service Failures on Their Recovery Effort Evaluations and Satisfaction Judgements," *Journal of the Academy of Marketing Science*, Winter 2002, p. 5; Michael Brady, "Improving Your Measurement of Customer Satisfaction: A Guide to Creating, Conducting, Analyzing, and Reporting Customer Satisfaction Measurement Programs," *Journal of the Academy of Marketing Science*, Spring 2000, p. 315; David M. Szymanski, "Customer Satisfaction: A Meta-Analysis of the Empirical Evidence," *Journal of the Academy of Marketing Science*, Winter 2001, p. 16; Thorsten Hennig-Thurau and Alexander Klee, "The Impact of Customer Satisfaction and Relationship Quality on Customer Retention: A Critical Reassessment and Model Development," *Psychology & Marketing*, December 1997, p. 737; Scott W. Hansen, Thomas L. Powers, and John E. Swan, "Modeling Industrial

Buyer Complaints: Implications for Satisfying and Saving Customers," *Journal of Marketing Theory & Practice*, Fall 1997, p. 12; Paul G. Patterson, Lester W. Johnson, and Richard A. Spreng, "Modeling the Determinants of Customer Satisfaction for Business-to-Business Professional Services," *Journal of the Academy of Marketing Science*, Winter 1997, p. 4; Stephen S. Tax, Stephen W. Brown, and Murali Chandrashekaran, "Customer Evaluations of Service Complaint Experiences: Implications for Relationship Marketing," *Journal of Marketing*, April 1998, p. 60; F. Gouillart and F. Sturdivant, "Spend a Day in the Life of Your Customers," *Harvard Business Review*, January–February 1994, p. 116.

4. Scott R. Colwell, "The Future of Marketing: Practical Strategies for Marketers in the Post-Internet Age," *Journal of the Academy of Marketing Science*, Winter 2003, p. 95; Kevin J. Clancy and Robert S. Shulman, *Marketing Myths that are Killing Business: The Cure for Death Wish Marketing* (New York: McGraw-Hill, 1994); Regina E. Herzlinger, "Can Public Trust in Nonprofits and Governments Be Restored?" *Harvard Business Review*, March–April 1996, p. 97; Michael S. Minor, "Relentless: The Japanese Way of Marketing," *Journal of the Academy of Marketing Science*, Spring 1998, p. 160; Charles C. Snow, "Twenty-First-Century Organizations: Implications for a New Marketing Paradigm," *Journal of the Academy of Marketing Science*, Winter 1997, p. 72; Frederick F. Reichheld, "Learning From Customer Defections," *Harvard Business Review*, March–April 1996, p. 56. For a classic discussion of the problem and mechanics of measuring the efficiency of marketing, see Reavis Cox, *Distribution in a High-Level Economy* (Englewood Cliffs, NJ: Prentice-Hall, 1965).

5. For more on criticisms of advertising, see David C. Vladeck, "Truth and Consequences: the Perils of Half-Truths and Unsubstantiated Health Claims for Dietary Supplements," *Journal of Public Policy & Marketing*, Spring 2000, p. 132; Barbara J. Phillips, "In Defense of Advertising: A Social Perspective," *Journal of Business Ethics*, February 1997, p. 109; Charles Trappey, "A Meta-Analysis of Consumer Choice and Subliminal Advertising," *Psychology & Marketing*, August 1996, p. 517; Karl A. Boedecker, Fred W. Morgan, and Linda B. Wright, "The Evolution of First Amendment Protection for Commercial Speech," *Journal of Marketing*, January 1995, p. 38; Thomas C. O'Guinn and L. J. Shrum, "The Role of Television in the Construction of Consumer Reality," *Journal of Consumer Research*, March 1997, p. 278; see also Robert B. Archibald, Clyde A. Haulman, and Carlisle E. Moody, Jr., "Quality, Price, Advertising, and Published Quality Ratings," *Journal of Consumer Research*, March 1983, p. 347.

6. Thomas O. Jones and W. E. Sasser, "Why Satisfied Customers Defect," *Harvard Business Review*, Novembe–December 1995, p. 88; "The Satisfaction Trap," *Harvard Business Review*, March–April 1996, p. 58.

7. "Can Money Buy Happiness?" *Adweek*, February 3, 2003, p. 26; James E. Burroughs and Aric Rindfleisch, "Materialism and Well-Being: a Conflicting Values Perspective," *Journal of Consumer Research*, Dec 2002, p. 348; John Watson, Steven Lysonski, Tamara Gillan and Leslie Raymore, "Cultural Values and Important Processions: a Cross-Cultural Analysis," *Journal of Business Research*, November 2002, p. 923; Roy F. Baumeister, "Yielding to Temptation: Self-Control Failure, Impulsive Purchasing, and Consumer Behavior," *Journal of Consumer Research*, March 2002, p. 670; Donald F. Dixon, "The Economics of Conspicuous Consumption: Theory and Thought Since 1700," *Journal of Macromarketing*, June 2001, Vol. 21, 1, p. 101; Guliz Ger, "Human Development and Humane Consumption: Well-Being Beyond the 'Good Life,'" *Journal of Public Policy & Marketing*, Spring 1997, p. 110; Ronald P. Hill and Sandi Macan, "Consumer Survival on Welfare With an Emphasis on Medicaid and the Food Stamp Program," *Journal of Public Policy & Marketing*, Spring 1996, p. 118; Dennis J. Cahill, "The Refinement of America: Persons, Houses, Cities," *Journal of Marketing*, October 1994, p. 121. See also Michael J. Barone, Randall L. Rose, Kenneth C. Manning, and Paul W. Miniard, "Another Look at the Impact of Reference Information on Consumer Impressions of Nutrition Information," *Journal of Public Policy & Marketing*, Spring 1996, p. 55; Thomas A. Hemphill, "Legislating Corporate Social Responsibility," *Business Horizons*, March–April

1997, p. 53; Priscilla A. La Barbera and Zeynep Gurhan, "The Role of Materialism, Religiosity, and Demographics in Subjective Well-Being," *Psychology & Marketing*, January 1997, p. 71; Dennis J. Cahill, "Consumption and the World of Goods," *Journal of Marketing*, April 1994, p. 131; Jacqueline K. Eastman, Bill Fredenberger, David Campbell, and Stephen Calvert, "The Relationship Between Status Consumption and Materialism: A Cross-Cultural Comparison of Chinese, Mexican and American Students," *Journal of Marketing Theory & Practice*, Winter 1997, p. 52; James A. Muncy and Jacqueline K. Eastman, "Materialism and Consumer Ethics: An Exploratory Study," *Journal of Business Ethics*, January 1998, p. 137; Donald P. Robin and R. Eric Reidenbach, "Identifying Critical Problems for Mutual Cooperation Between the Public and Private Sectors: A Marketing Perspective," *Journal of the Academy of Marketing Science*, Fall 1986, p. 1. See also Terrence H. Witkowski, "The Early American Style: A History of Marketing and Consumer Values," *Psychology & Marketing*, March 1998, p. 125; Arnold J. Toynbee, *America and World Revolution* (New York: Oxford University Press, 1966), p. 144; John Kenneth Galbraith, *Economics and the Public Purpose* (Boston: Houghton Mifflin, 1973), p. 144.

8. For more on global social responsibility, see Chapter 1, endnote 10, and Chapter 5, endnote 5.

9. For other environmental issues, see "The Race to Save a Rainforest," *Business Week*, November 24, 2003, p. 125; "Cellphone Makers Connect for Recycling Program," *USA Today*, October 22, 2003, p. 6B; "The Information Age's Toxic Garbage," *Business Week*, October 6, 2003, p. 54; "Offsetting Environmental Damage by Planes," *The New York Times*, February 18, 2003, p. C6; "Behind Roses' Beauty, Poor and Ill Workers," *The New York Times*, February 13, 2003, p. A1; "Industrial Evolution," *Business Week*, April 8, 2002, p. 70; "Green Sales Pitch Isn't Moving Many Products," *The Wall Street Journal*, March 6, 2002, p. B1; "Brazilian Mahogany: Too Much in Demand," *The Wall Street Journal*, November 14, 2001, p. B1; "How Much Power Do You Use?" *The Wall Street Journal*, August 16, 2001, p. B1; "Choice of Evils: As a Tropical Scourge Makes a Comeback, So, Too, Does DDT," *The Wall Street Journal*, July 26, 2001, p. A1; "It May Be Time to Toss Old Ideas on Recycling," *USA Today*, July 2, 2001, p. 7D; "As BP Goes Green, the Fur Is Flying," *The Wall Street Journal*, April 16, 2001, p. A10; "Once Is Not Enough," *Business Week*, April 16, 2001, p. 128B; "EarthShell Saw Big Macs and Big Bucks—Got Big Woes," *The Wall Street Journal*, April 10, 2001, p. B2; "Recycling Redefined," *The Wall Street Journal*, March 6, 2001, p. B1; "More Gas-Powered Autos on 'Green' List," *USA Today*, February 9, 2001, p. 3B; "Nonprofits—and Landfills—Deluged with Old PCs," *Investor's Business Daily*, November 27, 2000, p. A6; "Conservation: Been There, Doing That," *Business Week*, November 27, 2000, p. 194F; "Recycler's Nightmare: Beer in Plastic," *The Wall Street Journal*, November 16, 1999, p. B1; "As Old Pallets Pile Up, Critics Hammer Them as a New Eco-Menace," *The Wall Street Journal*, April 1, 1998, p. A1. See also Lynette Knowles Mathur and Ike Mathur, "An Analysis of the Wealth Effects of Green Marketing Strategies," *Journal of Business Research*, November 2000, p. 193; Subhabrata Bobby Banerjee, Easwar S. Iyer, and Rajiv K. Kashyap, "Corporate Environmentalism: Antecedents and Influence of Industry Type," *Journal of Marketing*, April 2003, p. 106; Anil Menon and Ajay Menon, "Enviropreneurial Marketing Strategy: The Emergence of Corporate Environmentalism As Market Strategy," *Journal of Marketing*, January 1997, p. 51; William E. Kilbourne, "Green Advertising: Salvation or Oxymoron?" *Journal of Advertising*, Summer 1995, p. 7.

10. "The Good News: No More Coke in School. The Bad News: Snapple Is Replacing It," *The Wall Street Journal*, January 13, 2004, p. D1; "Coke's Guidelines for Soft Drinks in Schools Faces Some Criticism," *The Wall Street Journal*, November 17, 2003, p. A6; "New in School Vending Machines: Yogurt, Soy," *The Wall Street Journal*, October 15, 2003, p. B1; "A Real Food Fight Breaks Out in Schools," *Investor's Business Daily*, September 22, 2003, p. A8; "Head of the Class: Don't Spare the Brand," *Brandweek*, March 10, 2003, p. 20; "Cafeteria Food Fight,"

The Wall Street Journal, June 14, 2002, p. B1; "Coke Finds Its Exclusive School Contracts Aren't So Easily Given Up," *The Wall Street Journal*, June 26, 2001, p. B1; "Web-Filter Data from Schools Put Up for Sale," *The Wall Street Journal*, January 26, 2001, p. B1; "On Many Campuses, Big Brewers Play a Role in New Alcohol Policies," *The Wall Street Journal*, November 2, 2000, p. A1; "Pepsi Hits High Note with Schools," *Advertising Age*, October 9, 2000, p. 30; "If It's Marketing, Can It Also Be Education?" *Fortune*, October 2, 2000, p. 274; "AOL to Announce This Week the Launch of Free Online Service Aimed at Schools," *The Wall Street Journal*, May 16, 2000, p. B6; "Mouse-Trapping the Student Market," *American Demographics*, May 2000, p. 30; "Grad Students Match Wits in Marketing Competition," *The Wall Street Journal*, February 9, 2000, p. S1; "Pitching Saturns to Your Classmates—for Credit," *The Wall Street Journal*, January 31, 2000, p. B1; "Marketers on Campus: A New Bag of Tricks," *The Wall Street Journal*, January 31, 2000, p. B1; "Tobacco Money Sparks a New Fight," *The Wall Street Journal*, December 10, 1999, p. B1; "Schools for Sale," *Advertising Age*, October 25, 1999, p. 22; "Big Cards on Campus," *Business Week*, September 20, 1999, p. 138; "Cola Contracts Lose Fizz in Schools," *USA Today*, August 18, 1999, p. 9D; "Ads in Schools: Lesson in Failure?" *Advertising Age*, June 7, 1999, p. 26; "Classrooms for Sale," *Time*, April 19, 1999, p. 44; "Big Car on Campus?" *Business Week*, August 31, 1998, p. 32; "Are We Selling Our Students?" *Raleigh News & Observer*, August 2, 1998, p. 25A; "This School Was Sponsored by . . . ," *Parenting*, March 1998, p. 23; "Channel One Taps Principals as Promoters," *The Wall Street Journal*, September 15, 1997, p. B1; "School's Back, and So Are the Marketers," *The Wall Street Journal*, September 15, 1997, p. B1; "Hey Kid, Buy This!" *Business Week*, June 30, 1997, p. 62; "This Class Brought to You by . . . ," *USA Today*, January 3, 1997, p. 3A; "New Ad Vehicles: Police Car, School Bus, Garbage Truck," *The Wall Street Journal*, February 20, 1996, p. B1.

11. For more on privacy, see Chapter 14, footnote #12. See also "You're on Candid Cellphone!" *The Wall Street Journal*, September 30, 2003, p. B1; "Stalk Market: New Battleground in Web Privacy War, Ads that Snoop," *The Wall Street Journal*, August 27, 2003, p. A1; "Online Shopper Still Fear Security Issues," *Investor's Business Daily*, June 3, 2003, p. A4; "Privacy in an Age of Terror," *Business Week*, November 5, 2001, p. 83; "Internet Insecurity," *Time*, July 2, 2001, p. 44; "Privacy Options Are a Blur," *USA Today*, April 10, 2001, p. 3D; "The Battle Over Web Privacy," *The Wall Street Journal*, March 21, 2001, p. B1; "Network Solutions Sells Marketers Its Web Database," *The Wall Street Journal*, February 16, 2001, p. B1; "Continental Air Loses Some Accounts after Data-Disclosure Demand," *The Wall Street Journal*, February 6, 2001, p. B1; "Special Report: Privacy," *Business Week*, April 5, 1999, p. 84. See also Curt J. Dommeyer and Barbara L. Gross, "What Consumers Know and What They Do: an Investigation of Consumer Knowledge, Awareness, and Use of Privacy Protection Strategies," *Journal of Interactive Marketing*, Spring 2003, p. 34; John A. McCarty, "Data Privacy in the Information Age," *Journal of Public Policy & Marketing*, Fall 2002, p. 336; George R. Milne and Andrew J. Rohm, "Consumer Privacy and Name Removal Across Direct Marketing Channels: Exploring Opt-In and Opt-Out Alternatives," *Journal of Public Policy & Marketing*, Fall 2000, p. 238; Joseph E. Phelps, Giles D'Souza and Glen J. Nowak, "Antecedents and Consequences of Consumer Privacy Concerns: an Empirical Investigation," *Journal of Interactive Marketing*, Autumn 2001, p. 2; Ellen R. Foxman and Paula Kilcoyne, "Information Technology, Marketing Practice, and Consumer Privacy: Ethical Issues," *Journal of Public Policy & Marketing*, Spring 1993, p. 106; Robert E. Thomas and Virginia G. Maurer, "Database Marketing Practice: Protecting Consumer Privacy," *Journal of Public Policy & Marketing*, Spring 1997, p. 147; Marren J. Roy, "Regulation of Automatic Dialing and Announcing Devices Upheld," *Journal of the Academy of Marketing Science*, Summer 1997, p. 269.

12. For more on online fraud, see "Scammed! Web Merchants Use New Tools to Keep Buyers from Ripping Them Off," *The Wall Street Journal Reports*, January 27, 2003, p. 16; "E-Commerce Report: Crime Is Soaring in Cyberspace," *The New York Times*, January 27, 2003, p. C4;

"Credit-Card Scams Bedevil E-Stores," *The Wall Street Journal*, September 19, 2000, p. B1; "Fraud on the Internet," *Business Week E.Biz*, April 3, 2000, p. EB58; "Online Scambusters," *Business Week E.Biz*, April 3, 2000, p. EB66; "Card Sharps," *Business Week E.Biz*, April 3, 2000, p. EB68. For more on in-store fraud, see "Stores Battle Employee Theft," *Raleigh News & Observer*, October 15, 2000, p. 1E; "As Thievery by Insiders Overtakes Shoplifting, Retailers Crack Down," *The Wall Street Journal*, September 8, 2000, p. A1; "Electronic Tags Are Beeping Everywhere," *The Wall Street Journal*, April 20, 1998, p. B1; "A Time to Steal," *Brandweek*, February 16, 1998, p. 24.

13. For more on socially responsible and ethical behavior, see "Teaching the Wrong Lesson," *Business 2.0*, November 2003, p. 60; "Food Sellers Push Animal Welfare," *USA Today*, August 13, 2003, p. 1D; "In the Name of Responsibility," *Brandweek*, May 12, 2003, p. 32; "For MBAs, Soul-Searching 101," *Business Week*, September 16, 2002, p. 64; "Wanted: Ethical Employer," *The Wall Street Journal*, July 9, 2002, p. B1; "I Take Thee . . . Back to the Store," *The Wall Street Journal*, May 30, 2002, p. D1. See also John C. Kozup, Elizabeth H. Creyer, and Scot Burton, "Making Healthful Food Choices: the Influence of Health Claims and Nutrition Information on Consumers' Evaluations of Packaged Food Products and Restaurant Menu Items," *Journal of Marketing*, April 2003, p. 19; Sankar Sen, Zeynep Gurhan-Canli, and Vicki Morwitz, "Withholding Consumption: a Social Dilemma Perspective on Consumer Boycotts," *Journal of Consumer Research*, December 2001, p. 399; Steve Hoeffler and Kevin Lane Keller, "Building Brand Equity Through Corporate Societal Marketing," *Journal of Public Policy & Marketing*, Spring 2002, p. 78; Dwane Hal Dean, "Associating the Cooperation with a Charitable Event Through Sponsorship: Measuring the Effects on Corporate Community Relations," *Journal of Advertising*, Winter 2002, p. 77; Richard Pearce and Maria Hansson, "Retailing and Risk Society: Genetically Modified Food," *International Journal of Retail & Distribution Management*, (11) 2000, p. 450; W. P. Cunningham, "The Golden Rule As Universal Ethical Norm," *Journal of Business Ethics*, January 1998, p. 105; "Ethnic Pricing' Means Unfair Air Fares," *The Wall Street Journal*, December 5, 1997, p. B1, William P. Cordeiro, "Suggested Management Responses to Ethical Issues Raised by Technological Change," *Journal of Business Ethics*, September 1997, p. 1393; Eli P. I. Cox, Michael S. Wogalter, Sara L. Stokes, and Elizabeth J. T. Murff, "Do Product Warnings Increase Safe Behavior? A Meta-Analysis," *Journal of Public Policy & Marketing*, Fall 1997, p. 195; "On the Net, Anything Goes," *Newsweek*, July 7, 1997, p. 28; "'Levi's As Ye Sew, So Shall Ye Reap," *Fortune*, May 12, 1997, p. 104; "48% of Workers Admit to Unethical or Illegal Acts," *USA Today*, April 4, 1997, p. 1A; H. R. Dodge, Elizabeth A. Edwards, and Sam Fullerton, "Consumer Transgressions in the Marketplace: Consumers' Perspectives," *Psychology & Marketing*, December 1996, p. 821; David W. Stewart, "Internet Marketing, Business Models, and Public Policy," *Journal of Public Policy & Marketing*, Fall 2000, p. 287; Albert A. Foer, "E-commerce Meets Antitrust: A Primer," *Journal of Public Policy & Marketing*, Spring 2001, p. 51; "Ethics for Hire," *Business Week*, July 15, 1996, p. 26; "How a Drug Firm Paid for University Study, Then Undermined It," *The Wall Street Journal*, April 25, 1996, p. A1; James A. Roberts, "Will the Real Socially Responsible Consumer Please Step Forward?" *Business Horizons*, January–February 1996, p. 79; John Priddle, "Marketing Ethics, Macromarketing, and the Managerial Perspective Reconsidered," *Journal of Macromarketing*, Fall 1994, p. 47; Bernard Avishai, "What is Business's Social Compact?" *Harvard Business Review*, January–February 1994, p. 38; Paul N. Bloom, George R. Milne, and Robert Adler, "Avoiding Misuse of New Information Technologies: Legal and Societal Considerations," *Journal of Marketing*, January 1994, p. 98; James A. Muncy and Scott J. Vitell, "Consumer Ethics: An Investigation of the Ethical Beliefs of the Final Consumer," *Journal of Business Research*, June 1992, p. 297; Gene R. Laczniak and Patrick E. Murphy, "Fostering Ethical Marketing Decisions," *Journal of Business Ethics*, April 1991, p. 259.

Illustration Credits

CHAPTER 1

Exhibits: Exhibit 1-2, adapted from William McInnes,"A Conceptual Approach to Marketing,"in *Theory in Marketing*, 2d ser., ed. Reavis Cox, Wroe Alderson, and Stanley J. Shapiro (Homewood, IL: Richard D. Irwin, 1964), pp. 51–67. Exhibit 1-3, model suggested by Professor A. A. Brogowicz, Western Michigan University. Exhibit 1-5, adapted from R. F. Vizza, T. E. Chambers, and E. J. Cook, *Adoption of the Marketing Concept—Fact or Fiction* (New York: Sales Executive Club, Inc., 1967), pp. 13–15. Exhibit 1-6, this exhibit is different from, but stimulated by, a graph that appears on the Satisfaction Management Systems, Inc., website <http://www.satmansys.com>. Exhibit 1-8, adapted from discussions of an American Marketing Association Strategic Planning Committee.

Photos/ads: Zuma Press/Marianna Day Massey; GLAD and STAND & ZIP are trademarks of The Glad Products Company. Advertisement ©2000 The Glad Products Company. Used with permission; Courtesy Pfizer, Inc.; Courtesy SAP AG; ©2003 PeopleSoft, Inc. PeopleSoft is a registered trademark of PeopleSoft, Inc.; Courtesy L.L.Bean; Courtesy Girl Scouts of Northern California and Nevada; Courtesy of Obata Design & Emerson Electric Co.; Agency: Hal Riney & Partners; Art Director: Chris Chaffin; Copywriter: Tony Barlow; Photographer: Bob Mizono; Courtesy Maryland Aviation Administration; Courtesy AllBusiness; ©William D. Perreault, Jr., Ph.d.; CLOROX® is a registered trademark of The Clorox Company. Used with permission. ©1994 The Clorox Company. Reprinted with permission; Courtesy Toyota Motor Sales, U.S.A., Inc.; agency: Oasis Advertising/New York.

CHAPTER 2

Exhibits: Exhibit 2-9, Copernicus: The Marketing Investment Strategy Group, Inc., 450 Lexington Street, Auburndale, MA 02166. Exhibit 2-11, Igor Ansoff, *Corporate Strategy* (New York; McGraw-Hill, 1965).

Photos/ads: AP Photo/Harry Cabluck. All Courtesy Penzoil-Quaker State Co.to/Car @ Jiffy Lube. All Courtesy Toddler University.sity ad. Courtesy Timex Corporation. Courtesy of Zippo Manufacturing Company, Inc. Courtesy Sara Lee Bakery Group. Courtesy of Audi of Norway; Agency: Bates Reklamebyra/ Oslo. Used with permission from McDonald's Corporation. Used with permission from McDonald's Corporation; Agency: DDB Chicago. Courtesy Unilever P.L.C. ©1999 Barry Lewis/Network.

CHAPTER 3

Exhibits: Exhibit 3-12, Russell I. Haley,"Benefit Segmentation: A Decision-Oriented Research Tool,"*Journal of Marketing*, July 1968, p. 33.

Photos/ads: ©William D. Perreault, Jr., Ph.D. Courtesy Olympus America, Inc; Courtesy of Vivitar Corporation; Polter, Katz, Postal & Ferguson; MGI Software, Inc. Courtesy Samsung Electronics America. Courtesy Hallmark Cards, Inc. Courtesy Claritas. Courtesy Maplinx Corp. CLOROX CLEAN-UP® is a registered trademark of The Clorox Company. Used with permission. ©2002 The Clorox Company. Reprinted with permission. READYMOP® is a registered trademark of The Clorox Company. Used with permission. ©2002 The Clorox Company. Courtesy CNBC, Inc. Courtesy CNN. ©The Procter & Gamble Company. Used by permission. Courtesy Del Laboratories. Photographer: Steve Bonini; Courtesy Orange Glo International; Courtesy Sara Lee Bakery Group.; Courtesy Grey Worldwide/Thailand; Courtesy Target Stores.

CHAPTER 4

Exhibits: Exhibit 4-7, adapted from M. G. Allen,"Strategic Problems Facing Today's Corporate Planner,"speech given at the Academy of Management, 36th Annual Meeting, Kansas City, Missouri, 1976.

Photos/ads: Courtesy United Parcel Service of America, Inc.; Courtesy REI; Courtesy Harley-Davidson Motor Company; Courtesy Hurd Windows; Agency: Carmichael Lynch; Photo: ibid; Courtesy of Dutch Boy Paint Company a division of Sherwin-William Company; Courtesy Royal Appliance Mfg. Co.; Courtesy Accenture; Courtesy Smart Money; Ad created by: DiMassimo Brand Advertising/New York; Courtesy MSNBC; Microsoft Corporation; Courtesy Springer & Jacoby UK Ltd.; Photography by: F.A. Cesar; Courtesy Adero, Inc.; Courtesy adidas America; Photo by: Bob Allen; Nutri-Grain® is a registered trademark of Kellogg Company. ©2003 Kellogg Co.; Courtesy Con Agra Foods, Inc. – Snack Foods Group; Both Courtesy American Honda Motor Co.; Courtesy Honda North America, Inc.; Courtesy Baldor Electric; Courtesy Click 2 Asia.

CHAPTER 5

Exhibits: Exhibit 5-1, map developed by the authors based on U.S. Census data including, *Global Population Profile: 2000* and *World Population Profile: 1998* and *World Population at a Glance: 1998 and Beyond, IB/98–4* and *World Population Profile: 1994, WP/94 and WP/94-DD* (Washington, DC: U.S. Government Printing Office). Exhibit 5-2, table based on U.S. Census data, including"International Data Base"available from World Wide Web: http://www.census.gov/cgi-bin/ipc/idbsum?cty=?? and other U.S. Census data including *An Aging World: 2001, P95/01-1* and *World Bank data including, World Development Indicators: 2003* (Washington, DC: International Bank for Reconstruction and Development/The World Bank, 2003) and available from World Wide Web: <http://devdata.worldbank.org/data-query>; Central Intelligence Agency data and available from World

Wide Web: <http://www.odci.gov/cia/publications/factbook>; Population Reference Bureau data, including *2002 World Population Data Sheet* (Washington, DC: Population Reference Bureau, 2002) and available from World Wide Web: http://www.prb.org/pubs/wpds2002. Exhibit 5-3, map developed by the authors based on U.S. Census data including U.S. Bureau of the Census, *Statistical Abstract of the United States 2002* (Washington, DC: U.S. Government Printing Office, 2001), p. 22 and available from World Wide Web: http://www.census.gov/statab. Exhibit 5-4, map developed by the authors based on U.S. Census data including U.S. Bureau of the Census, *Statistical Abstract of the United States 2002* (Washington, DC: U.S. Government Printing Office, 2001), p. 23 and available from World Wide Web: <http://www.census.gov/statab>and "Special Report: Counting Change," *Advertising Age*, July 8, 2002, pp. S1-S12. Exhibit 5-5, graph developed by the authors based on U.S. Census data including U.S. Bureau of the Census, *Statistical Abstract of the United States 2002* (Washington, DC: U.S. Government Printing Office, 2001), p. 9 and p. 59 and available from World Wide Web: http://www.census.gov/statab. Exhibit 5-6, graph developed by the authors based on U.S. Census data: including U.S. Bureau of the Census, *Statistical Abstract of the United States 2002* (Washington, DC: U.S. Government Printing Office, 2001), p. 18 and p. 25 (for 2000 figures) and p. 20 (for 2010 figures) and available from World Wide Web: <http://www.census.gov/statab>. 1990 figures from U.S. Census Bureau, *Current Population Reports*, P25-917 and P25-1095 and unpublished data and available on World Wide Web: <http://www.census.gov/population/www/estimates/popest> and <http://www.census.gov/statab/freq/ 99s0014>. Exhibit 5-7, graph developed by the authors based on U.S. Census data including "Table F-6. Regions-Families (All Races) by Median and Mean Income: 1953 to 2001" and available from World Wide Web: <http://www.census.gov/ hhes/income/hitinc/f06.html>. Exhibit 5-8, graph developed by the authors based on U.S. Census data including "Table F-1. Income Limits for Each Fifth and Top 5 Percent of Families (All Races): 1947 to 2001" and available from World Wide Web: <http:// www.census.gov/hhes/income/histinc/f01.html>, "Table F-2. Share of Aggregate Income Received by Each Fifth and Top 5 Percent of Families (All Races): 1947 to 2001" and available from World Wide Web: <http://www.census.gov/hhes/income/ histinc/f02.html>. Exhibit 5-9, adapted from Patrick E. Murphy and William A. Staples, "A Modern Family Life Cycle," *Journal of Consumer Research*, June 1979, p. 17.

Photos/ads: Courtesy Charles Schwab & Co.; Courtesy SRC; Courtesy Leo Burnett Advertising Sdn Bhd; ©Setboun Michel/Corbis Sygma; Courtesy Accenture; Courtesy Turner Broadcasting System; Courtesy DiMassimo Brand Advertising; Creative Director: Mark DiMassimo; Art Director: Christian Hasford; Courtesy of CBS Television Network; Courtesy Bell South Advertising Group; Courtesy element79partners; Photographer: Guzmans/New York City, NY; Courtesy National Fluid Milk Processor Promotion Board; Agency: Bozell Worldwide.

CHAPTER 6

Exhibits: Exhibit 6-2, adapted from C. Glenn Walters, *Consumer Behavior*, 3d ed. (Homewood, IL: Richard D. Irwin, 1979). Exhibit 6-5, Joseph T. Plummer, "The Concept and Application of Life-Style Segmentation," *Journal of Marketing*, January 1974, pp. 33–37.

Photos/ads: Copyright 2001 USA TODAY. Reprinted with permission; The Wendy's name, design and logo are registered trademarks of Oldemark, LLC and are licensed to Wendy's International, Inc.; Courtesy of ConAgra Foods; Courtesy DDB Singapore. FRESH STEP® is a registered trademark of The Clorox Pet Products Company. Used with permission. ©2002 The Clorox Pet Products Company. Reprinted with permission; Courtesy Bates Hong Kong Ltd.; Courtesy Stride Rite Corporation; Lifestyle Photo: Peggy Sirota; Product Photo: John Lawler; All ©The Procter & Gamble Company. Used by permission; Courtesy Harley-Davidson, Inc.; Agency: Carmichael Lynch/Minneapolis; Photo: ©Chris Wimpey; ©M. Hruby; ©2000 Jockey International, Inc. World Rights Reserved; Courtesy of the General Mills Archive; Courtesy A.T. Cross Company; AP Photo/Hasan Jamali; Christopher Morris/VII Photo Agency.

CHAPTER 7

Exhibits: Exhibit 7-1, U.S. Bureau of the Census, *Statistical Abstract of the United States 2000*; U.S. Bureau of the Census, *County Business Patterns 1998, United States* (Washington, DC: U.S. Government Printing Office, 2000). Exhibit 7-5, adapted from Rowland T. Moriarty, Jr., and Robert E. Spekman, "An Empirical Investigation of the Information Sources Used During the Industrial Buying Process, *Journal of Marketing Research*, May 1984, pp. 137–47. Exhibit 7-8, data adapted from U.S. Bureau of the Census, *Statistical Abstract of the United States 2000*; U.S. Bureau of the Census, *County Business Patterns 1998, United States*; U.S. Bureau of the Census, *1997 Census of Manufacturers, Subject Series, General Summary* (Washington, DC: U.S. Government Printing Office, 2001). Exhibit 7-9, available from World Wide Web: http://www.naics.com.

Photos/ads: Photo courtesy of Deere & Company/Moline, Illinois; Courtesy Dow Agro Sciences; Agency: Bader Rutter & Associates/Brookfield, WI; Courtesy Arlington Industries, Inc.; Courtesy International Truck & Engine Corp.; Agency: Fallon/Minneapolis; Both ©Roger Ball Photography; Courtesy Yellow Freight Systems, Inc.; Courtesy Canon USA, Inc.; Courtesy Ingersoll-Rand; Courtesy Rockwell International Corporation; Reproduced with permission of Yahoo! Inc. ©2003 by Yahoo! Inc. YAHOO! and the YAHOO! logo are trademarks of Yahoo! Inc. Photo: Doug Adesko; Courtesy Google; Courtesy DoveBid.com; Courtesy National Semiconductor; Courtesy Hertz Corporation; Courtesy American Express; Agency: Ogilvy & Mather/New York; Photographer: Micheal McLaughlin; All photos: Courtesy of Alcoa; Courtesy Savin Corporation; Courtesy SDI Technologies; Courtesy Cisco Systems, Inc.

CHAPTER 8

Exhibits: Exhibit 8-5, adapted from Paul E. Green, Frank J. Carmone, and David P. Wachpress,"On the Analysis of Qualitative Data in Marketing Research," *Journal of Marketing Research*, February 1977, pp. 52–59.

Photos/ads: ©The Procter & Gamble Company. Used by permission; Courtesy Oracle; Courtesy of MapInfo; Courtesy Find/SVP; Created by Sonnenberg, Haviland & Partners,

Ridgewood, N.J.; Courtesy JRP Marketing Research Services; Courtesy Google. Reprinted with permission from Northern Light Technology, Inc. Copyright 1999; Courtesy Decision Analyst, Inc.; Courtesy Focus Vision Worldwide, ™Inc.; Courtesy Focus World International; Courtesy Zero knowledge Systems, Inc.; Courtesy Greenfield Online; Courtesy Royal Appliance Mfg. Co.; Courtesy Office Depot, Inc.; ©John Harding; Both Courtesy Simmons Company; Courtesy Abacus B2B/A Division of DoubleClick, Inc.; Courtesy Catalina Marketing Corporation; Courtesy SPSS, Inc.; Copyright2002, SAS Institute Inc., Cary, NC, USA. All Rights Reserved. Reproduced with permission of SAS Institute Inc. Cary, NC, USA; Courtesy Survey Sampling, Inc.; Courtesy Simmons Custom Research; Courtesy P. Robert & Partners; Courtesy Quality Controlled Services – St. Louis, MO.

CHAPTER 9

Exhibits: Exhibit 9.5 Timberland logo reprinted with the permission of The Timberland Company. Timberland and 🌳 are trademarks or registered trademarks of The Timberland Company; [eBay Mark] is a trademark of eBay, Inc. These materials have been reproduced with the permission of eBay Inc. COPYRIGHT ©EBAY INC. ALL RIGHTS RESERVED; Courtesy Boys & Girls Clubs of America; Courtesy Dole Food Company, Inc.; Courtesy Volkswagen of America; Agency: arnoldworldwide/ Boston; Courtesy American Red Cross; Courtesy Sprint Communications Company L.P.; Michelin and the Tire Man logo are registered trademarks of Michelin North America, Inc. and are used here by permission; Courtesy FedEx Services; Linux: Created by Larry Ewing and The Gimp. Courtesy Nestlé Waters North America, Inc.

Photos/ads: Courtesy Segway LLC; Courtesy burst.com; Courtesy Garrity Industries; Reproduced courtesy of the Workrite Uniform Company/Oxnard, CA.; Agency: Applied Concepts/Ventura, CA; Courtesy The Hertz Corporation; Copyright, State Farm Mutual Automobile Insurance Company, 1996. Used by permission; Courtesy Orbitz; Courtesy 3M; Both Courtesy Allen-Edmonds Shoe Corporation; Courtesy Crate & Barrel; Courtesy GE Plastics; Courtesy PerkinElmer, Inc.; Courtesy ADP; Courtesy of The Service Master Company; Stone/Getty Images; Both Courtesy Unilever United States, Inc.; Courtesy Del Monte Fresh Produce N.A., Inc.; Courtesy GE Lighting; Courtesy Saatchi & Saatchi/Paris; Art Director: Benoit Raynert; Copywriter: Jean-Francois Fournon; ©M. Hruby; ©2003 KCWW Reprinted with Permission; Courtesy Colgate-Palmolive Company; These materials have been reproduced with the permission of eBay Inc. COPYRIGHT© EBAY INC. ALL RIGHTS RESERVED; Courtesy Sears Roebuck & Co.

CHAPTER 10

Exhibits: Exhibit 10-4, adapted from Frank R. Bacon, Jr., and Thomas W. Butler, *Planned Innovation* (Ann Arbor: University of Michigan Institute of Science and Technology, 1980). Exhibit 10-5, adapted from Philip Kotler, "What Consumerism Means for Marketers," *Harvard Business Review*, May–June 1972, pp. 55–56.

Photos/ads: Courtesy Frog Design; Courtesy Samsung Electronics America; Courtesy TransitionsOptical, Inc.;

Dennis Chamberlain/Black Star; Courtesy Braun, Inc.; Courtesy Inditex S.A.; Courtesy DuPont Textiles & Interiors' LYCRA®; Agency: Saatchi & Saatchi/Zurich; Courtesy Unilever; Image courtesy of Kanguru Solutions; ©The Procter & Gamble Company. Used by permission; Reynold Wrap®Release® courtesy of REYNOLDS Consumer Products, a business of Alcoa, Inc.; ©The Procter & Gamble Company. Used by permission; Courtesy Sauder Woodworking Company; Courtesy Underwriters Laboratories, Inc.; Courtesy CSA International; Courtesy Zenith Electronics Corporation; Courtesy Porsche Cars North America; ©Caroline Parsons.

CHAPTER 11

Exhibits: Exhibit 11-2, adapted from D. J. Bowersox and E. J. McCarthy, "Strategic Development of Planned Vertical Marketing Systems," in *Vertical Marketing Systems*, ed. Louis Bucklin (Glenview, IL: Scott, Foresman, 1970).

Photos/ads: ©William D. Perreault, Jr., Ph.D.; Courtesy Footlocker, Inc.; Courtesy Esprit International; Courtesy Colgate-Palmolive Company; ©William D. Perreault, Jr., Ph.D.; ©William D. Perreault, Jr., Ph.D.; Courtesy Office Depot; ©William D. Perreault, Jr., Ph.D.; Kellogg's is a trademark of Kellogg Company. All rights reserved. Used with permission; Courtesy Peterson Manufacturing Company; Reprinted with Permission from Pactiv Corporation; Photo by Tim Boyle/Getty Images; Courtesy Pro-Line International; Courtesy Experian; Courtesy Reebok International Ltd.; Courtesy Unilever, P.L.C.; Courtesy Unilever, P.L.C.; Courtesy Unilever, P.L.C.; Photographer: Bill Prentice; Courtesy Office Depot, Inc.

CHAPTER 12

Exhibits: Exhibit 12-4, adapted from B. J. LaLonde and P. H. Zinzer, *Customer Service: Meaning and Measurement* (Chicago: National Council of Physical Distribution Management, 1976); and D. Phillip Locklin, *Transportation for Management* (Homewood, IL: Richard D. Irwin, 1972). Exhibit 12-7, adapted from Louis W. Stern and Adel I. El-Ansary, *Marketing Channels* (Englewood Cliffs, NJ: Prentice Hall, 1977), p. 150.

Photos/ads: AP Photo/Natalee Waters; Courtesy Great Plains Software, Inc; Courtesy IBM Corporation; Agency: Ogilvy & Mather/New York; Courtesy Prince Castle; Courtesy Business Objects; Courtesy Sauder Woodworking Company; Courtesy CNF, Inc; ©2002 Menlo Worldwide, LLC; Courtesy BAX Global; ©Allan Hunter Shoemake Photography, Inc; ©Steve Smith; All courtesy DHL; Photo by David McNew/ Getty Images; ©The Procter & Gamble Company. Used by permission; Advertisement provided courtesy of Frito-Lay, Inc; ©Stephen Begleiter; Courtesy GE Information Services; Courtesy Frog Design.

CHAPTER 13

Exhibits: Exhibit 13-5, available from World Wide Web: <http://www.census.gov>. U.S. Bureau of the Census, *County Business Patterns 1998, United States*; U.S. Bureau of the Census, *1997 Census of Retail Trade, Subject Series, Establishment and Firm Size* (Washington, DC: U.S. Government Printing Office, 2000).

P. Exhibit 13-6, available from World Wide Web: <http://www.census.gov>. U.S. Bureau of the Census, *County Business Patterns 1998, United States*; U.S. Bureau of the Census, *1997 Census of Wholesale Trade, Geographic Area Series, United States* (Washington, DC: U.S. Government Printing Office, 2000).

Photos/ads: Photo: Karen Capland; Courtesy Frieda's, Inc; All ©2003 Lands' End, Inc. Used with permission; The New York Times/Ritz Sino; Courtesy of Office Depot; ©Marty Katz; Reproduced courtesy of Exxon Mobil Corporation; www.themojogroup.com; Courtesy Barnes & Noble, Inc; Courtesy Jersey Gardens Outlet Mall; Courtesy Wyler Werbung/Zurich; Courtesy UGA Media.com; Courtesy Unilever, P.L.C; ©Barbel Schmidt; ©Steve Niedorf; Advance Bar Code Technology, Inc; These materials have been reproduced with the permission of eBay Inc. COPYRIGHT ©EBAY INC. ALL RIGHTS RESERVED.

CHAPTER 14

Photos/ads: ©2003. Used with permission MINI Cooper USA; Photo by: Sean Gallup/Getty Images; Courtesy of Featherlite, Inc; Courtesy FLOORgraphics, Inc; All Courtesy Stanley Works; Courtesy Colgate-Palmolive Company; Courtesy Beech Nutrition Corporation; Courtesy JVC Company of America; Agency: e2amp, inc; Courtesy Overture; Agency: Overture Creative Development; Photographer: Zachary Scott; Both Courtesy Sara Lee Corporation; Courtesy LivePerson, Inc; Courtesy LG Electronics US; Advertisement courtesy of the California Pistachio Commission; Courtesy Alice/Paris; Courtesy Reily Foods Company; ©2000 Network Solutions, Inc; ©Yahoo, Inc.

CHAPTER 15

Exhibits: Exhibit 15-3, exhibit suggested by Professor A. A. Brogowicz, Western Michigan University.

Photos/ads: ©Timothy Archibald; Photograph Courtesy of Glaxo Holdings, p.l.c; Copyright, State Farm Mutual Automobile Insurance Company, 1996. Used by permission; Courtesy of Sauder Woodworking Company; ©2004. The Charles Schwab Corporation; Courtesy CDW; Courtesy General Electric Company; Photo by: Brownie Harris; ©1996 Vickers & Beechler; Courtesy Alcoa; Photo by: Robert Feldman; Courtesy The Clorox Company; Photo by: Lisa Papel; Courtesy Allegheny Power; Courtesy SalesDriver; Courtesy salesforce.com; Robert Wahrenburg, Rental Advertising Manager, Caterpillar, Inc; Courtesy Boise Cascade Office Products; Courtesy Eiki International, Inc; Courtesy Keebler.

CHAPTER 16

Exhibits: Exhibit 16-2, "2001 Advertising to Sales Ratios for the 200 Largest Ad Spending Industries," *Advertising Age*, September 17, 2001, and available from World Wide Web: <http:// www.adage.com>. Exhibit 16-4, cost data from *Standard Rate and Data*, 2000, and sales estimates are a compilation by the authors from "Special Report: Media Outlook 2003," *Adweek*, September 29, 2003; "Ad Industry Looks Ahead with Cautious Optimism," *Advertising Age*, December 16, 2002, p. 4; "Domestic Advertising Spending Totals," available from World Wide Web: <http:// www.adage.com>. Exhibit 16-5, compila-

tion by the authors from online sources including adage.com and nine agencies' websites.

Photos/ads: Courtesy Subway Restaurants/Doctor's Associates, Inc; ©Michael Goldwater/Network; ©The Procter & Gamble Company. Used by permission; Courtesy Hoechst AG; CLOROX® is a registered trademark of The Clorox Company. Used with permission. ©2002 The Clorox Company. Reprinted with permission; Courtesy Del Pharmaceuticals, Inc; Courtesy of Brown Shoe Co., Inc; Courtesy of Campbell Soup Company; Courtesy New York Interconnect; Courtesy Tierney Agency/Philadelphia; David Taylor/Allsport; Courtesy Unilever United States, Inc; Courtesy Taxi/Toronto; Creative Directors: Zak Mroueh & Paul Lavole; Courtesy Colorado Wildlands; Courtesy Adobe Systems, Inc; Courtesy Bates USA South/Miami; Courtesy Greenfield Online, Inc; Courtesy Circuit City; Photographer: Jeff Zaruba; Courtesy Insignia Systems, Inc; Courtesy Promo Edge; Agency: Bader Rutter & Associates/Brookfield, WI.; Art director: Sarah Kmet-Hunt; Copywriter: Dennis Cook; Photo: Getty Images; All ©The Procter & Gamble Company. Used by permission.

CHAPTER 17

Exhibits: Exhibit 17-6, exchange rate data is available from the Federal Reserve Bank; see also International Monetary Fund data available from World Wide Web: <http://www.imf.org/external/np/tre/sdr/drates> and Universal Currency Converter available from World Wide Web: <http://www.x-rates.com>.

Photos/ads: ©William D. Perreault, Jr., Ph.d; Courtesy Clarke Goward Agency; Courtesy Merck Co., Inc; Norbert Schwerin/The Image Works; Courtesy Hydra Pools; Courtesy Arch Chemicals; Courtesy Carnival Corporation; Courtesy National Trade Publications, Inc; Courtesy Dupont Surfaces; All rights reserved, Palm, Inc; Courtesy 8 in 1 Pet Products, Inc; Ad photo courtesy of Nestle, USA, Inc. LEAN CUISINE® is a registered trademark of Societe des Products Nestle S.A; These materials have been reproduced with the permission of PayPal, Inc. COPYRIGHT ©2003 PAYPAL, INC. ALL RIGHTS RESERVED; Courtesy The Richards Group; Copywriter: Chris Smith; Art Director: Warren Lewis; Mike Williams/Mercury; Courtesy Con Agra Foods, Inc. – Grocery Products Division; Courtesy Dollar Thrifty Automotive Group, Inc; Both ©The Procter & Gamble Company Used by permission; ©Fritz Hoffman.

CHAPTER 18

Exhibits: Exhibit 18-12, this exhibit is different from, but stimulated by, a graph that appears on the Satisfaction Management Systems, Inc., website <http://www.satmansys.com>.

Photos/ads: AP Photo/Chris O'Meara; Courtesy Kohler, Co; BIC, the BIC Logo, BIC COMFORT 3, and SOFT FEEL are trademarks and registered trademarks of the BIC Group and are reproduced with permission; Don Smetzer/Tony Stone; ©William D. Perreault, Jr., Ph.d; Courtesy Owens Corning; Mark Henley/Impact; Courtesy Hallmark Cards, Inc.; Agency: Leo Burnett/Chicago, IL; Courtesy Euro RSCG Worldwide/London; Courtesy Metform, L.L.C; Courtesy Emerson Electric

Company; Courtesy eCampus.com; Agency: Devito-Verdi Advertising; Courtesy Orbitz; Courtesy Affordable Furniture; Courtesy The Diamond Trading Company; Agency: J. Walter Thompson U.S.A., Inc; Courtesy Audio Stream; Courtesy Worldbid.com; Courtesy Jaffe Software Systems.

CHAPTER 19

Exhibits: Exhibit 19-2, Marie Gaudard, Roland Coates, and Liz Freeman, "Accelerating Improvement," *Quality Progress*, October 1991, pp. 81–88. Exhibit, 19-3, Marie Gaudard, Roland Coates, and Liz Freeman, "Accelerating Improvement," *Quality Progress*, October 1991, pp. 81–88.

Photos/ads: ©William D. Perreault, Jr., Ph.d; Courtesy GE Company; Courtesy Lotus Development Corporation, an IBM Company; Courtesy FedEx Services; ©2004 Hertz System, Inc. Hertz is a registered service mark and trademark of Hertz System, Inc; Courtesy Kenwood Communications; Courtesy WebEx; Agency: Antenna Group Public Relations/San Francisco; Courtesy Toyota Motor Company; Courtesy Pozzi; Courtesy Balboa Instruments, Inc; Courtesy The Timken Company; Courtesy Information Resources, Inc; Courtesy Allen Canning Company; Courtesy Hoborama LLC; Courtesy Acco Brands Inc.

CHAPTER 20

Photos/ads: Used with the permission of Inter IKEA Systems B.V.; Courtesy T-Mobile; Agency: Publicis Agency/Seattle; Network/SABA; Courtesy Key Corp; Courtesy CIT Group, Inc; Photo by: Will Faller/Word Management Group; Both Kellogg's® RICE KRISPIES TREATS® is a trademark of Kellogg Company. All rights reserved. Used with permission; Courtesy Unilever United States, Inc; Courtesy Oral-B/The Gillette Company; Both Courtesy Lear Corporation; Courtesy Springer & Jacoby/Hamburg; Courtesy Claritas; Courtesy Business Objects Americas, Inc; Courtesy SMART Technologies, Inc; Courtesy Sears Roebuck & Co; ©2003 Air Products and Chemicals, Inc; ©2003. Siemens Corporation; ©William D. Perreault, Jr., Ph.d; ©William D. Perreault, Jr., Ph.d.

CHAPTER 21

Exhibits: Exhibit 21-5, "2003 Survey of Buying Power," *Sales & Marketing Management*, Supplement, 2003. Exhibit 21-6, based on data reported in *Fiber Box Industry Statistics*, Fiber Box Association and NAICS codes available from World Wide Web: <http://www.naics.com>.

Photos/ads: Courtesy Maytag Corporation; Courtesy Lindsay, Stone & Briggs, Inc./Madison, WI.; Photography: Vedros & Associates Photography; ©The Procter & Gamble Company. Used by permission; Courtesy Duracell; ©2002 Time Warner Cable; Courtesy Trief USA, Inc; Courtesy Rubin Postaer & Assoc.; Photography: Stock; ©The Procter & Gamble Company. Used by permission; Courtesy Garmin International; Courtesy Sunlite Casual Furniture; Courtesy of Third Wave Research Group, Ltd; KELLOGG's® and SNACK 'UMS™ are trademarks of Kellogg Company. All rights reserved. Used with permission; Courtesy Greenfield Online, Inc; Courtesy Hershey Foods Corporation; Courtesy Eckerd Food Stores; Courtesy Land Rover; Agency: Rainey Kelly Campbell Roalfe Y&R/London; Courtesy Frieda's, Inc; Courtesy Haier America; Courtesy Lowe's Companies; Courtesy Planet HVAC.

CHAPTER 22

Exhibits: Exhibit 22-1, adapted and updated from discussions of an American Marketing Association Strategic Planning Committee.

Photos/ads: ©Lauren Fleishman; ©Robin Moyer; Courtesy Planetfeedback; Courtesy Carlson Hospitality Worldwide; Courtesy J.D.Power & Associates; Courtesy New Products Works; ©2004 Hertz System, Inc. Hertz is a registered service mark and trademark of Hertz System, Inc; Courtesy Johnson & Johnson; Photo by: Bob Wolter & Associates; Courtesy McAfee Security; Agency: Grey Advertising/San Francisco; Courtesy Zippo Manufacturing Company, Inc; Courtesy Princeton Video Image.

APPENDIX C

Photos/ads: Courtesy General Motors.

Author Index

Company Index

Subject Index

Glossary

Accessories Short-lived capital items—tools and equipment used in production or office activities.

Accumulating Collecting products from many small producers.

Administered channel systems Various channel members informally agree to cooperate with each other.

Administered prices Consciously set prices aimed at reaching the firm's objectives.

Adoption curve Shows when different groups accept ideas.

Adoption process The steps individuals go through on the way to accepting or rejecting a new idea.

Advertising Any *paid* form of nonpersonal presentation of ideas, goods, or services by an identified sponsor.

Advertising agencies Specialists in planning and handling mass-selling details for advertisers.

Advertising allowances Price reductions to firms in the channel to encourage them to advertise or otherwise promote the firm's products locally.

Advertising managers Managers of their company's mass-selling effort in television, newspapers, magazines, and other media.

Agent middlemen Wholesalers who do not own (take title to) the products they sell.

AIDA model Consists of four promotion jobs: (1) to get *Attention,* (2) to hold *Interest,* (3) to arouse *Desire,* and (4) to obtain *Action.*

Allowance (accounting term) Occurs when a customer is not satisfied with a purchase for some reason and the seller gives a price reduction on the original invoice (bill), but the customer keeps the goods or services.

Allowances Reductions in price given to final consumers, customers, or channel members for doing something or accepting less of something.

Assorting Putting together a variety of products to give a target market what it wants.

Attitude A person's point of view toward something.

Auction companies Agent middlemen that provide a place where buyers and sellers can come together and complete a transaction.

Automatic vending Selling and delivering products through vending machines.

Average cost (per unit) The total cost divided by the related quantity.

Average-cost pricing Adding a reasonable markup to the average cost of a product.

Average fixed cost (per unit) The total fixed cost divided by the related quantity.

Average variable cost (per unit) The total variable cost divided by the related quantity.

Bait pricing Setting some very low prices to attract customers but trying to sell more expensive models or brands once the customer is in the store.

Balance sheet An accounting statement that shows a company's assets, liabilities, and net worth.

Basic list prices The prices that final customers or users are normally asked to pay for products.

Basic sales tasks *Order-getting, order-taking,* and *supporting.*

Battle of the brands The competition between dealer brands and manufacturer brands.

Belief A person's opinion about something.

Benchmarking Picking a basis of comparison for evaluating how well a job is being done.

Bid pricing Offering a specific price for each possible job rather than setting a price that applies for all customers.

Birthrate The number of babies per 1,000 people.

Brand equity The value of a brand's overall strength in the market.

Brand familiarity How well customers recognize and accept a company's brand.

Brand insistence Customers insist on a firm's branded product and are willing to search for it.

Brand managers Manage specific products, often taking over the jobs formerly handled by an advertising manager—sometimes called *product managers.*

Brand name A word, letter, or a group of words or letters.

Brand nonrecognition Final customers don't recognize a brand at all—even though middlemen may use the brand name for identification and inventory control.

Brand preference Target customers usually choose the brand over other brands, perhaps because of habit or favorable past experience.

Brand recognition Customers remember the brand.

Brand rejection Potential customers won't buy a brand—unless its image is changed.

Branding The use of a name, term, symbol, or design—or a combination of these—to identify a product.

Break-even analysis An approach to determine whether the firm will be able to break even—that is, cover all its costs—with a particular price.

Break-even point (BEP) The sales quantity where the firm's total cost will just equal its total revenue.

Breakthrough opportunities Opportunities that help innovators develop hard-to-copy marketing strategies that will be very profitable for a long time.

Brokers Agent middlemen who specialize in bringing buyers and sellers together.

Bulk-breaking Dividing larger quantities into smaller quantities as products get closer to the final market.

Business and organizational customers Any buyers who buy for resale or to produce other goods and services.

Business products Products meant for use in producing other products.

Buying center All the people who participate in or influence a purchase.

Buying function Looking for and evaluating goods and services.

Capital The money invested in a firm.

Capital item A long-lasting product that can be used and depreciated for many years.

Cash-and-carry wholesalers Like service wholesalers, except that the customer must pay cash.

Cash discounts Reductions in the price to encourage buyers to pay their bills quickly.

Cash flow statement A financial report that forecasts how much cash will be available after paying expenses.

Catalog wholesalers Sell out of catalogs that may be distributed widely to smaller industrial customers or retailers that might not be called on by other middlemen.

Chain of supply The complete set of firms and facilities and logistics activities that are involved in procuring materials, transforming them into intermediate and finished products, and distributing them to customers.

Channel captain A manager who helps direct the activities of a whole channel and tries to avoid, or solve, channel conflicts.

Channel of distribution Any series of firms or individuals who participate in the flow of products from producer to final user or consumer.

Close The salesperson's request for an order.

Clustering techniques Approaches used to try to find similar patterns within sets of data.

Combination export manager A blend of manufacturers' agent and selling agent—handling the entire export function for several producers of similar but noncompeting lines.

Combined target market approach Combining two or more submarkets into one larger target market as a basis for one strategy.

Combiners Firms that try to increase the size of their target markets by combining two or more segments.

Communication process A source trying to reach a receiver with a message.

Comparative advertising Advertising that makes specific brand comparisons using actual product names.

Competitive advantage A firm has a marketing mix that the target market sees as better than a competitor's mix.

Competitive advertising Advertising that tries to develop selective demand for a specific brand rather than a product category.

Competitive barriers The conditions that may make it difficult, or even impossible, for a firm to compete in a market.

Competitive bids Terms of sale offered by different suppliers in response to the buyer's purchase specifications.

Competitive environment The number and types of competitors the marketing manager must face, and how they may behave.

Competitive rivals A firm's closest competitors.

Competitor analysis An organized approach for evaluating the strengths and weaknesses of current or potential competitors' marketing strategies.

Complementary product pricing Setting prices on several related products as a group.

Components Processed expense items that become part of a finished product.

Concept testing Getting reactions from customers about how well a new product idea fits their needs.

Confidence intervals The range on either side of an estimate from a sample that is likely to contain the true value for the whole population.

Consideration set The list of potential choices that a consumer will actually consider buying.

Consultative selling approach A type of sales presentation in which the salesperson develops a good understanding of the individual customer's needs before trying to close the sale.

Consumer panel A group of consumers who provide information on a continuing basis.

Consumer Product Safety Act A 1972 law that set up the Consumer Product Safety Commission to encourage more awareness of safety in product design and better quality control.

Consumer products Products meant for the final consumer.

Consumer surplus The difference to consumers between the value of a purchase and the price they pay.

Consumerism A social movement that seeks to increase the rights and powers of consumers.

Containerization Grouping individual items into an economical shipping quantity and sealing them in protective containers for transit to the final destination.

Continuous improvement A commitment to constantly make things better one step at a time.

Contract manufacturing Turning over production to others while retaining the marketing process.

Contractual channel systems Various channel members agree by contract to cooperate with each other.

Contribution-margin approach A cost analysis approach in which all costs are not allocated in *all* situations.

Control The feedback process that helps the marketing manager learn (1) how ongoing plans and implementation are working and (2) how to plan for the future.

Convenience (food) stores A convenience-oriented variation of the conventional limited-line food stores.

Convenience products Products a consumer needs but isn't willing to spend much time or effort shopping for.

Cooperative advertising Middlemen and producers sharing in the cost of ads.

Cooperative chains Retailer-sponsored groups, formed by independent retailers, to run their own buying organizations and conduct joint promotion efforts.

Copy thrust What the words and illustrations of an ad should communicate.

Corporate chain A firm that owns and manages more than one store—and often it's many.

Corporate channel systems Corporate ownership all along the channel.

Corrective advertising Ads to correct deceptive advertising.

Cost of sales Total value (at cost) of the sales during the period.

Cues Products, signs, ads, and other stimuli in the environment.

Cultural and social environment Affects how and why people live and behave as they do.

Culture The whole set of beliefs, attitudes, and ways of doing things of a reasonably homogeneous set of people.

Cumulative quantity discounts Reductions in price for larger purchases over a given period, such as a year.

Customer relationship management (CRM) An approach where the seller fine-tunes the marketing effort with information from a detailed customer database.

Customer satisfaction The extent to which a firm fulfills a consumer's needs, desires, and expectations.

Customer service level How rapidly and dependably a firm can deliver what customers want.

Customer value The difference between the benefits a customer sees from a market offering and the costs of obtaining those benefits.

Data warehouse A place where databases are stored so that they are available when needed.

Dealer brands Brands created by middlemen—sometimes referred to as *private brands*.

Debt financing Borrowing money based on a promise to repay the loan, usually within a fixed time period and with a specific interest charge.

Decision support system (DSS) A computer program that makes it easy for marketing managers to get and use information *as they are making decisions*.

Decoding The receiver in the communication process translating the message.

Demand-backward pricing Setting an acceptable final consumer price and working backward to what a producer can charge.

Demand curve A graph of the relationship between price and quantity demanded in a market, assuming all other things stay the same.

Department stores Larger stores that are organized into many separate departments and offer many product lines.

Derived demand Demand for business products derives from the demand for final consumer products.

Determining dimensions The dimensions that actually affect the customer's purchase of a *specific* product or brand in a *product-market*.

Differentiation The marketing mix is distinct from and better than what's available from a competitor.

Direct marketing Direct communication between a seller and an individual customer using a promotion method other than face to face personal selling.

Direct type advertising Competitive advertising that aims for immediate buying action.

Discount houses Stores that sell hard goods (cameras, TVs, appliances) at substantial price cuts to customers who go to discounter's low-rent store, pay cash, and take care of any service or repair problems themselves.

Discounts Reductions from list price given by a seller to buyers, who either give up some marketing function or provide the function themselves.

Discrepancy of assortment The difference between the lines a typical producer makes and the assortment final consumers or users want.

Discrepancy of quantity The difference between the quantity of products it is economical for a producer to make and the quantity final users or consumers normally want.

Discretionary income What is left of disposable income after paying for necessities.

Disposable income Income that is left after taxes.

Dissonance Tension caused by uncertainty about the rightness of a decision.

Distribution center A special kind of warehouse designed to speed the flow of goods and avoid unnecessary storing costs.

Diversification Moving into totally different lines of business—perhaps entirely unfamiliar products, markets, or even levels in the production-marketing system.

Door-to-door selling Going directly to the consumer's home.

Drive A strong stimulus that encourages action to reduce a need.

Drop-shippers Wholesalers that own (take title to) the products they sell but do not actually handle, stock, or deliver them.

Dual distribution When a producer uses several competing channels to reach the same target market—perhaps using several middlemen in addition to selling directly (sometimes called *multichannel distribution*).

Dumping Pricing a product sold in a foreign market below the cost of producing it or at a price lower than in its domestic market.

Early adopters The second group in the adoption curve to adopt a new product; these people are usually well respected by their peers and often are opinion leaders.

Early majority A group in the adoption curve that avoids risk and waits to consider a new idea until many early adopters try it and like it.

E-commerce Exchanges between individuals or organizations—and activities that facilitate those exchanges—based on applications of information technology.

Economic and technological environment Affects the way firms, and the whole economy, use resources.

Economic buyers People who know all the facts and logically compare choices to get the greatest satisfaction from spending their time and money.

Economic needs Needs concerned with making the best use of a consumer's time and money—as the consumer judges it.

Economic system The way an economy organizes to use scarce resources to produce goods and services and distribute them for consumption by various people and groups in the society.

Economies of scale As a company produces larger numbers of a particular product, the cost for each of these products goes down.

Elastic demand If prices are dropped, the quantity demanded will stretch enough to increase total revenue.

Elastic supply The quantity supplied does stretch more if the price is raised.

Electronic data interchange (EDI) An approach that puts information in a standardized format easily shared between different computer systems.

Emergency products Products that are purchased immediately when the need is great.

Empowerment Giving employees the authority to correct a problem without first checking with management.

Empty nesters People whose children are grown and who are now able to spend their money in other ways.

Encoding The source in the communication process deciding what it wants to say and translating it into words or symbols that will have the same meaning to the receiver.

Equilibrium point The quantity and the price sellers are willing to offer are equal to the quantity and price that buyers are willing to accept.

Everyday low pricing Setting a low list price rather than relying on frequent sales, discounts, or allowances.

Exclusive distribution Selling through only one middleman in a particular geographic area.

Expectation An outcome or event that a person anticipates or looks forward to.

Expense item A product whose total cost is treated as a business expense in the period it's purchased.

Expenses All the remaining costs that are subtracted from the gross margin to get the net profit.

Experience curve pricing Average-cost pricing using an estimate of *future* average costs.

Experimental method A research approach in which researchers compare the responses of two or more groups that are similar except on the characteristic being tested.

Export agents Manufacturers' agents who specialize in export trade.

Export brokers Brokers who specialize in bringing together buyers and sellers from different countries.

Exporting Selling some of what the firm produces to foreign markets.

Extensive problem solving The type of problem solving consumers use for a completely new or important need—when they put much effort into deciding how to satisfy it.

Facilitators Firms that provide one or more of the marketing functions other than buying or selling.

Factor A variable that shows the relation of some other variable to the item being forecast.

Factor method An approach to forecast sales by finding a relation between the company's sales and some other factor (or factors).

Fad An idea that is fashionable only to certain groups who are enthusiastic about it—but these groups are so fickle that a fad is even more short-lived than a regular fashion.

Family brand A brand name that is used for several products.

Farm products Products grown by farmers, such as oranges, sugar cane, and cattle.

Fashion Currently accepted or popular style.

Federal Fair Packaging and Labeling Act A 1966 law requiring that consumer goods be clearly labeled in easy-to-understand terms.

Federal Trade Commission (FTC) Federal government agency that polices antimonopoly laws.

Financing Provides the necessary cash and credit to produce, transport, store, promote, sell, and buy products.

Fishbone diagram A visual aid that helps organize cause and effect relationships for "things gone wrong."

Fixed-cost (FC) contribution per unit The selling price per unit minus the variable cost per unit.

Flexible-price policy Offering the same product and quantities to different customers at different prices.

F.O.B. A transportation term meaning free on board some vehicle at some point.

Focus group interview An interview of 6 to 10 people in an informal group setting.

Foreign Corrupt Practices Act A law passed by the U.S. Congress in 1977 that prohibits U.S. firms from paying bribes to foreign officials.

Form utility Provided when someone produces something tangible.

Franchise operation A franchisor develops a good marketing strategy, and the retail franchise holders carry out the strategy in their own units.

Freight-absorption pricing Absorbing freight cost so that a firm's delivered price meets the nearest competitor's.

Freight forwarders Transportation wholesalers who combine the small shipments of many shippers into more economical shipping quantities.

Full-cost approach All costs are allocated to products, customers, or other categories.

Full-line pricing Setting prices for a whole line of products.

Functional accounts The categories to which various costs are charged to show the *purpose* for which expenditures are made.

General merchandise wholesalers Service wholesalers that carry a wide variety of nonperishable items such as hardware, electrical supplies, furniture, drugs, cosmetics, and automobile equipment.

General stores Early retailers who carried anything they could sell in reasonable volume.

Generic market A market with *broadly* similar needs—and sellers offering various and *often diverse* ways of satisfying those needs.

Generic products Products that have no brand at all other than identification of their contents and the manufacturer or middleman.

Gross domestic product (GDP) The total market value of all goods and services provided in a country's economy in a year by both residents and nonresidents of that country.

Gross margin (gross profit) The money left to cover the expenses of selling the products and operating the business.

Gross sales The total amount charged to all customers during some time period.

Heterogeneous shopping products Shopping products the customer sees as different and wants to inspect for quality and suitability.

Homogeneous shopping products Shopping products the customer sees as basically the same and wants at the lowest price.

Hypermarkets Very large stores that try to carry not only food and drug items but all goods and services that the consumer purchases *routinely* (also called *supercenters*).

Hypotheses Educated guesses about the relationships between things or about what will happen in the future.

Iceberg principle Much good information is hidden in summary data.

Ideal market exposure When a product is available widely enough to satisfy target customers' needs but not exceed them.

Implementation Putting marketing plans into operation.

Import agents Manufacturers' agents who specialize in import trade.

Import brokers Brokers who specialize in bringing together buyers and sellers from different countries.

Impulse products Products that are bought quickly as *unplanned* purchases because of a strongly felt need.

Indices Statistical combinations of several time series used to find some time series that will lead the series to be forecast.

Indirect type advertising Competitive advertising that points out product advantages—to affect future buying decisions.

Individual brands Separate brand names used for each product.

Individual product A particular product within a product line.

Inelastic demand Although the quantity demanded increases if the price is decreased, the quantity demanded will not stretch enough to avoid a decrease in total revenue.

Inelastic supply The quantity supplied does not stretch much (if at all) if the price is raised.

Innovation The development and spread of new ideas, goods, and services.

Innovators The first group to adopt new products.

Installations Important capital items such as buildings, land rights, and major equipment.

Institutional advertising Advertising that tries to promote an organization's image, reputation, or ideas rather than a specific product.

Integrated marketing communications The intentional coordination of every communication from a firm to a target customer to convey a consistent and complete message.

Intensive distribution Selling a product through all responsible and suitable wholesalers or retailers who will stock or sell the product.

Intermediary Someone who specializes in trade rather than production, sometimes called a *middleman*.

Internet A system for linking computers around the world.

Intranet A system for linking computers within a company.

Introductory price dealing Temporary price cuts to speed new products into a market and get customers to try them.

Inventory The amount of goods being stored.

ISO 9000 A way for a supplier to document its quality procedures according to internationally recognized standards.

Job description A written statement of what a salesperson is expected to do.

Joint venturing In international marketing, a domestic firm entering into a partnership with a foreign firm.

Jury of executive opinion Forecasting by combining the opinions of experienced executives, perhaps from marketing, production, finance, purchasing, and top management.

Just-in-time delivery Reliably getting products there *just* before the customer needs them.

Laggards Prefer to do things the way they have been done in the past and are very suspicious of new ideas; sometimes called *nonadopters*—see *adoption curve*.

Lanham Act A 1946 law that spells out what kinds of marks (including brand names) can be protected and the exact method of protecting them.

Late majority A group of adopters who are cautious about new ideas—see *adoption curve*.

Law of diminishing demand If the price of a product is raised, a smaller quantity will be demanded—and if the price of a product is lowered, a greater quantity will be demanded.

Leader pricing Setting some very low prices—real bargains—to get customers into retail stores.

Leading series A time series that changes in the same direction but *ahead of* the series to be forecast.

Learning A change in a person's thought processes caused by prior experience.

Licensed brand A well-known brand that sellers pay a fee to use.

Licensing Selling the right to use some process, trademark, patent, or other right for a fee or royalty.

Lifestyle analysis The analysis of a person's day-to-day pattern of living as expressed in that person's Activities, Interests, and Opinions—sometimes referred to as *AIOs* or *psychographics*.

Limited-function wholesalers Merchant wholesalers that provide only *some* wholesaling functions.

Limited-line stores Stores that specialize in certain lines of related products rather than a wide assortment—sometimes called *single-line stores*.

Limited problem solving When a consumer is willing to put *some* effort into deciding the best way to satisfy a need.

Logistics The transporting, storing, and handling of goods to match target customers' needs with a firm's marketing mix—both within individual firms and along a channel of distribution (i.e., another name for *physical distribution*).

Long-run target return pricing Pricing to cover all costs and over the long run achieve an average target return.

Low-involvement purchases Purchases that have little importance or relevance for the customer.

Macro-marketing A social process that directs an economy's flow of goods and services from producers to consumers in a way that effectively matches supply and demand and accomplishes the objectives of society.

Magnuson-Moss Act A 1975 law requiring that producers provide a clearly written warranty if they choose to offer any warranty.

Major accounts sales force Salespeople who sell directly to large accounts such as major retail chain stores.

Management contracting The seller provides only management skills—others own the production and distribution facilities.

Manufacturer brands Brands created by producers.

Manufacturers' agents Agent middlemen who sell similar products for several noncompeting producers for a commission on what is actually sold.

Manufacturers' sales branches Separate warehouses that producers set up away from their factories.

Marginal analysis Evaluating the change in total revenue and total cost from selling one more unit to find the most profitable price and quantity.

Marginal cost The change in total cost that results from producing one more unit.

Marginal profit Profit on the last unit sold.

Marginal revenue The change in total revenue that results from the sale of one more unit of a product.

Markdown A retail price reduction that is required because customers won't buy some item at the originally marked-up price.

Markdown ratio A tool used by many retailers to measure the efficiency of various departments and their whole business.

Market A group of potential customers with similar needs who are willing to exchange something of value with sellers offering various goods or services—that is, ways of satisfying those needs.

Market development Trying to increase sales by selling present products in new markets.

Market-directed economic system The individual decisions of the many producers and consumers make the macro-level decisions for the whole economy.

Market growth A stage of the product life cycle when industry sales grow fast—but industry profits rise and then start falling.

Market information function The collection, analysis, and distribution of all the information needed to plan, carry out, and control marketing activities.

Market introduction A stage of the product life cycle when sales are low as a new idea is first introduced to a market.

Market maturity A stage of the product life cycle when industry sales level off and competition gets tougher.

Market penetration Trying to increase sales of a firm's present products in its present markets—probably through a more aggressive marketing mix.

Market potential What a whole market segment might buy.

Market segment A relatively homogeneous group of customers who will respond to a marketing mix in a similar way.

Market segmentation A two-step process of (1) *naming* broad product-markets and (2) *segmenting* these broad product-markets in order to select target markets and develop suitable marketing mixes.

Marketing audit A systematic, critical, and unbiased review and appraisal of the basic objectives and policies of the marketing function and of the organization, methods, procedures, and people employed to implement the policies.

Marketing company era A time when, in addition to short-run marketing planning, marketing people develop long-range plans—sometimes five or more years ahead—and the whole company effort is guided by the marketing concept.

Marketing concept The idea that an organization should aim *all* its efforts at satisfying its *customers*—at a *profit*.

Marketing department era A time when all marketing activities are brought under the control of one department to improve short-run policy planning and to try to integrate the firm's activities.

Marketing ethics The moral standards that guide marketing decisions and actions.

Marketing information system (MIS) An organized way of continually gathering, accessing, and analyzing information that marketing managers need to make decisions.

Marketing management process The process of (1) *planning* marketing activities, (2) directing the *implementation* of the plans, and (3) *controlling* these plans.

Marketing mix The controllable variables that the company puts together to satisfy a target group.

Marketing model A statement of relationships among marketing variables.

Marketing orientation Trying to carry out the marketing concept.

Marketing plan A written statement of a marketing strategy *and* the time-related details for carrying out the strategy.

Marketing program Blends all of the firm's marketing plans into one big plan.

Marketing research Procedures to develop and analyze new information to help marketing managers make decisions.

Marketing research process A five-step application of the scientific method that includes (1) defining the problem, (2) analyzing the situation, (3) getting problem-specific data, (4) interpreting the data, and (5) solving the problem.

Marketing strategy Specifies a target market and a related marketing mix.

Markup A dollar amount added to the cost of products to get the selling price.

Markup chain The sequence of markups firms use at different levels in a channel—determining the price structure in the whole channel.

Markup (percent) The percentage of selling price that is added to the cost to get the selling price.

Mass customization Tailoring the principles of mass production to meet the unique needs of individual customers.

Mass marketing The typical production-oriented approach that vaguely aims at everyone with the same marketing mix.

Mass-merchandisers Large, self-service stores with many departments that emphasize soft goods (housewares, clothing, and fabrics) and staples (like health and beauty aids) and selling on lower margins to get faster turnover.

Mass-merchandising concept The idea that retailers should offer low prices to get faster turnover and greater sales volume by appealing to larger numbers.

Mass selling Communicating with large numbers of potential customers at the same time.

Merchant wholesalers Wholesalers who own (take title to) the products they sell.

Message channel The carrier of the message.

Metropolitan Statistical Area (MSA) An integrated economic and social unit with a large population nucleus.

Micro-macro dilemma What is good for some producers and consumers may not be good for society as a whole.

Micro-marketing The performance of activities that seek to accomplish an organization's objectives by anticipating customer or client needs and directing a flow of need-satisfying goods and services from producer to customer or client.

Middleman An intermediary.

Mission statement Sets out the organization's basic purpose for being.

Missionary salespeople Supporting salespeople who work for producers by calling on their middlemen and their customers.

Modified rebuy The in-between process where some review of the buying situation is done—though not as much as in new-task buying or as little as in straight rebuys.

Monopolistic competition A market situation that develops when a market has (1) different (heterogeneous) products and (2) sellers who feel they do have some competition in this market.

Multichannel distribution When a producer uses several competing channels to reach the same target market—perhaps using several middlemen in addition to selling directly (sometimes called *dual distribution*).

Multinational corporations Firms that have a direct investment in several countries and run their businesses depending on the choices available anywhere in the world.

Multiple buying influence Several people share in making a purchase decision—perhaps even top management.

Multiple target market approach Segmenting the market and choosing two or more segments, then treating each as a separate target market needing a different marketing mix.

Nationalism An emphasis on a country's interests before everything else.

Natural accounts The categories to which various costs are charged in the normal financial accounting cycle.

Natural products Products that occur in nature—such as timber, iron ore, oil, and coal.

Needs The basic forces that motivate a person to do something.

Negotiated contract buying Agreeing to a contract that allows for changes in the purchase arrangements.

Negotiated price A price that is set based on bargaining between the buyer and seller.

Net An invoice term meaning that payment for the face value of the invoice is due immediately—also see *cash discounts*.

Net profit What the company earns from its operations during a particular period.

Net sales The actual sales dollars the company receives.

New product A product that is new *in any way* for the company concerned.

New-task buying When an organization has a new need and the buyer wants a great deal of information.

New unsought products Products offering really new ideas that potential customers don't know about yet.

Noise Any distraction that reduces the effectiveness of the communication process.

Nonadopters Prefer to do things the way they have been done in the past and are very suspicious of new ideas; sometimes called *laggards*—see *adoption curve*.

Noncumulative quantity discounts Reductions in price when a customer purchases a larger quantity on an *individual order*.

Nonprice competition Aggressive action on one or more of the Ps other than Price.

North American Free Trade Agreement (NAFTA) Lays out a plan to reshape the rules of trade among the U.S., Canada, and Mexico.

North American Industry Classification System (NAICS) codes Codes used to identify groups of firms in similar lines of business.

Odd-even pricing Setting prices that end in certain numbers.

Oligopoly A special market situation that develops when a market has (1) essentially homogeneous products, (2) relatively few sellers, and (3) fairly inelastic industry demand curves.

One-price policy Offering the same price to all customers who purchase products under essentially the same conditions and in the same quantities.

Open to buy A buyer has budgeted funds that he can spend during the current time period.

Operating ratios Ratios of items on the operating statement to net sales.

Operating statement A simple summary of the financial results of a company's operations over a specified period of time.

Operational decisions Short-run decisions to help implement strategies.

Opinion leader A person who influences others.

Order getters Salespeople concerned with establishing relationships with new customers and developing new business.

Order-getting Seeking possible buyers with a well-organized sales presentation designed to sell a good, service, or idea.

Order takers Salespeople who sell to regular or established customers, complete most sales transactions, and maintain relationships with their customers.

Order-taking The routine completion of sales made regularly to target customers.

Packaging Promoting, protecting and enhancing the product.

Pareto chart A graph that shows the number of times a problem cause occurs, with problem causes ordered from most frequent to least frequent.

Penetration pricing policy Trying to sell the whole market at one low price.

Perception How we gather and interpret information from the world around us.

Performance analysis Analysis that looks for exceptions or variations from planned performance.

Performance index A number that shows the relation of one value to another.

Personal needs An individual's need for personal satisfaction unrelated to what others think or do.

Personal selling Direct spoken communication between sellers and potential customers, usually in person but sometimes over the telephone or even via a video conference over the Internet.

Phony list prices Misleading prices that customers are shown to suggest that the price they are to pay has been discounted from list.

Physical distribution (PD) The transporting, storing, and handling of goods to match target customers' needs with a firm's marketing mix—both within individual firms and along a channel of distribution (i.e., another name for *logistics*).

Physical distribution (PD) concept All transporting, storing, and product-handling activities of a business and a whole channel system should be coordinated as one system that seeks to minimize the cost of distribution for a given customer service level.

Physiological needs Biological needs such as the need for food, drink, rest, and sex.

Piggyback service Loading truck trailers or flatbed trailers carrying containers on railcars to provide both speed and flexibility.

Pioneering advertising Advertising that tries to develop primary demand for a product category rather than demand for a specific brand.

Place Making goods and services available in the right quantities and locations—when customers want them.

Place utility Having the product available *where* the customer wants it.

Planned economic system Government planners decide what and how much is to be produced and distributed by whom, when, to whom, and why.

Population In marketing research, the total group you are interested in.

Portfolio management Treats alternative products, divisions, or strategic business units (SBUs) as though they are stock investments to be bought and sold using financial criteria.

Positioning An approach that refers to how customers think about proposed or present brands in a market.

Possession utility Obtaining a good or service and having the right to use or consume it.

Prepared sales presentation A memorized presentation that is not adapted to each individual customer.

Prestige pricing Setting a rather high price to suggest high quality or high status.

Price The amount of money that is charged for "something" of value.

Price discrimination Injuring competition by selling the same products to different buyers at different prices.

Price fixing Competitors illegally getting together to raise, lower, or stabilize prices.

Price leader A seller who sets a price that all others in the industry follow.

Price lining Setting a few price levels for a product line and then marking all items at these prices.

Primary data Information specifically collected to solve a current problem.

Primary demand Demand for the general product idea, not just the company's own brand.

Private brands Brands created by middlemen—sometimes referred to as *dealer brands*.

Private warehouses Storing facilities owned or leased by companies for their own use.

Product The need-satisfying offering of a firm.

Product advertising Advertising that tries to sell a specific product.

Product assortment The set of all product lines and individual products that a firm sells.

Product-bundle pricing Setting one price for a set of products.

Product development Offering new or improved products for present markets.

Product liability The legal obligation of sellers to pay damages to individuals who are injured by defective or unsafe products.

Product life cycle The stages a new product idea goes through from beginning to end.

Product line A set of individual products that are closely related.

Product managers Manage specific products, often taking over the jobs formerly handled by an advertising manager—sometimes called *brand managers*.

Product-market A market with very similar needs—and sellers offering various *close substitute* ways of satisfying those needs.

Production Actually *making* goods or *performing* services.

Production capacity The ability to produce a certain quantity and quality of specific goods or services.

Production era A time when a company focuses on production of a few specific products—perhaps because few of these products are available in the market.

Production orientation Making whatever products are easy to produce and *then* trying to sell them.

Professional services Specialized services that support a firm's operations.

Profit maximization objective An objective to get as much profit as possible.

Promotion Communicating information between seller and potential buyer or others in the channel to influence attitudes and behavior.

Prospecting Following all the leads in the target market to identify potential customers.

Psychographics The analysis of a person's day-to-day pattern of living as expressed in that person's Activities, Interests, and Opinions—sometimes referred to as *AIOs* or *lifestyle analysis*.

Psychological pricing Setting prices that have special appeal to target customers.

Public relations Communication with noncustomers—including labor, public interest groups, stockholders, and the government.

Public warehouses Independent storing facilities.

Publicity Any *unpaid* form of nonpersonal presentation of ideas, goods, or services.

Pulling Using promotion to get consumers to ask middlemen for the product.

Purchase discount A reduction of the original invoice amount for some business reason.

Purchasing managers Buying specialists for their employers.

Purchasing specifications A written (or electronic) description of what the firm wants to buy.

Pure competition A market situation that develops when a market has (1) homogeneous (similar) products, (2) many buyers and sellers who have full knowledge of the market, and (3) ease of entry for buyers and sellers.

Pure subsistence economy Each family unit produces everything it consumes.

Push money (or prize money) allowances Allowances (sometimes called *PMs* or *spiffs*) given to retailers by manufacturers or wholesalers to pass on to the retailers' salesclerks for aggressively selling certain items.

Pushing Using normal promotion effort—personal selling, advertising, and sales promotion—to help sell the whole marketing mix to possible channel members.

Qualifying dimensions The dimensions that are relevant to including a customer type in a product-market.

Qualitative research Seeks in-depth, open-ended responses, not yes or no answers.

Quality A product's ability to satisfy a customer's needs or requirements.

Quantitative research Seeks structured responses that can be summarized in numbers—like percentages, averages, or other statistics.

Quantity discounts Discounts offered to encourage customers to buy in larger amounts.

Rack jobbers Merchant wholesalers that specialize in hard-to-handle assortments of products that a retailer doesn't want to manage—and they often display the products on their own wire racks.

Random sampling Each member of the research population has the *same* chance of being included in the sample.

Raw materials Unprocessed expense items—such as logs, iron ore, and wheat—that are moved to the next production process with little handling.

Rebates Refunds to consumers after a purchase.

Receiver The target of a message in the communication process, usually a potential customer.

Reciprocity Trading sales for sales—that is, "if you buy from me, I'll buy from you."

Reference group The people to whom an individual looks when forming attitudes about a particular topic.

Reference price The price a consumer expects to pay.

Regrouping activities Adjusting the quantities or assortments of products handled at each level in a channel of distribution.

Regularly unsought products Products that stay unsought but not unbought forever.

Reinforcement Occurs in the learning process when the consumer's response is followed by satisfaction—that is, reduction in the drive.

Reminder advertising Advertising to keep the product's name before the public.

Requisition A request to buy something.

Research proposal A plan that specifies what marketing research information will be obtained and how.

Resident buyers Independent buying agents who work in central markets for several retailer or wholesaler customers based in outlying areas or other countries.

Response An effort to satisfy a drive.

Response rate The percent of people contacted in a research sample who complete the questionnaire.

Retailing All of the activities involved in the sale of products to final consumers.

Return When a customer sends back purchased products.

Return on assets (ROA) The ratio of net profit (after taxes) to the assets used to make the net profit—multiplied by 100 to get rid of decimals.

Return on investment (ROI) Ratio of net profit (after taxes) to the investment used to make the net profit—multiplied by 100 to get rid of decimals.

Reverse channels Channels used to retrieve products that customers no longer want.

Risk taking Bearing the uncertainties that are part of the marketing process.

Robinson-Patman Act A 1936 law that makes illegal any price discrimination if it injures competition.

Routinized response behavior When consumers regularly select a particular way of satisfying a need when it occurs.

Rule for maximizing profit The highest profit is earned at the price where marginal cost is just less than or equal to marginal revenue.

Safety needs Needs concerned with protection and physical well-being.

Sale price A temporary discount from the list price.

Sales analysis A detailed breakdown of a company's sales records.

Sales decline A stage of the product life cycle when new products replace the old.

Sales era A time when a company emphasizes selling because of increased competition.

Sales forecast An estimate of how much an industry or firm hopes to sell to a market segment.

Sales managers Managers concerned with managing personal selling.

Sales-oriented objective An objective to get some level of unit sales, dollar sales, or share of market—without referring to profit.

Sales presentation A salesperson's effort to make a sale or address a customer's problem.

Sales promotion Those promotion activities—other than advertising, publicity, and personal selling—that stimulate interest, trial, or purchase by final customers or others in the channel.

Sales promotion managers Managers of their company's sales promotion effort.

Sales quota The specific sales or profit objective a salesperson is expected to achieve.

Sales territory A geographic area that is the responsibility of one salesperson or several working together.

Sample A part of the relevant population.

Scientific method A decision-making approach that focuses on being objective and orderly in *testing* ideas before accepting them.

Scrambled merchandising Retailers carrying any product lines that they think they can sell profitably.

Search engine A computer program that helps a marketing manager find information that is needed.

Seasonal discounts Discounts offered to encourage buyers to buy earlier than present demand requires.

Secondary data Information that has been collected or published already.

Segmenters Aim at one or more homogeneous segments and try to develop a different marketing mix for each segment.

Segmenting An aggregating process that clusters people with similar needs into a market segment.

Selective demand Demand for a company's own brand rather than a product category.

Selective distribution Selling through only those middlemen who will give the product special attention.

Selective exposure Our eyes and minds seek out and notice only information that interests us.

Selective perception People screen out or modify ideas, messages, and information that conflict with previously learned attitudes and beliefs.

Selective retention People remember only what they want to remember.

Selling agents Agent middlemen who take over the whole marketing job of producers, not just the selling function.

Selling formula approach A sales presentation that starts with a prepared presentation outline—much like the prepared approach—and leads the customer through some logical steps to a final close.

Selling function Promoting the product.

Senior citizens People over 65.

Service A deed performed by one party for another.

Service mark Those words, symbols, or marks that are legally registered for use by a single company to refer to a service offering.

Service wholesalers Merchant wholesalers that provide all the wholesaling functions.

Shopping products Products that a customer feels are worth the time and effort to compare with competing products.

Simple trade era A time when families traded or sold their surplus output to local middlemen who resold these goods to other consumers or distant middlemen.

Single-line (or general-line) wholesalers Service wholesalers that carry a narrower line of merchandise than general merchandise wholesalers.

Single-line stores Stores that specialize in certain lines of related products rather than a wide assortment—sometimes called *limited-line stores*.

Single target market approach Segmenting the market and picking one of the homogeneous segments as the firm's target market.

Situation analysis An informal study of what information is already available in the problem area.

Skimming price policy Trying to sell the top of the market—the top of the demand curve—at a high price before aiming at more price-sensitive customers.

Social class A group of people who have approximately equal social position as viewed by others in the society.

Social needs Needs concerned with love, friendship, status, and esteem—things that involve a person's interaction with others.

Social responsibility A firm's obligation to improve its positive effects on society and reduce its negative effects.

Sorting Separating products into grades and qualities desired by different target markets.

Source The sender of a message.

Specialty products Consumer products that the customer really wants and makes a special effort to find.

Specialty shop A type of conventional limited-line store—usually small and with a distinct personality.

Specialty wholesalers Service wholesalers that carry a very narrow range of products and offer more information and service than other service wholesalers.

Spreadsheet analysis Organizing costs, sales, and other information into a data table to show how changing the value of one or more numbers affects the other numbers.

Standardization and grading Sorting products according to size and quality.

Staples Products that are bought often, routinely, and without much thought.

Statistical packages Easy-to-use computer programs that analyze data.

Status quo objectives "Don't-rock-the-*pricing*-boat" objectives.

Stock A share in the ownership of a company.

Stocking allowances Allowances given to middlemen to get shelf space for a product—sometimes called *slotting allowances*.

Stockturn rate The number of times the average inventory is sold during a year.

Storing The marketing function of holding goods.

Storing function Holding goods until customers need them.

Straight rebuy A routine repurchase that may have been made many times before.

Strategic business unit (SBU) An organizational unit (within a larger company) that focuses its efforts on some product-markets and is treated as a separate profit center.

Strategic (management) planning The managerial process of developing and maintaining a match between an organization's resources and its market opportunities.

Substitutes Products that offer the buyer a choice.

Supercenters Very large stores that try to carry not only food and drug items, but all goods and services that the consumer purchases routinely (also called *hypermarkets*).

Supermarkets Large stores specializing in groceries—with self-service and wide assortments.

Supplies Expense items that do not become part of a finished product.

Supply curve The quantity of products that will be supplied at various possible prices.

Supporting salespeople Salespeople who help the order-oriented salespeople but don't try to get orders themselves.

S.W.O.T. analysis Identifies and lists the firm's strengths and weaknesses and its opportunities and threats.

Target market A fairly homogeneous (similar) group of customers to whom a company wishes to appeal.

Target marketing A marketing mix is tailored to fit some specific target customers.

Target return objective A specific level of profit as an objective.

Target return pricing Pricing to cover all costs and achieve a target return.

Task method An approach to developing a budget—basing the budget on the job to be done.

Task transfer Using telecommunications to move service operations to places where there are pools of skilled workers.

Task utility Provided when someone performs a task for someone else—for instance, when a bank handles financial transactions.

Team selling Different sales reps working together on a specific account.

Technical specialists Supporting salespeople who provide technical assistance to order-oriented salespeople.

Technology The application of science to convert an economy's resources to output.

Telemarketing Using the telephone to call on customers or prospects.

Telephone and direct-mail retailing Allows consumers to shop at home—usually placing orders by mail or a toll-free long-distance telephone call and charging the purchase to a credit card.

Time series Historical records of the fluctuations in economic variables.

Time utility Having the product available *when* the customer wants it.

Total cost The sum of total fixed and total variable costs.

Total cost approach Evaluating each possible PD system and identifying *all* of the costs of each alternative.

Total fixed cost The sum of those costs that are fixed in total—no matter how much is produced.

Total quality management (TQM) A management approach in which everyone in the organization is concerned about quality, throughout all of the firm's activities, to better serve customer needs.

Total variable cost The sum of those changing expenses that are closely related to output—such as expenses for parts, wages, packaging materials, outgoing freight, and sales commissions.

Trade (functional) discount A list price reduction given to channel members for the job they are going to do.

Trade-in allowance A price reduction given for used products when similar new products are bought.

Trademark Those words, symbols, or marks that are legally registered for use by a single company.

Traditional channel systems A channel in which the various channel members make little or no effort to cooperate with each other.

Transporting The marketing function of moving goods.

Transporting function The movement of goods from one place to another.

Trend extension Extends past experience to predict the future.

Truck wholesalers Wholesalers that specialize in delivering products that they stock in their own trucks.

2/10, net 30 Allows a 2 percent discount off the face value of the invoice if the invoice is paid within 10 days.

Unfair trade practice acts Put a lower limit on prices, especially at the wholesale and retail levels.

Uniform delivered pricing Making an average freight charge to all buyers.

Unit-pricing Placing the price per ounce (or some other standard measure) on or near the product.

Universal functions of marketing Buying, selling, transporting, storing, standardizing and grading, financing, risk taking, and market information.

Universal product code (UPC) Special identifying marks for each product readable by electronic scanners.

Unsought products Products that potential customers don't yet want or know they can buy.

Utility The power to satisfy human needs.

Validity The extent to which data measures what it is intended to measure.

Value in use pricing Setting prices that will capture some of what customers will save by substituting the firm's product for the one currently being used.

Value pricing Setting a fair price level for a marketing mix that really gives the target market superior customer value.

Vendor analysis Formal rating of suppliers on all relevant areas of performance.

Vertical integration Acquiring firms at different levels of channel activity.

Vertical marketing systems Channel systems in which the whole channel focuses on the same target market at the end of the channel.

Virtual corporation The firm is primarily a coordinator—with a good marketing concept—instead of a producer.

Voluntary chains Wholesaler-sponsored groups that work with independent retailers.

Wants Needs that are learned during a person's life.

Warranty What the seller promises about its product.

Wheel of retailing theory New types of retailers enter the market as low-status, low-margin, low-price operators and then, if successful, evolve into more conventional retailers offering more services with higher operating costs and higher prices.

Wheeler Lea Amendment Law that bans unfair or deceptive acts in commerce.

Wholesalers Firms whose main function is providing *wholesaling activities*.

Wholesaling The *activities* of those persons or establishments that sell to retailers and other merchants, or to industrial, institutional, and commercial users, but who do not sell in large amounts to final consumers.

Wholly owned subsidiary A separate firm owned by a parent company.

Working capital Money to pay for short-term expenses such as employee salaries, advertising, marketing research, inventory storing costs, and what the firm owes suppliers.

Zone pricing Making an average freight charge to all buyers within specific geographic areas.

TO THE STUDENT

STUDENT CD-ROM

Everyone learns in different ways (lecture, reading, self-study, interactive quizzing, hands-on exercises). That's why we've included this Student CD-ROM with every new copy of **Basic Marketing, 15/e**. What is the Student CD-ROM? It's an interactive learning tool, expressly built for YOUR use and built for the ways YOU learn—whether it's by seeing, listening, self-testing, or a combination of the three.

The power of this CD-ROM is that it supports the text and the lecture, gives you the opportunity to get additional help on more difficult concepts, and drills basic concepts in each chapter. This CD-ROM offers the following resources:

- The entire text in hypertext format
- Computer-Aided Problem software
- Chapter quizzes with feedback for each response
- 8 narrated slide shows focus on key topics in marketing
- 7 video clips to accompany the written cases in the appendix
- Links to companies discussed in the text
- Sample advertisement with caption from each chapter